MW01259886

ArtScroll Tanach Series®

A traditional commentary on the Books of the Bible

Rabbi Nosson Scherman/Rabbi Meir Zlotowitz
General Editors

Iyov

JOB / A NEW TRANSLATION WITH A COMMENTARY ANTHOLOGIZED FROM TALMUDIC, MIDRASHIC, AND RABBINIC SOURCES.

Published by

Mesorah Publications, ltd

Translation and commentary by
Rabbi Moshe Eisemann

Overview by
Rabbi Moshe Eisemann
with Rabbi Nosson Scherman

FIRST EDITION
First Impression . . . March 1994

Published and Distributed by
MESORAH PUBLICATIONS, Ltd.
4401 Second Avenue
Brooklyn, New York 11232

Distributed in Europe by
J. LEHMANN HEBREW BOOKSELLERS
20 Cambridge Terrace
Gateshead, Tyne and Wear
England NE8 1RP

Distributed in Israel by
SIFRIATI / A. GITLER – BOOKS
4 Bilu Street
P.O.B. 14075
Tel Aviv 61140

Distributed in Australia & New Zealand by
GOLD'S BOOK & GIFT CO.
36 William Street
Balaclava 3183, Vic., Australia

Distributed in South Africa by
KOLLEL BOOKSHOP
22 Muller Street
Yeoville 2198, Johannesburg, South Africa

THE ARTSCROLL TANACH SERIES
IYOV / JOB

ISBN
0-89906-015-3 (hard cover)
0-89906-016-1 (paperback)

Typography by CompuScribe at ArtScroll Studios, Ltd.
4401 Second Avenue / Brooklyn, N.Y. 11232 / (718) 921-9000

Printed in the United States of America by Moriah Offset
Bound by Sefercraft Quality Bookbinders, Ltd., Brooklyn, NY

◆§ Publisher's Preface

The story of Iyov/Job has inspired wonder and discussion among every shade of person for millennia. It is the classic text on the subject of why righteous people suffer. The complexities of its language and philosophical disputations have baffled students and scholars alike, and classic commentators have taken varying approaches to the Book.

We are proud that one of the distinguished thinkers of our generation has undertaken to compose this truly seminal translation and commentary. RABBI MOSHE EISEMANN has been well-known to ArtScroll readers since his acclaimed commentary on the Book of *Yechezkel/Ezekiel* and *Divrei HaYamim/Chronicles*. His mastery of such classic sources as Maharal, Ramchal, and Hirsch lend profundity to all of his writings, and his own depth of insight adds refreshing and stimulating leaven to his masterly blend of authoritative comments. It has been a privilege for us to bring this outstanding author to the attention of the broad Torah public.

We are indebted to MR. AND MRS. WILLIE ROSENFELD and MR. AND MRS. SHMUEL BORUCH WILHELM, who dedicated this work. Old and respected friends, they are people of sensitivity who decided several years ago that they would like to help support a work on this subject.

We are grateful also to all the dedicated members of our staff who extended themselves to make this publication possible. We are confident that many people will find it both stimulating and comforting.

Rabbi Meir Zlotowitz / Rabbi Nosson Scherman

Adar, 5754
February, 1994

ותפארת בנים אבותם

And the splendor of children are their parents

This volume is dedicated to our parents:

. . . To the memory of

ר׳ ישעיה בן ר׳ משה דוד בראון ע״ה

נפ׳ ב׳ סיון, תשל״ה

חיה דוסיא בת ר׳ שמואל ברוך ווילהעלם ע״ה

נפ׳ י״א אייר, תשל״ה

תנצב״ה

. . . And in honor of

ר׳ חיים יהושע ווילהעלם עמו״ש

שרה גאלדה כהן עמו״ש

If our generation produces fruit,
it is because our parents planted seeds,
and sacrificed to nurture them,
with loyalty to the mesorah of their parents.

Shmuel Boruch and Feigie Wilhelm

הודו לה' כי טוב
כי לעולם חסדו

Give thanks to Hashem for He is good;

His kindness endures forever!

Karen and Dovid Deutsch

Amy and Moshe Goldman

Dina and Binyomin Kessler

Aharon Rosenfeld

and families

Dedicated with gratitude by

Janet and Willie Rosenfeld

◆§ Author's Preface

The publication, after many years of effort and preparation, of the ArtScroll *Iyov* gives me particular satisfaction. Certainly I also felt wonderful when I was able to offer the Commentaries on *Ezekiel* and *Divrei HaYamim* to the public. But, something tells me, that *Iyov* will reach a wider audience than either of these and that it will, in certain ways, fill a different kind of need.

It is truly significant that this book may be studied even on *Tishah B'Av* and during the *shiva* period, when we are enjoined from learning Torah. We look to it for help in understanding what we may, in accepting the often incomprehensible, and for the solace which can be our's if we permit ourselves to enter *Iyov's* thought-world.

I hope that this commentary will prove helpful to anyone who uses it. I pray sincerely that it will not dissappoint those who turn to *Iyov* in their time of need. As Iyov did before them, may they set out upon a quest for answers and end up by finding God.

Many thanks to my good friends at Mesorah Publications, Rabbis Meir Zlotowitz and Nosson Scherman, for making this adventure possible. Their patience was sorely tried while we all attempted to find a formula which would accomodate the need of standardization with the rest of the ArtScroll Tanach Series and my own creative urges, without which I could not have undertaken so difficult a work. I hope that the end result justifies all the rocky roads which we had to traverse in order to get there.

I owe a large debt of gratitude to Rabbi Moshe Lieber, who shepherded this work through to publication. My greatest thanks is reserved for Mrs. Ethel Gottlieb and Mrs. Bassie Gutman. What these wonderful ladies went through in their selfless attention to the minutest details in this large and intimidating work can only be imagined. Thank you both very much.

A special word for Rabbi Eliyahu Meir Klugman who kindly

consented to serve as my editor for this work. It was a thankless task for him as he coolly and firmly insisted on protecting me — and the reading public — from my own excesses and occasional flights of fancy. In that difficult task, his sometimes collaborator and guide was my dear friend, Rabbi Yehezkel Danziger, who has frequently assisted me in the past. Although along the way I struggled mightily for almost each original comma, I recognize that the work is tighter, more valuable and, in the end, more true for his efforts.

The book will not be easy reading. The elegance and simple beauty with which Rabbi Sheah Brander and his graphics staff have produced it, will at least make the going more pleasant.

Then there are the largely anonymous people who each by their own invaluable contributions, make an enterprise as large and significant as Mesorah Publications possible. I appreciate each one of you immensely.

There are other thanks and other thoughts which are best expressed in silence. My feelings, I know, will reach their intended destination.

Moshe M. Eisemann

❧ Table of Contents

An Overview / Iyov The Man And Iyov The Book

I. An Oral Tradition Not Reflected in the Text

The guiding principle that must always accompany one in his study of *Tanach* is the need — if we are to achieve our goal of instruction and enlightenment — to seek out the wisdom and the insights of the Sages. This is doubly essential when we set out to tackle issues as sensitive and potentially explosive as those that make up the book of *Iyov*. Our תּוֹרָה שֶׁבִּכְתָב, *Written Torah*, and תּוֹרָה שֶׁבְּעַל פֶּה, *Oral Torah*, form an indivisible whole which alone, in the comprehensiveness of its vision, can lead us to the truth.

Our Written Torah, and Oral Torah, form an indivisible whole which alone, in the comprehensiveness of its vision, can lead us to the truth.

This essential unity guides us effectively when these two Torahs function in tandem, complementing, broadening and deepening one another, but we are perplexed when the Written and Oral Torahs appear to be at odds with one another.

Such seems to be the case with *Iyov*.

Was Iyov as innocent as he claimed to be? Did God really inflict unbearable suffering upon him for no reason other than to satisfy the Satan? Does it make sense that a totally innocent man should suffer so terribly — and, for all that we can understand, senselessly? In a footnote to 1:6-12 we have attempted to address this issue, but after all has been said, we are left with a nagging feeling of unease. The concept seems too big for us. Something within us rebels at such seemingly arbitrary vulnerability.

In this most fundamental of all questions surrounding the Iyov saga, there appears to be a contradiction between the written record and the tradition preserved orally by the Sages.

In this most fundamental of all questions surrounding the Iyov saga, there appears to be a contradiction between the written record and the tradition preserved orally by the Sages.

We can read the story from beginning to end without encountering even a whisper of guilt imputed to Iyov. God's own testimony to the Satan makes Iyov's blameless perfection unequivocally clear. If we need confirmation, it comes from the most unexpected source, the Satan himself. Never in any way does he dispute the facts as laid down by God. In loyal discharge of his duties, he merely demands a test. Never does he even suggest that Iyov might have done anything to deserve punishment. This is the picture we see in the book of *Iyov.*

But in *Sotah* 11a, the Sages present a different picture:

> R' Chiyah bar Abba taught in R' Simai's name: Three men were involved with [Pharaoh's] plan [to destroy Israel]: Balaam, Iyov and Jethro. Balaam, who advised [Pharaoh to destroy the Jews], was killed; Iyov, who kept silent, was stricken by suffering; Jethro, who fled [rather than dispute or participate in the plot], was rewarded by having his descendants seated in the Chamber of Hewn Stone [as judges in the Sanhedrin].

Clearly, the Sages felt that Iyov's suffering must be justified by some cause other than the Satan's indictment.

Clearly, the Sages felt that Iyov's suffering must be justified by some cause other than the Satan's indictment.

How, in this case, do תּוֹרָה שֶׁבִּכְתָב and תּוֹרָה שֶׁבְּעַל פֶּה relate to one another?[1]

A similar problem comes to mind in *Genesis* chapter 15. In the vision that presages the Egyptian exile, Abraham is told that his descendants — the Jewish people — would be exiled and enslaved in a strange land for four hundred years. A simple reading of *Genesis* does not yield any motive for this decree, but the Sages clearly felt that some explanation was required. In *Nedarim* 32a they offer three possible reasons, none of which are explicated in the text as causes for the decree.

For several reasons, however, that situation is different from ours. All three incidents involving Abraham are taken from stories that are recorded in the Torah. This means that a careful reading of the *Genesis* text — given the profound wisdom and insights of the Sages — can yield a satisfactory understanding of the causes of the Egyptian exile. In the case of Iyov, however, the connection between cause and effect — as far as the written text is concerned — is non-existent.

In the case of Iyov, however, the connection between cause and effect — as far as the written text is concerned — is non-existent.

The difference is even more profound. The entire tension of the Iyov saga centers upon the issue of seemingly

1. It is not our contention that every story with which the Sages flesh out our knowledge of Biblical subjects and personalities must have its source in the text. Examples abound of biographical and historical material with which every Jewish child is intimately familiar and which are based entirely on oral tradition.

In our case, however, the problem is a different one. If, indeed, the implication of the Sages' tradition is as we read it — that Iyov's suffering would never have come about if it had not been preceded by some guilt — then a vital element is missing from the story, for the story as it stands is incomprehensible without even a suggestion of a sin that justified Iyov's suffering.

undeserved suffering. Iyov maintains that he is the victim of manifest injustice — his friends claim that he must have sinned. In the end Iyov is vindicated, the friends refuted. But if the Sages' tradition bears out the friends' contention, then the story is turned upside down. Iyov had truly sinned and deserved to be punished, and the friends have been standing throughout upon solid ground.

With such a crucial element missing, we are bound to misconstrue the story as it is written in Scripture.

Whatever the solution to this problem might be, one thing is clear: with such a crucial element missing, we are bound to misconstrue the story as it is written in Scripture. All this is in addition to the fact that God's testimony and the Satan's evident acquiescence seem to stand in direct contradiction to the Sages' assertion.

A more oblique, if no less unambiguous, indication of the direction of the Sages' thinking in this matter comes from *Bava Basra* 15a and b.

There we have a number of different opinions apparently concerning the historical setting of Iyov. We quote at considerable length because the passage has much to teach us concerning the view which our Sages took of the saga.

> R' Levi bar Chama said: Iyov lived in Moses' days . . . for in *Iyov* we find the word, אֵפוֹ (19:23) as also in connection with Moses, . . . וּבַמֶּה יִוָּדַע אֵפוֹא (*Exodus* 33:16). But perhaps he lived in Isaac's time, for in connection with Isaac, too, we find the same word, מִי אֵפוֹא הוּא הַצָּד צַיִד (*Genesis* 27:33) . . .
>
> Rava said: Iyov lived in the period of the spies . . . [The Gemara bases Rava's opinion on the assumption that when Moses asked the spies to check for עֵץ, *trees*, he meant them to see whether there was among the Canaanites someone righteous enough so that his merits would protect them, as a tree's shade protects those underneath it. This is assumed to refer to Iyov, based on the textual allusion of his native land: Iyov was from the land of עוּץ, *Utz*, which can be related to the word עֵץ, *trees.*]
>
> R' Yochanan said: Iyov was among those who returned from the Babylonian exile, and his *Beis HaMidrash* is situated in Tiberias. [*Bereishis Rabbah* 57:3 adds: And thus they were able to learn from his actions (1:20-21) that a mourner is obliged to tear his clothes and bless God.]
>
> A *Baraisa* taught: R' Elazar said: Iyov lived in the

period of the Judges, for he accused the friends of indulging in *folly* (הֶבֶל; 27:2), and the period of the Judges can be described as a time of כֻּלּוֹ הֶבֶל, *absolute folly.*

R' Yehoshua ben Korcho said: Iyov lived in the days of Ahasuerus, for in *Iyov* we are told that throughout the land no women as beautiful as Iyov's daughters could be found (42:15), and it was during Ahasuerus's reign that efforts were made to find the most beautiful women.

R' Nassan said: Iyov was contemporary with the Queen of Sheba (מַלְכַּת שְׁבָא), for at 1:15 we are told that Sabeans (שְׁבָא) fell upon Iyov's oxen and she-asses.

The *Chachamim* said: Iyov lived in the time of the Chaldeans [*Rashi*: during the days of Nebuchanezzar], as it is written, *The Chaldeans fielded three divisions ...* (1:17).

Others hold: Iyov lived in the days of Jacob, and married his daughter Dinah. This because it is written, *You talk as any senseless woman* (אַחַת הַנְּבָלוֹת; 2:10), while in the matter of Jacob's daughter Dinah it is written, *... For an abomination* (נְבָלָה) *had been done in Israel* (*Genesis* 34:7).

None of the discussants mean to place a specific historical figure into a precise historical context as we would normally understand such an exercise.

A careful examination of this passage makes it abundantly clear that none of the discussants mean to place a specific historical figure into a precise historical context as we would normally understand such an exercise.[1]

The proofs for this assertion are as follows:

1. *The nature of the textual allusions upon which some of the opinions are based:* Even a cursory glance at the textual allusions makes clear that they are more in the nature of acoustic congruencies that suggest mental associations, than solid backing for a historical claim. Let us take, for example the opinion of the *Baraisa* that places Iyov in the time-frame of the Judges because he accused the friends of speaking הֶבֶל *folly*. This is based upon the assessment of the Sages — for which there is no textual basis — that the era of the Judges is best described as כֻּלּוֹ הֶבֶל, *absolute folly*. Now, clearly there is

1. In footnote 1 to 1:1 we cite *Rambam* in *Moreh Nevuchim* that the disparate time-frames suggested by the various sages itself indicate that he was only a *mashal*, a parable, rather than a narrative.

In the light of our discussion here it seems possible that *Rambam* means, as we will now argue, that the word-associations upon which the various judgments are based — yielding the wide range of periods under discussion — themselves imply that all agree with the essential concept that Iyov was only a *mashal*. Whatever the intention of the discussants — see inside for *Maharal's* thinking — they make no attempt at writing history.

no apparent compelling reason to associate the one הֶבֶל with the other. Nevertheless the association is made.

It can be readily seen that the other allusions, too, are not more compelling than this one.

2. *The identity of the discussants*: Opinions are recorded by sages ranging from rather early *Tannaim* to late *Amoraim*, a spread of several hundred years. Among them are R' Yehoshua ben Korcho, who belongs to the generation immediately after R' Akiva (see *Rashi*, *Shavuos* 6a), to Rava, who belongs to the penultimate generation of the *Amoraim*.

Normally *Amoraim* [in this case: R' Levi bar Chamah, Rava, and R' Yochanan], do not argue with *Tannaim* [in this case: R' Elazar, R' Yehoshua ben Korcho, R' Nassan, and the *Chachamim*].

In the rare cases where we find that an *Amora* disagrees with a *Tanna*, that *Amora* is privy to a tradition with a *Tannaic* source. If such were the case with Rava's contention, the problem would be alleviated. However, it appears unlikely that a late *Amora* like Rava should be aware of a *Tannaic* tradition of which R' Yochanan, four generations earlier, was not aware.

3. *R' Yochanan's opinion:* Among all the opinions recorded, that of R' Yochanan appears to be unique: *Iyov was among those who returned from the Babylonian exile, and his Beis HaMidrash is situated in Tiberias.* No attempt is made here to associate this assertion with any Scriptural basis; R' Yochanan states a fact: he knows who Iyov is, knows the precise location of his *Beis HaMidrash*, and, according to *Bereishis Rabbah* cited above, he knows that certain halachic traditions are traceable to Iyov.

R' Yochanan appears to be testifying to the facts as he knows them. After such an unambiguous assertion, what possible basis could Rava have had for attempting a different identification?

From the foregoing it is obvious that this subject is far removed from historical assessments. Clearly all the various opinions are compatible in that they are mutually tolerant notions of the various historical periods each of which could have had its own 'Iyov.'

4. *Rava's opinion:* Rava disagrees with R' Levi bar Chama and asserts that Iyov was not *in the time of Moses,* but *in the time of the spies.* These two times, however, are congruent, since it was Moses who appointed the spies (*Maharal*).

From the foregoing it is obvious that this subject is far removed from historical assessments. Clearly all the various opinions are compatible in that they are mutually tolerant notions of the various historical periods each of which *could* have had its own 'Iyov.' R' Yochanan may know of such a flesh and blood 'Iyov' who happened to live in Tiberias. Rava is not fazed. The *time of the spies* may very well have had its own.

Maharal (Chidushei Aggadah, Bava Basra) helps us understand this concept.

No power in heaven or on earth, no Satan, could, under normal circumstances, have the power that Satan in the Iyov story seems to have enjoyed.

All the discussants begin from a common premise: No power in heaven or on earth, no Satan, could, under normal circumstances, have the power that Satan in the Iyov story seems to have enjoyed. Such authority can be imagined only during a period of unmitigated מִדַּת הַדִּין, *the Attribute of stern uncompromising Justice*, rather than מִדַּת הַחֶסֶד, *the Attribute of Mercy.*

If, then, a book is to be written which has such a Satan as a central figure, its historical setting must be one in which a figure with such authority might be appropriate.

If, then, a book is to be written which has such a Satan as a central figure, its historical setting must be one in which a figure with such authority might be appropriate. The discussion in the *Gemara* centers around the question of which historical period might have been most prone to such unbridled sway of the Attribute of Justice.[1]

For the purpose of our own discussion, this *Gemara* is profoundly significant. Once more, just as in the discussion in *Sotah*, the Sages insist on an explanation for the suffering with which Iyov was afflicted. They refuse to countenance the idea that the narrative can be taken at face-value. Just as *Sotah* postulates a sin which needed to be expiated — in this case Iyov's silence when Pharaoh's diabolical plan was being debated — so too does *Bava Basra* demand an extraneous circumstance which could explain the Satan's power.

But, of all this, the text says nothing at all.

What conclusions are we to draw from this discrepancy

1. *Maharal's* explanations for each of the various opinions — why the particular period which is identified is most prone to the exercise of the מִדַּת הַדִּין — go beyond the scope of this Overview, but we offer one example:

The time of Moses is the time when God gave the Torah to Israel, the historical moment in which Israel is irrevocably elevated to the unique state of being God's chosen people. Such an elevation must, in justice, be warranted. Does Israel deserve such a standing? Are its people sufficiently righteous?

It is by questions such as these, that the Attribute of Justice is energized.

God offers the Satan power of Iyov [in this opinion Iyov is Jewish] in order to test these assumptions.

According to the explanation which we have offered, all the discussants agree to the essential notion that Iyov is not a historical figure — only a *mashal*, a parable. The difference between them and the single opinion (not cited above) recorded in the *Gemara* that states explicitly that Iyov was a *mashal* is this: The *Tannaim* and *Amoraim* cited here believe that some historical setting is required to explain the story. Each chose, for his theoretical 'Iyov,' the period which he considered most suitable. Those who hold differently, deny this need. According to them, the story can stand on its own, without ascribing a historical context.

between the Scriptural text and the Talmudic tradition?

There is a cryptic passage in *D'var Eliyahu*, the commentary to *Iyov* ascribed to the *Gaon of Vilna*. To 1:8, *Have you taken note of my servant, Iyov? For there is no one like him on earth, a man of unquestioning integrity coupled with a probing mind, who fears God and eschews evil!*, he remarks:

> Consider how admirable were Iyov's deeds, that even the Satan had absolutely nothing to say against him, until God Himself brought up the matter by asking, *Have you taken note of My servant Iyov ... a man of unquestioning integrity* ... God Himself testified for him ... And it was for that reason that Iyov cried out so bitterly against his suffering, for he knew himself to be totally innocent ...
>
> But, after God debated him and asserted His rectitude, then he brought offerings [Iyov brought offerings to atone for the friends, not for himself] prayed and regretted deeply that he had originally cried out without justification against the God Who[m he now knew to be] righteous in all His ways.
>
> This is what the Sages meant when they said that Iyov was only a *mashal*. This means that he existed only for this — that people should take him as an example not to question God's ways, for all His ways are just ... [For *Gra's* understanding of *mashal*, see below.]

Gra begins his comment with the assertion that both in his own eyes and in God's, Iyov was totally innocent of any wrongdoing. He ends by asserting that after the debate Iyov was convinced that he had, in fact, deserved his fate. How are the two halves of this comment to be harmonized?

The answer may lie in a difficult passage in Tzophar's first speech. *That He would inform you of the hidden recesses of wisdom, that sagacity has double folds. Know then, that God grants you accommodation from some of your sins!* (11:6) Here Tzophar, as both *Rashi* and *Ramban* understand him, is enunciating a doctrine that is difficult to understand: God is so exalted, the obligation to serve Him so demanding, that by definition, no human being can ever really do enough. There will always be sins of omission or commission of which he is not even aware. As Bildad did before him, Tzophar postulates that Iyov's suffering must be traced to a shortfall in his righteousness. Tzophar's contribution consists of minting the concept that man can sin and be deserving of punishment

Tzophar's contribution consists of minting the concept that man can sin and be deserving of punishment — without even being able to know what he had done wrong.

— without even being able to know what he had done wrong.

In the commentary there we wondered why a person should be punished for sins of which he does not, indeed cannot, know.

We may surmise as follows: Our question would indeed be justified if we looked upon such suffering as purely punitive. It certainly goes against our sense of fairness, that man should be held responsible for sins of which he is not even aware.

But perhaps suffering has a different function. Perhaps it is meant to stimulate a search.

But perhaps suffering has a different function. Perhaps it is meant to stimulate a search. Perhaps, when Tzophar says that we are called to suffer for sins of which we cannot know, he means only that we cannot know of them as long as we live superficial lives. Perhaps, goaded by pain, we can become aware of new vistas, deeper, more intimate visions of ourselves, our responsibilities and abilities. Perhaps, through them, we may even aspire to meet our God anew. Perhaps the light from such an encounter can cast its probing beam into the dark and hidden crevices of our own personality. Perhaps, in the end, by meeting our God — we meet ourselves!

Perhaps this is what *Gra* meant.

Iyov, the old Iyov, was indeed blameless. So he felt about himself, and so did God testify. Had he asked himself about his silence as he sat in on Pharaoh's deliberations he would have experienced no sense of compunction, would have found a hundred different reasons why just this reaction was, under the circumstances, correct. He feels no guilt and — at this stage of his development — Satan may not impute any.

But, in times when an uncompromising Attribute of Justice holds sway, more is demanded.

Iyov is dragged through searing crucibles of agony and despair. Layer by layer the trappings of a support system that has allowed him to live a life not plagued with excessive self- criticism are peeled away. He is left with only himself — and his God.

Iyov is dragged through searing crucibles of agony and despair. Layer by layer the trappings of a support system that has allowed him to live a life not plagued with excessive self-criticism (see particularly ch. 29), are peeled away. He is left with only himself — and his God.

What will he do now? That is the test.

Iyov turns to God, loves Him, prays to Him and cajoles Him, remonstrates with Him, challenges Him, is angered by Him — and, by dint of superhuman trust, determination, and tenacity, eventually beholds Him.

Hearing gives way to seeing (42:5), intellect begets experience. The light by which Iyov sees his God serves also to illuminate hidden crevices in his own soul. By looking outwards Iyov learns to see inwards. Ugly, jagged, danger-infested crags appear where, before, everything had seemed smooth and safe. A darker, more complex, more vulnerable Iyov moves yesterday's hero aside.

In the scheme we have now recognized, neither the ideational underpinnings for the Satan's authority — the historical reality that posits an ambience in which Justice preponderates; nor the immediate justification for his indictment — Iyov's sin of omission during Pharaoh's deliberations — exist at the surface level of the story.

'Iyov' *could* have lived — indeed might live at this very moment — in any historical setting; the dark secrets lurking beneath the surface of his consciousness might have taken any form. The dynamics of the saga demand that the particular form not be known. It is from the very ignorance of these conditions that the stuff of the drama is made.

The dynamics of the saga demand that the particular form not be known. It is from the very ignorance of these conditions that the stuff of the drama is made.

Because of this, the book is silent on any but the surface events. If we are to learn from Iyov's struggles, if we are to plunge to the depths of his despair, if we are to accompany him as slowly and painfully he drags himself out of the morass of his broken spirit, if our ears are to pick up the seismic rumblings of a world beyond our comprehension, if our eyes are to behold the wonders of nature that will point us upon our way back to God — then it is best that we, like him, should be ignorant of any but the immediate experience.

The book tells the story in such a way that we can use it as a guide to navigate the tortuous labyrinths of our own lives. The oral tradition provides the theological infrastructure.

And so, Iyov turns into 'Iyov.' Everyman quarreling against incomprehensible fate.

II. Mashal or LeMashal

Was Iyov a historical figure? [See at 1:1 for discussion.] As we have seen above, it hardly seems to matter. Certainly, whether or not there was ever a man called Iyov who suffered grievous losses, maintained his faith throughout his travail, and ultimately was granted a vision of God — his story was recorded for us only because of its value as a *mashal,* a parable that will illuminate our own lives.

Iyov's story was recorded for us only because of its value as a mashal, a parable that will illuminate our own lives.

We will learn that ultimately — somehow, somewhere — there is an answer to our questions. We will not expect God to appear to us from out of the whirlwind as He did to Iyov. We will not expect to discover the precise reason for the fates that befall us — Iyov, we recall, never did learn the truth (see Introductory Remarks to ch. 38). But all that is unnecessary. Enough that one man found the path to perfect submission and renewed happiness. No sufferer, after that, will ever need to feel forsaken (see Introductory Remarks to ch. 32).

Enough that one man found the path to perfect submission and renewed happiness.

These thoughts may underlie an unusual reading in *Bava Basra* 15a, which appears to have found some currency.

As noted above, the *Gemara* there listed a number of different opinions concerning the historical setting in which Iyov might be placed. In the course of that passage, we read as follows:

> A certain *talmid chacham* sat before R' Shmuel bar Nachmeini and asserted: Iyov never was nor was he ever created (לֹא הָיָה וְלֹא נִבְרָא). He was only a *mashal.* [The latter objected,] if so, why would his name and the name of his city be recorded? [No answer is given to this question.]

It requires only that there be some motive for writing such a mashal.

The concept seems simple enough. It requires only that there be some motive for writing such a *mashal,* and we discuss this aspect of the issue, particularly *Rashi's* opinion, in the *Introduction to the Iyov Commentary.* The unanswered question about the reason for recording the names of the protagonist and his city seems also less than absolutely problematic. In the *Introduction to the Iyov Commentary,* we show that both *R' Saadyah Gaon* and *Rambam* assume that, even in Scriptural writing, *meshalim* are expanded to "flesh out" the details. We assume that this is why the *Gemara* offers no answer to this question.

Nevertheless, there is a record of a different reading of the opinion of the *certain talmid chacham. Pachad Yitzchak* tells that in the tractate of *R' Hai Gaon,* the reading of the relevant phrase was: אִיּוֹב לֹא נִבְרָא אֶלָּא לְמָשָׁל, *Iyov was created only in order to serve as a mashal.* [A ל is added to מָשָׁל and the word הָיָה is eliminated.]

III. The Commentary as It Depicts the Personalities and the Story-Line of the Saga

In the commentary we make certain assumptions about the characters of the various protagonists, and also about the development of the saga's story-line. Though these positions may appear new and unsupported, we take them because they seem to be yielded by internal evidence. We have assumed that there is validity to the pictures projected by the unvarnished text, quite independent of the Rabbinic traditions preserved in various Midrashic or Talmudic texts. We predicate this license upon the assumption that *aggadic* interpretations are often meant to illuminate only one characteristic of a person, rather than to provide an all-embracing portrait. Thus, a Rabbinic inference from a particular expression or turn of phrase may indicate only one aspect among many of the protagonists' personality.[1]

Rabbinic inference from a particular expression or turn of phrase may indicate only one aspect among many of the protagonists' personality.

With this in mind, we review some of our assumptions.

Iyov: As is to be expected, Iyov himself is the greatest enigma with which the book tantalizes the reader. Love and hate, death-wish and passionate affirmation of life, blasphemy and adoration, submission and defiance chase each other in dizzying counterpoint across the ruggedly uneven terrain of his tortured soul. [We have discussed this point on numerous occasions in the commentary. For a partial listing of sources see fn. 1 to Introductory Remarks to ch. 26. See, also, particularly the discussion at 19:27.]

To discover the inner harmony that ultimately makes peace among these and other seemingly dissonant themes, we base the commentary upon Rava's teaching at *Bava Basra* 16b, that אֵין אָדָם נִתְפָּס בִּשְׁעַת צַעֲרוֹ, *No man is held accountable for words uttered during the time of his agony.* This allowed us to view Iyov as a perfectly righteous person whose occasional lapses into near-blasphemy are not expressive of his true feelings and are therefore not to be held against him. Thus, we are able to view Iyov as an unblemished, untarnished hero whose tenacious search for the truth is contrasted to the

This allowed us to view Iyov as a perfectly righteous person whose occasional lapses into near-blasphemy are not expressive of his true feelings and are therefore not to be held against him.

1. A case in point is the issue, raised by the *Tannaim* at *Sotah* 27b, whether Iyov, in his service of God, was motivated by love or by fear. The Mishnah indicates that there are two opinions on this matter, each based upon textual proofs, and this is reinforced by the *Yerushalmi Sotah* 25a which cites Iyov as an example of one who serves God out of fear, even though a number of references had been adduced previously clearly indicating that he was motivated by love.

In actual fact, it is quite clear that taking the book as a whole, there are many ambiguities concerning this matter. In the commentary to 2:3 and, particularly, in the footnote there, we noted that *Ramban* holds that Iyov underwent a religious progression, moving from a relationship based upon fear, to one sustained by love. See also fn. to 9:14 where we demonstrate that there was a constant oscillation between the poles of love and fear, which animates Iyov's thought.

Clearly, then, the proofs adduced by each of the protagonists in the debate are not meant to be absolute. It is more likely that the argument revolves around the question of which of the two motivations seems to preponderate in Iyov's thought.

ineffectiveness and theological naiveté of the friends.

While Rava's insight helped to remove the difficulty of Iyov's extremes of vilification, it was left to us, as readers of the text, to determine the rationale for Iyov's constant questioning, challenging and hectoring of God. We discovered this in the tension between the poles of *temimus* and *chanufah*, which we found to be one of the major themes of the book. [We have come back to this idea again and again throughout the commentary. It is discussed in greatest detail at 6:13.] Iyov asserts that *temimus* — which we have rendered as *unquestioning integrity* — occasionally not only tolerates but even mandates trenchant challenges. The very integrity of absolute faith confers the right, as it were, to insist upon an explanation when God, by the way He acts (and what man perceives) seems not to fit in some recognizable category, such as His claim to be a Just King and a Loving Father. [For elaboration, see also at 6:5-6 and 7:11.]

Iyov asserts that temimus — which we have rendered as unquestioning integrity — occasionally not only tolerates but even mandates trenchant challenges.

With all this well established, we nevertheless found that Iyov's reaction is not the only possible one, nor even the best. Throughout the book, especially in the commentary to 6:2, we have compared his attitude to catastrophe with that of Nachum Ish Gamzu (*Taanis* 21a). We found that Iyov's challenges were more suited to the gentile world that had greeted God's offer to give them the Torah, with the demand to know, מַה כְּתִיב בָּהּ, *What does it contain*?, than to the Jewish people whose, נַעֲשֶׂה וְנִשְׁמַע, *We undertake to do. Let us then hear what our duties are to be*! became for all times the paradigm for perfect submission to God's will. [This theme recurs throughout the commentary. It is first broached in fn. 2 to 1:1.]

These, are the ideas which have informed our approach to the character of Iyov. The thrust of this approach leaves us with the feeling — which cannot be traced to any specific quote in the book — that Iyov passed the test that, at the Satan's urging, had been imposed upon him.

We may say with some confidence that the approach delineated here is based upon the classical commentators to *Iyov*. It is not, apparently, universally accepted. Thus at *Bava Basra* 15b, we have a *Baraisa*, as follows:

> There was once, among the gentile people, a *chassid* whose name was Iyov. He was placed into this world with only the purpose that he might earn his just reward. God exposed him to suffering and [rather than submitting quietly] he began to curse and to blaspheme. Because of

this, God doubled his reward in This World so that he might be driven out of the World to Come.

[We have discussed Iyov as a man of This World rather than of the World to Come in fn. 2 to 1:3.]

The Friends: It is not easy to assign a clearly defined role to the friends. The problem is exacerbated by the fact that their portrait as depicted by the Sages seems quite different from the one which is yielded by the text.

Their portrait as depicted by the Sages seems quite different from the one which is yielded by the text.

If Iyov is indeed the hero of the piece, it would be natural to see the friends as villains, or, at best, as pietists whose one-dimensional world-view is inadequate for the purpose at hand. Iyov's deeply probing, agony-driven, intellect functions at a level far beyond their's.

Though it seems unlikely that the Author would use simpletons as a foil for Iyov's incisive thinking, the text leaves room for such a perception. Beyond the explicit condemnations — by the Author's description of Elihu's thinking at 32:3 and explicitly by God at 42:8 — the friends are treated so disdainfully by Iyov — condoned as it were by the Author who does not criticize him, and on the contrary appears to collude with him as we shall see below — as to leave very little room for respect.

Iyov's cavalier treatment of the friends is manifest in the following areas:

In the first place, from the very beginning, he ignores them completely. They have come from afar, have sat silently for seven days in an expression of solidarity, an effort to share the burden of his agonies, and Iyov does not even acknowledge their presence. Worse, by implication, he insults them. His first speech consists of but a single theme: The wish that he had never been born, or that now that the fact of his existence is beyond repair, he might make his way to the grave without delay. Has he then nothing to live for? Does the love of three such friends mean nothing to him?

For all the role they play in Iyov's thought, the friends might as well not have existed.

By implication the answer is, No! For all the role they play in Iyov's thought, the friends might as well not have existed. This utter disregard of the value of their friendship is not a momentary aberration brought on by the sheer horror of his new situation, but is replayed in a context in which we could have expected otherwise. In chapters 29 and 30 Iyov casts a nostalgic eye upon his past, allows the memory of better days to tantalize him. He talks of the power he had once wielded, the respect which he had once enjoyed, the secure home suffused by the bright light of God's presence that had once been his — but never about friends whose love and companionship had sustained him. Our Sages teach, או חַבְרוּתָא או מִיתוּתָא, *either companionship or death* (*Taanis* 23a); Rava (*Bava Basra* 16b) quotes a popular saying that, *Let a man have friends like those of Iyov, or choose death* — yet there is still not a word from Iyov himself — not one word about how the friendship of these three had filled his life with substance and meaning.

There is still not a word from Iyov himself — not one word about how the friendship of these three had filled his life with substance and meaning.

More. In Introductory Remarks to chapter 29 we examine that speech carefully and take note of its apparent redundancy. Iyov had already won the debate, the friends had already bowed out of the discussion. Why, we wondered, did Iyov feel constrained to go over all the old ground once more? We concluded that the answer may be that, in a sense, there could have been no more unequivocal refutation of the friends than to say that, after the avalanche of words and thoughts they had shared, after three rounds of fierce give and take — absolutely nothing had changed. Iyov's complaints, the intensity of his suffering, are precisely the same as they had been all along. The friends had not, by even one iota, been able to change anything at all.

Iyov's complaints, the intensity of his suffering, are precisely the same as they had been all along. The friends had not, by even one iota, been able to change anything at all.

Iyov does not bother to tell them in so many words, but the import of the speech is clear. You have been no use to me at all, and for all the help you have given me, might just as well not have existed.

Even in the heat of the debate Iyov seems to ignore what the friends have to say. We have noted this throughout the book, but it can best be illustrated from the structure of the second round. As can be seen from the relevant speeches, all three friends, at this stage of the debate, make the same point: the tranquility of the wicked is illusory; justice does or will prevail and either now or later they will suffer for their wrongdoing. In his responses to Eliphaz and Bildad, Iyov ignores this theme completely. To Eliphaz he reacts by bemoaning his fate, and to Bildad, by pleading passionately for understanding. He seems to have been absolutely deaf to their arguments. Only after Tzophar's speech does Iyov take up the issue. Surely, if Iyov had taken either of the first two friends seriously we could have expected some attempt to rebut the points they had so carefully presented.

The Author himself, as it were, assists in the effort by giving the friends patently weak arguments to counter Iyov's legitimate complaints.

The belittling of the friends is not limited to Iyov. The Author himself, as it were, assists in the effort by giving the friends patently weak arguments to counter Iyov's legitimate complaints. Once more, we can draw one of the most graphic examples from the second round. Each of the three friends makes essentially the same point. The problem of רָשָׁע וְטוֹב לוֹ, *the tranquility of the wicked,* simply does not exist — the wicked do not live tranquil lives. No arguments are presented, no proofs mustered. The idea is presented starkly — as a matter of fact. In his response to Tzophar's speech (ch. 21), Iyov states quite simply that the opposite is true. With graphic clarity he paints the picture — familiar to all of us — of just how happy and solidly ensconced the wicked often are. Instinctively, the reader agrees; his own experiences bear him out. Iyov seems to offer his friends no argument of any substance. They have erected straw men, and it takes little to knock them down.

With graphic clarity he paints the picture of just how happy and solidly ensconced the wicked often are.

Perhaps the clearest example of this weighting of the ambience of the debate against the friends can be found in Eliphaz's third speech (ch. 22): *Clearly your evil is overwhelming, there is no end to your iniquities. For without any justification do you take pledges from your brothers, tear off the garments from the naked. You would never give an exhausted man water to drink, would withhold bread from the starving ... You have driven away widows emptyhanded, broken the strength of orphans.*

Eliphaz says this to a man concerning whom God had said to the Satan, *Have you taken note of my servant, Iyov? For there is no one like him on earth, a man of unquestioning integrity coupled with a probing mind, who fears God and eschews evil!* In Eliphaz's denunciation there seems to be a vindictive spitefulness, in which the need to assert his theological position has blinded him to reality. There simply is no truth to anything of which he accuses Iyov.

Thus the impression projected by the narrative.

The tradition of the Sages preserved in Midrashic and aggadic literature paints a quite different picture.

The tradition of the Sages preserved in Midrashic and *aggadic* literature paints a quite different picture.

In the first place, *Bava Basra* 16b lists the three friends among the seven prophets whose prophecy was directed to the gentile nations. Now while the gift of prophecy does not necessarily indicate that the recipient is righteous — Balaam is among the seven — it certainly seems to preclude the picture of bumbling naiveté which we have traced from the narrative.

Other Rabbinic sources say much the same thing. Thus *Koheles Rabbah* 7 teaches that the three friends were imbued with רוּחַ הַקּוֹדֶשׁ, the *Divine spirit.* Furthermore, we have the tradition that Eliphaz was a *tzaddik*, a righteous man who had completely disassociated himself from his evil father, Esau (*Yalkut Iyov*, 897) and who, ... *because he had been reared upon Isaac's lap, merited that the Divine spirit rest upon him* (*Rashi* 4:1).

The Rabbinic tradition seems to be in absolute conflict with the impressions created by the simple meaning of the text.

In effect, with regard to the friends this leaves us in the same predicament we noted earlier about Iyov. In both instances the Rabbinic tradition seems to be in absolute conflict with the impressions created by the simple meaning of the text. In the case of Iyov the tradition changes him from hero to something considerably less. The friends, by contrast, are elevated from inept bunglers to Divinely inspired saints. What are we to make of this?

IV. Surface and Sub-Surface in the Iyov Saga

We can readily see that the two areas in which the Rabbinic tradition appears to differ from the written record are interconnected. The written record which makes Iyov the hero of the drama must, of necessity, present the friends as failures. Conversely, the tradition which portrays Iyov as a disappointment will portray the friends positively.

But, are the two compatible? It goes without saying that we cannot countenance a real contradiction between the written record and the Rabbinic tradition.

The answer is that the two are indeed compatible if we postulate, as we have done so many times throughout the commentary, and as discussed above, that the book's purpose is to present the correct approach to suffering from the point of view of the this-worldly man, of the gentile nations who insisted upon examining the Torah's demands before declaring themselves willing to accept it.

The answer is that the two are indeed compatible if we postulate, as we have done so many times throughout the commentary, and as discussed above, that the book's purpose is to present the correct approach to suffering from the point of view of the this-worldly man, of the gentile nations who insisted upon examining the Torah's demands before declaring themselves willing to accept it. As such, it recognizes that Iyov's is by no means the only, nor even the best, of possible attitudes. [See, at this point, particularly Introductory Remarks to 42:10.]

Once we grant this thesis, we may propose the existence, as it were, of two entirely discrete, self-contained worlds. The postulates and assumptions of the one are not only different but antagonistic to those of the other.

In the world portrayed in the simple text of the book, the one in which Iyov moved, thought and lived, his philosophy holds unchallenged sway. He is the undisputed hero; the friends merely props or foils against which his superior understanding and bearing might the better be brought into sharp relief. In the other world, however, the one the Sages detected at the sub-surface level, the tables are turned. There, truth is more subtle, appearances less persuasive. There, the ineptitude of the friends turns into passionate preachings that lay bare the emptiness of Iyov's protests. There, his argumentativeness is revealed as blasphemy, his values as shallow surface-simplicities that lack the infinitely nuanced truths of a more profound, less physical world. These worlds do not contradict one another any more than the roiling vital life of the sea-bed contradicts the deceptive calm of the surface waters. They coexist, each granting the other validity within its own sphere. But — and this is vital — mutual tolerance is not synonymous with an identity of values. Where values are concerned, each world is jealous and uncompromising. The denizens of the one are strangers in the other.

Where values are concerned, each world is jealous and uncompromising. The denizens of the one are strangers in the other.

Let us begin our analysis with Eliphaz's third speech. Above, we noted the patent falseness of his accusations, that they had no basis in reality. Had God Himself not testified that Iyov was beyond any possible reproach?

Perhaps, after all, Eliphaz's allegations were not as unfounded as they originally sounded to us.

Then Reuben went and lay with Bilhah, his father's concubine (*Genesis* 35:22). A straightforward enough statement. Nevertheless, as is well known, the Sages do not take it at face value. In their tradition, he never violated his father's wife. Rather, in protest at what he perceived as Jacob's cavalier treatment of his mother, Reuben moved his father's bed into her tent.

We have here entered a world in which actions are defined by their essence rather than by their outer contours. With uncompromising honesty, the Torah cuts through the outer layer of Reuven's "commendable" deed and reveals the deeply embedded character-fault which made possible his unpardonable interference in his father's intimate affairs. Taken a little further that flaw could have led Reuben to violate Bilhah. The two usurpations of what should by right be his father's prerogative — worlds apart in the world of action — are identical in essence.

What appears as unblemished innocence at one level may well be viewed as actionable transgression at another.

Above, we discussed the relationship between the tradition of the Sages that Iyov was punished for having kept silent during Pharaoh's deliberations, and the text that makes no mention of this at all. We traced the solution to the doctrine of the *double folds* with which Tzophar endows *sagacity*. We noted that what appears as unblemished innocence at one level may well be viewed as actionable transgression at another. We can now enlarge this scheme and have it encompass the whole gamut of Eliphaz's accusations. It is true that God had testified to Iyov's blameless life. But, Eliphaz tells Iyov, that blamelessness holds good only in the world in which you have made your home — the gentile, surface world of action. Do you not realize, Eliphaz urges passionately, that many of your ostensible charities — to the extent that they were performed out of a sense of *noblesse oblige* rather than out of genuine love for your fellow man (see fn. 1 to 29:2 and commentary to 31:1) — could really be conceived as acts of cruel indifference?

Let us reconsider the *Baraisa* from *Bava Basra* 15b, which we quoted above, and which we can see to open new vistas upon the Satan's incitement. *There was once, among the gentile people, a chassid whose name was Iyov. He was placed into this world with only the purpose that he might earn his just reward.*

What precisely is the meaning of this phrase? In what sense was Iyov placed in this world, *to earn his just reward*? *Rashi* is silent.

Iyov, a gentile whose rightful place is within the here and now of Olam Hazeh, had been sent into the world to see whether, perhaps, he could lift himself beyond the limitations which his nature imposes upon him and to become a creature of the World to Come.

From the context we might suggest the following meaning. Iyov, a gentile whose rightful place is within the here and now of *Olam Hazeh*, had been sent into the world to see whether, perhaps, he could lift himself beyond the limitations which his nature imposes upon him and to become a creature of the World to Come. Perhaps it is there in the land of the spirit, that his *just reward* is located? This is the ultimate meaning of the contrast that the Satan draws between Iyov and Abraham. The two occupy two discrete worlds. Is the one not vastly superior to the other? The Satan demands a test. Can Iyov rise to the occasion?

Iyov fails, but not within the context of his *own* reality. There, in truth, he passes his tests with flying colors. That is the story with which the open text deals. But, at the level of the potential that he might have made his own, in terms of the new world that he could have conquered ... *he began to curse and to blaspheme. Because of this, God doubled his reward in this world so that he might be driven out of the World to Come.* From Nachum Ish Gamzu's standpoint, Iyov's questings for understanding were blasphemous.

A detailed exposition of all the ramifications which the

suggested theory might have for all the sections of the book lies beyond the scope of this Overview. However, the interested reader will have no difficulty in working out for himself how the radically different world-views of the respective protagonists will yield vastly different perspectives upon such issues as the apparent tranquility of the wicked. The justification from the friends' perspective takes the long-term view in which justice prevails inevitably. By contrast, Iyov the this-worldly man must view matters as they appear in the short run.

The study of the book demands a constant vigilance so that we are awake to the double meaning of every passage.

The study of the book demands a constant vigilance so that we are awake to the double meaning of every passage. There is the plain meaning of the text — it is that which has been the basis for our commentary — and there is the underlying tension that is produced as we recognize the friends attempting to help Iyov transcend himself and find his place in a new, more wonderful world.

Indeed we now understand Rav's popular saying, *Let a man have friends like those of Iyov, or choose death* (*Bava Basra* 16b). In the text, as it stands, these friends had appeared to us as dismal failures — insensitive, locked into single-minded, single-dimensional simplicities, unloving, and ultimately reduced to open distortions in the defense of the defenseless. In reality, as we now realize, they were the best friends a man could have. They steeled themselves from excessive pity so that they might goad Iyov to the greatness that beckoned him. They talked of depths he could not plumb, of heights he could never scale. He did not understand them. Nor did we who, tied as we were to the mode in which the book is written, saw only the horizons that bounded Iyov's world.

Now we know better. There is a more authentic truth. It was he — not they — who failed.

Adar 5754

Rabbi Moshe Eisemann
with Rabbi Nosson Scherman

◆§ Introduction To The Iyov Commentary

Within the truly vast body of Iyov commentary, greater probably than that for any other of the Biblical books, there are essentially two approaches to the interpretation and understanding of the Iyov story.

The majority of both earlier and later commentators feel that the purpose of the book is to elucidate one or another of the great theological issues which must engage the mind of any thinking man. These concern matters such as the nature and degree of God's providence, the concepts of reward and punishment and the nagging problem of why the righteous occasionally suffer and the wicked frequently live tranquil lives. These commentators view the speeches as components of a debate in which positions are staked out, points made and refuted, with victory expected to go to one or another of the contestants. The hallmark of this approach is the tendency to provide, either at the beginning or at the end of every speech, summations of the motifs which have been touched, what has been conceded and what disputed, and where, at this or that given point, the discussion stands. *Ramban* is representative of this approach as are *Ralbag* and *Metzudos*. *Rambam* too, although he delineates his ideas in the *Moreh Nevuchim* rather than in a verse by verse commentary on the book, belongs to this group. Of the later commentators *Malbim*, among many others, takes this approach.

Other commentators, among them *Rashi*, *R' Yosef Kara* and *Rabbeinu Meyuchas* offer no summations as part of their commentary, nor do they ever hint at a formal theological debate. They limit themselves to the interpretation of individual words and phrases, guide us by indirection rather than by explication, and let the story speak to us at the multitude of levels which we would expect of *Kisvei HaKodesh* (Sacred Writings). They trust us, the students, to listen attentively to what the book has to teach us.

It seems likely that they see the book as having an altogether different agenda. It does not at all purport to elucidate the theological problems of the philosopher but tells a human story. It is a saga of crashing pains, well-meaning, fumbling and ultimately ineffectual attempts at comforting, of friendship gone awry, of sublime religious ecstasy warring with bitter disillusion in a God Who refuses to allow Himself to be understood, of erratic leaps between submission and rebellion, of sensitive empathizing, of revelation and reconciliation. It wishes to teach us how to deal with people — not with problems.

The nature of debate — as the book is seen by the commentators belonging to the first genre — requires that each speech be carefully structured, and that, moreover, a logical and consistent progression lead from speech to speech, and from protagonist to protagonist. Because of this, individual verses can never be understood independently, but must be interpreted within the system which the particular commentator has worked out for himself. This, for practical purposes, makes the task of the anthologizer impossible. Where in other Biblical books, the unit under consideration might be a small passage, a chapter or, sometimes even a series of chapters — in the case of *Iyov* it has to be the whole complex book! For each sentence the entire gamut of available commentary would have to be made available since the interpretation of this particular sentence would depend upon what — in the eyes of this or that particular commentator — was said before, and would — once more in each respective system — in turn, influence what comes after. If a reasonably complete survey of the available literature were undertaken we would, in place of an anthology, have a listing — from beginning to end — of entire commentaries.

Because of these very real considerations it was decided to concentrate upon just two commentators.

Rashi would of course provide the base for the commentary. The close scrutiny of his ideas which we will provide later in these Introductory Remarks, particularly his gloss to *Bava Basra* 15a, will yield that in all likelihood he would subscribe to the second of these two possibilities. However, as is his custom throughout his commentary to *Tanach*, his remarks are relatively sparse, and this forces us to look to the text itself and to allow its nuances to guide us through the complexities of the book. Our reading of these nuances can certainly not be ascribed to *Rashi*. The most that can be said is that he has left us the room to read the sacred text closely and allow it to speak to us.

We will go to *Ramban* to be representative of the first approach.

Obviously, throughout the commentary we will draw upon a wide range of other commentators — to flesh out, to augment, to clarify, to yield insights where *Rashi* and *Ramban* either remain silent or are unclear.

Both the approach of *Rashi* and that of *Ramban* require further analysis, and we shall give them our careful attention in the course of these Introductory Remarks. In the meanwhile, however, since it is unthinkable that any *Iyov* commentary would ignore luminaries like *R' Saadyah Gaon*, *Rambam*, and among the later commentators, *Malbim*, we shall devote a short survey to the ideas of each of them.

Our all-too-brief encounter with the immortal creations of these three commentators, affords us an opportunity to discuss a fundamental issue in the field of *Parshanus HaMikra*, the interpretation and elucidation of Biblical texts. It is an issue which cuts to the core of our perception of *Kisvei HaKodesh* as *holy* writ, that is, as Divinely dictated, or at the very least, Divinely inspired compositions which — because they are not human creations — ought not to be subject to human shortcomings or foibles.

The Sacred Writings: It was *Malbim* who dedicated the awesome power of his creative genius to the proposition that *Kisvei HaKodesh* cannot be viewed from the same perspective which we use when judging other literary compositions. His credo is stated forthrightly and unambiguously in a three-point exposition of the principles upon which his commentary is to be based (Introduction to *Isaiah*). They are:

1. The poetry of the prophets will never contain redundancies inserted simply for the sake of beauty [כֶּפֶל עִנְיָן בְּמִלּוֹת שׁוֹנוֹת] . . . There will never be two sentences which have identical meanings, no two metaphors designed to describe the same matter, no synonyms without subtle differences between them.
2. No words are ever chosen arbitrarily. Whenever a particular word is used we can be certain that this word, and only this word, can fulfill the task assigned to it. No other expression could have been substituted.
3. We must never expect a shell which is empty or a body which is not animated by a soul. No single phrase appears that does not contain some deep and meaningful message. Thus, and only thus, can we approach the words of the Living God.

Malbim holds fast to these ideas in his gigantic commentary to *Iyov*. But, in addition to the requirements which adherence to these principles imposes, the format in which *Iyov* is written creates some conditions all its own. We quote:

> Clearly, a book which is written in the form of a dialogue in which a number of people debate one another, must project a number of positions equal to the number of the protagonists — each disputant defending one particular point of view in his presentation. For, if the issue under debate, could be viewed from only two perspectives, the author would have limited the debate to two discussants. Manifestly, then, since there are three friends arguing with Iyov, each of them must have a position which is different from those defended by his colleagues. And so, too, the fourth protagonist [Elihu] who comes last, must have a unique contribution to make. Thus did *Rambam* in his *Moreh Nevuchim*, followed by all straight-thinking men, attempt to assign discrete ideas to each of the discussants . . .

Now it is true that, as we shall see below, *Rambam* does, indeed, have each of the protagonists project a discrete view. However, he, in common with *R' Saadyah Gaon*, certainly does not share *Malbim's* view of the economy of Scriptural writing.

Thus, we quote the famous passage in the prologue to the *Moreh HaNevuchim*, in which *Rambam* discusses the use of *mashal* (parable) — the major pedagogical tool of any competent instructor, as *Rambam* sees it — in the prophetic books.

> Know then, that two different kinds of *meshalim* are used in the prophetic literature. There are those *meshalim* in which every single word has a positive function, and there are those in which the *mashal* in its

totality sheds light upon the *nimshal* (lesson to be conveyed) but contains many words which have no parallel in the *nimshal* but were added only to beautify the *mashal* or contribute to its inner logic [וְיָבוֹאוּ בְּאוֹתוֹ מָשָׁל מִלִּים רַבּוֹת מְאוֹד שֶׁאֵין כָּל מִלָּה מֵהֶן מוֹסִיפָה דָּבָר בְּאוֹתוֹ עִנְיָן הַנִּמְשָׁל אֶלָּא נֶאֶמְרוּ לְיַפּוֹת הַמָּשָׁל וְהַסְדָּרַת הַדְּבָרִים בּוֹ] ... Given this, there is no reason at all, when confronted with *meshalim* of this second category, to worry over the use of this or that phrase [... אַל תַּטְרִיד אֶת מַחֲשַׁבְתְּךָ לוֹמַר וּמַה עִנְיָן ...] ... For it has no function other than to create an appropriate ambience ... [... כִּי כָּל זֶה הֶמְשֵׁךְ לְפִי פְּשַׁט הַמָּשָׁל ...]

And more to the point, from *Rambam's* analysis of the book of *Iyov* in his *Moreh HaNevuchim* 3:22:

> ... It is my desire to make Iyov's ideas and those of his friends clear to you. I will do this through proofs which I will *collect from within each of their speeches*. Do not concern yourself with all the rest of the things which they say. These are said only because the context requires them as I have explained to you earlier. [אֲבָל רְצוֹנִי לְבָאֵר לְךָ הַהַשְׁקָפָה הַמְיוּחֶסֶת לְאִיּוֹב וְהַהַשְׁקָפָה הַמְיוּחֶסֶת לְכָל אֶחָד מֵחֲבֵרָיו מַה הִיא, בִּרְאָיוֹת אֲלַקְּטֵם מִדִּבְרֵי כָּל אֶחָד מֵהֶם, וְאַל תִּפְנֶה לְכָל יֶתֶר הַדְּבָרִים שֶׁחִיֵּיב אֲמִירָתָם שֶׁטֶף הַלָּשׁוֹן כְּמוֹ שֶׁבֵּאַרְתִּי לְךָ ...]

In accordance with this view, we find both *R' Saadyah Gaon* and *Rambam* isolating key phrases in each of the speeches of the various protagonists, because the ideas expressed in them are the ones which are central to the position of this particular discussant, and relegating large sections of each of the speeches to a secondary rank. To illustrate, we quote *R' Saadyah Gaon* in his introduction to *Iyov*.

> [One of the difficulties which people find in understanding this book derives from] the need to isolate those verses which are the essence of each speech ... My own commentary will] begin with the pilot verse in every speech which I will elucidate in such a way that it is separated from the subsidiary verses ...

In addition, we will find that *R' Saadyah Gaon* — in contradistinction to the point made by *Malbim* — has the three friends defending only one position.

R' Saadyah Gaon: *R' Yosef Kapah*, the contemporary translator and interpreter of *R' Saadyah Gaon*, has some ambivalence about how he should translate R' Saadyah Gaon's Arabic title of the book. He reports that, originally he had felt that the correct translation would be, סֵפֶר הָאִזּוּן, the *Book of Balance*, because its function is, indeed, to lend balance and direction to man's outlook on life. It aims to create harmony among human drives and to help us to subordinate our ego-drives to a higher goal. Upon reflection, however, he decided that a more correct rendering would be, סֵפֶר הַצִּדּוּק, the *Book of Justification*, because its fundamental purpose is to demonstrate the essential justice which informs God's stewardship of human affairs and to make clear that none of His actions are the result of arbitrariness.

R' Saadyah Gaon takes as his point of departure the assumption that God's relationship to the world is one of all-encompassing and unstinting חֶסֶד, *altruistic goodness*. Clearly then some explanation for the reality of suffering is required. He isolates three possible causes: Suffering can serve as an educational tool much as a father chastises his son in order to make him learn; it can be a punishment and cleansing agent where sin has been committed; and it can be used to test one's faith in God — so that when it is borne as it should be borne, it might bring great reward in this world and the next.

But, people find it difficult to cope with pain. When exposed to suffering they become confused and rebellious, are unable to apply their theoretical knowledge to the reality of their agony. Because of this, God found it helpful to provide us with a role-model — one righteous man who refused to be cowed or disoriented by his terrible fate, so that we might learn the art of life from him. This is the reason why the saga of Iyov was preserved for us in Scripture.

When Iyov was smitten, unaware of the third alternative — that his travail might be the very means by which he would be able to earn untold bliss — and fully convinced that he neither needed the educational nor deserved the punitive mode of suffering, he was forced to the conclusion that God's omnipotence entitled Him to cause suffering not because it was deserved but simply because He willed it [9:12]. The friends — rightly — refused to countenance such an assumption but could think of no explanation other than that Iyov must have sinned grievously and that his suffering belonged to the punitive mode [for Eliphaz, 4:7-9; for Bildad, 8:11-13; for Tzophar, 11:20]. It took Elihu to suggest the truth — that suffering may be justified as a test of the victim's relationship to his God [33:30].

In the event, Iyov triumphed over the Satan's challenge, and was duly rewarded.

Rambam: In contrast to *R' Saadyah Gaon* who, as we saw above, thinks that the aim of the book is to help people cope with life's vicissitudes, by providing Iyov as a role-model, *Rambam* sees the book as a systematic presentation of various attitudes towards Divine Providence [מָשָׁל לְבֵאוּר הַשְׁקָפוֹת בְּנֵי אָדָם בְּהַשְׁגָּחָה] in the face of the observed fact that many righteous people suffer and many wicked people live happy and tranquil lives [צַדִּיק וְרַע לוֹ, רָשָׁע וְטוֹב לוֹ].

This problem had caused many thinkers to conclude (erroneously) that God has no knowledge of human affairs — a concept which, once they had adopted it they proceeded to buttress by means of all kinds of erroneous philosophical legerdemain. They had reached this conclusion because of the perceived unacceptability of any alternative. For, if God does have knowledge of this world, we would, in consideration of the injustice which prevails, have to conclude either that He is willing to countenance these horrors — He just does not care — or, that He is impotent and cannot change things if He would. Both these alternatives were deemed unacceptable, and willy-nilly it (erroneously) follows that God must be ignorant of what is happening.

The book of *Iyov* is meant, in part, to dispel these false ideas.

The five protagonists were all towering figures, paragons of piety and wisdom. Each felt the need to grapple with the intractable reality of a world apparently run amok, in which there is no discernible pattern which might point to a just and caring God. Each presents his own solution. Among them they represent all the ideas which reasonable men had worked out for themselves. The differences between them are profound. But, as significant as those differences are, there are among them common assumptions which are no less important. These are the absolute conviction that God knows everything and that God is just. The thoughts of those other philosophers — that God is ignorant of human affairs — is not even considered.

Of the first four protagonists — Iyov and the three friends — only Eliphaz is privy to the truth as the Torah teaches it. His contention is that all that happens to man, be it bliss or suffering, is determined only by his own actions. There is reward, there is punishment — and there is nothing else [22:5].[1]

Iyov, writhing in agony while supposing himself to be innocent of any wrongdoing, cannot accept this thesis. Since he will not even consider the possibility that God might not be aware of what transpires in this world, he can find no explanation for his fate other than that God is simply too exalted to care about what happens to man. As we humans are unconcerned about the fate of the insects which crawl around upon our floor, so too, Iyov claims at several points, is God uninterested in our fate. It is not that He does not know, but that He does not care [9:22-23, 21:23-26 and elsewhere]! By the end of the book, Iyov will, of course, have discarded these pernicious ideas — else he could not have been described as having triumphed over his adversities. But, within the debate, it is this position which he defends.

Bildad believes that a perfectly just God might yet expose an innocent man to suffering, because this would be a means of increasing his subsequent reward [8:6-7], while Tzophar believes that God's omnipotence is sufficient reason for anything which happens. The cause invariably lies within His inscrutable will [... כִּי הַכֹּל נוֹהֵג כְּפִי הָרָצוֹן הַמּוּחְלָט וְאֵין לְחַפֵּשׂ לְמַעֲשָׂיו סִבָּה כְּלָל, וְאֵין לוֹמַר לָמָּה עָשָׂה זֶה וְלֹא מַדּוּעַ ...] [11:5-7]. [This is the opinion which *R' Saadyah Gaon* ascribed to Iyov — see above.]

These, then are the options which the book sets before the reader. Contrary to our expectations, no judgment is made which forces us to side with Eliphaz [representative of the Torah's view] over any of the others. By having Iyov live in the land of עוּץ, which word, while in the context it is clearly a proper noun, nevertheless resonates in our mind with the concept of, עֵצָה, *profound and*

1. *Rambam*, in his short synopsis of the book, does not state expressly how Eliphaz — or the Torah — will address those instances in which it is clearly impossible to say that suffering is the fruit of sin.

This issue is discussed in various places in *Moreh Nevuchim*. See particularly the fifty-first chapter of the third part.

productive thinking, the author challenges us to reach our own conclusion [וּכְאִילוּ יֹאמַר לְךָ חֲשֹׁב בְּמָשָׁל זֶה וְהִתְבּוֹנֵן בּוֹ וְדַע עִנְיָנוֹ וְהָבֵן הַהַשְׁקָפָה הַנְּכוֹנָה אֵיזוֹ הִיא].

This, because the author has in store for us a lesson that is more important than even the knowledge of which of the four models which have been presented is the correct one.

That message is the soul of first Elihu's and then God's speeches, and it constitutes the real goal of the book [וְזוֹ הָיְתָה מַטְּרַת סֵפֶר אִיּוֹב בִּכְלָלוּתוֹ]. It is not so important that Iyov should receive the correct answer to his questions. Eliphaz is the repository of this answer, and it is hoped that the reader will be aware of this. It is vastly important that he know that the question ought not, in the first place, to have been asked. The one, major and unforgivable error that Iyov — and indeed the three friends — had made, was to trivialize God, to create Him, as it were, in their own image. Misled by the limitations of language which force us to use terms which describe human involvement and human stewardship for God's relationship with man, they had made the mistake of thinking that God's ways can be understood — and therefore challenged — by the human mind. By pointing to the wonders of nature — so clearly beyond human ken or grasp — Elihu, and later God, demonstrate Iyov's folly.

The *denoument* of the saga comes at the moment that Iyov grasps this truth:

> Once man realizes this, it will be simple for him to bear any and all suffering. His agonies will not generate doubts concerning God — whether He is aware or is not aware, whether He watches over us or doesn't. They will, on the contrary, only serve to increase his love of God as we read at the end of this vision, *Therefore I revile* [all that I valued before] *and have reconciled myself to the dust and ashes* [in which, because of my illness, I wallowed]. [See comm. there.] And this accords with the teaching of the Sages [concerning the religious grandeur of those who] . . . Serve [God] out of love, and rejoice in suffering (*Shabbos* 88b).

Here *Rambam* leads us to the triumphant ending of the Iyov saga as he perceives it. God gifted us with this tale of struggle and ultimate victory so that we might aspire to the highest pinnacle of religious fulfillment. A love of God which will blanket out all doubts and questions and leave only the joy which even suffering can bring when we know that it comes from a caring, loving God.

Malbim: As we have seen, *R' Saadyah Gaon* and *Rambam* share the opinion that in a work such as *Iyov* we must not expect that every passage, let alone every word, contribute to the main theme. Pilot phrases are sifted out which reveal the true and central thinking of the speaker.

Such a system is clearly not without its pitfalls. How, from among the avalanche of words, are we to isolate which is the particular phrase which carries the weight of the argument? We need only think of Iyov and Tzophar to see that the method, by no means, produces even results. *R' Saadyah Gaon* had seen 9:12 — the concept that God's Will is self-justifying — as the key-phrase in Iyov's thinking, while *Rambam* gives pride of place to 9:22-23 and the like, which explain suffering on the basis of God's lack of concern. What *R'Saadyah Gaon* had defined as the main thrust of Iyov's thought, *Rambam* assigns to Tzophar, while *R' Saadyah Gaon's* understanding of Tzophar's argument — 8:11-13, suffering comes as the wages of sin — *Rambam* assigns to Eliphaz.

But, even apart from this difficulty, *Malbim* cannot make peace with the thought that *Kisvei HaKodesh* should contain any words which are not essential to the message. As the passages which we quoted from him, above, make clear, he is committed to an interpretation of *Iyov* which not only accounts for every single word, but which will explain that word as it functions within the thinking of the particular protagonist in whose speech it occurs.

Malbim's system is too intricate to reproduce here in even a shortened form. We mention him in these Introductory Remarks only in order to explain why such an important commentator has not been given his due in our commentary. The explanation lies in the stern structure, the rigid, unbending insistence that the book is a mathematical edifice in which the logic of each piece depends utterly upon the logic of the whole, which his thinking imposes upon him. One cannot anthologize *Malbim* to *Iyov* — no single piece makes sense without all the rest — one can only translate the entire work.

Rashi: As stated above, the basis for the commentary will, of course, be *Rashi.*[1]

The school of thought of which we believe *Rashi* to be representative, is one which views the Iyov saga not as a debate of theological issues, but as a drama detailing — for reasons which will become clear — the interactions between the various protagonists. It is important to examine whether, indeed, such a school exists, and whether *Rashi* has this view of the book.

We go first to the latter of these two issues.

As in all his commentaries to *Nach*, *Rashi's* remarks and elucidations to our book are very sparse. In contrast to many other commentators, he never seems to examine the book as a whole, never attempts to offer an overview of what has transpired or of what we are to expect. This makes it difficult to use his commentary as a basis for a judgment in this matter.[2]

---

1. See Appendix on The Authorship of the Rashi Commentary p. 378 for a discussion as to the authorship of the commentary printed in the standard edition under the name of *Rashi*.

2. We use the word, *difficult* because careful analysis of the commentary can — if only in a negative sense, that is, by way of analyzing what *Rashi* does *not* do — lead us to certain conclusions.

A case in point would be *Rashi's* approach to Iyov's very first speech. Here we have a series of imprecations flung against the nights and days involved in Iyov's conception and birth. *Ramban*, as do many other commentators, makes a major point of the fact that, at least at this

As it happens, *Rashi* has, after all, left us with a statement which defines his vision.

At *Bava Basra* 15a we have a discussion concerning the dating of our story. Among the various opinions which are listed we have one which denies that Iyov was even a historical figure: אִיּוֹב לֹא הָיָה וְלֹא נִבְרָא אֶלָּא מָשָׁל הָיָה, *Iyov never really existed — his story is only a parable*. Now obviously if a Scriptural book is written as a parable it must have some clearly defined educational purpose, and thus this statement provides an opportunity for a commentator to say in a nutshell what the objective of this מָשָׁל might be.

Rashi writes as follows: מָשָׁל הָיָה, לִלְמוֹד מִמֶּנּוּ תְּשׁוּבוֹת לַמְקַטְרְגִים [נ״א עַיֵּין דִּקְדּוּקֵי סוֹפְרִים, לַמְקַנְטְרִין] עַל מִדַּת הַדִּין וְשֶׁאֵין אָדָם נִתְפָּס עַל צַעֲרוֹ. *It is a mashal [written] so that we might learn from it [appropriate] responses to those who condemn [or grumble about] the manifestations of God's stern justice [which might overtake them], and [further, to teach us] that no man is blamed for words that he utters because of his agony*.

Now as the only statement which we have from *Rashi* concerning the purpose of the book, these words deserve careful analysis.

For a better understanding of his precise meaning in this passage, we should examine it together with *Rashi's* remarks to 42:7 where God castigates the friends by telling Eliphaz: ... *My anger is seething against you and against your two friends, because, in your defense of Me, you did not speak as appropriately as did My servant Iyov.* Because of the extreme significance of this *Rashi* in understanding his remarks in *Bava Basra*, we quote it in full in the original Hebrew and in translation.

כִּי לֹא דִבַּרְתֶּם: שֶׁהֲרֵי לֹא דִבַּרְתֶּם אֵלַי טַעֲנָה נְכוֹנָה, כְּעַבְדִּי אִיּוֹב שֶׁהֲרֵי הוּא לֹא פָּשַׁע בִּי, כִּי אִם עַל אֲשֶׁר אָמַר תָּם וְרָשָׁע הוּא מְכַלֶּה . . . וְאִם הוֹסִיף לְדַבֵּר, מִפְּנֵי קוֹשִׁי יִסּוּרִין אֲשֶׁר כָּבְדוּ וְחָזְקוּ עָלָיו דִּבֵּר. אֲבָל אַתֶּם פְּשַׁעְתֶּם, עַל אֲשֶׁר הִרְשַׁעְתֶּם אוֹתוֹ לֵאמֹר . . . וְהֶ(ת)חֱזַקְתֶּם אוֹתוֹ בְּחֶזְקַת רָשָׁע, וּלְבַסּוֹף הֱיִיתֶם מְשׁוּתָּקִים וּמְנוּצָּחִים לְפָנָיו. וְהָיָה לָכֶם

---

point, Iyov denies Divine Providence and ascribes man's fate to the heavenly constellations — certainly a theological position, one that can be and ought to be, debated. Indeed, as *Ramban* interprets Eliphaz's first speech, it is precisely to this point that he addresses himself. *Rashi* says nothing of all this. Nowhere does he indicate that Iyov believes that human fate lies in the hands of the constellations and he interprets the relevant verses in Eliphaz's speech differently than does *Ramban* — see commentary there.

It would seem that *Rashi* does not view Iyov, in this first speech, as staking out a theological position. Rather, his silence makes it possible to read the passage as simply an expression of the kind of profound anguish which wishes — irrationally — but wishes still, that the past could be erased and with it the dreadful experiences which simply overwhelm in their horror.

Throughout the book there are numerous examples of this kind. Of these, because it is profoundly significant for the understanding of the basic structure of the book, we mention one.

It concerns the function of Elihu in the saga. In contrast to *Ramban*, *Rashi* makes no attempt at all to isolate any new contribution which Elihu might be making to the debate. We discuss this phenomenon in Introductory Remarks to 33:14, and conclude that this too is a function of the divergent attitudes which these two commentators have to the dynamics of the story — see there.

לְנַחֲמוֹ כַּאֲשֶׁר עָשָׂה אֱלִיהוּ. וְלֹא דַי לְאִיּוֹב בְּצָרָתוֹ וְיִסּוּרָיו כִּי גַם הוֹסַפְתֶּם עַל חַטֹּאתֵיכֶם פֶּשַׁע לְהַקְנִיטוֹ.

For you did not speak: For you did not confront me with as good a claim as My servant, Iyov. He never sinned against Me except that he said, 'He destroys the constant with the wicked' . . . and if he spoke too much, that was only because of the dreadfulness of his pains which weighed heavily upon him and drove him to speech. But you were guilty by accusing him of wickedness by saying . . . and you declared him to be wicked. But in the end you were silenced and defeated by him. Instead you should have comforted him as Elihu did. As though his sorrows were not enough for Iyov, you added guilt to your sins by upsetting him!

The entire tenor of the friends' approach is called into question here. It is not a case of an occasional insensitive remark or inappropriate accusation intermingled among essentially acceptable arguments. Nothing appears to be salvageable. They were *silenced and defeated* by Iyov. Not only were they wrong but they were cruel as well. For they did not comfort Iyov as Elihu did, but upset him mercilessly where they should have empathized with his unbearable misfortune.

Most strikingly, *Rashi* goes out of his way to contrast the friends unfavorably with Elihu although the verse says nothing at all about him. And, note well, Elihu is praised not for the superior cogency of his arguments, but for his simple humanity in comforting a sufferer.

Iyov does not escape criticism entirely. Certainly some of his accusations had better been left unsaid. But he is excused, as *Rashi* says in *Bava Basra*, because it was his unbearable pain which drove him to these excesses.

If we now turn to *Rashi* in *Bava Basra* and ask ourselves what precisely *Rashi* meant when he writes that the purpose of the book is to help us, *learn appropriate responses . . .*, we are hard-put to determine who among the book's protagonists is to instruct us? The friends are totally discredited and Elihu is singled out for praise not for the arguments which he made but for the sensitivity which he brought to bear.

We may perhaps conjecture, and it is no more than conjecture, that *Rashi* subscribes to the opinion of the *Zohar* which we quote at the beginning of ch.4, that the friends had many correct and potent arguments to offer, but failed, by being inadequately prepared, to couch them in terms which would be acceptable to Iyov. We feel that when *Rashi* says that we are to learn how to respond to a sufferer who rebels against his fate, this means too, that we are to learn how *not* to respond. The book of *Iyov*, as we saw so plainly in the *Rashi* which we analyzed above, is about friendship and its limitations, about sensitivity and insensitivity, about empathy and love, about disappointment and reconciliation. When he says that the purpose of the book is to help us learn appropriate responses he may be referring not so much to the philosophical content of the answers which we give, but to the tone which we use, the attitude and empathy which we project. **More than we learn *what* to answer we learn *how* to answer — and, most importantly how *not* to answer.**

The book is also about human frailty. The final phrase in *Rashi* is remarkable. *And [further, to teach us] that no man is blamed for words that he utters because of his agony*. This is a lesson which Rava, at *Bava Basra* 16b, derives from 34:35, אִיּוֹב לֹא בְדַעַת יְדַבֵּר וּדְבָרָיו לֹא בְהַשְׂכֵּל, which Rava renders, *Iyov is not to be blamed for what he said. Because of his pain it is to be viewed as though he had said it unwittingly. His words came without the benefit of considered thought*. Now, clearly this is an important insight. But, on what basis does *Rashi* pick it from the many other teachings which are recorded in two large folio pages dealing with our book, as being central to the whole enterprise? What made *Rashi* say that this whole complex *mashal* was written expressly that we should learn this particular homily?

Clearly, as *Rashi* reads the story, and, once more, as seems borne out by the *Rashi* which we analyzed above, it is this, and specifically this, which is the crucial element in the saga. Why is it so important that those who shoulder the responsibility of attempting to comfort a sufferer should do so only after adequate preparation? It is because of the dreadful vulnerability of the broken. When we are healthy and strong we should all be able to take our knocks, must be able to bear up under the small *faux-pas* of which even the best friends will occasionally be guilty. But one who is bereaved, shattered in body and battered in spirit, has the right to be treated with greater consideration. As we understand the *Rashi*, the second part of his gloss is connected to the first. We must learn well how to comfort *because* no man can be held accountable for the excesses of his agony.

This, then, may be the story of Iyov as *Rashi* sees it.

We may surmise that *Rashi* chose this approach to the book rather than viewing it as a debate as some of the other commentators did, for some of the following reasons:

Firstly there is the matter of the style in which the book is written. *Rashi* may well have felt that debate requires clarity born of conciseness, not the florid poetry in which all the speeches are couched. *Rambam* himself writes in his Introduction to the *Moreh Nevuchim* that a prerequisite for sensible dialogue is that there be agreement concerning the meaning of specific terms, a lucidity of expression which leaves no room for ambiguity. Poetry — and especially poetry as complex as that used in our book — by its very nature leaves room for all kinds and levels of nuance and meaning. It stirs the emotions much more than it stimulates the mind. It is, of all styles, the least suited to intellectual debate.

Again, *Rashi* may agree in principle with *Malbim* that we should not expect redundancies and literary embellishments in *Kisvei HaKodesh*. Now, all those commentators who view the dialogue as debate, are hard put to justify the need for much of what each of the protagonists has to say. We have already seen the ideas of *R' Saadyah Gaon* and *Rambam* in this matter. In our analysis of

Ramban we will see that he frequently writes that this or that speech contains nothing that has not been said before, without however dealing with the obvious difficulty: If it adds nothing, why record it? None of this is problematic if we do not accept that the protagonists are debating. In real life, in the hurly-burly of actual confrontation, there is never an excessive economy of expression. People come back again and again to the thoughts that roil their emotions. Pain, anger, pity, disdain, all seek expression, all insist upon bursting through the restraints of orderly, logical discourse. In the course of the commentary we shall have frequent occasion to note how entirely appropriate many of the apparent redundancies really are, once we accept the view that we are not dealing with an actual debate.

In addition, what is true of redundancies is true also of inconsistencies and contradictions. Again and again we shall see that, throughout his speeches, Iyov espouses ideas which are antagonistic to one another and cannot, by any stretch of logic coexist. See, for example in Introductory Remarks to ch.12, and commentary to 16:14. Again at 9:31 and elsewhere we have recognized the literary lurches in which Iyov frequently indulges. Instead of following one consistent line of argument, he tends to interrupt a certain train of thought with some ideas which, on the surface, are totally extraneous to it, only to pick it up again a few verses later. These are all matters which have no place in an orderly debate but are natural and expected in the anguished cries of a broken man whose soul is crying not with reasoned arguments but with a desperate plea for understanding.

There is also another point. If we are dealing with a debate — let us say on the model of *Rambam* — then each protagonist is presumed to adhere to a certain stance concerning the issue under discussion, and we would expect consistency. Iyov, for example, believes this and that, questions such and such. In such a scheme there is no room for the shocking blasphemies of, say, 9:22-24 as Rava interprets these verses — see commentary there. However, if we are dealing with the portrait of a broken man whose cries of pain are not designed for an academic presentation of some nice theological point, there is no difficulty at all. There are times when Iyov simply drops into the pits of despair and words escape him which, in saner moments he would not even have dreamed of thinking. At other times he soars to untold heights of adoration — and there is no contradiction at all. That is just the way people are.

Can *Rashi* be said to be representative of a school? Is his opinion shared by others?

As we have indicated above, we feel that there is a strong supposition that those commentators who do not supply the reader with a summation of the points made within each speech — as do most others — would probably share the view which we have now worked out in *Rashi* — that the Iyov saga is not, primarily, a debate.

Now were it not for the two *Rashis* which we have now examined, we would have been hesitant to base such a far-reaching theory upon the rest of

Rashi's commentary to *Iyov*. We know from *Rashi* to the rest of *Nach* that he tends to be very brief, concentrating upon the meaning of individual words or phrases, and not, except on rare occasions, treating or analyzing entire units.

However, *R' Yosef Kara* — *Rashi's* contemporary — is a different matter. As *Moshe Arend* in his Introduction to the *R' Yosef Kara* commentary to *Iyov* points out, it was this commentator's pride that he did consider each section in the context of the entire unit. Again and again he writes that he offers his interpretations, לְפִי הִלּוּךְ הַמִּקְרָאוֹת לְחַבֵּר אֶת הָעִנְיָן לִהְיוֹת אֶחָד (7:21), or, לְחַבֵּר אֶת הָעִנְיָן לִהְיוֹת אֶחָד (17:6-8) and the like. Surely, then, we would have expected from this author that he make some attempt to specify the direction which the debate is taking, which points are being made or challenged, as do so many other commentators. That he does not do so leads us to suspect that perhaps he — as well as others whose commentaries have a similar structure such as *R' Meyuchas* — share *Rashi's* approach to the book.

Ramban: The *Book of Iyov*, as *Ramban* sees it, has a single purpose. It tackles head-on the one seemingly intractable riddle which has bedeviled man from, literally, the first Sabbath of creation. Why, in a world governed by a benign God, a God of truth, a God of justice, should every form of pernicious unfairness seem to run rampant? Why should good people writhe in agony? Why should the wicked gloat in the abundance of health, wealth, power and joy which life seems to heap upon them with such a liberal hand?[1]

There are four major sources from which we should be able to glean some idea of *Ramban's* understanding of the book. We have, besides his verse to verse commentary, his *Introduction* to the book, a long and detailed analysis in his *Toras HaAdam* and a less detailed one in his *Derashah al Koheles*. There are some minor inconsistencies among these four sources [see, for example, footnote 1 to 11:13-15] but, by and large, we have a consistent approach.

To understand the thrust of our book correctly, we must examine it against

1. We say that the question began on the first Sabbath of creation. Impossible as that may sound, it is clearly the tradition of the Sages. As the first Sabbath came in, as Adam wearied and dispirited from the grinding experiences of that first terrible Friday — the soaring exhilaration of meeting his God; the searing agony of failure, sin, shame and terror; the curse; the expulsion; the first tentative steps towards rehabilitation — felt the healing balm of its sanctity wash over him, he broke into song, מִזְמוֹר שִׁיר לְיוֹם הַשַּׁבָּת.

That song speaks of only one topic. Our's. Somehow — in ways which need not concern us here — Sabbath taught him that if the wicked seem to flourish it is only so that their triumphs may lead them to ultimate destruction. That the righteous, appearing now to be crushed and broken, will yet blossom into a majestic palm tree and become strong and invincible as the cedar.

Why this, of all messages, on that first Sabbath?

Whichever other profound lesson may be hidden in this tradition of the Sages — and we may be sure that there are many — at the very least it seems to imply the following: The problem is endemic to the human condition. Not a single day passed but that it required a solution.

the background of a considerable literature which deals with the same issue. Indeed *Ramban* [*Toras HaAdam*] takes note that *Berachos* 7a teaches that Moses himself asked God this very question. As the Talmud records the conversation, God answered Moses that suffering strikes only the less than perfect *tzaddik* [צַדִּיק שֶׁאֵינוֹ גָּמוּר], and only a *rasha* with some merits which deserve reward [רָשָׁע שֶׁאֵינוֹ גָּמוּר], will experience well-being. This answer, *Ramban* notes, assumes that the true and final reckoning is made in עוֹלָם הַבָּא [*Olam Haba*], the *World to Come*. The not- quite-perfect man is punished for his minor shortcomings in this world so that his ultimate reward might be perfect; the wicked man is rewarded in the sorry currency of this world for the few merits which he may have accrued.

Now, *Ramban* points out, adequate as this answer may be for some cases — clearly most people are neither completely good nor completely bad —it does not cover the totality of the problem [*Introduction, Iyov*]. There are, manifestly, people who are innocent of even minor infractions, who by every measure of justice ought to live lives of bliss in both worlds, who still must drink the dregs of bitterness; and there are those who lead pleasant lives although they have no redeeming characteristics at all.

Ramban's question makes it clear that he does not consider the answer offered by the *Gemara* in *Berachos* to be meant as *the* ultimate explanation beyond which no problems can arise and no solutions are required. R' Yannai taught in *Avos* 4:15: It is not in our power to grasp either the tranquility of the wicked or the suffering of the righteous. Apparently no single answer can fit every single circumstance. Only this can explain the fact that throughout *Nach* — *Tehillim, Koheles, Eichah* and *Habbakuk* are examples — the question is taken up repeatedly and other explanations are offered.

But all this ambiguity, all this tolerance of the uncertain and the ill-defined, is true only up to the *Book of Iyov*. Here *Ramban* demands that the ultimate answer, the one which leaves no residue of doubt or unease, must be given.

In the opinion of some of our Sages, Moses wrote this book after having received it from God's mouth as he had received the book of *Genesis*. He was commanded to record it in writing because:

> . . . Its subject matter is the very root of faith, the foundation upon which the Torah rests. Know then that in this book all the questions concerning this matter, which might ever occur to anyone are asked, *and in it, of necessity, the absolute answer must be found*.

And later, at 33:30:

> . . . See now, that I have elucidated this matter . . . the argument is sound, the ideas, correct. *After this no possible question could conceivably remain in anyone's mind*.

The ultimate answer, as *Ramban* perceives it, is the mystery of *Gilgul*

HaNeshamos which, in *Ramban's* view, is the heart of Elihu's contribution to the saga.[1]

Why is *Iyov* different? Why was the same Moses who was granted only a partial answer when he asked in his own behalf, given so much more when God revealed the Iyov saga to him?

Ramban does not say. We may surmise as follows:

Why, we may ask, has God elected that such a crucial issue — *Ramban calls it* the most fundamental component of any man's faith-world — should so bedevil us. Could not God exercise His stewardship over human affairs in such a way that we could understand?

The answer may well lie in God's response to Habbakuk's anguished cry of confusion: *How long, O HASHEM, must I cry out, when You do not listen, call out "Violence!' when You do not help? . . . Does this not weaken Torah, is justice not eternally deferred when the wicked encircle the righteous. What a perversion of justice*!

Here is God's answer.

> *The future holds a vision, he who announces the end does not lie. It may tarry, but do you wait for it. Be assured it will come, it will not overstay its time. See! He who is arrogant, his nature is perverse. But as for the righteous man, he lives through his faith*!

וְצַדִּיק בֶּאֱמוּנָתוֹ יִחְיֶה, *But as for the righteous man, he lives through his faith!* — that may be the answer. The one thing that really matters to us will remain forever hidden — so that אֱמוּנָה, might become our life-force, the air which we breathe, the food which sustains us. If we could understand God's ways, if His stewardship of our affairs held no mystery for us, then indeed we would be wise — but not of strong faith. Faith presupposes the inscrutable — something that the mind cannot grasp but upon which the soul can fasten.

We recall the *chassid* of whom *Chovos HaLevavos* speaks. He rose up at night and called out, 'My God! You have left me hungry and naked, have forsaken me to the terrors of the night — but have also taught me how mighty You are, how great! Were You now to burn me in fire — it would only increase my love of You and my joy in Your proximity' (*Shaar HaAhavah* 1).

Why? Would this *chassid* love more, rejoice more if God tortured him? Why would he not, as Iyov did, accuse God of wanton injustice, attempt to summon Him to a court of justice?

Clearly, the crucial element here is faith. The *chassid*, in his abiding faith, has no problems. He sees his suffering as only one other opportunity — and

---

1. See ch.33 Introductory Remarks to v.14 and the long discussion in commentary to v.30 for the place which the revelation of this mystery occupies in Elihu's thought.

The discussion there is crucial to a correct perception of *Ramban's* understanding of the book. Here we limit ourselves to a discussion of the unique place which the *Book of Iyov* appears to play in *Ramban's* thought-world.

because of the difficulty involved, a significant one — of giving expression to his overwhelming love of God.

This is the Jewish way of relating to life's trials [see commentary to 6:2 on Nachum Ish Gamzu]. The absence of clarity concerning an issue as central as God's stewardship of human affairs is not a necessary evil — it is, on the contrary, an ideal for a people whose lifeblood is אֱמוּנָה. The objective of the Jew is not to know but to serve. The need for clarity lies in the breast of those who asked מַה כְּתִיב בָּהּ; the ability to live with ambiguities is the skill of those who declared, נַעֲשֶׂה וְנִשְׁמַע! (see ch. 1 fn. #2 to v. 1; comm. to 7:11, Introductory Remarks to ch. 9; Introductory Remarks to ch. 38; and Introductory Remarks to 42:10).

The *Book of Iyov*, as *Bava Basra* 15b appears to teach, is addressed to the gentile nations [הָכָא עִיקַר נְבִיאוּתַיְיהוּ לְאוּמּוֹת הָעוֹלָם. . .] — see fn. to 1:1. *Ramban* himself subscribes to the concept that Iyov was a gentile — see 42:17. For them, and for those among us who find themselves unduly influenced by their way of thinking, answers are indeed of paramount importance.

Iyov

א אִישׁ הָיָה בְאֶרֶץ־עוּץ אִיּוֹב שְׁמוֹ וְהָיָה | הָאִישׁ הַהוּא

I.

1. אִישׁ הָיָה — *There was a man.* The stark featurelessness of this statement — nothing is said which would place Iyov in any known time-frame, or familiar setting — seems to mark him as timeless and supra-historical. Our phrase perhaps means to say that Iyov is a מָשָׁל [*mashal*], *parable*. Make no attempt to place him in any known period, among any known people. He is too big to be contained in this or that context. Do not diminish him by placing limitations of time or place upon him.[1]

It is true that at *Bava Basra* 15a a number of attempts are made to place Iyov in a particular historical context. But, *Rambam* in *Moreh Nevuchim* 22 thinks that the very fact that such disparate time-frames are suggested — they range from patriarchal times to the return from the Babylonian exile — argues for the assumption that Iyov is not a historical figure.[2]

There are, however, midrashic sources which refuse to accept the idea that Iyov was not a historical figure. Thus we have *Midrash HaGadol, Vayikra* listing a number of things which *never were and never will be,* with *R'*

1. In *Introduction to the Iyov Commentary* we surveyed a number of commentators for their view of what the purpose of the book of *Iyov* might be. All appear to agree with our assessment here. If there were a historical context, then surely, that should play some role in the interpretation of the book. None of the commentators surveyed make any attempt to read anything of the sort into the text. *Rambam* explicitly, the others tacitly, seem to accept — at least for the purpose of their commentaries — that Iyov functions in a world of his own, unattached to any period or personality.

2. Even though there seems much to commend the opinion that the book is a parable, such an assumption is not without difficulties. Chief among these is the argument that if indeed it is a tale which has no basis in actual events, we would have expected the author (whom *Bava Basra* 14b and 15a identifies as Moses) to have chosen Jews as his protagonists, and the Torah as the thought-world within which the ideas of Iyov and his friends are formed. (In fact, though, all the people in the book seem to be non-Jewish (*Yad Ramah, Bava Basra* 15b), and neither the laws nor the values of the Torah are in evidence.

Following are some of the indications that the book's frame of reference is patriarchal, that is, pre-Torah:

a. The friends can find no cause for Iyov's suffering other than that he must have lived by unethical standards (22:6ff.). Nowhere do they suggest that perhaps Iyov had transgressed some of the Torah's laws. Furthermore, Iyov, in his defense, mentions only such actions and attitudes as might be expected from any good human being. Nothing is mentioned of those social obligations which derive from Torah law. Moreover we note that *Yad Ramah* to *Bava Basra* 15b and 16a points out that Iyov takes credit for actions which would have been interdicted by the Torah. To 29:13, *I received the blessing of the wretched*, the Sages (*Bava Basra* 16a) comment that it was his custom to 'steal' property from orphans, work it and then return it to them improved. The Torah forbids stealing even when undertaken for the benefit of the victim.

b. That the wicked must ultimately suffer is assumed on the basis of tradition (8:8), wisdom (15:18), or the tidings brought by wayfarers (21:29). The Torah's teachings on the subject are not mentioned.

c. The names עוּץ, בּוּז (הַבּוּזִי), אֱלִיפַז, תֵּמָן (הַתֵּמָנִי), and שׁוּחַ (הַשּׁוּחִי) all come from the families of Abraham and Nahor. (See *Ramban* in commentary to עוּץ.)

d. The coinage used is the קְשִׂיטָה (42:11) which is found only in connection with the patriarch Jacob (*Genesis* 33:19).

Would we not have expected a parable, thought out by Moses, to be constructed quite differently?

There is one thought which might eliminate much of this difficulty. *Bava Basra* 15b teaches that the main thrust of the prophecy of Iyov and that of his friends was directed to the gentile nations [. . . the main portions of the prophecies of (the other prophets) was directed to Israel, but the main portions of the prophecy (of Iyov and his friends) was directed to the nations of the world.] The commentators are silent on this issue and do not explain why the main portions of this book, which is part of כְּתְבֵי הַקּוֹדֶשׁ, *the holy writ*, is not addressed to Israel.

Perhaps, then, we are to conclude that the lessons of the book are indeed directed more to the nations than they are to Israel. Israel has its Torah and can learn the truth concerning God's providence from its teachings. Not so, the nations of the world. They must find their way to God along the tortuous highways and byways by which Iyov eventually learned the truth. The Torah which Moses gave to Israel was the Torah which had been accepted with נַעֲשֶׂה וְנִשְׁמַע, with total unquestioning subjugation to God's will. A people with such a Torah may safely bypass Iyov's agonized searchings.

The nations, on the other hand, wanted to know מַה כְּתִיב בָּהּ?, *What does the Torah contain*, what does it demand of us? For them, the book of *Iyov* is needed. It teaches that God can be found through search and struggle.

If this is indeed so, then we can well understand why, even if Moses wrote the book, and even if it is a parable, he chose to create the background and the identity of the protagonists in a non-Jewish, non-Torah context. It is an ambience which is most suited to the nations of the world to whom, as *Bava Basra* teaches, it is mainly directed.

1 There was a man in the land of Utz, Iyov was his name. Now,

Nosson in each case claiming that not only had they existed but that he had somehow been personally involved with them. They are: the בֵּית הַמְּנוּגָּע, *the house smitten with leprosy* [R' Nosson said, 'I personally removed the stones (from such a house)]; *the* עִיר הַנִּדַּחַת, *the city condemned to total destruction* because the majority of its inhabitants had served idols ['I personally have stood on the hill (upon which such a city had been built)]; the בֵּן סוֹרֵר וּמוֹרֶה, *the rebellious son* ['I sat in the court which judged him and stood at his grave']; the great eagle (described in *Ezekiel* 17:3) ['I saw its young ones']; and Iyov ['I encountered his grandchildren'].[1]

Moreover, we have a tradition preserved by *R' Meir Aramah* in *Meir Iyov* which reads as follows: *It is well known, even today, in the kingdom of Togarma, that the righteous Iyov was buried in the city of Kostantina and that great honor was paid him; burning lights, a hospice for all travelers and a monument on his grave* ... The author concludes: וְאִם קַבָּלָה הִיא נְקַבֵּל, 'if this is the tradition then we must accept it.'

Ibn Ezra maintains that Iyov must have been a historical personage since *Ezekiel* (14:14, 20) brackets him together with Noah and Daniel as examples of extremely righteous people.

It is of course possible that even if we assume that the book is a *mashal* there is nevertheless a historical core from which the parable was adapted. Thus the circumstances and persona of the drama were given. The book is a *mashal* only in the sense that the author fleshed out the bare outlines which were available to him — a righteous man had suffered greatly for no discernible reason — and used it as the vehicle through which he was able to present his teachings (*R' Meir Aramah* in *Meir Iyov*).

בְּאֶרֶץ־עוּץ — *In the land of Utz.* We remarked before that the stark phrase with which the book opens appears to argue for the assumption that Iyov was not a historical figure and that, consequently, he ought not to be tied to a particular time or place.

Why, then, the identification of the place in which he lived? Indeed, *Bava Basra* 15a asks this very question on the Sage who had suggested that Iyov was not a historical personage. No answer is given. It is possible that even a *mashal* might assign a fictitious place, either as simple fleshing out (see *Rambam's* view on this matter, explicated in *Introduction to the Iyov Commentary*) or, because it evokes certain associations — see below to verse 3.

Accordingly, we need to know the meaning of אֶרֶץ עוּץ even if we subscribe to the opinion that Iyov is only a *mashal.*

Rashi suggests that Utz is the son of Abraham's brother Nahor (*Genesis* 22:21) and that consequently the land of Aram is meant.[2]

Ibn Ezra and *Ramban* both cite *Eichah* 4:21, where Utz is described as the homeland of the *daughter of Edom* to indicate that Iyov was a descendent of Esau — that is, that he belonged to Abraham's direct family. *Ramban* goes on to show that the friends, too, belonged to the same clan: Eliphaz is described as the Temanite, and Teman was a son of Esau's son Eliphaz (*Genesis* 36:11); one of Abraham's children from Keturah was Shuah (*Genesis* 25:2) and this would be the ancestor of Bildad the Shuhite. The connection of Tzophar is less clear, but *Ramban* believes that it is not too farfetched to associate him with the Tzepho who is given as another son of Esau's son Eliphaz (*Genesis* 36:15).[3]

אִיּוֹב שְׁמוֹ — *Iyov was his name.* If the name is a Hebrew one, then the root would be איב, *to be hostile to,* and the structure would be similar to גִּבּוֹר from גבר, *to be strong,* or שִׁכּוֹר from שכר,

1. It is clear that this Midrash is couched in *aggadic* idiom and lends itself to various possible interpretations. Nevertheless, at the very least it must mean that at least in R' Nosson's view, Iyov did in fact exist.

2. We quote *Midrash Yelamdenu*: Our Rabbis taught: All the prophets of the gentile nations were descended from Milkah [Nahor's wife]. As it is written, *Utz, his firstborn;* this is Iyov, as it is written, *There was a man in the land of Utz; his name was Iyov.* And his brother Buz, that is Elihu the son of Berachel the Buzite. And Kemuel, that is Bilam.

3. *Ramban* goes on to show that the fifth actor in the narrative — Elihu the Buzite (chapter 32ff.) was descended from Abraham's brother Nahor who had a son called Buz (*Genesis* 22:21).

Ramban sees the significance of the fact that the narrative takes place among the family of Abraham, because he assumes that it was from him that they inherited the strong faith in God which so obviously informs all their thinking: ... *The man who was the root of faith, whose children adhered to his teachings.*

In light of our thoughts (in footnote above), that the book of *Iyov* might have been written by Moses for the nations of the world, there may be an added significance to the fact that the main protagonists are all descended from Abraham. He had, after all, been declared by God to be the אַב הֲמוֹן גּוֹיִם, *the father of a multitude of nations.* Even non-Jewish mankind would be led to God through his teachings as they were perpetuated in his children.

ב תָּם וְיָשָׁר וִירֵא אֱלֹהִים וְסָר מֵרָע: וַיִּוָּלְדוּ לוֹ שִׁבְעָה בָנִים

to be drunk. Indeed *Bava Basra* (16a) points out the similarity between the two forms: [Iyov] said to God: *Master of the world! Could it be that a whirlwind passed by You and You became confused between* אוֹיֵב *and* אִיּוֹב?[1]

However, *Ibn Ezra* at 2:11 suspects that the saga had its origins in a different language and that it was translated into Hebrew. If so, the name need have no significance. [*Daas Mikra* points out that, although the name does not occur anywhere else in Scripture, there is archaeological evidence that it was common in patriarchal and pre-patriarchal times.]

This may indeed be the meaning of the passage in *Bava Basra* where Iyov asks God whether perhaps He had become confused between אִיּוֹב and אוֹיֵב, between the name Iyov and the Hebrew word for *enemy*. Iyov, as we assume throughout this commentary, was a non-Jew and his name was therefore without any significant connotation. Accordingly, he may well have meant to ask the following question of God: Have You forgotten that I am not Jewish, that within the duties which are expected of me as a non-Jew I have performed well. Do You see me as a Jew, whose name, derived from the Hebrew, would connote *enemy*, and therefore deem me to have fallen short of my obligations?

The sequence, אִיּוֹב שְׁמוֹ, *Iyov was his name*, instead of the possible, וּשְׁמוֹ אִיּוֹב, *whose name was Iyov*, appears significant. Midrashim (cf. *Esther Rabbah* 6:3) make the point that in the case of righteous people their *name* precedes them — for example וּשְׁמוֹ מָרְדְּכַי, *whose name was Mordechai* (*Esther* 2:5). In this they are like God concerning whom it says, וּשְׁמִי ה׳, *by My Name* HASHEM (*Exodus* 6:3). By contrast, the wicked precede their *name*: Thus, נָבָל שְׁמוֹ, *Nabal was his name* (*I Samuel* 25:25) and other examples. Given this, the implication of the wording in our verse is that Iyov is to be seen as wicked (the Midrashim do not adduce this example). *Ibn Ezra* notes the wording but feels that there is no need to attach any importance to it. He suggests that the Sages of Midrash did not mean to formulate a hard and fast rule but pointed only to a generally valid usage. He adduces ה׳ שְׁמוֹ, *His Name is* HASHEM (*Exodus* 15:3) to demonstrate the limited applicability of the ruling.[2]

תָּם וְיָשָׁר — *Of unquestioning integrity coupled with a probing mind*. For תָּם [*tam*], *Rashi* writes: שָׁלֵים בְּמַעֲשָׂיו, *perfect in his actions*. We believe this to imply a life lived in congruence with the ideals and principles which guide it. There are no aberrations; everything contributes to a totally integrated picture.

However, throughout Scripture, *tam* also carries another connotation, that of an undevious simplicity, a willingness to accept things, unquestioningly, as they are. Thus, for example, *Rashi* (to *Genesis* 25:27) writes that in contrast to Esau the cunning trapper, the Patriarch Jacob is described as a *tam*. He says that a *tam* knows nothing of such wiles, speaking only that which is in his heart. He is one who cannot deceive easily.

Thus, also *Gra* (to *Proverbs* 2:7, where the Torah is described as proffering *advice* to the *yashar* and as *shielding* the *tam*) writes: The *yashar* is a man whose intellect directs his steps

1. This astounding statement in *Bava Basra* is ascribed to Rabba. However, *Mesores HaShas* suggests that this, together with certain other assertions on this page, be instead ascribed to Rava, as it is indeed ascribed at *Niddah* 52a.

This change is significant since it is Rava who teaches (*Bava Basra* 16b) that אֵין אָדָם נִתְפָּס בִּשְׁעַת צַעֲרוֹ, *no man should be blamed for outrageous statements uttered in the throes of his agony*.

The *Gemara* does not, of course, endorse Iyov's words. Indeed they are described as a חִרוּף, *blasphemy*. However, they are a very clear reflection of many of the sentiments which Iyov will express throughout the book — see particularly in chapter 9. We shall deal with each of these cases in the commentary and try to understand them in the context in which they occur.

2. *R' E.E. Dessler* in *Michtav Me'Eliyahu* explains the difference between the two types of formulation. The *name* of a person can be seen as defining his essence and God-determined destiny. When the *name* precedes *them* the implication is that the life of the righteous person was entirely congruent with the destiny which had been laid down for him by God. When *they* precede their name,this means that the life which the wicked make for themselves is of their own design and does not coincide with that which God had planned for them. They, as it were, create their own *name*.

Perhaps, taken thus, the formulation used with Iyov is appropriate, even if he was a righteous person. The turns which his life took were not predetermined. The cruel suffering to which he fell victim and the ebb and flow of his reactions came as a result of the Satan's challenge to God's assessment of Iyov's character. As a result of his spiritual grandeur in the face of his sorrows the man Iyov turned into *Iyov* the paradigm of the man who, in spite of feeling himself wronged can still turn humbly to his God. Iyov did, indeed, forge a new life for himself.

that man was of unquestioning integrity coupled with a probing mind; he stood in awe of God and eschewed evil. [2] *Seven sons*

and human qualities into the straight and virtuous paths laid down by God. He requires the *advice* of the Torah so as not to err in his understanding. The *tam,* on the other hand, walks on a more simple, unquestioning path, not deviating right nor left from the Torah's prescriptions, and also in his human qualities he does not rely on his intellect but does everything from simple faith. He needs no *advice* since his understanding is not the determining factor in his way of life, and he need prepare himself for no battles of the mind ... but, he may well stumble ... and thus he needs a *shield* to protect him from faltering.

Our rendering of תָּם combines *Rashi's* definition with that of *Gra.* For יָשָׁר we have followed *Gra.*

Is תְּמִימוּת, as we have defined it, and as Iyov displays it at verse 21 and at 2:10, compatible with the probing, questing mind implied by the term יָשָׁר?

Indeed, later as the ill-fated debate develops, Iyov talks very differently than we would expect from a *tam.* Far from a self-negating acceptance of his lot, we have him belligerently imputing indifference, and worse, to God, challenging Him to justify events and consistently and pugnaciously refusing to make peace with what has occurred.

Is there no inconsistency here? Can the man who had bowed to the Divine will with the profound religious faith expressed in verse 21, then turn around, berate God, and presume to summon Him to the bar of justice?

This problem seems, indeed, to have troubled the friends. They are unable to reconcile Iyov's initial submissiveness with the aggressive self righteousness which he displays in his arguments with them. They have only one explanation: Iyov's first reaction was one of *chanufah,* a fawning favor-currying religiosity which has nothing at all to do with the inner man. Iyov stands revealed in his true colors only later, as blasphemy following upon appalling blasphemy tumbles forth from his anguished mouth.

Iyov, on the other hand, will stoutly and consistently maintain that his is an unblemished integrity. The *temimus* of his initial reaction — in which he confirms God's right to take back that which is His to grant or withhold, and which expresses his determination to continue, in spite of everything, to bless and to adore Him — is the religious stance with which he identifies (see particularly 9:21,22, and 27:5 and 31:6, for the stubborn assertion that in spite of the pounding to which God inexplicably exposes him, he is a *tam*). His anguished questings and questionings, far from standing in contradiction to *temimus,* are one of its functions. If he is to submit to God's providence — and he craves only to do that — he must not be faced with contradictions which the human mind cannot reconcile. God cannot, he attempts to say, have it both ways. He cannot appear to be despotic, arbitrary and cruel, and have man accept Him as all-just and all-good.[1]

וִירֵא אֱלֹהִים וְסָר מֵרָע — *He stood in awe of God and eschewed evil. Malbim* believes that Iyov's qualities are described here in order to serve as background to the problem of Iyov's suffering which forms the core of the book. We are told from the very start that there was nothing in Iyov's spiritual standing which was reprehensible; nothing that could make his terrible fate understandable in terms of conventional explanations. Thus, this phrase completes the thoughts begun earlier. Even one who is a *tam* or a *yashar* might be exposed to suffering if his actions do not conform to the Torah's requirements. In Iyov's case there was no such shortcoming. In spirit and action he lived a perfectly exemplary life.

Ramban writes: ... He knew his Creator and served Him with his intellect, in matters involving *temimus* and *yashrus* as also in avoiding harm (סָר מֵרָע) to his fellowman.

Bava Basra 15b teaches: Greater is that which is written in connection with Iyov, than that which is written in connection with Abraham. In connection with Abraham the wording is, *That you fear God* (*Genesis* 22:12), but in connection with Iyov the wording is, *of unquestioning integrity coupled with a prob-*

1. There are, of course, levels of faith which are not disturbed by seemingly insoluble contradictions. There was no way in which Abraham was able to reconcile the command to sacrifice Isaac with God's promise that it would be through this son, and no other, that his future was to be assured. Nevertheless, Abraham went to Moriah, not only uncomplainingly but also unquestioningly.

The difference between Abraham's relationship to God and that of Iyov's is one of the great *aggadic* themes with which the Sages embellish our book. See especially chapter 42, Introductory Remarks to verse 10.

ג וְשָׁלוֹשׁ בָּנוֹת: וַיְהִי מִקְנֵהוּ שִׁבְעַת אַלְפֵי־צֹאן וּשְׁלֹשֶׁת
אַלְפֵי גְמַלִּים וַחֲמֵשׁ מֵאוֹת צֶמֶד־בָּקָר וַחֲמֵשׁ מֵאוֹת
אֲתוֹנוֹת וַעֲבֻדָּה רַבָּה מְאֹד וַיְהִי הָאִישׁ הַהוּא גָּדוֹל
ד מִכָּל־בְּנֵי־קֶדֶם: וְהָלְכוּ בָנָיו וְעָשׂוּ מִשְׁתֶּה בֵּית אִישׁ

ing mind, he feared God and shunned evil.[1]

Rambam (*Moreh Nevuchim* 3:22) makes the point that wisdom is not one of the qualities with which Iyov was endowed. He was good but lacked deep insight into the nature of God and His relationship to man. Had he been granted such acumen he would surely have reacted quite differently to his suffering. But see below, commentary to verse 3, s.v. וְהָיָה הָאִישׁ הַהוּא . . .

2. שִׁבְעָה בָנִים וְשָׁלוֹשׁ בָּנוֹת — *Seven sons and three daughters. Metzudos* suggests that in line with the next verse which details how blessed Iyov was in earthly possessions, this verse, too, shows how favored he was: It is perceived as a sign of good fortune to have more than double as many sons as daughters.

Gra makes the point that seven and three together make ten, a number always associated with completeness. He had as many children as one could possibly desire.

The recurrence of the numbers three and seven [there were also seven thousand sheep and three thousand camels] creates a sense of artificiality and tends to support the idea that the book is a *mashal* rather than the record of an actual event (*R' Zerachiah*).

3. . . . וַיְהִי מִקְנֵהוּ — *His possessions consisted of* . . . We have translated *possessions,* rather than herds or flocks, because the broader expression is more suited to include the עֲבֻדָּה רַבָּה at the end of the verse.

A vast wealth is described here. Later (v. 10) Satan is going to use these riches as a significant part of his cavils, . . . *his possessions spread out in the land.*[2]

1. Here we have another instance where Iyov and Abraham are brought together. But what could be the intention of the Sages when they compare, apparently unfavorably, Abraham with Iyov?

Maharsha explains that there is no real implication that Iyov was in fact greater than Abraham. God was talking to Abraham directly when he called him a God-fearing person while the assessment of Iyov is not made to him personally. The Sages teach that only partial praise may be said in a person's presence (*Eruvin* 18b), and we may therefore assume that when God called Abraham a *Yerei Elokim* this was only a fraction of what might have been said. Thus, Abraham is not inferior to Iyov.

Maharal has an entirely different understanding of the passage. More qualities are listed for Iyov than were given for Abraham, because Iyov was a composite man. The four qualities listed for him are each akin to one of those which earmarked the three patriarchs and King David. He was a *Yerei Elokim* as Abraham had been; a *yashar* as Isaac had been (*Maharal* takes this as given and does not adduce a source); his *Temimus* came to him from Jacob (*Genesis* 25:27); while the quality of eschewing evil was shared with David (again no source is adduced).

Maharal's interpretation seems to place Iyov in a patriarchal frame. In his person are contained those qualities which together are the spiritual building blocks of which Israel was formed. Iyov, then, is the *father* of the gentile nations. Such a patriarchal role for Iyov is further attested to by *Pesikta Rabbosi* (*Acharei Mos*), which teaches that had Iyov withstood the test of his suffering without making bitter accusations against God (see particularly chapter 9), then in our prayers we would not only address God as the God of Abraham, Isaac and Jacob, but also as the God of Iyov. See further in *Overview, Iyov and Abraham.*

2. The Sages (*Bava Basra* 15b) attach great importance to this immense wealth. They offer a novel interpretation to the phrase from verse 10, quoted in the commentary: וּמִקְנֵהוּ פָּרַץ בָּאָרֶץ, *his possessions spread out in the land.*

פָּרַץ is rendered in its meaning, *to breach*: His flocks breached the normal standards of the world. Normally we expect wolves to devour goats, but those of Iyov were so strong that they killed the wolves.

Later, in verse 14, they remark that the blessings bestowed on Iyov were akin to those of *Olam Haba,* the *World to Come* (see there for their understanding of the verse). *Maharal* there understands this teaching of the Sages to mean that Iyov was granted such great blessings in *olam hazeh, This World* [akin to those of the *World to Come*] because indeed he was not to have a share in the *World to Come.* Iyov is a man of the here and now.

We understand the idea to be conveyed by these teachings as follows: In various footnotes above, we have noted that Iyov's prophecies were entirely directed to the nations of the world and that, indeed, he is to be regarded as a kind of patriarch to the gentile people. Thus the story of Iyov is to take place in a setting that projects those nations in a state that is ideal to their role in history. There is an ideal form for *This World,* one that is akin to *the World to Come;* and the drama of the man who had been granted all, lost everything, and because of a tenacious love of truth, regained what had been taken, takes place against the background of that ideal.

and three daughters were born to him. [3] *His possessions consisted*
of seven thousand small-stock, three thousand camels, five hundred span of oxen and five hundred she-asses. And, of many different enterprises. That man was greater than anyone who dwelled in the East. [4] *His sons would go to revel, each on his special*

שִׁבְעַת אַלְפֵי־צֹאן וּשְׁלֹשֶׁת אַלְפֵי גְמַלִּים — *Seven thousand small-stock, three thousand camels.* צֹאן is a term that includes both sheep and goats (see *Leviticus* 1:10).

Daas Mikra makes the point that the proportion of small-stock to camels is quite different than that which we find in the case of Jacob's gift to Esau (*Genesis*, chapter 32). There Jacob sent two hundred and forty small-stock and thirty camels — a proportion of 1:8 — while in Iyov's flock we have a 3:7 relationship. This probably points to a greater wealth on Iyov's part, since camels are much more precious than the smaller animals.[1]

וַחֲמֵשׁ מֵאוֹת . . . וַחֲמֵשׁ מֵאוֹת — *Five hundred . . . and five hundred.* From verse 14 it appears that the she-asses were grazing in the vicinity in which the oxen worked. *Daas Mikra* surmises that the asses were used to carry the ploughing utensils used by the span of oxen to the place where the ploughing was being done. Apparently this is still practiced in various primitive societies. This would explain why there were exactly as many asses as there were span of oxen.

וַעֲבֻדָּה רַבָּה מְאֹד — *And of many different enterprises.* The translation follows *Rashi* to *Genesis* 26:14.

Other interpretations are: Many servants (*Ibn Ezra*); fields, gardens and orchards [so called because they yield their produce as a result of the labor (עֲבוּדָה from עָבַד, *to work*) invested in them] (*Sforno, Metzudos* and others).

וַיְהִי הָאִישׁ הַהוּא גָּדוֹל מִכָּל־בְּנֵי־קֶדֶם — *That man was greater than anyone who dwelled in the East.* Haran lies to the east of *Eretz Yisrael* and if, indeed, Iyov, lived in that land, this would be the meaning of the phrase. He was wealthier than any of the people among whom he dwelled. However, if he came from the land of Edom, which lies more to the north, then the meaning of the phrase is as follows: The land of the East was rich in pasture lands and the people there had great flocks (*Ezekiel* 27:21). Utz, to the contrary, was a more arid land, not suited for the raising of small-stock. Nevertheless, Iyov was so blessed that even in these circumstances he was wealthier than any of the people who lived in the East (*Ramban*; for his assumptions concerning the locations of the lands of Haran and Utz [Edom] respectively, see his commentary to *Genesis* 32:2 and *Chavel* there).

When we take into consideration that in Scripture, בְּנֵי קֶדֶם are considered to be the repository of *wisdom* (see *I Kings* 5:10: *The wisdom of Solomon exceeded that of all the* בְּנֵי קֶדֶם), then *R' Yosef Kimchi's* explanation of גָּדוֹל seems most appropriate: Iyov was greater in wisdom than all the בְּנֵי קֶדֶם who were the wisest in the world. If we combine this with *Rambam's* assertion in *Moreh Nevuchim* that the name עוּץ hints at the ideas of *advice* and *conjecture*, then these descriptions are vital to the setting of the book: Iyov lived in a land in which wisdom was held in high esteem and among people who were the very epitome of wisdom. That *land of wisdom* supported the conventional wisdom that good acts must invariably be followed by good fortune — the theory which the three friends relentlessly press. Iyov, the major denizen of this *land of wisdom*, originally subscribes to these ideas and is torn loose from them only by his terrible experiences.

However, *R' Yosef Kimchi's* suggestion that Iyov's *greatness* expressed itself in his wisdom runs counter to *Rambam* in *Moreh Nevuchim*, quoted in commentary to verse 1, s.v. וִירֵא.

4. וְהָלְכוּ בָנָיו וְעָשׂוּ מִשְׁתֶּה . . . . — *His sons would go to revel . . .* The past tense is used here to describe something that was habitually done, for

R' Nochum Lansky has suggested that given this, we can understand the suffering to which Iyov was exposed within the context of the comparison between Iyov and Abraham which we have recognized as being central to the book. Abraham's all was in the spiritual realm and was vested in the future of which Isaac was the repository. He was called upon to sacrifice this only son, in a way which totally defied reason. To sacrifice that reason and submit himself unquestioningly to God's command was the test of the *Akeidah*. In much the same way, Iyov had to sacrifice all that he had been given, the utopian *Olam Hazeh* which marked the perfection of that of which he was capable, and also come to the realization that ultimately we do not ask questions of God.

1. If, indeed, the choice of the numbers is significant, then this would be part of the general picture which we traced above, in which Iyov is the man of *Olam Hazeh*. When the world was divided between Jacob and Esau, the former was given *Olam Haba;* the latter, *Olam Hazeh* (see *Gur Aryeh* to *Genesis* 15:22). In the

א/ה יוֹמוֹ וְשָׁלְחוּ וְקָרְאוּ לִשְׁלֹשֶׁת אַחְיֹתֵיהֶם לֶאֱכֹל
ה וְלִשְׁתּוֹת עִמָּהֶם: וַיְהִי כִּי הִקִּיפוּ יְמֵי הַמִּשְׁתֶּה וַיִּשְׁלַח
אִיּוֹב וַיְקַדְּשֵׁם וְהִשְׁכִּים בַּבֹּקֶר וְהֶעֱלָה עֹלוֹת מִסְפַּר כֻּלָּם
כִּי אָמַר אִיּוֹב אוּלַי חָטְאוּ בָנַי וּבֵרְכוּ אֱלֹהִים בִּלְבָבָם

which the use of the future tense would also be appropriate — see כָּכָה יַעֲשֶׂה אִיּוֹב in verse 5 (*Metzudos*).

וְעָשׂוּ מִשְׁתֶּה — *To revel.* If the verse is to be taken literally, that indeed, every day was a feast day for Iyov's children, then we have a usage here which is hard for us to understand. How can a man as righteous as Iyov have educated his children to such profligacy? What possible merit could there be in such usage, and why would they have *blasphemed* God in their hearts (v. 5)?

Perhaps we may understand this in the light of what we have suggested above (see footnote 2 p. 6), that Iyov was granted a perfect *Olam Hazeh* in his role as the paradigm of the gentile nations. The nations' fulfillment and *raison d'etre* was in the here and now, rather than in the redemptive future. *Bamidbar Rabbah* 21 tells us: There was a certain gentile who invited the entire city to a banquet. R' Dustai related that he had been invited together with all of them. No luxury was missing from the tables, save only nuts from Perech. What did the host do? He took a table top worth six talents of silver and smashed it in the presence of his guests. [A wild fit of profligacy and abandon in order to demonstrate his wealth and how little he cared for anything.] R' Dustai asked him, 'Why do you do this?' He answered, 'You [Jews] teach that *Olam Hazeh* is ours and *Olam Haba* is yours. If we do not make full use of our portion now, then when will we be able to do so?'

We see, then, that this is the ethos of the man of *Olam Hazeh*. In its purest form, it demands total immersion into hedonism. Perhaps such a path, too, can lead ultimately to God. But there is a danger. Steeped in this-worldly pleasures, a terrible sense of meaninglessness may well up inside the heart; a feeling of rebellion against a God Who has ordained this to be my lot. Iyov feared that his sons might become confused by this terrible paradox: The all-consuming delight of senses aroused and fulfilled, which must coexist with the searing frustrations of a life lived without spiritual content. Iyov brought offerings lest his children *blaspheme* God in their hearts.

בֵּית אִישׁ יוֹמוֹ — *Each on his special day in his own home.* There were seven sons, so we assume that the oldest would have the banquet in his house on Sunday, the next on Monday, and so on throughout the week, till Shabbos (*Ma'ayon Gannim*).

וְשָׁלְחוּ וְקָרְאוּ — *And they would send word.* Although the past tense is used, a continuous usage is meant (*Rashi*).

5. וַיְהִי כִּי הִקִּיפוּ — *When ... had made their rounds.* As the week came to an end and a new round of banquets was about to begin (*Rashi* and *Metzudos*). הִקִּיפוּ, from נָקַף, *to encircle.*

וַיְקַדְּשֵׁם — *To summon them.* The translation follows *Targum* and is accepted by *Rashi* and *Metzudos. Rashi* adduces *Numbers* 11:18. See *Rashi* there.

He summoned them so that they would come to him so that he could offer them guidance on following the straight path of Godliness (*Metzudos*).

מִסְפַּר כֻּלָּם — *One for each of them.* He brought as many sacrifices as he had children — his sons and his daughters (*Rashi* and *Metzudos*).

וּבֵרְכוּ — *And blasphemed.* See commentary to verse 4.

בֵּרֵךְ, which usually means *to bless,* is used throughout as a euphemism to describe an act of blasphemy.

6-12. Unwittingly, and through no fault of his own — the introductory sentences have made this clear — Iyov now becomes an apparently hapless and helpless pawn in a confrontation between God and the Satan.

Many early thinkers have found great difficulties in understanding this confrontation in light of Hashem being all-good and all-powerful. The former quality appears compromised by a seemingly unethical acquiescence to an unconscionable challenge made by the Satan — by what right is Iyov to be deprived of the happy and satisfying life which he had earned for himself by his blameless conduct?

R' Saadyah Gaon moves the entire scene from heaven to earth: The *B'nei HaElokim*, of verse 6 are righteous humans who gathered periodically in order to discuss matters of

context of an *Olam Hazeh* which is akin to *Olam Haba* there would be greater wealth. Jacob, the man of *Olam Haba*, is therefore less blessed in wealth than Iyov.

day in his own home; and they would send word to invite their
three sisters to eat and drink with them. 5 *When the days of*
revelry had made their rounds, Iyov would send word to summon
them, would rise early in the morning, and sacrifice burnt
offerings, one for each of them; for Iyov thought, 'Perhaps my
children have sinned and blasphemed God in their hearts.'

spirituality and to put their religious houses in order. Satan is one of their number, a man as they are men, who, in the course of the debates, raises the matter of Iyov's righteousness. *Rambam* employs an allegorical explanation in which the *B'nei HaElokim* are the spiritual forces which animate man's inner life, while the Satan is the physical part of man from which all his weaknesses derive.

Ramban, in his preface to the book, goes to some length to demonstrate that the Satan is, in fact, an angel, and in his commentary to our verse proves from the description of the Heavenly tribunal that the book must have been written by prophetic inspiration. No human could have known what transpired among God and His angels without the gift of prophecy. Apparently he has no difficulty in understanding the passage as a literal portrayal of an actual event.

R' Meir Aramah also accepts this position: *... For it is the understanding of the Sages that the Heavenly governance is of the same nature as earthly governance: There is justice and there are judges above, records are kept, there are angels whose duty it is to vindicate the accused and there is a prosecutor — in precisely the same fashion as in a human court. Thus we read in Daniel 7:9-10: ... 'I watched till thrones were set up and the Ancient of Days sat ... the judgment was set and the books were opened.'*

Since this seems to be the understanding of the Sages in a variety of Midrashic sources, it will be the basis of our commentary.[1]

Those commentators who are untroubled by *Rabbeinu Saadyah Gaon's* concerns with an apparently independent Satan can find ample support for their position. Every nuance in the description of the Heavenly tribunal clearly precludes the existence of some coercive, malevolent power. God's hand will not

1. What of the question of the ethics of God's response to the Satan's challenge, and Satan's apparent power to impose his will on that of God — those issues which cause *R' Saadyah Gaon* and *Rambam* to deviate from the simple meaning?

We propose the following solutions:

a) *Rambam* (*Moreh Nevuchim* 3:24) discusses the *nisyonos, tests,* which, as the Torah teaches, are occasionally imposed on people and which cause them apparently undeserved suffering. He concludes that these *nisyonos* are only justified as means by which mankind is to be educated. Individuals of special spiritual stature are challenged, seemingly beyond reasonable expectations, in order that others should draw conclusions from their heroic acts: This is how God should be served!

Apparently, then, the individual is obliged to accept undeserved hardships if these have an educational function.

An analogy can perhaps be found in *Ezekiel* chapter 24. There, the prophet is told that his beloved wife is to die so that he, in his mourning, should be able to serve as a symbol of Israel's sorrow when the Temple will have been destroyed. Nowhere is there any indication that this wife had done any wrong for which she deserved to die. Rather, it seems that Ezekiel's role as mentor to his people imposed upon him and his immediate family the duty to sacrifice even their lives if through this the people would be brought to their senses (See fn. to *ArtScroll, Ezekiel* Vol. 2, p. 420).

The philosophical underpinnings for God's *right* to withhold earned *Olam Hazeh* for these or other purposes would be as follows: In the ninth chapter of *Hilchos Teshuvah, Rambam* teaches that the promises which the Torah makes of this-world rewards for a life dutifully lived, are not to be seen as an indication that such is in fact the ultimate reward which the righteous are to expect. The true and final reward for the performance of *mitzvos* is reserved for *Olam Haba, the World to Come.* Temporal rewards are only promised, and bestowed, in order to provide a framework within which further service of God can be most readily undertaken. *Rabbeinu Bachya* to *Pirkei Avos* makes the point that this-worldly reward is referred to by *Chazal* as פְּרָס, a kind of bonus, rather than an award actually earned.

Thus it transpires that we have no real claim upon the pleasures which *Olam Hazeh* has to offer. The good and tranquil life which the Torah promises to those who fulfill God's wishes is not their due, but one more aspect of God's all encompassing goodness.

As such, we can understand that when there is an overriding need to deny the person those beneficial results of his righteousness, then that which is withheld from him is nothing to which he has an actual claim. God will deny him those fruits of his labor when a compelling consideration makes this necessary.

ו כָּכָה יַעֲשֶׂה אִיּוֹב כָּל־הַיָּמִים׃ וַיְהִי הַיּוֹם וַיָּבֹאוּ
בְּנֵי הָאֱלֹהִים לְהִתְיַצֵּב עַל־יהוה וַיָּבוֹא גַם־הַשָּׂטָן
ז בְתוֹכָם׃ וַיֹּאמֶר יהוה אֶל־הַשָּׂטָן מֵאַיִן תָּבֹא וַיַּעַן הַשָּׂטָן

be forced; He acts only as He would wish to act.

In the first place, we note the use of the Tetragammaton, the *Shem Havayah,* throughout the introductory story — noteworthy because, overwhelmingly, the protagonists themselves use *El* and *Shaddai.* This Name conveys God's absolute omnipotence. *There is none besides Him* (*Deuteronomy* 4:35), our Sages teach, *including even the occult forces,* which also have their role to play in the affairs of man (*Sanhedrin* 67b). None have any independent existence; all derive only from His will. *Rashi* there adds: When the Holy One Blessed is He gave the Torah, He opened all the seven heavens to them. Even as He exposed the upper spheres, so too did He expose the lower spheres — and they saw that He is the only One.

As we see in the commentary to verse 7, Satan cannot even begin to speak until invited to do so by God — a clear indication that what he has to say derives exclusively from Divine mandate. Indeed, Satan's right, or better, obligation, to indict is attested to in both Scriptural and Rabbinic sources, with no hint of opprobrium attached to the exercise of that function. Thus at *Zechariah* 3:1ff. we have Satan, quite properly, functioning as prosecutor. True, there God silences him — as He does not in the case of Iyov — but for a specific reason, as explicated there.

Jewish tradition knows nothing of a force of evil functioning independently of the Divine determination that the world be ... *exceedingly good* (*Genesis* 1:31). There is no force propagating evil for evil's sake.

The point is made very clearly by *R' E.E. Dessler* in *Michtav MeEliyahu* vol. 4, p. 190: *Shabbos* (88b) teaches that after Moses persuaded the angels that the Torah should be given to man, the angels, Satan among them, befriended him and gave him presents. The Angel of Death, made him a gift of *ketores,* incense — the very means by which death may be defied. *R' Dessler* explains: Satan, himself, wants nothing so much as that he should be defeated. He functions within God's vision of an ideal world within which, ... *He will destroy death forever* (*Isaiah* 25:8). He incites, accuses and deals death — by Divine fiat — not because he craves evil, but because ultimate good demands that he fill that role.

Satan, challenged as it were by God, raises a reasonable question. Can Iyov's sterling qualities — which he does not dispute — withstand a crucial test? It is true, that *Iyov fears God.* Satan wonders whether that pious stance is *for nothing* (v. 9). Does it hold good only for a benign God, easily understood and as easily loved, or will it stand by him even when faced by apparently uncaring, willful cruelty? Will it buckle under the intense strain of a dreadful feeling of isolation born of incomprehension?

It should be borne in mind that the confrontation in the Heavenly court is taking place on Rosh Hashanah — the day of judgment (v. 6). In the context of God's justice, it is legitimate to demand that character traits, resident within the personality, be subjected to the crucible of action. As *Ramban* (to *Genesis* 22:1) writes in his famous rationale for the tests to which God exposes the righteous: ... *the matter must be moved from the latent to the actual, reward is to follow meritorious action, rather than be granted to the [potentially] good heart.*

Always, it is action which counts. There is a telling passage at the end of the *Kuzari,* in which the *Chaver* apprises the king of his intention to go to *Eretz Yisrael,* to better serve God there.

The king wonders why it is necessary for the *Chaver* to undertake such an arduous journey. His beliefs were so strong, his religious commitment so firm; was this not enough for God, Who in the final analysis is interested in our hearts. Why the need to actualize that which was so patently present in his soul?

The *Chaver* answers: [The heart is enough only] when action is, for some reason, impossible. But man is positioned between his aspirations and his practical realization. [If he does not act when opportunity bids, then those aspirations are not real.]

This, then, is Satan's claim. Iyov ought not be defined — even upon God's own testimony — as one who is, *of unquestioning integrity coupled with a probing mind, fears God and shuns evil,* unless those qualities have been *moved from the latent to the actual.* Until they have been put to the cruelest of tests they remain in the heart — and God's justice must demand more than that (*Pachad Yitzchak, Yom Kippur,* 24:3).

6. וַיְהִי הַיּוֹם — *On a certain day.* Our translation reflects the tradition of the Sages that the

This is what Iyov always did. [6] *On a certain day the angels came*
to stand before H*ASHEM and the Satan, too, came along with them.*
[7] H*ASHEM said to the Satan, 'From where do you come?' Satan*

session of the Heavenly Court took place on Rosh Hashanah. On this day the angels are charged with presenting the merits and faults of everyone before the Divine bar of justice (*Rashi* and *Metzudos*).

Alternatively, the phrase could be rendered simply as *one day* — the day upon which the events about to be described took place (*Ramban*).

בְּנֵי הָאֱלֹהִים — *The angels.* The translation follows *Ramban* in his preface. *Metzudos* thinks that the *B'nei HaElokim* are those angels charged with presenting the merits of the accused.

לְהִתְיַצֵּב עַל־ה׳ — *To stand before* H*ASHEM*. The translation follows *Ramban*. As does *Metzudos* above, he thinks that these angels came to act as accusers and defenders in the Heavenly court.

R' Moshe Kimchi thinks that these angels presented themselves before God that He might send them where He wished, and to render a report of what they had done in His behalf.

Rashi, apparently troubled by the unusual combination of נִצָּב עַל, interprets homiletically: The angels came to argue with God (*Rashi* adduces *Isaiah* 3:13. See also *Rashi* to *Numbers* 16:27). *Rashi* seems to feel that all the angels — not only the Satan — had the task of challenging God's assertions.

וַיָּבוֹא גַם־הַשָּׂטָן בְּתוֹכָם — *And the Satan, too, came along with them.* Satan from שָׂטַן, *to be,* or *act as an adversary,* or *an obstacle.* Thus, the angel whose duty it is to be the accuser in the Heavenly court.

Rambam in *Moreh Nevuchim* makes the point that our phrase seems to imply that Satan is not part of the *B'nei HaElokim*. He comes along with them but does not really belong among them. In *Rambam's* understanding of our passage the Satan represents the physical force which drags man downward, as opposed to his spirituality [the *B'nei HaElokim*] which alone has the right to stand before Hashem.

The Sages, too, see the Satan as the source and cause of evil and suffering in the world: A *Baraisa* taught: He comes down [from heaven] to incite [his intended victim, to sin]; he then ascends [back to heaven] to generate [God's] wrath [against the sinner]; he receives authorization [from God] and takes the [sinner's] soul.

Or, as *Reish Lakish* taught: Satan [himself] is the יֵצֶר הָרָע [*Yetzer Hara*], *Evil Inclination* [that incites man to sin], and the angel of death (*Bava Basra* 16a).

Thus, we can agree with *Rambam's* reading of the implications of our phrase, even though we interpret the *B'nei HaElokim* and the Satan as angels. Clearly the Satan, the *Yetzer Hara* and the *Malach Hamaves* are means, not ends, in the Divine plan. They may come *along* with the *B'nei HaElokim* and may be necessary to guarantee a correct balance between good and evil, but they are not in themselves *B'nei HaElokim*.

7. מֵאַיִן תָּבֹא — *From where do you come?* Satan would not have been able to speak if he had not first been addressed by God (*Metzudos*).

Where have you found sins which you would wish to report to Me? (*Daas Mikra*).

מִשּׁוּט בָּאָרֶץ וּמֵהִתְהַלֵּךְ בָּהּ — *From exploring the earth and wandering about there. Rashi* to *Numbers* 11:8 writes that the term implies an effortless roaming around. But the context here seems to imply a more purposeful peregrination, and so we have followed *Ramban* who associates the word with searching something out, or *Radak* (*Shorashim*) who reads a connotation of spying.

From *Rashi's* remarks here, it would also seem that perhaps he would agree that the word in our context has a different meaning than in *Numbers*. He writes: It is my wont to roam around to observe the wicked and the righteous. I have roved throughout the world and have found none like Abraham, concerning whom it says, 'Arise and wander (הִתְהַלֵּךְ, as in our verse) in the land.' Our Sages have taught that the Satan's motivation [in inciting God against Iyov] was grounded in good intentions (לְשֵׁם שָׁמַיִם), so that Abraham's merits might not be forgotten by God (see further at v. 9).

Rashi, then, apparently agrees that מִשּׁוּט is not to be taken as an aimless roaming, but rather that its purpose was to ascertain the spiritual state of the world.

It seems significant that even before God's query in the next verse, the Sages find a hint of the Satan's praise for Abraham. We would not have expected that an angel whose sole purpose, as defined by his name, is to act as an accuser, would find it appropriate to say anything good about anyone. Even if we grant that he found nothing evil to report, he should

ח אֶת־יהוה֒ וַיֹּ֫אמֶר מִשּׁ֫וּט בָּאָ֫רֶץ וּמֵהִתְהַלֵּ֫ךְ בָּהּ: וַיֹּ֫אמֶר
יהוה֒ אֶל־הַשָּׂטָ֫ן הֲשַׂמְתָּ לִבְּךָ֫ עַל־עַבְדִּ֫י אִיּ֫וֹב כִּ֫י אֵ֫ין
כָּמֹ֫הוּ֒ בָּאָ֫רֶץ אִ֫ישׁ תָּ֫ם וְיָשָׁ֫ר יְרֵ֫א אֱלֹהִ֫ים וְסָ֫ר מֵרָֽע:
ט וַיַּ֫עַן הַשָּׂטָ֫ן אֶת־יהוָ֫ה וַיֹּאמַ֫ר הַֽחִנָּ֫ם יָרֵ֫א אִיּ֫וֹב אֱלֹהִֽים:
י הֲלֹא־אַ֫תָּ שַׂ֫כְתָּ בַֽעֲדוֹ וּבְעַד־בֵּיתוֹ וּבְעַ֫ד כָּל־אֲשֶׁר־
ל֫וֹ מִסָּבִ֫יב מַעֲשֵׂ֫ה יָדָיו֒ בֵּרַ֫כְתָּ וּמִקְנֵ֫הוּ פָּרַ֫ץ בָּאָֽרֶץ:

have kept silent. The statement that he found no one to equal Abraham seems to fall outside the purview of his competence or interest.

It would appear that a lesson of great importance is being taught. Although, as the story develops, great power is granted to the Satan — an apparently blameless man is given over into his hands — there are limits to what he may do. There is an incorruptible, irreducible, core of sanctity — Abraham — which he cannot touch. He himself, as a function of his mission, is forced to delineate the boundaries within which his activities must be confined. He is granted control over Iyov's destiny, for the very reason that Iyov lies outside the Abraham who is beyond his reach. Thus the stage is set for the contrasting of Iyov with Abraham which we have traced above, and to which we will continue to turn.

8. הֲשַׂמְתָּ לִבְּךָ עַל־עַבְדִּי אִיּוֹב — *Have you taken note of My servant, Iyov?* What was God's purpose in asking this question?

Ramban suggests that all along, it was God's intention to put Iyov to the test. He draws the Satan's attention to him so that the latter might undertake the process of attempting to destroy him. Given this assumption, we understand the Satan's incitement in its own most simple and straightforward terms. God had meant him to play precisely the role which he in fact assumed.

It would appear that the Sages understood God's question in a different light. We recall their statement that the Satan's incitement was well-intentioned — לְשֵׁם שָׁמַיִם [*lesheim shamayim*]. He feared that Iyov might replace Abraham in God's affections. When the Satan saw that God seemed to be inclining towards Iyov, he said, *Perhaps, Heaven forbid, He will forget Abraham's goodness!*

What, in the view of the Sages, was the point of God's query, and how did the Satan react to it?

Maharal explains the basis of the assertion that the Satan was motivated by considerations which were *lesheim shamayim* as follows: It is inconceivable that the destruction of a perfectly innocent and righteous person should fall within the purview of the Satan's mission. Just as we noted above that even a *Satan* must proclaim the limitations of his own sphere of activity and admit that he cannot touch an Abraham, so too Iyov, in his own right, would have been beyond the Satan's reach. It was only as symbol of a form of Divine worship which stands in opposition to that of Abraham, that he was vulnerable.

That form is as we have defined it above. Iyov was a man of the here and now, Abraham was the man of the future. Iyov's world was the outer one, the physical and tangible. Abraham lived with the inner, the essential, the sub-surface reality. Iyov's was the service of God within the context of *Olam Hazeh*; Abraham knew only the verities of *Olam Haba*.

When God asked whether the Satan had considered 'My servant Iyov,' the implication seemed clear. God had not asked after Abraham. Did this not mean that the one mode of service seemed to be the better one, that *Iyov* was to replace *Abraham*?

As the angel charged with putting appearances to the test, the Satan's task was now clear. He would demonstrate that an external righteousness was not righteousness at all. He would expose Iyov to pressures which would force his inner shortcoming to the surface. Abraham would be vindicated.

אִישׁ תָּם וְיָשָׁר — *A man of unquestioning integrity coupled with a probing mind....* See commentary to verse 1 for an explanation of these terms.

With these words the assessment made in verse 1, by the anonymous author, is confirmed by God Himself. Here we have Divine testimony that indeed Iyov was all that had been claimed for him.

If, in spite of this testimony, the Satan still has the right to demand proof, then this can only be explained as we saw above: Qualities of the soul, be they even the most noble, must be tested in the crucible of action before they have any real meaning.

9. הַחִנָּם — *Is it for nothing.* Did Your bounty not precede his righteousness? (*Metzudos*).

answered HASHEM, *and said, 'From exploring the earth and wan-*
dering about there.' [8] HASHEM *said to Satan, 'Have you taken note*
of my servant, Iyov? For there is no one like him on earth, a man of
unquestioning integrity coupled with a probing mind, who fears
God and eschews evil!' [9] *The Satan answered* HASHEM, *saying, 'Is*
it for nothing that Iyov fears God? [10] *Have You not protected him,*
his household and all that he has. You have blessed whatever he has
undertaken, and his possessions are spread throughout the land.

Metzudos seems to think that the Satan is denying any validity to Iyov's righteousness. To be good when fortune smiles upon one means nothing at all. *Ramban* does not go so far. Good fortune, as well as suffering, can be a challenge to one's religious sensibilities. It is just that the two conditions test different spiritual muscles. Iyov had shown high constancy in the years of his happiness. Would he, asks the Satan, do as well when his benign world collapses around him?

Ramban makes a further point. With all the Satan's implacable determination to find the worst in Iyov, he does not state, nor even hint, that God's testimony is not accurate. He agrees that Iyov has led a totally blameless life, claiming only that his sterling qualities must undergo testing before they can be truly evaluated. Thus, the stage is set for Iyov's arguments. He will claim that he is innocent, his suffering has no justification. The friends will accuse him of all manner of wrongdoing. By having the Satan silent on this score, Iyov is vindicated. He is right, his friends are wrong.

וַיֹּאמַר הַחִנָּם יָרֵא אִיּוֹב אֱלֹהִים — *Is it for nothing that Iyov fears God?* The upshot of the Satan's argument is, that Iyov's fear of God is superficial. Fortune is smiling upon him, and under such circumstances it is easy enough to be good. Were he to be deprived of all the things that now spell success for him, he would show himself in his true colors: Goaded by agonies beyond endurance, he would lash out at the source of his torment. He would *blaspheme* God (v. 11).

The implication of the Satan's wording is that of the four qualities ascribed to Iyov (vs. 1 and 8), particularly the last one, *fear of God*, would be put to the test. If authentic, it would erect a bulkhead against the torrents of frustrations to which he would be subject; if it has no more than a surface validity, it would crumble.

But this would seem to contradict the apparent meaning of 2:3 and 9 which imply that it was Iyov's *temimus*, his constancy, which restrained him from sinning.

Perhaps the two qualities function at two different levels. The *tam* is totally accepting of his fate; nothing in the deep inner harmony which informs his being is disturbed [though he may question, as Iyov does later in the book], and the idea of striking out at God does not even occur to him.

But even when *temimus* is not enough to see the sufferer through his purgatory, when the pain is simply too great, the sorrow too deep, and a hatred wells up inside him which calls for the surcease of the release granted by blasphemy, the *fear of God* will protect him from himself.

This, then, is the answer to our problem. The Satan claims that Iyov will actually blaspheme. Nothing, certainly not the superficial fear of God, will hold him back. In the event, both God and Iyov's wife realized that far from actually uttering the terrible words, Iyov had not even questioned. He had clung to his constancy and accepted his fate.

10. הֲלֹא אַתָּ שַׂכְתָּ בַעֲדוֹ — *Have You not protected him?* You have guarded him as though You had built a wall around him (*Metzudos*).

שַׂכְתָּ from שׂוּךְ, *to fence up* or *about*. See *Isaiah* 5:5.

מַעֲשֵׂה יָדָיו בֵּרַכְתָּ וּמִקְנֵהוּ פָּרַץ בָּאָרֶץ — *You have blessed whatever he has undertaken and his possessions are spread throughout the land.* We have seen and discussed above how the Sages view phrases such as these as indicating the immense wealth of Iyov and the degree to which he enjoyed a perfect this-worldly life.

Concerning these two phrases we find in *Bava Basra* 15b: *You have blessed whatever he has undertaken* — Whoever took even a single coin from Iyov found himself blessed [i.e. the small coin grew into huge amounts of money]. And, ... *his possessions spread out in the land* — Iyov's flocks breached normal usage [פָּרַץ, *to breach*]. Normally wolves kill goats, but the goats of Iyov's flock killed wolves. See footnote 2 p. 6 to verse 3 for the meaning of these concepts.

יא וְאוּלָם שְׁלַח־נָא יָדְךָ וְגַע בְּכָל־אֲשֶׁר־לוֹ אִם־לֹא עַל־
יב פָּנֶיךָ יְבָרְכֶךָּ׃ וַיֹּאמֶר יהוה אֶל־הַשָּׂטָן הִנֵּה כָל־אֲשֶׁר־לוֹ
בְּיָדֶךָ רַק אֵלָיו אַל־תִּשְׁלַח יָדֶךָ וַיֵּצֵא הַשָּׂטָן מֵעִם פְּנֵי

11. אִם־לֹא — *If he does not.* The words *and see* are implied. See whether he will not blaspheme You to Your face (*Ramban*).

Metzudos thinks there is an implied oath here. May something terrible happen to me if Iyov does not blaspheme You to Your face.

עַל־פָּנֶיךָ — *To Your face.* The literal translation of the words follows *Gra*. He understands פָּנִים as *presence*. [He adduces expressions like מִקְצָת שְׁבָחוֹ בְּפָנָיו in Rabbinic Hebrew. *Rashi* occasionally offers a similar interpretation. See, for example, *Deuteronomy* 5:7.] He makes the point that most of our prayers are worded in the third person out of respect to God. Even in prayer we ought not to speak to Him directly. In the frenzy of his fury Iyov will break through all bounds of propriety and blaspheme God, addressing Him directly in the second person.

Malbim understands the word פָּנֶיךָ to mean God's providence. Not satisfied with throwing off the yoke of Heaven, Iyov will also rebel against the perceived arbitrariness of a Divine providence run awry.

Rashi does not offer any explanation here. However, we may surmise as follows: *Rashi* frequently renders פָּנִים as indicating either anger (see, e.g. *Genesis* 32:21, *Jeremiah* 21:10), or pleasure (see e.g. *Numbers* 6:25). We assume that the word takes these meanings since these emotions are reflected in the expression of the face. Perhaps, then, the meaning of our phrase might be that Iyov will blaspheme because of the apparent capriciousness with which God relates to him. The sudden change from a benign radiance to a dark and threatening mien will throw Iyov off balance and call forth a curse from the deepest recesses of his soul.

עַל־פָּנֶיךָ יְבָרְכֶךָּ — *Blaspheme You to Your face.* The Satan's challenge seems to lack an inner logic.

Previously we have been told that Iyov lived a blameless life; every facet of his being demonstrated one of the four qualities with which he had been described by the author (v. 1) and by God (v. 8). The Satan claimed that this was not surprising in view of the favors which God had showered upon him. Thus, logic would demand that the Satan should wish to demonstrate that once troubles overtook him, Iyov would act differently than he had done up to now. No more would he be the kindly benefactor of all with whom he came into contact, no more would his bearing exemplify the man of God (see chapters 30 and 31 for Iyov's own description of his life). Abandoned by a heretofore benign Deity, victim of seemingly blind, vindictive forces which overwhelmed him with careless, unfeeling cruelty, thrown — as he would think — upon his own resources, he would become the petty, selfish, grabbing and grubbing brute whom Eliphaz describes in chapter 22.

All this we would have expected the Satan to argue. But why blasphemy? Why would this follow from Iyov's suffering?

Malbim apparently was troubled by this question, and suggests that the reaction which we have described is self-understood. The meaning of the verse is that not only would Iyov stop serving God, but he would even blaspheme against Divine providence [*Malbim* understands פָּנֶיךָ to mean God's providence] which he would now perceive to be unfair and pernicious.

Alternatively, we may suggest that the blasphemy of which the Satan talks is an instinctive reaction which, if the Satan's perception that Iyov's piety is only skin-deep is correct, would slip out of Iyov's mouth immediately when tragedy strikes. No need to wait and see how his religious life will develop. A man of shallow or spurious religiosity must blaspheme (see below) when hit by the kind of catastrophe which the Satan has in mind.

עַל־פָּנֶיךָ יְבָרְכֶךָּ — *Blaspheme You to Your face.* Never, throughout all Iyov's tribulations, is there any question of his denying God. The act of cursing, as defined in halachah, is יַכֶּה יוֹסֵי אֶת יוֹסֵי, *May Yose* [God as expressed in one of His Names] *smite Yose* [as expressed in another of His Names]. The name *Yose* was substituted for the Name of Hashem (see Mishnah *Sanhedrin* 7:5 and *Rambam, Avodah Zarah* 2:7). This should certainly not be viewed as a repudiation of God. Rather, it is a furious lashing out, born of impotence and frustration, at a seemingly malevolent Deity intent on wreaking mayhem and destruction.

See verse 5 for בֵּרֵךְ as an euphemism for blasphemy.

Ramban appears to have a different understanding of יְבָרְכֶךָּ. No act of cursing is meant. Rather it is an expression of disappointment and disillusion. We quote: *From out of his knowledge of You he will denigrate the value*

[11] *But stretch out Your hand and afflict all that he has, [and
see] if he does not blaspheme You to Your face.'* [12] *HASHEM
said to Satan, 'See, all that he has is yours to dispose, only do
not lay a hand on him.' Satan departed from the presence of*

of serving You. He will say, 'It is useless to serve God, and what have I gained from having been true to His covenant, and from having walked in darkness before Him. For it is beyond God's ability, or outside His interest, [to save] those who do His will. For we see that their loyalty has not helped them.'

12. הִנֵּה כָל־אֲשֶׁר־לוֹ בְּיָדֶךָ — *See, all that he has is yours to dispose.* The translation attempts to accommodate *Radak* who takes יָד here as עֵצָה, *scheme* or *connivance. Radak* adduces *II Samuel* 14:19, which *Rashi* also interprets in the same way (see *Rashi, Ezra* 10:9).

We find *Rashi* also rendering יָד as רְשׁוּת, *control* or *possession* (cf. *Genesis* 32:14), or as כֹּחַ, *dominion* (cf. *Joshua* 8:20). Either translation would apparently be appropriate here too, but see below.

God's apparent capitulation to the Satan's demands poses an ethical problem. Can it be justified to destroy an innocent man's life, to kill his children, simply in order to test his religious standing? There is something within us which finds it difficult to accept such a concept. *R' Zerachia* articulates the problem in the sharpest possible language and pours out his scorn on anyone who would presume to take the passage literally.

We have already noted above that *Ramban* does seem to favor a literal understanding of the entire incident.

At the end of the book he suggests a novel interpretation of our passage. He notes that God had only said, *All that he has is yours;* He had not said, *Do with him as you would wish.* The implication is that the Satan was only given the right to deceive Iyov; the animals and children were not destroyed at all but were taken to a secret place and returned to him at the end of the book.

This interpretation would eliminate the ethical problem and also explain *Radak's* rendering of יָד as עֵצָה rather than as רְשׁוּת or כֹּחַ. The Satan did not, in fact, receive authority over Iyov's possessions.

רַק אֵלָיו אַל־תִּשְׁלַח יָדֶךָ — *Only do not lay a hand on him.* Iyov's travail is not flung upon him all at once. In this first round, the Satan is not permitted to lay hands upon his person. Only Iyov's property and children are to be victimized.

Why the two stages? Why the requirement that Iyov's person be handed over to the Satan in only the second round?

Daas Mikra suggests that there was simply no need to offer the Satan more at this stage. Had the Satan not been sanguine that Iyov would succumb, he would surely have asked to be granted greater latitude. He did not do so because he was certain that the loss of wealth and children would be enough to show Iyov in his true colors.

Rambam in *Moreh Nevuchim* 3:22, makes the point that Iyov was tested in all those areas which could break down a man's defenses: There are those who would crumble immediately upon losing their wealth, while others could accept such a loss with equanimity, but would be unable to stand strong in the face of their children's death. Again there are those who would not be moved by even such a tragedy, but even they would be unable to bear the torments of a putrid, dying body. Perhaps, then, we may suppose that the Satan's purposes would have been better served with a narrower mandate. Iyov's failure would have been greater if even the lesser pressure would have called forth a blasphemy. The second round, at which he is granted control over Iyov's body, becomes necessary only because Iyov, by his steadfastness, confounded the Satan's calculations.

We may surmise that there is a qualitative difference between the loss of wealth and children in the first round and the wasting of Iyov's body in the second.

It is instructive to contrast his reactions to the two sets of blows. After the first round losses we read: *Then Iyov arose, tore his robe, cut off his hair and threw himself on the ground and prostrated himself. He said, 'I was naked when I came out from my mother's womb and naked shall I return there, HASHEM has given, HASHEM has taken away: Blessed be the name of HASHEM.'*

No hint, here, of desperation or even of a passive resignation. Iyov throws himself upon the ground. Not because his suffering overpowers him, but in order to worship. God's taking is on a par with God's giving. Both elicit a religious reaction. Iyov is in total control (vs. 20 and 21).

By contrast, when Iyov is struck by leprosy he says nothing at all. *He took some potsherd to scrape himself as he sat in ashes* (2:8). It is his wife who breaks the silence with her preposter-

יג יהוה: וַיְהִי הַיּוֹם וּבָנָיו וּבְנֹתָיו אֹכְלִים וְשֹׁתִים יַיִן בְּבֵית
יד אֲחִיהֶם הַבְּכוֹר: וּמַלְאָךְ בָּא אֶל־אִיּוֹב וַיֹּאמַר הַבָּקָר הָיוּ
טו חֹרְשׁוֹת וְהָאֲתֹנוֹת רֹעוֹת עַל־יְדֵיהֶם: וַתִּפֹּל שְׁבָא וַתִּקָּחֵם
וְאֶת־הַנְּעָרִים הִכּוּ לְפִי־חָרֶב וָאִמָּלְטָה רַק־אֲנִי לְבַדִּי
טז לְהַגִּיד לָךְ: עוֹד | זֶה מְדַבֵּר וְזֶה בָּא וַיֹּאמַר אֵשׁ אֱלֹהִים
נָפְלָה מִן־הַשָּׁמַיִם וַתִּבְעַר בַּצֹּאן וּבַנְּעָרִים וַתֹּאכְלֵם
יז וָאִמָּלְטָה רַק־אֲנִי לְבַדִּי לְהַגִּיד לָךְ: עוֹד | זֶה מְדַבֵּר וְזֶה בָּא
וַיֹּאמַר כַּשְׂדִּים שָׂמוּ | שְׁלֹשָׁה רָאשִׁים וַיִּפְשְׁטוּ עַל־
הַגְּמַלִּים וַיִּקָּחוּם וְאֶת־הַנְּעָרִים הִכּוּ לְפִי־חָרֶב וָאִמָּלְטָה
יח רַק־אֲנִי לְבַדִּי לְהַגִּיד לָךְ: עַד זֶה מְדַבֵּר וְזֶה בָּא וַיֹּאמַר

ous suggestion, and it is to answer her that Iyov speaks up. Even then he says only, *Should we accept such good from God, but not accept evil?* No worshipful prostration here, no blessing of God for a *taking* which, no less than His *giving*, manifests His goodness. Here we have *good* and *bad*; Iyov's illness is an unrelieved evil; he will live with it because he must, but it is no more than a passive submission. Iyov's spirit has been broken. [We cannot, of course, ignore the possibility that Iyov's quite different reaction after the second round results from a cumulative effect. It is not that his sickness is qualitatively different than the previous losses, but that, together with what went before, it was enough to break Iyov's spirit. Nevertheless there is a good possibility that our surmisal is correct and that it is the fact of the personal illness which broke Iyov. See more in commentary there.]

The Sages teach that *a leper is akin to a corpse* (*Nedarim* 64b). As long as Iyov has his health, he stands straight before God. He is a strong and independent human being, a servant of God, who weighs each circumstance carefully and decides what he is called upon to do. He is active, not passive. Once broken in body, all this changes. In a sense he has already died. All he can offer is a weary submission. The two stages of the story reflect this qualitative difference.

וַיֵּצֵא הַשָּׂטָן — *The Satan departed.* In order to destroy Iyov's family and property (*Metzudos*).

13. וַיְהִי הַיּוֹם — *It was on a certain day.* It was once more the turn of the oldest son to invite his brothers and sisters to a feast. Iyov, as was his custom (v. 5), had brought sacrifices on that very day to atone for anything his children might have done. If at no other time, on this of all days they were without spiritual blemish; on this of all days they should be safe.

With fiendish cunning, the Satan chose the one day on which Iyov would not be able to admit any justification for his children's agony. On this, of all days, he must surely blaspheme in the face of such blatant wrong (*Metzudos*).

14. וּמַלְאָךְ בָּא — *A messenger came.* We hear only of a messenger coming to bring the catastrophic tidings; nowhere are the actual events described. From this *Ramban* concludes that in reality, the Satan had never been given a mandate to actually destroy Iyov's property or to kill his children. All were removed to a secret place from which they were eventually returned to Iyov.

Ramban writes that his contention is borne out by the use of the term *messenger*, rather than *man*. It makes no sense to talk of a *messenger* unless we know who sent him — but this is never told in the text. Rather, the *Ramban* concludes, we should assume that these were messengers sent by Satan himself in order to deceive Iyov into thinking that all these terrible things had happened.

As noted above, *Ramban's* suggestion goes far to lay to rest the ethical problem of how an innocent person could be made to suffer, simply in order to put him to a test.

הַבָּקָר הָיוּ חֹרְשׁוֹת — *The oxen were plowing.* See above, in commentary to verse 3, for *Daas Mikra's* explanation of the fact that the she-asses were grazing in the vicinity of the plowing oxen.

As noted above, in the footnote to verse 3, the Sages (*Bava Basra* 15b) deduce from this phrase that the blessings which God bestowed upon Iyov were akin to those of the World to Come.

This, as follows:

Rashi: While the oxen were still plowing, the asses were already grazing off the produce that was sown in the furrows which had only now been cut. As will be the case in Messianic times,

HASHEM. 13 *It was on a certain day, as his sons and daughters were eating and drinking wine in the house of their eldest brother.* 14 *A messenger came to Iyov and said, 'The oxen were plowing and the she-asses were grazing close by.* 15 *When Sabeans laid siege upon them and took them captive, and killed the servants by the sword; I alone have escaped [and have come] to tell you.'* 16 *This one was still speaking when another came and said 'God's fire fell from heaven, raged among the small-stock and the servants and consumed them; I alone have escaped [and have come] to tell you.'* 17 *This one was still speaking when another came and said, 'The Chaldeans fielded three divisions who deployed themselves against the camels and took them, and killed the servants by the sword; I alone have escaped [and have come] to tell you.'* 18 *Once he had spoken, another came and said,*

there was no time lapse between planting and reaping, effort and fruition.

Maharal: Perfect peace reigned between the oxen and the asses — a peace akin to that universal harmony which will be the hallmark of the Messianic era.

The implications of the qualitative perfection of Iyov's blessings have been discussed in the footnote to verse 3, above.

15. וַתִּפֹּל שְׁבָא — *When Sabeans laid siege upon them.* The translation follows *Rashi,* who often makes the point that the root נפל can have the meaning *to camp* or *come to rest* (see, for example, *Rashi* to *Genesis* 24:64, *Judges* 7:12, *Ecclesiastes* 11:3).

Maayan Gannim, based on *Targum,* renders, *When Sabeans attacked them suddenly.*

וָאִמָּלְטָה רַק־אֲנִי לְבַדִּי — *I alone have escaped.* The messenger was one of the workers who had been looking after the animals (*Ramban*).

Pesikta d'R'Kahana sees significance in the use of רַק, which usually carries an exclusionary connotation. Even this messenger who had escaped had been badly wounded, and in fact, fell dead the moment that he had delivered his message.

לְהַגִּיד לָךְ — *[And have come] to tell you.* The translation follows *Ramban.* The messenger does not mean that he escaped the Sabean sword so that he could take the tidings to Iyov, but rather that he was enabled to do so because he had remained alive.

16. אֵשׁ אֱלֹהִים נָפְלָה מִן־הַשָּׁמַיִם — *God's fire fell from heaven.* The Sages (*Pesikta Rabbosi* 17, and *Vayikra Rabbah* 17) teach that at first, when Iyov heard that his flocks had been under attack, he began to round up his retainers in order to do battle. When he heard that God's fire had come down from heaven to destroy him, he desisted. He realized that he was in the grips of something with which he was unable to contend.

We have translated in accordance with *Pesikta.* However, אֵשׁ אֱלֹהִים could also mean *a great fire.* See *ArtScroll* commentary to *I Chronicles* 12:23 for examples of such usage. See also *Jonah* 3:3.

17. כַּשְׂדִּים שָׂמוּ שְׁלֹשָׁה רָאשִׁים — *The Chaldeans fielded three divisions.* ראש as a military grouping occurs frequently in Scripture. See, for example, *Judges* 9:34 (*Metzudos*).

וַיִּפְשְׁטוּ עַל־הַגְּמַלִּים — *Who deployed themselves against the camels.* The translation follows *Rashi.* פָּשַׁט, similar to פָּרַץ, *to burst forth, to breach* (*Radak, Shorashim*) is used here in the sense *to plunder,* because while a band of marauders will cluster together for protection while *en route* to their objective, once they arrive they will split up into smaller groups so that they may surround their quarry, the more easily to abduct it.

וְאֶת־הַנְּעָרִים — *The servants.* The shepherds who were looking after the camels (*Rashi*).

18. עַד זֶה מְדַבֵּר — *Once he had spoken. Maayan Gannim* takes עַד as synonymous with עוֹד, and then the translation should be, *This one was still talking.* But *Gra* believes that the עוד was changed to עַד here with a purpose. The pain of hearing of his children's death would be much greater than the chagrin which Iyov must have felt at the loss of his property. The fourth messenger purposely bided his time so that he arrived after the third had delivered his news. Iyov would have had a few moments in which to recover from his shock, and thus the tidings of his children's death would hit him that much harder. He had thought his travail at an end — and still it continued. All this had been worked

בָּנֶיךָ וּבְנוֹתֶיךָ אֹכְלִים וְשֹׁתִים יַיִן בְּבֵית אֲחִיהֶם הַבְּכוֹר׃
יט וְהִנֵּה רוּחַ גְּדוֹלָה בָּאָה ׀ מֵעֵבֶר הַמִּדְבָּר וַיִּגַּע בְּאַרְבַּע
פִּנּוֹת הַבַּיִת וַיִּפֹּל עַל־הַנְּעָרִים וַיָּמוּתוּ וָאִמָּלְטָה רַק־אֲנִי
כ לְבַדִּי לְהַגִּיד לָךְ׃ וַיָּקָם אִיּוֹב וַיִּקְרַע אֶת־מְעִלוֹ וַיָּגָז אֶת־
כא רֹאשׁוֹ וַיִּפֹּל אַרְצָה וַיִּשְׁתָּחוּ׃ וַיֹּאמֶר עָרֹם יָצָתִי מִבֶּטֶן אִמִּי

out by the Satan so that the agony — and thus the likelihood of blasphemy — would be maximized.

19. וְהִנֵּה רוּחַ גְּדוֹלָה בָּאָה . . . וַיִּגַּע . . . — *When lo, a mighty wind came . . . It struck . . .* The Sages (*Bereishis Rabbah* 24:4) believe this to have been a miraculous wind. As in the case of the storm which threatened to capsize the boat which was carrying Jonah, the waters which surrounded the ship remained untouched and calm. So too the wind, which smashed the house in which Iyov's children held their revelry, left the surrounding areas undisturbed.

This may be indicated by a grammatical irregularity. בָּאָה is in the feminine form, וַיִּגַּע is in the masculine. *Maayan Gannim* notes this but makes no issue of it. He adduces *I Kings* 19:11, where we find the same usage. However, in the context of the tradition of the Sages we may say as follows: As the wind approached the house it was a weak ineffective (feminine form) wind, which was incapable of harming anything. Only the house itself was attacked by the full and mighty fury of a storm (masculine).

עַל־הַנְּעָרִים — *Upon the young men.* There is no need to mention the daughters (*Rashi*) because they are weaker and would surely also have been killed (*Metzudos*).

Ramban maintains that נְעָרִים includes the girls, because it is customary in Hebrew to use the masculine form when both males and females are involved (*Maayan Gannim*).

20. וַיָּקָם אִיּוֹב — *Iyov arose.* The translation does not reflect the total meaning of the Hebrew word.

Moed Kattan 20b attempted to show from this phrase that, when a mourner rends his garment, as required by the *halachah*, he must do this from a standing position. The *Gemara* rejects the proof. Iyov may have wanted to go beyond the strict requirements of the *halachah*, just as he also plucked out his hair, although a mourner has no obligation to do so.

What, then, is the point of standing up? What is this *extra* (מִלְּתָא יְתֵירָא) gesture which Iyov undertook?

Gra to *I Chronicles* 28:2 demonstrates that the root קום is not generally used to describe the act of getting up on one's feet. For this, the correct word is עָמַד. Rather קום describes a reorientation, a change of attitude or position. Only this can explain phrases such as in *Genesis* 27:19, where קום is used in conjunction with sitting down (קוּם נָא שְׁבָה).

Thus, we assume that Iyov's physical act of rising to his feet [even if he actually rose, which, as *Gra* understands it, may not necessarily be true] denoted that he was willing to shoulder an entirely different way of life, or better, a new relationship with God. He recognized that a new world was opening before him. He had served God, and served Him well, out of a state of peaceful well-being; he would now show that he could serve Him with equal devotion from the depth of suffering.

In rising to his feet Iyov spoke volumes concerning his reaction to his personal tragedy. Far from being a broken, passive victim, he would accept the challenge, would prostrate himself before God, would defy the forces which sought to drag him down by rising to new heights — of perfect submission.

Our understanding of this phrase may help us to solve a problem. In verse 22 we read, *For all that, Iyov did not sin nor did he ascribe caprice to God.* But should Iyov's reaction be expressed in such negative terms — that he cast no aspersions on God? Did he not actively prostrate himself, and in perfect humility express total submission and acceptance of his fate, in the affirmation of verse 21? In 2:10, the assertion that Iyov did not *sin with his lips* is appropriate. There, as we saw above, he had remained silent in the depth of his agony, and had spoken — and that in an extremely restrained manner — only in reply to his wife's preposterous suggestion. But surely here Iyov deserves better.

Perhaps the solution lies in regarding verse 22 as providing the background to our verse. Only because Iyov cast no aspersions on God, only because it did not occur to him, at this stage, to question the workings of Divine justice, was the positive attitude expressed here possible. One may tear one's clothes and pluck one's hair without feeling any particular submissiveness. But the change of attitude, the willingness to shoulder the new challenges,

'Your sons and daughters were eating and drinking wine in the
house of their eldest brother. 19 *When, lo, a mighty wind came from*
the wilderness. It struck the four corners of the house so that it
collapsed upon the young men and they died. I alone have escaped
[and have come] to tell you.' 20 *Iyov arose, tore his shirt, plucked*
out his hair, threw himself upon the ground, and prostrated
himself. 21 *He said, 'I was naked when I came out from my*

can derive only from an unquestioning acceptance of the essential rightness of Divine providence.

וַיִּקְרַע אֶת־מְעִלוֹ — *Tore his shirt.* An expression of suffering and mourning (*Metzudos*).

The rending of garments is one of the practices prescribed by the *halachah* for a mourner (*Yoreh De'ah* 340).

וַיָּגָז אֶת־רֹאשׁוֹ — *Plucked out his hair.* גָּזַז is often used for *shearing,* presumably done with an instrument. However, *Rashi* maintains that here the meaning is that Iyov plucked out his hair by hand. Perhaps he thought that cutting the hair with a pair of scissors would not be considered to be an act expressing mourning.

Gra believes that the hairs were not completely severed — the Torah forbids balding oneself as a sign of mourning (*Deuteronomy* 14:1 — but see *Michah* 1:16). [It is evident from *Gra's* remark that he thinks that Iyov would have conformed to the Torah law — but see footnote to verse 1 for proofs that the story seems placed in patriarchal times and that there are many apparent instances in which Torah law seems to be ignored.]

Since the hairs, not the head, are plucked, *Ramban* suggests that the phrase is to be read as though the word *hairs* were added. Alternatively, based on *Jeremiah* 7:29, he feels that גָּזַז can be used with head as the object.

וַיִּשְׁתָּחוּ — *And prostrated himself.* The worshiper lies flat upon the ground with hands and feet spread out (*Rashi* to *Genesis* 42:6).

The act of prostrating oneself denotes submission, and that submission is expressed in words by the worshiper. What Iyov spoke is given in the next verse (*Daas Mikra*).

21. וַיֹּאמַר — *He said. Ramban* offers two ways in which Iyov's musings may be understood: Though I was born naked, I had hoped to leave this world rich in family and possessions. Now I know that this is not to be. The same God who granted me my wealth, has seen fit to take it back.

Alternatively, Iyov is seeking to comfort himself: It was always clear to me that I would leave the world naked, as I had entered it. The fact that all that I had treasured was taken from me earlier than I had anticipated is no tragedy.

Gra offers: There is no reason why I should be broken by my losses. My existence is independent of my possessions — I was born naked. I would eventually have lost them anyway — I will die naked. God gave them to me and therefore, when He chooses to take them back once more, there can be no pain.

We can think of no more sublime acceptance of a calamitous fate than that which Iyov displays here. A lesser man, when faced with unbearable loss, would tend to seek to assuage his pain through defenses which deaden his sensitivities and leave him unhurt but unhelped. He might seek to blank out the joys of the past from his memory, or deceive himself into believing that things had, after all, not been so very wonderful. He may pretend that the loss is of no consequence, or foolishly try to deny its finality — I can make it all up in no time. Such a one is left with a surly, unloving surrender; and somewhere deep inside, where sure self-knowledge refuses to yield to deceit, a festering hatred of an unaccepted fate will begin to spread its silent, vicious tentacles to crush all hope, stifle all joy, and ultimately destroy any remnant of living, loving, humanity.

Iyov did none of these. Not for one moment did he permit himself the spurious luxury of denial. He did not need or seek to anesthetize his senses; he stood, unbowed and unbroken, because he knew himself to be in the hands of his God.

עָרֹם יָצָתִי מִבֶּטֶן אִמִּי — *I was naked when I came out of my mother's womb.* The next phrase, וְעָרֹם אָשׁוּב שָׁמָּה, *and naked shall I return there,* seems to point to a metaphorical use of *womb. Rashi* surmises that the earth is meant. Man was originally created from the earth, and it is there that he will eventually be buried. However, *Rashi* concedes that it is also possible to take the term literally.

What, then, is the meaning of the second phrase?

Two possibilities suggest themselves. *Ibn Ezra* believes that שָׁמָּה is not to be taken as the adverb modifying, *shall I return,* but as a euphemism for grave. He adduces *Ecclesiastes*

א/כב וְעָרֹם אָשׁוּב שָׁמָּה יהוָה נָתַן וַיהוָה לָקָח יְהִי שֵׁם יהוָה
כב מְבֹרָךְ׃ בְּכָל־זֹאת לֹא־חָטָא אִיּוֹב וְלֹא־נָתַן תִּפְלָה
ב/א־ג א לֵאלֹהִים׃ וַיְהִי הַיּוֹם וַיָּבֹאוּ בְּנֵי הָאֱלֹהִים לְהִתְיַצֵּב
עַל־יהוָה וַיָּבוֹא גַם־הַשָּׂטָן בְּתֹכָם לְהִתְיַצֵּב עַל־יהוָה׃
ב וַיֹּאמֶר יהוה אֶל־הַשָּׂטָן אֵי מִזֶּה תָּבֹא וַיַּעַן הַשָּׂטָן
ג אֶת־יהוה וַיֹּאמַר מִשֻּׁט בָּאָרֶץ וּמֵהִתְהַלֵּךְ בָּהּ׃ וַיֹּאמֶר
יהוָה אֶל־הַשָּׂטָן הֲשַׂמְתָּ לִבְּךָ אֶל־עַבְדִּי אִיּוֹב כִּי
אֵין כָּמֹהוּ בָּאָרֶץ אִישׁ תָּם וְיָשָׁר יְרֵא אֱלֹהִים וְסָר מֵרָע

3:16 for a similar usage. *Ramban* thinks that the grave could be imagined as the *womb* of the earth. Hence the meaning would be, I left one womb naked and will return to another womb, naked.

ה׳ נָתַן — *HASHEM has given.* This was his first thought. Lovingly, and with unstinting gratitude, he allows his mind's eye to rest upon his erstwhile riches. It had all been so beautiful — and so right, because it had been granted by God. Flocks and fields, sons and daughters, all had served him well, all had led towards an experiencing of God's caring proximity, His limitless bounty. Yes, all had been God's gifts, means not ends. They were dispensable now, because they could fulfill their purpose when wrested from him as well as when he had basked in their delights. *HASHEM has given* yields readily to *HASHEM has taken.* God is no less evident in the one than in the other. God's smile or God's frown; it is all one. For the one, all pervasive, totally absorbing truth is — God Himself, and His willingness to let us experience Him. *Blessed be the name of HASHEM!*

יְהִי שֵׁם ה׳ מְבֹרָךְ — *Blessed be the name of HASHEM.* The Satan's challenge had been couched in the words: אִם לֹא עַל פָּנֶיךָ יְבָרְכֶךָּ, *If he does not blaspheme You to Your fac* (v. 11). That is, he used the root ברך to express a curse (see commentary there for the euphemistic use of this root). Iyov does indeed do what Satan had predicted. He is מְבָרֵךְ God, but what a difference! Instead of blasphemy his entire being expresses adoration (*Meir Weiss*).

22. בְּכָל־זֹאת — *For all that.* Iyov had been left totally bereaved. Reason enough, we would have supposed, to wonder and then to rebel at the seemingly mindless destruction of his world. Nevertheless, not a single sinful thought even crossed his mind (*Gra*). Surely, his children had been taken for their sins — perhaps they had indeed blasphemed in their hearts — and he had been punished because he, too, was not guiltless. They had grown up in his home, seen him as the model upon which to pattern their lives. If they were willful and arrogant, must the source of their malaise not lie in his own bearing?

Thus, are the thoughts of the perfect *tzaddik* (*Ramban*). God had been vindicated, the Satan had failed.

וְלֹא־נָתַן תִּפְלָה לֵאלֹהִים — *Nor did he ascribe impropriety to God. Rashi* here seems to read תִּפְלָה as עָוֶל, *unseemliness.* However, at 6:6 he defines תָּפֵל as *unseasoned, tasteless,* and it is thus that *Ramban* takes it here. Iyov did not suspect that God had acted arbitrarily, that he or his children had been made to suffer for no fault. It would require the horrors to which he would be exposed in the next round to shake his faith and to let him see anarchy where, at this moment, all still seems ordered and benign.

II.

1. וַיְהִי הַיּוֹם — *On a certain day.* See commentary to 1:6. *Targum,* who translates there, . . . *on the day of judgment, on Rosh Hashanah,* writes here, . . . *on the day of the great judgment, on the day when sins are forgiven.* This second confrontation, then, took place on Yom Kippur.

[If Iyov was not a Jew, it is difficult to see what significance Yom Kippur would have had for him. Rosh Hashanah, the day the world was created, has universal meaning — all of mankind passes in judgment before Him. But Yom Kippur is a specifically Jewish day of atonement, commemorating the day on which God granted forgiveness for the Jewish sin of having made the Golden Calf.]

לְהִתְיַצֵּב עַל־ה׳ — *To argue with HASHEM.* The translation follows what appears to be *Ramban's* understanding of the phrase. He notes that at 1:6, where we have the almost identical verse, the Satan is not described as coming

1/22 *mother's womb and naked shall I return there.* HASHEM *has given,*
HASHEM *has taken away, blessed be the name of* HASHEM.' [22] *For all*
that, Iyov did not sin nor did he ascribe impropriety to God.

2/1-3 [1] *On a certain day the angels came to stand before* HASHEM, *and*
Satan, too, came along to argue with HASHEM. [2] HASHEM *said*
to the Satan, 'From where do you come?' The Satan answered
HASHEM, *'From exploring earth and wandering about, there.'*
[3] HASHEM *said to the Satan, 'Have you observed My servant Iyov?*
For there is no one like him on earth, a man of unquestioning
integrity coupled with a probing mind, who fears God and eschews

לְהִתְיַצֵּב עַל ה'. *Ramban's* explanation: At that point, the Satan had no cause to argue with God. He had not yet been challenged by Iyov's perfection. Consequently, had the expression been used it would have had to be rendered as it is when describing the coming of the other angels — that he, as they, was coming to stand before God. This would have put the Satan on an equal footing with the other heavenly beings — and that is not so, as we see from *Rambam* (*Moreh Nevuchim*) quoted to that verse.

Not so in our verse. Surely after his defeat, the Satan would be coming equipped with fresh arguments with which to make a case against Iyov. לְהִתְיַצֵּב עַל, as it relates to the Satan, can thus be taken as we have rendered it, which differentiates it from the same expression used to describe the angels.

This translation is akin to the one suggested by *Rashi* at 121:6.

2. אֵי מִזֶּה תָּבֹא — *From where do you come?* אֵי, *where is the place concerning which you would say,* מִזֶּה, *it is from here that I am coming* (*Metzudos*).

In 1:7 the expression was מֵאַיִן. One would be inclined to think that מֵאַיִן is a more general question. There is no assumption that there is a זֶה, a specific place of interest, but that אֵי מִזֶּה does postulate such a point. If correct, this thesis would explain the change in language between the two chapters. On the second occasion there is an expectation that the Satan would have something specific to report.

However, they appear to be used interchangeably in Scripture. Compare, for example, *Joshua* 2:4 to *I Samuel* 25:11. It seems likely that the two expressions, מֵאַיִן and אֵי מִזֶּה, really have identical meanings.

וּמֵהִתְהַלֵּךְ בָּהּ — *And wandering about, there.* In the commentary to 1:7 we saw that the Sages felt that this wording hinted at Abraham (קוּם הִתְהַלֵּךְ בָּאָרֶץ). The Satan was making the point that in all his peregrinations around the world he had found none to equal Abraham in his service of God. See there for a discussion.

While *Rashi* says nothing to this verse, consistency would seem to demand that here, too, we should see the same reference. The Satan would then be saying that nothing in his perception of the relative merits of Abraham and Iyov had changed. The former was still unique. This becomes significant in light of *Ramban's* assertion (see commentary to next verse) that in the course of his suffering Iyov had risen to a level of serving God out of love rather than out of fear.[1]

3. הֲשַׂמְתָּ לִבְּךָ אֶל־עַבְדִּי אִיּוֹב — *Have you observed My servant Iyov?* We have changed the translation from the rendering in chapter 1. It seems obvious that the query carries a different weight here. There, the question was a neutral one, *Have you taken note . . .*, is there anything special about Iyov. Here, as the end of the sentence makes clear, God is confronting the Satan with his failure. Have you observed how Iyov, far from losing his integrity, has even grown from the terrible experiences which you forced him to undergo?

1. We have seen in the commentary and footnotes to chapter 1 that the Satan's concern was that God might be rejecting Abraham in favor of Iyov; Israel, in favor of the other nations — see particularly commentary to verse 8.

Thus, we may say that in this confrontation, the choice of Israel as God's particular people is hanging in the balance.

It is particularly apt that this confrontation should take place on Rosh Hashanah (commentary 1:1) and Yom Kippur (commentary v. 1), since the Sages teach that on those days God, in fact, sits in judgment concerning this very issue. Each year the choice of Israel from among the nations must be, and is, reaffirmed. See *Vayikra Rabbah* 21:3 and 30:2.

ד וְעֹדֶנּוּ מַחֲזִיק בְּתֻמָּתוֹ וַתְּסִיתֵנִי בוֹ לְבַלְּעוֹ חִנָּם׃ וַיַּעַן
הַשָּׂטָן אֶת־יהוה וַיֹּאמַר עוֹר בְּעַד־עוֹר וְכֹל אֲשֶׁר לָאִישׁ
ה יִתֵּן בְּעַד נַפְשׁוֹ׃ אוּלָם שְׁלַח־נָא יָדְךָ וְגַע אֶל־עַצְמוֹ

וְעֹדֶנּוּ מַחֲזִיק בְּתֻמָּתוֹ — *He still keeps his unquestioning integrity*. See commentary to 1:9 for a discussion of which of Iyov's qualities was being put to the test.

וַתְּסִיתֵנִי בוֹ לְבַלְּעוֹ חִנָּם — *And now you have incited Me against him to destroy him for no good reason*. The idea of the Satan *inciting* God seems to have troubled the Sages. R' Yochanan taught: Were it not written plainly, we could never have said it on our own. [God was] like a man who submitted to incitement (*Bava Basra* 16a).

Perhaps the point which called forth R' Yochanan's wonderment was the seemingly irresistible power of the Satan. God did not want to be turned against Iyov [otherwise no *incitement* would be necessary] and nevertheless allowed Himself to be coerced!

The concept is hard for us to grasp. Perhaps it involves the system of law and justice which underlies God's governance of the world — *By justice a king sustains the land* (*Proverbs* 29:4). Once God creates a force in the world, the purpose and function of which is to act as accuser, that force has a right to exist, which in terms of its own reality means that it can demand a hearing. This may be the understanding of *Maharal* who explains the passage which we have quoted by saying: For He, blessed be, created a Satan to point out the faults of mankind ... He permits Himself to act upon Satan's findings.

Ramban also seems to deem the expression inappropriate as a description of that which happened between God and the Satan. He sees its use as an example of the Torah's usage, to speak *in the language of man* — as a king would address his servants. However, he adds that the *destruction* which God undertook *for no apparent reason* was really not a destruction at all. That which the Satan had hoped would break Iyov proved, on the contrary, to stimulate him to scale heights of spirituality, hitherto too great for him. Where till now he had served God only out of fear, he would be, in the end, counted among those who are motivated by love.

With this remark *Ramban* seems to be relegating the inappropriate phrase to the realm of appearances. It looked as though God had been incited to do an idle thing. In reality, the experiences to which Iyov was exposed were not wasted. God's willingness to make Iyov suffer becomes the most positive and significant event in his life, and it was the Satan whose efforts turned out to be in vain.[1]

חִנָּם — *For no good reason*. He had not sinned, which would have been reason enough to make him suffer, but was simply being put to a test (*Metzudos*).

Surely the חִנָּם here is meant to echo Satan's rhetorical question הַחִנָּם יָרֵא אִיּוֹב אֱלֹהִים, *Is it for nothing that Iyov fears God*? The term is now turned against Satan.

4. עוֹר בְּעַד־עוֹר — *Limb for limb*. One limb may be sacrificed to protect another. If a person sees a sword descending upon his head he will raise his arm so that it may take the blow (thus exposing it to mutilation). Certainly, then, a man who knows himself to be deserving punishment would be prepared to sacrifice anything he has [in this case, property and children] if thereby he himself can remain untouched (*Rashi*).

[*Rashi* appears to take עוֹר, *skin*, as synonymous with limb. Perhaps this naming of a unit by the word which describes its appearance would be analogous with the use of תְּכֵלֶת, a color, to describe wool dyed with that color (see *Exodus* 25:4).

Again the word עוֹר may have the meaning of, *that which protects or holds something together, supports or services it*. Thus we have *Iyov* 19:20 talking of *the skin of my teeth*, which, as *Rashi* explains there, refers to the gums. Perhaps, then, any limb could be described as the עוֹר of the body.]

Ramban suggests that the first עוֹר may be describing the bodies of Iyov's children. Any man would be prepared to sacrifice his children if thereby he could save his own skin.

Malbim thinks that the first עוֹר may be describing a garment made of skin or fur. Anyone would be willing to sacrifice his clothing in order to save his own body. Similarly Iyov ultimately absorbs the loss of wealth and children,

1. *Chavel* points out that *Ramban's* assertion that as a result of his suffering, Iyov changed from service motivated by fear to service motivated by love, is a combination of two opinions cited in *Sotah* 27b. There we learn that *R' Yochanan ben Zakkai* maintains that Iyov served God out of fear, while *R' Yehoshua ben Horkenus* thinks that he was motivated by love. We shall have occasion to return to this dispute at relevant places in the commentary.

evil. He still keeps his unquestioning integrity. And now you have
incited Me against him, to destroy him for no good reason.' 4 *The*
Satan answered HASHEM, *'Limb for limb all that a man has he will*
give up for his life. 5 *But, stretch out Your hand and smite his bones*

since these do not touch his own person.

בְּעַד־עוֹר . . . בְּעַד נַפְשׁוֹ — *For limb . . . for his life.* בְּעַד is most frequently used in Scripture in the sense of praying for someone; see for example *Genesis* 20:7. Its meaning is, therefore, *for the sake of, in behalf of*. Thus, the sense of our two phrases is that he will sacrifice one *skin* for the sake of another, or all that he has for the sake of his life.

נַפְשׁוֹ — *His life.* נֶפֶשׁ describes the entire person — body and soul together, not only the soul. *Leviticus* 7:20 speaks of a נֶפֶשׁ eating, and *Numbers* 6:6 speaks of a נֶפֶשׁ dying (*Mahari MiTrani, I Samuel* 25:29). Hence, *his life*.

5-6. שְׁלַח־נָא יָדְךָ — *Stretch out Your hand.* The language used by the Satan here is identical with that used in his request at 1:11. It is significant in that he recedes entirely into the background. In his thought-world it is God, not he, who is the active agent in causing man's suffering.

There is, however, a substantive change in the language which God uses to answer the Satan. At 1:12 He says, *See all that he has is yours to dispose, only do not lay a hand on him.* The wording is very precise: הִנֵּה כָל־אֲשֶׁר־לוֹ בְּיָדֶךָ [the phrase which we have rendered idiomatically, *See all that he has is yours to dispose*]. It is not a question of My laying a hand. He is in your hands (בְּיָדֶךָ). Only, do not lay a hand on his person. Once more, it is you, not I, who is the active agent in Iyov's suffering.

Here, God's answer does not parallel the one in chapter 1 precisely. Once more we have הִנּוֹ בְיָדֶךָ, *See he is yours to dispose*, just as in the earlier conversation, but the next phrase is different: We have אַךְ אֶת־נַפְשׁוֹ שְׁמֹר, *only spare his life*, where we would have expected רַק אֶל נַפְשׁוֹ אַל תִּשְׁלַח יָדֶךָ.

Perhaps we have here the key to the truths which we learned in the commentary to 1:12. There is a qualitative difference between attacking Iyov's property but sparing his person, and attacking his person while sparing his life — a difference which expressed itself in the radically dissimilar way in which Iyov reacted to the second catastrophe. In chapter 1 Iyov himself was truly beyond the Satan's reach, ' . . . only do not lay a hand on him.' Iyov is not among that which is now בְּיַד of the Satan. But once Iyov's body is given בְּיַד of the Satan, then the obligation to spare his life is only a quantitative inhibition. As we learned above, the מְצוֹרָע, *leper*, is akin to a corpse; death to a degree has set in. The Satan, in a real sense, is laying a hand upon his victim's very life. The language which we suggested above would not have been appropriate.[1]

And so, we enter upon a new phase of Iyov's travails. A painful, revolting and totally debilitating form of death sets in, leaving a physically broken shell where once a proud and happy man had stood.

Earlier we saw that God had characterized the Satan's first incitement as חִנָּם, *for no good reason*. We saw that *Ramban* goes out of his way to show that this definition conformed only to the appearance. In reality the terrible experiences to which Iyov was exposed changed him from one who fears God into one who loves Him.

What of this newest torment? Was this really חִנָּם, or did it have positive ramifications for the hapless victim?

It may well be that Iyov's ultimate triumph, his personal epiphany, his loving acceptance of God's will however it may have been expressed, which in the end made his rehabilitation possible, may well have been a direct re-

1. Our insight can help us to understand an otherwise difficult passage in *Bava Basra* 16a. *R' Yitzchak* taught: The Satan (who was not allowed to kill Iyov) suffered more than Iyov himself. His frustrations are akin to those of a servant who is told to break open a barrel of wine but forbidden to drink any.

In the light of what we have learned from the wording of the phrase, we can readily understand the high frustration level of the Satan. He was allowed to kill, really to kill, and yet had to keep Iyov alive!

But how are we to understand the concept being taught? The Satan after all had no interest in killing Iyov. He had wanted to show that under severe pressure his piety would break down and he would blaspheme God. Why then the chagrin at not being allowed to kill?

It would appear that the Sages are teaching us the essential evil of the Satan who, as we saw above (1:6), is not only accuser but also inciter and the angel of death. With a victim's life actually within his grasp, his original purpose becomes blurred. The essential, death-dealing, intractable force of evil preempts the role of the accuser, which can have its benign side (as we saw from the teaching of the Sages that the Satan's original intentions were good).

ו וְאֶל־בְּשָׂרוֹ אִם־לֹא אֶל־פָּנֶיךָ יְבָרְכֶךָּ: וַיֹּאמֶר יְהוָה
ז אֶל־הַשָּׂטָן הִנּוֹ בְיָדֶךָ אַךְ אֶת־נַפְשׁוֹ שְׁמֹר: וַיֵּצֵא הַשָּׂטָן
מֵאֵת פְּנֵי יְהוָה וַיַּךְ אֶת־אִיּוֹב בִּשְׁחִין רָע מִכַּף רַגְלוֹ °עַד °וְעַד ק'
ח קָדְקֳדוֹ: וַיִּקַּח־לוֹ חֶרֶשׂ לְהִתְגָּרֵד בּוֹ וְהוּא יֹשֵׁב בְּתוֹךְ־
ט הָאֵפֶר: וַתֹּאמֶר לוֹ אִשְׁתּוֹ עֹדְךָ מַחֲזִיק בְּתֻמָּתֶךָ בָּרֵךְ
י אֱלֹהִים וָמֻת: וַיֹּאמֶר אֵלֶיהָ כְּדַבֵּר אַחַת הַנְּבָלוֹת תְּדַבֵּרִי

sult of the physical purgatory through which he had to pass.

Later, in Elihu's speech (33:15-22), we shall learn more about the educating properties of physical suffering. Here we note only that in many of our sources it is perceived as a means of breaking down impediments to a greater spiritual awareness and experience. Thus, for example, we have *Gra* advising his wife to use corporal punishment in bringing up their children because: '... sometimes seeds may be sown on stony ground, a stony heart, which they are unable to penetrate. Such a stone must be beaten, eventually to be broken open [so that the seed may enter, and flowering become possible].' *R' E. E. Dessler* (*Michtav MeEliyahu* vol. 3, Letters), based on *RaMCHaL*, understands *Gra's* ideas as equating physical suffering with the removal (circumcising) of the עָרְלַת הַלֵּב, *the dulling, numbing, deadening 'foreskin' of the heart*, and with חִבּוּט הַקֶּבֶר, *the smashing or wearing away of physicality associated with death and the grave*, both designed to release one's spiritual potential. [See also *Zohar* 2:198: ... The righteous one craves that he be broken, breakage piled on breakage, all for the sake of Hashem, his God.]

We may surmise that the heights to which Iyov ultimately rose, the vision of God which in the end was granted him, became accessible only after he had traversed a valley of bitter suffering. As we shall see at 42:5, Iyov's problems stemmed from the fact that although he had indeed *heard* of God he had not yet *seen* Him. The clarity of vision by which he would perceive God thus, that no questions could ever trouble him again, would not come easily. It is a function of deeply recessed founts of spirituality which must await their release in the searing flames of Iyov's agony.

Thus, here too there was no question of a real חִנָּם in God's acquiescence to the Satan's challenge.

אֶל־עַצְמוֹ וְאֶל־בְּשָׂרוֹ — *His bones and his flesh.* The translation is literal. In this we follow *Gra* as he interprets *Genesis* 29:14. See *ArtScroll* commentary there. We could, of course, also assume that the expression is idiomatic and render the phrase, *his own flesh and blood*.

7. וַיֵּצֵא הַשָּׂטָן — *The Satan departed*. With his departure from the Divine Presence, bent on afflicting Iyov (*Metzudos*), the Satan recedes entirely from our field of interest. Nowhere in the book is he mentioned again, nowhere is the point made that he had lost his wager.

By the method of ignoring the Satan completely except to the extent that he impinges directly upon the story of Iyov, the author teaches an important lesson.

In 1:6-12 we learned from *Ramban* that the Satan is an angel (מַלְאָךְ, *messenger*, from לאך, *to send*), one whose entire being is exhausted in his capacity of being a functionary for the fulfillment and actualization of God's will. Judaism knows of no evil power, locked in some cosmic struggle with the forces of good. Thus, once his task is fulfilled, he does not even *exist* in any real sense — his being is congruent with his specific charge. Having done what God wished him to do, he is no more.

בִּשְׁחִין רָע — *A severe inflammation*. שְׁחִין occurs in *Leviticus* 13:18 as an infection (caused by anything other than a burn — *Negaim* 9:1) upon which, after it heals, צָרַעַת may develop. *Rashi* at *Exodus* 9:9 and elsewhere has the word implying heat (חֲמִימוּת). Hence, an inflammation.

שְׁחִין רָע is the most painful kind of this שְׁחִין (*Metzudos*).

8. לְהִתְגָּרֵד בּוֹ — *To scrape himself*. *Gra* explains that the אֵפֶר in which Iyov sat, as described in the latter part of this verse, is the pile of dead skin that flaked off Iyov's body because of the שְׁחִין.

וְהוּא יֹשֵׁב בְּתוֹךְ־הָאֵפֶר — *As he sat in ashes*. *Rashi* (*Taanis* 15a) points out that אֵפֶר, *ashes*, and עָפָר, *dust*, are interchangeable in Scripture. Accordingly, the translation could well be, *in dust*.

He sat in the ashes either as a sign of mourning (*Ibn Ezra* and others), or to cool the inflammation (*Metzudos* and others). [*Daas Mikra* makes the point that he did not sit *on*, but *in*, the ashes; his sorrow was so intense that he felt

and his flesh, and he will surely blaspheme You to Your face.'
[6] HASHEM said to the Satan, 'See, he is yours to dispose; only
spare his life.' [7] The Satan departed from the presence of HASHEM
and inflicted a severe inflammation on Iyov from the sole of his
foot till the crown of his head. [8] He took some potsherd to scrape
himself as he sat in ashes. [9] His wife said to him, 'Are you still
maintaining your unquestioning integrity! Blaspheme God and
die!' [10] He said to her, 'You talk as any senseless woman might talk.

he had to pile up the symbol of his agony all around himself.]

Malbim quotes a midrash in which Iyov is depicted as suffering from two kinds of שְׁחִין. The upper part of his body was afflicted with a dry variety which required scratching or scraping, while the lower part was covered by a moist kind, and there it was necessary to drain off the excess liquid. This was accomplished by sitting in the ashes.

9. וַתֹּאמֶר לוֹ אִשְׁתּוֹ — *His wife said to him. R' Zerachiah* raises the question of why the author (if we are to deem the book a מָשָׁל) found it necessary to introduce Iyov's wife. He rejects the idea that she may be used simply to act as a foil for Iyov's rejoinder, to give us a chance to learn of Iyov's righteousness through the answer that he gives her, because we have had ample proof of his goodness from the reaction to his suffering which is recorded in the first chapter.

His solution is that just as the Satan stands for man's physicality, so too is Iyov's wife symbolic of the יֵצֶר הָרַע, *the evil inclination* which seduces man to do that which is wrong in the eyes of God. He feels that her role in the story is analogous to that of Eve in Eden. In both instances the wives stand as temptresses, wishing to introduce death, where obedience to God's wishes would guarantee life.

We may suggest a different motive for the introduction of Iyov's wife into the story. It may well be that she appears with her preposterous suggestion in order, as it were, to rub salt into Iyov's wounds. His agony is to be total. Even though, as we have seen above, the sickness which smote his body was already a kind of dying, no man is ever completely forsaken as long as a loving and supportive wife is at his side. By demonstrating her complete inability to understand her husband's desperate need to maintain his integrity in the face of unassailable evidence that this integrity seemed meaningless, she dealt him the final blow. Now, indeed, he stood alone.

בָּרֵךְ אֱלֹהִים וָמֻת — *Blaspheme God and die!* There is no point in prolonging such a life of agony. Blaspheme God now, and you will die right away (*Metzudos*).

Ramban objects: There is no reason to suppose that even the most terrible of sins would be followed by immediate death. What right had she to assume that Iyov could end his agony at will? Rather, we must assume that this woman was unable to conceive of an altruistic service of God. Surely, she reasoned, if Iyov had maintained his integrity up to this point, that would only be because he hoped thereby to earn a long life as a reward. She argues that under the circumstances, this would be the worst thing that could happen. Much better to make an end of it. Let Iyov sin, and then, at least, he will not be made to bear the agony longer than necessary.

Iyov's rejoinder will be that his service of God is not conditioned by any expectation of reward. He is motivated by pure love (see above, v. 3).

Malbim sees a biting and bitter sarcasm in the woman's words. בָּרֵךְ means *to bless*, not to blaspheme. When the calamities of chapter 1 had come upon him, Iyov had blessed God: *Blessed be the name of HASHEM* (1:21). This supreme act of submission had been *rewarded* by the vile שְׁחִין which was, even now, torturing him. Let him once more maintain his integrity, let him again bless God. What *reward* will there be left to give? Surely the next thing that God can do in reaction to his constancy will be to kill him.

10. אַחַת הַנְּבָלוֹת — *Any senseless woman*. נָבָל appears in Scripture with many different nuances. *Metzudos* here renders *lowly*, *ignoble*, and this would reflect the meaning in *Isaiah* 32:5 where the word is contrasted with נָדִיב, *a noble-minded person*. This, too, is how *Rashi* renders the verb נבל at *Deuteronomy* 32:15.

However, we have translated *senseless*, in accordance with *Rashi* to *Ezekiel* 13:3 where he uses שׁוֹטִים, *fools*. This meaning seems appropriate here, where Iyov accuses his wife of a lack of religious sophistication. This rendering accords with *Deuteronomy* 32:6 where the word is contrasted to חָכָם, one who is wise.

גַּם אֶת־הַטּוֹב נְקַבֵּל מֵאֵת הָאֱלֹהִים וְאֶת־הָרָע לֹא נְקַבֵּל
בְּכָל־זֹאת לֹא־חָטָא אִיּוֹב בִּשְׂפָתָיו׃
יא וַיִּשְׁמְעוּ שְׁלֹשֶׁת ׀ רֵעֵי אִיּוֹב אֵת כָּל־הָרָעָה הַזֹּאת
הַבָּאָה עָלָיו וַיָּבֹאוּ אִישׁ מִמְּקֹמוֹ אֱלִיפַז הַתֵּימָנִי וּבִלְדַּד

גַּם אֶת־הַטּוֹב — *Such good*. Commentators are troubled by the word גַּם, which does not readily fit the syntax. Our rendering attempts to reflect *Rashi's* understanding, although the wording is not easily given in the English idiom. *Rashi* thinks that the גַּם is there to underline the qualitative greatness of God's goodness, so that a refusal to submit to His providence when it imposes suffering becomes an even more heinous crime: The fact that we owe our very existence to God makes any additional (גַּם) favors doubly great.

Ramban sees the גַּם as dealing with the entire concept dealt with in Iyov's statement. A willingness to accept God's favors, coupled with (גַּם) a refusal to submit to His providence when that expresses itself in harshness, constitutes a sin that is greater than a total denial of Divine Providence.

As we saw above, *Ramban* sees this statement as a ringing affirmation of Iyov's love for God.

לֹא־חָטָא אִיּוֹב בִּשְׂפָתָיו — *Iyov did not sin by his mouth*. But in his heart he sinned (*Rashi*, based on *Bava Basra* 16a, and *Targum*, here).

Above, at 1:12, we noted the apparent passivity of Iyov's reaction to the שְׁחִין, when contrasted to his active prostration and worship at the time when he lost all his possessions. Our verse, as interpreted by the Sages, explains his silence. Already at this stage, doubts about the logic and fairness of Divine Providence play havoc with his preconceived notions of a neatly arranged and benign world order. Iyov, the relentless seeker of truth as he perceives it (see specifically at 13:15-17), is beginning to replace Iyov the humble and accepting servant of God.

Both *Ibn Ezra* and *Ramban* perceive the thrust of the phrase somewhat differently. Even at this point [עַד הֵנָּה = בְּכָל־זֹאת (*Ramban*)] Iyov was not yet speaking rebelliously. The implication is that as time would pass, when he would be talking with his friends (*Ramban*), he would indeed be sinning with his lips.

We have, then, a progression in Iyov's reactions: From worship, to a silent questioning, to articulated insubordination. We have already attempted to understand the movement from the first to the second state at 1:12. We must analyze the dynamics which led to Iyov's open rebellion, as part of our discussion of the role which the three friends play in his saga. See below.

11-13. There are three significant points which we can isolate about the friends of Iyov and their role in the saga.

1. The friendship between these four men is perceived by the Sages as ideal. Rava taught: There is a proverb which says: Death is preferable for a person who does not have friends such as those which Iyov had.

As the Sages teach, the four friends lived very far apart [*three hundred leagues* — a number denoting great distance in *aggadic* literature]. How then did they know of Iyov's troubles. Either they had crowns [upon which the faces of the other three were pictured. When something untoward happened to one of them, his likeness on the crowns would change and all the friends would know that they were needed (*Rashi*)] or they had trees [of which the leaves would wither when one of them was in trouble. *Rashi* implies that on the trees, too, the three images were engraved] (*Bava Basra* 16b).

Maharal understands the *crowns* as symbolizing a degree of nobility which bound these friends together and separated them from all others. The *trees* are a metaphor for four entities, each maintaining its own integrity while nevertheless being joined by a common base, in much the same way that four distinct trees are nevertheless joined by the fact that they all grow from the same ground. Even without understanding the precise symbolism of *crown* and *tree* we can still appreciate the fact that by means of these ideas the Sages are pointing to the unusual and perhaps unique ties of friendship which bound these four men together.

2. Their efforts at helping Iyov failed miserably. Not only were they not of any comfort, but gradually their friendship turned to sour hatred (see especially, Eliphaz's third speech in chapter 22), which, in smug self-righteousness, drained them of any feeling of empathy or understanding for a comrade suffering in agony.

To appreciate the extent of their abject failure we need only listen to Iyov's anguished cry: *Pity me, pity me! You are my friends; for the hand of God has struck me! Why do you pursue me like God? Is my [putrid] flesh not enough [suffering] for you?* (19:21-22). God Himself is repelled by their harsh insensitivity: *My anger*

Should we accept such good from God and not accept evil?' For all that Iyov did not sin by his mouth.

11 *Iyov's three friends heard about all these calamities which had befallen him, and each came from his home — Eliphaz the Temanite,*

is seething against you and against your two friends, because in your defense of Me you did not speak as appropriately as did My servant Iyov (42:7).

Indeed, when *Bava Metzia* 58b wishes to illustrate the kind of talk which is interdicted under the rubric *Ona'as Devarim*, the use of speech to subject a person to suffering, the example is drawn from the friends' approach to Iyov's troubles: If a man is exposed to suffering or illness, or if he was called upon to bury his children, do not say to him *as Iyov's friends said* to him: *Was then your reverence not your folly, so too your hopes and the constancy of your bearing. Do recall I beg you: Who is the innocent that was ever left without a trace.*

Clearly if the friends have become the paradigm of what *not* to say to a sufferer, their failing must have been great indeed.

3. In some unexplicated way, the friends exercise a deleterious effect upon Iyov. From the moment that they come, and progressing as debate turns into argument and finally into recrimination, his stance undergoes a metamorphosis. From silent if uncomprehending acceptance, Iyov moves to belligerent and indeed bellicose confrontation. True, actual words of blasphemy never cross his lips but, as frustration and anger pile upon frustration and anger, he permits himself expression of sentiments which, in implication if not in form, come perilously close.

What went wrong? Why were the friends such an abysmal failure?

Since the book presents the story on its own terms and offers no explanations, we are thrown upon our own critical faculties and must read the text in such a way that it provides us with the answers which we are seeking.

The secret may lie in a correct perception of the role which Elihu (chs. 32-37) plays in the saga. An exhaustive analysis must be left for later in the book, but even now we can make the following observations.

1. Elihu directs only his opening remark (chapter 32) to Iyov. After those, he turns to wise men in general (34:2), presumably those standing around listening to the debate, and ignores Iyov as a person, quoting him (e.g. 34:5) but not engaging him in the discussion. Apparently his concern is less with Iyov the man than with *Iyov* the problem.

2. He does not in any way attack Iyov as a person. He offers explanations for the suffering which, occasionally, is the lot of man (e.g. 33:14ff.), but does not in any way attempt to blame Iyov for what has happened to him.

3. Apparently, as a result of this objective and uninvolved approach, Iyov does not feel called upon to answer Elihu in any way. He was attacked by the friends and could not let their charges and insinuations go unchallenged. By contrast, he can listen quietly to Elihu, and judge the arguments on their merits. Later, at an appropriate place, we shall discuss what in fact Iyov's reactions to Elihu were, and how the ideas offered by him mesh with those taught by God when He ultimately appears to Iyov.

All this seems to point to what may be an important theme in the book: Friends, particularly very good friends, may not make the best comforters. They cannot, by their very nature, be dispassionate, cannot distance themselves in order to make sure that their perceptions are not distorted. Their very familiarity, they feel, entitles them to be critical and brutally honest, where instead, a more circumspect respect would have been in order.

It remains possible to wonder how successful the friends would have been if instead of debating Iyov they would have loved him, if instead of trying to explain suffering — with all the good intentions of stimulating their comrade to repentance — they would have made it bearable by being supportive. If they would have helped Iyov to accept rather than to question, to concentrate on ways to cope rather than upon recriminations, they may have met with greater success.

11. שְׁלֹשֶׁת רֵעֵי אִיּוֹב — *Iyov's three friends*. Iyov must, of course, have had more than three friends. The others, however, distanced themselves from him as soon as troubles overtook him — see 19:13-19 and 42:11. The meaning is — three friends who had remained loyal to him (*Daas Mikra*).

Alternatively, we can interpret: The three special friends — those who had the qualities of friendship described above.

אֱלִיפַז ... וּבִלְדַּד ... וְצוֹפַר ... — *Eliphaz ... and Bildad ... and Tzophar*. See commentary 1:1 for *Ramban's* identification of these men.

וַיִּוָּעֲדוּ יַחְדָּו — *And met together*. Although they came from homes which were far removed

הַשּׁוּחִי וְצוֹפַר הַנַּעֲמָתִי וַיִּוָּעֲדוּ יַחְדָּו לָבוֹא לָנוּד־לוֹ
יב וּלְנַחֲמוֹ׃ וַיִּשְׂאוּ אֶת־עֵינֵיהֶם מֵרָחוֹק וְלֹא הִכִּירֻהוּ וַיִּשְׂאוּ
קוֹלָם וַיִּבְכּוּ וַיִּקְרְעוּ אִישׁ מְעִלוֹ וַיִּזְרְקוּ עָפָר עַל־רָאשֵׁיהֶם
יג הַשָּׁמָיְמָה׃ וַיֵּשְׁבוּ אִתּוֹ לָאָרֶץ שִׁבְעַת יָמִים וְשִׁבְעַת לֵילוֹת
וְאֵין־דֹּבֵר אֵלָיו דָּבָר כִּי רָאוּ כִּי־גָדַל הַכְּאֵב מְאֹד׃ אַחֲרֵי־
יד כֵן פָּתַח אִיּוֹב אֶת־פִּיהוּ וַיְקַלֵּל אֶת־יוֹמוֹ׃

from one another, they all entered the city in which Iyov lived by the same gate, as if instinctively drawn together (*Bava Basra* 16b, and *Maharsha*, there).

לָנוּד־לוֹ — *To mourn with him*. The translation attempts to conform to *Rashi*, who at *Jeremiah* 15:5 and 16:5 renders the word with מְקוֹנֵן, *to sing a dirge or an elegy*.

Metzudos thinks that the meaning is to shake one's head, as one who wishes to show solidarity with his friends' suffering would do. [When the word is used in the התפעל (see *Jeremiah* 48:27), *Rashi* too renders, *to shake the head*, as does *Metzudos*.]

וּלְנַחֲמוֹ — *And to comfort him*. In the event, the friends did not really find the words to comfort Iyov effectively — see above. *Daas Mikra* believes that their ineptness was itself a result of the Satan's wiles. Under other circumstances, perhaps they would have done better.

12. וְלֹא הִכִּירֻהוּ — *But could not recognize him*. His face had changed because of his suffering (*Rashi*).

Another explanation may be possible. See *Targum* to *Proverbs* 26:24: בְּשִׂפְתָא יִנָּכֵר שׂוֹנֵא, *An enemy may be recognized by his speech*. Thus we have נכר used, not to describe the recognizing of an identity, but of a nature. Perhaps the friends could not *recognize* Iyov in the sense that his face projected a look of bitterness and disillusion, quite different from anything to which they had been used. This was not the old Iyov whom they knew. See further at *The First Round*, between chapters 14 and 15.

עַל־רָאשֵׁיהֶם הַשָּׁמָיְמָה — *Into the air over their heads*. It is *Metzudos* who renders הַשָּׁמָיְמָה as [the air] of the heavens.

13. וַיֵּשְׁבוּ אִתּוֹ לָאָרֶץ — *They sat with him on the ground*. In order to share in his pain (*Rashi*).

The use of אִתּוֹ instead of עִמּוֹ is no doubt significant. There appears to be differences of opinion among linguists as to which of the two expressions denotes absolute equality and which a simple joining, a togetherness born of circumstances rather than a real affinity.

Wertheimer (*Biur Sheimos HaNirdafim B'Tanach*) quotes *Ibn Janah* that אֶת is used for נִטְפָּל, *the subordinate*, while עִם is used for שָׁוִוי, *the equal*. He adduces many examples and also quotes *Zohar* to *Genesis* 32:29 [it does not say אֶת but עִם — an expression of being (absolutely) joined and of being a twosome] to support his thesis.

However, *HaKesav VeHaKabbalah* to *Genesis* 24:32 maintains the exact opposite, also adducing a number of proofs.

The implications for our verse are obvious. The expression will convey either a total identification with Iyov's pain or a mere formality. If the latter is true, then already at this point the insensitivity which the friends displayed afterward is foreshadowed.

שִׁבְעַת יָמִים וְשִׁבְעַת לֵילוֹת — *Seven days and seven nights*. We are familiar with the *shivah*, the seven days of mourning institutionalized by the Sages. The custom of assigning seven days to mourning is an early one, dating back all the way to Joseph in Egypt (*Genesis* 50:10) (*Daas Mikra*).

וְאֵין־דֹּבֵר אֵלָיו דָּבָר — *None spoke a word to him*. They realized the depth of his pain and were, as yet, unable to find an appropriate path to his heart that they might comfort him (*Metzudos*).

Perhaps, too, they were so deeply shocked by the human wreckage before them that they simply could find no words to express their feelings. Again, they may simply have wished to permit Iyov himself to take the initiative of opening the conversation. They would not impose their thoughts upon him until he was ready (*Daas Mikra*).

Indeed, the Sages (*Moed Kattan* 28b) deduce from the fact that the friends first allowed Iyov to have his say, that comforters are not allowed to say anything to the mourner until he himself begins to speak.

14. אַחֲרֵי־כֵן — *Afterward*. *Daas Mikra* suggests that this phrase may be highly significant in understanding Iyov's frustrations. During the seven days, it had not seemed in any way strange that the friends had not spoken. We saw above that such silence showed sensitivity toward the feelings of the sufferer. But when he saw that they said nothing even after the seven

and Bildad the Shuhite, and Tzophar the Naamathite — and met
together, to mourn with him and to comfort him. 12 *They looked from*
a distance but could not recognize him. So they broke into loud
weeping; each one tore his garment and they threw dust into the air
over their heads. 13 *They sat with him on the ground for seven days*
and seven nights. None spoke a word to him for they saw that the
pain was very great. 14 *Afterward Iyov began to speak and cursed*
the day of his birth.

days had elapsed, he realized that they simply had no words of comfort for him. Now, indeed, the terror of his solitude hits him, and he begins the futile tirade of the next chapter.

וַיְקַלֵּל אֶת־יוֹמוֹ — *And cursed the day of his birth.* Thus, *Ibn Ezra* and *Metzudos*. See commentary to next chapter for an analysis, and see further in commentary to verse 7, s.v. יִקְּבֻהוּ אֹרְרֵי יוֹם.

III.

⋖§ Iyov's First Speech

We take *Rashi* and *Ramban* as representative of two possible approaches to this chapter.

Ramban has Iyov, already at this point, taking a theological position: It is inconceivable that a benign God should allow injustice to prevail in His world. The only possible conclusion is that it is not He who controls life, but the heavenly constellations. The celestial bodies which hold sway at the moment of conception and birth determine each individual's fate and in the face of this predestination, God must be impotent.

From within his suffering Iyov has erected a world-system which, if it seems depressing in the extreme, can at least be handled intellectually. A confrontation with unreasonable and implacably malign forces must result in endless sorrow, but has the merit of leaving one's religious integrity intact. It is not a system to which he had ascribed when all went well with him (see 31:26-27), but for the moment, it makes life bearable.

We have assumed that *Rashi,* by not even hinting at such ideas, shows that he does not resort to them in interpreting this speech. We have no expression of any theological stand, but rather a primordial cry of anguish rising from the depths of Iyov's frustrations. Not till almost the end of his musings do the first theological issues begin to surface (see commentary to v. 19). Even then, we have only questions. The bitter conclusions to which these will lead become articulated only in later speeches as Iyov reacts to the apparent obduracy of his would-be comforters.

What thoughts passed through Iyov's mind during the seven days of silence?

At 1:12 we noticed that after he had been struck by the inflammation, a noticeable change in attitude set in. Where earlier Iyov had seen God's taking as no less a cause for blessing than His giving, he now recognizes that there is bad as well as good. They are both to be accepted, but at this stage, weary submission has replaced the earlier religious ecstasy.

Are we now at a third stage of Iyov's development?

A careful reading of this speech would seem to so indicate.

The justification for Iyov's longing never to have been born, or if born to have died immediately, seems to be contained in the last two verses: *For, I was greatly frightened — and it has overtaken me, that which I dreaded has come to me. Never did I feel secure, never quiet, never at peace; and now — torment.* The sense appears to be that even when times were good, there was a nagging fear that it could not last. Looking back, Iyov realizes that he had never been truly happy. No life that is lived in constant terror is worth living — would it not, indeed, have been better if he had never been born?

We can thus trace three distinct developments in Iyov's attitude: 1. Even the bad is cause for blessing — the bad is really good. 2. The bad is indeed bad and is to be decried although it must be accepted, but there was also good — in itself, cause for gratitude. 3. Even the good was never wholly good; there was never a real sense of security — there can be no justification at all for his life.

What brought about the change?

Perhaps it was the continued, stony silence of the friends (see above 2:14 for *Daas Mikra's* understanding of, *Afterward . . .*). We may surmise that Iyov had hoped to hear words of love and comfort from the three men, who had not forsaken him in the moment of his travail (see above at 2:11).

א־ב וַיַּעַן אִיּוֹב וַיֹּאמַר: יֹאבַד יוֹם אִוָּלֶד בּוֹ וְהַלַּיְלָה אָמַר הֹרָה
ג גָבֶר: הַיּוֹם הַהוּא יְהִי חֹשֶׁךְ אַל־יִדְרְשֵׁהוּ אֱלוֹהַּ מִמָּעַל

Certainly his pathetic cry at 19:21, *Pity me, pity me! You are my friends . . .*, gives eloquent expression to his piteous craving for a kind word.

But not a sound escapes their lips. They too, apparently, have been thinking during the seven days of silence. We recall that, . . . *they could not recognize him* (2:12, and see commentary there). The Iyov whom they had known, the man who carried himself with such earnest and pious demeanor, whose inner being they had never found necessary to probe, was no more. Instead, they see a broken spirit in a broken body — they are assailed by the stench of a putrid sickness which, they suspect, is only the outer form of an inner fouling: God's accusing finger, pointing at a life lived as a sham.

And so, Iyov has lost his friends. Lost his friends — and with them any will to live, or to even admit to ever really having lived.

For this is what *Bava Basra* 16b teaches: Let a man have friends as Iyov had — or else let him choose death. Iyov was utterly alone. His children have been taken; his wife can offer no companionship; a God Whom he can no longer understand, Who appears capricious at best, cruel at worst, can provide no spiritual anchorage; and now — his friends are gone.

Small wonder that Iyov sees his whole life stretched before him — a dark chasm of futility.

1. וַיַּעַן אִיּוֹב וַיֹּאמַר — *Iyov declaimed, saying.* *Rashi* renders וַיַּעַן, *to call out,* adducing sources which indicate that עָנָה connotes *declaiming something in a loud voice.*

2. יֹאבַד יוֹם אִוָּלֶד בּוֹ — *O that the day upon which I was to be born might never have been* [lit. *Let the day be destroyed*].

What does Iyov mean in this passage?

At 2:14 we learned that Iyov ... *cursed the day of his birth.* What is implied in such an action, what motivations would stir a man to do this?

Radak (to *Jeremiah* 20:14) writes: From a feeling of bitterness the righteous will curse the day of their birth, even though having passed into history, it is immune from any hurt.

This because Jeremiah, too, saw himself frustrated at every turn in his valiant attempts to stem the tide of spiritual disintegration which was engulfing his people. Finally he broke out in bitter maledictions against the day upon which he had been born.

However, *Ramban* points out that Iyov's curses belong to a different category. Where Jeremiah simply reacted, by giving way to momentary despair, to the bitter negativism of the people's obstructionism which blighted every hope, stunted every promise of growth, Iyov's intent cannot be excused. His words are prompted by a fundamental denial of the doctrine of Divine Providence.

In his *D'rashah on Koheles, Ramban* deduces this attitude from the inordinate length of the passage, and the care Iyov takes in detailing all the different components: *day; night; twilight stars* and *blush of dawn.* Surely, then, this is not a passionate, temporary and therefore superficial lashing out, but a reasoned theological stance which the friends recognize and forthwith attack.

How, then, are we to understand this passage?

Ramban may be taken as representative of a school of commentators who see Iyov as resorting to astrology to explain his sufferings. The blind forces of the heavenly constellations are at work here, not God — for He could never wreak such palpable evil. We quote: "When Iyov observed the great and evil troubles that overtook him, knowing all along that he was innocent of any wrongdoing, he considered that perhaps God has no knowledge of or interest in human affairs, and that His providence is removed from them. He begins his argument by saying that the control which the stars and the constellations exercise during the days of birth and the moments of conception (thus in *Kad HaKemach*) generate evil and beneficence for the child that is born. Thus he inclined towards the thinking of the nonsensical astrologers. Because of this he opens with, *O that the day on which I was born* . . . and cursed the day and night . . ."[1]

Ramban adduces numerous other verses throughout the book to bolster the theory of Iyov's dependence upon the theories of *mazal* — the assumption that man's fate can be directed by the influence of the heavenly spheres. The commentary will note the verses which carry such connotations as we get to them.

However *Rashi*, at least in the context of this section, sees no need to resort to such an expla-

1. Note that *Ramban,* in contrast to *Rashi* (see below), sees the future form of אִוָּלֶד as insignificant. The simple past is meant, although the future is used. He adduces other places in which this is done.

1 Iyov declaimed, saying: 2 O that the day upon which I was to be born
might never have been, nor the night fallen, in which it was said:
A man has sired. 3 May that day be darkness. Let God pay it no heed

nation. On the basis of the future, passive form of אִוָּלֶד, the day upon which *I was to be born,* he places Iyov *before* the event. Iyov did not curse the past from the vantage point of his present troubles, but expresses the wish that the day of his birth might never have come. If that day *had never been,* he would never have been born. We are, in fact, not dealing with a curse in the formal sense of the word.[1]

Rashi's rendering fits well with the assessment which Eliphaz makes of Iyov's first speech. At 4:5 he accuses him of demonstrating — apparently by what he said — *weariness* and *confusion.* These descriptions would be more appropriate in describing a futile and ultimately meaningless lashing out at fate — see below — than a misguided, but nevertheless considered, imprecation hurled at a known astrological reality.

We should understand Iyov's action, as *Rashi* sees it, as follows:

At 1:11 we saw that Satan was certain that under pressure, Iyov would blaspheme, ... *to Your face.* We found this to mean that in spite of normal human reticence which hesitates to address God in the second person — even in prayer — Iyov in the frenzy of his pain will make God the object of his imprecations.

In fact, Iyov will never do this. But when the provocation is great and the source of one's troubles is beyond reach, it is natural to turn frustrated rage against the agent — the immediate, most available, symbol of one's pain who through no fault of his own, was the direct cause of the suffering endured. Iyov will not, indeed cannot, blaspheme against God. But how he wishes, impotently and uselessly — out of the utter *weariness* and *confusion* of his tortured mind — that the day of his birth could be excised from history!

Blasphemy, *R' Isaac Breuer* writes, is the palpable expression of impotent, frustrated, hatred. As Iyov continues to struggle with his tormented feelings, as thoughts, suspicions, hopes, disappointments, defiance and rage, tumble and jostle for expression in the speeches which are to follow, that hatred will occasionally be directed against God Himself. As yet, he cannot articulate as much. What he has to say, he will not fling *at the face* of God.

וְהַלַּיְלָה אָמַר הֹרָה גָבֶר — *Nor the night fallen, in which it was said: A man has sired* [lit. *in which he said*]. The text uses, ... *he said,* without specifying a subject. It is self-understood that the subject is whoever would be in a position to be aware that conception had taken place (*Metzudos*) (*Rashi*). See further at verse 9 on, *For that He did not shut ...*

Ramban, apparently unwilling to introduce an unspecified subject, and moreover, in view of the unlikelihood of anyone being aware that conception had taken place (but see below, on *sired*), assumes *the night* to be the subject: ... *the night which decreed that a man would sire.*

הֹרָה גָבֶר — *A man has sired.* The translation follows *Rashi,* who takes הֹרָה as the *hiphil,* causative, of הָרָה. In the *kal,* simple form, this root has the meaning *to conceive.* Therefore, in the causative — *to cause to conceive.* See *Rashi* to *Genesis* 49:26. See further at *Genesis* 4:18.

Ramban renders, *a male child was conceived.* He also considers the possibility that הֹרָה might be used for *being born.* Iyov did not know whether he was born by day or by night. Consequently, he curses both. Hence, *Or the night ...*

3. הַיּוֹם הַהוּא יְהִי חֹשֶׁךְ — *May that day be darkness.* Here *Rashi* moves to the future. Henceforth, may this day, as it comes back every year, *be darkness.*[2]

חֹשֶׁךְ is a noun, not an adjective. Iyov's imprecation is not that the day should be *dark,* but that it should be a unit of *darkness.* See below, s.v. יִגְאָלֻהוּ חֹשֶׁךְ וְצַלְמָוֶת, for the significance of this usage.

אַל־יִדְרְשֵׁהוּ אֱלוֹהַּ מִמָּעַל — *Let God pay it no heed from above.* May God not shower His goodness upon it (*Rashi*); or, may He not concern himself

1. That, indeed, is the basis for *Ramban's* argument with *Rashi.* He feels that וַיְקַלֵּל in 2:14 indicates an actual curse. Moreover, he shows from verse 9, *For that it did not shut the portals of my womb,* that the vantage point from which Iyov speaks is from the present, looking back.

In view of the fact that Jeremiah (*Jeremiah* 20:14ff.) clearly cursed the day of his birth, it is difficult to see why *Rashi* does not wish to view Iyov's action in the same light.

2. When we consider the structure of Iyov's incantation against the day, we find two verses of three stiches each. Of these six stiches four involve some reference to a darkness which apparently is meant to smother the light of day; the fifth, to the demons which cause turmoil and havoc. We would expect that our phrase, too, would bear on matters which have a positively deleterious effect upon the day rather than upon a withholding of God's providence.

The tenor of the blessing over the lights which we say at *Shacharis* is of God lovingly casting light, each

ד וְאַל־תּוֹפַע עָלָיו נְהָרָה: יִגְאָלֻהוּ חֹשֶׁךְ וְצַלְמָוֶת תִּשְׁכָּן־עָלָיו
ה עֲנָנָה יְבַעֲתֻהוּ כִּמְרִירֵי יוֹם: הַלַּיְלָה הַהוּא יִקָּחֵהוּ אֹפֶל אַל־
ו יִחַדְּ בִּימֵי שָׁנָה בְּמִסְפַּר יְרָחִים אַל־יָבֹא: הִנֵּה הַלַּיְלָה הַהוּא
ז יְהִי גַלְמוּד אַל־תָּבֹא רְנָנָה בוֹ: יִקְּבֻהוּ אֹרְרֵי־יוֹם הָעֲתִידִים

with human needs in order to act with beneficence towards those who deserve it (*Ramban*).[1]

וְאַל־תּוֹפַע עָלָיו נְהָרָה — *So that dawn may not break upon it.* נְהָרָה in the sense of *light* occurs elsewhere as a verb (see *Isaiah* 60:5, and *Psalms* 34:6) but never as a noun.

Targum here renders, שְׁפַרְפְּרָא, a term which normally implies, *dawn* (see *Aruch HaShalem*, and *ArtScroll, Daniel* 6:20). Apparently, then, he understands the phrase to mean, . . . *may dawn never break upon this day.* This would tend to confirm the suggestion made above, that this last phrase is a continuation of the earlier one. God is asked to withhold His consideration from this accursed day in the sense that He should not prepare the morning light as He usually does. The result will be that dawn will never break.

4. יִגְאָלֻהוּ חשֶׁךְ וְצַלְמָוֶת — *May it be sullied by murkiness and dread shadows.* גאל, *to be filthy* (*Rashi*) — see *Isaiah* 59:3, *Malachi* 1:7,12.

What does our verse add to the previous one, in which Iyov already asked that the anniversary of his birth should be *shrouded in darkness?*

The apparent redundancy of our phrase may confirm our perception of the meaning of the previous verse. We had thought that the thrust of that part of the incantation was that the day would remain dark, since no dawn would ever break upon it. The use of יְהִי חשֶׁךְ in this context seems particularly apt. חשֶׁךְ is a noun. Translated literally, the phrase means: *Let that day be a darkness!* The night, as it were, swallows up the day. It never becomes day but remains instead eternal night.

This is Iyov's initial wish. In his frustration he wishes it would be so. Deep in his heart he knows that it cannot be. Every night eventually turns into day. Accordingly, he now shapes his wish into a more reasonable form. Even if I have to admit that I am asking the impossible, I would still wish that the day which must in-

morning, over the earth: *The Beneficent One prepared and worked on the rays of the sun. Avudraham* and others suggest that the beginning of this blessing — *He Who illuminates the earth* — is based on *Iyov* 25:3: *On whom does His light not shine.* Apparently, then, *Iyov* views each breaking dawn as a new act of beneficence borne of God's concern for . . . *the earth and all those who dwell in it.*

Accordingly, we may suppose that reference in our phrase is to God's careful preparation, during the night hours, of the morning light. Taken thus, this phrase leads straight into the next: May God pay no attention to the [coming day], prepare no light to shine upon it, so that indeed no dawn will ever break. The darkness of the night will continue throughout the day.

See commentary to the next phrase where we pursue the suggestion that, indeed, reference may be to the breaking dawn.

1. Our suggestion for the interpretation of this verse rests upon the assumption of a uniformity of expression and spirit throughout the poetic imagery of Iyov's speech.

However, it seems clear that in fact Iyov's speech is riddled with rough verbal lurches from topic to topic. A good example of this is verse 15, which will be discussed in the commentary there, but which at this point can already serve to illustrate our thesis.

Verses 9 through 11 had bemoaned the fact that Iyov had been born. In verse 9 he apparently considers the possibility that no conception would have taken place at all, while in verses 10 and 11 he muses about the pity that he had not succumbed at birth. From there, in verses 12 through 14, he pictures the perceived peace which comes with the grave, where all, even those who lead the most turbulent lives, are at rest.

The description of the grave is picked up once more at verses 16 through 18, from a slightly different perspective.

Verse 15 — Iyov's querulous longing that he had been stillborn seems disjunctive here. As an idea, it belongs together with those expressed in verses 9-11. Instead, it comes in the precise center of the description of the grave — out of place, and, disruptive. [See below at verse 12 for an analysis.]

Certainly we may suppose that such disjunctions are the function of the distraught mind of the sufferer. In *Introduction to the Iyov Commentary* we have argued that the poetic form in which the speeches are written makes it unlikely that the book is to be understood as a philosophical debate. Nothing is more indicative of the free, unstructured — and therefore totally unsuited to philosophical discourse — nature of the discussion than the lurching tendency. Here we have — as is natural — an emotionally dictated sequence of ideas, associations and resonances, which take the speaker where they may. Earlier, we described Iyov's first speech as an impassioned primordial scream of fury. Strict adherence to a formal structure would be inappropriate to the language of despair.

from above, so that dawn may not break upon it. [4] *May it be sullied by murkiness and dread shadows, enveloped in lowering clouds, petrified by the demons who stalk by day.* [5] *May gloom snatch that night, joyless midst the days of the year, uncounted among the months.* [6] *Mark well! that night shall be forlorn, no sounds of cheer shall obtrude upon it.* [7] *Let those who curse their fate, those who stand ready*

evitably dawn should be stained by murkiness.

We can detect such a progression from the unreasonable to the possible in the rest of the Iyov's speech, too. From the wish that the day of his birth might have been expunged from the calendar (v. 2, see above for *Rashi's* perception), an unreasonable wish, he moves on to regret that he was not stillborn (v. 15) — something that could well have happened.

We can readily understand such progressions. The immediate frustration expresses itself in totally unreasonable forms. The imprecation itself acts as a form of catharsis, and the sufferer can now lower his sights to the more possible and therefore more reasonable options.

צַלְמָוֶת — *Dread shadows. Rashi* generally renders צַלְמָוֶת as simply, *darkness.* See, *Jeremiah* 2:6 and *Psalms* 23:4. Here, he renders: ... *shadow of death* [from צֵל, *shadow*, and מָוֶת, *death*] *which never again becomes light.*

It is likely that here, too, *Rashi* understands the term as a synonym for *darkness.* He simply makes the point that this darkness is different. It is the kind that is permanent. In terms of our earlier discussion, this is another change of direction. Once more the impossible and therefore the unreasonable, breaks into the sufferer's thoughts.

כִּמְרִירֵי יוֹם — *By the demons who stalk by day.* We follow *Rashi*, as understood by *Mabit.* In general, demons roam only at night. There is one particularly ferocious one, the ... *ravager who stalks in the afternoon* (*Psalms* 91:6), who is afraid of nothing. Iyov here invokes all demons who are as courageous as that one to come and petrify the accursed day.[1]

Rashi adduces *Deuteronomy* 32:24 where we have the expression, קֶטֶב מְרִירִי. There, *Rashi* maintains that מְרִירִי is a proper noun — the name of a particular demon. Perhaps, then, we should render here: *Meriri [the demon] who stalks by day.*

Alternative renderings are: *the day's searing heat* (*Metzudos*), and *air carrying the plague* (*Ramban*).

5. הַלַּיְלָה הַהוּא יִקָּחֵהוּ אֹפֶל — *May gloom snatch that night.* Iyov's speech appears to be structured logically. In verse 2 he had decried both the day of his birth and the night of his conception — in that order. Verses 3 and 4 then centered upon the imprecations which he uttered against the day. Our verse now turns to the night. What idea is expressed in gloom *snatching* the night?

If our perception of verse 3, *May that day be darkness,* is correct — that Iyov was wishing at that stage that dawn might never break, allowing the night simply to engulf the day — then our verse would be a precise parallel. The day on which he was born would be swallowed up by the previous night; the night in which he was conceived would be snatched by אֹפֶל, a more profound darkness than that expressed by חֹשֶׁךְ. See *Malbim* to *Isaiah* 8:22. [But see, *Wertheimer's, Biur Sheimos HaNirdafim B'Tanach.*]

אַל־יִחַדְּ בִּימֵי שָׁנָה — *Joyless midst the days of the year.* The translation follows *Rashi* who takes the root חדה, to mean, *to rejoice.* He adduces *Exodus* 18:9. *Metzudos* sees the word related to אֶחָד, *one.* Thus: *Let it not become one with the other days of the year.* Let it not be counted among them.

6. הִנֵּה הַלַּיְלָה הַהוּא יְהִי גַלְמוּד אַל־תָּבוֹא רְנָנָה בוֹ — *Mark well! That night shall be forlorn, no sounds of cheer shall obtrude upon it. Metzudos* takes the two phrases together. The darkness in which the night is to be enveloped is to be so forbidding that no group of people will venture forth in it [it will be *forlorn*]. Therefore, the sound of joyful song which normally accompanies a group traveling together will not be heard.

7. יִקְּבֻהוּ אֹרְרֵי־יוֹם — *Let those who curse their fate ... imprecate it.* We have rendered יוֹם as

1. We note *Gra* to *Yoreh Deah* 179:6. Quoting *Rambam*, the *Shulchan Aruch* writes there: Someone who was bitten by a scorpion may utter a spell over it even on Shabbos, *in spite of the fact that it will help nothing at all ...*

To this *Gra* writes: This is *Rambam's* opinion, stated also in commentary to chapter 4 of *Avodah Zarah.* But all who came after him disagree with him, for many spells are mentioned in the *Gemara.* However, he allowed himself to be influenced by philosophy and therefore writes that sorcery, the use of names, spells, demons and amulets are all falsehood. But this opinion has been violently disputed ... for even the Torah

ח עֹרֵר לִוְיָתָן: יֶחְשְׁכוּ כּוֹכְבֵי נִשְׁפּוֹ יְקַו־לְאוֹר וָאַיִן וְאַל־
ט יִרְאֶה בְּעַפְעַפֵּי־שָׁחַר: כִּי לֹא סָגַר דַּלְתֵי בִטְנִי וַיַּסְתֵּר
י עָמָל מֵעֵינָי: לָמָּה לֹּא מֵרֶחֶם אָמוּת מִבֶּטֶן יָצָאתִי
יא וְאֶגְוָע: מַדּוּעַ קִדְּמוּנִי בִרְכָּיִם וּמַה־שָּׁדַיִם כִּי אִינָק:

fate rather than *day* since it is often used in Scripture to denote a point of destiny rather than an actual day — see for example, 18:20 below — and our context seems to demand it. If correct, this rendering produces a striking and effective play on words. Those who curse their יוֹם, *fate,* are called upon to imprecate the יוֹם, *day* which Iyov is trying to anathematize.

Those who curse their fate do so because of the intense suffering which they undergo (*Rashi*).

הָעֲתִידִים עֹרֵר לִוְיָתָן — *Those who stand ready to keen at their dirges.* The monster known to us as *Leviathan* from *Isaiah* 27:1 and *Psalms* 74:14 plays an important role in *Iyov* from 40:25 onwards. Certainly, then, here too we would be inclined to assume that its reference is to that terror of the sea. The more so, since at 41:2 the same verb ערר, used here, is applied to that monster: Indeed, in his second interpretation *Ramban* offers: *Let those same upper forces which can hurl imprecations against accursed days, who are one day destined to rouse the Leviathan whom none other are fierce enough to rouse, curse the day . . .*

However, many commentators appear to be disinclined to assign this meaning. *Rashi* offers two possible explanations: The first is that לִוְיָתָן is related to לֹיוֹת in *I Kings* 7:29, which in *Rashi's* opinion there is to be understood as the *union between man and wife.* עֹרֵר has the meaning which it usually carries in Scripture: *to be childless.* Thus the phrase is to be understood: *Those whose conjugal union is destined to end in barrenness.* [These unfortunates are the ones who tend to curse their fate.]

In this rendering, הָעֲתִידִים is to be taken as, *. . . who are destined,* based on the feminine form, עֲתִידָה, which in Scriptural Hebrew means *the future.* See, for example, *Deuteronomy* 32:35. In the following rendering we take it as, *to stand ready* (*Ibn Ezra*, based on *Proverbs* 24:27).

In our translation we have elected to follow *Rashi's* second explanation, partly because he adduces *Yerushalmi, Moed Kattan* 1, and partly because it appears to be favored by the majority of commentators. לִוְיָתָן is a dirge, and the verb לוה is understood as keening. Hence, our translation.

8. יֶחְשְׁכוּ כּוֹכְבֵי נִשְׁפּוֹ — *O, that its twilight stars be dimmed.* נֶשֶׁף connotes *darkness* (*Rashi*, here and at *Jeremiah* 13:16). However, as *Berachos* 3b teaches, it is also a name given to specific periods of the day. Thus, based on *Proverbs* 7:9, there is a *neshef of the evening* [*Rashi*: נֶשֶׁף is the name given to that time of the day which turns into evening], and based on *I Samuel* 30:17, there is also one for the morning. This almost certainly implies *the morning and evening twilight.* [From *Rashi* to *Berachos*, there, it appears that he associates the meaning of נֶשֶׁף the noun with that of נשף the verb, which means, *to move.* This would be an excellent term for twilight, the point at which the movement towards day or night is most apparent.] Thus, if we combine this with the meaning *darkness* ascribed by *Rashi*, the correct meaning would probably be, *the darkest moment during the morning and evening twilights.*

Daas Mikra makes the suggestion that the three phrases in this verse relate respectively to the three watches of the night. The first phrase hopes that the darkening twilight, which ushers in the night should not be brightened by the early stars.

יְקַו־לְאוֹר וָאַיִן — *Let it crave light — but there is none.* According to *Daas Mikra* above, this phrase has the middle watch of the night in mind. The *light* which it craves would, accordingly, have to be that of the stars which would normally brighten its darkest hours. *Metzudos*, however, takes this phrase as referring to daylight, thus introducing the next phrase: The night anticipates the daylight, but it never comes, since even dawn will never break.

וְאַל־יִרְאֶה בְּעַפְעַפֵּי־שָׁחַר — *May it not see the blush of dawn.* Thus, *Rashi* here and at 41:10 [*. . . the reddening morning sky*]. See also *Radak, Sefer HaShorashim.*

Metzudos takes the word in its more general meaning, *eyelids.* The intimations of light which brighten the east before the sun rises are reminiscent of the opening eye.

9. כִּי לֹא סָגַר דַּלְתֵי בִטְנִי — *For that he did not shut the portals of my womb.* Once more, as in verse 2, the subject is not mentioned (*Rashi*).

itself [mentions such creatures] . . . but philosophy led him astray . . . But as for me . . . I accept it all at face value . . .

to keen at their dirges, imprecate it. [8] *O that its twilight stars be*
dimmed, let it crave light — but there is none, may it not see the blush
of dawn. [9] *For that he did not shut the portals of my womb, thereby*
hiding weariness from my sight. [10] *Why would I not die straight*
from the womb, come forth from the belly and expire? [11] *Why did*
the lap welcome me, what purpose the breasts that I should suckle?

In *Genesis* 29:31 and 30:22 the term, ... *He opened her womb,* appears to refer to conception. Thus, we are justified in assuming that in our phrase, too, Iyov is wishing that he might never have been conceived. It seems reasonable, then, that the implied subject would be he who normally brings about conception. Iyov here seems to be allowing himself the first stirring of anger against God Himself. Would that He had not permitted conception to take place.

Metzudos takes the *portal of the womb* to be the umbilicus by way of which food reaches the fetus. If this had been closed off by the heavenly constellations whom Iyov is here cursing (in the opinion of various commentators, see above), then he would have starved within the womb.

דַּלְתֵי בִטְנִי — *The portals of my womb.* Obviously, in this context, *my mother's womb.*

וַיַּסְתֵּר עָמָל מֵעֵינָי — *Thereby hiding weariness from my sight. Targum* tends to render עָמָל, with לָעָה, *weariness,* and this appears to be the appropriate rendering in our context.

Rashi occasionally equates עָמָל with *sin* (see *Rashi* to *Numbers* 23:21 and *Koheles* 4:4). This, because sins which humans commit tend to *weary* God, as it were. It seems barely possible that Iyov intends such a word-play. Evidently God views him as a sinner — a man who wearies Him. Otherwise, why would He torture him so? If indeed God is wearied by him, why did He not cause that Iyov never be conceived? *From my sight* would then be a euphemism for, *from His sight.* [There would seem to be some justification for this interpretation: Only God *looks upon* weariness (see *Psalms* 10:14), man *experiences* it.]

10. לָמָּה לֹא מֵרֶחֶם אָמוּת — *Why would I not die straight from the womb.* Iyov once more places himself before the event. I would have been prepared to die immediately upon my birth (*Rashi*).[1]

11. מַדּוּעַ קִדְּמוּנִי בִרְכָּיִם — *Why did the lap welcome me.* It seems simplest to understand the phrase as does *Metzudos.* The lap is that of the midwife, upon which she receives the baby as it is born.

However, *Rashi* writes: My mother's lap. What could this mean?

At *Isaiah* 66:12 we have the lap as we know it — a place for nurturing and loving the child. Indeed, that is how *Rashi* appears to understand the cryptic phrases at *Genesis* 30:3 and 50:23. In the one case, Rachel suggests that Jacob marry her maid-servant Bilhah so that, ... *she will bear upon my knees,* and in the other we are told that great grandchildren of Joseph, ... *were born upon his knees.* In both instances *Rashi* cites *Targum,* that the phrase is idiomatic and implies the raising of the child.

Iyov had been an eagerly anticipated and adored child, dangled upon the lap, in the loving interplay which bonds mother to child. Thus, both lap and bosom are means of nurturing the child, and Iyov bemoans the fact that they were so readily available to him. Had he been unwanted and left to his own devices he would surely have succumbed. [Thus, also *Mabit.*]

1. We note that from verses 9 through 11, the perspective changes three times: In verse 9 Iyov looks backwards: Why did *He* not close the portals of the womb? In our verse he places himself before the event. I was looking forward to dying immediately upon birth. In the next verse, he looks back once more: Why was there a welcoming lap when I was born: without it I would surely have died. In the final phrase he is once more before the event (*Rashi*). He views the tendered bosom with horror. Why are these offered to me when I would so much rather die!

There is more here than the distraught meandering of a sufferer in the travail of his agony. Initially, Iyov wishes that he had never been conceived. He would then never have come into existence at all, and consequently there is no perspective from which he could have looked ahead. Once conceived, however, he exists as a fetus. By placing himself ahead of the event, he gives graphic reality to his death-wish: My wish to die defined my entire being. Even as a fetus, I was filled with only that one wish. In the event, he was born alive — and learned quickly that there was to be no respite. The midwife stands ready to receive him. Looking back he cannot conceive why this was necessary. Could he not have been let alone? But now he has a new existence. Not a fetus anymore, but a living person, he stands before the prospect of the nursing and nurturing which his mother is prepared to shower upon him. What positive purpose can this bosom serve?

יב־יג כִּֽי־עַתָּה שָׁכַבְתִּי וְאֶשְׁקוֹט יָשַׁנְתִּי אָז ׀ יָנוּחַ לִי׃ עִם־
יד מְלָכִים וְיֹעֲצֵי אָרֶץ הַבֹּנִים חֳרָבוֹת לָמוֹ׃ אוֹ עִם־שָׂרִים זָהָב
טו לָהֶם הַֽמְמַלְאִים בָּתֵּיהֶם כָּסֶף׃ אוֹ כְנֵפֶל טָמוּן לֹא אֶהְיֶה
טז כְּעֹלְלִים לֹא־רָאוּ אוֹר׃ שָׁם רְשָׁעִים חָדְלוּ רֹגֶז וְשָׁם יָנוּחוּ
יז יְגִיעֵי כֹחַ׃ יַחַד אֲסִירִים שַׁאֲנָנוּ לֹא שָׁמְעוּ קוֹל נֹגֵשׂ׃

12. כִּי־עַתָּה שָׁכַבְתִּי וְאֶשְׁקוֹט — *For now I would have lain supine — untroubled.* Iyov, agitated beyond bearing by the horrors which life has heaped upon him, sees the grave as a place of rest — of utter peace.[1]

13. עִם־מְלָכִים וְיֹעֲצֵי אָרֶץ — *Together with kings and world planners . . .* The combination יֹעֵץ — אָרֶץ does not recur. To take the word in its usual sense of *counselor* would not explain the association, and moreover would not fit smoothly into the context. It is not the counselors who build up the ruins. However, we find יוֹעֵץ paralleling *king* at *Michah* 4:9, and *judge* at *Isaiah* 1:26. Thus, people who exert power — but through a deep and fundamental perception of the issue. Hence, those rulers and empire-builders whose accomplishments are the crowning glory of their careful planning are termed יוֹעֵץ.

Metzudos understands the sentence as describing the leveling effect of the grave. There all, the great and the small, are equal.

But the inequality of society had not been part of Iyov's complaint. Why covet the grave for its obliteration of social differences, when these had never seemed a problem? *Daas Mikra* explains as follows: Iyov is anticipating an argument. How could he wish for death; would he then not lose his chance of amassing wealth and all the other amenities which life offers? He answers that once in the grave, nothing that was accomplished in this world would make any difference. Kings and commoners are all alike there. *Daas Mikra* goes on to suggest that in this context, the phrase, . . . *who build up ruins for their fame,* may well be meant ironically. Indeed, the kings build up huge edifices, but they will not last. The most beautiful palace is in reality only a ruin.

הַבֹּנִים חֳרָבוֹת לָמוֹ — *Who build up ruins for their fame.* This follows *Rashi* and *Metzudos.* A ruler who builds his palace or his empire upon ruins will be particularly remembered for his prowess.

14. אוֹ עִם־שָׂרִים — *Or with princes . . .* Both the powerful (v. 13) and the wealthy share the untroubled and peaceful ambience of the grave.

1. This passage, which describes the grave, requires careful analysis, both regarding its internal structure and its place within the larger context of Iyov's musings.

Five verses describe those with whom Iyov expects to share the grave: In verses 13 and 14 he sees the proud rulers of the world in simple repose, while in verses 16, 17 and 18 his mind's eye turns to the spent, the downtrodden and the oppressed who will at long last be beyond the reach of those at whose orders they had once trembled.

Between these two segments, we have verse 15, in which Iyov bemoans the fact that he was not stillborn.

At first glance, this verse appears to be out of place. It would more naturally have fitted with verses 9 through 11. Like them, it expresses Iyov's vain fury at his very existence. [But see commentary to verse 15 for *Rashi's* interpretation.] Moreover, by what logic does this verse interrupt the description of the grave's denizens?

With our perception of the meaning of verse 11, as *Rashi* understood it, the following pattern emerges.

Verses 11 through 14 are to be viewed as belonging together. There is, indeed, a seductive comfort and sense of security for the infant cuddling in its mother's arms. But that is all a sham! Only the grave can offer true and lasting repose. Even kings and princes, who one might suppose led lives of luxury which left nothing at all to be desired, are truly at peace only there. Their perceived experiences can testify to the truth of Iyov's assertions.

From his contrasting of the mother's embrace with that of the grave, Iyov now returns to his musings of the might-have-been.

Verse 9 had toyed with the idea that he might never have been conceived. Verses 10 and 11 dealt with the possibility of having been born, but not lived. There is a third alternative: He might have died within the womb.

It is an attractive thought. The agitation of the contracting womb, the trauma of expulsion from known and protective surroundings into the threatening and overwhelming light of day — all the attendant dislocations of birth might have been avoided. In Iyov's mind the fetus is a prisoner and slave of inexorable, unbending laws of nature.

Once more the grave appears as a beguiling alternative — no task masters or slave owners there. Having died within the womb, Iyov would have been freed from the demanding disciplines of reality.

[12] *For now I would have lain supine — untroubled, I would have slum-*
bered — then would there be rest for me. [13] *Together with kings*
and world planners who build up ruins for their fame. [14] *Or with*
princes rich in gold, who fill their treasure houses with silver.
[15] *Or why could I not have been stillborn? — concealed, as infants*
who never saw the light. [16] *There, the wicked cease their agitations,*
and there those whose strength is spent, find repose. [17] *There the cap-*
tives, all together, are at rest, they cannot hear the taskmaster's voice.

15. או כְנֵפֶל טָמוּן לֹא אֶהְיֶה — *Or why could I not have been stillborn? — concealed.* In our discussion above, we assumed that in this verse Iyov is once more voicing a death-wish — within the context of those expressed in verses 9 and 10. This is indeed how *Metzudos* understands our verse.

Rashi, however, sees it as a continuation of the previous verse. Iyov is still dealing with the grave. He would have lain together with the kings and world movers — the famous, or with the totally unknown stillborn children who lie there.

The word *concealed* means something different according to *Rashi* than it does according to *Metzudos.* In *Rashi's* view it describes the *anonymous* stillborn in contrast to the famous people mentioned in the previous verses. *Metzudos* understands it as a description of the imperfectly formed fetus. It is folded upon itself and parts of its body are therefore concealed.

בְּעֹלְלִים לֹא־רָאוּ אוֹר — *As infants who never saw the light.* עֹלֵל is usually a nursing child (*Rashi* to *Jeremiah* 6:11). Its use to describe a stillborn is unexpected. The explanation may be as follows: *Rashi* explains that the root עלל has the basic meaning of *filth.* The small child is called עֹלֵל because ... *its whole being is one of folly and filth.* Thus the stillborn fetus, bloodied by birth, may also be described by that name.

16. שָׁם — *There.* This is a euphemism for the grave (*Ramban*).

שָׁם רְשָׁעִים חָדְלוּ רֹגֶז — *There, the wicked cease their agitations.* רֹגֶז is a noun. Does it mean the agitations which the wicked inflict upon others, or that which they, by their nature, undergo?

Rashi, Metzudos and *Ramban* (in one interpretation) assume the former. In that case, it seems likely that *those whose strength is spent* are the former victims of the machinations of the *wicked* ones. In that case we have the grave as the refuge of three different categories of victims: those who were formerly at the mercy of the wicked, in our verse; the prisoners freed from their taskmasters, in the next; and, finally, the slave who is no longer subjugated to his master, in verse 18.[1]

Ibn Ezra, however (quoted by *Ramban*), takes רֹגֶז as describing the state of mind of the wicked man, rather than his effect upon society. While in the context of the section as a whole, this interpretation would not produce the pleasing congruence with the following two verses, it has the advantage of treating the word in the same way as it is used throughout the book; moreover, it reflects Iyov's perception of the kind of life which the wicked live, as expressed in 15:20ff.

In this interpretation, the two halves of the verse do not relate to one another as do cause and effect, but are a repetition of the same thought (*Ramban*). The wicked — that is, those *whose strength is spent* — will find repose in the grave.

17. יַחַד אֲסִירִים שַׁאֲנָנוּ — *There the captives, all together, are at rest.* The purpose of stressing ... *all together* is not clear. Two possibilities suggest themselves: Perhaps prisoners are usually locked up in separate cells. In the grave this unnatural denial of human contact will cease. Alternatively, prisoners may be categorized by the crimes which they had committed. Once they are totally ... *at rest,* these divisions will lose their meaning.

לֹא שָׁמְעוּ קוֹל נֹגֵשׂ — *They cannot hear the taskmaster's voice.* The voice of the official who summons them to do the king's word (*Metzudos*).

1. Comparison with the previous section describing the comforts of the grave yields as follows: Either there, too, we have three categories: kings, world planners, and princes; or, if kings and world planners which are juxtaposed in the same verse are to be taken as one grouping, only two.

In the latter case, the imbalance can be readily explained. The categories of the oppressed are more numerous than those who find pleasure in this world. This itself is, of course, part of Iyov's complaint. This idea is given graphic expression by giving two examples of the latter, three of the former.

יח־יט קָטֹן וְגָדוֹל שָׁם הוּא וְעֶבֶד חָפְשִׁי מֵאֲדֹנָיו׃ לָמָּה יִתֵּן לְעָמֵל אוֹר
כ וְחַיִּים לְמָרֵי נָפֶשׁ׃ הַמְחַכִּים לַמָּוֶת וְאֵינֶנּוּ וַיַּחְפְּרֻהוּ
כא־כב מִמַּטְמוֹנִים׃ הַשְּׂמֵחִים אֱלֵי־גִיל יָשִׂישׂוּ כִּי יִמְצְאוּ־קָבֶר׃ לְגֶבֶר
כג אֲשֶׁר־דַּרְכּוֹ נִסְתָּרָה וַיָּסֶךְ אֱלוֹהַּ בַּעֲדוֹ׃ כִּי־לִפְנֵי לַחְמִי אַנְחָתִי
כד תָבֹא וַיִּתְּכוּ כַמַּיִם שַׁאֲגֹתָי׃ כִּי פַחַד פָּחַדְתִּי וַיֶּאֱתָיֵנִי וַאֲשֶׁר
כה יָגֹרְתִּי יָבֹא לִי׃ לֹא שָׁלַוְתִּי וְלֹא שָׁקַטְתִּי וְלֹא־נָחְתִּי וַיָּבֹא רֹגֶז׃

18. קָטֹן וְגָדוֹל שָׁם הוּא — *Small and great are there.* *Rashi* understands this phrase in a way that seems unconnected with the rest of Iyov's thoughts here. In the grave it will be clearly seen who is truly great and who truly small. That is because nothing can change anymore. Whatever position a person occupies is forever.

In context, it is easier to understand *Metzudos*, who interprets this phrase so that it leads into the next: In the grave all are equal; there is no difference between the great and the small. Because of this, the slave will be free of his master.

19. לָמָּה יִתֵּן לְעָמֵל... לְמָרֵי נָפֶשׁ — *Why should [He] grant to the weary ... embittered.* The change from the singular עָמֵל to the plural מָרֵי נָפֶשׁ seems significant. Evidently, in the first phrase Iyov is thinking about himself, and from there he moves on to include himself with all the world's embittered souls (*Ramban*).

If so, this passage would be a watershed in the book. From expressions of personal frustration Iyov has now progressed to criticizing God's providence. [The neutral, undefined *He* clearly refers to God (*Ramban*).] From his experiences he has learned that oblivion is much to be preferred to the debilitating agonies to which he has become heir. Would others not feel the same? Why then force them into a life against which their very being rebels?

Iyov has begun to question![1]

We have taken *Ramban's* insight into the wording of our verse and drawn conclusions from it within the framework of our perception of *Rashi's* understanding of the speech. However, *Ramban* himself, though he does not say so in his remarks to this verse, probably understands this section quite differently than does *Rashi*.

We recall that *Ramban's* interpretation of our chapter has Iyov subscribing to the views of the astrologers, that man's fate is in the hands of the heavenly spheres. (See Prefatory Remarks and commentary to verse 2, s.v. יֹאבַד יוֹם אִוָּלֶד בּוֹ.) Throughout the presentation of his thoughts, *Ramban* makes the point that Iyov reaches his conclusions not out of disrespect for God, but from deep feelings of reverence. God's providence would express itself only in the most benign manner. If we can observe chaotic caprice in place of a fair, consistent and systematic intelligible order, that can only be because God has no hand in that which occurs.

In his concluding remarks, *Ramban* encapsulates this thought in the following sentence: The evil that occurs in the world convinces Iyov that providence is not in the hands of the Creator, *for it is not in the nature of a benign director to create beings for the purpose of harming them.*

Accordingly, we may assume that *Ramban* interprets this section not as part of an anguished cry — a rhetorical question — but instead, as a reasoned argument to bolster his theological position. God would certainly not want to grant life

1. From *Ramban's* interpretation it is clear that Iyov's empathy for his fellow sufferers has derived solely out of his own bitter experiences. Surely, even before his tragedy, he had been aware that there was suffering in the world. Indeed, he had always been there to extend words of comfort to those who were buckling under the weight of their sorrows (see 4:3-4). But we may safely assume that what he had to say was closely akin to the thoughts which the friends will project so forcefully in their vain efforts to help him. Perhaps, more sensitively, in the past he shared some of his own insights — that God's taking may be as much of a blessing as His giving (1:21), or that one has to be prepared to accept the bad as well as the good at God's hands (2:10).

Now, however, everything has changed. Iyov has lost the faculty to comfort others. Only death holds promise for him.

At 2:3 we learned from *Ramban* that as Iyov withstands the tests to which he is put, his relationship to God changes. From having served *out of fear,* he begins to relate to God *out of love.*

We understand the meaning of this as follows: In the neat thought-world of the friends — and presumably also of Iyov before he learned better — well-being invariably followed righteousness, suffering, evil. God acts in a predictable fashion. Logic dictates that such a God be served — with an expectation of reward and an acceptance that misdeeds will be punished. This is a *service out of fear.*

A new world is now beginning to open. A world of apparent caprice and unpredictability. Such a world can break the spirit — or exalt it. He who serves *in spite of . . . ,* instead of *because . . . ,* serves out of love.

With Iyov's first questioning a beginning has been made. The book ends with his triumph over adversity.

[18] *Small and great are there, the slave freed from his owner.* [19] *Why should light be granted to the weary, life to the embittered,* [20] *Who crave death but it eludes them, seek it more eagerly than hidden treasures;* [21] *who rejoice at good fortune, delight when they find the grave.* [22] *The man who has lost his bearings, against whom God has raised a wall.* [23] *For my sighing ushers in my meal, my groans gush forth like water.* [24] *For, I was greatly frightened — and it has overtaken me, that which I dreaded has come to me.* [25] *Never did I feel secure, never quiet, never at peace; and now torment.*

to anyone who would only be wearied by it. Surely then, that part of existence is not in His hands.

20-21. With these verses, Iyov takes a more realistic view of what these wearied and embittered people want. They do not seek to expunge the day of their birth from the calendar — they wish, simply, that they would die, sooner rather than later.

20. הַמְחַכִּים לַמָּוֶת וְאֵינֶנּוּ — *Who crave death, but it eludes them.* They bemoan the fact that it eludes them (*Rashi*).

21. הַשְּׂמֵחִים אֱלֵי־גִיל — *Who rejoice at good fortune.* The combination between אֱלֵי and גִּיל is, besides here, found only at *Hosea* 9:1. The simplest way to understand this obscure phrase would seem to be how *Ibn Ezra* takes it. גִּיל is apparently a joyous occasion, one which would produce merriment or exhilaration. שָׂמֵחַ אֱלֵי גִיל would mean *to react joyously to such an occasion.* The *joyous occasion* in our verse would be the finding of the grave.

Rashi may agree to this interpretation. He renders the unusual אֱלֵי as בִּשְׁבִיל, *because of.* Thus, they are in a state of שִׂמְחָה, *because of* a גִּיל.

אֱלֵי is the poetic form of אֶל — found only in *Iyov* (5:26, 15:22 and 29:19) — which usually connotes, *motion in a direction.*

22. לְגֶבֶר אֲשֶׁר־דַּרְכּוֹ נִסְתָּרָה — *The man who has lost his bearings.* The phrase is in apposition to verse 19. Who is *weary,* who *embittered*? The man . . . (*Mabit*).

We have translated in accordance with *Ramban* and *Mabit. Rashi,* adducing *Isaiah* 40:27, renders: *A man whose good deeds are hidden [from God],* that is, that God seems unaware of all the good things that he has done. But there, the phrase does indeed read, נִסְתְּרָה דַרְכִּי מֵה׳. God is specifically mentioned.

וַיָּסֶךְ אֱלוֹהַּ בַּעֲדוֹ — *Against whom God has raised a wall* (*Rashi*). Making him unable to move around freely (*Ramban*); or, making him unable to enjoy anything (*Mabit*).

Clearly, this phrase is meant to pick up that of the Satan at 1:10, *Have You not built a fence around him.* Two interpretations seem possible: If Iyov is now describing his present situation, the implication is: The fence that You once erected to protect me has now turned into a stockade which locks me in.

If, as verses 24 and 25 seem to indicate, Iyov now looks back critically at the good times and tells himself that even then he was never really happy, then the meaning would be: The very wall which You erected to protect me, was the cause of my misery. My riches were so overwhelming that fear of losing them soured any joy I might have had.

23. כִּי־לִפְנֵי לַחְמִי אַנְחָתִי תָבֹא — *For my sighing ushers in my meal.* My sorrow is always with me. Even the prospect of a good meal does nothing to assuage my pain (*Metzudos*).

וַיִּתְּכוּ כַמַּיִם שַׁאֲגֹתָי — *My groans gush forth like water.* We have translated in accordance with *Rashi,* although he himself usually renders נָתַךְ as *to reach* or *to cast* (see *Rashi* to *Exodus* 9:33).

Ramban seems to render וַיִּתְּכוּ as *to melt* (see *Ezekiel* 22:22): *My groans have been melted down into constant tears.*

24. כִּי פַחַד פָּחַדְתִּי — *For I was greatly frightened.* Even during the best of times I was constantly worried that my children might sin. My worst fears have now been realized (*Rashi* and *Mabit*). *Ramban* points out that Iyov would not have been afraid on his own account since he considered himself righteous and assumed that suffering could only overtake the wicked.[1]

25. לֹא שָׁלַוְתִּי וְלֹא שָׁקַטְתִּי וְלֹא נָחְתִּי וַיָּבֹא רֹגֶז — *Never did I feel secure, never quiet, never at peace; and now — torment.* As we pointed out at the beginning of this chapter, Iyov has now moved away from the positions which he held in the first two chapters. From within the throes of his agony he is unable to admit that there was ever any real joy in his life.

1. From *Rashi* and *Mabit* it appears that Iyov is, at least, toying with the idea that his suffering may have come about because of his children's transgressions.

It seems possible, too, that at this moment, his mind is only on his children's death. That, at least, he can ascribe to their shortcomings.

IV.

◆§ Eliphaz's First Speech

The central thrust of this speech, in *Ramban's* view, is to challenge Iyov's assertion that man's fate is determined by the heavenly constellations. Proofs are marshalled and arguments made that ultimately — and to this everyone must agree — it is God alone who orders the affairs of man.

There is a significant admission, that not every human experience can be categorized as either the prosperity deserved by the righteous or the punishment due the wicked. There are situations which seem to fly in the face of our belief in a world-order reflecting the stewardship of a just God. However, our inability to understand these must be laid at the door of the limits of human understanding. Certainly, they are the exception and not the rule.

Consequently, Iyov is to accept the terrible fate which has befallen him in spite of his righteousness as chastisement from God. As such it is surely motivated by good and sufficient reasons.

We have assumed that in *Rashi's* view, Iyov never asserted an astrological base for human experiences, and consequently, there can be no need to refute such assumptions.

The thrust of Eliphaz's speech is to voice disappointment at Iyov's reaction to his fate and to suggest an alternative, legitimate, response to suffering. Instead of lashing out impotently at meaningless targets when, in any case, intractable realities are firmly in place, the sufferer is exhorted to sublimate, and thus ultimately overcome, his pain.

Iyov should look inward rather than outward. His goal should be to be good rather than to be cured. His experiences should be turned into a goad to growth, rather than be dissipated in futile railing.

In the subjugation of self, implicit in such a response, a relationship to God is established which will, in the end, guarantee a happy and blessed life.

At 2:11-13 we began to analyze the function and contribution of the three friends. As we turn now to Eliphaz, the first among them to react to Iyov's speech, we must, once more, consider their position. What were they attempting to do?

We begin with a quote from *Zohar* to *Korach* (3:176-177):

Rav Yehudah opened his remarks: O wise men, listen to my words, and you who have knowledge, lend me your ear (34:1 from Elihu's speech). *This verse was said by Elihu. Come see! What is written* (at 32:3): *And, too, against his friends His anger flared, for that they were unable to find an appropriate answer . . . For they had said that which they had to say — but Iyov was not comforted by them. From here we learn: One who sets out to comfort a mourner must first organize his thoughts, for Iyov's friends had sensible things to say, but could not comfort him. They would have needed arguments to which he could have agreed, to accept the heavenly judgment upon himself, and thank the Holy King for it. Now, what is written* (32:4), *Elihu bided his time to address Iyov . . . that afterwards he thanked the Holy One Blessed is He, and accepted the heavenly judgment upon himself.*

In the assessment of Rav Yehudah, then, the friends had much to say that was good — but failed to understand Iyov's mentality. Their theology was sound — their human instinct, faulty. [See above at 2:11-13 for the Talmud's use of the friends as a paradigm for abusive language.]

We assume that the *Zohar's* perception of the friends would not apply to at least some of the latter speeches. As we shall see, all the friends, but especially Eliphaz, ultimately descended to angry diatribes in place of reasoned arguments or simple words of comfort. We can sympathize. Iyov had refused to accept any of the valid points which they had made. Perhaps they perceived him as spurning their proffered concern. So friendship turns to censure and ultimately, apparently, to hatred.

But all this lies in the future. We must certainly assume that in this first speech, Eliphaz has only Iyov's good in mind.

What is he saying?

Ramban, in accordance with his understanding of Iyov's first speech — that, in spite of his bias against such an assumption, he had concluded that man's fate lies in the hands of the heavenly constellations — has Eliphaz debate that issue. He paints a picture of the world in which the righteous find success and happiness, while the wicked invariably are punished.

This could only be true if it is God, not astrological forces, who controls human destiny.

The key phrase in *Ramban's* system is: *It is God's breath which destroys them* (4:9); we have rendered the verse here as *Ramban* would. Our translation of 5:8 follows *Rashi*: *But as for me, I would search out the Almighty* . . . Both make the point that what happens is determined by God and is not the result of happenstance.

As we saw in the previous chapter, *Rashi* does not agree with *Ramban's* system. Indeed, he understands 4:9 quite differently — see commentary there.

What idea is Eliphaz attempting to convey to Iyov?

We begin with a general remark concerning the style in which Eliphaz couches his teaching.

There appears to be a tendency towards poetic embellishment. In contrast to Iyov's speech, which although also expressed in poetic language displays an economy of expression — each phrase is made to tell — that of Eliphaz contains whole sections of descriptive material which appear to add little to any argument he might be making.

We could argue that of the forty-eight verses which make up Eliphaz's speech, only nine can be defined as actual debating points; the rest are descriptive.

Herewith, the nine verses which seem to make up the argument:

4:7. *Do recall I beg you: Who is the innocent who was ever lost without a trace, who the upright ones, who were blotted out.*
4:8. *Even as I observed, those who plow sin and plant weariness must harvest it.*
5:1. *Cry out, I beg you — will any answer you, to whom among the saintly can you turn?*
5:2. *For frustration will kill the fool, anger will slay the simple-minded.*
5:6. *For injury does not spring from the dust, nor does the earth bring forth weariness.*
5:7. *For man is born to weariness, while the spirits soar in flight.*
5:8. *But as for me, I would search out the Almighty, direct my speech to God.*
5:17. *See, how happy the man whom God disciplines, never loathe the chastisement of Shaddai.*
5:18. *For He inflicts pain — but will assuage wounds, but His hands will heal.*

The other passages fall into the following categories:

4:1-6. Disappointment at Iyov's reaction to suffering.
4:9-11. How the sinners are destroyed.
4:12-21. The vision; the message; the contrast between the angels and man.
5:3-5. Eliphaz observes and describes how the wicked always suffer.
5:9-16. God is all-powerful and Eliphaz describes how He frustrates the designs of the wicked.
5:19-26. Description of the good fortune which befalls a man who gladly submits to God's discipline.

The impression is of a less focused, more verbose presentation than that of Iyov. It may well be that with this style, the ground-work for the denouement at the end of the book is being laid. It is as though we are being shown that Eliphaz is more enamored with an idea than with the person of his stricken friend. The grand word-pictures which he paints are just that — pictures of an idealized world, which has no reality. Such sophistry cannot compete with Iyov's dogged and desperate pursuit of the truth — which, in the end, will carry the day.

But that is a matter of style. Surely there is also sound theological substance. What, then, is the gist of Eliphaz's argument?

The nine verses which we have identified as presenting Eliphaz's substantive arguments may be divided into two parts: The two verses from chapter 4, and the seven from chapter 5. Verses 7 and 8 in chapter 4 project a world-view: The pure do not perish, those who nurture evil will eventually be caught up in it. In the commentary we shall see that as *Ramban* understands it, the vision which was granted him acts as a slight modification to this thesis. But the essential system remains untouched — it is the credo upon which Eliphaz intends to build.

Given the essential justice of this perceived world-order, the question is now: What does the good man do when he is struck by suffering. What, in short, should have been Iyov's response. Eliphaz is not yet making any suggestion that Iyov is wicked — but he is firmly convinced that his reaction was wrong (4:2-6). Why?

Eliphaz's answer is given in the remaining seven verses.

א־ב וַיַּעַן אֱלִיפַז הַתֵּימָנִי וַיֹּאמַר: הֲנִסָּה דָבָר אֵלֶיךָ
ג תִּלְאֶה וַעְצֹר בְּמִלִּין מִי יוּכָל: הִנֵּה יִסַּרְתָּ רַבִּים

Caught in straits of agony, man can turn outward or inward. All depends on the focus of his concern. There are those for whom the urgency of removing the pain preempts all other considerations. The objective fact of the pain is their only reality. Such a one will shout for help, turn in every direction for a sympathetic ear — his salvation can only come from without (5:1). Absent a helping hand, his frustrations and anger must ultimately kill him (5:2).

But there is another way. There is the man to whom pain and comfort, sorrow and joy have no reality of their own. Central to his concern — really his only interest — is his personal integrity; how and where does he stand in his relation to God (5:8). For him the issue of whether he is suffering or at peace is of only relative importance. Both are challenges — each presents its own problems — which, if met, yield that purity of soul which alone has objective significance. He would wish to be cured, but that desire is subordinate to the craving to be good.

Such a one will rejoice at the discipline to which he is exposed, will treasure God's chastisement (5:17). He knows that while the innocent never perish (4:7), sin is still a part of the human condition — bringing injury and weariness in its wake (5:6-7).

These, as *Zohar* points out, are positive and constructive ideas. If Eliphaz erred it was in the way he expressed them. He had not grasped sufficiently the exquisite sensitivity which is born of absolute vulnerability. In the words of the *Zohar*, he had not prepared himself as carefully as his daunting task demanded. In his profligate use of words — the vivid and seemingly pointed description of the downfall of the wicked and the guaranteed tranquility of the righteous — Iyov was bound to hear only criticism of himself. He feels attacked, and the profound theological insights which Eliphaz has to offer are lost to him. The downward spiral in the relationship has begun.

1. וַיַּעַן אֱלִיפַז הַתֵּימָנִי — *Eliphaz, the Temanite, responded.* He is the Eliphaz who was Esau's son. Because he was raised in Isaac's lap, he became great enough for the Divine spirit to rest upon him (*Rashi*).

See fn. on 1:1, s.v. בְּאֶרֶץ עוּץ, for our discussion of the fact that all the protagonists in this drama are descendants of Abraham.

If the Sages make a point of teaching that the Eliphaz of our book is the same one who was Esau's son (see *Targum Yonassan* to *Genesis* 36:12), there must surely be something about him which made him uniquely suitable for the role he is to play here.[1]

We may surmise that Eliphaz's life experiences contributed to his theological insights, as we have understood them in the Prefatory Remarks to this chapter. Eliphaz, the Sages teach, was a *tzaddik*, a righteous man (*Midrash Torah* 2) who had completely disassociated himself from his evil father (*Yalkut Iyov*, 897). He was thus able, as it were, to stand back and draw lessons from that which he had observed of God's dealings within his own family.

Eliphaz saw this: The evil Esau is luxuriating among Seir's hills, secure in his possessions, in control of his life. Yaakov, God's beloved, is groaning under Egypt's heavy yoke. [See *Joshua* 24:4: ... *I gave Esau the hill country of Seir as a possession, while Yaakov and his sons descended to Egypt.*]

For Yaakov, the horrors of slavery are the gates to destiny. Egypt is to be the crucible in which Israel is formed.

Clearly, then, suffering in itself is neither evil nor an indication of caprice or lack of caring. There is a right way to react to it, to sublimate it, and ultimately to overcome it.

Eliphaz is, indeed, the ideal man to convey these ideas to Iyov. His tragedy is that he does not command the skills to do it correctly.

From the fact that Eliphaz waited with his speech until after Iyov had spoken, *Moed Kattan* 28b deduces that people who come to comfort a mourner may not begin to speak before he does. *Aruch HaShulchan* (*Yoreh Deah* 374) suggests that the reason is so that the mourner should first go through a

1. It would be wrong to see the book of *Iyov* as an objective entity, divorced of any historic framework. The mere fact that the Sages go out of their way to identify the period in which the drama took place — *Bava Basra* 15a and b, and see fn. to 1:1, s.v. אִישׁ הָיָה — indicates that they see the historical background as being significant to the understanding of the book.

Indeed, *Yalkut* to our chapter reads any number of historical allusions into Eliphaz's presentation.

[1] Eliphaz the Temanite responded and spoke: [2] Do you tire of
of one hurdle set against you; who would be capable
of withholding speech. [3] Mark well! You have chided many,

צִדּוּק הַדִּין, *an acceptance of God's justice,* and only then would words of comfort be in place. Indeed, *Beis Yosef* (there) adduces a custom that the mourner opens with the words בָּרוּךְ דַּיַּן הָאֱמֶת, *Blessed is the true Judge.*

For an analysis of the implications of the fact that this *halachah* is derived from the Iyov saga — see *The First Round,* between chapters 14 and 15.

2. הֲנִסָּה דָבָר אֵלֶיךָ תִּלְאֶה — *Do you tire of one hurdle set against you. Rashi* takes הֲנִסָּה from נָסָה, *to test.* However, we see from *Rashi* to *Exodus* 20:17 that he associates this root with נָסֹה, *to raise up.* Apparently, *Rashi* views a test as a kind of hurdle to be crossed. Our translation attempts to reflect this nuance.

לָאָה, as *being weary,* is used particularly in situations in which burdens which are simply too heavy have to be borne. See, for example, *Isaiah* 1:14. It is noteworthy that Iyov picks up this expression from Eliphaz at 16:7, in answer to Eliphaz's second speech. He seems to be saying: You accuse me of excessive weariness? Indeed I am weary — my burdens are entirely unreasonable.

וַעְצֹר בְּמִלִּין מִי יוּכָל — *Who would be capable of withholding speech.* Now [that you tired so easily] it is necessary to react to your speech (*Rashi*).

It seems clear from *Rashi* that the urge to answer was prompted by Iyov's impatience and weariness. This is a quite different perception from that of *Ramban* who, as we saw above, believes that the intent of Eliphaz's speech was to disagree with Iyov's premise of a world subject to the influence of the heavenly constellations. Indeed, *Ramban* disagrees, too, with *Rashi's* interpretation of the first phrase in this verse. He renders: *If one were to venture a word with you* [נִסָּה, *to attempt*] *you would surely tire.* Or, *Has God indeed tested you with something that tires you out?*

3. הִנֵּה יִסַּרְתָּ רַבִּים — *Mark well! You have chided many.* You upbraided and spoke sternly to those who had much to say for themselves (*Rashi*).

וְיָדַיִם רָפוֹת תְּחַזֵּק — *Steadying hands that were weak.* You would encourage those that were weak and terrified by the punishments that overtook them, telling them not to be afraid since this was God's justice in action (*Rashi*).

Rashi does not explain who the one who *stumbled* and whose *knees buckled,* in the next verse, is referring to. However, from the context we can deduce, and *Metzudos* expresses as much, that these too are people whose belief in Divine Providence was shaken by their experiences.

We have, then, a picture of Iyov as the stern admonisher of those whose faith is troubled — bracing them to face their terrible fate with fortitude.

It is interesting to note that Iyov's memories of the golden days when, ... *His lantern would gleam over my head* (29:3) were quite different. True, he was a persuasive speaker: *When I would leave for the gate, to the canopied throne, when I would set up my seat in the street. Youngsters would glimpse me — and hide, the aged would rise and remain standing. Princes would withhold their speech, place hands upon their mouths. The powerful whose voice would normally be heard concealed themselves, their tongue cleaved to their palate. When any ear that heard of me would applaud, any eye that saw, would affirm my worth* (29:7-11).

But that was during debates at the city gates. His listeners were the elders and the nobles.

His relationship to the sufferers was one of uncritical help. Never a word concerning their fate. Only deeds — that changed lives: *When I would quiet the cries of the poor, the orphan whom none would help. The blessing of the wretched was directed to me, I brought joy to the widow's heart ... I served as eyes to the blind, the feet of the lame. I made myself father to the benighted, if I knew nothing of the nature of their claims, I would investigate them.*

The Sages (*Yalkut*) have a different tradition of how Iyov used to comfort the broken in body. He would go to someone who was blind and ask him: Would you, if you were a builder, wish to build a house without windows? So too, will HASHEM one day cure you, as it is written, ... *then the eyes of the blind will be opened* (*Isaiah* 35:5). And so on for the dumb and the lame.

It is not God's wish that anyone should suffer: each individual is His *house,* for each He wants only the best. Witness, that in an ideal state, when the Messianic era will have come, there will be no more disabilities, no

ד וְיָדַיִם רָפוֹת תְּחַזֵּק: כּוֹשֵׁל יְקִימוּן מִלֶּיךָ וּבִרְכַּיִם
ה כֹּרְעוֹת תְּאַמֵּץ: כִּי עַתָּה ׀ תָּבוֹא אֵלֶיךָ וַתֵּלֶא תִּגַּע
ו עָדֶיךָ וַתִּבָּהֵל: הֲלֹא יִרְאָתְךָ כִּסְלָתֶךָ תִּקְוָתְךָ וְתֹם
ז דְּרָכֶיךָ: זְכָר־נָא מִי הוּא נָקִי אָבָד וְאֵיפֹה יְשָׁרִים
ח נִכְחָדוּ: כַּאֲשֶׁר רָאִיתִי חֹרְשֵׁי אָוֶן וְזֹרְעֵי עָמָל יִקְצְרֻהוּ:

more pain. Therefore, accept your suffering. If God, the all powerful, Who does not wish to hurt anyone, afflicts you, it must be for some significant purpose — surely because you need it.

If this was Iyov's mode of comforting, then it is entirely apt that Eliphaz should bring it up at this point. As we have shown, this is precisely his argument in this speech — sublimate your suffering instead of lashing out! Why could Iyov not help himself, as he had so often helped others?

5. וַתֵּלֶא . . . וַתִּבָּהֵל — *Weary . . . confused.* We have noted above that taken at its simplest, this verse demonstrates that Eliphaz accuses Iyov of a faulty reaction rather than of deviant theology. Why was he not able to rally that inner strength which he had so often commended to others?

6. הֲלֹא יִרְאָתְךָ כִּסְלָתֶךָ — *Was then your reverence not your folly.* Thus, *Rashi*. [However, the two other times that the root כסל occurs in the book (8:14 and 31:24) he renders, *trust*. Perhaps the two ideas are related. The folly of the כְּסִיל may derive from an unwarranted and excessive self-reliance which refuses to admit the possibility of error.]

The thought is to be understood as follows: You always encouraged people who were suffering by expounding a certain value system to them — see above. Evidently, then, this value system has the ability to lend strength and confidence where, without it, there would be despair. Why do these same convictions not help you in your own troubles? It follows that you yourself never really subscribed to them. You deceived yourself by mouthing superficial platitudes — never allowing them to inform your whole being with a true reverence for God. Had you done so, surely you would have become neither wearied nor confused.

At 2:11 we learned that the friends had set out from their homes, *to mourn with him and to comfort him.* Certainly, it is scant comfort to tell someone that his actions make his life into a lie and that he is now, and has always been, a hypocrite. Wouldn't our perception of comforting words be to assure the mourner that in spite of everything that was happening, his integrity and worth in our eyes remains unimpaired?

Two explanations seem possible: Perhaps Eliphaz thought, mistakenly, that he could best draw Iyov out of his destructive negativity by shock. A warm, friendly and loving approach might have tended to reinforce the self-righteous, understandable, but ultimately nonproductive recriminations in which he was wallowing. Only the painful jolt which Eliphaz's biting rejection would bring about could move Iyov to a new and more constructive path.

Alternatively, we may consider the possibility that the three friends underwent a change of heart during the seven days of silence during which they sat with Iyov. We recall that 2:12 had taught that when they first came, *they did not recognize him.* We surmised that this implies that they detected a change of nature. Instead of the righteously confident Iyov whom they had known, they saw a mask of disillusion and bitterness. Perhaps they had expected some indication of joy or appreciation at their coming. Iyov did not even acknowledge their presence. We may surmise that during the seven days of silence they sat, expecting to catch a glimpse of the old Iyov whom they had known and loved. Perhaps once he started talking he would be himself once more. Instead, ignoring them completely he moves straight into his diatribe of curses. When Eliphaz saw this, he knew that his duty is now to instruct, rather than to comfort.

As we have understood Eliphaz's criticism of Iyov, *Ramban's* interpretation seems particularly apt. He takes כִּסְלָה in the sense of *trust,* and renders: Why do you become weary and confused? Surely your reverence for God can support you, in it you can find *trust, hope* and *constancy.* This is precisely the point which, as we have understood it, Eliphaz is making: There is a correct way to react to tragedy. It is to muster all of your spiritual resources to help you to sublimate your experience. This is the very opposite of the mindless despair which you have evinced.

Ramban differs from *Rashi* in that he takes our verse as leading into the next: Your

steadying hands that were weak. [4] *Your words would raise*
him who had stumbled, you would brace buckling knees. [5] *So*
now do you weary when it befalls you, it touches you, and
you become confused? [6] *Was then your reverence not your folly,*
so too your hopes and the constancy of your ways. [7] *Do recall I*
beg you: Who is the innocent who was ever lost without a
trace, who the upright ones, who were blotted out. [8] *Even as I*
observed those who plow sin and plant weariness must harvest it.

reverence can support you because if you observe carefully, you will see that no one innocent was ever lost without a trace, no one upright was ever blotted out; but rather that sinners invariably had to live with the fruits of their evil lives. Clearly, then, it is God Whose providence reigns, not the immutable unknowing and uncaring fate which derives from the constellations.

Rashi clearly takes the next verses as a new phase in the argument. See the analysis of Eliphaz's speech in the prefatory remarks.

תִּקְוָתְךָ וְתֹם דְּרָכֶיךָ — *So too your hopes and the constancy of your ways.* We have interpolated *so too*, in accordance with *Rashi*. All has been shown to be folly: Your *reverence*, your *hopes* and your *unquestioning integrity*.

For our rendering of תֹּם as *constant*, see commentary to 1:1, s.v. תָּם וְיָשָׁר.

7. זְכָר־נָא — *Do recall I beg you.* Eliphaz is consistent with his previously stated assumptions. The ideas which Iyov espoused in the past are to be ignored. They are, he thinks, useless platitudes which help least when they are most needed. But it is not too late. Draw now upon your experiences; think well; a just and understandable world-order will rise from your memories.

If we should judge the appropriateness of Eliphaz's suggestion by the reactions it evokes in Iyov — we must conclude that it was insensitive to the real issue. In the speech which follows that of Eliphaz — it cannot really be described as a rejoinder — Iyov appears to completely ignore the theoretical model of the world which Eliphaz projects. He knows only his own agonies, can look only inward.

מִי הוּא נָקִי אָבָד — *Who is the innocent who was ever lost without a trace.* We have translated *lost without a trace*, to parallel the *blotted out* at the end of the verse. Clearly, Eliphaz is not saying that good people never suffer at all. But he does claim that they are never totally obliterated (*Metzudos*).

While commentators do not make the following point, we feel it is legitimate, can well be read into the words, and within the context of Eliphaz's thinking may well be what he means: Eliphaz does not maintain that in a physical sense, no innocent people ever perish: Solomon had said, ... *Sometimes a righteous man perishes for all his righteousness* (*Koheles* 7:15), and, ... *Sometimes there are righteous men who are treated as if they had done according to the deeds of the wicked* (*Koheles* 8:14). Why would Eliphaz declare as a fact something which we all know not to be so. Rather, he may well mean that even when the righteous man is called upon to suffer, he does not permit his agony to force him into oblivion. By responding as God would wish him to respond, he forges immortality from out of his pain.[1]

8. כַּאֲשֶׁר רָאִיתִי חֹרְשֵׁי אָוֶן וְזֹרְעֵי עָמָל יִקְצְרֻהוּ — *Even as I observed those who plow sin, and plant weariness must harvest it.* Here, apparently, Eliphaz does not feel that he can ask Iyov to search his own memory in order to discover the same conclusion. As Iyov makes abundantly clear in his rebuttal to Tzophar's second speech (chapter 21), observation can yield ample evidence of the wicked leading lives which seem quite successful.

[The fact that Eliphaz assumes Iyov's agreement to the thesis that the innocent are never blotted out, but feels the need to convince him that the wicked can never really prosper, could explain the imbalance between the two sections of his argument — one sentence against four. That to which they both agree manifestly requires less elaboration than does a thesis of which Iyov has yet to be convinced.]

1. We quote *Chovos HaLevovos, Sha'ar Ahavas HaShem* chapter 1:

> It is told about a certain *chassid*, that he used to arise in the middle of the night and say: My God, You have made me go hungry, and left me naked, and made me dwell in the darkness of the night. But, You have [also] taught me of Your might and Your greatness. Were You now to consume me in fire it could only increase my love for You and the happiness which I feel in Your closeness.

ט־י מִנִּשְׁמַת אֱלוֹהַּ יֹאבֵדוּ וּמֵרוּחַ אַפּוֹ יִכְלוּ׃ שַׁאֲגַת אַרְיֵה
יא וְקוֹל שָׁחַל וְשִׁנֵּי כְפִירִים נִתָּעוּ׃ לַיִשׁ אֹבֵד מִבְּלִי־טָרֶף
יב וּבְנֵי לָבִיא יִתְפָּרָדוּ׃ וְאֵלַי דָּבָר יְגֻנָּב וַתִּקַּח אָזְנִי שֵׁמֶץ
יג מֶנְהוּ׃ בִּשְׂעִפִּים מֵחֶזְיֹנוֹת לָיְלָה בִּנְפֹל תַּרְדֵּמָה עַל־
יד־טו אֲנָשִׁים׃ פַּחַד קְרָאַנִי וּרְעָדָה וְרֹב עַצְמוֹתַי הִפְחִיד׃ וְרוּחַ
טז עַל־פָּנַי יַחֲלֹף תְּסַמֵּר שַׂעֲרַת בְּשָׂרִי׃ יַעֲמֹד ׀ וְלֹא־
אַכִּיר מַרְאֵהוּ תְּמוּנָה לְנֶגֶד עֵינָי דְּמָמָה וָקוֹל אֶשְׁמָע׃

Eliphaz, then, must mean something else: Inevitably the wicked will reap the fruits of their wickedness. A soul that has been plowed by sin — deep furrows reaching down into its essence — so that the seeds of weariness and sin seep into the very marrow of existence, such a soul is beyond the innocent joy of accomplishment, the sense of being blessed, that lights the path of success of those who have not blighted their lives.

This thought would parallel precisely the earlier one concerning the innocent. In each case, the assertions do not deal with overt realities, but with the effect which experiences have upon the soul. The innocent will generate light out of darkness, the wicked, gall from sweetness.

The translation follows *Ramban. Rashi* reads the beginning of our verse together with the previous one, as follows: [Who the upright one who was blotted out.] Even as I observed that those who plow sin [are blotted out], while those that plant weariness must harvest it.

9. מִנִּשְׁמַת אֱלוֹהַּ יֹאבֵדוּ — *Just a puff from God, and they perish.* The translation follows *Metzudos.* The point is being made that the success of the wicked is illusory. It takes just a very small puff of God's fury to collapse the empire which he has built for himself.

According to this interpretation, there is no assertion that the wicked will inevitably lose his wealth; just that its foundations are weak and are therefore easily smashed. We can understand this in a physical sense — he has no firm grasp on his riches; or from a psychological standpoint — with his sense of inner worth eroded by his self-disgust, he has no stomach to defend himself against the blows of misfortune.

We have noted above that in *Ramban's* view, this verse is central to Eliphaz's thesis. The destruction of the wicked comes from God, not from the heavenly bodies.

10-11. שַׁאֲגַת אַרְיֵה וְקוֹל שָׁחַל וְשִׁנֵּי כְפִירִים נִתָּעוּ. לַיִשׁ אֹבֵד מִבְּלִי־טָרֶף וּבְנֵי לָבִיא יִתְפָּרָדוּ — *By the lion's roar, the lionet's yelp, the fangs of the cub, they lose their bearings. By the lion straying without a kill, by the lion's whelps who roam loose.* The translation follows *Ramban* who understands these two verses as describing how the destruction wrought by God (v. 9) will come about.

◆§ The Vision

Rashi and *Ramban* have radically different perceptions of the vision which Eliphaz reports. We have translated in accordance with *Rashi* although, as we shall explain, *Ramban's* explanation can be more readily understood in the context.

In *Rashi's* view, the vision reveals that no man can be perfect in God's sight. If He is able to, and does, find fault even with His angels, then what can be said of a mere mortal?

Rashi's interpretation is not without difficulty. Why should this teaching be conveyed by way of a vision from above? The reasoning itself seems to be self-sufficient — as witness that Eliphaz himself makes the point once more at 15:15ff. and Bildad, a very similar one at 25:4ff., both without the benefit of revelation. Certainly, the fear and trembling which precedes the vision, and the mere fact of a heavenly presence being sent, would seem to imply that Eliphaz was about to be made privy to some deep secret. The lesson, as *Rashi* understands it, would not seem to require the solemn framework in which it was taught (but see our analysis at 15:14-16).

Ramban, however, interprets the passage in a way which does indeed bring us face to face with what is perhaps the profoundest of all of life's mysteries: the inscrutability of God's providence. There is an admission, as it were, that the neat picture painted above in verses 7 and 8, is not always true. The world occasionally looks chaotic, indeed. We *do* find that the innocent suffer; we *do* see the wicked prosper. We do, in short, observe facts which appear to

9 Just a puff from God, and they perish; by the breath of His nos-
trils they come to their end. 10 By the lion's roar, the lionet's yelp,
the fangs of the cub, they lose their bearings. 11 By the lion straying
without a kill, by the lion's whelps, who roam loose. 12 As for me, a
message stole up upon me, my ear picked up just a mite of it.
13 During the ruminations of the night's visions, as slumber des-
cends upon men. 14 Terror seized me, and trembling; it petrified the
mass of my limbs. 15 A spirit brushed past my face; the hair of my
flesh stood on end. 16 He stood, but I could make nothing of his ap-
pearance; an image was before my eyes; I heard a sound of silence.

fly in the face of our notions of a just and ordered world. It is to this issue that the vision addresses itself — though, in the end, for us, at least, the truth remains shrouded in the inaccessibility of God's wisdom.

The role which such an insight would play in Eliphaz's presentation, seems to be as follows: He wishes to persuade Iyov that his reaction to his fate — the total frustration which he had displayed — had been in error. Pain is sent — even to the innocent — in order to elicit a response which will, in the end, sublimate the suffering and exalt the sufferer. This, in itself, would be ample justification for the horrors which he had experienced. There is every reason that Iyov should accept such an explanation for what had happened. For, even though it is true that there *are* occasionally situations which defy any explanation — the subject of the vision — these are only a small minority. Why should Iyov assume that his experiences belong to that small category.

12. וְאֵלַי דָּבָר יְגֻנָּב — *As for me, a message stole up upon me.* Thus, *Rashi.* Eliphaz is a non-Jew. Accordingly prophecy, which to the Jewish prophet comes openly and proudly, as a man would go to his wife, slinks up to him secretly, as a man would go to his concubine.

Ramban, as we saw above, has a radically different interpretation for this verse. He takes אֵלַי, in the first part of this verse, as a synonym for מִמֶּנִּי, *from me.* The meaning is: Although my observations confirm that we live in an essentially just and well-ordered world, in which the innocent are never blotted out and in which the wicked reap the fruits of their evil, there is nevertheless something that I do not fully understand [it is *stolen from me*]. For, truth be told, there are occasionally wicked people who to all appearances are firmly *rooted* (5:3) and successful.

This is a deeply serious problem, but a part of the solution [the *mite* which his *ear picked up*] was revealed to me in prophetic vision.

See below for *Ramban's* explanation of the following verses.

As indicated above, this explanation carries abiding implications for the understanding of the book of *Iyov.* For here we have an admission from one of the friends that all is not as cut and dried as they claim in most of their speeches. There are aspects to Divine Providence which appear to us to be capricious. The ramifications will be noted throughout the book.

◆§ The Encounter With The Heavenly Messenger

13-16. Taken together with the previous verse, we have five verses describing Eliphaz's reaction to the appearance of the heavenly messenger — the precise number of verses devoted to the actual message. We may wonder whether this is another example of the insensitivity with which *Zohar* accuses the friends. It seems a self-centered approach, unsuitable to the occasion. It would seem that the mourner, not the comforter, should occupy center stage.

13. בִּשְׂעִפִּים — *During the ruminations.* שְׂעִף, as *thoughts* or *ruminations,* occurs only in *Iyov* (see also at 20:2), although with a *samech* we have it also at *Psalms* 119:113. See *Radak, Shorashim.*

14. פַּחַד קְרָאַנִי — *Terror seized me.* Fear of the *spirit* of verse 15 — which denotes an angel (*Rashi*).

15. תְּסַמֵּר שַׂעֲרַת בְּשָׂרִי — *The hair of my flesh stood on end.* תְּסַמֵּר, from מַסְמֵר, *a nail* (*Metzudos*).

16. דְּמָמָה וָקוֹל אֶשְׁמָע — *I heard a sound of silence.* The words were uttered so quietly that they could be described as an admixture of sound and silence (*Metzudos*).

ד/יז־כא יז־יח הַאֱנוֹשׁ מֵאֱלוֹהַּ יִצְדָּק אִם־מֵעֹשֵׂהוּ יִטְהַר־גָּבֶר: הֵן בַּעֲבָדָיו
יט לֹא יַאֲמִין וּבְמַלְאָכָיו יָשִׂים תָּהֳלָה: אַף ׀ שֹׁכְנֵי בָתֵּי־
כ חֹמֶר אֲשֶׁר־בֶּעָפָר יְסוֹדָם יְדַכְּאוּם לִפְנֵי־עָשׁ: מִבֹּקֶר
כא לָעֶרֶב יֻכַּתּוּ מִבְּלִי מֵשִׂים לָנֶצַח יֹאבֵדוּ: הֲלֹא־נִסַּע
ה/א־ב א יִתְרָם בָּם יָמוּתוּ וְלֹא בְחָכְמָה: קְרָא־נָא הֲיֵשׁ עוֹנֶךָּ
ב וְאֶל־מִי מִקְּדֹשִׁים תִּפְנֶה: כִּי־לֶאֱוִיל יַהֲרָג־כָּעַשׂ וּפֹתֶה

◆§ The Message:

17. הַאֱנוֹשׁ מֵאֱלוֹהַּ יִצְדָּק אִם־מֵעֹשֵׂהוּ יִטְהַר־גָּבֶר — *Can mortals be deemed righteous before God, could man be considered pure before his Creator?* The prefix *mem* must be understood as *before,* as in *Numbers* 32:22 (*Daas Mikra*).

As *Rashi* understands it, this verse states the general proposition that no mortal can be deemed more righteous than God. The next four verses then develop this theme by presenting a *kal vachomer.* The mortal's vulnerability to criticism follows absolutely from the fact that even the angels themselves are not perfect in His sight.

Ramban appears to translate the verse as does *Rashi,* but the intent is quite different. The issue is not whether man is blameless in the formal sense of whether or not he commits sins and should be punished for them. Rather, the point is that imperfect man has no right to expect to understand the workings of God's providence. True, there are inconsistencies which we can observe — but their explanation is beyond our ken.

This proposition is then supported in the next four verses. Even the angels are not privy to God's thinking; how then can mortals summon the temerity to pretend to understand?

18. הֵן בַּעֲבָדָיו לֹא יַאֲמִין — *See! Even His servants He does not trust.* In a sentence structured like ours: ... *His servants* ... *His angels* ..., it would be usual to take *servants* as synonymous with *angels,* with the verse repeating the same thought with a slightly heavier emphasis in the second stich: Not only does He not trust his ministering angels, He even ascribes frivolity to them. *Rashi,* however, renders *servants* as *righteous people.* He does not trust them in the sense that He causes them to die before their time, in order to make sure that they die innocent. With longer years they would be apt to sin.

Ramban, consistent with his understanding of the whole passage, and adducing *Numbers* 12:7, renders: He does not even *entrust* His servants and angels with the mysteries of His providence. Ultimately, what God does is locked in the impenetrable essence of His being.

תָּהֳלָה — *Frivolity.* As in הֹלֵלוֹת, (*Koheles* 1:17 and elsewhere) (*Rashi*).

19. אַף שֹׁכְנֵי בָתֵּי־חֹמֶר — *Surely, then, those that dwell in houses of clay. Ibn Ezra* and *Ramban* both take the expression metaphorically — mortals who are locked into their physical bodies, *houses of clay,* in contrast to the spiritual beings of the previous verse.

אֲשֶׁר־בֶּעָפָר יְסוֹדָם — *Destined to a grave of dust. Rashi* renders thus [although it is not clear why יְסוֹד, usually *base* or *source,* should come to mean *grave*]. *Ramban* renders in the more usual manner: *Whose beginnings are from the dust.*

יְדַכְּאוּם לִפְנֵי־עָשׁ — *Whom they crush for the maggots.* The subject would be *agents from heaven* (*Rashi*); *the angels of death* (*Ramban*); or an unidentified agency [as in 3:2, see there] (*Ramban*).

The maggots are the ones who will consume them in death (*Rashi*).

20. מִבֹּקֶר לָעֶרֶב יֻכַּתּוּ — *From just morning to night they are ground down. Rashi*: The sense is that their destruction takes no time at all.

Ramban: From having been whole and strong in the morning, they will be ground down by evening.

מִבְּלִי מֵשִׂים — *Without considering.* Without taking their situation to heart and taking the opportunity to repent (*Rashi*).

21. הֲלֹא־נִסַּע יִתְרָם בָּם — *Clearly the pride which had been theirs deserts them. Rashi* suggests *pride* and *wisdom* for יִתְרָם, adducing *Isaiah* 15:7. The base meaning for נסע is *to uproot* — see, for example, *Judges* 16:14.

וְלֹא בְחָכְמָה — *No wiser. Rashi* offers no explanation. *Ramban* offers: They die without ever understanding their death — for it overtakes them suddenly.

[If we take the whole passage as does

4/17-21 [17] *Can mortals be deemed righteous before God, could man be*
considered pure before his Creator? [18] *See! Even His servants He*
does not trust, ascribes frivolity to His very angels. [19] *Surely, then*
those that dwell in houses of clay, destined to a grave of dust,
whom they crush for the maggots. [20] *From just morning to night*
they are ground down, without considering — lost forever.
[21] *Clearly the pride which had been theirs deserts them; they die —*
no wiser.

5/1-2 [1] *Cry out, I beg you — will any answer you, to whom among the*
saintly can you turn? [2] *For frustration will kill the fool; anger*

Ramban (see above), it would perhaps have been possible to explain this phrase: They die without ever understanding the secrets which guide God's providence.]

V.

1. קְרָא־נָא הֲיֵשׁ עוֹנֶךָּ וְאֶל־מִי מִקְּדֹשִׁים תִּפְנֶה — *Cry out, I beg you — will any answer you, to whom among the saintly can you turn?* Eliphaz has finished with his account of the prophecy. He now returns once more to his reasoning (*Rashi*).

The first part of the verse is clear enough: Scream as much as you want (*Rashi*); or, make your complaints known in order to find someone who would support you in your contentions (*Ramban*). Nobody will sympathize or even answer.

But what of the second part. Who are these *saintly* ones?

Rashi: Against whom among the *saintly*, who decreed that these troubles overtake you, will you fight?

[The thought is not entirely clear. Who are these *saintly* ones; in what sense do they decree that people suffer? If reference is to the heavenly constellations, Iyov (as *Rashi* has understood him) has never indicated that these were the source of his troubles.]

Ramban: To whom among the *saintly* will you turn for an answer? Not one among them will support you in your resistance to suffering.

[In *Ramban's* view, the *saintly* ones might well be pious people (*Psalms* 89:6 and elsewhere) whose approbation Iyov would value. None would agree with his negative attitude.]

Ramban's view, then, is precisely that which we would have expected as we have understood Eliphaz's thinking. He is uncompromisingly critical of what he perceives as Iyov's negativism — proposing instead that suffering can, and therefore should, be sublimated.

For the crucial significance of this and the next verse to Eliphaz's ideas as we have understood them — see Prefatory Remarks to chapter 14.

2. כִּי־לֶאֱוִיל יַהֲרָג־כָּעַשׂ וּפֹתֶה תָּמִית קִנְאָה — *For frustration will kill the fool; anger will slay the simple-minded.*

Rashi comments: If you had kept silent, perhaps God would once more have shown you mercy.

The introductory word, *For . . .*, in our verse clearly ties it to the previous one which addresses Iyov directly. It follows that it is Iyov, rather than a theoretical class of people, who here is being described as *fool* and *simple minded*. It seems noteworthy that these descriptions do not recur in the book. The friends, in the course of their speeches, accuse Iyov of a great many shortcomings, but never, after this one occasion, of stupidity.

Perhaps this would tend to reinforce our understanding of Iyov's first speech as unique in that it projects no theological stance but simply rails against a reality which, by its very nature, is intractable and immutable. It is easily understandable that Eliphaz would consider such a giving way to frustration as folly.[1]

1. At 4:6 we discussed the question whether כִּסְלָתֶךָ, in that verse, is to be understood as *folly* or as *trust*.

That Eliphaz here describes Iyov as an אֱוִיל may argue in favor of the meaning *folly*. Throughout *Proverbs* the ideas of כְּסִלוּת and אֱוִילוּת are closely related. For some examples among many, see 14:8 and 26:4.

The same association would be accomplished by the use of the two terms in concert, in Eliphaz's speech.

ג תָּמִית קִנְאָה: אֲנִי־רָאִיתִי אֱוִיל מַשְׁרִישׁ וָאֶקּוֹב נָוֵהוּ

כַּעַשׂ . . . קִנְאָה — *Frustration . . . anger.* כַּעַס is frequently used to describe the anger and frustrations which derive from unhappy relationships from which one had the right to expect more. Thus, the feelings of a father suffering from a stupid son (*Proverbs* 17:25), or of the husband of a contentious wife (21:19, there). So, also, God's reaction to the idol worshiping disloyalty of His sons and daughters (*Deuteronomy* 32:19). Accordingly, it is an appropriate term to describe Iyov's disappointment at a seemingly capricious God Who he felt had deeply wronged him.

The basic meaning of קִנְאָה is to act with *zeal* or *ardor*. Hence, a *burning anger* or *fury*. We find its use parallel to כַּעַס, as, for example, at *Deuteronomy* 32:16.[1]

◆§ An Interpolation:

Verses 3-7: A careful analysis of this chapter seems to yield that verses 3-7 are an interpolation, the kind of lurching which we detected in Iyov's first speech (see 3:3, footnote 1, p. 32). There we attributed this unexpected usage to the sufferer's distraught state of mind; here we must assume that Eliphaz is suddenly gripped by an anger which, as the Sages teach (*Sifre, Matos* 48), brings error in its wake.

We explain.

In verse 1, Eliphaz had sarcastically challenged Iyov, *Cry out, I beg you — will any answer you!* There seems little doubt that verse 8, *But as for me, I would search out the Almighty . . .* , is meant to present a contrast: You address your cries to those who will not care, I call upon God. That section continues through verse 16. [Thread I]

Verse 2 had made the point that, . . . *frustration will kill the fool . . .* . Certainly the section beginning with verse 17, *See how happy the man whom God disciplines . . .* , is meant to be placed in contrast to such folly. [Thread II]

The almost perfect symmetry between these two passages appears to bear out this parallelism. Verse 8, which makes the statement that it is best to turn to God, is followed by eight verses which describe all the advantages which accrue to one who puts his trust in God. Verse 17 notes the folly of allowing oneself to be frustrated by suffering imposed by God, and is then followed by nine verses which describe the advantages which accrue to the person who rejoices in God's discipline. However,of these nine verses, one, verse 19, is really an introductory statement to the next section. Accordingly, there are precisely eight verses which are operative — precisely the number in the earlier section. We have, then, a perfectly balanced system. (See Chart below.)

Thread I	Thread II	Interpolation
1. Cry out, I beg you — will any answer you — to whom among the saintly can you turn? **8.** But, as for me, I would search out the Almighty, direct my speech to God. **9.** Who performs great deeds beyond understanding, wonders beyond numbering . . . **12.** He frustrates the plottings of the cunning, so that their hands will not produce results . . . **15.** He delivers from the sword — their mouths, the destitute from the hands of the powerful. **16.** For the miserable it constitutes hope; wrongdoing must clamp up its mouth.	**2.** For frustration will kill the fool, anger will slay the simple minded. **17.** See, how happy the man whom God disciplines, never loathe the chastisement of Shadai. **18.** For He inflicts pain — but will assuage, wounds, but His hands will heal. **19.** From six straits He will save you, and at the seventh, no harm shall come to you . . .	**3.** As for me, I saw a fool strike roots, but presaged an instant bane upon his home. **4.** May fortune elude his children; let them be crushed at the gate with no one to help. **5.** May the famished consume his harvest; gathering it from among the brambles, the parched will gulp their riches. **6.** For injury does not spring from the dust, nor does the earth bring forth weariness. **7.** For man is born to weariness, while the spirits soar in flight.

1. For our purpose, the following passage from *Proverbs* 14:29-30 is particularly apt: *Patience results in much understanding; impatience exalts folly* (אִוֶּלֶת). *A healing heart is good for the body; passion rots the bones.*

Gra remarks: *A healing heart is good for the body,* because it helps one to understand the justification of another's anger and to find healing in that appreciation of a position other than one's own. Thus, his silence is a healing one, balm to his body. But, *furious rage* at another's [annoyance] *rots the bones.*

Clearly, this is precisely the idea expressed in our verse. Iyov is called upon to seek to understand God's actions.

will slay the simple-minded. 3 *As for me, I saw a fool strike roots,*

1 . . . 8-16 = 2 . . . 17-26

This pattern established, it is clear that the entire passage from verse 8 onwards is the logical continuation of verses 1 and 2. Clearly, verses 3-7 are an interpolation.

Why would Eliphaz veer from his chosen and so carefully structured pattern?

We suspect that we have here the beginnings of an anger which, more and more, will color Eliphaz's attitudes as the discussions unfold. In verse 2 Eliphaz had, probably for the first time, seen Iyov for a *fool*, or one who is *simple-minded*. He simply had no understanding of Iyov's attitude which seemed to fly in the face of everything for which he had previously stood. With the אֱוִיל, *the fool*, in his mind, he suddenly remembers his own reaction to seeing a *fool* who had *struck roots*. He recalls, what were to him, inevitable disasters which had overtaken that one.

Could it be that Iyov's experiences were due to such self-same folly? Eliphaz, as yet, makes no such accusation — but the drift of his thinking is clear.[1]

3. אֲנִי־רָאִיתִי אֱוִיל מַשְׁרִישׁ וָאֶקּוֹב נָוֵהוּ פִתְאֹם — *As for me, I saw a fool strike roots, but presaged a curse upon his home.* The translation follows *Ramban*, see below.

Rashi appears to take וָאֶקּוֹב as a curse uttered by Eliphaz.

Rashi does not explain why Eliphaz would curse the wicked, or what the point was in telling this to Iyov.

We may perhaps surmise that he is contrasting himself to his hapless friend. I did not waste my curses in useless and therefore meaningless diatribes against the inevitable. In contrast to you I used them for good effect against the wicked.

Ramban believes that this passage goes back to the vision which Eliphaz had previously described.

We recall that this vision had come in reaction to Eliphaz's observation that the cut and dried system in which the innocent always prosper and the wicked always suffer has its exceptions. The wicked, occasionally, do very well indeed. The vision had suggested that man cannot expect to understand the mysteries of God's providence when these are hidden from even His angels.

Eliphaz now returns to this issue. In the vision he did, indeed, see wicked people prosper. However, he saw too that an instant curse would descend upon them. [*Ramban* takes וָאֶקּוֹב unconventionally, as *I saw prophetically that a curse would descend*, rather than, *I cursed* (see also *Metzudos*).]

The sense seems to be as follows:

Earlier, the wicked had been described as those who *plow sin and plant weariness.* Here, they are seen as *fools.* There is certainly an echo here of the *fool* (Iyov) of verse 2. Iyov is a fool for allowing himself to be overwhelmed by his misfortunes; but no less is the wicked man *a fool* who allows himself to be lulled into a sense of security by his successes.

This, the vision made clear.

It taught that the apparent invincibility implied in *taking root* is illusory. It will not last — sudden destruction will overtake it. [The meaning does not appear to be that the successes will last for only a short time (— מִיָּד

1. Our thesis may help to answer the following difficulty:

If, indeed, Eliphaz is now taking up the issue of those instances in human experience which allow for no rational explanation, why does he deal only with the problem of the prospering wicked, and not with that of the suffering saint? Surely this latter is more germane to Iyov's dilemma?

Indeed, when *Ramban* in his *Toras HaAdam* discusses the fact that there are human experiences which defy explanation, he specifically adduces an example from the suffering saint rather than from the prospering wicked man.

Because of its importance to understanding the basics of the book of *Iyov* as *Ramban* develops them, we quote:

> . . . However there are totally righteous people who, in defiance of any logical system still suffer . . . and this is the basis for Iyov's arguments . . . But for this matter there is no answer which humans can grasp — the explanation is reserved for God's mind alone.
>
> Thus did they say concerning R' Akiva who was shown to Moses in prophetic vision. Moses asked: 'You have shown me his Torah — show me now his reward!' He saw them cutting up his flesh in the marketplace. He said to God: 'Is this the reward for the Torah?' God answered: 'Silence, thus has My mind decreed.'
>
> The meaning of this passage is that R' Akiva's sufferings could not be explained as a means of generating atonement for some minor sins which he had committed — for he was entirely pure. But — the matter is mystery. Such are the thoughts of Him Who is the source of all thought . . .

Thus, we would have expected this problem, too, to be raised by Eliphaz. However, if the whole passage was generated only by the thought-association from the mention of the אֱוִיל, there is no difficulty.

ד פִּתְאֹם׃ יִרְחֲקוּ בָנָיו מִיֶּשַׁע וְיִדַּכְּאוּ בַשַּׁעַר וְאֵין מַצִּיל׃
ה אֲשֶׁר קְצִירוֹ ׀ רָעֵב יֹאכֵל וְאֶל־מִצִּנִּים יִקָּחֵהוּ וְשָׁאַף
ו צַמִּים חֵילָם׃ כִּי ׀ לֹא־יֵצֵא מֵעָפָר אָוֶן וּמֵאֲדָמָה
ז לֹא־יִצְמַח עָמָל׃ כִּי־אָדָם לְעָמָל יוּלָּד וּבְנֵי־רֶשֶׁף יַגְבִּיהוּ
ח עוּף׃ אוּלָם אֲנִי אֶדְרֹשׁ אֶל־אֵל וְאֶל־אֱלֹהִים אָשִׂים
ט דִּבְרָתִי׃ עֹשֶׂה גְדֹלוֹת וְאֵין חֵקֶר נִפְלָאוֹת עַד־אֵין מִסְפָּר׃

פִּתְאוֹם, *immediately*; see *Metzudos*) — witness that the next two verses speak about the debacle overtaking the children — but that when destruction ultimately comes it will be *sudden*. It will come about in a way which will underline that it is not a natural erosion of wealth — which could still leave us with the idea that the original success was a natural state of affairs — but that even while it lasted, it was an aberration.]

Why the wicked should be granted such temporary prosperity is not said. That is part of the mystery of God's providence to which we can never become privy. We recall that Eliphaz had only been vouchsafed a *mite* of understanding. But the *sudden* destruction which overtakes them will have the effect of preserving the truth that the *normal* state of affairs is one in which, indeed, the good prosper and the wicked suffer.

Eliphaz seems to be saying: By and large, the world is run by a system of justice which even we can observe. There are exceptions, but these are minor — and themselves contain elements which tend to confirm our basic belief in an ordered world. Therefore, you, Iyov, must assume purpose to your troubles — and forthwith set out to sublimate them.

4. יִרְחֲקוּ בָנָיו מִיֶּשַׁע — *May fortune elude his children.* This is the curse which Eliphaz would hurl against the fools (*Rashi*). In *Ramban's* approach, this is the fate which he foresees for them.

The object of the imprecation, or the subject of Eliphaz's look into the future, is *his children*. The implication accords with what we saw above: There is no assumption that the prospering of the wicked man must be short-lived. In God's inscrutable providence, there may be times that the success which he enjoys seems firmly entrenched indeed. But at some point, possibly only during the life of his descendants [בָּנָיו need not mean literally *children*; later generations could also be meant], the evil which he perpetrated will catch up with him.

Translated literally, the verse would read: *His sons will distance themselves from fortune.* Indeed, that is how *Ramban* understands it: They, themselves, will act in such a way that fortune will certainly elude them. Evil, Eliphaz says, is self-destructive. It is a cancer that lies embedded within the soul; eventually, virulently, it bursts forth and encompasses all.

וְיִדַּכְּאוּ בַשַּׁעַר וְאֵין מַצִּיל — *Let them be crushed at the gate, with no one to help.* Throughout Scripture the *gate* is the seat of the court. Thus, they will be crushed in sight of the community's elders and of all the people. No one will raise a hand in their defense (*Ramban*).

From the next verse it is clear that the wicked man envisioned here was both wealthy and powerful. We must assume that his was a voice which carried much weight in the community. All this will be shown to have been illusory. No one ever really cared for him. No one cares at all for his children.

5. אֲשֶׁר קְצִירוֹ רָעֵב יֹאכֵל וְאֶל־מִצִּנִּים יִקָּחֵהוּ וְשָׁאַף צַמִּים חֵילָם — *May the famished consume his harvest; gathering it from among the brambles, the parched will gulp their riches.* The sense is that the impotence of the sons will make it possible for the famished people who had been victims of the father's greed to repossess that which had been taken from them (*Rashi*).

We have translated the next phrase in accordance with *Metzudos*. The famished will collect even those parts of the harvest which grow among the brambles. That is, there will be no sense of haste. They do not fear that anyone will chase them away. The children are weak and can do nothing to protect their fields.

The final phrase continues with the same thought. Those who became parched during the father's lifetime because of that which he had robbed from them will now gulp down the wealth which is rightfully theirs.

6. כִּי לֹא־יֵצֵא מֵעָפָר אָוֶן וּמֵאֲדָמָה לֹא־יִצְמַח עָמָל — *For injury does not spring from the dust, nor does the earth bring forth weariness.*

7. כִּי־אָדָם לְעָמָל יוּלָּד וּבְנֵי־רֶשֶׁף יַגְבִּיהוּ עוּף — *For man is born to weariness, while the spirits soar*

but presaged a curse upon his home. [4] *May fortune elude*
his children; let them be crushed at the gate with no one to
help. [5] *May the famished consume his harvest; gathering it*
from among the brambles, the parched will gulp their riches.
[6] *For injury does not spring from the dust, nor does the*
earth bring forth weariness. [7] *For man is born to weariness,*
while the spirits soar in flight. [8] *But as for me, I would search*
out the Almighty, direct my speech to God. [9] *Who performs*
great deeds beyond comprehension, wonders beyond numbering.

in flight. The sense of these two verses, according to *Rashi*, is as follows: The suffering to which man is prone [אָוֶן here means שֶׁבֶר, *brokenness*, as in *Jeremiah* 4:14] does not come of itself — it does not, so to speak, sprout from the earth. *Man is born to weariness* in the sense that inevitably he will sin and, in consequence, be overtaken by punishment. This is in contrast to spiritual beings [*Rashi* renders: angels and spirits] who can soar ever upwards, unencumbered by the troubles which will always dog man made of flesh.

Ramban adds that given this truism, it is clear that the prospering of the wicked can, in the final analysis, not last. These two verses are the philosophical underpinnings for the observations recorded in the last three verses.

He renders the second phrase as follows: [Trouble is as endemic to the human condition] *as flight is to birds.* [בְּנֵי רֶשֶׁף are *birds*, as in *Deuteronomy* 32:24.]

If our understanding of Eliphaz's thrust in this first speech is correct — that he is arguing in favor of sublimating suffering rather than permitting it to frustrate — then another explanation of verse 7 seems possible.

A בֶּן רֶשֶׁף might well be a *man of the spirit*, in contrast to the אָדָם, the *earth-man*, of the earlier part of the verse (cf. *Song of Songs* 8:6). If we then take the *vav* as *but*, rather than as *and*, the sense would be as follows: Indeed, man must inevitably meet up with suffering. But whereas *earth-man* will allow the pain to crush him, the *man of spirit* will convert the experience into an opportunity to raise himself to ever new heights.

8. אוּלָם אֲנִי אֶדְרֹשׁ אֶל־אֵל וְאֶל־אֱלֹהִים אָשִׂים דִּבְרָתִי — *But as for me, I would search out the Almighty, direct my speech to God.* If this suffering had overtaken me, I would have reacted by turning to God in prayer and entreaty (*Rashi*).

See Prefatory Remarks to chapter 4 where we note that in *Ramban's* view this verse is central to Eliphaz's speech. It makes the point that suffering comes not from the heavenly constellations, but from God. In this context, he takes דִּבְרָתִי as הַנְהָגָתִי, the *direction in which God takes my life*, adducing *I Kings* 5:23. The sense is: *I ascribe the direction of my life to God*, not to the influence of the planets.

Above, s.v. *An Interpolation*, we made the point that this verse introduces a section (up to v. 16), which elaborates on what was said in verse 1 of this chapter. The correct reaction to suffering is not to lash out impotently at forces which influence nothing at all, but to turn to God, the source and justification of all of life's vagaries, as described in the next few verses.

9-11. *Ramban* takes these three verses together and sees them as an introduction to verses 12-16, as follows:

From God's providence as it manifests itself in the broad brush strokes for which whole countries and continents provide the canvas, we can draw the conclusion that individual fates, too, are in His hands. And, in the large picture, it is through the provision and dispensation of rainfall that we can observe Him best. Sun and moon, myriad contributors to earth's survival, are all constant, predictable, undeviating. Only rainfall is sporadic, only of the gift of water can we never be sure.

And thus, it is in rainfall (v. 10), which has the power to *raise the lowly* and to *uplift the shriveled*, parched and thirsty masses (v. 11), in which we recognize *deeds beyond comprehension, wonders beyond numbering* (v. 9).

9. עֹשֶׂה גְדֹלוֹת וְאֵין חֵקֶר נִפְלָאוֹת עַד־אֵין מִסְפָּר — *Who performs great deeds beyond comprehension, wonders beyond numbering.* As we saw above, *Ramban* takes this verse together with the next. In verse 10 is defined the *deeds* and *wonders* in terms of the rain which God brings upon the earth.

Indeed *Taanis* 2a appears to understand our passage in just that way. The *mishnah* there, 1:1, refers to גְּבוּרַת גְּשָׁמִים, *the might of God as manifested through the bringing of rain*, and the *Gemara* adduces our passage as a source for this perception. Rainfall, in the

י הַנֹּתֵן מָטָר עַל־פְּנֵי־אָרֶץ וְשֹׁלֵחַ מַיִם עַל־פְּנֵי חוּצוֹת׃
יא־יב לָשׂוּם שְׁפָלִים לְמָרוֹם וְקֹדְרִים שָׂגְבוּ יֶשַׁע׃ מֵפֵר
יג מַחְשְׁבוֹת עֲרוּמִים וְלֹא־תַעֲשֶׂינָה יְדֵיהֶם תֻּשִׁיָּה׃ לֹכֵד
יד חֲכָמִים בְּעָרְמָם וַעֲצַת נִפְתָּלִים נִמְהָרָה׃ יוֹמָם יְפַגְּשׁוּ־
טו חֹשֶׁךְ וְכַלַּיְלָה יְמַשְׁשׁוּ בַצָּהֳרָיִם׃ וַיֹּשַׁע מֵחֶרֶב מִפִּיהֶם
טז וּמִיַּד חָזָק אֶבְיוֹן׃ וַתְּהִי לַדַּל תִּקְוָה וְעֹלָתָה קָפְצָה פִּיהָ׃
יז הִנֵּה אַשְׁרֵי אֱנוֹשׁ יוֹכִחֶנּוּ אֱלוֹהַּ וּמוּסַר שַׁדַּי אַל־תִּמְאָס׃

thought-world of the Sages, is of a kind with creation itself. No less than that greatest of all God's marvels, does it point to the total inscrutability of Divine wisdom.

However, in terms of the simple meaning of the passage, we could, with *Daas Mikra*, understand this verse as following the previous one. Eliphaz claims that had he found himself in Iyov's situation, he would have turned to God. He now explains: He would not have permitted himself to slip into hopelessness even though his troubles appeared without cure, since God, in His peerless wisdom, would certainly find a way to turn his fate around.

Verses 10 and 11 would then be adduced as proofs of God's might. If he can dispense rain to all who need it (v. 10), and by this means rejuvenate entire societies (v. 11), then surely he can help the suffering individual out of his troubles.

10. הַנֹּתֵן מָטָר עַל־פְּנֵי־אָרֶץ וְשֹׁלֵחַ מַיִם עַל־פְּנֵי חוּצוֹת — *Who brings rain upon the earth, sends waters over the open country. Daas Mikra* points out that rain is often used as an example of God's omnipotence. Cf. *Jeremiah* 10:12-13.

The sending of *waters over the open country* may refer to the wells and streams which, replenished by the rain, can now spread their bounty over wide areas. The expression recalls *Proverbs* 5:16, *May your wells spread out over the open country.*

11. לָשׂוּם שְׁפָלִים לְמָרוֹם וְקֹדְרִים שָׂגְבוּ יֶשַׁע — *So that the lowly will be raised on high, the shriveled uplifted by deliverance.* By judicious placing of the rainfall, those who might otherwise have been sunk in abject destitution can be raised to riches and power (*Ramban*).

We have rendered קֹדְרִים as *shriveled* in accordance with *Rashi*, here. Usually (cf. *Rashi* to *Psalms* 35:14) he renders *blackened* or *darkened*, as does *Metzudos* here. Thus: *Those whose faces have become blackened by hunger.*

12-16. Once more we follow *Ramban*. We now move from the general to the particular, from entire societies rising and falling at God's will, to the solitary individual who, no less than the family of man, is the object of Divine Providence and concern.

The conclusions to which these thoughts of Eliphaz will lead are expressed in verse 17: *See, how happy the man whom God disciplines.*

12. מֵפֵר מַחְשְׁבוֹת עֲרוּמִים וְלֹא־תַעֲשֶׂינָה יְדֵיהֶם תֻּשִׁיָּה — *He frustrates the plottings of the cunning, so that their hands will not produce results.* The *cunning* in this verse are those who attempt all manner of schemes to rid themselves of troubles to which Divine Providence had subjected them. God, Who fashioned their fate in accordance with His own inscrutable knowledge, Who knows that this suffering is to their advantage, frustrates their machinations (*Ramban*).

עֲרוּמִים, as *cunning*, is well attested. Cf. *Genesis* 3:1. תֻּשִׁיָּה derives from יֵשׁ, *there is, there exists*; thus something that is *solid in achievement* (*Ramban*). *Rashi* generally takes תֻּשִׁיָּה as a synonym for עֵצָה, *counsel*, and is consistent here: Their hands will not be able to bring the *plans* which they had laid to fruition.

13. לֹכֵד חֲכָמִים בְּעָרְמָם וַעֲצַת נִפְתָּלִים נִמְהָרָה — *He traps the wise in their trickery, and the plans of the devious turn to folly.* These *wise* are astrologers who seek to turn their knowledge of the constellations to their own advantage — to trap the *destitute* and the *miserable* in their wiles. God will frustrate their plans — for, in fact, no power is vested in the stars; all is in His hands (*Ramban*).

וַעֲצַת נִפְתָּלִים נִמְהָרָה — *And the plans of the devious turn to folly.* We have translated נִפְתָּלִים as *devious* in accordance with *Rashi* to *Genesis* 30:8; פָּתִיל is something that is *twisted*; נִמְהָרָה derives from מַהֵר, *to hasten.* Any decision made in haste is bound to be a bad one and result in folly (*Rashi*).

14. יוֹמָם יְפַגְּשׁוּ־חֹשֶׁךְ וְכַלַּיְלָה יְמַשְׁשׁוּ בַצָּהֳרָיִם — *Even by day they encounter darkness, grope around at midday, as in the night.* The plans

[10] *Who brings rain upon the earth, sends waters over the open coun-*
try. [11] *So that the lowly will be raised on high, the shriveled uplifted*
by deliverance. [12] *He frustrates the plottings of the cunning, so that*
their hands will not produce results. [13] *He traps the wise in their*
trickery, and the plans of the devious turn to folly. [14] *Even by day*
they encounter darkness, grope around at midday, as in the night.
[15] *He delivers from the sword — [from] their mouths, the destitute*
from the hands of the powerful. [16] *For the miserable it constitutes*
hope; wrongdoing must clamp up its mouth. [17] *See, how happy*
the man whom God disciplines, never loathe the chastisement of

which these plotters laid so carefully will not succeed. The light of their wisdom turns to darkness (*Rashi*).

Perhaps we may add another dimension. These people sought to be more clever than anyone else. They were sure that their knowledge of astrology (see v. 11) would put them in a position of power — in control of those who know less than they. In the end the tables will be turned. It takes no special wisdom to be able to see by daylight — the simplest people can do that. For the plotters, even the day will turn to darkness, even the midday sun will not light their way. They will have totally lost their bearings.

15. וַיֹּשַׁע מֵחֶרֶב מִפִּיהֶם וּמִיַּד חָזָק אֶבְיוֹן — *He delivers from the sword — their mouths, the destitute from the hands of the powerful. Rashi* takes *their mouths* in apposition to *the sword*. The sword is a metaphor for the mouths of the wicked who seek to swallow up those weaker than they.

16. וַתְּהִי לַדַּל תִּקְוָה וְעֹלָתָה קָפְצָה פִּיהָ — *For the miserable it constitutes hope; wrongdoing must clamp up its mouth. Daas Mikra* points out that תִּקְוָה in Scripture is not used exclusively to denote *hope*, but can also mean the fulfillment of hope (cf. *Jeremiah* 31:16). Thus, we should perhaps render: *For the miserable, it constitutes vindication.*

This verse seems to be a return to Eliphaz's earlier thesis: No one should allow himself to break under suffering. Since all comes from God, we must assume that the time will come in which *wrongdoing must clamp its mouth shut*, that the *miserable* who have been subject to so much pain will know vindication.

As mentioned above, the next section would now flow naturally from these premises.

17. הִנֵּה אַשְׁרֵי אֱנוֹשׁ יוֹכִחֶנּוּ אֱלוֹהַ וּמוּסַר שַׁדַּי אַל־תִּמְאָס — *See, how happy the man whom God disciplines, never loathe the chastisement of Shaddai.* Eliphaz has made the point that God's providence extends to every individual, and that consequently, there is hope and happy anticipation for even those who are now destitute and miserable. It follows that suffering should be viewed as God's *discipline* — and as a source of happiness, while every effort is made to sublimate His *chastisement* into a positive experience (*Ramban*).

Above, s.v. *An Interpolation*, we suggested that this verse introduces a section (up to verse 26) which elaborates upon the point made in verse 2. Only *fools* and the *simple-minded* will allow their suffering to frustrate them. The truth is that such tribulations can be a source of joy and the key to untold happiness, as described in the next few verses.

In what sense are we to understand this passage? How does the discipline and hurt to which God subjects one, open the gates for the blissful existence described below?

Our verse recalls an almost identical one in *Proverbs* 3:11 which can help us understand the passage here.

We quote verses 11 and 12 there, together with *Gra's* commentary:

Verse 11: *My son, do not loathe* H*ASHEM's chastisement, nor abhor His rebuke.*

H*ASHEM's chastisement*: These are the sufferings which come upon one. *My son do not loathe* them, but accept them with love and delight.

Verse 12: *For* H*ASHEM rebukes him whom He loves, and will make up to him as a father to a son.*

> *For* H*ASHEM rebukes him whom He loves*: The natural way is to rebuke only someone for whom one cares a great deal, and who seems to be going on a wrong path. Thus, if God is chastising you, it can be assumed that He cares for you very much.
>
> *And will make up to him as a father to a son*: This phrase goes back to the exhortation not to loathe God's discipline. For a father would normally rebuke only his son, but if a stranger ignores his rebukes,

יח־יט כִּי הוּא יַכְאִיב וְיֶחְבָּשׁ יִמְחַץ וְיָדָו תִּרְפֶּינָה׃ בְּשֵׁשׁ צָרוֹת
כ יַצִּילֶךָּ וּבְשֶׁבַע ׀ לֹא־יִגַּע בְּךָ רָע׃ בְּרָעָב פָּדְךָ מִמָּוֶת
כא וּבְמִלְחָמָה מִידֵי חָרֶב׃ בְּשׁוֹט לָשׁוֹן תֵּחָבֵא וְלֹא־תִירָא
כב מִשֹּׁד כִּי יָבוֹא׃ לְשֹׁד וּלְכָפָן תִּשְׂחָק וּמֵחַיַּת הָאָרֶץ
כג אַל־תִּירָא׃ כִּי עִם־אַבְנֵי הַשָּׂדֶה בְרִיתֶךָ וְחַיַּת הַשָּׂדֶה
כד הָשְׁלְמָה־לָךְ׃ וְיָדַעְתָּ כִּי־שָׁלוֹם אָהֳלֶךָ וּפָקַדְתָּ נָוְךָ וְלֹא
כה תֶחֱטָא׃ וְיָדַעְתָּ כִּי־רַב זַרְעֶךָ וְצֶאֱצָאֶיךָ כְּעֵשֶׂב הָאָרֶץ׃

he will just let him go on the path which he has chosen. No father would ever ignore a son who does not listen, but will discipline him until he is willing to hear. This is because of his overwhelming love expressed by the pain which he feels at his son's waywardness, and his strong desire to lead him on the right path. The proof that he is motivated by a father's love is that after he has put away his stick, he will want to do him all kinds of favors, and moreover, talks soothingly to him so that he will be comforted. Thus — do not loathe His discipline! For surely, if He causes you pain, it is because He loves you like a son; and afterwards, in a fatherly manner, he will wish to make up to you and to grant all your wishes.

All this appears to be expressed clearly in this section of Eliphaz's argument.

The use of the terms *discipline* and *chastisement* indicates that Eliphaz is considering the possibility that the suffering to which Iyov was subject may have come about as a response to sins he had committed. If so, this would be a change of direction at this stage. Up to this moment, his arguments have centered around the assumption that Iyov's experiences belonged to that category which had been dealt with in the vision — those which defy explanation completely.

Even so, we cannot, for this assumption alone, fault Eliphaz with insensitivity. Everyone, even the very greatest among us, has some shortcomings. Iyov, however, will argue (chapter 7) that the suffering is excessive. No sin which he might have committed could possibly justify such a pouring out of wrath.

18. כִּי הוּא יַכְאִיב וְיֶחְבָּשׁ יִמְחַץ וְיָדָו תִּרְפֶּינָה — *For He inflicts pain — but will assuage; wounds, but His hands will heal. Metzudos* suggests: The *pain* and the *wound* themselves will exercise the healing function. The agony which they cause is a healing one — it atones for the sins to which they were a response.

19. בְּשֵׁשׁ צָרוֹת יַצִּילֶךָּ וּבְשֶׁבַע לֹא־יִגַּע בְּךָ רָע — *From six straits He will save you, and at the seventh, no harm shall come to you. Daas Mikra* points to the common Scriptural usage of a progression of numbers such as the one used here. For example, we have a whole series at the beginning of *Amos* (1:3): *For three transgressions . . . for four . . .* We have the use of the progression, six to seven, in *Proverbs* 6:16-19: *There are six which HASHEM hates, seven which He abominates . . .*

Seven is a number often used in Scripture to denote *totality*, such as *Deuteronomy's* (28:7) promise that our enemies will . . . *flee from you in seven directions*, or (*Proverbs* 24:16), *The righteous man can fall down seven times — and yet rise again*. Accordingly, the use of this number here, particularly in the progressive form from six to seven which lends emphasis, suggests that you will be saved from a totality of all the evil things that could possibly happen (*Ramban*).

Understood thus, it is perhaps not necessary to attempt to find exactly six, and then a seventh, strait in the following list. The use of the numbers means simply — you will be saved from everything, with examples to follow (*Daas Mikra*). However, *Rashi* and *Metzudos* do suggest that there is a precise reckoning of six and seven. As we shall see, the text does not readily yield to such a system. In the commentary we shall use *Rashi's* system.

20. בְּרָעָב פָּדְךָ מִמָּוֶת וּבְמִלְחָמָה מִידֵי חָרֶב — *During famine he rescued you from death, during war — from the sword*. There is no problem in using these two examples, *famine* and *war*, as the first two in our list of six.

21. בְּשׁוֹט לָשׁוֹן תֵּחָבֵא וְלֹא־תִירָא מִשֹּׁד כִּי יָבוֹא — *When calumny roams, you shall be concealed, you need have no fear when destruction threatens. Rashi* takes these two as the next in the count of six, bringing it to four in our verse.

The *roaming tongue* is certainly a clear and present danger to a potential victim. Slander can easily bring to ruin. You will be *concealed*,

Shaddai. [18] *For He inflicts pain, but will assuage; wounds, but*
His hands will heal. [19] *From six straits He will save you, and at*
the seventh, no harm shall come to you. [20] *During famine*
he rescued you from death, during war — from the sword. [21] *When*
calumny roams, you shall be concealed, you need have no
fear when destruction threatens. [22] *You can smile at violence*
and famine, need have no fear of the wild beasts in the land.
[23] *For you have struck a treaty with the boulders of the field,*
the wild beasts of the field will be at peace with you. [24] *So you*
will be secure that there is peace in your tent, you will contem-
plate your home — and never err. [25] *You will know that your*
seed is manifold, your descendants as the grass of the field.

that is, protected, from its poison. No one will talk evil about you (*Metzudos*).

שֹׁד is used most frequently together with חָמָס (see, for example, *Jeremiah* 6:7, *Habakuk* 1:3). Thus, a destruction resulting from *violence.*

22. לְשֹׁד וּלְכָפָן תִּשְׂחָק וּמֵחַיַּת הָאָרֶץ אַל־תִּירָא — *You can smile at violence and famine, need have no fear of the wild beasts in the land. Rashi* does not explain כָּפָן here, but clearly understands our verse as dealing with *hunger*, as in *Ezekiel* 17:7. This is also the meaning of the word in Rabbinic usage. See, for example, *Targum* to *Ruth* 1:1.

Violence and *famine* should not be used in the count of six, since both were already listed in the previous verses — *famine* in verse 20 and *violence* in verse 21.

Why they should be listed in this verse for a second time is indeed puzzling. Perhaps we can read the verse as follows:

The key may lie in *Rashi's* interpretation of חַיַּת הָאָרֶץ in our verse. He is troubled by the fact that the next verse talks of חַיַּת הַשָּׂדֶה, and it is unlikely that wild animals would be listed twice. Accordingly, he explains that the expression here is to be taken metaphorically — *armed robbers* are meant. Given this, we may perhaps assume that famine and violence in our verses are mentioned merely as events which would cause brigands to come: You can smile at violence and famine — situations which are not only tragic in themselves, but tend to bring roaming bands of robbers in their wake — since such brigands carry no fear for you.

We assume that the *wild beasts/armed robbers* of our verse are the fifth in the list of six straits.

23. כִּי עִם־אַבְנֵי הַשָּׂדֶה בְרִיתֶךָ וְחַיַּת הַשָּׂדֶה הָשְׁלְמָה־לָךְ — *For you have struck a treaty with the boulders of the field, the wild beasts of the field will be at peace with you.* In this verse we have translated differently than does *Rashi*, for two reasons:

Rashi understands אַבְנֵי הַשָּׂדֶה as *a kind of man,* equating it with the אַדְנֵי הַשָּׂדֶה of *Kilayim* 8:5, which appears to be a man-like animal. *Tiferes Yisrael* there, identifies it with the orangutan. For חַיַּת הַשָּׂדֶה, *Rashi* offers a French word גרוב״א (not גרוש״ה as in some editions) which is a transliteration of *garove*, the *werewolf* (*La'azey Rashi B'Tanach*). *Rashi* appears to bracket these two (orangutan and werewolf) together as paradigmatic *beasts of the field*, and this verse therefore provides us with the sixth strait.

24. וְיָדַעְתָּ כִּי־שָׁלוֹם אָהֳלֶךָ וּפָקַדְתָּ נָוְךָ וְלֹא תֶחֱטָא — *So you will be secure that there is peace in your tent, you will contemplate your home — and never err. Rashi* believes that this verse deals with the seventh strait from which the person who lives up to the demands of verse 17 will be protected.

The first phrase means: Wherever you are, even from far away, you will always have a sense of security that all is well at home.

In the second phrase *Ibn Ezra* takes וּפָקַדְתָּ as *coming home.* When you come home you will never be faced by unpleasant surprises. You will always find what you expected to find.

For חָטָא, to err, *Rashi* adduces *Judges* 20:16.

25. וְיָדַעְתָּ כִּי־רַב זַרְעֶךָ וְצֶאֱצָאֶיךָ כְּעֵשֶׂב הָאָרֶץ — *You will know that your seed is manifold, your descendants as the grass of the field.* Here we move from protection from untoward straits, to positive blessings. The person who subjugates himself unquestioningly to God's providence — suffering willingly in this knowledge that his all is in the hands of God — becomes an object of God's special concern. See *Rabbeinu Yonah, Shaarei Teshuvah, Third Principle* #13.

ה/כו־כז כו־כז תָּבוֹא בְכֶלַח אֱלֵי־קָבֶר כַּעֲלוֹת גָּדִישׁ בְּעִתּוֹ: הִנֵּה־זֹאת
ו/א־ב א חֲקַרְנוּהָ כֶּן־הִיא שְׁמָעֶנָּה וְאַתָּה דַע־לָךְ: וַיַּעַן אִיּוֹב
°וְהַוָּתִי ק׳ ב וַיֹּאמַר: לוּ שָׁקוֹל יִשָּׁקֵל כַּעְשִׂי °והיתי בְּמֹאזְנַיִם יִשְׂאוּ־

26. תָּבוֹא בְכֶלַח אֱלֵי־קָבֶר כַּעֲלוֹת גָּדִישׁ בְּעִתּוֹ — *You will go to the grave in ripe old age, as the sheaf is taken in, in its time.* כֶּלַח, *ripe old age,* does not recur outside this book. *Rashi* judges from the context — the metaphor of the sheaf which is gathered in only when it has ripened sufficiently — that it means *old age.*

Ramban offers an original interpretation. כֶּלַח is a composite word כְּאִלּוּ לַח, *as though it were still full of life's sap.* The sense is that when you will die in old age, you will still appear to be in your youthful vigor.

27. הִנֵּה־זֹאת חֲקַרְנוּהָ כֶּן־הִיא שְׁמָעֶנָּה וְאַתָּה דַע־לָךְ — *See, all this we have considered, it is so. O hear it. And, as for you — absorb it!* Eliphaz ends his speech on an exhortive note. He feels that he has offered Iyov a reasonable way to cope with his troubles. If Iyov will but absorb his teachings — all will be well. In the latter rounds we will observe how Iyov's rejection of these ostensibly sensible suggestions will serve to alienate this friend and turn him into a bitter enemy.

VI.

◆§ Iyov's Response to Eliphaz's First Speech

In *Ramban's* view, Iyov takes a momentous step forward in this speech. From having, in the first blush of his agony, ascribed his experiences to the influence of the heavenly constellations, he is now ready to affirm that God must be the Source of all that happens.

However, such a realization, far from softening his pain, pours salt into the open, festering wound of his perplexity. The move from an impotent deity to an uncaring one provides scant comfort. Inexorably, Iyov passes to another stage of denial: To protect God from the devastating accusation of callousness which His own actions would seem to hurl at Him, Iyov evolves a doctrine of transcendence. God's exaltedness lifts Him beyond interest in human affairs. His very greatness makes Him impervious and therefore indifferent to their suffering.

In our alternative analysis, we find Iyov rejecting Eliphaz's suggestion that the correct response to his suffering would be sublimation rather than rebellion. Every facet of his fate confirms his perception of God as an adversary Who seeks only to destroy, rather than as a benefactor Who seeks to uplift.

He looks at his past and sees only blight, his future is without hope. His lot, the dreadful unbearable present, could have been lightened if only his friends had bothered to understand. Totally alone, sunk in the dejection which only a life of utter uselessness can summon forth, he lashes out against an unreasonableness which is all the more terrible since it stems from the Fount of all reason.

In *Ramban's* view, this speech marks a significant reversal in Iyov's theological stance. As verse 4 indicates, he is now willing to see God — and not the heavenly constellations — as the source of his suffering.

But this recognition places him in a severe quandary. Why would God subject him to these horrors? He rejects, out of hand, the possibility that they are meant to chastise. The pain is just too great — out of proportion to any such purpose.

Moreover, he has trouble assimilating the world-view propounded by Eliphaz at 4:7-8. The short life-span allotted to man (7:1 and 6) makes the good times allegedly enjoyed by the righteous seem insignificant and thus inequitable recompense for their loyal service. Again, the sheer emptiness of life coupled with the inevitability of death (7:16, and elsewhere) seems a sufficiently harsh fate for the wicked — without the addition of more pain inflicted from on high.

Because of all this, Iyov begins to wonder whether God may be so exalted as to be totally indifferent to the affairs of man — indeed, the idea that human sin leaves God untouched and could therefore well be ignored forms a part of his thinking in this speech (7:20) — and that whatever happens to people is as unprovidential as are the vagaries of fate within the animal world.

Far from wishing to denigrate God with these heresies, Iyov sees them as vindicating Him. We

5/26-27 [26] *You will go to the grave in ripe old age, as the sheaf is taken in,*
in its time. [27] *See, all this we have considered, it is so. O hear it.*
And, as for you absorb it!

6/1-2 [1] *Iyov responded and said:* [2] *If only my frustration were to be*
weighed, or they were to place my trauma in its entirety, upon

cannot blame Him for life's unfairness — He is too far removed to care.

We shall note *Ramban's* ideas at the relevant verses, while continuing the commentary along the lines which we have perceived as possibly reflecting *Rashi's* understanding of the issues.

2. לוּ שָׁקוֹל יִשָּׁקֵל כַּעְשִׂי — *If only my frustration were to be weighed.* Most striking in Iyov's response is that in the formal sense, it is not really a response at all. Eliphaz is not mentioned as an individual. To the extent that the friends form a part of Iyov's musings, they are grouped together — *My brothers have betrayed me ...* — and are not even addressed directly until verse 21. Even then they are shadowy figures, engulfed as it were in the metaphor of the faithless river. They are more ideas than men; elusive ideas, hidden and inaccessible through ice and snow piled up atop them, or meandering among the wastelands where they can quench no thirst, gladden no heart.

This, perhaps, is the meaning of the *Zohar* with which we introduced our analysis of Eliphaz's first speech (chapter 4). The friends have, at least initially, good ideas and valid insights — but no understanding of Iyov the man. Consciously, he does not even recognize that they have taken a theological stance: *This, is what you have been, you saw brokenness and became terrified.* He sees them escaping into realms of theoretical conjecture, too frightened to tackle the tangible horror of Iyov's reality — the *worms* and the *mildew*, the *repulsiveness* that now contoured his world.

Nevertheless, although Eliphaz the man has, through his ineptness, made no individual impression, the ideas which he presented have left some mark. Iyov's feverish mind has picked them up. To these he addresses himself now.

Eliphaz had suggested that suffering need not break the victim — on the contrary, it can be sublimated, prompting him to ever more intimate relationships with his creator. True! Iyov seems to be saying — but not when the horrors encountered crush the victim beneath their sheer, smothering, unrelenting, weight. Pile wet sand atop someone, and you goad him not at all — you incapacitate him.

Later, Iyov returns to the metaphor of the sand — and in the same vein: *Am I, then, the sea ... that you should set guards against me!* (7:12). It is the sand which *guards* the sea. The prodigious effort of wave upon wave thrusting outward is always frustrated. Eventually the tide retreats, exhausted by its futile battling. Thus does Iyov perceive his own predicament. Even if he were to take Eliphaz's advice and would try to sublimate his sorrows, he would only meet frustrations. As the sand at the seashore beats back the impotently pounding waves, so the sheer weight of his sorrows would reduce attempts at growth, to impotent thrashings against an unyielding barrier.

At this point it is germane to quote *Taanis* 21a.

Nachum Ish Gamzu was blind in both eyes, had both his hands and both his feet cut off, and his whole body was covered by leprosy. He lay in a house which was about to collapse and the legs of his bed were placed in bowls of water so that the ants should not be able to creep up upon him. His students wanted to carry him out first [because the house was about to fall in] and only then to carry out the other things in the house.

He said to them, 'My sons, take out everything else and only then carry me out, for as long as I am in the house, it will not fall.'

They did as he said, and, when they carried him out, the house fell.

They asked him, 'Since you are so righteous why do you suffer so much?'

He answered, 'My sons, I brought this upon myself. For, once I was going along the way ... a poor man stopped me and asked for some food. I said, "Wait until I have unloaded the donkey." By the time I unloaded the donkey, he had died.

'I went and fell upon his face and said, "My eyes which had no mercy on yours should be blinded. My hands and feet which had no mercy on yours should be cut off." Even then I felt no relief, until I begged that my entire body should be covered by leprosy.'

They said, 'Woe to us that we have seen you thus.'

He said, 'Woe to me had you not seen me thus!'

The difference between Nachum's attitude to his suffering and that of Iyov is striking in-

ג-ד יָֽחַד׃ כִּֽי־עַתָּה מֵחוֹל יַמִּים יִכְבָּד עַל־כֵּן דְּבָרַי לָעוּ׃ כִּי
חִצֵּי שַׁדַּי עִמָּדִי אֲשֶׁר חֲמָתָם שֹׁתָה רוּחִי בִּעוּתֵי אֱלוֹהַּ
ה יַֽעַרְכוּנִי׃ הֲיִֽנְהַק־פֶּרֶא עֲלֵי־דֶשֶׁא אִם יִגְעֶה־שּׁוֹר עַל־בְּלִילוֹ׃
ו הֲיֵאָכֵל תָּפֵל מִבְּלִי־מֶלַח אִם־יֶשׁ־טַעַם בְּרִיר חַלָּמוּת׃

deed. It could be, of course, that in spite of the terrible circumstances in which Nachum found himself, they were still not as bad as Iyov's. But the sense of the story would seem to imply that things were as bad as they could have been. Nevertheless, Nachum is not crushed.

How are we to explain the difference?

To say that Nachum brought the suffering upon himself will not serve as an adequate answer. It is still clear that it is possible to bear up under even the very worst conditions. Why then could Iyov not rally the same degree of strength?

We feel that this bears out the thesis which we propounded in the footnote to 1:3 and expanded upon throughout the book — that Iyov was a man of *Olam Hazeh*, a utopian, this-worldly existence, and that it is within that framework that he had to struggle.

Nachum Ish Gamzu would have approached his problem from the point of view expressed by *Bereishis Rabbah* 84:3: Is it not enough for the righteous that they are destined to be at comfort in *Olam Haba*, that they also want to be at peace in *Olam Hazeh*? He had no great expectations of what this world has to offer, his reality lay in the future. But Iyov had no such comfort. By every rule within which he functioned, he should not have been subjected to such agonies. He felt crushed, impotent and betrayed.

וְהַוָּתִי — *My trauma.* הוה has a number of different meanings. *Rashi* here (as in *Psalms* 55:12) renders שֶׁבֶר, *that which is broken.* The meaning here would be both Iyov's broken body and his shattered spirit.

יָחַד — *In its entirety.* For יָחַד in this sense, *Daas Mikra* adduces *Isaiah* 27:4.

As we have translated the phrase, *trauma* is in apposition to *frustration.* If someone were to weigh Iyov's frustration and trauma against all the sands of the sea, the former would outweigh the latter.

Ramban suggests a different understanding of the phrase — and gives יַחַד a different meaning. Iyov is defending himself against Eliphaz's accusation (5:2), that he is a fool for giving way to anger. He now makes the point that however angry and frustrated he feels, that is nothing compared to the trauma of which he is a victim. If the *anger* were to be weighed against (that is, יַחַד, *together with*) the hurt of his breakage, then the anger would be infinitely lighter. His suffering would easily outweigh it.

3. כִּי־עַתָּה מֵחוֹל יַמִּים יִכְבָּד — *Now surely it would outweigh the sands of the seas.* See above, commentary to verse 2, for the implications of this metaphor.

עַל־כֵּן דְּבָרַי לָעוּ — *Therefore, my words [are uttered] stammeringly. Rashi* and *Metzudos* render thus. Significantly, *Metzudos* does not limit the *stammering* to the halting speech of the invalid, but expands it to encompass the mode of presentation: Because of the overwhelming pain my words are not well organized: Excessive complaints, doubts concerning God's providence, and saying sometimes this and sometimes that.

This would tend to confirm our thoughts at 3:5 concerning the verbal lurches which riddle Iyov's speeches.

4. כִּי חִצֵּי שַׁדַּי עִמָּדִי אֲשֶׁר חֲמָתָם שֹׁתָה רוּחִי בִּעוּתֵי אֱלוֹהַּ יַעַרְכוּנִי — *For the arrows of Shaddai are my companion, their poison saps my spirit, God's terrors do battle against me.* See Prefatory Remarks, that *Ramban* in this verse detects a change of position on Iyov's part. This is the first time that he admits that his troubles come from God — not from the heavenly constellations.

Significantly, for our perception, Iyov here makes use of metaphors from battle. His pains are God's poisoned arrows, flung at him in the heat of war.

This would be a devastating rejection of Eliphaz's contention that Iyov's suffering was brought upon him by a benign deity in order that he should sublimate it. Iyov maintains that, on the contrary, God perceives him as an enemy against whom He flings weapons.

This, then, is a second justification for Iyov's rejection of the concept that his experiences might be used positively. The first was that their sheer weight tends to smother rather than to elevate, the second that they seem to be directed from a spirit of enmity rather than from benign motivation. [See *Ramban* quoted at 13:26-27 on the enormity of Iyov's sin in considering God to be his enemy.]

There appears to be yet a third consideration:

a scale. 3 *Now surely it would outweigh the sands of the*
seas. Therefore, my words [are uttered] stammeringly. 4 *For the*
arrows of Shaddai are my companion, their poison saps my
spirit, God's terrors do battle against me. 5 *Does, then, the wild*
ass bray in the pastures, or the ox low at his fodder? 6 *Can*
bland food be eaten without salt, is there taste in healthy spittle?

that of the loss of human dignity. *That which I had once refused to touch, is now the cloth upon which I eat* (v. 7). No man can be expected to rise above his circumstances when, wherever he turns, he is repulsed and nauseated by sickening sights and smells — of which he is the source.

Manifestly, then, verse 7 seems to belong together with verses 3 and 4. See below for verses 5 and 6 which appear to interrupt the flow of Iyov's thoughts.

יַעַרְכוּנִי — ... *Do battle against me.* The base meaning of עָרַךְ is *to arrange.* Most frequently it is used to describe formations deployed on the field of battle. See, for example, *Judges* 20:22, *I Samuel* 17:8.

5-6. Do these two verses express one single, or two separate thoughts?

Clearly, verse 5 makes the point that Iyov's complaints are not gratuitous. Even a dumb animal does not complain when all is well. Verse 6 criticizes the friends. Their ideas are bland, unstimulating and ultimately useless.

The issue before us is to clarify whether verse 5 deals with Iyov's original complaints: Do not fault me for my frustrations — they are surely justified. If so, this verse is unconnected to the next one. Or, does it refer to Iyov's rejection of Eliphaz's presentation: Believe me, if it would have been able to satisfy my cravings I would have accepted your logic. I do not enjoy crying — even animals do not bellow without a cause. However, even after your speech my emotional hunger has remained unassuaged — the arguments you offer are bland and unsatisfying.

Further, verse 6 seems to express the identical thought which finds voice in verses 25 and 26. In what way is it different, and what is its function here?

The significant difference between the two passages would seem to be that where verses 25 and 26 are part of a speech which is expressed directly to the friends (from v. 21 onwards the friends are addressed directly), here we have a soliloquy. Iyov is talking to himself, more than to Eliphaz.

Why?

The answer will explain why these two verses — which we believe are indeed expressing one unified thought — interrupt between verses 3 and 7 which, as we demonstrated above, really seem to belong together.

Again and again we shall note that the one quality which gives Iyov the courage to fight the unknowable, instead of taking the easy — but dishonest — path of submission proposed by the friends, is his tenacious insistence upon unadulterated truth. He will not — indeed, cannot — admit to non-existent guilt in order to fit neatly into the superficially attractive but overly simplistic theological stance adopted by the friends.

However, to be truthful one must be ruthlessly self-critical. Iyov must assure himself that his unwillingness to accept guidance does not stem from some built-in obstinacy which rebels against a truth which did not have its source within his own soul.

Iyov wishes to marshal three arguments against Eliphaz's theory of sublimation. Three — which in Torah-thought establishes a proposition beyond the need of further proof. Before he voices the third argument, Iyov must justify himself before the bar of his own conscience.

This justification is the burden of verses 5 and 6. Iyov is convincing *himself,* rather than the friends, that surely he is not so foolish as to complain for the sake of complaining. Even brutish animals know better than that. His rejection, then, is not based on an unreasonable insistence that he be right at all costs, but upon a firm determination not to be swayed by the bland, conventional, and therefore unconvincing argument of the friends.

5. הֲיִנְהַק־פֶּרֶא עֲלֵי־דֶשֶׁא אִם יִגְעֶה־שּׁוֹר עַל־בְּלִילוֹ — *Does, then, the wild ass bray in the pastures, or the ox low at his fodder?* פֶּרֶא carries the connotation of *wildness* (see *Genesis* 16:12). For בְּלִיל, *Rashi* offers *produce,* at 24:6.

The sense of the verse is: My complaints are not gratuitous. Even dumb animals do not bellow without a cause (*Rashi*). See above for our analysis of this argument.

6. הֲיֵאָכֵל תָּפֵל מִבְּלִי־מֶלַח אִם־יֶשׁ־טַעַם בְּרִיר חַלָּמוּת — *Can bland food be eaten without salt, is there taste in healthy spittle?* Do you think that words without any significant content have any meaning? (*Rashi*).

ז־ח מְאֲנָה לִנְגּוֹעַ נַפְשִׁי הֵמָּה כִּדְוֵי לַחְמִי: מִי־יִתֵּן
ט תָּבוֹא שֶׁאֱלָתִי וְתִקְוָתִי יִתֵּן אֱלוֹהַּ: וְיֹאֵל אֱלוֹהַּ
י וִידַכְּאֵנִי יַתֵּר יָדוֹ וִיבַצְּעֵנִי: וּתְהִי־עוֹד | נֶחָמָתִי וַאֲסַלְּדָה
בְחִילָה לֹא יַחְמוֹל כִּי־לֹא כִחַדְתִּי אִמְרֵי קָדוֹשׁ:

[In his paraphrase *Rashi* appears to treat this sentence as though Iyov were addressing the friends directly. See above for our perception of this sentence together with the previous one. There we suggested that the text implies a soliloquy rather than a direct address.]

בְּרִיר חַלָּמוּת — *... in healthy spittle.* Thus *Metzudos.* The spittle of a sick person has some taste, but that of someone who is well is totally bland. *Ramban* suggests *egg-white,* because the yolk is called חֶלְמוֹן. The white, so to speak, is the liquid (ריר) surrounding the yolk.

Daas Mikra thinks that the word may be identical with the חַלְמִית of *Kilayim* 1:8, which is a *mallow,* a herb containing a great deal of mucilaginous — and bland — juice.

7. מֵאֲנָה לִנְגּוֹעַ נַפְשִׁי הֵמָּה כִּדְוֵי לַחְמִי — *That which I had once refused to touch, is now the cloth upon which I eat. Rashi* adduces *II Samuel* 10:4 where מַדְוֶה means *a garment.*

Ramban suggests an alternative: מַדְוֶה could be *a sickness* or *something that causes suffering,* as in *Deuteronomy* 28:60. The verse is a continuation from the previous one: Surely, I have the right to complain. When all was well with me, I would never have thought of touching bland tasteless foods. Now they are my daily — and painful — bread.

Taking the verse as does *Rashi* — that is, unconnected to the previous one, which is a metaphor for uninspired advice rather than a description of actual food — we have suggested above that the idea expressed in this verse is the third argument for rejecting Eliphaz's idea of sublimation. Iyov's sickness has not only caused him pain — which perhaps he might have been able to overcome — but has robbed him of his human dignity. It has filled him with disgust and loathing at the filth and stench which is his daily lot. If a man is deprived of his sense of self-respect, sublimation of his troubles becomes a virtual impossibility.

In summation of this section, we note that Iyov has marshalled three arguments to justify his rejection of Eliphaz's concept of sublimation.

1. His suffering is too great. It smothers rather than goads.
2. His troubles indicate God's enmity, rather than His benign concern.
3. Robbed of human dignity, spiritual growth is beyond him.

8-12. It would appear that having disposed of Eliphaz's suggestions to his own satisfaction, Iyov now returns to his original death-wish. How he wishes that God would kill him, and thus make an end of the travesty which his life has become.

However, this is not entirely true. We do not have a reverting to his original plea, but a progression. A careful reading of chapter 3 — Iyov's first speech — yields that he never actually asked to die. In the first part of that speech he muses how much better it would have been if he had never lived, and towards the end, he begins to allow uncertainties about the justice and logic of God's providence to make their first, still tentative appearance (see commentary to v. 19, there). He never, in so many words, challenges God to kill him now.

We may surmise that such a request runs perilously close to rebellion and blasphemy. There is a great difference between philosophical musings about the value of life for those who are weary and in pain, and an actual demand that life be terminated — now. If we view life as the greatest gift which God has to bestow upon us, then spurning that gift — hurling it back, as it were, in absolute disparagement of its value — constitutes a giant step towards insolent defiance.

So, Iyov has now crossed another barrier. There is an inner tension here between content and form. The words which Iyov uses are couched in the conventions of prayer — but that which he requests is far, far removed from the submissiveness which must be the hallmark of the supplicant. And so, content eventually overpowers form. Towards the end of the speech — 7:17ff. — even the tone will become belligerent and bitter.

Iyov has not yet turned to the friends. He is still soliloquizing. His feverish mind has picked up — and ultimately rejected — certain ideas from Eliphaz's speech, but no personal contact between friend and caring friend has been made. Eliphaz does not exist for Iyov at this stage. Later, in utter bemusement at his solitude, he will begin to wonder what has happened to the three men whose friendship had been so highly vaunted.

*7 That which I had once refused to touch, is now the cloth upon
which I eat. 8 O, Who will grant that my wish be fulfilled, that God
bestow that for which I hoped. 9 O that God would but wish to crush
me, let loose His hand, so that He would destroy me. 10 Moreover, I
could find comfort in this; tremblingly, I beg that He show no mercy,
for never have I fallen short of the demands of the Most Holy.*

8. מִי־יִתֵּן תָּבוֹא שֶׁאֱלָתִי וְתִקְוָתִי יִתֵּן אֱלוֹהַּ — *O, who will grant that my wish be fulfilled, that God bestow that for which I hoped. Ramban* specifically ties this verse to the earlier ones: What sense my life if I have to suffer so much!

Above, we noted that this request is a progression from the ones made in Iyov's earlier speech. Never before has he asked to die. We must indeed suppose that his earlier musings brought him to this point. From the three points which he made in rejection of Eliphaz's sublimation principle, he suddenly realizes the utter futility of his life. If, as the object of God's enmity, I am overwhelmed by unbearable loads of suffering, bereft of any shred of human dignity, why should I wish to continue living?

9. וְיֹאֵל אֱלוֹהַּ וִידַכְּאֵנִי יַתֵּר יָדוֹ וִיבַצְּעֵנִי — *O that God would but wish to crush me, let loose His hand, so that He would destroy me.* It seems clear that this thought is a continuation of verse 4. If indeed God views me as an enemy, why does He not go all the way. Instead of torturing me, why does he not kill me.

יֹאֵל, *to be willing.* Cf. *Exodus* 2:21.

דַּכָּא, *lowly,* as in *Isaiah* 57:15.

We have rendered יַתֵּר as *let loose* in accordance with *Metzudos,* because that is the usual meaning of the verb in the *hiphil* derived from מַתִּיר. See, for example, *Isaiah* 58:6. *Rashi,* however, renders *increase in size.* Let Him make His hand large. Apparently he relates the word to the Aramaic adjectival form meaning *great,* which otherwise occurs only in *Daniel.*

10. וּתְהִי־עוֹד נֶחָמָתִי וַאֲסַלְּדָה בְחִילָה לֹא יַחְמוֹל כִּי־לֹא כִחַדְתִּי אִמְרֵי קָדוֹשׁ — *Moreover, I could find comfort in this; tremblingly, I beg that He show no mercy, for never have I fallen short of the demands of the Most Holy.* We have translated this difficult verse in accordance with *Rashi.*

In the merit of his never having fallen short of his duties to God, Iyov feels that he has the right to approach Him in trembling trepidation to beg that He show no mercy, but do as Iyov had suggested in the previous verse — crush and destroy him.

Iyov can certainly not be faulted for the mode of his approach. He comes in the classic attitude of prayer — the trembling supplicant. But he cannot have remained unaware of the biting sarcasm of his words. To *beg* that there be *no* mercy is a contradiction in terms. Mercy is that quality which is always stimulated by a victim's plight — and craving for relief. Iyov seems to be saying: If what You are doing to me is a manifestation of Your mercy — I want none of it. Your 'mercy' is the source of all my agonies.

It may be that because Iyov realizes that notwithstanding his prayerful stance, his words are bitter and angry, he couches his words in the third person. He does not yet dare to address his scorn to God directly. That will come later in the speech.

וַאֲסַלְּדָה בְחִילָה — *Tremblingly, I beg. Rashi* notes that סלד does not recur in Scripture. In Rabbinic literature it has the meaning, *to recoil, to hold oneself back.* Accordingly it came to mean the kind of prayer which is informed by an overwhelming feeling of awe. Thus, for example: אֶנְקַת מְסַלְּדֶיךָ in the Ashkenazi rite of *Ne'ilah,* on Yom Kippur. See further below.

כִחַדְתִּי — *Fallen short.* This meaning for כחד is unusual. *Rashi* himself [at 4:7] renders *hidden and lost,* which we translated as *blotted out.*

אִמְרֵי קָדוֹשׁ — *The demands of the Most Holy.* Nowhere else does Iyov refer to God by this description. Perhaps its use here is of a piece with Iyov's *trembling* in the previous verse, as follows: At 2:3 and 3:19 we have discussed *Ramban's* assertion that in the course of the book, Iyov will grow from a relationship to God based on fear to one based on love.

Manifestly, at this stage, there is no love as yet — only the fear of the enduringly distant. That feeling seems to inform Iyov's approach at this stage. The understanding born of love is still beyond him. He does not really comprehend this capricious deity with Whom he has to deal. But — he fulfills His demands. Tremblingly, he approaches Him in the hope that in that merit his prayers might be answered.

That is the meaning of קָדוֹשׁ, the One Who

יא־יב מַה־כֹּחִי כִי־אֲיַחֵל וּמַה־קִּצִּי כִּי־אַאֲרִיךְ נַפְשִׁי: אִם־כֹּחַ
יג אֲבָנִים כֹּחִי אִם־בְּשָׂרִי נָחוּשׁ: הַאִם אֵין עֶזְרָתִי בִי וְתֻשִׁיָּה
יד נִדְּחָה מִמֶּנִּי: לַמָּס מֵרֵעֵהוּ חָסֶד וְיִרְאַת שַׁדַּי יַעֲזוֹב:

is ever *separate* [see *Rashi* to *Leviticus* 19:2] and frighteningly distant.

11-12. מַה־כֹּחִי כִי־אֲיַחֵל וּמַה־קִּצִּי כִּי־אַאֲרִיךְ נַפְשִׁי אִם־כֹּחַ אֲבָנִים כֹּחִי אִם־בְּשָׂרִי נָחוּשׁ — *How much strength do I have, that I should wait, what worth my end that I should draw out my existence? Is my strength the strength of stones, is my flesh made out of brass? Ramban* and *Metzudos* see these verses as reacting to Eliphaz's argument that Iyov's suffering will eventually give way to a pleasant life under God's direct protection, and that he can look forward to longevity, going to the grave in ripe old age (5:19-26).

Iyov's rejoinder is that the shortness of man's life-span makes such an argument specious. His body has been so weakened by his sickness that it can never recover sufficiently to enable him to enjoy his waning years, and the time which would be left him would be all too short.

In our perception, these two verses play much the same role as had verses 5 and 6. We thought there that Iyov was checking himself. Did he have the right to reject Eliphaz's arguments out of hand? Here too Iyov, struck by the enormity of his temerity in demanding that God take his life, is asking himself: Am I justified, am I being too impetuous?

Our two verses give the answer. Indeed there is nothing left to hope for. Under these circumstances, why not ask for immediate death!

13. הַאִם אֵין עֶזְרָתִי בִי וְתֻשִׁיָּה נִדְּחָה מִמֶּנִּי — *Am I then to have no help, is counsel to be withheld from me. Rashi* takes this verse as the beginning of Iyov's diatribe against the friends: *Am I then to have no help*: Am I to suffer even this ... that those friends who should have been my support, fail me! *Is counsel to be withheld from me*: The advice which good counselors might have given me — I do not have. You have raised yourselves up against me to goad me to anger and to repulse me.

Ramban, however, sees the verse quite differently. As he takes it, it is deeply significant for understanding Iyov's stance — which in the end is vindicated by God's approbation — throughout the long, arduous debates.

Because of its centrality to the understanding of the book, we quote *Ramban* on this verse, in its entirety.

We translate as he would:

> *Does my support not lie within myself!* This is a continuation of the earlier verses. *Does, then, the wild ass bray ..., Can bland food be eaten without salt ..., Does my support not lie within myself ...,* The meaning is: Can I not find strength and support within myself. Can I not find counsel and wisdom within my own being, that I should be able to discern between the truth, and the senseless ideas which you propagate?

As *Ramban* reads it, this verse is an assertion of Iyov's intellectual independence. He will not take the easy path of the weak man seeking at all costs — even at the expense of the integrity of his own mind — to be at peace with everyone, including God. He knows what he knows. And he knows that his experiences make no sense.

Already at 1:1 (s.v. תָּם וְיָשָׁר) we have noted that one of the tensions of the book is between the poles of *temimus*, constant and undeviating loyalty to God; and *chanufah*, simple dishonesty as the friends see it. As defined by Iyov, *chanufah* is the easy-come easy-go approach to life, clinging to conventional religious thought-patterns, even when these lead ultimately to the ridiculous. This approach imputes the most devastating of insults against the all-knowing, all-mighty, God. [See specifically 13:4ff.]

All three of the friends, at one time or another, hurl the *chonef* (practitioner of *chanufah*) epithet at Iyov: Bildad at 8:13; Eliphaz at 15:34; and Tzophar at 20:5. In turn, Iyov uses it against Tzophar at 13:16; against Eliphaz at 16:38; and in general terms at 27:8 [which may have had Bildad in mind, since he was the most recent of the friends to have addressed Iyov at that point].

What is the issue?

The friends' thinking is clear enough. They can find no bridge between the pious Iyov whom they had known and the bitter, unyielding, bitingly sarcastic, belligerent challenger whom they now see before them. They can suggest only one solution. The original piety was a sham — it reflected no reality. Iyov is a *chonef*, a hypocrite whose allegiance lasts only as long as he perceives it to be profitable.

Iyov sees things very differently.

At 2:5-6 we were introduced to the idea —

[11] *How much strength do I have, that I should wait, what worth my end that I should draw out my existence?* [12] *Is my strength the strength of stones, is my flesh made out of brass?* [13] *Am I then to have no help, is counsel to be withheld from me.* [14] *To him who denies kindness to a friend, who forsakes the fear of Shaddai.*

which will be further explicated at 42:5 — that Iyov's difficulties stemmed from the fact that he had *heard* of God, but had not *seen* Him. Once God is experienced, once He becomes absolute reality, all questioning — indeed the very urge to understand — becomes meaningless. But as long as God is perceived only through the intellect — as long as man *hears* of Him but does not *see* Him — questions not only may, but must be asked.

Our view of God is anthropomorphic. He proclaims Himself to us as King, as Father — לְשַׁבֵּר אֶת הָאוֹזֶן, that the *ear* might comprehend — ideas which we can perceive in human terms. But kings must govern wisely, fathers may be stern but must ultimately be loving — and thus, says Iyov, God must justify Himself, as it were, at the bar of our intellect.

The mind is God's greatest gift to man — and man dare not ever jettison it. If God projects Himself as an adversary to *hearing* man, then — proclaims Iyov throughout the book — there is only one religiously justified stance: to challenge, to demand, to rebel against perceived injustice.

There will be time later for *seeing* man to dispense with all this, to lose any sense of self in all-encompassing love. In the meanwhile, abdication of the responsibility which the possession of a mind imposes upon us, a facile assumption that all must surely fit into conventionally soothing patterns even when the facts scream in contradiction — that is *chanufah*. If God throws down the gauntlet to *hearing* man, He must wish him to take up the cudgels — to refuse to submit.

14. לַמָּס מֵרֵעֵהוּ חָסֶד וְיִרְאַת שַׁדַּי יַעֲזוֹב — *To him who denies kindness to a friend, who forsakes the fear of Shaddai. Rashi* does not make entirely clear how he understands this verse. It would seem that it is tied to the one before in one of two possible ways:

Either: *Help* and *counsel* ought not to be withheld from me. They ought to be withheld from one who denies kindness to a friend (*Ramban*).

Or: The *help* and *counsel* which I had the right to expect seems to be enjoyed instead by those who deserve it much less, those who deny kindness to a friend (*Daas Mikra*).

For לַמָּס, *Rashi* adduces *Exodus* 16:21, where the word means *to melt away, to disappear.*

◆§ The Faithless River

Slowly and painfully, Iyov is coming to grips with the realization that he is truly all alone. A sensitive reading of the text reveals to us the inner struggle, the efforts to deny that which, in the final analysis, will brook no denial. In verses 13 and 14 we have the first, tentative ruminations. The friends are not identified in any way, and there is the bitter awareness that all is not as it should be; a man in his situation surely deserves some *help, counsel* and *kindness*. In addition, Iyov allows himself a rueful reflection: Not everyone is bereft of these amenities; those who deserve them least seem to have no trouble in finding them. But withal, nothing is said about the friends.

Verses 15-20 constitute a progression. His earlier thoughts have apparently stirred him to a smoldering anger. Why have his *brothers* used him so shamefully! How despicable their behavior! But still he does not address them directly. It is as though there is still a faint hope that these three, the closest and most truly loving of all his former friends, will come through. He is still ready to take them to his heart if they will but give a sign. The diatribe contained in these verses will then remain true only of those others who did not even trouble to come to visit him in his travail [see 2:11].

It is only in verse 21 that his pent up fury really breaks out, and he turns to them directly with his recriminations.

What had Iyov expected from his friends?

At 2:11-13, we suspected that what he had wanted was, ... to have someone who could lend a sympathetic ear, could convey the message that he was not alone; that despite being crushed by debilitating illness and prostrated by the loss of all he had, he was nevertheless a man of goodness and integrity, and, above all, of worth.

We should now analyze whether these assumptions are borne out by the metaphor of the faithless river.

We suspect that they are the truth, but not the whole truth.

In *Ezekiel* chapter 47, we find the river as source of blessing and abundance. *Psalms* 36:9

טו־טז אַחַי בָּגְדוּ כְמוֹ־נָחַל כַּאֲפִיק נְחָלִים יַעֲבֹרוּ׃ הַקֹּדְרִים
יז מִנִּי־קָרַח עָלֵימוֹ יִתְעַלֶּם־שָׁלֶג׃ בְּעֵת יְזֹרְבוּ נִצְמָתוּ
יח בְּחֻמּוֹ נִדְעֲכוּ מִמְּקוֹמָם׃ יִלָּפְתוּ אָרְחוֹת דַּרְכָּם
יט יַעֲלוּ בַתֹּהוּ וְיֹאבֵדוּ׃ הִבִּיטוּ אָרְחוֹת תֵּמָא הֲלִיכֹת
כ שְׁבָא קִוּוּ־לָמוֹ׃ בֹּשׁוּ כִּי־בָטָח בָּאוּ עָדֶיהָ וַיֶּחְפָּרוּ׃

talks of the stream of God's delights, and *Isaiah* 35:6-7 foresees the time in which the waters flowing through the *Aravah* will turn wilderness and desert into gardens rich with vegetation. In such a capacity, the river would surely serve as metaphor for all that we have suggested above.

However, we also find the river used as a metaphor for wisdom: *The words a man speaks are deep waters, a flowing stream, a source of wisdom* (*Proverbs* 18:4). We must certainly assume that this, too, Iyov had wished to hear from the friends. Had they provided insights to help him understand his plight, surely that would have been a balm upon his wounds.

But none was forthcoming. Too often, a river disappoints [see *Isaiah* 58:11, and *Jeremiah* 15:18], and this river was no exception. The ways in which the friends failed him will come through as we study the different parts of the metaphor.

15. אַחַי בָּגְדוּ כְמוֹ־נָחַל כַּאֲפִיק נְחָלִים יַעֲבֹרוּ — *My brothers have betrayed me like a stream, pass me by as does the streams' flow.* Verse 16 will describe how, during the winter colds, the water which one would want to drink hides beneath layers of ice and snow; while verses 17-20 talk of the summer heats which drive the river flow into unproductive paths, leaving only dried out beds where thirsty travelers had hoped for cooling waters.

It seems probable that each of these two sections describes one of the terms, *betrayed* and *pass me by*, respectively.

Since *pass me by* clearly deals with the waters taking a different, unproductive route, *betrayed* would be the term describing the waters lurking under the winter ice.

To *betray* describes a positive disloyalty. I am here, I have obligations — and I avoid them. To *pass by* simply implies an absence. When most needed, I am not there.

In the Prefatory Remarks to this section we noted that Iyov would have had two expectations from the friends: their guidance and their love. The first is an obligation. Wisdom bestows obligations, to share and to instruct — see below on verse 24. The second is either there or not — one cannot demand true love.

Thus, the betrayal practiced by the winter waters is the metaphor for the friend's withholding of wisdom; the absence of the summer streams, for their unloving, judgmental stance.

Given this, we note that four verses are devoted to the meandering summer streams, as against only one for the hiding winter waters. This proportion is reflected once more below. For verses 22 and 23, in which Iyov is telling the friends that he wanted nothing concrete from them — only their love and understanding [see our understanding of that passage there] — are two verses, as against verse 24 which challenges them to instruct him.

The implication is clear. Iyov the sufferer needs love a great deal more than he needs wisdom.

Daas Mikra makes the point that Iyov is here addressing all the friends — *My brothers* — although only Eliphaz has spoken. He ascribes this to 5:27 where Eliphaz had said, *See, all this we have considered* ... The implication is that he is the spokesman for all three friends.

כַּאֲפִיק נְחָלִים יַעֲבֹרוּ — *Pass me by as does the streams' flow.* For this phrase we have followed *Ramban's* rendering since it accords with the cantillation which reads the verse as a balanced couplet: My brothers have betrayed me like a river — pass me by as does a river's flow. *Rashi*, as he does in the rest of Scripture [see, for example at *Isaiah* 8:7], takes אֲפִיק as *source*. Now a source does not flow, and *Rashi* is therefore forced to read the verse as follows: My brothers have betrayed me like a river, like a source of water — they have passed [from acting in a friendly fashion, to acting traitorously].

16. הַקֹּדְרִים מִנִּי־קָרַח עָלֵימוֹ יִתְעַלֶּם־שָׁלֶג — *Tucking itself beneath the ice, hiding under concealing snow.* Above, we worked out that this is the *betrayal* of which verse 15 speaks. The wise insights which he had expected to hear from his friends are hidden and inaccessible under piles of verbiage which, for practical purposes, make it useless. See also in commentary to verse 2.

*15 My brothers have betrayed me like a stream, pass me by as
does the streams' flow. 16 Tucking itself beneath the ice, hiding under concealing snow. 17 As they are burned up, they are
no more, in the heat they forsake their place. 18 They make
their own paths on their way, disappear into the wastes, and
are lost. 19 They set their eyes to the paths of Teima, draw lines
toward the roads of Sheba. 20 They were mortified, for they had
committed their trust, they approached it and were humiliated.*

We suspect that *ice* and *snow* may both have their specific function within the metaphor. Ice is formed from the water itself. A portion of the life-giving water becomes hard, cold and unyielding, thereby not only eroding its own usefulness, but denying access to that which flows underneath. Snow, on the other hand, is frozen rainfall, an extraneous force, which makes the water beneath the ice even more remote.

From the *Zohar* which we quoted at the beginning of chapter 4 we recall that much of what the friends had to say could have been helpful to Iyov in his travail. But they had not troubled to think through how they could share their insights without hurting his sensibilities.

We quote from our discussion in the Prefatory Remarks to chapter 4.

> If Eliphaz erred it was in the way he expressed them. He had not grasped sufficiently the exquisite sensitivity which is born of absolute vulnerability. In the words of the *Zohar*, he had not prepared himself as carefully as his daunting task demanded. In his profligate use of words — the vivid and seemingly pointed description of the downfall of the wicked and the guaranteed tranquility of the righteous — Iyov was bound to hear only criticism of himself. He feels attacked, and the profound theological insights which Eliphaz has to offer are lost to him.

This would be the *ice* of the metaphor. Sweet, life-giving water representing profound ideas — turned to distasteful, unresponsive dogma by insensitive phrasing and presentation.

The *snow* would be the useless, self- indulgent profligacy of language which we also found in Eliphaz's speech — see at 4:13-16.

As he does at 5:11, *Rashi* takes קָדַר as *shriveled* or *folded* and seems to understand the phrase as we have translated it. The waters *tuck* themselves beneath the ice.

Rashi's understanding of the second phrase is difficult. At *Deuteronomy* 22:1 and 3 he renders the *hispael* of עלם as *turning away the eye*, that is, *hiding himself from the object*, or *making it so that the object is hidden from him*. Here, he seems to take the word as *turning oneself into something that hides something else*. The snow becomes that which hides the ice-covered water.

17. בְּעֵת יְזֹרְבוּ נִצְמָתוּ בְּחֻמּוֹ נִדְעֲכוּ מִמְּקוֹמָם — *As they are burned up, they are no more, in the heat they forsake their place. Rashi* relates זָרַב, to צָרַב, which he normally renders *a scald — something shriveled* [by heat] (*Ezekiel* 21:3). The base meaning of זָרַב appears to be *to contract* or *shrivel* [see *Rashi* to *Bava Kama* 85b, s.v. צמחה and, hence, *to cook*, at *Pesachim* 40b. In the *hiphil*, *Rashi* renders it *to cut off* (*Psalms* 101:8). דָעַךְ always means *to move abruptly from one place to another* (*Rashi*, *Psalms* 118:12).

See above where we understood this part of the metaphor to describe the disappointment born of simple absence. The river is not where the thirsty had hoped it would be. There is some aspect to the friend's personality [we thought, it was their caring love] which was simply not there when it was needed most.

18. יִלָּפְתוּ אָרְחוֹת דַּרְכָּם יַעֲלוּ בַתֹּהוּ וְיֹאבֵדוּ — *They make their own paths on their way, disappear into the wastes, and are lost. Rashi* renders לָפַת as *to take hold of*. Thus, to make their own path.

19. הִבִּיטוּ אָרְחוֹת תֵּמָא הֲלִיכֹת שְׁבָא קִוּוּ־לָמוֹ — *They set their eyes to the paths of Teima, draw lines towards the roads of Sheba*. Teima is a low-lying land, a place where water would tend to gather (*Rashi*). קִוּוּ is a verb formed from קַו, *a line*.

20. בֹּשׁוּ כִּי־בָטָח בָּאוּ עָדֶיהָ וַיֶּחְפָּרוּ — *They were mortified, for they had committed their trust, they approached it and were humiliated*. The subject of this verse are the people who had hoped to drink from this faithless river. They come to it to quench their thirst, and are mortified and humiliated by the fact that it is not there.

ו / כא־כט

כא־כב כִּֽי־עַתָּה הֱיִיתֶם לֹו תִּרְאוּ חֲתַת וַתִּירָֽאוּ׃ הֲֽכִי־אָמַרְתִּי הָבוּ
כג לִי וּמִכֹּחֲכֶם שִׁחֲדוּ בַעֲדִֽי׃ וּמַלְּטוּנִי מִיַּד־צָר וּמִיַּד עָרִיצִים
כד תִּפְדּֽוּנִי׃ הֹורוּנִי וַאֲנִי אַחֲרִישׁ וּמַה־שָּׁגִיתִי הָבִינוּ לִֽי׃
כה־כו מַה־נִּמְרְצוּ אִמְרֵי־יֹשֶׁר וּמַה־יֹּוכִיחַ הֹוכֵחַ מִכֶּֽם׃ הַלְהֹוכַח
כז מִלִּים תַּחְשֹׁבוּ וּלְרוּחַ אִמְרֵי נֹאָֽשׁ׃ אַף־עַל־יָתֹום תַּפִּילוּ
כח וְתִכְרוּ עַל־רֵיעֲכֶֽם׃ וְעַתָּה הֹואִילוּ פְנוּ־בִי וְעַל־פְּנֵיכֶם
כט אִם־אֲכַזֵּֽב׃ שֻׁבוּ־נָא אַל־תְּהִי עַוְלָה °ושבו עֹוד צִדְקִי־בָֽהּ׃

°וְשֻׁבוּ ק׳

21. כִּי־עַתָּה הֱיִיתֶם לוֹ תִּרְאוּ חֲתַת וַתִּירָאוּ — *This, is what you have been, you saw brokenness and became terrified.* At last, Iyov turns directly to the friends. If they thought that they would be spared the fury of his abuse, they are to be disappointed. With abrupt directness he hurls an accusation of cowardice and hypocrisy at them.

In the light of our analysis above, that a central issue between Iyov and the friends is the question of who is the *chonef* [see commentary to v. 13, above], the language of *Rashi* here is significant: The sight of my sickness frightened you so that you feared to tell the truth, and instead, you fawn [*machanifim*] at my adversary.

22-23. הֲכִי־אָמַרְתִּי הָבוּ לִי וּמִכֹּחֲכֶם שִׁחֲדוּ בַעֲדִי. וּמַלְּטוּנִי מִיַּד־צָר וּמִיַּד עָרִיצִים תִּפְדּוּנִי — *Have I said 'Give me!' or, 'Use your might to bribe in my behalf. Thus saving me from an oppressor, reclaiming me from the hands of tyrants.'* We see these two verses as directed at the lack of any love or concern shown by the friends. Iyov is, in effect, saying: That which I want from you most of all would not cost you a penny. Is it so hard to try to understand my plight?

Iyov appears to be moving perilously close to blasphemy. If we take his words at face value, they could surely be understood to mean: Indeed I am in the hands of an *oppressor* and *tyrant*. But in this situation it is not money that is required. There is only one possible *oppressor* and *tyrant* Whom he could have in mind.

Might is used in the sense of *money* (*Rashi*).

24. הוֹרוּנִי וַאֲנִי אַחֲרִישׁ וּמַה־שָּׁגִיתִי הָבִינוּ לִי — *Instruct me, and I shall keep silent, let me understand how I have erred.* Here Iyov moves to the next of his complaints against the friends. He had hoped for insights which might guide him through his travail — they have offered nothing that he does not already know — see commentary to verse 13.

25-26. מַה־נִּמְרְצוּ אִמְרֵי־יֹשֶׁר וּמַה־יּוֹכִיחַ הוֹכֵחַ מִכֶּם. הַלְהוֹכַח מִלִּים תַּחְשֹׁבוּ וּלְרוּחַ אִמְרֵי נֹאָשׁ — *How eloquent is sensible talk, but what have any of you demonstrated? Do you really believe that words can convince, empty talk is so much wind.* Iyov is earnestly protesting his willingness to listen; his agonies have not made him unreasonable. But in place of *sensible talk*, which could have made its point, and shown him what to do with his life, he hears only *empty talk*, a *wind* blowing with much sound and movement, but no substance.

Certainly, Iyov's criticism seems to bear out the point which we made in the Prefatory Remarks to chapter 4 in the commentary to verse 10, there. There was just too much verbiage in Eliphaz's speech; the grain is overwhelmed by the chaff, the valid points drowned out in the wind.

Rashi leaves us with some lack of clarity concerning the precise meaning of נִמְרְצוּ. First he adduces נִמְרֶצֶת, at *I Kings* 2:8. *Rashi* there renders, *spelled out clearly.* He then continues by adducing *Proverbs* 25:11, דָּבָר דָּבֻר עַל אָפְנָיו, *. . . words spoken correctly* [*Rashi*: על כנו]. *Rashi* then goes on to adduce *Psalms* 119:103, מַה נִּמְלְצוּ לְחִכִּי, where *Rashi* renders *sweet.* We have rendered *eloquent*, which can perhaps accommodate the various shadings of meaning.

We have rendered אִמְרֵי נוֹאָשׁ as *empty talk* in accordance with *Rashi*, who writes: Which have no real content. Again, it is not clear whether this accords with *Rashi* at *Jeremiah* 2:25, where the word is used to describe the attitude which some people had towards prophecies which they chose to ignore. *Rashi* there takes the word as a verb, adducing a French word meaning *unconscious*, that is, indifference or unconcern, with the implication: *It is clear to me that your words have nothing to offer me.* Thus, אִמְרֵי נוֹאָשׁ should more properly be rendered: *Words that have nothing to offer to the listener.*

27. אַף־עַל־יָתוֹם תַּפִּילוּ וְתִכְרוּ עַל־רֵיעֲכֶם — *You hurl outrage upon an orphan, dig [pits into which to haul] your friend.* By choosing to make your response in terms of unbending justice, you pour out anger upon a poor sufferer such as I (*Rashi*).

6/21-29 [21] *This, is what you have been, you saw brokenness and became*
terrified. [22] *Have I said 'Give me!' or, 'Use your might to bribe*
in my behalf. [23] *Thus saving me from an oppressor, reclaiming*
me from the hands of tyrants.' [24] *Instruct me, and I shall*
keep silent, let me understand how I have erred. [25] *How eloquent*
is sensible talk, but what have any of you demonstrated? [26] *Do*
you really believe that words can convince, empty talk is so
much wind. [27] *You hurl outrage upon an orphan, dig [pits into*
which to haul] your friend. [28] *And, now, be so good as to turn to*
me, see whether I will be untrue to your faces. [29] *Come*
now, change your ways so that there will be no evil, consider
once more and notice that I am innocent of any wrongdoing.

Rashi appears to take *orphan* as a synonym for *poor*. It seems possible to understand it in its original sense. Iyov has lost his bearings. None of the verities in which he had found anchorage in the past seem to hold true any more. He is adrift in a sea of broken trust, buffeted by ever more threatening breakers of disillusion. He is a true orphan, fatherless and motherless in the sense that father and mother provide stability and security.

How can you pour out anger against such a one!

Rashi understands תִּכְרוּ, in the second half of the sentence, to mean *you dig*. The sense is that Iyov is accusing the friends of digging a pit into which to throw their friend. It is difficult to see why such an accusation would be laid at the friends' door. They have certainly shown themselves to be insensitive, but not (at least not as yet) vindictive.

Metzudos understands the entire verse differently: You have shown yourself to be so unfeeling, that I am justified in supposing that you would even set out to harm an orphan, even dig a pit to trap your friend. We assume that *Rashi* rejected this interpretation because it does not really belong in the context of the speech. Verse 28 could very well follow onto verse 26, and verse 27 seems, gratuitously, to interrupt the flow.

28-30. The words sound placating and conciliatory, but they do, in their own way, continue the biting criticism which Iyov is leveling at the friends. The key phrase appears to be the opening one: *And now, be so good as to turn to me.* The implication is: You have not been listening to me at all! Your windy rhetoric has latched onto an idea — and you have lost the all important . . . man!

28. וְעַתָּה הוֹאִילוּ פְנוּ־בִי וְעַל־פְּנֵיכֶם אִם־אֲכַזֵּב — *And, now, be so good as to turn to me, see whether I will be untrue to your faces.* The root יאל is given a number of different connotations by the commentators, the main ones are *to begin* and *to desire*. *Rashi* himself is not entirely consistent, occasionally using the former [cf. *Deuteronomy* 1:5], but mostly the latter [cf. *Genesis* 18:31 and elsewhere]. Here, *Rashi* renders *to desire*, and we have translated accordingly.

Mabit translates, *to begin.*

In the context of the Prefatory Remarks to this section, either of the meanings would seem to fit well. According to *Rashi* and *Ramban* the sense is: Summon up your will to see things as they are. That you have failed to do so up to now has been because you simply have not cared enough.

In *Mabit's* view the sense is: Let the past be the past. You have, up to now, misunderstood me completely. Try from now on to be more sensitive to my vulnerability.

We could have rendered אֲכַזֵּב as *lie*. We did not do so because Iyov's honesty, at this point at least, seems not to have been at issue. But כזב also has the meaning *to disappoint, not to produce that which could have been expected* [cf. *Isaiah* 58:11], and this may well be the meaning here. In the commentary to verse 13 above, we saw that the friends considered Iyov to be a *chonef*, a hypocrite, whose carping, belligerent attitude under stress could not be squared with his meek acceptance when tragedy first struck. Iyov's point is that if the friends will just try and see things as they are, they will learn that there is no contradiction at all between his present and his former stance. He has not been untrue to himself.

29. שֻׁבוּ־נָא אַל־תְּהִי עַוְלָה וְשֻׁבוּ עוֹד צִדְקִי־בָהּ — *Come now, change your ways so that there will be no evil, consider once more and notice that I am innocent of any wrongdoing.* We have translated according to *Ramban*. שֻׁבוּ is taken

ו/ל
ז/א־ד

ל־א הֲיֵשׁ־בִּלְשׁוֹנִי עַוְלָה אִם־חִכִּי לֹא־יָבִין הַוּוֹת: הֲלֹא־
ב צָבָא לֶאֱנוֹשׁ עֲלֵי־אָרֶץ וְכִימֵי שָׂכִיר יָמָיו: כְּעֶבֶד יִשְׁאַף־
ג צֵל וּכְשָׂכִיר יְקַוֶּה פָעֳלוֹ: כֵּן הָנְחַלְתִּי לִי יַרְחֵי־שָׁוְא
ד וְלֵילוֹת עָמָל מִנּוּ־לִי: אִם־שָׁכַבְתִּי וְאָמַרְתִּי מָתַי אָקוּם

as *repent*, and the sense is: Repent on your earlier attitudes and eradicate, from within yourselves, the *evil* which was there.

In the second phrase we have also followed *Ramban*. The word בָּהּ is an irregular form of מִמֶּנָּה, *from it*. Hence, You will observe such righteousness in me as is far removed from any evil.

30. הֲיֵשׁ־בִּלְשׁוֹנִי עַוְלָה אִם־חִכִּי לֹא־יָבִין הַוּוֹת — *Is there evil on my tongue, can my palate not detect folly.* Understand correctly, and with a modicum of good will, and you will see that there was nothing evil in what I said. Certainly, here and there there were phrases which, taken in one way, would sound heretical. But if you will just understand my situation, you will see that I meant nothing bad. Trust me enough, on the basis of your knowledge of me from the past, that I would instinctively avoid uttering any *folly*.

It would have been possible to interpret these last three verses differently than we have done. The language would lend itself to a defense of an intellectual position, as much as to the excuse that Iyov had simply given verbal expression to his suffering.

We chose the one interpretation over the other, because in the next chapter Iyov appears once more to revert to a description of his unbearable pain. What he says there, he is inviting the friends to consider here. Accordingly, we assume that Iyov's meaning is as we have understood it.

VII.

1. הֲלֹא־צָבָא לֶאֱנוֹשׁ עֲלֵי־אָרֶץ וְכִימֵי שָׂכִיר יָמָיו — *Clearly, there is a fixed service-term for man upon earth, his days are like those of a hired man. Rashi* here and at various other places renders צָבָא as *time. Ibn Ezra* has *fixed time.*

We have rendered *service-term*, because the context seems to demand it — see below.

What is Iyov saying in this verse?

Rashi confirms the thoughts which we developed in the last chapter. Iyov is reaffirming his right to the utter frustration which had been expressed in what we have called his primordial scream: ... For, how can I not *cry out* as a result of my brokenness! After all, you know that man's life on earth is limited ... (see below to the next verse).

Ramban sees this verse as beginning the second stage of Iyov's quarrel with the ideas expressed by Eliphaz (see Prefatory Remarks to chapter 6): Iyov complains that his days are numbered and that he longs for them to end, as would a hired man. He knows well that life is measured, that those months which he can count his own are a stretch of futility, and that only few nights — and those full of travail — have been allotted him. Nights stretch endlessly before him, and when day breaks at last, there is nothing but debilitating activity till he, once more, seeks release in darkness. Day and night are one long span of deadening sorrow. [Accordingly, the world view expressed by Eliphaz at 4:7-8 is to be rejected.]

A careful analysis of our verse in conjunction with the next three will place it squarely within the context of Iyov's thoughts as we have understood them up to this point.

We have translated צָבָא as *fixed service-term* for two reasons. The parallelism in which much of *Iyov* is written gives us an *a priori* assumption that the two parts of our verse express similar thoughts [*Days ... of a hired man* = *service-term*], and the juxtaposition of *slave* and *hired man* in the next verse makes it likely that it is a follow-on of ours. Thus:

1. הֲלֹא־צָבָא לֶאֱנוֹשׁ עֲלֵי־אָרֶץ *Clearly there is a fixed service-term for man upon earth.*	2. כְּעֶבֶד יִשְׁאַף־צֵל *Like a slave he longs for shade.*
וְכִימֵי שָׂכִיר יָמָיו *His days are like those of a hired man.*	וּכְשָׂכִיר יְקַוֶּה פָעֳלוֹ *Like a hired man he anticipates his wages.*

Verse 3 begins with, *Thus* ... , clearly making it a direct continuation of what was said before.

The sense of the section appears to be as follows:

The indolent slave and the grasping hired

6/30 *[30] Is there evil on my tongue, can my palate not detect folly?*
7/1-4 *[1] Clearly, there is a fixed service-term for man upon earth,*
his days are like those of a hired man. [2] Like a slave he
longs for shade, like a hired man he anticipates his wages.
[3] Thus have I been assigned months of frustration, nights of
misery have been allotted to me. [4] When I lay down I would
say, 'When, as darkness moves on, will I be able to get up?'

man of verse 2 fall far short of the ideal. Iyov holds them forth as an object of disgust. When man was given his life as a *service-term*, and when his days were to have the character of those of a *hired man*, the intention was certainly not that his time be spent in wishing that he could be relieved of his obligations. On the contrary — as Iyov makes very clear in the later chapters in which he details the full and happy life which he used to live — hard work and heavy duties can be pleasurable and rewarding.

But when one's *flesh is clothed by worms and mildew*, when one's *skin is wrinkled and repulsive* (v. 5) then all joy in life dissipates. Nights are then defined as periods fully exhausted in a craving for morning, days are filled with futile thrashings to pass the time till night (v. 4). Months become stretches of futility; life, just so much misery (v. 3).

The relationship between verses 1 and 2 is as follows: Man — in his best sense, free and responsible — is given life as a *service-term*, as a time to be filled with significant and constructive labor (v. 1a). *However*, he can approach it as does a *slave*, indolent and uncaring — wanting only to avoid the burning sun by lying in the shade (v. 2a). *His days are like those of a hired worker* — he himself is not a hired worker — in which every second has to count since he is expected to deliver a reckoning for his wages (v. 1b). *However*, he can act as actual day-laborers do, uninterested and uninvolved — seeing only the pay they are to receive, never the dignity of the work they do (v. 2b).

To Iyov's distress this is precisely the point to which he has come. His agonies have robbed his life of content.

2. כְּעֶבֶד יִשְׁאַף־צֵל וּכְשָׂכִיר יְקַוֶּה פָעֳלוֹ — *Like a slave he longs for shade, like a hired man he anticipates his wages. Rashi* sees this verse as a continuation of the previous one: I spend the fixed amount of time that has been given me, as a slave who longs for the shade ...

Rashi takes *shade* as the evening shadows. In this way the first phrase parallels the second one precisely.

If our perception of the relationship of this verse to the previous one is correct (see commentary to v. 1), a better translation might be: *Like a slave he may long for shade, like a hired worker he may anticipate his wage.*

3. כֵּן הָנְחַלְתִּי לִי יַרְחֵי־שָׁוְא וְלֵילוֹת עָמָל מִנּוּ־לִי — *Thus have I been assigned months of frustration, nights of misery have been allotted to me.* This is how it was decided in heaven that the *service-term given to me on earth* should be spent (*Rashi*).

How do months and nights fit together in our verse?

Along with the identification of months by their position vis-a-vis *Nissan — Chodesh HaRishon, Chodesh HaSheini* and so on — we come across months which were, in Biblical times, known by other names: Thus, at *I Kings* 6:38, we have *Marcheshvan* referred to as *Yerach Bul* [a word apparently meaning *produce*; see *Iyov* 40:20]. At *I Kings* 6:1, *Iyar* is called *Chodesh Ziv* [apparently because of the bright light of the sun at that time of the year]. There is, thus, a valid assumption that the agricultural year was divided into months, each named after its particular contribution to the produce.

If so, and bearing in mind that Iyov is comparing himself to the slave and the hired worker, whose work units would accordingly have been reckoned in months, the verse is self explanatory. My work-time — the various *yerachim* — was a constant *frustration*; my resting times — the *nights* when I should have been sleeping — were *misery*.

4. אִם־שָׁכַבְתִּי וְאָמַרְתִּי מָתַי אָקוּם וּמִדַּד־עָרֶב וְשָׂבַעְתִּי נְדֻדִים עֲדֵי־נָשֶׁף — *When I lay down I would say, 'When, as darkness moves on, will I be able to get up?' I satiate myself on thrashings till nightfall.* This verse explains the previous one — it describes why life had become a constant frustration and misery.

The structure of the two verses is chiastic. The second verse picks up what was mentioned last in the previous one, and then moves on to what was said there first.

Rashi takes מִדַּד as derived from נָדַד, *to flee, stray*, or *wander away*. He waits for the night to give way to day in the vain hope that things will be better then. *Ramban* derives the word

ה וּמִדַּד־עָרֶב וְשָׂבַעְתִּי נְדֻדִים עֲדֵי־נָשֶׁף׃ לָבַשׁ בְּשָׂרִי
ו רִמָּה °וגיש עָפָר עוֹרִי רָגַע וַיִּמָּאֵס׃ יָמַי קַלּוּ מִנִּי־אָרֶג
ז וַיִּכְלוּ בְּאֶפֶס תִּקְוָה׃ זְכֹר כִּי־רוּחַ חַיָּי לֹא־תָשׁוּב עֵינִי
ח לִרְאוֹת טוֹב׃ לֹא־תְשׁוּרֵנִי עֵין רֹאִי עֵינֶיךָ בִּי וְאֵינֶנִּי׃

°וְגוּשׁ ק׳

from מָדַד, *to measure*. When will the night have run its full measure so that it will be time to arise?

The next phrase describes what happens during the day. He *thrashes* about upon his bed, waiting for night to come, unable to find the surcease of sleep because of his constant misery, as described in the next verse.

For נֶשֶׁף, see 3:8.

5. וְגוּשׁ עָפָר — . . . *and mildew*. גּוּשׁ is a *clod of earth* (*Rashi* to *Bava Metzia* 101a). Such clods of earth tend to become moist and, consequently, to grow mildew (*Rashi*).

Metzudos suggests that *clods of earth* is to be taken literally. Iyov's flesh was *clothed* in earth because, as told at 2:8, he *sat in the earth*. Thus *Metzudos*, there.

Ramban suggests that Iyov may be looking ahead to his death, when indeed his body will be *clothed* in the earth of the grave.

עוֹרִי רָגַע וַיִּמָּאֵס — *My skin is wrinkled and repulsive*. *Rashi*, who renders *wrinkled* here, must be understood in terms of *Rashi* to *Jeremiah* 31:34. There, to רֹגַע הַיָּם, he writes: He breaks up the sea, moves it around and causes its waters to seethe so that it appears wrinkled. He adduces our phrase.

Metzudos adduces רָגַע from *Psalms* 35:20, to yield *clefts*. Thus, . . . *my skin is split*.

We have rendered וַיִּמָּאֵס, from מָאַס, *to reject* or *despise*. *Ramban* believes that the word may derive from נָמַס, *to flow*, or from מָסַס, *to melt*. The word describes the blood and filth that flow from Iyov's body.

The sense of the passage, up to this point, has been that Iyov denies the possibility of sublimating his suffering. Because his experiences are so horrible, far from constituting a goad to growth, they are simply the cause of a frustrating sense of futility.

From the quality of his life, Iyov now turns to its transience.

6-10. *Rashi* and *Ramban* part ways in the interpretation of this passage. In the commentary to the individual verses we shall follow *Rashi*, so in these Prefatory Remarks we offer *Ramban's* synopsis of this section:

> The sense of this entire passage is that man's life is short and filled with trouble and, moreover, must inevitably end with death.
>
> Now, inasmuch as his merits do not save him from death, nor will they bring him back home from the grave, it stands to reason that he deserves no additional punishment for his sins.
>
> Because of this, justice would demand that God cease to cause him to suffer, for his life is as nothing at all.

6. יָמַי קַלּוּ מִנִּי־אָרֶג וַיִּכְלוּ בְּאֶפֶס תִּקְוָה — *My days fly faster than the weaver's shuttle, they end without any hope*. My days of happiness went by very fast (*Rashi*).

We suppose that *Rashi* interprets this verse as referring to Iyov's happy days, rather than to life in general (as does *Ramban*), because in contrast to verses 9-10, which are in the third person and do indeed seem to deal with human existence rather than with Iyov's personal experiences, our verse and the next are in the first person. Iyov is talking of his own life.

In the context of our understanding of verse 1 and the following four verses, we interpret this thought as follows: Man is certainly created with a very definite task to fulfill on earth (v. 1). My frustrations stem from the fact that from the point of view of accomplishing anything useful, the days of my suffering are a total loss (verses 2-5). Do not condemn my attitude with the reasoning that at least my life up to now had been happy, and therefore constructive, in terms of my allotted task. That is not so. The days of my happiness were really only a fleeting moment.

See below for the meaning of the next phrase.

וַיִּכְלוּ בְּאֶפֶס תִּקְוָה — *They end without any hope*. I do not hope for any further good [times to happen to me] (*Rashi*).

A superficial reading of *Rashi* would seem to yield that the first part of this verse described the happy past — it went by all too fast, and now that Iyov looks to the future, he sees no hope of any improvement.

However, this reading is impossible from a grammatical standpoint. וַיִּכְלוּ must have the same subject as קַלּוּ, and if the latter talked of the good days which have passed, so must the former.

Correctly rendered the verse must read: My days of happiness went by very fast, and *they* ended without any promise of hope.

I satiate myself on thrashings till nightfall. [5] *My flesh is clothed*
by worms and mildew, my skin is wrinkled and repulsive.
[6] *My days fly faster than the weaver's shuttle, they end*
without any hope. [7] *O remember that my life is just a wind,*
never will my faculties return, enabling me to live a life of
fulfillment. [8] *The eyes of those who seek to gaze upon me will*
never see me. Your eyes were upon me, and I am no more.

The sense is that the happy times ended in such an unnatural and abrupt way, that they must be viewed as a kind of death (see below). Nothing can ever be the same — it is senseless to talk of my suffering as a transitional period. At one particular moment my life ended — irrevocably.

In this context, we can make good use of *Ramban's* alternative suggestion for the rendering of the word תִקְוָה, which in accordance with *Rashi* we have translated *hope*. *Ramban*, however, in the context of the *weaver's shuttle*, suggests that it may be rendered *thread* (as in *Joshua* 2:18 and 21). This would paint a very graphic picture. As the shuttle is hurled back and forth, it does indeed seem to have a life of its own. But let the thread run out, and immediately everything ceases. The instrument is put aside with no use at all.

With the insights gained here, we shall continue the interpretation of the next two verses. For the moment we shall leave *Rashi* aside, for reasons which will be explained at the end of the commentary to verse 8.

7. זְכֹר — *O remember*. As is yielded by the end phrase of verse 8, Iyov is here addressing God.

The contrast with verse 3 is striking. There, in discussing the poor quality of Iyov's life, we have a conspicuous use of the passive: *I have been assigned ... have been allotted to me*. There appears to be a conscious effort to avoid addressing the criticisms directly to God.

Yet here, when the transience of the good times is under discussion, Iyov turns directly to God.

Perhaps it is the metaphor of the weaver's shuttle which wrought the change. When that picture rises before Iyov's eye, he sees the shuttle being hurled back and forth, an absolutely passive and helpless tool in the hands of the all-powerful, all-able, weaver. Once that relationship has been established, it is impossible to see his fate as divorced from God's direct interference. The Cause of his miseries must, inevitably, impinge upon the picture.

Once this first step has been taken, Iyov's speech will quickly deteriorate into the belligerence which we will trace towards the end of this chapter.

זְכֹר כִּי־רוּחַ חַיָּי לֹא־תָשׁוּב עֵינִי לִרְאוֹת טוֹב — *O remember that my life is just a wind, never will my faculties return, enabling me to live a life of fulfillment*. Translated literally, the second half of the sentence would read: *Never will my sight return enabling me to see good.*

We have translated as we have done, for the following reasons:

1. We begin with the assumption that *life*, in this verse, parallels *My days* in the previous one. The subject, then, is the good times which Iyov experienced before his troubles overtook him.

2. We assume that טוֹב, in the second half of the verse, parallels *life* in the first half. This would be analogous to *Psalms* 34:13, מִי הָאִישׁ הֶחָפֵץ חַיִּים אֹהֵב יָמִים לִרְאוֹת טוֹב, *Which man desires life, who loves days of seeing good?*, where that same parallelism is quite clear. When we analyze the very few places in Scripture in which the combination רָאָה — טוֹב occurs (*Psalms* 4:7; 34:13, *Koheles* 3:13), it is clear that the phrase is an idiom, not to be translated literally. Clearly, it conveys the idea of *life* lived in a full and happy way.

Thus also, עֵינִי, *my eyes* or *sight*, must not be translated literally. עֵינַיִם are used in Scripture to describe spiritual and mental faculties (cf. *Genesis* 3:5 and many others).

The sense of the verse is as follows: As in the previous verse, reference is to the good times which Iyov had experienced. Earlier, he had compared them to a weaver's shuttle in order to describe the speed with which they passed.

Now another aspect engages his mind. Those times were like the wind which, once it blows itself out, never comes back again. It is the result of a confluence of forces which are unique to that moment. It passes by — and simply ceases to exist. So does Iyov perceive the good life which he used to live. It was a one-time, unique experience which disappeared permanently when it came to an end. Something has died, and life can never be fulfilling again.

8. לֹא־תְשׁוּרֵנִי עֵין רֹאִי עֵינֶיךָ בִּי וְאֵינֶנִּי — *The eyes of those who seek to gaze upon me will never see me. Your eyes were upon at me, and I am no*

ט־י כָּלָה עָנָן וַיֵּלַךְ כֵּן יוֹרֵד שְׁאוֹל לֹא יַעֲלֶה: לֹא־יָשׁוּב עוֹד

more. As we understand this phrase: Those who look at me now, thinking they see the old Iyov whom they knew, are mistaken. They will never again see *me,* the Iyov with whom I truly identify myself. He is gone, because You have set Your eyes against him — he is no more.

Thus, we have the second part of Iyov's complaint. It is useless to talk of sublimation for two reasons: Life has lost any meaning, for it is spent entirely in wishing for the relief of death; secondly, the Iyov to whom it had been possible to talk of reacting positively to adversity is long gone. He has died, never to return.

We mentioned above that in the commentary to these two verses we have left *Rashi* aside. We shall now quote the relevant comments of *Rashi* and discuss them:

On the words, *Never will my faculties return . . .* (v. 7) [or, as they are to be translated literally, *Never will my eyes,* or *sight, return . . .*], *Rashi* remarks: This refers to returning after death. Here Iyov denies the doctrine of *T'chiyas HaMeisim, resurrection of the dead,*

On the words in verse 8, *. . . will never see me, Rashi* says: The eyes that would wish to see me after my death will never be able to do so.

And on the words, *Your eyes are* [we translated, *were*] *upon me and I am no more,* he writes: Iyov is addressing God: Why do You need to hurt and to crush me through suffering. All You need to do is to glance at me once, and I am gone from the world.

Clearly, *Rashi* does not accept the assertion which we made above, that the entire passage deals with the good times which Iyov had experienced before his troubles began. From the second half of verse 7 onwards, he has Iyov looking ahead from his present position. And we assume that already at verse 6 he reads the end phrase, *. . . they end without hope,* in the same way. Iyov sees no hope in the future.

We feel that *Rashi* does not mean his interpretation to be taken as the simple meaning (*p'shat*) of the section. Rather he is teaching us, for very significant considerations, the *d'rashah* which the Sages saw in the text (see fn. to 28:4). For this reason we have chosen first to present the simple meaning, and this we have done by interpreting the passage to refer entirely to the earlier times, so that now we can absorb the teachings of the *d'rashah.*

We assume then that Rava's statement that our verse teaches that Iyov denied *T'chiyas HaMeisim* (*Bava Basra* 16a) is to be understood as a *d'rashah,* based on the wording of the verse which certainly conveys such a surface meaning. As in countless other *d'rashos,* the phrase is taken *out of context* in order to yield the important lesson which it does.

What is that important lesson, and why did *Rashi* consider it sufficiently significant to quote it here, even at the cost of ignoring the *p'shat*?

To understand this well, we should attempt to understand Rava's approach to the interpretation of the book of *Iyov.*

In *Bava Basra* 16a there is a series of seven statements, all apparently made by Rava — all extremely critical of Iyov.[1]

1. To 2:10: Iyov did not sin with his mouth — but in his heart he sinned.
2. To 9:24: Iyov wanted *to turn the dish over on its mouth.* [*Rashi*: To destroy every vestige of respect (towards God).] [Rava assumes that reference in that verse is to God.]
3. To 10:7: Iyov denies free choice. [Man is predestined to good or to evil.]
4. To 6:2: Let Iyov's mouth be stuffed with dirt. Can he put himself in one category with God? [The implication of the verse is that God and Iyov have obligations to one another and that a weighing should take place to determine whether each of the parties had fulfilled his duty.]
5. To 9:33: Let Iyov's mouth be stuffed with dirt. Can we imagine a slave upbraiding his master?
6. To 31:1: Let Iyov's mouth be stuffed with dirt. He did not look upon a woman that was not his. Abraham did not look even at his own.
7. To 9:17: Iyov blasphemed in the context of a storm . . .

Now, it is surely significant that Rava takes such a negative view of much that Iyov said — particularly since we see that at least in one instance, the verse lends itself to another interpretation. In example #2, Abaye disagrees with Rava. He believes that the *wicked one* of that verse refers not to God, but to Satan. The *Gemara,* moreover, traces this disagreement to an earlier source and demonstrates that the same two possibilities for understanding that

1. We say *apparently* made by Rava, because a number of them are attributed to other *Amoraim.* However, most manuscript readings, adduced by *Mesores HaShas,* ascribe them all to Rava.

[9] *As a cloud disintegrates and is gone, so he that goes down*
to the grave shall never come back. [10] *Never will he return*

verse were the subject of an argument between the *Tannaim* R' Eliezer and R' Yehoshua. Had Rava wished, he could presumably have accepted the more lenient interpretation.

We assume that Rava was interested in finding the most negative interpretation to Iyov's words, because of his understanding of the basic teaching of the book. At *Bava Basra* 16b he deduces from 34:35 and from 42:7 (see *Dikdukei Soferim*) that: Man is not to be blamed for belligerent statements which he makes under circumstances of extreme distress. Elsewhere (Introduction to the *Iyov* Commentary) we have noted that *Rashi* to *Bava Basra* 15a s.v. מָשָׁל הָיָה, believes this proposition to be one of the most central lessons of the book.

Accordingly, we may assume that Rava was willing to impute even the most negative ideas to Iyov, because he believes — and the book so teaches — that however far Iyov sank in the liberties which he permitted himself, he is never to be blamed. The book's message comes out more clearly if Iyov's words were very rebellious indeed.

In addition, there is another consideration which argues against the assumption that the only valid interpretation of our section is that in it, Iyov denies the doctrine of *T'chiyas HaMeisim*. We assume that such a denial would be significant only if Iyov was a Jew and was thus bound to that belief. However, as we sought to demonstrate in the footnote to 1:1, there is much evidence that the book's frame of reference is patriarchal, and this would presumably free Iyov from the obligation to accept *T'chiyas HaMeisim* as a given.

9-10. If we study this metaphor carefully, we will see that its content parallels the earlier one precisely:

7. זְכֹר כִּי־רוּחַ חַיָּי *O remember that my life is just a wind,*	
לֹא־תָשׁוּב עֵינִי לִרְאוֹת טוֹב *never will my faculties return, enabling me to live a life of fulfillment.*	8. לֹא־תְשׁוּרֵנִי עֵין רֹאִי *The eyes of those who seek to gaze upon me will never see me . . .*
9. כָּלָה עָנָן וַיֵּלַךְ כֵּן יוֹרֵד שְׁאוֹל לֹא יַעֲלֶה *As a cloud disintegrates and is gone, so he that goes down to the grave shall never come back.*	10. לֹא־יָשׁוּב עוֹד לְבֵיתוֹ וְלֹא־יַכִּירֶנּוּ עוֹד מְקוֹמוֹ *Never will he return to his home, never more will his community know him.*

The differences between the two are only that where the first section chooses the wind as a metaphor, the second chooses a cloud; and that in the first metaphor Iyov speaks of his own life — *. . . my life is just a wind* — while in the second he talks in general terms — *. . . he that goes down to the grave.*

What does the second metaphor add to the first? Why repeat the same ideas twice?

It would seem that in this section we have confirmation of our understanding of the previous one. The sense of the entire piece is as follows: Iyov had seen his days of happiness as a fleeting moment, ending in a kind of death, as described in the first metaphor. In the second section he describes actual death in precisely the same terms — thus making the point which is important to him. In all the essential details he has gone through the same dying process as one who actually dies.

Therefore, the first metaphor talks of Iyov's own experiences, the second deals in general terms. When Iyov talks of his own earlier life, he compares it to the wind — in his mind it had no substance at all; life in general is more like a cloud, it has body and exists for measurable time.

9. כָּלָה עָנָן וַיֵּלַךְ כֵּן יוֹרֵד שְׁאוֹל לֹא יַעֲלֶה — *As a cloud disintegrates and is gone, so he that goes down to the grave shall never come back.* כָּלָה has many different connotations. For its use as indicating the disintegration of an entity, we can adduce, among other examples, *Ezekiel* 5:12.

As we noted above, the phrase, *. . . shall never come back*, does not necessarily, at the level of *p'shat*, mean a denial of the doctrine of *T'chiyas HaMeisim*. The issue of that doctrine is really not germane to Iyov's thinking at this point. Rather, he seems to mean that death brings down the curtain upon a man's existence in his present form. Life, as we know it, ends irrevocably. This interpretation seems borne out in the next verse, see below.

יא לְבֵיתוֹ וְלֹא־יַכִּירֶנּוּ עוֹד מְקוֹמוֹ: גַּם־אֲנִי לֹא אֶחֱשָׂךְ
יב פִּי אֲדַבְּרָה בְּצַר רוּחִי אָשִׂיחָה בְּמַר נַפְשִׁי: הֲיָם־
יג אָנִי אִם־תַּנִּין כִּי־תָשִׂים עָלַי מִשְׁמָר: כִּי־אָמַרְתִּי

10. לֹא־יָשׁוּב עוֹד לְבֵיתוֹ וְלֹא־יַכִּירֶנּוּ עוֹד מְקוֹמוֹ — *Never will he return to his home, never more will his community know him.* מְקוֹמוֹ is to be taken as a shortened form of, *the people of his former place,* the *community* within which he functioned (*Metzudos*).

As noted in the commentary to the previous verse, this sentence appears to exert a limiting function upon the statement that one who descends to the grave will never more rise. The meaning, as yielded by our verse, is that he will never again function within the social framework of his present existence. Life, as it is experienced now, is over once the person dies. There is no implication, at the level of *p'shat,* that the doctrine of *T'chiyas HaMeisim* is at issue.

11. גַּם־אֲנִי לֹא אֶחֱשָׂךְ פִּי אֲדַבְּרָה בְּצַר רוּחִי אָשִׂיחָה בְּמַר נַפְשִׁי — *I, too, will not muzzle my mouth, I shall speak in the affliction of my spirit, give expression in the bitterness of my soul.* What is the implication of the word גַּם, which clearly indicates that Iyov's decision to speak up is a result of something that was previously stated?

Rashi: Since You will not leave me alone, I, too, will not withhold my speech and will protest against what You do.

However, the idea of God's constant importuning, without any let-up, has not yet been mentioned. It first draws Iyov's attention in verse 18ff.

Perhaps, because of this consideration, *Metzudos* sees a different reasoning: Since suffering is my constant companion and I have no expectation of a better life, I will speak up to give vent to the bitterness which I feel. If I am to be punished for this, so be it!

Iyov risks nothing and therefore feels safe in expressing his bitterness. But why do it? What does he expect to gain? It seems unlikely that he simply wishes to relieve pent-up frustrations.

In Prefatory Remarks to 6:5-6 above, we began to discuss what appears to us to be the central drive of Iyov's tortured mind — his dogged pursuit of truth, the adamant refusal to twist facts in order to suit doctrine.

As noted, Iyov's determination will be vindicated at the end of the book. It was he, in his unbending integrity — not the friends in their doctrinaire blandness — who *spoke appropriately* (42:7) and earned God's approbation.

From where does Iyov take the theological license for his battling with God?

It seems that such a license inheres in the necessary boundaries which limit human perceptions of the Divine. By our very nature there must be a degree of anthropomorphism in our relationship with God. With the purpose of *accommodating the ear* (לְשַׁבֵּר אֶת הָאוֹזֶן), God projects Himself to us as father, judge, king and various other guises, all of which carry associations in our minds which in their totality create the imperfect image we have of God.

However, such *accommodation of the ear* places, so to speak, certain limitations upon God. Iyov's claim is that if we are to perceive Him as, let us say, a father, then He must act as one. He cannot, as it were, do such things as no father would do and still want us to look upon Him as a father. In practical terms, this means that in whichever way God chooses to reveal Himself, what we perceive must fit some recognizable category. Where it does not, questions have to arise.

What, then, is to be the theologically correct stance of a man who is faced with experiences which allow for no explanation? What, he must ask himself, does God want of me. What are the options which I have?

As suggested in the footnote to 1:1, there may well be a difference here between Israel, whose Torah is one of נַעֲשֶׂה וְנִשְׁמַע, an unquestioning acceptance of God's providence; and the nations, whose approach has always been מַה כְּתִיב בָּהּ, *What is written in it?* How are we to understand our obligations?

Within that frame of reference there is, indeed, only one possible response. By leaving no plausible explanation for His actions, God is manifestly goading the sufferer to challenge Him and demand an accounting. Such relentless determination to understand will ultimately bring about a confrontation with God, as it does in Iyov's case. That experience can prove sufficiently overpowering to swing the subject from an apprehension of God defined by a *hearing of the ear,* to one of a *seeing of the eyes* (42:5), with all that such a change implies. The suffering will have served its purpose — the sufferer can, after all, become reconciled to his fate.

to his home, never more will his community know him. [11] *I, too, will not muzzle my mouth, I shall speak in the affliction of my spirit, give expression in the bitterness of my soul.* [12] *Am I, then, the sea, or a sea monster, that you should set guards against me?* [13] *When I*

This would be the sense of our verse.

Since Iyov has demonstrated that there is no way at all in which his experiences can be sublimated, he concludes that they can only have one purpose. He hears a summons to the hardest task to which a human can be called. God challenges him! He, who lived his life as God's servant (1:8), must now become His adversary. The integrity of his beliefs allows for no other stance.

The base meaning of חָשַׂךְ is *to withhold.* It is used to describe a holding back of speech at *Proverbs* 10:19 and 17:27.

12. הֲיָם־אָנִי אִם־תַּנִּין כִּי־תָשִׂים עָלַי מִשְׁמָר — *Am I, then, the sea, or a sea monster, that you should set guards against me?* Once Iyov has made up his mind that he is now called upon to give vent to his bitterness, he leaves no holds barred. He challenges God to justify His actions.

The guard which God places around the sea, the boundary beyond which neither the crashing waves nor the mighty sea monsters may venture, is of course the sand.

The metaphor is clear, but we do not yet know which of Iyov's experiences it is meant to elucidate. In what sense does Iyov feel himself hemmed in, in much the same way that the sea and its monsters are imprisoned by the beach?[1]

Rashi thinks that Iyov is bemoaning his inability to die. His soul is trying to escape from his body, and Satan will not let it, in much the same way that the sand will not allow the sea to wash over it.

Ramban agrees with *Rashi* that that which is allowed no escape is Iyov's life. The span which has been allotted to him keeps him inexorably alive. However, *Ramban* takes the meaning of the verse one stage further. Iyov actually compares his life to a sea. He feels himself constantly buffeted and overwhelmed by mountainous waves which keep crashing over him and which allow him no respite. Day and night are all the same (vs. 13-14), and there is no let-up at all.

There is an additional resonance which this metaphor would seem to awaken in us. When we think of the sands of the seashore bounding the waters, we think of them as a wall which protects the surroundings from being engulfed (cf. *Psalms* 104:9). Certainly, preventing Iyov from dying cannot be viewed as protecting anyone from danger. If all that is being elucidated is the inability of the soul to depart from the body, then the metaphor seems to be saying too much.

Moreover, we cannot ignore the fact that the metaphor consists of two parts; sea and monster are both contained by the constraining sands. Now sand functions differently in containing the sea than it does in serving to imprison the monster. It is a natural barrier to the water; it lies in the character of the two that they interact as they do, the one straining ever outward, the other placing firm limits which may never be crossed. Not so in the case of the monster. The sand, as sand, could never impede its progress. It is only because it has no life outside its natural habitat that it may never roam beyond the walls that bound the sea.

Iyov protests that he is neither water nor sea monster. What does he mean?

At 6:2 we suggested that the metaphor in our verse may be of a kind with the one used there. To Iyov's mind his sufferings were so much wet sand, which smothered and inhibited by sheer dead weight and denied any

1. There may be any number of conscious or subconscious drives and associations which bring a particular metaphor to the mind of the speaker. By the same token it lies in the nature of a metaphor that it may contain many different layers of meaning (*Rambam,* Introduction to *Moreh Nevuchim*). We may therefore be incorrect in asking which is *the* experience which Iyov is trying to elucidate. There could be many different ones.

Thus, it may well be that at some level of consciousness, his futile attempts to make his implacable friends understand became to him furious breakers beating uselessly against indifferent and unmoving sands.

Again, there is the possibility that his own impotence against an all-powerful wholly free God, Who seems impervious to all entreaties, suggested the metaphor.

We may stand at the seashore and observe fierce, towering, seemingly invincible waves reduced to almost laughable frailty, lapping tamely at the sands as they meet up with the line beyond which they may never venture. Such an image may well have been conjured up in Iyov's mind when he recalled the heyday of his powers and had now to contemplate his reduced and broken state.

יד תְּנַחֲמֵנִי עַרְשִׂי יִשָּׂא בְשִׂיחִי מִשְׁכָּבִי: וְחִתַּתַּנִי בַחֲלֹמוֹת
טו וּמֵחֶזְיֹנוֹת תְּבַעֲתַנִּי: וַתִּבְחַר מַחֲנָק נַפְשִׁי מָוֶת מֵעַצְמוֹתָי:
טז מָאַסְתִּי לֹא־לְעֹלָם אֶחְיֶה חֲדַל מִמֶּנִּי כִּי־הֶבֶל יָמָי:

possibility of growth or expansion of the spirit.

Would this not be the meaning here, too?

In this whole chapter Iyov has constantly bemoaned the absolute senselessness of his hurts. They have no redeeming feature, contain no glint of hope to lighten their savage darkness; rather, they cruelly and thoughtlessly lay waste a life that could so easily have been blessed and productive.

Body and soul are both equally crushed. The body is the natural and passive victim of the sickness. It is the sea which, in spite of all its pulsating energy, must ultimately bow to the superior power of the sands. Within, though, there is a raging monster, a titan of force; a spirit which, could it but escape, would recognize no limits to its horizons — but which is now chained and impotent because it cannot break loose from a sickly, broken body.

Whom could I have harmed, Iyov asks bitterly. Is anyone the safer because my life has been robbed of meaning?

13-14. כִּי־אָמַרְתִּי תְּנַחֲמֵנִי עַרְשִׂי יִשָּׂא בְשִׂיחִי מִשְׁכָּבִי. וְחִתַּתַּנִי בַחֲלֹמוֹת וּמֵחֶזְיֹנוֹת תְּבַעֲתַנִּי — *When I said, 'My bed will comfort me, my couch will bear my woes.' Then You would smash me with dreams, terrorize me with visions.* Even a prisoner, hemmed in by walls which may never be scaled, can occasionally escape his agonies. He can lose himself in sleep, and on flights of dream-spun fancy, soar beyond his sordid confines. Not Iyov. He finds no surcease at night. What should be a time of blessed relief merely signals a change from the physical poundings of a pain-racked body, to the infinitely more terrible tortures of a fevered mind.

Thus would *Rashi* and *Ramban* understand the relationship of these two verses to the previous one. If Iyov is not to be granted the escape of death, he would still willingly have accepted the temporary relief of sleep. Even this is denied him.

As we have understood the previous verse, the thought process would be as follows: Iyov's spirit is indeed chained to his body — and is crushed together with it. But Eliphaz himself had taught that the soul can find release in dreams; that as the body lies quiescent the spirit can be touched by intimations of another reality. His seminal vision had come to him, *During the ruminations of the night's visions, as slumber descends upon men* (4:13). Bitterly, Iyov recognizes that even this avenue of growth is closed to him. No heavenly messengers people his dreams — his is a world of only darkness and terror.

עֶרֶשׂ is a *bed* (see Deuteronomy 3:11). It is used here as a synonym for *sleep*. The sense is: I would find comfort in sleep.

יִשָּׂא, from נָשָׂא, *to carry*. Suffering is seen as a burden to be carried; the sleep (made possible by the couch) as a help in bearing that burden.

חִתֵּת, *to smash*. See *Rashi* to *Isaiah* 8:9.

15. וַתִּבְחַר מַחֲנָק נַפְשִׁי מָוֶת מֵעַצְמוֹתָי — *My soul craved to be strangled, preferred death to being.* This verse seems to be a continuation of verse 13: I demanded very little from life, and could have, if necessary, been satisfied with the peace which a restful sleep might have granted me. It was only after I saw that even that modest request was refused, that even at night I was to be pounded and smashed, that I longed for death.

מַחֲנָק is a noun formed from חָנַק, *to strangle*. It does not recur in Scripture.

עַצְמוֹתָי, rendered literally, would be *my bones*. Here *limbs* are meant. In place of these limbs which delineate my being I would have wished for death.

16. מָאַסְתִּי לֹא־לְעֹלָם אֶחְיֶה חֲדַל מִמֶּנִּי כִּי־הֶבֶל יָמָי — *I am sickened; I shall not live forever, leave me be for my days are as nothing.* We quote *Ramban* — who sees this verse as the ending of the second stage of Iyov's argument — as presented in the commentary to the beginning of this chapter: "I am sick of my life which anyway will not last forever. Therefore, leave me alone and do not punish me in accordance with my sins. My days, after all, are nothing. They do not hold out any promise even if I were to mend my ways."

A more detailed analysis of this passage yields further insights.

Since this verse appears to lead into a consideration of the insignificance of man in general (vs. 17-18), we should examine it in that light.

What does Iyov mean by the phrase, *I shall not live forever*. That statement appears to be too self-evident to make a serious contribution to any argument that Iyov might be making.

A comparison with *Isaiah* 2:22 will, we think, place our verse in its correct perspective.

said, 'My bed will comfort me, my couch will bear my woes.' 14 *Then*
You would smash me with dreams, terrorize me with visions. 15 *My*
soul craved to be strangled, preferred death to being. 16 *I am sick-*
ened; I shall not live forever, leave me be for my days are as nothing.

Iyov 7:16	Isaiah 2:22
1. לֹא־לְעֹלָם אֶחְיֶה *I shall not live forever,*	1. חִדְלוּ לָכֶם מִן־הָאָדָם *Leave man be*
2. חֲדַל מִמֶּנִּי *leave me be*	2. אֲשֶׁר נְשָׁמָה בְּאַפּוֹ *who has only breath in his nostrils*
3. כִּי־הֶבֶל יָמָי *for my days are nothing.*	3. כִּי בַמֶּה נֶחְשָׁב הוּא *for by what does he merit esteem?*

Iyov's statement, *I shall not live for ever,* (1) parallels *who has only breath in his nostrils* (2) (*Isaiah* 2:22). The difference in position derives from the context, as will become clear below.

The *Isaiah* phrase is the key to understanding our's. No undue importance ought to be attached to mortal man, for in truth he does not merit it. But where *Isaiah* deals with man in general, Iyov comes to this realization from within himself (our verse), and from there moves on to his thoughts about the human condition in general (in the next two verses).

How does this idea belong in Iyov's thought at this stage?

The key lies in the opening word of the sentence, *I am sickened!*

Iyov has examined his life, searching for a glimmer of meaning in the oppressive bleakness of his life and mood. He has found nothing — no joy, no hope, and ultimately no justification for living. A strangling disgust wells up inside him. He wants no part of such a travesty.

Now it is a truism that man, despite all the evidence of mind and senses, tenaciously holds on to a sense of his own immortality. Cognitively he well knows that he will die; emotionally he will not accept this. Every fiber of his being joins in generating a denial of reality which becomes the focal reality of his life.[1]

However, all this is true only as long as life holds meaning for him. He wants desperately to live — and his will becomes for him truth. But when, filled with loathing, he looks upon life as an insupportable burden and wants nothing more than to rid himself of it, he becomes able to distance himself and permit his emotions to come to grips with the facts which his mind had known all along: *I am sickened; I shall not live forever!*

Aware now — really aware — of how fleet-

1. This facet of our condition plays a role in shaping responses to a wide range of human experiences. We cite examples ranging from the wicked, to the unthinking, and finally, to even the best among us.

The Wicked: *Shabbos* 31b.: The wicked know that their ways lead to death — but their loins are encased in fat [and deaden their feelings so that they refuse to think about the future — *Rashi*].

The Unthinking: The *Mirrer Mashgiach,* R' Yeruchem Levovitz, *zt'l,* illustrates the illogic of our mindless pursuit of luxuries by a parable told by R' Chaim of Volozhin (*Limudei Musrei HaTorah* to *Bo*).

An ordinary mortal once met a citizen of the city of Luz — where, tradition teaches, no one ever dies. In the course of their conversation the mortal, after much difficulty, succeeds in explaining the idea of death to the Luzite.

The latter, fascinated by such a novel concept, asks to be told something about the mores of life in such a strange and short-lived society. Surely, he supposes, no one dreams of eating anything but the simplest vegetables, of dwelling in anything but caves, or dressing in anything but rags. Obviously it would be the height of folly to invest efforts directed to enhancing a life which is so ridiculously short.

To his surprise he is told that, on the contrary, the quality of food, housing and clothes are central to human concerns . . .

R' Yeruchem explains this phenomenon in terms of our unwillingness to come to grips with the reality of death. We know that we will die — but do not really believe it.

The Best Among Us: *Ramban,* in *Toras HaAdam,* wonders at man's reaction to death. Why are we invariably shocked when someone passes on, why do we mourn over something which we always knew to be our inescapable lot?

Ramban's solution is that with all our knowledge of the realities, we still cling to the initial concept of life which, as God had willed it, would have known no death. Had Adam not sinned, then indeed we would all have been immortals. Such is life in its purest form, and it is this concept of life which animates our reactions.

ז/יז־כא יז־יח מָה־אֱנוֹשׁ כִּי תְגַדְּלֶנּוּ וְכִי־תָשִׁית אֵלָיו לִבֶּךָ: וַתִּפְקְדֶנּוּ
יט לִבְקָרִים לִרְגָעִים תִּבְחָנֶנּוּ: כַּמָּה לֹא־תִשְׁעֶה מִמֶּנִּי לֹא־
כ תַרְפֵּנִי עַד־בִּלְעִי רֻקִּי: חָטָאתִי מָה אֶפְעַל ׀ לָךְ נֹצֵר הָאָדָם
כא לָמָה שַׂמְתַּנִי לְמִפְגָּע לָךְ וָאֶהְיֶה עָלַי לְמַשָּׂא: וּמֶה ׀
לֹא־תִשָּׂא פִשְׁעִי וְתַעֲבִיר אֶת־עֲוֺנִי כִּי־עַתָּה לֶעָפָר אֶשְׁכָּב
ח/א־ב א־ב וְשִׁחֲרְתַּנִי וְאֵינֶנִּי: וַיַּעַן בִּלְדַּד הַשּׁוּחִי וַיֹּאמַר: עַד־אָן

ing life actually is, he is suddenly struck by its sheer insignificance. Can this be all there is — and if so, why would God care?

17-18. מָה־אֱנוֹשׁ כִּי תְגַדְּלֶנּוּ וְכִי־תָשִׁית אֵלָיו לִבֶּךָ. וַתִּפְקְדֶנּוּ לִבְקָרִים לִרְגָעִים תִּבְחָנֶנּוּ — *What is man that You exalt him, that You turn Your thoughts towards him. Considering him each morning, testing him each second?* As long as Iyov had thought of his own life in positive terms, he did not question God's concern with man. His own life lived in integrity, dignity and rectitude was ample proof that if indeed man's feet stood on the ground, his soul might yet reach heavenward. He had no difficulty in perceiving mankind as the crown of creation — a fitting focus of God's interest and providence.

Now all this had changed. If the value which he had thought to detect in his own life meant so little; if all that he had — with a degree of justified pride — done and wrought could mean so little; if a deity, seemingly oblivious to the pain and dislocations which His actions cause, could in one moment smash such accomplishment into nothingness — then this could only mean that man, in the totality of the Divine scheme, is so puny and insignificant as to have no standing at all.

If so, Iyov wonders, why should God care what man does? Why place such a nonentity into the very center of His concerns?[1]

19. כַּמָּה לֹא־תִשְׁעֶה מִמֶּנִּי לֹא־תַרְפֵּנִי עַד־בִּלְעִי רֻקִּי — *It is so long since You have averted Your gaze from me. Can You not let me be while I swallow my spittle.* Iyov's full resentment now surfaces. On the one hand God obviously cares nothing for him. He has, without any compunction, laid a flowering life waste — and on the other hand He leaves him no respite at all ... *Considering him each morning, testing him each second.*

שָׁעָה means *to turn towards*; ... שָׁעָה מִ , *to*

1. If these thoughts are more than just a cry of anguish, if indeed they are offered as a serious theological stance, then we would need to know how Iyov, at this stage of his thoughts, perceives the role of man among the teeming myriads of earth's creatures.

Presumably, Iyov does not deny the story of creation — neither here nor anywhere else in the book is there as much as a hint that would justify such an assumption. If so, he knows that man was introduced into a completed and expectant world, at the very last moment before the Sabbath, as the goal, crown and therefore justification for all that God had wrought.

Could he be as insignificant then as Iyov makes him out to be?

Both in form and content, Iyov's cry here parallels that of the psalmist at *Psalms* 8:5: *What is the frail man that You should remember him, and mortal man that You should be mindful of him?*

In the tradition of the Sages, these words were uttered by the angels when they protested God's intention to entrust His Torah to man. Can mortal man be given such responsibilities? Will he use or misuse this greatest of all gifts?

The angels, then, wished to keep the Torah in heaven. Well and good! But what of man? Is he to be written off? If he is not to receive the Torah, is any role left to him?

It is significant that the angels objected only to man's receiving the Torah. There was no protest against the seven Noachide laws, which had imprinted the Divine image upon human endeavors since the very beginning of time.

Manifestly, then, there is an essential difference between the two codes. The Torah places each individual — as an individual — into a direct relationship to God. To this the angels objected. No one person should be trusted with such an awesome responsibility. Let the unit (mankind) be formed, guided and polished by the demanding standards of the Noachide laws — but never solitary man! The Torah must be kept in heaven!

This may be the thrust of Iyov's argument. God, evidently, has no truck with the individual. The human race may well be a different story. With its centrality to God's plans, Iyov has no quarrel.

The proposition that God does not care about the individual seems to stand in contradiction to Iyov's assertion, at 6:4, that God treats him as an enemy — see *Ramban* to 35:2. This inconsistency is brought to its sharpest focus in chapters 12-14, Iyov's further speech, made in response to Tzophar. See Prefatory Remarks to that speech.

7/17-21 17 *What is man that You exalt him, that You turn Your thoughts
towards him. 18 *Considering him each morning, testing him each
second? 19 *It is so long since You have averted Your gaze from me.
Can You not let me be while I swallow my spittle. 20 *Have I sinned,
*how does that touch You, Watcher of man! Why do You set me up
as a target, so that I have become a burden to myself. 21 *How is it
*that You cannot forgive my sin and erase my transgression — for
*then I would have lain in the dust. Even should You search for me
— I am no more.

8/1-2 1 **B***ildad the Shuhite responded and spoke:* 2 *How long will*

turn away from (*Rashi, Genesis* 4:4 — but see also *Rashi* to *Exodus* 5:9).

תַרְפֵּנִי is from רָפָה, *to loosen.* (See *Rashi* to *Moed Kattan* 10a.)

While I swallow my spittle, does not recur in Scripture. It is obviously meant to describe an extremely short time. There is not a moment in Iyov's life in which he does not feel himself under surveillance.

20. חָטָאתִי מָה אֶפְעַל לָךְ — *Have I sinned, how does that touch You.* The translation follows *Metzudos. Ramban* renders: If I have sinned, what can I do to make up for it to You. How might I obtain atonement?

נֹצֵר הָאָדָם — *Watcher of man!* נֹצֵר means *to watch* (*Rashi, Jeremiah* 31:5), but it also means *to lay siege* (*Rashi* there, 4:16). The context here appears to demand a belligerent exclamation — and that is how we have rendered it [that is, closer to the second meaning].

This also appears to be *Ramban's* understanding in his initial rendering: שׁוֹמֵר אוֹרְחוֹתָיו. [If so, we assume that he would have understood the previous phrase as does *Metzudos.*]

However, *Ramban* has a change of heart — perhaps he feels that Iyov, in all his frustrations, would still not have permitted himself such a familiarity; or because the more usual meaning of נצר would be a caring, protective watching rather than one motivated by enmity.

Thus: Why would You *Who grant and nurture life,* punish me so cruelly. Have I sinned? How can I make it up to You? (See above and see further at 35:3.)

לָמָּה שַׂמְתַּנִי לְמִפְגָּע לָךְ — *Why do You set me up as a target.* פָּגַע, *to meet.* Thus: As someone who meets another while very angry, and pours out his fury upon him (*Rashi*).

וָאֶהְיֶה עָלַי לְמַשָּׂא — *So that I have become a burden to myself. Rashi* writes that here we have a euphemism (תִּקּוּן סוֹפְרִים). The meaning is really: Why do You treat me as though I were a burden to *You.*

Metzudos points out that we can make sense of the phrase even as it stands. I am so disgusted with my life that I have become a burden to myself. Would that I could be relieved of having to live!

21. וּמֶה לֹא־תִשָּׂא פִשְׁעִי וְתַעֲבִיר אֶת־עֲוֹנִי כִּי־עַתָּה לֶעָפָר אֶשְׁכָּב וְשִׁחַרְתַּנִי וְאֵינֶנִּי — *How is it that You cannot forgive my sin and erase my transgression — for then I would have lain in the dust. Even should You search for me — I am no more.* This thought follows directly from the previous one. Iyov looks upon life as a punishment — he would so much rather be dead. Thus, he asks God to forgive his sins so that he might, at last, die in peace.

שׁחר would usually mean *to search for something* in a positive sense — see, for example, *Proverbs* 11:27. The sense of the phrase would then be that even if You were to look for me in order to make up for all my suffering, it would be too late — *I would be no more.* Apparently, Iyov means that he would gladly opt now for death, even though that would make it impossible for God ever to make his suffering up to him. He prefers immediate relief to the possibility of eventual reparation.

VIII.

⊲§ Bildad's First Speech

In *Ramban's* view Bildad supports Eliphaz in his rejection of Iyov's stance but, at the same time, moves beyond him. Where Eliphaz's tone had been placatory, Bildad's is accusatory. He dismisses Iyov's children out of hand. They were irredeemably wicked — and deserved to die.

With regard to Iyov's own suffering, Bildad feels that he can understand that too. He accepts

ג תְּמַלֶּל־אֵלֶּה וְרוּחַ כַּבִּיר אִמְרֵי־פִיךָ: הַאֵל יְעַוֵּת מִשְׁפָּט
ד וְאִם־שַׁדַּי יְעַוֵּת־צֶדֶק: אִם־בָּנֶיךָ חָטְאוּ־לוֹ וַיְשַׁלְּחֵם

Iyov's contention that it cannot have been meant to inspire and to bring him closer to God. There is too much of it, it is too intense, too overwhelming. If so, Bildad reasons, its purpose must be one of cleansing and atonement. Iyov must have sinned — not as grievously as his children, but sufficiently to require a purification by the fire of his agonies.

For Bildad, the problem is solved.

In our alternative analysis, Bildad does indeed move beyond Eliphaz's stance, but is much more restrained than he is in *Ramban's* view. He introduces the concept that Iyov's suffering may be the wages of sin, but allows for the possibility that it may not be. Rather than accusing, he challenges. Let Iyov himself examine his past. Does it bear up under his scrutiny? If he truly lived a life of constancy and purity, then the suffering is a temporary aberration, and the future beckons bright. He is master of his fate — let him pray and all will be well once more.

But let Iyov beware! There is, too, the other possibility. If his pieties were a sham, his life a lie, then he is indeed doomed. For the hypocrite there will be no mercy.

Bildad, then, is at this point still reticent about making any judgments. The full fury of the erstwhile friends has not yet been released.

In this, Bildad's first speech, *Ramban* detects a movement away from Eliphaz's placatory tone. Bildad is the first among the friends to accuse Iyov of wrongdoing.

Paradoxically, this is because he accepts at least a part of Iyov's argument. The suffering is too great to be sublimated. However, where Iyov stops there and lashes out with bewildered fury against a fate which he knows to be without explanation, Bildad draws quite a different conclusion.

Sin brings destruction in its wake. Absolute wickedness brings absolute destruction — death — and that is what happened to Iyov's children. But, even lesser transgressions need to be expiated. Iyov is suffering because he deserves to suffer — let him turn to God in prayer, and he will be cured.

Rashi disagrees with *Ramban* in the interpretation of a number of key phrases, and it seems likely that he sees the thrust of the speech differently.

We shall trace the development of his thesis in the commentary to the individual verses.

2-3. עַד־אָן תְּמַלֶּל־אֵלֶּה וְרוּחַ כַּבִּיר אִמְרֵי־פִיךָ. הַאֵל יְעַוֵּת מִשְׁפָּט וְאִם־שַׁדַּי יְעַוֵּת־צֶדֶק. *How long will you say such things; your speech is just an avalanche of words. Would God pervert justice, would Shaddai pervert righteousness?* Bildad attempts to pull Iyov up short. True, he had never said in so many words that God was acting unjustly. But, Bildad points out, rhetorical questions do not simply float. They imply an answer — one, to be sure, assumed to be too obvious to require explication — but, nonetheless, clear and unequivocal. Is Iyov willing to declare, in so many words, that God has betrayed justice? Bildad suspects not. Iyov is spewing forth an *avalanche of words* which tie him to a position which he would not care to defend.

But, if so, what is the explanation for Iyov's misfortunes? Does not the good fortune which once smiled upon all his endeavors indicate that he deserves a better fate? Can the violent dislocation of apparently well-earned tranquility be squared with justice? Bildad plans to present some answers to this question.

It is instructive to contrast *Rashi's* interpretation of רוּחַ with that of *Metzudos*.

Metzudos takes רוּחַ as *anger* and כַּבִּיר as *mighty*. Thus: What you have said constitutes *mighty anger*. It is rebellion, pure and simple. It generates anger and condemnation.

Now, *Rashi* could have agreed: At *Koheles* 7:8, he too renders רוּחַ as *anger*, and in *Iyov* 34:17 he renders כַּבִּיר as *very great*. His explanation is thus contextual and not linguistic. He creates a much softer tone by taking רוּחַ as *speech* and כַּבִּיר as *much*.

Rashi and *Metzudos* may be influenced by their respective understanding of Bildad's words in verse 4. These might be read as an outright condemnation of Iyov's sons. If so, already in our two verses, Bildad limbers up for the attack. He knows precisely where Iyov stands. His judgment is incisive and uncharitable. (Thus, *Metzudos* and, as indicated in Prefatory Remarks, *Ramban*.)

We shall point out, below, that this need not be the meaning of verse 4. It may well be that by softening the implications of our verse, *Rashi* is creating the ambience for a less judgmental stance.

you say such things; your speech is just an avalanche of words.
3 *Would God pervert justice, would Shaddai pervert righteousness?*
4 *If, because your sons sinned against Him, He sent them away*

For the two sections of the second sentence (v. 3), *Ramban*, wishing to avoid redundancy, suggests two possible interpretations: *Would God pervert justice*: by repaying the righteous with suffering. *Would Shaddai pervert righteousness*: by failing to reward them, and leaving them to the vagaries of fate. Or, *would God pervert justice*: by failing to punish the wicked. *Would Shaddai pervert righteousness*: by failing to reward the righteous.[1]

4. אִם־בָּנֶיךָ חָטְאוּ־לוֹ וַיְשַׁלְּחֵם בְּיַד־פִּשְׁעָם — *If, because your sons sinned against Him, He sent them away at the hands of their iniquity.* As noted above, *Ramban* understands this verse as an absolute condemnation of Iyov's sons. He writes: [Bildad] judged the sons to be completely wicked, culpable of having their lives taken, and this is the reason why they already died.

Metzudos adds the thought that it was their constant feasting which led them along the path of unseemly levity — which in its turn leads to more serious transgressions. They were killed in the house in which the current feast was taking place, in order to underline this point.

We assume that these commentators understand the אם with which the verse starts as *when* (cf. *Numbers* 36:4 and elsewhere), rather than as the more usual *if*.[2]

1. *Ramban's* second interpretation has the merit of introducing the issue of the seeming good fortune of the wicked — a theme which apparently occupies Bildad at the end of this chapter (see there).

However, it must be noted that nowhere, up to this point, has Iyov questioned the apparent prospering of the wicked — see commentary to 4:8. It is not easy to see why Bildad would feel called upon to address this question. See the commentary to verse 22.

2. In Introductory Remarks we saw that in *Ramban's* view, Bildad is suggesting a new explanation for Iyov's suffering. He must have sinned [Eliphaz made no such assertion], and his pains have a cleansing and atoning function. Now, this thought is never explicated by Bildad in this speech. We must assume that *Ramban* sees it implicit in our verse. From the fate that overtook your children you can see that the wage of sin is death. Granted that you were less wicked than your sons — you were not killed — but you must read your suffering as constituting a small death.

The bridge to the next verse is explained by *Metzudos*: From this you may conclude that if you were to turn to God in prayer, He would show mercy to you.

A careful analysis of the points which Bildad appears to be making throughout his speech can yield another meaning for our verse. This would retain the more usual meaning, *if*, for אם, and also create a more direct connecting link to the next verse.

What is the unifying theme in Bildad's speech?

The metaphor of the reeds (v. 11ff.) provides the answer.

As *Rashi* interprets the two sets, vs. 11-12 and 16-18, they appear to deliver similar messages: Good fortune can be short-lived indeed. Where well-being depends upon an outside source it must be expected that when that source is cut off, erosion and eventual death results. Deny the reeds the water which is their lifeblood, and their amazing growth and robust strength becomes a thing of the past.

Bildad's thesis is clear: If the happiness of the early years was indeed a reflection of a *pure* and *constant* life, if the source lay within his own being, then Iyov can expect that his present setbacks are only temporary. But if it was never self-sustaining, if it was an infusion from without — if, essentially, he was one *who forgets God*, a *hypocrite* whose pieties were a sham — then he must not be surprised at his downfall.

However, which of the two is the truth? Throughout, Bildad makes no judgment. He presents the two alternatives, but leaves it to Iyov to draw the correct conclusions.

As a test, he directs Iyov's thoughts to the death of his children.

Let us analyze Bildad's thinking.

The idea of the *home* appears to be very central to Bildad's thought. In the twenty-one verses of his speech, he resorts three times — in three unconnected passages — to this theme. Verse 6 has the *home — locus of [Iyov's] righteousness*, verses 14-15 talk of the homes of *those who forget God* and of the *hypocrite*, and verse 22 predicts that the *tent of the wicked* will be *no more*.

What defines a home? Let Eliphaz speak: *As for me, I saw a fool strike roots, but presaged an instant bane upon his home. May fortune elude his children, let them be crushed at the gate with no one to help* (5:3-4). *Rashi*, there, makes clear that the *bane* is the fact that *fortune eludes his children*. A home is only truly a home when it is blessed with children.

When Iyov's children died in the storm, his home crumbled. That he still had a roof over his own head matters not at all. Loss of livestock and wealth is unimportant in Bildad's eyes. He does not

ה בְּיַד־פִּשְׁעָם: אִם־אַתָּה תְּשַׁחֵר אֶל־אֵל וְאֶל־שַׁדַּי תִּתְחַנָּן:
ו אִם־זַךְ וְיָשָׁר אָתָּה כִּי־עַתָּה יָעִיר עָלֶיךָ וְשִׁלַּם נְוַת צִדְקֶךָ:
ז־ח וְהָיָה רֵאשִׁיתְךָ מִצְעָר וְאַחֲרִיתְךָ יִשְׂגֶּה מְאֹד: כִּי־שְׁאַל־נָא
ט לְדֹר רִישׁוֹן וְכוֹנֵן לְחֵקֶר אֲבוֹתָם: כִּי־תְמוֹל אֲנַחְנוּ וְלֹא
י נֵדָע כִּי צֵל יָמֵינוּ עֲלֵי־אָרֶץ: הֲלֹא־הֵם יוֹרוּךָ יֹאמְרוּ לָךְ
יא וּמִלִּבָּם יוֹצִאוּ מִלִּים: הֲיִגְאֶה־גֹּמֶא בְּלֹא בִצָּה יִשְׂגֶּא־אָחוּ
יב בְּלִי־מָיִם: עֹדֶנּוּ בְאִבּוֹ לֹא יִקָּטֵף וְלִפְנֵי כָל־חָצִיר יִיבָשׁ:

5-6. אִם־אַתָּה תְּשַׁחֵר אֶל־אֵל וְאֶל־שַׁדַּי תִּתְחַנָּן. אִם־זַךְ וְיָשָׁר אָתָּה כִּי־עַתָּה יָעִיר עָלֶיךָ וְשִׁלַּם נְוַת צִדְקֶךָ — *If you would just supplicate God, entreat Shaddai. Then, if indeed you are pure and upright, even now He will invoke these for you, crown your home — locus of your righteousness with perfection.* If your contention is true, if indeed you are wholly righteous, then surely God will wish to restore you to your original tranquility. But, if that is what you wish, you must desist from your pugnacious challenges. Instead, supplicate God and entreat Him, and you will see that all will be well.

He will invoke these for you, refers to Iyov's purity and uprightness. It will be these which will ultimately bring healing to his home.

וְשִׁלַּם — *Crown your home . . . with perfection.* Thus *Rashi* and *Ramban.* The perfection will be explicated in the next verse. By comparison to what will be, his earlier happiness will seem to have been as nothing.

As we have understood the thrust of Bildad's thought, the meaning could be as follows: We find שִׁלַּם, in the sense of making up something that had been taken away, at *Joel* 2:25. Accordingly, he would be telling Iyov that if he had prayed to God, all the losses which he had sustained would be made up to him.

Indeed, this is precisely what eventually happened to Iyov. As we learn at 42:10ff., all that he had lost was eventually returned. In the event, this came about through prayer, as Bildad predicted, but not through the form of prayer which he had anticipated. God returned all that Iyov had lost *when he prayed for his friends.*

נְוַת צִדְקֶךָ — *Your home — locus of your righteousness. Ramban,* consistent with his perception that Bildad has made an unequivocal judgment on Iyov's past, understands *locus of your righteousness* to lie in the future. In contrast to the home of the past, which was full of sin, your new one, in which righteousness will reign, will know greater bliss.

According to the interpretation which we suggested above: The home which, in the event, will have been shown to be *locus of your righteousness,* as you have consistently claimed.

7. וְהָיָה רֵאשִׁיתְךָ מִצְעָר וְאַחֲרִיתְךָ יִשְׂגֶּה מְאֹד — *Then, though your beginnings were insignificant, your latter years will flourish exceedingly.* Relative to the joys that await you, your past will seem of no significance at all (*Rashi*).

In *Ramban's* perception this would perhaps be because the true penitent is to be rewarded.

According to the alternative interpretation which we offered: Perhaps, to make up for the pain which Iyov had to suffer through no fault of his own, he *will flourish exceedingly.*

8-10. כִּי־שְׁאַל־נָא לְדֹר רִישׁוֹן וְכוֹנֵן לְחֵקֶר אֲבוֹתָם — *Inquire, I beg you, concerning the earlier generation, set yourself to absorb that which they learned from their fathers.* כִּי־תְמוֹל אֲנַחְנוּ וְלֹא נֵדָע כִּי צֵל יָמֵינוּ עֲלֵי־אָרֶץ — *For we are but yesterday's creatures, unable to comprehend, our lives are a shadow upon the earth.* הֲלֹא־הֵם יוֹרוּךָ יֹאמְרוּ לָךְ וּמִלִּבָּם יוֹצִאוּ מִלִּים — *Surely they will instruct you and tell you, extract words from within their hearts. Ramban* takes these three verses together: Our lives are very short, and we may occasionally see the wicked flourish and believe that this will last forever

even mention it. Iyov's tragedy is that he is homeless.

But why?

This is the question which Bildad poses in the next few verses.

Were the children destroyed because of their own iniquity, in which case Iyov is not to blame, or is it not they who sinned but he? If the former, then Iyov need simply turn to God in prayer and all will be made up to him. His latter years will even be much better than his earlier ones (vs. 5 and 6).

But if his home was never a real home, if his own shortcomings never gave his children a chance, if all that he had was an artificial infusion from without, but never a reflection of a strong and complete inner purity — then indeed, history and experience must teach that Iyov is doomed (vs. 8-19).

at the hands of their iniquity. 5 *If you would just supplicate God, en-*
treat Shaddai. 6 *Then, if indeed you are pure and upright, even now*
He will invoke these for you, crown your home — locus of your right-
eousness — with perfection. 7 *Then, though your beginnings were*
insignificant, your latter years will flourish exceedingly. 8 *Inquire,*
I beg you, concerning the earlier generation, set yourself to absorb
that which they learned from their fathers. 9 *For we are but yester-*
day's creatures, unable to comprehend, our lives are a shadow
upon the earth. 10 *Surely they will instruct you and tell you, extract*
words from within their hearts. 11 *Can reeds flourish without a*
marsh, a meadow shoot up without water? 12 *As long as it is still*
fresh it will not be snapped, but, ahead of all herbage, it will dry out.

(v. 9). However, if we ask our elders to share their experiences and traditions with us (v. 8) and also to draw upon the wisdom stored up in their own hearts (v. 10), we will surely learn that the well-being of the wicked must eventually come to an end. The metaphor of the reeds (vs. 11 and 12), as *Ramban* interprets it (see below), will bear this out.

This principle is essentially the same as that taught by Eliphaz at 4:8. There, Eliphaz had drawn upon his own experience to confirm it. By contrast, Bildad invokes history. Perhaps both Bildad and Iyov are younger than Eliphaz; their lives have not spanned as long a period.

But why repeat a teaching which Iyov had already once ignored? Moreover, at least up to this point, Iyov has not seemed at all troubled by the good fortune which occasionally smiles upon the wicked. His entire horizon seems emblazoned with just one word — pain; his own and that of all the world's unfortunates. To this he comes back relentlessly. He has sought relief more than understanding, craved peace more than knowledge. Why, then, concentrate on an issue which seems to concern him not at all?

As we understand Bildad's speech, the issue is a different one: Up to this point he had given Iyov the benefit of the doubt. Perhaps, indeed, his sons had been wicked, and he is not to be blamed for their death. Let him just pray and he may expect his fortunes to be restored.

Now he turns to the alternative and invokes history to bear out his grim thesis. What if Iyov was really at fault? His earlier good fortune proves nothing about his personal integrity. Experience teaches us, our observations confirm, that not all success is self-sustaining. Much that once flowered in profusion and seeming strength, eventually dries up and leaves no mark. Many a fortress has proved to be no stronger than a spider's web. Iyov's losses are permanent — his good fortune was as much of a hypocrite as he. Both at one time displayed a smiling visage, in both is masked — bankruptcy.

It seems significant that Bildad spends just four verses (4-7) to describe what will happen if Iyov is in fact pure and upright, but requires twelve (8-19) to picture the realities of destruction which he will face if he is one of those who forget God and who are hypocrites. This imbalance alone would seem to indicate to which of the two options Bildad lends more credence.

This would place Bildad within the progression from compassionate (if slightly insensitive) understanding, to ultimately no-holds-barred criticism of Iyov, which marks the attitudes of the friends.

Nevertheless, it should be noted that in spite of the sheer weight of words on the side of the option which seeks to condemn Iyov, Bildad does end his speech on a conciliatory note (vs. 20-22). This would tend to stand as a corrective of the imbalance.

11-12. הֲיִגְאֶה־גֹּמֶא בְּלֹא בִצָּה יִשְׂגֶּא־אָחוּ בְלִי־מָיִם — *Can reeds flourish without a marsh, a meadow shoot up without water?* עֹדֶנּוּ בְאִבּוֹ לֹא יִקָּטֵף וְלִפְנֵי כָל־חָצִיר יִיבָשׁ — *As long as it is still fresh it will not be snapped, but, ahead of all herbage, it will dry out. Ramban* and *Rashi* part ways in the rendering and interpretation of this metaphor — and derive vastly different lessons from it.

Our translation follows *Rashi*, and we will explain the meaning below.

Herewith, *Ramban*: The ה in הֲיִגְאֶה is not to be understood as interrogative. It is to be rendered, *if*. Accordingly:

Reeds grown outside a marsh, or a meadow planted without sufficient water, would dry

יג־יד כֵּן אָרְחוֹת כָּל־שֹׁכְחֵי אֵל וְתִקְוַת חָנֵף תֹּאבֵד: אֲשֶׁר־יָקוֹט
טו כִּסְלוֹ וּבֵית עַכָּבִישׁ מִבְטַחוֹ: יִשָּׁעֵן עַל־בֵּיתוֹ וְלֹא יַעֲמֹד
טז יַחֲזִיק בּוֹ וְלֹא יָקוּם: רָטֹב הוּא לִפְנֵי־שָׁמֶשׁ וְעַל־גַּנָּתוֹ
יז יֹנַקְתּוֹ תֵצֵא: עַל־גַּל שָׁרָשָׁיו יְסֻבָּכוּ בֵּית אֲבָנִים יֶחֱזֶה:

out and die in the very earliest stages of their development, even if no human hand would pluck it.

We are offered a simple metaphor for the inevitable destruction of the wicked. As surely as plants which are denied their proper nourishment must die, so, inevitably, the wicked will be destroyed.

Rashi understands the second verse as follows: As long as they are moist and fresh the reeds are safe. But deny them water — and they shrivel up faster than any other plant.

[The function of the first verse is to provide the rationale for the point which the second one makes. Since reeds cannot grow without a swamp . . ., it follows clearly that once water is denied, they must die.]

The lesson is quite different from that of *Ramban*. To the extent that strength and resilience seem to promise longevity, they can be deceiving. Today, swift ruin may make short shrift of that which, but yesterday, seemed destined to last forever.

The next verses will draw the requisite conclusions.

13. כֵּן אָרְחוֹת כָּל־שֹׁכְחֵי אֵל וְתִקְוַת חָנֵף תֹּאבֵד — *Such are the paths of all those who forget God, the hope of the hypocrite is doomed.* The lesson from the forgoing metaphor is drawn. As *Ramban* understood it, it is that the wicked are destined to destruction.

As we have understood it, the message is more nuanced. The moment of truth must ultimately overtake those whose successes were not due to an inner strength, but to artificial infusions from without.

Is there a difference between *paths* and *hope*? Does *those who forget God* carry a different connotation to *hypocrite*? Can we fine-tune the lesson of the metaphor?

We note a perplexing structural oddity: The metaphor of the reeds is picked up once more in verses 16-18. Verses 13-15 interrupt by applying the lessons of verses 11-12 to the homes of the wicked.

Why should the drawing of lessons not wait until the entire metaphor is complete? Moreover, at the end of the second half of the metaphor, there seems to be no parallel to our verse — no drawing of conclusions, no deriving of lessons to be learned.

A careful reading of the two halves of the metaphor yields that each treats a different aspect of the debacle of the reeds. The first — of their premature death; the second — of the oblivion which follows.

Everyone must eventually die. If death strikes early, that is not in itself outside nature. But everyone has the hope, indeed the need, to leave a mark — to have mattered to someone, to have his significance acknowledged. To die and to leave no trace — that is unrelieved tragedy. No more terrible fate can await man than that his place, the framework within which he had lived and functioned, should, after his uprooting, call out: *I have never seen you!*

Here we have the ideas of *path* and *hope* of which our verse speaks.

A *path* is present reality, a *hope* looks into the future. At 7:6 Iyov had moaned: *My days fly faster than a weaver's shuttle, they end without any hope.* What *hope* had Iyov meant, in what way would his future be blighted? The meaning is obvious — Iyov's children were his "hope," their death destroyed his future. Not only had he been felled by his own agonies, but he had been robbed of the expectation that the meaning of his life would outlive his battered and debilitated self.

This aspect of Iyov's tragedy — the death of the children above all others — is what had engaged Bildad's attention, as we saw at verse 4.

We may now understand our verse, and with it the structure of the speech, as follows:

Iyov is faced with two tragedies: His own death-through-pain (see at 7:6 how, in his own eyes, he has already died), and the oblivion which follows as a result of the loss of his children. The one, as we have seen above, is sad but not unnatural, a *path* of sorrow; the other is unnatural, a blighted *hope*.

The first is to be expected for those who *forget God*. They live a life closed off from heaven, bearing no responsibility, no accountability, not caring at all. God responds by affirming their stance. He removes His providence and leaves them to the vagaries of fate. This, inevitably, becomes the *path* of sorrow along which they must drag out their lives.

But what are we to make of a life that ends without *hope*, without a future? There we deal not only with a sapping of vitality, but with an erosion of meaning. Nothing, not all the myri-

*13 Such are the paths of all those who forget God, the hope
of the hypocrite is doomed. 14 That in which he had placed
his faith will be cut away, that upon which he had relied
— a spider's web. 15 He may trust his house — but it will
not last; seek support in it — but it will not stand. 16 Before the
heat — it is moist, its tendrils spread out in its garden. 17 Its
roots take hold by a stream, it searches out a stone fortress.*

ads of projects which occupy man's time and effort, which infuse his being with feelings of self-respect and confidence, mean anything at all. All is lost. It was, after all, a sham — stick-figures without substance, form without essence, a hypocrisy.

To die without *hope* — that is the fate of the *chonef*!

We understand the structure of Bildad's presentation as follows:

The first half of the metaphor deals with premature death. It is the *path of all those who forget God*. The next two verses will illustrate the lesson.

The second half of the metaphor deals with the oblivion which can follow upon a seemingly useful life. It demonstrates that *the hope of the hypocrite is doomed*.

Because the two halves of the metaphor deal with totally different aspects of Iyov's tragedy, Bildad interrupts the presentation by first drawing conclusions from the first half. The lessons which the second half yields are self-evident — we have already been introduced to the death of the children in Bildad's thought at verse 4. The second part of our sentence, which anticipates the second half of the metaphor, requires no further elaboration.

14-15. אֲשֶׁר־יָקוֹט כִּסְלוֹ וּבֵית עַכָּבִישׁ מִבְטַחוֹ — *That in which he had placed his faith will be cut away, that upon which he had relied — a spider's web.* יִשָּׁעֵן עַל־בֵּיתוֹ וְלֹא יַעֲמֹד יַחֲזִיק בּוֹ וְלֹא יָקוּם — *He may trust his house — but it will not last; seek support in it — but it will not stand.* Verse 15, and the second half of verse 14 which introduces the spider's web as metaphor, make clear that the first phrase in verse 14, *that in which he had placed faith*, also refers to a home.

Thus, these two verses illustrate what are the experiences of one who *forgets God*. The house, which by its solidity and imperviousness to the threatening elements, had seemed to promise security and permanence, is seen to be no more than a mirage. Solidly reassuring beams turn out to be as vulnerable as the filaments of a spider's web. Lean on them, and they buckle; steady yourself against them, and they collapse.

We have seen above that Bildad, as Eliphaz before him, feels that it is in the children that the home is truly embodied.

Earlier, we equated children with the future — the assurance that one's existence can and will extend beyond death.

In Torah thought they also fulfill another function. When Ruth bore a son to Boaz, the women congratulated Naomi because God had granted her one *who will sustain her old age* (*Ruth* 4:15).

Children, then, are a support for their parents as these reach their old age, links in the ongoing chain of mutual dependence. Parents who are blessed with children have every right to look forward to their advanced years with equanimity. Their frailty will be borne on strong and willing shoulders. When the children are torn away, when the nest empties before its time — a home has disintegrated.

Look well, Bildad seems to be saying to Iyov, and see whether you do not recognize your own experiences in this description.

יָקוֹט, from קוט, which *Rashi* here understands as *to cut off*. See commentary 4:6 for כֶּסֶל, as *trust*. [There *Rashi* renders, *folly*.] עַכָּבִישׁ is elsewhere found only at *Isaiah* 59:5.

16-18. This second part of the metaphor climaxes with the words: *I have never seen you*! Its object is to describe the fate of a life lived in luxury [. . . *its tendrils spread out in its garden. Its roots take hold by a stream* . . .], strong and secure [. . . *it searches out a stone fortress*].

16. רָטֹב הוּא לִפְנֵי־שָׁמֶשׁ וְעַל־גַּנָּתוֹ יוֹנַקְתּוֹ תֵצֵא — *Before the heat — it is moist, its tendrils spread out in its garden.* Our translation follows *Rashi*, upon whose reading our entire perception of Bildad's speech is based. *Metzudos* understands the sense differently: It is moist *even* in the fierce heat of the sun.

The subject of the sentence seems to be the *reeds* and *meadow* of verse 11 (*Rashi*).

17. עַל־גַּל שָׁרָשָׁיו יְסֻבָּכוּ בֵּית אֲבָנִים יֶחֱזֶה — *Its roots take hold by a stream, it searches out a stone fortress. Rashi* is silent on גַּל, but we have rendered *stream* in accordance with *Metzudos*. This, since *Rashi* to *Shir HaShirim* 4:12 appears to agree. *Ramban* renders *a pile of stones*. It appears that he understands the phrase together

ח/ יח־יט אִם־יְבַלְּעֶנּוּ מִמְּקֹמוֹ וְכִחֶשׁ בּוֹ לֹא רְאִיתִיךָ: הֶן־הוּא
יח־כב כ מְשׂוֹשׂ דַּרְכּוֹ וּמֵעָפָר אַחֵר יִצְמָחוּ: הֶן־אֵל לֹא יִמְאַס־
כא תָּם וְלֹא־יַחֲזִיק בְּיַד־מְרֵעִים: עַד־יְמַלֵּה שְׂחוֹק פִּיךָ
כב וּשְׂפָתֶיךָ תְרוּעָה: שֹׂנְאֶיךָ יִלְבְּשׁוּ־בֹשֶׁת וְאֹהֶל רְשָׁעִים
ט/א־ב א־ב אֵינֶנּוּ: וַיַּעַן אִיּוֹב וַיֹּאמַר: אָמְנָם יָדַעְתִּי כִי־כֵן וּמַה־

with the next one, as a description of the strength of the tendrils. They can take hold around a pile of stones, can penetrate into a fortress.

סָבַךְ, *to take hold*. See also *Rashi* to *Sotah* 43b.

יֶחֱזֶה is not easy. חָזָה usually means *to see*, but it is difficult to understand how that fits into the context. *Rashi* suggests: It *sees* a well protected place and chooses it as a fortress. *Ramban* thinks that it *sees* the stone house when its mighty tendrils penetrate the walls.

As an alternative, *Metzudos* suggests *a boundary*. It stands close to a stone house, and that lends it beauty. See *Rashi* to *Isaiah* 28:15.

18. אִם־יְבַלְּעֶנּוּ מִמְּקֹמוֹ וְכִחֶשׁ בּוֹ לֹא רְאִיתִיךָ — *But, let him uproot it from its place, it will disavow it: I have never seen you*! *Rashi* believes that the subject is not given. If whoever uproots it does so . . .

Ramban believes that the subject is the *sun* of verse 16 — and this fits well with the meaning of that verse. There, it had been said that the plant is only moist so long as the sun does not come out to burn it. Our verse now describes what happens when the sun does appear.

Nothing, neither root nor branch, is left of it; it is as though it had never been. The falling [of the wicked person] is not like that of a righteous person, who may fall but will always rise again. This one will fall — and never rise (*Rashi*).

19. הֶן־הוּא מְשׂוֹשׂ דַּרְכּוֹ — *Such are his joyous ways*. Such is the happiness of the wicked. All his joys and successes have no future at all (*Rashi*).

וּמֵעָפָר אַחֵר יִצְמָחוּ — *From the earth, others will sprout*. *Other* people, who up to now had been trodden into the earth by the wicked person, will now flourish in his place (*Rashi*).

20. הֶן־אֵל לֹא יִמְאַס־תָּם וְלֹא־יַחֲזִיק בְּיַד־מְרֵעִים — *Surely God will not disdain those who are constant, will not support evildoers*. Bildad has now presented the two alternatives to Iyov — while indicating his own leanings by the disproportionate amount of space which he allows for the description of the fate of the truly wicked. Nevertheless, although he is more inclined to see Iyov at fault, he is not yet willing to condemn him out of hand. He ends his speech with the reassurance that if, after all, Iyov had all along been *constant* with God, he has nothing to fear.

It is extremely significant that Bildad chooses the *tam* as the example of him whom God will not disdain. As we pointed out at 1:1 (s.v. תָּם) and discussed in detail at 6:13, much of the tension of the book revolves around just this issue — is Iyov a *tam* or a *chonef*. Is he one who stands constantly and undeviatingly with his God, or is he an opportunist whose pieties were nothing more than the smug platitudes of a hypocrite who knew well on which side his bread was buttered. By using *chonef* as the paradigm of him who *has no hope* (v. 13), as opposed to the *tam* of our verse, Bildad is placing this tension into sharp relief.

Ramban says at *Numbers* 35:33: *Chanufah* is doing the opposite of what appearances would have led us to expect. Bildad cannot shake off the feeling that *appearances*, Iyov's original pietistic response to his losses, would have indicated a willingness to accept the ideas with which the friends sought to comfort him. That Iyov has now vehemently spurned all the ideas that have been offered him indicates, to Bildad's mind, that the original submissiveness was only a surface reaction. He fails to comprehend the very real difference between the instinctive grasping at deeply cherished verities which are given to the man of faith, and the subsequent need to engage the intellect under the constant pounding of realities, which seem to make a mockery of theoretical positions and tear not only the outer but also the inner person apart. In Bildad's mind, Iyov's belligerence runs counter to expectations and thus marks his original reaction as hypocrisy.

He is, however, still willing to consider Iyov's own interpretation — the great theme of his response in the next chapter — that on the contrary, his agonized grapplings for the truth are themselves the highest form of *temimus*. Accordingly he ends his speech with the concession that perhaps Iyov is right. Perhaps he really is a *tam*. If so, he ought not to worry. All should turn out well.

8/18-22 [18] *But, let him uproot it from its place, it will disavow it: I have*
never seen you! [19] *Such are his joyous ways; from the earth, others*
will sprout. [20] *Surely God will not disdain those who are constant,*
will not support evildoers. [21] *Shortly, He will fill your mouth with*
9 *laughter, your lips with shouts of joy.* [22] *Those who hate you will be*
1-2 *garbed in shame, the tent of the wicked — is no more.*

[1] *Iyov responded and said:* [2] *Truly, I know that it is so; but how*

Who are the *evildoers* in the second part of the verse?

If our understanding of the first phrase is correct — if it describes Iyov as he appears in his own eyes — then these *evildoers* are placed in contrast to him — those who wish him evil. This is also clear from the next two verses, in which verse 21 describes Iyov's vindication, and verse 22 talks of the troubles which will overtake *those who hate you.*

Iyov, then, has enemies who will be clothed in shame when he becomes vindicated

But who are these enemies? Iyov's problems are with his losses and his agonies; nowhere have we found people who wish him ill.

There appears to be only one possible solution. The *evildoers* and the *ones who hate him* are the three friends whose original loving concern has even now begun to turn into the implacable enmity which will become more and more apparent as the speeches wax ever harsher, ultimately to lose all sense of reality in the vituperation which they heap upon their erstwhile friend.

If you are right, Bildad is saying, then we are wrong — and will be made to pay for it.

Iyov himself had picked up this tragic change of heart in his speech at 6:13, had mused upon it in the metaphor of the faithless river and had finally given it expression in verse 27 there.

At 6:13 we noted that Iyov will, in the course of the book, accuse each of the friends of the very same *chanufah* of which they find him guilty. And so, the stage is set for the underlying dynamics of the confrontation. One or another of the two opposing views is false. One or another of the parties is guilty of the unforgivable — dishonesty before God. One or another of them will be punished severely.

In the event, Bildad's words proved to be prophetic. From 42:7ff. it is clear that had it not been for the sacrifices which the three friends brought and for Iyov's prayerful intercession in their behalf, they would indeed have been made to suffer.

21-22. עַד־יְמַלֵּה שְׂחוֹק פִּיךָ וּשְׂפָתֶיךָ תְרוּעָה — *Shortly, He will fill your mouth with laughter, your lips with shouts of joy.* שֹׂנְאֶיךָ יִלְבְּשׁוּ־בֹשֶׁת וְאֹהֶל רְשָׁעִים אֵינֶנּוּ — *Those who hate you will be garbed in shame, the tent of the wicked — is no more.* Verse 21 carries overtones of a victory to be won. שְׂחוֹק can be a *derisive* laugh (*Jeremiah* 20:7), and תְּרוּעָה is often *a shout of triumph over one's enemies* (*Jeremiah* 50:15).

Thus, these verses continue the prediction of a vindication. If indeed you are a *tam*, the time will come when you will be able to crow over those who would not have it so.

The *shame* which will cover *those who hate* Iyov, will derive from the fact that they will have been proven wrong. Their vaunted wisdom will not have protected them from making the most terrible misjudgment in the most basic of human obligations. Their most beloved friend — they did not know at all!

The *tent of the wicked* is clearly meant to stand in opposition to the *home — locus of your righteousness* of verse 6. Iyov's home — that which he had perceived as *locus of his righteousness* — had been destroyed through the death of his children (v. 4). When he will have been vindicated, when his home will have been restored, then that of his enemies will be destroyed.

IX.

◆§ Iyov's Response to Bildad's First Speech

Ramban isolates three separate points which Iyov makes in this, his third speech:

1. He is unable to detect any difference between the fate of the righteous and the wicked. Both, as time takes its course, are destroyed.
2. He demands a go-between who could mediate the claims he wishes to press against God. He can find no logic to his suffering. There can be no justification for punishing an innocent

ג יִצְדַּק אֱנוֹשׁ עִם־אֵל׃ אִם־יַחְפֹּץ לָרִיב עִמּוֹ לֹא־יַעֲנֶנּוּ

man — evil thoughts which inevitably passed through his mind ought not to be counted as sin, nor will the idea that he is being tested answer the issue. God, unlimited by human frailties, surely knows what is in Iyov's mind, and has neither the need to test Iyov nor the wish to demonstrate His might. These are claims which a go-between could take up with God.

3. He can find no real justification for making the wicked suffer. A fleeting life which will, inevitably, end in the darkness of the grave ought to be enough punishment for anyone. (See at 7:6-10.)

In our alternative analysis, Iyov indignantly rejects Bildad's assessment of his predicament. His deeply rooted conviction that he is the innocent victim of malevolent cruelty, coupled with the frustration caused by his absolute impotence in effecting a correction or even being granted a hearing, goads him to throw all caution and reverence to the winds. Sacrilege follows upon the heel of sacrilege, insults and taunts are hurled indiscriminately against God. In Iyov's vision, fatally flawed and distorted in the searing flames of his agony, God has been reduced to the dimension of a human antagonist — pernicious and despotic.

It is only at the end of the speech, when emotional exhaustion steps in to take the place of biting fury, that Iyov comes to himself and, almost one might say, in a whimper, repeats his wish that he might never have been born alive.

And then, totally unexpectedly, comes a ringing affirmation of the sweetness of life — and an entreaty that God spare him further pain so that his remaining time on earth, might be spent in tranquility, before he will be swallowed up into the darkness of the grave.

In this, Iyov's third speech, we find sentiments expressed and ideas promulgated which — if taken at their face value — can only be described as sacrilege at its most appalling. How could Iyov have dared — and how, if he did dare, could there ever be forgiveness!

Rashi and *Ramban* part ways radically in their interpretations. *Rashi*, as do the Sages in *Bava Basra* 16a, allows the text to speak for itself — let the chips fall where they may. Even within this approach there is room for softening the impact, and this *Rashi* opts to do in his commentary; although, as we shall see below, the *Amora* Rava, there, does not shy away from the very harshest alternative.

Ramban chooses to understand Iyov's arguments in a way which avoids the whole issue.

Ramban has Iyov going back once more to the ideas which he expressed in his earlier speech — see Prefatory Remarks to chapter 6. God is too exalted to care about man's fate, and as a result the righteous and the wicked suffer equally — there simply is no justice or fairness in the fate to which man is subject.

This approach affects the interpretation of almost every verse in this long speech, and the commentary will consistently draw attention to *Ramban's* reading.

Rashi clearly does not agree with *Ramban*. At every crucial point he interprets the text in such a way that a totally different picture emerges — a picture of an Iyov deeply enmeshed in perceptions of the Divine-human relationship.

At 7:8 we quoted the various criticisms of Iyov which the *Amora* Rava makes at *Bava Basra* 16a. Among them were: putting himself into one category with God (to 6:2), and the propagating of the idea that a slave might be in a position to upbraid his master (to 9:33). Both are a staggering diminishing of God's image to human dimensions.

What could have caused such error?

At 31:26-28 we have Iyov priding himself upon the fact that he never gave way to the lure of worshiping the sun and other heavenly bodies. In a footnote to 1:1 we advanced this as one of the indicators that Iyov lived in Patriarchal times, before the Torah was given, when such a boast would have been meaningful. Idol worship was the accepted form of religious expression. The perceptions of God upon which it was based were universally assumed (see *Rambam, Avodah Zarah* ch. 1), and therefore, certainly formative in Iyov's own thought-world.

Iyov's God was One to Whom human categories could be applied. Iyov had discovered Him, not through revelation but through speculation. Inevitably, He was subject to the limitations of human conceptualization. Iyov, in short, created a God in his own image.

This is the God Who is worshiped in the mode of, מַה כְּתִיב בָּהּ, *What is written in it?* Those who demand to understand His demands before they accept them wish, too, to understand their God. But that which the human mind seeks to grasp it can also distort. A deity created in man's image can become the grotesque caricature which Iyov's fevered mind ultimately produced.

It will only be at the end of the book, when God reveals Himself to Iyov in all His inscrutability, that this perverted vision of the Divine will finally be laid aside. We will see that, likely, this progression in theological sophistication is itself the underlying dynamic of the book. Iyov — and through him all the nations of the world to whom his prophecy is addressed (*Bava Basra* 15b, and see above at 1:1) — must, and will learn that there is a God, infinitely beyond human perception, beyond challenge and question, to be accepted and adored, but never to be understood.

At that point Iyov, freed from the crushing need to understand and to justify, will make peace with his fate; profoundly comforted not because he has been answered, but because, in the overwhelming light of this revelation, answers become irrelevant.

This, then, is to be the path leading to understanding for those who persist in asking מַה כְּתִיב בָּהּ. To them, too, God reveals Himself. True that He will not challenge them to sanctity. That was the call at Sinai, and it was directed to those whose נַעֲשֶׂה וְנִשְׁמַע typed them as a people of *Olam Haba*, for whom this world is no more than an antechamber. Rather, He will show Himself as the God of nature, will demonstrate that *The voice of God is in the force, the voice of God is in the form* (*Bieberfeld's* rendering of *Psalms* 29:4).[1]

Such a revelation comes hard. A world whose soul is shrouded by the forces of nature does not lightly or readily yield the secret of its vitality. It must be wrested from out of the darkness — and only a heroic and tenacious determination to find the truth, such as animated Iyov, will bring it about.

At that time, the primitive groping, which resulted in so much distortion, will have been vindicated as the indispensable steps towards revealed truth.

2. אָמְנָם יָדַעְתִּי כִי־כֵן וּמַה־יִּצְדַּק אֱנוֹשׁ עִם־אֵל — *Truly, I know that it is so; but how can man expect to best God? Rashi* is silent, thus permitting us to read our own interpretation to this introductory sentence.

But, first *Ramban*: I know well that God will destroy those who hate Him, and that He will doom the hopes of the hypocrite. But, granting all this, how can the righteous man expect to demonstrate his goodness, if God refuses to argue with him? When trouble overtakes [the righteous], God does not explain his fate, does not point to a transgression — does not, in fact, because of man's insignificance, bother with him at all.

At this point Iyov accepts the fact that God destroys the sinners. Iyov observes, though, that He will nevertheless not explain the troubles that overtake the righteous. Thus, the victim believes those troubles to be undeserved and therefore views them as acts of indefensible violence. If so, he must reason, the destruction of the wicked also comes to them gratuitously. All evidently share one fate. All — from the very beginning — are vanity.

In accordance with his understanding, that the central issue of Iyov's admission is the fact that God destroys the wicked, *Ramban* now reads the next section, up to verse 14, as an expansion upon that theme: The mountains of verse 5 are the fortresses within which the wicked would seek to find strength; the earth of verse 6 is the place within which they might have wished to seek refuge; the sun of verse 7 is the kingship of the vicious, which God can readily deny them; the planets mentioned in verse 8 are the astrological entities within which the power of the wicked is rooted; and the passage, as a whole, describes how surely they will be lost.

We feel that *Rashi* would disagree with *Ramban* for the following reasons: Firstly, *Rashi* takes the entire section as leading up to verse 14 in the sense of *kal vachomer* — If God has the power to do all this, then surely I have no chance to win an argument with Him. Thus he does not take this section, as does *Ramban*, to be a description of the destruction of the wicked.

Secondly, it is clear from *Ramban's* language in his first sentence [God *destroys* those who hate Him and *dooms* the *hypocrite*] that

1. And so, too, it is remarkable that when God finally appears to Iyov, it is from out of a raging whirlwind. At *I Kings* 19:11ff. Elijah had learned that God does not appear to the individual in *great and mighty winds that split mountains and shatter rocks*, nor yet in *earthquakes* nor in *fires*. He is to be discovered only in the *soft voice of silence*.

But that was for Elijah, great scion of a people who had partaken of Sinaitic revelation. To the people of מָה כְּתִיב בָּהּ, who must learn of the reality of God within nature, the whirlwind is the appropriate medium.

ד אַחַת מִנִּי־אָלֶף: חֲכַם לֵבָב וְאַמִּיץ כֹּחַ מִי־הִקְשָׁה אֵלָיו

he takes the first phrase of Iyov's response to refer back to verse 13 of Bildad's speech in chapter 8. [*Such are the paths* (they are destroyed or uprooted, see verse 12) *of those who forget God, (those who hate Him) the hope of the hypocrite is doomed.*] This picks just one point from Bildad's long speech — and that, not the main one.[1]

Why then would Iyov say simply: *I know that it is so,* without specifying which of Bildad's ideas he accepts.

It would seem that we should rather take Iyov's acceptance [*I know that it is so*] to refer to the totality of Bildad's speech.

Bildad had pointed out to Iyov that his experiences might be explained in one of two ways. His home might have been destroyed through no direct fault of his own — and will surely be restored to him if only he will turn his entreaty to God. Alternatively, he might be truly wicked — in which case he must resign himself to absolute destruction.

Iyov responds: Indeed I know that it is so. Doubtless my terrible experiences demanded of me that I confront my past, that I probe mercilessly to see whether perhaps there was not a deeply rooted cancer eating away at the seemingly blameless externals of my life. But what use is there in such a self-examination when, were I to assert my innocence, I could never hope for a fair hearing?

Here we have a significant departure from the suggestion which Bildad had made: Bildad, at 8:5, counseled prayer. If Iyov's sons had been sent away because of their own sins, such that their untimely death did not reflect badly upon Iyov, then all he had to do was to *supplicate God, entreat Shaddai.*[2]

Iyov indignantly turns aside that suggestion. If indeed he is innocent, he should not have to resort to prayer. He views himself as a litigant rather than as a supplicant, wishes to present a claim rather than to plead for mercy.[3]

This difference in approach may have its root in the contrasting views of the two men regarding the way Iyov had carried himself during the period of his trials. Bildad, as we have seen above, saw only the *chonef,* the hypocrite whose earlier pieties had been a sham. Iyov himself will say later, *for no hypocrite will come before Him.* Accordingly, Bildad can see hope only in submissive prayer. Even if he is innocent, Iyov has much ground to make up.

Iyov, on the other hand, who sees no contradiction between his earlier passivity and his present pugnaciousness — who, on the contrary, feels that his restless quest for truth against all convention is the only true *temimus* — feels that he has every right to come before God demanding rights rather than pleading for favors. In his own eyes he is a *yashar,* one who need have no fear of presenting his case before

1. This is so even in *Ramban's* own view: He explained that Bildad was offering a new explanation for Iyov's suffering — that it had a cleansing function designed to lessen Iyov's guilt. If so, the destruction of the wicked is peripheral to Bildad's thought.

2. This is another example of the essentially good advice which the friends had to offer. As the *Zohar* which we quoted at the beginning of Eliphaz's first speech teaches, it was not the ideas of the friends which should be faulted, but the insensitivity with which they presented them.

We may surmise that Bildad erred by blurring his urging to pray, with the vivid but deeply offensive description of what would befall Iyov if he was really wicked. Granted that Bildad was biased towards this interpretation of events — we showed that from the imbalance in the amount of space allowed the presentation of the two alternatives — but why not give prayer a chance? Why launch immediately into the graphic portrayal of impending tragedy?

By his eagerness to confront Iyov with a worst-case scenario, Bildad soured Iyov's attitude. The thoughtful, genuinely well-meant and excellent suggestion that Iyov might find surcease in prayer became lost in the welter of recriminations.

3. *Berachos* 17b, on the basis of *Isaiah* 46:12 which speaks of the *strong of heart, far removed from charity,* talks approvingly of righteous people who demand God's sustenance as a right and spurn His charity. Apparently, then, Iyov's attitude is not to be condemned out of hand. However, it is doubtful whether even these *strong of heart* would have couched their claims in terms of familiarity such as Iyov uses throughout this chapter [e.g. *There is no arbitrator between us who might lay his hands on us both*]. Iyov's demand for justice is inappropriate. It derives from a primitive and ultimately distorted view of God which places Him on an equal footing with himself — an aggrieved rival. No such sacrilege underlies the claims of the righteous. Fully aware of the true nature of God — to the extent that such awareness is possible for man — they also know, and know deeply, to what grandeur the truly righteous man can rise. The Rabbis are called kings (*Gittin* 61a) . . . ministering angels (*Nedarim* 20b). Men such as they may stand up straight before their God, confident in the rights which goodness and purity confer — because God Himself, as it were, looks with wonder on the truly great: See this creature which I have created, this being which I have formed! (*Bereishis Rabbah* 12).

he could not reply to one in a thousand. [4] *Wise of heart and mighty in power, who stubbornly opposed Him and remained sound?*

God (23:3ff. and especially v. 6, there.)

We have rendered וּמַה יִּצְדַּק אֱנוֹשׁ עִם אֵל, as *but how can man expect to best God?* Thus יִצְדַּק, in the sense of winning a case at court, as in *Deuteronomy* 25:1. We cannot exclude the possibility that Iyov chooses this particular formulation as a play on Eliphaz's rhetorical question, הַאֱנוֹשׁ מֵאֱלוֹהַּ יִצְדָּק, *Can mortals be deemed righteous before God* (4:17). Iyov may be using a play on words: I am less interested in being deemed a צַדִּיק, *righteous man*, by God, than in winning my case against Him.

3. אִם־יַחְפֹּץ לָרִיב עִמּוֹ לֹא־יַעֲנֶנּוּ אַחַת מִנִּי־אָלֶף — *If He would agree to wrangle with him, he could not reply to one in a thousand.* The use of pronouns in this sentence makes it difficult to determine the subjects of the respective predicates. Neither *Rashi* nor *Ramban* offer any interpretation of the verse.

Metzudos renders: If the righteous man would wish to wrangle with God concerning the denial of his just rewards, God would not answer even one question in a thousand.

We have chosen the opposite meaning for mainly contextual considerations: In the first place, our and the following verses all seem to lead up to verse 15 where Iyov bemoans the fact that even if he were proven to be right, he would still feel so overwhelmed by the sheer power of God's presence, that he would be, for all purposes, struck dumb.

The same fear is once more repeated at verse 32. It appears likely that our verse has the same meaning.

Again, only if we ascribe the meaning which we have suggested, is there a really smooth transition from the previous verse.

The earlier verse had said that it is impossible for a mortal to best God in a suit. This is simply a recognition of man's puny weakness in contrast to an all-mighty God. [Note the use of אֵל as God's name in this context. It is a name which denotes might.] This indeed is the theme of all the following verses in this section, which picture God's might as manifest in His total mastery over the titans of nature. In this context, nothing is said which would lead us to suppose that God would be unwilling to answer charges brought against Him. But if the sense of the verse is that man would be frightened into silence by the terror of a confrontation with God, then this follows directly from the previous thought.

4. חֲכַם לֵבָב וְאַמִּיץ כֹּחַ מִי־הִקְשָׁה אֵלָיו וַיִּשְׁלָם — *Wise of heart and mighty in power, who stubbornly opposed Him and remained sound? Wise of heart* in arguing a case, and *mighty in power,* to punish those who oppose Him (*Rashi*).

קשה in the *hiphil* form is almost always used transitively: *To harden a spirit* (*Deuteronomy* 2:30); or, *a yoke* (*I Kings* 12:4). We have it intransitively at *Exodus* 13:15, where the subject is Pharaoh's stubborn refusal in the face of God's constant demands to let the Israelites go. We assume a similar meaning here: Even if God were to consent to a confrontation, Iyov feels he could not win. A spirited defense would surely be construed as a stubborn refusal to bow before God's will. No one could come out sound (*Rashi*) from such an encounter.

5-13. We have noted above that *Rashi* and *Ramban* have widely divergent interpretations for this section. In *Ramban's* view, we have a series of metaphors for God's untrammeled power to subdue the wicked; in *Rashi's* view it is a description of God's mastery over nature, from which Iyov concludes that he has no chance at all to come out victoriously from a confrontation.

It is instructive to examine the type of examples from nature which Iyov marshals to demonstrate God's might. We might gainfully compare these, for example, with *Psalms* 104, where we have another (albeit much larger) listing of God's prowess. We are immediately struck by the contrast in tone. Where David sings of a caring God, who manifests His concern for His creatures in the infinitely wonderful, infinitely variegated panorama of the living world, Iyov's view is unrelievedly negative. The God Whom he describes is one of disharmony and chaos, One Who tears up mountains, sets the earth to trembling and darkens the sky — Who plays havoc with His own creation.

When God reveals Himself to Iyov from out of the whirlwind (chapter 38ff.), it is also as creator and sustainer; all-wise, all-powerful, and all-able; lord of a cosmos of such mind-boggling variety and complexity, that Iyov's mind must reel before such omnipotence. It is a description in the mode of the psalm — generous in scope, unsparing in the vivid images with which it paints the canvas of God's goodness — quite different from the parsimonious, single faceted (and that, negative) listing which Iyov uses here.

Surely Iyov, too, knew that there are other, more positive, facets to God's stewardship over

ה וַיַּשְׁלֵם: הַמַּעְתִּיק הָרִים וְלֹא יָדָעוּ אֲשֶׁר הֲפָכָם בְּאַפּוֹ:
ו־ז הַמַּרְגִּיז אֶרֶץ מִמְּקוֹמָהּ וְעַמּוּדֶיהָ יִתְפַּלָּצוּן: הָאֹמֵר
ח לַחֶרֶס וְלֹא יִזְרָח וּבְעַד כּוֹכָבִים יַחְתֹּם: נֹטֶה שָׁמַיִם
ט לְבַדּוֹ וְדוֹרֵךְ עַל־בָּמֳתֵי יָם: עֹשֶׂה־עָשׁ כְּסִיל וְכִימָה
י וְחַדְרֵי תֵמָן: עֹשֶׂה גְדֹלוֹת עַד־אֵין חֵקֶר וְנִפְלָאוֹת
יא עַד־אֵין מִסְפָּר: הֵן יַעֲבֹר עָלַי וְלֹא אֶרְאֶה וְיַחֲלֹף
יב וְלֹא־אָבִין לוֹ: הֵן יַחְתֹּף מִי יְשִׁיבֶנּוּ מִי־יֹאמַר אֵלָיו
יג מַה־תַּעֲשֶׂה: אֱלוֹהַּ לֹא־יָשִׁיב אַפּוֹ תַּחְתָּו שָׁחֲחוּ
יד עֹזְרֵי רָהַב: אַף כִּי־אָנֹכִי אֶעֱנֶנּוּ אֶבְחֲרָה דְבָרַי עִמּוֹ:

nature. [See his response to Bildad's third speech at chapter 26.] At this point, the bitterness of his spirit did not permit him to dwell upon them. It will take the exultation born of direct revelation from God to restore a sense of balance.

5. הַמַּעְתִּיק הָרִים וְלֹא יָדָעוּ אֲשֶׁר הֲפָכָם בְּאַפּוֹ — *He uproots mountains — they know not, upturning them in His fury.* In *Ramban's* view, these are the mountain strongholds in which the wicked sought to protect themselves.

In *Rashi's* view, this is an example of God's untrammeled power. Mountains are frequently seen as symbols of almost eternal fastness and security — the *titans upon whom the earth was built* (*Micah* 6:2). That God can uproot them at will — and with such effortless speed that they never know from where this terror overtakes them — is evidence of God's might.

Isaiah, too, talks of God destroying mountains (*Isaiah* 42:15). But, what a difference! There these mountains symbolize the power of the wicked whom God will eliminate in order to make room for His people:

> I will burn up the mountains and the hillocks, cause all their vegetation to wither. I will turn rivers into islets, dry up the swamps. Thus will I lead the blind along roads they never knew, I will take them by paths that are strange to them. Before them I shall turn darkness to light, straighten out all that is crooked . . .

The difference in perception lies in the attitude. At this moment, Iyov is in no mood to see anything beyond the immediate destruction.

6. הַמַּרְגִּיז אֶרֶץ מִמְּקוֹמָהּ וְעַמּוּדֶיהָ יִתְפַּלָּצוּן — *He agitates the earth to move from its place, so that its very pillars quiver.* God moves the earth around at will so that the mighty have no place to which to flee (*Ramban*).

As *Rashi* understands it, this is one other example of God's might. Again, it is not dissimilar to other Scriptural passages (such as, in this case, *Psalms* 18:8ff.) but, once more, there is a difference in thrust. There, David sees God as unleashing His fury against the wicked, so that His servant might be saved. Here Iyov just sees violence.

7. הָאֹמֵר לַחֶרֶס וְלֹא יִזְרָח וּבְעַד כּוֹכָבִים יַחְתֹּם — *He orders the sun — and it does not shine, He seals off the stars.* חֶרֶס, as, *sun*, occurs in Scripture. See, for example, *Judges* 14:18.

Ramban interprets: The darkening of the sun is a metaphor for the downfall of one kingdom and the rise of another. The sealing of the stars implies the frustration of the plans laid by those who seek guidance from the heavenly constellations. Thus, our verse describes the downfall of the kings and their counselors.

In *Rashi's* view, we have another example of God's might. The darkening of the sun at midday [presumably through an eclipse], a time at which we would expect it to shine in all its power, occurs frequently in Scripture. See, for example, *Isaiah* 13:10 and 59:10. See also above at 5:14.

8. נֹטֶה שָׁמַיִם לְבַדּוֹ וְדוֹרֵךְ עַל־בָּמֳתֵי יָם — *On His own He spreads out the heavens, tramples upon the crests of the sea.* *Ramban* writes: He is able to do as He wishes with the sun and the stars (previous verse) because He alone spreads out the heavens. (This is how *Ramban* would render נֹטֶה, see below.) Also, He treads upon the heights of the sea, that is, the crests of the waves, thereby quieting the stormy waters.

As a description of God's might (*Rashi*), the verse seems out of character if we render נֹטֶה as *to spread out*, and understand it to be a metaphor for the creation of the sky. In a listing of apparently malevolent acts, such a statement of God's benign prowess seems inappropriate. Nevertheless, this is how *Rashi* understands it here.

We may suggest an alternative. In *Psalm* 18

[5] He uproots mountains — they know not, upturning them in His
fury. [6] He agitates the earth to move from its place, so that its very
pillars quiver. [7] He orders the sun — and it does not shine, He seals
off the stars. [8] On His own He spreads out the heavens, tramples
upon the crests of the sea. [9] He sets up Osh, K'sil and Chimah,
and the chambers of the south. [10] He performs great deeds beyond
ken, wonders beyond numbering. [11] He could pass me by and I
would not see, glide by and I would not notice Him. [12] He smites
suddenly — who can hold Him back, who can challenge Him:
'What are You doing?' [13] God will never call back His fury, those
who arrogantly seek to help are prostrate beneath Him. [14] Could I
then possibly respond to Him, choose words to argue with Him?

which we quoted above, we have a very similar sentence in a parallel context. Verse 8 there describes God roiling up the earth and causing its pillars to tremble; verse 9 pictures smoke rising up in His nostrils, fire billowing from His mouth, and burning coals smoldering within Him. Verse 10 then goes on: וַיֵּט [from נטה] שָׁמַיִם וַיֵּרַד, *He inclined the heavens and descended upon them. Rashi* explains this to mean that it was as though God had inclined the heavens downward so as to descend upon them in order to inflict the punishments which are described in that passage. It seems possible to assign the same meaning here. God inclines the heavens so that He might descend by them in order to trample the crescending waves.

9. עֹשֶׂה־עָשׁ כְּסִיל וְכִימָה וְחַדְרֵי תֵמָן — *He sets up Osh, K'sil and Chimah, and the chambers of the south.* These are the signs of the zodiac under which the mighty evildoers function. Since God masters these constellations, he is able to exercise control over the wicked (*Ramban*).

The *chambers of the south* are the rooms in which the storms are kept (*Rashi*). Compare 37:9 and *Zechariah* 9:14.

10. עֹשֶׂה גְדֹלוֹת עַד־אֵין חֵקֶר וְנִפְלָאוֹת עַד־אֵין מִסְפָּר — *He performs great deeds beyond ken, wonders beyond numbering.* This is an exact repetition of Eliphaz's cry of wonder at 5:9. It seems quite certain that Iyov is quoting his antagonist. Yes, he seems to be saying, indeed God does all kinds of wonderful things — all destructively!

11. הֵן יַעֲבֹר עָלַי וְלֹא אֶרְאֶה וְיַחֲלֹף וְלֹא־אָבִין לוֹ — *He could pass me by and I would not see, glide by and I would not notice Him.* He can do whatever He wants, never visible by the human eye (*Rashi*). It is quite impossible to take precautions against Him (*Ramban*).

12. הֵן יַחְתֹּף מִי יְשִׁיבֶנּוּ מִי־יֹאמַר אֵלָיו מַה־תַּעֲשֶׂה — *He smites suddenly — who can hold Him back, who can challenge Him: 'What are You doing?'* Thus *Rashi. Ramban* renders: He can rob suddenly [יַחְתֹּף is the same as יַחְטֹף, the *ches* and *tes* being interchangeable], and who can make Him return that which He has taken.

13. אֱלוֹהַּ לֹא־יָשִׁיב אַפּוֹ תַּחְתָּו שָׁחֲחוּ עֹזְרֵי רָהַב — *God will never call back His fury, those who arrogantly seek to help are prostrate beneath Him.* No human agency will ever force God to withdraw His anger (*Rashi*). The rest of the translation follows *Rashi. Ramban* renders: . . . *those who seek to help the arrogant.*

Up to this point Iyov has shown that the wicked are powerless before God. Now he once more takes up his own concerns (*Ramban*). *Rashi* would say that up to this point Iyov has demonstrated God's untrammeled might, and from this Iyov will now draw the conclusion that he can hope for little in a direct confrontation. The all-powerful presence of God would surely overwhelm him.

14. אַף כִּי־אָנֹכִי אֶעֱנֶנּוּ אֶבְחֲרָה דְבָרַי עִמּוֹ — *Could I then possibly respond to Him, choose words to argue with Him?* See the commentary to verses 2 and 3. Iyov draws the obvious conclusion from the picture which he has drawn of God's might. A God to Whom the titans of nature are mere playthings, is not likely to be impressed by the importuning of one such as he.

A careful analysis of the passage, beginning with our verse and ending with verse 20, yields an unexpected structure. Verses 19 and 20 seem a clear continuation from verse 16 — they too deal with Iyov's despairing of ever achieving a true "man to man" confrontation with God — with verses 17 and 18, which describe the terrible sufferings which Iyov has

טו־טז אֲשֶׁר אִם־צָדַקְתִּי לֹא אֶעֱנֶה לִמְשֹׁפְטִי אֶתְחַנָּן: אִם־
יז קָרָאתִי וַיַּעֲנֵנִי לֹא־אַאֲמִין כִּי־יַאֲזִין קוֹלִי: אֲשֶׁר־

had to undergo at God's hands, interrupting the smooth flow. (See Chart p. 107)

Why does Iyov allow his thoughts to veer away from the subject at hand?

The impression gained is that while both sections 14-16 and 19-20 deal with Iyov's frustrations as a potential litigant, they deal with different aspects of the same problem.

We can recognize this on the basis of a marked similarity between verses 15 and 20.

15. אֲשֶׁר אִם־צָדַקְתִּי לֹא אֶעֱנֶה לִמְשֹׁפְטִי אֶתְחַנָּן *Even if I were right, I could never assert it, could I entreat Him Who judges me?*	20. אִם־אֶצְדָּק פִּי יַרְשִׁיעֵנִי תָּם־אָנִי וַיַּעְקְשֵׁנִי *Even if I were in the right — my mouth would pronounce me guilty, if I were innocent, it would proclaim me* crooked.

There is another similarity in expression which we must not overlook. Verse 4 had described God as אַמִּיץ, *mighty in power,* and this identical word is used once more in verse 19: *Is it to be brawn? — See, He is the stronger* (אַמִּיץ).

We understand the structure of the entire passage as follows:

We have seen earlier that verse 14ff. states the conclusion to be drawn from the earlier passage, which in itself is the proof which Iyov offers for the assertion made in verse 4: God is so *wise of heart and mighty in power,* that no one *stubbornly opposed Him and remained sound.* Examples of this untrammeled might are then drawn from nature. At verse 14 the argument is complete: Iyov can see no hope that a confrontation might prove beneficial to him.

This thought is further developed in verse 15: Even if Iyov were in the right, he is lost. He would be afraid to assert his innocence or even to ask for mercy from his tormentor. God has shown Himself to be an implacable opponent (see 6:4) and, when such an opponent is also all-mighty, then indeed all is lost. Iyov is so convinced of God's overbearing and purposeful savagery that he would deny his very senses: Even if God were to answer him, he would be unable to bring himself to believe that he would have a hearing.[1]

1. We have used strong — indeed sacrilegious — expressions in describing Iyov's perception of God in the context of this passage. We have done this in order to establish an ambience within which the shocking calumnies of verses 22-24 could find some justification.

Still, some explanation is necessary. How can we square an Iyov, capable of the exquisite adoration expressed in verses like 1:21 or 13:15, with the vicious deiphobe who emerges from this speech?

There is an illuminating passage in *Yerushalmi, Sotah* 5:5, which can help us understand.

The *Mishnah* there discusses the question of whether Iyov served God out of love or out of fear. Various verses are adduced to illustrate the respective opinions.

In the *Gemara* there the following lesson is taught: . . . Serve God out of love, and serve Him also out of fear. Serve Him out of love — for, should you feel inclined to hate, you will remember that you love. Serve Him also out of fear — for, should you be inclined to strike out at Him — he that fears does not strike out.

Clearly, the *Yerushalmi* believes that fear can easily degenerate into hatred. Fear demands, fear threatens, and, ultimately fear crushes. Only when tempered by love — the healing balm which smooths rough edges, blunts sharp and hurtful thrusts and suffuses the harshest experience with healing, energizing light and warmth — can fear be sublimated to find its place, in healthy proportion, within the totality of man's relationship to God.

Did Iyov serve out of a love of God, or was he animated only by dull, stultifying fear? The *Tannaim,* as we saw above, dispute the point. Surely we may assume that *these and those are the words of the living God.* (See footnote to 2:3 where we confirm this from *Ramban.*) No man, and certainly none who are exposed to the roiling experiences to which Iyov was subject, maintains one, steady, unvarying relationship with God. All, in the words of one contemporary Mussar teacher, experience *Days of Love* and *Days of Hatred* (see *R' Shlomo Wolbe's, Alei Shas,* Part I, Section I, Chapter V).

Thus, we should not be surprised to find conflicting nuances within the many speeches which Iyov makes. Certainly, even in his travail, there will be times in which the light of love breaks through to cast its healing rays upon the shadows of his despondency. We must expect, though, that at other times and in other passages, his frustrations block out any but the soberest awareness of his terrible vulnerability. Then fear preponderates and, as it does in our passage, brings hatred in its wake.

Certainly, this was a serious failing on Iyov's part. As *Pesikta Rabbasi,* quoted at 1:1, teaches: Had Iyov not given way to his frustrations and instead accepted God's judgment in total humility, then in our prayers we would not only have spoken of the God of Abraham, Isaac and Jacob, but also of the God of Iyov.

15 Even if I were right, I could never assert it, could I entreat Him
who judges me? 16 Even were I to call and He would answer me, I
could not believe that He would listen to my voice. 17 For He has

In the next two verses, Iyov defends his cynicism. Is he himself not the uprooted mountain, the trembling earth, the eclipsed sun? What in his experience would encourage him to think otherwise — in spite of everything, to hope. God has smashed him without mercy — why should Iyov suppose that he could ever achieve redress?

The first part of verse 19 now sums up this section. *Is it to be brawn? — See, He is the stronger.* Iyov has every justification to be afraid. But, what of the other aspect of Godliness of which verse 4 had spoken. God is mighty — but He is also *wise of heart.* Would God's wisdom not leave some room for hope?

It is to this that the second half of verse 19 turns. What of the God of the wise and understanding heart? Can Iyov not pin his expectations on such a God?

But this, too, leaves Iyov unhelped and uncomforted. The benign God of wisdom is almost harder to face than the God of power. It is so easy for puny man to be overwhelmed in the presence of such awful majesty. Suddenly he wants nothing so much as to lose himself in that bright light, to render himself up in a total, all-encompassing giving — even of his integrity. Let his lips shriek 'Guilty, guilty,' even though the heart feels that there is no guilt — it is, he feels, a small enough price to pay.

But Iyov knows that he is not willing to pay it. He has lost all — except his determination to spurn the easy path of capitulation.

Impaled upon the horns of this dilemma, knowing that he can gain nothing except by losing all — Iyov turns to the bitter denunciations of the next passage.

15. אֲשֶׁר אִם־צָדַקְתִּי לֹא אֶעֱנֶה לִמְשֹׁפְטִי אֶתְחַנָּן — *Even if I were right, I could never assert it, could I entreat Him who judges me?* As we explained above, Iyov is here bemoaning his impotence in the face of God's overwhelming power. He is simply afraid [not overwhelmed by God's grandeur as in verse 20] to assert himself.

It is not easy to pin down the precise meaning of the second phrase. *Rashi* and *Ramban* are silent, and so we have translated as does *Metzudos*, although we cannot use his interpretation. He assumes that Iyov is still asserting that his fate lies in the hands of the constellations, and accordingly understands as follows: I cannot turn with my entreaties to Him Who judges me, since my fate is decided by the uncaring and inaccessible heavenly spheres.

The commentary, however, following *Ramban,* has assumed that Iyov already rejected this idea at 6:3. He would not be reverting to it here.

Perhaps the term מְשֹׁפְטִי should be taken, not as one who judges (in the sense of deciding a controversy), but as one who executes punishment and suffering (as in *Ezekiel* 7:3 and many other places). The sense would then be: It is useless to expect that one who punishes me so severely would listen to my entreaties. Thus, both avenues which would normally be open to an innocent man asserting his rights or begging for consideration are closed to Iyov.

An alternative translation would take the לֹא of the first phrase and read it into the second one, too: . . . *could never assert it, could never entreat Him Who judges [punishes] me.*

16. אִם־קָרָאתִי וַיַּעֲנֵנִי לֹא־אַאֲמִין כִּי־יַאֲזִין קוֹלִי — *Even were I to call and He would answer me, I could not believe that He would listen to my voice.* Iyov has reached such a state of depression that he could even believe that his own senses are deceiving him. If God were to answer, Iyov would not trust his ears.

Ramban detects a theological stance in this verse, which will influence much of what Iyov has to say throughout his long speech. Iyov cannot believe that God would answer his entreaties, because he does not accept that Divine Providence extends to the individual. In the next few verses, he observes that disasters strike the righteous as much as they do the wicked, leading him to conclude that the individual cannot hope for fair treatment at God's hands.

17. אֲשֶׁר־בִּשְׂעָרָה יְשׁוּפֵנִי וְהִרְבָּה פְצָעַי חִנָּם — *For He has shattered me in a tempest, multiplied my wounds for no good reason. Ramban*, as we have seen in the previous verse, understands this as an assertion that God's providence does not extend to the individual. If a storm were to come, Iyov claims, he, the righteous man, would be crushed the same as his wicked neighbors. The furious — and blind — hurricane will tear the fruits off the tree as surely as it strips off the leaves!

From *Rashi* at 38:1, we suspect that he understands the verse as we have done. There, God appears to Iyov from out of a *whirlwind*, bringing the story to its dramatic climax.

יח בִּשְׂעָרָה יְשׁוּפֵנִי וְהִרְבָּה פְצָעַי חִנָּם׃ לֹא־יִתְּנֵנִי הָשֵׁב רוּחִי
יט כִּי יַשְׂבִּעַנִי מַמְּרֹרִים׃ אִם־לְכֹחַ אַמִּיץ הִנֵּה וְאִם־לְמִשְׁפָּט
כ מִי יוֹעִידֵנִי׃ אִם־אֶצְדָּק פִּי יַרְשִׁיעֵנִי תָּם־אָנִי וַיַּעְקְשֵׁנִי׃
כא־כב תָּם־אָנִי לֹא־אֵדַע נַפְשִׁי אֶמְאַס חַיָּי׃ אַחַת הִיא עַל־כֵּן

Rashi, based on the midrash, writes: From the very whirlwind which you used to calumniate Me (our verse), I will answer you!

From the association which the Sages see here, it seems likely that they think of the whirlwind in our verse as being a metaphor for all the terrible troubles which had overtaken Iyov. His life had been laid waste as by the brutal, non-discriminating savagery of a hurricane. At 38:1, God reveals to him that the very storm which he had seen as his nemesis was in truth the source of his salvation. The ecstasy of basking in God's revelation would never have been his if he had not first gone through the purgatory of his agonies. (See there, and at Introductory Remarks to chapter 29, for a development of this theme.)

The phrase, *You multiplied my wounds for no good reason*, is highly significant in this context. We recall that at 2:3, God had used the same expression in His rebuke to Satan, *You have incited Me for no good reason*. In the commentary to that verse we cited *Ramban* who notes that the suffering to which Iyov was exposed was *for no good reason* only at the level of surface appearances. In fact, his agonies had a salutary effect in that by reacting to them correctly, and ultimately being rewarded by a vision of God, he raised his level of service from fear to love (see there).

Thus, when *for no good reason* is used here, we are meant to understand it with bitter irony: Indeed my suffering has been totally useless. Mired as I am now in the hatred engendered by fear of God untempered by love for Him, it has served only to drag me downward.

יְשׁוּפֵנִי is derived from שָׁפִי, *to grind down*. See *Rashi* to *Genesis* 3:15.

18. לֹא־יִתְּנֵנִי הָשֵׁב רוּחִי כִּי יַשְׂבִּעַנִי מַמְּרֹרִים — *He will not suffer me to catch my breath, for He gluts me with bitterness*. The rendering, *catch my breath*, accords with *Ramban* and *Metzudos*. The idea of the verse is clear enough; buffeted and crushed by the virulence of the tempest which God has unleashed against him, Iyov cannot find even a moment's relief. Bitterness fills every nook and cranny of his being, and he cannot forget it even for a moment.

Rashi is silent and leaves room for the following conjecture. The combination of שוב [in the *hiphil*] and רוּחַ occurs only once more in Scripture — in Eliphaz's second speech at 15:13. There, it parallels *speak* [*wind*] — *words from your mouth*], and thus, according to all the commentators, means to *fling one's innermost thoughts* at someone. This would be a singularly felicitous meaning in our context. I know, says Iyov, that God will never give me the chance to share my thoughts with Him. He makes His attitude to me clear by glutting me with bitterness.

19. אִם־לְכֹחַ אַמִּיץ הִנֵּה וְאִם־לְמִשְׁפָּט מִי יוֹעִידֵנִי — *Is it to be brawn? — See, He is the stronger, if, due process, who will set a time for it?* The translation follows *Rashi*. In which arena, Iyov asks, am I to do battle with God? If it is to be a test of strength, I have already demonstrated [this is the implication of הִנֵּה, *See*!] that I have no chance. Everything I have said until now makes it abundantly clear that God is immeasurably stronger.

Yet — a wistful and fleeting dream — perhaps, after all, there might be some justice. God is not only the *mighty in power*, but also the *wise of heart*. Would He meet me in court?

But this too, Iyov knows for sure, is only an illusion. *Who will set a time for it?* Who will fix a time for such a confrontation [יוֹעִידֵנִי, from יָעַד, *to appoint a time*] which will be meaningful for me? I could, indeed, come to the trial, but the avowal of my innocence would die within my throat. Blameless though I am, I would pronounce my own guilt. I simply cannot face the grandeur of the all-wise God.

20. אִם־אֶצְדָּק פִּי יַרְשִׁיעֵנִי תָּם־אָנִי וַיַּעְקְשֵׁנִי — *Even if I were in the right — my mouth would pronounce me guilty, if I were innocent, it would proclaim me, crooked*. The translation follows *Rashi*, who takes the subject of וַיַּעְקְשֵׁנִי as פִּי, *my mouth*, of the earlier phrase. In this context תָּם parallels אֶצְדָּק and should thus be rendered *innocent* (as in *Psalms* 19:14), rather than as *unquestioning integrity*, as we have taken it in the rest of the book. See next verse.

However, *Metzudos* takes the subject of וַיַּעְקְשֵׁנִי as God. Iyov accuses God of bringing out the worst in him by exposing him to undeserved suffering. See further, below, at verses 30-31.

21. תָּם־אָנִי לֹא־אֵדַע נַפְשִׁי אֶמְאַס חַיָּי — *I am constant but at a loss how to find rest, I am*

shattered me in a tempest, multiplied my wounds for no good rea-
son. 18 *He will not suffer me to catch my breath, for He gluts me with*
bitterness. 19 *Is it to be brawn? — See, He is the stronger, if, due pro-*
cess, who will set a time for it? 20 *Even if I were in the right — my*
mouth would pronounce me guilty, if I were innocent, it would pro-
claim me, crooked. 21 *I am constant, but at a loss how to find rest,*
I am disgusted with my life. 22 *There is a thing — because of which*

disgusted with my life. The proclamation, *I am constant*, echoes the ending of the previous verse. There, the same phrase had paralleled, *I am in the right*, and thus had meant, *I am innocent*. But having used the term, Iyov recalls its more fundamental meaning in relation to his problems. With firm determination, Iyov rejects the idea propagated by the friends, that his belligerent questioning makes him a *chonef* (hypocrite), the very opposite of a *tam*.

Notwithstanding appearances, *I am a tam*! The very constancy of my devotion to God entitles me — nay, forces me — to question. (See commentary to 6:13 for a wide-ranging discussion of this issue.)

The second phrase is translated in accordance with *Rashi*, who equates נַפְשִׁי with נוֹפֵשׁ, *rest*. The word נוֹפֵשׁ does not occur in Scripture. *Rashi* at *Exodus* 31:17 makes clear that the concepts of *soul* and *resting* are closely related [much as the English idiom, *to come to oneself*]; and thus, his rendering here falls well within the range of the possible.

However, it is difficult to see a really compelling thought-development between the first and second phrases. How does the proclamation that Iyov is a *tam*, lead to his bemoaning his inability to find rest? We must assume that it provides the ground for his anguished question: Why, since I am constant, do I suffer so much?

There seems to be another possibility: The combination of ידע נפש, *to know a soul*, occurs in two other places. *Exodus* 23:9 uses the expression to demand from us an understanding of the גֵּר, *the stranger*, whose *soul we know* from our experiences in Egypt; and *Proverbs* 12:10 describes the righteous man who *knows the soul* [nature] of his animal and, thus, understands precisely what it needs.

The idiom, then, implies an intimate knowledge and understanding of the nature of man or beast.

Taken thus, the phrase would mean: I do not recognize myself. I am a *tam*, totally devoted to God. What, then, is it that makes me so rebellious and angry?

Iyov knows the thoughts that are roiling inside him — the resentment which, in the next few verses will boil over into such appalling calumnies. Iyov wonders how this could have happened to him. He is horrified at his attitude, looks with loathing upon a life which has come to this.

22-24. אַחַת הִיא עַל־כֵּן אָמַרְתִּי תָּם וְרָשָׁע הוּא מְכַלֶּה — *There is a thing — because of which I said: 'He destroys the constant with the wicked!'* אִם־שׁוֹט יָמִית פִּתְאֹם לְמַסַּת נְקִיִּם יִלְעָג — *When Satan goes for the sudden kill — he mocks the rotting of the innocent.* אֶרֶץ נִתְּנָה בְיַד־רָשָׁע פְּנֵי־שֹׁפְטֶיהָ יְכַסֶּה אִם־לֹא אֵפוֹא מִי־הוּא — *The land is in the hands of the wicked one, he sheaths the faces of its judges. If not, then who is it?* Much of our understanding of the book of *Iyov* hinges upon a correct understanding of this astounding passage. We must submit it to careful analysis.

At the outset, it should be noted that *Rashi*, at 40:5, has Iyov regretting what he said in verse 22, the introductory verse to this passage. He undertakes never to repeat such thoughts.

Evidently, then, this passage brings Iyov to the brink of the unthinkable.

We have translated the passage in accordance with *Rashi*. However, it lends itself to at least four interpretations, each of which we must consider. We shall see below that *Rashi's* assertion (at 40:5), that Iyov regrets having said what he said here, probably assumes a different translation than the one he offers here.

The most innocuous one is suggested by *Daas Mikra*. At 8:20 Bildad had maintained that: *Surely God will not disdain those who are constant, will not support evildoers*. The assumption is that the righteous will not be *disdained*, will not be made to suffer. Iyov refutes this assertion, in accordance with the well-known dictum that once the destroyer has been set loose, he makes no distinction between the righteous and the wicked (*Mechilta* 11, quoted by *Rashi* to *Exodus* 12:22). Iyov illustrates this from both the natural and the social spheres. A raging storm (v. 23) smashes everything in its path, and a wicked ruler can do as he wishes by undermining the judicial system in his realm (v. 24).[1]

Rambam and *Ramban* start out from the same premise, but interpret the individual verses in marginally different ways.

Both believe that verse 21 makes the statement that there is no essential difference between the fate that befalls the righteous and that which is the lot of the wicked man. This, because God is so exalted that He is indifferent to man's fate. We recall that in *Ramban's* view, this was already said in verses 16-17.

According to *Ramban* the two following verses have this to say: It can be shown that God is elevated beyond caring for man's fate. For, if we were to say that what happens comes about because God wills it, then it would be He Who sets out on a rampage of sudden death, He Who mocks the destruction of the innocent (v. 23). He would then have to be described as a wicked king who wreaks his will by emasculating the judicial system in his realm (v. 24). Manifestly, this latter option is more denigrating of God than the first. Much better to say that God is not involved.

By reading the latter two verses as he does, *Ramban* avoids the need to have verses 23 and 24 actually describing God. They say only what would have been had the premise laid down in verse 22 not been true.

Rambam, Moreh Nevuchim 3:23, goes one step further. Verse 23 describes God as being seemingly indifferent to man's fate. He looks disparagingly (יְזַלְזֵל, in Kapach's rendering) upon the woes of the innocent.

Rambam gives no interpretation for the all-important verse 24.

Although *Rambam* goes further than *Ramban* in that he has verse 23 actually describing God, he avoids interpreting the verse in such a way that God is perceived as inflicting the suffering callously upon an innocent victim.[2]

Here we are at the very crux of the issue of how the book of *Iyov* is to be understood. Is it to be viewed as a debate between the various protagonists concerning the problems of suffering, reward and punishment, God's providence and the like; or is it an existential account of one human being grappling, not always successfully, with his own private hell, interacting as best he can with the importunings of an obtuse wife and well meaning but blundering friends, all the while struggling to maintain the integrity which alone can be his anchorage.

As we have pointed out in *Introduction to the Iyov Commentary*, we perceive this issue as dividing *Rashi* from the other classical commentators.

In an existential struggle, which purports to portray no single theological stance, but just the reality of one man's purgatory, we need expect no single, consistent line of argument or thought. Indeed we will expect wild fluctuations of demeanor, from the deepest depression to the highest exultation — all true, none absolute. We will not be shocked to hear Iyov blaspheme (as he does in our passage as Rava sees it). There is no other word for it; it is a blasphemy of desperation, robbed of its sharpness by the fact that the same man, occasionally within the same speech, will feel and express the highest, most moving flights of love. It is not — cannot be — the evil, hating and destructive blasphemy which the Satan had hoped to elicit.

In short, we need not fear even the most preposterous ideas, since, as Rava himself (*Bava Basra* 16b) teaches: No man can be punished for speech uttered in the throes of his agony. Iyov says terrible things and may even for the moment subscribe to them, but he remains the same constant and upright servant of God that he always was.

If, however, we are dealing with carefully considered philosophical positions, then there is no room for such violent mental and emotional dislocations. Any *a priori* suppositions concerning the religious stance of the various protagonists must assure a uniformity of religious assumptions which preclude the possibility of the excesses which Rava lays to Iyov's door.

To that extent, then, we see Rava's statements in the *Gemara* as supportive of *Rashi's* general approach.

1. To the best of my knowledge, this principle has never been questioned as being unjust or as reflecting an uncaring God. It is based on the assumption that God's justice deals not only with the individual, but also with the community at large. In such a context, the individual — unless he is a man of such stature that he merits an open miracle — will be subsumed within his community.

If a righteous man dwells among wicked people who are to be punished by drought, there will be no rain falling upon his field, even though he is not deserving of punishment.

The assumption is that God will somehow compensate for such inevitable seeming miscarriages of justice. *R' Elchanan Wasserman* discusses this concept in detail in an essay, reprinted in *Kovetz Ma'amarim*.

2. It seems clear that *Rambam* and *Ramban* interpret as they do in order to avoid placing in Iyov's mouth the terrible blasphemies which, as we can see from the commentary, Rava does not hesitate to ascribe to him.

It should be added that to the modern mind, unschooled in the philosophical niceties with which the medieval greats grappled, the idea of an uninvolved God Who cares nothing for man because of the latter's sheer insignificance, is as difficult to grasp as a vindictive God who sees man as the plaything of His casual, uncaring cruelty.

But Rava (in *Bava Basra* 16a) does just that. In a remarkable passage relating to verse 24, *The land is in the hands of the wicked one*, he says: 'Iyov attempted to turn the dish upside down upon its opening' [an idiom which likely means: To rob the world of any meaning. Just as a dish, which is used to store things within it, becomes useless once it is turned upside down, so too a world with a cruel, capricious God means nothing at all.] Abaye said to him, [You are wrong] — the verse is to be read with reference to the Satan. The *wicked one* into whose hands the world is given is not a capricious God, but rather Satan].

Rashi here takes Abaye's approach and interprets the verses as referring to the Satan. But that does not relieve us of dealing with Rava's understanding — the more so, since the *Rashi* at 40:5 quoted above (which maintained that our passage is one of those which, in the end, Iyov regretted having said) presumably is based on Rava's opinion.

In the first place we must ask: If indeed these thoughts which Iyov expresses are *taunts and blasphemy* (as *Rashi* defines them), then has Satan not been vindicated? He maintained that Iyov would blaspheme under the pressure of his agonies, and indeed, has he not done so? In the footnote (p. 96) we have suggested one possible answer: Iyov's excesses at this point are not expressions of rejection, but of caring — so much of what he says is love at its most exalted (see, for example 13:15). In totally human reaction, his fevered mind lifts him to the highest ecstasies at one moment, only to plunge him to the depths of despair in the next. Love and hatred, hope and resignation, death wishes and life-affirming schemes, chase each other in and out and ever around in the black hole of his despair. As Rava himself teaches, he will not be held accountable for them, for they are utterances born of agonies.

However, even given all this, there is something in us which rejects the possibility that Iyov could actually have expressed the thoughts which Rava attributes to him. The very fact that none of our classical commentators brings himself to render the words in the mode in which Rava seems to interpret them, demonstrates with absolute clarity that Iyov cannot possibly have said them.

Rather, we suggest as follows: The all-important verse 24 reads: אֶרֶץ נִתְּנָה בְיַד רָשָׁע, *the land is in the hands of the wicked one.* Now the combination of נָתַן בְּיַד occurs frequently in Scripture — almost always in the sense that a people or an army are given into the hands of a conqueror. The only example we might adduce which is similar to the usage in our verse is *Genesis* 9:2, which talks of God subjugating the animal world under man — all are given over into his hands. But, by whom?

The narrative tone used in *Genesis* makes it abundantly clear that it is God by Whom the animal world is *placed* under man's dominion. The passive form of נִתָּנוּ, while not explicating a subject, clearly implies one. In verse 24, though, if the *rasha* to whom the world is given is God Himself — who has given it over into His hands? Clearly, if the meaning of the verse was that which Rava appears to assign to it, the formulation is infelicitous. נִתְּנָה should not have been used.

We suspect that Rava's interpretation of the verse is not meant as a literal rendering. Iyov's words may well lend themselves to other meanings. Perhaps, if we had to choose, *Daas Mikra's* reading — that of an uncaring human ruler into whose hand power had slipped — comes closest to the simple, unadorned text. However, the tone of resentful belligerence which marks the whole speech (as we have interpreted it) persuades Rava that Iyov had a double meaning in mind. Beneath the innocuous words lay a darker, more terrible meaning — one which Iyov did not quite dare to articulate, but which is the natural outgrowth of all that he has said and thought up to this point.

22. אַחַת הִיא עַל־כֵּן אָמַרְתִּי תָּם וְרָשָׁע הוּא מְכַלֶּה — *There is a thing — because of which I said: 'He destroys the constant with the wicked!'* We follow *Rashi* who writes: There is one matter in life, and it is concerning it that I said, *He destroys the constant with the wicked*. That matter is ... [the subject of the next verse].

Ramban has: The fate of the righteous and the wicked *is all one*. For this reason I maintain that He [permits] both the constant and the wicked to be destroyed. Man is too insignificant for Him to care.

Daas Mikra: *It is a matter of absolute clarity to me*, that situations arise (see Prefatory Remarks above and commentary to the next two verses) in which the righteous are destroyed together with the wicked.

כד לְמַסַּת נְקִיִּם יִלְעָג: אֶרֶץ ׀ נִתְּנָה בְיַד־רָשָׁע פְּנֵי־שֹׁפְטֶיהָ
כה יְכַסֶּה אִם־לֹא אֵפוֹא מִי־הוּא: וְיָמַי קַלּוּ מִנִּי־רָץ בָּרְחוּ
כו לֹא־רָאוּ טוֹבָה: חָלְפוּ עִם־אֳנִיּוֹת אֵבֶה כְּנֶשֶׁר יָטוּשׂ
כז עֲלֵי־אֹכֶל: אִם־אָמְרִי אֶשְׁכְּחָה שִׂיחִי אֶעֶזְבָה פָנַי
כח וְאַבְלִיגָה: יָגֹרְתִּי כָל־עַצְּבֹתָי יָדַעְתִּי כִּי־לֹא תְנַקֵּנִי:

23. אִם־שׁוֹט יָמִית פִּתְאֹם לְמַסַּת נְקִיִּם יִלְעָג — *When Satan goes for the sudden kill — he mocks the rotting of the innocent*. We follow *Rashi* who takes שׁוֹט as connoting שָׂטָן, the Satan. The translation of the rest of the verse follows automatically. Thus, we see that *Rashi* chooses to interpret the passage as does Abaye in *Bava Basra*. The subject is not God but the Satan. Needless to say, this interpretation avoids some of the difficulties with which we have dealt above. However, we have already pointed out that *Rashi* to 40:5 appears to consider Rava's understanding as well.

Ramban does not indicate what he thinks is the meaning of שׁוֹט. Perhaps he takes it as does *Rambam* in *Moreh Nevuchim*, as *flood*. As we saw above, he takes the sentence to be a proof to the proposition of the previous verse — that God is too exalted to care for man's fate. Were we to say that God Himself is the source of human fate, then we would have to say that when a flood wipes out the righteous with the wicked, it is *He who mocks the suffering of the innocent*. Far better to deny Him involvement in the matter.

Daas Mikra sees the verse simply as affirming the fact that occasionally natural disasters will indiscriminately destroy everything in their path, making no difference between the good and the bad. Whoever allows these disasters to happen [by implication, God] evidently is not concerned with the destruction of the innocent.

24. אֶרֶץ נִתְּנָה בְיַד־רָשָׁע פְּנֵי־שֹׁפְטֶיהָ יְכַסֶּה אִם־לֹא אֵפוֹא מִי־הוּא — *The land is in the hands of the wicked one, he sheaths the faces of its judges. If not, then who is it? Rashi*: The *wicked one* is Satan. All is in his power. He is able to confuse the judges so that they are unable to discern differences, and thus will never know the truth. This is the only possible explanation for all the evil in the world. *If not*, if Satan is not behind all the suffering, *then who is it*?

Ramban: This continues the argument begun in the previous verse. If we were to ascribe the indiscriminate destruction which occasionally takes place to God, that would mean that *the land is in the hands of the wicked one* [God] who *sheaths the faces of the judges*, and thus is able to practice all kinds of injustice. Such an assumption about God is clearly untenable. But, if it were not so, if God did indeed deal with the affairs of man, to whom else could we ascribe evil?

Daas Mikra: Not only do the natural forces not discriminate between good and evil people, but in the social sphere too this can be found. An evil king who controls the judiciary can wreak a great deal of harm on his subjects — the good and the bad. Manifestly, God permits such things to happen. If it is not His responsibility, then whose is it?

25-26. וְיָמַי קַלּוּ מִנִּי־רָץ בָּרְחוּ לֹא־רָאוּ טוֹבָה — *My days were more fleet of foot than a runner, they have escaped me, never experiencing joy*. חָלְפוּ עִם־אֳנִיּוֹת אֵבֶה כְּנֶשֶׁר יָטוּשׂ עֲלֵי־אֹכֶל — *They went past like the ships of Eiveh, like a vulture swooping over prey*. *Rashi* to verse 25: My days ran out on me together with those of all the other innocents who suffered unjustly.

Clearly, *Rashi* is attempting to bridge between the earlier passage and this.

Ramban, too, has the thoughts expressed in these two verses following loosely on what went before. The earlier section had, in his interpretation, made the point that God must be too exalted to care for man; else we would have to ascribe all the injustice in the world to Him — and that would be intolerable. Iyov now brings proof from his own life experience.[1]

He knows that he is righteous, and nevertheless has lived an absolutely frustrating life. Clearly none of this should be ascribed to God.

In spite of these reasonable connecting links, we cannot but notice that there seems to be a certain incongruence here. The complaints about a life that is over all too fast conformed well to the tenor of Iyov's speech in chapters 6 and 7. Here, however, the subject both before and after these two verses is God's seemingly

1. *Ramban* notes that whenever Iyov wants to make the point that the righteous occasionally suffer, he does so in the first person and draws upon his own experiences. This, because in contrast to the observation that the wicked often lead happy lives, which can be established objectively — we can see when a person acts wickedly — one can never know for sure whether another man is truly virtuous, and for all we know his sufferings may result from some secret vice.

goes for the sudden kill — he mocks the rotting of the innocent.
24 The land is in the hands of the wicked one, he sheaths the faces
of its judges. If not, then who is it? 25 My days were more fleet
of foot than a runner, they have escaped me, never experiencing
joy. 26 They went past like the ships of Eiveh, like a vulture
swooping over prey. 27 If I decided to abandon my grousing,
forgo my anger and show fortitude, 28 Were I to rein in my mis-
eries — yet I know that You would not proclaim me innocent.

uncaring inaccessibility, and the wanton destruction which can engulf all beings — including the innocent man. In such a context our verses seem too bland — particularly since they seem to be only a repetition of thoughts which Iyov had previously expressed in his response to Eliphaz.

When we consider the next section, running from verse 27 through verse 35, we may have a solution to the insertion of these two verses here. Verse 27 has Iyov toying with the wistful thought that it would be so good if he could perhaps bring himself to forget his murmuring, and verse 35 is a defiant assertion of his right to speak out.

Evidently, then, Iyov is agonizing over whether or not he should express his feelings and frustrations. He wishes that he could keep silent, but concludes that he cannot — he has the duty of defending his integrity.

We are now ready to understand the insertion of our two verses.

The hair-raising sacrilege of the previous three verses has brought on a reaction of horror. Iyov is appalled at his own temerity. He has gone too far — and he knows it. Accordingly, he seeks refuge in the more familiar, blander complaints of his earlier speech. They express his dissatisfaction with his lot without goading him beyond the acceptable.

However, he notices immediately that the stage is past in which the controlled expression of such reasonable grievances could have given some surcease to his agonies. It was adequate before; it cannot serve any more. This is what he says in verse 25. I know that I ought not have talked as I did; indeed in the last two verses I have tried to tone down my belligerence. But, I just cannot. You give me no chance to act as I know I should act. Therefore, unhappily, I will speak that which I must (v. 35).

Iyov gives three metaphors for the speed with which his good days have passed him by: [We say *good days*, on the basis of the very similar verse at 7:6 — see commentary there.] The runner [on land], the boat [on the sea], and the swooping vulture [in the air] (*Daas Mikra*).

We imagine that there is more here than the simple expedience of increasing impact by using a variety of metaphors. We may surmise as follows. The runner is sent by someone — the impetus for his haste comes from the need to do as he was told. The boat passes the bystander — he sees only the speed with which it plies the waves — but he cannot tell its origin or goal. The vulture is single-mindedly in pursuit of his prey. Iyov sees every aspect of his former life directed only towards his tragedy. It is as though the thoughts of Him Who sent him on his journey, the swiftly passing years, and the point to which they were making their headlong rush, all led inexorably to — disaster.

For the rendering of נֶשֶׁר as *vulture* rather than as the more usual eagle, see at 39:27.

אֳנִיּוֹת אֵבֶה — *The ships of Eiveh*. The name of a swift river (*Rashi*). *Ramban* quotes a *Targum* [not ours]: Swift boats of the enemies, intent upon capturing spoils. He understands אֵבֶה to be related to אֵיבָה, *hatred*. Our *Targum* has ships bearing luxuries, taking the word from אִבֵּי הַנָּחַל, *the fresh produce of the valley* (*Shir HaShirim* 6:11).

Daas Mikra, on the basis of etymological similarity to the Arabian and Accadian, suggests *reeds*. Thus, *boats made out of reeds*. Such boats are still in use in Ethiopia today.

27-28. אִם־אָמְרִי אֶשְׁכְּחָה שִׂיחִי אֶעֶזְבָה פָנַי וְאַבְלִיגָה — *If I decided to abandon my grousing, forgo my anger and show fortitude*, יָגֹרְתִּי כָל־עַצְּבֹתָי, יָדַעְתִּי כִּי־לֹא תְנַקֵּנִי — *Were I to rein in my miseries — yet I know that You would not proclaim me innocent*. See above for our perception of these two verses. Shocked at the excesses of which he had seen himself capable, Iyov had tried to mute his complaints, in verses 25-26. Now he recognizes that such reticence will not work for him. His frustration runs too deep — and so (as verse 35 determines), he must speak.

We have rendered פָּנַי as *anger* in accordance with *Rashi*. *Ibn Ezra* adduces *I Samuel* 1:18.

On עַצְּבֹתָי, which we have rendered *miseries*, *Rashi* remarks: Those which will not let me keep silent.

יָדַעְתִּי כִּי־לֹא תְנַקֵּנִי — *Yet I know that You would not proclaim me innocent*. The implication —

כט־ל אָנֹכִי אֶרְשָׁע לָמָּה־זֶּה הֶבֶל אִיגָע: אִם־הִתְרָחַצְתִּי
°בְּמֵי ק׳ לא °בְמוֹ־שָׁלֶג וַהֲזִכּוֹתִי בְּבֹר כַּפָּי: אָז בַּשַּׁחַת תִּטְבְּלֵנִי וְתִעֲבוּנִי
לב שַׂלְמוֹתָי: כִּי־לֹא־אִישׁ כָּמֹנִי אֶעֱנֶנּוּ נָבוֹא יַחְדָּו בַּמִּשְׁפָּט:

reinforced by the first phrase of the next verse, *I will anyway be guilty* — is that here Iyov is picturing himself as standing at the bar of justice before God, the judge. No more is he a litigant (as in the earlier part of this ch.), who wishes to summon God to answer for His actions. Rather he is a supplicant, begging God for justice — and knowing that it will be denied. Not until v. 32 does he once more take up the earlier theme — see there (also Chart p. 107).

We may suppose that this image was born in his mind when, in verse 24, he talked of the wicked one who *sheathes the faces of the judges*. Whatever the true meaning of the phrase — see above — there is clearly the picture of judges averting their gaze from the truth and, in consequence, perverting justice. At some level of his consciousness, Iyov is struck by the aptness of this description for his own situation.

29. אָנֹכִי אֶרְשָׁע לָמָּה־זֶּה הֶבֶל אִיגָע — *I will anyway be guilty — why should I weary myself uselessly?* It is useless to go to court and to supplicate for vindication, when the guilty verdict is a foregone conclusion (*Rashi*).

Neither my silence (vs. 27 and 28) nor my speech (v. 29) will help me in the least. There is nowhere that I can turn, nothing that I can do (*Ramban*).

30-31. אִם־הִתְרָחַצְתִּי בְמֵי־שָׁלֶג וַהֲזִכּוֹתִי בְּבֹר כַּפָּי — *Though I washed in melted snow, cleansed my hands with soap.* אָז בַּשַּׁחַת תִּטְבְּלֵנִי וְתִעֲבוּנִי שַׂלְמוֹתָי — *You would dunk me in the muck, my very clothes would loathe me.* What are these two verses saying, at this point of the argument? Verses 27 to 29 had depicted God as a tainted judge from whom no fairness could be expected. Verse 32 goes back to the earlier parts of the chapter where God was to be a party in litigation. Our two verses do not fit easily into either of the two sections, nor is it readily apparent how they are to bridge between them.

Rashi is silent, and *Ramban* remarks as follows: Verse 30 is a metaphor which depicts Iyov as one who is clean of hand and pure of heart. Verse 31 describes the day of Iyov's death when he anticipates that God will submerge him in the slimy depths of the grave. Iyov's clothes will shame him; he is not sufficiently clean to appear before the king for judgment. The passage teaches that a death is followed by judgment — a proposition which Iyov accepts as true.

Still, there appears to be no compelling link to either the passage that went before, or the one which follows.

If indeed verse 30 — that is, the description of one who has washed himself clean — is a metaphor for innocence, then verse 31, which depicts God as dunking Iyov into the muck, would have to be understood as having God accuse Iyov and burden him with sins which he had never committed. However, nowhere has Iyov claimed that God would do such a thing. Certainly he has expressed outrage at being made to suffer without good reason, but he has not said that God would accuse him unfairly of sins which he had never committed.

If, as illustrated by the Chart (p. 107) we can understand these two verses as following directly onto verse 20, we will have no difficulty in gauging their meaning.

But first, a brief analysis of the structure of Iyov's speech.

At verse 21 we recognized one of the literary lurches which we have come to expect in Iyov's cries from the heart. As we explained there, the mention of the *tam* concept in verse 20 had recalled to him his claim to *temimus*, in the face of the belligerent questioning which had made the friends accuse him of being a *chonef*. His proud assertion, *I am a tam*! had then led to the next passage in which his bitterness finally spilled over into the dreadful accusations that we analyzed above. Then, at verses 25-26, there was the short-lived attempt to mute his pugnaciousness; this brought him in turn to the painful realization that in truth, there was no avenue open to him at all. Neither silence nor the pressing of his claim would help (vs. 27-29).

He now goes back to his thoughts of verse 20, which had been interrupted there.

In verse 20 Iyov had reflected upon the futility of attempting to press his case against an all-wise God. As *Rashi* had interpreted that verse, it contained no negative reference to God. The subject of יַרְשִׁיעֵנִי was *my mouth*. However, we quoted *Metzudos* who saw that phrase as a condemnation of a God Who proclaims Iyov crooked, in spite of his constancy.

The thought-progression of our two verses recalls *Psalms* 73:13-14:

29 I will anyway be guilty — why should I weary myself use-
lessly? 30 Though I washed in melted snow, cleansed my
hands with soap. 31 You would dunk me in the muck, my
very clothes would loathe me. 32 For You are not a mortal as I
am, that I could answer You, that we could wrangle together.

Job (chapter 9)	*Psalms (chapter 73)*
30. אִם־הִתְרָחַצְתִּי בְמֵי־שָׁלֶג וַהֲזִכּוֹתִי בְּבֹר כַּפָּי. *Though I washed in melted snow, cleansed my hands with soap.*	13. אַךְ רִיק זִכִּיתִי לְבָבִי וָאֶרְחַץ בְּנִקָּיוֹן כַּפָּי. *In vain have I cleaned my heart and washed my hands spotless.*
31. . . . אָז בַּשַּׁחַת תִּטְבְּלֵנִי *You would dunk me in the muck . . .*	14. . . . וָאֱהִי נָגוּעַ כָּל הַיּוֹם *Still I was plagued all day long . . .*

The term which *Psalms* uses in verse 14 is נָגוּעַ. This expression has a simple meaning, but also resonates with an implied association. נָגַע means *to touch*, and is used throughout Scripture to denote *smiting* of any kind. It is most naturally associated with *leprosy* because it is a key word in *Leviticus* chapter 13.

Now, leprosy — an evil filth from which people tend to recoil in disgust — is seen by the Sages as the outer form of an inner erosion of sanctity. It is visible sin, the tangible ugliness of a tarnished soul. Thus, *Still I was plagued all day long . . .*, really paraphrases quite accurately the dirt and squalor of, *You would dunk me in the mud . . . .*

What is the precise symbolism of that phrase?

The שַׁחַת of our verse, which we have translated *muck*, also carries a variety of meanings: It is frequently used to denote simply a hole in the ground, *a pit* (see, for example, *Jeremiah* 18:20), but there is also the association with *death* through its use for *grave* (see, for example, *Psalms* 30:10). Thus, the *muck* of our phrase carries the stench of death.

When we consider further that in the thought-world of our Sages, leprosy is regarded as a form of death [a leper is considered as one dead (*Nedarim* 64b)], the parallelism becomes clear.

Iyov's mind focuses upon the putrification of his entire body, is obsessed by the filth and smell oozing from it. He realizes that it has become an object of loathing to those who meet him but, more importantly, to himself. He sees himself as he must surely appear to others — the personification of an evil, revolting personality that has burst out, to reveal itself in all its horror, upon his body. He is walking malevolence, living death.

And none of it is true. Iyov has, on the contrary, . . . *washed in melted snow, cleansed his hands with soap*. He knows himself to be innocent. In spite of his inner purity and constancy, God has branded him a sinner in the eyes of the entire world.

What chance has he in litigation, against one who does not hesitate to twist his innocence into crookedness (v. 20), to take what was pure and shining and dunk it into a death-pit filled with the muck-stink of evil!

בְּבֹר — *With soap*. *Rashi* equates בֹּר with *cleanliness*. But *Metzudos* believes it is a herb which can be used for cleaning, akin to our soap.

וְתִעֲבוּנִי שַׂלְמוֹתָי — *My very clothes would loathe me*. The idea is difficult for us to grasp. What exactly does Iyov mean by saying that his clothes would loathe him?

The simple meaning would be that he is, metaphorically, endowing his clothes with human feelings. The clothes lie right next to the body and normally do not balk at this intimate proximity. Iyov's putrid flesh would disgust even his clothes.

If we are correct in understanding the filth of which Iyov talked in the previous verse as referring to the inflammation and the boils which covered his body, then the phrase might be meant to describe the irritation of his clothes rubbing against these open sores — even my clothes join in torturing me.

32. כִּי־לֹא־אִישׁ כָּמוֹנִי אֶעֱנֶנּוּ נָבוֹא יַחְדָּו בַּמִּשְׁפָּט — *For You are not a mortal as I am, that I could answer You, that we could wrangle together*. The commentary to verse 3 should be studied together with this verse.

As we have understood the structure of the speech, this verse grows out of Iyov's complaints as expressed in verse 20 and in the previous two verses. God's perceived overbearing demeanor as a litigant is possible only because He is no mortal, and therefore, immeasurably stronger than Iyov. Iyov wishes vainly that there were greater equality between himself and his Divine opponent. See next verse.

ט/לג־לה לג־לד לֹא יֶשׁ־בֵּינֵינוּ מוֹכִיחַ יָשֵׁת יָדוֹ עַל־שְׁנֵינוּ: יָסֵר
לה מֵעָלַי שִׁבְטוֹ וְאֵמָתוֹ אַל־תְּבַעֲתַנִּי: אֲדַבְּרָה וְלֹא
י/א־ב א אִירָאֶנּוּ כִּי־לֹא־כֵן אָנֹכִי עִמָּדִי: נָקְטָה נַפְשִׁי בְּחַיָּי
ב אֶעֶזְבָה עָלַי שִׂיחִי אֲדַבְּרָה בְּמַר נַפְשִׁי: אֹמַר אֶל־אֱלוֹהַּ

33. לֹא יֶשׁ־בֵּינֵינוּ מוֹכִיחַ יָשֵׁת יָדוֹ עַל־שְׁנֵינוּ — *There is no arbitrator between us who might lay his hands on us both*. The מוֹכִיחַ, according to *Rashi*, is one who points out the merits and faults in the positions of each one of the litigants. He *lays his hands* in the sense that he is able to impose his authority upon both, thus making sure that the stronger one does not overwhelm the weaker.

At 7:8 we quoted Rava in *Bava Basra* 16a, who remarks to this verse: Let Iyov's mouth be stuffed with dirt. Can we imagine a slave upbraiding his master?

What is Rava criticizing?

The correct interpretation apparently depends upon understanding the relationship between our verse and the next. *Ramban* offers two possibilities. The first, that the wish expressed in the next verse flows from this one, but is not a direct continuation. Iyov wishes that there were an arbitrator between him and God. Once fairness is assured, God, of His own accord, would surely lay aside His cudgel.

The second possibility is that the arbitrator himself is the subject of the next verse. His function will be to make God lay aside His cudgel.

If the first interpretation is the correct one, it is difficult to see how Iyov's temerity in making the suggestion that an arbitrator be appointed would be expressed as a servant upbraiding his master. It would seem that Rava's abhorrence of this idea might be better worded in the form of the earlier criticism voiced there: Can Iyov put himself in one category with God?

Accordingly, it would seem that Rava is more likely to understand the verse according to the second alternative. His criticism is leveled at Iyov for thinking that a slave [the arbitrator] could upbraid God and force Him to relinquish His cudgel.

34. יָסֵר מֵעָלַי שִׁבְטוֹ וְאֵמָתוֹ אַל־תְּבַעֲתַנִּי — *That He might remove His cudgel from me, that fear of Him would cease to terrify me*. See commentary above for the relationship of this verse to the earlier one.

35. אֲדַבְּרָה וְלֹא אִירָאֶנּוּ כִּי־לֹא־כֵן אָנֹכִי עִמָּדִי — *I shall speak and not fear Him, for this is not how I perceive myself*. Iyov has now decided that the silence which he attempted to impose upon himself in verse 27 cannot serve. He must speak, must give voice to the torments which leave him no peace. He knows that he is innocent, knows that the friends do not perceive him as he really is (*Metzudos*). He will take God to task and attempt to force Him, ultimately, to justify Himself.

X.

1. נָקְטָה נַפְשִׁי בְּחַיָּי אֶעֶזְבָה עָלַי שִׂיחִי אֲדַבְּרָה בְּמַר נַפְשִׁי — *My very soul protests life, even were I to suppress my grousing, I would speak out in the bitterness of my soul*. In the final verse of the previous chapter, we found Iyov expressing his determination to speak out at all costs. We would suppose that the logical follow-up from that decision would be our verse 2, which, beginning as it does with the words *I say . . .*, is clearly born of that decision.

What, then, is the function of our verse?

In human terms, it is easy to understand. Iyov is about to embark on a daring venture, indeed. As belligerent as were his thoughts in the previous chapter, they were in a large part said *about* God, not *to* Him. Iyov is about to harangue God Himself, to accuse Him directly of the distortions of justice which his ruminations in the previous chapter had yielded.

It is natural enough that in the last moment, there should be some hesitation, some need to absolve himself from the obligation to rein in his feelings. Iyov's bitterness is just too great; it demands release.

In this sense, our verse parallels 7:11 which also precedes a direct address to God. Here, however, Iyov goes much further than he does in that speech. While there he protests vigorously against the constant pounding to which he is being subjected, he does not yet summon the temerity of openly accusing God of perverting justice. In the current speech there are no such inhibitions.

נָקְטָה derives from קוט, which *Rashi* to

9/33-35 [33] *There is no arbitrator between us who might lay his hands on us*
both. [34] *That He might remove His cudgel from me, that fear of Him*
would cease to terrify me. [35] *I shall speak and not fear Him, for this*
is not how I perceive myself.

10/1-2 [1] *My very soul protests life, even were I to suppress my grousing,*
I would speak out in the bitterness of my soul. [2] *I say to God,*

Thread I	Thread II	Thread III
14. Could I then possibly respond to Him, choose words to argue with Him? **15.** Even if I were right, I could never assert it, could I entreat Him who judges me? **16.** Even were I to call and He would answer me, I could not believe that He would listen to my voice.		
	17. For He has shattered me in a tempest, multiplied my wounds for no good reason. **18.** He will not suffer me to catch my breath, for He gluts me with bitterness.	
19. Is it to be brawn? — See, He is the stronger, if, due process, who will set a time for me? **20.** Even if I were in the right — my mouth would pronounce me guilty, if I were innocent, it would proclaim me, crooked.		
		21. I am constant, but at a loss how to find rest, I am disgusted with my life. **22.** There is a thing — because of which I said: 'He destroys the constant with the wicked!' **23.** When Satan goes for the sudden kill — he mocks the rotting of the innocent. **24.** The land is in the hands of the wicked one, he sheaths the faces of its judges. If not, then who is it?
	25. My days were more fleet of foot than a runner, they have escaped me, never experiencing joy. **26.** They went past like the ships of Eiveh, like an eagle swooping over prey.	
		27. If I decided to abandon my grousing, forgo my anger and show fortitude, **28.** Were I to rein in my miseries — yet I know that You would not proclaim me innocent. **29.** I will anyway be guilty — why should I weary myself uselessly?
30. Though I washed in melted snow, cleansed my hands with soap. **31.** You would dunk me in the muck, my very clothes would loathe me. **32.** For You are not a mortal as I am, that I could answer You, that we could wrangle together.		

ג אַל־תַּרְשִׁיעֵנִי הוֹדִיעֵנִי עַל מַה־תְּרִיבֵנִי: הֲטוֹב לְךָ | כִּי־
תַעֲשֹׁק כִּי־תִמְאַס יְגִיעַ כַּפֶּיךָ וְעַל־עֲצַת רְשָׁעִים הוֹפָעְתָּ:
ד־ה הַעֵינֵי בָשָׂר לָךְ אִם־כִּרְאוֹת אֱנוֹשׁ תִּרְאֶה: הֲכִימֵי אֱנוֹשׁ
ו יָמֶיךָ אִם־שְׁנוֹתֶיךָ כִּימֵי גָבֶר: כִּי־תְבַקֵּשׁ לַעֲוֹנִי וּלְחַטָּאתִי
ז תִדְרוֹשׁ: עַל־דַּעְתְּךָ כִּי־לֹא אֶרְשָׁע וְאֵין מִיָּדְךָ מַצִּיל:

Psalms 95:10 takes to mean *quarrel*, synonymous with ריב. See 8:14, above, where the same root has the meaning, *to cut off*.

2. אֹמַר אֶל־אֱלוֹהַּ אַל־תַּרְשִׁיעֵנִי הוֹדִיעֵנִי עַל מַה־תְּרִיבֵנִי — *I say to God, 'Do not condemn me. Tell me, why do You pick a fight with me?* אַל is not as absolute as לֹא. It is a softer negation, usually carrying the connotation of request or entreaty (see *Wertheimer's, Biur Sheimos HaNirdafim B'Tanach*). Thus, even though Iyov has determined to give expression to his bitterness, he begins on a conciliatory note.

For a precise understanding of the first phrase, we must combine it with verse 7 in which Iyov states absolutely that God knows that he does not bear any guilt. Thus: Please, do not condemn me out of hand. It is not fitting that You should declare as wicked someone whom You know to be innocent.

Within this context we have rendered the second phrase, *why do You pick a fight with me?* ריב can have a fairly wide range of meanings. Closest to what we have in mind as being within the spirit of our verse is *Psalms* 103:9, where it is used to parallel נָטַר, *to bear a grudge.*

3. הֲטוֹב לְךָ כִּי־תַעֲשֹׁק כִּי־תִמְאַס יְגִיעַ כַּפֶּיךָ וְעַל־עֲצַת רְשָׁעִים הוֹפָעְתָּ — *Does it feel good to plunder, to despise the labor of Your hands, having smiled upon the plots of the wicked.* With mounting bitterness, Iyov begins to lash out. At 9:23 he had suggested that God *mocks the rotting of the innocent.* (See commentary there that in *Rava's* view, that passage has God as the subject.) He now has found the courage to fling that accusation at God Himself in the rhetorical question which makes up our verse.

A better rendering of תַּעֲשֹׁק, according to the simple meaning of the verse, might have been *persecute.* However, we have used *plunder* in order to accommodate *Rashi's* understanding of the phrase. God has robbed the righteous man of his righteousness.

The theme that God apparently *despises* the innocent [here referred to as *the labor of Your hands,* in order to set the tone for verses 8-12 which elaborate on this idea — see commentary to verses 6-7 for further analysis], while encouraging the wicked, is Bildad's thought at 8:20, turned inside out. Bildad had assured Iyov that, *God will not disdain those who are constant, will not support evildoers.* Iyov feels that his experience shows him otherwise.

Iyov, who by this time has totally reduced God to human dimensions — see next verse — sees the vindictive pursuit of His own handiwork as a particularly heinous act. Here we do not have only callous disregard, but a crime against nature itself. How could God wantonly destroy that which He had formed with so much love and care?

In accordance with our analysis in the commentary to 8:20, we assume that the *wicked* of our verse are the three friends.

הוֹפָעְתָּ comes from יָפַע, *to shine upon.* We have taken the idiom, *to smile upon,* from *Rashi.*

4-5. הַעֵינֵי בָשָׂר לָךְ אִם־כִּרְאוֹת אֱנוֹשׁ תִּרְאֶה — *Do You have eyes of flesh, do You see as man does?* הֲכִימֵי אֱנוֹשׁ יָמֶיךָ אִם־שְׁנוֹתֶיךָ כִּימֵי גָבֶר — *Are Your days like those of a mortal, Your years as the years of man? Rashi* and *Ramban* part ways radically in the interpretation of these verses. Each is consistent with his approach to the entire speech.

Rashi sees Iyov throwing restraint to the wind and recklessly accusing God of reducing Himself to human frailty. You have lowered Yourself to my level, Iyov accuses. You are picking a fight and pursuing me as though You were of my own kind.

In Introductory Remarks to this speech, in chapter 9, we recognized that the tendency to reduce God to human dimensions underlies much of Iyov's thinking. None of the truly outlandish ideas which he expresses in this, his third speech, would have been possible if there were not this fundamental flaw in his perception of the Divine. In a sense, it is this primitive idea of the nature of God which agitates Iyov so. If God can be contained in a human mold, then His ways must be understandable in human terms. It will take the revelation from the whirlwind to introduce Iyov to the idea of a God Who is inscrutable

'Do not condemn me. Tell me, why do You pick a fight with me?
3 Does it feel good to plunder, to despise the labor of Your hands,
having smiled upon the plots of the wicked. 4 Do You have eyes of
flesh, do You see as man does? 5 Are Your days like those
of a mortal, Your years as the years of man. 6 That You search
out my transgression, look for my sin? 7 You know that I will
not be guilty — but there is none that can save from Your hand.

and utterly beyond human understanding. That understood, Iyov can desist from his restless searching.

In *Ramban's* view, Iyov is asking reasonable questions: Are You as shortsighted as a human that You would have the need to test me to see whether I love You with all my might? Are You as short-lived as man that You have to punish me now, and are unable to wait until I die?

We have rendered יְמֵי גָבֶר as *years of man,* instead of as *days,* in accordance with *Rashi* to *Leviticus* 25:29 (and other places) that יָמִים can be rendered *years*.

6-7. כִּי־תְבַקֵּשׁ לַעֲוֹנִי וּלְחַטָּאתִי תִדְרוֹשׁ — *That You search out my transgression, look for my sin.* עַל־דַּעְתְּךָ כִּי־לֹא אֶרְשָׁע וְאֵין מִיָּדְךָ מַצִּיל — *You know that I will not be guilty — but there is none that can save from Your hand. Rashi* does not explain these two verses.

Within the context of his understanding of the earlier verses, we would be inclined to take verse 6 separately from verse 7 and to translate it: *That You search out my transgression, look for my sin.* The meaning would be that Iyov accuses God of pouncing upon his slightest transgression in order that he might be punished. The idea would be much the same as that expressed by, *Watcher of man!* at 7:20.

However, verse 7 would then be difficult to understand. The first phrase does not lend itself readily to: *You know that I will not be guilty,* since אֶרְשָׁע is in the imperfect. Furthermore, there is no very clear connection between the first and the second parts of the verse.

Accordingly, it seems more likely that *Rashi,* as does *Ramban,* would combine verses 6 and 7, understanding them as we have rendered them. Iyov feels that God is making him suffer *in order* to goad him into an act of blasphemy and sin.[1]

[תְּבַקֵּשׁ is used in the sense of *wanting to bring something about,* as in *Psalms* 34:15. So too, תִּדְרֹשׁ, as in *Micah* 6:8.] But, Iyov claims (v. 7), there is little purpose in that. You, God, know that I will pass the test, that I will not be found guilty. He is stricken by the sheer waste of his agonies, but what can he do — *None can save from God's hand.*

A careful analysis of verse 3 and its relationship to our verses yields another possibility. Verse 3 makes the point that it is not right that God should *despise the labor of [His] hands.* This theme is clearly taken up in verses 8-12, a fact which raises a question of why Iyov mentions it at verse 3, drops it, and then picks it up once more.

The following structural scheme seems likely.

Verse 3 reads: *Does it feel good to plunder, to despise the labor of Your hands.* We noted that *Rashi* explains *plunder* in the sense that God seems to wish to rob the righteous of his righteousness.

We suggest the following scheme: The first phrase, *Does it feel good to plunder,* is then expanded upon in verses 4-7; the second phrase, *To despise the labor of Your hands,* in verses 8-13.

This new insight into the structural scheme will not alter our understanding of verses 4-5. As before, these decry God's lowering Himself to Iyov's level in order to accomplish his destruction. Verses 6 and 7 then continue: Your purpose in denying me the fruits of my righteousness is surely in order that my transgressions should be highlighted: *That You search out my transgression, look for my sin* (v. 6). But You know very well that whatever You do, I shall never be truly wicked (v. 7a). Hiding my merits and stressing my shortcomings does not change the facts. Moreover, why should it *feel good* to do this to me? Is it to demonstrate Your strength? But, You are all-powerful, *None can save from Your hands,* so what are You proving by subjecting me to this violation of my rights (v. 7b).

The next section will now begin to enlarge upon the second theme in verse 3.

Rava, in *Bava Basra* 16a, appears to have a different perception of our verse 7.

1. In the event, that was not far from the truth; except that it was Satan, not God, who was torturing him in order to cause him to blaspheme.

ח־ט יָדֶיךָ עִצְּבוּנִי וַיַּעֲשׂוּנִי יַחַד סָבִיב וַתְּבַלְּעֵנִי׃ זְכָר־נָא כִּי־
י כַחֹמֶר עֲשִׂיתָנִי וְאֶל־עָפָר תְּשִׁיבֵנִי׃ הֲלֹא כֶחָלָב תַּתִּיכֵנִי
יא וְכַגְּבִינָה תַּקְפִּיאֵנִי׃ עוֹר וּבָשָׂר תַּלְבִּישֵׁנִי וּבַעֲצָמוֹת
יב וְגִידִים תְּשֹׂכְכֵנִי׃ חַיִּים וָחֶסֶד עָשִׂיתָ עִמָּדִי וּפְקֻדָּתְךָ
יג שָׁמְרָה רוּחִי׃ וְאֵלֶּה צָפַנְתָּ בִלְבָבֶךָ יָדַעְתִּי כִּי־זֹאת עִמָּךְ׃

He renders עַל־דַּעְתְּךָ כִּי־לֹא אֶרְשָׁע, as, *If You would wish it, I would not be wicked,* and teaches as follows:

> Iyov wished to free the whole world from responsibility. He said to God: Master of All, You created the ox with split hoofs, You created the donkey with hoofs that are in one piece; You created the Garden of Eden and You created *Gehinnom;* You made people be righteous and You made people be wicked. Who can stop You from doing as You wish?

This verse, then, constitutes a denial of the doctrine of free will and of consequent accountability.

At 7:8 we had a similar instance, where the Talmudic tradition reads a verse in Iyov's speech as constituting a denial of the doctrine of the *Resurrection of the Dead.* There, for both textual considerations and also because such a theological stance seemed irrelevant to that part of the speech, we suggested that the Sages did not claim their interpretation to be the simple meaning of the verse, but rather discovered it in Iyov's words at the level of *d'rash.*

We suggest the same to be true here. A denial of the doctrine of free will does not fit readily into the flow of Iyov's speech at this point. Rather, the Sages detected a sub-surface tension because of the most unusual form עַל דַּעְתְּךָ for *You know.* The phrase seems to convey the idea, *It is up to You,* and its use here would not have been coincidental. In Iyov's agitated frame of mind, many of the verities upon which, unquestioningly, he had based his life, began to seem less certain. If God was indeed as petty as Iyov, in his fevered mind, now envisioned Him, then it is possible that all human life is without meaning; and that man, who we might have supposed to be the crown of creation, is really nothing more than an automaton.

8. יָדֶיךָ עִצְּבוּנִי וַיַּעֲשׂוּנִי יַחַד סָבִיב וַתְּבַלְּעֵנִי — *Your hands aligned me and fashioned me: as one, round about . . ., and thus, You consume me.* Iyov goes back to the second thought expressed in verse 3: How could God *despise the labor of [His] hands?*

The form which this *despising* takes is, in *Rashi's* view, the subject of the second half of our verse.

We must understand the difficult phrase, *as one round about . . .,* in the context of the next one: *and thus, You consume me.* To this latter phrase, *Rashi* remarks: These are the worms. To the earlier one, he remarks: . . . and now, Your armies, as one, are round about [me].

Iyov is sitting in the dust (see 2:8) and feels the worms gnawing away at the dead skin on his body. These are the legions which with single-minded determination are ranged around him. Choked with outrage and disgust, he cannot bring himself to mention them by name. All he can articulate is the strangled accusation: You made me with so much love and care — how could You have let it come to this?

We have rendered עִצְּבוּנִי, *aligned,* in accordance with *Rashi* to *Shabbos* 147a, s.v. וְאֵין. It describes the ordering of the bones in relation to the spine.

Ramban suggests various ways of interpreting this difficult verse. Among them is that of *Targum,* who takes the words עִצְּבוּנִי וַיַּעֲשׂוּנִי, *aligned me and fashioned me,* together with יַחַד סָבִיב, *as one, round about,* and renders: *Your hands have formed me, and fashioned me all round about, now You have consumed me.*

9. זְכָר־נָא כִּי־כַחֹמֶר עֲשִׂיתָנִי וְאֶל־עָפָר תְּשִׁיבֵנִי — *O remember that You fashioned me as from clay, and that You will return me to the dust.* The entire sentence can be paraphrased simply, *I am only mortal!* That appears to be the idea expressed in having been formed from clay (see 33:6), and that is certainly implied in the statement that one day he will be returned to the dust.

Ramban explains: You have invested labor into creating me to live for a given time-span. To cut off my days now would spell a waste of all Your efforts.

This explanation does not, however, flow well from the previous verse as *Rashi* understood it. The train of thought begun there would seem to continue smoothly in verse 10. Our verse appears out of place.

[8] Your hands aligned me and fashioned me: as one, round about ..., and thus, You consume me. [9] O remember that You fashioned me as from clay, and that You will return me to the dust. [10] You pour me out like milk, congeal me like cheese. [11] You clothe me with skin and flesh, protect me with bones and sinews. [12] You granted me life and kindness, and my spirit submitted to Your guardians. [13] But You harbored these in Your heart, though I know that this is in Your mind.

Perhaps, Iyov is sidetracked by his reference to the gnawing worms. Their attacks on him are premature. Having been formed from the earth and destined to return to the dust, he realizes that he is destined one day to fall prey to them. But to face them now — that goes against nature.

10-12. הֲלֹא כֶחָלָב תַּתִּיכֵנִי וְכַגְּבִינָּה תַּקְפִּיאֵנִי — *You pour me out like milk, congeal me like cheese.* עוֹר וּבָשָׂר תַּלְבִּישֵׁנִי וּבַעֲצָמוֹת וְגִידִים תְּשֹׂכְכֵנִי — *You clothe me with skin and flesh, protect me with bones and sinews.* חַיִּים וָחֶסֶד עָשִׂיתָ עִמָּדִי וּפְקֻדָּתְךָ שָׁמְרָה רוּחִי — *You granted me life and kindness, and my spirit submitted to Your guardians.* From his visions of the grave, his ultimate destination, Iyov's thoughts turn to his beginnings — within his mother's womb. See 1:21 for the thought-association between these two concepts.

[If there were no such thought-association, then the picture which Iyov paints would be flawed. In verse 8 he had already described how God had shaped his skeleton. Why now go back to his very beginning?]

Verse 10 describes the moment of conception. *You pour me out like milk* (תַּתִּיכֵנִי, from נָתַךְ, *to pour out,* see 3:23) refers to the drop of semen (*Rashi*); while *congeal me like cheese* is a metaphor describing the beginnings of the fetus (*Metzudos*).

The *protection* in verse 11 presumably refers to the rib cage which protects the vital organs (*Metzudos*). Accordingly, it would perhaps be better to render the second half of the verse, ... *having protected me* ... *Metzudos* understands the function of the *sinews* as binding the bones together.

The *life* in verse 12 is the life granted the fetus inside its mother. It is described as *kindness,* since no merit on the part of the child preceded it (*Metzudos*). The *spirit* of the child *submits to the guardians* [פְּקֻדָּתְךָ, a *cadre of sentries* (*Rashi*)] which God places around it, in the sense that it remains inside the mother's womb for the term which is determined for it (*Rashi* and *Metzudos*).

13. וְאֵלֶּה צָפַנְתָּ בִלְבָבֶךָ יָדַעְתִּי כִּי־זֹאת עִמָּךְ — *But You harbored these in Your heart, though I know that this is in Your mind.* You harbored plans for my destruction in Your mind, although I am quite sure that You remember all the effort which You put into me when You first formed me (*Rashi* and *Ramban*).

In consideration of the next two verses, and bearing in mind our interpretation of verses 6-7, we may suggest an alternative explanation.

Our second phrase: *I know that this is in Your mind,* goes back to what was said in verses 6-7. There, Iyov had accused God of wanting to trap him into sin, of relishing the expectation of discovering his iniquity. Now that Iyov has traced the loving care with which God had initially formed him, and drawn the conclusion that He must consciously be suppressing these memories in order to enable Himself to cause all this anguish — Iyov feels that this thesis is proven. There must be a quality of vindictiveness in God — there is no other explanation.

An analysis of verses 14-15 in relation to verses 6-7 reinforces the connection. Verse 6 speaks of God searching out Iyov's *transgressions* and *sins*; verse 14 uses the same terms, chiastically. Verse 7 asserts that Iyov will not be found *guilty,* and verse 15 speaks of his *guilt.* The congruence is absolute.

We understand the relationship as follows: Verses 6-7 had claimed that God was purposely attempting to trap Iyov into sin, knowing all the time that he would never be found guilty. Verse 13b reaffirms this proposition: Iyov simply *knows that this is in Your mind.*

Verses 14-15 then go on to say: If it had been different, if indeed you had discovered *sins* and *transgressions,* and had then punished my *guilt,* then, *woe is to me.* I would have no justification for my complaints. But if I am innocent, as indeed I am, why should I have shame heaped upon me?

יד־טו אִם־חָטָאתִי וּשְׁמַרְתָּנִי וּמֵעֲוֺנִי לֹא תְנַקֵּנִי: אִם־רָשַׁעְתִּי
אַלְלַי לִי וְצָדַקְתִּי לֹא־אֶשָּׂא רֹאשִׁי שְׂבַע קָלוֹן וּרְאֵה
טז עָנְיִי: וְיִגְאֶה כַּשַּׁחַל תְּצוּדֵנִי וְתָשֹׁב תִּתְפַּלָּא בִי:
יז תְּחַדֵּשׁ עֵדֶיךָ ׀ נֶגְדִּי וְתֶרֶב כַּעַשְׂךָ עִמָּדִי חֲלִיפוֹת
יח וְצָבָא עִמִּי: וְלָמָּה מֵרֶחֶם הֹצֵאתָנִי אֶגְוַע וְעַיִן לֹא־
יט תִרְאֵנִי: כַּאֲשֶׁר לֹא־הָיִיתִי אֶהְיֶה מִבֶּטֶן לַקֶּבֶר אוּבָל:

14-15. אִם־חָטָאתִי וּשְׁמַרְתָּנִי וּמֵעֲוֺנִי לֹא תְנַקֵּנִי — *If I have sinned, and You scrutinize me, refuse to cleanse me of my transgression.* אִם־רָשַׁעְתִּי אַלְלַי לִי וְצָדַקְתִּי לֹא־אֶשָּׂא רֹאשִׁי שְׂבַע קָלוֹן וּרְאֵה עָנְיִי — *If, then, I have been guilty — woe is to me. But if I am innocent should I not be able to raise my head? Surfeited with shame, confronted by my misery!* We have rendered these difficult verses in accordance with our suggestion in the commentary to the previous verse. They consider what would have been had God really found the sins which, Iyov believes, He would have wanted to find.

For וּשְׁמַרְתָּנִי, *Rashi* has: You watch me constantly refusing to be forgiving and to look away.

שְׂבַע קָלוֹן is literally, *sated with shame.* We have rendered *surfeited,* a stronger word, to reflect Iyov's frustration at the unfairness of it all.

Rashi points out that וּרְאֵה is not to be understood as the imperative, *See!,* but that the phrase is to be rendered as a noun: One who constantly sees his misery.

See at 35:3 for *R' Yosef Kara's* understanding of this verse.

16. וְיִגְאֶה כַּשַּׁחַל תְּצוּדֵנִי וְתָשֹׁב תִּתְפַּלָּא בִי — *It became too much that You set traps for me as for a lion, so You returned again and again to render punctilious judgment against me.* We have rendered this cryptic verse as does *Rashi.* His reading here confirms our understanding of verses 6-7, and the structure of the rest of the passage up to this point. It can only mean: The agonies to which You exposed me in the hope that I would become ensnared in sin, are the equivalent of traps set to catch a mighty lion. However, when I stood firm and refused to be dragged into blasphemy, You tired of the test, and instead, You now expose my every action to exacting and finicky judgment [so that the slightest infringement is severely punished].

יִגְאֶה, from גָּאָה, *to grow big.* See above at 8:11.

For וְתָשֹׁב, *Rashi* adds: [*You returned*] day after day.

For תִּתְפַּלָּא, *Rashi* writes: To be punctilious and exacting in judgment. He adduces כִּי יַפְלִא, which could refer either to *Leviticus* 27:2 or to *Numbers* 6:2. In both those places *Rashi* renders יַפְרִישׁ, *to make clear.*[1]

17. תְּחַדֵּשׁ עֵדֶיךָ נֶגְדִּי וְתֶרֶב כַּעַשְׂךָ עִמָּדִי חֲלִיפוֹת וְצָבָא עִמִּי — *You constantly revitalize those that attest for You against me, piling up Your anger against me. Mine are relays and measured time-spans.* As we shall see in the commentary to the next verse, ours seems to be the final one in the main part of this, Iyov's third, and up to this point, most caustic, speech. Accordingly, we would expect it to sum up all the bitter feelings which, throughout, have animated him.

However, the verse is difficult. What is its precise meaning, and what does it add to what has been said before?

On עֵדֶיךָ, *Rashi* writes: To bear witness concerning the relays of the sicknesses and the pains. This, in contrast to *Ramban* who thinks that the sickness itself is the *witness* to Iyov's alleged wickedness.

Who are these witnesses? What is their function? To what do they testify, and for what purpose?

We have rendered תְּחַדֵּשׁ as *revitalize,* and עֵדֶיךָ as *Those that attest for You against*

1. At first sight, *Rashi's* comparison to the use of the word in *Leviticus* and *Numbers* seems farfetched. There seems little connection between clarity of expression and punctilious and exacting justice.

However *Chizkuni,* one of the great exponents of *Rashi,* lends new insights to *Rashi's* meaning in those two places. In both instances he points out that פלא belongs to that group of words which can be used for opposites. He cites *Deuteronomy* 17:8, כִּי יִפָּלֵא מִמְּךָ דָבָר, where פלא is used to describe a judgment that is unclear or hidden from the judges. Apparently, then, he understands *Rashi's* use of יַפְרִישׁ in those two instances not to mean simply, clarity of expression, but a thoughtful and caring analysis of the situation which clearly indicates the desirability of making the respective vows with which the passages there deal.

[14] *If I have sinned, and You scrutinize me, refuse to cleanse me*
of my transgression. [15] *If, then, I have been guilty — woe is to*
me. But if I am innocent should I not be able to raise my head?
Surfeited with shame, confronted by my misery! [16] *It became*
too much that You set traps for me as for a lion, so You re-
turned again and again to render punctilious judgment against
me. [17] *You constantly revitalize those that attest for You against*
me, piling up Your anger against me. Mine are relays and
measured time-spans. [18] *Now why did You bring me out from*
the womb, would that I had died so that no eye would see me.
[19] *It would then have been as though I had never existed,*
would that I had been carried from the womb to the grave.

me, rather than, *Your witnesses against me*, for the following reasons:

The verb חִדֵּשׁ, in the *piel*, is never used to describe the action of producing something new, but rather, as *renewing* and giving new life to that which had already existed earlier. For one example, see *I Samuel* 11:14, and *Rashi* there.

The use of the personal pronoun together with עֵד is rare. When it occurs at all (in *Isaiah* chapters 33 and 34) it always means those who bear witness *concerning* the person indicated by the pronoun; the meaning is never, the witnesses brought by that person against another.

Never once in Scripture is the preposition נֶגֶד used to describe the bearing of witness *against* someone, the correct form for this is לְהָעִיד בְּ . . . . נֶגֶד, usually means, *in the presence of*.

Accordingly, we understand the meaning as follows:

In one last shriek of utter impotence, Iyov pictures himself, the helpless quarry, in the hands of an all-powerful, cruel and implacable God — Who, inexplicably, sees frail mortals as fair game over which to demonstrate His superiority (vs. 4-5). Iyov's unspeakable experiences are *witnesses* testifying to God's ability to make man squirm, and leave no doubt in Iyov's mind that he is destined to suffer ever more relays of agonies washing over him. With exquisite cruelty, each new wave of pain comes with fresh vigor — no waning strength, no spent energy, there. Moreover, God's wrath seems never satiated, it constantly reuses itself with overwhelming vindictiveness.

By contrast to this constantly self-replenishing source of power, Iyov sees himself as utterly without help, as a pawn who exercises no influence over his own fate. If new tortures are considered appropriate, they smash down upon him in waves — he can do nothing to stop them. If one particular pain seems to torture with greater force than the other, then it is allowed to play itself out in *measured time-span*. All that is left to him is to suffer.

18-19. וְלָמָּה מֵרֶחֶם הֹצֵאתָנִי אֶגְוַע וְעַיִן לֹא־תִרְאֵנִי — *Now why did You bring me out from the womb, would that I had died so that no eye would see me.* כַּאֲשֶׁר לֹא־הָיִיתִי אֶהְיֶה מִבֶּטֶן לַקֶּבֶר אוּבָל — *It would then have been as though I had never existed, would that I had been carried from the womb to the grave.* Iyov's fury has finally spent itself. There is a part of him which knows well that none of what he has said is really true. The God Whom he has faithfully worshiped all his life is not, cannot be, the ogre whom he has painted here. It will not be long — it will be in his response to Tzophar in chapter 13 — that the same Iyov who has, in this speech, apparently sunk to the depths of blasphemy, will soar to the most sublime adoration of God.

Clearly, then, it was not the real Iyov who was speaking here. It was a man, almost crazed by agony, who allowed his surface emotions to run away with him. In the end, God will understand. As *Rava* teaches in *Bava Basra* 16b, no man is blamed for the thoughtless words which he utters under the goading of unrelieved pain.

But, for now, Iyov is tired. Rebellion is drained from him. Wistfully he returns to the impossible dream which has tantalized him since his world came tumbling down around him. How beautiful it would have been if he could just simply have died at birth. What horrors would have been spared him!

י/כ-כב כ הֲלֹא־מְעַט יָמַי °יחדל °ישית מִמֶּנִּי וְאַבְלִיגָה מְּעָט׃
°וְחָדַל ק׳ כא בְּטֶרֶם אֵלֵךְ וְלֹא אָשׁוּב אֶל־אֶרֶץ חֹשֶׁךְ וְצַלְמָוֶת׃
°וְשִׁית ק׳ כב אֶרֶץ עֵפָתָה ׀ כְּמוֹ אֹפֶל צַלְמָוֶת וְלֹא סְדָרִים וַתֹּפַע
יא/א-ב כְּמוֹ־אֹפֶל׃ א-ב וַיַּעַן צֹפַר הַנַּעֲמָתִי וַיֹּאמַר׃ הֲרֹב דְּבָרִים

20-22. הֲלֹא־מְעַט יָמַי וַחֲדָל וְשִׁית מִמֶּנִּי וְאַבְלִיגָה מְּעָט — *My days are so few — leave off, distance Yourself from me so that I can come to myself a little.* בְּטֶרֶם אֵלֵךְ וְלֹא אָשׁוּב אֶל־אֶרֶץ חֹשֶׁךְ וְצַלְמָוֶת — *Before I depart never to return, to a land of gloom and the shadows of death.* אֶרֶץ עֵפָתָה כְּמוֹ אֹפֶל צַלְמָוֶת וְלֹא סְדָרִים וַתֹּפַע כְּמוֹ־אֹפֶל — *A land darkened as the murkiness of death's shadows, chaos, its brightest spots — grim darkness.'*

Chapter 10	Chapter 7
20. הֲלֹא־מְעַט יָמַי וַחֲדָל . . . וְשִׁית מִמֶּנִּי וְאַבְלִיגָה מְּעָט *My days are so few — leave off, distance Yourself from me so that I can come to myself a little.*	16. מָאַסְתִּי לֹא־לְעֹלָם אֶחְיֶה חֲדַל מִמֶּנִּי כִּי־הֶבֶל יָמָי *I am sickened; I shall not live forever, leave me be for my days are as nothing.*

Verse 20 is sufficiently similar in tone to 7:16 and 19 to make the differences between the remainders of the two passages striking. There we saw that the musings of verse 16 led from Iyov's preoccupation with his own troubles to an examination of the human condition in general. This was then followed by an expression of surprise at God's apparently relentless fixation with Iyov's shortcomings, and the wish, so often prominent in Iyov's thinking, that he might die and thus escape his troubles.

Here, we have, instead, the anticipation of the unrelieved darkness of the grave.

We should note further that our verses 18-19 are almost identical with 3:10 and 12.

Chapter 10	Chapter 3
18. וְלָמָּה מֵרֶחֶם הֹצֵאתָנִי אֶגְוַע וְעַיִן לֹא־תִרְאֵנִי *Now why did You bring me out from the womb, would that I had died so that no eye would see me.*	10. לָמָּה לֹּא מֵרֶחֶם אָמוּת מִבֶּטֶן יָצָאתִי וְאֶגְוָע *Why would I not die straight from the womb, come forth from the belly and expire.*
19. כַּאֲשֶׁר לֹא־הָיִיתִי אֶהְיֶה מִבֶּטֶן לַקֶּבֶר אוּבָל *It would then be as though I had never existed, would that I had been carried from the womb to the grave.*	12. כִּי־עַתָּה שָׁכַבְתִּי *For now I would have lain supine . . .*

Further, our verse 20 is noteworthy for the fact that it is read differently than it is written (*k'ri-k'siv*). The written forms are יַחְדָּל and יָשִׁית which are in the third person — that is, that Iyov's direct speech to God has ended, and these final three verses are in the form of soliloquy. The form in which they are read yields, וַחֲדָל and וְשִׁית, forms which carry no connotation that the direct address to God is ended. [We have indicated the ambivalence by omitting the quotation marks.]

Crucial to the understanding of our passage is the unrelievedly gloomy picture of the grave which it paints, in sharp contrast to 3:12ff. and particularly 3:16ff., where the grave is depicted as a place of peace and tranquility.

We suggest the following interpretation for this passage:

The marked similarity between verses 18-19 and the earlier verses, which we have indicated above, are certainly meant to awaken an association with that passage. Iyov expresses the forlorn wish that he might have died at birth — and gone to the idyllic resting place which he described in chapter 3.

But verse 20 veers off in a different direction. The indication lies in the *k'ri-k'siv.* It indicates that although Iyov is still addressing God (the *k'ri*), these are really thoughts which, more properly, belong in his own mind.

We have here another of the mental lurches

10/20-22 [20] *My days are so few — leave off, distance Yourself from me so that I can come to myself a little.* [21] *Before I depart never to return, to a land of gloom and the shadows of death.* [22] *A land darkened as the murkiness of death's shadows, chaos, its brightest spots — grim darkness.'*

11/1-2 [1] *Tzophar the Naamathite responded and said:* [2] *Should one*

which we have observed before. The meaning of the passage is that suddenly Iyov longs terribly to live, and to live happily. His meaning here is not as it was at 7:16, that his life is too insignificant to warrant God's attention, but on the contrary life is sweet and desirable; and Iyov, with all his heart, wishes that God would relieve him of his agonies, so that he could enjoy the short time that is left to him on earth.

The attitude toward the grave depends upon whether or not there is a will to live. When Iyov wanted nothing better than to die, the grave looked attractive. He would, at last, find repose from all his troubles. Now that he wants desperately to live after all, the grave takes on the ominous, threatening dimension of darkness and gloom.

He is hesitant about saying all this to God. He had, after all, always begged for the opposite — death as quickly as possible, the faster to escape his fate. He is diffident about changing direction now, and asking for life. Hence the *k'ri-k'siv*, which indicates an ambivalence about addressing this request to God. It is more properly a thought which belongs in his own mind, to be shared with no one.

As we have noted often, such switches in perspective are perfectly normal for a person in the throes of suffering. Life, after all, *is* sweet; and in spite of agonizing pain, men tend to cling to it with all their might. The sudden change in direction is not in consonance with any particular philosophical position, but it is intensely human.

However, we must ask why this sudden affirmation of life should appear specifically at the end of this particular speech. Clearly, it is unacceptable to argue that Iyov just happened to think this particular thought at this point.

We suggest that this sudden swing is a function of the vehemently aggressive tone of the rest of the speech. Iyov, as it were, has become shocked by the vehemence of his diatribes. He knows that what he has said, the appalling accusations which he has hurled at God, are not really his ideas. He has allowed his suffering to goad him to unacceptable lengths. In reaction, he swings to the other extreme.

This tacit admission of excess appears to lay the ground for Tzophar's speech, which at its very beginning recognizes Iyov's speech as merely an *abundance of words* and as the fulminations of a *garrulous man* — see commentary there. Our passage marks Iyov for what he really is — an essentially good man, crazed by pain and frustration.

וְשִׁית, from שִׁית, *to place* (*Rashi* to *Exodus* 10:1). Literally, *Place Yourself away from me* (*Rashi*).

עֵפָתָה is *darkness*. See *Amos* 4:13, and *Rashi* there.

תֹּפַע from יָפַע, *to shine forth*.

Ramban (*Toras HaAdam*) believes that אֶרֶץ עֵפָתָה is a reference to *Gehinnom*. See the footnote to Introductory Remarks to 36:9.

XI.

☙ Tzophar's First Speech

Tzophar's aim, as *Ramban*, and possibly *Rashi*, see it, is similar to that of Bildad: Iyov must be brought to a realization that suffering is the wage of sin. Neither of the two can conceive of a world-order — under God — which would allow for any other explanation. Iyov's protestations notwithstanding, there must, there simply must, be a cankerous worm of evil gnawing within the seemingly wholesome exterior of his blameless life.

But where Bildad paints a canvas in which blighted hopes and false expectations are calculated to break the spirit, in which the fortress is stripped away to reveal the spider's web beneath, Tzophar guides Iyov's eyes upwards. In lyric exultation he sings of greater wisdoms, of hidden worlds, of a might and an exaltedness which belie even the possibility of human innocence. Iyov must have sinned in ways which he himself cannot have appreciated. Let him but focus on man's inherent shortcomings, let him admit the truth, correct past mistakes and turn to God in contrition and prayer — the dreadful past will slip away into the mists of

ג לֹא יַעֲנֶה וְאִם־אִישׁ שְׂפָתַיִם יִצְדָּק׃ בַּדֶּיךָ מְתִים יַחֲרִישׁוּ

forgetfulness, a renewed and invigorated future beckons.

The commentary offers an alternative interpretation. Tzophar does not discuss Iyov's suffering at all. He offers no explanations, does not discuss whether or not Iyov had sinned. His entire focus is upon the dreadful blasphemies of the previous two chapters. With exquisite sensitivity he lets it be known that he realizes that Iyov had spoken only out of the throes of an unbearable agony and had never meant the calumnies which he had uttered. Nevertheless, he will not let them pass in silence.

First, he establishes how far God is removed from the base motives which Iyov had ascribed to Him. Surely, Iyov must realize that the mighty God of nature cannot be cut down to human dimensions. From there, he turns to Iyov's rehabilitation. With keen psychological insight he lets Iyov know that his loss of control derived from the brokenness that is the function of impurity. Let Iyov put his spiritual house in order, and all the malignant pettiness which had caused his bitterness will dissipate.

Ramban places Tzophar within the motif begun by the other friends. As Bildad did before him, he takes it for granted that Iyov must have sinned [thus *Ramban's* perception of Bildad's theological stance — see chapter 8], but he is willing to recognize the difficulties which Iyov has in accepting this, and to address them.

His solution is that in view of the profound and impenetrable wisdom and goodness of God, Iyov may well be erring when he considers himself a *tzaddik*. Who can claim righteousness before such a great God? On the contrary, it is likely that God is overlooking some of Iyov's transgressions, and punishing him for only part of them.

Tzophar buttresses this position on philosophical grounds. He offers a breakthrough explanation for the tranquility in which many wicked find themselves — a problem that has troubled Iyov sorely.[1]

1. Iyov does indeed tackle this question in later speeches, particularly at 21:7ff. However, up to this point he has not really raised the issue, and it is not easy to see why *Ramban* identifies it here as Iyov's 'great question.' In his commentary to 9:1, *Ramban* specifically states that for now, Iyov agrees to Bildad's assertion that the wicked are destroyed.

This same problem has troubled us earlier, in the commentary to 8:8-10. There, too, *Ramban* sees the thrust of Bildad's argument as making the point that the well-being of the wicked cannot last, and that eventually their wickedness will reap its just punishment. But again, this is an issue which seems not to have troubled Iyov at all in the first round.

We suspect that *Ramban's* interpretations may be influenced by his understanding of the purpose for which the book of *Iyov* was written. In his Introduction to the book, he isolates the problems which people have with the observable suffering of the innocent and well-being of the wicked (צַדִּיק וְרַע לוֹ רָשָׁע וְטוֹב לוֹ) as being the one main cause for denial of God's benign providence over the affairs of man. He asserts that it was with the view of providing answers for these vexing difficulties that the book was written.

In the course of his commentary, he ascribes to Iyov the various attitudes [or variations of them] which, as he reports in his Introduction, the ancients espoused in their attempts to grapple with this difficulty. In sum, these maintain that God, for one reason or another, is not involved in the affairs of man. This might be because human fate lies with the heavenly constellations (see Prefatory Remarks to chapter 3): God is impotent; or because God is so exalted as to be utterly indifferent to what happens on earth (see Prefatory Remarks to chapter 6): God is uncaring.

Since this is Iyov's theological stance, it stands to reason that the friends would address this theological problem. Indeed, in *Ramban's* view this is the thrust of all the arguments. God knows; God cares; God is able; and God actively intervenes in human affairs. (See *Ramban* to *Exodus* 13:16 which should be studied in conjunction with the beginning of his Introduction to *Iyov*.)

Given these assumptions concerning the structure and dynamics of the book, it is not surprising that the friends should interchange the problem of the wicked man's apparent tranquility, with that of the righteous man's suffering. They are, after all, two sides of the same coin, and to the extent that Iyov is troubled by the one, he would also be troubled by the other, although he does not actually express this side of the problem.

However, in *Rashi's* view, as we have understood it throughout — that the book is an existential account of human suffering rather than a presentation of theological arguments — none of this would hold true. Iyov's immediate concern is with his own suffering. The problem of the tranquil wicked — one which is purely theoretical within the context of his present experiences — does not impinge upon his fevered agonies until, in the course of the conversation, it becomes a part of the agenda.

It is, however, noteworthy that in *Toras HaAdam*, where *Ramban* gives a brief overview of the book of *Iyov*, he states that Tzophar has supplied an answer to the 'great and well-known problem' of the tranquil wicked, without identifying it (as he does in his commentary) as Iyov's great question.

of abundant words not be answered, should the eloquent man be in the right? [3] *Your fabrications strike men dumb,*

God in His mercy is granting them time to repent. If they do not, their wickedness will certainly overtake them and they will be punished. This assumption being accepted, it clearly demonstrates God's concern for even the wicked. From that point we are ready to progress with a *kal vachomer*. If God is so long-suffering and loving even to the wicked, then clearly he would not make the innocent suffer.

Thus, Tzophar's point is proven: Iyov's suffering is not in vain. It comes to prod him towards penitence. Let him take the lesson, divest himself of sinful gains, pray to God and all will be well.[1]

In essential details *Rashi* appears to agree with *Ramban*. Where the two diverge, the commentary will point this out.

2. הֲרֹב דְּבָרִים לֹא יֵעָנֶה וְאִם־אִישׁ שְׂפָתַיִם יִצְדָּק — *Should one of abundant words not be answered, should the eloquent man be in the right?* As Eliphaz did before him (4:2), Tzophar begins his speech by stating that he feels constrained to an answer to Iyov's speech.[2]

However, whereas Eliphaz's urge to speak derived from the impatience which Iyov had displayed (see commentary there for *Rashi's* interpretation), Tzophar seems to feel prompted to reply simply by the abundance of words which Iyov had uttered, the eloquence with which he makes his points.

It appears that by isolating this aspect of Iyov's speech rather than feeling called upon to refute the dreadful blasphemies which he had spoken, Tzophar expresses an understanding for the truth which Iyov himself had recognized at the end of the last chapter — see towards the end of the commentary to verses 20-22. The dreadful things which he had said were not really an expression of his true feelings. They had been wild fulminations, forced from him by his agonies — a torrent of words which, after all, were only words. Tzophar, as it were, confirms *Rava's* statement (*Bava Basra* 16b) that no man should be held responsible for what he said in the throes of suffering.

1. Bildad, too, has suggested that Iyov turn to God in prayer, see at 8:5. Whether or not Eliphaz made the same suggestion, would depend on the rendering of 5:8. As we saw in the commentary there, *Ramban* understands that phrase not as recommending prayer but as expressing Eliphaz's conviction that all that happens is to be ascribed to God's providence rather than to the influences of the heavenly constellations.

In *Ramban's* view, then, Bildad and Tzophar both urge Iyov to pray, while Eliphaz does not.

This highlights *Ramban's* understanding of the different ideas expressed by the three friends:

Eliphaz had offered no suggestions for explaining Iyov's suffering, had accused him of no wrongdoing. He simply suggested that with the situation given, it would be wise for Iyov to sublimate his experiences, use them as a goad to better himself, and thus turn them into a positive good (see commentary to 5:1 and 2).

Bildad is the first to suggest that Iyov must have sinned, and he therefore offers another idea concerning his suffering: It has a cleansing and atoning function. Iyov's sons have been absolutely wicked and so had to die. Iyov himself was less culpable, but had to pass through a small death — his agonies — in order to achieve atonement (see Introductory Remarks to chapter 8 and commentary to v. 4, there).

Tzophar, as we shall see in the commentary to this chapter, offers another explanation for the suffering. Indeed, Iyov had sinned, and thus God is sending him his agonies so that they should drive him towards repentance. See below to verses 13 and 14.

Thus, it is clear why both Bildad and Tzophar call Iyov to prayer, while Eliphaz does not. Each of the latter two had explained the suffering as being related to Iyov's shortcomings, and as having the purpose of correcting them in one of the two suggested forms. Once Iyov understands this, its purpose will have been served. Newly cleansed, he can turn to God in prayer, and He will then cause the pain to cease. In Eliphaz's thought, there is no room for this kind of prayer. [But see the commentary, where we find *Ramban* himself explaining Tzophar's call to prayer somewhat differently.]

2. Bildad, in chapter 8, does not seek to justify himself for responding to Iyov.

Each of the friends may be introducing his words in a way which is appropriate to the contents of the speech to which he is responding.

Eliphaz and Tzophar must both have been outraged by the thoughts which Iyov had expressed. Eliphaz needed to react to Iyov's contention that man's fate was decided by the heavenly constellations (*Ramban*), or to the total disillusion which he expressed in his diatribe. Tzophar's speech comes after Iyov has hurled accusations against God which must have assaulted the listener's ears.

Both, therefore, make the point that they simply could not remain silent.

Not so Bildad. In his response to Eliphaz, Iyov had said nothing which could have provoked such a sense of outrage. Bildad could make no claim that he felt himself forced to respond.

ד וַתִּלְעַג וְאֵין מַכְלִם: וַתֹּאמֶר זַךְ לִקְחִי וּבַר הָיִיתִי בְעֵינֶיךָ:
ה־ו וְאוּלָם מִי־יִתֵּן אֱלוֹהַ דַּבֵּר וְיִפְתַּח שְׂפָתָיו עִמָּךְ: וְיַגֶּד־לְךָ ׀
תַּעֲלֻמוֹת חָכְמָה כִּי־כִפְלַיִם לְתוּשִׁיָּה וְדַע ׀ כִּי־יַשֶּׁה לְךָ

We have rendered אִישׁ שְׂפָתַיִם as *an eloquent man*, as does *Metzudos*, and this appears to be *Targum's* understanding too. He renders: A man who is *master* of the lips. *Ramban* offers no explanation for the term. It could perhaps be understood as simply a parallelism to רב דְּבָרִים, and be rendered *a loquacious* or a *garrulous* man. The correct understanding of the term will affect the meaning of the next verse.

3. בַּדֶּיךָ מְתִים יַחֲרִישׁוּ וַתִּלְעַג וְאֵין מַכְלִם — *Your fabrications strike men dumb, you ridicule and no one confounds you. Rashi* offers no explanation for the second part of the verse, and so, in translating it, we have followed *Metzudos. Ramban* understands it to mean: *You have uttered words which deserve to be ridiculed.*

The difference is profound.

Ramban's understanding is as follows: On a number of occasions he makes the point that the problem of the tranquility of the wicked is far more difficult to deal with than that of the suffering of the righteous. This, because we can all judge objectively when a person acts in an evil manner. If he lives a happy life in spite of his manifest wickedness, God's justice must be questioned. Not so in the case of the suffering *tzaddik*. We can never know for sure whether a person is truly righteous. Even though he appears to act in an exemplary way, his thoughts may be evil. When we see an ostensibly righteous man suffer, we can always tell ourselves that he must have done something of which we do not know, to deserve his fate. Only the person himself, who knows himself to be absolutely good, has the right to question God's providence when suffering strikes.

It is against the background of this truism that *Ramban* understands this and the next verse.

Tzophar is addressing himself to Iyov's claim that his suffering is unjustly imposed upon him. He has deserved better at God's hands. But Tzophar, who is convinced of God's justice, sees this claim as an untruth. Clearly, Iyov must have sinned. Yet no man can prove Iyov wrong. All are struck dumb (our verse) by his forceful assertion of innocence (next verse), because in his public life he has indeed acted well. However, without his protestations people would have told themselves that he must have harbored some hidden vice within himself. It is his false claim to total goodness which silences men.

Now this claim of innocence cannot be defined as an act of ridiculing. Accordingly, *Ramban* explains the second half of the verse as we have seen above. Iyov's claims deserve to be ridiculed.

Iyov's assertion of innocence did not require any particular eloquence. Accordingly, it is likely that *Ramban* understands אִישׁ שְׂפָתַיִם of the previous verse as one who is loquacious rather than as one who has shown remarkable eloquence.

We believe that *Rashi* has an entirely different understanding of the verse. On בַּדֶּיךָ, he writes: [The fabrications] which you devise in your heart. Now, by adding the words, *in your heart, Rashi* appears to make the point that although בַּדֶּיךָ is an expression of falsehood (see *Rashi* to *I Kings* 12:33), it is a special type of falsehood. The root בדה is used twice in Scripture as a verb: once at *I Kings* 12:33, and once at *Nehemiah* 6:8. In both instances it describes the investing of a given phenomenon with a meaning that is foreign to it. In the former case, a month which has no sanctity is treated as though it has; in the latter case, innocent building activities are construed as acts of rebellion. In a very similar vein, *Rashi* to *Isaiah* 44:25 explains that star-gazers, whose interpretations are frequently false, are called בַּדִּים. Once more, we have the same idea. Heavenly constellations are invested with meanings which they do not really have.

Accordingly, *Rashi's* meaning, here too, is that בַּדֶּיךָ does not describe simple falsehoods — such as would have been the case if, as *Ramban* understands it, the issue would have been Iyov's freedom from sin — but rather the interpretation of events by ideas which have their source in the observer's heart, but never in objective truth.

In short, the *fabrications* which strike men dumb are Iyov's interpretation of the way in which God deals with man. The terrible accusations which he has made are, Tzophar asserts, unrelated to the truth. They have their genesis — and their only reality — in Iyov's own heart.

How did Iyov *ridicule*? Certainly, the simple meaning of it is *you ridicule*, rather than, as *Ramban* takes it, *you have uttered words which deserve to be ridiculed.*

In the commentary to 9:22-24 we suggested that in verse 24, Iyov is saying one thing —

11
4-6

you ridicule and no one confounds you. 4 *So that you say, 'My*
doctrine is impeccable, for I have been pure in Your eyes!'
5 *However, would that God would speak, open His lips to you.*
6 *That He would inform you of the hidden recesses of wisdom, that*
sagacity has double folds. Know then, that God grants you

such as, that occasionally there is a wicked King whose unjust laws make both the righteous and the innocent suffer — but that his choice of words indicates that he really means another — that God Himself is that wicked king. Such a double entendre might well be described as engaging in *ridicule.* It would certainly be a usage to which Tzophar might well take exception.

The ability to silence his audience by propounding theories which have no basis in reality but are in fact wholly produced within his own heart, to be able to convey subliminal meanings within an apparently innocent text — these are skills of *eloquence,* and we assume that this is how *Rashi* takes the phrase in the previous verse.

4. וַתֹּאמֶר זַךְ לִקְחִי וּבַר הָיִיתִי בְעֵינֶיךָ — *So that you say, 'My doctrine is impeccable, for I have been pure in Your eyes!'* As we saw above, *Ramban* reads this verse together with the earlier one. The fabrications which had silenced critics were the assertions of innocence which Iyov had always made. We assume that *Ramban* would render the beginning of our verse: *That you say . . . ,* rather than as we have done.

To the second part of the sentence *Ramban* adds: *From my very beginnings I have been pure in Your eyes.*

But why לֶקַח, *doctrine*? The issue revolves not around Iyov's teachings, but his actions.

As we have understood *Rashi* the question of *doctrine* is relevant indeed. Iyov's *fabrications* concerned the *doctrine* which he insisted upon propounding — his assessment of God's relationship to humanity, His unfeeling and uncaring despotism which delights in the suffering of the innocent and apportions agonies to righteous and wicked alike. Iyov maintains that this doctrine is absolute truth, cannot be faulted (see *Proverbs* 16:2 for a similar use of זַךְ). This, because of his assertion that he had always been *pure in [God's] eyes* and therefore deserved no punishment.

5. וְאוּלָם מִי־יִתֵּן אֱלוֹהַּ דַּבֵּר וְיִפְתַּח שְׂפָתָיו עִמָּךְ — *However, would that God would speak, open His lips to you.* In *Ramban's* view this verse flows from the previous one. No human can really pass judgment upon your claim of innocence. Only God Himself can refute it.

Rashi, from his perspective, would understand the verse in a similar way. Only God, by revealing to you the truths taught in the next verse, can wean you away from your false perceptions.

6. וְיַגֶּד־לְךָ תַּעֲלֻמוֹת חָכְמָה כִּי־כִפְלַיִם לְתוּשִׁיָּה וְדַע כִּי־יַשֶּׁה לְךָ אֱלוֹהַּ מֵעֲוֹנֶךָ — *That He would inform you of the hidden recesses of wisdom, that sagacity has double folds. Know then, that God grants you accommodation from some of your sins! Rashi* ties the two parts of the sentence together as cause and effect. Once God has revealed the *hidden recesses of wisdom* to you, you will realize that *sagacity has double folds* — the Torah [thus he appears to take תּוּשִׁיָּה] places many more obligations upon you than you previously realized, double those which you have fulfilled. Contrary to your assertions, you fall far short of that which is demanded of you.

Far from being punished too harshly, you yet owe God much for sins which, in ignorance of your obligations, you have committed. [יַשֶּׁה, the *hiphil* of נשה, *to be owed,* means *to be a creditor to someone.*]

Ramban understands the thrust of the argument in much the same way, although he renders the words quite differently. He assumes that תּוּשִׁיָּה is related to יֵשׁ *that which exists,* and understands the phrase to mean that all existence has a dual nature: the part of it which we apprehend, and the part which must forever remain hidden from us. Through these two facets of being, Divine wisdom functions as both the revealed and concealed mover of human fate. In the parts which we can observe we find His stewardship over our affairs to be wholly good; we conclude that this holds true in even greater measure in those aspects of the Divine Providence which is beyond our ken.

From this accolade to God's benevolence, the second half of the verse flows naturally. How can anyone possibly serve such a God adequately? Clearly, Iyov's shortcomings are legion, and the punishments which God is inflicting upon him leave countless other sins unrequited.

The thrust, then, of both *Rashi's* and *Ramban's* understanding of the verse is that Iyov's

ז אֱלוֹהַ מֵעֲוֺנֶךָ: הַחֵקֶר אֱלוֹהַ תִּמְצָא אִם עַד־תַּכְלִית שַׁדַּי
ח תִּמְצָא: גָּבְהֵי שָׁמַיִם מַה־תִּפְעָל עֲמֻקָּה מִשְּׁאוֹל מַה־תֵּדָע:
ט־י אֲרֻכָּה מֵאֶרֶץ מִדָּהּ וּרְחָבָה מִנִּי־יָם: אִם־יַחֲלֹף וְיַסְגִּיר
יא וְיַקְהִיל וּמִי יְשִׁיבֶנּוּ: כִּי־הוּא יָדַע מְתֵי־שָׁוְא וַיַּרְא־אָוֶן וְלֹא

suffering is to be traced to shortcomings of which he himself is not even aware.

But, why should Iyov be punished so severely for sins which he had committed unwittingly? And moreover, why he, of all people? Tzophar is surely not suggesting, at this point, that Iyov is more wicked than the average man. What Iyov did not know about God, we may safely assume that very few others knew. Nevertheless, no one else suffers as he does. How does Tzophar presume to comfort Iyov with these words?

If we read verses 6-11 as one unit and, for the moment, leave aside the second halves of verses 6 and 11, which deal with man's sin, then the entire section is a paean to God's inscrutable wisdom as it is manifest in the wonders of nature. As such, it is strikingly similar to the thrust of God's speech from the whirlwind. Tzophar, who in verse 5 had expressed the wish that God might communicate with Iyov directly, has in fact gauged correctly what the burden of such a communication would be.

Tzophar would be addressing himself directly to those elements of Iyov's previous speech which, as we have isolated above, he found to be so objectionable. If only, he seems to be saying, if only you could have a glimpse of God's true greatness, you would never have hurled all those dreadful accusations against Him!

Verse 12 tends to confirm this thesis precisely. *That the hollow man might win a heart, that a wild ass might yield a man.* This, is to be the result of learning the truths described in the previous few verses. But, what is being said in this verse? What is a *hollow man*, what *heart* is he destined to acquire, and who is described as a *wild ass*?

As we understand the section, this is indeed an ideal description of the Iyov of the foregoing speech. He was indeed *hollow* in the sense that he lacked the *heart* to comprehend the true majesty of God, and acted like a *wild ass*, in lashing out without any restraint against the God Whom he did not understand at all.

How, then, are we to understand the second halves of verses 6 and 11 within such a context?

The phrase כִּי יַשֶּׁה לְךָ אֱלוֹהַ מֵעֲוֺנֶךָ is an extremely difficult one to understand. As we saw above, both *Rashi* and *Ramban* take the word from נָשָׁה, *to be a creditor to someone*, and understand the meaning to be that there are many sins which Iyov still 'owes' to God in the sense that he has not yet been punished for them.

Ibn Ezra writes that this is an unlikely meaning for the word. He does not explain why, but perhaps he reasons from the fact that invariably, when the word is so used in Scripture, it appears with the preposition . . . ב, rather than with . . . ל. See, for one example among many, *Deuteronomy* 24:11.

Ibn Ezra suggests that the meaning of the word is to be taken from נשה, *to forget*; thus, in the *hiphil*, *to cause to forget*. But, he does not make clear what precisely is being said. In fact, the form . . . יַשֶּׁה ל, is anyway problematic since normally this root meaning takes . . . אֶת, rather than . . . ל. For example, see *Genesis* 41:51.

In short, . . . יַשֶּׁה ל is unique in that nowhere else do we find נָשָׁה, in any of its possible meanings, used with . . . ל.

In *Iyov* we have נשה in the *hiphil* used in yet another sense. At 39:17, in the description of the stork, its meaning is that God *denied* this bird wisdom. On the assumption that the use of a root within the same book might indicate a congruence of meaning, we should examine that possibility.

The interpretation of מֵעֲוֺנֶךָ as meaning, *from some of your sins*, also appears strained in the context.

We might consider that the prefix, . . . מ here, has the meaning *because of . . .* , as, for example, in *Eichah* 4:13.

If so, the sense of the phrase, within the larger context of the verse, would be: Know that because of your sins (מֵעֲוֺנֶךָ) God causes you ignorance [deprives you (יַשֶּׁה לְךָ)] of [the understanding] concerning the hidden recesses of wisdom, the double folds of sagacity. You simply have no perception of God's true greatness!

Given this interpretation, the root נשה would here, uniquely, be used intransitively. This could well explain the use of the . . . ל, instead of the usual, אֶת.

The second part of verse 11 lends itself to a simple explanation within the spirit of the passage as we have understood it: God is so

11
7-11
accommodation from some of your sins! 7 Can you attain a
thorough knowledge of God, could you penetrate to the uttermost
reaches of Shaddai? 8 The very heights of heaven — what can you
do, deeper than the nethermost pit — what can you know? 9 Its
length — greater than the earth, and it is wider than the sea. 10 If
He were to pass by, and suppress, and gather in — who could turn
Him back? 11 For He knows futile man, sees iniquity and does not

overwhelmingly aware of man's pettiness and *futility*, that He can observe sin without ever giving it serious consideration. He is in no way touched by your shortcomings.

Interpreted thus, Tzophar in no way accuses Iyov of sin. The whole thrust of the passage is, simply, to show how ridiculous Iyov's assumptions about the nature and motivations of God were. How can you talk disparagingly about a God, Tzophar asks, Whose greatness you cannot even imagine and Who is far removed from the ignoble motives which you ascribed to Him?

7. הַחֵקֶר אֱלוֹהַּ תִּמְצָא אִם עַד־תַּכְלִית שַׁדַּי תִּמְצָא — *Can you attain a thorough knowledge of God, could you penetrate to the uttermost reaches of Shaddai?* You understand nothing of the real God. How, then, can you be sure that you have fulfilled all your duties towards Him?

This appears to be *Rashi's* understanding. *Ramban* translates each of the two phrases more specifically as relating to Iyov. He would render תַּכְלִית as *purpose*: Can you possibly know the *thorough knowledge* which God has of you? [תַּכְלִית is not that which man knows of God, but that which God knows of man.] Could you ever appreciate the purposes for which He brings suffering upon you?

In the alternative interpretation suggested in the commentary to the previous verse, we would understand the verse as does *Rashi*, but without the conclusion that because of God's inscrutability, Iyov is meant to conclude that he had sinned. Tzophar is chiding Iyov for the accusations he has made against God. How could you reduce a God Who is so great, to human dimensions?

חֵקֶר, from חקר, *to search out.* תַּכְלִית is a noun formed from the root כלה, *to bring to an end.*

8. גָּבְהֵי שָׁמַיִם מַה־תִּפְעָל עֲמֻקָּה מִשְּׁאוֹל מַה־תֵּדָע — *The very heights of heaven — what can you do, deeper than the nethermost pit — what can you know?* That which is as high as the heavens (*Rashi*), that is, God's wisdom (*Ramban*), what can you do — to attain it (*Ramban*). God's wisdom is deeper than the nethermost pit (*Rashi*), to which it penetrates (*Ramban*). What can you know of it?

9. אֲרֻכָּה מֵאֶרֶץ מִדָּה וּרְחָבָה מִנִּי־יָם — *Its length — greater than the earth, and it is wider than the sea.* God's wisdom is being described (*Ramban*).

10-11. אִם־יַחֲלֹף וְיַסְגִּיר וְיַקְהִיל וּמִי יְשִׁיבֶנּוּ — *If he were to pass by, and suppress, and gather in — who could turn Him back?* כִּי־הוּא יָדַע מְתֵי־שָׁוְא וַיַּרְא־אָוֶן וְלֹא יִתְבּוֹנָן — *For he knows futile man, sees iniquity and does not consider. Rashi* takes these two difficult verses together, and renders as follows: [*If He were to pass by,* is left untranslated], and [if He were] to *suppress,* by suffering, whomever He chose to, and were to *gather* His entire Heavenly Court to debate that suppression, then *who* among them *could turn Him back* by pointing out that His dealings are unfair? [And if we were to object on the basis of the fact that until now Iyov had lived a tranquil life, apparently indicating that he is a righteous person, this too cannot help at all.] *For,* though *He knows* well all the deeds performed by *futile man,* He may yet appear as though *He does not consider,* knows nothing of their sins, since He will hold back His anger and not punish them immediately [in order to give them time to repent].

Ramban, too, takes the two verses together and understands the second one precisely as does *Rashi.* His rendering of the first verse is radically different. יַחֲלֹף hints at *humankind* (*Proverbs* 31:8) and the verse is to be understood as follows: If God were to create many humans (יַחֲלֹף), and hand over the earth to them (יַסְגִּיר), and increase them (יַקְהִיל), then who could stay His hand [if they were wicked]?

Above, we suggested an alternative interpretation to that which sees Tzophar as accusing Iyov of sin. We saw him as attacking Iyov on his presumption in whittling God down to human dimensions, of accusing Him of cruel despotism, of challenging Him to justify Himself before the bar of Iyov's intellect. In the previous verses, Tzophar has described God in His inscrutable wisdom. He now turns to detailing His all-might in relation to man. He will demonstrate how patently ridiculous is

יב־יג יִתְבּוֹנָן: וְאִישׁ נָבוּב יִלָּבֵב וְעַיִר פֶּרֶא אָדָם יִוָּלֵד: אִם־אַתָּה
יד הֲכִינוֹתָ לִבֶּךָ וּפָרַשְׂתָּ אֵלָיו כַּפֶּיךָ: אִם־אָוֶן בְּיָדְךָ
טו הַרְחִיקֵהוּ וְאַל־תַּשְׁכֵּן בְּאֹהָלֶיךָ עַוְלָה: כִּי־אָז | תִּשָּׂא פָנֶיךָ

the idea that God is the celestial bully of Iyov's fulminations.

We have three verbs in our verse, יַחֲלֹף, יַסְגִּיר, and יַקְהִיל, each of which requires elucidation.

Iyov has used יַחֲלֹף at 9:11 — there too in the context of a description of God's all-might — with a meaning parallel to יַעֲבֹר עָלַי. The sense of those two phrases (we translated the second one *[He] glides past*) is that God works His will in the twinkling of an eye. Man is not even aware of Him as He exercises control over human destiny.

The speed with which God is able to do that which He sets out to do is then, in Iyov's thought-world, an indication of His incalculable might.

There seems no reason why the same meaning cannot be assigned in our verse, the more so since the context is identical — a description of God's might.

At *Psalms* 35:3 we have the root סגר used, as *Rashi* understands it, to describe the erection of a barrier between two entities. This usage would make it an antonym of קהל, which describes a *gathering together*.

Our verse is saying that mankind is totally helpless against God. In one second (יַחֲלֹף) He can either divide people from one another (יַסְגִּיר) or gather them together (יַקְהִיל), and there is absolutely no one who can deny Him his wish (וּמִי יְשִׁיבֶנּוּ). God is absolute master over the affairs of man!

In this context the expression, מְתֵי שָׁוְא, for describing man, is singularly apt. God is fully aware when puny man, in his futile thrashing, in the midget rebellions of his insignificance, seeks to defy Him (וַיַּרְא אָוֶן), but He does not pay any attention to these iniquities (וְלֹא יִתְבּוֹנָן). He is above them and consequently not touched by them. [This is akin to Elihu's argument at 35:6.]

Tzophar has eloquently made his point. Iyov has overstepped the boundaries of the acceptable, by putting himself in one category with God (see at 8:8, for this as one of the criticisms which *Rava*, at *Bava Basra* 16a, levels at Iyov).

12. וְאִישׁ נָבוּב יִלָּבֵב וְעַיִר פֶּרֶא אָדָם יִוָּלֵד — *That the hollow man might win a heart, that a wild ass might yield a man.* The translation follows *Rashi*. *Ramban* believes that יִלָּבֵב belongs to that group of words which are used to describe both a given concept and its opposite. Thus יִלָּבֵב, *to be without a heart*, to lack wisdom.

The meaning of the verse changes with the two modes of interpretation.

In *Rashi's* view the verse seems to follow directly upon the previous one. There, Tzophar had said that God occasionally disregards the wicked man's sins, so as to grant him time for repentance. Our verse then describes what will occur if man takes advantage of this dispensation. The emptiness within will be replaced by a receptive and discriminating understanding. He will discover a man where, before, there appeared to be only a wild ass.

In *Ramban's* view, the verse stands in sorrowful contrast to what was described before. God is good in that He grants the sinner time to repent. From this we are to deduce that He certainly would not harm the righteous person. But ... the hollow man has no heart — he understands nothing of all this. He is akin [יִוָּלֵד, *is born*] to the wild ass which charges around in uncontrolled abandon, totally unaware of its potential to wreak harm. The wicked man cannot assess his own wickedness and will remain ignorant of his true standing unless he can correct himself, as described in the next verse.

In the alternative interpretation which we have offered above, our verse goes back to verse 5 in which Tzophar had expressed the wish that God might indeed appear to Iyov in His overwhelming grandeur. If only this were to happen, the shallow ignorance which made Iyov's tragic misunderstandings possible, would be replaced with an understanding heart; the uncontrolled fury which had hurled such cruel and unfounded accusations against a wholly benign God would be softened. Man would replace the wild ass of Iyov's passion.

13-15. אִם־אַתָּה הֲכִינוֹתָ לִבֶּךָ וּפָרַשְׂתָּ אֵלָיו כַּפֶּיךָ — *If you were but to set your heart, if you would spread out your hands to Him.* אִם־אָוֶן בְּיָדְךָ הַרְחִיקֵהוּ וְאַל־תַּשְׁכֵּן בְּאֹהָלֶיךָ עַוְלָה — *If there is iniquity in your hands — you were to distance it, were not to permit sin to settle in your dwelling.* כִּי־אָז תִּשָּׂא פָנֶיךָ מִמּוּם וְהָיִיתָ מֻצָק וְלֹא תִירָא — *For then, free from blemish, you could look up, stand strong and never fear.* We have combined these three verses in accordance with *Rashi's* understanding. *Ramban*, as we shall see, reads them differently.

Rashi's understanding is as follows: If, after

consider. [12] *That the hollow man might win a heart, that a wild ass might yield a man.* [13] *If you were but to set your heart, if you would spread out your hands to Him.* [14] *If there is iniquity in your hands — you were to distance it, were not to permit sin to settle in your dwelling.* [15] *For then, free from blemish, you could look up,*

your suffering, you were to set your heart to repentance, turn to God in prayer, divest yourself of any ill-gotten gains and make sure that your dwelling is clean from any sinful profit — if, in short, you were indeed to turn to God in penitence — then all would be well with you.

Ramban, as we saw above, reads verse 13 together with the preceding one: Man, born like a wild ass, will never comprehend the subtle nuances of God's providence unless he sets his heart to examine his deeds as a prelude to true penitence, and then entreats God to open his eyes so that he might fathom the depths of his obligations.

With his new-found understanding, he will then be able to summon up the energy to distance any iniquity from his hands, and to cleanse his abode from any wrongdoing.

After that, no blemish will disfigure him anymore.[1]

The phrase כִּי אָז תִּשָּׂא פָנֶיךָ מִמּוּם is difficult. *Rashi* is unclear (see below), so we have translated in accordance with *Ramban*: One whose body is blemished tends to feel embarrassment and to bend his head downward in shame. Freed from such compromising disabilities, you will, once more, be able to lift your face and, so to speak, look people in the eye. [For such a usage of the phrase תִּשָּׂא פָנֶיךָ, that is, that it describes an actual lifting up of the face rather than that it serves as an idiomatic expression, we may adduce *II Samuel* 2:22. There, too, it is used to describe the inability to look an offended party in the eye.] *Ramban* takes the second half of the sentence in the same vein: You will *never* have to *fear* a return of your sickness.

However, it seems legitimate to wonder whether Iyov's broken physical state would be described as מוּם, a *blemish*. Nowhere else in the book is this expression used, and indeed it seems inappropriate in a situation in which an entire body is covered with the loathsome filth which Iyov has described in the earlier speeches — see especially at 7:5.

Perhaps, then, we should take מוּם as describing Iyov's sins (see *Deuteronomy* 32:5 and *Proverbs* 9:7) which were mentioned in the previous verse. If, indeed, Iyov will make the effort to distance iniquity from his hands, to make sure that no sin sully his abode, then he will be able to stand up straight, unburdened by the weight of evil. This may be how *Rashi* understands the phrase.

In the context of the alternative interpretation which we have offered for this speech, the meaning is as follows: Tzophar is making the point that Iyov's rebellion in his previous speech was the function of an alienation from the self, an erosion of awareness of worth, which is born of the weariness (v. 16) and fear (our verse), which are the bitter fruits of sin. Once Iyov gets his spiritual house in order, there will be light where now there is only a cloying darkness (v. 17); he will learn to trust, instead of to hate (v. 18); and, most important, others will regain their trust in him (v. 19).

1. In footnote (p. 117) we traced the progression which *Ramban* sees in the suggestions made by the three friends: Eliphaz offers no explanation for Iyov's suffering — he only calls upon him to sublimate them; Bildad ascribes a cleansing function to them; while Tzophar sees them as a goad to repentance.

Now this system seems an eminently logical one, and would, indeed, explain the distinct contribution made by each of the three friends in the first round of the debate.

It seems desirable to ascribe a discrete position to each of the three friends, for if the story of Iyov is a *mashal*, we would need to justify the fact that three protagonists were chosen to represent the opposition to Iyov's own stance. Why not just one? Why not more than three?

Indeed, this is a distinct advantage which *Ramban's* approach to the book has over that which we traced in *Rashi*, or the alternative ideas which we have discussed here and there. While we have isolated different thrusts in each of the speeches of the three friends, we do not have the same clear-cut, threefold progression: sublimation; cleansing; goad to penitence.

The more so, we wonder why *Ramban*, in his synopsis of the book offered in the *Toras HaAdam*, does not mention this aspect of Tzophar's contribution. He notes only that Tzophar provides a new idea in his assertion of a hidden aspect to Divine wisdom (v. 6), and an answer to the nagging problem of the tranquility of the wicked — that God occasionally allows a sin to go unpunished for a while in order to give the sinner a chance to repent (v. 11).

Ramban there makes no mention of the point which he stresses in his commentary — that Tzophar has a different explanation for Iyov's suffering.

טו מִמּוּם וְהָיִיתָ מֻצָק וְלֹא תִירָא: כִּי־אַתָּה עָמָל תִּשְׁכָּח
יז כְּמַיִם עָבְרוּ תִזְכֹּר: וּמִצָּהֳרַיִם יָקוּם חָלֶד תָּעֻפָה
יח כַּבֹּקֶר תִּהְיֶה: וּבָטַחְתָּ כִּי־יֵשׁ תִּקְוָה וְחָפַרְתָּ לָבֶטַח
יט־כ תִּשְׁכָּב: וְרָבַצְתָּ וְאֵין מַחֲרִיד וְחִלּוּ פָנֶיךָ רַבִּים: וְעֵינֵי
רְשָׁעִים תִּכְלֶינָה וּמָנוֹס אָבַד מִנְהֶם וְתִקְוָתָם מַפַּח־נָפֶשׁ:

Buoyed by a feeling of spiritual well-being, basking in the warm, life-dispensing rays of the midday sun (v. 17), knowing that fate once more is smiling upon him (*Rashi*, there), the need to lash out against God will be wholly dissipated.

We have rendered מִמּוּם, *free from blemish.* The *free* is implied rather than stated.

מֻצָק, from יָצַק, *to pour out* or *cast. Strong* as something cast from metal (*Metzudos*).

16. כִּי־אַתָּה עָמָל תִּשְׁכָּח כְּמַיִם עָבְרוּ תִזְכֹּר — *You would forget weariness, remember it only as waters which have passed. Ramban* understands the *weariness* meant here as the pain which Iyov suffered because of his illness. That is the meaning which the word had at 7:3.

However, עָמָל frequently has the meaning of *sin*, and that is how it has been used in *Iyov.* See, for example, at 4:8 and 5:6. This could well be the meaning in our phrase. The debilitating weariness which came about as the result of a sinful life will become a thing of the past.

This latter explanation appears the more likely one. The wording of our verse strikes a jarring note. In the first phrase Tzophar tells Iyov that he will *forget* the עָמָל, while the second phrase talks of *remembering* it — albeit as a dim and distant recollection. We do not normally talk of forgetting and remembering the same thing in one context.

However, שָׁכַח does not only mean *to forget.* It is also used in the sense: *to disregard, to pay no attention to something.* Thus, for example, at *Jeremiah* 29:14. The meaning of verse would then be: You will be able to disregard the sins of the past; they will exercise scant influence upon you; eventually they will remain only a dim memory.

The metaphor, *as waters which have passed,* requires some elucidation. Do such waters leave a mark or don't they? *Metzudos* appears to think that they do. The earth remains sodden. You will remember the suffering of the past just sufficiently to prevent you from returning to your earlier, flawed, state.

However, when we recall the metaphor of the faithless river (see 6:15ff.) where the same root עבר was used (v. 15) to describe the river which forsakes its place in the summer months, leaving only a parched and dry bed where refreshing waters could have done so much good, it seems likely that Tzophar is picking up the same metaphor which Iyov had previously used against him and the other friends. You will no longer have to complain of our disloyalty, he seems to be saying. It is not we who are not where you expected us to be. You will look around for your familiar agonies and not find them. They will have passed into the world of memory.

17. וּמִצָּהֳרַיִם יָקוּם חָלֶד תָּעֻפָה כַּבֹּקֶר תִּהְיֶה — *Fate will become like the afternoon, darkness will be as the morning. Rashi* renders חָלֶד either as *fate* or as *dark, rusty blotches. Ramban* thinks it may describe man in his state of suffering (see *Aruch HaShalem* under חלד). In any event, according to both, the meaning of the verse is the same. Tzophar assures Iyov of a bright future. His luckless existence, the murky darkness of experience and the agonies of his poor racked body, will give way to the bright, healthful afternoon sunshine.

תָּעֻפָה is taken as *darkness.*

But, it seems noteworthy that neither חָלֶד, nor תָּעֻפָה, has the possessive pronoun. Verses 16 and 18 address themselves directly to Iyov. Our verse appears to be a statement of neutral fact. Not Iyov's fate, not his darkness will change to light. Rather, a general destiny, a universal malaise, seems to be meant.

In the context of our alternative interpretation, the meaning is clear. As Tzophar made clear in the earlier verses, he sees the brazenness of Iyov's accusations against God as deriving from the frustrations of his own shortcomings. In a joyless world, engulfed in the lowering clouds of evil which block out the sun's healing rays, it is easy to hate, easy to lash out against — even God. Repent, Tzophar exhorts Iyov, and your entire world will take on a more cheerful nature. From hatred, you will turn to trust.

18-19. וּבָטַחְתָּ כִּי־יֵשׁ תִּקְוָה וְחָפַרְתָּ לָבֶטַח תִּשְׁכָּב — *You will trust — for there is hope, you will dig [a moat] so that you will lie without fear.* וְרָבַצְתָּ וְאֵין מַחֲרִיד וְחִלּוּ פָנֶיךָ רַבִּים — *You shall settle down — and none will frighten you, many will*

stand strong and never fear. 16 *You would forget weariness,*
remember it only as waters which have passed. 17 *Fate will become*
like the afternoon, darkness will be as the morning. 18 *You will trust*
— for there is hope, you will dig [a moat] so that you will lie without
fear. 19 *You shall settle down — and none will frighten you, many*
will wait upon your presence. 20 *The eyes of the wicked will be*
strained with longing, haven will be denied them, their hope —
deep frustration.

wait upon your presence. חָפַר is rendered *to dig*. You will be as trusting as though you had dug a deep moat around yourself for your protection (*Metzudos*). See further at 39:21.

Rashi and *Ramban* offer no commentary to these verses. They take them as a general description of the well-being which will be Iyov's if he listens to Tzophar's advice.

In our alternative interpretation — in which Tzophar addresses the accusations which Iyov had made against God — the concepts of *trust, hope*, and *safety* are particularly appropriate. Iyov had felt himself a hapless pawn in the hands of God. What hope is there for the righteous man when indiscriminate destruction reigns supreme? In whom can one trust, when the all-mighty seems to gloat over the agonies of the innocent? Is there a corner in which one can hide before a juggernaut ploughing, unconcerned, over everything?

All this will change, Tzophar assures Iyov, with your perception of the world. Once more you will know yourself to be safely cradled in God's loving concern.

Tzophar's promise that *many will wait upon [Iyov's] presence*, is particularly insightful. He must have known Iyov in the heyday of his popularity and influence when, indeed, his counsel was sought assiduously:

> *People listened to me with anticipation, waited in silence for my guidance. Once I had spoken they would not ask again, to them my words were prophecy. They would long for me as for rain, wait long for themselves to have their say. Were I to smile upon them — they would not believe it, had not the courage to presume to take advantage of my pleasant demeanor. I would determine their life's path, ensconced like a king among his soldiers. I was regarded as one who offers comfort to mourners.*

With deep and exquisite sensitivity, Tzophar realizes that the loss of his community's confidence which came in the wake of his downfall, must have been particularly painful to Iyov. The very fact that Iyov would describe the position of influence which he had enjoyed in such loving detail, shows clearly how much it had meant to him. Evidently, it contributed measurably to his feeling of self-worth. Bereft of this supportive assurance, he might well see his life as having been emptied of any meaning. Enough reason to lash out against the apparently malevolent cause of his anguish!

Tzophar feels that by holding out the promise of restoration he may well be able to galvanize Iyov into the repentance which he sees as crucial to his rehabilitation.

20. וְעֵינֵי רְשָׁעִים תִּכְלֶינָה וּמָנוֹס אָבַד מִנְהֶם וְתִקְוָתָם מַפַּח־נָפֶשׁ — *The eyes of the wicked will be strained with longing, haven will be denied them, their hope — deep frustration. Rashi* has this description referring to Iyov's personal enemies. There was a time in which they enjoyed gloating over Iyov's discomfiture. Once he will have repented and returned to his former happy state, they will look in vain for the anguish which they long to see. The *haven* from their own inadequacies which they found in observing Iyov's lowly state will henceforth be denied them. The hope which they nurtured that they might yet see him downtrodden once more, will prove to be nothing but deep-cutting frustration.

But, Iyov has made no mention of enemies who take perverse joy in his agonies. Why would Tzophar mention them?

Ramban prefers to see this phrase as a general reference to those wicked people who, unlike Iyov, will not repent. They will look in vain for salvation. Nothing but the deepest frustration awaits them.

In the alternative interpretation which we have offered, we may suggest that reference is to the wicked of the world, with whose fate Iyov had tried to bracket the righteous. All, together, would eventually be destroyed!

Tzophar has denied this. Iyov, if he will only listen, will find his former happiness restored. Only the truly wicked will be utterly without hope.

א־ב וַיַּעַן אִיּוֹב וַיֹּאמַר: אָמְנָם כִּי אַתֶּם־עָם וְעִמָּכֶם תָּמוּת
ג חָכְמָה: גַּם־לִי לֵבָב | כְּמוֹכֶם לֹא־נֹפֵל אָנֹכִי מִכֶּם וְאֶת־
ד מִי־אֵין כְּמוֹ־אֵלֶּה: שְׂחֹק לְרֵעֵהוּ | אֶהְיֶה קֹרֵא לֶאֱלוֹהַּ
ה וַיַּעֲנֵהוּ שְׂחוֹק צַדִּיק תָּמִים: לַפִּיד בּוּז לְעַשְׁתּוּת שַׁאֲנָן

XII.

⋄§ Iyov's Response to Tzophar's First Speech

Ramban begins his commentary to this chapter by remarking that it does not really contain anything new. It raises the question of רָשָׁע וְטוֹב לוֹ, the apparent tranquility in which the wicked appear to pass their lives — a problem that has disturbed Iyov from the very beginning — and reasserts his contention that he is guiltless of any wrongdoing.

If there are no new arguments, there is still much to be learned concerning some of Iyov's earlier thoughts. In this speech positions are staked out which cannot comfortably coexist with one another. Confidently asserted ideas reveal fissures of ambivalence and inconsistency; are shown to be really no more than tentative probings into uncharted and mutually exclusive areas of theological conjecture, to which he is driven by the relentless pressure of his agony. The dreadful storm-winds of his inner turbulence do not always blow in only one direction. Each of these apparently contradictory positions have figured in earlier perorations, but never have they appeared juxtaposed so closely.

The antagonistic ideas are, on the one hand, the assertion of God's absolute exaltedness which makes Him indifferent to individual man's fate; and, on the other hand, the concept that God sees Iyov as an enemy and treats him accordingly. These two propositions cannot both be true (see *Ramban* to 35:2), but both receive play in this exceedingly long and complicated speech.

As *Rashi* interprets this speech, it is here that Iyov scales the heights of exultation in his adoration of God, plumbs the depths of the human soul in his longing for requital. He has lost his friends. They will not, cannot, grasp the music of the exquisitely fine-tuned harp-strings pulsating in Iyov's heart — know nothing of belligerence borne of love, of unrelenting, pugnacious demanding growing out of passionate caring.

And so, after all the three friends have had their say, Iyov stands alone. Nonetheless, he still stands straight, has not grovelled along the beguiling path of hypocrisy — and, in the splendor of his isolation, he waits expectantly for vindication.

It is interesting to note that where each of the three would-be comforters had less to say than the previous one [Eliphaz's first speech spread over forty-eight verse, Bildad's, over twenty-two, and Tzophar's, over twenty], Iyov's speeches increase in length. The first consisted of just twenty-five verses, the second went up to fifty-one, the third to fifty-seven, while this, his fourth speech, spreads over seventy-five verses.

It seems likely that this increase in words is due to Iyov's growing frustration with his friends' obduracy. He wants so much that they should understand him — and they seem to hear him not at all.

Nevertheless, at first glance there seem to be hardly any fresh thoughts in this, Iyov's fourth speech. Indeed, at the end of his commentary to Tzophar's speech, *Ramban* writes that at that point the friends have staked out their essential positions, and that in the rest of their speeches they add only proofs and support to what has already been said. *Ramban* does not make the same assertion for Iyov, but it seems to be implied in his approach to the commentary. Thus, in his introductory remarks to this fourth speech, he says only that Iyov will raise the question of רָשָׁע וְטוֹב לוֹ, the vexing question of the tranquility in which many wicked people live, and continue to assert his own innocence. All this has been said before.

There is, however, one point which Iyov will make — and which *Ramban* considers crucial to Iyov's stand. At verse 7 Iyov derives from his observation of the animal world that God does indeed exercise stewardship over the world, but that his concern is extended only to the species, not to the individual. Henceforth, Iyov will apparently regard this as the key to his suffering — and his justification for rejecting the world-view of the friends. They claim that all that happened to him was the function of God's providence. Iyov maintains — based on both his own experiences

[1] *Iyov responded and said:* [2] *Truly, you are the many, and at your*
passing wisdom will die. [3] *I too, as you do, possess understand-*
ing, nowise do I fall short of you. Who does not have the like of
these! [4] *A butt for his friend's banter, I will call out to God, and He*
will grant — laughter to him who is whole in his righteousness. [5] *A*
debasing torch for those who live in a dream-world of security —

and his observations — that the individual is left to the vagaries of accident. See further at 13:3.

Rashi's commentary to this speech is extremely sparse. However, it allows room for the exploration of the possibility that Iyov's response is not just a restatement of earlier positions, but that it is tightly tailored to the precise points which Tzophar made. We shall attempt to work out such an approach in the commentary.

2. אָמְנָם כִּי אַתֶּם־עָם וְעִמָּכֶם תָּמוּת חָכְמָה — *Truly, you are the many, and at your passing wisdom will die. Rashi* does not explain the first phrase. The translation follows *Metzudos.* It seems likely that Iyov used this expression because now all the three friends have had their say. Since not a single one among them has agreed with him, he now sees himself ranged against a majority.

Ramban understands עָם as describing an aristocracy among mankind. You are the ones, relative to whom all other men are as animals.

The next phrase has the meaning: Acumen and discernment are identified with you. At your passing no wise men will remain. Wisdom will die with you.

In contrast to *Metzudos* who takes the phrase as being sarcastic [Do you really believe that with your passing all wisdom will die?] *Rashi* and *Ramban* appear to take it at face value. Iyov admits the superior wisdom of the friends. However, he argues that for the question at hand, no great wisdom is required. I, too, have the requisite understanding. His thoughts will develop in the next few verses.

3. גַּם־לִי לֵבָב כְּמוֹכֶם לֹא־נֹפֵל אָנֹכִי מִכֶּם וְאֶת־מִי־אֵין כְּמוֹ־אֵלֶּה — *I too, as you do, possess understanding, nowise do I fall short of you. Who does not have the like of these!* It would have been illogical to say, in the previous verse, that the three friends were the sole repositories of wisdom — that it would die with their death — and then to claim that Iyov himself was as wise as they. Accordingly, we understand this verse to mean that while I may not be as wise as you, I too have understanding. To say what you have said — useless ideas, put forward only with the purpose of making fun of me (next verse) — needs no deep wisdom. Anyone could have mouthed the same platitudes.

On, *Who does not have the like of these, Rashi* remarks: That God is in control and can [if He wishes] allow the wicked to have long-lasting times of tranquility. This, apparently, is in reference to Tzophar's argument at 11:11 — see commentary there.

The contrast in wording between our verse, *. . . the like of these,* and the first phrase in verse 9, *Who does not know through all these,* suggest bitter sarcasm as the true ambience of our phrase. The ideas which you have put forward are false and irrelevant, you are quacks who heal nothing at all (13:4). It is very hard to find the truth, but it is very easy to offer cliches. There are many more which might have been suggested — by anyone — and all would be equally useless. All would have had only the purpose of deriding my agony (v. 4). Iyov will develop his rejection of Tzophar's thought from verse 5 onwards. Verse 4 continues straight from the thoughts expressed in our verse.

4. שְׂחֹק לְרֵעֵהוּ אֶהְיֶה קֹרֵא לֶאֱלוֹהַּ וַיַּעֲנֵהוּ שְׂחוֹק צַדִּיק תָּמִים — *A butt for his friend's banter, I will call out to God, and He will grant — laughter to him who is whole in his righteousness.* There is wide divergence between *Rashi* and *Ramban* in this and the next two verses — a divergence which sets the tone for two totally different perspectives upon this speech.

We go first to *Ramban,* who would translate this verse differently than we have done. The major structural difference is that he takes אֶהְיֶה together with the first phrase, thus eliminating any reference to a prayer which Iyov intends to offer up.

He views this verse, together with the next two, as a restatement of the problems of צַדִּיק, the suffering *tzaddik,* and of רָשָׁע וְטוֹב לוֹ, וְרַע לוֹ, the wicked man who lives a life of tranquility, as follows:

Verses 4 and 5 deal with the problem of the suffering *tzaddik,* thus: *I have become a butt for my friends' banter.* I [who used to be loved by God, in that I] *would call to God and He would answer.* [My friends' laughter is thus directed at] *one who is whole in his righteousness.* [This righteous man] *who* [formerly] *thought*

ו נָכוֹן לְמוֹעֲדֵי רָגֶל: יִשְׁלָיוּ אֹהָלִים | לְשֹׁדְדִים וּבַטֻּחוֹת
ז לְמַרְגִּיזֵי אֵל לַאֲשֶׁר הֵבִיא אֱלוֹהַּ בְּיָדוֹ: וְאוּלָם שְׁאַל־נָא
ח בְהֵמוֹת וְתֹרֶךָּ וְעוֹף הַשָּׁמַיִם וְיַגֶּד־לָךְ: אוֹ שִׂיחַ לָאָרֶץ
ט וְתֹרֶךָּ וִיסַפְּרוּ לְךָ דְּגֵי הַיָּם: מִי לֹא־יָדַע בְּכָל־אֵלֶּה כִּי
י יַד־יהוה עָשְׂתָה זֹּאת: אֲשֶׁר בְּיָדוֹ נֶפֶשׁ כָּל־חָי וְרוּחַ

tranquil thoughts [is now engulfed in] *burning embarrassment and destined to be among those whose feet flounder.*

This poses the problem of the suffering *tzaddik.*

Verse 6 then turns to the issue of the wicked *robbers* and *those who anger God,* who live out their lives in apparent tranquility.

See below to verses 7 and 8, how *Ramban* deals with the progression from verses 4-6 to verse 7.

Rashi reads the verse as we have rendered it — אֶהְיֶה goes together with the phrase which follows. The verse evidently relies upon a play on the word שְׂחוֹק, which can mean both *derisive laughter* and *the sound of joy.* Iyov is saying: Indeed I have been an object of banter for the friends. But he who laughs last, laughs longest! I will turn to God in prayer, and He will answer by granting me the joy which can only be experienced by a fully righteous person, the true *tzaddik.*

This jubilant assurance of ultimate vindication informs the entire speech. In the next chapter we shall see how central to Iyov's thinking is his uninhibited condemnation of what he views as the friends' hypocrisy, as opposed to his own unadulterated quest for truth. This he sees as an expression of the most sublime love for God — see 13:15. [And see there, that *Ramban,* who does not share *Rashi's* insight into our verse, disagrees with him, there, too.] Thus, already here the mood is set. Iyov is going over to the attack — not only against a Divine Providence to which he denies any logical validity (see below), but also against the friends. They have shot their bolt — and lost! The ideas which they espouse are untenable — and Iyov, resorting to cutting and incisive irony, will show them why.

Tzophar had maintained that if only Iyov could have access to the *hidden recesses of [God's] wisdom,* if only he could bring himself to realize that *sagacity has double folds,* then he himself would realize how groundless the terrible accusations which he has hurled against God really were.

Iyov's response, simply stated, is this: Your ideas are not borne out by reality. In contrast to the logical, well balanced and readily understandable world of nature (vs. 7 and 8), human affairs seem chaotic and unpredictable — the fate to which man is exposed appears to be blind to fault or merit (vs. 5 and 6).

Clearly, then, the honest man must question. There simply is no other way. Thus, this first chapter leads into the next, in which Iyov belabors the friends for their facile and ultimately hypocritical espousal of cliches, which cannot really satisfy. Only his way, a rebellion born of love (13:15), can be justified.

Thus, two worlds are set against one another. There is one in which humankind appears to be the plaything of chaos, and another in which a well-ordered animal kingdom disports itself. The contrast between is implied in the word וְאוּלָם, with which verse 7 begins. Animals and birds have something to teach us which stands in sharp contrast with that which is described in verses 5 and 6.

Thus, we now have the key to understanding these two verses. They describe the chasm which divides ideal from reality, between that which the friends claim to be the truth, and that which our eyes observe.

As *Rashi* (in contrast to *Ramban*) interprets this verse, Iyov's problem, as expressed in verses 5-6, is limited to the apparent tranquility of the wicked. He does not raise the question of the suffering of the righteous. This is understandable in view of Tzophar's assertion that no human can ever claim righteousness — God's exaltedness creates obligations which no one can ever really fulfill. Iyov can only refute this by indirection. If the wicked would also suffer — then I could accept your thesis. But since they are tranquil, I must conclude that there is no justice at all. The suffering of the righteous also remains unexplained. Given this assumption we can really understand why, in the second round, all the friends address only the question of the tranquility of the wicked. Iyov's arguments stand or fall upon only this issue. See further at chapter 15.

5. לַפִּיד בּוּז לְעַשְׁתּוּת שַׁאֲנָן נָכוֹן לְמוֹעֲדֵי רָגֶל — *A debasing torch for those who live in a dreamworld of security — they are destined to be among those whose feet flounder.* Here we have the theoretical ideal: The wicked are those who say, 'All will be well with me!' (*Rashi* on עַשְׁתּוּת

they are destined to be among those whose feet flounder. [6] *The tents of the robbers are at ease, there is tranquility for those who anger God, to whomever God grants by His hand.* [7] *However, I beg you, ask the beasts — and they will instruct you, the birds of the sky — and they will tell you.* [8] *Or, speak to the earth — it will teach you, the fish of the sea will recount it to you.* [9] *Who does not know through all these — that it is the hand of* H*ASHEM which wrought all this.* [10] *In Whose hand is the life-force of all living creatures, the*

שַׁאֲנָן; עַשְׁתּוּת from עשת, *to think*). They will be engulfed in flames (לַפִּיד) which consume them with contempt (בּוּז; *Rashi* renders *hell-fire*). Certainly, they will one day be among those whose wickedness will trip them up (נָכוֹן לְמוֹעֲדֵי רָגֶל).

So much for theory. Verse 6 describes the reality.

R' Meyuchas offers a radically different interpretation for this verse. He had understood verse 4 as has *Ramban*, and reads this one to continue smoothly with the same thought:

The ל of לַפִּיד is a prefix — not a part of the root. פִּיד is *calamity*, as it is used in *Proverbs* 24:22 and also in our book at 30:24 and 31:29. The verse is to be understood as follows: In the opinion of those who are *secure in their opinions* (לְעַשְׁתּוּת שַׁאֲנָן), the unfortunate ones, i.e., *those whom calamity overtakes* (לַפִּיד) *are an object of contempt* (בּוּז). Thus also do *those who are well established* (נָכוֹן) look upon people *whose foot has slipped* (לְמוֹעֲדֵי רָגֶל).

6. יִשְׁלָיוּ אֹהָלִים לְשֹׁדְדִים וּבַטֻּחוֹת לְמַרְגִּיזֵי אֵל לַאֲשֶׁר הֵבִיא אֱלוֹהַּ בְּיָדוֹ — *The tents of the robbers are at ease, there is tranquility for those who anger God, to whomever God grants by His hand.* The gift of tranquility is bestowed by God indiscriminately to both good and bad (*Rashi* to לַאֲשֶׁר הֵבִיא אֱלוֹהַּ בְּיָדוֹ). Therefore, even *robbers* and those who *anger God* appear to live at peace.

Verse 7 then goes on to contrast this chasm between the ideal and the real, with the consistency to be found in the world of nature.

7-8. וְאוּלָם שְׁאַל־נָא בְהֵמוֹת וְתֹרֶךָּ וְעוֹף הַשָּׁמַיִם וְיַגֶּד־לָךְ — *However, I beg you, ask the beasts — and they will instruct you, the birds of the sky — and they will tell you.* אוֹ שִׂיחַ לָאָרֶץ וְתֹרֶךָּ וִיסַפְּרוּ לְךָ דְּגֵי הַיָּם — *Or, speak to the earth — it will teach you, the fish of the sea will recount it to you. Rashi* is silent on these two verses. *Ramban* does explain them, within his understanding of the previous ones, and we can borrow his general approach for the place which they might have in *Rashi's* scheme.

Ramban believes that in these two verses, Iyov asserts the absoluteness of Divine Providence over the species, even though individual members of the group are subject to capricious fate. That the various species seem to exist eternally certainly indicates an intelligent concern for their preservation. That their individual members are left to the vagaries of their particular, specific, and of course accidental circumstances, is a given.

He appears to understand the structure of Iyov's thought as follows: In verses 5 and 6, Iyov had demonstrated that the righteous often become the laughingstock of the wicked, that evildoers frequently prosper. However, he hastens to assert, this observation does not constitute a denial of Divine Providence. It must be explained on the basis of our observations of nature. Divine Providence, the existence of which is indeed undisputed, deals exclusively with the generality, never with the individual. See further at 13:3.

We assume that *Rashi* takes the meaning of the two verses in a similar vein. Observation of the animal world does, indeed, yield that there must be a caring providence which nurtures, protects and preserves. In contrast to the chaos which appears to hold sway in human affairs, it is a world of balance and harmony, of logic and consistency.

And there lies the source of Iyov's frustrated anger and pugnacious belligerence. Why, he seems to cry out, why, when the whole of nature bears such eloquent testimony to God's caring stewardship, must just human experience be so riddled with problems and contradictions?

Tzophar had maintained that God's works were too profound to be grasped by man. But, Iyov argues, it is easy enough to comprehend them as they relate to the animal world. It follows, then, that his problems are not a function of some hidden dimension of wisdom, but of an essential lawlessness which cannot be defended. He will develop this thought from verse 14 onward.

9-10. מִי לֹא־יָדַע בְּכָל־אֵלֶּה כִּי יַד־ה׳ עָשְׂתָה זֹּאת — *Who does not know through all these — that it is the hand of* H*ASHEM which wrought all this.*

יא כָּל־בְּשַׂר־אִישׁ׃ הֲלֹא־אֹזֶן מִלִּין תִּבְחָן וְחֵךְ אֹכֶל יִטְעַם־
יב־יג לוֹ׃ בִּישִׁישִׁים חָכְמָה וְאֹרֶךְ יָמִים תְּבוּנָה׃ עִמּוֹ חָכְמָה
יד וּגְבוּרָה לוֹ עֵצָה וּתְבוּנָה׃ הֵן יַהֲרוֹס וְלֹא יִבָּנֶה יִסְגֹּר
טו עַל־אִישׁ וְלֹא יִפָּתֵחַ׃ הֵן יַעְצֹר בַּמַּיִם וְיִבָשׁוּ וִישַׁלְּחֵם
טז־יז וְיַהַפְכוּ־אָרֶץ׃ עִמּוֹ עֹז וְתוּשִׁיָּה לוֹ שֹׁגֵג וּמַשְׁגֶּה׃ מוֹלִיךְ
יח יוֹעֲצִים שׁוֹלָל וְשֹׁפְטִים יְהוֹלֵל׃ מוּסַר מְלָכִים פִּתֵּחַ וַיֶּאְסֹר
יט אֵזוֹר בְּמָתְנֵיהֶם׃ מוֹלִיךְ כֹּהֲנִים שׁוֹלָל וְאֵתָנִים יְסַלֵּף׃
כ־כא מֵסִיר שָׂפָה לְנֶאֱמָנִים וְטַעַם זְקֵנִים יִקָּח׃ שׁוֹפֵךְ בּוּז

אֲשֶׁר בְּיָדוֹ נֶפֶשׁ כָּל־חָי וְרוּחַ כָּל־בְּשַׂר־אִישׁ — *In Whose hand is the life-force of all living creatures, the spirit within all of mankind.* The rhetorical question with which verse 9 begins finds its basis and justification in verse 11: *Can the ear not discern words ....* It seems clear that this verse carries on the metaphor which was begun in verses 7 and 8, in which the denizens of the world of nature were, so to speak, endowed with the faculty of speech. Verse 11 demands that their speech be understood. You should be able to discern what all these are telling you. You have been given a discriminating ear, to comprehend just such messages!

Therefore, reasons our verse, even the meanest intellect must be aware of those truths which observation of the animal world yields: God is clearly He Whose mighty hand has brought all this about. Just as He controls the animal world [*In Whose hand is the life-force of all living creatures*], so too, though man is obviously imbued with spirit [*The spirit ...*], still it resides in a physical body [*... all of mankind*], and it too is therefore in His control.

11. הֲלֹא־אֹזֶן מִלִּין תִּבְחָן וְחֵךְ אֹכֶל יִטְעַם־לוֹ — *Can the ear not discern words, as the palate delights in food.* The translation follows *Rashi* who takes the second phrase as a comparative clause. *Ramban* views the two phrases as independent of one another. Man was given the means to be discriminating: He has the ear for the purpose of discerning speech, the palate for recognizing taste. Should he then not be able to understand the simple truths which Iyov perceives as so obvious?

12-13. בִּישִׁישִׁים חָכְמָה וְאֹרֶךְ יָמִים תְּבוּנָה — *Wisdom resides with the oldsters, with length of days — understanding.* עִמּוֹ חָכְמָה וּגְבוּרָה לוֹ עֵצָה וּתְבוּנָה — *He possesses wisdom and might, His are counsel and insight. Rashi* appears to understand these two verses together: Those who have lived a long life have garnered enough wisdom to realize that wisdom and might, counsel and insight, reside with God.

Once more, *Rashi's* remarks are sparse and he does not explain the place which this thought has in the general argument.

Ramban understands the first verse differently than does *Rashi*, but we may use his understanding of the second verse to attempt to fathom *Rashi's* perception. The first verse refers to Iyov himself: He had attained old age and felt that experience had ripened into wisdom. His claim that the *tents of the wicked are at ease* is based not on hearsay, but on his own observations.

For verse 13, he writes: Since God *possesses wisdom and might*, man has no chance at all to protect himself from Divine decrees: Inevitably he is too weak and too foolish. God has *counsel and insight*, can do whatever He wishes to subject man to the fate which He chooses for him.

We assume that *Rashi* takes verse 13 in a similar vein. In the earlier verses he had complained of the contrast between the well-ordered world of nature, and the chaotic affairs of man. In our two verses he maintains that people who have grown old, who have followed the system over a long period and have thus been able to discern that there is a constant pattern, will recognize the truth of what he has said. Their observations of the animal world will confirm that all is in the hands of God — they must then also admit that the chaos in human affairs is also His doing. Clearly He has the wisdom and the power to do as He wishes; none can escape from that which He determines shall happen (v. 13).

Given all this, we are willy-nilly faced with the terrible questions and doubts which have racked Iyov all along. Why would the Master of order and harmony wish to wreak such havoc in human lives?

These constant dislocations are then de-

spirit within all of mankind. 11 *Can the ear not discern words, as*
the palate delights in food. 12 *Wisdom resides with the oldsters,*
with length of days — understanding. 13 *He possesses wisdom and*
might, His are counsel and insight. 14 *See, He will demolish — and*
it will nevermore be built up, lock up upon a man — it will never be
opened. 15 *See, He dams up the waters — causing aridity, He sends*
them forth — and they overturn the land. 16 *He possesses power*
and resourcefulness, His are the erring victim and he who leads
astray. 17 *He leads the counselors into folly, brings the judges to*
stupidity. 18 *He loosens the yoke of kings, though He girded a belt*
upon their loins. 19 *He causes princes to walk in folly, subverts the*
mighty. 20 *He distorts the utterances of even those who are loyal to*
Him, deprives the elders of cogency. 21 *He pours scorn over nobles,*

scribed in the following verses.

14. הֵן יַהֲרוֹס וְלֹא יִבָּנֶה יִסְגֹּר עַל־אִישׁ וְלֹא יִפָּתֵחַ — *See, He will demolish — and it will nevermore be built up, lock up upon a man — it will never be opened.* From here until the end of the chapter we have a list of ways in which Divine Providence takes a hand in the affairs of man. All the examples which are given appear to be negative in their results.

Our understanding of the passage is that it is meant to contrast the harmonious balance in nature — to which Iyov referred in verses 7 and 8 — with the turbulent negativism which seems to govern human experience.

The problem, as stated, will then serve as justification for Iyov's persistent and insistent questioning of God's justice. This he will contrast to the passive (and in Iyov's view, hypocritical) acceptance evinced by the friends. This is the subject of the following chapter.

15. הֵן יַעְצֹר בַּמַּיִם וְיִבָשׁוּ וִישַׁלְּחֵם וְיַהַפְכוּ־אָרֶץ — *See, He dams up the waters — causing aridity, He sends them forth — and they overturn the land.* Iyov's gaze is riveted to the abnormal. He does not see the peaceful rivers winding their way to the sea, the life-giving rain dispensing blessing to the crops. Such is their nature, this is what we may expect. But why, on occasion, does God bring about the untold misery of drought; why, too often, the lashing torrents which wreak destruction?

16. עִמּוֹ עֹז וְתוּשִׁיָּה לוֹ שֹׁגֵג וּמַשְׁגֶּה — *He possesses power and resourcefulness, His are the erring victim and he who leads astray.* For תוּשִׁיָּה, see at 5:12. *Ramban*, here too, renders *all existence* instead of *resourcefulness.*

The sense of the verse, as *Ramban* understands it, is that since God is master over all [*He possesses power and resourcefulness*], He is able to trap people into fooling themselves [*His are the erring victim*], and to maneuver them into a position from which they will deceive others [*and he who leads astray*].

Rashi understands the last phrase, *he who leads astray*, to refer to Satan, the universal cozener. However, we may assume that he understands the sentence as a whole, as does *Ramban*. Both victim and tormentor are in God's hands. He can, so to speak, turn the screws whenever He wishes.

17. מוֹלִיךְ יוֹעֲצִים שׁוֹלָל וְשֹׁפְטִים יְהוֹלֵל — *He leads the counselors into folly, brings the judges to stupidity.* Those who are supposed to guide the kings are trapped into giving bad advice. Judges, as they attempt to administer justice, instead hand down rulings which are ridiculous (*Ramban*).

18. מוּסַר מְלָכִים פִּתֵּחַ וַיֶּאְסֹר אֵזוֹר בְּמָתְנֵיהֶם — *He loosens the yoke of kings, though He girded a belt upon their loins.* The translation follows *Rashi*. God forcibly takes away the rulership from the very kings whom He had established upon the throne.

Ramban thinks of the belt in the second half of the verse as a symbol of servitude. God throws kings off the throne, and then forces them to be vassals of the rulers who replace them.

19. מוֹלִיךְ כֹּהֲנִים שׁוֹלָל וְאֵיתָנִים יְסַלֵּף — *He causes princes to walk in folly, subverts the mighty.* כֹּהֲנִים is used to describe people of substance, *the aristocracy*. Examples are, *Exodus* 3:1 and *II Samuel* 8:18 (*Rashi* and *Ramban*).

20. מֵסִיר שָׂפָה לְנֶאֱמָנִים וְטַעַם זְקֵנִים יִקָּח — *He distorts the utterances of even those who are loyal to Him, deprives the elders of cogency.* We have rendered the first phrase in accor-

יב/כב־כה כב עַל־נְדִיבִים וּמְזִיחַ אֲפִיקִים רִפָּה: מְגַלֶּה עֲמֻקוֹת מִנִּי־חֹשֶׁךְ
כג וַיֹּצֵא לָאוֹר צַלְמָוֶת: מַשְׂגִּיא לַגּוֹיִם וַיְאַבְּדֵם שֹׁטֵחַ לַגּוֹיִם
כד וַיַּנְחֵם: מֵסִיר לֵב רָאשֵׁי עַם־הָאָרֶץ וַיַּתְעֵם בְּתֹהוּ לֹא־
יג/א־ג כה־א דָרֶךְ: יְמַשְׁשׁוּ־חֹשֶׁךְ וְלֹא־אוֹר וַיַּתְעֵם כַּשִּׁכּוֹר: הֶן־כֹּל
ב רָאֲתָה עֵינִי שָׁמְעָה אָזְנִי וַתָּבֶן לָהּ: כְּדַעְתְּכֶם יָדַעְתִּי
ג גַּם־אָנִי לֹא־נֹפֵל אָנֹכִי מִכֶּם: אוּלָם אֲנִי אֶל־שַׁדַּי אֲדַבֵּר

dance with *Rashi*, for the sake of consistency. In fact, if this is what it says, it is not easy to understand the thought expressed in it, nor why it has a place in the litany of human suffering which appears to be the theme of this section.

Rashi comments: Even those who are loyal to Him sometimes have their utterances confused, in that they slander Him. Thus Abraham, concerning whom it is written, *He believed in* H*ASHEM*, nevertheless asked, *How shall I know*?

But why should Abraham's sin be laid to God's door? It is not God Who made him speak as he did! [But see footnote at 28:4.]

Ramban offers two possible explanations for נֶאֱמָנִים. Either it is related to אָמַן, *trust*, in which case the phrase should be rendered: *He thwarts the eloquence of those in whom the people place their trust*; or it comes from נְאֻם, *to speak*, in which case its meaning is: *He thwarts the eloquence of orators.*

21. שׁוֹפֵךְ בּוּז עַל־נְדִיבִים וּמְזִיחַ אֲפִיקִים רִפָּה — *He pours scorn over nobles, loosens the belt of the powerful.*

The commentators render מְזִיחַ as *belt*. This seems clear from the context in *Psalms* 109:19 where the very similar מֵזַח is used.

אֲפִיקִים is rendered, *the powerful* or *mighty ones*. The root אפק means *to be strong*, and is found in words such as וַיִּתְאַפַּק, at *Genesis* 43:31.

22. מְגַלֶּה עֲמֻקוֹת מִנִּי־חֹשֶׁךְ וַיֹּצֵא לָאוֹר צַלְמָוֶת — *He bares schemings from within darkness, brings the deepest gloom, out to light. Rashi* and *Ramban* do not offer any explanations. *Metzudos* renders: He helps man to understand deep wisdom which would otherwise be covered in darkness, throws light on even such truths as would normally be totally inaccessible.

However, such an interpretation would make this verse an anomaly among the litany of descriptions which paint God's stewardship of human affairs in a negative light.

We have thus translated according to *Malbim*, that עֲמֻקוֹת refers to the hidden plots which the poor harbor against the wealthy. He understands the verse as being a continuation of the previous one: The powerful are toppled by having the ordinary people rebel against them. God aids the insurgents to bring their schemes to reality.

Daas Mikra, too, argues that by context, we ought to assume negative connotations for this verse. He has it refer to the baring of state secrets. God will ruin whole nations by baring their best-kept secrets.

עֲמֻקוֹת, as *plans*, can be adduced from verses such as *Isaiah* 29:15.

23. מַשְׂגִּיא לַגּוֹיִם וַיְאַבְּדֵם שֹׁטֵחַ לַגּוֹיִם וַיַּנְחֵם — *He lifts up nations only to destroy them, spreads out the nations and leads them away. Spreads out the nations* means that God increases their number, spreading them over huge tracts of land, only ultimately to lead them to destruction (*Rashi* and *Ramban*).

Targum has *spreads out*, describing the laying of a trap. God lays out traps for the nations, and then leads them to the trap so that they might be caught in it.

24. מֵסִיר לֵב רָאשֵׁי עַם־הָאָרֶץ וַיַּתְעֵם בְּתֹהוּ לֹא־דָרֶךְ — *He takes away wisdom from the leaders of the people, causes them to stray in a pathless void.* He takes away the wisdom of the generals who lead the people in war (*Ramban*).

Rashi to *Genesis* 1:2 renders תֹהוּ with the French, *etourdissement*, which describes a state of being dazed.

The syntax of the second phrase is irregular. The phrase should be read as though the לֹא had a שׁ, prefixed: A void which is really no path at all (*Rashi*).

25. יְמַשְׁשׁוּ־חֹשֶׁךְ וְלֹא־אוֹר וַיַּתְעֵם כַּשִּׁכּוֹר — *They tap around in darkness — never in light, He confuses them as one intoxicated.* Iyov has now come to the end of his accusatory litany. The incongruence between the orderliness of the natural world, and the distressing series of tragedies which seems to be the lot of man, makes it necessary to question God. To pretend that all is well is simply pious fraud and hypocrisy. This is the theme which he will now take up.

1. הֶן־כֹּל רָאֲתָה עֵינִי שָׁמְעָה אָזְנִי וַתָּבֶן לָהּ — *See,*

12/22-25 *loosens the belt of the powerful.* 22 *He bares schemings from within*
darkness, brings the deepest gloom, out to light. 23 *He lifts up*
nations only to destroy them, spreads out the nations and leads
them away. 24 *He takes away wisdom from the leaders of the*
people, causes them to stray in a pathless void. 25 *They tap around*
in darkness — never in light, He confuses them as one intoxicated.

13/1-3 1 *See, my eye has seen all, my ear has heard, and understood*
it. 2 *As you understand, so do I, too, understand, I do not,*
at all, fall short of you. 3 *But, it is to Shaddai that I would speak,*

XIII.

my eye has seen all, my ear has heard, and understood it. In contrast to the friends, who have allowed the siren-song of comforting platitudes to deafen them to the lessons which nature — when contrasted to human society — can whisper to the discerning ear, Iyov has remained alert. He has seen, has heard, and above all, has understood the implications of what he has observed. He will not flinch from the inescapable conclusions. He will turn away from sterile discussions with the friends. They offer bland palliatives where sharp, biting, but ultimately, healing medicines are needed (v. 4). He will demand satisfaction from the one source that can guarantee it. He will confront God Himself and demand surcease from the agonies of his questing.

It appears significant that Iyov speaks of having seen with his eye. The thrust of the challenge which he threw before the friends in the previous chapter, that they learn what nature has to teach so that they might draw conclusions, was couched in terms of *hearing*. The animals were to be *asked* so that they might *instruct*, the birds would *tell* what needs to be told. The earth would *teach*, the fish *recount*. In frustration Iyov had wondered why the *ear* could not discern *words*. Nothing at all had been said concerning the eye.

It may be argued that the difference between lessons learned from the observant eye and those picked up by the vigilant ear, lies at the very fulcrum of the concerns of our book. At 42:5, the point at which Iyov finally allows himself to bask in the redeeming light of understanding, he lays his previous obduracy to the fact that his perception of God had come to him only through the *hearing* of the ear. Having been permitted to *see* the truth with his eyes, his terrible experiences have at last found sublimation.

If so, we may understand our verse as follows: Iyov is stressing the terrible clarity with which he has seen — and understood — the inequities in human experience. He could not — and did not — demand the same degree of lucid comprehension from the friends. But if they had not been able — or perhaps had refused — to see, they should at least have listened!

2. כְּדַעְתְּכֶם יָדַעְתִּי גַם־אָנִי לֹא־נֹפֵל אָנֹכִי מִכֶּם — *As you understand, so do I, too, understand, I do not, at all, fall short of you.* This verse is an almost verbatim repetition of 12:3. Together these two verses bracket the arguments which Iyov has marshalled in support of the position, that logic justifies and integrity demands that he reject the vapid cliche-ridden thought-world of the friends.

You have nothing to teach me, he tells the friends. Only God Himself can help me in my dilemma.

3. אוּלָם אֲנִי אֶל־שַׁדַּי אֲדַבֵּר וְהוֹכֵחַ אֶל־אֵל אֶחְפָּץ — *But, it is to Shaddai that I would speak, it is with God that I would remonstrate.* יכח is one of those roots which has many different nuances. Thus, for example, the second part of verse 15, in our chapter, almost certainly carries the connotation of *demonstrating* the essential rightness of Iyov's ways. At 40:2 *Rashi* takes the *hiphil* form, מוֹכִיחַ, in the *hispael*, as though מִתְוַכֵּחַ would have been used, and renders *one who argues.*

In our phrase we have rendered *remonstrate*, because when Iyov finally turns directly to God, at verse 20, he seems to be *remonstrating* with Him, rather than attempting to justify his own ways — see particularly from verse 25 onwards, and throughout the next chapter.

Ramban thinks that Iyov's rejection of the friends' position — that there is some plausible explanation for his suffering — is based on their assertion that God's providence extends not only to the species but also to the

ד וְהוֹכֵחַ אֶל־אֵל אֶחְפָּץ׃ וְאוּלָם אַתֶּם טֹפְלֵי־שָׁקֶר רֹפְאֵי
ה אֱלִל כֻּלְּכֶם׃ מִי־יִתֵּן הַחֲרֵשׁ תַּחֲרִישׁוּן וּתְהִי לָכֶם
ו לְחָכְמָה׃ שִׁמְעוּ־נָא תוֹכַחְתִּי וְרִבוֹת שְׂפָתַי הַקְשִׁיבוּ׃
ז־ח הַלְאֵל תְּדַבְּרוּ עַוְלָה וְלוֹ תְּדַבְּרוּ רְמִיָּה׃ הֲפָנָיו תִּשָּׂאוּן
ט אִם־לָאֵל תְּרִיבוּן׃ הֲטוֹב כִּי־יַחְקֹר אֶתְכֶם אִם־
י כְּהָתֵל בֶּאֱנוֹשׁ תְּהָתֵלּוּ בוֹ׃ הוֹכֵחַ יוֹכִיחַ אֶתְכֶם אִם־
יא בַּסֵּתֶר פָּנִים תִּשָּׂאוּן׃ הֲלֹא שְׂאֵתוֹ תְּבַעֵת אֶתְכֶם
יב וּפַחְדּוֹ יִפֹּל עֲלֵיכֶם׃ זִכְרֹנֵיכֶם מִשְׁלֵי־אֵפֶר לְגַבֵּי־חֹמֶר
יג גַּבֵּיכֶם׃ הַחֲרִישׁוּ מִמֶּנִּי וַאֲדַבְּרָה־אָנִי וְיַעֲבֹר עָלַי מָה׃

individual. This flies in the face of the conclusions which he drew from his observation of the animal-world — see Introductory Remarks to chapter 12 and commentary to 12:7.

4. וְאוּלָם אַתֶּם טֹפְלֵי־שָׁקֶר רֹפְאֵי אֱלִל כֻּלְּכֶם — *You, however, mass deceit, all of you are worthless physicians.* This verse, together with those which follow, is to be seen as a continuation of verse 2 in which Iyov totally rejects that which the friends have to offer. With trenchant, bitter incisiveness he now proceeds to apply the scalpel of his intellect, the bludgeon of his emotions, to a merciless examination of their motives and attitudes.

Verse 3 was parenthetical to this passage.

Rashi takes the root, טפל, as denoting the *joining together* of various components. The sense of our phrase [which is the basis of the stich, טָפַלְנוּ שֶׁקֶר, in the אָשַׁמְנוּ confession of Yom Kippur] is that the friends have built an edifice of falsehoods. Each of the arguments which they have marshalled and joined to one another is just one more brick in a castle of air.

In the phrase רֹפְאֵי אֱלִל, *Rashi* takes אֱלִל as a form of אַל, which connotes *non-existence, something without substance. Ramban* understands it literally — *idols.* Your efforts at healing my pain are akin to those which idols make for those that look to them for help. Nothing that they could do would ever alleviate any pain.

In this speech this is the only barb which Iyov looses at the friends from his personal standpoint. It is as though he has been hurt so much by their insensitive obduracy, that he simply cannot appeal to them anymore. What he has to say to them as a disappointed friend, he has said in the metaphor of the faithless river at 6:15ff. From now on, he will stand back and view them dispassionately. They have failed as comforters; how do they measure up as advocates for God's cause? With biting honesty, he examines their performance. They have not only failed to understand Iyov — they have hopelessly misconstrued their God, His purpose, and their role.

5. מִי־יִתֵּן הַחֲרֵשׁ תַּחֲרִישׁוּן וּתְהִי לָכֶם לְחָכְמָה — *Who will grant that you keep utterly silent — that would be deemed wisdom for you.* The only hope a fool has of being deemed wise is to keep silent (*Metzudos*). Certainly, what the friends had said did them no credit.

6. שִׁמְעוּ־נָא תוֹכַחְתִּי וְרִבוֹת שְׂפָתַי הַקְשִׁיבוּ — *Hear, I beg of you, my remonstration, attend to the contention of my lips.* Having rid himself of all personal interest in the friends (see to verse 4, above), Iyov now takes up the cudgels for God. True, there is much that he, himself, holds against Him. Towards the end of this speech he will state his case and his complaint — without perceptible restraint. But, withal, he never compromises his perception of God as the repository of unadulterated truth. Indeed, it is that unshakable faith which, to his mind, mandates his uncompromising insistence that he has the right to understand. But, the friends have created a puny God, in their own, cramped image. A God who will feel flattered by their insincerities, Who will wish to hide behind the wall of bland theology which they have erected for His protection. This Iyov will not condone.

7. הַלְאֵל תְּדַבְּרוּ עַוְלָה וְלוֹ תְּדַבְּרוּ רְמִיָּה — *Will you represent God with wickedness, would you speak falsehoods for Him?* It is clear that the friends perceive themselves as advocates for God's cause. One who undertakes to represent God must be specially careful not to ascribe wickedness to Him, or to seek to justify His actions with lies (*Rashi*).

The *wickedness* and *falsehoods* implied by the friends' defense of God would be the pretense that Iyov is guilty of sins which, in fact, he had never committed. The logic is simple: Suffering comes to a person only in punishment for sin; Iyov is suffering; therefore Iyov has sinned. But Iyov knows that he has not

it is with God that I would remonstrate. [4] *You, however, mass*
deceit, all of you are worthless physicians. [5] *Who will grant that*
you keep utterly silent — that would be deemed wisdom for you.
[6] *Hear, I beg of you, my remonstration, attend to the contention of*
my lips. [7] *Will you represent God with wickedness, would you*
speak falsehoods for Him? [8] *Do you expect to flatter Him, is it for*
God that you contend? [9] *Would it be good were He to inquire into*
you, would you treat Him with derision as you would, a man?
[10] *Surely He will remonstrate with you. Will you assert veneration*
in the private chambers? [11] *Will His exaltedness not terrify you, His*
fear not fall upon you? [12] *When you are recalled it will be in the*
likeness of ashes, your imposing height is but a pile of clay. [13] *Do not*
respond to me — I will have my say. Let what may, come upon me!

sinned. Evidently then, he stands falsely accused, he is a victim of fraud. For God to perpetrate fraud would be both wicked and false.

In what way, however, is this worse than the dreadful accusations which Iyov himself had hurled at God, in chapter 9? Is the idea of a fraudulent God more sacrilegious than one of a God taking malicious pleasure in the suffering of the innocent?

Iyov will give the answer to this question in verse 15. His is a true love of God — stronger, fiercer than even his love for life. Truly he has said much that had better never been said, but that was only under the ruthlessly demanding pressure to find surcease from overpowering agony. Man cannot be held to task for what bursts forth from his mouth in moments of unbearable stress. No such excuse can be made for the friends. They are at ease. Nothing forces them to speak except their own determination that Iyov not be in the right. And so, they weave their theological fantasies — small thoughts by small men — tragically producing a small God in their own image.

8. הֲפָנָיו תִּשָּׂאוּן אִם־לָאֵל תְּרִיבוּן — *Do you expect to flatter Him, is it for God that you contend?* To *lift up one's own face* to someone means *to show him favor* — see, for example, *Numbers* 6:26. To *lift someone else's face* would be *to cause him to show favor,* thus, *to flatter.* See, for example, 34:19 and *Proverbs* 18:5.

9. הֲטוֹב כִּי־יַחְקֹר אֶתְכֶם אִם־כְּהָתֵל בֶּאֱנוֹשׁ תְּהָתֵלּוּ בוֹ — *Would it be good were He to inquire into you, would you treat Him with derision as you would, a man?* It is not impossible that Iyov is playing on Tzophar's phrase at 11:7. Tzophar had said, הַחֵקֶר אֱלוֹהַּ תִּמְצָא, *Can you attain a thorough knowledge of God?* Iyov now mocks him: What will you do if God were to turn his חֵקֶר upon you. What if He should wish to have *thorough knowledge* of the motives which drive you! If you were to claim that you had spoken in order to defend His honor, He would recognize your words for what they are — a mark of *derision,* not to be taken seriously.

10. הוֹכֵחַ יוֹכִיחַ אֶתְכֶם אִם־בַּסֵּתֶר פָּנִים תִּשָּׂאוּן — *Surely He will remonstrate with you. Will you assert veneration in the private chambers?* Surely He will charge you with the slanders with which you have besmirched Him. When you are finally arraigned before Him in the privacy of His chambers, will you claim then too that it was your purpose to exalt Him? (*Rashi*).

11. הֲלֹא שְׂאֵתוֹ תְּבַעֵת אֶתְכֶם וּפַחְדּוֹ יִפֹּל עֲלֵיכֶם — *Will His exaltedness not terrify you, His fear not fall upon you? Targum* renders: Should you not be terrified as God sits upon His throne of justice?

Rashi suggests that שְׂאֵת could also be rendered, *His flame.* So also *Metzudos,* based on *Nahum* 1:4. Thus: *Does His burning flame not terrify you?*

12. זִכְרֹנֵיכֶם מִשְׁלֵי־אֵפֶר לְגַבֵּי־חֹמֶר גַּבֵּיכֶם — *When you are recalled it will be in the likeness of ashes, your imposing height is but a pile of clay.* You are only human, how can you not tremble before exalted God? (*Ramban*)

Once more, Iyov appears to be turning Tzophar's arguments against the friends. The entire thrust of Tzophar's speech had been to point to the chasm that must exist between human perceptions and the Divine reality. Iyov now taunts the friends with this very insight: If God is indeed so exalted, how can you presume to talk for Him in the ill-considered fashion which you have chosen!

13. הַחֲרִישׁוּ מִמֶּנִּי וַאֲדַבְּרָה־אָנִי וְיַעֲבֹר עָלַי מָה — *Do not respond to me — I will have my say. Let what may, come upon me!* Iyov wishes to hear no more from the friends. He perceives their

יד־טו עַל־מָה ׀ אֶשָּׂא בְשָׂרִי בְשִׁנָּי וְנַפְשִׁי אָשִׂים בְּכַפִּי: הֵן יִקְטְלֵנִי
טז °לֹא אֲיַחֵל אַךְ־דְּרָכַי אֶל־פָּנָיו אוֹכִיחַ: גַּם־הוּא־לִי — לוֹ ק׳
יז לִישׁוּעָה כִּי־לֹא לְפָנָיו חָנֵף יָבוֹא: שִׁמְעוּ שָׁמוֹעַ מִלָּתִי
יח וְאַחֲוָתִי בְּאָזְנֵיכֶם: הִנֵּה־נָא עָרַכְתִּי מִשְׁפָּט יָדַעְתִּי כִּי־אֲנִי
יט אֶצְדָּק: מִי־הוּא יָרִיב עִמָּדִי כִּי־עַתָּה אַחֲרִישׁ וְאֶגְוָע:

speeches as serving only to run destructive interference to the torrent of feelings to which he knows that he must give vent. Unable to be constructive, they had best be quiet.

חָרַשׁ means *to be silent.* In our verse, the translation of הַחֲרִישׁוּ מִמֶּנִּי would be literally, *Be silent from me.* מִמֶּנִּי plays a similar role to that of the לָהּ of, for example, *Numbers* 30:15. That is, *to keep silent in the face of something another had said.* In our case: Do not react anymore to anything I have said or might say. You have nothing of any value to contribute.

The words, *Let what may, come upon me*! seem to imply that Iyov anticipates that what he has to say may be sinful, but that he is willing to shoulder any consequences. However, as *Rashi* understands verse 15, it appears that Iyov feels certain that his honest bluntness will not be faulted. We may therefore understand our phrase in one of two ways. Either he is talking from the point of view of the friends: Even though you think that I have no right to speak as I do, do not seek to protect me from myself. I must speak; the thought of punishment cannot sway me. In fact, though, he knows himself to be free from blame.

Or, this passage shows Iyov, once more, in the throes of his existential dilemma of uncertainty. He knows only one thing with utmost certainty — he must speak. Silence would be a greater torture than the pains which, up till now, he has been called upon to bear (next verse). He fears that he might be punished, but hopes against hope that perhaps his forthright honesty will be judged against the background of his love for God — and that, after all, it will not be viewed as sinful. Hope and fear play upon his distraught person in constant, inescapable counterpoint — but he will not be silenced!

14. עַל־מָה אֶשָּׂא בְשָׂרִי בְשִׁנָּי וְנַפְשִׁי אָשִׂים בְּכַפִּי — *Why should I clamp down with my teeth upon my flesh, place my life in my hands?* *Rashi* and *Ramban* approach this and the next verse in fundamentally different ways. In *Rashi's* view they form the very linchpin of Iyov's self-justification. His forthright refusal to bow to manifest injustice is not only defensible but necessary. There exists a self-evident right for the sufferer to relieve his pain. No logic can require him to keep silent.

Ramban takes them simply as a fine-tuning of Iyov's ideas concerning Divine Providence.

First *Ramban*: *Why should I clamp down with my teeth upon my flesh* — from excessive pain. *Place my life in my hands* — in that I am dangerously ill. I deserve none of this because . . ., and *Ramban* moves on to the next verse which will show him to be strong and true in his belief in a Providence which is concerned with the soul if not with the body — see further below. Our verse, then, is simply one more cry of outrage at the fate which has befallen an innocent man.

Rashi sees the verse as a direct follow-up and development of the defiant cry with which the previous verse ended. There Iyov had proclaimed: *I will have my say. Let what may, come upon me*! He now proceeds to justify himself: *Why should I clamp down my teeth upon my flesh* — to chastise myself and force me to silence. *Place my life in my hands* — to risk death through the agony which silence imposes upon me.

The next verse will explain why Iyov has the right to speak.

15. הֵן יִקְטְלֵנִי לוֹ אֲיַחֵל אַךְ־דְּרָכַי אֶל־פָּנָיו אוֹכִיחַ — *Were He to kill me — I would still yearn for Him, but I will justify my ways to His face.* We have translated the verse as *Rashi* would. We shall discuss his understanding below.

Ramban would translate as follows: *Once He has killed me I shall have expectations of Him.* The sense is as follows: In the previous verse Iyov, as understood by *Ramban*, had complained of his suffering; he feels that he does not deserve it. Here, he explains: He believes in Divine Providence — has never and would never deny it — to the extent that it deals with the soul. He knows that after his death he will come to his just reward. However, he cannot believe that God is concerned with man's physical being. The body, he thinks, is exposed to the exigencies of happenstance, as much as is any other in the animal

[14] *Why should I clamp down with my teeth upon my flesh,*
place my life in my hands? [15] *Were He to kill me — I would*
still yearn for Him, but I will justify my ways to His face. [16] *Still,*
He will prove to be my salvation — for no hypocrite will come before
Him. [17] *Hear well my words, let my speech enter your ears.* [18] *See,*
I have composed a brief, I know that I shall win the case. [19] *Who*
dares to wrangle with me, were I to keep silent now, I would die.

world. This is not fair — and this is the thought expressed in the second half of the verse. Why should he — innocent as he is — be subjected to any kind of punishment!

It is against this background that *Ramban* understands verses 20 and 21. He begs that God not do two evils to him. He feels dreadfully wronged in this world — this is the first evil. If now, God were to make him suffer also in the World to Come — the second evil — then indeed there would be no hope. If, however, God will grant him relief in the after-life, then at that point, he will be able to present his case before his maker.

This is quite different than *Rashi's* interpretation of these two verses. For that, see below.

Rashi would translate as we have done. Iyov's love for God is total and unconditional (see *Sotah* 27b and 31a). Even were God to do His very worst to him, he would continue to adore Him and yearn for His closeness. God knows this and will view his belligerence within that context. Iyov cannot, and therefore will not, remain silent. God will not hold it against him. He has nothing to fear.

16. גַּם־הוּא־לִי לִישׁוּעָה כִּי־לֹא לְפָנָיו חָנֵף יָבוֹא — *Still, He will prove to be my salvation — for no hypocrite will come before Him.* In the first part of this verse, *Rashi* and *Ramban* close ranks. God will prove to be my salvation — He will not hold my words against me.

In the second part of the sentence, too, they agree as to the general thrust, although there is a slight difference in their interpretation. *Ramban* believes that the *hypocrite* would be Iyov himself, had he kept silent. *Rashi* has it refer to the friends. Iyov maintains that it is only his relentless search after the truth which is pleasing to God. The friends with their bland pastiche of baseless theories are *hypocrites* who will find no welcome before God. (See above at 1:1 and 6:13.)

17. שִׁמְעוּ שָׁמוֹעַ מִלָּתִי וְאַחְוָתִי בְּאָזְנֵיכֶם — *Hear well my words, let my speech enter your ears.* The *words* which Iyov is about to speak are addressed to God, not to the friends. This is evident from the wording of verse 20 and onwards. If he wishes the friends to listen to what he has to say [although they are to remain silent (v. 13)] it can only be so that they might be instructed in the correct way to approach God. Iyov is, as it were, turning the tables upon them. They had presumed to teach him — without even understanding the dimensions and contours of the issue. He will now become the teacher and lead them to the truth.

Ramban renders, אַחְוָתִי as *teaching. Rashi* is silent here, but at 36:2 (and at *Psalms* 19:3) he understands the word simply as *telling,* or *that which is told.* Nevertheless, this root certainly carries the particular nuance of *imparting knowledge,* as at 32:6,10 and 17.

18. הִנֵּה־נָא עָרַכְתִּי מִשְׁפָּט יָדַעְתִּי כִּי־אֲנִי אֶצְדָּק — *See, I have composed a brief, I know that I shall win the case.* עָרַךְ often means *to organize something, to set it forth.* Thus at 23:4 it clearly means, to present a brief in court. Here, however, *Rashi* understands the phrase to mean, I have composed a brief in my heart. I have thought through my case, all its ramifications are clear to me — and I am convinced that I can win my case.

Rashi in various places (9:32, *Exodus* 28:15, *Isaiah* 32:7) notes that the word מִשְׁפָּט can have three different meanings: the arguments of the litigants; the decision of the court; and, the actualizing of the judgment. Here, then, *Rashi* is taking the word according to the first of these meanings.

Ramban appears to take the word in its more usual sense: *the entire procedure before the court.* The sentence means: By bringing my court case before God Himself I can feel confident of being vindicated. God is just and will not accuse me of sins which I did not commit.

19. מִי־הוּא יָרִיב עִמָּדִי כִּי־עַתָּה אַחֲרִישׁ וְאֶגְוָע — *Who dares to wrangle with me, were I to keep silent now, I would die.* If anyone were to attempt less than potent arguments to dissuade me from pressing my case, he would cause my death. No one dare stop me from seeking justice, for my very life is at stake (*Metzudos*).

כ־כא אַךְ־שְׁתַּיִם אַל־תַּעַשׂ עִמָּדִי אָז מִפָּנֶיךָ לֹא אֶסָּתֵר: כַּפְּךָ
כב מֵעָלַי הַרְחַק וְאֵמָתְךָ אַל־תְּבַעֲתַנִּי: וּקְרָא וְאָנֹכִי
כג אֶעֱנֶה אוֹ־אֲדַבֵּר וַהֲשִׁיבֵנִי: כַּמָּה לִי עֲוֹנוֹת וְחַטָּאוֹת
כד פִּשְׁעִי וְחַטָּאתִי הֹדִיעֵנִי: לָמָּה־פָנֶיךָ תַסְתִּיר וְתַחְשְׁבֵנִי
כה לְאוֹיֵב לָךְ: הֶעָלֶה נִדָּף תַּעֲרוֹץ וְאֶת־קַשׁ יָבֵשׁ תִּרְדֹּף:

20. אַךְ־שְׁתַּיִם אַל־תַּעַשׂ עִמָּדִי אָז מִפָּנֶיךָ לֹא אֶסָּתֵר — *If only You would not do these two to me, then I will not conceal myself from Your presence.* The next verse will enumerate the two things which Iyov hopes that God will not do to him (*Metzudos*).

This introduction to Iyov's litany of complaints to God is almost identical to the one at 9:33 — see there. The fact that Iyov uses it here, too, tends towards the first interpretation that we offered there.

The sense of our verse is that Iyov insists that he cannot freely present his case unless God will grant him the respite requested in the next verse.

For *Ramban's* interpretation of this and the next verse, see above to verse 15.

21. כַּפְּךָ מֵעָלַי הַרְחֵק וְאֵמָתְךָ אַל־תְּבַעֲתַנִּי — *Distance Your coercion from upon me, let fear of You not terrify me!* The earlier verse had requested that God *not* do these two things to Iyov. Accordingly, the first part of our verse, *Distance Your coercion from me,* must be understood as though it were written: Do not crush me with Your anger.

כַּף would normally be translated as *hand.* However, *Rashi* notes that כַּף as *hand* is always used in a protective sense, never as a metaphor for punishment. He therefore prefers to associate it with כָּפָּה at 33:7, which has the meaning of *force* or *coercion.*

Iyov appears to be requesting respite in two areas. The first phrase seeks relief from his physical pains; the second, for his crushed spirit. To stand up and argue his case he must be strong of body and of mind.

22. וּקְרָא וְאָנֹכִי אֶעֱנֶה אוֹ־אֲדַבֵּר וַהֲשִׁיבֵנִי — *Then call out, and I shall respond, or, let me speak, and give me an answer.* If only God would grant him some respite, Iyov feels confident that he can made a convincing case in his defense. He asks no advantage from God, leaves the format of the debate to Him. If God chooses, let Him list His accusations, and Iyov will respond. Alternatively, Iyov is willing to make his case first, and then hear God's answer.

All this is, of course, wishful thinking. The formal litigation process which Iyov craves so much will never come about — and Iyov knows it. And so, from the confident challenge which he voices in this verse — itself predicated upon the granting of the relief requested in verse 21, which Iyov cannot believe will come — he turns once more to the sour reflections which have plagued him in all his earlier speeches: Why the unrelenting hounding and enmity; why the dignifying of puny, fleeting man into an adversary worthy of God's attention; why the blowing up of minor peccadillos into major crimes; why the persistent dogging of his footsteps, the determined probing into every cranny of his life, as though God delights in the discovery of some fault?

Indeed, all this has been said before — in the appropriate verses we shall make reference to parallels, particularly in chapters 7 and 10. It is true, as we shall see, that the thrust of Iyov's protests runs along somewhat different lines than did the earlier ones — but it is also true that from the point of view of a strictly structured debate or discussion, not sufficient new ground is broken to warrant this speech.

But just this seems to be the point of this speech. Iyov is talking not as a philosopher, but as a hurting, perplexed human being, whose cry comes more from the heart than from the mind. By repeating himself, by returning again and again to the same themes which had earlier burst the dams of his control, Iyov is eloquently pointing to the utter futility of the friends well-meaning but misguided efforts. Nothing has changed — the pain is no whit smaller. The primordial cry of pain, demanding surcease, cannot be soothed or stilled!

23. כַּמָּה לִי עֲוֹנוֹת וְחַטָּאוֹת פִּשְׁעִי וְחַטָּאתִי הֹדִיעֵנִי — *How many are my sins and transgressions, inform me of my iniquity and my transgression.* Iyov begins his diatribe in much the same way as he began that section of his third speech, at 10:2: *Tell me, why do You pick a fight with me!*

The second part of the verse turns the first section into a rhetorical question. Iyov does not really expect an answer, for he knows himself to be perfectly innocent (*Metzudos*).

20 If only You would not do these two to me, then I will not conceal
myself from Your presence. 21 Distance Your coercion from upon
me, let fear of You not terrify me! 22 Then call out, and I shall
respond, or, let me speak, and give me an answer. 23 How many are
my sins and transgressions, inform me of my iniquity and my
transgression. 24 Why do You hide Your face, consider me Your
enemy? 25 Will you frighten a driven leaf, pursue dry stubble?

24. לָמָּה־פָנֶיךָ תַסְתִּיר וְתַחְשְׁבֵנִי לְאוֹיֵב לָךְ — *Why do You hide Your face, consider me Your enemy? Rashi* interprets the first phrase as accusing God of averting His eyes from Iyov's merits. Because God, unwilling to consider any of Iyov's good points, is unaware of his righteousness, He has come to look upon him as an enemy.

Ramban first suggests another meaning: *Why do You hide Your face* — from my cries? And for the second half of the verse: *Consider me Your enemy* — in that You inflict cruel suffering upon me.

However, he rejects this rendering in favor of *Rashi's* interpretation, which he considers the better of the two because implied in it is Iyov's rejection of Divine Providence — at least as regards the individual. *Ramban* has previously isolated this rejection as central to Iyov's thinking (see at 12:7).

At 33:11 *Ramban* explains the connection to the second part of the verse, [You] *consider me Your enemy,* as follows: Inasmuch as You do not concern Yourself with individuals, You cannot know me as I really am. Thus, You mistakenly consider me to be Your enemy, when in fact, I am righteous — a friend.

[Although *Ramban* cites *Rashi* approvingly inasmuch as his interpretation tends to confirm *Ramban's* ideas concerning Iyov's rejection of Divine Providence, it does not follow that *Rashi* himself subscribes to this opinion. He may take the verse as indicating simply that Iyov suspects God of intentionally averting His eyes from his merits, as part of a pattern of unfair practices which Iyov has claimed in earlier speeches and will yet detail below. See further, below, concerning *Ramban's* assessment of these accusations.]

That God does, indeed, view Iyov as an enemy, Iyov will demonstrate in verses 26 and 27, see below (see also above at 6:4).

At *Bava Basra* 16a the Sages have Iyov complaining to God about his suffering, in the following words: O Master of the world! Is it possible that a hurricane passed in front of You causing You to become confused between [my name] אִיּוֹב, and [the term] אוֹיֵב [*enemy*]. It seems likely that this play of words on Iyov's name was suggested to them by our phrase: You consider me an אוֹיֵב rather than an אִיּוֹב. [See above, at 1:1, for the possible derivation of Iyov's name from the root, איב, *to be hostile to.*]

25. הֶעָלֶה נִדָּף תַּעֲרוֹץ וְאֶת־קַשׁ יָבֵשׁ תִּרְדֹּף — *Will You frighten a driven leaf, pursue dry stubble?* The sense is: What satisfaction can the assertion of power over an opponent as puny as I, possibly give You? What have You demonstrated by frightening a driven leaf, by flexing Your muscles against dry stubble which can so easily be burned? (See 10:4-5 and especially, 17.)

This verse appears to be out of place at this point. To appreciate the structure of this section of Iyov's speech, we quote Elihu's strictures as he paraphrases this speech 33:10-11.

> *'See, He seeks to find pretexts against me, considers me to be His enemy.Places my feet in the stocks, stalks my every path.'*

Clearly, Elihu understands verses 26 and 27 as following directly upon verse 24. God's perception of Iyov as an enemy is demonstrated by the relentless persistence with which He stalks his every move, and by the fact that He places Iyov's feet in stocks. Verse 25, then, seems to interrupt this thought.

Moreover, *Ramban* points out that verse 28, which once more takes up man's fleeting transitoriness, appears to be a direct continuation from verse 25. If so, we would have expected a sequence such as this: 24, 26, 27, 25, 28.

Here again we appear to have not the reasoned, dispassionate ruminations of the philosopher, but the mercurial, emotion-laden cry of the human heart. Perhaps, rather than translate the second phrase of verse 24 as: *consider me Your enemy?*, we should have rendered it more literally as, *consider me an enemy — of One as You!*

The sheer enormity of being considered to be an enemy of God arrests the flow of Iyov's thought. Is it really conceivable that God should dignify a *driven leaf,* a pile of *dry stubble,* by His enmity?

יג/כו־כח כו־כז כִּי־תִכְתֹּב עָלַי מְרֹרוֹת וְתוֹרִישֵׁנִי עֲוֹנוֹת נְעוּרָי: וְתָשֵׂם בַּסַּד
ו רַגְלַי וְתִשְׁמוֹר כָּל־אָרְחֹתָי עַל־שָׁרְשֵׁי רַגְלַי תִּתְחַקֶּה:
יד/א־ב כח־א וְהוּא כְּרָקָב יִבְלֶה כְּבֶגֶד אֲכָלוֹ עָשׁ: אָדָם יְלוּד אִשָּׁה קְצַר
ב יָמִים וּשְׂבַע־רֹגֶז: כְּצִיץ יָצָא וַיִּמָּל וַיִּבְרַח כַּצֵּל וְלֹא

But, ludicrous or not, Iyov's experiences — as delineated in verses 26 and 27 — leave him no alternative. Indeed God appears to hate him — fiercely! And so, at verse 28 and onwards, he returns to the theme which he had touched upon gingerly at verse 25. He just cannot grasp the meaning of a Deity Who would joust — with a mirage!

We have rendered תַּעֲרוֹץ together with the interrogatory, ...הֶ, as, *Will You frighten*, in accordance with *Rashi*. This, although *Rashi* generally understands the root as *to smash* (see, for example, at *Deuteronomy* 1:29). It would have seemed possible to render this verse: *Will You smash a driven leaf, pursue dry stubble?* as does *Metzudos*.

נִדָּף has the base meaning, *to move*. It is frequently used to describe something that is wind-blown. See, for example, *Psalms* 1:4.

26-27. כִּי־תִכְתֹּב עָלַי מְרֹרוֹת וְתוֹרִישֵׁנִי עֲוֹנוֹת נְעוּרָי — *That You record my rebellions, impose the sins of my youth upon me.* וְתָשֵׂם בַּסַּד רַגְלַי וְתִשְׁמוֹר כָּל־אָרְחֹתָי עַל־שָׁרְשֵׁי רַגְלַי תִּתְחַקֶּה — *That You place my feet in the stocks, stalk my every path, investigate my very footsteps.* We have seen above that at 33:10-11, Elihu refers to this speech and takes Iyov to task for the temerity which it displays.

His paraphrasing shows that he views these two verses as an explanation for Iyov's earlier assertion that God views him as an enemy. Only such a perception of Iyov could explain the ugly usages described here.

Why, of all the many things that Iyov has said, does Elihu choose just these two verses as his target?

We quote *Ramban*: [These matters] have angered Elihu more than anything else that Iyov has said. For his [earlier] denial of Divine Providence over lowly man, derives from his perception of the Blessed Creator as too exalted and great [for such concerns. It was consequently, not as reprehensible]. But when Iyov, in his recriminations, claims that [God] considers him an enemy, stalking his paths that He might falsely accuse him, that is absolute heresy and a *blaspheming of God* ... Surely one who asserts such things has *blasphemed God* ...

Ramban's language, ... *blaspheming of God*, is highly significant. He is actually using the same words, בִּרְכַּת ה׳, as the Satan used in making his original challenge. If we take *Ramban* literally, this would appear to mean that Iyov in fact succumbed and *blasphemed* God, as Satan had predicted that he would.

But are Iyov's assertions here substantively worse than those which he uttered at 9:22ff.? As the commentary there makes clear, what he said in that speech, particularly, as understood by *Rava* at *Bava Basra* 16a, seems immeasurably more heinous:

> 22. *There is a thing — because of which I said: 'He destroys the constant with the wicked!'*
> 23. *When Satan goes for the sudden kill — he mocks the rotting of the innocent.*
> 24. *The land is in the hands of the wicked one, he sheaths the faces of its judges. If not, then who is it?*

Perhaps the explanation is as follows: As we saw repeatedly in the commentary to chapter 9, Iyov, at that moment, had been in the throes of a fury which, seething inside this frustrated and broken man, finally smashed all dams of self restraint and expressed itself in the appalling words quoted above. Clearly, a just and benign God would not hold Iyov to task for those words. Surely, when *Rava* in *Bava Basra* teaches that man cannot be blamed for that which bursts forth from him under unbearable stress, he must have had in mind just such a speech as the one in chapter 9.

But, Elihu reasoned, the speech with which our chapter deals is being said in defense of the earlier one. Already at 10:18 we observed a shift of emphasis which showed that Iyov's rage had spent itself. Indeed, the speech with which we are dealing now is, in every respect, more measured and restrained than the earlier one.

However, in that very restraint lies Iyov's disgrace, as Elihu sees it. The sentiments to which Iyov gives vent here were never forged in the searing kiln of uncontrolled and uncontrollable anguish. That lies in the past. The Iyov who speaks here is quite another man: still desperate, still smarting under the lashings of a fate which he cannot grasp, but withal, in full possession of his faculties. From the mouth of such a one, the diatribe in which

13/26-28 26 *That You record my rebellions, impose the sins of my youth upon*
me. 27 *That You place my feet in the stocks, stalk my every path,*
investigate my very footsteps. 28 *When, after all, it is destined to*
waste away like a rotting mass, like a garment consumed by the
moth.

14/1-2 1 *Man born of woman, a short life-span, sated with frustration.*
2 *A shoot came up and withered, fleeing as a shadow, never*

he indulges can only be defined — as Elihu sees it — as blasphemy.

If, in the end, God is willing to excuse even this, then that shows only that His magnanimity exceeds Elihu's grasp. He is willing to make allowance for even the very human tendency of defending the indefensible, rather than to admit the failing of error.

28. וְהוּא כְּרָקָב יִבְלֶה כְּבֶגֶד אֲכָלוֹ עָשׁ — *When, after all, it is destined to waste away like a rotting mass, like a garment consumed by the moth.* The description is of the human body (*Rashi*). At verse 25 (see commentary there) Iyov had begun to allow himself to dwell upon the sheer insignificance of puny humanity, and to wonder why God would bother to see man as His enemy. This theme is now picked up once more and will be developed further in the next chapter.

XIV.

1. אָדָם יְלוּד אִשָּׁה קְצַר יָמִים וּשְׂבַע־רֹגֶז — *Man born of woman, a short life-span, sated with frustration.* Iyov continues with the theme which he began at the end of the previous chapter. He just cannot conceive how God can look upon man as a worthy adversary. Short-lived and ineffectual, utterly insignificant and puny, he is just not worthy of God's attention!

Iyov's harsh assessment of humanity is, of course, not absolute. When we read chapter 29 — Iyov's description of his better days — the picture is one of a substantial and revered leader, whose influence reaches from the highest level of society where his weighty opinions are eagerly sought out, to the weak and the indigent, for whom, with a highly developed sense of *noblesse oblige,* he cares with feeling and sensitivity. No *rotting mass* there, no *garment consumed by the moth,* but a good and worthwhile life, lived with ability and responsibility.

But Iyov there makes it clear that the source of all that was worthwhile and admirable in his life was God's benign interest and help. All this took place during, ... *those days when God would watch over me when His lantern would gleam over my head, when God's mysteries permeated my home.* Here, his argument runs that without God's help, when indeed God views man as an *enemy,* man is a puny chunk of nothingness. For all his grandeur when God smiles upon him, he is nothing at all on his own.

What led Iyov's thought into this direction? Two possible avenues suggest themselves.

Perhaps, his thoughts were stimulated by Tzophar's words. It was he who had so eloquently pointed to the chasm which divides man from the Divine. His hope had been that Iyov's acceptance of this truism would effectively place God beyond questioning. In the event, it had just the opposite effect. As we saw above, Iyov is sure that his relentless probing is mandated by God Himself. Accordingly, the awareness of man's relative insignificance simply pours more fuel onto the fire. It makes God's apparently implacable enmity even more incomprehensible to him.

Alternatively, Iyov's musings upon man's frailty may be the reaction to the frustration of his craving that he might demand an accounting from God at some bar of justice. As we noted at 13:22, there was a part of him which knew well that this hope would never be realized, that it was no more than wishful thinking. Man is simply too small; he cannot hope to litigate as an equal with God. But if so, Iyov's anguished heart cries out, why does God bother with him at all. How can God seemingly feel Himself threatened by such a nonentity?

2. כְּצִיץ יָצָא וַיִּמָּל וַיִּבְרַח כַּצֵּל וְלֹא יַעֲמוֹד — *A shoot came up and withered, fleeing as a shadow, never tarrying.* A shoot bursting through the ground, fresh and daring, wakens within us a sense of anticipation and hope for a future of beauty and accomplishment. Soon enough, it withers and is no more. How rarely, Iyov reflects, is potential fulfilled, are the euphoric promises of childhood kept!

Even when something is accomplished, it

ג יַעֲמוֹד: אַף־עַל־זֶה פָּקַחְתָּ עֵינֶךָ וְאֹתִי תָבִיא בְמִשְׁפָּט
ד־ה עִמָּךְ: מִי־יִתֵּן טָהוֹר מִטָּמֵא לֹא אֶחָד: אִם־חֲרוּצִים | יָמָיו
ו מִסְפַּר־חֳדָשָׁיו אִתָּךְ חֻקָּו עָשִׂיתָ וְלֹא יַעֲבֹר: שְׁעֵה מֵעָלָיו
ז וְיֶחְדָּל עַד־יִרְצֶה כְּשָׂכִיר יוֹמוֹ: כִּי יֵשׁ לָעֵץ תִּקְוָה
ח אִם־יִכָּרֵת וְעוֹד יַחֲלִיף וְיֹנַקְתּוֹ לֹא תֶחְדָּל: אִם־יַזְקִין
ט בָּאָרֶץ שָׁרְשׁוֹ וּבֶעָפָר יָמוּת גִּזְעוֹ: מֵרֵיחַ מַיִם יַפְרִחַ וְעָשָׂה
י קָצִיר כְּמוֹ־נָטַע: וְגֶבֶר יָמוּת וַיֶּחֱלָשׁ וַיִּגְוַע אָדָם וְאַיּוֹ:
יא־יב אָזְלוּ־מַיִם מִנִּי־יָם וְנָהָר יֶחֱרַב וְיָבֵשׁ: וְאִישׁ שָׁכַב
וְלֹא־יָקוּם עַד־בִּלְתִּי שָׁמַיִם לֹא יָקִיצוּ וְלֹא־יֵעֹרוּ

has little substance or permanence. No status is long maintained. There is constant flux, constant movement, always closer — to death (*Malbim*).

3. אַף־עַל־זֶה פָּקַחְתָּ עֵינֶךָ וְאֹתִי תָבִיא בְמִשְׁפָּט עִמָּךְ — *Do You cast Your eyes upon even this, bring such as I to judgment with You?* Here Iyov, as *Rashi* interprets this phrase, gives vent to weary disgust with the frailty and insubstantiality which appear to be both his lot and his curse. He can no longer even talk about himself in human terms. He has become, simply, *this*! The *rotting pile of nothingness* which he described above. What possible interest can God have to examine, and bring to justice, such a nonentity? [For an analysis of the theological stance implied in these thoughts — see footnote to 7:17.]

Ramban's interpretation is somewhat softer: *This* is to be understood as, *A man who is thus*, that is, one whose life is so short and insignificant. Iyov is returning to the point which he made at 13:15 (see commentary there) that man's physical being — though not his existence in the after-life — is beneath God's notice. It is too fleeting, too meaningless, to be the object of Divine Providence. Iyov is arguing, first and foremost, that he has not sinned. However, even if God could succeed in imputing some wrongdoing to him, there is still no reason why he should be made to suffer for it in this world.

4. מִי־יִתֵּן טָהוֹר מִטָּמֵא לֹא אֶחָד — *Who could bring forth purity from filth? There is not a single one.* Man, formed from his father's unclean semen, nourished by his mother's unclean menstrual blood (*Malbim*), cannot be expected to live an unblemished, pure life. No one has ever shown that this could be done (*Rashi* and *Ramban*).

5-6. אִם־חֲרוּצִים יָמָיו מִסְפַּר־חֳדָשָׁיו אִתָּךְ חֻקָּו עָשִׂיתָ וְלֹא יַעֲבֹר — *If his days are precisely measured, his months numbered with You, You have determined a fixed time which can never be altered, for him.* שְׁעֵה מֵעָלָיו וְיֶחְדָּל עַד־יִרְצֶה כְּשָׂכִיר יוֹמוֹ — *Then, turn away from him, so that he will be relieved, until — like a hired man — he will crave his day. Rashi* takes these two verses as one continuous thought, and, together, as leading into the next section of Iyov's speech. The sense is as follows: If indeed You, God, consider man Your enemy; if, for some reason which I cannot fathom, You wish to hurt him — then, is the shortness of his allotted life-span, the iron-clad boundary of time beyond which he can never hope to pass, not enough torture for him? He is hurting enough! Why not just leave him to his own resources. Soon enough, tired and debilitated by his toils, he will look forward to and gratefully anticipate his death, much as a hired worker craves the end of his working day.

In the next passage, Iyov will demonstrate that the terrible finality of death, that element of man's existence which, Iyov feels, is pain enough, is limited to the human experience. Other forms of life can defy extinction, can perpetuate themselves beyond their own exit from the stage of life. Only puny man is inexorably shackled by his mortality. Why expose him to pain beyond this greatest of all terrors?

We have rendered חֲרוּצִים, *precisely measured*, as *Rashi* and *Ramban* appear to take it. *Radak*, in *Sefer HaShorashim*, takes note of the more frequent use of this root as connoting a *passing of judgment* or an *apportioning*. Thus, *If his days are apportioned to him.*

We have rendered שְׁעֵה מֵעָלָיו, *turn away from him*, in accordance with *Rashi* to *Isaiah* 22:4.

7-9. כִּי יֵשׁ לָעֵץ תִּקְוָה אִם־יִכָּרֵת וְעוֹד יַחֲלִיף וְיֹנַקְתּוֹ לֹא תֶחְדָּל — *For there is hope for a tree — even if it were to be cut off, it will once more renew*

tarrying. 3 Do You cast Your eyes upon even this, bring such as I to
judgment with You. 4 Who could bring forth purity from filth?
There is not a single one. 5 If his days are precisely measured, his
months numbered with You, You have determined a fixed time
which can never be altered, for him. 6 Then, turn away from him,
so that he will be relieved, until — like a hired man — he will crave
his day. 7 For there is hope for a tree — even if it were to be cut off,
it will once more renew itself, its sapling will not cease. 8 Even if its
roots were to grow old in the ground, its trunk to die in the earth.
9 With just a whiff of water it will send out shoots, sprout branches
like a tree. 10 But, when man dies, he languishes, man breathes his
last — where is he? 11 As waters from the sea depart, turning rivers
arid and dry. 12 So man, having lain down will never rise. They
will not wake up until the heavens are no more, will not be roused

itself, its sapling will not cease. אִם־יַזְקִין בָּאָרֶץ שָׁרְשׁוֹ וּבֶעָפָר יָמוּת גִּזְעוֹ — *Even if its roots were to grow old in the ground, its trunk to die in the earth.* מֵרֵיחַ מַיִם יַפְרִחַ וְעָשָׂה קָצִיר כְּמוֹ־נָטַע — *With just a whiff of water it will send out shoots, sprout branches like a tree.* The sense of these three verses is clear. A tree, in contrast to man whose death is absolute, will always be able to renew itself.

For יֹנֵק, as a *branch*, see *Psalms* 80:12. In translating, עֵץ as *tree*, we follow *Ramban*.

We may wonder at Iyov's choice of the metaphor of the tree as an illustration that even death need not always write *finis* to growth and purpose. Bildad, at 8:16-18, had used the metaphor of a tree-like plant to illustrate the absolute finality of death: *But let him uproot it from its place, it will disavow it: I have never seen you!*

10. וְגֶבֶר יָמוּת וַיֶּחֱלָשׁ וַיִּגְוַע אָדָם וְאַיּוֹ — *But, when man dies, he languishes, man breathes his last — where is he?* The sequence of expression seems puzzling. Surely man languishes before he dies?

However, when we consider that this verse is contrasting man after his death to the tree which has expired, the wording is exact. A tree, even after it has ceased to live, can still renew itself. Not so, man. What is left of him after death, languishes and is unable to produce other life.

11-12. אָזְלוּ־מַיִם מִנִּי־יָם וְנָהָר יֶחֱרַב וְיָבֵשׁ — *As waters from the sea depart, turning rivers arid and dry.* וְאִישׁ שָׁכַב וְלֹא־יָקוּם עַד־בִּלְתִּי שָׁמַיִם לֹא יָקִיצוּ וְלֹא־יֵעֹרוּ מִשְּׁנָתָם — *So man, having lain down will never rise. They will not wake up until the heavens are no more, will not be roused from their sleep.* Earlier, at 7:9, Iyov had used another metaphor to illustrate the finality of death: *As a cloud disintegrates and is gone, so he that goes down to the grave shall never come back.* We must assume that our metaphor of the departed waters has something different to say.

We have translated verse 11 in accordance with *Rashi.* The sense is that when the waters — which come there from the sea — desert the river's source, then the river, which relies upon them for its life, will become arid and dry.

Manifestly, the metaphor seems to be less concerned with the fact that the waters will not return, than with the negative results of their absence. We mourn, not the waters, but the river that is no more.

This is a radically different perspective than the one evoked by the disintegrated cloud. There, the stress is entirely upon the transience of such an existence. The cloud is there for a very short period of time — and then is gone, forever. No issue is made of the fact that it will be missed.

The difference may be explained on the basis of the context in which our metaphor appears. As we saw above, *Rashi* seems to have Iyov argue that the insignificance and transience of human life is hurtful enough to satisfy even a vengeful and vindictive God Who is seeking to inflict pain. Thus, the focus here is not upon the fact that human life is short, but upon the misery which that shortness brings about. That is doubtless increased by the thought of unfinished business. There is so much more that could have been accomplished. With death comes the frustration of many hopes and expectations. This thought is expressed by the picture of the dry and arid river-bed, waiting vainly for the waters which will come no more.

Indeed, we have here a very different

יג מִשְׁנָתָם: מִי יִתֵּן ׀ בִּשְׁאוֹל תַּצְפִּנֵנִי תַּסְתִּירֵנִי עַד־שׁוּב
יד אַפֶּךָ תָּשִׁית לִי חֹק וְתִזְכְּרֵנִי: אִם־יָמוּת גֶּבֶר הֲיִחְיֶה כָּל־
טו יְמֵי צְבָאִי אֲיַחֵל עַד־בּוֹא חֲלִיפָתִי: תִּקְרָא וְאָנֹכִי
טז אֶעֱנֶךָּ לְמַעֲשֵׂה יָדֶיךָ תִכְסֹף: כִּי־עַתָּה צְעָדַי תִּסְפּוֹר
יז לֹא־תִשְׁמוֹר עַל־חַטָּאתִי: חָתֻם בִּצְרוֹר פִּשְׁעִי וַתִּטְפֹּל
יח עַל־עֲוֹנִי: וְאוּלָם הַר־נוֹפֵל יִבּוֹל וְצוּר יֶעְתַּק מִמְּקֹמוֹ:

picture than the one at 7:9. There, the cloud dissipates and there is nothing at all left. Here, in verse 12, we have the slumbering dead, who could theoretically be woken up, but aren't; and in verse 13 we even have the whimsical wish that God would cache Iyov in the grave for a temporary period, after which he could rise once more. Evidently, then, in contrast to the cloud metaphor, we picture something remaining after death — something that the dead could accomplish if only they could be brought back to the land of the living.

That this will never be is the tragedy of the human condition — a tragedy, Iyov argues, which should free man from any other suffering.

The subject of the final sentence, *They will not wake up . . .*, is, all the people who die.

13. מִי יִתֵּן בִּשְׁאוֹל תַּצְפִּנֵנִי תַּסְתִּירֵנִי עַד־שׁוּב אַפֶּךָ תָּשִׁית לִי חֹק וְתִזְכְּרֵנִי — *If only You could cache me in the grave, hide me until Your anger turned away, set me a fixed time — and remember me. Ramban* explains as follows: If death could be a temporary state, it could be measured out precisely to serve as a suitable punishment. Such and such a sin; so and so much death. But now that death is permanent, it must always be out of proportion to any sin that has been committed. If so, it ought to obviate the need for any additional suffering.

14-15. אִם־יָמוּת גֶּבֶר הֲיִחְיֶה כָּל־יְמֵי צְבָאִי אֲיַחֵל עַד־בּוֹא חֲלִיפָתִי — *When man dies, can he ever live again? Throughout the days of my service-term, I long — until the time of my passing comes.* תִּקְרָא וְאָנֹכִי אֶעֱנֶךָּ לְמַעֲשֵׂה יָדֶיךָ תִכְסֹף — *Call out! I will answer You. O crave the work of Your hands. Rashi* and *Ramban* have radically different approaches to these two verses. In *Rashi's* view, the burning love which Iyov feels for God despite — or because of (see footnote below) — his tribulations, once more finds lyrical expression. *Ramban*, as he did at 13:15 where *Rashi* first discovered Iyov's adoration, offers a different interpretation.

First *Ramban*: Already at 13:15, Iyov (as understood by *Ramban*) had stated his belief that Divine justice was limited to the soul after it had departed the body. In our physical world he can detect only the vagaries of blind happenstance. This section continues in the same vein: *Ramban* would translate as follows: *If, when man dies, he could live once more, then throughout my assigned life I would long for death. For, then You would call, and I would respond, when You long for the work of Your hands.*

Iyov longs for a confrontation with God. He knows that this can only occur after he had died. No one wants to die. But this is because of the dreadful finality of death. If only death would not have to be so final, then Iyov would wish to die, would willingly answer God's call, made from His longing for the creature of His handiwork, so that he would have the opportunity of presenting his case.

Our translation follows *Rashi*.

In the first verse, Iyov confronts the finality of death. But rather than allowing the knowledge that he cannot live forever to break him, he learns to imbue each second of his existence with infinite value. Each second is precious — because it is irreplaceable. Every moment of his life, up to the very moment of death, he craves just one thing — life itself!

However, the meaning which life has for Iyov is circumscribed by his relationship to God. For him it has purpose and focus only to the extent that it is lived in the benign glow of God's concern. And so, in the second verse, he entreats God to care. Why do You not call out to me, why do You not *crave the work of Your hands* sufficiently to be interested in what I have to say? If only You could bring Yourself to care, to call upon me — how readily would I answer, how eagerly explain and justify my claims! [1]

1. Iyov is, of course, mistaken in his perception, and in the general thesis expressed in this part of the speech.

It is true that life is short and fleeting, death inevitable and final. All that, however, holds good only in

14/13-18 *from their sleep.* [13] *If only You could cache me in the grave, hide
me until Your anger turned away, set me a fixed time — and
remember me.* [14] *When man dies, can he ever live again?
Throughout the days of my service-term, I long — until the time
of my passing comes.* [15] *Call out! I will answer You. O crave
the work of Your hands.* [16] *For now You number my footsteps,
have no patience with my sins.* [17] *My iniquities are sealed in
a bundle, You cling to my transgressions.* [18] *But, a mountain that
falls may yet produce grain, as also a rock torn from its place.*

16-17. כִּי־עַתָּה צְעָדַי תִּסְפּוֹר לֹא־תִשְׁמֹר עַל־חַטָּאתִי — *For now You number my footsteps, have no patience with my sins.* חָתֻם בִּצְרוֹר פִּשְׁעִי וַתִּטְפֹּל עַל־עֲוֹנִי — *My iniquities are sealed in a bundle, You cling to my transgressions.* As *Rashi* understands these two verses, Iyov is bemoaning the dreadful contrast between what might have been and what is. Instead of the loving concern for which Iyov has expressed such longing in the previous verse, he sees God perversely and vindictively dogging his every footstep, pounding zealously upon every sin, so that punishment can be exacted at the earliest possible moment. Nothing is overlooked, no shortcoming allowed to sink into oblivion. Each is jealously wrapped and guarded, to be used against the hapless Iyov as opportunity permits.

Ramban interprets in similar fashion, but within the context of his understanding of the previous section. Iyov had longed for death so that he might be granted the opportunity of presenting his case. This, because he knows that *now*, in this world, God will never give him a chance to vindicate himself. Here, all that God does is to hound him mercilessly, as described in these two verses. *Ramban* here does not explain וַתִּטְפֹּל, but at 33:10 he makes clear that he understands it as a finding of a pretext against Iyov: You seek to make sins *stick to* me.

18-19. וְאוּלָם הַר־נוֹפֵל יִבּוֹל וְצוּר יֶעְתַּק מִמְּקֹמוֹ — *But, a mountain that falls may yet produce grain, as also a rock torn from its place.* אֲבָנִים שָׁחֲקוּ מַיִם תִּשְׁטֹף־סְפִיחֶיהָ עֲפַר־אָרֶץ וְתִקְוַת אֱנוֹשׁ הֶאֱבַדְתָּ — *Stones, worn away by water — their growth! It abrades them into dust of the earth.*

an absolute sense. Out there, with infinite, omnipotent God as unique and absolute truth, man is indeed beneath caring. A putrid speck of insignificance, unworthy of attention in the vast oceans of a reality which neither needs nor notices him.

But relative to life as we humans know it, the seventy or eighty years allotted us (*Psalms* 90:10) are significant, indeed. Every moment of every day we are confronted with challenges and opportunities to create, if nothing else, at least our own lives, to give them content and meaning. There are endless chances to leave our mark, our footsteps in the sands of time. Even if we are immobilized by suffering we can choose to bear it with grace and dignity as an inspiration to others; or, even if it is our fate to writhe in our agonies in solitude, we can still affirm our worth as human beings created in the image of God.

Iyov has missed an important insight. His desperate plea that God care enough to call out to him, ignores the eloquence of God's impenetrable silence. From the first moment in which Iyov's world disintegrated, when wealth, children, wife and finally friends deserted him, the focus of every waking thought, the center of every torturous nightmare, has been God — the only sure anchorage in the maelstrom of his terrors. Unrealized and unbeknown to Iyov, a link is being forged, a oneness created, infinitely stronger and more meaningful than the less intense needs of a placid life could ever have produced (see commentary to 9:17).

As we have seen above (at 7:8 and footnote to 9:2) Iyov, before the revelation from within the whirlwind, is bedeviled by the tragic error of placing himself on one level with God. His preoccupation with the vain pipe-dream of summoning God to the bar of justice is ample evidence of such a distorted perception. When God is defined in such severely reduced terms, it is understandable that the quality of the relationship should be measured by the intensity of communication between the two parties. The idea that a constantly sustained love, maintained in the face of silence, ignored and unrequited, could be its own reward, is out of the range of such limited religious sophistication.

We may well surmise that indeed, the revelation from within the whirlwind was granted Iyov as a direct result of the unshakable steadfastness of his love — revealed, paradoxically, by his cantankerous insistence upon satisfaction of his claim. Such passionate longing will not go unrewarded. He who insists on tracking God through the cold, dark wastelands of His awesome silence will eventually find Him.

יט אֲבָנִים ׀ שָׁחֲקוּ מַיִם תִּשְׁטֹף־סְפִיחֶיהָ עֲפַר־אָרֶץ וְתִקְוַת
כ אֱנוֹשׁ הֶאֱבַדְתָּ׃ תִּתְקְפֵהוּ לָנֶצַח וַיַּהֲלֹךְ מְשַׁנֶּה פָנָיו
כא וַתְּשַׁלְּחֵהוּ׃ יִכְבְּדוּ בָנָיו וְלֹא יֵדָע וְיִצְעֲרוּ וְלֹא־
כב יָבִין לָמוֹ׃ אַךְ־בְּשָׂרוֹ עָלָיו יִכְאָב וְנַפְשׁוֹ עָלָיו תֶּאֱבָל׃

But, man's hope — You have destroyed. Rashi relates יבול to יְבוּל, *produce*, and understands verse 18 as we have rendered it. The sense is that, collapse, for a mountain, does not spell the end. It will be crumbled into earth and thus will still be able to produce grain. So too the rock, torn away from its foundations, will eventually disintegrate into dust, which can yet be productive.

The same idea is expressed in the next verse, though the language of the second half is obscure in the extreme:

סְפִיחַ is defined by *Rashi* as produce that grows spontaneously from grain which was dropped at the time of the harvest (*Rashi* to *Leviticus* 25:5). The subject of תִּשְׁטֹף [literally, to *flood*] is the [implied, but not specified] stream of water which wears away the stone. עֲפַר אָרֶץ, *the dust of the earth*, is the object of the predicate, שָׁחֲקוּ. The sentence is to be paraphrased as follows: When waters wear away stone, then the stream of water will turn the stone into dust of the earth, thus making sure that the erstwhile stone will have its own produce — the spontaneous growth which will spring up in that dust.

All this is contrasted to *man's hope*. For man, death truly spells the end.

This appears to be precisely the same idea as was previously expressed in the metaphor of the dead tree in verses 7-10, above. Why should it be repeated here?

A careful reading of the next few verses yields the answer. Iyov bemoans the fact that the dead have no contact with their children. These will succeed or fail within the orbit of their own lives. Their dead parents remain unaware of, and untouched by, their fate. This is a different perspective than his complaint in the earlier section. That centered upon the finality of death in relation to the person himself.

Thus, we understand our passage as follows: The mountain, the rock, and the stone all retain their own effectiveness even after they have undergone death. They themselves, albeit in a new form, will still be useful and productive. Man is different. After death, he himself is no more. He must live on through his children — and that, for him, is no life at all.

Ramban reads essentially the same message into these verses, though his rendering differs from that of *Rashi*. He suggests that נוֹפֵל might be an adjective connoting *gigantic* (*Genesis* 6:4) and reads יְבוּל, as formed from נָבַל, *to wither away*, and interprets as follows: Gigantic mountains may wither, even solidly implanted rocks may eventually fall, and stones may be eroded by water. Everything, even such as appear securely entrenched, can eventually undergo some change for better or worse. Only death is absolute.

Ramban, too, has trouble with the second phrase in verse 19. He suggests that the sense may be as follows: Water will erode stones into dust, and this will eventually produce a plant. But the very water which generated the possibility that this plant might grow, will eventually sweep it away. The plant will thus be lost — but man's hope is lost even more.

The difficulties which *Rashi* and *Ramban* encountered derived from their interpretation of סְפִיחַ as *a plant*. *Radak*, in *Sefer HaShorashim*, suggests that סְפִיחַ might be an inversion of סחף, a verb used to describe the sweeping power of the flood. The phrase would thus be rendered: *The sweeping power of its flood produces dust of the earth.*

20. תִּתְקְפֵהוּ לָנֶצַח וַיַּהֲלֹךְ מְשַׁנֶּה פָּנָיו וַתְּשַׁלְּחֵהוּ — *You overpower him — so that he must go to eternity, transform his visage — and send him off.* We have translated the first part of the verse in accordance with *Ramban*, and this may also well be *Rashi's* interpretation.

The *transformed visage* could refer to the aging face (*Malbim*) which has lost the glow (*Bereishis Rabbah* 11:2) of youth.

22. אַךְ־בְּשָׂרוֹ עָלָיו יִכְאָב וְנַפְשׁוֹ עָלָיו תֶּאֱבָל — *O but his flesh will smother him in pain, his soul will be in mourning over itself. Rashi* sees reference here to the agony which the body suffers as it is devoured by worms in the grave. This, however, may not be the simple meaning of the verse. *Ramban* thinks that the pain and sorrow of approaching death is meant.

19 *Stones, worn away by water — their growth! It abrades them*
into dust of the earth. But, man's hope — You have destroyed!
20 *You overpower him — so that he must go to eternity, transform*
his visage — and send him off. 21 *His sons may be wealthy — he*
will not know; they may suffer — but he will have no
understanding for them. 22 *O but his flesh will smother him in pain,*
his soul will be in mourning over itself.

◆§ The First Round

We look back onto the first round of the debate and find that we are able to make certain observations, but also that there is much that remains obscure.

In the first place, neither the precise structure of the debate, nor, indeed, the point from which it begins, are readily defined. Are we to read Iyov's first speech as the opening salvo, and relegate the friends to the position of reacting to his ideas? Or is it Eliphaz who is determined to open a dialogue, and who, by the power of his hectoring, forces Iyov into a defense of his position?

The difficulty is acute because, in point of fact, the speeches can be viewed as a debate only if we take that term in the loosest possible sense (*Rambam,* in *Moreh Nevuchim* 3:23, ed. *Kapach,* uses *viku'ach* to describe the discussion). This, because while each of the friends, in this first round, addresses Iyov directly, Iyov himself hardly turns to them at all. His speeches appear to be more in the form of soliloquies, punctuated occasionally with short snatches of direct speech, but these are addressed to God as frequently as to the friends. Certainly, there is nothing even akin to a reasoned argument or refutation of ideas put forward by his disputants — such as we would have expected in a debate, as we know it.

We cannot know why such a loose format was chosen; why, if indeed, as so many commentators assume, each of the protagonists expresses formal theological positions (which by their nature could be attacked and would need to be defended), there is not a more rigorous structure which would force a point for point analysis of each assertion as it is made. But, the fact remains that it is so. Perhaps by this means the absolute impotence of the friends is brought into sharp relief. They might as well have saved themselves their impassioned perorations; Iyov remains unmoved, unchanged, and ultimately unhelped.

Therefore, we cannot know with any certainty what is the precise role of Iyov's first speech (chapter 3). Is it to be reckoned as part of the debate, or is it rather a primordial scream of agony, a release of the pent-up devils which had churned within Iyov during the seven days of silent, addressed to no one — indeed made without the awareness of any presence save that of the crushing, horrible realities of his existence.

It may be that the answer to this question would depend upon the two possible interpretations of this chapter which we discussed in the commentary. If, as *Ramban* maintains, Iyov is already here staking out a theological position — that man's fate is governed not by God, but by the heavenly constellations — then there appears to be little reason why we should not regard this speech as the beginning of the debate. Indeed *Ramban* makes clear that much of what Eliphaz says in his first speech is in direct refutation of Iyov's position in this matter. If, however, as we surmised might be *Rashi's* opinion, the curses which Iyov flings at the night of his conception and the day of his birth, are simply the expressions of a frustration which quite naturally tends to lash out at the nearest, most tangible, cause of suffering — then it is quite possible that this speech ought not to be considered a part of the debate.

We should discuss this question in the context of a closer analysis of the role of *comforters* which the book ascribes to the friends (see 2:11). Certainly what they say appears to be oriented more towards criticism of Iyov's attitude, and assertions of the essential justice which underlies God's stewardship of human affairs, than to comfort in the conventional sense.

Let us examine, once more, the account of the friends' coming and their initial contact with Iyov:

> *When Iyov's friends heard about all these calamities which had befallen him, each came from his home — Eliphaz . . ., Bildad . . ., and Tzophar . . . — and met together, to mourn with him and to comfort him. When they saw him from the distance they could not recognize him and they broke into loud weeping . . . They sat with him on the ground seven days and seven nights. None spoke a word to him for they saw that his suffering was very great. Afterwards Iyov began to speak and cursed the day of his birth.*

See commentary to 4:1, that from the fact that the friends first kept silent, and that Eliphaz began to speak (chapter 4) only after Iyov's first speech (chapter 3), *Moed Kattan* 28b deduces the *halachah* that at a place of *shivah,* the comforters are to keep silent until the mourner himself has begun to speak. As the commentators understand this requirement, it is to give the mourner the chance to express his *tziduk hadin,* his acceptance of the fate to which Divine Providence has subjected him.

It is difficult to see how such an assertion can be made in view of verse 13 which states explicitly: *None spoke a word to him for they saw that his suffering was very great.* Surely, there is an implication that if his hurt had not been so overwhelming, the friends would indeed have addressed him even before he began to speak.

There is another difficulty: At 2:11-13 we quoted *Rava* who taught that: Let a man choose death unless he has friends such as those which Iyov had. The Sages, then, make an issue of the fact that the relationship between Iyov and these three was at the very acme of what friendship should be. But, why is this significant for the dynamics of the story. If this unusually close friendship would somehow have been crucial to the type of comfort they gave him, then indeed we ought to be told of it. On the contrary, however, we see that the friends fell woefully short of the sensitive empathy which might have made them true comforters.

Why then make an issue of the fact that originally, they were such wonderful friends?

All this leads us to wonder whether perhaps there is a deeper significance to verse 12. Why does the story require that: *When they saw him from the distance they could not recognize him*? Does it matter? If not, why should an apparently useless embellishment be added?

At 2:12 we thought that, . . . *they could not recognize him,* meant that the look of bitterness and disillusion which they saw upon his face was quite different from anything that they had seen before. This was not the Iyov whom they knew!

Perhaps, then, we are being told that there was here a total change of heart. When originally they left their homes to come to the succor of one who was as flesh of their flesh, blood of their blood, when instinct brought them together with one heart, so that they entered by the same gate (2:11), they had intended to act quite differently than they eventually did. Had they 'recognized' Iyov, they would have come not as philosophers but as friends, showered him with the affection which he craved so much and which, in the event, they denied him (see the parable of the *faithless river* at 6:15ff.). There would have been no formal rules for the comforter, no artificial etiquette for the mourner's house. Rather they would have acted with the spontaneity of natural love — and taken the stricken Iyov to their hearts.

But, they came and could not recognize him! For seven days they sat silent, observing, hoping that they could catch a glimmer of the familiar well-loved Iyov. Had there been a flicker of recognition, they would not have stood on formality, would have spoken before he spoke — would, in short, have acted as friends such as they would act.

Taken thus, it is indeed of utmost importance to point out what a unique friendship these four men had. Significantly, we know only that, . . . *they could not recognize him*! How did Iyov look upon himself? Of this we know nothing. Certainly from his piteous cries in the later speeches, from the bewilderment at their desertion which he expresses, it is clear enough that he had expected better at their hands. He knew himself to be essentially unchanged, knew the mighty strength and resilience which yet buoyed up his broken body, knew himself ready to love and to be loved as in the past — and found no resonance in the stony, obtuse hearts of those who had become his last support. He, too, sat silent for seven days; he too hoped and hoped, and sat still, and hoped; until hope gave way to despair, until he could not avoid the dreadful conclusion — *My brothers have betrayed me like a river*! (6:15).

Here was the final indignity: Iyov, the true Iyov, had become invisible to the world — irredeemably alone! Even to those who, among all men, might have been expected to see beneath the outer shell, there was only the grotesque caricature of the man whom they had once known and loved.

And so, from now on, only formalities were possible. This much they would yet do for him. Let him humble himself and listen; they will instruct him in God's ways. Still, form must be followed — Iyov must, by etiquette, be the one to speak first. Small matter that in place of the expected *tziduk hadin* (see at 4:1), curses and maledictions spurted out from that poor mouth. The niceties had been observed.

Did they perceive their perorations as comfort?

To answer this question, we would first have to define the concept of *nichum aveilim* more precisely. How are we to help mourners to bear their loss?

Kesubos 8b teaches that one of the great *Amoraim* would address mourners thus: Brothers, wearied and crushed by this loss, O consider the following carefully! It is established for all eternity [that all must die, and that, therefore you should not cry excessively (*Rashi*)] a path [laid down] since the six days of creation. Many have drunk [from the cup of suffering] and many are yet to drink; the drinking of the latter ones will be just the same as that of the earlier ones. O brothers, may He Who is the Master of comfort, comfort you!

Apparently, then, it is the feeling of being a part of the eternal, universal, and inevitable rhythms of life which in the long run assuages pain. I am not unique, others have suffered and will suffer as I do now. I submerge my sorrows into the maelstrom of all human woe and thus, presumably, will ultimately learn, too, to taste of the abundance of all human joy.

Perhaps such a comforting must be denied Iyov. His troubles were unique. Nothing the friends could have said could possibly have persuaded him that his was just another of humanity's private sorrows.

What then would have been appropriate comfort for him? And how did the friends perform on that score?

Let us examine the relationship of the three speeches to one another, both according to *Ramban,* and according to the system which we have suggested according to *Rashi*:

Ramban	*Rashi*
Eliphaz: The central thrust of this speech is to challenge Iyov's assertion that man's fate is determined by the heavenly constellations. Proofs are marshalled, and arguments made, that, ultimately — and to this everyone must agree — it is God alone Who orders the affairs of man.	**Eliphaz:** The thrust of this speech is to voice disappointment at Iyov's reaction to his fate — and to suggest an alternative, legitimate response. Instead of lashing out, impotently, at meaningless targets, when in any case intractable realities are firmly in place, the sufferer is exhorted to, sublimate, and thus ultimately overcome, his pain.
Bildad: Bildad supports Eliphaz in his rejection of Iyov's stance, but, at the same time, moves beyond him. Where Eliphaz's tone had been placatory, Bildad's is accusatory. He dismisses Iyov's children out of hand. They were irredeemably wicked — and deserved to die. With regard to Iyov's own suffering Bildad feels that he can understand that, too. He accepts Iyov's contention that it cannot have been meant to inspire and to bring him closer to God. There is too much of it, it is too intense, too overwhelming. If so, Bildad reasons, its purpose must be one of cleansing and atonement. Iyov must have sinned — not as grievously as his children, but sufficiently to require a purification by the fire of his agonies.	**Bildad:** In our alternative analysis, Bildad does indeed move beyond Eliphaz's stance — but is much more restrained than he is in *Ramban's* view. He introduces the concept that Iyov's suffering may be the wages of sin — but allows for the possibility that it may not be. Rather than accusing, he challenges. Let Iyov himself examine his past. Does it bear up under his scrutiny? If he truly lived a life of constancy and purity, then the suffering is a temporary aberration, and the future beckons bright. He is master of his fate — let him pray and all will be well once more. But let Iyov beware! There is, too, the other possibility. If his pieties were a sham, his life a lie, then he is, indeed doomed. For the hypocrite there will be no mercy.

Tzophar: Tzophar's aim, as *Ramban* and possibly *Rashi* see it, is similar to that of Bildad: Iyov must be brought to a realization that suffering is the wages of sin. Neither of the two can conceive of a world-order — under God — which would allow for any other explanation. Iyov's protestations notwithstanding, there must, there simply must, be a cancerous worm of evil gnawing within at the seemingly wholesome exterior of his blameless life.

But where Bildad paints a canvas in which blighted hopes and false expectations are calculated to break the spirit, in which the fortress is stripped away to reveal the spider's web beneath, Tzophar guides Iyov's eyes upwards. In lyric exultation he sings of greater wisdoms, of hidden worlds, of a might and an exaltedness which belie even the possibility of human innocence. Iyov must have sinned in ways which he himself cannot have appreciated. Let him but focus on man's inherent shortcomings, let him admit the truth, correct past mistakes and turn to God in contrition and prayer — the dreadful past will slip away into the mists of forgetfulness, a renewed and invigorated future beckons.

The commentary offers an alternative interpretation. Tzophar does not discuss Iyov's suffering at all:

He offers no explanations, does not discuss whether or not Iyov had sinned. His entire focus is upon the dreadful blasphemies of the previous two chapters. With exquisite sensitivity he lets it be known that he realizes that Iyov had spoken only out of the throes of unbearable agony and had never meant the calumnies which he had uttered. Nevertheless, he will not let them pass in silence.

First, he establishes how far God is removed from the base motives which Iyov had imputed to Him. Surely, Iyov must realize that the mighty God of nature cannot be cut down to human dimensions. From there, he turns to Iyov's rehabilitation. With keen psychological insight he lets Iyov know that his loss of control derived from the brokenness of spirit that is the function of impurity of the spirit. Let Iyov put his spiritual house in order, and all the malignant pettinesses which had caused his bitterness will dissipate.

We can say with some degree of accuracy that according to both interpretations, the underlying thrust of all the three speeches is to help Iyov cope with his problems in a positive way. Certainly it is accurate to say that even the realization that all suffering must ultimately derive from sin, is a positive step towards rehabilitation, in that such an awareness is essential if the healing road of penitence is to be trodden. If helping the sufferer to take such actions as might be expected to cure him can be described as a kind of comfort, then indeed we would be able to describe this set of speeches as being undertaken in the spirit of *nichum aveilim.*

There is, however, an interesting observation which we must make in this connection.

We shall see that in the second round, all the speeches of the three friends are directed towards describing the evil that must, in one form or another, overtake the evildoer. There can never be a wicked man who prospers in a meaningful way. We shall have to analyze what role this second round — these speeches — play in Iyov's saga. Not only do they seem to fly in the face of reality — a case which Iyov makes most forcefully in his response to Tzophar in chapter 21 — but they seem irrelevant to Iyov's dilemma.

Certainly we would be hard put to describe them as speeches of comfort.

Nevertheless, it is only in this second round, in reaction to these seemingly irrelevant speeches, that Iyov uses the word *nechamah* (comfort). True, the word is used in a spirit of derision: the friends are *wearying comforters* (16:2); they *comfort uselessly* (21:34); and they are urged to *comfort* by listening rather than by speaking (21:2). The implication is, nonetheless, that deluded as they are, the friends see themselves even in this context as comforters.

Not so in the first round. Not once is the word *nechamah* invoked in either a positive or a negative sense.

In spite of all this, it does seem clear that the *Gemara,* which deduces from our passage the *halachah* that those who visit at a place of *shivah* are not permitted to begin their comforting until the mourner has spoken, clearly assumes that even the first speeches were meant to comfort. In such a context, Iyov's first speech would fill the requirement that the mourner speak first — though in this case it would have been a far cry from the *tziduk hadin* which is expected of him — and there would be no assumption that it was the first salvo in a debate.

There is, though, also the possibility that *Ramban* would understand the requirement that the mourner speak first differently than we have interpreted it. Perhaps the *halachah* requires the comforters to wait and see what the needs of the mourner are, as they are expressed in the first words that he utters. It is no easy matter to relieve another's severe distress, and there is certainly no formula that will serve in every case. If so, then Iyov's outburst of maledictions would have indicated to the friends the direction in which they must go. Given such an interpretation, Iyov's first speech ought to be considered the beginning of the first round of the debate.

◆§ Eliphaz's Second Speech

The first round is over. Each of the friends has tried, in his own way, to help Iyov in his travail. None has made the slightest impact. Iyov seems not even to have heard what they had to say. When he reacts to them at all, it is to the betrayal which he detects in their bearing towards him, never really to their thoughts. It is as though his agony has shrouded him in a haze through which only an occasional phrase can penetrate. The impression is of tiny, inadequate, darts of well-meant but conventional wisdom being hurled impotently against the massive armor of pain-generated indifference to the niceties of theological conjecture. Iyov is impervious to anything but the straight path of his own pain-driven cravings for relief.

And, so, this second round of speeches takes a different turn. The three speeches are so similar in structure as to seem artificially stylized. Each begins with an almost *pro forma* condemnation of

Iyov's obduracy, and then swings into a vivid description of the fate that will inevitably overtake the wicked. Now, the perceived tranquility of the wicked has not been central to Iyov's concerns. Why should the entire second round be devoted to it? It would seem that the friends, frustrated at their own impotence (see 32:3 where Elihu faults the friends for, . . . *that they were unable to find an argument [to satisfy Iyov]*), are taking refuge in flights of oratory which deal with a theoretical — and therefore safe — topic, thus saving themselves the ignominy of failure in a more direct and meaningful approach.

Perhaps they intend an oblique thrust at Iyov's perceived self-righteousness. You, they are saying, are the wicked one whose agonies we are describing. If so, they do not yet dare to make their accusations openly. This Eliphaz will do in his third speech.

Ramban introduces the chapter by noting the reasons for Eliphaz's change of heart. In his first speech he had been willing to grant Iyov the benefit of the doubt, had satisfied himself with urging him to sublimate his suffering instead of rebelling against it. Now, however, having heard Iyov's obstinate assertion of innocence — his folly-ridden insistence upon meeting God, head on, in legal confrontation — he has become convinced that Iyov really is wicked. For the rest, our analysis above applies to *Ramban's* perception of the second half of this speech.

Rashi understands the description of the suffering of the wicked, not as an objective analysis of a theoretical question, but as a threat of what will happen if Iyov will not admit guilt. He understands verse 18 as advocating the free concession of having sinned. The rest of chapter fifteen is devoted to describing the dire consequences of obstinacy.

XV.

Eliphaz has been hearing Iyov's speeches but has not really been listening. Again and again, we will find him using phrases which clearly echo words and thoughts from Iyov's response to Tzophar, but we look in vain for a grasp of the roiling emotions, the deep caring, the love and the hate clamoring for expression in harshly clashing counterpoint of hope and despair, which, so clearly, agitated Iyov as he spoke. He is reacting to a one-dimensional cardboard man; he pounces upon perceived heresies but misses the profoundly human, profoundly complex, needs which animate them (see fn. to 9:22-24). He fixes upon the unsubstantial wind-character of some of Iyov's agony-driven mental meanderings (verses 12 and 13), but remains unmoved by the hurricane of passionate religious feeling which drives Iyov relentlessly into differing and often contradictory directions.

And so, unaware of (and uninterested in) the wild beauty and savage forces which pulsate with vital energy beneath, he follows a path of his own mapping. We can almost observe him ticking off points for rebuttal as he listens to Iyov speak: Iyov is self-righteous — his vanity must be pricked by sarcastic taunts; he errs in his observation that often the wicked seem tranquil and at ease — he will be set straight.

Issues are addressed, never the man!

And which are the issues which Eliphaz tackles? From Iyov's response it would appear that the one substantive theme in Eliphaz's speech — that the wicked never prosper — is totally irrelevant to his concerns. He does not even bother to refute it — that he leaves to chapter 21.

Why, if the book of *Iyov* is a *mashal*, a parable, does the author put into Eliphaz's mouth a speech which seems to be so inadequate to the needs which he is trying to fill?[1]

At 2:11-13 we suggested that part of the author's intention may have been to teach us how *not* to comfort. We recognized that friends, particularly friends as close as those of Iyov, might be too intimately and emotionally involved to be able to see the needs of the sufferer accurately.

Eliphaz's failure to help Iyov at all might be a case in point. He moves from a positive approach in the first round — an attempt to persuade Iyov that the correct reaction to pain is sublimation — to accusations in the second round (vs. 5 and 6), to outright and vicious slander in the third (see chapter 22).

---

1. We do assume that even at this stage Eliphaz considers his words to have the function of *comforting* Iyov. This we can deduce from 16:2 where, in reaction to Eliphaz's words, Iyov describes all the friends as empty comforters.

We are hard put to see what element of comfort there might be in this speech.

Perhaps Eliphaz believes that Iyov might feel better in the knowledge that after all, justice prevails in human affairs. If, inevitably, the wicked suffer, then his troubles too are not the result of arbitrary caprice. He will examine his past, and armed with new awareness of his shortcomings, he will be able to take the first step towards rehabilitation (see commentary 20-23, below).

א־ב וַיַּעַן אֱלִיפַז הַתֵּימָנִי וַיֹּאמַר: הֶחָכָם יַעֲנֶה דַעַת־רוּחַ
ג וִימַלֵּא קָדִים בִּטְנוֹ: הוֹכֵחַ בְּדָבָר לֹא יִסְכּוֹן וּמִלִּים
ד לֹא־יוֹעִיל בָּם: אַף־אַתָּה תָּפֵר יִרְאָה וְתִגְרַע שִׂיחָה
ה לִפְנֵי־אֵל: כִּי יְאַלֵּף עֲוֺנְךָ פִיךָ וְתִבְחַר לְשׁוֹן עֲרוּמִים:

We may perhaps have a clue for what went wrong, in verse 6: *Your mouth declares you wicked — not I.* As *Ramban* interprets this verse the meaning is: For my part, in my first speech I was willing to give you the benefit of the doubt. I did not accuse you of sin, but instead attempted to guide you to a positive method of dealing with pain — sublimation. Instead of accepting this well-meant and constructive advice, you chose to accuse God of injustice and challenged Him to appear before a court of justice. Thus, your own mouth *declared you wicked.*

Why the stress on, *Not I*? Here, indignation spurred on by rejection creeps in. Eliphaz is hurt. He had meant well, had sincerely wished to help his beloved friend. The sense of having been spurned, rankles. Gradually, sincere (if somewhat obtuse) love turns to resentment, which ultimately poisons until it generates the patent distortions of chapter 22.

But one who sets out to comfort must not allow himself to be hurt. True empathy will always find excuses for illogical, belligerent, pain-driven responses which do not reflect the real man at all, but are a function of the psychological dislocations experienced as a result of profound, shattering loss.

The author has Eliphaz going off on an irrelevant tangent in order to underline his total inadequacy in the role which he has chosen to assume. Nothing can express that failure more than the preoccupation with theological niceties, which have no bearing at all upon the very real agonies of a very real friend who is writhing in the throes of dreadful loss, now compounded by the rejection and misunderstanding of those for whom he had cared most.

Eliphaz, plastering platitudes upon open and festering wounds, has become detached from reality. Iyov, in his response, will completely ignore his thesis.

2. הֶחָכָם יַעֲנֶה דַעַת־רוּחַ וִימַלֵּא קָדִים בִּטְנוֹ — *Would a wise man hold forth with bluster, fill his belly with the east wind? Rashi* and *Ramban* differ in their interpretation of יַעֲנֶה. *Rashi,* whom we have followed, takes the word in its meaning of *declaiming, stating with conviction.* Why would a wise man declaim *wind-opinions,* ideas which have no real substance, with such conviction?

This verse begins an argument which reaches its unfolding in verse 4. You, Iyov, are wise. People who hear you will justifiably assume that such a one as you would not offer specious arguments. Accordingly, they will take your position as representing the truth. The result will be a subverting of the awe in which people stand before God.

Ramban takes the word in the softer sense, *to answer.* Why would a wise man answer those who argue with him, with hollow ideas? And why would his own thoughts, those which he keeps to himself [*fill his belly . . .*], be empty of any real import?

Eliphaz seems totally to miss the point of Iyov's speech. He is so busy picking holes in the theological positions which Iyov seems to espouse, that he does not notice the raging inner tumult, the emotions of love nd hate, fear and hope, which leave Iyov no peace, making well nigh impossible any judicious weighing of ideas.

Iyov's words ought not to be taken as the reasoned, seasoned credo of the philosopher. They are searing sparks leaping in unchoreographed abandon from the cauldron of his agony.

Daas Mikra suggests that this opening salvo is in reaction to Iyov's claim to wisdom, made in his most recent speech: *I too, as you do, possess understanding . . .* If so, Eliphaz sneers, why so much bluster, why so little of any substance?

3. הוֹכֵחַ בְּדָבָר לֹא יִסְכּוֹן וּמִלִּים לֹא־יוֹעִיל בָּם — *Indulge in arguments from which he will gain nothing, in words which help him not at all.* Even impassioned arguments, when made by the wise, will be so inflected as to reflect well upon the disputant. Yours only draw suspicion upon yourself and serve to mislead those who listen (*Ramban*).

For סָכַן, as *that which brings gain* or *pleasure, Rashi* adduces *I Kings* 1:2.

Daas Mikra points out the parallel expression at 13:3. There Iyov had expressed the wish that, ... *it is with God that [he] would remonstrate* (וְהוֹכֵחַ אֶל אֵל אֶחְפָּץ). Eliphaz asks: Are the useless arguments which you are making, really the type of remonstration which you had in mind?

15/1-5 [1] Eliphaz the Temanite responded and said: [2] Would a wise man
man hold forth with bluster, fill his belly with the east wind?
[3] Indulge in arguments from which he will gain nothing, in words
which help him not at all. [4] Certainly you will subvert awe, through
that you inflate speech before God. [5] It is the evil within you which
coaches your mouth, you should have chosen the language of the wise.

4. אַף־אַתָּה תָּפֵר יִרְאָה וְתִגְרַע שִׂיחָה לִפְנֵי־אֵל — *Certainly you will subvert awe, through that you inflate speech before God. Rashi* and *Ramban* interpret גרע in diametrically opposite ways, and thus read the verse in two different ways.

Rashi, consistent throughout the book (see at verse 8 and at 36:27) takes the word as *increase.* Thus: With the avalanche of words which you pour out before God, you will undermine the awe in which people stand before the Divine. This is the end of the argument begun in verse 2.

Ramban prefers to take the word as *to withhold.* The import of the second phrase is thus: You hurl accusations against God which He cannot possibly answer [thus, *withholding speech . . .*]. The first phrase now lends itself to two possible interpretations: Either it can be taken as does *Rashi*: [By making these accusations] you subvert the natural awe which people would tend to feel for the Divine. Or: [By making these accusations] you show that you were never truly a God fearing person. Your actions now expose your earlier life as having been a fraud.

Daas Mikra, on the basis of *Psalms* 102:1, understands שִׂיחָה as *prayer.* People who hear what you are saying will find it difficult to pray to God. This is a particularly apt accusation when we consider Iyov's assertion (see commentary to 12:7-8) that God's providence is limited to the species but does not concern itself with the individual. Given such an outlook, it would be difficult indeed for the individual to turn to God in prayer.

5. כִּי יְאַלֵּף עֲוֹנְךָ פִיךָ וְתִבְחַר לְשׁוֹן עֲרוּמִים — *It is the evil within you which coaches your mouth, you should have chosen the language of the wise.* The translation follows *Rashi.* עָוֹן is not the sin itself, but its cause: the יֵצֶר הָרַע, *evil inclination,* which resides within each person. The sense of the verse is, to continue the thoughts expressed in the previous ones. That one as wise as Iyov could have spoken in a manner which would cause such havoc in people's minds, could only come about because he had handed the reigns of his mouth to the *yetzer hara.* This force within him, this drive towards evil, was generating Iyov's destructive speech.

Targum renders the second phrase as: *You should have chosen the language of the wise.* This accords with the Sages' interpretation at *Pesachim* 3a, and *Rashi* accepts it here.

R' Meyuchas objects, apparently because וְתִבְחַר does not normally translate to denote something that *should* be done, but is rather a statement of fact: *You chose to speak in the language of the crafty* (עָרוּם, as in the description of the snake at *Genesis* 3:1).

Ramban, too, leans towards this meaning and renders in accordance with his second interpretation of the previous verse: Your own mouth shows everyone that you have always been wicked. In your constant questioning of God you chose your words cunningly, in order to convey the impression that you were sincerely on the quest for truth, that you really wanted to understand why the righteous sometimes suffer and the wicked occasionally prosper. However, you have deceived no one. It is clear to all that your motives were not pure.

This accusation clearly seems meant to refute Iyov's oft repeated claim to *temimus,* constancy of thought and deed characterized by a complete lack of guile. The use of the *language of the crafty,* would place Iyov squarely among the חֲנֵפִים, the *hypocrites* whom the book constantly sets up in contradistinction to the *temimim* (see at 1:1 and 6:13).

We wonder whether, on this basis, we should understand the חָנֵף of verse 34 as referring to Iyov himself?

This question is part of the more general one which ought to be asked in connection with Eliphaz's long description of the woes which befall the wicked. Is this speech a presentation of a theoretical model meant to illustrate the ultimate fairness of God's stewardship of human affairs, or is it meant, albeit obliquely, to accuse Iyov of wickedness? He, if the truth be admitted, is the wicked man described here; his troubles are the actualization of the adversity which, Eliphaz claims, must inevitably overtake those who lead evil lives.

Certainly, our verse appears to pull no punches. Iyov is squarely accused of hypocrisy. After such an introduction we would seem justified in assuming that the rest of the speech would be devoted to elaborating

ו־ז יַרְשִׁיעֲךָ פִיךָ וְלֹא־אָנִי וּשְׂפָתֶיךָ יַעֲנוּ־בָךְ: הֲרִאישׁוֹן אָדָם
ח תִּוָּלֵד וְלִפְנֵי גְבָעוֹת חוֹלָלְתָּ: הַבְסוֹד אֱלוֹהַּ תִּשְׁמָע וְתִגְרַע
ט אֵלֶיךָ חָכְמָה: מַה־יָּדַעְתָּ וְלֹא נֵדָע תָּבִין וְלֹא־עִמָּנוּ
י־יא הוּא: גַּם־שָׂב גַּם־יָשִׁישׁ בָּנוּ כַּבִּיר מֵאָבִיךָ יָמִים: הַמְעַט
יב מִמְּךָ תַּנְחֻמוֹת אֵל וְדָבָר לָאַט עִמָּךְ: מַה־יִּקָּחֲךָ לִבֶּךָ
יג וּמַה־יִּרְזְמוּן עֵינֶיךָ: כִּי־תָשִׁיב אֶל־אֵל רוּחֶךָ וְהֹצֵאתָ
יד מִפִּיךָ מִלִּין: מָה־אֱנוֹשׁ כִּי־יִזְכֶּה וְכִי־יִצְדַּק יְלוּד אִשָּׁה:

on this theme, that in fact it is Iyov himself who is being described in the latter part of the speech.

But if so, why does Eliphaz, in verses 7-9, challenge Iyov's wisdom? The thrust of his argument is that Iyov is wicked — not that he lacks understanding. If he is accused in one breath of being a glib schemer, then he ought not, in the next sentence, be held to task for lack of theological subtlety.

Perhaps, at this stage, Eliphaz is still ambivalent about his attitude toward his erstwhile friend. The very fact that he refrains from leveling direct and specific accusations — as he does unflinchingly in his last speech — shows that he is not yet ready for the complete break which such an approach would imply. For this same reason he will also allow for the possibility that Iyov may not have practiced cunning at all. Perhaps, after all, he simply failed to understand the full implication of his actions.

6. יַרְשִׁיעֲךָ פִיךָ וְלֹא־אָנִי וּשְׂפָתֶיךָ יַעֲנוּ־בָךְ — *Let your mouth pronounce you wicked — not I, let your lips testify against you. Rashi* has this verse leading into the next one. Eliphaz is about to pose some questions to Iyov. He anticipates that the answers to these questions will incriminate Iyov, and make it unnecessary for Eliphaz to declare him wicked.

Ramban translates: *Your mouth pronounces you wicked — not I, your lips have testified against you.* Eliphaz reminds Iyov that in his original speech he had been willing to assume Iyov's innocence. By not a single word had he implied that Iyov was anything but righteous. He had simply suggested that Iyov might do better by attempting to sublimate his experiences, than by railing against them. Iyov, however, by his intemperate tirades, had shown himself to be wicked.

Daas Mikra sees Eliphaz's taunt as reacting to Iyov's plaint at 13:23: *How many are my sins and my transgressions* ... Eliphaz retorts: You yourself are the most potent witness against your claim to innocence.

7. הֲרִאישׁוֹן אָדָם תִּוָּלֵד וְלִפְנֵי גְבָעוֹת חוֹלָלְתָּ — *Were you the first man ever to be born, were you formed before the hills? Daas Mikra* suggests that here we have a double entendre. The phrase could be understood: Are you the first *man* ever to be born . . .? meaning, were all those who were born before you animals, so that their ideas carry no weight with you at all? Or, we could understand it [and so, *Rashi*]: Were you perhaps born before Adam, so that by the sheer weight of your experience, you are wiser than anyone else?

Metzudos suggests that this taunt is in reaction to 12:12 where Iyov appears to throw Tzophar's youth in his face. The sense would be: Granted that you are older — and therefore more experienced — than some of us. But, your age is not such that it gives you the right to claim that you are the sole repository of truth.

For the second phrase, ... *were you formed before the hills?, Daas Mikra* offers an ingenious explanation. Eliphaz is asking: Are you, perhaps the very embodiment of wisdom? For it is concerning *wisdom* that *Proverbs* 8:25 teaches, that it came into being before the very hills were formed.

In *Ramban's* view, Eliphaz had something very specific in mind when he asked Iyov whether he claimed to have been born before the very world had been created. Only then would he have the right to state with the certainty which he had mustered in some of his speeches, that God's providence extends only to the community, but that the individual is beyond the pale of His concern.

8. הַבְסוֹד אֱלוֹהַּ תִּשְׁמָע וְתִגְרַע אֵלֶיךָ חָכְמָה — *Are you privy to God's mysteries, appropriating all wisdom for yourself?* The taunts from the previous verse continue. In wake of *Targum, Rashi, Ramban* and *Metzudos* all take סוד as *something secret* or *mysterious*, as in *Proverbs* 11:13. *R' Meyuchas* renders the word *council*, as in *Proverbs* 15:22. *Daas Mikra* suggests that there is no need to limit the word to any one of its definitions. We may safely assume that each of the various possibilities was meant to

[6] Let your mouth pronounce you wicked — not I, let your lips testify against you. [7] Were you the first man ever to be born, were you formed before the hills? [8] Are you privy to God's mysteries, appropriating all wisdom for yourself? [9] What can you know that we do not know, what fathom that we do not possess? [10] We have among us such as have white hairs, even such as are very aged, with many more days than even your father. [11] Do you deem God's consoling gestures, inadequate? His serene bearing towards you? [12] Whither does your heart prompt you, what do your eyes intimate? [13] That you respond to God with wind-thoughts, speak [wind]-words from your mouth. [14] What power can man command that he could ever win his case? Could he who is born of woman ever be in the right?

be a separate dagger piercing Iyov's heart.

Daas Mikra thinks that this verse comes as a reaction to 10:13: *But You harbored these in Your heart ...* Iyov, there, had apparently claimed to be privy to God's inner thoughts. Eliphaz is asking: Are you an expert on God's thinking as far back as the creation? Do you really believe that you understand everything?

As at verse 4, *Rashi* takes גרע as *to increase.*

The thrust of these two verses is very much the same as that in God's speech from the whirlwind at 38:4ff. However, where God's speech ultimately assuages Iyov's pain, Eliphaz will succeed only in provoking Iyov more, in inflaming his anger more fiercely. The failure of Eliphaz's thoughts to penetrate becomes clear in the next verse. Iyov is arrogant because he holds himself to be privy to truths which the friends do not know — not because he dares to fling challenges against an unknown and unknowable God. Iyov perceives the argument to be self-serving. Such a speech can never move him to the humility which must precede acceptance.

10. גַּם־שָׂב גַּם־יָשִׁישׁ בָּנוּ כַּבִּיר מֵאָבִיךָ יָמִים — *We have among us such as have white hairs, even such as are very aged, with many more days than even your father.* This, evidently in reaction to 12:12: *Wisdom resides with the oldsters . . .* (*Ramban*).

11. הַמְעַט מִמְּךָ תַּנְחוּמוֹת אֵל וְדָבָר לָאַט עִמָּךְ — *Do you deem God's consoling gestures, inadequate? His serene bearing towards you? Metzudos* explains as follows: The many good times which you had before tragedy struck, could, and ought, to be viewed as a consolation for your suffering. It is only reasonable that if you were so amply rewarded for the good which you have done, you should now be called to justice for your sins.

לָאַט is a verb describing slow, tranquil, movement (*Rashi*).

12. מַה־יִּקָּחֲךָ לִבֶּךָ וּמַה־יִּרְזְמוּן עֵינֶיךָ — *Whither does your heart prompt you, what do your eyes intimate? Rashi* adduces *Deuteronomy* 32:2 for לקח, as *teaching. Ramban* (*Numbers* 16:1) understands the word as describing *ideas* and *thoughts* which occupy the mind: With what subversive ideas does your heart attempt to mislead you? In your innermost thoughts — such as you will reveal to no one — you toy with the idea that the world is subject to caprice — there is neither judge nor justice. The look in your eyes makes it clear that you deny God's providence.

Rashi points out that יִרְזְמוּן is an inversion of רָמַז, *to hint.*

R' Meyuchas offers the following interpretation for our verse: To what straits have your sufferings brought you? How can your eyes flash with so much arrogance?

13. כִּי־תָשִׁיב אֶל־אֵל רוּחֶךָ וְהֹצֵאתָ מִפִּיךָ מִלִּין — *That you respond to God with wind-thoughts, speak [wind]-words from your mouth. Rashi* is silent to this verse. The translation follows *Ramban. Ibn Ezra* takes רוּחַ as *anger.* Thus: That you fling your fury at God.

From the next few verses it would seem that the *wind-thoughts* which Eliphaz is objecting to here are Iyov's assertions (13:18-19) that he is armed with a brief that could guarantee him victory over God before a court of law. In Eliphaz's mind there can be no substance to such a claim. It is pure bombast, an empty posturing which has no meaning at all. Verses 14-16 will explain why.

14-16. מָה־אֱנוֹשׁ כִּי־יִזְכֶּה וְכִי־יִצְדַּק יְלוּד אִשָּׁה — *What power can man command that he could ever win his case? Could he who is born of woman ever be in the right?* הֵן בִּקְדֹשָׁו לֹא יַאֲמִין וְשָׁמַיִם לֹא־זַכּוּ בְעֵינָיו — *See! Even*

טו־טז הֵן בִּקְדֹשָׁו לֹא יַאֲמִין וְשָׁמַיִם לֹא־זַכּוּ בְעֵינָיו: אַף כִּי־נִתְעָב
יז וְנֶאֱלָח אִישׁ־שֹׁתֶה כַמַּיִם עַוְלָה: אֲחַוְּךָ שְׁמַע־לִי וְזֶה־חָזִיתִי

his holy ones, He does not trust, the very heavens are not unsullied in His eyes. אַף כִּי־נִתְעָב וְנֶאֱלָח אִישׁ־שֹׁתֶה כַמַּיִם עַוְלָה — *Certainly, then, one who is loathsome and tainted, who drinks iniquity like water.* See commentary to verse 13. Eliphaz is offended by the fact that Iyov feels that could he but summon God before some objective tribunal, he would surely be vindicated. Such claims, Eliphaz feels, are *wind-thoughts* and *wind-words*; sheer bombast which defies all reason.[1]

Chapter 15	*Chapter 4*
14. What power can man command that he could ever win his case? Could he who is born of woman ever be in the right?	17. Can mortals be deemed righteous before God, could man be considered pure before his Creator?
15. See! Even his holy ones, He does not trust, the very heavens are not unsullied in His eyes.	18. See! Even His servants He does not trust, ascribes frivolity to His very angels.
16. Certainly, then, one who is loathsome and tainted, who drinks iniquity like water.	19. Surely, then, those that dwell in houses of clay, destined to a grave of dust, whom they crush for the maggots.
	20. From just morning to night they are ground down, without considering — lost forever.
	21. Clearly the pride which had been theirs deserts them; they die — no wiser.

If our passage were, indeed, no more than a repetition of that which Eliphaz had already said, we would have to clarify the reason for such a duplication; and, moreover, to wonder why, if these ideas originally required a vision — presumably because the truth they express is too profound for a human to have worked out for himself — they are now presented as simple logic.

However, a close reading yields that in spite of the similarity in form, the intent of our passage is different from that expressed in the vision.

Our analysis will be based on *Rashi's* interpretation of chapter 4. We shall first attempt to define the difference in intent between the two passages, and then to see how the respective wording and structure of each is particularly suited to its theme.

As *Rashi* understands the vision, it makes the point that no mortal can possibly lay claim to absolute righteousness. The mere fact that humans dwell in *houses of clay*, are locked into the limitations of physical existence (see commentary there), guarantees that they will ever fall short of perfection. God even takes the extremely righteous to their graves early so that they may die innocent (*Rashi* to v. 18), *ascribes frivolity* to even *His very angels.* It is presumptuous arrogance to claim, as Iyov had done, that he is deserving of no punishment.

By contrast, our passage points to the patent folly of summoning God to a bar of justice. Man, powerless and sinful, can never hope to be successful in such litigation. The logic which it summons to support this thesis — that man is, by definition, *loathsome and tainted*, that he *drinks iniquity like water* — is based on the message of the earlier vision, that humans are by their very nature sinful.

This, as follows:

The idea that no man can be considered blameless by God, could not have been propounded without Divine confirmation in the form of a vision. We meet up with saintly people and are hard-put to find any fault in them. That the mere fact of dwelling *in houses of clay* guarantees imperfection, is not something which we would know intuitively.

Accordingly, the heavenly messenger came to Eliphaz to apprise him of this fact.

However, once this is accepted as given, the

1. The formulation is very similar to the nocturnal vision which Eliphaz reported at 4:17ff. In order to compare the two passages effectively, we present them side by side.

[15] *See! Even His holy ones, He does not trust, the very heavens are not unsullied in His eyes.* [16] *Certainly, then, one who is loathsome and tainted, who drinks iniquity like water.* [17] *I will instruct you. Hear me! I have observed this and will*

futility of summoning God to justify Himself before a tribunal follows logically. If even the most, apparently, righteous man is *tainted* and *loathsome*, then he cannot hope to muster a winning case against God.

That Eliphaz chose to couch his logical argument, in the precise form in which the vision, which he had earlier shared with Iyov, had been vouchsafed him, can be explained by his negative approach throughout this second speech. He allows himself to sink to sour sarcasm. He seems to be saying: What I have said before, when I was trying to be positive and supportive — and which you rejected — is coming back to haunt you now. Had you listened then, you would not have come to a pass in which you toy with the ridiculous. What I say now should not be new to you. Why were you so obdurate?

Given the disparate thrust of the two arguments, the differences in expressions used and in the general structure are readily understandable. The key lies in the fact that the vision talks of God's point of view — how He looks upon man. By contrast, Eliphaz is describing how man ought to view himself in relation to God.

Thus, we understand why man's lowliness is much more sharply expressed in Eliphaz's argument than in the vision: In the argument we have מָה אֱנוֹשׁ, which, while it is certainly a rhetorical question, also carries the connotation of an unadorned statement — man is absolutely nothing. [Compare, *Exodus* 16:7-8.] In the vision, we have simply the description, *Man*. This man is granted a certain level of accomplishment — admittedly insignificant in contrast to God's grandeur — but there is no attempt to deny him any standing whatever. Again, the יְלוּד אִשָּׁה of the argument has a more denigrating connotation than the simple גָּבֶר of the vision.

The same contrast is evident in the descriptions contained in verse 15 (of our chapter) and verse 18 (of chapter 4), respectively. The vision, which had a more measured perception of man's lowliness, is less lavish in its praise. *Servants* is more restrained than *holy ones*; and so too is the use of *angels*, when contrasted with *the very heavens*, where *the hosts of the heavens, the angels*, are meant.

The explanation is simple enough. In the vision, the point is being made that God must look upon even the most righteous human being as falling short of perfection. True! But God has no need to exaggerate the differences between mortals and immortals. That difference is real enough, without embellishment. By contrast, in the argument, Eliphaz is demanding that Iyov himself realize the enormity of the conceit, that he might summon God to stand before a bar of justice. Eliphaz's point is strengthened by taking the poles of his contrast to their absolute extremes.

The differences between verse 16 (our chapter) and verse 19 (chapter 4) are self-explanatory. In the vision the point is to demonstrate that man, by the very limitations imposed by his physical reality, must fall short of perfection. It is not only his actual sins which are germane, but his propensity to sin. Thus, the important thing is to underline that he is forced to live his life in *houses of clay*, and this concept is embellished in verses 20 and 21. But, in the argument, it serves Eliphaz's purpose to stress the actual sinfulness of man [and this requires no further embellishment], to drive home the futility of Iyov's fantastic illusion.

שָׁמַיִם, in verse 15, is to be taken as short for *the hosts of heaven* (*Rashi*).

For נֶאֱלָח, in verse 16, *Rashi* offers מְעוּרְבָּב, *impure, it has something else mixed into it*. He adduces *Psalms* 53:4.[1]

◆§ Eliphaz's Second Speech

17-19. אֲחַוְךָ שְׁמַע־לִי וְזֶה־חָזִיתִי וַאֲסַפֵּרָה — *I will instruct you. Hear Me! I have observed this and will recount.* אֲשֶׁר־חֲכָמִים יַגִּידוּ וְלֹא כִחֲדוּ מֵאֲבוֹתָם — *That the wise are willing to tell, will not conceal from their fathers.* לָהֶם לְבַדָּם נִתְּנָה

1. In verse 14 we have rendered יִזְכֶּה as, . . . *win his case*, and in verse 15 we have זַכּוּ as *unsullied*. The second rendering accords with *Rashi*, who apparently derives the word from the root זכה, *to be pure*. He would have chosen this connotation because of the association of שָׁמַיִם, *heavens*, with the concept of purity (see *Exodus* 24:10). *Rashi* is silent on the יִזְכֶּה of verse 14, but we chose to render it as we have done because that is clearly its meaning when it parallels יִצְדַּק. See, for example, *Psalms* 51:6. Certainly in Rabbinic Hebrew the word carries this meaning. See *Rashi* to *Sanhedrin* 15b.

טו/יח־כג יח־יט וַאֲסַפֵּרָה: אֲשֶׁר־חֲכָמִים יַגִּידוּ וְלֹא כִחֲדוּ מֵאֲבוֹתָם: לָהֶם
כ לְבַדָּם נִתְּנָה הָאָרֶץ וְלֹא־עָבַר זָר בְּתוֹכָם: כָּל־יְמֵי רָשָׁע
כא הוּא מִתְחוֹלֵל וּמִסְפַּר שָׁנִים נִצְפְּנוּ לֶעָרִיץ: קוֹל־פְּחָדִים
כב בְּאָזְנָיו בַּשָּׁלוֹם שׁוֹדֵד יְבוֹאֶנּוּ: לֹא־יַאֲמִין שׁוּב מִנִּי־חֹשֶׁךְ
כג °וצפו הוּא אֱלֵי־חָרֶב: נֹדֵד הוּא לַלֶּחֶם אַיֵּה יָדַע ׀ כִּי־ °וְצָפוּי ק׳

הָאָרֶץ וְלֹא־עָבַר זָר בְּתוֹכָם — *To them alone will the land have been given, no interloper will pass through it.* *Rashi* and *Ramban* diverge radically in their interpretation of these verses and, in turn, this leads to differing approaches to the rest of this chapter. The differences appear to be rooted in conflicting interpretations to a number of earlier passages in the book.

Briefly: In *Rashi's* view, our three verses tell that the wise are generally willing to admit sin and error — and find themselves richly rewarded for their courage. The rest of the chapter then goes on to describe the fate of those who, although culpable, insist upon asserting their innocence.

Ramban, as we shall see below, renders these verses differently than we have translated them and sees them as an introduction to the rest of the chapter which deals with the problem of רָשָׁע וְטוֹב לוֹ, the perceived tranquility of the wicked.

Ramban is certainly justified in terms of his interpretation of many other passages in the book. We have frequently noted (see commentary 8:8-10 and, particularly, the footnote to the introductory passage to chapter 11; see also commentary to 9:2ff.) that in his view the problem of the tranquility of the wicked is central to Iyov's concerns. Within such an agenda it would be logical for Eliphaz to take up the matter in detail. In fact, this would place Eliphaz into one logical pattern with Bildad and Tzophar, both of whom, in this second round, appear to concentrate on that issue.

Moreover, from a tactical standpoint it would make sense to have the friends, in this second round, move from direct counsel to a more general examination of God's providence. Their every effort at personal guidance has been totally frustrated; Iyov has not only ignored their ideas, but has even, except for a cursory word here or there, failed to acknowledge their very existence. A theoretical discourse upon the fate of the wicked — one which would nevertheless, albeit obliquely, let Iyov know their true opinion of him — might indeed appear to be the less threatening course.[1]

Rashi may well have been disinclined to follow this line.

Nowhere has he attached that importance, which we have observed in *Ramban*, to the problem of the tranquility of the wicked. As we have noted a number of times, this issue appears to be peripheral to Iyov's concerns. His questions are screamed out as he slowly turns upon the spit of his incomprehensible fate, they crash through his battered body as the existential response of a writhing victim — never as the cool questing of the philosopher. He demands to know the secret of righteous — his own — suffering. There is no room in his concerns for searchings after the niceties of God's providence. The theoretical problem of the tranquility of the wicked concerns him not at all. However, at 12:4 we have suggested that after Tzophar's first speech, wherein the point is made that no one can ever be truly righteous, Iyov himself has to locate his arguments at the

1. It has been observed that, in general, the speeches of the three friends can be broken down into two elements [each of which can, of course, be refined further]: The personal, which can take the form of criticism or exhortation; and the substantive, which is the statement of the particular theological or philosophical position which is being presented. In the speeches of all the three friends, the proportion between the two changes radically from the first round to the second.

Thus, in the forty-eight verses of Eliphaz's first speech, at least seven verses could reasonably be considered personal (4:2-7; 5:17 and 27), while in this second speech, which runs for thirty-five verses, only two (2-3) can be defined as personal.

Similar relationships are discernible in the second round speeches of both Bildad and Tzophar.

This pattern would seem to bear out the thesis which we have suggested. It seems likely that the friends have simply given up the hope of being able to sway Iyov by frontal attack. They hope that in the cooler more intellectual climate of the second round, more headway can be made.

In the third round, at least as far as Eliphaz is concerned, we will be able to observe a return to the original confrontational style. That, however, must be attributed to the radical change of direction in the third round. There, as we shall see, every pretense of real friendship will be dropped, and Eliphaz will resort to open, no-holds-barred invective.

15/18-23 *recount* — [18] *That the wise are willing to tell, will not conceal from their fathers.* [19] *To them alone will the land have been given, no interloper will pass through it.* [20] *But all the days of the wicked are spent in fretting, the sum of the years allotted to the oppressor.* [21] *The sounds of terror are in his ears, even in times of tranquility he anticipates the pillager.* [22] *He cannot believe that he will escape the dark, [knows] that he is destined for the sword.* [23] *[Knows] that he must roam [to find] where bread might be, knows that*

problem of the tranquility of the wicked. If so, it is logical that the speeches of the friends in this second round should center upon this issue.

To, *I have observed* . . ., of verse 17, *Ramban* remarks: What I tell you is not born of my imagination. I have observed it myself [and can, therefore attest to its truth].

In verse 18, *Ramban* translates differently than does *Rashi*: [Those things which I have seen] are told by the wise [who also had observed them] and, moreover, [the very earliest generations] had not withheld this information from the fathers [of these wise men, so that the teachings which they passed on to me had come to them not only from their own observations but also through traditions passed on to them by their fathers, who in turn had been taught these lessons by the earliest generations].

Ramban has verse 18 flow on to verse 19: [Because of their superior wisdom, these wise men] were given rulership over the world. No one, not of their number, would presume to encroach upon their authority. [These wise men have taught . . ., and now, on to the next section which details the terrible fate of the wicked. These do not, contrary to Iyov's assumptions, live out their lives in tranquility.]

Rashi interprets verse 19 as describing the rewards which are in store for those men who are wise enough to admit their errors. As we saw above, this is meant in contrast to the sufferings which the next section predicts for the obstinate, who insist upon asserting their own innocence.

20-23. כָּל־יְמֵי רָשָׁע הוּא מִתְחוֹלֵל וּמִסְפַּר שָׁנִים נִצְפְּנוּ לֶעָרִיץ — *But all the days of the wicked are spent in fretting, the sum of the years allotted to the oppressor.* קוֹל־פְּחָדִים בְּאָזְנָיו בַּשָּׁלוֹם שׁוֹדֵד יְבוֹאֶנּוּ — *The sounds of terror are in his ears, even in times of tranquility he anticipates the pillager.* לֹא־יַאֲמִין שׁוּב מִנִּי־חֹשֶׁךְ וְצָפוּי הוּא אֱלֵי־חָרֶב — *He cannot believe that he will escape the dark, [knows] that he is destined for the sword.* נֹדֵד הוּא לַלֶּחֶם אַיֵּה יָדַע כִּי־נָכוֹן בְּיָדוֹ יוֹם־חֹשֶׁךְ — *[Knows] that he must roam [to find] where bread might be, knows that he is fated for a day of darkness.* In *Rashi's* view, this passage describes the life of the wicked [those who adamantly maintain their innocence and refuse to admit fault — see above] during even such times when fortune seems to smile upon them. They are never truly happy, since they live in constant fear that terror will strike.

In *Ramban's* view, the argument is meant to tear apart the fallacious assumption — based on superficial observation — that the wicked often lead tranquil lives. [*Ramban* (beginning of next chapter) believes that awareness of ultimate retribution for the wicked would tend to comfort Iyov, inasmuch as it would indicate that contrary to our short-term impressions, there is justice in the world. See footnote 1 p. 151] It is true, *Ramban* maintains, that when things are going well, they believe themselves immune from trouble. But the collapse of their fool's paradise is just around the corner. If they could but know what the future has in store for them, their lives would be filled with anticipatory fear.

Rashi and *Ramban* have different interpretations for the various verses. Herewith, a presentation of the two approaches. The translation follows *Rashi*.

Rashi [here, but nowhere else] takes מִתְחוֹלֵל as an expression of אֲנִינוּת, *worrying* or *fretting*. Furthermore, the second phrase stands in apposition to the first, reinforcing the thought that had already been expressed. The sense is that all *the days of the wicked*, even those periods of their lives which appear to be happy and unthreatened, are spent in *fretting* and worry in anticipation of calamity; and, moreover, this sense of impending disaster is a constant presence throughout *the sum of the years allotted to the oppressor*.

While *Rashi* does not say so expressly, it appears from his commentary that he understands מִסְפַּר שָׁנִים as *the span of life* — מִסְפָּר being understood in its root sense, as *number*. However, מִסְפַּר שָׁנִים seems equivalent to, for example, יָמִים מִסְפָּר (*Numbers* 9:20), where

טו/כד־לא
כד נָכ֖וֹן בְּיָד֣וֹ יוֹם־חֹֽשֶׁךְ׃ יְֽ֭בַעֲתֻהוּ צַ֣ר וּמְצוּקָ֑ה תִּ֝תְקְפֵ֗הוּ
כה כְּמֶ֤לֶךְ ׀ עָתִ֬יד לַכִּידֽוֹר׃ כִּֽי־נָטָ֣ה אֶל־אֵ֣ל יָד֑וֹ וְאֶל־שַׁ֝דַּ֗י
כו־כז יִתְגַּבָּֽר׃ יָר֣וּץ אֵלָ֣יו בְּצַוָּ֑אר בַּ֝עֲבִ֗י גַּבֵּ֥י מָגִנָּֽיו׃ כִּֽי־כִסָּ֣ה
כח פָנָ֣יו בְּחֶלְבּ֑וֹ וַיַּ֖עַשׂ פִּימָ֣ה עֲלֵי־כָֽסֶל׃ וַיִּשְׁכּ֤וֹן ׀ עָ֘רִ֤ים
נִכְחָד֗וֹת בָּ֭תִּים לֹא־יֵ֣שְׁבוּ לָ֑מוֹ אֲשֶׁ֖ר הִתְעַתְּד֣וּ לְגַלִּֽים׃
כט לֹֽא־יֶ֭עְשַׁר וְלֹא־יָק֣וּם חֵיל֑וֹ וְלֹא־יִטֶּ֖ה לָאָ֣רֶץ מִנְלָֽם׃
ל לֹֽא־יָס֙וּר ׀ מִנִּי־חֹ֗שֶׁךְ יֹֽ֭נַקְתּוֹ תְּיַבֵּ֣שׁ שַׁלְהָ֑בֶת וְ֝יָס֗וּר בְּר֣וּחַ
לא פִּֽיו׃ אַל־יַאֲמֵ֣ן בַּשָּׁ֣ו נִתְעָ֑ה כִּי־שָׁ֝֗וְא תִּהְיֶ֥ה תְמוּרָתֽוֹ׃

Rashi renders *a few days*, in accordance with the common usage of מִסְפַּר as *few*, in the sense that it is an amount that is easily counted.

It is closer to this usage that *Ramban* takes the word. Moreover, he differs with *Rashi* in his interpretation of מִתְחוֹלֵל, taking it as deriving from חִיל, *to writhe in agony*. The two phrases are not in apposition, but say two different things: The days of the wicked are [or, would, if they but knew what lay in store for them] spent writhing in agony: There is a clearly fixed [and, by implication, a short] time allotted to him for his tranquility. [It cannot, and will not, last.]

Rashi takes verse 20, too, as describing the anticipatory fear of the wicked. He constantly hears voices [*Ramban's* remark to the plural פְּחָדִים: *Fear following upon fear*] which tell him that the time for payment is near.

The future form of יְבוֹאֶנּוּ would seem to indicate that this, too, describes his fear of some undetermined catastrophe that is destined to overtake him. *The pillager* has not yet come — but is just around the corner.

Rashi and *Ramban* part ways in their interpretation of the next two verses. *Rashi* still reads them as describing the anticipatory woes of the wicked: He feels that if ever darkness were to overtake him, he will be unable to escape it; knows that he can hope for no end other than by the sword; knows that he will one day have to roam the streets for bread; knows that the overwhelming darkness which he anticipates is close at hand.

Ramban believes that these two verses deal with darkness which has already overtaken the wicked: He does not believe that he will ever be able to extricate himself from it; knows that his only escape will be by the sword; knows himself to be friendless, and therefore condemned to roam the streets for bread; and, finally, knows that this darkness is now his natural and permanent state. He will never break out from it.

24. יְבַעֲתֻהוּ צַר וּמְצוּקָה תִּתְקְפֵהוּ כְּמֶלֶךְ עָתִיד לַכִּידוֹר — *Distress and straits frighten him, overpower him, like a king destined to the flames.* כִּידוֹר is unique. *Rashi* suspects that the final ר might be in place of a ד, in which case the word would derive from יָקַד, *to burn*. The verse hints at Nebuchadnezzar who, in spite of his earlier prowess, ended up in the flames (but see fn. at 28:4).

Ramban thinks that the word carries the connotation of כַּדּוּר, *surrounding*. Thus: Distress and straits surround the wicked man in much the same way as a king is surrounded by his legions when he goes out to battle.

25-27. כִּי־נָטָה אֶל־אֵל יָדוֹ וְאֶל־שַׁדַּי יִתְגַּבָּר — *For he turned his hand against God, [wished] to rear himself up over Shaddai.* יָרוּץ אֵלָיו בְּצַוָּאר בַּעֲבִי גַּבֵּי מָגִנָּיו — *Dashed against Him with neck [held high], [secure] in the massive bulk of his shields.* כִּי־כִסָּה פָנָיו בְּחֶלְבּוֹ וַיַּעַשׂ פִּימָה עֲלֵי־כָסֶל — *For his face is covered by his fat, it was [folded] mouth-like over his loins.* The connecting *For* . . ., is to be understood in terms of the final verse of Eliphaz's speech: *To conceive sin is to bear iniquity, their womb prepares — deceit*! Evil will, inevitably, bring about its own just desserts. The terrors which haunt the wicked are the direct results of their evil lives.

Within our section, verse 27 appears to be given as the cause of that which the previous two describe. The self-indulgence which covers him with the folds of fat and blubber, ultimately intoxicates him with a crazed sense of invulnerability. He can quarrel against the Almighty — overpower Him!

The two expressions for God in verse 25 are particularly apt within the context. אֵל has a base meaning of *strong one*, (cf. *Ezekiel* 17:13) and describes God in His all-might. Hence the utter ludicrousness of *turning one's hand* [attempting to provoke anger with one's actions (*Ramban*)] against such a mighty adversary. שַׁדַּי is interpreted by the Sages as connoting, *He who cries out to the [expanding] world, 'Enough!'* (See *Rashi*, *Genesis* 43:14.)

he is fated for a day of darkness. [24] *Distress and straits frighten*
him, overpower him, like a king destined to the flames. [25] *For*
he turned his hand against God, [wished] to rear himself up
over Shaddai. [26] *Dashed against Him with neck [held high],*
[secure] in the massive bulk of his shields. [27] *For his face is covered*
by his fat, it was [folded] mouth-like over his loins. [28] *He dwelt in*
cities which had been laid waste, in houses which had
no inhabitants — had been destined to be mounds. [29] *He will never*
be wealthy, his possessions will not endure, their aspirations
will never reach earth. [30] *He will never shake off darkness, a*
flame will dry out his sapling so that it will be gone by the breath
of His mouth. [31] *He who meanders around to no good purpose*
will never believe that his exertions will produce — vanity.

The wicked man wishes to *rear himself up* over One who can and does cow the very cosmos into curbing its ambition to unfurl itself into infinity.

The ... *neck [held high]* of verse 26 is a symbol of conceit, and has a parallel in *Psalms* 75:6. *Massive bulk* is a paraphrase of עָב, *thickness*, and גַּב, *height*. *Ramban* thinks that the *shields* are the arms of the wicked person. The bulging, menacing muscles of the fighter are being described.

Verse 27 appears to echo *Deuteronomy* 32:15. Becoming gross [the ballooning fat is folded over, appearing like so many *mouths* (*Rashi*)] is the sure forerunner of insolence and rebellion.

28. וַיִּשְׁכּוֹן עָרִים נִכְחָדוֹת בָּתִּים לֹא־יֵשְׁבוּ לָמוֹ אֲשֶׁר הִתְעַתְּדוּ לְגַלִּים — *He dwelt in cities which had been laid waste, in houses which had no inhabitants — had been destined to be mounds. Rashi*, in accordance with *Targum*, understands as follows: It appeals to the wicked man's conceit to build up ruins which had been thought to be beyond human occupancy. He also likes to live in houses which, it had been thought, would remain mounds forever. [This latter explanation is according to *Metzudos* — *Rashi* is silent.]

Ramban translates: He dwells in cities which — when his wickedness finally catches up with him — will be laid waste, in houses which will end up without inhabitants, will eventually be nothing but mounds.

29. לֹא־יֶעְשַׁר וְלֹא־יָקוּם חֵילוֹ וְלֹא־יִטֶּה לָאָרֶץ מִנְלָם — *He will never be wealthy, his possessions will not endure, their aspirations will never reach earth.* מִנְלָם is difficult. *Rashi* suggests that we have a contraction of two words. מֶן לָהֶם, from יִמֵּן, *to prepare*, together with לָהֶם, *their*. The sense is: That for which they had mentally prepared themselves — *their aspirations.* יִטֶּה from נָטָה, *to incline*. Their aspirations will not be sent down to them from heaven to earth.

30. לֹא־יָסוּר מִנִּי־חֹשֶׁךְ יֹנַקְתּוֹ תְּיַבֵּשׁ שַׁלְהָבֶת וְיָסוּר בְּרוּחַ פִּיו — *He will never shake off darkness, a flame will dry out his sapling so that it will be gone by the breath of His mouth.* He will never shake off the darkness to which his wicked deeds have condemned him. Even if a plant manages to take root in his land, a flame will surely scorch it dry. This hints at the death of the wicked man's children (*Ramban*).

We have capitalized, ... *the breath of His mouth*, in accordance with *Rashi* who, with *Targum*, believes that the subject is God. *Ramban* prefers to see the subject as the wicked man himself. Whatever tragedy overtakes his home and family is by *the breath of his mouth*; it is the result of his own misdeeds.

31. אַל־יַאֲמֵן בַּשָּׁו נִתְעָה כִּי־שָׁוְא תִּהְיֶה תְמוּרָתוֹ — *He who meanders around to no good purpose will never believe that his exertions will produce — vanity.* The translation follows *Rashi*. The subject of יַאֲמֵן is the בַּשָּׁו נִתְעָה, *the one who meanders to no good purpose*. For תְּמוּרָה, *Rashi* suggests *exertions*. He adduces *Ruth* 4:7, although there he renders the word חֲלִפִין, in accordance with the teachings of the Sages.

Ramban, too, sees נִתְעָה as describing one who meanders along the path of life. But he takes בַּשָּׁו as the equivalent of שָׁוֶה, a term describing the stability and normalcy of a regular life: Let the one who strays not believe that his life will be lived out in a normal, undisturbed fashion. The change [תְּמוּרָה has its more usual meaning, *something that is exchanged for another*] that will overtake his life will be for the worse. A meaningless and purposeless existence.

טו/לב־לה לב־לג בְּלֹא־יוֹמוֹ תִּמָּלֵא וְכִפָּתוֹ לֹא רַעֲנָנָה: יַחְמֹס כַּגֶּפֶן
לד בִּסְרוֹ וְיַשְׁלֵךְ כַּזַּיִת נִצָּתוֹ: כִּי־עֲדַת חָנֵף גַּלְמוּד וְאֵשׁ
לה אָכְלָה אָהֳלֵי־שֹׁחַד: הָרֹה עָמָל וְיָלֹד אָוֶן וּבִטְנָם תָּכִין
טז/א־ב א־ב מִרְמָה: וַיַּעַן אִיּוֹב וַיֹּאמַר: שָׁמַעְתִּי כְאֵלֶּה רַבּוֹת

32. בְּלֹא־יוֹמוֹ תִּמָּלֵא וְכִפָּתוֹ לֹא רַעֲנָנָה — *Before its time it will be stunted, no freshness in its bower.* The translation follows *Rashi.* תִּמָּלֵא is taken as *completed,* in the sense that the efforts of the wicked man (תְּמוּרָתוֹ) will become stunted and not develop any more.

The *bower* is called כִּפָּה because it resembles a dome. *Ramban* believes that reference is to a child who might outlive the wicked man. There will be no freshness, no permanence. Quickly, this remnant too will dry out.

33. יַחְמֹס כַּגֶּפֶן בִּסְרוֹ וְיַשְׁלֵךְ כַּזַּיִת נִצָּתוֹ — *He will cut off — as the vine its unripe grapes, throw off — as the olive tree its flowers.* It takes very little to shake off (חמס can mean *to cut off,* see *Rashi* to *Eichah* 2:6) the unripe grapes (בּוֹסֶר) from the vine, or the petals off the olive tree [that is the produce of the trees before they have reached completion]. So will the children of the wicked man — even if they be a hundred — die before they reach manhood (*Ramban*; *Rashi* is silent.)

34. כִּי־עֲדַת חָנֵף גַּלְמוּד וְאֵשׁ אָכְלָה אָהֳלֵי־שֹׁחַד — *For the hypocrite's clan will be forlorn, fire will consume tents [built from] bribes.* Once more *Rashi* is silent. In *Ramban's* view, *clan* presumably refers to the wicked man's children who had been mentioned in the previous few verses. The home is described as a *tent* because, made from cloth, it will burn more readily.

35. הָרֹה עָמָל וְיָלֹד אָוֶן וּבִטְנָם תָּכִין מִרְמָה — *To conceive sin is to bear iniquity, their womb prepares — deceit!* Inevitably we reap the fruits of the seeds which we have sown. It is preposterous to imagine that iniquity could be rewarded with a happy and tranquil life. If it appears so — it is only in our eyes. In the end it will become apparent that it was all — *deceit.* The wicked will receive their just desserts. [See Appendix p. 379 for further clarification of Eliphaz's two speeches.]

XVI.

⇐§ Iyov's Response to Eliphaz's Second Speech

There is nothing new in this speech. Iyov tells the friends that their words are empty of meaning; that in order to comfort him they concoct lies — specifically that because God is just, the wicked are doomed to destruction. He complains about his wounds and illness, affirming his opinion that they are undeserved and that therefore there is, manifestly, no Divine Providence or indeed interest in human affairs. He complains that his friends are denying his righteousness. In his own eyes he is a *tzaddik* (*Ramban*).

While there may not be any new arguments in this speech, we can nevertheless isolate a new dimension to the disintegration of Iyov's world.

Suddenly, he sees himself surrounded and hounded on all sides by hostile hordes intent, by vicious torture, to wrack his poor body; by cruel mockery and derision, to destroy his spirit. Not only God (16:7, 8, 9, 12, 13; 17:4, 6), Satan (16:9), the friends (16:11,20; 17:2, 4, 5, 10, 11), and all manner of bystanders (16:7, 9, 10, 11) are counted among his foes — his very wounds are anthropomorphized (16:7, 8, 11, 13) and become active participants in the conspiracy of which he is the hapless victim.[1]

We suspect that Iyov may have become so sensitive to his vulnerability because of Eliphaz's description, in the previous chapter, of the fate of the wicked. Surrounded by enemies, hounded and pursued, they are doomed to ultimate destruction (vs. 20-24).

With fascinated horror, Iyov sees a stunning role-reversal. Totally innocent of any wrongdoing, he is nevertheless being stalked by malevolent forces. Has there not been some terrible mistake? Has God really confused אִיּוֹב with אוֹיֵב (*Bava Basra* 16a)? Has he, for no reason that he can discern, become God's enemy?

1. For the purpose of this survey, we have taken all the various opinions and suggestions listed in the commentary together. Strictly speaking, some of the references are true only according to *Rashi,* some according to *Ramban.* The purpose here is simply to demonstrate the ambience generated in the speech by the many references to hostile forces which Iyov perceives as victimizing him.

15/32-35 [32] *Before its time it will be stunted, no freshness in its bower.* [33] *He*
will cut off — as the vine its unripe grapes, throw off — as the olive
tree its flowers. [34] *For the hypocrite's clan will be forlorn, fire will*
consume tents [built from] bribes. [35] *To conceive sin is to bear*
iniquity, their womb prepares — deceit!

16/1-2 [1] *Iyov responded and said:* [2] *Of such I have heard a great deal;*

Iyov's first response in the second round is built along the same structural pattern as was that of Eliphaz. After a short passage in which he disparages the friends' hapless attempts at comforting, he swings into his main topic — the bemoaning of his fate — first with Satan (see below to v. 9), then God, and then the friends as targets for his complaints.

An analysis of the speeches of the three friends in the second round yields that in essence, they all convey the same message: The apparent tranquility of the wicked is deceiving — in one way or another their lives are, or shortly will be, a shambles. With *Ramban* we assume that these presentations are meant to comfort Iyov — in the sense that if justice reigns, his suffering too must have a rationale.

The essential sameness of the ideas put forward by each of the friends makes the very real differences in the content of Iyov's three rejoinders, significant. A careful reading yields that his response to Eliphaz consists entirely of a bemoaning of his fate; that to Bildad is a heart-rending plea for understanding — addressed to all the friends; and finally, that which follows Tzophar's presentation is a rebuttal of the thesis which each of the three had propounded. Iyov claims that the wicked do indeed live happy and fulfilling lives.

Why, if Iyov feels able to discredit the theory which asserts the necessary and real blight which informs the life of the wicked, does he not do so immediately in answer to Eliphaz's contention?

We feel that this may be one more instance in which it appears that the book of *Iyov* is not meant to be the record of a dispassionate debate of reasoned theological position, but rather, that it wishes to present the existential dilemma of one suffering man, caught between the horrifying reality of his tortures and the bungling efforts of well-meaning but inept friends to help.

When Eliphaz first propounds his theory, Iyov, as it were, cannot believe his ears. Again and again, during the first round, he had made clear — to his own satisfaction — that his experiences cannot possibly be attributed to any reasonable stewardship. Had his friends, he wonders, heard nothing at all? Why would Eliphaz, at this late stage, still spin his web of theory — which Iyov knows to be false — to assert a point which has long ago been so effectively refuted?

He reaches the only possible conclusion: God has entrusted the task of comforting him to buffoons (16:11), to mockers who want only to taunt him (17:2). Accordingly, he ignores Eliphaz's thesis entirely and turns inward, once more, to bemoan his fate.

To his consternation, Bildad takes up the argument where Eliphaz had left off. Once more an avalanche of eloquence is brought to bear — to prove what Iyov believes to be patent nonsense. His worst suspicions are confirmed. The friends are trying to torture him with their obduracy. Pathetically he turns to them, crying for mercy (19:21).

It is only after Tzophar, too, reverts to the same ideas as the other two had presented, that it dawns upon Iyov that the friends in fact believe in their suggestion — and mean it to be a comfort to him. In disgust he tells them that if indeed they want to help, they had best be silent and listen to what he has to say (21:2). There can be no comfort at all in the insubstantial, utopian dream-castle which they have built. The bitter truth is that the wicked wax fat and enjoy life. There is as little logic or justice in their fate as there is in his!

In his introductory remarks to this speech, *Ramban* writes that it contains no new positions, but that in the course of his remarks, Iyov bemoans his fate and opines that his suffering is undeserved, *and this would be a proof that there is no Divine Providence.*

Now, in our Introductory Remarks to chapters 12-14, we noted that in *Ramban's* opinion there are inconsistencies and even contradictions among Iyov's assertions. Occasionally he seems to claim that God is too exalted to care about humankind at all, and at other times he sees God pursuing him as an enemy. The two ideas are obviously not compatible. If we are to take what *Ramban* says here literally, then our speech would be one in which that opinion which sees God as too exalted to care about human affairs, holds sway. However, there seem to be a number of verses which imply that Iyov sees himself relentlessly pursued by God, Who acts towards him as an enemy. We shall deal with these issues in the commentary.

ג מְנַחֲמֵי עָמָל כֻּלְּכֶם: הֲקֵץ לְדִבְרֵי־רוּחַ אוֹ מַה־יַּמְרִיצְךָ
ד כִּי תַעֲנֶה: גַּם | אָנֹכִי כָּכֶם אֲדַבֵּרָה לוּ יֵשׁ נַפְשְׁכֶם
תַּחַת נַפְשִׁי אַחְבִּירָה עֲלֵיכֶם בְּמִלִּים וְאָנִיעָה עֲלֵיכֶם
ה־ו בְּמוֹ רֹאשִׁי: אֲאַמִּצְכֶם בְּמוֹ־פִי וְנִיד שְׂפָתַי יַחְשֹׂךְ: אִם־
ז אֲדַבְּרָה לֹא־יֵחָשֵׂךְ כְּאֵבִי וְאַחְדְּלָה מַה־מִּנִּי יַהֲלֹךְ: אַךְ־

2. שָׁמַעְתִּי כְאֵלֶּה רַבּוֹת מְנַחֲמֵי עָמָל כֻּלְּכֶם — *Of such I have heard a great deal; you are all empty comforters.* What you, Eliphaz, have now said, is of a piece with all the other arguments which I have already heard from all three of you. Having nothing meaningful to say, you think that you can substitute quantity for substance (*Ramban*).

We have rendered עָמָל as *empty*, in accordance with *Ramban* and *R' Meyuchas* who equate the term with הֶבֶל. Significantly, at 21:34, at the end of Iyov's final speech in the second round — his response to Tzophar — he asks rhetorically: *How can you comfort me with emptiness* (הֶבֶל)! This, after he has shown that contrary to the assertions of the friends, the wicked do in fact prosper. It seems likely that he has this repudiation of the thesis in mind already at this stage. True that for now he will not address the issue directly, but in general terms, he rejects Eliphaz's contention at the very outset of his words.

3. הֲקֵץ לְדִבְרֵי־רוּחַ אוֹ מַה־יַּמְרִיצְךָ כִּי תַעֲנֶה — *Is there any end to wind-words, what is it that drives you to answer?* The *wind-words* appear to be in direct response to the *wind-thoughts* in Eliphaz's speech (15:13).

To explain יַמְרִיצְךָ, *Rashi* uses יְשַׁטֶּרְךָ, formed from the Scriptural term שׁוֹטֵר, *an official with power to enforce.* Iyov finds it hard to understand what makes Eliphaz want to speak. Solid reasoning would have supplied its own motivation. But why should he feel himself obliged to gush forth a series of platitudes which he himself must know cannot convince? *R' Meyuchas* appears to have the same understanding: What in my suffering causes you pain, that you [insist upon] speak[ing] words of comfort.

Ramban and *Metzudos* explain יַמְרִיצְךָ as *to strengthen*, or *encourage.*

4. גַּם אָנֹכִי כָּכֶם אֲדַבֵּרָה לוּ יֵשׁ נַפְשְׁכֶם תַּחַת נַפְשִׁי אַחְבִּירָה עֲלֵיכֶם בְּמִלִּים וְאָנִיעָה עֲלֵיכֶם בְּמוֹ רֹאשִׁי — *I am as able to hold forth as you are. Were you in my place, I would string words together over you[r predicament], would shake my head over you[r troubles].* It is not from lack of understanding that I refuse to accept your facile solutions. I too know all the easy answers, could hector you as readily as you now hector me (*Rashi*). On the contrary, it is you who fail to empathize with my predicament.

To *shake one's head* is a sign of joining in mourning. See commentary to 2:11.

5. אֲאַמִּצְכֶם בְּמוֹ־פִי וְנִיד שְׂפָתַי יַחְשֹׂךְ — *I would lend you encouragement with my mouth, would [then] withhold the workings of my lips.* The first part of the verse is a continuation of the thoughts expressed in the previous one: Were you in my place I would find the words to lend you support, even as you imagine that you are able to help me. I would tell you, 'Keep silent and find the strength to bear your pains' (*Rashi*).

Ramban declares *Rashi's* interpretation of the second half of the verse to be incorrect. *Rashi* reads: The complaints and cries to which I give voice now would then cease. I would neither complain nor cry out any more.

What, indeed, can be *Rashi's* meaning. Surely the implication of the entire passage is that Iyov is imagining what would have transpired had the shoe been on the other foot, had the friends been the sufferers and he the comforter. What can possibly be meant by saying that in such a role he would not have been crying nor complaining as he is doing now?

Perhaps the meaning is that had he had to fill the role of the comforter, he would have so convinced himself of the efficacy of the platitudes which he would have uttered, that they would have assuaged even his own pain, had he then been in a position of needing comfort. Thus, he is saying, he understands to some extent why the friends are so convinced of the correctness of their approach. They are carried along by the sheer force of their own eloquence.

This leads him into the thought expressed in the next verse. Granted that he too, had he been cast in the role of comforter, might have been convinced by his own persuasiveness, but as it stands now that is not the case. His vision is unclouded by any need to impose his ideas upon another, and so what he has to say in the next verse follows.

you are all empty comforters. 3 *Is there any end to wind-words,*
what is it that drives you to answer. 4 *I am as able to hold forth as*
you are. Were you in my place, I would string words together over
you[r predicament], would shake my head over you[r troubles.]. 5 *I*
would lend you encouragement with my mouth, would [then]
withhold the workings of my lips. 6 *Were I to speak — my pain*
would not subside, and so, if I keep silent, what will I lose? 7 *O but*

6. אִם־אֲדַבְּרָה לֹא־יֵחָשֵׂךְ כְּאֵבִי וְאַחְדְּלָה מַה־מִּנִּי יַהֲלֹךְ — *Were I to speak — my pain would not subside, and so, if I keep silent, what will I lose?* See commentary to verse above. *Rashi* does not explain this verse, but we can assume that he takes it as we have rendered it: Totally convinced that I have nothing to gain from debating with you, I know that I stand to lose nothing by desisting. Accordingly, I will waste no more time in speaking to you. Rather, I will now follow my thoughts, without reference to your arguments.

7-14. The section beginning with verse 7 and ending with verse 14 is structurally difficult.

Herewith, a breakdown of some of the problems:

1. Verse 7 begins in the third person and ends in the second.
2. Verse 8 reverts once more to the second person and is presumably addressed to the same subject as the previous verse.
3. Verse 9 describes some undefined *enemy*, in the third person.
4. Verse 10 is a description of how an undefined group of people [third person plural] reacted to Iyov's suffering.
5. Verse 11 tells what *God* did. The precise meaning of יִרְטֵנִי is difficult to determine.
6. Verses 12-14 are once more in the third person and seem to be a direct continuation of verse 9.
7. Unexpectedly, some of the verses in this section have three stiches instead of two. They are: Verses 8, 9, 10, 12, and 13. Verses 11 and 14 have the usual two stiches.

We suggest the following interpretation for this section. It is based on the assumption that Iyov, in two separate poems, is bemoaning two aspects of his fate. One, the terrible suffering which God is imposing upon him; and two, his loss of standing within his community. There, he had once been looked upon as a worthy person; now all regard him as wicked.

We postulate further that when Iyov talks about the pains which God has inflicted upon him, he uses the third person. He will not, as it were, attack God directly.

Thus, we assume that verse 7 introduces both themes: The first phrase describes how he has become exhausted by the suffering which God has imposed upon him; the second phrase describes the astonishment felt at his downfall by all those who observe him.

Verse 8 is the introductory (three stich) line of the poem indicated in the second half of verse 7; verse 9 is the introductory (three stich) line of the one indicated in the first.

Verses 10 (three stich) and 11 (two stich) then end the poem which was begun in verse 8, while verses 12 (three stich), 13 (three stich) and 14 (two stich), complete the poem begun in verse 9. The body of both poems is written in verses of three stiches, except that in each case, the ending verse reverts to two stiches. The poem dealing with Iyov's suffering at God's hands is one line longer than the other one, because his personal suffering is more painful to him than the changed attitudes of the community.

We may structure the two poems thus:

7. *You have shocked my entire company into silence . . .* 8. *You have wizened me — it has become a witness, my wasted body rises up against me, denounces me to my face . . .* 10. *They accused me with their mouths, disdainfully they smote my cheeks, thronged, all of them together, against me.* 11. *God has handed me over to a buffoon, wishes to comfort me at the hands of the wicked.*

7. *O but now, He has wearied me:* 9. *His anger has slashed me — he hates me; he has gnashed his teeth against me; my foe casts barbed glances at me.* 12. *I was composed but He ground me up, grabbed me by the throat and mangled me, stood me up as a target* 13. *His archers gather round about me, He cleaves open my kidneys — shows no mercy, pours out my gall upon the ground.* 14. *He breaks me open, breach upon breach, dashes upon me like a warrior.*

We suspect that if our analysis is correct, we would have to understand verse 11 as follows: Iyov is bemoaning the fact that he is exposed to the derision of the crowds. He sees these crowds

ח עַתָּה הֶלְאָנִי הֲשִׁמּוֹתָ כָּל־עֲדָתִי: וַתִּקְמְטֵנִי לְעֵד הָיָה וַיָּקָם
ט בִּי כַחֲשִׁי בְּפָנַי יַעֲנֶה: אַפּוֹ טָרַף ׀ וַיִּשְׂטְמֵנִי חָרַק
י עָלַי בְּשִׁנָּיו צָרִי ׀ יִלְטוֹשׁ עֵינָיו לִי: פָּעֲרוּ עָלַי ׀ בְּפִיהֶם
יא בְּחֶרְפָּה הִכּוּ לְחָיָי יַחַד עָלַי יִתְמַלָּאוּן: יַסְגִּירֵנִי אֵל
יב אֶל עֲוִיל וְעַל־יְדֵי רְשָׁעִים יִרְטֵנִי: שָׁלֵו הָיִיתִי ׀ וַיְפַרְפְּרֵנִי
יג וְאָחַז בְּעָרְפִּי וַיְפַצְפְּצֵנִי וַיְקִימֵנִי לוֹ לְמַטָּרָה: יָסֹבּוּ
עָלַי ׀ רַבָּיו יְפַלַּח כִּלְיוֹתַי וְלֹא יַחְמֹל יִשְׁפֹּךְ לָאָרֶץ
יד מְרֵרָתִי: יִפְרְצֵנִי פֶרֶץ עַל־פְּנֵי־פָרֶץ יָרֻץ עָלַי כְּגִבּוֹר:

as people who wish him ill. In the uniformity of their reaction they take on the form of a single עֲוִיל, an evildoer. We would translate as follows: *God has handed me over to an evildoer, has placed me at the mercy of the wicked.*

We offer this interpretation of the section as an attempt to deal with the structural problems enumerated above. The commentators take each verse individually, and we have followed them in the commentary.

7. אַךְ־עַתָּה הֶלְאָנִי הֲשִׁמּוֹתָ כָּל־עֲדָתִי — *O but now, He has wearied me: You have shocked my entire company into silence.* The initial impression, from the change from third to second person, is that the two sections are not connected.

Ramban quotes *Ibn Ezra,* that Iyov's wounds are the subject of the entire sentence. They have wearied him, and they are [figuratively] addressed in the second part. The sense of that phrase is: You have desolated *my company*, that is, those that mourn for my losses. From *Ramban* it appears that the next sentence too, according to this point of view, would be addressed to the wounds.

It seems unlikely that had *Rashi* agreed with this position, he would have said nothing to explain this sentence. Certainly, it cannot be said that such an interpretation is self-evident. It seems more likely that *Rashi* (together with *R' Meyuchas* and, perhaps, *Metzudos*) sees God as the subject of the entire verse. [*R' Meyuchas* points out that the change in person (in our case, from third to second) within one sentence is not unusual.]

The *company* would be the people who gathered around in order to observe what was happening to Iyov. See further in *Ramban's* interpretation to verse 9 and onwards.

Our verse now follows naturally upon the previous one. Disillusioned by the friends insensitivity, Iyov turns to God. See further at verse 9, below.

8. וַתִּקְמְטֵנִי לְעֵד הָיָה וַיָּקָם בִּי כַחֲשִׁי בְּפָנַי יַעֲנֶה — *You have wizened me — it has become a witness, my wasted body rises up against me, denounces me to my face.* My wizened, shrivelled appearance, the gauntness of my wasted body, appear to the observer to attest my guilt.

Rashi equates תִּקְמְטֵנִי with קָדַרְתִּי, *darkened.* See at 5:11. כַּחַשׁ means *to be thin* or *weakened.*

9. אַפּוֹ טָרַף וַיִּשְׂטְמֵנִי חָרַק עָלַי בְּשִׁנָּיו צָרִי יִלְטֹשׁ עֵינָיו לִי — *His anger has slashed me — he hates me; he has gnashed his teeth against me; my foe casts barbed glances at me.* According to our understanding of verse 7, that the third person referred to there is God, we would have to assume that here we have a case of outright blasphemy. Based on this assumption, the pronouns should be capitalized: ... *He hates me; He has gnashed His teeth ...*

However, *Rashi* states explicitly that the *foe* at the end of the verse is Satan, not God. *Rashi* may have decided this on the basis of feeling that it is just not possible that Iyov would dare, or wish, to describe God in the terms used in this verse. [Although it is not really clear in what way the ideas expressed here would be more offensive than the descriptions contained in verses 12-14, which clearly refer to God.] Or, the explicit mention of God in verse 11, ... *God has handed me over* ..., makes it unlikely that He would be the subject of our verse.

However, see carefully the commentary to 9:22-24 where we also find *Rashi* — in accordance with the opinion of Abaye at *Bava Basra* 16a — softening the impact of that difficult passage by having it refer to Satan rather than to God. We noted there that we cannot escape the fact that *Rava* (*Bava Basra* there) does in fact interpret that passage as referring to God. We may wonder whether here, too, *Rava* would read our passage, blasphemous as it would be, in the same way. If so, he would no doubt excuse Iyov (as he does there), since no man can be blamed for the excesses to which he gives voice while writhing in the throes of unbearable agony

now, He has wearied me: You have shocked my entire company
into silence. 8 *You have wizened me — it has become a witness,*
my wasted body rises up against me, denounces me to my face.
9 *His anger has slashed me — he hates me; he has gnashed*
his teeth against me; my foe casts barbed glances at me. 10 *They*
accused me with their mouths, disdainfully they smote my
cheeks, thronged, all of them together, against me. 11 *God has*
handed me over to a buffoon, wishes to comfort me at the hands
of the wicked. 12 *I was composed but He ground me up, grabbed*
me by the throat and mangled me, stood me up as a target. 13 *His*
archers gather round about me, He cleaves open my kidneys —
shows no mercy, pours out my gall upon the ground. 14 *He breaks*
me open, breach upon breach, dashes upon me like a warrior.

(see, particularly, fn. 2, p. 100 to chapter 9).

Ramban has the verse referring to any one of the *company* of verse 7 who might wish Iyov ill.

The base meaning of לָטַשׁ is *to sharpen.* We have tried for a similar idiom in English.

10. פָּעֲרוּ עָלַי בְּפִיהֶם בְּחֶרְפָּה הִכּוּ לְחָיָי יַחַד עָלַי יִתְמַלָּאוּן — *They accused me with their mouths, disdainfully they smote my cheeks, thronged, all of them together, against me.* *Rashi* renders פָּעַר with פָּתַח, *they opened. Ramban* explains: That they [presumably, the disdainful throngs] opened their mouths in order to affirm that Iyov had in fact sinned.

For יִתְמַלָּאוּן, *Rashi* and *Ramban* both suggest *to gather. Isaiah* 31:4 is adduced. *R' Meyuchas* suggests, *... are filled with anger against me.*

11. יַסְגִּירֵנִי אֵל אֶל עֲוִיל וְעַל־יְדֵי רְשָׁעִים יִרְטֵנִי — *God has handed me over to a buffoon, wishes to comfort me at the hands of the wicked.* The fact that God is here mentioned as the subject, casts some doubt upon the correct understanding of verse 8, see commentary there.

Reference is apparently to Eliphaz, or to the friends as a whole. Iyov believes that they are not taking him seriously, are simply making fun of his predicament.

Ramban takes עֲוִיל as *enemy.* He suggests that this *enemy* might be the wounds to which Iyov is subject (see above at verse 7), the friends whom Iyov now considers as his foes, or some of the bystanders who wish him ill. See at 8:20, above.

For יִרְטֵנִי, *Rashi* offers two possible interpretations. Either, *to cure* [and this would be the root of the Talmudic, *plaster* or *compress*] — thus, *... wishes to cure me ...* Or, *to comfort.* We have chosen the latter, because it is attested by *Rashi* at *Numbers* 22:32.

12. שָׁלֵו הָיִיתִי וַיְפַרְפְּרֵנִי וְאָחַז בְּעָרְפִּי וַיְפַצְפְּצֵנִי וַיְקִימֵנִי לוֹ לְמַטָּרָה — *I was composed but He ground me up, grabbed me by the throat and mangled me, stood me up as a target.* In this verse, the subject is certainly God, Who was mentioned in the previous verse (*Ramban*).

Rashi associates וַיְפַרְפְּרֵנִי with פֵּירוּרִין, *crumbs.* Thus, *to crumble up.*

מַטָּרָה is *a target.*

13. יָסֹבּוּ עָלַי רַבָּיו יְפַלַּח כִּלְיוֹתַי וְלֹא יַחְמֹל יִשְׁפֹּךְ לָאָרֶץ מְרֵרָתִי — *His archers gather round about me, He cleaves open my kidneys — shows no mercy, pours out my gall upon the ground.* The symbolism is drawn from the battlefield. It recalls 6:4, where (as discussed in the commentary there) we first have Iyov regarding God not so much as a concerned mentor who imposes suffering as a goad to improvement, but as an opponent who wages war against him. See commentary to 13:26-27.

The arrows which the archers are shooting are presumably the pains which are crashing through Iyov's poor body.

רַבָּיו are *archers,* from רֹבֶה, at *Genesis* 21:20.

For פָּלַח, *to cleave,* see also at 39:3.

Ramban points out that the Sages take the latter part of our verse literally (*Chullin* 43:1). They assert that Iyov had actually lost his kidneys and gall and should, by any medical standards, have been dead. He remained alive miraculously, because God had forbidden Satan to take his life.

14. יִפְרְצֵנִי פֶרֶץ עַל־פְּנֵי־פָרֶץ יָרֻץ עָלַי כְּגִבּוֹר — *He breaks me open, breach upon breach, dashes upon me like a warrior.* Once more, the picture is taken from the battlefield. פָּרֶץ is most often used in the sense of breaching a wall. See, for one example among many, *Nehemiah* 2:13. Within this context we have rendered גִּבּוֹר as *warrior,* although at *Psalms* 19:6 we find the

טו־טז שַׂק תָּפַרְתִּי עֲלֵי גִלְדִּי וְעֹלַּלְתִּי בֶעָפָר קַרְנִי: פָּנַי °חמרמרה
°חֳמַרְמְרוּ ק׳ יז מִנִּי־בֶכִי וְעַל עַפְעַפַּי צַלְמָוֶת: עַל לֹא־חָמָס בְּכַפָּי וּתְפִלָּתִי
יח־יט זַכָּה: אֶרֶץ אַל־תְּכַסִּי דָמִי וְאַל־יְהִי מָקוֹם לְזַעֲקָתִי: גַּם־
כ עַתָּה הִנֵּה־בַשָּׁמַיִם עֵדִי וְשָׂהֲדִי בַּמְּרוֹמִים: מְלִיצַי רֵעָי אֶל־
כא אֱלוֹהַּ דָּלְפָה עֵינִי: וְיוֹכַח לְגֶבֶר עִם־אֱלוֹהַּ וּבֶן־אָדָם לְרֵעֵהוּ:

combination, גִּבּוֹר — רוּץ, in a context in which an athlete is apparently meant.

We can only surmise why, just in this speech, Iyov draws such expansive pictures of God as a ruthless enemy. The more so, since in the next passage (v. 19), he asserts with absolute conviction that God, in heaven, will testify to his innocence. Granted that we expect a certain amount of ambivalence within Iyov's speeches — and are prepared for even outright contradictions (see Introductory Remarks to chapters 12-14) — there is still something striking in the starkness of imagery and the sharpness of the contradiction.

A solution may lie in *Ramban's* suggested reading of verse 17: *This, without robbery in my hands, my prayers are beyond reproach. Ramban* thinks that this may have been said sarcastically: These terrible things must be happening to me, *because* I have always been righteous. Manifestly, they do not happen to the wicked. Iyov's frame of mind is one of total confusion. He is good — and suffers as the most wicked person ought to suffer; God is absolutely true and just (verse 19) — and acts as would the worst enemy of all that is admirable and worthy. How, asks Iyov, is one to react to all this?

In such a context we can readily understand why Iyov wishes to portray God's perceived enmity in such vivid terms. It is in stark contrast to the picture of suffering which Eliphaz had drawn of the wicked. He had said that appearances deceive. Even though the wicked seem to live tranquil enough lives, this will not last. In the end they will be made to pay. Moreover, even during the best of times their happiness is not complete. Iyov reacts in total disgust: My suffering is real and unambiguous. It needs no one to explain it to me. If this is how God acts to the righteous, I would much rather have been counted among the wicked!

15-16. שַׂק תָּפַרְתִּי עֲלֵי גִלְדִּי וְעֹלַּלְתִּי בֶעָפָר קַרְנִי — *I have stitched sackcloth for my scars, have dirtied my visage in the dust.* פָּנַי חֳמַרְמְרוּ מִנִּי־בֶכִי וְעַל עַפְעַפַּי צַלְמָוֶת — *My face has become seamed from weeping, there is darkness upon my eyelids.* We have the distinct impression that verse 17 is the real and direct continuation from verse 14, and that our two verses are meant as a kind of parenthesis. This, because the sense of verse 17: All this is happening to me through no fault of my own ... seems more appropriate to the earlier passage, which describes terrors which are thrust upon Iyov through an agency outside himself, than to our verses which tell of discomforts provoked of his own volition. [Verse 15 is actually couched in the first person; verse 16 describes the results of the tears which he chose to shed, the gloom which he permitted to rest upon his eyelids.]

Certainly, our two verses appear to have more in common with 17:1 than they have with any of the remaining verses in our chapter.

It would appear that we are once more dealing with one of the verbal lurches which seem to be endemic to Iyov's style. [We first observed this tendency in Iyov's first speech, at 3:5]. Iyov seems to be interrupting his thoughts, as it were, shaking his head in wonder at the enormous energy expended in pursuing one as frail and broken as he. He is a shattered man, reduced to binding his wounds with material more likely to exacerbate than to soothe, bereft of even a modicum of human dignity, weeping uncontrollably and permanently sunk into deep depression. Is there any need, he wonders, to breach such a one further, to pursue him with the unflagging zeal of the relentlessly persistent warrior? The mood is reminiscent of 13:25.

Rashi renders עֹלַּלְתִּי, as *dirtied*, adducing *Judges* 19:25, which he understands as an expression of *dealing shamefully with someone.* [It is not entirely clear how such an interpretation of the expression there would yield *dirtied* here. At *Eichah* 1:22, *Rashi* renders נִוּוּל, *contemptibility*, adducing our verse.]

For חֳמַרְמְרוּ, *Rashi* here offers נִקְמְטוּ, *folded.* At *Eichah* 1:20 he has *shrunk*, which appears to have a different connotation.

We have rendered צַלְמָוֶת as *darkness.* It is a meaning which surely appears implied in the term, in the present context. *Rashi* writes: His features were darkened through his weeping and his tears.

[15] *I have stitched sackcloth for my scars, have dirtied my*
visage in the dust. [16] *My face has become seamed from weeping,*
there is darkness upon my eyelids. [17] *This, without robbery in*
my hands, my prayers are beyond reproach. [18] *O earth, do not*
cover up my blood, let there be no cache for my cries. [19] *Even*
now, see! My witness is in heaven, He Who attests for me is
on high. [20] *O my friends, who ply me with sophistry! As for me,*
it is to God that my eyes shed tears. [21] *O that He permit a human*
to wrangle with God, even as man, wrangles with his fellow.

17. עַל לֹא־חָמָס בְּכַפָּי וּתְפִלָּתִי זַכָּה — *This, without robbery in my hands, my prayers are beyond reproach. Rashi* comments ... *my prayers are beyond reproach*: I did not curse my friend, nor did I wish him evil. He does not explain the thrust of the verse as a whole.

Ramban offers two possible explanations: one that is a straightforward statement; the other, that Iyov intends a sarcastic sneer.

In the first possibility we must invert the words as though they were written, לֹא עַל חָמָס בְּכַפָּי. The meaning is: My problems are certainly not due to any shortcomings on my part. I have always been innocent of any wrongdoing.

The alternative is to read the verse sarcastically: A fate such as mine never seems to be the lot of the wicked. Manifestly I must be suffering because of my righteousness. It would have been far better for me to have lived a less good life!

We have noted above that this verse may well be a continuation from verse 14, in which case the two intervening verses would be parenthetical. Verse 18 follows on from this one.

18. אֶרֶץ אַל־תְּכַסִּי דָמִי וְאַל־יְהִי מָקוֹם לְזַעֲקָתִי — *O earth, do not cover up my blood, let there be no cache for my cries.* My blood, which was shed upon you, was innocent blood. Make sure that it is not forgotten (*Ramban*).

In addition, Iyov exhorts the earth not to provide a hiding place for his cries. He means them to ascend to heaven (*Rashi*).

19-20. גַּם־עַתָּה הִנֵּה־בַשָּׁמַיִם עֵדִי וְשָׂהֲדִי בַּמְּרוֹמִים — *Even now, see! My witness is in heaven, He Who attests for me is on high.* מְלִיצַי רֵעָי אֶל־אֱלוֹהַּ דָּלְפָה עֵינִי — *O my friends, who ply me with sophistry! As for me, it is to God that my eyes shed tears. Rashi* is silent on the thrust of these two verses. *Ramban* takes them together and reads them as a contrast between God and the friends. God, my creator (*Rashi*), the all-knowing One (*Ramban*), will attest to my innocence. This is in contrast to you, my friends, who insist upon wrangling with me.

We are initially perplexed by the apparent dissonance between the absolute reliance upon God's fairness which is expressed in this verse, and the passage in verses 11-14, where God is projected as a merciless hunter, pursuing Iyov with single-minded fixation.

However, we must recall that Iyov, in spite of his tormented questing and questioning, in spite of being bedeviled by a never relenting need for confrontation, is never for even one moment shaken from his adoration of the God Whom he has known and loved throughout his life (see at 13:15 and 14:15). There is no question here of rebellion or denial; just an obstinate and non-compromising insistence that problems must be faced, questions asked, and reality not glossed over by simplistic pieties. His restless searching, far from implying disloyalty or rejection, is never perceived by him as anything other than a simple religious duty. He cannot reconcile an apparently vindictive torturer with his picture of an upright and just God. But — he will not, because of this, deny either the one or the other.

Rashi is silent on the difficult, מְלִיצַי רֵעָי. Our translation follows *Ramban*.

Our rendering: *As for me, it is to God that my eyes shed tears,* follows *Ramban*. He suggests that Iyov may be weeping before God in order to entreat His mercy, or in accusation against the friends.

21. וְיוֹכַח לְגֶבֶר עִם־אֱלוֹהַּ וּבֶן־אָדָם לְרֵעֵהוּ — *O that He permit a human to wrangle with God, even as man, wrangles with his fellow.* The translation follows *Rashi*. Iyov once more indulges himself in the pipe-dream with which he has sought to comfort himself in the past. If only God could be reduced to human terms. If only He would be accessible at court!

If the tears of the previous verse were shed in entreaty, then our verse presents the subject of those prayers. Aware that the friends have nothing but sophistry to offer, Iyov turns

טז/כב כב כִּי־שְׁנוֹת מִסְפָּר יֶאֱתָיוּ וְאֹרַח לֹא־אָשׁוּב אֶהֱלֹךְ׃
יז/א־ה א־ב רוּחִי חֻבָּלָה יָמַי נִזְעָכוּ קְבָרִים לִי׃ אִם־לֹא הֲתֻלִים
ג עִמָּדִי וּבְהַמְּרוֹתָם תָּלַן עֵינִי׃ שִׂימָה־נָּא עָרְבֵנִי עִמָּךְ
ד מִי הוּא לְיָדִי יִתָּקֵעַ׃ כִּי־לִבָּם צָפַנְתָּ מִּשָּׂכֶל עַל־כֵּן
ה לֹא תְרֹמֵם׃ לְחֵלֶק יַגִּיד רֵעִים וְעֵינֵי בָנָיו תִּכְלֶנָה׃

away from them to God, to reveal to Him the innermost cravings of his heart.

If the tears were angry ones, shed in frustration at the friends' obduracy, then our verse is in reaction to the previous one. Knowing himself to be utterly alone, Iyov wearily takes up his old refrain. Vainly — or perhaps even with a glimmer of hope that God may accede to his request after all — he begs God to listen. There is so little time left! (See next verse.)

22. כִּי־שְׁנוֹת מִסְפָּר יֶאֱתָיוּ וְאֹרַח לֹא־אָשׁוּב אֶהֱלֹךְ — *For the years apportioned to me will surely come to an end, and then I will embark upon a path from which I will not return. Rashi* does not explain how this verse ties in to the context. Perhaps the meaning is as we have understood it in the previous verse. Iyov stresses the urgency of his craving. Something just must be done. My life is flowing away. If You will not answer me now — it will be too late. (See commentary to 10:20 for Iyov's passionate love of life.)

Ramban reads the argument as he has also done on previous occasions. Why subject to punishment one whose days are anyway so short? (see 7:6-10).

XVII.

1. רוּחִי חֻבָּלָה יָמַי נִזְעָכוּ קְבָרִים לִי — *My spirit is lacerated, my days have rushed past, I expect only — the grave*. At the end of the previous chapter we found that Iyov's passionate love of life imbued his entreaty, that he be given a chance to wrangle with God, with the urgency of desperation. There is so little time left before the dreadful finality of death; will You not answer my call while there is yet something to salvage!

This attitude appears to be in stark contradiction to the end of our chapter (the final verses of Iyov's rejoinder to Eliphaz), where his death-wish is expressed with as deep a longing — the grave described in vivid and positive terms — as we are likely to find in any record of man's absolute despair.

The movement from the one extreme to the other must be understood as coming about from the appalling contrast between Iyov's dream of the might-have-been and the stark reality of a world in which God is God and man is man, and a confrontation on equal terms will simply not come about.

As long as Iyov had allowed himself to conjure up a world contoured to his own wistful desires, life had indeed beckoned alluringly — its joys and triumphs seemingly within grasp. But it required only a glance at the mocking, uncomprehending faces of his supposed friends (v. 2) to bring the truth sharply — and painfully — into focus.

It would seem that our verse forms the bridge between these two worlds.

In the context within which it appears, there is some ambiguity in the final phrase of our verse: *I expect only — the grave*. Is this said in sorrow, or in happy anticipation? If we look to the part of the speech immediately preceding our verse, we would read it as an expression of despair. Where life could have been so beautiful, the only reality for Iyov now, is — death. However, as we have seen above, the final verses of the speech make it amply clear that the grave can be regarded as a welcome relief from an unbearably difficult life.

The immediate context within which the verse appears argues in favor of the first option. Iyov is mourning the pervasive imminence of the grave. However, we suspect that at the very moment in which he bemoans this ubiquitous specter, the thought begins to germinate that perhaps it is not all bad. At the mercy of people who refuse to understand, he realizes that, after all, life has little to offer.

The rest of the chapter has Iyov spelling out his sorry state, until, at the end of his peroration, he states explicitly what is only hinted at in the ambiguity of our verse. The nethermost depths are really the very best place for him.

For זָעַךְ, *Rashi* offers קָפַץ, *to leap* or *to jump*. *Ramban* prefers, *to be extinguished*.

For the plural, קְבָרִים, *Metzudos* remarks: I am close to death wherever I walk. Consequently, each place at which I stand is a

16/22 [22] *For the years apportioned to me will surely come to an end, and*
then I will embark upon a path from which I will not return.

17/1-5 [1] *My spirit is lacerated, my days have rushed past, I expect*
only — the grave. [2] *Assuredly I am exposed to mockers,*
their taunts accompany me to sleep. [3] *O place [a bond], contract*
Yourself to me — with You; for who [among these] will grasp my
hand? [4] *See! You have blocked their heart from comprehension*
— therefore You can never be exalted. [5] *Each talks glibly to*
his friends; the eyes of his children will be strained with longing.

potential grave for me.[1]

2. אם־לא הֲתֻלִים עִמָּדִי וּבְהַמְּרוֹתָם תָּלַן עֵינִי — *Assuredly I am exposed to mockers, their taunts accompany me to sleep.* אם לא is commonly an expression of *assurance*. See, for example, *Isaiah* 5:9. *Ramban* explains this usage as being the tail end of an implied oath. May this and this happen, if such and such is not so.

For *Ramban's* understanding of this verse together with the next one, see commentary there.

For הָתֵל, *to mock*, see *I Kings* 18:27.

For the second phrase *Rashi* is not entirely clear and we have gone to *Ramban* (and *Ibn Ezra*) since it is possible that his understanding is also that of *Rashi*. The idea expressed is that Iyov can never go to sleep without previously having been exposed to the friends' antagonism. *Rashi* and *Ramban* (with *Ibn Ezra*) differ in their understanding of הַמְּרוֹתָם. *Rashi* renders with הַקְנָטָה, *hectoring* or *provoking*. *Ramban* suggests *embittering*, from מָרַר.

3. שִׂימָה־נָּא עָרְבֵנִי עִמָּךְ מִי־הוּא לְיָדִי יִתָּקֵעַ — *O place [a bond], contract Yourself to me — with You; for who [among these] will grasp my hand? Rashi* believes that God is being addressed; *Ramban*, that it is Eliphaz, the friend to whom Iyov is now responding.

First *Rashi*: For עָרְבֵנִי, we go to *Rashi* to *Isaiah* 38:14, where he equates the word with *to guarantee*. In that context — to extend salvation to me. But what are we to make of the עִמָּךְ? From the usage there, it is clear that no further object is required. *Rashi* seems to feel this problem and to solve it by adding the words: *To wrangle together*. Thus: *Contract Yourself* — to permit me to wrangle *with You*. The second part of the sentence is then explained: I turn to You because none among my friends would be willing to guarantee me anything. The combination, יָד and תָּקַע, always means, *to shake hands in order to guarantee something*. See, for example, *Proverbs* 6:1 where it is paralleled to עָרַב.

Within the given context, it is difficult to see why Iyov would come back once more to his demand for a confrontation with God. The following verses all seem directly connected with verse 2, and this request seems an uncalled for interruption of an otherwise natural flow.

Perhaps it is for this reason that *Ramban* chooses a different interpretation. The verse is to be read together with the previous one, and in a sense precedes it. In verse 3 Iyov is, as it were, challenging Eliphaz (שִׂימָה נָּא ...) or anyone else (מי הוא ...) to contest his assertion from the previous verse that he is *exposed to mockers*. In this context, the אם לא ... of the previous verse is to be translated literally: *Is it not true . . .!?*

4-5. כִּי־לִבָּם צָפַנְתָּ מִשָּׂכֶל עַל־כֵּן לֹא תְרוֹמֵם — *See! You have blocked their heart from comprehension — therefore You can never be exalted.* לְחֵלֶק יַגִּיד רֵעִים וְעֵינֵי בָנָיו תִּכְלֶנָה — *Each talks glibly to his friends; the eyes of his children will be strained with longing.* We follow *Rashi*: God is being addressed. He has blocked (צָפַן, *to hide*) the hearts of (probably, as in v. 2) the friends; they understand nothing whatever of Iyov's travail. In consequence He can never become exalted through them.

We can understand the reasoning well. Iyov

1. That the plural, קְבָרוֹת, is also used at 21:32, suggests that the form belongs to that group of words known to grammarians as *plurals of extension*, of which an example would be עוֹלָמִים, for *eternity*. (See *Gesenius* #124b.) The idea of this usage is to provide a sense of amplification over the single unit of that which is being discussed. קְבָרִים would thus denote *the world of graves*, or, perhaps, *graveyard*.

We wonder, too, whether the phrase קְבָרִים לִי might not be a direct continuation of יָמַי נִזְעָכוּ. The idea would be that each of the days which are rushing past me have become a 'grave' for some of my ambitions and potentials. There is so much that I could have done if I had been allowed to live a normal life.

ו־ז וְֽהִצִּיגַנִי לִמְשֹׁל עַמִּים וְתֹפֶת לְפָנִים אֶהְיֶה׃ וַתֵּכַהּ מִכַּעַשׂ
ח עֵינִי וִיצֻרַי כַּצֵּל כֻּלָּם׃ יָשֹׁמּוּ יְשָׁרִים עַל־זֹאת וְנָקִי עַל־
ט חָנֵף יִתְעֹרָר׃ וְיֹאחֵז צַדִּיק דַּרְכּוֹ וּֽטֳהָר־יָדַיִם יֹסִיף אֹמֶץ׃
י וְֽאוּלָם כֻּלָּם תָּשֻׁבוּ וּבֹאוּ נָא וְלֹא־אֶמְצָא בָכֶם חָכָם׃

is repeating his thoughts from 13:7-12. The friends may, in all honesty, be trying to help God by protecting Him from Iyov's bitter slurs. But, because their hearts are choked up, because they are insensitive to the very real problems which he raises, they voice bland and predictable platitudes, which are irrelevant and which therefore, far from vindicating God, really degrade Him.

Of interest is the fact that Iyov talks *about* the friends, but does not talk *to* them. This, in contrast to chapter 13 where he criticizes them to their faces. We see confirmed what we surmised in our remarks at the beginning of this speech. Iyov has lost interest in communicating with the friends. They are mockers and buffoons — what can possibly be gained by haranguing them?

We have rendered, וְעֵינֵי בָנָיו תִּכְלֶנָה, *the eyes of his children will be strained with longing*, in accordance with *Rashi* to 11:20. He writes that this is invariably the meaning when the root כלה is combined with עַיִן. We think that the meaning of the verse may be as follows: Friends may need one another and rely upon each other for help. But, if one of them feels let down, there will always be someone else to whom to turn. Not so, children. They must look to their parents for guidance. When they are offered hackneyed banalities in place of loving and concerned understanding, then indeed, their eyes are strained by longing. They have nowhere else to turn.

Rashi renders חֵלֶק with חֲלַקְלַקּוֹת. Both derive from חָלַק, *to be smooth*. Thus, *smoothness, flattery, glibness* and the like.

6. וְהִצִּיגַנִי לִמְשֹׁל עַמִּים וְתֹפֶת לְפָנִים אֶהְיֶה — *He has made a popular adage of me, I am perceived as a kind of drum* [lit. *He has set me up as a byword of the people*].

Rashi remains silent concerning the identity of the subject of the first phrase. It seems legitimate to assume that as in verse 3, it is God. However, *Ramban* identifies the subject as Eliphaz [though he too considers the possibility that it might be God], and *Metzudos* thinks that it is Iyov's pain which has made him into an adage.

Ramban understands the *adage* as follows: Iyov is generally used as an example to curse those who pretend to a saintliness which they have not truly attained. People will say to them, 'You are acting just like Iyov!' *Metzudos* interprets: When catastrophe strikes someone, people will say: 'What has happened to you is similar to the fate which overtook Iyov.'

Rashi's rendering of תֹּפֶת as *drum* is not easy to accommodate in this context. *Ramban* also entertains this possibility. However, he renders לְפָנִים as *in the past*, and this makes the sense of the entire verse understandable. The meaning is: In bygone days people used to rejoice at meeting me as they would be happy to hear the music of the drum; now I have become an adage in their mouths.

But *Rashi* has לְפָנִים mean *to people's faces*, which we take as meaning as we have rendered it: *I appear to people as a drum*. But, what could this possibly mean? We may surmise that Iyov has the monotonous pounding of a drum in mind. My words have ceased to impress people. I have had to say so much that by now, people only hear a background rumble. Again reference may be to the drum's insistent noise which importunes those that are exposed to it. I have become a nuisance to people. They do not really wish to hear any more what I have to say.

However, neither of these explanations sits comfortably when we consider that without exception, the word תֹּפֶת meaning *drum*, occurs in Scripture in the context of making music in a joyful sense.

There is, perhaps, one other possibility. In *Nahum* 2:8 we have the verb תָּפַף in the sense of *beating one's breast*. Perhaps Iyov means: When I beat my breast in anguish, it makes as little impression upon the people as though I were beating a drum.

Ramban adduces *Targum* for a rendering of תֹּפֶת as *Gehinnom* — hell fires (see *Isaiah* 30:33). לְפָנִים means *inside*, and the meaning is: I am suffering so much that, though I am still alive, I feel as though I were in some inner hell. *Metzudos* has the same general idea: My pains are so great and varied, that people see in me the suffering of *Gehinnom*.

7. וַתֵּכַהּ מִכַּעַשׂ עֵינִי וִיצֻרַי כַּצֵּל כֻּלָּם — *My eyes have dimmed from frustration, all my limbs have become a shadow*. The frustration is caused either by the friends' obduracy, or by the pain of the wounds (*Ramban*).

For the dimming of the eye as a sign of debilitation, see *Zechariah* 11:17.

[6] *He has made a popular adage out of me, I am perceived as a kind of drum.* [7] *My eyes have dimmed from frustration, all my limbs have become a shadow.* [8] *Let the fair-minded be shocked at this, let the innocent bestir themselves against the hypocrite.* [9] *Let he who is righteous hold fast to his path, the one with clean hands, fortify himself.* [10] *However! All of them! You will return [to the fray]. Come, I beg you. But — I will not find a wise man among you.*

Targum renders יְצֻרַי as *limbs*. The word is derived from יָצַר, *to form*. Thus, those parts of me which have been formed.

8-9. יָשֹׁמּוּ יְשָׁרִים עַל־זֹאת וְנָקִי עַל־חָנֵף יִתְעֹרָר — *Let the fair-minded be shocked at this, let the innocent bestir themselves against the hypocrite.* וְיֹאחֵז צַדִּיק דַּרְכּוֹ וּטֳהָר־יָדַיִם יֹסִיף אֹמֶץ — *Let he who is righteous hold fast to his path, the one with clean hands, fortify himself.* *Rashi*, and to a lesser extent *Ramban*, see these two verses as a summons to the fair-minded, calling them to battle against those who would falsify the truth.

Rashi does not tell us how he understands the *this* of verse 8. *Ramban* thinks that it means: Let the fair-minded be shocked at the thought that their righteous lives will not necessarily save them from suffering. We feel that had *Rashi* agreed to this explanation — or read a similar one into the *this* — he would have had to spell it out. In the event it seems more likely that he understands the word to refer to the subject matter of the latter part of the verse — the taunting derision of the friends.

Accordingly we read *Rashi* to verse 8 as follows: Let the fair-minded be shocked at the way I am being treated by my friends. Let those who are innocent bestir themselves to do battle with the[se] hypocrites who seek to curry favor with God by denouncing me. Verse 9 then continues: Let he who is righteous hold fast to his path of steadfast opposition to the falsifiers, and the one who is clean of hands fortify himself so that he will be able to maintain his fight.

Ramban, whose understanding of the first phrase we saw above, continues as follows: Let all who know perfectly well that they undergo suffering in spite of leading blameless lives, argue against Eliphaz who is seeking to curry favor with God by condemning Iyov. Verse 9: Let those who are righteous and clean of hand be consistent and strong in their fight against the prevaricators, so that truth may be known from falsehood.

We offer an alternative interpretation from *Daas Mikra*, because there is a degree of difficulty in reading the *this* of verse 8 (according to *Rashi*), and the section as a whole (according to both *Rashi* and *Ramban*) as referring to the hypocrisy of the comforters which was last mentioned in verse 2. The intervening passage deals with other issues.

We note further that verse 9 would lend itself readily to an interpretation which has nothing at all to do with fighting the hypocrites.

We address ourselves first to the phrase: *Let he who is righteous hold fast to his path*. What, precisely, is the meaning of this idiom? Judging from the almost identical usage at 23:11, we would conclude that it describes the life-style of the *tzaddik*, a steady clinging to a path of righteousness, and carries no implication of his relationship to the wicked.

The noun אֹמֶץ is unique in Scripture, but the verb אמץ is frequently used. It is true that it often connotes the overpowering or subduing of another (see, for example, *Genesis* 25:23), but it is also frequently used to describe inner strength, unrelated to the vanquishing of a foe (see, for example, *Joshua* 1:7).

Accordingly, the whole passage may be read as a call of encouragement to the righteous bystanders. Indeed there is much in Iyov's experiences that is truly shocking. Indeed there is much that is anger-provoking in Eliphaz's obdurate myopia. But, in spite of all this, they are not to be swayed from their true and straight path. Let them, on the contrary, fortify themselves in their determination to do that which is right. A righteous life is its own justification; that it often goes unrewarded, should make no difference at all.

10. וְאֻלָּם כֻּלָּם תָּשֻׁבוּ וּבֹאוּ נָא וְלֹא־אֶמְצָא בָכֶם חָכָם — *However! All of them! You will return [to the fray]. Come, I beg you. But — I will not find a wise man among you*. Iyov has had his say, and now wishes to invite a reaction from the friends. The syntax clearly indicates his hesitancy in approaching them. He begins in the third person — *All of them*. He progresses to the second person — *You will return* — but still shies away from the imperative. It is only at a third attempt — *Come I beg you* — that he manages to actually request them to make some advance towards him (*Daas Mikra*).

יז/יא־טו יא־יב יָמַי עָבְרוּ זִמֹּתַי נִתְּקוּ מוֹרָשֵׁי לְבָבִי: לַיְלָה לְיוֹם
יג יָשִׂימוּ אוֹר קָרוֹב מִפְּנֵי־חֹשֶׁךְ: אִם־אֲקַוֶּה שְׁאוֹל
יד בֵּיתִי בַּחֹשֶׁךְ רִפַּדְתִּי יְצוּעָי: לַשַּׁחַת קָרָאתִי אָבִי
טו אָתָּה אִמִּי וַאֲחֹתִי לָרִמָּה: וְאַיֵּה אֵפוֹ תִקְוָתִי וְתִקְוָתִי
טז מִי יְשׁוּרֶנָּה: בַּדֵּי שְׁאֹל תֵּרַדְנָה אִם־יַחַד עַל־עָפָר
יח/א־ב א־ב נָחַת: וַיַּעַן בִּלְדַּד הַשֻּׁחִי וַיֹּאמַר: עַד־אָנָה ׀

In spite of the awkwardness in the English rendering as we have it, we have decided to translate literally, in order to retain this significant progression.

Almost immediately — before they have any chance to respond — Iyov is once more filled with utter dejection. What, after all, is the use of inviting them to speak. He has lost any real hope of eliciting true wisdom from them.

But — a dashed hope leaves a greater void than there would have been if no expectation had ever been raised. Accordingly, Iyov now sinks into the despondency which finds expression in the following final sentences of his speech.

11. יָמַי עָבְרוּ זִמֹּתַי נִתְּקוּ מוֹרָשֵׁי לְבָבִי — *My days, my aspirations have slipped away; my heart's ambitions are thwarted*. We have translated the sentence as *Rashi* appears to take it. The cantillation would seem to indicate a different division: *My days have slipped away; my aspirations, my hearts ambitions are thwarted*.

זִמֹּתַי derives from זָמַם *to intend*. מוֹרָשֵׁי, from יָרַשׁ, *to inherit*. Thus: My heart had assured me that I could anticipate the fulfillment of certain hopes. These hopes and that anticipation has now been thwarted.

12. לַיְלָה לְיוֹם יָשִׂימוּ אוֹר קָרוֹב מִפְּנֵי־חֹשֶׁךְ — *They turn my night into day; as darkness falls, it seems that only now had it become light*. We have translated according to *Rashi*. With their lack of understanding, the friends have turned Iyov's life into a greater misery than have his physical suffering. Nights have become a torture. The otherwise welcome embrace of darkness offers the solace of sleep as little as the brightest day.

Under these circumstances Iyov has come to prefer the day. Then, at least, he does not have to make the pretense of trying to fall asleep. But these periods of relative relief are all too short. Every evening, as night begins to fall, it seems to him as though it had only just become light.

For קָרוֹב as describing something that had only recently happened, *Rashi* adduces a number of examples, among them *Genesis* 19:20.

13. אִם־אֲקַוֶּה שְׁאוֹל בֵּיתִי בַּחֹשֶׁךְ רִפַּדְתִּי יְצוּעָי — *Inasmuch as I crave the nethermost depths as my home, I spread my mattress in the dark*. *Rashi* offers מֵאַחַר for אִם, and it therefore appears that he takes the second phrase as following upon the first one as we have translated it.

The meaning of the entire verse seems to be as follows: I am so eager to call the grave my home, that in my mind's eye, I have already spread my mattress in the darkness.

14. לַשַּׁחַת קָרָאתִי אָבִי אָתָּה אִמִּי וַאֲחֹתִי לָרִמָּה — *I called to the pit, 'You are my father!', to the worms, 'My mother, my sister!'* At 10:20-22 we saw that Iyov had anticipated the grave in two vastly different ways. In chapter 3 — his first speech — he had looked towards it as a place of ultimate repose, a welcome refuge from the injustice and inequity which break the spirit of the downtrodden and brutalize the mighty. By contrast, in chapter 10 it had awakened in him a feeling of unrelieved gloom.

We had thought that his attitude would be substantially influenced by the degree to which he felt attached to life. In chapter 3, at the first flush of his agony, he wanted nothing so much as to make an end to it all. In such a frame of mind, the thought of the grave was beguiling. It appeared to present an excellent alternative to his miseries. In chapter 10, however, life had suddenly appeared very sweet. In the light of its attractions, the dark terrors of the grave seemed threatening indeed.

Here we have a third — and different — perspective. Just as he was in chapter 3, Iyov now seems to be filled with eager anticipation of the grave. He craves the nethermost depths; and is, in his mind's eye, already setting up his pallet in the darkness. But — it is not serene repose which he contemplates, not the egalitarian system which he idealized in his earlier speech. The pit itself, the gnawing worms, have now become father, mother and sister to him. The murky blackness, far from posing a lowering threat, now beckons him into its welcoming embrace.

We understand this transformation from his earlier attitude in the light of what had taken place in chapter 10. During that short moment, when life really did seem worth living, he was

17/11-16 [11] *My days, my aspirations have slipped away; my heart's ambitions are thwarted.* [12] *They turn my night into day; as darkness falls, it seems that only now had it become light.* [13] *Inasmuch as I crave the nethermost depths as my home, I spread my mattress in the dark.* [14] *I called to the pit 'You are my father!', to the worms, 'My mother, my sister!'* [15] *Where then is my hope, who will diligently extend to me that which I hoped for?* [16] *Those grave-limbs that will sink, that they might rest together in the dust.*

18/1-2 [1] *Bildad the Shuhite responded and spoke:* [2] *How long! Make*

forced to face the ultimate falsehood of the benign picture with which he had managed to deceive himself in his original speech. Black, futile, emptiness suddenly stared him in the face — and he became afraid. Indelibly this picture became etched in his mind.

And so, now that his terrible loneliness makes him, once more, hope for death, it is with this image of the grave that he must cope. And in the depth of his despair, even this dreadful reality becomes the object of his craving.

15. וְאַיֵּה אֵפוֹ תִקְוָתִי וְתִקְוָתִי מִי יְשׁוּרֶנָּה — *Where then is my hope, who will diligently extend that which I hoped for, to me?* The hope expressed in the previous verses — that he might soon merit to lie in the grave (*Rashi*).

Rashi, at *Hosea* 13:7, renders שור as *lie in wait and observe diligently*. It appears that here too, he takes the word with that meaning.

The sense of the whole passage is very much the same as that of 6:8-9. Iyov does not really believe that God will grant him even this modest request. Apparently even the favor of dying must be earned. With desperate rhetoric, born of bitterness and disillusion, Iyov casts around — vainly — for help which, deep down, he knows will not be forthcoming.

16. בַּדֵּי שְׁאֹל תֵּרַדְנָה אִם־יַחַד עַל־עָפָר נָחַת — *Those grave-limbs that will sink, that they might rest together in the dust.* The extension from *branch*, the usual meaning of בַּד, to *limbs* is easy to understand. בַּדֵּי שְׁאֹל, then, are *limbs that are destined to go down to the grave*. The hopes concerning which Iyov felt so frustrated in the previous verse, were centered upon death. He cannot wait for the day on which the limbs — his body — which even now are so clearly destined for the grave, will indeed sink down so that they, all together, might at last lie in the dust which will become their eternal resting place.

XVIII.

◆§ Bildad's Second Speech

In this, Bildad's second speech, he follows Eliphaz's lead in that he hardly talks to Iyov at all. After the initial sparse, almost *pro forma* rebuke that Iyov ought to listen carefully to the friends' theological expositions, he launches into a lyric description of the utter devastation which awaits the wicked person. He seems totally oblivious to the fact that in front of him there is a living, suffering human being, who is less concerned with the theoretical fate of the theoretical sinner, than — to judge from his next speech — his utter alienation from former verities and anchorages, and his vulnerability to the onslaughts of his merciless lacerations.

Additionally, Bildad appears to be totally insensitive to the agony which he must be causing Iyov by his constant reference to the blighted hopes of the wicked — the inevitable death of his children. Only recently, Iyov himself had to come to grips with the thought that the future, for him — held nothing at all. His children — his grasp on immortality — lay beneath the rubble of the collapsed home of his firstborn.

Earlier, in his first speech, Bildad had already been ready to write off Iyov's children. God, as far as Bildad was concerned, had sent them away because of their wickedness. But there, the children themselves had been the focus of his concern; here it is the bereaved father over whose loss — as it were — Bildad gloats.

Small wonder that in his next speech, Iyov gives vent to the cry of agony that wells up in his heart: "Pity me, O pity me, my friends!"

ג תְּשִׂימוּן קִנְצֵי לְמִלִּין תָּבִינוּ וְאַחַר נְדַבֵּר: מַדּוּעַ נֶחְשַׁבְנוּ
ד כַבְּהֵמָה נִטְמִינוּ בְּעֵינֵיכֶם: טֹרֵף נַפְשׁוֹ בְּאַפּוֹ הֲלְמַעַנְךָ תֵּעָזַב
ה אָרֶץ וְיֶעְתַּק־צוּר מִמְּקֹמוֹ: גַּם אוֹר רְשָׁעִים יִדְעָךְ וְלֹא־
ו־ז יִגַּהּ שְׁבִיב אִשּׁוֹ: אוֹר חָשַׁךְ בְּאָהֳלוֹ וְנֵרוֹ עָלָיו יִדְעָךְ: יֵצְרוּ
ח צַעֲדֵי אוֹנוֹ וְתַשְׁלִיכֵהוּ עֲצָתוֹ: כִּי־שֻׁלַּח בְּרֶשֶׁת בְּרַגְלָיו

2. עַד־אָנָה | תְּשִׂימוּן קִנְצֵי לְמִלִּין תָּבִינוּ וְאַחַר נְדַבֵּר — *How long! Make an end to speeches. First understand and then, let us talk!* Bildad's first speech also began with the words, עַד אָנָה. However, the מַהְפָּךְ לְגַרְחֵיה [the standard *mahpach* followed by a vertical stroke], with which אָנָה is accentuated, suggests that here, in contrast to their use there, these words stand on their own. Thus, apparently, *Rashi.*

R' Meyuchas makes reference to the parallelism with the earlier speech and, in deference to that similarity, renders the two first phrases together: How long will you inhibit [the effect which] our speeches ought to have on you. [You do this by answering each of our arguments immediately, without giving yourself a chance to think over what we have said.] You should first attempt to understand, and only then debate us!

Rashi, as understood by *R' Yosef Kara*, has Bildad addressing the friends: Why do you cut Iyov short! You should attempt to understand fully what he has to say, and only then to answer him. *R' Yosef Kara* objects to this: Nowhere do the friends interrupt Iyov. Each time they answer him only after he has stopped speaking on his own. Therefore he offers: Why do we constantly listen to Iyov and then give him our answers. In this way the debate can continue indefinitely. Rather, he should listen carefully to what I will now say and then the argument will be closed.

Ramban, too, has this verse addressed to the friends. Bildad is chiding his colleagues for cutting short their presentations in order to give Iyov a chance to have his say: How long will you continue to rein in your words so that you might understand Iyov's position, and only then do you continue. [It would be much better if all of us spoke one after the other, without allowing Iyov the chance to interrupt us with his thoughts.]

3. מַדּוּעַ נֶחְשַׁבְנוּ כַבְּהֵמָה נִטְמִינוּ בְּעֵינֵיכֶם — *Why should we be considered as cattle? [Why], are we stupid in your eyes?* The more similar the earlier verse is to the introductory sentence in Bildad's first speech, the more striking is the difference between the follow-on verse there, and the one we have here. There, Bildad was outraged at Iyov's perception of God: *Would God pervert justice, would Shaddai pervert righteousness?* Here, his anger is directed at Iyov for denigrating himself and his colleagues.

The exasperation of being completely ignored by the erstwhile friend whom he would so much wish to help, is clearly showing through.

נִטְמִינוּ, from טָמַם, *to be blocked up.*

4. טֹרֵף נַפְשׁוֹ בְּאַפּוֹ הַלְמַעַנְךָ תֵּעָזַב אֶרֶץ וְיֶעְתַּק־צוּר מִמְּקֹמוֹ — *[O you] who, in his rage, tears his very being asunder, should the earth be abandoned just to please you, [should] the rock be dislodged from its place?* The combination טֹרֵף נֶפֶשׁ, in this context, is unique. It would seem to describe the dreadful violence which Iyov is doing to his own being. Whether in frustrated anger, or with residual feelings of friendliness — it is hard to tell which — Bildad expresses his chagrin at Iyov's perceived obduracy. Can't you see — he seems to be saying. Can't you see that you are ruining yourself by your unceasing cavilling. You could so easily find inner peace, if you would only agree to our propositions.

Ramban interprets as follows: It is God's usage, because He is inclined to be merciful to all His creatures, to allow the wicked some short time of tranquility before they are served their just desserts. Such is the system with which He exercises His stewardship of human affairs. It is a good system — there is no reason why human society [*the earth*] should be bereft of it [*be abandoned*]. It is firmly established — solid as the *rocks*; why should it be uprooted? There is no reason why God should change the form of His stewardship just because it obscures your perception of Him as a just God.

It is not quite clear how *Rashi* understands the latter part of the verse. He may mean the same as *Ramban*, except that he takes צוּר as *creator* rather than as *rock*, and accordingly, מְקֹמוֹ is not a physical place but *a stand taken.* God will not be bullied into changing the form of His stewardship.

5-6. גַּם אוֹר רְשָׁעִים יִדְעָךְ וְלֹא־יִגַּהּ שְׁבִיב אִשּׁוֹ — *Surely the light of the wicked will leap away, no brilliance to his fire's sparks.* אוֹר חָשַׁךְ בְּאָהֳלוֹ וְנֵרוֹ עָלָיו יִדְעָךְ — *Light turns to darkness in his*

18/3-8 *an end to speeches. First understand and then, let us talk!* 3 *Why*
should we be considered as cattle? [Why], are we stupid in your
eyes? 4 *[O you] who, in his rage, tears his very being asunder,*
should the earth be abandoned just to please you, [should] the rock
be dislodged from its place? 5 *Surely the light of the wicked will*
leap away, no brilliance to his fire's sparks. 6 *Light turns to*
darkness in his tent, and, near him, his lamp will be extinguished.
7 *His strides, taken in confidence, will become constricted; his own*
schemes will discard him. 8 *For he is cast upon a net by his feet,*

tent, and, near him, his lamp will be extinguished. What, precisely, is verse 5 saying, and is verse 6 simply a repetition in different words?

What is *the light of the wicked?* At 38:15 this concept is mentioned in connection with a vivid description of the breaking day. As dawn breaks, the *light of the wicked is withheld from them.* But, how are we to understand this? In what sense does the dawn 'withhold' light from anybody? It has been suggested that the phrase is to be understood on the basis of 24:13-16, which describes how the wicked, because they perform all their nefarious deeds at night, tend to shun the light of day. Thus the 'light' of the wicked, the time at which they are active, is really the night. Its protective blanket of darkness serves them as the light of day would serve those who have nothing to hide. The dawn does, indeed, effectively *withhold their light* from them. Here, Bildad looks to the time when the night will refuse the wicked its protection.

So much for *the light of the wicked.* What can be meant by *his fire?*

We suggest that this phrase might refer to the moon. It is *his fire* in contrast to the innocent who, because they function during the day, have the sun to serve them. The sparks of the moon (*Rashi* renders שְׁבִיב, with the French, *eatincelles,* sparks) could perhaps be the stars. In the poet's sight these might well appear like sparks springing forth from the moon. In the past the wicked man had been able to make use of the light cast by the moon and stars to follow his desires. The time will come in which they will no more light his way.

In the next verse, we move into the home of the wicked. There too, light will be extinguished. But this time, the word is used metaphorically to describe the success which, in the past, may have been his lot (*Metzudos*).

It is difficult to know the precise meaning of עָלָיו in this context. *Metzudos* takes it together with *his lamp.* That is, the lamp which had been shining over him.

However, we find על used to denote *proximity,* as for example at *Genesis* 16:7, and in this sense the word may well mean something akin to *in his presence.* That is, while he is in the act of using the lamp and enjoying its light, it will become extinguished.

With the failure of his various enterprises (v. 5), darkness and misery will enter his house. As we discuss in our analysis of the relationship between Bildad's first two speeches, it is the home which is the main focus of his interest.

7. יֵצְרוּ צַעֲדֵי אוֹנוֹ וְתַשְׁלִיכֵהוּ עֲצָתוֹ — *His strides, taken in confidence, will become constricted; his own schemes will discard him.* At *Proverbs* 4:12, where the promise is made that one who is reared in the paths of wisdom, will never have his steps constricted as he walks, *Rashi* remarks: One who does not widen his steps can readily fall. At *II Samuel* 22:37, David thanks God for having *widened his steps* — that is, prevented him from falling.

אוֹן is usually translated as *strength* (but see further at verse 12). Thus, *steps taken with strength.*

The subject of תַּשְׁלִיכֵהוּ is *scheme.* His scheme will throw him over or out. The meaning is that his plans will go awry and thus precipitate him to the lowest depths (*Metzudos*).

8. כִּי־שֻׁלַּח בְּרֶשֶׁת בְּרַגְלָיו וְעַל־שְׂבָכָה יִתְהַלָּךְ — *For he is cast upon a net by his feet, he will wander onto [a pit covered by] a latticework [of branches].* The *pual* form of שֻׁלַּח and the *hispael* of יִתְהַלָּךְ indicate a kind of passivity. Without his wishing it, his feet will carry him onto the entangling net; as he wanders around, he will willy-nilly stumble upon the deceptive latticework of branches which covers the pit into which he will — inevitably — fall. It is a similar thought to the one expressed in the previous verse. Just as his own plans will prove to be his undoing, so too his own feet will carry him to disaster (*Ramban*).

שְׂבָכָה is used for anything interlaced or netlike. Thus, for example, the mesh-work decorating Solomon's Temple at *I Kings* 7:17.

ט וְעַל־שְׂבָכָה יִתְהַלָּךְ: יֹאחֵז בְּעָקֵב פָּח יַחֲזֵק עָלָיו
י צַמִּים: טָמוּן בָּאָרֶץ חַבְלוֹ וּמַלְכֻּדְתּוֹ עֲלֵי נָתִיב:
יא־יב סָבִיב בִּעֲתֻהוּ בַלָּהוֹת וֶהֱפִיצֻהוּ לְרַגְלָיו: יְהִי־רָעֵב
יג אֹנוֹ וְאֵיד נָכוֹן לְצַלְעוֹ: יֹאכַל בַּדֵּי עוֹרוֹ יֹאכַל בַּדָּיו
יד בְּכוֹר מָוֶת: יִנָּתֵק מֵאָהֳלוֹ מִבְטַחוֹ וְתַצְעִדֵהוּ לְמֶלֶךְ
טו בַּלָּהוֹת: תִּשְׁכּוֹן בְּאָהֳלוֹ מִבְּלִי־לוֹ יְזֹרֶה עַל־נָוֵהוּ גָפְרִית:

9. יֹאחֵז בְּעָקֵב פָּח יַחֲזֵק עָלָיו צַמִּים — *A trap will grab him by the heel, highwaymen will overpower him.* צַמִּים is difficult. Above at 5:5 we rendered *parched,* in accordance with most commentators who read the word as though it were written with an *aleph,* צְמֵאִים, *those that are thirsty.* Indeed this is how *Ramban* takes it here: Those that are thirsty to drink his blood, or those who wish to gulp down his wine and his milk, that is, his property.

Radak in *Sefer HaShorashim* thinks that the word is related to צמם, which he renders: *plaited hair.* The צַמִּים, are highway robbers whose practice it was to plait their hair and allow it to hang behind them. We have translated in accordance with *Radak* because then the word is of one piece with the various traps mentioned in these verses — that is, a danger lurking along the path which the wicked man is walking.

R' Meyuchas renders, דוּחָקוֹת וְצָרוֹת. Apparently, then, he understands the word as connoting something restricting or constricting. If so, it might be possible to understand the word as describing the clamping jaws of a closing trap. Perhaps even a noose closing in upon its victim. If this were indeed so, then the word would be entirely apt within this section which deals with the various snares which are ready to entrap the wicked on his way.

10. טָמוּן בָּאָרֶץ חַבְלוֹ וּמַלְכֻּדְתּוֹ עֲלֵי נָתִיב — *The rope which will catch him is hidden in the ground, the snare which will hold him lies on his path.* We have inserted, *... which will catch him, which will hold him,* because of the possessive pronouns, *his rope, his snare.*

See *Bildad's Two Speeches* (p. 182) for our analysis of how this section, which discusses the dangers lurking along the road which the wicked man has to take, grows out of the thoughts expressed in Bildad's earlier speech.

11. סָבִיב בִּעֲתֻהוּ בַלָּהוֹת וֶהֱפִיצֻהוּ לְרַגְלָיו — *Specters terrify him on all sides, they beat him to the ground.* The use of בַלָּהוֹת seems to tie this verse to the section which follows (see v. 14) rather than to the foregoing. See further below. See also, at verse 18.

Rashi invariably renders בַּלָּהוֹת with שֵׁדִים, *specters,* whose function it is to harm men. See, for example, *Isaiah* 17:14. He renders וֶהֱפִיצֻהוּ with יְחַבְטוּהוּ, *to smash down. Ramban* prefers to take it as נָפַץ, *to scatter,* in our context, *to break into small pieces.* רַגְלָיו is to be understood, *the place upon which his feet stand.* That is, *the ground.*

12. יְהִי־רָעֵב אֹנוֹ וְאֵיד נָכוֹן לְצַלְעוֹ — *His child will go hungry, catastrophe lies in wait for his wife.* Although אוֹן, in verse 7, clearly meant *strength* (or, as we rendered it, *confidence*), we have translated it here as *child* (taking *Rashi* who gives this interpretation as *p'shat* rather than *d'rash*), since in the context of going hungry, this seems to be the likely meaning. For the same *p'shat* meaning, we may adduce *Proverbs* 11:7.

For the same reason we have used *Rashi's* rendering of צַלְעוֹ as *wife,* although he usually renders this root as *breakage* (*Psalms* 38:18).

13. יֹאכַל בַּדֵּי עוֹרוֹ יֹאכַל בַּדָּיו בְּכוֹר מָוֶת — *He will consume the children born of his body, the Prince of Death will devour his branches.* See commentary to 17:16 that בַּד, which often translates as *branch,* can by extension be readily used for *limbs.* Accordingly, we could well understand the verse to say that the Prince of Death will eventually devour the body [that is, the sum-total of the limbs] of the wicked. However, if that were the case, the verse would be out of place between verses 12 and 14, which both deal with the home-relatives of the wicked man — his wife and his children.

Because of this, *Rashi* chooses to understand בַּדֵּי עוֹרוֹ to refer to the children of the wicked man. In the previous verse, *Rashi* had rendered אֹנוֹ as *child.* Now *Targum,* too, understood the term in this way — but specifies that it refers to the firstborn child — the most immediate manifestation of the father's אוֹן, *strength.* (See *Genesis* 49:3.) Accordingly, the בַּדִּים of our verse would be the younger children — those not included in the threats of the previous verse.

We take עוֹרוֹ, literally *skin,* to stand for *body.* This in accordance with *Rashi* at 2:4, where he renders עוֹר בְּעַד עוֹר as *limb for limb.* Apparently, then, *skin* can be viewed as describing that which it covers — namely, the body.

he will wander onto [a pit covered by] a latticework [of branches].
9 A trap will grab him by the heel, highwaymen will overpower
him. 10 The rope which will catch him is hidden in the ground, the
snare which will hold him lies on his path. 11 Specters terrify him
on all sides, they beat him to the ground. 12 His child will go hungry,
catastrophe lies in wait for his wife. 13 He will consume the
children born of his body, the Prince of Death will devour his
branches. 14 He will be torn from the wife whose bastion he had
been, she will walk him to the King of the Specters. 15 She will dwell
in his tent without him, sulfur will be scattered over his abode.

The second part of the verse is apparently in apposition to the first part. Who will consume *his body's parts*? The *Prince of Death*.

Rashi points out that בְּכוֹר, the base-meaning of which is *first-born*, can also denote someone of high standing, *a prince*. He adduces *Psalms* 89:28. The Prince of Death is the mightiest of all who kill; none can escape him (*Ramban*).

14. יִנָּתֵק מֵאָהֳלוֹ מִבְטַחוֹ וְתַצְעִדֵהוּ לְמֶלֶךְ בַּלָּהוֹת — *He will be torn from the wife whose bastion he had been, she will walk him to the King of the Specters*. The translation follows *Rashi*.

The use of אֹהֶל, *tent*, to describe she who lives in the tent — the wife — recalls R' Yose's statement in *Shabbos* 118b that he would invariably refer to his wife as his *house*! It is the wife who turns the house into the home.

צָעַד means *to take a step*. *Rashi* here takes the word as synonymous with *to send away, to throw out*.

The rendering of מֶלֶךְ בַּלָּהוֹת as *the King of the Specters* accords with *Rashi*. See above, in verse 11.

Ramban renders: He will be torn away from the home in which he had placed his trust; that very trust will, instead of granting him fulfillment, walk him to the King of Specters.

Bildad's view of the house as a bastion in which one can place one's trust, recalls 8:14 where he talked of the disappointment to which the hypocrite is doomed. The fortress in which he had placed his confidence will turn out to have been no stronger than a spider's web.

15. תִּשְׁכּוֹן בְּאָהֳלוֹ מִבְּלִי־לוֹ יְזֹרֶה עַל־נָוֵהוּ גָפְרִית — *She will dwell in his tent without him, sulfur will be scattered over his abode*. The translation follows *Rashi*. The verse refers back to the wife who had been hinted at in the previous verse.

The use of, בְּאָהֳלוֹ, to describe the empty home is particularly poignant when we recall that in the previous verse, the identical word had been used to depict the wife in her capacity of lending content and meaning to her husband's life. The אֹהֶל, which had once been suffused with warm and vibrant personality, will have been reduced to a shell.

We recall that *Ramban* does not read the previous verse as referring to the wife. Accordingly he believes that our verse describes the soul, the life-force of the wicked man. It will live in the tent which — because robbers will have taken it over — is no longer his.

Ramban points out that although the soul is not mentioned specifically in our verse we are expected to fill it in on our own. He adduces *I Samuel* 24:11 where, he believes, the word soul is also left out on the assumption that the reader will supply it.[1]

יְזֹרֶה, in the second half of the verse, is in

1. From the fact that *Ramban* adduces an example of another instance in which the word *nefesh* is left out, it is clear that he regards this as a usage which is specifically associated with that word — not as an example of the Scriptural custom that words which are self-understood are occasionally omitted on the assumption that the reader can supply them on his own.

It is of particular interest that on the verse which *Ramban* adduces, *Rashi* too comments that the word *nefesh* is omitted, and he too adduces another example of this usage — this one from *II Samuel* 13:39.

From this it is clear that *Rashi*, too, believes that the word *nefesh* has its own rules in this regard.

We may consider the following explanation:

The word *nefesh*, when it means *soul*, connotes the essential, vibrant presence which we sense when we are together with another human being. It is not a physical quality — it is clearly absent from one who has died — nor can it be quantified nor measured. But — it is there. It is elusive, but real. It is the humanity within each of us.

David had long been endangered by Saul's hatred. He chanced upon the king while the latter was asleep. He could easily have killed him. But — there was something within him, elusive and intangible, which stayed his hand. Somehow, a surge of mercy welled up within his . . . soul!

The *nefesh* — source of this human feeling — is not identified. As David himself could not clearly define

טז-יז מִתַּחַת שָׁרָשָׁיו יִבָשׁוּ וּמִמַּעַל יִמַּל קְצִירוֹ: זִכְרוֹ־אָבַד מִנִּי־
יח אָרֶץ וְלֹא־שֵׁם לוֹ עַל־פְּנֵי־חוּץ: יֶהְדְּפֻהוּ מֵאוֹר אֶל־חֹשֶׁךְ

the passive, *pu'al* (*R' Meyuchas*).

The structure of the verse seems irregular. We have come to expect a degree of parallelism between the two stiches of any given verse — and here, there seems no connection at all between the first and the second halves of the verse.

An examination of the use of נָוֶה throughout Scripture yields that, overwhelmingly, it tends to describe a home of peace and tranquility. Certainly that is the connotation it has carried so far in the book of *Iyov*, at 5:3 in Eliphaz's speech, and for us more importantly, in Bildad's first speech, at 8:6.

Accordingly, we may suppose that we have here a metaphor within a metaphor. Certainly, even at a simple level, the sulfur being poured out upon the house is not to be taken literally. Rather we have a metaphor for total destruction. But, as we shall demonstrate below, Bildad, in this part of the speech, addresses himself to the essence rather than to the form of the subjects with which he deals. Thus, he may not even mean a physical destruction, but rather, the absolute desolation that surrounds the widow as she ekes out an empty life at the cold hearth of her solitude.

The *naveh* of the wicked man, the tranquil home to which his presence had once lent dignity and meaning — will henceforth be as though laid waste by an avalanche of sulfur. The acrid smell of destruction wafts from every corner of the house which had once been a home.

Based on the analysis which we offer in *Bildad's Two Speeches*, we suggested in the commentary to verse 10 that the section of the traps (vs. 7-10) is an extension of the thoughts which Bildad expressed in verse 13 of his first speech (chapter 8). There he had mused upon the *path* which the wicked must tread, and here Bildad describes vividly just how much danger lurks along that road.

It would seem to follow logically that the next section in this second speech — verses 11-15 which we have now learned — should relate to the other topic with which verse 13 there deals — the frustrated *hope* of the wicked — see commentary there. Indeed, this appears to be the case. There, we identified that *hope* as that which is vested in a man's children — his future. And it is that future which, in Bildad's vivid word-picture, crumbles before our eyes.

Bildad uses exquisite finesse in wielding the knife with which he tears the dreams of the wicked man to shreds. The passage — stylistically unique in his three speeches — is couched in pure poetry, in which always the essence — never the form, is supreme. The children are אוֹנוֹ or בַּדָּיו; the wife, צַלְעוֹ or אָהֳלוֹ; the grave is personified as בְּכוֹר מָוֶת or as מֶלֶךְ בַּלָּהוֹת. Bildad knows well that the dreadful prospect which his words paint, becomes that much more threatening when the elements from which it is formed are reduced to their essence. The son who is to be lost stands for life-power (אוֹן) and future growth (בַּדִּים); the wife who will remain a widow is flesh of your flesh (צֶלַע), the warmth and light of your home (אֹהֶל); the grave — not blessed oblivion, but the trap which delivers you to the vindictive forces of darkness.

16. מִתַּחַת שָׁרָשָׁיו יִבָשׁוּ וּמִמַּעַל יִמַּל קְצִירוֹ — *From beneath, his roots will dry out; above, his branches will be lopped off.* The wicked man is here compared to a tree. He himself is represented by the roots, his children by the branches. He is to die, his children are destined to be destroyed (*Ramban*).

The translation of יִמַּל as . . . *will be lopped off* is based on *Rashi* to *Psalms* 37:2.

what it was that stopped him, so the text does not amplify. We sense the reality of a hidden something. To have explicated it would have been a distortion (*I Samuel* 24:11).

Tragedy had struck David's house. Fratricide had shattered the peace of his family, when, in the wake of Tamar's violation at Amnon's hands, Absalom had caused him to be killed. In disgrace at that bloody act, Absalom fled to his grandfather, Talmay. After three years David found himself longing for his son — whom, in spite of everything, he loved. There was a yearning inside him, something that longed, something that craved, something that filled his entire being. It was a vital force — a *nefesh* — which, in the face of logic which demanded that a murderer not be tolerated, would still not be denied. Perhaps, if David would have been asked outright how he could so love a son who had basely betrayed him, he could not have explained it. Again the *nefesh* was too elusive to be tied down — or to be explicated in the text (*II Samuel* 13:39).

And so it is, here too. It is not the physical presence, now languishing in the house turned prison, which disturbs Bildad in his description of the wicked. It is the life-force — the soul — that which had once pulsated with vibrant energy to imbue every family experience with meaning, which had once turned house into home, and which now still fills every nook and cranny (but in sorrow rather than in joy) — that he bemoans. That intangible presence is felt rather than observed. The text reflects that truth by allowing us to imagine it on our own.

[16] *From beneath, his roots will dry out; above, his branches will
be lopped off.* [17] *His memory will be lost from earth, no fame
for him, abroad.* [18] *They will drive him from light to darkness,*

In itself, the comparison of man to a tree, and his destruction to the cutting off of roots and branches, can be attested from many places — see, for example, *Amos* 2:9 — and poses no problem. However, in the context of Bildad's speech, it seems out of place. At the *Amos* location, indicated above, and as another example at *Psalms* 37:2, the metaphor stands on its own and as such lends vividness and immediacy to the message. Here, however, the death of the wicked and the disintegration of his home and family has received extensive and eloquent treatment in the earlier passage. Moreover, the themes which run through the earlier part of the speech — light and darkness, loss of hope, destruction of the home — are picked up once more immediately after our verse. Thus, the metaphor of the tree here not only seems redundant in that it appears to add no readily apparent dimension to what was said before; it also blatantly interrupts the flow of thoughts which give the speech, as a whole, cohesion and structure.

Clearly, as we suggest in *Bildad's Two Speeches*, we must assume that this word-picture is meant to be a development of the plant metaphor which occupies such an important role in the earlier Bildad speech.

17. זִכְרוֹ־אָבַד מִנִּי־אָרֶץ וְלֹא־שֵׁם לוֹ עַל־פְּנֵי־חוּץ — *His memory will be lost from earth, no fame for him, abroad.* Clearly, this verse is meant as an explanation of the previous one (*Metzudos*).

18. יֶהְדְּפֻהוּ מֵאוֹר אֶל־חֹשֶׁךְ וּמִתֵּבֵל יְנִדֻּהוּ — *They will drive him from light to darkness, hustle him off the earth. Ramban* identifies the subject of יֶהְדְּפֻהוּ as the בַּלָּהוֹת mentioned earlier in the chapter. The *terrors* [or as we rendered according to *Rashi, the specters*] will drive the wicked man from light to darkness.

An analysis of *Ramban's* position lends us insight into the difficult structure of our chapter. *Ramban* can only mean the בַּלָּהוֹת mentioned in verse 11, and this would mean that our verse is a direct continuation of that one. This would place the intervening verses — verses 12-17 — into a kind of parentheses.

This insight, in turn, can help us solve the difficulty of verse 19, which seems redundant in that it appears to add nothing to what has already been said in verses 12-17.

The following chart will illustrate the structure of this whole segment, and we will then attempt to understand it:

11. Specters terrify him on all sides, they beat him to the ground.	
	12. His child will go hungry, catastrophe lies in wait for his wife. 13. He will consume the children born of his body, the Prince of Death will devour his branches. 14. He will be torn from the wife whose bastion he had been, she will walk him to the King of the Specters. 15. She will dwell in his tent without him, sulfur will be scattered over his abode . . . 17. His memory will be lost from earth, no fame for him, abroad.
18. They will drive him from light to darkness, hustle him off the earth. 19. Neither son nor grandson has he among his people, no one remains in his dwelling.	

If we take verses 11,18 and 19 together, they can clearly be read as a cohesive and logically structured unit. Bildad sees the *terrors* banding together to hound the wicked man; they drive him from light to darkness and wreak destruction upon his family. This last, was to be the terrifying end of his dire predictions.

We suggest that Bildad, as he began this vision, was so overwhelmed by the picture of destruction which he was about to paint — we recall from chapter 8 how much the idea of a tranquil home meant to him — that in verses 12-17 he jumped ahead of himself and described that disintegration of the family

יח/יט־כא יט וּמִתֵּבֵל יְנִדֻּהוּ: לֹא נִין לוֹ וְלֹא־נֶכֶד בְּעַמּוֹ וְאֵין שָׂרִיד
כ בִּמְגוּרָיו: עַל־יוֹמוֹ נָשַׁמּוּ אַחֲרֹנִים וְקַדְמֹנִים אָחֲזוּ
כא שָׂעַר: אַךְ־אֵלֶּה מִשְׁכְּנוֹת עַוָּל וְזֶה מְקוֹם לֹא־יָדַע־
יט/א־ב א־ב אֵל: וַיַּעַן אִיּוֹב וַיֹּאמַר: עַד־אָנָה תּוֹגְיוּן

life in detail. Only after he has ended that description can he bring himself to return to his original ideas. He does this at verse 18 and completes the thought as he had planned it.

19. לֹא נִין לוֹ וְלֹא־נֶכֶד בְּעַמּוֹ וְאֵין שָׂרִיד בִּמְגוּרָיו — *Neither son nor grandson has he among his people, no one remains in his dwelling.* In *Bildad's Two Speeches* we have drawn attention to the similarity between the loss of all hope for the future contained in this verse, and the similar thought expressed at 8:18.

See commentary to verse 18 for the relationship between this verse and verses 12, 13 and 17, above.

20. עַל־יוֹמוֹ נָשַׁמּוּ אַחֲרֹנִים וְקַדְמֹנִים אָחֲזוּ שָׂעַר — *The latter ones will be astounded by his fate, the earlier ones are as buffeted by a storm.* In later years people will look back in astonishment at the absolute oblivion which was the fate of the wicked person. The shock-waves of his suffering buffet his contemporaries (thus *Ibn Ezra*), as would a whirlwind.

For שָׂעַר as *storm,* see for example *Ezekiel* 27:35.

21. אַךְ אֵלֶּה מִשְׁכְּנוֹת עַוָּל וְזֶה מְקוֹם לֹא־יָדַע־אֵל — *Such are the dwelling places of the sinner, such the place of him who knows not God.* As at chapter 8, Bildad ends his speech with a glance at the homes of the wicked.

◆§ Bildad's Two Speeches

The structural affinity which we traced above, between Eliphaz's first and second speeches, is not duplicated in Bildad's case. Nevertheless, in terms of its thought-world, its word-pictures and its metaphors, this second of Bildad's speeches stands in total consonance with his first.

Analysis yields the following breakdown:

After the initial, introductory verses (1-4) we can clearly recognize a number of different, but related, themes.

Firstly, there is the picture of *light* turning into *darkness.* This first appears in verses 5 and 6 and is then picked up once more at verse 18. Then, verses 7-11 talk of the *traps* which are strewn along the path of the wicked. Verses 12-15 deal with the disintegration of *family* and the *home,* and this theme is picked up once more in verses 19 and 21. Verses 16 and, perhaps, 17 is based on the metaphor of a *plant,* although this seems out of place within the context of the chapter.

We may begin our analysis by noting the important position which the disintegration of family and home occupies. In the commentary to 8:4 we recognized that in that first speech, there are, within the relatively short space of twenty-one verses, three unconnected references to the home. Moreover, we showed conclusively that in Bildad's mind the idea of *home* is inextricably tied up with children. The home is the place in which the future — vested in one's children — is nurtured. In verse 13, where we learn that, . . . *the hope of the hypocrite is doomed,* we saw that the *hope* is to be defined in terms of the future which every man promises himself — the prolonging and projecting of his own life into that of his progeny. We saw further at verse 18 that the second half of the *metaphor of the reeds* details the terrible finality of the father's frustrated expectations when his children die and drag all that he had hoped to be — through living in them — into the grave: *But, let him uproot it from its place, it will disavow it: I have never seen you!*

There seems little doubt that the many verses which, in this second speech, are devoted to that same theme — see particularly verse 19 as it relates to verse 13 there — constitute a logical extension to those thoughts.

While the theme of change from light to darkness, which plays such a prominent role in this second speech, has no overt anchorage in the earlier one, it does seem that this too belongs to that of home and family. This is made quite clear in verse 6, . . . *in his tent,* and the association is well grounded in the thought-world of *aggadah.* We know, for example, that the Shabbos lights are kindled so that they might increase the *shalom bayis,* the harmony and tranquility which, ideally, informs the spirit of the happy home. When light *in the tent* is plunged into darkness, then the stage is set for the chaos and dislocations which presage total disintegration.

The passage detailing the *traps* which lie in wait for the wicked, also has its source in the earlier speech. Verse 13 there, besides telling that *the hope of the hypocrite is doomed,* talks also of the

18/19-21 *hustle him off the earth.* [19] *Neither son nor grandson has he among*
his people, no one remains in his dwelling. [20] *The latter ones will be*
astounded by his fate, the earlier ones are as buffeted by a storm.
[21] *Such are the dwelling places of the sinner, such the place of him*
who knows not God.

19/1-2 [1] *Iyov responded and said:* [2] *How long will you cause me*

fact that *such are the paths of all those who forget God.* In the commentary there, we worked out that these *paths* refer to the road of life which every man has to travel, and that it is used in contrast to the *hope* of that verse, which deals with his vision of the future as vested in his children. Clearly, our passage elaborates upon this theme, telling how many traps and snares lie along the path which the wicked man has to follow.

The *plant* theme is clearly related to the very thorough treatment given in chapter 8 to the *metaphor of the reeds.*

There are less general points of contact between the two speeches which are noted in the commentary to the individual verses. These, together with the broader themes discussed here, clearly mark this speech as closely related to Bildad's earlier one.

⇐§ Iyov's Response to Bildad's Second Speech

Bildad has not taken Iyov seriously.

He appears to have been totally deaf to the desperate words of the quarry scuttling in a vain search for refuge, driven, at last, to see his hope only in the grave.

For all Bildad seems to have heard, Iyov and the friends might have been arguing a fine point of theology in the quiet halls of academe. He chides Iyov with speaking before he has fully understood all the points which had been made. He feels hurt that the friends are not given the respect which age and wisdom ought to command.

All this, while Iyov is groveling in filth and agony, smarting under the pain of the deserted, learning the terrible solitude of him who finds no answers to his questions, no understanding from those he loves.

And so, Iyov does not even hear Bildad's finely wrought word-picture of the dreadful fate which awaits the wicked. He experiences only his own humiliation. Bildad the ostensible comforter has done nothing but cause Iyov grief, has drained his already depleted reserve of energy with — poetry of the absurd.

And so, in disgust, Iyov once more, in chapter 19, turns inward.

God, he says, has pummeled him physically and mentally; and in the end, worst of all, has driven him into a social exile in which, unloved and unrespected, he stands alone.

In spite of all, he has not lost hope. Never for even one moment does he doubt that there is a benign God, a personal Redeemer, through Whom he will one day find vindication.

But, after the momentary glance toward that beguiling future, he sinks once more into moroseness. His pain is too great. The exultation of the awareness that a light, outside his present reality, is beckoning in the future, gives way to a stultifying preoccupation with the all-pervasive catastrophe of the moment. From the glory of his vision he shrinks into the petulant prediction that punishment will one day overtake his tormentors.

XIX.

We have discussed the structure of Iyov's second round responses in the Introductory Remarks to chapter 16.

While Iyov does not, in this speech, appear to be responding directly to Bildad's thoughts, we can nevertheless trace a perhaps subliminal reaction to them.

Bildad had made much of the utter desolation which would engulf the home of the wicked. He had described the cheerless hearth which would one day succumb to the relentless onslaught of sulfuric disintegration; the forsaken widow, bereft of support or hope; and the fatherless children who, as their own turn comes, would also be uprooted and finally destroyed.

With bitter irony, Iyov proclaims that there is more than one way to destroy a home. I did not have to die, he cries, in order for my world to disintegrate and finally, to fall apart. I am very

ג נַפְשִׁי וּתְדַכְּאוּנַנִי בְמִלִּים: זֶה עֶשֶׂר פְּעָמִים תַּכְלִימוּנִי
ד לֹא־תֵבֹשׁוּ תַּהְכְּרוּ־לִי: וְאַף־אָמְנָם שָׁגִיתִי אִתִּי תָּלִין
ה מְשׁוּגָתִי: אִם־אָמְנָם עָלַי תַּגְדִּילוּ וְתוֹכִיחוּ עָלַי חֶרְפָּתִי:
ו־ז דְּעוּ־אֵפוֹ כִּי־אֱלוֹהַּ עִוְּתָנִי וּמְצוּדוֹ עָלַי הִקִּיף: הֵן אֶצְעַק
ח חָמָס וְלֹא אֵעָנֶה אֲשַׁוַּע וְאֵין מִשְׁפָּט: אָרְחִי גָדַר וְלֹא
ט אֶעֱבוֹר וְעַל־נְתִיבוֹתַי חֹשֶׁךְ יָשִׂים: כְּבוֹדִי מֵעָלַי הִפְשִׁיט
י וַיָּסַר עֲטֶרֶת רֹאשִׁי: יִתְּצֵנִי סָבִיב וָאֵלַךְ וַיַּסַּע כָּעֵץ תִּקְוָתִי:

much alive, wishing only to find comfort in the bosom of my loving family, respect from the members of my household, and strength in the solid, supportive relationships which I have built up within the wider community — and all that is denied me.

As a bitter, rejected outsider, I can observe a society that functions efficiently — without me. Here, indeed, is a living death!

2. עַד־אָנָה תּוֹגְיוּן נַפְשִׁי וּתְדַכְּאוּנַנִי בְמִלִּים — *How long will you cause me grief, drain me with words?* תּוֹגְיוּן is *hiphil* of יָגָה. Thus, *cause to suffer.*

We have previously (4:19, 6:9) rendered דִּכָּא as *to crush,* because the context seemed to require it. However, we note that *Rashi* usually understands the word in the sense, *to weaken.* See, for example, at *Psalms* 90:3. Accordingly, we have chosen to translate here as *drained* — of strength. We feel that this word, projecting as it does a sense of despair and impotence, best expresses the mood which would give rise to the heart-rending cry of verse 21.

The words עַד אָנָה, with which the speech begins, seem to have been chosen in reaction to Bildad's opening salvo. Bildad had started with the challenge, 'How long!' (see commentary to 18:2). Iyov turns the question around, and in the process changes it from a rhetorical to a real one. Why do you not ask yourself, how long will you continue to cause me grief?

3. זֶה עֶשֶׂר פְּעָמִים תַּכְלִימוּנִי לֹא־תֵבֹשׁוּ תַּהְכְּרוּ־לִי — *Ten times have you humiliated me! Are you not ashamed to act as strangers toward me? Rashi* wishes to take the number *ten* literally. Counting Iyov's initial lament, there have been altogether ten speeches up to this point (Iyov, Eliphaz, Iyov, Bildad, Iyov, Tzophar, Iyov, Eliphaz, Iyov, Bildad). The *humiliation* which Iyov suffered when the friends spoke is readily apparent. However, even his own speeches turn out to have been an embarrassment to him, since the friends, evidently preoccupied by and enamored with their own theories, did not even bother to listen to him.

Ramban rejects this interpretation and feels that the number ten is simply chosen to describe a great number of times. As an example of such usage he adduces *Leviticus* 26:26.

We have understood the second half of the verse as a rhetorical question in accordance with *Metzudos.*

הכר does not recur in Scripture. The translation follows *Rashi.*

Ramban adduces *Genesis* 42:7, וַיִּתְנַכֵּר אֲלֵיהֶם, which describes Joseph's actions towards his brothers when he wanted to hide his identity from them. It is interesting to note that *Ramban* there offers two possible explanations. One, that Joseph covered his face with his hat so that they should not recognize him (וַיִּתְנַכֵּר, *he made himself appear to them as a stranger*), and secondly, that he talked roughly to them, as a *stranger* would.

Ramban does not indicate which of the two interpretations he has in mind here. Either would fit the sense of our verse. Iyov could be complaining that he cannot even recognize his former friends. These three self-righteous people were not the kind and caring friends whom he had known. Alternatively, he could be objecting to the mode of speech which the friends had employed. No softness there, no love — only accusatory polemic.

4. וְאַף־אָמְנָם שָׁגִיתִי אִתִּי תָּלִין מְשׁוּגָתִי — *Granted that I may have erred — it is I to whom the results of my folly are constant companions.* The translation follows *Rashi.* תָּלִין is derived from לון, *to stay overnight;* thus, to be in a given place for a long period of time. מְשׁוּגָתִי is to be taken as, . . . *the results* of my folly.

The sense is that Iyov is claiming that even if he were to grant that he had sinned, albeit unwittingly, he has by now been amply punished. There is no reason why the friends should act toward him as though he were still wicked.

Ramban believes that *erred* refers to Iyov's philosophy, not to his actions. I may be wrong in the way that I am thinking, Iyov says, but if I am, my mistakes will stay with me. You

19/3-10 *grief, drain me with words?* 3 *Ten times have you humiliated me!*
Are you not ashamed to act as strangers toward me? 4 *Granted*
that I may have erred — it is I to whom the results of my folly
are constant companions. 5 *Inasmuch as you seek to overwhelm*
me, throwing my disgrace to my face. 6 *Know, that God has*
wronged me, has ringed me around with His siege-works. 7 *See,*
I call out, 'Robbery!' but will not be answered, I scream — but
there is no justice. 8 *He has fenced in my path so that I cannot pass,*
has plunged my road into darkness. 9 *He has stripped me of my*
honor, has taken off my crown. 10 *He has broken me down from all*
sides, and thus I go; has uprooted my hope as one would, a tree.

will never convince me of my errors or instruct me in the truth. You have lost your right to my respect. You are not wise, but foolish.

5-6. אִם־אָמְנָם עָלַי תַּגְדִּילוּ וְתוֹכִיחוּ עָלַי חֶרְפָּתִי — *Inasmuch as you seek to overwhelm me, throwing my disgrace to my face.* דְּעוּ־אֵפוֹ כִּי־אֱלוֹהַּ עִוְּתָנִי וּמְצוּדוֹ עָלַי הִקִּיף — *Know, that God has wronged me, has ringed me around with His siege-works.* Verses 5 and 6 appear to go together, and then, from verse 7 onwards, Iyov demonstrates how *God has wronged* him.

We have translated in accordance with *Ramban*, who renders, ... *seek to overwhelm me* [by your speech].

In the second phrase we have followed *Rashi*. For *Rashi* would render: *While it is you who load me* [*with troubles*]. The next verse should then be rendered: *know that God*, too, *has wronged me* ... For וְתוֹכִיחוּ, which literally means *to demonstrate*, he offers: *You show and demonstrate my disgrace to my face.*

In verse 6, Iyov reverts to the theme that he has been wronged by God. He will elaborate on this in verse 22 where he describes God as one who pursues him. Once more, Iyov appears to teeter on the brink of real blasphemy (see footnote to 9:14, commentary to verses 22-24 there, and in chapter 16, commentary to verses 19 and 20).

מְצוּדָה has a number of different meanings: fortress; trap; net; and siege-works. This latter, at *Koheles* 9:14. We have chosen this rendering because it seems most nearly to give a graphic picture of an implacable enemy who — as Iyov describes below, and as we work out at the end of the commentary to verse 12 — allows no respite to his foe, guiding his attack to any point of vulnerability.

7. הֵן אֶצְעַק חָמָס וְלֹא אֵעָנֶה אֲשַׁוַּע וְאֵין מִשְׁפָּט — *See, I call out, 'Robbery!' but will not be answered, I scream — but there is no justice. Ramban* sees this as an example of the *wrong* which God has done to Iyov, as we learned in the previous verse. It is certainly not fair that Iyov's prayer for redress not be answered.

The text does not explicate which *robbery* Iyov has in mind. From the context it would seem that he is not thinking of the bands of robbers who fell upon his flocks and carried them away, but rather, that his complaint is leveled at God Himself who has 'robbed' him of all that had once made him happy and fulfilled.

8. אָרְחִי גָדַר וְלֹא אֶעֱבוֹר וְעַל־נְתִיבוֹתַי חֹשֶׁךְ יָשִׂים — *He has fenced in my path so that I cannot pass, has plunged my road into darkness.* He has frustrated my every wish. I cannot do anything which I would wish to do (*Metzudos*).

9. כְּבוֹדִי מֵעָלַי הִפְשִׁיט וַיָּסַר עֲטֶרֶת רֹאשִׁי — *He has stripped me of my honor, has taken off my crown.* We cannot know precisely to what כְּבוֹדִי refers. It seems likely, though, that the standing which Iyov had in his community — which is described in graphic detail at 29:8-25 — would be the *honor* to which he refers.

עֲטֶרֶת רֹאשִׁי, literally *the crown of my head*, while idiomatically correct in Hebrew, would be a redundancy in English. Accordingly, we have rendered simply, *my crown*.

10. יִתְּצֵנִי סָבִיב וָאֵלַךְ וַיַּסַּע כָּעֵץ תִּקְוָתִי — *He has broken me down from all sides, and thus I go; has uprooted my hope as one would, a tree. Rashi* and *Ramban* are silent on this verse. *Metzudos* renders: He has smashed [my person — see, for example, *Psalms* 52:7] from all sides, and thus — wounded — I have to make my way through life.

Daas Mikra suggests that the thought expressed here is meant to contrast what had been said in verse 8. There, Iyov had accused God of fencing in his path so that he could go nowhere at all. Here he says that if, perchance, there was some protective fencing around me — He would break it down so that I might the better be able to go toward destruction.

יא־יב וַיִּחַר עָלַי אַפּוֹ וַיַּחְשְׁבֵנִי לוֹ כְצָרָיו: יַחַד ׀ יָבֹאוּ גְדוּדָיו
יג וַיָּסֹלּוּ עָלַי דַּרְכָּם וַיַּחֲנוּ סָבִיב לְאָהֳלִי: אַחַי מֵעָלַי הִרְחִיק
יד וְיֹדְעַי אַךְ־זָרוּ מִמֶּנִּי: חָדְלוּ קְרוֹבָי וּמְיֻדָּעַי שְׁכֵחוּנִי:

According to both interpretations, the second half of the verse would have the same meaning. A tree which is *cut down* can grow once more — there is still hope (14:7); but once it is *uprooted* it can never sprout forth again. Thus the tree, torn out by its roots, becomes the symbol of blighted hopes.

However, neither of these two interpretations allow for any parallelism between the two stiches of the verse. A careful reading of the other verses in this section shows that in every case, the second half of the verse expresses a similar idea to the first. The uprooting of hope seems in no way to parallel either the smashing of the body, nor the breaking down of protective walls.

Perhaps, then — particularly when we recall the sense of alienation which pervades such large parts of this speech — we can understand the sense of this verse as portraying the unanchored wandering of the eternal outsider who has been dislodged from his familiar, non-threatening surroundings.

Both stiches of the verse describe the trauma of dislocation. The first compares Iyov to a structure that has been broken down (as, for example, at *Isaiah* 22:10), the second to a tree which has been uprooted. Both have lost the security which allowed them to function and to flourish.

It is true that, . . . *and thus I go,* seems a poor word-picture for a destroyed building. But clearly, even as Iyov makes liberal use of metaphor, he never allows his own predicament to stray far from the surface of his consciousness.

11. וַיִּחַר עָלַי אַפּוֹ וַיַּחְשְׁבֵנִי לוֹ כְצָרָיו — *He has kindled His anger against me; has considered me His foes. Daas Mikra* notes that וַיִּחַר is in the *hiphil,* causative form. The implication is that God did not really have any reason to be angry with me. He intentionally brought Himself to anger. This would certainly be one of the ways in which, Iyov says, God has *wronged* him (v. 6).

The plural form of *foes* is again noted by *Daas Mikra.* Iyov feels that God is not satisfied with looking upon him as a simple enemy. He regards the hapless Iyov as a conglomeration of all possible enemies.

12. יַחַד יָבֹאוּ גְדוּדָיו וַיָּסֹלּוּ עָלַי דַּרְכָּם וַיַּחֲנוּ סָבִיב לְאָהֳלִי — *Together, His regiments come, making their way against me, encamping around my tent.* Once more we go to *Daas Mikra* for an insightful interpretation. The verse is to be understood as standing in sharp contrast to what is to come. Iyov is isolated and alienated from everyone — except the attacking regiments who, far from distancing themselves from him, are all too eager to approach him from all sides.

[In the footnote to 16:7 we noted a tendency to end a section with a sentence made up of a different number of stiches than the rest of that section. There, we dealt with poems the lines of which were made up of tri-stiches and which ended with a di-stich. If *Daas Mikra's* perception of this verse as the ending of the first section of the speech is correct, then the fact that this verse is a tri-stich is readily understood. The section as a whole is made up of di-stiches. A differently balanced verse would be an appropriate ending.]

We recall *Rashi* at 10:8 describing the worms which were eating away at Iyov's dead skin, as an attacking army. Perhaps here, too, he would understand the *regiments* as a metaphor for these worms.

וַיָּסֹלּוּ is related to the word מְסִילָּה, *path* (*Rashi*).

Before we move to what appears to be the main section of the speech — the tragic litany of rejection piled upon rejection which describes the contours of Iyov's present isolation — we make a further attempt to understand the structure and thrust of the preceding few verses. It seems imperative to find some order in what would, superficially, seem to be a disjointed and unconnected list of complaints.

We will take verses 7-12, one by one, and subject each to a brief analysis [see chart on facing page].

13. אַחַי מֵעָלַי הִרְחִיק וְיֹדְעַי אַךְ־זָרוּ מִמֶּנִּי — *He has driven my brothers away from me, those who knew me have cruelly distanced themselves.* Iyov's social world has collapsed. He has been turned into a pariah, as in universal, instinctive revulsion, more and more of his colleagues have turned their backs upon him.

14. חָדְלוּ קְרוֹבָי וּמְיֻדָּעַי שְׁכֵחוּנִי — *Those close to me have ceased; those whom I have known have forgotten me.* For *have ceased, Metzudos* writes: They have ceased to visit me.

11 *He has kindled His anger against me, has considered me His foes.*
12 *Together, His regiments come, making their way against me, en-*
camping around my tent. 13 *He has driven my brothers away from*
me, those who knew me have cruelly distanced themselves. 14 *Those*
close to me have ceased; those whom I have known have forgotten

7. *See, I call out, 'Robbery!' but will not be answered, I scream — but there is no justice.*	To call out and not be answered erodes the feeling of self-worth which alone can support man in the time of his tribulations. He is being told: Your ideas and feeling are of no value or interest to anyone. Iyov, in particular, has measured his significance by the attention which people paid to what he had to say. To ignore his call is the fastest way to destroy his self.
8. *He has fenced in my path so that I cannot pass, has plunged my road into darkness.*	Iyov has not been able to make himself heard. Does this mean that all communication between him and the outside world is cut off? Perhaps, if instead of calling out, he attempts to go to people, will they listen? This too will not work for him. He is unable to move from his place. He has become truly isolated.
9. *He has stripped me of my honor, has taken off my crown.*	Willy-nilly, Iyov has been forced to stop assessing himself on the basis of his relationship to others. The avenues of communication have been effectively blocked. He must now look inward in order to locate his value as a human being. But — and this he has often remarked earlier — his disgust with his putrid, feverish, worm-ridden body, makes it hard to respect himself. He is left with neither honor nor crown with which to assuage his self-loathing.
10. *He has broken me down from all sides, and thus I go; has uprooted my hope as one would, a tree.*	Even after man is bereft of both honor and crown, there is always the hope of rebirth and rejuvenation as long as there is some anchorage in a familiar and supportive environment. Under such circumstances, life can always reassert itself. But once a person is uprooted from everything which contributed to a positive identity, and is set adrift in a non-knowing, non-caring world, hope and expectations wither and die.
11. *He has kindled His anger against me, has considered me His foes.* 12. *Together, His regiments come, making their way against me, encamping around my tent.*	Not satisfied with denying my humanity by isolating me from any possibility of communication, and then systematically draining from me any sense of self-worth or expectation, God has also decided to attack from without. I am an enemy, nay, I am the sum of all possible enemies, and I must be destroyed. God's regiments will do what my own sense of failure has been unable to accomplish.

13-14. A careful reading of the passage appears to yield a gradual narrowing of concentric circles. The betrayal — as Iyov sees it — moves inward, from the outer rim of distant acquaintances, to the most dreadful moment of all — when his children, flesh of his flesh, blood of his blood, spurn his entreaties.

We begin by examining the relationship between verses 13 and 14:

טו גָּרֵי בֵיתִי וְאַמְהֹתַי לְזָר תַּחְשְׁבֻנִי נָכְרִי הָיִיתִי בְעֵינֵיהֶם:
טז־יז לְעַבְדִּי קָרָאתִי וְלֹא יַעֲנֶה בְּמוֹ־פִי אֶתְחַנֶּן־לוֹ: רוּחִי זָרָה
יח לְאִשְׁתִּי וְחַנֹּתִי לִבְנֵי בִטְנִי: גַּם־עֲוִילִים מָאֲסוּ בִי אָקוּמָה
יט וַיְדַבְּרוּ־בִי: תִּעֲבוּנִי כָּל־מְתֵי סוֹדִי וְזֶה־אָהַבְתִּי נֶהְפְּכוּ־
כ בִי: בְּעוֹרִי וּבִבְשָׂרִי דָּבְקָה עַצְמִי וָאֶתְמַלְּטָה בְּעוֹר שִׁנָּי:

13. He has driven my brothers away from me, those who knew me have cruelly distanced themselves.	14. Those close to me have ceased; those whom I have known have forgotten me.

The two verses appear to parallel one another: *Brothers — Those close to me*, and, *those who knew me — those whom I have known.*

Let us begin by examining the first relationship: אָח, which often translates as *brother*, is also used to describe people who are close to one another in other ways. See, for example, *Genesis* 31:37. In *Proverbs* 27:10 the word is used disparagingly to describe how the אָח may often be unreliable in a pinch, and that a neighbor who is *close* is to be much preferred to him.

Accordingly, we may safely assume that the *brothers* of verse 13 are further removed from Iyov, than *those close to me* of verse 14.

For the second relationship we note as follows: יוֹדְעַי of verse 13 derives from the *kal*, יָדַע, and means, *those who knew me*. On the other hand, מְיֻדָּעַי, of verse 14, derives from the *pual, to be known*, hence *those who were known by me*. We may safely assume that the ones who knew Iyov, but whom apparently Iyov did not know, are people who moved in his orbit but whom he was not interested in knowing.

Thus, it seems reasonable to assume that verse 13 deals with the outer rings of Iyov's acquaintanceship, people with whom there was contact but no intimate relationship. Verse 14 moves closer and leads into verse 15.

There we have those guests to whom Iyov had extended hospitality, and his maid-servants. Certainly these are closer to him than the general community with which he came into contact, but they are not as close as the man-servant described in verse 16.

Verse 17 then goes on to Iyov's wife, and from there to his children — his own flesh and blood.

We may discern the same pattern in the next section which describes, first the distancing of the youngsters (v. 18), and only then that of the intimates (v. 19) with whom Iyov used to confer.

We have rendered the second phrase, ... *have cruelly distanced themselves*, in accordance with *Rashi*. He picks up the phonetic relationship between אַךְ זָרוּ and the word אַכְזָר, meaning *cruel*.

15. גָּרֵי בֵיתִי וְאַמְהֹתַי לְזָר תַּחְשְׁבֻנִי נָכְרִי הָיִיתִי בְעֵינֵיהֶם — *My very guests, even my very maid-servants — have come to consider me a stranger, I am an outsider in their eyes.* Iyov had always prided himself upon his hospitality. His house had ever been open to those who wished to enter (31:32); indeed, his household would resent the extra work which his ever-willingness to grant shelter to the needy imposed upon them (31:31). *Avos d'R' Nasan* 7:1 tells how he had entrances on all four sides of his house in order that the poor would not have to go to the trouble of walking around to find the door. Moreover, it was his practice to offer each guest such fare as he was used to at home. Those in the habit of eating meat were served meat, those who would drink wine at home were offered wine.

He was a just master. Neither servant nor handmaid ever needed to fear that their just claims would be ignored (31:13).

But — for this very reason — there is a special bitterness when these beneficiaries of his largess and his sense of justice, turn the tables and regard him as a stranger in his own home.

16. לְעַבְדִּי קָרָאתִי וְלֹא יַעֲנֶה בְּמוֹ־פִי אֶתְחַנֶּן־לוֹ — *I called to my servant — he will not answer, even though I beg him with words.* A very special intimacy can develop between master and servant (*Berachos* 24b). Still — it is certainly the master who issues orders, the servant who obeys. It must cost a master dearly when he has to admit that he needs his servant's fellowship. Certainly, when it reaches a point at which hints are not enough, and he must actually beg for a kind word.

17. רוּחִי זָרָה לְאִשְׁתִּי וְחַנֹּתִי לִבְנֵי בִטְנִי — *My breath is abhorrent to my wife, I have to ingratiate myself to my children.* We have

19/15-20 *me.* 15 *My very guests, even my very maid-servants — have come*
to consider me a stranger, I am an outsider in their eyes. 16 *I called*
to my servant — he will not answer, even though I beg him with
words. 17 *My breath is abhorrent to my wife, I have to ingratiate*
myself to my children. 18 *Even youngsters despise me; I rise and*
they talk against me. 19 *My intimates look upon me with disgust,*
those that I loved have turned against me. 20 *My bones cling to my*
skin and my flesh, I have escaped with only the gums of my teeth.

used *Radak* in *Sefer HaShorashim,* for רוּחַ. *Rashi* is silent, and *Ramban* is not completely clear. He talks about Iyov's appearance which, because of his sickness, sickens those who see him. Perhaps he, too, understands the word as does *Radak,* and the sense according to both of them is that the bad smell of Iyov's breath is abhorrent to his wife.

R' Meyuchas takes רוּחִי as *personality*: My ideas and my speech seem distant from my wife — she refuses to accept them.

Metzudos understands the word to refer to Iyov's *desires* for conjugal relations: She does not respond to his wants even though he *entreats her so that he might have children* [*Metzudos's* understanding of the second phrase in this verse].

The *children* of the second half of the verse present some difficulties: All Iyov's children had been killed in the disaster described in chapter 1. *Rashi's* solution is to take *children* metaphorically — those whom I have raised in my house as though they were my children. *Ramban* suggests either: Even if I had children I would have to ingratiate myself to them, or that Iyov means grandchildren. It is quite possible that Iyov's sons already had children and that these grandchildren were not killed together with their parents.

18. גַּם־עֲוִילִים מָאֲסוּ בִי אָקוּמָה וַיְדַבְּרוּ־בִי — *Even youngsters despise me; I rise and they talk against me.* At 16:11, we took עֲוִילִים as *enemies,* based on *Ramban* there. Here he, together with most commentators [but *R' Meyuchas* renders, *the wicked*] takes the word to mean *youngsters* as at 21:11.

The sense of the verse is that Iyov has lost all respect even among the untried youngsters [and certainly among the princes of the realm (*Rashi*)], so that even when he rises in order to do them honor, they make fun of him, paying no heed at all to the respect which he is showing them (*Metzudos*).

19. תִּעֲבוּנִי כָּל־מְתֵי סוֹדִי וְזֶה־אָהַבְתִּי נֶהְפְּכוּ־בִי — *My intimates look upon me with disgust, those that I loved have turned against me.* מְתֵי means *men.* סוֹד may mean either *secret* or *company.* Either meaning would make good sense in this context: We could understand the phrase as describing either the men with whom, in the past, Iyov had shared his secrets, or those with whom he had kept company. *Targum* takes the word in the former meaning.

The וְזֶה in the second stich is difficult. *Metzudos* has it refer to the people who are standing around listening to Iyov. These very people who are listening, and whom I used to love, have now turned against me.

20. בְּעוֹרִי וּבִבְשָׂרִי דָּבְקָה עַצְמִי וָאֶתְמַלְּטָה בְּעוֹר שִׁנָּי — *My bones cling to my skin and my flesh, I have escaped with only the gums of my teeth.* Iyov's entire body was filled with the sores of his leprosy and the worms which fed upon his wasted, dying skin. Only his gums were free from the incursions of his sickness (*Rashi*).

After the litany of soured relationships which has been the subject of the last few verses, we would have expected verse 21, the desperate call for fellowship, to follow immediately.

Why then does this verse, which seems not to be related at all, come in the middle?

Perhaps it is meant to describe the ultimate alienation. Even once a person has lost all social contact, he is not yet, necessarily, entirely alone. He can, as it were, step outside his own skin, look upon himself objectively, be pleased with what he sees, and derive at least some comfort from the fact that here is a worthwhile person with whom he, the essential personality, can identify. If he is alone in the social sense, there is still a sense of companionship with a personality projected into reality by memories and present perceptions.

Iyov looks upon his physical emaciation as a metaphor for an inner wasting. I — my real essential being — am totally alone. I am — both physically, emotionally and spiritually — a bag of skin and bones. There is nothing left of me, nothing to which I can relate, nothing to give me even a modicum of comfort!

כא־כב חָנֻּנִי חָנֻּנִי אַתֶּם רֵעָי כִּי יַד־אֱלוֹהַּ נָגְעָה בִּי: לָמָּה תִּרְדְּפֻנִי
כג כְמוֹ־אֵל וּמִבְּשָׂרִי לֹא תִשְׂבָּעוּ: מִי־יִתֵּן אֵפוֹ וְיִכָּתְבוּן מִלָּי
כד מִי־יִתֵּן בַּסֵּפֶר וְיֻחָקוּ: בְּעֵט־בַּרְזֶל וְעֹפָרֶת לָעַד בַּצּוּר
כה יֵחָצְבוּן: וַאֲנִי יָדַעְתִּי גֹּאֲלִי חָי וְאַחֲרוֹן עַל־עָפָר יָקוּם:

21. חָנֻּנִי חָנֻּנִי אַתֶּם רֵעַי כִּי יַד־אֱלוֹהַּ נָגְעָה בִּי — *O Pity me, pity me, you who are my friends; for the hand of God has afflicted me.* חָנֻּנִי from חֵן, *favor*, from which חִנָּם, *without cost*, is built (*Radak, Sefer HaShorashim*). Thus, the sense of the word is, a free granting of favor — neither deserved nor to be requited. In our context the meaning is clear. I have nothing left at all, nothing which might be attractive to you, nothing from which you would stand to make any gain. Even so, I dare to throw myself upon your mercy because I am totally alone. Out of desperation I beg you for your freely bestowed kindness.

Or, perhaps not.

The correct interpretation of this verse will depend upon our understanding of the relationship in which it stands to the next; *Why do you pursue me ...* If we are correct that in our verse Iyov is asking for freely bestowed kindness, then the next verse is a fall-back position. Sure that the friends will not heed his cry, he begs them at least not to pursue him. If they will not be his friends, let them, at least, not be his enemies.

There is, though, the possibility that verse 22 is to be understood as an explanation of our's. Iyov's entreaty that the friends show him mercy may well focus on the rhetorical question with which he challenges them there: 'Have mercy upon me, my friends. Ask yourselves why you pursue me so!'

If this is the case, Iyov's expectations are much more narrow than we had thought.

Now that Iyov is reduced to this heart-rending plea for understanding, it is appropriate for us to review, briefly, the various postures which he has taken towards the friends from the time of their arrival.

We have noted again and again that we ought not to expect consistency in the ideas which this torn and broken man wrests from the turmoil of his agony. Thus, for example, his troubled and ambivalent feelings about God. We have observed Iyov in moments of the darkest despair during which God appeared to him as an implacable and cruel enemy; and seen him, too, exulting in passionate adoration of Him Who, without any doubt, will ultimately prove to be both refuge and vindicator.

Thus, we will not be surprised if the feelings which animate his attitude toward the friends are also marked by wildly gyrating ambivalence.

Iyov first allows resentment to spill over into his speeches in chapter 6. There, we have the metaphor of the faithless river, in which he castigates the friends — albeit only in the third person — for disloyalty and insensibility. Then, from verses 21 till verse 27 he turns his anger at them directly, accusing them of real cruelty. Nevertheless, once his fury is spent, he tries, from verse 28 onwards, to cajole them to be reasonable.

In chapter 8, verses 20-22, we hear from Bildad's mouth how Iyov had come to regard the former friends as bitter foes. When in the end he would be vindicated, he would be able to gloat over the destruction which would overtake them.

In chapter 12, verses 2-4, we find Iyov derisive and sarcastic. He mocks the friends for the sanctimonious blandness and predictability of their ideas, and seeks comfort in the thought that surely God would eventually vindicate him.

At chapter 13, verses 4-12, Iyov takes the friends to task for the irresponsibility with which they undertake their self-ordained task of playing advocate for God. Far from explaining the seemingly inexplicable, they seem to suggest that He is capable of wickedness and deceit.

At chapter 16, verses 11 and 20, Iyov accuses the friends of buffoonery and sophistry. Throughout chapter 17, he continues to portray them negatively: in verse 2, as mockers; in verse 4, as obtuse; in verse 5, as glib talkers; in verse 10, as lacking wisdom; and in verse 12, as people who hound him, turning his life to misery.

In verses 2-3, and then again in verse 5 of our own chapter, the litany of accusations continues: The friends are bullies who should feel ashamed of their disloyalty and cruel insensitivity.

In spite of all these negative perceptions, Iyov now — in desperation — calls upon the friends to have mercy on him. He realizes that after all, they are the only ones to whom he can turn.

We recall from the commentary to chapter 2 that in the view of the Sages, Eliphaz, Bildad and Tzophar serve as paradigms for what, ide-

21 O pity me, pity me, you who are my friends; for the hand of
God has afflicted me. 22 Why do you pursue me, as does God?
Are you not satisfied with my flesh? 23 Would that my words
could be written down, would that they could be hewn into a
record. 24 With an iron stylus and with lead, permanently
engraved in rock. 25 But, I know that my Redeemer lives, as
the very last one He will remain, beyond the dwellers on earth.

ally, friends should be: Let a man choose death, *Rava* taught, unless he has friends such as those which Iyov had. In *The First Round,* we wondered at this assessment. Manifestly, their efforts at comforting Iyov were a sad and total failure. They displayed none of the empathy which we would have expected from men who are truly driven by love. If so, why make an issue of the closeness of the original relationship. It helped not at all, so why is it significant?

Our passage may help. We have here a cry welling up from the deepest recesses of the heart. Clearly, in spite of the fierce savaging of past speeches, there is still a solid core of love which has remained untouched. Iyov's mind has weighed the friends' performance and found it trite, thoughtless and ineffective; but his soul still craves their companionship and understanding. This, *Rava* feels, is true friendship: a bonding which will not allow itself to become dislodged by even the buffeting of bitter disappointment.

22. לָמָּה תִּרְדְּפֻנִי כְמוֹ־אֵל וּמִבְּשָׂרִי לֹא תִשְׂבָּעוּ — *Why do you pursue me, as does God? Are you not satisfied with my flesh?* The translation of the first phrase follows *Ramban* and *Metzudos.*

אֵל is God, and the tone is ironic: Do you believe that it is necessary to follow God's lead in the way you treat me? Is it not enough that He wrongs me?

R' Saadyah Gaon and *Ralbag* take אֵל as though it were written אֵלֶּה, *these.* Reference is to the *youngsters* of verse 18. Why do you pursue me as they do?

We have followed *Metzudos* in rendering the second phrase: Are you not satisfied with the agonies which I bear in my flesh? Must you add to my suffering?

Daas Mikra suggests a different rendering for the second half of the verse: *My flesh will not satisfy you.* The phrase is a metaphor and imagines an animal pleading with the hunter: There is no reason for you to pursue me so that you can use me for food. I am thin and puny, and will never be able to satisfy your hunger.

23-24. מִי־יִתֵּן אֵפוֹ וְיִכָּתְבוּן מִלָּי מִי־יִתֵּן בַּסֵּפֶר וְיֻחָקוּ — *Would that my words could be written down, would that they could be hewn into a record.* בְּעֶט־בַּרְזֶל וְעֹפָרֶת לָעַד בַּצּוּר יֵחָצְבוּן — *With an iron stylus and with lead, permanently engraved in rock.* There should be a permanent record of my words because, although you refuse to understand me, there will be others who will find it in their hearts to pity me (*Ramban*).

We may perhaps surmise that Iyov has a different thought in mind. At 16:3 he had accused the friends of talking *wind-words,* in response to Eliphaz's accusation at 15:13 that Iyov's ideas were *wind-thoughts.* These expressions evoke images of flightiness and impermanence — thoughts and words which ought not to be preserved.

By contrast, Iyov claims that his ideas are substantial and inviolable. They should be preserved for posterity because they proclaim significant truths.

We have rendered סֵפֶר as *record* rather than as book, in accordance with *Daas Mikra* who adduces archaeological evidence for the usage of סֵפֶר to describe engraved writing. Given the legitimacy of such a rendering, it appears likely that the בַּסֵּפֶר of our verse should be read as paralleling the בַּצּוּר of the next.

We have rendered *... and with lead,* in accordance with *Rashi.* He reasons that it is not the pen or stylus that is made from lead, since that would be too soft to make an impression in rock. Rather the lead is used to blacken the letters which were first engraved into the rock by means of an iron stylus.

25. וַאֲנִי יָדַעְתִּי גֹּאֲלִי חָי וְאַחֲרוֹן עַל־עָפָר יָקוּם — *But, I know that my Redeemer lives, as the very last one He will remain, beyond the dwellers on earth. Rashi* believes that this verse begins with a *vav,* so that it be read as a continuation of verse 22: You may well be pursuing me, Iyov says, but I know that I have a Redeemer, one Who will, one day, punish you. The passage of time is no problem for Him, for He will continue to be long after all of mankind [those that *dwell on earth*] will have ceased to exist.

Ramban ties this verse to the two previous ones. Iyov had yearned that his words might be engraved in stone. Surely, he had reasoned, the future must bring someone who would be sym-

כו־כז וְאַחַר עוֹרִי נִקְּפוּ־זֹאת וּמִבְּשָׂרִי אֶחֱזֶה אֱלוֹהַּ: אֲשֶׁר אֲנִי ׀
כח אֶחֱזֶה־לִּי וְעֵינַי רָאוּ וְלֹא־זָר כָּלוּ כִלְיֹתַי בְּחֵקִי: כִּי תֹאמְרוּ

pathetic to his cause. But — reality pays little heed to wishful dreamings. No one is engraving his words in stone, and his case, he knows, will likely die with him; there can be little expectation that his vindication will come from man. Rather, he realizes now, his hope lies with his Redeemer — God, eternal, Who must in the end reveal the truth.

Once more we are confronted with a shocking change of mood. In verses 6-13 we have unbridled invective, in which bitterness brims over into blasphemous recrimination; and here with no bridge to span the chasm, we have lyric affirmation of unbounded trust and adoration.

We have discussed a similar phenomenon at 16:19. See further in commentary to verse 27.

There does, however, appear to be a progression between what Iyov said in his response to Eliphaz at 16:19, and what he says here as he reacts to Bildad's speech. There, he spoke of God as his *witness*, here as his *redeemer*. The two are different. The witness stands, dispassionately, to the side, important and useful to the accused, but uninvolved. The redeemer deals with people — not with facts. He saves, rather than informs.

Apparently, as Iyov becomes more and more disappointed in his friends, he turns to God — the only One in Whom he can place his trust — with ever-increasing intensity.

26. וְאַחַר עוֹרִי נִקְּפוּ־זֹאת וּמִבְּשָׂרִי אֶחֱזֶה אֱלוֹהַּ — *But — they cut away at my skin. From out of my flesh I must behold God.* We have translated according to *Rashi*, although it is difficult to see how his rendering accounts for the two words, וְאַחַר and זֹאת which complicate the syntax of this verse.

The subject of the verse, in this view, are the friends. In the previous verse Iyov had summoned them to contemplate the inevitable outcome of their cruelty: justice would catch up with them, there is a Redeemer Who would one day avenge Iyov's suffering. They continue hounding Iyov, cutting away at his skin, so that from his very flesh — from the agonies which rack his poor body — he is forced to come to grips with the stern image of God as a strict, unbending judge.

At *Isaiah* 10:34 and 17:6, *Rashi* renders נִקֵּף as *to cut off*.

Ramban thinks that the subject of the verse is the dreadful sickness that is plaguing Iyov, and which, not satisfied with disfiguring his skin, eats away behind it (אַחַר), attacking the flesh which is invisible to the eye. Iyov is pointing to some putrid flesh or bone (זֹאת), and saying: 'See! Even this, deep inside me, is dying, being slashed by my agonies. Under such circumstances, surely, only the Redeemer of the previous verse can help me.'

From this insight, Iyov moves to a lyric paean of praise to this God, Who — in spite of everything — will prove to be his salvation: From my flesh I will behold God!

The meaning, as *Ramban* understands it, is as follows: My body is slowly dying — and yet, I am alive! My very flesh, rotting inside me, testifies to an all-powerful God, Who can take man to the very brink of destruction — and yet . . . grant life!

27. אֲשֶׁר אֲנִי אֶחֱזֶה־לִּי וְעֵינַי רָאוּ וְלֹא־זָר כָּלוּ כִלְיֹתַי בְּחֵקִי — *It is I who beholds. My eyes — not those of a stranger — see. My kidneys, within me, are no more. Rashi* is silent on this verse. It seems likely — and this is borne out by the use of אֶחֱזֶה, as in verse 26 — that we have a continuation of what was said in the previous verse. There, Iyov had bemoaned the fact that he had been forced to apprehend the stern punishing face of God from out of his own flesh. Here he develops this theme.

A careful analysis of the entire passage from verse 25 through the end of this chapter will, we think, yield the correct understanding of the point which Iyov is making in this verse. Moreover, it will allow us insights into one of the most perplexing issues in the Iyov saga — his complex relationship to God which, as we have seen, seems to vacillate between surly hostility and the most exalted heights of exulting adoration.

First, then, let us see what our verse appears to be saying, and then we shall try to gauge its significance within the larger context.

In the previous verse Iyov bemoaned the fact that he had been forced, by his own flesh, to meet up with the God of justice. Our verse stresses the profound impact which this apprehension must have had upon him. The sense is: My perception of the God of justice came about not through hearsay but through experience. It has been sharply etched into my consciousness. It has become the great reality of my religious ethos. I have paid dearly for this perception. My very kidneys were destroyed in the process.

What does this mean in the context of the passage?

We will briefly paraphrase the verses from verse 25 through verse 28:

[26] *But — they cut away at my skin. From out of my flesh I must be-*
hold God. [27] *It is I who beholds. My eyes — not those of a stranger*
— see. My kidneys, within me, are no more. [28] *Do you ever say,*

25. There is a Redeemer who will one day exact payment for the wrongs which the friends have done me.
26. [a] The friends refuse to consider the existence of this Redeemer.
    [b] Through my suffering I have learned to know the God of justice.
27. My knowledge of the God of justice is deeply ingrained within my religious consciousness. It cost me dearly.
28. You, my friends do not pause for even a moment to wonder whether you are right in pursuing me, whether, indeed, I am deserving of my agonies.

The sense of the passage appears to be as follows: Iyov wishes to demonstrate a contrast — in his favor — between himself and the friends.

There would have been every reason to believe — indeed the logic of human nature would have demanded — that Iyov's bitter experiences at God's hands (26b and 27) would have blocked out any belief in, or relationship to, a God of love and caring. Nevertheless, Iyov proudly points out, I have not permitted my outlook and religious standards to become jaundiced. I know that in spite of everything, God is still my Redeemer (v. 25), and that through Him I will ultimately be vindicated.

By contrast, you, my friends, who have suffered nothing at all, are nevertheless so hidebound in your beliefs that not only do you refuse to countenance the reality of my Redeemer (26a), but you refuse me even the common decency of examining your motives and actions (v. 28).

Given this interpretation of the passage we have the key to the apparent ambivalence in Iyov's relationship to God. Indeed he resents — and, indeed, he loves! There is the Redeemer — and there is the God of justice — and Iyov reacts differently to each.

This concept require careful elucidation.

Commentators who have grappled with the dissonances between Iyov the petulant malcontent, and Iyov the exalted visionary of God's love, have sought insight from the famous passage in *Ibn Gabirol's, Keser Malchus*:

> If the burden of my sin is too great, O Lord, How will You protect Your glorious Name?
>
> If I may not hope for Your mercies From whom, beside You, can I expect pity?
>
> And so, were You to kill me I would still yearn for You,
>
> Were You to search out my sin, I would flee *from You to You,*
>
> Seeking protection *from You, in Your shadow.*

From You to You! There lies the secret. From the God of Justice, to the loving caring Redeemer.

But — there is a difference. Not in *Ibn Gabirol*, nor in any other source, do we find even a trace of Iyov's truculent resentment. Awe and fear, goads to seek protection at the hands of the God of Love from the God of Justice — yes. But, never the belligerent rejection which we find in Iyov's speeches.

Here, once more, we may have a confirmation of the thesis which we propounded in the footnote to 1:3 and again in the footnote to 6:2, and throughout the book — that Iyov is to be seen as paradigm of the non-Jewish, this-worldly servant of God, the man of מַה כְּתִיב בָּהּ (*what is written in it*) more than the man of נַעֲשֶׂה וְנִשְׁמַע (*unquestioning obedience*) [see also footnote 1:1].

The first of the Ten Commandments reads: *I am HASHEM your God Who took you out of the land of Egypt.* To this, *Rashi* remarks: Because at the sea God appeared to them as a warrior engaged in battle, and here, as an elder, full of mercy ... since I appear to you in various guises, do not say: 'There are two authorities.' I [Who appear to you now as the elder] and He Who took you out of Egypt [and was with you] at the sea [in the guise of the warrior, are one].

The lesson that all our perceptions of God, in the various guises in which He chooses to reveal Himself to us, are to be subsumed under one absolute and indivisible oneness is a lesson which was taught at Sinai — to Israel. In this mode it would be inconceivable that anyone could rail against the God of Justice while adoring the God of Love. The most radical formulation of the idea that God indeed reveals Himself to us in different ways, would be the one which *Ibn Gabirol*, in his consummate poetry, bequeathed to us.

However, for Iyov, this idea would not be as clear. One who did not stand at Sinai would have an entirely more ambivalent attitude toward a God Who sometimes appears as a warrior and sometimes as an elder, sometimes as a strict and unbending judge and sometimes as a loving father.

כט מַה־נִּרְדָּף־לוֹ וְשֹׁרֶשׁ דָּבָר נִמְצָא־בִי: גּוּרוּ לָכֶם ׀
מִפְּנֵי־חֶרֶב כִּי־חֵמָה עֲוֺנוֹת חָרֶב לְמַעַן תֵּדְעוּן
שַׁדּוּן ק׳
°שדין:
א־ב וַיַּעַן צוֹפַר הַנַּעֲמָתִי וַיֹּאמַר: לָכֵן

28. כִּי תֹאמְרוּ מַה־נִּרְדָּף־לוֹ וְשֹׁרֶשׁ דָּבָר נִמְצָא־בִי — *Do you ever say, 'Why do we pursue him?' What are the causes which lie within me?* See commentary to previous verse. Iyov is taxing the friends with inexcusable obduracy. It does not even occur to them to examine their motives, or indeed, to wonder why Iyov should be suffering so much. This, in contrast to himself, who has not allowed his agony to blind him to a God of love — One Who will, in the end, be his Redeemer.

29. גּוּרוּ לָכֶם מִפְּנֵי־חֶרֶב כִּי־חֵמָה עֲוֺנוֹת חָרֶב לְמַעַן תֵּדְעוּן שַׁדּוּן — *Tremble before the sword, for your sins generate the fury of the sword — so that you may know, punishment!* The friends' obduracy will bring terrible punishment in its wake. *Leviticus* 26:25 speaks of an *avenging sword, avenging the breaking of a covenant,* and it is of just such disloyalty that the friends are guilty (*Daas Mikra*).

On שַׁדּוּן we follow *Rashi* who, in accordance with the way the word is read (קְרִי), renders פּוּרְעָנוּת, *punishment* or *reprisal.* The friends would find out the severity with which wrongdoing is visited. Indeed, at the end of the book, after Iyov has won vindication, God commands him to bring sacrifices for the friends. The implication is clear. Without atonement they would be destroyed.

However, *Rashi* points out that the way the word is written (כְּתִיב), שַׁדִּין, can also be fitted well into the text. דין is *justice,* and the phrase is rendered, *So that you may know that there is justice in the world.* Your sins will not go unrequited.

XX.

◆§ Tzophar's Second Speech

Tzophar does not, in this speech, intend to introduce any new ideas. Rather, he wishes to describe in the most graphic terms the inevitable destruction of the wicked. There is, after all, no need for any of the friends to add any new arguments — each has already offered his thoughts to Iyov. Therefore they do nothing other than describe the downfall of the wicked and of their descendants.

Thus, *Ramban.*

There is, however, something very special in this speech: It is Tzophar's farewell to Iyov. In the third round, he will be silent.

On what note does Tzophar make his exit? What final impression does he wish to leave with Iyov?

Certainly, it is very different from the farewells which each of the other two friends will make in the third round.

Eliphaz (ch. 22) will lash into Iyov with unprecedented fury, project him as an ogre capable of the utmost depravity, and then tantalize him with the beauty of what the future can hold for him — if he repents. He has not lost sight of his original purpose. He means to guide Iyov through the valley of his travail. His assessment of his erstwhile friend has changed, but according to his own lights, he has remained loyal and caring.

Bildad (chapter 25) will ignore Iyov completely. He will lose himself in an ecstatic vision of the heavenly grandeur which is God's. He has little use for anything else. He makes his departure with the final thought that man is no more than rottenness, is indeed no better than the worm. Perhaps he meant this to be a comfort to Iyov, or perhaps he had forgotten him.

And what of Tzophar?

We may surmise that Tzophar wishes to leave Iyov with the gift of simple unassuming friendship. In the Introductory Remarks to this chapter we shall see that he has already distanced himself from the group. He has renounced his formal role as mentor to his stricken friend. He eschews both the bombast of Eliphaz's accusations and the irrelevance of Bildad's rapture. He speaks as an individual who has some significant thoughts to share. He has observed, he has cogitated, and he has reached the conclusion that there is justice and order in the world.

He will leave Iyov with this thought.

19/29 *'Why do we pursue him?' What are the causes which lie within me? [29] Tremble before the sword, for your sins generate the fury of the sword — so that you may know, punishment!*

20/1-2 [1] *Tzophar the Naamathite responded and said: [2] Therefore*

Ramban remarks that Tzophar presents no new ideas in this speech. It is no more than a lyric description of the devastation that will overtake the wicked.

That is true in a strictly literal sense. It does seem that Tzophar says nothing that has not, in one form or another, been said before.

Nevertheless, the two introductory verses create a unique ambience, and this infuses the ideas expressed in the rest of the speech with a flavor all of their own.

We have noted earlier that the second speeches of both Eliphaz and Bildad have obvious, and clearly intended, ties to their earlier ones. It is impossible to detect any affinity between Tzophar's two speeches, either in structure or content.

Are we to assume that we have here a break in this carefully nurtured and eminently reasonable pattern? How are we to understand Tzophar if there is to be no traceable system to his thought?

Tzophar is unique among the friends in that in the third round he is completely silent. His second speech is his last. This places him on the opposite pole to Eliphaz, whose third speech achieves an obvious escalation from his two previous ones, but it does not make him so very different from Bildad. For Bildad, while he does speak in the third round, says very little indeed, and that on a different plane than any of the earlier speeches. His speech is no more than a very short paean of praise to God.

It would appear that, at least as regards these two, Iyov's impassioned plea for mercy in his last speech has left a mark. Both, but especially Tzophar, have some regrets, and these contour their speeches and their silences.

An analysis of Tzophar's two introductory verses yields some remarkable insights:

1. On all previous occasions the friends justified their involvement on the basis that Iyov's fulminations called for a response: Eliphaz, 4:2; 15:2. Bildad, 8:2; 18:2. Tzophar, 11:2. Eliphaz, and only he, uses a similar opening in his third-round speech at 22:2. Here it is Tzophar's own cogitations, not Iyov's errors, which force his involvement.
2. The friends, an occasional use of the first person notwithstanding, look upon themselves as a group. Eliphaz: *What can you know that* **we** do not know (15:9). Bildad: *Why should* **we** *be considered as cattle . . .* (18:3). The brief justificatory remarks at the beginning of the various speeches are always couched in general terms: Someone ought to respond to Iyov. Here Tzophar talks in the first person. He is apparently speaking for himself, not as representative of the group.
3. Particularly significant is Tzophar's reference to *my silence* (v. 2). What is this silence which rankles within him?

It would appear that this silence foreshadows his retirement from the debate in the next round. Iyov's pathetic entreaties of the previous chapter have engulfed him with a deep feeling of shame — the sense of his earlier, unfeeling self-righteousness lacerates him and forces silence upon him. He has already disassociated himself from the group. He wants no more part in their insensitivity. If he speaks at all — and this time for himself — it will be only because, in spite of the self-imposed silence which must from now on remove him from the stage, there is still one more thought which he must share. His insights will out, they force themselves to his lips.

Bildad has been similarly affected. He too wants out. He will still speak in the third round, but not from a sense of outrage, and not, as in his previous speeches, as a purveyor of ideas similar to those expressed by Eliphaz. It is more in the sense of a gentle farewell to Iyov, a loving exhortation to look upward rather than inward.[1]

---

1. The insight that both Bildad and Tzophar allowed themselves to be softened by Iyov's impassioned outburst can help us to understand two difficult passages:

1. Verses 4-6 in Bildad's last speech (chapter 25) are a repetition of the vision which Eliphaz had reported in his first speech. Why would Bildad repeat — without benefit of a Divine revelation — what Eliphaz had, on higher authority, already said?

Perhaps, Bildad is disassociating himself from Eliphaz's intemperate third speech. He is begging Iyov: Do

ג שְׂעִפַּי יְשִׁיבוּנִי וּבַעֲבוּר חוּשִׁי בִי: מוּסַר כְּלִמָּתִי אֶשְׁמָע
ד וְרוּחַ מִבִּינָתִי יַעֲנֵנִי: הֲזֹאת יָדַעְתָּ מִנִּי־עַד מִנִּי שִׂים אָדָם
ה עֲלֵי־אָרֶץ: כִּי רִנְנַת רְשָׁעִים מִקָּרוֹב וְשִׂמְחַת חָנֵף עֲדֵי־
ו־ז רָגַע: אִם־יַעֲלֶה לַשָּׁמַיִם שִׂיאוֹ וְרֹאשׁוֹ לָעָב יַגִּיעַ: כְּגֶלְלוֹ
ח לָנֶצַח יֹאבֵד רֹאָיו יֹאמְרוּ אַיּוֹ: כַּחֲלוֹם יָעוּף וְלֹא יִמְצָאֻהוּ
ט וְיֻדַּד כְּחֶזְיוֹן לָיְלָה: עַיִן שְׁזָפַתּוּ וְלֹא תוֹסִיף וְלֹא־עוֹד
י תְּשׁוּרֶנּוּ מְקוֹמוֹ: בָּנָיו יְרַצּוּ דַלִּים וְיָדָיו תָּשֵׁבְנָה אוֹנוֹ:

2. לָכֵן שְׂעִפַּי יְשִׁיבוּנִי וּבַעֲבוּר חוּשִׁי בִי — *Therefore do my cogitations prod me to respond, for that my silence rankles within me.* שְׂעִיף is also a *branch.* Thought relates to the heart as does the branch to the tree (*Ramban* and *Radak*).

שוב, in the *hiphil, to cause to answer.*

For חוּשִׁי, we have followed *Rashi* who interprets the word as derived from חָשָׁה, *to be silent.* The interpretation offered in Introductory Remarks above derives from the assumption that this is the meaning of the word. This root does not, apparently, recur in Scripture with this meaning.

Other commentators render the word as *sense.* The meaning of the phrase is that all Tzophar's senses join his cogitations in urging him to respond to Iyov.

3. מוּסַר כְּלִמָּתִי אֶשְׁמָע וְרוּחַ מִבִּינָתִי יַעֲנֵנִי — *I constantly hear the painful insults which are addressed to me, but a will, born of my insights, makes me declare. Rashi* takes כְּלִימָה as the shame which you thrust upon me. Hence, *insult.* מוּסָר from יָסַר, *to chastise,* hence, the chastisement which you inflict upon me by your insults.

In the Introductory Remarks to these two verses, we have suggested another possible translation: כְּלִמָּה can be taken as the shame which I feel (*Jeremiah* 51:51 and elsewhere), hence, *my disgrace*. The verse would then be rendered: *The castigations to which my disgrace makes me subject, ring constantly in my ear.*

4. הֲזֹאת יָדַעְתָּ מִנִּי־עַד מִנִּי שִׂים אָדָם עֲלֵי־אָרֶץ — *Do you know that which has held true since time began, since man was placed upon the earth?* — Tzophar's argument will be that whatever joy falls to the lot of the wicked is short-lived and, ultimately, destructive to them.

What is gained by claiming that this is, as it were, a law of nature, a truth as old as man himself?

The explanation may be as follows:

There appears to be an inner weakness in an argument which posits that the success of the wicked is short-lived. In a world of absolute justice — such as one must expect from a Just God — even a short period of tranquility for the wicked seems unjustifiable. Tzophar is not, after all, suggesting any of the arguments with which thinkers have, throughout the ages, sought to explain the apparent miscarriage of justice when evildoers flourish. No word here of, for example, the possibility that a temporal reward for minor good deeds might be given in this world, so that God's full wrath might have free reign in the next. Brevity of duration is here offered as its own justification.

But, how are we to understand this?

The metaphor of the ordure in verse 7 is particularly evocative and compelling. Ordure is the offensive, malodorous substance which remains after the life-giving nutritional force has been separated from the food and absorbed into the body, there to work its wonders.

If this is a true word-picture of the wicked man in the aftermath of his fall from the heady soaring, depicted in verse 6, then indeed we have an answer to our question. The very transience of his affluence is designed to instruct. *When the wicked flower like grass, when evildoers sprout forth — it is to destroy them for all eternity.* After the lesson has been learned — the moral, absorbed — the wicked man becomes so much offal, to be discarded in disgust without a thought.

Such lessons, Tzophar says, have been needed since the dawn of creation. The

not permit yourself to be alienated by Eliphaz's intransigence. The Eliphaz you see before you now is not the friend of your past. Recall what he said in his earlier speech. It was there, before frustration took its toll, that he told you a profound truth that you would do well to ponder.

2. At 42:7 God expresses special anger against Eliphaz: My anger is kindled against you and against your two friends (see commentators there for explanations). This singularization can be readily explained on the basis of our theory. Eliphaz, alone among their friends, allowed his anger to escalate into the third round.

do my cogitations prod me to respond, for that my silence rankles
within me. 3 *I constantly hear the painful insults which are*
addressed to me, but a will, born of my insights, makes me dec-
lare. 4 *Do you know that which has held true since time began,*
since man was placed upon the earth? — 5 *That the joyous shout*
of the wicked is but of recent standing, the happiness of the
hypocrite lasts only a moment. 6 *Let his eminence rise up to*
heaven, let his head touch the clouds. 7 *Like so much ordure he*
will be destroyed forever, those who had seen him will ask, 'Where
is he?' 8 *He will be like a dream which takes wing, they will not*
be able to find him; he will be hustled away, be like a vision of
the night. 9 *The eye had seen him — but no longer, his community*
will not look upon him any more. 10 *His children must mollify the*
poor, his very hands must make restitution of his violent gain.

taunting mystery of God's seeming detachment from the human weal has tantalized the first man — and continues to baffle as the world grows old. Always there have been the wicked who flourished — but success was constantly short-lived, so that all might know that it is no more than an aberration.

5. כִּי רִנְנַת רְשָׁעִים מִקָּרוֹב וְשִׂמְחַת חָנֵף עֲדֵי־רָגַע — *That the joyous shout of the wicked is but of recent standing, the happiness of the hypocrite lasts only a moment.* At no time, during the period of tranquility, will one be able to say, 'This happiness began long ago' (*Rashi*).

6. אִם־יַעֲלֶה לַשָּׁמַיִם שִׂיאוֹ וְרֹאשׁוֹ לָעָב יַגִּיעַ — *Let his eminence rise up to heaven, let his head touch the clouds.* שִׂיאוֹ is derived from נָשָׂא, *to lift up.*

7. כְּגֶלְלוֹ לָנֶצַח יֹאבֵד רֹאָיו יֹאמְרוּ אַיּוֹ — *Like so much ordure he will be destroyed forever, those who had seen him will ask, 'Where is he?'* See commentary to verse 4.

Ramban derives גֶּלְלוֹ from גָּלַל, *to roll.* The wicked man hardly has time to roil around, to move from side to side, before catastrophe overtakes him.

8. כַּחֲלוֹם יָעוּף וְלֹא יִמְצָאֻהוּ וְיֻדַּד כְּחֶזְיוֹן לָיְלָה — *He will be like a dream which takes wing, they will not be able to find him; he will be hustled away, be like a vision of the night.* עוּף and נוּד, or נָדַד, are frequently used to parallel one another. See, for example, *Proverbs* 26:2. However, here יֻדַּד is in the passive voice. Since *visions of the night* would fly away on their own rather than be chased away, we have not rendered: ... *be moved away like a vision of the night,* but have, instead, divided the second part of the verse into two phrases. The wicked man will be hustled off the stage of life. Once gone, he will have left as little mark as a vision of the night.

The metaphor of the dream probably wishes to teach that there will be nothing left of all the wealth and power that the evildoer had controlled. All will turn out to have been insubstantial and illusory.

9. עַיִן שְׁזָפַתּוּ וְלֹא תוֹסִיף וְלֹא־עוֹד תְּשׁוּרֶנּוּ מְקוֹמוֹ — *The eye had seen him — but no longer, his community will not look upon him any more. Rashi,* in common with many other commentators (cf. *Radak* and *Ibn Janah* in their respective *Sefer HaShorashim*), renders שָׁזַף, *to see.*

Thus, apparently: *The eye had seen him — but no more.*

The second part of the verse recalls 7:10 and, just like there, *Metzudos* points out that מְקוֹמוֹ is to be understood as a shortened form of אַנְשֵׁי מְקוֹמוֹ, the people who live in his home-town — *his community.* Thus: *His community will not look upon him any more.*

10. בָּנָיו יְרַצּוּ דַלִּים וְיָדָיו תָּשֵׁבְנָה אוֹנוֹ — *His children must mollify the poor, his very hands must make restitution of his violent gain.* In the end none of his ill-gotten gains will help him in the least. They will all have to be returned.

The verse is to be understood as follows: In the long run, his children will certainly have to make restitution. It may even be that his success will be so short-lived, that he himself will have to compensate his victims for their loss (*Metzudos*).

אוֹן is *strength.* Hence, *That which he took because he was strong.*

יא־יב עַצְמוֹתָיו מָלְאוּ עֲלוּמָו וְעִמּוֹ עַל־עָפָר תִּשְׁכָּב׃ אִם־
יג תַּמְתִּיק בְּפִיו רָעָה יַכְחִידֶנָּה תַּחַת לְשׁוֹנוֹ׃ יַחְמֹל עָלֶיהָ
יד וְלֹא יַעַזְבֶנָּה וְיִמְנָעֶנָּה בְּתוֹךְ חִכּוֹ׃ לַחְמוֹ בְּמֵעָיו נֶהְפָּךְ
טו מְרוֹרַת פְּתָנִים בְּקִרְבּוֹ׃ חַיִל בָּלַע וַיְקִאֶנּוּ מִבִּטְנוֹ יֹרִשֶׁנּוּ
טז־יז אֵל׃ רֹאשׁ־פְּתָנִים יִינָק תַּהַרְגֵהוּ לְשׁוֹן אֶפְעֶה׃ אַל־יֵרֶא
יח בִפְלַגּוֹת נַהֲרֵי נַחֲלֵי דְּבַשׁ וְחֶמְאָה׃ מֵשִׁיב יָגָע וְלֹא יִבְלָע
יט כְּחֵיל תְּמוּרָתוֹ וְלֹא יַעֲלֹס׃ כִּי־רִצַּץ עָזַב דַּלִּים בַּיִת גָּזַל
כ וְלֹא יִבְנֵהוּ׃ כִּי ׀ לֹא־יָדַע שָׁלֵו בְּבִטְנוֹ בַּחֲמוּדוֹ לֹא
כא יְמַלֵּט׃ אֵין־שָׂרִיד לְאָכְלוֹ עַל־כֵּן לֹא־יָחִיל טוּבוֹ׃
כב־כג בִּמְלֹאות שִׂפְקוֹ יֵצֶר לוֹ כָּל־יַד עָמֵל תְּבֹאֶנּוּ׃ יְהִי ׀ לְמַלֵּא
בִטְנוֹ יְשַׁלַּח־בּוֹ חֲרוֹן אַפּוֹ וְיַמְטֵר עָלֵימוֹ בִּלְחוּמוֹ׃

11. עַצְמוֹתָיו מָלְאוּ עֲלוּמָו וְעִמּוֹ עַל־עָפָר תִּשְׁכָּב — *His youthful vitality permeates his being, with him it must lie upon the dust.* עֶלֶם is a *young man.* Hence עֲלוּמָו, the period in which he was a young man, *his youth.*

The translation follows *Rashi* who reads the verse as expressing the sorrow and the pity of the blighted life of the wicked. He will die early, dragging his youthful vigor into the grave.

Metzudos equates עֲלוּמָו with *the sins of his youth.* These have become a part of his very being, and will accompany him to the grave, because he will not repent for them.

12. אִם־תַּמְתִּיק בְּפִיו רָעָה יַכְחִידֶנָּה תַּחַת לְשׁוֹנוֹ — *If his mouth carries the sweet taste of evil, he will conceal it under his tongue.* תַּמְתִּיק derives from מָתַק, *to be sweet.*

The wicked man savors the taste of evil, being careful to keep it to himself — *concealing it under his tongue* — until the precise moment in which it can do the most harm (*Rashi* and *Metzudos*).

13. יַחְמֹל עָלֶיהָ וְלֹא יַעַזְבֶנָּה וְיִמְנָעֶנָּה בְּתוֹךְ חִכּוֹ — *He will treasure it — never letting it go, will hold it back under his palate.* A continuation of the thought expressed in the previous verse. יַחְמֹל from חָמַל, *to take pity.*

14. לַחְמוֹ בְּמֵעָיו נֶהְפָּךְ מְרוֹרַת פְּתָנִים בְּקִרְבּוֹ — *His food will twist in his belly, a serpent's bile in his innards.* הָפַךְ, *to turn around, to go backward.* The food, which is wracking his innards as though it were a *serpent's bile,* will turn around, to be vomited out by way of the mouth.

Whatever the wicked man undertakes will, as it were, double back upon his intentions, to leave him frustrated (*Metzudos*).

15. חַיִל בָּלַע וַיְקִאֶנּוּ מִבִּטְנוֹ יֹרִשֶׁנּוּ אֵל — *He devoured riches — will disgorge them, God will purge them from his gut.* The metaphor is graphic, indeed. The tossing, heaving stomach disgorges its contents without any volition. Never is man so helpless as when his insides spew forth the bitter malodorous rot which his body refused to accommodate.

Nevertheless, the verse is quick to point out that the writhing body is not its own master. It is God Who purges it of the malignant presence.

16. רֹאשׁ־פְּתָנִים יִינָק תַּהַרְגֵהוּ לְשׁוֹן אֶפְעֶה — *He will suck the serpent's venom, the cobra's tongue will slay him.* The milk which he suckled from his mother will turn to venom, and into the forked tongue of the cobra.

All his efforts, even those undertaken in the innocence of youth, will ultimately turn back upon him and and contribute to his downfall (*Ramban*).

17. אַל־יֵרֶא בִפְלַגּוֹת נַהֲרֵי נַחֲלֵי דְּבַשׁ וְחֶמְאָה — *He will never behold the branching waters, rivers, streams of honey and butter.* The wicked man will be denied any and all the pleasures of this world (*Ramban*), or of the Garden of Eden (*Rashi*).

18. מֵשִׁיב יָגָע וְלֹא יִבְלָע כְּחֵיל תְּמוּרָתוֹ וְלֹא יַעֲלֹס — *He will have to reinstate, may never swallow up, the fruits of labor. His retribution will be commensurate with his wealth. No happiness for him.* יָגָע, that which is gained through labor (יגע, *to exhaust oneself*).

The wicked man has stolen the fruits of other people's work. He will not be allowed to enjoy his ill-gotten gains. Even if he has already put food into his mouth, he will not be permitted to swallow it (*Ramban*).

For the second part of the verse we follow *Metzudos.* חֵיל is wealth, and תְּמוּרָה, from מור,

[11] His youthful vitality permeates his being, with him it must lie upon the dust. [12] If his mouth carries the sweet taste of evil, he will conceal it under his tongue. [13] He will treasure it — never letting it go, will hold it back under his palate. [14] His food will twist in his belly, a serpent's bile in his innards. [15] He devoured riches — will disgorge them, God will purge them from his gut. [16] He will suck the serpent's venom, the cobra's tongue will slay him. [17] He will never behold the branching waters; rivers, streams of honey and butter. [18] He will have to reinstate, may never swallow up, the fruits of labor. His retribution will be commensurate with his wealth. No happiness for him. [19] Because he smashed the poor and laid them waste, he will not build up the house which he stole. [20] Because his stomach would leave him no rest, he will not escape with his comeliness intact. [21] His sustenance will go to no survivor, none anticipates his goods. [22] When his expectations are fulfilled — then misfortune will strike, he will be exposed to the power of the villainous. [23] He will let loose His rage against him — it will stuff his belly. In the fury of battle He will shower upon him.

to exchange, is that which comes to him in the place of the wealth which he was forced to return. Literally: As great as the stolen wealth was, so great will be the poverty which will replace it.

19. כִּי־רִצַּץ עָזַב דַּלִּים בַּיִת גָּזַל וְלֹא יִבְנֵהוּ — *Because he smashed the poor and laid them waste, he will not build up the house which he stole.* We have translated in accordance with *R' Meyuchas*, who adduces proof that עָזַב can be used in the sense, *to lay waste.*

Other commentators assume the more usual meaning, *to forsake.* Possibilities are: Having smashed the poor, he will have to forsake them — since he will die (*Rashi*); or, he will not leave the poor people alone until he has smashed them (*Metzudos*).

The cohesion between the two parts of the verse is best understood according to *R' Meyuchas.* Because he laid the destitute waste, that is, he destroyed their homes, he will not be granted the opportunity to build up any houses which he may have acquired in the course of his depredations.

20. כִּי לֹא־יָדַע שָׁלֵו בְּבִטְנוֹ בַּחֲמוּדוֹ לֹא יְמַלֵּט — *Because his stomach would leave him no rest, he will not escape with his comeliness intact.* His stomach would leave him no rest, because it always longed for more and more satisfaction. He could not steal enough to satisfy its cravings. Because of this, he will die starved and emaciated. His body will have lost the pleasing contours of a well-fed man (*Rashi* and *R' Meyuchas*).

21. אֵין־שָׂרִיד לְאָכְלוֹ עַל־כֵּן לֹא־יָחִיל טוּבוֹ — *His sustenance will go to no survivor, none anticipates his goods.* The translation follows *Ramban.* He takes שָׂרִיד in its usual meaning of *survivor.* See also at 18:19. Alternative renderings are: He did not share the remnants of his food with the poor (*Rashi*); or, he never bothered to leave over any food for the next day, secure in his knowledge that he could always steal more (*Metzudos*).

חיל can have the meaning, *to wait anxiously, to hope* (cf. *Genesis* 8:10), or *to be successful* (*Psalms* 10:5). *Ramban*, consistent with his interpretation of the first part of the verse, assumes the former. Since there will be no survivors, there will be no sense of happy anticipation for the wicked man's goods. *Rashi* and *Metzudos* assume the latter meaning. Because of his wickedness, his endeavors will never know success.

22. בִּמְלֹאות שִׂפְקוֹ יֵצֶר לוֹ כָּל־יַד עָמֵל תְּבֹאֶנּוּ — *When his expectations are fulfilled — then misfortune will strike, he will be exposed to the power of the villainous.* His troubles will begin when he is at the very peak of his success. שָׂפַק, *to be sufficient* [cf. *I Kings* 20:10] (*Rashi* and *Metzudos*).

The translation of the second half of the verse follows *Metzudos.*

23. יְהִי לְמַלֵּא בִטְנוֹ יְשַׁלַּח־בּוֹ חֲרוֹן אַפּוֹ וְיַמְטֵר עָלֵימוֹ בִּלְחוּמוֹ — *He will let loose His rage against him — it will stuff his belly. In the fury of*

כ/ כד־כה יִבְרַח מִנֵּשֶׁק בַּרְזֶל תַּחְלְפֵהוּ קֶשֶׁת נְחוּשָׁה: שָׁלַף וַיֵּצֵא
כד־כט כו מִגֵּוָה וּבָרָק מִמְּרֹרָתוֹ יַהֲלֹךְ עָלָיו אֵמִים: כָּל־חֹשֶׁךְ טָמוּן
כז לִצְפּוּנָיו תְּאָכְלֵהוּ אֵשׁ לֹא־נֻפָּח יֵרַע שָׂרִיד בְּאָהֳלוֹ: יִגֶל
כח שָׁמַיִם עֲוֹנוֹ וְאֶרֶץ מִתְקוֹמָמָה לוֹ: יִגֶל יְבוּל בֵּיתוֹ נִגָּרוֹת
כט בְּיוֹם אַפּוֹ: זֶה ׀ חֵלֶק־אָדָם רָשָׁע מֵאֱלֹהִים וְנַחֲלַת אִמְרוֹ
כא/א־ב א־ב מֵאֵל: וַיַּעַן אִיּוֹב וַיֹּאמַר: שִׁמְעוּ שָׁמוֹעַ מִלָּתִי

battle He will shower upon him. God had been mentioned in verse 15, and there is no need to identify Him once more by name (*Ramban*).

Perhaps, God's rage is designed to stuff the wicked man's stomach because it was that stomach, with its insatiable craving (v. 20), which drove him to his evil ways.

Rashi understands לְחוּם as the *fury of battle* (from לָחַם, *to fight*). God will, as in battle, shower fire and sulfur upon the evildoer.

Ramban offers *his body* or *his food.* God will shower His rage upon either the wicked man or his sustenance.

24. יִבְרַח מִנֵּשֶׁק בַּרְזֶל תַּחְלְפֵהוּ קֶשֶׁת נְחוּשָׁה — *He will flee from iron armor. The copper bow will pierce him.* Nothing will help him. As he flees from one set of weapons, the other will catch up with him. Even as he runs away, the pursuing arrow pierces and fells him (*Metzudos*).

25. שָׁלַף וַיֵּצֵא מִגֵּוָה וּבָרָק מִמְּרֹרָתוֹ יַהֲלֹךְ עָלָיו אֵמִים — *He has drawn it out ... it has already left the scabbard. A lightning flash, born of stark terror, overwhelms him with fear. Ramban* has this verse refer back to the arrows of the previous verse. He would render גֵּוָה as *quiver* rather than *scabbard.* We have followed *Rashi* and *Metzudos* who interpret the description as referring to a sword.

גֵּוָה is related to גְּוִיָּה, *body.* The scabbard or quiver relates to its contents as the body does to the soul (*Metzudos*). *Radak* in his *Sefer HaShorashim* also relates the word to *body,* but appears to understand the verse thus: *He withdrew [the arrow from its quiver] and now it comes out of the body of the evildoer.* Consistent with this interpretation, he renders מְרוֹרָה as *gall,* thus: *... and the lightning [-like sword] comes out of the victim's gall.*

For our rendering of this word, we have followed *Metzudos,* who offers *bitter fear.*

אֵמִים can be either *fear,* as we have rendered it (*Metzudos*), or *frightening hordes* (*Ramban*).

26. כָּל־חֹשֶׁךְ טָמוּן לִצְפּוּנָיו תְּאָכְלֵהוּ אֵשׁ לֹא־נֻפָּח יֵרַע שָׂרִיד בְּאָהֳלוֹ — *Total darkness lies in wait for his hidden treasures. Hell's fire — never in need of a bellows — will consume him, those in his home who will outlive him will fare badly.* צְפוּנָיו, from צָפַן, *to hide.*

We have followed *Targum* in including *Hell's fire* into the translation. *Ramban,* too, implies here and states specifically in *Toras HaAdam,* that reference here is to *Gehinnom.* See further in footnote to Introductory Remarks to 36:9.

Metzudos interprets differently: No bellows will be used to blow upon the fire that is to consume the wicked man. This, in order that it should burn more slowly, subjecting him to greater agony.

27. יְגַלּוּ שָׁמַיִם עֲוֹנוֹ וְאֶרֶץ מִתְקוֹמָמָה לוֹ — *The heavens will make known his sins, the earth rises up against him.* By the sheer weight of the misery which will descend upon him from the heavens, all will know that he is wicked (*Metzudos*).

28. יִגֶל יְבוּל בֵּיתוֹ נִגָּרוֹת בְּיוֹם אַפּוֹ — *The harvest which his family had produced will be carried away, trampled contemptuously on the day of His anger.* יִגֶל, from גָּלָה, *to go into exile* (*Rashi*).

Where נָגַר occurs in Scripture, *Rashi* associates it with a flowing, downward motion. Here he renders, *that which is downtrodden and treated with contempt.*

29. זֶה חֵלֶק־אָדָם רָשָׁע מֵאֱלֹהִים וְנַחֲלַת אִמְרוֹ מֵאֵל — *This is the wicked man's portion from God, his verdict, assigned him from the Almighty.* Tzophar has had his say. He has observed the ways of the world and is satisfied with what he has seen. The successes of the wicked do not faze him. Invariably they are short-lived, themselves a part of the lesson which God wishes to teach man — see commentary to verse 4. He leaves the scene, sorry to have pained his friend, but secure in his beliefs.

His final words say it all: an objective and honest appraisal of the fate which befalls the wicked makes it clear that all is ordained by God. There is no accident, no happenstance. Iyov will have to make his peace with the realization that what has happened to him must have an explanation within a matrix of providence and justice.

20/24-29 24 *He will flee from iron armor. The copper bow will pierce him.*
25 *He has drawn it out ... it has already left the scabbard. A*
lightning flash, born of stark terror, overwhelms him with fear.
26 *Total darkness lies in wait for his hidden treasures. Hell's fire —*
never in need of a bellows — will consume him, those in his home
who will outlive him will fare badly. 27 *The heavens will make*
known his sins, the earth rises up against him. 28 *The harvest which*
his family had produced will be carried away, trampled contemp-
tuously on the day of His anger. 29 *This is the wicked man's portion*
from God, his verdict assigned him from the Almighty.

21/1-2 1 *Iyov responded and said:* 2 *Listen carefully to my words; let*

XXI.

◆§ Iyov's Response to Tzophar's Second Speech

In this, his last speech in the second round, Iyov finally demolishes the utopian fantasies conjured up by the friends. Where they — because their theories demanded it — saw frustration, terror and destruction as the lot of the wicked, he insists that reality, with all its bewildering ambiguities, all its shocking inconsistencies and injustices, must be faced. It is outrageous, it is unnerving (v. 6), but it is the truth: More often than not the evildoers lead perfectly happy lives, secure in health and power, surrounded by the joyous sounds of laughing, playing children, unmoved by any pangs of conscience, brazen-faced in their refusal to bow before God.

How, in the face of these undeniable truths, can the friends continue to prattle platitudes and betrayals (v. 34)!

But with all the rage which animates him, Iyov, in this speech, seems more circumspect, more attuned to facts and issues, than he was in his two previous second round speeches. There is no echo here of the dreadful death wishes of his response to Eliphaz [I called to the pit, *'You are my father!' to the worms, 'My mother, my sister!'* (17:14)]; nor of the threats hurled at the friends [*Tremble before the sword, for your sins generate the fury of the sword — so that you may know, devastation* (19:29)] with which he closed his response to Bildad. He is disappointed — but not broken.

The difference may have its source in the tenor of Tzophar's speech. As we saw in the Introductory Remarks to chapter 20, it was meant to be conciliatory rather than confrontational. And though, as we discuss in the commentary to verse 34, Iyov concludes that in the end Tzophar too must bear the collective guilt for the impotence of the hapless comforters, it at least had the effect of putting Iyov into a more hopeful mood.

The second speeches of each of the three friends have been devoted to demonstrating that the tranquility enjoyed by the wicked is insubstantial and of short duration. Calamity must soon overtake them or their children.

It is only now, after Tzophar's speech, that Iyov rebuts this argument.

In the Introductory Remarks to chapter 16 we suggested that, at first, Iyov had not been able to bring himself to believe that the friends actually gave credence to their patently ridiculous contentions. It was so clear to him that, indeed, many wicked men lead happy and prosperous lives, that he felt forced to conclude that the friends were spinning their webs of fantasy simply in order to mock and taunt his misery. Only after Tzophar's speech does he realize that the friends are actually propounding a serious theological stance.

This can be more readily understood in the light of the insights which we gained in the last chapter concerning Tzophar's thinking in this, his final speech. We found that he had already distanced himself from the friends, and that what he had to say now he said as an individual who felt that he simply must unburden himself of a deeply felt truth. Iyov must have realized that here was an honest attempt to portray the reality as Tzophar perceived it. Such a presentation calls for a rebuttal, and Iyov is prepared to make one.

Ramban notes that in this speech, Iyov makes one significant new point. All the friends have

ג וּתְהִי־זֹאת תַּנְחוּמֹתֵיכֶם׃ שָׂאוּנִי וְאָנֹכִי אֲדַבֵּר וְאַחַר
ד דַּבְּרִי תַלְעִיג׃ הֶאָנֹכִי לְאָדָם שִׂיחִי וְאִם־מַדּוּעַ לֹא־
ה תִקְצַר רוּחִי׃ פְּנוּ־אֵלַי וְהָשַׁמּוּ וְשִׂימוּ יָד עַל־פֶּה׃
ו־ז וְאִם־זָכַרְתִּי וְנִבְהָלְתִּי וְאָחַז בְּשָׂרִי פַּלָּצוּת׃ מַדּוּעַ רְשָׁעִים
ח יִחְיוּ עָתְקוּ גַּם־גָּבְרוּ חָיִל׃ זַרְעָם נָכוֹן לִפְנֵיהֶם עִמָּם
ט וְצֶאֱצָאֵיהֶם לְעֵינֵיהֶם׃ בָּתֵּיהֶם שָׁלוֹם מִפָּחַד וְלֹא שֵׁבֶט
י אֱלוֹהַּ עֲלֵיהֶם׃ שׁוֹרוֹ עִבַּר וְלֹא יַגְעִל תְּפַלֵּט פָּרָתוֹ
יא וְלֹא תְשַׁכֵּל׃ יְשַׁלְּחוּ כַצֹּאן עֲוִילֵיהֶם וְיַלְדֵיהֶם יְרַקֵּדוּן׃

maintained that even if the wicked do occasionally experience lives of peace and tranquility, this will not continue for any length of time. If not they, then their children or descendants will swallow the bitter fruits of evil. Iyov questions this logic. His own observations have shown that the happy lives of the wicked can span a number of generations. Even if we grant that hundreds of years later, justice will claim its due, this would not constitute a fitting punishment for the wicked.

2. שִׁמְעוּ שָׁמוֹעַ מִלָּתִי וּתְהִי־זֹאת תַּנְחוּמֹתֵיכֶם — *Listen carefully to my words; let that be the comfort you extend to me.* The best comfort which you can give me is to listen to what I have to say (*Rashi*).

We have rendered, *'Listen carefully ...'* because this seems implied by the doubled שִׁמְעוּ שָׁמוֹעַ. Certainly the friends have been hearing his words, but intent upon their own theories, they have not really been listening.

The doubled שִׁמְעוּ שָׁמוֹעַ may have another purpose. There is a message beneath the simple words of this speech. Outwardly, Iyov's arguments address the narrow issue of the occasional tranquility of the wicked man. Iyov demonstrates from countless examples within all their experiences, that the wicked do prosper. But then, how is one to understand the friends who have unanimously asserted the opposite? Clearly they are swayed by theoretical constructs of an ideal world, which are not grounded in reality. But if by listening to Iyov's argument in this narrow issue they will realize this, then the entire structure of their earlier ideas will unravel. They will be forced to admit the justice of all of Iyov's complaints. The echoes of what they hear now will reverberate throughout the imposing structure of their religious philosophy — and lay it low.

3. שָׂאוּנִי וְאָנֹכִי אֲדַבֵּר וְאַחַר דַּבְּרִי תַלְעִיג — *Bear with me that I might speak; after I have had my say, you may deride me. Ramban* and *Metzudos* both explain that שָׂאוּנִי refers to Iyov's words: Before you deride me, you should have the patience to listen to what I have to say.

But *Rashi* renders simply, *Have patience with me.* There is a subtle rebuke here: If you feel unable to accept my arguments, is it not possible that this is so because you have no love or patience for me as a person?

There is a sad tone of resignation to this verse. Iyov has no real hope that his argument will be accepted. He anticipates nothing but derision. However, *R' Yosef Kara* understands the phrase positively: Listen to me and you will find that there is nothing to deride!

He notes further that תַּלְעִיג is in the singular. Iyov is addressing each of the friends as an individual. If indeed Iyov is turning to the friends' better nature, then we can readily appreciate this approach. We saw in the previous chapter that once Tzophar had broken rank and thus had removed himself from the need of presenting a united front, he had begun to take Iyov seriously. This has kindled a hope in Iyov. Perhaps, if he can break through the tyranny of the group — if he can find the human face behind the cold unbending facade of common self-righteousness — perhaps then, after all, there is the possibility that he may yet be understood.

4. הֶאָנֹכִי לְאָדָם שִׂיחִי וְאִם־מַדּוּעַ לֹא־תִקְצַר רוּחִי — *Am I then dealing with a human being? Why do I not have the right to lose my patience!* If my quarrel were with a human being who overwhelms me with his power, so that I cannot expect to get satisfaction from him, I could always comfort myself that his son will be more amenable to my claims. But I am being punished by God and have no hope at all for ultimate vindication. Why then am I not justified in my frustrations? (*Ramban*).

5. פְּנוּ־אֵלַי וְהָשַׁמּוּ וְשִׂימוּ יָד עַל־פֶּה — *Concentrate upon me and you will be astounded, then hold your hand in front of your mouth.* Once more, a plea to renounce sterile sophistry in favor of a personal involvement. If only you would focus upon me rather than upon my theology,

21/3-11 *that be the comfort you extend to me.* 3 *Bear with me that I might*
speak; after I have had my say, you may deride me. 4 *Am I then*
dealing with a human being? Why do I not have the right to lose
my patience! 5 *Concentrate upon me and you will be astounded,*
then hold your hand in front of your mouth. 6 *Whenever I think*
about it I feel unnerved, trembling takes hold of me. 7 *Why should*
the wicked endure, attain old age and accomplish mightily! 8 *They*
yet experience their children well established, can watch even
their grandchildren. 9 *No terror disturbs the peace of their homes,*
the rod of God is not upon them. 10 *His ox impregnates [its seed] not*
rejected; his cow calves, never losing her young. 11 *They rear their*
young freely like so many sheep, their children frisk cheerfully.

you would come to understand the correctness of my claim.

6. וְאִם־זָכַרְתִּי וְנִבְהָלְתִּי וְאָחַז בְּשָׂרִי פַּלָּצוּת — *Whenever I think about it I feel unnerved, trembling takes hold of me.* Iyov appears to have in mind that which is about to follow. When he contemplates the tranquil lives of the wicked he is deeply disturbed. Perhaps it is the feeling that there is no justice in the world, and that, necessarily, everyone's fortune is in the grip of blind happenstance, which robs him of his equanimity.

7. מַדּוּעַ רְשָׁעִים יִחְיוּ עָתְקוּ גַּם־גָּבְרוּ חָיִל — *Why should the wicked endure, attain old age and accomplish mightily!* Iyov does not even bother to refute the assertion of the friends that, in fact, the wicked lead miserable lives. In his mind it is self-evident that this is not the case. It is the *why!*, the unfairness of it all, which allows him no rest.

We assume that the *why* of this verse carries over to the series of verses which follows: Why should the wicked have their children settled with them? Why does no terror grip their homes? and so on.

We have translated עָתַק, *to grow old*, in accordance with *Metzudos*. However, *R' Yosef Kara* renders, *to be strong and to accumulate wealth.*

8. זַרְעָם נָכוֹן לִפְנֵיהֶם עִמָּם וְצֶאֱצָאֵיהֶם לְעֵינֵיהֶם — *They yet experience their children well established, can watch even their grandchildren.* The translation follows *R' Yosef Kara*. The wicked live to see their children and grandchildren flourish.

9. בָּתֵּיהֶם שָׁלוֹם מִפָּחַד וְלֹא שֵׁבֶט אֱלוֹהַּ עֲלֵיהֶם — *No terror disturbs the peace of their homes, the rod of God is not upon them.* This thought appears to react to Eliphaz's assertion that even the days during which the wicked live outwardly tranquil lives, are filled with fear about what the future might bring (15:20-23).

10. שׁוֹרוֹ עִבַּר וְלֹא יַגְעִל תְּפַלֵּט פָּרָתוֹ וְלֹא תְשַׁכֵּל — *His ox impregnates [its seed] not rejected; his cow calves, never losing her young.* עִבֵּר in the *piel, to make pregnant,*, here, to pass the semen into the cow. גָּעַל, in Rabbinic usage: *to exude.* Here, it is descriptive of the cow's rejection of inadequately projected semen. פָּלַט, *to escape*; in the *piel, to deliver*; here, *to calve.* שָׁכֹל, *to be bereaved.*

It seems clear that verse 11, which describes the carefree upbringing which the wicked are able to give their children, would properly belong directly after verse 9 which speaks of the tranquility of the home. We would not have expected Iyov's mind to veer to the herd, away from the home.

Our suggestion that verse 9 is in reaction to Eliphaz's second speech may provide a solution. That speech ends with the assertion that, *To conceive sin is to bear iniquity, their womb prepares — deceit!* His thoughts intent upon Eliphaz's words, this final thought engenders bitter reflections in Iyov's mind. The birthing process is a singularly inapt metaphor for the alleged suffering of the wicked man. His very oxen belie its assertions. Unerringly, they bring forth their young!

11. יְשַׁלְּחוּ כַצֹּאן עֲוִילֵיהֶם וְיַלְדֵיהֶם יְרַקֵּדוּן — *They rear their young freely like so many sheep, their children frisk cheerfully.* In his response to Bildad's second speech Iyov had described the terrible loneliness of society's outcasts, had reflected bitterly that the respect which he shows to even the עֲוִילִים, *youngsters*, is repaid by the cold shoulder which only the firmly entrenched know how to turn upon the vulnerable (19:18). Here, from the outside, he jealously observes these same youngsters frisking freely, without a care in the world, in the loving embrace of their parents in the homes of the wicked!

יב־יג יִשְׂאוּ כְּתֹף וְכִנּוֹר וְיִשְׂמְחוּ לְקוֹל עוּגָב: °יבלו בַטּוֹב יְמֵיהֶם
יד וּבְרֶגַע שְׁאוֹל יֵחָתּוּ: וַיֹּאמְרוּ לָאֵל סוּר מִמֶּנּוּ וְדַעַת דְּרָכֶיךָ
טו לֹא חָפָצְנוּ: מַה־שַּׁדַּי כִּי־נַעַבְדֶנּוּ וּמַה־נּוֹעִיל כִּי נִפְגַּע־בּוֹ:
טז־יז הֵן לֹא בְיָדָם טוּבָם עֲצַת רְשָׁעִים רָחֲקָה מֶנִּי: כַּמָּה ׀ נֵר־
יח רְשָׁעִים יִדְעָךְ וְיָבֹא עָלֵימוֹ אֵידָם חֲבָלִים יְחַלֵּק בְּאַפּוֹ: יִהְיוּ
יט כְּתֶבֶן לִפְנֵי־רוּחַ וּכְמֹץ גְּנָבַתּוּ סוּפָה: אֱלוֹהַּ יִצְפֹּן־לְבָנָיו
כ אוֹנוֹ יְשַׁלֵּם אֵלָיו וְיֵדָע: יִרְאוּ עֵינָו כִּידוֹ וּמֵחֲמַת שַׁדַּי יִשְׁתֶּה:
כא־כב כִּי מַה־חֶפְצוֹ בְּבֵיתוֹ אַחֲרָיו וּמִסְפַּר חֳדָשָׁיו חֻצָּצוּ: הַלְאֵל
כג יְלַמֶּד־דָּעַת וְהוּא רָמִים יִשְׁפּוֹט: זֶה יָמוּת בְּעֶצֶם תֻּמּוֹ כֻּלּוֹ
כד שַׁלְאֲנַן וְשָׁלֵיו: עֲטִינָיו מָלְאוּ חָלָב וּמֹחַ עַצְמוֹתָיו יְשֻׁקֶּה:

°יְכַלּוּ ק׳

12. יִשְׂאוּ כְּתֹף וְכִנּוֹר וְיִשְׂמְחוּ לְקוֹל עוּגָב — *They make music with drum and harp, rejoice at the flute's sound.* נָשָׂא, *to lift up,* therefore to raise one's voice in song, and in general, to make music.

We have translated עוּגָב as *flute,* on the basis of *Targum* who renders אֲבוּבָא which is a wind instrument — see *Arachin* 2:3.

13. יְכַלּוּ בַטּוֹב יְמֵיהֶם וּבְרֶגַע שְׁאוֹל יֵחָתּוּ — *They spend their days happily to old age, then, they do not linger as they go down to the grave.* יְבַלּוּ, from בָּלָה, *to grow old and worn out.* See, for example, *Genesis* 18:12.

יֵחָתּוּ, from נָחַת, *to go down.* Literally: *They go down to the grave in one second* (*Metzudos*). Or, *They go down to the grave in tranquility* [רֶגַע from רָגַע, *to be at rest, repose*] (*Ramban*).

14. וַיֹּאמְרוּ לָאֵל סוּר מִמֶּנּוּ וְדַעַת דְּרָכֶיךָ לֹא חָפָצְנוּ — *Though they say to the Almighty, 'Leave us be! We have had no wish to know* Your *paths.* This verse and the next appear to continue the thought expressed in verse 7: *Why should the wicked endure* and enjoy all the advantages listed in the intervening verses, when they have no interest at all in following the Almighty's paths?

15. מַה־שַּׁדַּי כִּי־נַעַבְדֶנּוּ וּמַה־נּוֹעִיל כִּי נִפְגַּע־בּוֹ — *'What is Shaddai that we should serve Him? What would we gain if we were to turn to Him in prayer?'* The wicked are continuing to talk. But where in verse 14 they addressed God directly, they have now changed to the third person. Thus, the form which their speech takes, suits its content. There is nothing, they claim, to gain from turning to God in prayer. Accordingly, we will not do so.

The wicked see no purpose in prayer other than to fill their needs. If, erroneously, they feel themselves able to cope on their own, they see no need to have any relationship with God. This contrasts sharply with Iyov's own attitude. *Were He to kill me — I would still yearn for Him*! (13:15).

For פָּגַע, *to meet,* as an expression denoting prayer, see *Berachos* 26b.

16. הֵן לֹא בְיָדָם טוּבָם עֲצַת רְשָׁעִים רָחֲקָה מֶנִּי — *Indeed, do they not control their own well-being! But, far from me the wiles of the wicked*! The translation follows *Rashi* and *Metzudos.* The sense is that although the wicked seem in absolute control of their lives, Iyov will not be persuaded to throw in his lot with them. He will maintain his own path of righteousness.

Or: The success of the wicked is clearly not their own doing. It must come to them from heaven. How then can the friends claim that invariably the wicked suffer (20:29)? I, on the other hand, have never walked in the path of the wicked — and still the hand of God is upon me! (*R' Yosef Kara*).

17. כַּמָּה נֵר־רְשָׁעִים יִדְעָךְ וְיָבֹא עָלֵימוֹ אֵידָם חֲבָלִים יְחַלֵּק בְּאַפּוֹ — *How long? May the lamp of the wicked sputter so that their fate come upon them. Let Him dispense their due in His fury.* The translation follows *Rashi. R' Yosef Kara* and *R' Meyuchas* have essentially the same understanding of the verse but offer different interpretations for חֲבָלִים. *R' Yosef Kara*: *May God inflict* pain *upon them. R' Meyuchas*: *May God* divide their property *to others.*

Ramban points out that כַּמָּה may mean, *How little*! just as it can mean, *How much*! Thus: *How inadequate is the sputtering flame of the wicked*! They should be punished much more severely than they are.

18. יִהְיוּ כְּתֶבֶן לִפְנֵי־רוּחַ וּכְמֹץ גְּנָבַתּוּ סוּפָה — *Let them be like straw in the face of the wind, like so much chaff snatched up by the whirlwind.* This may be a continuation of the imprecations which Iyov voiced in the previous verse: *Let Him dispense . . . Let them be . . .* (*Ramban*).

Metzudos reads this verse as a continuation

12 *They make music with drum and harp, rejoice at the flute's
sound.* 13 *They spend their days happily to old age, then, they do
not linger as they go down to the grave.* 14 *Though they say to the
Almighty, 'Leave us be! We have had no wish to know Your
paths.'* 15 *'What is Shaddai that we should serve Him? What
would we gain if we were to turn to Him in prayer?'* 16 *Indeed, do
they not control their own well-being! But, far from me the wiles of
the wicked!* 17 *How long? May the lamp of the wicked sputter so
that their fate come upon them. Let Him dispense their due in His
fury.* 18 *Let them be like straw in the face of the wind, like so much
chaff snatched up by the whirlwind.* 19 *Should God store up his evil
for his children? Let Him requite him — so that he may know!*
20 *Let his own eyes behold his breakage, let him drink of Shaddai's
anger!* 21 *What does he care for the home which he will leave behind, once he has received the allotted number of months?* 22 *Could
anyone be expected to offer explanations for the Almighty? His
judgments are beyond ken.* 23 *This one dies his perfection
unimpaired, in absolute peace and tranquility.* 24 *His breasts are
full of milk, the marrow of his bones, constantly replenished.*

of the first phrase of the previous one, which he understood as did *Ramban*: *How few are the wicked whose light sputters . . . how few who are as the straw in the face of the wind*!

19. אֱלוֹהַ יִצְפֹּן־לְבָנָיו אוֹנוֹ יְשַׁלֵּם אֵלָיו וְיֵדָע — *Should God store up his evil for his children? Let Him requite him — so that he may know*! Here Iyov rejects the possibility that justice is meted out to the wicked by having their children suffer. It would seem to be much more fair to have the perpetrator of evil, himself, punished (*Rashi*).

20. יִרְאוּ עֵינָו כִּידוֹ וּמֵחֲמַת שַׁדַּי יִשְׁתֶּה — *Let his own eyes behold his breakage, let him drink of Shaddai's anger*! *Rashi* cites no source for his rendering of כִּיד,as *breakage*. He believes that this translation is required by the context. *Radak* (*Shorashim*) suggests that the word may be related to אֵיד, *fate* (verse 17).

21. כִּי מַה־חֶפְצוֹ בְּבֵיתוֹ אַחֲרָיו וּמִסְפַּר חֳדָשָׁיו חֻצָּצוּ — *What does he care for the home which he will leave behind, once he has received the allotted number of months*? The thought that it makes no sense to explain the tranquility of the wicked by the suffering of their children, continues.

Rashi relates חָצַץ to קָצַץ, *to make an end*. *Radak* (*Shorashim*) relates it to חָצָה, *cut in half*. In our context, presumably, to be given a precise portion.

22. הַלְאֵל יְלַמֶּד־דָּעַת וְהוּא רָמִים יִשְׁפּוֹט — *Could anyone be expected to offer explanations for the Almighty? His judgments are beyond ken*. Thus, *Metzudos*. Or: *Could one such as I possibly arrogate to myself the right to teach the Almighty — He whose judgments encompass even the most exalted*? (*Ramban*).

23. זֶה יָמוּת בְּעֶצֶם תֻּמּוֹ כֻּלּוֹ שַׁלְאֲנַן וְשָׁלֵיו — *This one dies his perfection unimpaired, in absolute peace and tranquility*. This verse is to be read together with the next three. Together they demonstrate the inscrutability of God's judgments.

For עֶצֶם, *Rashi* offers *appearance*. This, in accordance with his rendering at *Genesis* 17:23 and *Exodus* 24:10. Other commentators, including *Radak* (*Shorashim*), render *strength* or *life-force*. Thus, at the time of his death, his appearance or energy were unimpaired.

The *lamed* in שַׁלְאֲנָן is added as a literary accouterment for beauty [תִּפְאֶרֶת הַלָּשׁוֹן] (*R' Meyuchas*). The word has the same meaning as שַׁאֲנָן (*Rashi*).

24. עֲטִינָיו מָלְאוּ חָלָב וּמֹחַ עַצְמוֹתָיו יְשֻׁקֶּה — *His breasts are full of milk, the marrow of his bones, constantly replenished*. מַעֲטָן is the vat in which olives are stored so that their oil may collect. Here it is used as a synonym for the breasts which contain the fat milk. [Perhaps *his breasts* can be understood as, the breasts which are his concern; that is, his wife's breasts are filled with milk so that his children lack nothing.]

The meaning of the second phrase is not clear. *Rashi* to *Proverbs* 3:8 appears to take

כה־כו וְזֶה יָמוּת בְּנֶפֶשׁ מָרָה וְלֹא־אָכַל בַּטּוֹבָה׃ יַחַד עַל־עָפָר
כז יִשְׁכָּבוּ וְרִמָּה תְּכַסֶּה עֲלֵיהֶם׃ הֵן יָדַעְתִּי מַחְשְׁבוֹתֵיכֶם
כח וּמְזִמּוֹת עָלַי תַּחְמֹסוּ׃ כִּי תֹאמְרוּ אַיֵּה בֵית־נָדִיב וְאַיֵּה
כט אֹהֶל ׀ מִשְׁכְּנוֹת רְשָׁעִים׃ הֲלֹא שְׁאֶלְתֶּם עוֹבְרֵי דָרֶךְ
ל וְאֹתֹתָם לֹא תְנַכֵּרוּ׃ כִּי לְיוֹם אֵיד יֵחָשֶׂךְ רָע לְיוֹם
לא עֲבָרוֹת יוּבָלוּ׃ מִי־יַגִּיד עַל־פָּנָיו דַּרְכּוֹ וְהוּא־עָשָׂה מִי
לב יְשַׁלֶּם־לוֹ׃ וְהוּא לִקְבָרוֹת יוּבָל וְעַל־גָּדִישׁ יִשְׁקוֹד׃
לג מָתְקוּ־לוֹ רִגְבֵי נָחַל וְאַחֲרָיו כָּל־אָדָם יִמְשׁוֹךְ וּלְפָנָיו אֵין
לד מִסְפָּר׃ וְאֵיךְ תְּנַחֲמוּנִי הָבֶל וּתְשׁוּבֹתֵיכֶם נִשְׁאַר־מָעַל׃

יְשֻׁקֶּה to refer to the process of making marrow for the bones. *Targum* renders the phrase: His bones' marrow is *fat. Ramban* and *Metzudos* take יְשֻׁקֶּה to mean, *are given to drink.* That is, the marrow of his bones is constantly fresh and moist as though it had only just been infused with life-giving liquid.

25. וְזֶה יָמוּת בְּנֶפֶשׁ מָרָה וְלֹא־אָכַל בַּטּוֹבָה — *The other dies, profoundly bitter, never having tasted delight.* This could well be someone who has never sinned (*R' Yosef Kara*). Iyov's disillusionment and conviction that all is happenstance, with no connection at all to the person's action, are expressed in the next verse.

26. יַחַד עַל־עָפָר יִשְׁכָּבוּ וְרִמָּה תְּכַסֶּה עֲלֵיהֶם — *Together, they will lie in the dust, worms will blanket them.* The righteous and the wicked can both expect the same fate (*Rashi*).

27. הֵן יָדַעְתִּי מַחְשְׁבוֹתֵיכֶם וּמְזִמּוֹת עָלַי תַּחְמֹסוּ — *See, I know your thoughts, the ideas which you withhold from me. Metzudos,* whose system we will follow in the next few verses, takes חמס in the sense, *to withhold.* Iyov accuses the friends of marshalling only such arguments as tend to support their thesis. They *withhold* any facts which contradict their ideas.

Rashi renders: *The schemes which do me violence.* You are so full of your discredited theories that you deny me the one thing that is my right — a caring and friendly empathy in my predicament.

28. כִּי תֹאמְרוּ אַיֵּה בֵית־נָדִיב וְאַיֵּה אֹהֶל מִשְׁכְּנוֹת רְשָׁעִים — *That you say, 'I challenge you to show me the secure house of those that act nobly; I challenge you to show me the fragile tent of the wicked!'* We continue with *Metzudos*'s interpretation: The arguments which tend to bolster your position are: People who act nobly have no need to build secure houses for themselves. They feel perfectly safe in a fragile tent. The wicked must protect themselves in fortresses.

29. הֲלֹא שְׁאֶלְתֶּם עוֹבְרֵי דָרֶךְ וְאֹתֹתָם לֹא תְנַכֵּרוּ — *But is it not true that you have inquired of the wayfarers, those whose clearly demonstrated truths you dare not reject.* The things which you refuse to mention are the truths which you have learned from the wayfarers; people wise in the ways of the world. They offer proofs (אֹת, *a sign*) for their assertions, which you can in no way deny.

The observations of the wayfarers will be quoted in the next few verses.

30. כִּי לְיוֹם אֵיד יֵחָשֶׂךְ רָע לְיוֹם עֲבָרוֹת יוּבָלוּ — *That the evil man is spared the day of calamity, the day upon which the furies are summoned.* חָשַׂךְ, *to withhold.* In this context, *to withhold involvement, to spare.*

31. מִי־יַגִּיד עַל־פָּנָיו דַּרְכּוֹ וְהוּא־עָשָׂה מִי יְשַׁלֶּם־לוֹ — *Who dares chide him to his face? Though he has transgressed, who will requite him?* The wicked man would laugh at anyone attempting to castigate him for his evil ways. Experience has shown him that he has nothing to fear.

32. וְהוּא לִקְבָרוֹת יוּבָל וְעַל־גָּדִישׁ יִשְׁקוֹד — *He will be taken to the burial ground, be hastened to the mound.* When he dies, he will be treated with respect and carried to burial with appropriate speed.

גָּדִישׁ is a pile of sheaves. It is borrowed here as a metaphor for the grave, called a mound because of the earth which will have been piled up upon it after the interment.

33. מָתְקוּ־לוֹ רִגְבֵי נָחַל וְאַחֲרָיו כָּל־אָדָם יִמְשׁוֹךְ וּלְפָנָיו אֵין מִסְפָּר — *The earth-clods of the valley will seem sweet to him, all will be drawn after him, those who go before him are without number.* The burial itself will be a sweet experience. He will be followed by crowds of people, eager to show him the last respect. And he will have been preceded by many people who will have vied for the honor of preparing his grave for him.

25 The other dies, profoundly bitter, never having tasted delight.
26 Together, they will lie in the dust, worms will blanket them.
27 See, I know your thoughts, the ideas which you withhold from
me. 28 That you say, 'I challenge you to show me the secure house
of those that act nobly; I challenge you to show me the fragile tent
of the wicked!' 29 But is it not true that you have inquired of the
wayfarers, those whose clearly demonstrated truths you dare not
reject. 30 That the evil man is spared the day of calamity, the day
upon which the furies are summoned. 31 Who dares chide him to
his face? Though he has transgressed, who will requite him? 32 He
will be taken to the burial ground, be hastened to the mound. 33 The
earth-clods of the valley will seem sweet to him, all will be drawn
after him, those who go before him are without number. 34 How can
you attempt to comfort me with platitudes, all your justifications
are no more than betrayals.

34. וְאֵיךְ תְּנַחֲמוּנִי הָבֶל וּתְשׁוּבֹתֵיכֶם נִשְׁאַר־מָעַל — *How can you attempt to comfort me with platitudes, all your justifications are no more than betrayals.* I have clearly demonstrated that the world is not governed by Divine Providence. Everything that happens results from blind happenstance. Accordingly, your promises that if I were to repent all would be well, are no more than empty platitudes. Nothing can make any difference to what happens to me.

In Iyov's final sentence, he once more treats the friends as a group. At verse 3 we saw that for a brief moment, he had hoped that their united front might be broken, and that as individuals, they would empathize more lovingly with his terrible plight. His anticipation was short-lived.

We cannot know the source of his disillusionment. Perhaps he saw from Tzophar's face that his impassioned description of the sleek and successful evildoers left no impression at all.

The speech which had begun in high hope, ends in disappointment.

◆§ The Second Round

We are hard put to find the precise function, in the Iyov saga, of this second round of speeches. It will be instructive to quote *Ramban* in his compact introductions to the six speeches which comprise it:

1. Eliphaz: The content [of Eliphaz's second speech] is as follows: When Eliphaz first heard Iyov curse the day of his birth, he chided him by pointing out that the heavenly constellations play no function in determining evil or good. All derives only from the wish of the Almighty — all is justice and righteousness. Eliphaz did not [then] accuse Iyov of any wrongdoing, but only encouraged him to sublimate his sufferings. Now, however, that Iyov defended himself and challenged God to debate, Eliphaz tells him, 'Till now I had thought that your suffering had the purpose, not of punishing you for a heinous crime, but of chastising you so that you might improve yourself. But now, your own mouth testifies that, all along, you were wicked, without any fear of God.'

   For the rest of this speech, it denies that some wicked men have a good life; for all of them will eventually perish. This is the position of all the friends.
2. Iyov: In this speech no new ground is broken. Iyov says to the friends only that their attempts at comforting are meaningless, and that in order to help him they fabricate lies — specifically that the wicked are destined to be destroyed. He bemoans his wounds and illnesses and opines that they have come upon him undeserved. This proves that there is no Divine Providence. He complains of his friends who deny his righteousness, for in his own eyes he is a righteous man.
3. Bildad: Bildad adds nothing new in this speech, concentrates only upon a graphic description of the destruction of the wicked. This is advanced as incontestable proof that suffering comes only as judgment.
4. Iyov: In this speech, Iyov breaks no new ground. He only describes his pains and evil fortune

graphically and claims that they come upon him for no good reason and in contravention of justice. His intention is to contradict the assertion that they are meant to chastise and to guide. He bemoans his fate, as do all those who writhe in pain. The degree of his suffering serves as proof that God protects no one. In the end, he adds that the friends will all be punished for not empathizing with him in his pain.

5. Tzophar: This man teaches nothing in this speech. All he does is to paint graphic pictures and expound upon the destruction of the wicked. This, because all the friends have already given Iyov answers to his problems, each in his own first speech. They have nothing more to do now than to speak of the destruction of the wicked and that their descendants will be cut off.
6. Iyov: In this speech Iyov goes to great lengths to assert that there are wicked people who live happy lives, endowed with wealth, blessed with children and tranquility. He derides the friends who claim that justice is served by the fact that, ultimately, the seed of the wicked will be destroyed. His intention is to destroy their arguments with incontrovertible proofs. This is all he does, because he had already tried to convince them of his righteousness and had not succeeded; because the suffering of the righteous is never an insurmountable problem, for we are always able to assume that, in reality, he is a sinner . . .

In numbers 5 and 6, *Ramban* makes clear that the first round has exhausted the substantive arguments in the debate. The friends have made their respective points, and Iyov has offered his defense — and has had it rejected. In effect then, beside indicating a change in direction on the part of Eliphaz [1] and a spirited rebuttal of the doctrine of the inevitable destruction of the wicked by Iyov [6], there is really nothing new in this round [2,3,4 and 5].

How, then, are we to understand its purpose?

This problem arises only if we look upon the book as a record of a theological debate, designed to elucidate differing points of view concerning the burning issues of human suffering and Divine concern or indifference. If this is the purpose, then we should expect that each speech make a distinct and discrete contribution to the subject at hand.

But, if there is another design; if we are to study human nature and to learn how to go about, or not go about, the comforting of another human being, then this second round has much to teach us.

Each of the three friends has reacted differently to the frustrations of the first round.

In *Eliphaz's Second Speech* (chapter 15) we were troubled by the fact that the entire second round is devoted to the problem of the perceived tranquility of the wicked — a problem which had never been uppermost in Iyov's mind. We suggested that, . . . *frustrated at their own impotence . . . [the friends] are taking refuge in flights of oratory which deal with a theoretical — and therefore safe — topic, thus saving themselves the ignominy of failure in a more direct and meaningful approach.*

This is certainly true for Eliphaz. Indeed this greatest of the three friends seems to have suffered most from the frustration born of Iyov's perceived obduracy. He alone, in the third round, will accuse Iyov of the vilest transgressions, will not have been moved at all by Iyov's piteous cry, *O pity me, pity me, you who are my friends!* (19:21). He is, then, the prototype of the ineffective comforter of whom the *Zohar* talks (see Introductory Remarks to chapter 4). In him we see the danger of being unprepared to deal with human suffering. From well-meant but ill-conceived concern, he moves to insensitive and uncaring polemic, to outright cruelty, in the third round.

Bildad appears as both worse and better than Eliphaz. In the second round he follows the latter's lead, but surpasses him in his lack of tact. He chides the grovelling and tortured Iyov with ignoring the niceties of formal debate, and is so insensitive as to describe in the most vivid terms how the wicked man can expect to have his children die, never remembering that only now had Iyov himself had to face the blight of his own future as his sons lay beneath the rubble of his firstborn's house.

But, and this is to his credit, he is not deaf to Iyov's pathetic cry. He does not go as far as Tzophar who already in his second speech distances himself from the group (see Introductory Remarks to chapter 20), but he does not, either, follow Eliphaz's lead in the third round — is apparently unwilling to condemn Iyov further. He turns to God in ecstasy — not against Iyov in imprecation.

Perhaps, the key element in understanding Bildad is that he was a follower, not a leader. Where Eliphaz, in the second round, was circumspect, Bildad ebulliently threw any inhibition to the wind and went much further. But, there was a point beyond which he would not follow. Where Eliphaz

1 Eliphaz the Temanite responded and said: 2 Can a mere human

refused to be deflected from the road that he had chosen, Bildad allowed himself to be moved by Iyov's agony to the extent that after he has had his say in this second round he will not condemn Iyov anymore.

Tzophar, already in his first speech, had lacked the condemnatory spirit. As we have discussed in *Tzophar's First Speech* (chapter 11), he was interested not in explaining Iyov's suffering, but in helping him over his propensity to vilify God. He shows sensitivity and deep psychological insight in recognizing the causes of Iyov's brokenness of spirit and gently chides him to put his own house in order so that he might conquer the spirit of bitterness which caused him to blaspheme. With such a disposition to see the positive in his friend, it is no surprise that he would pick up on Iyov's plea for mercy and disassociate himself from the group which had erred so badly in its attempts at comforting.

And so, this second round leads into the third. There, Eliphaz will lose all sense of proportion in a sweeping, and totally unfounded, condemnation of Iyov; Bildad will sing a song of jubilation to God, perhaps hoping to sweep up Iyov in his ecstasy; and Tzophar will not appear at all — a chastened spirit, aware of his failings and unwilling to take up the cudgels anymore.

◈ Eliphaz's Third Speech

Did Eliphaz mean this (chapter 22) to be his last speech? Did he think that with it, he would finally convince Iyov? Was it Iyov's rejection which persuaded him not to continue? Was it Bildad's clear change of direction? Was it Tzophar's silence?

For these questions we will find no answers. It seems certain, at least when read superficially, that there is nothing to differentiate this speech from any of the others, nothing which would give us any intimation that with it, Eliphaz will disappear from the stage.

And yet — there is, after all, something special.

In Eliphaz's first two speeches we applied a careful structural analysis to those two speeches. We found significance in both the amount of space which was devoted to each of the various topics, and also in their positioning within the speeches.

If we then subject this third speech to the same tests, we find within it a remarkable symmetry. The first thirteen verses (A: 2-14) are devoted to a description of Iyov's alleged wickedness. Then we have four verses (B: 15-18) in which the wicked are described. These are followed by another twelve (C: 19-30) which talk of the bliss which will be the lot of the righteous.

If we apply the criteria of our earlier analysis, then clearly the (C) section is, both by dint of its position and its relative length when compared with (B), by far the more significant in Eliphaz's mind. If, however, we compare it to (A), then each has a very slight advantage over the other. The description of Iyov's perceived wickedness is marginally longer, the description of the bliss of the righteous is more advantageously positioned.

What is being said by this?

Perhaps Eliphaz wishes to leave us with a feeling of ambiguity. By content, as we have analyzed the speech in the commentary, it is certainly unrelievedly and — as we believe, unreasonably — negative. By skillful and felicitous structuring however, Eliphaz allows us to retain doubts. Iyov was after all his friend. Although convinced of his unconscionable wickedness (A), he would nevertheless be happier if it were different. He wishes to leave Iyov with a picture of what might have been because — he still hopes — it may yet come about.

XXII.

1-5. Most striking about this, Eliphaz's last speech, is the opening passage. Each of the friends' earlier speeches had begun with some remark, addressed to what Iyov had said immediately before. Thus, to take the examples from Eliphaz himself, his first speech opens: *If you tire of one hurdle set against you; who would be capable of withholding speech* (4:2). This is said in reaction to the imprecations to which Iyov had given vent in chapter 3. The second speech opens: *Would a wise man hold forth with bluster, fill his belly with the east wind?* (15:2), which clearly, as the remainder of his remarks makes clear, reacts to what Iyov had said in his earlier reply to Tzophar.

Here, Eliphaz's opening salvo finds no point of reference in the ideas which Iyov has just expressed. Verse 2 is obscure, but there is no doubt that it belongs together with verses 3 and 4, and that the sense of this cluster of

ג עָלֵימוֹ מַשְׂכִּיל: הַחֵפֶץ לְשַׁדַּי כִּי תִצְדָּק וְאִם־בֶּצַע
ד כִּי־תַתֵּם דְּרָכֶיךָ: הֲמִיִּרְאָתְךָ יֹכִיחֶךָ יָבוֹא עִמְּךָ
ה בַּמִּשְׁפָּט: הֲלֹא רָעָתְךָ רַבָּה וְאֵין־קֵץ לַעֲוֹנֹתֶיךָ:

verses is to assert that God owes nothing at all to man, and that He will be neither bribed nor bullied into a personal confrontation. Verse 5 hurls a general accusation of evildoing against Iyov, of which verses 6-14 spell out the details. In the speech which Iyov has just now completed in answer to Tzophar or, more correctly, in answer to all the three friends in the second round, there is no mention at all of any wish to confront God at a bar of justice, nor of any claim to personal righteousness. It is devoted entirely to a refutation of the doctrine espoused by the friends — that the wicked invariably are punished for their evil.

The two points which Eliphaz makes here would be entirely appropriate in answer to Iyov's reply to Tzophar in round 1 (chapters 12-14); would, in fact, appear to be a logical continuation of Eliphaz's answer to that speech (chapter 15).

In that speech, Iyov does challenge God to a confrontation [*But it is to Shaddai that I would speak, it is with God that I would remonstrate* (13:3). *See I have composed a brief, I know that I shall win the case* (13:18)], and does also assert his own righteousness [*How many are my sins and my transgressions, inform me of my sins and my transgressions!* (13:23)].[1]

There seems to be no doubt at all that even the form of the four verses which open Eliphaz's remarks here, is designed to match Iyov's words in that speech:

Chapter 13	*Chapter 22*
7. הַלְאֵל תְּדַבְּרוּ עַוְלָה וְלוֹ תְּדַבְּרוּ רְמִיָּה *Will you represent God with wickedness, would you speak falsehoods for Him?*	2. הַלְאֵל יִסְכָּן־גָּבֶר כִּי־יִסְכֹּן עָלֵימוֹ מַשְׂכִּיל *Can a mere human be of any help to the Almighty! Surely one who lives his life with understanding, helps only himself.*
8. הֲפָנָיו תִּשָּׂאוּן אִם־לָאֵל תְּרִיבוּן *Do you expect to flatter Him, is it for God that you contend?*	3. הַחֵפֶץ לְשַׁדַּי כִּי תִצְדָּק וְאִם־בֶּצַע כִּי־תַתֵּם דְּרָכֶיךָ *What does Shaddai care if you are righteous, what gain if you were to perfect your ways?*
9. הֲטוֹב כִּי־יַחְקֹר אֶתְכֶם אִם־כְּהָתֵל בֶּאֱנוֹשׁ תְּהָתֵלּוּ בוֹ *Would it be good were He to inquire into you,would you treat Him with derision as you would, a man?*	4. הֲמִיִּרְאָתְךָ יֹכִיחֶךָ יָבוֹא עִמְּךָ בַּמִּשְׁפָּט *Would fear of you inveigle Him into a confrontation, cause Him to appear with you at the bar of justice?*
11. הֲלֹא שְׂאֵתוֹ תְּבַעֵת אֶתְכֶם וּפַחְדּוֹ יִפֹּל עֲלֵיכֶם *Will His exaltedness not terrify you, His fear not fall upon you?*	5. הֲלֹא רָעָתְךָ רַבָּה וְאֵין־קֵץ לַעֲוֹנֹתֶיךָ *Clearly your evil is overwhelming, there is no end to your iniquities.*

The parallelism does not exhaust itself in the language of the two passages [Both begin with, . . . הַלְאֵל, continue with two sentences both beginning with the interrogative . . . הֲ, and are followed by a sentence beginning with, . . . הֲלֹא (although the earlier passage has one intervening verse)], but extends to the content. In the earlier passage, Iyov uses the first three verses to chide the friends for their erroneous understanding of God — they believe that they serve Him well by obfuscating the issues; while here, in the parallel three verses, Eliphaz attempts to set Iyov straight about his assumptions about Divine-human relationships — God gains nothing from human wisdom or righteousness. In the fourth verse of the earlier passage, Iyov tells the friends some home-truths about themselves — they are destined to be terrified by the consequences of their temerity; and in our section Eliphaz turns the tables with his dissection of Iyov's character.

We conclude that Eliphaz has not even been listening to the intervening debate. His mind

1. At this point we note that our verse 4 appears to pick up expressions from 13:3 and 18 respectively. הֲמִיִּרְאָתְךָ יֹכִיחֶךָ recalls, . . . וְהוֹכֵחַ אֶל אֵל אֶחְפָּץ, while יָבוֹא עִמְּךָ בַּמִּשְׁפָּט . . . echos, הִנֵּה נָא עָרַכְתִּי מִשְׁפָּט.

be of any help to the Almighty! Surely one who lives his life
with understanding, helps only himself. [3] *What does Shaddai*
care if you are righteous, what gain if you were to perfect your
ways? [4] *Would fear of you inveigle Him into a confrontation,*
cause Him to appear with you at the bar of justice? [5] *Clearly*
your evil is overwhelming, there is no end to your iniquities.

is still on Iyov's earlier speech — the one that he was last called upon to answer. As we indicated in *The Second Round*, he among all the friends seems to have failed Iyov most dismally. His mind has veered away from his erstwhile love and now knows nothing but the theological dream-castles which he has built.

In *Ramban's* thought, there is another, extremely significant point of reference to Iyov's speech in chapter 13.

At 13:15 Iyov had, as *Ramban* there understood him, affirmed his belief in Divine Providence and justice in the afterlife. He had simply argued that even granting this, it could not excuse the suffering of the righteous in this physical, albeit temporary, world. Why, he demanded, could God not provide the righteous with the bliss which they merited, in both worlds? It is to this argument that Eliphaz responds here. He argues that from the fact that God gains nothing at all from man's good deeds, it follows that His purpose in demanding anything at all is only to benefit us. Clearly, even man's fate in this world is governed by God's beneficence. If Iyov is suffering, it can only be because he was, in fact, a sinner.

Ramban views this theological position of Iyov — that justice prevails in the afterlife but not in this world — as being absolutely fundamental to Iyov's thought. As *Ramban* interprets it, this thought permeates the entire *mashal* which Iyov delivers in chapters 27-28, see there.

It should be noted, though, that this thesis is yielded by only *Ramban's* reading of 13:15. *Rashi* never makes this point, and consequently diverges from *Ramban* in key sections of the book.

2. הַלְאֵל יִסְכָּן־גָּבֶר כִּי־יִסְכֹּן עָלֵימוֹ מַשְׂכִּיל — *Can a mere human be of any help to the Almighty! Surely one who lives his life with understanding, helps only himself.* We have rendered the verse as does *Metzudos*. Taken thus, it fits in smoothly with the next two verses.

Ramban suggests: [We disagree with you, not in order to curry favor with God.] Our human efforts can never help God in any way. That a wise person (מַשְׂכִּיל) refutes your arguments (עָלֵימוֹ) will never in any way give pleasure to God (כִּי יִסְכֹּן). [Therefore it is only for the sake of truth that we argue with you.]

Targum: Could man ever teach God anything (סכן, *to teach*). And if he were to attempt such a thing, would God ever listen to him?

3. הַחֵפֶץ לְשַׁדַּי כִּי תִצְדָּק וְאִם־בֶּצַע כִּי־תַתֵּם דְּרָכֶיךָ — *What does Shaddai care if you are righteous, what gain if you were to perfect your ways?* Your righteousness could in no way persuade God to enter into an argument with you (*Rashi*).

4. הֲמִיִּרְאָתְךָ יֹכִיחֶךָ יָבֹא עִמְּךָ בַּמִּשְׁפָּט — *Would fear of you inveigle Him into a confrontation, cause Him to appear with you at the bar of justice*? Would fear that you might otherwise act wickedly bring God to the bar of justice? Your wickedness could in no way harm Him (*Metzudos*).

5. הֲלֹא רָעָתְךָ רַבָּה וְאֵין־קֵץ לַעֲוֺנֹתֶיךָ — *Clearly your evil is overwhelming, there is no end to your iniquities*. God must know that you have perpetrated great evil (*Rashi*) [and it must be for this reason that He brings suffering upon you. He need feel no compunction for refusing to justify Himself in front of a bar of justice.]

Rashi, by interpreting, . . . הֲלֹא, *Clearly, He knows . . .*, appears to be softening Eliphaz's apparently preposterous statement. If, as the simple translation of the phrase would have seemed to yield, Eliphaz is making a statement of fact — Iyov is very evil — then we would have had to ask: How does Eliphaz know this? Up to the moment of his coming to comfort him, Eliphaz had lived far away, had indeed regarded Iyov as a close friend. If from his personal observation he would have known that Iyov is the cruel ogre whom he now depicts, he would surely have broken off that friendship.

But, even given all this, *Rashi's* explanation holds good only for this verse. If Eliphaz had made only this general statement, then indeed we would have seen it as justified under the circumstances. But what of the litany of sins which follows? Why the graphic depiction of heinous crimes which cannot be more than figments of Eliphaz's imagination?

We must conclude that Eliphaz is allowing

ו־ז כִּֽי־תַחְבֹּ֣ל אַחֶ֣יךָ חִנָּ֑ם וּבִגְדֵ֖י עֲרוּמִּ֣ים תַּפְשִֽׁיט: לֹא־
ח מַ֭יִם עָיֵ֣ף תַּשְׁקֶ֑ה וּ֝מֵרָעֵ֗ב תִּֽמְנַֽע־לָֽחֶם: וְאִ֣ישׁ זְ֭רוֹעַ ל֣וֹ
ט הָאָ֑רֶץ וּנְשׂ֥וּא פָ֝נִ֗ים יֵ֣שֶׁב בָּֽהּ: אַ֭לְמָנוֹת שִׁלַּ֣חְתָּ רֵיקָ֑ם
י וּזְרֹע֖וֹת יְתֹמִ֣ים יְדֻכָּֽא: עַל־כֵּ֭ן סְבִיבוֹתֶ֣יךָ פַחִ֑ים וִ֝יבַהֶלְךָ֗
יא פַּ֣חַד פִּתְאֹֽם: אוֹ־חֹ֥שֶׁךְ לֹֽא־תִרְאֶ֑ה וְֽשִׁפְעַת־מַ֥יִם
יב תְּכַסֶּֽךָּ: הֲֽלֹא־אֱ֭לוֹהַּ גֹּ֣בַהּ שָׁמָ֑יִם וּרְאֵ֤ה רֹ֖אשׁ כּוֹכָבִ֣ים
יג כִּי־רָֽמּוּ: וְֽ֭אָמַרְתָּ מַה־יָּ֣דַע אֵ֑ל הַבְעַ֖ד עֲרָפֶ֣ל יִשְׁפּֽוֹט:

his condemnatory spirit to run away with him. He has become completely caught up in his thesis, theory has entirely replaced reality. It is small wonder that God's anger was kindled against him and his friends (42:7).

Metzudos, again apparently with the object of softening the statement, suggests: God will certainly not agree to a confrontation with you. However, I will answer in His stead: He has been justified in sending these troubles upon you because, as a role-model from whom people will learn, your smallest transgressions loom large. There is no end to your iniquity because it does not stop with you. It continues to make waves as more and more people learn to act as you have done.

6. כִּי־תַחְבֹּל אַחֶיךָ חִנָּם וּבִגְדֵי עֲרוּמִּים תַּפְשִׁיט — *For without any justification do you take pledges from your brothers, tear off the garments from the naked.* חבל, *to bind*, thus, *to take* or *give a pledge. Without any justification* seems to imply that Iyov would take pledges from his brothers [friends?, relatives?], even when they owed him no money at all.

In chapter 24, Iyov describes the practices of wicked people. The taking of pledges from defenseless people is mentioned twice: once from the widow (v. 30) and once from the destitute (v. 9). It is instructive that never does Iyov accuse even the most wicked of taking pledges חִנָּם, *without any justification*. Once more we see a propensity on Eliphaz's part to exaggerate Iyov's purported wickedness.

Metzudos points out that clothes are not torn off people who are already naked. They become naked because their clothes are taken. But, he says, such is the usage of Hebrew that people and things are described עַל שֵׁם סוֹפָן, as they will be as a result of a given action.

7. לֹא־מַיִם עָיֵף תַּשְׁקֶה וּמֵרָעֵב תִּמְנַע־לָחֶם — *You would not give an exhausted man water to drink, and withheld bread from the starving.* Iyov himself paints a different picture about his attitude toward the poor: *I would save the groaning poor, the orphans whom none would help. The blessings of the destitute were mine, I would give cheer to widows. I would don righteousness so that it became my very garment, my sense of justice became shirt and crown to me. I became eyes for the blind, legs for the lame. I am a father for the destitute, made it my business to acquaint myself with quarrels of which I knew nothing* (29:12-16).

8. וְאִישׁ זְרוֹעַ לוֹ הָאָרֶץ וּנְשׂוּא פָנִים יֵשֶׁב בָּהּ — *Does then the world belong to him who would strong-arm others, does he who is looked up to have a permanent lease upon it?* The translation follows *Rashi*. Eliphaz is taunting Iyov as the bully who thinks that he owns the world.

Metzudos has: While you always took advantage of the poor and defenseless, you would toady to the rich. As far as you were concerned it was as though the strong men owned the world; the powerful ones might, for all you cared, live there permanently.

9. אַלְמָנוֹת שִׁלַּחְתָּ רֵיקָם וּזְרֹעוֹת יְתֹמִים יְדֻכָּא — *You have driven away widows empty-handed, broken the strength of orphans.* In contrast to your treatment of the powerful, you were merciless to the widows. If you became aware of even a slight infraction of any rule, you would drive them out, even taking from them the little that they possessed. In doing so you broke the strength of their children, the orphans. With their mothers gone, there was no one to help them. (*Metzudos*).

10. עַל־כֵּן סְבִיבוֹתֶיךָ פַּחִים וִיבַהֶלְךָ פַּחַד פִּתְאֹם — *Therefore are you surrounded by snares, sudden terror will confuse you.* Clearly the sense of this verse and the next is that the troubles described in them are Iyov's punishment for the wrongdoings listed in the earlier verses.

But, if this is the case, would we not have expected Eliphaz to describe the actual suffering to which Iyov had been subjected? Why does he not say that because of his wickedness his wealth had been decimated, his family destroyed, his health ruined? Why the snares, the terror, the darkness, the water?

Perhaps this would indicate that the accusa-

6 For without any justification do you take pledges from
your brothers, tear off the garments from the naked. 7 You
would not give an exhausted man water to drink, and withheld
bread from the starving. 8 Does then the world belong to him who
would strong-arm others, does he who is looked up to have a per-
manent lease upon it? 9 You have driven away widows empty-
handed, broken the strength of orphans. 10 Therefore are you
surrounded by snares, sudden terror will confuse you. 11 Or dark-
ness through which you cannot see, till torrents of water engulf
you. 12 Is not God high in the heaven? You have set your sights
above the vaulting stars. 13 That you say, 'What can the Almighty
know, can He make judgments through the intense darkness?'

tions of the previous verses are not to be taken literally. Eliphaz was not describing Iyov, the man, but talked of him as a paradigm of a wicked person who, having done all the evil things described, would be punished as set forth here. This interpretation would certainly tend to mitigate the harsh picture of Eliphaz's unreasoning animosity, as we have analyzed it in the commentary above.

However, there is also another possibility. Eliphaz is describing Iyov's present situation, not what has happened to him in the past. He is explaining why Iyov cannot find peace from his restless questings, why now, that nothing can be undone anymore, he cannot make peace with himself and simply learn to live positively in his reduced state. For this he uses the metaphor of the frightened animal dashing in every which direction in order to escape some unknown terror, always driven back by obstacles which it cannot overcome, darkness which it cannot penetrate, waters which are too deep to ford. So too is Iyov. Unwilling to live with the horror of his reality, striking out in all directions for some solution to his predicament, he is always being beaten back by truths against which his intellectual vigor beats itself to exhaustion.

11. אוֹ־חֹשֶׁךְ לֹא־תִרְאֶה וְשִׁפְעַת־מַיִם תְּכַסֶּךָּ — *Or darkness through which you cannot see, till torrents of water engulf you.* We follow *Ramban*. The earlier verse had talked of sudden terrors which constantly plague the wicked Iyov. Our verse describes the other possibility. He may be totally unaware, and therefore unafraid, of the lowering clouds and darkness until the downpour which engulfs him takes him by surprise.

12. הֲלֹא־אֱלוֹהַּ גֹּבַהּ שָׁמָיִם וּרְאֵה רֹאשׁ כּוֹכָבִים כִּי־רָמּוּ — *Is not God high in the heaven? You have set your sights above the vaulting stars.* If you are so wicked and still have the temerity to maintain your innocence, this can only be because you believe God to be so far removed from the affairs of man, that He simply is unaware of what they do. This, will be made clear in the next verses (*Rashi, Ramban* and *Metzudos*).

13. וְאָמַרְתָּ מַה־יָּדַע אֵל הַבְעַד עֲרָפֶל יִשְׁפּוֹט — *That you say, 'What can the Almighty know, can He make judgments through the intense darkness?'* The thought begun in the previous verse continues here and carries on into the next verse.

Again, one has to wonder at Eliphaz's contention. Can he really believe that Iyov thinks that God is unaware of what goes on in this world? Even if such an opinion held sway among some groups of heretics [see *Ramban* (Introduction to *Iyov*) on *Psalms* 73:10: *Then they say, 'How could God know, does the Most High have knowledge?'*], Iyov certainly does not subscribe to it: *Who does not know through all these — that it is the hand of God which wrought all this. In Whose hand is the life-force of all living creatures, the spirit within all of mankind* (12:9-10). And even if, with *Ramban*, we were to assert that Iyov's first speech indicates a similar line of thought, it is clear that already at chapter 6, when he responds to Eliphaz's first speech, he has conceded his error — see Introductory Remarks to that chapter.

Now it is true that throughout Iyov's many speeches, there is a degree of ambivalence concerning God's involvement in the affairs of man (see *Iyov's Response to Tzophar's First Speech* in chapter 12, and *Ramban* to 35:2), but to say that he denies God's *knowledge* flies in the face of most of his contentions — chief among them, that God somehow takes pleasure in the tortures which he is undergoing (see particularly chapter 9).

יד־טו עָבִים סֵתֶר־לוֹ וְלֹא יִרְאֶה וְחוּג שָׁמַיִם יִתְהַלָּךְ: הַאֹרַח
טז עוֹלָם תִּשְׁמוֹר אֲשֶׁר דָּרְכוּ מְתֵי־אָוֶן: אֲשֶׁר־קֻמְּטוּ וְלֹא־
יז עֵת נָהָר יוּצַק יְסוֹדָם: הָאֹמְרִים לָאֵל סוּר מִמֶּנּוּ
יח וּמַה־יִּפְעַל שַׁדַּי לָמוֹ: וְהוּא מִלֵּא בָתֵּיהֶם טוֹב וַעֲצַת
יט רְשָׁעִים רָחֲקָה מֶנִּי: יִרְאוּ צַדִּיקִים וְיִשְׂמָחוּ וְנָקִי יִלְעַג־
כ־כא לָמוֹ: אִם־לֹא נִכְחַד קִימָנוּ וְיִתְרָם אָכְלָה אֵשׁ: הַסְכֶּן־
כב נָא עִמּוֹ וּשְׁלָם בָּהֶם תְּבוֹאָתְךָ טוֹבָה: קַח־נָא מִפִּיו
כג תּוֹרָה וְשִׂים אֲמָרָיו בִּלְבָבֶךָ: אִם־תָּשׁוּב עַד־שַׁדַּי תִּבָּנֶה
כד תַּרְחִיק עַוְלָה מֵאָהֳלֶךָ: וְשִׁית־עַל־עָפָר בָּצֶר וּבְצוּר
כה נְחָלִים אוֹפִיר: וְהָיָה שַׁדַּי בְּצָרֶיךָ וְכֶסֶף תּוֹעָפוֹת לָךְ:

How indeed can Eliphaz, in this very speech, deride Iyov's longing to stand with God before the bar of justice — a claim which would be absolutely meaningless once God's *knowledge* is denied — and then claim that Iyov challenges that very knowledge?

Once more we must conclude that Eliphaz, in this last speech, has lost his sense of proportion and is willing not only to accuse Iyov of wrongdoings which he clearly never committed, but also of opinions to which, manifestly, he does not subscribe.

14. עָבִים סֵתֶר־לוֹ וְלֹא יִרְאֶה וְחוּג שָׁמַיִם יִתְהַלָּךְ — *The clouds hide Him so that He cannot see, He travels around the circle of the heavens.* His sphere of interest is limited to the heavens; He knows nothing of what transpires upon the earth (*Rashi*).

15. הַאֹרַח עוֹלָם תִּשְׁמוֹר אֲשֶׁר דָּרְכוּ מְתֵי־אָוֶן — *Do you recall the ways of old, the ways trodden by the sinners?* Translation follows *Ramban* and *Radak*. [*Rashi* and *R' Yosef Kara* read the ensuing passage as referring to the fate of, either the people of Sodom, or to the generation of Noah which was inundated by the Flood. Since we feel that this is true at the *aggadic* level, but is not meant as the simple meaning of the text, we have elected to follow those commentators who go with the plain meaning of the verses; see footnote to 28:4.] The heresies described in the previous verses are not new. There have always been people who denied God's knowledge, but these have been speedily destroyed as described in the next verse. Surely, Iyov does not want to be a part of this.

16. אֲשֶׁר־קֻמְּטוּ וְלֹא־עֵת נָהָר יוּצַק יְסוֹדָם — *Who were cut off before their time, torrents poured down upon their foundations.* קָמַט as *cut off* follows *Ramban* and *Radak* in *Shorashim*. The meaning, according to the latter, could either be borrowed from the meaning, *to be wrinkled*, in which case it would be a metaphor for old age, and therefore, approaching death; or קָמַט might be an inversion of קָטַם, *to pluck*.

The torrents of water inundating the foundations are a metaphor for speedy destruction (*Ramban*). *Rashi* and various other commentators see the phrase as a reference to the people who were swept away by the flood in Noah's time.

17. הָאֹמְרִים לָאֵל סוּר מִמֶּנּוּ וּמַה־יִּפְעַל שַׁדַּי לָמוֹ — *They, who say to the Almighty, 'Leave us be!' And what will Shaddai do to them? Ramban* and *Metzudos* read סוּר as though it were written, סָר, *He has turned away*. They say about God that He has forsaken them. We have translated the form as an imperative, as it is written.

18. וְהוּא מִלֵּא בָתֵּיהֶם טוֹב וַעֲצַת רְשָׁעִים רָחֲקָה מֶנִּי — *But He had filled their homes with all manner of good, surely the thoughts of the wicked are beyond me!* God had filled the homes of the wicked with all the beautiful things which they possess. Why, then, would they wish to deny Him? Eliphaz professes not to understand their thinking.

19. יִרְאוּ צַדִּיקִים וְיִשְׂמָחוּ וְנָקִי יִלְעַג־לָמוֹ — *The righteous watched and rejoiced, the pure derided them.* We follow *Ramban* that this verse is to be read together with the next: The righteous of the world will be pleased by their vindication, the pure will have occasion to deride the wicked when their downfall becomes obvious.

20. אִם־לֹא נִכְחַד קִימָנוּ וְיִתְרָם אָכְלָה אֵשׁ — *That our world has not been destroyed, but their pride was burned by fire.* Taking קִימָנוּ as an unusual form of יְקוּמֵינוּ, *our world* (*Radak, Shorashim*), the translation follows *Ramban*. The righteous mentioned in the previous verse see that in spite of all vicissitudes, their world

[14] The clouds hide Him so that He cannot see, He travels around
the circle of the heavens. [15] Do you recall the ways of old, the
ways trodden by the sinners? [16] Who were cut off before their
time, torrents poured down upon their foundations. [17] They,
who say to the Almighty, 'Leave us be!' And what will Shaddai
do to them? [18] But He had filled their homes with all manner
of good, surely the thoughts of the wicked are beyond me! [19] The
righteous watched and rejoiced, the pure derided them. [20] That
our world has not been destroyed, but their pride was burned
by fire. [21] Acquire, then, the habit of being with Him as He would
wish — and you shall be at peace, by such methods you shall be
granted happiness. [22] Allow, I beg you, His words to instruct
you, place His sayings in your heart. [23] If you but turn back
to Shaddai you will be re-established, but, distance iniquity
from your heart. [24] You will raise up strongholds upon the earth,
rocks in the valleys will contain your gold. [25] Then Shaddai will
turn against your enemies, mountains of silver will be yours.

continues to flourish, and this imbues them with joy. They look askance upon the wicked who, in spite of initial gains, will eventually lose everything.

We have rendered יִתְרָם as *their pride*, in accordance with *Rashi* who offers גֵּאוּתָם, *gain*, which would be a more literal translation from יָתֵר, *to add* on.

21. הַסְכֶּן־נָא עִמּוֹ וּשְׁלָם בָּהֶם תְּבוֹאָתְךָ טוֹבָה — *Acquire, then, the habit of being with Him as He would wish — and you shall be at peace, by such methods you shall be granted happiness.* We have followed *Metzudos*. סָכַן as the *acquisition of a habit* is attested by him from *Psalms* 139:3.

We have expanded the simple עִמּוֹ, *with Him*, to *being with Him as He would wish*, in accordance with *Rashi's* understanding.

From here onward, Eliphaz exhorts Iyov to strike out in a new direction, to become righteous where earlier, as perceived by Eliphaz, he had been wicked.

The first step would seem to be the acceptance of God's direct providence as a given (*Metzudos*).

22. קַח־נָא מִפִּיו תּוֹרָה וְשִׂים אֲמָרָיו בִּלְבָבֶךָ — *Allow, I beg you, His words to instruct you, place His sayings in your heart*. Once Iyov will have accepted the given of God's direct providence, he will be vitally interested in discovering the ways in which God wishes him to go.

23. אִם־תָּשׁוּב עַד־שַׁדַּי תִּבָּנֶה תַּרְחִיק עַוְלָה מֵאָהֳלֶךָ — *If you but turn back to Shaddai you will be re-established, but, distance iniquity from your heart*. Your rehabilitation is up to you. You need only repent and all will be well — but your repentance must be an honest one. You must not hold on to any of your past transgressions. Were you to do so, you would be like one who immerses himself in a *mikveh* while holding on to the source of his uncleanliness. Needless to say, his immersion will be useless (*Metzudos*).

24. וְשִׁית־עַל־עָפָר בָּצֶר וּבְצוּר נְחָלִים אוֹפִיר — *You will raise up strongholds upon the earth, rocks in the valleys will contain your gold*. If you but return to God, you will be both mighty and wealthy.

Ramban understands *upon the earth*, that you will be so strong that you will not find it necessary to build your fortresses among the rocks. You will not have to fear many threats, and therefore it will not be necessary that your fortresses be impregnable.

For צוּר נְחָלִים we have followed *Rashi*. Strong rocks located in deep valleys, protected by the mountains which surround them, are the safest place to keep one's treasures (*Metzudos*). אוֹפִיר is short for זְהַב אוֹפִיר, *the gold from Ophir*, which is the highest quality gold (*Metzudos*).

Targum, apparently followed by *Ramban* and *R' Meyuchas*, read as though the phrase were written, . . . וּכְצוּר נְחָלִים. The sense is: Your gold will be as plentiful [or as cheap] as stones piled up in the river.

25. וְהָיָה שַׁדַּי בְּצָרֶיךָ וְכֶסֶף תּוֹעָפוֹת לָךְ — *Then Shaddai will turn against your enemies, mountains of silver will be yours*. The translation

כו־כז כִּי־אָז עַל־שַׁדַּי תִּתְעַנָּג וְתִשָּׂא אֶל־אֱלוֹהַּ פָּנֶיךָ: תַּעְתִּיר
כח אֵלָיו וְיִשְׁמָעֶךָּ וּנְדָרֶיךָ תְשַׁלֵּם: וְתִגְזַר־אֹמֶר וְיָקָם
כט לָךְ וְעַל־דְּרָכֶיךָ נָגַהּ אוֹר: כִּי־הִשְׁפִּילוּ וַתֹּאמֶר גֵּוָה
ל וְשַׁח עֵינַיִם יוֹשִׁעַ: יְמַלֵּט אִי־נָקִי וְנִמְלַט בְּבֹר כַּפֶּיךָ:

follows *Ramban*. For the first phrase he offers an alternative: Shaddai will feel with you in your troubles [from צָרַר, *to be in difficult straits*].

יָעֵף, *to be tired;* תּוֹעָפוֹת, *mountain peaks* [perhaps because of the weariness of the mountain climber attempting to scale the peaks — see *Hirsch, Numbers* 23:22].

26. כִּי־אָז עַל־שַׁדַּי תִּתְעַנָּג וְתִשָּׂא אֶל־אֱלוֹהַּ פָּנֶיךָ — *For then you will find delight in Shaddai, will be able to lift your face to God*. The second phrase means that Iyov will have established a trusting relationship with God (*R' Meyuchas*).

27. תַּעְתִּיר אֵלָיו וְיִשְׁמָעֶךָּ וּנְדָרֶיךָ תְשַׁלֵּם — *You will pray to Him and He will listen to you, you will be able to fulfill your oaths*. When in trouble, it is normal to make conditional commitments. If God will help me, then I undertake to do such and such, or to bring these or those sacrifices. You will be in a position to have *to fulfill your oaths,* means that God will always help — your stipulations will have been met, and you will have to honor your commitments (*Metzudos*).

28. וְתִגְזַר־אֹמֶר וְיָקָם לָךְ וְעַל־דְּרָכֶיךָ נָגַהּ אוֹר — *You will make plans which will succeed, your paths will be bathed in light*. The light of success (*Metzudos*).

29. כִּי־הִשְׁפִּילוּ וַתֹּאמֶר גֵּוָה וְשַׁח עֵינַיִם יוֹשִׁעַ — *Should there be lowly ones, you will command, 'Arise!', will save those whose eyes are low*. Not only you, but all with whom you come into contact will benefit from your new closeness to God. God will raise the lowly, save the broken, simply because you wish it (*Metzudos*).

גֵּוָה, from גַּאָה, *to be proud*. *Vav* and *aleph* are interchangeable.

30. יְמַלֵּט אִי־נָקִי וְנִמְלַט בְּבֹר כַּפֶּיךָ — *Even the guilty will escape, be freed by the purity of your hands*. Your merits will extend even to helping someone who is really guilty, so great will be your purity (*Metzudos*).

◈ Iyov's Response to Eliphaz's Third Speech

Angry at the friends for suspecting him of being evilly disposed toward God and man, Iyov does not react in any way to what they have said. Instead, he gives voice to his longing for a confrontation with God. Surely he would be able to win final vindication for himself (*Ramban*).

In chapter 26:2-4, in response to Bildad's final speech, Iyov addresses him in the singular — as an individual. Previously, in all his responses, he had invariably used the plural — aiming his remarks at the group. Clearly, by the time that Bildad addressed him for the last time, Iyov realized that the association between the friends had disintegrated, that both Eliphaz and Tzophar had dropped out of the debate.

Accordingly, it is clear that when Iyov began this, his third response to Eliphaz, he already knew that it would be his last.

What, in these circumstances, would we have expected in terms of tone and content?

Iyov had never been reticent in condemning the friends. Again and again he had let them know, in no uncertain terms, that he regarded them as ineffective, disloyal, unfeeling and cruel. Indeed, in his final speech to Bildad he will continue in this mode: Bildad, he says clearly, has helped not at all, has brought no wisdom to bear upon the solution of the problem, has failed in this last attempt at comfort as he had failed in the earlier ones.

We would have expected nothing different in his response to Eliphaz.

Eliphaz in his recent speech has done what neither he nor any of the other friends had done before. He has accused Iyov of the vilest sins — with absolutely no basis in reality. If ever Iyov would have been justified in expressing his pique in a personal attack, it would have been now. But, he does nothing of the sort. In this speech, he addresses no single word to either Eliphaz individually or to the friends as a group. Even verse 2, in which he bemoans the ineffectiveness of comfort which he had been offered, is addressed to no one; it is spoken in the form of a soliloquy.

The lesson seems clear. Iyov will criticize, and criticize sharply, only those who have not forfeited their claim upon his friendship. None of the previous speeches had put any of the friends totally beyond the pale. They may have ceased to love Iyov, but Iyov had not ceased to love them.

22/26-30 *26 For then you will find delight in Shaddai, will be able to lift your*
face to God. 27 You will pray to Him and He will listen to you, you
will be able to fulfill your oaths. 28 You will make plans which will
succeed, your paths will be bathed in light. 29 Should there be lowly
ones, you will command, 'Arise!', will save those whose eyes are
low. 30 Even the guilty will escape, be freed by the purity of your
hands.

He felt the obligation to pull them up short, to halt their rush into self-deception upon which they seemed bent.

Not so Eliphaz. He has finally, and irrevocably, lost Iyov. Iyov feels no obligation to set him straight, will not dignify his scurrilous attacks with any answer at all.

And so, Iyov is subject to yet another loss. If family wealth and standing had all disappeared in the whirlwind of God's displeasure, there had always been the comforting knowledge that he was yet blessed with friends. We can imagine the terrible feeling of loneliness and alienation which must have overtaken Iyov at the moment in which he realized that Eliphaz, too, was gone.

And so, we are not surprised that in this speech Iyov says nothing of his pains, of his loss of standing in society, of the disintegration of his family and home, in short, of all the dreadful realities upon which his fevered mind had seized in his earlier speeches.

At this point he is overwhelmed by a different realization. He has not only lost his friend, he is even unable to find — his God. In one of the most poignant passages in the book, we have Iyov launching an abortive search along all the points of the compass for some glimpse of the Divine purpose, for some understanding of his predicament. But, there is nothing. Nothing at all except a power seemingly set upon smashing his world. With exquisite poignancy Iyov expresses a longing for the simple verities of earlier generations — it was so easy to comprehend the fate of the *Dor HaMabul, the generation of the Flood.*

Iyov ends this sad speech with a pathetic attempt to elicit confirmation for his thesis. Everyone, he feels, must agree with him. But, we are left wondering. What will Iyov really gain if he is right? For him there seems nothing left but a world in shambles.

XXIII.

Ramban asserts that Iyov has nothing new to say in this speech. He is angry at the friends for suggesting that he is an evil person, and therefore does not bother to answer them. He does express his desire to discuss his own righteousness with God, and to question Him about the wickedness which the evildoers practice — apparently with impunity. These are two issues which are uppermost in his mind.

While it is true that the speech breaks no new philosophical or theological ground, it is nevertheless profoundly revealing when read with what we have understood to be *Rashi's* approach to the book in mind. It is significant, more for what Iyov does not say, than for what he says.

Eliphaz's speech had ended with a ringing call for *teshuvah* (repentance). It had held out beguiling prospects of boundless bliss and even power to elicit grace for others — if only Iyov would be willing to change. We would have supposed that Iyov would have been moved. Is not, after all, even the greatest *tzaddik* a *baal teshuvah* (repentant)? Do we not all, even the holiest among us, pray daily that God accept our penitence? Why then should Iyov, even if he is right and therefore righteous, spurn this heartfelt plea? Why do we hear only a bellicose challenge hurled at God, instead of a silent whisper of contrition?

Clearly, Eliphaz has failed in even this, his most reasonable attempt at helping Iyov. A speech begun with thirteen verses of recrimination and false accusation cannot hope to redeem itself with a friendly ending. With his first words, Eliphaz, instead of eliciting interest, curiosity and an inclination toward the positive, had by his groundless attack stoked Iyov's fury. Nothing that he could say afterward would make any difference. Once more we can understand the *Zohar's* condemnation — good thoughts cloaked in hopelessly inadequate garb. The friends, insufficiently prepared for their exquisitely difficult task, were doomed to failure.

א־ב וַיַּעַן אִיּוֹב וַיֹּאמַר: גַּם־הַיּוֹם מְרִי שִׂחִי יָדִי כָּבְדָה עַל־
ג אַנְחָתִי: מִי־יִתֵּן יָדַעְתִּי וְאֶמְצָאֵהוּ אָבוֹא עַד־תְּכוּנָתוֹ:
ד־ה אֶעֶרְכָה לְפָנָיו מִשְׁפָּט וּפִי אֲמַלֵּא תוֹכָחוֹת: אֵדְעָה
ו מִלִּים יַעֲנֵנִי וְאָבִינָה מַה־יֹּאמַר לִי: הַבְּרָב־כֹּחַ יָרִיב
ז עִמָּדִי לֹא אַךְ־הוּא יָשִׂם בִּי: שָׁם יָשָׁר נוֹכָח עִמּוֹ
ח וַאֲפַלְּטָה לָנֶצַח מִשֹּׁפְטִי: הֵן קֶדֶם אֶהֱלֹךְ וְאֵינֶנּוּ
ט וְאָחוֹר וְלֹא־אָבִין לוֹ: שְׂמֹאול בַּעֲשֹׂתוֹ וְלֹא־אָחַז
י יַעְטֹף יָמִין וְלֹא אֶרְאֶה: כִּי־יָדַע דֶּרֶךְ עִמָּדִי בְּחָנַנִי כַּזָּהָב
יא אֵצֵא: בַּאֲשֻׁרוֹ אָחֲזָה רַגְלִי דַּרְכּוֹ שָׁמַרְתִּי וְלֹא־אָט:
יב מִצְוַת שְׂפָתָיו וְלֹא אָמִישׁ מֵחֻקִּי צָפַנְתִּי אִמְרֵי־פִיו:

2. גַּם־הַיּוֹם מְרִי שִׂחִי יָדִי כָּבְדָה עַל־אַנְחָתִי — *After all this, my speech is just as bitter, the hand that afflicts me is heavier than my cries.* After all your many speeches I remain uncomforted, and therefore feel bitter against you (*Ramban*). Nothing that any of you has said has assuaged my pain.

Or: Even after all the bitter thoughts that I have uttered ... (*Metzudos*).

יָדִי is taken, not as *my hand*, but as *the hand that afflicts me.* The sense is that either, after all your useless attempts at comfort, or even after all the bitterness which I have expressed, my cries are still very much less than might have been warranted by the degree of my suffering.

3. מִי־יִתֵּן יָדַעְתִּי וְאֶמְצָאֵהוּ אָבוֹא עַד־תְּכוּנָתוֹ — *Would that I would know so that I might find Him, I would go right up to the very base of His throne.* Iyov roughly rejects Eliphaz's call to *teshuvah*. He is looking not for penitence but for confrontation (*Daas Mikra*).

תְּכוּנָה, from כּוּן, *to establish.* Here, hinting at מְכוֹן כִּסְאוֹ, *the base of God's throne* (*Psalms* 97:2), where He sits in judgment (*Rashi*).

4. אֶעֶרְכָה לְפָנָיו מִשְׁפָּט וּפִי אֲמַלֵּא תוֹכָחוֹת — *Would lay out my claims before Him, would fill my mouth with arguments.* מִשְׁפָּט is frequently used to denote a *right, something which is due.* See, for example, *Exodus* 23:6, *the right of the destitute*, or *Deuteronomy*, *the right of the orphan.*

תּוֹכָחָה from יָכַח, *to demonstrate.*

5. אֵדְעָה מִלִּים יַעֲנֵנִי וְאָבִינָה מַה־יֹּאמַר לִי — *At least I would know the words by which He will answer me, understand what He will say to me.* The translation follows *Rashi*. Even if He will not allow me to speak, I will at least hear what He has to say. *Ramban* believes that Iyov is contrasting God to the friends. I have no knowledge or understanding of what you are trying to say to me. I am quite sure that, were I to hear from God Himself, I would comprehend His meaning.

6. הַבְּרָב־כֹּחַ יָרִיב עִמָּדִי לֹא אַךְ־הוּא יָשִׂם בִּי — *Will He battle me with exaggerated force? Surely not! Of only this will He accuse me.* The syntax is difficult. Following are some of the suggested interpretations.

Our translation follows *Rashi*. The sense of the final phrase is that God will accuse me only of such sins as I have actually committed, He will not confront me with spurious accusations.

R' Yosef Kara has the same general understanding, but reads the phrase: *He will not bring false accusations against me.*

Ramban: Would He personally wrangle with me so that He might demonstrate His superior strength? Surely not. Instead He will appoint an impartial judge over me, who will not frighten me and in front of whom my righteousness will come into its own (next verse).

Or: Instead of flaunting His superior strength, He will devote His concentration upon my case to see what I have really done. Once this happens, I will surely be judged innocent (next verse).

7. שָׁם יָשָׁר נוֹכָח עִמּוֹ וַאֲפַלְּטָה לָנֶצַח מִשֹּׁפְטִי — *There, my forthrightness will confront Him, once and for all I will escape my accuser. There* refers to the *base of His throne* in verse 3, where the confrontation is to take place.

The translation follows *Metzudos*. Iyov's forthrightness is anthropomorphized. My good deeds will argue for me — and I will certainly be vindicated.

Ramban (see commentary to v. 6) reads: There, the impartial, non-threatening judge whom God will have appointed (יָשָׁר) will

23/1-12 [1] *Iyov responded and said: [2] After all this, my speech is just as
bitter, the hand that afflicts me is heavier than my cries.
[3] Would that I would know so that I might find Him, I would go
right up to the very base of His throne. [4] Would lay out my claims
before Him, would fill my mouth with arguments. [5] At least I
would know the words by which He will answer me, understand
what He will say to me. [6] Will He battle me with exaggerated
force? Surely not! Of only this will He accuse me. [7] There, my
forthrightness will confront Him, once and for all I will escape my
accuser. [8] But, I walk to the East, He is not there, to the West and
cannot perceive Him. [9] The North He created — but I cannot
glimpse Him, He has concealed the South so that I cannot see.
[10] For He knows the path which I have followed, were He to
test me — I would come out as gold. [11] My legs have followed His
footsteps, I have kept to His path and have not strayed. [12] The
commands uttered by His lips — I would not defect from them, His
mouth's utterances were more precious than my daily bread.*

be available to me, and I will be able to argue my case before him, sure that I will be vindicated.

8. הֵן קֶדֶם אֶהֱלֹךְ וְאֵינֶנּוּ וְאָחוֹר וְלֹא אָבִין־לוֹ — *But, I walk to the East, He is not there, to the West and cannot perceive Him.* קֶדֶם, *that which lies in front*, and אָחוֹר, *that which lies behind*, are East and West respectively. This in Scriptural usage, which describes the cardinal points from the point of view of one who is facing East. For this reason, North and South are described as left and right, respectively (next verse).

Iyov is reacting to Eliphaz's accusation at 22:14. Far from believing that God's interest is limited to the *circle of the heavens*, he knows Him to be a very real presence upon earth. It is just that his best efforts to find God are constantly being frustrated (*Daas Mikra*).

9. שְׂמֹאול בַּעֲשֹׂתוֹ וְלֹא־אָחַז יַעְטֹף יָמִין וְלֹא אֶרְאֶה — *The North He created — but I cannot glimpse Him, He has concealed the South so that I cannot see.* The first phrase is difficult. Some possibilities:

Rashi: When He created the North, He did not place His throne there. Therefore I cannot find Him there.

Ramban: Even though He created the North, I cannot find Him there.

אָחַז, a shortened form of אֶחֱזֶה from חָזָה, *to see.* עָטַף, *to envelop*. See, for example, *Psalms* 65:14, *The valleys cover themselves with corn.*

10. כִּי־יָדַע דֶּרֶךְ עִמָּדִי בְּחָנַנִי כַּזָּהָב אֵצֵא — *For He knows the path which I have followed, were He to test me — I would come out as gold. Rashi* reads this as going back to verse 6. God has no intention of doing battle with me, because He knows that my path has been blameless, that were He to test me I would prove to be as pure as gold.

Eliphaz had accused Iyov of thinking that he could force God into a confrontation with him: *Would fear of you inveigle Him into a confrontation, cause Him to appear with you at the bar of justice?* (22:4). Here Iyov contradicts this assertion. On the contrary, God will not consent to a confrontation because He knows my innocence (*Daas Mikra*).

11. בַּאֲשֻׁרוֹ אָחֲזָה רַגְלִי דַּרְכּוֹ שָׁמַרְתִּי וְלֹא־אָט — *My legs have followed His footsteps, I have kept to His path and have not strayed.* אָשַׁר, *to go straight*, thus, אֲשׁוּר, *footstep*.

The idiom, 'to walk in God's footsteps,' is unusual. Perhaps it is intended to convey the idea which the Sages derive from the expression, *And you shall walk in His paths* (*Deuteronomy* 28:9): That we are bidden to attempt to emulate God's own goodness, to act in all cases as God would act. Even as He is merciful so we too should be merciful, and the like.

12. מִצְוַת שְׂפָתָיו וְלֹא אָמִישׁ מֵחֻקִּי צָפַנְתִּי אִמְרֵי־פִיו — *The commands uttered by His lips — I would not defect from them, His mouth's utterances were more precious than my daily bread.* חֻקִּי echoes *Proverbs* 30:8, לֶחֶם חֻקִּי, *my daily bread.* חוֹק from חָקַק, *to decree*, means *something prescribed.*

כג/יג־יז יג־יד וְהוּא בְאֶחָד וּמִי יְשִׁיבֶנּוּ וְנַפְשׁוֹ אִוְּתָה וַיָּעַשׂ: כִּי יַשְׁלִים
טו חֻקִּי וְכָהֵנָּה רַבּוֹת עִמּוֹ: עַל־כֵּן מִפָּנָיו אֶבָּהֵל אֶתְבּוֹנֵן
טז־יז וְאֶפְחַד מִמֶּנּוּ: וְאֵל הֵרַךְ לִבִּי וְשַׁדַּי הִבְהִילָנִי: כִּי־לֹא
כד/א־ז א נִצְמַתִּי מִפְּנֵי־חֹשֶׁךְ וּמִפָּנַי כִּסָּה־אֹפֶל: מַדּוּעַ
ב מִשַּׁדַּי לֹא־נִצְפְּנוּ עִתִּים וְיֹדְעָו לֹא־חָזוּ יָמָיו: גְּבֻלוֹת
ג יַשִּׂיגוּ עֵדֶר גָּזְלוּ וַיִּרְעוּ: חֲמוֹר יְתוֹמִים יִנְהָגוּ יַחְבְּלוּ
°עֲנִיֵּי ק׳ ד שׁוֹר אַלְמָנָה: יַטּוּ אֶבְיֹנִים מִדָּרֶךְ יַחַד חֻבְּאוּ °ענוי־
ה אָרֶץ: הֵן פְּרָאִים ׀ בַּמִּדְבָּר יָצְאוּ בְּפָעֳלָם מְשַׁחֲרֵי לַטָּרֶף
°יִקְצוֹרוּ ק׳ ו עֲרָבָה לוֹ לֶחֶם לַנְּעָרִים: בַּשָּׂדֶה בְּלִילוֹ °קצירו וְכֶרֶם
ז רָשָׁע יְלַקֵּשׁוּ: עָרוֹם יָלִינוּ מִבְּלִי לְבוּשׁ וְאֵין כְּסוּת בַּקָּרָה:

13. וְהוּא בְאֶחָד וּמִי יְשִׁיבֶנּוּ וְנַפְשׁוֹ אִוְּתָה וַיָּעַשׂ — *But, he is single-minded, who can sway Him, He wanted — and so He did.* Although God knows that I am innocent, He is single-minded in His insistence upon subjecting me to all manner of suffering. There is nobody who can gainsay Him, He is all-powerful and can do what He wants.

14. כִּי יַשְׁלִים חֻקִּי וְכָהֵנָּה רַבּוֹת עִמּוֹ — *He is determined to impose full measure upon me, many such as this can be traced to Him.* There appears to be an intentional play on the חֻקִּי of verse 12. We both have our fixed agenda. Mine is the need for my daily bread, His is to make sure that I am exposed to a measure of suffering.

The second phrase justifies the first. His determination to harm me comes as no shock to me. He has done the same to me in the past, others too have suffered from Him.

15. עַל־כֵּן מִפָּנָיו אֶבָּהֵל אֶתְבּוֹנֵן וְאֶפְחַד מִמֶּנּוּ — *Therefore I am confused before Him, when I consider — I am frightened of Him.* Confusion and terror result from arbitrariness. If there were some logic to the way God treats me, I would more readily be able to cope. But, if even a life lived in absolute purity cannot protect me from suffering — then indeed I am terrified.

16. וְאֵל הֵרַךְ לִבִּי וְשַׁדַּי הִבְהִילָנִי — *For the Almighty has made me faint of heart, Shaddai has confounded me.* Iyov's problems go beyond the actual suffering to which he is exposed. His whole personality has changed. Where before he was an upstanding, confident person, he is now easily afraid and bitterly confused (*Metzudos*).

17. כִּי־לֹא נִצְמַתִּי מִפְּנֵי־חֹשֶׁךְ וּמִפָּנַי כִּסָּה־אֹפֶל — *For I had never been cut off because of darkness, He was wont to cover up the dense gloom from before me.* The translation follows *Metzudos*. Iyov suffers all the more from his disorientation, because of the sheltered life which he had led when fortune still smiled upon him. Never before did he have to fear darkness; always, when gloom threatened, did God protect him. This makes him all the more vulnerable to his current uncertainties.

Ramban interprets: If only I had been cut off before all this darkness descended, if only You had protected me from my present gloom by letting me die early!

XXIV.

1. מַדּוּעַ מִשַּׁדַּי לֹא־נִצְפְּנוּ עִתִּים וְיֹדְעָו לֹא־חָזוּ יָמָיו — *Why? No time-span is, after all, hidden from Shaddai; moreover even those who know Him best, know nothing of His days.* We have followed *R' Meyuchas* in the translation of this very difficult verse. The opening question — or exclamation — goes back to the end of the previous chapter, *For the Almighty has made me faint of heart* . . .. Why is He able to do this? Because He knows, and therefore controls, everything; and no one, even those who know Him best, can have any idea of His true being.

Rashi: Would that God were not aware of the time at which a person is destined to die. If He did not know this for sure, then He would not be in so much of a hurry to bring suffering upon him, and then there would be a chance that the person might die before he was exposed to troubles. Why should it be that even those who know Him best, know so very little about the real God?

R' Yosef Kara: Why did God not hide away the times allotted to my suffering, for the wicked people who are going to be described

23/13-17 13 *But, he is single-minded, who can sway Him, He wanted — and
so He did. 14 *He is determined to impose full measure upon me,
many such as this can be traced to Him.* 15 *Therefore I am confused
before Him, when I consider — I am frightened of Him.* 16 *For the
Almighty has made me faint of heart, Shaddai has confounded me.*
17 *For I had never been cut off because of darkness, He was wont to
cover up the dense gloom from before me.*

24/1-7 1 *Why? No time-span is, after all, hidden from Shaddai;
moreover even those who know Him best, know nothing
of His days.* 2 *They move back boundary markers, have stolen
flocks and take them out to graze.* 3 *Drive the orphan's donkey,
take the widow's ox in pledge.* 4 *Drive the destitute from the
road, together, the poor of the land go into hiding.* 5 *See, they are
the wild asses of the desert going out to do their work, lying
in ambush for prey, the plain serves as breadbasket for his
accomplices.* 6 *They reap the harvest in the fields, the very
vineyard, the wicked will denude.* 7 *They allow the naked to
spend the night unclothed, no garments to shield against the cold.*

in the following verses. Had He done so, then those who know Iyov would never have had to see him in the terrible straits within which he finds himself now.

2. גְּבֻלוֹת יַשִּׂיגוּ עֵדֶר גָּזְלוּ וַיִּרְעוּ — *They move back boundary markers, have stolen flocks and take them out to graze.* Although the wicked have not been mentioned, the context itself makes clear to whom Iyov is referring.

Metzudos interprets the second phrase: They take out the stolen flocks to graze in the very fields which they obtained through moving the boundary markers, thus compounding their offense.

3. חֲמוֹר יְתוֹמִים יִנְהָגוּ יַחְבְּלוּ שׁוֹר אַלְמָנָה — *Drive the orphan's donkey, take the widow's ox in pledge.* They steal the donkey of the orphan, and then lead it around, brazenly, in public. They take the widow's ox as pledge for non-existing debts (*Metzudos*).

4. יַטּוּ אֶבְיֹנִים מִדָּרֶךְ יַחַד חֻבְּאוּ עֲנִיֵּי־אָרֶץ — *Drive the destitute from the road, together, the poor of the land go into hiding.* Everyone is afraid of them. The destitute will, in their weakness and fear, elect to dare the dangers and pitfalls of back-roads and byways rather than risk a confrontation. If there is no other way of avoiding a meeting, they will even go into hiding (*Metzudos*).

5. הֵן פְּרָאִים בַּמִּדְבָּר יָצְאוּ בְּפָעֳלָם מְשַׁחֲרֵי לַטָּרֶף עֲרָבָה לוֹ לֶחֶם לַנְּעָרִים — *See, they are the wild asses of the desert going out to do their work, lying in ambush for prey, the plain serves as breadbasket for his accomplices.* A graphic metaphor! The wild asses are indigenous to the desert, feel entirely at home in its inhospitable environment. The robbers, too, feel unthreatened by any difficult conditions. They go about their task, always ready to pounce upon their defenseless prey. They have turned the plains, through which wayfarers must pass, into a source of sustenance for their bands. נַעַר is often used in the sense of *servant* or *retainer* (see, for example, *Genesis* 14:24).

6. בַּשָּׂדֶה בְּלִילוֹ יִקְצוֹרוּ וְכֶרֶם רָשָׁע יְלַקֵּשׁוּ — *They reap the harvest in the fields, the very vineyard, the wicked will denude.* They go into the fields of the poor (*R' Yosef Kara*) and reap the harvest as though it were their own.

In the second phrase, the cantillation (*trop*) sets us on the right course. It separates כֶּרֶם from רָשָׁע, thus yielding our translation (*R' Yosef Kara*).

לֶקֶשׁ is the sprouting of growth — see *Amos* 7:1. Thus, לִקֵּשׁ is used for the removal of that growth. Accordingly, *to despoil* or *denude* (*Rashi*).

7. עָרוֹם יָלִינוּ מִבְּלִי לְבוּשׁ וְאֵין כְּסוּת בַּקָּרָה — *They allow the naked to spend the night unclothed, no garments to shield against the cold.* Without pity they plunder the poor, take even their clothes away, even though this will mean that they have to spend the night naked, with nothing to protect them from the cold (*Metzudos*).

ח־ט מִזֶּרֶם הָרִים יִרְטָבוּ וּמִבְּלִי מַחְסֶה חִבְּקוּ־צוּר׃ יִגְזְלוּ
י מִשֹּׁד יָתוֹם וְעַל־עָנִי יַחְבֹּלוּ׃ עָרוֹם הִלְּכוּ בְּלִי לְבוּשׁ
יא וּרְעֵבִים נָשְׂאוּ עֹמֶר׃ בֵּין־שׁוּרֹתָם יַצְהִירוּ יְקָבִים דָּרְכוּ
יב וַיִּצְמָאוּ׃ מֵעִיר מְתִים ׀ יִנְאָקוּ וְנֶפֶשׁ־חֲלָלִים תְּשַׁוֵּעַ
יג וֶאֱלוֹהַּ לֹא־יָשִׂים תִּפְלָה׃ הֵמָּה ׀ הָיוּ בְּמֹרְדֵי־אוֹר
יד לֹא־הִכִּירוּ דְרָכָיו וְלֹא יָשְׁבוּ בִּנְתִיבֹתָיו׃ לָאוֹר יָקוּם
טו רוֹצֵחַ יִקְטָל־עָנִי וְאֶבְיוֹן וּבַלַּיְלָה יְהִי כַגַּנָּב׃ וְעֵין נֹאֵף ׀
שָׁמְרָה נֶשֶׁף לֵאמֹר לֹא־תְשׁוּרֵנִי עָיִן וְסֵתֶר פָּנִים יָשִׂים׃

8. מִזֶּרֶם הָרִים יִרְטָבוּ וּמִבְּלִי מַחְסֶה חִבְּקוּ־צוּר — *They become drenched from the mountain streams, embracing the rock for lack of shelter.* Left without shelter, they are at the mercy of the elements. They cling even to inhospitable rocks in the hope that they might offer at least a little protection.

9. יִגְזְלוּ מִשֹּׁד יָתוֹם וְעַל־עָנִי יַחְבֹּלוּ — *They tear the orphan from the breast, snatch the poor man's child as pledge.* Translation of the first phrase follows *Rashi* and *Ramban*. For שׁוֹד as *breast, Isaiah* 60:16 is adduced.

In the second phrase we have followed a suggestion by *Malbim*. עַל for *child* would be related to עֲוִיל at 16:11, 19:18 and 21:11. This interpretation makes it unnecessary to have עַל, *on*, stand for, *that which is on the poor person* — his clothes. Thus *Metzudos*.

10. עָרוֹם הִלְּכוּ בְּלִי לְבוּשׁ וּרְעֵבִים נָשְׂאוּ עֹמֶר — *They permit them to go naked — for they are without clothes, those who carried the sheaves — hungry.* The first phrase seems to be an almost exact repetition of verse 7. *Daas Mikra*, based on *Malbim's* interpretation of עַל in the previous verse, suggests as follows: Verse 7 describes the suffering imposed upon the poor at night, while they are at rest. Here, our verse and the next deal with the unconscionable labor practices of the powerful rich. They steal the children of the poor (v. 9), enslave them and make them work under dreadful conditions. They have to work without adequate clothing, hungry even while they are carrying sheaves of plenty — they are not permitted to eat of the produce (v. 10). Moreover, even while they work at pressing oil and treading grapes for wine, they are still thirsty — they are not permitted to slake their thirst from the fruits of their labor (v. 11).

Rashi, who seems untroubled by the apparent redundancy from verse 7, offers two possible interpretations for the second phrase. Either, *[the rich] steal the pitiful sheaves which the starving poor had been allowed to collect from the fields* (לֶקֶט). Or, *[the poor] starve because [the rich] steal their sheaves from them.*

11. בֵּין־שׁוּרֹתָם יַצְהִירוּ יְקָבִים דָּרְכוּ וַיִּצְמָאוּ — *They cause the oil to flow among the rows, tread for the wine vats — and yet, are thirsty.* See commentary to previous verse.

Rashi and *Metzudos* interpret: *Even though the poor may produce oil and wine, they nevertheless go thirsty, because the rich steal it all from them.*

יַצְהִירוּ, *to make oil*, from יִצְהָר, *oil.*

For *rows*, *Rashi* surmises that in the place where olives are pressed, these are stored in rows, and that the oil, as it comes out from the fruit, flows between these rows.

12. מֵעִיר מְתִים יִנְאָקוּ וְנֶפֶשׁ־חֲלָלִים תְּשַׁוֵּעַ וֶאֱלוֹהַּ לֹא־יָשִׂים תִּפְלָה — *From the city come the groans of its men, the dying rattle of the slain. In spite of all, God does not attach blame.* The rendering, *dying rattle of the slain*, reflects *Ramban's* second interpretation. חָלָל is a *corpse*. How then can we speak of the cry (שׁוע) of the חָלָל? *Ramban's* suggestions are, either to say that חָלָל is used in the sense, *those that are about to become corpses*, or, that reference is to the sound that issues forth at the moment of death.

We have rendered תִּפְלָה as *blame* in accordance with *Rashi* and *Targum*. However, the word usually means something *tasteless* or *insubstantive*. Accordingly *Ramban* understands the phrase: *Yet God, instead of making sure that the deeds of the wicked should be insubstantive [seems to imbue them with unlimited power]*.

Metzudos understands the term as does *Ramban* and renders: *How can you claim that God never does anything without reason? [Would it not make more sense to save the lives of many by having the few wicked people die?]*

13-24. In this passage *Rashi* and *Ramban* part ways radically. The different interpretations

8 They become drenched from the mountain streams, embracing
the rock for lack of shelter. 9 They tear the orphan from the
breast, snatch the poor man's child as pledge. 10 They permit
them to go naked — for they are without clothes, those who carried
the sheaves — hungry. 11 They cause the oil to flow among the
rows, tread for the wine vats — and yet, are thirsty. 12 From the
city come the groans of its men, the dying rattle of the slain.
In spite of all, God does not attach blame. 13 They belong to the
ranks of those that resist the light, unwilling to know its ways,
unwilling to dwell in its paths. 14 By day the murderer must
take over, killing the poor and the destitute; at night he can become
a robber. 15 The philanderer's eye anticipates the night, saying,
'No eye shall watch me, it shall provide covering for my face!'

are felt particularly in verses 22-24, the finale of Iyov's speech.

Rashi has verses 13-23 describe the wickedness of the *Dor HaMabul,* the generation which was wiped out in Noah's time. Verses 22-24 then describe their punishment — and with this Iyov ends his speech.

Rashi does not make clear how this passage fits into the speech. If, indeed, the *Dor HaMabul* was as severely punished as is described in the ending passage of the speech, then evidently there is justice in the world. This seems completely to negate the point which Iyov made in verses 2-12 of our chapter.

Perhaps Iyov means to use the experiences of the *Dor HaMabul* as foil for his complaint. God is not unable to punish — witness the severity with which He reacted to the wickedness of this earlier generation. If so, why does He now permit the evildoers to prosper?

This would follow logically upon the ending phrase of verse 12: *In spite of all this God does not attach blame.* That is to say, that Iyov ends that part of the speech with a question. The wicked prosper and God does not do anything about it! This question is now fleshed out with a description of the experiences of the *Dor HaMabul* as we have understood it.[1]

Ramban, in his interpretation, says nothing of the *Dor HaMabul.* Accordingly he takes the entire passage, including verses 22-24, as a description of the successes of the wicked. It is simply a continuation of what was being said in verses 2-12.

13. הֵמָּה הָיוּ בְּמֹרְדֵי־אוֹר לֹא־הִכִּירוּ דְרָכָיו וְלֹא יָשְׁבוּ בִּנְתִיבֹתָיו — *They belong to the ranks of those that resist the light, unwilling to know its ways, unwilling to dwell in its paths. Rashi* sees a reference to the generation that was wiped out by the Flood. They rebelled against God [the *light*] because of a sense of self-sufficiency. *Ramban,* in his second interpretation, favors this explanation because מָרַד, *to rebel* or *resist,* is particularly apt in this context.

Targum renders: *They rebelled against the Torah.* He too appears to understand *light* as a metaphor.

Ramban, in consonance with the following verses which seem to extol the darkness from the point of view of the criminal, takes the verse at face value. The wicked people prefer the dark woods and caves to the light of day, as it makes their nefarious activities that much more simple.

14. לָאוֹר יָקוּם רוֹצֵחַ יִקְטָל־עָנִי וְאֶבְיוֹן וּבַלַּיְלָה יְהִי כַגַּנָּב — *By day the murderer must take over, killing the poor and the destitute; at night he can become a robber.* We have translated in accordance with *Ramban,* as he takes the previous verse. Light is no friend of the criminal. It forces him to violence which he would rather avoid. By day he has no alternative but to kill in order to attain his ends. At night, unobserved, he can simply take what he wants.

15. וְעֵין נֹאֵף שָׁמְרָה נֶשֶׁף לֵאמֹר לֹא־תְשׁוּרֵנִי עָיִן וְסֵתֶר פָּנִים יָשִׂים — *The philanderer's eye anticipates the night, saying, 'No eye shall watch me, it shall provide covering for my face!'* The night itself will hide me from prying eyes (*Metzudos*).

1. This analysis of the chapter would not hold valid for *R' Yosef Kara,* who in all essential points interprets our section as does *Rashi,* but in contrast to *Rashi* who sees the first reference to the *Dor HaMabul* in verse 13, he has verse 12 already dealing with that generation.

טז חָתַר בַּחֹשֶׁךְ בָּתִּים יוֹמָם חִתְּמוּ־לָמוֹ לֹא־יָדְעוּ אוֹר:
יז כִּי יַחְדָּו ׀ בֹּקֶר לָמוֹ צַלְמָוֶת כִּי־יַכִּיר בַּלְהוֹת צַלְמָוֶת:
יח קַל־הוּא ׀ עַל־פְּנֵי־מַיִם תְּקֻלַּל חֶלְקָתָם בָּאָרֶץ לֹא־יִפְנֶה
יט דֶּרֶךְ כְּרָמִים: צִיָּה גַם־חֹם יִגְזְלוּ מֵימֵי־שֶׁלֶג שְׁאוֹל חָטָאוּ:
כ יִשְׁכָּחֵהוּ רֶחֶם ׀ מְתָקוֹ רִמָּה עוֹד לֹא־יִזָּכֵר וַתִּשָּׁבֵר כָּעֵץ
כא עַוְלָה: רֹעֶה עֲקָרָה לֹא תֵלֵד וְאַלְמָנָה לֹא יְיֵטִיב:
כב וּמָשַׁךְ אַבִּירִים בְּכֹחוֹ יָקוּם וְלֹא־יַאֲמִין בַּחַיִּין: יִתֶּן־
כג־כד לוֹ לָבֶטַח וְיִשָּׁעֵן וְעֵינֵיהוּ עַל־דַּרְכֵיהֶם: רוֹמּוּ מְּעַט ׀
כה וְאֵינֶנּוּ וְהֻמְּכוּ כַּכֹּל יִקָּפְצוּן וּכְרֹאשׁ שִׁבֹּלֶת יִמָּלוּ: וְאִם־

16. חָתַר בַּחֹשֶׁךְ בָּתִּים יוֹמָם חִתְּמוּ־לָמוֹ לֹא־יָדְעוּ אוֹר — *In the darkness he burrows under houses, but by day they seal themselves shut, never knowing light.* The burglar, too, favors the night. By day he prefers to lock himself into his lair in order to avoid meeting people who might recognize him (*Metzudos*).

17. כִּי יַחְדָּו בֹּקֶר לָמוֹ צַלְמָוֶת כִּי־יַכִּיר בַּלְהוֹת צַלְמָוֶת — *To both of them the morning is a dense darkness, the time that men recognize one another, a frightening gloom.* In contrast to other people to whom the coming of the morning light is a time of relief and joy, these two, the philanderer and the robber, see the morning light as a threatening darkness. The translation follows *Metzudos.*

18. קַל־הוּא עַל־פְּנֵי־מַיִם תְּקֻלַּל חֶלְקָתָם בָּאָרֶץ לֹא־יִפְנֶה דֶּרֶךְ כְּרָמִים — *Lightfooted he, as upon the waters, their portion of the land accursed, he does not turn aside to the vineyards.* The translation follows *Ramban.* As something swept along by a water current, so too the wicked make their way swiftly from place to place in order that they should not be caught. Their lands deteriorate, their vineyards are not attended. They have no time for them at all. Their only wish is to rob and to oppress.

19. צִיָּה גַם־חֹם יִגְזְלוּ מֵימֵי־שֶׁלֶג שְׁאוֹל חָטָאוּ — *As parching heat snatches the melting snow, so the grave, those that have sinned.* The translation follows *Metzudos.* As the dryness and heat make short shrift of the waters left by the snow, so the grave snatches up the wicked. There is no pain or prolonged illness. Everything goes easy for them.

We can well understand how Iyov, in his intense suffering, would be particularly upset by the ease with which the wicked are able to leave this world.

Rashi and *R' Yosef Kara,* in accordance with their view that our passage is a description of the *Dor HaMabul* (see commentary 13-24), read our verse as follows: In the tradition of the Sages (*Bereishis Rabbah* 34:11), the solar and lunar systems were thrown into confusion during the period of the Deluge. For an entire year, the orderly sequence of the seasons was not operative. Thus: *They stole the dryness and the heat, so too did they steal the waters caused by the snow.* Nature had lost its bearings, and none of the expected changes in the climate took place.

20. יִשְׁכָּחֵהוּ רֶחֶם מְתָקוֹ רִמָּה עוֹד לֹא־יִזָּכֵר וַתִּשָּׁבֵר כָּעֵץ עַוְלָה — *His very mother will forget him, he is delectable to the worms, he shall no more be remembered, the sinner will be snapped like a twig.* The translation follows *Metzudos.* The verse continues the thought of the previous one. It describes the speed and painlessness with which the wicked die. The faster and the less complicated the dying process, the less will anyone, even his own mother, remember him, and the more will the worms enjoy feeding upon him. His body, not emaciated, will have retained its fat.

רֶחֶם, *the womb,* is used as a metaphor for mother.

21. רֹעֶה עֲקָרָה לֹא תֵלֵד וְאַלְמָנָה לֹא יְיֵטִיב — *He coddles the barren woman who can bear no children, but begrudges kindness to the widow.* The translation follows *Rashi.* People would marry two wives, one for their pleasure, the other one to bear children. The first one would be rendered sterile, indulged in all her wishes, clothed like a princess, in order to make her beautiful. The child-bearing woman would be starved and dressed in widow's clothes. This was the practice, according to the tradition of the Sages, during the *Dor HaMabul,* and *Rashi* is consistent with his earlier interpretation in quoting it here.

Other commentators take רֹעֶה from רָעַע, *to smash.* Thus, he smashes the most defenseless women, the childless whose sons cannot protect her, the widows whose husbands cannot stand at their sides (*Metzudos*).

[16] *In the darkness he burrows under houses, but by day they seal*
themselves shut, never knowing light. [17] *To both of them the*
morning is a dense darkness, the time that men recognize one
another, a frightening gloom. [18] *Lightfooted he, as upon the waters,*
their portion of the land accursed, he does not turn aside to the
vineyards. [19] *As parching heat snatches the melting snow, so the*
grave, those that have sinned. [20] *His very mother will forget him, he*
is delectable to the worms, he shall no more be remembered, the
sinner will be snapped like a twig. [21] *He coddles the barren woman*
who can bear no children, but begrudges kindness to the widow.
[22] *But, by dint of His power he drew these colossi forward, each*
would be petrified in place, unable to summon faith in life. [23] *He*
would grant protection to each so that he would feel secure; then
He turned His attention upon their ways. [24] *They were removed in*
a flash — and were no more, were pulverized and, as happens to all,
were snatched away, ground up as are the tops of grain-stalks. [25] *If*

22. וּמָשַׁךְ אַבִּירִים בְּכֹחוֹ יָקוּם וְלֹא־יַאֲמִין בַּחַיִּין — *But, by dint of His power he drew these colossi forward, each would be petrified in place, unable to summon faith in life.* As we saw above in commentary 13-24, *Rashi* and *Ramban* part ways radically in the interpretation of this and the next two verses.

Rashi: In spite of the forbearance which God had displayed for so many years, the time would come when He would drag the violent criminals of the *Dor HaMabul* to their destruction. A moment would come in which, wherever they would be standing (*R' Yosef Kara*), they would suddenly realize that they had no hold at all upon life.

Ramban: The evildoers brutalize even the most mighty. They rise up against them (יָקוּם) so that the victims have no hope at all that they might continue to live.

23. יִתֶּן־לוֹ לָבֶטַח וְיִשָּׁעֵן וְעֵינֵיהוּ עַל־דַּרְכֵיהֶם — *He would grant protection to each so that he would feel secure; then He turned His attention upon their ways.* In *Rashi's* view the description of the *Dor HaMabul* continues: God, as it were, gave them a long leash, but in the end, turned His face upon them in the full measure of His fury.

Ramban: The wicked man feels secure and reliant upon the strength of his previous triumphs, knows full well that the deceit which he practices invariably brings success [*His past successes allow him to live secure and to rely upon them for the future*]. All this happens while God is fully aware of what is happening [*While His eyes are upon their ways*]. God appears to be completely unresponsive to the dreadful things that are happening. *Ramban* points out that the second phrase repeats the thought expressed in verse 12, *Yet God, instead of making sure that the deeds of the wicked should be insubstantive [seems to imbue them with unlimited power].* (Thus, according to *Ramban*, see there.) Accordingly, the entire intervening passage seems to be an extension of that thought: Why does God do nothing at all in the face of the triumphs which the wicked experience?

24. רוֹמּוּ מְעַט וְאֵינֶנּוּ וְהֻמְּכוּ כַּכֹּל יִקָּפְצוּן וּכְרֹאשׁ שִׁבֹּלֶת יִמָּלוּ — *They were removed in a flash — and were no more, were pulverized and, as happens to all, were snatched away, ground up as are the tops of grain-stalks.* In *Rashi's* view the description of the destruction of the *Dor HaMabul* continues. He appears to take רוֹמּוּ as the *pual* of רום, *to be lifted up* (*Heichal Rashi, Milon HaPeirushim*). Here, *to be taken away from the world.* הֻמְּכוּ is the *hophal* of מכך which *Rashi* usually renders, *to be low* (see, for example at *Psalms* 106:43), but here, as, *to be ground up.* קָפַץ is usually rendered by *Rashi* as *to close* (see, for example, *Isaiah* 52:15, סָגַר, and *Psalms* 107:42, סָתַם). Here, in the *niphal*, *Rashi* uses תַּמּוּ כְּרֶגַע, *to be suddenly consumed.*

Ramban takes the verse as describing the ultimate downfall of the wicked, but hastens to point out that this is not in contradiction to his interpretation of the earlier verses. First the translation: *They are uplifted for only a short while — and then disappear, thrown down [to the earth]. In common with all men they will be cut off, will be ground up like the tops of grain-stalks [leaving no roots or branches].* *Ramban* continues: Now Iyov has

כה־א לֹ֥א אֵ֭פוֹ מִ֣י יַכְזִבֵ֑נִי וְיָשֵׂ֖ם לְ֝אַ֗ל מִלָּתִֽי׃ וַ֭יַּעַן
ב בִּלְדַּ֥ד הַ֝שֻּׁחִ֗י וַיֹּאמַֽר׃ הַמְשֵׁ֣ל וָפַ֣חַד עִמּ֑וֹ עֹשֶׂ֥ה שָׁ֝ל֗וֹם
ג בִּמְרוֹמָֽיו׃ הֲיֵ֣שׁ מִ֭סְפָּר לִגְדוּדָ֑יו וְעַל־מִ֝֗י לֹא־יָק֥וּם אוֹרֵֽהוּ׃
ד וּמַה־יִּצְדַּ֣ק אֱנ֣וֹשׁ עִם־אֵ֑ל וּמַה־יִּ֝זְכֶּ֗ה יְל֣וּד אִשָּֽׁה׃

no intention here of hyperbolically describing the destruction of the wicked [since this would stand in contradiction to the earlier verses], but, he wishes to point out that there are wicked people who have no desire to have either children or property, they wish only to kill, to fornicate and to steal. They do this all their lives and then die as does everyone else. Now if they are then permanently cut off, what harm does it do them? This is precisely that to which they strive and this is their desire ...

25. וְאִם־לֹא אֵפוֹ מִי יַכְזִיבֵנִי וְיָשֵׂם לְאַל מִלָּתִי — *If all this is not so, who is there that can demonstrate my falsehood, show my words to be empty?* All that I have said is demonstrably true. The righteous, for whom I serve as paradigm, suffer agonies and wish for nothing more than death — which does not come to them soon enough — and the wicked flourish undisturbed.

XXV.

◆§ Bildad's Third Speech

Bildad, chastened and changed by Iyov's earlier plea for mercy, makes a final attempt to help his erstwhile friend. As presented in the commentary, the tenor of this speech, its content, thrust and motivation, make it unique. If Iyov would have been of a mind to be helped by any form of persuasion, this would have been the speech which would have turned the tide of his despair.

In fact, it touches Iyov not at all. His response in the next chapter is in no way different to all his previous reactions. Full of bitter disdain for all the friends, he makes short shrift equally of Bildad the man and his message.

We may speculate about what would have occurred if this would have been the first, instead of the last speech offered by the friends. Perhaps Iyov would have succumbed to its tone if not to its message. Certainly when the friends first came, he was predisposed to regard them and what they had to say positively. Perhaps the need for friendship and understanding would have persuaded him to compromise his position. But not any more! From the first he has had to contend valiantly to maintain his view of the truth. Every tiny component of it has become dear to him in the struggle. He is not about to give up anything of his hard-won integrity.

And therefore, in a book dedicated to teaching that the truth is valuable beyond all else, that facile but false solutions are to be eschewed at even the cost of agonizing loneliness and alienation, this speech was indeed left to the last. It falls short of that standard of truth which Iyov — ultimately vindicated in his position by God Himself — refuses to compromise.

Iyov will emerge victorious from the most terrible of all his losses — the loss of his treasured friends.

Bildad, as did Eliphaz before him, makes a third and last attempt at communication. In this he parts ways with Tzophar who, as we saw in Introductory Remarks to chapter 25, had been sufficiently impressed by Iyov's heart-rending plea in chapter 24 to have determined that his second speech would be his last.

But Bildad, too, perhaps as a result of that self-same plea which Iyov had made in response to Bildad's second speech, has not remained unmoved. He appears to have turned into a changed person. The difference between this speech and Bildad's earlier ones is almost as striking as is Tzophar's silence. He, as much as Tzophar, has ceased to be a debater. In place of abuse [*How long will you say such things, your speech is just an avalanche of words* (8:2)], and self-importance [*Why should we be considered as cattle? [Why] are we stupid in your eyes?* (18:3)] we have unabashed adoration of a God before Whom all human pretensions are meaningless and foolish. Bildad has become a visionary, who now, in one last desperate effort, seeks to carry Iyov along in his own religious ecstacy.

2. הַמְשֵׁל וָפַחַד עִמּוֹ עֹשֶׂה שָׁלוֹם בִּמְרוֹמָיו — *Dominion and awe are His, He makes peace in His high places.* The fact that here Bildad does not begin by addressing Iyov directly, as he did in

24/25 *all this is not so, who is there that can demonstrate my falsehood,*
show my words to be empty?

25/1-4 [1] *Bildad the Shuhite responded and said:* [2] *Dominion and awe*
are His, He makes peace in His high places. [3] *Can His*
regiments be numbered? Upon whom does His light not shine?
[4] *Can a [frail] mortal expect to best the Almighty? What power can*
one born of woman command that he would ever win his case?

his earlier speeches, is in tune with our analysis in the Introductory Remarks and argues in favor of reading this verse as an expression of pure adoration rather than as a direct response to Iyov's previous speech. This accords with *R' Meyuchas* to this verse.

Rashi, by way of contrast, suggests that this verse does indeed react to Iyov's wishful dream at 23:4: He had wanted to confront God with his innocence: *Would that I would know so that I might find Him, I would go right up to the very base of His throne. Would lay out my claims before Him, would fill my mouth with arguments.* Bildad tells him, *Dominion and awe are His*! *Dominion* refers to the angel Michael, *awe* to the angel Gabriel. Could you face even one of them? [How much more then, that you can have no hope of vindicating yourself before God.]

For the second phrase *Rashi* writes: Since each of the heavenly constellations rises alone there is no jealousy among them, since each believes himself to be first. *Rashi* does not explain how this thought ties in with the first phrase, nor what is the continuing thought expressed in the next verse.

Ramban, too, takes the passage as a reaction to Iyov's speech. He writes: Unable to find any flaws in Iyov's arguments, Bildad decides once more to justify his thinking by contrasting man's lowly state to God's exaltedness. Hapless man is simply too foolish to understand the absolute rectitude of Divine justice. Therefore Bildad derides Iyov, who believes that his sufferings are the result of blind happenstance.

He renders this and the next verse as follows: *Dominion and awe are His*: He is able to bring even the most mighty to justice. Accordingly, they all stand in awe of Him. *He makes peace in His high places*: Among God's servants there is peace and harmony. They are subject to none of the failings and foibles of man. *Can His regiments be numbered*: Even though they are so numerous, there is no dissonance among them. *Upon whom does His light not shine*: None of them have light independently of Him. Only He gives them existence.

The sense is that in the face of God's overwhelming power and rectitude, no mere human could ever be considered blameless.

3. הֲיֵשׁ מִסְפָּר לִגְדוּדָיו וְעַל־מִי לֹא־יָקוּם אוֹרֵהוּ — *Can His regiments be numbered? Upon whom does His light not shine?* *Rashi* is silent on this verse. We have seen *Ramban*'s interpretation in the commentary to the previous verse.

In contrast to *Ramban*'s interpretation of the second half of the verse (see above), *R' Meyuchas* interprets it as follows: *Who can hide himself from His light?* In this interpretation the phrase is similar in meaning to *Psalms* 19:7: *Nothing can be hidden from His sun.* The entire verse, then, is to be read as a description of God's might. God's regiments, those whom He sends to do His bidding, are without number. He is, therefore, all-powerful. Moreover, there is no one who can hide himself from God's scrutiny. Therefore, everyone is vulnerable.

4. וּמַה־יִּצְדַּק אֱנוֹשׁ עִם־אֵל וּמַה־יִּזְכֶּה יְלוּד אִשָּׁה — *Can a [frail] mortal expect to best the Almighty? What power can one born of woman command that he would ever win his case?* Both halves of the verse have occurred in other parts of the book, the first at 9:2 in Iyov's response to Bildad's first speech. This makes its use by Bildad particularly evocative. He has, as it were, appropriated Iyov's own words — while attaching his own meaning to them. Iyov had used them to bemoan the unfairness of his situation. What hope has he that an apparently uncaring God would listen to his claims of innocence. Bildad turns the meaning of the phrase around: Indeed there is no hope, but not because God is not fair, but because you must, as indeed would any mortal, fall far short of your obligations.

There could be another explanation for the choice of a phrase which Iyov himself had used earlier. We examine this together with an analysis of the use of the second phrase.

This second phrase, as indeed the entire argument offered here in verses 4-6, echoes Eliphaz's thoughts at 15:14.

Why would Bildad repeat the point which Eliphaz had already made?

In Introductory Remarks to chapter 20 we

כה/ה־ו ה־ו הֵן עַד־יָרֵחַ וְלֹא יַאֲהִיל וְכוֹכָבִים לֹא־זַכּוּ בְעֵינָיו: אַף
כו/א א כִּי־אֱנוֹשׁ רִמָּה וּבֶן־אָדָם תּוֹלֵעָה: וַיַּעַן אִיּוֹב וַיֹּאמַר:

suggested one explanation — see there. We might also consider the following: It is clear that the tenor of each of the friend's speeches — except only Tzophar's second one — up to this last of them all, has been hostile. We have proposed a possible explanation for this in the commentary to 4:6. Clearly, this tone of negativism toward Iyov's legitimate concerns contributed to the failure of the friends to make any headway in their attempts at comforting. Bildad, as we have seen throughout this chapter, has struck out in a new direction. There is nothing in his words here that could be construed as critical of Iyov — it is in every way a speech that any good and wise friend might have made. Accordingly, Bildad reaches back to the profound truth which Eliphaz had earlier established, in the hope that in the new ambience created by the more friendly atmosphere, Iyov might now be willing to accept what he had earlier rejected.

This, then, might also explain why the first phrase in the sentence is a borrowed one. Bildad seems to be telling Iyov: It is time to forget past rancors. Let us go over some of the old ground. New attitudes will uncover fresh implications in the old phrases.

5. הֵן עַד־יָרֵחַ וְלֹא יַאֲהִיל וְכוֹכָבִים לֹא־זַכּוּ בְעֵינָיו — *See the moon passed by, but was not able to cast a light, the very stars are not deserving in His sight.* In *Rashi's* interpretation עַד is a verb, meaning *to pass by.* See *Rashi* to *Numbers* 21:30, and to *Rosh Hashanah* 16a and *Kiddushin* 33a. The sense of the verse seems to be based on the assumption that for the heavenly bodies to cast the light which is expected of them, they must deserve to do so. If occasionally the moon passes without giving light, as for example during a lunar eclipse, or if light of the stars is blocked off by the clouds, then this means that they have fallen short in God's eye. The next verse will draw conclusions about man's inevitable foibles and failings.

The thoughts expressed in this verse are once more a reworking of Iyov's own ideas at 9:7: *He orders the sun — and it does not shine, He seals off the stars.* Again, Bildad uses Iyov's reasoning to show the opposite. Iyov had seen the unnaturally darkened sky as one more example of God's untrammeled destructive power, one more instance of God playing havoc with His own world — see commentary to 9:5-13. For Bildad it is a manifestation of the Divine passion for absolute justice, an illustration of the exhilaratingly demanding standards expected of God's servants.

6. אַף כִּי־אֱנוֹשׁ רִמָּה וּבֶן־אָדָם תּוֹלֵעָה — *How much more a frail, rotting, mortal, the son of man — a worm.* The אֱנוֹשׁ רִמָּה of our verse is clearly meant to echo the אֱנוֹשׁ of verse 4, while the בֶּן־אָדָם of our verse parallels the יְלוּד אִשָּׁה of that verse.

Clearly then, we can structure Bildad's speech as follows: There is the initial paean contained in verse 2, and this is followed by two self-contained couplets, each setting up two units in relationship to one another. Verses 3 and 4 (the first couplet) contast lowly man with exalted God. God controls countless legions, His searching piercing light makes any hope of hiding from Him pointless, while man is frail and mortal — and clearly no match for Him.

Verses 5 and 6 (the second couplet) set up man against the heavenly bodies. If these latter, in all their majesty, can never be considered deserving, then surely rotting worm-like mortals must be positively weighed down by guilt.

But still, the structure is surprising. Would we not have expected the insight that man is worm-like to have been used in the comparison to God (the first couplet), rather than in the assertion of man's inescapable culpability (the second couplet)? Surely the *a fortiori* argument from the fact that even the heavenly bodies are undeserving in God's sight would have been effective even without the awareness of man's absolute nothingness, while the comparison to God would certainly have been that much more graphic.

We conclude that in addition to the two doublet structure, we also have a progression. At first Bildad sees man as lowly, but not as totally without merit (v. 4). But, as he ponders the ridiculous presumption of the challenge to God implied in the stated wish to find vindication, his mind turns to the impossibility of escaping guilt in God's eyes. It occurs to him that even the heavenly bodies are undeserving and this convinces him that he has been too lenient in his judgment. Man is not only lowly, but also a mass of rotting putrefaction.

Bildad, then, has used his awareness of God's overwhelming grandeur to reach a conclusion about man. Worm-like and rotting, he is beneath contempt.

It is instructive to contrast Bildad's conclusion to that of the singer in *Psalms* 8:4ff.: *When I behold Your heavens, the work of Your fingers, the moon and the stars which You have set*

25/5-6 [5] *See the moon passed by, but was not able to cast a light, the very*
stars are not deserving in His sight. [6] *How much more a frail,*
rotting, mortal, the son of man — a worm.

26/1-2 [1] *Iyov responded and said:* [2] *What assistance have you been,*

in place ... What is the frail human that You should remember him? And what is the son of man that You should be mindful of him? Yet You have made him only a little less than the angels, and crowned him with a soul and a splendor. You gave him dominion over the works of Your hand. You placed everything under his feet. Sheep and cattle, everything, even the beasts of the open field; the birds of the sky and the fish of the sea ... HASHEM our Master, how mighty is Your Name throughout the earth!

What a difference! The singer begins with precisely the same thought as does Bildad. Contemplation of the heavenly spheres seems to yield that puny man is, indeed, nothing at all (מָה אֱנוֹשׁ ...). But, instead of leaving it at that, he surprises us with a complete turnabout: *Yet* ... Quite the opposite of what we thought, is true. Far from being an impotent worm, man is the very master of the universe. God's greatness, far from devaluing man, lifts him to the most stupendous heights. And, what is more, this human grandeur diminishes God's greatness not one whit. The final verse of the psalm is a repetition of the first. The singer still proclaims in all his earlier fervor: *HASHEM our Master, how mighty is Your Name throughout the earth!*

Is Bildad correct, or, more precisely, is his stance a theologically valid one which can stand side by side with that of the psalmist?

Perhaps not. We do not find his precise conclusion mirrored anywhere in Scripture. Even *Psalms* 22:7: *But I am a worm, not even human, scorned by men, despised by people,* is not offered as an objectively reached, philosophically correct, conclusion, but rather it is a subjective cry of despair uttered at a moment in which the psalmist felt himself deserted by God. Quickly this black mood is dissipated and gives way to exultation: ... *For he did not scorn, He did not spurn the plea of the lowly ... Let the lowly eat and be satisfied ... Always be of good cheer!*

It is perhaps for this reason that Iyov will reject even this last, well-meant speech. We have frequently quoted the *Zohar* that the friends had essentially valid advice to give, but that their failure came about because they were not sufficiently well prepared to offer it in the right way. They were not well attuned to Iyov's sensitivities, rode rough-shod over his vulnerability. Would we not have thought that by this time, after so much has been said, so much learned, that the friends would have picked up that which was wrong with their approach — particularly Bildad in his new-found goodwill?

But it is possible that at this point, indeed, the shoe has changed to the other foot. Bildad has indeed found the right tone, but in the end, his argument has become unsound. Iyov does not want to hear himself described as a rotting worm. He knows, as he has known throughout, that if he is to retain his integrity, if he is to remain a *tam* and not become a *chonef*, he must not lose his self-respect. It is true that deep down he realizes that his constant demand of a face to face confrontation with God, as an equal or as almost an equal, is not realistic. But, if it is true that it can never come about, it is not because he is a rotting worm. He is an upright human being, worthy of respect and recognition for what he has accomplished. His limitations are inherent in his mortality. But that is not the same as saying that he is a worm.

This may be the key to understanding the tenor of Iyov's rejection speech in the next chapter. There he accuses Bildad of lack of wisdom and then goes on to describe God's undisputed prowess. He appears to be chiding Bildad for his mistaken conclusions: Half of what you said, Bildad, is correct. God is indeed mighty beyond all human ken. But that is obvious. No one needs to be told any of this (v. 4). With the other half I do not agree. I describe God's omnipotence, but say nothing of man's frailty. The one does not follow from the other.

XXVI.

◆§ Iyov's Response to Bildad's Third Speech

When we compare this, Iyov's last speech in the debate, to his earlier ones, we can detect a substantive difference in tone. Until now he has been, with the rare exception of the occasional phrase, unrelievedly critical of God, has indeed been engaged in vehement invective which, if it was not actual blasphemy, certainly bordered dangerously close upon it.

ג מֶה־עָזַרְתָּ לְלֹא־כֹחַ הוֹשַׁעְתָּ זְרוֹעַ לֹא־עֹז׃ מַה־יָּעַצְתָּ
ד לְלֹא חָכְמָה וְתֻשִׁיָּה לָרֹב הוֹדָעְתָּ׃ אֶת־מִי הִגַּדְתָּ מִלִּין
ה וְנִשְׁמַת־מִי יָצְאָה מִמֶּךָּ׃ הָרְפָאִים יְחוֹלָלוּ מִתַּחַת מַיִם

Here Iyov speaks only favorably of God's might and accomplishments. Indeed, if the speech had not been expressly attributed to Iyov, we would have been able to ascribe it to any of the friends.

That is not to say that Iyov has abandoned previous positions. In the soliloquies that follow, he will continue to proclaim stoutly the incomprehensibility and unfairness of his predicament. Indeed, all along, his contention has been that the arguments made by the friends explain nothing at all. Now that he has adopted some part of their position, we need not expect him to have solved his problems. Still, and this is important, he does show us that his attitudes are not monolithic. He knows full well that there is a God Whose might places Him infinitely beyond our ken, Whom he would willingly adore and venerate. His problem is that that same God appears to him as vindictive, a phenomenon which he describes in such graphic detail in the earlier speeches.

Why does Iyov, at this point in the narrative, allow himself to move so close to the friends' position?

We suspect that the change is a result of Bildad's more positive tone. With Eliphaz's unreasonable accusations behind him, with Tzophar already won to his side, with Bildad now so eminently reasonable — if not in his conclusions which Iyov refuses to accept, then at least in his tone — Iyov is ready to jettison the unrelieved blackness of his earlier visions.

We have, throughout the commentary, assumed the *Zohar's* position — that much of what the friends had said was wise and useful, and could indeed have helped Iyov. They erred in not being well enough prepared to be able to couch their thoughts in a form which would be palatable to Iyov. According to *Rashi,* upon whose idea (that the purpose of the book is to instruct us about how to react to one who rebels against his lot) we have based much of the commentary, this is extremely significant. By having Iyov take such a positive turn at the end of the debate, when it is already too late, we become aware of what might have been. Who knows but that a more thoughtful and empathetic approach might have saved the friends from their abject failure.

Iyov rejects Bildad's thoughts completely. At the end of the last chapter we surmised that in this he might be motivated by his refusal to accept Bildad's view of man as a disgusting and rotting worm.

If we are correct in this surmisal, we may have the key to the solution of an enigma posed by this, Iyov's last speech in response to the friends. After the *pro forma* condemnation of Bildad with which the speech opens, Iyov moves on to a description of God's prowess. In effect, he is telling Bildad that the latter's ecstasy at discovering God's might was misplaced. None of what he said was new. Indeed he, Iyov, could describe many more wonders.

Now at chapter 9, in Iyov's response to Bildad's first speech, Iyov also has a passage describing the many aspects of God's power. In commentary 5-13 there, we noted that all the examples which Iyov lists are unrelievedly negative. They depict a powerful God, Who can and does wreak havoc throughout nature. Here the list is much more positive. We observe God in the mighty acts of creation — building, spreading, firming — but never smashing (except only the wicked, at v. 12), darkening or destroying.

Why the change?

It may be that Iyov was offended by Bildad's conclusions, that if God is all-mighty, then man is beneath disgust.

We had surmised that by omitting any *a fortiori* conclusions about man's lowliness in the face of the manifest grandeur which Iyov had observed, he is subtly chiding Bildad for his reasoning. The God Whom I know, says Iyov, is as omnipotent as yours. However this does not yield, for me, that man is a worm.

With this end in mind, Iyov may have chosen to slant his list toward the positive. Iyov may be telling Bildad: You reached your erroneous conclusion because you concentrated on the wrong aspects of God's power. You saw Him as a fierce Judge from Whom no one can hide (v. 3), one with uncompromising demands which no one can be expected to deliver (v. 5). It is such harsh omnipotence which reduces man to insignificance.

But, Iyov suggests, let us, without reducing by one whit the awe in which we regard Him, see God somewhat differently. Let us see an all-might which shrouds itself in mystery (v. 9), which

inasmuch as you have no strength? In what sense has your arm —
which is powerless — helped? [3] *What have you advised those*
without wisdom? As for counsel, how liberally have you divulged!
[4] *Whom have you told anything at all? Whose ideas have issued*
forth from you? [5] *The dead tremble, even those that dwell deep*

engages in acts of creativity, balancing a cosmos in a vacuum (v. 7), lending the vaporous clouds the strength to bear the waters (v. 8), girding the oceans (v. 10) and supporting the heavens (v. 11). An all-might which, if it interferes at all in the affairs of man, does so only to dash the arrogant spirits of the proud upon the sea's crashing waves.

Before such a God we may indeed tremble, without, at the same time, devaluing man.

Does this picture which Iyov now draws contradict his earlier visions of a God seemingly bent upon destroying His own world? How does the God who smashes the arrogant, coexist with One Who permits the wicked to flourish, thereby confounding every tenet of justice or fairness (chapters 23-24)?

Such questions will trouble only those who expect a wasting, suffering Iyov, deserted by society, bereft of both past and future, sickened and disgusted with his putrefying body, frustrated beyond bearing by an apparently indifferent Deity of Whose love or even caring he has despaired, to produce an integrated, strictly reasoned, fully harmonious world-view. But that is precisely what Iyov has not done, in all the avalanche of words which he has poured out up till now. He has fluctuated wildly between hope and despair, pugnacious confrontation and pathetic dependence, depressed denial and soaring affirmation of life — and much more.[1]

Clearly, Iyov knows that God's indivisible unity notwithstanding, He can appear to us in a bewildering multiplicity of images (see *Rashi* to *Exodus* 20:2). Even in moments in which he felt himself the victim of incomprehensible vindictiveness, he knew that somewhere, apparently aloof and inaccessible, there was a God of love to Whom — could he but know how — he could flee for comfort from his torments. Iyov, even in his worst moments, never made the terrible mistake of reducing God to a monochromatic blandness easily grasped and neatly definable by philosophical enterprise. It is just this propensity for simplistic apprehension of the infinitely variegated Divine, which Iyov so decried in the friends.

And so, we should not be surprised when now, that the need arises, Iyov is able to produce a vision of God which is quite different to that which on earlier occasions he has been able to conjure up. It will not serve to comfort him — he knows only too well that others, too, exist. However, it serves to free him from the pernicious conclusions of Bildad's logic. Iyov knows one thing very clearly — he is not a worm.

2. מֶה־עָזַרְתָּ לְלֹא־כֹחַ הוֹשַׁעְתָּ זְרוֹעַ לֹא־עֹז — *What assistance have you been, inasmuch as you have no strength? In what sense has your arm — which is powerless — helped? Rashi* is silent to this and the next verse. We have followed *Targum. Ramban*, as do most other commentators, render as follows: *What assistance have you been to those who have no strength [to understand God on their own]? How have you helped him whose arm has no power?* In explanation, *Ramban* adds: Those who believe that they are the victims of happenstance do so for the very reason that they think God too great and themselves too insignificant. You have only confirmed them in their folly.

3. מַה־יָּעַצְתָּ לְלֹא חָכְמָה וְתֻשִׁיָּה לָרֹב הוֹדָעְתָּ — *What have you advised those without wisdom? As for counsel, how liberally have you divulged*! The meaning of the first phrase depends upon the rendering of the previous verse. We have once more followed *Targum.* The second phrase is to be taken sarcastically. You appear to think that you have been generous in sharing your helpful insights. The truth is that there is no one who will derive any benefit from your largess.

4. אֶת־מִי הִגַּדְתָּ מִלִּין וְנִשְׁמַת־מִי יָצְאָה מִמֶּךָּ — *Whom have you told anything at all? Whose ideas have issued forth from you*? Who could possibly have placed such patently obvious thoughts in your mouth. Who could have thought that they would serve any useful purpose?

5. הָרְפָאִים יְחוֹלָלוּ מִתַּחַת מַיִם וְשֹׁכְנֵיהֶם — *The dead tremble, even those that dwell deep down beneath the waters.* We have followed *R'*

1. Herewith, a partial listing of sources: footnote to 9:14; footnote to 9:22-24; commentary to 10:20-22; 13:15 and 14:15; commentary to 16:19; commentary to 19:26, and especially to 19:27 where we quote the famous *From You to You* passage from *Ibn Gabirol's Keser Malchus.*

ו־ז וְשֹׁכְנֵיהֶם: עָרוֹם שְׁאוֹל נֶגְדּוֹ וְאֵין כְּסוּת לָאֲבַדּוֹן: נֹטֶה צָפוֹן
ח עַל־תֹּהוּ תֹּלֶה אֶרֶץ עַל־בְּלִימָה: צֹרֵר מַיִם בְּעָבָיו וְלֹא־
ט־י נִבְקַע עָנָן תַּחְתָּם: מְאַחֵז פְּנֵי־כִסֵּה פַּרְשֵׁז עָלָיו עֲנָנוֹ: חֹק־
יא חָג עַל־פְּנֵי־מָיִם עַד־תַּכְלִית אוֹר עִם־חֹשֶׁךְ: עַמּוּדֵי שָׁמַיִם
°וּבִתְבוּנָתוֹ ק׳ יב יְרוֹפָפוּ וְיִתְמְהוּ מִגַּעֲרָתוֹ: בְּכֹחוֹ רָגַע הַיָּם °ובתובנתו
יג מָחַץ רָהַב: בְּרוּחוֹ שָׁמַיִם שִׁפְרָה חֹלְלָה יָדוֹ נָחָשׁ בָּרִחַ:

Meyuchas, as being closest to the simple meaning of the verse. רְפָאִים is used as a synonym for מֵתִים, *the dead* (*Isaiah* 26:14), and that seems to be its plain meaning throughout Scripture. יְחוֹלָלוּ, from חיל, *to tremble,* as in *Psalms* 29:9.

Rashi takes רְפָאִים as *Gehinnom,* and יְחוֹלָלוּ from חלל, *to make a hole.* Thus, reference is to the seven holes or *caverns* associated with *Gehinnom.*

The sense of the verse is the same according to both interpretations: Bildad had said that God's light shines upon everyone — that is, that there is no hiding from God (25:3). Iyov replies that if this were of any significance, one could take it much further. Not only the living but even the dead (*R' Meyuchas*), not only this world but even *Gehinnom,* is exposed to God's unforgiving vision. Even those who live in the earth's deepest depths, that is, beneath the waters, are not protected.

6. עָרוֹם שְׁאוֹל נֶגְדּוֹ וְאֵין כְּסוּת לָאֲבַדּוֹן — *Before Him the grave is naked, the consuming depths have no cover.* The thought is continued from the next verse. The lowest depths are open to God's scrutiny. Nothing can protect itself from them.

According to the analysis which we offered in the Introductory Remarks to this chapter, these last two verses relate to that which comes later, as follows: If indeed it were useful to stress the all-knowing aspect of God's omnipotence, then it is possible to go much further than Bildad did. However I, Iyov, prefer to perceive God's might in different terms, and it is these that I will now depict.

7. נֹטֶה צָפוֹן עַל־תֹּהוּ תֹּלֶה אֶרֶץ עַל־בְּלִימָה — *He spreads man's habitation over a void, suspends the earth upon nothingness.* Iyov will now show how God's might can be demonstrated from the wonders of creation and nature, without denigrating man into a worm.

The sense of the verse is that the earth, suspended in the atmosphere, rests upon nothing but *the strong arms of the Holy One, Blessed is He* (*Rashi*). It is certainly an indication of His might.

צָפוֹן, which normally translates as *north,* is used here as a synonym for the earth, since mainly the northern part of the earth is occupied by man (*Ramban* and *Metzudos*).

In this interpretation, the second phrase is an elaboration of the first. *R' Saadyah Gaon* prefers to have the two halves of the verse say different things. He takes צָפוֹן as *heavens.* For this rendering, *Daas Mikra* adduces *Isaiah* 14:13-15.

בְּלִימָה is a contraction of two words: בְּלִי מָה, *without anything* (*Metzudos*).

8. צֹרֵר מַיִם בְּעָבָיו וְלֹא־נִבְקַע עָנָן תַּחְתָּם — *He bundles waters in His thick vapors, the cloud does not split under them.* We would have expected the fragile cloud to break under the weight of the water, so that it would all fall down together. Instead, it comes down drop by drop (*Rashi*).

9. מְאַחֵז פְּנֵי־כִסֵּה פַּרְשֵׁז עָלָיו עֲנָנוֹ — *He places an enclosure around the throne, spreads His cloud over it.* כִּסֵּה can either be taken to describe God's throne (*Rashi*), or as a synonym for heaven (*Ramban* and *Metzudos*).

First *Rashi*: *Rashi's* rendering is in the tradition of the *Targum*: *He wraps His throne in darkness so that the angels should not be able to see Him, places a screen around Himself — the clouds of Glory.*

The positioning of this sentence is difficult. Verses 7 and 8 describe the wonders of creation, and so do verses 10 and 11. Thus our verse, which cannot be said to be part of that description, seems to interrupt a flow of thought which would seem to belong together.

According to *Ramban* and *Metzudos* who take כִּסֵּה as a synonym for *heaven,* the verse is of a piece with the whole series beginning with verse 7. The sense is either: He occasionally holds back the heavens [so that it does not rain], and on other occasions spreads His cloud over the sky [so that it should rain] (*Ramban*); or, He [collects moisture in the atmosphere thereby making it palpable] so that the heavens can [almost] be held, and by that process is able to spread His clouds over the heavens (*Metzudos*).

10. חֹק־חָג עַל־פְּנֵי־מָיִם עַד־תַּכְלִית אוֹר עִם־חֹשֶׁךְ — *He has rounded off a border around the waters, until light and darkness will come to*

26/6-13 *down beneath the waters.* 6 *Before Him the grave is naked, the*
consuming depths have no cover. 7 *He spreads man's habitation*
over a void, suspends the earth upon nothingness. 8 *He bundles*
waters in His thick vapors, the cloud does not split under them.
9 *He places an enclosure around the throne, spreads His cloud over*
it. 10 *He has rounded off a border around the waters, until light and*
darkness will come to an end. 11 *The pillars of the heavens were*
unsteady, they were frozen in place by His restraining rebuke. 12 *In*
His might He folded up the waters, in His wisdom He smashed
the arrogant ones. 13 *By His word He spread out the heavens*
like a canopy, His hand caused distress to the straight serpent.

an end. For חֹק as *boundary, Daas Mikra* adduces *Isaiah* 5:14. The sense of the verse is that God surrounded the sea with sand which binds the water and does not permit it to overflow. This is portrayed as an act of particular prowess, because surely we would have supposed that the mighty waves would easily crash past the fragile sands.

The combination אוֹר עִם חשֶׁךְ is unique, and moreover, the phrase, *until light and darkness will come to an end* as a description of *eternity,* does not recur in Scripture. Perhaps its use here can be explained as follows: The ideas of *light* and *darkness* have been used throughout the book to describe not only the times of the day, but also as metaphors for joy and sorrow. Iyov may want our inner thoughts to pick up the sense of God's inscrutable might which takes no cognizance of man's puny temporality. Long after light and darkness, happiness and pain, will have ceased to have any meaning, the sand will still impose its iron hand upon the roaring seas.

11. עַמּוּדֵי שָׁמַיִם יְרוֹפָפוּ וְיִתְמְהוּ מִגַּעֲרָתוֹ — *The pillars of the heavens were unsteady, they were frozen in place by His restraining rebuke.* There are many different interpretations to this verse. Our translation follows *Rashi.* Reference is to the time of creation. The pillars upon which the world is supported were initially unsteady. The world had no firm base. God's restraining rebuke steadied these pillars and the world stood firm.

Ramban: The verse continues on from the previous one. There we saw that the water, the nature of which is to be constantly on the move, is nevertheless inhibited by the fragile sand. Here we learn that the pillars of heaven which, in contrast to the water, we would expect to stand firm, occasionally tremble (יְרוֹפָפוּ) in uncertainty (וְיִתְמְהוּ), as would a person in fear of a loud noise. Reference is to the world shaking at the sound of thunder — God's rebuke.

R' Yosef Kara: The verse is a progression from verses 5 and 6. There we learned how even the nethermost depths stand in fear of God's discovery. Here we move to the greatest heights, *the pillars of the heavens,* that is, the heavenly Hosts. These also tremble (תמה, *to tremble,* as in *Genesis* 43:33) before God's rebuke.

Metzudos: The *pillars of the heavens* is a way of describing the earth. This occasionally trembles — reference is to an earthquake — and comes to rest only when God with His restraining rebuke chooses to control it.

12. בְּכֹחוֹ רָגַע הַיָּם וּבִתְבוּנָתוֹ מָחַץ רָהַב — *In His might He folded up the waters, in His wisdom He smashed the arrogant ones.* The translation follows *Rashi,* who reads a reference to the drowning of the Egyptians at the Sea of Reeds. [רַהַב, the *arrogant ones,* is used for the Egyptians at *Isaiah* 30:7 and, as *Rashi* takes it, at *Psalms* 87:4.] God first folded up the water in order to solidify it into one place so that it could tower over the Egyptians like a wall. Then, by releasing the water, He smashed His arrogant foes.

Ramban sees this verse as a continuation of the thought expressed in verse 10. There we saw the wild sea bounded by the seemingly fragile sands, forced willy-nilly into the bounds which nature set for it. Here we have God, at will, splitting the sea — against its nature. The *arrogant ones* are the mighty sea-monsters whom God, when He wishes, can smash against the waters (compare *Psalms* 74:13).

13. בְּרוּחוֹ שָׁמַיִם שִׁפְרָה חֹלְלָה יָדוֹ נָחָשׁ בָּרִחַ — *By His word He spread out the heavens like a canopy, His hand caused distress to the straight serpent.* Our translation follows *Rashi.* We render בָּרִחַ as *straight* in accordance with *Hirsch* (*Collected Writing* vol. II p.

 יד הֶן־אֵ֗לֶּה ׀ קְצ֬וֹת דְּרָכָ֗ו וּמַה־שֵּׁ֣מֶץ דָּ֭בָר נִשְׁמַע־בּ֑וֹ וְרַ֥עַם
 א גְּ֝בוּרֹתָ֗ו מִ֣י יִתְבּוֹנָֽן׃ וַיֹּ֣סֶף אִ֭יּוֹב

113). This, because at *Isaiah* 27:1 it is conformed to the נָחָשׁ עֲקַלָּתוֹן, the *coiled serpent.* בָּרִחַ is a *bolt,* normally, *straight.* The *straight serpent* is Pharaoh, and that phrase appears to be a continuation of what was said in the previous verse.

But, what of the first phrase? What is the unifying theme in our verse, and how does it fit into the general picture?

We may surmise that, since this is the final sentence in Iyov's paean of praise, he wishes to combine in it the two threads which have run through his description of God's prowess — God as creator, nurturer and master of nature, and God as the one in Whose hand the destiny and fate of nations is vested. By means of this combination, another aspect of God's greatness will become apparent. God not only controls the titans of nature — heaven, earth and seas — but at the very same time that He spreads out the canopy of the heavens, he has the time, as it were, to be also the God of history, drowning Pharaoh and his hordes in the sea. Man is not so puny that he does not warrant God's concern.

Ramban takes שִׁפְרָה from שָׁפַר, *to be beautiful.* God cleans the clouds away from the sky so that the turbulent waters can come to rest. Once there is more peace below, the huge sea-monsters can be born (חוֹלְלָה from חולֵל, *to give birth*).

R' Yosef Kara takes נָחָשׁ בָּרִחַ as one of the heavenly constellations. Accordingly, the whole verse is of one piece. God made the heavens into a canopy in which He placed the constellations which He had created (חָלַל = יָצַר).

14. הֶן־אֵלֶּה קְצוֹת דְּרָכָו וּמַה־שֶּׁמֶץ דָּבָר נִשְׁמַע־בּוֹ וְרַעַם גְּבוּרֹתָו מִי יִתְבּוֹנָן — *See these are the smallest of His ways, how can we presume to understand even a mite of Him? Who can contemplate His thundering force?* The first part of this final sentence follows logically upon all that went before. In effect, Iyov has been saying that if a description of God's greatness and power could have yielded a solution to his problems — as seems to have been Bildad's thinking in his last speech — then that description could have been taken much further than did Bildad. But — the implication is — all this solves nothing at all. Bildad had supposed that from the recognition of God's all-might it would follow that man must be a rotting worm and that, in consequence, any suffering to which he would be exposed would be understandable. Iyov, who clearly refuses to draw the conclusion concerning man's lowliness, is left with his quandary.

But, what of the last phrase? As another aspect of God's might — as expressed through the awesome rumbles of the thunder — it would belong together with the earlier section. What can be its function here?

We must recall that these are the very last words which Iyov will say to the friends. The speeches which follow appear to be soliloquies to which Iyov was inspired by the debate, but which are not a part of it. We would certainly expect that somehow they would sum up, as much as is possible in such a short frame, the burden of Iyov's contentions in the hard-fought battle which he has been waging in defense of his religious integrity.

Let us then assume that the *thundering force* of which Iyov speaks, is meant as a description of his dreadful experiences at God's hand. It is God's רַעַם which has destroyed his wealth, snatched his children and smitten him with his hideous sores. A roaring, terrifying, show of force!

If so, the phrase has significance at two levels. In the first, and more immediate sense, it is a final rejection of Bildad's thesis: My troubles are to be traced to God's all-might, not to my rotten worm-like insignificance!

Now this is not just a fine point — a theological nicety — but a devastating assertion of rejection. The difference is a bottomless chasm of perplexity. If Iyov could have accepted Bildad's thesis, then he would have had an answer to all his problems. Having rejected it, he is left with all the former turbulence in his heart and mind: *Who can contemplate His thundering force?*

And this phrase, in its curt finality, becomes the ultimate justification for Iyov's restless questings, alienation and loneliness, pugnacious challenging and despairing death-wishes. For, if there is no understanding of the thunder's crashes, then its victim is left to flounder in his helpless, unenlightened humanity. Every one of his reactions — be they ever so extreme, ever so inconsistent with one another, ever so blasphemous while at the same time permeated with a dreadful, aching, love and longing, ever so incomprehensible to the cold, orderly, theologically sophisticated friends — can find ground and justification in the endless complexities of the human mind and soul. If God will not instruct me, Iyov is saying in one last retort — then I am right in being afraid, angry, demanding and rebellious.

The debate has ended.

14 *See these are the smallest of His ways, how can we presume to understand even a mite of Him? Who can contemplate His thundering force?*

XXVII.

◆§ The First Mashal

The debate is over. Iyov has won the argument but lost his friends. There is much on his mind. His triumph must be savored — though a victory which leaves his problems unsolved and his questings unrequited must — as the next *mashal* will show — have been scant comfort.

Iyov feels the need to consolidate his present by looking back over the past and making judgments. Where does he stand as a loyal servant of a God Who seems to care for him not at all. Has his course been correct? He has dared much, risked much, in his desperate determination to hold on to his integrity. Could he have been justified? Should he change course for the future? Iyov does not know — as we, the readers do — that there is an Elihu waiting in the wings, that God Himself is prepared to lead him to the truth. He is, as far as he knows, entirely alone. Must he condemn his solitude to the bitter unrest of struggle? Is it maybe time to give up?

What of the friends? Discredited, adrift in a sea of theological confusion, bereft of anchors which had only recently seemed so secure, what does the future hold for them? Can they be defended? Must they be condemned?

What of God and His omnipotence? What does God want from us? Can we understand — if so, why don't we? Is it that we *can't* understand? Ought we to try, to struggle, knowing that, perhaps, only frustration awaits us? Or will the quest generate its own answer? Is there perhaps a truth, the nature of which we cannot even guess at, which will be granted to the stubborn souls who refuse to give up on their God?

All these thoughts engage Iyov's mind as he launches upon the first of his great *meshalim.*

The following two *meshalim*, chapters 27-28 and 29-31, respectively, appear to be a bridge between the debate and the appearance of the mysterious Elihu. They are clearly marked as separated from that which went before, by the verse which introduces each of them, but which appears in none of the earlier speeches: *Iyov then continued to take up his cogitations, and said* ... On the other hand, the verse which really closes the debate, *Now these three men desisted from answering Iyov ...*, occurs only at 32:1, after the two *meshalim* have been completed. Clearly, then, they stand on their own: not as a *response* as Iyov's earlier speeches had been (... וַיַּעַן), but as a reworking, and subsequently a restating — partly for himself, partly for the friends, partly for the listeners crowding around from whose ranks Elihu will step forth — of the positions and ideas to which Iyov had held so tenaciously throughout the debate. Now, he knows quite clearly, his beliefs are vindicated by the abdication of the friends.

Certainly, it is entirely human to wish, to muse just once more, upon ideas, the defense of which had been undertaken at such cost and heroism. But even from a purely didactic point of view, it makes sense to highlight once more the main points to be taken out from the welter of words and ideas which, in the nature of things, had poured from the suffering Iyov in the heat of debate.

In the first *mashal* we learn of three issues which, Iyov realizes in retrospect, ought to be viewed as the pillars upon which his philosophy rests.

Most significant among these is the contrasting between תְּמִימוּת, *temimus* (v. 5), and חֲנוּפָה, *chanufah* (v. 8). As we have worked out in detail in the commentary to 1:1 and 6:13, it is this issue, more than any other, which divides Iyov's philosophy from that of the friends. They have maintained throughout that *temimus* should demand a docile submission to God's decrees, and feel that Iyov's belligerence belies his original acceptance (see at 1:21) and brands him as a *chonef.* This, Iyov categorically denies. He feels that his uncompromising quest for the truth is entirely in consonance with the demands of *temimus* — God, after all, wishes us to have some conception of Him, and if He acts in ways other than those in which He chooses to describe Himself, He leaves us no alternative to rigorous questioning. On the contrary, a mindless white-washing which has no basis in reality, is the epitome of *chanufah.*

As a necessary corollary of his thesis, Iyov then turns to the second issue of this soliloquy. He

ב שְׂאֵת מְשָׁלוֹ וַיֹּאמַר: חַי־אֵל הֵסִיר מִשְׁפָּטִי וְשַׁדַּי
ג הֵמַר נַפְשִׁי: כִּי־כָל־עוֹד נִשְׁמָתִי בִי וְרוּחַ אֱלוֹהַּ בְּאַפִּי:

must declare the friends wicked and culpable. He cannot simply leave them as wrong. If their's were a position which was in any way defensible, then he would never have had the courage, nor indeed the right, to embark upon the terrible path which he, throughout, felt himself forced to take. His relentless questing has brought him to the very brink of unforgivable blasphemy — may even, on occasion, have pushed him across the line, and that cannot be taken lightly. The other path, passive submission against his better judgment — nay, against his firm and healthy theological knowledge and intuition — would have been so much more congenial, had it been possible. Nothing will do but to say the absolute truth. Comfortable self-delusion is inexcusably wicked and will, indeed must, meet its punishment. The time will come at which Iyov will be able to lift himself beyond this narrow view. He will grow to a point at which he can feel more forgiving — will indeed be able to pray for the friends (see at 42:10). But that will occur only after he has been vouchsafed his vision of God. As yet, this is beyond him.[1]

The third, and most extensively treated, topic in the soliloquy is Iyov's paean to wisdom. In the sense in which we understand Iyov's musings at this point, it is entirely appropriate that this jubilant affirmation of the equation, *fear of God = wisdom*, be a part of them.

The friends have, after all, predicated all their arguments upon the premise of their superior wisdom — see for example 15:8-10. That is, they have equated wisdom with their facile — ultimately discredited — theological assumptions. But, Iyov is convinced, someone who truly stands in awe of the Almighty can never satisfy himself with superficial platitudes. He who knows that one day he will be called upon to answer for himself would rather remain eternally in a theological limbo, twisting and turning, subject to constant frustration, occasional rage, frequent despair — but, withal, engaged in honorable quest — than to deaden his mind to the relentless, intractable problems which beset thinking man. True wisdom respects the problems with which it must wrangle. Respect goads and challenges, respect demands engagement. Respect despises the lassitude induced by inappropriate and misplaced certainties.

'Hear I beg you, my remonstration, attend to the contention of my lips. Will you represent God with wickedness, would you speak falsehoods for Him? Do you expect to flatter Him, is it for God that you contend? Would it be good if He were to inquire into you, would you treat Him with derision as you would a man? Surely He will remonstrate with you. Will you assert veneration in the private chambers? Will His exaltedness not terrify you, His fear not fall upon you?' (13:6-11).

Here we have Iyov's credo, summoned forth in rough, accusatory spurts of invective, by the friend's merciless insensitivity and condescension in the earlier portion of the debate. Now, with his adversaries routed, Iyov allows himself to luxuriate in poetic musings upon the same topic. Wisdom, as expressed in firmly cast verities, is eternally beyond us. If we can partake of it at all, it will be in the awe-struck wonder of the eternal quest.

Ramban sees the thrust of this speech quite differently. He bases his understanding upon his perception of Iyov's theological stance, which he first enunciated in his commentary to 13:15 (see there), and expanded in his introduction to chapter 22 — see our Introductory Remarks there. Iyov, he maintained, never denies Divine Providence and fairness, as it relates to the afterlife. His only quarrel with God's stewardship of human affairs centers upon human fate in this, our physical world. He cannot make peace with the idea that the righteous should ever, even temporarily, be denied their just desserts.

These points have been established in the earlier speeches. Here, Iyov reaches the conclusion that the logic behind God's action, lies forever beyond human ken. Divine wisdom cannot be

---

1. Needless to say, Iyov's prediction that the friends are to be punished does not contradict his earlier assertions that the wicked live happy lives, untroubled by any consequences of their evil deeds — see particularly in chapter 21.

Iyov's contention had never been that no wicked person is ever punished. His constant longing for a confrontation with God before some competent bar of justice indicates beyond any shadow of doubt that he believes in God's ultimate fairness and justice. What Iyov does contend, and did not hesitate to spell out in graphic eloquence, is that in spite of all this, terrible miscarriages of justice do occur. There are many many wicked people whom the arm of retribution seems never to overtake. Against this seeming arbitrariness and unpredictability, he feels called upon to struggle, and struggle mightily. This, however does not prevent him from expecting, and predicting, that the individual evildoer will be punished.

For *Ramban's* response to the apparent contradiction, see commentary to verse 14.

[1] *Iyov then continued to take up his cogitations, and said.* [2] *As the*
Almighty lives! He has withheld my rights, Shaddai has embit-
tered me. [3] *But, as long as my soul is within me, as long as God's*

plumbed by our intellects and, accordingly, the friends err in attempting to justify Iyov's horrible fate in terms which we can understand. Far better, Iyov claims, to remain silent, admit that we comprehend nothing, and leave it at that (commentary to vs. 13 and 14).

Now, it is not strictly true that we can know nothing at all of Divine wisdom. One tiny facet has God made known to us — that wisdom imposes upon us the obligation to stand in awe of God, and to turn aside from vil (28:28). Beyond that, it is true, that all is hidden; but this, in itself, is profoundly significant. For if indeed God wishes us to fear Him, wishes us to do good, then there must be Divine Providence and justice. Else we would be of no interest to Him. This, in *Ramban's* thinking at chapter 22, is the basis for Iyov's belief that in the afterlife, justice is to be expected.

Ramban's analysis of this *mashal* leaves us with an important question: If Iyov realizes that it is impossible to understand the motives which move God, then why, in all his previous speeches has he so relentlessly cried out against the perceived injustices which have been directed against him? Why has he accused, supplicated, challenged, when the key to his experiences was so close at hand? It all has an adequate explanation — we are just not wise enough to grasp it. Why did Iyov not impose the silence upon himself which he recommends here to the friends?

Clearly, in *Ramban's* interpretation of the book, the human element of Iyov's experiences is given play. Iyov screamed because his pain demanded to be somehow assuaged, not because he held to a theological stance which justified it.

1. וַיֹּסֶף אִיּוֹב שְׂאֵת מְשָׁלוֹ וַיֹּאמַר — *Iyov then continued to take up his cogitations, and said.* If the congruence between the introductory verses to our two *meshalim,* and those which open Balaam's visions at *Numbers* 23:7 and onward, is significant, then we should conclude that the *meshalim* here were not addressed directly to the friends, any more than were Balaam's prophetic visions addressed directly to Balak. Rather, they are soliloquies in which Iyov allows the highlights of the debate to pass once more before his mind's eye, reaffirming his own position and reiterating his unqualified condemnation of the friends.

For מָשָׁל we go to *Hirsch* on *Genesis* 4:7. The base meaning of the word is, *to declare what something is and should be; to give it character and design.* By extension: *to command, to rule.* Thus also, מִשְׁלֵי שְׁלֹמֹה, which tell us the true nature of men and things. So too the use of מָשָׁל as *metaphor:* It addresses *the ought* rather than *the is,* the essence rather than the form. It is a parable.

Accordingly, מָשָׁל is a precisely appropriate word to describe Iyov's musings. His assertions concerning who, between himself and the friends, ought to be regarded as a *tam* or *chonef,* respectively, what can and cannot be described as true חָכְמָה, indeed, even his contention that the friends must be regarded as wicked and liable to punishment — all these fit the idea of מָשָׁל perfectly. Through Iyov's teachings, we learn to be מֹשֵׁל (rule) over these categories.

2. חַי־אֵל הֵסִיר מִשְׁפָּטִי וְשַׁדַּי הֵמַר נַפְשִׁי — *As the Almighty lives! He has withheld my rights, Shaddai has embittered me. Rashi* quotes *Yerushalmi, Sotah* 5:5, that from the fact that Iyov swears by God's life, it is clear that his religious stance was prompted by love of God: No man would swear by the king's life if he would not love him. See above at 13:15.

That Iyov should express his love for God in this particular verse is highly significant. Clearly his love does not, by one whit, prevent him from expressing his dissatisfaction at the way he has been treated. God has withheld his rights, God has embittered him — and still Iyov loves Him! There can be no clearer statement than this of Iyov's philosophy that *temimus* does not demand mindless acquiescence to seeming miscarriages of justice.

For מִשְׁפָּט as a *right,* see, for example, *Exodus* 23:6.

3. כִּי־כָל־עוֹד נִשְׁמָתִי בִי וְרוּחַ אֱלוֹהַ בְּאַפִּי — *But, as long as my soul is within me, as long as God's breath is in my nostrils.* Nowhere else has Iyov used this precise formulation. In verse 5 he expresses the same thought — that throughout his life he will never compromise his integrity — with עַד אֶגְוָע, the much more prosaic, *up to my very death.* Iyov clearly wishes to underline what we already saw in the previous verse. His determination to argue for his rights, far from standing in contradiction to venerating God, is a necessary outcome of such a stance. Iyov is fully aware that his entire existence is no more than an expression

ד אִם־תְּדַבֵּרְנָה שְׂפָתַי עַוְלָה וּלְשׁוֹנִי אִם־יֶהְגֶּה רְמִיָּה׃
ה חָלִילָה לִּי אִם־אַצְדִּיק אֶתְכֶם עַד־אֶגְוָע לֹא־אָסִיר
ו תֻּמָּתִי מִמֶּנִּי׃ בְּצִדְקָתִי הֶחֱזַקְתִּי וְלֹא אַרְפֶּהָ לֹא־
ז יֶחֱרַף לְבָבִי מִיָּמָי׃ יְהִי כְרָשָׁע אֹיְבִי וּמִתְקוֹמְמִי כְעַוָּל׃
ח כִּי מַה־תִּקְוַת חָנֵף כִּי יִבְצָע כִּי יֵשֶׁל אֱלוֹהַּ
ט נַפְשׁוֹ׃ הֲצַעֲקָתוֹ יִשְׁמַע ׀ אֵל כִּי־תָבוֹא עָלָיו צָרָה׃

of God's will. His soul is that which God blew into him (נָשַׁם, *to blow*), his very nostrils are filled with God's breath. Despite that — or, more correctly, because of that — his lips will speak no evil, his tongue, no fraud.

4. אִם־תְּדַבֵּרְנָה שְׂפָתַי עַוְלָה וּלְשׁוֹנִי אִם־יֶהְגֶּה רְמִיָּה — *My lips shall speak no evil, my tongue shall utter no fraud.* Verse 5 makes clear that the *evil* and *fraud* would be an admission that the friends are correct in their contentions. Throughout the debate Iyov has maintained not only the integrity of his person, but also that of his views of God and man.

5. חָלִילָה לִּי אִם־אַצְדִּיק אֶתְכֶם עַד־אֶגְוָע לֹא־אָסִיר תֻּמָּתִי מִמֶּנִּי — *Far be it from me — up to my very death — to proclaim you to be in the right, I refuse to let go my claim to unquestioning integrity.* The translation to the second phrase follows *Rashi.* Not, *my unquestioning integrity*, but *my claim to unquestioning integrity*: I will never agree to your contention that I am not a *tam.*

6. בְּצִדְקָתִי הֶחֱזַקְתִּי וְלֹא אַרְפֶּהָ לֹא־יֶחֱרַף לְבָבִי מִיָּמָי — *I have held on to my integrity, I will not loosen my grip. My heart has never made me swerve.* Throughout the book, לִבִּי is used six times, לְבָבִי only twice (see at 17:11). The Sages teach that לֵבָב indictates a *two-heartedness.* Its use in this sense here is extremely apt. There must have been many times at which Iyov was of two minds whether to continue his lonely struggle in search of a truth with which he could live. Often, he must have thought, that it would be easier just to give in and admit to a guilt which he in no wise felt. But, these thoughts were always only momentary. Ultimately, Iyov always remained true to the verities which had always sustained him.

We have followed *Rashi* for חָרַף as *to swerve* [from the path]. Other interpretations are: I have not allowed my heart to indulge the follies of *youth* [חֹרֶף is the *winter* when life has its first stirrings, *old age* is compared to קַיִץ, *the summer*] (*Ramban*); my heart has had to feel shame [חָרַף, *to shame*] (*R' Yosef Kara*).

7. יְהִי כְרָשָׁע אֹיְבִי וּמִתְקוֹמְמִי כְעַוָּל — *May the lot of the wicked overtake my enemy, may those that rise up against me share the fate of the evildoer. Rashi* is silent to this verse, but reads verse 8 as a continuation of verse 6. Evidently our verse is to be subsumed under verse 6. Accordingly, we render this verse as does *R' Yosef Kara* who follows *Rashi*'s lead in connecting verses 6 and 8. The sense of the entire section is as follows: In verse 6 Iyov stoutly asserts his unshakable attachment to the principles which have guided his life; he has not deserted them in the past and does not intend to do so in the future. Verse 7 develops this theme: I am righteous, therefore may he who is my enemy — he who denies me this quality and accuses me of being wicked — himself share the fate of the wicked. Verse 8 till the end of the chapter then explains the statement in verse 6 by justifying Iyov's adherence to a path of righteousness. The fate of the wicked is so dreadful, that it would be absolute folly for him to throw in his lot with them.

Now, who is this enemy who, in our verse, accuses Iyov of being wicked? While the commentators do not spell this out, the thrust of the passage, following as it does upon verse 5 which addresses the friends directly, would surely point to the friends, or at the very least to Eliphaz who in his last speech (chapter 22) made no bones about accusing Iyov of every imaginable wickedness. Now the use of the singular (אֹיְבִי) would perhaps make it likely that only Eliphaz is meant. However, since Eliphaz has not been the last speaker, and since moreover, Iyov has in the past viewed all his erstwhile friends as enemies (see Introductory Remarks, *The Faithless River*, to 6:15ff., v. 27 there, and commentary to 8:20), it seems probable that he brackets all the three together. The use of the singular would then indicate that from Iyov's point of view, Tzophar's total and Bildad's partial reversal have come too late. None of them has weathered the storms which battered their relationship. All have become his foes.

Let us then draw conclusions: Iyov will never pretend that the friends are in any way correct (v. 5). This refusal he sees as evidence of an integrity which he will not give up under any circumstances (v. 6). This, because giving

breath is in my nostrils. 4 *My lips shall speak no evil, my tongue*
shall utter no fraud. 5 *Far be it from me — up to my very death — to*
proclaim you to be in the right, I refuse to let go my claim to unques-
tioning integrity. 6 *I have held on to my integrity, I will not loosen my*
grip. My heart has never made me swerve. 7 *May the lot of the*
wicked overtake my enemy, may those that rise up against me
share the fate of the evildoer. 8 *For, what hope of gain has the hyp-*
ocrite — certainly God will discard his life. 9 *Is it to be supposed that,*
when troubles overtake him, the Almighty will hear his screams?

up his position would be the equivalent of joining the ranks of the wicked, who are destined to a dreadful fate (v. 8ff.). This fate should indeed overtake those who accuse Iyov of wickedness (v. 7). Since it is the friends who accuse him of wickedness, the implication is clear that it is they who are destined to suffer in the ways which the rest of the chapter describes. With exquisite sensitivity Iyov does not make this explicit. But, the implication is clear. [See commentary to verse 12 for confirmation that it is indeed the friends who are accused of wickedness and hypocrisy.]

That indeed the friends deserved punishment is made clear at the end of the book (42:8), where Iyov's intercession for the friends is required if they are to be spared.

8. כִּי מַה־תִּקְוַת חָנֵף כִּי יִבְצָע כִּי יֵשֶׁל אֱלוֹהַּ נַפְשׁוֹ — *For, what hope of gain has the hypocrite — certainly God will discard his life.* See discussion in Introductory Remarks to this chapter for the use of חָנֵף, *chonef*, here. *Metzudos*, however, does not attach this significance to the expression and interprets it in a narrower sense: The *chonef* is one who panders to his evil inclinations and steals.

יִבְצָע from בָּצַע, *to take dishonest profit, to steal.*

יֵשֶׁל from נָשַׁל, *to throw off.*

Ramban, unlike *Rashi* and *R' Yosef Kara*, reads this verse together with the previous one: Let my enemy not take his accusations lightly. One who steals a person's reputation is as blameworthy as one who steals his money!

The phrase, ... כִּי מַה־תִּקְוַת חָנֵף, recalls Bildad's second speech in which, at 8:13 we read: כֵּן אָרְחוֹת כָּל־שֹׁכְחֵי אֵל וְתִקְוַת חָנֵף תֹּאבֵד. There, we understood תִּקְוָה as standing for all the hopes and dreams which might animate a normal person, and of which the *chonef*, who spends his time cheating life, will himself be cheated. We may conclude that, in our chapter too, the idea expressed in the phrase, *For what hope of gain has the hypocrite* ... is that of a blighted future in which all expectations are choked. A careful reading of the chapter yields a highly structured description of the blighted life which the *chonef* will certainly live. There are altogether six doublets, each consisting of two verses, which deal with the various areas in which the *chonef* will meet up with frustration. They are: His relationship with God (vs. 9-10); his hope of outliving his own death through his children (vs. 14-15); his greedy delight in his wealth (vs. 16-17); the sense of security engendered by his home and possessions (18-19); his relationship to natural forces (20-21); and his relationship to his community (22-23).

The first of these doublets — the one dealing with the wicked man's relationship to God — is separated from the others by verses 11-13 which are an introduction to what follows, in much the same way that verses 7 and 8 are an introduction to the couplet, 9-10. This separation, too, is eminently logical. The first and most immediate pillar of support for any man is God. That God will not be accessible to the wicked man's prayers, is the most devastating result of his evil ways. He is, as it were, left to flounder for himself in a world bereft of God's grace.

Forsaken by God, he finds himself in radically changed circumstances. But, even here, there are some anchorages to which he might look for support. It is to disabuse him of his attachment to these that the five couplets, 14-23, are devoted.

If the thesis to which we have adhered throughout the commentary to this chapter is correct — if, indeed, Iyov has the friends in mind when he describes the dreadful fate of the *chonef* — then the thrust of Iyov's predictions is entirely apt. From his point of view, their overriding crime had been their disloyalty to him — see *The Faithless River* in chapter 6. Iyov predicts that even as they had forsaken him, so too will they be bereft of every possible source of support.

9. הֲצַעֲקָתוֹ יִשְׁמַע אֵל כִּי־תָבוֹא עָלָיו צָרָה — *Is it to be supposed that, when troubles overtake him, the Almighty will hear his screams?* Of the

י־יא אִם־עַל־שַׁדַּי יִתְעַנָּג יִקְרָא אֱלוֹהַּ בְּכָל־עֵת: אוֹרֶה אֶתְכֶם
יב בְּיַד־אֵל אֲשֶׁר עִם־שַׁדַּי לֹא אֲכַחֵד: הֵן אַתֶּם כֻּלְּכֶם
יג חֲזִיתֶם וְלָמָּה־זֶּה הֶבֶל תֶּהְבָּלוּ: זֶה ׀ חֵלֶק־אָדָם רָשָׁע ׀
יד עִם־אֵל וְנַחֲלַת עָרִיצִים מִשַּׁדַּי יִקָּחוּ: אִם־יִרְבּוּ בָנָיו לְמוֹ־
טו חָרֶב וְצֶאֱצָאָיו לֹא יִשְׂבְּעוּ־לָחֶם: שְׂרִידָיו בַּמָּוֶת יִקָּבֵרוּ
טז וְאַלְמְנֹתָיו לֹא תִבְכֶּינָה: אִם־יִצְבֹּר כֶּעָפָר כָּסֶף וְכַחֹמֶר
יז־יח יָכִין מַלְבּוּשׁ: יָכִין וְצַדִּיק יִלְבָּשׁ וְכֶסֶף נָקִי יַחֲלֹק: בָּנָה כָעָשׁ
יט בֵּיתוֹ וּכְסֻכָּה עָשָׂה נֹצֵר: עָשִׁיר יִשְׁכַּב וְלֹא יֵאָסֵף עֵינָיו
כ פָּקַח וְאֵינֶנּוּ: תַּשִּׂיגֵהוּ כַמַּיִם בַּלָּהוֹת לַיְלָה גְּנָבַתּוּ סוּפָה:

litany of woes which are to overtake the *chonef*, the first one is that God will not listen to his cries. This seems particularly apt. The friends had, as Iyov sees it, attempted to curry favor with God by defending His justice (see 13:6-11). Do not think, says Iyov, that God appreciates your efforts. Far from favoring you, he will not even hear your screams when you call most loudly.

10. אִם־עַל־שַׁדַּי יִתְעַנָּג יִקְרָא אֱלוֹהַּ בְּכָל־עֵת — *Would he be able to live a life of luxury before Shaddai, and still expect to be able to call upon God whenever he wishes?* *Rashi* points out that this rhetorical question is to be seen as a repetitive strengthening of the one in the previous verse. It is Biblical usage in such instances to have the first question begin with . . . הַ, and the second one with, . . . אִם.

11. אוֹרֶה אֶתְכֶם בְּיַד־אֵל אֲשֶׁר עִם־שַׁדַּי לֹא אֲכַחֵד — *I will instruct you in the Almighty's ways, will not withhold from you that which is Shaddai's wont.* Iyov appears to be saying, 'The shoe is on the other foot. Rather than have you tell me how God runs His world, I will teach you that which, apparently, you do not know.'

12. הֵן אַתֶּם כֻּלְּכֶם חֲזִיתֶם וְלָמָּה־זֶּה הֶבֶל תֶּהְבָּלוּ — *Have not all of you observed, why then indulge in folly?* You yourselves know the fate that awaits the wicked (v. 13). Why have you not learned from your own wisdom? Why then are you wicked and hypocritical? (*Rashi*).

Here we have clear confirmation for the thesis suggested above. Iyov considers the friends to be wicked, and the punishments set out in the next section are his description of what lies in store for them.

Ramban, in accordance with his approach to this speech which we delineated in the Introductory Remarks to this chapter, has our verse refer to the friend's theological stance. Why do you talk nonsense (הֶבֶל תֶּהְבָּלוּ) when all our experiences show that the wicked do frequently prosper [v. 13 — *That success is often the allotment of the wicked from God* . . .], and so the only conclusion available to us is that we cannot understand. See further at verse 14.

13. זֶה חֵלֶק־אָדָם רָשָׁע עִם־אֵל וְנַחֲלַת עָרִיצִים מִשַּׁדַּי יִקָּחוּ — *That what follows is the allotment which the wicked man can expect from the Almighty, the endowment which oppressors must accept from Shaddai.* *Rashi* ties this verse to the previous one. There the object had been missing: *Have not all of you observed . . .,* but nothing is said of what they have seen. Our verse provides the answer: They have observed that all the dreadful things described in the following section are the wicked man's allotment from God.

עָרִיצִים from עָרַץ, *to cause to tremble.*

It is of particular interest that this verse echoes, almost verbatim, the closing sentence of Tzophar's second and last speech (20:29) in which he had described the fate of the wicked. Iyov appears to be appropriating Tzophar's very words for his own purposes — with Tzophar the erstwhile philosopher in the unfamiliar role of victim.

14. אִם־יִרְבּוּ בָנָיו לְמוֹ־חָרֶב וְצֶאֱצָאָיו לֹא יִשְׂבְּעוּ־לָחֶם — *Let his sons be many — they are destined to the sword, his descendants will want for food.* One wonders whether, in this verse, Iyov had his own children in mind. Is he perhaps telling the friends that they too may find out what it means to have one's family destroyed, one's wealth and power, wasted.

See above at verse 8 for the structure of Iyov's speech. Our verse begins the second couplet — the one which warns that the *chonef* will not be able to cheat death by living on through his children.

Ramban continues with his interpretation: It would be so much better for you to admit to ignorance of a wisdom which you can never grasp, than to attempt futile justifications for that which can never, in human terms, be

[10] *Would he be able to live a life of luxury before Shaddai, and
still expect to be able to call upon God whenever he wishes?* [11] *I
will instruct you in the Almighty's ways, will not withhold from
you that which is Shaddai's wont.* [12] *Have not all of you observed,
why then indulge in folly?* [13] *That what follows is the allotment
which the wicked man can expect from the Almighty, the
endowment which oppressors must accept from Shaddai.* [14] *Let his
sons be many — they are destined to the sword, his descendants
will want for food.* [15] *Those who remain to him will be buried in
the throes of death, his widows will not mourn them.* [16] *Let him
pile up money like dust, set aside clothes like so much clay.* [17] *He
will set aside, but the righteous man will wear them, as for the
money — He will apportion it to the innocent.* [18] *He has built — his
home is fragile like that of a moth, like a booth erected by a
watchman.* [19] *The opulent may die and not even be buried, he
should have opened his eyes — but is no more.* [20] *Fright overpowers
him like gushing water, the whirlwind snatches him in the night.*

justified. For, even if all the descriptions in the following verses were accurate, that is, even if, for argument's sake, I were to admit to your contention that the children of the wicked will eventually suffer, all that explains nothing at all. For, as Iyov has repeatedly argued before (see at 21:21), the wicked man cares not one whit about what happens after his death. The only meaningful punishment would be one that attacks him — not his children.

15. שְׂרִידָיו בַּמָּוֶת יִקָּבֵרוּ וְאַלְמְנֹתָיו לֹא תִבְכֶּינָה — *Those who remain to him will be buried in the throes of death, his widows will not mourn them.* The translation follows *Rashi.* Even those who do not die by the sword will suffer such tortures as they die, that their widows will rejoice at their death, which they view as a relief.

Or: The rest of his children — those that do not fall by the sword — will die on their beds. Their widows will be happy that at least this was granted them; that they did not fall on the battlefield to lie there like so much ordure (*Ramban*).

16. אִם־יִצְבֹּר כֶּעָפָר כָּסֶף וְכַחֹמֶר יָכִין מַלְבּוּשׁ — *Let him pile up money like dust, set aside clothes like so much clay. Clay* is used as something that is common and to be found in abundance.

Here we begin the second couplet in the second group. The wealth which the *chonef* has gleefully piled up will not be available to gladden him when he needs it.

17. יָכִין וְצַדִּיק יִלְבָּשׁ וְכֶסֶף נָקִי יַחֲלֹק — *He will set aside, but the righteous man will wear them, as for the money — He will apportion it to the innocent.* We have capitalized, *He will apportion . . .* in accordance with *Rashi,* who has God as the subject of the phrase.

18. בָּנָה כָעָשׁ בֵּיתוֹ וּכְסֻכָּה עָשָׂה נֹצֵר — *He has built — his home is fragile like that of a moth, like a booth erected by a watchman.* The thought recalls Bildad's at 8:14. See above at verse 8.

This verse begins the third couplet. The home and possessions of the *chonef* will prove to have been a mirage.

19. עָשִׁיר יִשְׁכַּב וְלֹא יֵאָסֵף עֵינָיו פָּקַח וְאֵינֶנּוּ — *The opulent may die and not even be buried, he should have opened his eyes — but is no more.* The translation draws upon *Rashi* and *R' Yosef Kara.* The sense is as follows: The wicked man may be struck by illness, taking to his bed while he is still wealthy, but losing his wealth so suddenly that by the time he dies during the night, there is already no money to use for his burial. By morning, when he should have opened his eyes to a new day, he will already be dead.

20. תַּשִּׂיגֵהוּ כַמַּיִם בַּלָּהוֹת לַיְלָה גְּנָבַתּוּ סוּפָה — *Fright overpowers him like gushing water, the whirlwind snatches him in the night.* It is possible to learn this verse as a continuation of the previous one: The wicked man never wakes up in the morning because he is overtaken by terrible confusions and snatched up by the whirlwind. This is in fact how *R' Yosef Kara* understands it, and accordingly, he would not agree with our perception of this and the next verse as the next couplet, which deals with Iyov's relationship to the natural forces.

However, in *Rashi* there is no indication that this and the next verse do not stand together as a discrete entity, and therefore, taking into consideration the very clear structure of the entire *mashal* as we have delineated it above, we take it to be, indeed, a separate couplet.

Now *Rashi* takes בַּלָּהוֹת as שֵׁדִים, *demons.* The exact meaning of the phrase is not entirely clear. However, when we take into account that in this and the next verse three stiches deal with natural forces, the *whirlwind*, the *east wind*, and the hurricane force with which this wind blows, we tend to understand the first phrase, too, as dealing with some manifestation of natural forces. The sense of the two verses would be that the *chonef* will find that nature, far from being his friend, buffets him around with scant concern for his well-being. It attacks him with the force and implacable determination of demons, snatches him up and disposes of him as it sees fit.

21. יִשָּׂאֵהוּ קָדִים וְיֵלַךְ וִישָׂעֲרֵהוּ מִמְּקֹמוֹ — *The east wind carries him away and he wanders off, it blasts him from his home. He wanders off,* never to return to his home (*Metzudos*).

וִישָׂעֲרֵהוּ, from שָׂעַר, *to sweep away.* Thus, שְׂעָרָה, *a storm* which sweeps away everything in its path.

22. וְיַשְׁלֵךְ עָלָיו וְלֹא יַחְמֹל מִיָּדוֹ בָּרוֹחַ יִבְרָח — *Mercilessly He inundates him, he flees desperately from his hand.* For a smooth rendering of this verse, we would have followed *Ramban*, who takes it as a continuation from the previous verse. *The [storm] pursues him without mercy, but he will escape it* [because he will die before the wind ever has a chance to catch up with him]. However, our translation follows *Rashi* who clearly opts for a less smooth syntax [three pronouns, *he*, of which only the middle one refers to a subject — the *chonef* — who has just been mentioned. The first, to be capitalized, refers to God, the last to the hypocrite's adviser who has not been mentioned at all.] It would appear that *Rashi* is determined to see these last two verses as a discrete entity, in accordance with the couplet structure which we have followed throughout this chapter.

Accordingly, this verse opens the last couplet, which deals with the hypocrite's relationship to his fellow men. The verse, as *Rashi* understands it, is to be understood as follows: God mercilessly pours out suffering upon the *chonef*, so that even his closest adviser will flee from any association with him.

23. יִשְׂפֹּק עָלֵימוֹ כַפֵּימוֹ וְיִשְׁרֹק עָלָיו מִמְּקֹמוֹ — *They will clap their hands over him, his community will hiss at him.* For מָקוֹם as a shortened form of אַנְשֵׁי מְקוֹמוֹ, *the people of his place*, his community, see 7:10.

Iyov has now ended his graphic description of the desolation to which the friends, who had forsaken him in his time of need, will in their turn be subjected. It is left to him to explain where they went wrong. This he will do in the next chapter, the connection to our chapter being established by the opening כִּי, *For*, by indicating that they had erred in their conception of true wisdom. They had thought it expressed in a slavish defense of the indefensible, while Iyov locates it in the *fear of God* which drives man to the dreadful extremes which he, in his loyalty to principles, had dared.

XXVIII.

As most commentators understand this paean to wisdom, its purpose is to demonstrate that there are limits beyond which humans cannot expect to understand God's ways. We have already seen *Ramban's* ideas in the Introductory Remarks and in the commentary to various verses, in the previous chapter.

Here, it is worthwhile to present *Ibn Ezra's* thoughts concerning this chapter, offered in his summation at the end of his commentary to the book: For God acts in accordance with His will, He will occasionally afflict both the wicked and the righteous, and occasionally grant both the righteous and the wicked anything that they might wish for . . .. To understand this system is beyond man's abilities. Accordingly [Iyov reasons], . . . is it not possible that the suffering that came upon me had some good reason, and *was not the result of any sin that I might have committed*? [This appears also to be the thrust of God's speeches to Iyov — see chapter 38ff. —

27/21-23 [21] *The east wind carries him away and he wanders off, it blasts him*
from his home. [22] *Mercilessly He inundates him, he flees desper-*
ately from his hand. [23] *They will clap their hands over him, his*
community will hiss at him.

28/1 [1] *For silver can be wrested from the mines, gold has a place from*

and it is not entirely clear why there was a need to repeat this lesson if Iyov, at this point, had already absorbed it.]

Rashi sees the passage differently. The subject is not the inscrutability of God's thoughts and intentions, but the unique worth of wisdom. In all of creation there is nothing that approaches it in value. Iyov will never give it up. Neither the alienation inherent in lost friendships (27:6ff.) nor the blandishments of wealth (our chapter) can shake his determination to maintain his intellectual integrity.

The difference in approach between *Rashi* and *Ramban* significantly affects their understanding of much of what this chapter has to say. We will point out divergent interpretations in the commentary to the individual verses.

In the Introductory Remarks to the previous chapter we have presented an alternative interpretation. Iyov is disabusing the friends of their conceit that their shallow theories — because they purport to defend God — are, somehow, a mark of superior wisdom. Since, Iyov argues, true wisdom can only be defined as fear of God, his own refusal to make do with superficial platitudes is much closer in spirit to what is expected of us.

We feel that the form in which Iyov couches his lesson, argues in favor of this last interpretation. As just one more argument in the long list of disagreements which Iyov has had with the friends, it would not have required such a long, beautiful, intricately wrought ode to wisdom, as we have here. There have been innumerable occasions when no less significant points have been made in one or two sharply pointed sentences. The profligacy of images, the majestic language, the soaring mood, all bespeak a triumphant victory hymn, a personal vindication at the profoundest level. 'I, not you,' Iyov jubilates, 'have found the ultimate key to the worthwhile life. I glory in the turbulence of my agonies, despise the tranquility of your supercilious certainties. Wisdom, to the extent that it is granted to humans to possess, is mine!

1. כִּי יֵשׁ לַכֶּסֶף מוֹצָא וּמָקוֹם לַזָּהָב יָזֹקּוּ — *For silver can be wrested from mines, gold has a place from which it can be isolated.* At the end of the commentary to the previous chapter, we suggested that the opening כִּי, *For*, indicates a continuation of the thoughts enunciated there. This appears to be *Rashi's* opinion. He writes: *This is another explanation for Iyov's assertion at 27:6: 'I have held on to my integrity, I will not loosen my grip.' For, why should I become wicked? If, for the sake of winning gold or silver, ... wisdom is much more precious than these* (see commentary to 27:7).

There is, however, another possible way of understanding the opening, כִּי. It is to be combined with the opening *vav* of verse 12. It is common Scriptural usage that when contrasting two units with each other, the first is introduced with כִּי and the second with a *vav*. As an example he adduces *Isaiah* 60:2. Thus we should translate, *Even though ... still.*

This appears to be *Ramban's* understanding. He writes: This passage is tied to that which is to come later, *But as for wisdom, where is it to be found.* He chides the friends: *Why then indulge in folly* ... (27:12) to ascribe useless explanations to the fates of the righteous and the wicked. For God has given man the ability to trace everything to its source, everything, besides the source of wisdom ... for that He hid from all creatures ... [See above in Introductory Remarks to chapter 27, where we discuss *Ramban's* understanding of our speech. What we have quoted here is in accord with his general approach.]

We have rendered the first phrase, *For silver can be wrested* ..., to emphasize this contrast to wisdom. If you try hard enough, you can find silver and even gold. Wisdom, try you ever so hard, will forever be beyond you.

We have rendered מוֹצָא as *mine*, that is, a place from which it can be extracted, from יָצָא, *to go out*. However, bearing in mind the connection of our verse to verse 12, וְהַחָכְמָה מֵאַיִן תִּמָּצֵא ..., *Daas Mikra* suggests that it may also be related to מָצָא, *to find*.

In the second phrase we have followed *Rashi*. יָזֹקּוּ, from זָקַק, *to cleanse*, that is, to separate the gold from the rocks in which it is contained. The phrase describes the mining of

ב־ג יָזֹקּוּ׃ בַּרְזֶל מֵעָפָר יֻקָּח וְאֶבֶן יָצוּק נְחוּשָׁה׃ קֵץ ׀ שָׂם
ד לַחֹשֶׁךְ וּלְכָל־תַּכְלִית הוּא חוֹקֵר אֶבֶן אֹפֶל וְצַלְמָוֶת׃ פָּרַץ
ה נַחַל ׀ מֵעִם־גָּר הַנִּשְׁכָּחִים מִנִּי־רָגֶל דַּלּוּ מֵאֱנוֹשׁ נָעוּ׃ אֶרֶץ
ו מִמֶּנָּה יֵצֵא־לָחֶם וְתַחְתֶּיהָ נֶהְפַּךְ כְּמוֹ־אֵשׁ׃ מְקוֹם־סַפִּיר
ז אֲבָנֶיהָ וְעַפְרֹת זָהָב לוֹ׃ נָתִיב לֹא־יְדָעוֹ עָיִט וְלֹא שְׁזָפַתּוּ
ח עֵין אַיָּה׃ לֹא־הִדְרִיכֻהוּ בְנֵי־שָׁחַץ לֹא־עָדָה עָלָיו שָׁחַל׃

gold in exact parallel to the first phrase's description of the taking of silver.

Rashi, apparently based upon his understanding of the function of verse 3 (see there), makes the point that implicit in the fact that silver and gold have a tangible beginning, is the truism that they also have an end. Quite clearly, they have a limit; the mines from which they are taken can become depleted. In his commentary to verse 11, *Rashi* will make the point that wisdom is not subject to the same inhibiting conditions. Its source lies in God, and it has no limits. It is therefore uniquely precious.

As pointed out in the Introductory Remarks, *Ramban* has a different approach. He reads this and the following verses as describing the accessibility of all that the world has to offer. Nothing — other than wisdom — is beyond human reach and grasp.

2. בַּרְזֶל מֵעָפָר יֻקָּח וְאֶבֶן יָצוּק נְחוּשָׁה — *Iron can be taken from the ground, rocks are smelted into copper.* Once more, *Rashi* stresses that since iron and copper have a source, they must necessarily also come to an end at a certain point.

3. קֵץ שָׂם לַחֹשֶׁךְ וּלְכָל־תַּכְלִית הוּא חוֹקֵר אֶבֶן אֹפֶל וְצַלְמָוֶת — *He has assigned an end-point for the advent of darkness, has precisely fathomed a limit for all things. There is a destructive source spewing forth gloom and murky darkness.* God has assigned a point at which the physical world as we know it will come to an end, and all will be plunged into darkness. Nothing that has its source in the physical can be eternal. Only wisdom, which comes from God Himself, is free of any limitations. In this sense, *Rashi* views our verse as complementing the previous two.

אֶבֶן usually means *stone.* Here *Rashi* assigns a metaphorical meaning. People can easily trip over a stone and hurt themselves on it. In that sense a stone can be viewed as a source of trouble or tragedy. It can thus be used metaphorically to describe any fount which spews forth hurtful elements. In this case, it is the fountainhead from which the darkness — destined to envelop the world — flows.

Ramban, consistent with his approach to the whole chapter, reads this verse differently: God knows where to find even the very end of darkness, has fathomed the location of the *stone of gloom.* [Here the meaning is unclear. Perhaps he understands אֶבֶן as does *Rashi.*] All this knowledge He has passed on to man. Only the source of wisdom remains hidden.

4. פָּרַץ נַחַל מֵעִם־גָּר הַנִּשְׁכָּחִים מִנִּי־רָגֶל דַּלּוּ מֵאֱנוֹשׁ נָעוּ — *Streams burst out of their normal flow, are lost to trodden paths, removed from humanity — gone. Rashi* to this verse brings the *aggadic* teaching of the Sages, that reference is to the people of Sodom and Amora. These had deserved destruction because they had driven guests out of their town (הַנִּשְׁכָּחִים מִנִּי רָגֶל, literally, *[Their town] had been forgotten by the wanderer's feet*). They were consequently destroyed.

In the context of the rest of the passage, we assume that at the *p'shat* level, *Rashi* would read this verse as describing something which God had brought to an end.[1]

Accordingly, in our translation we have followed *Metzudos*: Streams frequently disappear. They crash out of the river beds which normally control their flow (גָּר from נִגַּר, *to flow*), and will no longer be found by the people who were wont to tread a path in order to draw water from them. These streams were

1. There are also other passages which *Rashi* interprets in accordance with the *aggadah* of the Sages — see for example at 22:15ff. It seems clear that *Rashi* does not mean these interpretations to represent the literal meaning of the verses.

As proof, we may adduce *Rashi* to verse 11. There he begins by citing the tradition of the Sages that בְּכִי is to be taken in the sense, *to cry,* and that the verse has in mind the complaints of the *nether waters* at creation. Immediately following this, without any indication of a change of direction, he interprets the word in the sense that it is used at 38:16, where he takes it as meaning, the inner enclosed parts of the sea.

Clearly, *Rashi* assumes that we would understand that his initial interpretation is meant to inform us of the *aggadic* tradition of the Sages, but that it is not presented as the literal meaning of the verse.

which it can be isolated. 2 Iron can be taken from the ground, rocks
are smelted into copper. 3 He has assigned an end-point for the
advent of darkness, has precisely fathomed a limit for all things.
There is a destructive source spewing forth gloom and murky
darkness. 4 Streams burst out of their normal flow, are lost to
trodden paths, removed from humanity — gone. 5 Land from which
bread comes forth has, in its stead, turned into scorched earth. 6 Its
very stones yielded sapphires, its very dust was gold. 7 It has
become a path not known by even the eagle, which even the eye of
the buzzard has not observed. 8 The mighty beasts have not made
their way through them, not even the lion has passed through them.

withdrawn from human accessibility (דַּלּוּ from דָּלָה, *to raise up*), and moved away.

Ramban, consistent with his approach to the whole chapter, reads the verse quite differently: Iyov continues to describe God's great wisdom and ability, which in the previous verse had expressed itself in His knowledge of the place where darkness ends. Here we learn that God causes rivers to burst out of their subterranean sources and, because of the mighty movements of the water, steal whole areas away from human feet.

5. אֶרֶץ מִמֶּנָּה יֵצֵא־לָחֶם וְתַחְתֶּיהָ נֶהְפַּךְ כְּמוֹ־אֵשׁ — *Land from which bread comes forth has, in its stead turned into scorched earth.* This is another example of God bringing things to an end. Fertile earth which at one time provided bread can, when its time comes, become dry as though scorched by fire (*Metzudos*). At the *aggadah* level, *Rashi* appears to continue with the description of Sodom's downfall. It had been such a fertile land, now it is burned up!

Ramban sees the verse as another example of God's all-might. Dig a little further into the earth, which at its surface provides bread, and you will find the very opposite of fertile, nutrient-providing material. In the bowels of the earth are salt and sulfur — sapphires and gold-dust (next verse). Thus, to get at the sapphires one needs to penetrate these inhospitable regions — but it is within the range of the possible. Only wisdom is ever beyond us.

6. מְקוֹם־סַפִּיר אֲבָנֶיהָ וְעַפְרֹת זָהָב לוֹ — *Its very stones yielded sapphires, its very dust was gold. Metzudos* takes this and the next two verses together. There are places which once carried untold wealth within themselves. Later they became desolate so that they are shunned even by birds of prey and wild beasts.

Rashi, continuing with the downfall of Sodom, sees this verse as a description of its erstwhile wealth. The next two verses will continue to describe the land in its heyday.

Ramban, as we saw above, reads this verse together with the previous one. The next verse begins a new thought.

7. נָתִיב לֹא־יְדָעוֹ עָיִט וְלֹא שְׁזָפַתּוּ עֵין אַיָּה — *It has become a path not known by even the eagle, which even the eye of the buzzard has not observed.* We continue with *Metzudos*. When its time comes, the area which had once yielded so many riches, will become so desolate that even the eagle and the buzzard will not fly by there.

Rashi has the verse describe the days of Sodom's tranquility. No robber had ever passed through it (עַיִט from עִיט, *to dart greedily*), no spies ever pried out its secrets (אַיָּה, the *buzzard*, also known as רָאָה because of its keen eyesight, is a metaphor for spies).

According to *Ramban* the passage begins a description of an extremely remote land, in which God is nonetheless able to work His will.

We have used *eagle* and *buzzard* for the two bird-names in our verse, in accordance with *Dr. Yehudah Feliks* in *The Animal World of the Bible*. [See below at 39:27, that the נֶשֶׁר, commonly translated as *eagle*, is in reality the *vulture*.] Both the eagle and buzzard have exceptionally strong eyesight, and concerning the buzzard, *Chullin* 63b reports that, *It could be standing in Babylon but still be able to spy out carrion in the land of Israel.* In this sense we can understand why our verse used just these birds in its word-picture. The paths are so desolate that even these sharp-eyed creatures would fail to detect it.

8. לֹא־הִדְרִיכוּהוּ בְנֵי־שָׁחַץ לֹא־עָדָה עָלָיו שָׁחַל — *The mighty beasts have not made their way through them, not even the lion has passed through them.* The three commentators, *Metzudos, Rashi* and *Ramban*, whom we have traced throughout this passage remain consistent in their interpretation of this verse.

שַׁחַץ from שחץ, *to be arrogant.*

ט־י בַּחַלָּמִישׁ שָׁלַח יָדוֹ הָפַךְ מִשֹּׁרֶשׁ הָרִים: בַּצּוּרוֹת יְאֹרִים
יא בִּקֵּעַ וְכָל־יְקָר רָאֲתָה עֵינוֹ: מִבְּכִי נְהָרוֹת חִבֵּשׁ וְתַעֲלֻמָהּ
יב יֹצִא אוֹר: וְהַחָכְמָה מֵאַיִן תִּמָּצֵא וְאֵי זֶה מְקוֹם
יג בִּינָה: לֹא־יָדַע אֱנוֹשׁ עֶרְכָּהּ וְלֹא תִמָּצֵא בְּאֶרֶץ הַחַיִּים:

9. בַּחַלָּמִישׁ שָׁלַח יָדוֹ הָפַךְ מִשֹּׁרֶשׁ הָרִים — *He wielded power over the very rocks, overturned mountains from their foundation. Metzudos* sees this as another example of things coming to an end. When the rocks have outlived their usefulness, God destroys them.

In the *aggadic* view presented by *Rashi,* we have now reached the point at which Sodom is destroyed. The past tense used in this verse might appear to argue in favor of this interpretation.

Ramban sees this verse and the next as still continuing the previous picture. In the earlier verses we had the description of totally desolate places. Our verse and the next make the point that even there, God does as he wishes, overturning mountains and calling forth streams from the rocks.

10. בַּצּוּרוֹת יְאֹרִים בִּקֵּעַ וְכָל־יְקָר רָאֲתָה עֵינוֹ — *He cracked the rocks so that streams might flow, observed carefully all that is precious.* With this verse, *Rashi* returns to the plain meaning of the text. Our verse returns us to the beginning of the passage where we saw that all physical things have a clearly defined source. Streams, too, can be traced to their headwaters among the rocks; God knows clearly whence to produce all manner of precious commodities for His creatures.

Metzudos, for the first part of the sentence, continues with the previous thought. When the time comes for the rocks to be smashed, God brings out streams in their stead. In the second phrase, he joins in *Rashi's* interpretation. Everything of worth in this world has a beginning and an end. We may not always know where to find it, but God knows.

In *Ramban's* view, this verse continues to describe God's prowess in working His will in even the most desolate places.

11. מִבְּכִי נְהָרוֹת חִבֵּשׁ וְתַעֲלֻמָהּ יֹצִא אוֹר — *From the depths of the rivers he held back the water, that which is most hidden He brings to light.* For בְּכִי *Rashi* adduces 38:16, where he renders נִבְכֵי as *that which is enclosed.* Hence, apparently, the innermost depths of the water. For חִבֵּשׁ he adduces *Genesis* 22:3, חָבַשׁ, *to saddle* or to *tie.* It is difficult to fathom *Rashi's* precise meaning. We have interpreted as does *R' Meyuchas,* who writes: From the depths of the water He fashioned the dry land at the time of creation. *R' Chavel* in his glosses understands him to take חִבֵּשׁ as synonymous with עָצַר, *to hold back.* Hence, *He held back the waters so that dry land might be formed.* This could well be what *Rashi* had in mind.

For the second phrase we have followed most of the commentators. *Rashi* brings from *Pirkei d'R' Eliezer*: In the heavens there is an opening named *Taalumah.* From it the sun, in all its seasons, emerges.

Rashi concludes his interpretation to this difficult passage with the words: Everything, then, has a beginning and an end. Only wisdom has no source other than His mouth, and, to all eternity, no end.

❦ ❦ ❦

We have traced *Rashi* and *Ramban* through this difficult piece, and have seen that they do not agree in its interpretation. For *Rashi* the point of Iyov's argument is that wisdom alone, in an otherwise finite world, has no beginning and no end. It is infinitely precious because it comes from God Himself, and there are no limits to its reach. Iyov will never, under any circumstances, relinquish its quest. For *Ramban,* the point is that while God has granted man the ability to understand all other things, He has set aside the knowledge of wisdom for Himself. His thoughts are consequently inscrutable and it behooves man to shy away from any attempt to understand God.

Neither system seems to accommodate all the verses smoothly. Thus, in *Rashi's* system, if silver and gold (v. 1) are held up as examples of things which, though precious, are finite, we would have expected that this would somehow be demonstrated in relation to those metals. The fact that fertile land occasionally dries up (v. 6), or that places where sapphires and gold were once mined, can turn into absolutely desolate wastelands, seems irrelevant to the argument. In *Ramban's* system too, it is difficult to accommodate the section concerning God's absolute power (vs. 7-9), when the whole point of the earlier verses was to teach that God makes the understanding of nature accessible to man.

It is hard to see how each of the sections

*[9] He wielded power over the very rocks, overturned mountains
from their foundation. [10] He cracked the rocks so that streams
might flow, observed carefully all that is precious. [11] From the
depths of the rivers he held back the water, that which is most
hidden He brings to light. [12] But, as for wisdom, where is it to be
found, where is understanding to be located? [13] Man cannot know
its worth, its equivalent cannot be found in the physical world.*

contributes to a cohesive whole in which the contrast to wisdom which we are about to begin is sharply enunciated.

There is, perhaps, another possibility of interpreting the section in a way that preserves the spirit in which *Ramban* takes the section, but demonstrates the argument by another route.

We might postulate that this ode draws a picture of the universe as a series of challenges to man's curiosity and ingenuity. Mysteries are piled upon mysteries, each beckoning man to apply his insatiable appetite for knowledge, each promising that, after due effort, his quest will be rewarded.

Thus, man knows that if he is but willing to put in the effort, he may find the source from which gold, silver, iron and copper might be wrested. He knows that God has decreed a point at which darkness recedes before the coming light, knows that God has finely tuned the limits of all natural phenomena. The whole cosmos opens up before his questing mind. It is a subject which he can grasp. The discovery of the sources from which rivers flow, the point, far removed from human traffic, at which they burst out of the ground, has always piqued man's curiosity. His explorer's instinct is teased by the possibility of locating the salient points which open to him the geography of his environment. Husbandry, the secrets of agronomy, the qualities which make a piece of land fertile and which, in turn, can burn it out, must, if only out of an instinct of self-preservation, awaken his interest. The processes by which the earth yields its precious stones and minerals begs for discovery. Desolate lands wait to be found and colonized. Earthquakes and the movement of land masses open up the world of geological wonder, daring man to understand.

All this, God has given us. Nothing is barred, nothing is out of bounds. We are limited only by our intellectual awareness, our energy and our thirst for knowledge. Only wisdom is different. By its nature, it will not yield its secrets. To pursue it is futile.

12. וְהַחָכְמָה מֵאַיִן תִּמָּצֵא וְאֵי זֶה מְקוֹם בִּינָה — *But, as for wisdom, where is it to be found, where is understanding to be located?* For חָכְמָה, *Rashi* offers *Torah.* It seems likely that this is an *aggadic* interpretation (see fn. to v. 4 above). This would certainly be so according to those opinions that Iyov was a gentile — see commentary to 1:1. Rather, at the *p'shat* level, wisdom — the deep truths which lie beyond the exploration of physical phenomena — is meant. *Rashi* clearly understands the sense of the verse in consonance with what he has said before. Wisdom is so precious, that there is nothing in the world which would persuade him to part with it.

According to *Ramban* the verse means simply — as does the entire ode — that the motives behind God's providence are inscrutable. Man must satisfy himself with living a righteous life, and not seek out that which will forever lie beyond him.

Metzudos writes: but wisdom is not so readily accessible. Where, after all is it to be found? It does not derive from a physical source so that we might suppose that when that comes to an end, so too will wisdom.

As *Metzudos* understands it, the end of the argument will be that, indeed, there is no way that man on his own would ever be able to find wisdom. God Himself will grant him understanding — in reward for a life righteously lived.

13. לֹא־יָדַע אֱנוֹשׁ עֶרְכָּהּ וְלֹא תִמָּצֵא בְּאֶרֶץ הַחַיִּים — *Man cannot know its worth, its equivalent cannot be found in the physical world. Rashi* continues with his *aggadic* commentary. For the second phrase he writes: [Torah] will never be found among those who pamper themselves [*the land of the living* means those for whom the quality of their physical life is central], only among those who strain and starve themselves for it.

Accordingly, we have translated with *Metzudos.* Since wisdom alone is infinite, it can never be measured against anything else. If one were to attempt to find it anywhere in the physical world, one would meet with frustration.

יד־טו תְּהוֹם אָמַר לֹא בִי־הִיא וְיָם אָמַר אֵין עִמָּדִי: לֹא־יֻתַּן
טז סְגוֹר תַּחְתֶּיהָ וְלֹא יִשָּׁקֵל כֶּסֶף מְחִירָהּ: לֹא־תְסֻלֶּה בְּכֶתֶם
יז אוֹפִיר בְּשֹׁהַם יָקָר וְסַפִּיר: לֹא־יַעַרְכֶנָּה זָהָב וּזְכוֹכִית
יח וּתְמוּרָתָהּ כְּלִי־פָז: רָאמוֹת וְגָבִישׁ לֹא יִזָּכֵר וּמֶשֶׁךְ חָכְמָה
יט מִפְּנִינִים: לֹא־יַעַרְכֶנָּה פִּטְדַת־כּוּשׁ בְּכֶתֶם טָהוֹר לֹא
כ תְסֻלֶּה: וְהַחָכְמָה מֵאַיִן תָּבוֹא וְאֵי זֶה מְקוֹם בִּינָה:
כא־כב וְנֶעֶלְמָה מֵעֵינֵי כָל־חָי וּמֵעוֹף הַשָּׁמַיִם נִסְתָּרָה: אֲבַדּוֹן וָמָוֶת
כג אָמְרוּ בְּאָזְנֵינוּ שָׁמַעְנוּ שִׁמְעָהּ: אֱלֹהִים הֵבִין דַּרְכָּהּ וְהוּא

14. תְּהוֹם אָמַר לֹא בִי־הִיא וְיָם אָמַר אֵין עִמָּדִי — *The depths declare, 'It is not in me,' the sea asserts, 'It is not with me.'* Torah cannot be found by the deep sea-divers who spend their days dredging pearls up from the depths, nor by the merchants who ply the seas. They understand only such merchandise as can be bought for money (*Rashi*, consistent with his *aggadic* interpretation).

There is also the possibility that *Rashi's* offering here is consistent with the plain meaning of the verse. As our analysis at verse 20 will yield, the section beginning at verse 12 exactly parallels the one beginning at verse 20. The subject of the first part is the incomparable value of wisdom, while the subject of the second is its inaccessibility to anyone other than God. Because of this, our section is almost completely given over to contrasting wisdom to various precious metals and stones. In this context it makes sense to make the point that wisdom cannot be found with those people whose lives center upon mining gold and diamonds from the deep.

Or: Even if someone were to dare the depths to try to find wisdom there, he would be disappointed, as would someone who imagines that he could find it by traveling the seas (*Metzudos*).

15. לֹא־יֻתַּן סְגוֹר תַּחְתֶּיהָ וְלֹא יִשָּׁקֵל כֶּסֶף מְחִירָהּ — *Precious gold cannot be given in exchange for it, its price cannot be weighed in silver.* סָגַר, *to close. Rashi* explains: Gold which is so precious that when it comes upon the market, all other gold dealers are forced to *close* their doors.

Metzudos offers: Gold which was enclosed deep in the smelting furnace so that it was purified to a very high degree.

16. לֹא־תְסֻלֶּה בְּכֶתֶם אוֹפִיר בְּשֹׁהַם יָקָר וְסַפִּיר — *It is beyond comparison to Ophir gold,* to *precious diamonds or sapphires.* סָלָה or סָלָא means, either *to praise* (*Rashi* and *Metzudos*), or, *to weigh against* (*Radak, Shorashim*).

For כֶּתֶם, see further at verse 19.

17. לֹא־יַעַרְכֶנָּה זָהָב וּזְכוֹכִית וּתְמוּרָתָהּ כְּלִי־פָז — *Crystalline gold will not define its worth, the finest gold cannot yield a fair exchange. Rashi* appears to take זָהָב וּזְכוֹכִית together. Gold that shines like pearls.

18. רָאמוֹת וְגָבִישׁ לֹא יִזָּכֵר וּמֶשֶׁךְ חָכְמָה מִפְּנִינִים — *Coral and crystal cannot be mentioned together with it, the pursuit of wisdom is more precious than pearls. Rashi* identifies the precious stone mentioned here, as coming from the sea.

מָשַׁךְ, *to pull,* used here in the sense, *to extract.* The intellectual effort required to actualize wisdom from its potential to its realization, is the most worthwhile of all activities (*Metzudos*).

19. לֹא־יַעַרְכֶנָּה פִּטְדַת־כּוּשׁ בְּכֶתֶם טָהוֹר לֹא תְסֻלֶּה — *Emeralds from Kush cannot express its value, the purest bracelet cannot be likened to it.* We have rendered פִּטְדָה as *emerald* in accordance with *R' Aryeh Kaplan's, The Living Torah* at *Exodus* 28:17. He reaches his conclusion after extensive analysis of the sources. As an alternative, he offers *topaz.*

Rashi thinks that כֶּתֶם is a *grouping of ornaments,* used by women to bejewel themselves.

For סֶלָה, see commentary to verse 16.

20. וְהַחָכְמָה מֵאַיִן תָּבוֹא וְאֵי זֶה מְקוֹם בִּינָה — *As for wisdom, whence shall it come, where is understanding to be located?* This verse appears to parallel verse 12. A careful analysis of the two passages, introduced respectively by these two verses, yields great structural similarities. Each is followed by precisely seven verses. In our section this leads us up to verse 28 which is the climax of the entire poem and thus stands on its own, detailing the point that is being made.

In the first section, wisdom is shown to be more precious than the most precious objects which this world has to offer. Our section demonstrates that one cannot hope to attain it, except from God's own hand.

This explains the change of the one word which differentiates the two verses from one another:

[14] *The depths declare, 'It is not in me,' the sea asserts, 'It is not*
with me.' [15] *Precious gold cannot be given in exchange for it,*
its price cannot be weighed in silver. [16] *It is beyond comparison*
to Ophir gold, to precious diamonds or sapphires. [17] *Crystalline*
gold will not define its worth, the finest gold cannot yield a
fair exchange. [18] *Coral and crystal cannot be mentioned together*
with it, the pursuit of wisdom is more precious than pearls.
[19] *Emeralds from Kush cannot express its value, the purest*
bracelet cannot be likened to it. [20] *As for wisdom, whence shall*
it come, where is understanding to be located? [21] *It is hidden*
from the eyes of all living creatures, concealed from even the
birds of heaven. [22] *The consuming depths and Death admit to*
having heard its fame. [23] *Only God knows its paths, only He*

12. וְהַחָכְמָה מֵאַיִן תִּמָּצֵא *But as for wisdom, where is it to be found?*	20. וְהַחָכְמָה מֵאַיִן תָּבוֹא *As for wisdom, whence shall it come?*

In the earlier passage the speaker reaches the conclusion that there is no hope that man might ever be able to wrest wisdom from the elements in the same way that he can make them give up their physical wealth. Wisdom is nowhere to be *found*. No amount of effort will ever yield it.

In this second passage, that lesson has already been learned. But now the question arises: Is there perhaps someone who will grant wisdom to man. If he cannot take it for himself, is there a source from which it might perhaps *come*?

The answer will be, of course, that only God can grant wisdom and we can be privy to only such aspects as He is willing to have us attain.

Since both verses end with the identical phrase, וְאֵי זֶה מְקוֹם בִּינָה, *where is understanding to be located?* we feel justified in understanding the sense as follows. בִּינָה is a more advanced, more profound understanding, one which must build on the basis of the already acquired חָכְמָה. It would, in the context of Iyov's concerns, be that faculty which would enable him to grasp the terrible fate which had overtaken him. But, he bemoans, since חָכְמָה is beyond my grasp, I cannot wrest it from nature, and can turn to no one who might grant it to me, then from where can I expect to attain the understanding which I crave so much, but for which the unattainable wisdom is the prerequisite?

21. וְנֶעֶלְמָה מֵעֵינֵי כָל־חָי וּמֵעוֹף הַשָּׁמַיִם נִסְתָּרָה — *It is hidden from the eyes of all living creatures, concealed from even the birds of heaven.* Although birds can fly high in the sky and see much of the world stretched out beneath them, still they have no idea where to find wisdom (*Metzudos*).

The reference to the birds is clearly intended to create a contrast to God, Who *looks to the very ends of the earth, sees everything that is under the heavens* (v. 24). Fly the birds ever so high, their horizons are nevertheless limited. Only God, Who can comprehend the entirety of creation at one glance, knows the place of wisdom. See below, at verse 24, for the development of this thought.

Rashi assumes that the *birds of heaven* are the angels. Certainly that assumption, more than if actual birds were meant, serves to accentuate the uniqueness of God's cognition of wisdom. Even the angels lack God's comprehensive grasp of all reality.

22. אֲבַדּוֹן וָמָוֶת אָמְרוּ בְּאָזְנֵינוּ שָׁמַעְנוּ שִׁמְעָהּ — *The consuming depths and Death admit to having heard its fame.* Both אֲבַדּוֹן and מָוֶת are used in Scripture to parallel words denoting, *the grave.* The former together with קֶבֶר at *Psalms* 88:12, and with שְׁאוֹל at *Proverbs* 15:11 and at 26:26 above, the latter with שְׁאוֹל, at *Isaiah* 28:15. Accordingly we would be justified in assuming that the two terms are meant synonymously.

Rashi offers an *aggadic* rendering: Even those who wear themselves out (אִבֵּד, in the *piel, to destroy*), and court death in their pursuit of wisdom, know only that their efforts are rewarded. They know that their heroic efforts serve to preserve that which they have acquired of wisdom. But, that is all.

23. אֱלֹהִים הֵבִין דַּרְכָּהּ וְהוּא יָדַע אֶת־מְקוֹמָהּ — *Only God knows its paths, only He knows its place.* The next verse will explain why this is so.

כד יָדַע אֶת־מְקוֹמָהּ: כִּי־הוּא לִקְצוֹת־הָאָרֶץ יַבִּיט תַּחַת כָּל־
כה הַשָּׁמַיִם יִרְאֶה: לַעֲשׂוֹת לָרוּחַ מִשְׁקָל וּמַיִם תִּכֵּן בְּמִדָּה:
כו־כז בַּעֲשֹׂתוֹ לַמָּטָר חֹק וְדֶרֶךְ לַחֲזִיז קֹלוֹת: אָז רָאָהּ וַיְסַפְּרָהּ
כח הֱכִינָהּ וְגַם־חֲקָרָהּ: וַיֹּאמֶר | לָאָדָם הֵן יִרְאַת אֲדֹנָי הִיא
כט/א א חָכְמָה וְסוּר מֵרָע בִּינָה: וַיֹּסֶף אִיּוֹב

24. כִּי־הוּא לִקְצוֹת־הָאָרֶץ יַבִּיט תַּחַת כָּל־הַשָּׁמַיִם יִרְאֶה — *For He looks to the very ends of the earth, sees everything that is under the heavens.* God, through His comprehensive understanding, is the only One Who truly possesses wisdom.

The next two verses will describe some of the mighty deeds which God is able to perform because of His absolute command. It would certainly appear that we can infer from this, that this same omnipotence makes Him also privy to the secrets of Iyov's suffering.

25. לַעֲשׂוֹת לָרוּחַ מִשְׁקָל וּמַיִם תִּכֵּן בְּמִדָּה — *So that He can assign heft to the winds, precisely measure the waters.* When water is sent upon the earth Hashem takes into account the force with which the wind blows so that it might be appropriate to the needs of different locations; also the topography, aridity and moisture is taken into account when water is sent upon the earth (*Rashi* and *Metzudos*).

26. בַּעֲשֹׂתוֹ לַמָּטָר חֹק וְדֶרֶךְ לַחֲזִיז קֹלוֹת — *Can make the rain follow set paths, specify lanes for the thunder's roar among the clouds. Rashi* does not translate חֲזִיז as *path*, a meaning never assigned by him or any of the other classical commentators. Our translation is based on *Bava Basra* 16a, where our verse is rendered as follows: I have created numerous thunderclaps among the *clouds;* for each thunderclap I have assigned a separate path so that two should not travel by the same path, thus destroying the whole world.

Aruch suggests that חֲזִיז might be derived from חָזָה, *to see*, thus, *that which is seen in conjunction with the thunder's roar*, the *lightning.*

27. אָז רָאָהּ וַיְסַפְּרָהּ הֱכִינָהּ וְגַם־חֲקָרָהּ — *Then did He contemplate it and inscribe it, readied it and explored it.* Then, at the time of creation, He contemplated wisdom so that He might make use of it to bring forth His wondrous world. He inscribed it [סִפְּרָהּ from סֵפֶר, *book*, rather than from סָפַר, *to count* (*Ibn Ezra* and *Metzudos*)], that is, He gave it permanence; He organized it so that it might be used to the greatest advantage; and analyzed it so that nothing of it might remain hidden from Him (*Metzudos*).

28. וַיֹּאמֶר לָאָדָם הֵן יִרְאַת ה׳ הִיא חָכְמָה וְסוּר מֵרָע בִּינָה — *And told man, 'See the fear of God is wisdom, steering away from evil — understanding.'* The ode to wisdom has reached its climax. We have discussed its import above. Here we limit ourselves to quoting *Rashi* and *Ramban* in their respective commentaries:

This requires that [fear of God, and a determination to shy away from evil are necessary prerequisites for the acquisition of wisdom and understanding]. Wisdom has no allure unless prompted by the fear of God (*Rashi*).

He tells man that he should stand in awe before God — and that is all his wisdom. His shying away from evil is his understanding. For this is all of man — by this he shall be saved. Let him not seek that which must remain beyond him; let him not desire that which must remain hidden. God's mysteries are not his business (*Ramban*).

Thus, [Iyov] ends as Solomon did in *Koheles*: *The sum of the matter, when all has been considered: Fear God and keep His commandments, for that is all man's duty.*

This ending indicates Iyov's theological stance: All God's ways are benevolent in that He knows all, and provides for the soul. Only in this — physical — world, things appear to be unfair, thus providing the opportunity for complaint (*Ramban*).

As we have understood the passage, Iyov has now, finally, asserted the justification for his belligerent stance. If I cannot understand God's ways I will not, instead, accept platitudes which cope with no truth, deal with no reality. I can only demonstrate my loyalty to God by relentlessly challenging Him.

XXIX.

◆§ The Second Mashal

The exaltation of the final verse in the previous *mashal* could not be sustained. Pain and filth, loneliness and alienation, are too real to allow for more than a momentary flight into the heady spheres of freedom which Iyov's pursuit of wisdom through the cosmos permitted him. All too

28/24-28 *knows its place.* 24 *For He looks to the very ends of the earth, sees*
everything that is under the heavens. 25 *So that He can assign heft*
to the winds, precisely measure the waters. 26 *Can make the rain*
follow set paths, specify lanes for the thunder's roar among the
clouds. 27 *Then did He contemplate it and inscribe it, readied it and*
explored it. 28 *And told man, 'See the fear of God is wisdom,*
steering away from evil — understanding.'

quickly the grasping tentacles of horror constrict the heart, contain the vision, and demand their due.

Once more Iyov enters his own small world, bounded by the bittersweet recollections of a past that can no longer be summoned, a present that is too awful to contemplate, and a future which seems to hold no hope at all.

And yet — Iyov continues the struggle. What drives him to torture himself once more with the memories of a life that is no more? Why rehash the description of his present agonies when these same descriptions have so often before fallen on deaf ears? Why revert to the quixotic notion that he could summon God in front of some bar of justice?

Surely this seemingly superfluous speech lies at the very center of the lesson which our book seeks to convey. If Iyov is, in the end, granted the gift of prophecy, if he will after all find comfort in his experience of the Divine, this does not come of its own accord. It is the reward of a stubborn tenacity which refuses to make peace with silence.

This, Iyov's last speech, must have cost him dearly. He had every reason to give up, every motivation to sink into a bitter silence seeking what comfort he could find in a self-righteous rejection of God. It is Iyov's glory that he does not do so.

And so, this final speech contains the seeds of the comfort which Iyov so desperately seeks. His call for friends who will serve him better than the three who had failed him so badly (31:35-37) opens the door to Elihu's intervention — and the ultimate appearance of God, to which this intervention will lead.

After the friends had been silenced, Iyov's first instinct had been to speak a *mashal*, the enunciation of a credo of definition and assessment (see commentary to 27:1), concerning the salient features of the confrontation which had now — as far as he knew — ended. We have discussed this in detail in Introductory Remarks to chapter 27.

But now that that is done, Iyov's thoughts turn to a different direction. And we, as bystanders so to speak, are shocked by what we hear. The Iyov whom we even now heard jubilating in the exalted strains of the ode to wisdom, the Iyov who proudly and firmly attests to his vindication, changes back, before our very eyes, to the querulous, plaintive malcontent of the earlier rounds. Why cover the same ground that has been trodden so frequently before? Why stress once more the joys and virtues of his former life? Why, once more, challenge God to confrontation? Why wallow once more in the graphic description of his present dreadful predicament?

The answer may be that in a sense, there can be no more unequivocal refutation of the friends than to say that, after the avalanche of words and thoughts which they have shared, after all their attempts to make both friendship and enmity means by which the wall of Iyov's assurance might be breached, after three rounds of fierce give and take — absolutely nothing has changed.

We must recall that Iyov does not know at this point that his saga will continue. He knows nothing of Elihu, certainly does not anticipate that God Himself will, against all expectations, enter the debate. At this point he sees himself dragging on, his life trapped in a body which disgusts him, attacked by furies which leave him no rest, and above all, plagued by bitter disillusionment from which there can be no respite.

No wonder, then, that at this point he feels the need to rehash the realities of his existence. What, he seems to be asking, has really happened? What is there for me to hope for or to anticipate? I am what I am, left indeed with no expectations — but, challenging still — my integrity intact!

ב שְׂאֵת מְשָׁלוֹ וַיֹּאמַר: מִי־יִתְּנֵנִי כְיַרְחֵי־קֶדֶם כִּימֵי אֱלוֹהַּ
ג־ד יִשְׁמְרֵנִי: בְּהִלּוֹ נֵרוֹ עֲלֵי רֹאשִׁי לְאוֹרוֹ אֵלֶךְ חֹשֶׁךְ: כַּאֲשֶׁר
ה הָיִיתִי בִּימֵי חָרְפִּי בְּסוֹד אֱלוֹהַּ עֲלֵי אָהֳלִי: בְּעוֹד שַׁדַּי עִמָּדִי

1. וַיֹּסֶף אִיּוֹב שְׂאֵת מְשָׁלוֹ וַיֹּאמַר — *Once more, Iyov took up his cogitations and said. Metzudos* feels that the description, *mashal*, is appropriate for this speech, because many metaphors are used. As an example he cites, *When His lamp would gleam over my head,* in verse 3.

But clearly, if the use of metaphor justifies the description of the whole speech as a *mashal*, then there is not a single speech in the entire book which could not have been so called.

However, *mashal* in the Hirschian sense in which we took it in the commentary to 27:1 would be particularly appropriate to this and the previous speech. In contrast to all the others which we have had up to this point, which were responses within the context of a debate of sorts (וַיַּעַן), these last two speeches are soliloquies, uttered with the precise purpose of coming to grips, being מוֹשֵׁל (*ruling over*), controlling a situation by defining it.

2. מִי־יִתְּנֵנִי כְיַרְחֵי־קֶדֶם כִּימֵי אֱלוֹהַּ יִשְׁמְרֵנִי — *O who could change me back as I was in bygone times, those days when God would watch over me*! Iyov allows himself a nostalgic look backwards, recalling fondly the life that he had lived before tragedy struck. The vivid picture which he draws will serve as a foil to the bitter description of his present reality which follows, the contrast exacerbating the pain.

Iyov is human, and human hindsight is notoriously inaccurate. One may wonder whether the value scale revealed here accords with the facts or whether the passage of time has somehow played a role in distorting Iyov's memory of himself, causing him to color his past in hues more in the spirit of the picture of himself which he has painted in his impassioned arguments with the friends.

If Iyov's recollections are true to the reality, then the Satan, in his initial challenge, seriously misread him.

We quote from 1:9-10: *Is it for nothing that Iyov fears God? Have you not protected him, his household and all that he has? You have blessed whatever he has undertaken, and his possessions are spread throughout the land.*

Clearly, then, Satan saw Iyov's life centered upon his possessions. He served God only because it seemed useful to him to do so. Indeed, the ambience of that entire chapter suggests that once his flocks had been destroyed, his children snatched away from him, there would be nothing left for Iyov to lose.

An analysis of the second *mashal* leads to a quite different picture. In the long and extremely detailed overview of the happy life which preceded the downfall, Iyov's former wealth has just one verse (29:6) devoted to it. It does not enjoy pride of position — Iyov's first memories are of the sanctity in which his home was enveloped. Nor is it described in the same loving detail which is lavished upon the position of dignity which Iyov held within his community, see below.

We might say that had the Satan, as it were, seen this lament, his challenge to Iyov's religious standing might well have been couched in different terms.

What is Iyov's own view of his former life as depicted in this *mashal*?

A careful analysis of the structure leads to some unexpected conclusions.

Iyov's retrospect begins with four verses (2-5) in which the close proximity of God to his home is depicted. Clearly the fact that an aura of sanctity permeated his life (see various commentators to verse 4) is of major significance to him.

This is followed by precisely six verses (6-11), which depict how successful his life was at that time. Of these six verses only one — verse 6 — deals with the wealth which the Satan had placed at the center of Iyov's concerns. The other five describe the position of respect and the personal dignity which he enjoyed in his community.

These six verses are then followed by another six (12-17) which describe the many charitable acts which he performed while fortune was smiling upon him.

We ought surely to conclude that the precise congruence between the two sections — six describing Iyov's prominent standing, six, his responsible behavior — is intended. Iyov seems to be saying: Indeed I was blessed in enjoying such respect. But I, as it were, paid my dues. The community which granted me so much honor had no cause to regret it.

[1] *Once more, Iyov took up his cogitations and said. [2] O*
who could change me back as I was in bygone times,
those days when God would watch over me! [3] When His
lamp would shine over my head, when by His light I braved
the dark. [4] As I was in the days of my prime, when God's
mysteries permeated my home. [5] When Shaddai was still with me,

I made its well-being my concern.[1]

Then, there are three verses (18-20) which describe the expectations which Iyov had had for himself. He had thought that his exemplary life would find its reward in a tranquil and prosperous old age. Again, the number three seems propitious. His expectations were modest — only half of the good deeds which he had so liberally performed.

Up to this point we have observed a striking symmetry and a clearly calculated structure to the *mashal*. The more striking then is the next section (vs. 21-25) which, without any seeming logic, reverts to a description of the high standing which Iyov had enjoyed in his community. These verses seem to add nothing of substance to what he has already said in verses 7-11. What role do they play in Iyov's lament?

The impression is created that these five verses are like an unintended cry from the heart. Iyov may well have planned to finish his presentation after the artificially structured symmetry of the earlier section. But, something in him bursts forth and demands expression. Once more, the picture of his erstwhile dignity projects itself onto his mind. He remembers himself as a noble king among his cohorts, a kindly understanding elder to whom the bereaved looked for comfort (v. 25). The picture is too beguiling, and he cannot let it go. His preoccupation with this facet of his loss can also help to explain the surprising detail of his description of the utter insignificance of the fathers of the youngsters who now make sport of him (30:2-8). Such a lavish depiction of third parties who play no role at all in his saga is difficult to understand. It can make sense only in the context of an almost obsessive concentration upon the one loss which, at least in his present state, he views as the most tragic of all: that of his hard-earned and richly deserved human dignity.

3. בְּהִלּוֹ נֵרוֹ עֲלֵי רֹאשִׁי לְאוֹרוֹ אֵלֶךְ חֹשֶׁךְ — *When His lamp would shine over my head, when by His light I braved the dark.* הִלּוֹ is the *kal* form of הָלַל, *to shine.* The description is a metaphor for God's favor.

4. כַּאֲשֶׁר הָיִיתִי בִּימֵי חָרְפִּי בְּסוֹד אֱלוֹהַּ עֲלֵי אָהֳלִי — *As I was in the days of my prime, when God's mysteries permeated my home.* Our translation follows *Rashi* to *Bava Metzia* 106b who renders חָרְפִּי with חוזְקִי וְעִקְּרִי, *my strongest and best years,* rather than *Rashi* here, who renders בִּימֵי קַדְמוּתִי, *my early days.*

For סוֹד אֱלוֹהַּ we have used *Ramban's* interpretation: In accordance with the verse, *Those that fear God are privy to His secrets, He informs them of His covenant* (*Psalms* 25:14). The meaning of the verse is that God's mysteries were understood in Iyov's home, enabling him to prophesy concerning coming events so that he and his could protect themselves from all evil.

Alternatives are: The righteous people of Iyov's generation would gather in his house [סוֹד as *convocation* rather than as *secret* — see *Psalms* 111:1] to discuss matters of Torah, or to make decisions which were needed at any given time (*Rashi*). Or: The angels and the heavenly hosts would gather around his tent to shelter it from any evil.

R' Meyuchas equates, סוֹד אֱלוֹהַּ with רוּחַ הַקּוֹדֶשׁ, *Divine Inspiration.*

5. בְּעוֹד שַׁדַּי עִמָּדִי סְבִיבוֹתַי נְעָרָי — *When Shaddai was still with me, when my young men surrounded me.* נְעָרָי might refer to his servants (*Rashi*), or his sons (*Ramban*).

The juxtaposition appears discordant. If Shaddai was *with* him, why did Iyov feel the need to surround himself with his young men?

Perhaps we should understand the verse as follows: Even while I was surrounded by my young men, I felt God's presence intimately. I did not need to isolate myself from human contact in order to feel the wonderful proximity of the Divine.

1. The ambience of the passage expresses a sense of *noblesse oblige*. Iyov describes only what he did, not what he felt. The passage does not really portray him as a good person, only as one engaged in good activities.

It is only later in a different connection — and, in the context, unexpected, see there — that Iyov talks about his feelings for the poor: *Did I not weep for the one who was heavily burdened, was I not depressed at the fate of the destitute?* (30:25). At that point it is his nature as a kindly person rather than his contributions to his community which is at issue.

ו סְבִיבוֹתַי נְעָרָי: בִּרְחֹץ הֲלִיכַי בְּחֵמָה וְצוּר יָצוּק עִמָּדִי
ז פַּלְגֵי־שָׁמֶן: בְּצֵאתִי שַׁעַר עֲלֵי־קָרֶת בָּרְחוֹב אָכִין מוֹשָׁבִי:
ח־ט רָאוּנִי נְעָרִים וְנֶחְבָּאוּ וִישִׁישִׁים קָמוּ עָמָדוּ: שָׂרִים עָצְרוּ
י בְמִלִּים וְכַף יָשִׂימוּ לְפִיהֶם: קוֹל־נְגִידִים נֶחְבָּאוּ וּלְשׁוֹנָם
יא לְחִכָּם דָּבֵקָה: כִּי אֹזֶן שָׁמְעָה וַתְּאַשְּׁרֵנִי וְעַיִן רָאֲתָה
יב־יג וַתְּעִידֵנִי: כִּי־אֲמַלֵּט עָנִי מְשַׁוֵּעַ וְיָתוֹם וְלֹא־עֹזֵר לוֹ: בִּרְכַּת
יד אֹבֵד עָלַי תָּבֹא וְלֵב אַלְמָנָה אַרְנִן: צֶדֶק לָבַשְׁתִּי וַיִּלְבָּשֵׁנִי
טו כִמְעִיל וְצָנִיף מִשְׁפָּטִי: עֵינַיִם הָיִיתִי לַעִוֵּר וְרַגְלַיִם לַפִּסֵּחַ
טז אָנִי: אָב אָנֹכִי לָאֶבְיוֹנִים וְרִב לֹא־יָדַעְתִּי אֶחְקְרֵהוּ:

6. בִּרְחֹץ הֲלִיכַי בְּחֵמָה וְצוּר יָצוּק עִמָּדִי פַּלְגֵי־שָׁמֶן — *When my very feet were bathed in butter, where the rock that was with me gushed rivulets of oil.* Thus, *Rashi.* Alternatives are: When the paths I trod were awash with butter. Butter was so plentiful that if it spilled no one would bother to scoop it up (*Metzudos*). Or, the paths I walked were smooth and easy to traverse as though they were coated with butter (*R' Meyuchas*). Or, butter and honey would flow along the paths which I walked. The idea expressed is much the same as that when the land of Israel is described as, *... flowing with milk and honey* (*R' Yosef Kara*).

Oil is used as a metaphor for feelings of well-being and the fulfillment of all desires (*Rashi*).

יָצוּק from יָצַק, *to flow.*

7. בְּצֵאתִי שַׁעַר עֲלֵי־קָרֶת בָּרְחוֹב אָכִין מוֹשָׁבִי — *When I would leave for the gate, to the canopied throne, when I would set up my seat in the street. Rashi* ties this verse to the next. *Youths would glimpse me — and hide,* as I made my way to the courts of justice which were set up in the open by the city gates.

Rashi's interpretation of קָרֶת as *canopy* is consistent with his interpretation of *Proverbs* 8:3. Many commentators take the word as a synonym for *city* (*Metzudos,* here). Thus *Radak, Sefer HaShorashim,* who lists the word together with קִרְיָה, under קרה, and adduces the Aramaic קַרְתָּא.

8. רָאוּנִי נְעָרִים וְנֶחְבָּאוּ וִישִׁישִׁים קָמוּ עָמָדוּ — *Youths would glimpse me — and hide, the aged would rise and remain standing.* Even youths could tell that Iyov was someone whose personality demanded respect. They would be afraid to come too close.

R' Meyuchas renders נְעָרִים as *students* rather than as *young men.* Those with less knowledge stood in awe of Iyov. *Yerushalmi* (*Berachos* 2:1) reports that the *Amora,* Zeiri, would not greet his teacher Rabbah. He felt himself inadequate. For, in the schools of Babylonia the words of our verse, *Youths would glimpse me — and hide,* were applied in practice (*R' Chaim D. Chavel*).

9. שָׂרִים עָצְרוּ בְמִלִּים וְכַף יָשִׂימוּ לְפִיהֶם — *Princes would withhold their speech, place hands upon their mouths.* Nobody would speak before I had had my say (*Rashi*).

10. קוֹל־נְגִידִים נֶחְבָּאוּ וּלְשׁוֹנָם לְחִכָּם דָּבֵקָה — *The powerful whose voice would normally be heard, concealed themselves, their tongue cleaved to their palate.* We translate in accordance with *R' Meyuchas. Metzudos* has קוֹל נְגִידִים as the subject of נֶחְבָּאוּ. However this rendering cannot accommodate the plural form. In our rendering, the words *whose voice would normally be heard,* must be understood as being contained in the phrase, קוֹל נְגִידִים.

11. כִּי אֹזֶן שָׁמְעָה וַתְּאַשְּׁרֵנִי וְעַיִן רָאֲתָה וַתְּעִידֵנִי — *Any ear which heard of me would applaud, any eye that saw, would affirm my worth.* אַשֵּׁר, *to pronounce happy,* or *blessed,* as in אַשְׁרֵי.

12. כִּי־אֲמַלֵּט עָנִי מְשַׁוֵּעַ וְיָתוֹם וְלֹא־עֹזֵר לוֹ — *When I would quiet the cries of the poor, the orphan whom none would help.* The poor are particularly prone to oppression by bullies who have nothing to fear from them. In Iyov's golden-age heyday they were able to look to him for protection.

13. בִּרְכַּת אֹבֵד עָלַי תָּבֹא וְלֵב אַלְמָנָה אַרְנִן — *The blessing of the wretched was directed to me, I brought joy to the widow's heart.* We have followed *Metzudos* for the translation, as being closest to the simple meaning of the verse (אֹבֵד is one who is *lost* because of the terrible burden of his poverty).

Rashi first suggests that אֹבֵד might be a person who has died. He would bless Iyov,

when my young men surrounded me. 6 *When my very feet were*
bathed in butter, where the rock that was with me gushed rivulets
of oil. 7 *When I would leave for the gate, to the canopied throne,*
when I would set up my seat in the street. 8 *Youths would glimpse*
me — and hide, the aged would rise and remain standing. 9 *Princes*
would withhold their speech, place hands upon their mouths. 10 *The*
powerful whose voice would normally be heard concealed them-
selves, their tongue cleaved to their palate. 11 *Any ear which heard*
of me would applaud, any eye that saw, would affirm my worth.
12 *When I would quiet the cries of the poor, the orphan whom none*
would help. 13 *The blessing of the wretched was directed to me, I*
brought joy to the widow's heart. 14 *I clothed myself in righteous-*
ness — so that righteousness came and clothed me, my exercise of
justice was like a cloak, a turban. 15 *I served as eyes to the blind, the*
feet of the lame, I. 16 *I made myself father to the benighted, if I knew*
nothing of the nature of their claims, I would investigate them.

who made it his business to feed the widow and orphans who had been left behind.

Then, on the basis of *Bava Basra* 15a, *Rashi* suggests as follows: Iyov earned the blessing of the poor by stealing fields which belonged to orphans, improving them, and then returning them to their rightful owners. In this context, אֹבֵד would be one who had thought that his field was *lost* (*Rashi* to *Bava Basra*).[1]

The same Talmudic source suggests the following for the second half of the verse: Iyov would make widows happy by claiming them as his relative, so that others might wish to marry them, or even spreading rumors that he himself intended to marry them so that people should see them as desirable.

14. צֶדֶק לָבַשְׁתִּי וַיִּלְבָּשֵׁנִי כִמְעִיל וְצָנִיף מִשְׁפָּטִי — *I clothed myself in righteousness — so that righteousness came and clothed me, my exercise of justice was like a cloak, a turban.* *Metzudos* appears to take צֶדֶק as *charity.* He explains the first part of the verse as follows: I practiced charity so much that it became as much part of me as the clothes which I wore. Subsequently, I did not have to initiate my acts of charity. The poor people themselves came to solicit my help. It is as though my garments came of their own accord to clothe me (וַיִּלְבָּשֵׁנִי).

Metzudos believes that in the second phrase, *cloak* and *turban* were chosen because these are garments with a high visibility. People who wear them would want them to be particularly clean. Thus they serve as an appropriate metaphor for the justice which Iyov practiced. It delighted the eye with its purity.

R' Yosef Kara bases his interpretation upon the insight of the sages, quoted in *Yalkut*, here: There are judges whose judicial sense is impeccable, but the administration of justice does not become them — their own lives are filled with lawlessness. Then there are good people whose actions are beyond reproach, but who do not know how to judge correctly. But, Iyov says, 'As for me, *I clothed myself in righteousness,* that is, I administered justice, *and it became me,* because my actions did not belie my rulings.'

15. עֵינַיִם הָיִיתִי לַעִוֵּר וְרַגְלַיִם לַפִּסֵּחַ אָנִי — *I served as eyes to the blind, the feet of the lame, I.* Perhaps the אָנִי at the end of the verse is meant to underline the fact that Iyov did not delegate these tasks to others. He could easily have sent his servants to help the helpless. He chose to involve himself personally.

16. אָב אָנֹכִי לָאֶבְיוֹנִים וְרִב לֹא־יָדַעְתִּי אֶחְקְרֵהוּ — *I made myself father to the benighted, if I knew nothing of the nature of their claims, I would investigate them.* It is easy enough to do an isolated act of charity. It takes but a moment and leaves one with a glow of satisfaction. It is quite another thing to involve oneself in another's battles, caring enough to investigate unfamiliar legal territory. For this a father's concern is needed.

1. See at 1:1 that such a practice is interdicted by *halachah.* It is forbidden to steal with the intention of later returning the object. See there for our analysis.

כט/יז-כה יז-יח וָאֲשַׁבְּרָה מְתַלְּעוֹת עַוָּל וּמִשִּׁנָּיו אַשְׁלִיךְ טָרֶף: וָאֹמַר
יט עִם־קִנִּי אֶגְוָע וְכַחוֹל אַרְבֶּה יָמִים: שָׁרְשִׁי פָתוּחַ אֱלֵי־מָיִם
כ וְטַל יָלִין בִּקְצִירִי: כְּבוֹדִי חָדָשׁ עִמָּדִי וְקַשְׁתִּי בְּיָדִי תַחֲלִיף:
כא-כב לִי־שָׁמְעוּ וְיִחֵלּוּ וְיִדְּמוּ לְמוֹ עֲצָתִי: אַחֲרֵי דְבָרִי לֹא יִשְׁנוּ
כג וְעָלֵימוֹ תִּטֹּף מִלָּתִי: וְיִחֲלוּ כַמָּטָר לִי וּפִיהֶם פָּעֲרוּ
כד לְמַלְקוֹשׁ: אֶשְׂחַק אֲלֵהֶם לֹא יַאֲמִינוּ וְאוֹר פָּנַי לֹא
כה יַפִּילוּן: אֶבְחַר דַּרְכָּם וְאֵשֵׁב רֹאשׁ וְאֶשְׁכּוֹן כְּמֶלֶךְ בַּגְּדוּד
ל/א א כַּאֲשֶׁר אֲבֵלִים יְנַחֵם: וְעַתָּה | שָׂחֲקוּ עָלַי צְעִירִים מִמֶּנִּי

17. וָאֲשַׁבְּרָה מְתַלְּעוֹת עַוָּל וּמִשִּׁנָּיו אַשְׁלִיךְ טָרֶף — *I smashed the fangs of the evildoer, forced him to disgorge prey from between his teeth.* מְתַלְּעָה appears in *Psalms* 58:7, as מַלְתָּעָה. The form used here is the more usual one, see *Yoel* 1:6, *Proverbs* 30:14. *Metzudos* thinks that these are the *great teeth* — apparently the fangs with which animals tear their prey. *R' Meyuchas* writes that they are the grinding teeth.

The position of this verse suggests that it might be a continuation of the previous one. Iyov would investigate the claims of the poor and, if he found them to have merit, he would force their opponent to return that which he had taken.

18. וָאֹמַר עִם־קִנִּי אֶגְוָע וְכַחוֹל אַרְבֶּה יָמִים — *I had thought that death would come to me with my home intact, that my days would be as many as the sand.* Having listed his righteous actions, Iyov now spells out his modest expectations — see Introductory Remarks.

קֵן is a *nest*, and is used here as a synonym for *home* or for Iyov's children. He had thought that at his death they might still be alive, protected within his home as the tiny birds are protected by the nest (*R' Meyuchas* and *R' Yosef Kara*).

The translation of the second phrase follows *Metzudos* and accords with the simple meaning of the text. *Rashi* brings the tradition of the Sages that חול is the name of a bird which was rewarded with longevity as a reward for not having tasted from the Tree of Knowledge in the Garden of Eden.

R' Yosef Kara suggests that the use of קֵן in the first part of the verse would tend to bear out the Sages' interpretation. The entire verse deals with birds.

19. שָׁרְשִׁי פָתוּחַ אֱלֵי־מָיִם וְטַל יָלִין בִּקְצִירִי — *My roots opening upon the waters, dew moistening my branches overnight.* Iyov had thought that his blessings would come from below — *the waters* and from above — *dew. R' Yosef Kara* adduces *Deuteronomy* 33:13: *... with the sweetness of the heaven's dew, and the waters that lie below.*

20. כְּבוֹדִי חָדָשׁ עִמָּדִי וְקַשְׁתִּי בְּיָדִי תַחֲלִיף — *Always new modes of respect! My hand's strength guaranteeing always novel directions.* This is all still part of Iyov's expectations. He had thought that the respect which he enjoyed in the community would stay ever fresh. He had the power to make sure that it would constantly renew itself in all kinds of ways.

21. לִי־שָׁמְעוּ וְיִחֵלּוּ וְיִדְּמוּ לְמוֹ עֲצָתִי — *People listened to me with anticipation, waited in silence for my guidance.* See Introductory Remarks for our perception of why Iyov, once more at this point, takes up his nostalgic retrospect of the honor which had been granted him in his community.

Those that heard me would anticipate with certainty that my predictions would come about. In fact, they did. This was because my wisdom had been passed on to me by the wise (*Rashi*).

22. אַחֲרֵי דְבָרִי לֹא יִשְׁנוּ וְעָלֵימוֹ תִּטֹּף מִלָּתִי — *Once I had spoken they would not ask again, to them my words were prophecy.* The translation of the first phrase follows *Metzudos.* יִשְׁנוּ, from שָׁנָה, *to repeat.*

In the second phrase we have followed *Rashi* who takes נָטַף in the *hiphil*, as *to prophesy.* See *Rashi* at *Michah* 2:6.

Metzudos offers: That which I had said became a topic for conversation among them.

23. וְיִחֲלוּ כַמָּטָר לִי וּפִיהֶם פָּעֲרוּ לְמַלְקוֹשׁ — *They would long for me as for rain, wait long for themselves to have their say.* They would wait to hear my words with the same urgency that men wait for rain. They were willing to defer their own speech, be late in uttering their thoughts (לָקֵשׁ, *to be late*, as in מַלְקוֹשׁ, the *latter rains*), all for the sake of having me speak my piece (*Metzudos*).

24. אֶשְׂחַק אֲלֵהֶם לֹא יַאֲמִינוּ וְאוֹר פָּנַי לֹא יַפִּילוּן — *Were I to smile upon them — they would not believe it, had not the courage to presume to take advantage of my pleasant demeanor.*

29/17-25 17 *I smashed the fangs of the evildoer, forced him to disgorge prey
from between his teeth. 18 *I had thought that death would come to
me with my home intact, that my days would be as many as the
sand.* 19 *My roots opening upon the waters, dew moistening my
branches overnight.* 20 *Always new modes of respect! My hand's
strength guaranteeing always novel directions.* 21 *People listened to
me with anticipation, waited in silence for my guidance.* 22 *Once I
had spoken they would not ask again, to them my words were
prophecy.* 23 *They would long for me as for rain, wait long for
themselves to have their say.* 24 *Were I to smile upon them — they
would not believe it, had not the courage to presume to take
advantage of my pleasant demeanor.* 25 *Sitting at their head I would
determine their life's path, ensconced like a king among his soldiers.
I was regarded as one who offers comfort to mourners.*

30/1 1 *And now, those that are younger than I in days, such whose*

Iyov's exalted position demanded an earnest and grave bearing. He would not, as a rule, talk to people as equals or laugh with them.

For the second phrase, *Rashi* writes: They stood in such awe of me that they would not come close and would not feel at ease in my proximity. Perhaps he takes יַפִּילוּן as a truncated form of יַעְפִּילוּן, from עָפַל, *to act presumptuously*, as in *Numbers* 14:44.

We have elected to take אוֹר פָּנִים idiomatically, denoting a kind or pleasant demeanor.

Metzudos derives the word יַפִּילוּן from נפל, in its sense, *to lessen*. Hence: Even when I showed them a kindly demeanor, they would treat me with care in order not to lessen or inhibit the bright shine upon my face.

25. אֶבְחַר דַּרְכָּם וְאֵשֵׁב רֹאשׁ וְאֶשְׁכּוֹן כְּמֶלֶךְ בַּגְּדוּד כַּאֲשֶׁר אֲבֵלִים יְנַחֵם — *Sitting at their head I would determine their life's path, ensconced like a king among his soldiers. I was regarded as one who offers comfort to mourners.* Since my advice was precisely followed, I, in effect, was the one who determined what path those who consulted me should follow. When in company, I invariably sat at the head, just as a king among his soldiers (*Rashi*).

For the final phrase, *Rashi* says nothing, and we follow *Metzudos*: People would listen to my words with the same attention as mourners, eager to find comfort in their sorrow, would listen to one who had the ability to relieve them of their sorrow.

XXX.

The carefully organized symmetry which we traced in the last chapter (commentary v. 2), in the first part of this second of the two *meshalim*, seems to be continued in that section of the *mashal* which is contained in our chapter.

A careful reading will yield the following structure: Iyov bemoans three losses. To each of these losses he devotes precisely eight verses. After spelling them out, he concludes his elegy with the words: *My harp has turned to mourning, my lute to the sound of weeping.*

The first section of our chapter deals with the youngsters who undermine Iyov's dignity by jeering at him. This section runs from verses 1 through 14. But of these fourteen verses, six, verses 2-7, deal not with the youngsters themselves but with their lowly fathers. The enormity of Iyov's suffering at the hands of the youngsters is described in the remaining eight verses.

At verse 15, Iyov begins to describe his physical infirmities (see commentary to v. 15). This description runs through five verses, up to verse 19. At verse 20 Iyov begins to bemoan his new relationship with God. In contrast to the heady days of yore which were described in the beginning of the last chapter, when God was a loving and caring friend, there is now a Deity Who seems to hear no prayers and appears to delight in torturing His loyal servant. This description of a seemingly uncaring God continues for eight verses, through verse 27.

Verses 28-30 then pick up once more the story of Iyov's physical disabilities, adding three verses to the original five, for a total of eight.

לְיָמִים אֲשֶׁר־מָאַסְתִּי אֲבוֹתָם לָשִׁית עִם־כַּלְבֵי צֹאנִי׃
ב־ג גַּם־כֹּחַ יְדֵיהֶם לָמָּה לִּי עָלֵימוֹ אָבַד כָּלַח׃ בְּחֶסֶר וּבְכָפָן
ד גַּלְמוּד הַעֹרְקִים צִיָּה אֶמֶשׁ שׁוֹאָה וּמְשֹׁאָה׃ הַקֹּטְפִים
ה מַלּוּחַ עֲלֵי־שִׂיחַ וְשֹׁרֶשׁ רְתָמִים לַחְמָם׃ מִן־גֵּו
ו יְגֹרָשׁוּ יָרִיעוּ עָלֵימוֹ כַּגַּנָּב׃ בַּעֲרוּץ נְחָלִים לִשְׁכֹּן חֹרֵי
ז עָפָר וְכֵפִים׃ בֵּין־שִׂיחִים יִנְהָקוּ תַּחַת חָרוּל יְסֻפָּחוּ׃

We may sum up as follows: Verses 1 and 8-14 tell the story of the mocking youngsters; verses 15-19 and 28-30 describe Iyov's physical anguish; and verses 20-27 talk of the new and frightening distance between Iyov and his God.

The fact that the structure is not perfect in no way weakens our observation. On the contrary, it underscores the existential realism with which the story of Iyov has been told throughout the book. Here we have no objective debating of theological theories in the halls of academe, but the raw emotion-ridden suffering of a human being. Again and again, throughout the book, we have noted how Iyov refuses to be tied to his own carefully crafted and structured plans. If he is determined to spell out the sheer gall of the youngsters who make sport of him, he will be suddenly and deeply offended by the insignificance of their lineage — and will interrupt the flow of his thoughts in order to give play to this new insight. If he is intent upon describing the intensity of his physical suffering, this will suddenly wake in him the latent resentment against an apparently cruel God, and he will, though breaking the even flow of his rhetoric, follow where his heart leads him.

1. וְעַתָּה שָׂחֲקוּ עָלַי צְעִירִים מִמֶּנִּי לְיָמִים אֲשֶׁר־מָאַסְתִּי אֲבוֹתָם לָשִׁית עִם־כַּלְבֵי צֹאנִי — *And now, those that are younger than I in days, such whose fathers I would have regarded to be unworthy of serving with my sheep dogs, sneer at me.* One wonders why these youngsters sneered. It could be that they shared the opinion of the friends, that they assumed that Iyov must be a secret sinner, and they therefore lost all respect for him. This would have been painful enough for Iyov. Worse would be if their present disdain would indicate that they had earlier trembled, not before Iyov the man of honor, but before Iyov the man of power. Iyov suddenly realizes that he had lived in a dream world. He had thought that he had, by a life of probity, earned the respect of his community; he discovers now that he had earned nothing at all. He had been neither respected nor loved; only feared.

The question of whether Iyov, in his heyday, was truly loved, revolves to some extent around the question of whether he, himself, had loved.

What was Iyov's attitude toward his fellow man? On the one hand, he appears to subscribe to the concept of absolute equality of worth between humans — *Did not He Who formed me in the belly form him too? Was it not One, Who laid our foundations in the womb?* (31:15) — but, on the other hand, the diatribe against the fathers of the youths who now jeer him, seems to belie this sensitivity and, indeed, to color the account of his charitable deeds in the previous chapter with an aura of condescension.

At 19:19 Iyov does talk of, ... *those I had loved,* and this indicates that he had had friends within the community. Indeed it appears that it is just these friends who, upon his rehabilitation, came to feast with him and to comfort him and to leave him some small trinkets as a mark of their friendship (42:11). But, we certainly have the impression that these were not people who were capable of true love. One imagines that Iyov would have appreciated their company more while he was poor, suffering, ignored — and despised.

Can these insights in any way help us to a better understanding of the book?

Perhaps.

If indeed we may postulate that Iyov had not yet learned to love his fellow man well, we cannot avoid the conclusion that in his love of God, too, he was lacking. Hillel (*Shabbos* 31a) has taught us that the one depends upon the other. If our hearts are turned inward, with ourselves as the center of our interest, then we necessarily exclude not only our neighbors, but also God Himself, from our concern.

Indeed, throughout Iyov's many speeches, it is difficult to detect any love of God. It is true that there is the occasional flash (see at 13:15), but the general tenor of the speeches is one of fierce assertiveness, rather than of the softness and yearning of true love.

We might almost say that Iyov relates to God with the same stern demeanor with which he intimidated those people with whom he came into contact. If it is true that he sought justice for the weak and the downtrodden, he did no less for himself.

Now this insight may help us to solve one of the riddles in the book.

It is clear from the book's structure that it is the speeches which God delivers which ultimately help Iyov to find comfort. Why does God wait till the end — why could He not have set Iyov straight immedi-

30/2-7 fathers I would have regarded to be unworthy of serving with my
sheep dogs, sneer at me. 2 Their strength was useless to me, their old
age is a total loss. 3 Poverty and starvation drove them to solitude,
seeking escape in the barren wastelands, murky through the misty
fog. 4 Scraping moss from the trees, their bread — the roots of the
rasam tree. 5 Driven from the city, pursued like thieves by tumultuous cries. 6 Seeking shelter in the crevices of the valleys, in ditches
and in caves. 7 Braying among the trees, huddling among the

ately following upon the curses which Iyov uttered in chapter 3?

Perhaps it is not so easy to elicit God's response. Possibly the relentless questing and questioning upon which Iyov insisted so tenaciously is itself the cause for God's appearance. Perhaps, Iyov needed to hold his own against the terrible pressures to which he was subjected by the friends, before he could merit God's communication.

But, why did God not step in immediately after the present cogitation? Why did God wait until Elihu had had his say.

We suspect that beyond the heroic tenacity which Iyov displayed, which was certainly a necessary step toward meriting the ultimate revelation, there was one more lesson which Iyov had to learn. He would have to learn the lesson of love, so that he would become capable of a response other than the one that he had used up to this point. Iyov had perhaps been too pugnacious, had refused to grant any truth to even a single one of the friends' arguments. He had always argued back, often appearing not even to have listened to what they had to say.

In analyzing Elihu's contribution in the following chapters, we shall find that there is very little which is new in his speeches. Commentators are hard-put to understand what he adds to what has already been said by the friends, and, moreover, why Iyov apparently accepts his arguments after having so forcefully rejected those earlier ones. In the commentary to the Elihu chapters, we shall examine the possibility that, indeed, the difference between him and the friends is not in *what* was said, but in *how* it was said. Where the friends (according to the *Zohar* upon which we have based our entire commentary) had not taken the trouble to think out the best way to tell Iyov some unpalatable truths, so that he might be inclined to accept what they had to say, Elihu takes care to make the very same points in a much less offensive way. In short, Elihu breaks down Iyov's defenses with love and consideration.

Iyov's silence in the face of Elihu's arguments bears witness to the fact that he succeeded where the friends had so dismally failed.

2. גַּם־כֹּחַ יְדֵיהֶם לָמָּה לִּי עָלֵימוֹ אָבַד כָּלַח — *Their strength was useless to me, their old age is a total loss.* We follow *Metzudos.* Iyov looks with disdain upon the fathers of the youths who now jeer at him. He would not have had them join his sheep dogs because whatever strength they had to offer would have been inadequate to the task. They grew old without acquiring the wisdom which longevity usually bestows.

3. בְּחֶסֶר וּבְכָפָן גַּלְמוּד הַעֹרְקִים צִיָּה אֶמֶשׁ שׁוֹאָה וּמְשֹׁאָה — *Poverty and starvation drove them to solitude, seeking escape in the barren wastelands, murky through the misty fog.* The description of the fathers continues. They had none of the benefits bestowed by living together with civilized and cultured people. Lacking everything, they hid their shame in the wastelands, away from human contact.

That שׁוֹאָה is to be rendered *mist*, can be seen from *Tzephaniah* 1:15 where שׁוֹאָה וּמְשׁוֹאָה is paralleled with חֹשֶׁךְ וַאֲפֵלָה and עָנָן וַעֲרָפֶל.

4. הַקֹּטְפִים מַלּוּחַ עֲלֵי־שִׂיחַ וְשֹׁרֶשׁ רְתָמִים לַחְמָם — *Scraping moss from the trees, their bread — the roots of the rasam tree.* The translation follows *Rashi* who takes עֲלֵי as a poetic form of עַל, *on. Metzudos* and *R' Meyuchas* render, ... *who snatch up moss and tree leaves. Targum* and one suggestion in *R' Yosef Kara* take שִׂיחַ as *vegetation.* They eat inedible grasses in place of edible vegetation.

According to all of the opinions, this continues the description of the fathers of the youngsters. Driven into the wilderness by the famine, they subsist on animal fodder, with no remnant of human dignity.

5. מִן־גֵּו יְגֹרָשׁוּ יָרִיעוּ עָלֵימוֹ כַּגַּנָּב — *Driven from the city, pursued like thieves by tumultuous cries.* The description of the fathers continues. Iyov appears unable to break away from the contemplation of the sheer nothingness of the youths who now jeer at him.

6. בַּעֲרוּץ נְחָלִים לִשְׁכֹּן חֹרֵי עָפָר וְכֵפִים — *Seeking shelter in the crevices of the valleys, in ditches and in caves.* The base meaning of עָרַץ is *to break.* It is used for *fear* in a borrowed sense (see *Rashi* to *Deuteronomy* 1:29). Here the meaning is a break in the earth, *a crevice.*

7. בֵּין־שִׂיחִים יִנְהָקוּ תַּחַת חָרוּל יְסֻפָּחוּ — *Braying among the trees, huddling among the brambles.* The sub-humanity of the fathers is underlined by using terms which belong in the animal world. See 6:5 for נָהַק.

We cannot know the precise meaning of

ל/ח־יט ח־ט בְּֽנֵי־נָבָל גַּם־בְּנֵי בְלִי־שֵׁם נִכְּאוּ מִן־הָאָֽרֶץ׃ וְעַתָּה נְגִינָתָם
י הָיִיתִי וָאֱהִי לָהֶם לְמִלָּֽה׃ תִּֽעֲבוּנִי רָחֲקוּ מֶנִּי וּמִפָּנַי
°יִתְרִי ק׳ יא לֹא־חָשְׂכוּ רֹֽק׃ כִּֽי־°יתרו פִּתַּח וַיְעַנֵּנִי וְרֶסֶן מִפָּנַי שִׁלֵּֽחוּ׃
יב עַל־יָמִין פִּרְחַח יָקוּמוּ רַגְלַי שִׁלֵּחוּ וַיָּסֹלּוּ עָלַי אָרְחוֹת
°לְהַוָּתִי ק׳ יג־יד אֵידָֽם׃ נָֽתְסוּ נְתִיבָתִי °להיתי יֹעִילוּ לֹא עֹזֵר לָֽמוֹ׃ כְּפֶרֶץ
טו רָחָב יֶאֱתָיוּ תַּחַת שֹׁאָה הִתְגַּלְגָּֽלוּ׃ הָהְפַּךְ עָלַי בַּלָּהוֹת
טז תִּרְדֹּף כָּרוּחַ נְדִבָתִי וּכְעָב עָֽבְרָה יְשֻׁעָתִֽי׃ וְעַתָּה עָלַי
יז תִּשְׁתַּפֵּךְ נַפְשִׁי יֹאחֲזוּנִי יְמֵי־עֹֽנִי׃ לַיְלָה עֲצָמַי נִקַּר
יח מֵעָלָי וְעֹרְקַי לֹא יִשְׁכָּבֽוּן׃ בְּרָב־כֹּחַ יִתְחַפֵּשׂ לְבוּשִׁי כְּפִי
יט כְתָּנְתִּי יַאַזְרֵֽנִי׃ הֹרָנִי לַחֹמֶר וָאֶתְמַשֵּׁל כֶּעָפָר וָאֵֽפֶר׃

חָרוּל, but in *Proverbs* 24:31 the word is used to describe the weeds that overgrow the vineyard of the slothful farmer.

8. בְּנֵי־נָבָל גַּם־בְּנֵי בְלִי־שֵׁם נִכְּאוּ מִן־הָאָרֶץ — *Churls with no name to them, too lowly to have standing in the land!* From Iyov's graphic description of the fathers, he now turns once more to the jeering sons (*Metzudos*).

9. וְעַתָּה נְגִינָתָם הָיִיתִי וָאֱהִי לָהֶם לְמִלָּה — *And now I have become their ditty, provide conversation for them.* Their disrespectful attitude toward him seems to bother Iyov more than the physical abuse which he describes in the next verse.

10. תִּעֲבוּנִי רָחֲקוּ מֶנִּי וּמִפָּנַי לֹא־חָשְׂכוּ רֹק — *They have despised me, have distanced themselves from me, have not withheld their spittle from my face.* Not only did they talk about me among themselves, they even despised me to my face.

11. כִּי־יִתְרִי פִּתַּח וַיְעַנֵּנִי וְרֶסֶן מִפָּנַי שִׁלֵּחוּ — *He has loosened my bowstring, and afflicted me. They have thrown off their harness to my face.* None of this would have been possible if God Himself had not undermined my strength. It is as though he had loosened my bowstrings rendering me impotent. Once I was without power to restrain the youngsters, they threw off the harness that had bound them to me.

12. עַל־יָמִין פִּרְחַח יָקוּמוּ רַגְלַי שִׁלֵּחוּ וַיָּסֹלּוּ עָלַי אָרְחוֹת אֵידָם — *To my right unschooled youngsters make their place, pushing my feet aside. They beat out paths along which to bring about my downfall, against me.* Where in the past, only men of stature would stand at my right, now the lowest of the low will position themselves there. If there is not enough room for their comfort, they think nothing of pushing my feet aside.

אֵיד is a *destiny of destruction.* אָרְחוֹת אֵידָם are the paths along which they plan to bring this destiny upon me. סָלַל, from which מְסִילָה, *path*, is derived, denotes the *treading out of a path.*

13. נָתְסוּ נְתִיבָתִי לְהַוָּתִי יֹעִילוּ לֹא עֹזֵר לָמוֹ — *They have pulverized my road, brought on the shattering of my life, with no benefit to themselves.* The ס in נָתְסוּ replaces the צ from נָתַץ, *to destroy* (*Rashi*).

14. כְּפֶרֶץ רָחָב יֶאֱתָיוּ תַּחַת שֹׁאָה הִתְגַּלְגָּלוּ — *As through a wide breach they come pouring, under cover of the mist they make their way.* Our rendering, *As through a wide breach,* is not literal. The verbatim translation would read, *They come on like a wide breach.* In Iyov's distress, his enemies, and the breach in his defenses which makes their attack possible, are fused into one.

15. הָהְפַּךְ עָלַי בַּלָּהוֹת תִּרְדֹּף כָּרוּחַ נְדִבָתִי וּכְעָב עָבְרָה יְשֻׁעָתִי — *Malevolent spirits have turned upon me. You have chased away my noble bearing as by a storm. My salvation has drifted off like a cloud.* בַּלָּהוֹת has occured at 18:11 and 14, and at 27:20. In the earlier instances we followed *Rashi* who equates the term with שֵׁדִים, as we do here. At 27:20 the term seemed to require a different rendering — see commentary there.

Rashi equates נְדִיבָה, in our verse, with רוּחַ נְדִיבָה of *Psalms* 51:14. There *Rashi* renders קְצִינוּת, which means *royalty* or *empowerment.*

If the expression רוּחַ נְדִיבָה is a known idiom, then the combination in our verse, תִּרְדֹּף כָּרוּחַ נְדִבָתִי, is almost certainly meant as a play on words. Instead of the רוּחַ defining my נְדִיבוּת (רוּחַ נְדִיבוּת), it pursues it like an enemy.

We have rendered יְשֻׁעָתִי as *salvation* because that is the sense which the word usually conveys. In our context we suspect that it refers to Iyov's self-confidence, for it is that which is the source from which we draw our help in the face of adversity. This source would be the sense of power manifested within us, which

brambles. 8 *Churls with no name to them, too lowly to have*
standing in the land! 9 *And now I have become their ditty, provide*
conversation for them. 10 *They have despised me, have distanced*
themselves from me, have not withheld their spittle from my
face. 11 *He has loosened my bowstring, and afflicted me. They*
have thrown off their harness to my face. 12 *To my right*
unschooled youngsters make their place, pushing my feet aside.
They beat out paths along which to bring about my downfall,
against me. 13 *They have pulverized my road, brought on the*
shattering of my life, with no benefit to themselves. 14 *As through*
a wide breach they come pouring, under cover of the mist they
make their way. 15 *Malevolent spirits have turned upon me. You*
have chased away my noble bearing as by a storm. My salvation
has drifted off like a cloud. 16 *So now I feel distraught; I am caught*
up by sorrowful times. 17 *At night my bones are pecked clean, my*
sinews find no rest. 18 *Its mighty force has given me a different*
set of clothes. It encircles me as does the collar of my tunic.
19 *He has flung me into the clay, I have become like dust and ashes.*

enables us to deal with life's vicissitudes. The context of the verse, dealing as it does with Iyov's physical afflictions, appears to yield this interpretation.

Who are the *malevolent spirits* who have now turned upon Iyov? What has undermined Iyov's noble bearing, what has drained from him the feeling of confidence which, in earlier times, had helped him cope with adversity?

The context would seem to demand that we understand this verse as referring to Iyov's physical disabilities. It is these which occupy his mind in verses 17-19, and since, in our verse, Iyov appears to have moved away from his description of the jeering youngsters, it seems likely that it is meant to introduce the next section (see further in Introductory Remarks to this chapter). The illness appears to Iyov as the personification of so many malevolent spirits who are intent upon his destruction. Certainly one who has to struggle with Iyov's agonies, whose existence is circumscribed by the stench and ooze of a decaying body, will find it hard to carry himself nobly or to find within himself the sense of confidence required to deal with life's challenges.

16. וְעַתָּה עָלַי תִּשְׁתַּפֵּךְ נַפְשִׁי יֹאחֲזוּנִי יְמֵי־עֹנִי — *So now I feel distraught; I am caught up by sorrowful times.* Now that my יְשׁוּעָה, *my abilty to help myself,* is no more, I feel at the mercy of any troubles that might overtake me (*Metzudos*).

17. לַיְלָה עֲצָמַי נִקַּר מֵעָלָי וְעֹרְקַי לֹא יִשְׁכָּבוּן — *At night my bones are pecked clean, my sinews find no rest.* The worms peck my flesh off my bones (*Rashi*).

Both *Rashi* and *Metzudos* trace עֹרְקַי to an Arabic term meaning *sinew.*

18. בְּרָב־כֹּחַ יִתְחַפֵּשׂ לְבוּשִׁי כְּפִי כֻתָּנְתִּי יַאַזְרֵנִי — *Its mighty force has given me a different set of clothes. It encircles me as does the collar of my tunic.* We have translated the first part of the verse according to *R' Meyuchas.* The nature of my sickness has forced me to abandon my regular clothes and, instead, to cover myself with earth (2:8). *Rashi* and *Metzudos* have: Because of the sickness, the sweat and the extrusions, I constantly have to change my clothes. *R' Yosef Kara* takes *clothes* as a metaphor for the skin. The leprosy has changed the color of my skin.

כְּפִי could be rendered, *just like,* or *as the collar of ... Rashi* takes the latter meaning. The collar of the shirt fits snugly around the neck. In exactly the same way, my clothes, which usually hang loose, fit around my bloated body. *Daas Mikra,* taking into account that אֵזוֹר is a *belt,* which surrounds the widest part of the body, renders: I feel so constricted by my illness that it is as though my belt were no wider than my collar. *Metzudos* takes the former meaning: My sickness envelops me as does my garment.

19. הֹרָנִי לַחֹמֶר וָאֶתְמַשֵּׁל כֶּעָפָר וָאֵפֶר — *He has flung me into the clay, I have become like dust and ashes.* The translation follows *Metzudos* who takes הֹרָנִי from יָרָה, *to throw. Rashi* derives it from יֹרֶה, *to teach,* thus:

כ־כא אֲשַׁוַּע אֵלֶיךָ וְלֹא תַעֲנֵנִי עָמַדְתִּי וַתִּתְבֹּנֶן בִּי׃ תֵּהָפֵךְ
כב לְאַכְזָר לִי בְּעֹצֶם יָדְךָ תִשְׂטְמֵנִי׃ תִּשָּׂאֵנִי אֶל־רוּחַ
כג תַּרְכִּיבֵנִי וּתְמֹגְגֵנִי °תשוה׃ כִּי־יָדַעְתִּי מָוֶת תְּשִׁיבֵנִי וּבֵית
כד מוֹעֵד לְכָל־חָי׃ אַךְ לֹא־בְעִי יִשְׁלַח־יָד אִם־בְּפִידוֹ
כה לָהֶן שׁוּעַ׃ אִם־לֹא בָכִיתִי לִקְשֵׁה־יוֹם עָגְמָה נַפְשִׁי
כו לָאֶבְיוֹן׃ כִּי טוֹב קִוִּיתִי וַיָּבֹא רָע וַאֲיַחֲלָה לְאוֹר
כז וַיָּבֹא אֹפֶל׃ מֵעַי רֻתְּחוּ וְלֹא־דָמּוּ קִדְּמֻנִי יְמֵי־עֹנִי׃
כח־כט קֹדֵר הִלַּכְתִּי בְּלֹא חַמָּה קַמְתִּי בַקָּהָל אֲשַׁוֵּעַ׃ אָח הָיִיתִי
ל לְתַנִּים וְרֵעַ לִבְנוֹת יַעֲנָה׃ עוֹרִי שָׁחַר מֵעָלָי וְעַצְמִי־
לא חָרָה מִנִּי־חֹרֶב׃ וַיְהִי לְאֵבֶל כִּנֹּרִי וְעֻגָבִי לְקוֹל בֹּכִים׃

°תֻּשִׁיָּה ק׳

My leprosy has taught me how to sit in the clay.

20. אֲשַׁוַּע אֵלֶיךָ וְלֹא תַעֲנֵנִי עָמַדְתִּי וַתִּתְבֹּנֶן בִּי — *If I scream to You, You do not answer me, if I keep silent, You do not consider me.* Iyov now harks back to the beginning of this speech. There, he had begun his cogitations with fond memories of the close and loving relationship which he had had with his God (29:2-5). The contrast is shattering.

We have translated the verses in accordance with *Metzudos'* first rendering. The וְלֹא of the first phrase does double duty. It is to be read also with the second phrase, as though it were written, וְ[לֹא] תִּתְבֹּנֶן בִּי.

Rashi takes the verse as is: When I am silent you contemplate me with the aim of thinking up new horrors, planning ever new sicknesses.

21. תֵּהָפֵךְ לְאַכְזָר לִי בְּעֹצֶם יָדְךָ תִשְׂטְמֵנִי — *You have turned into my tormentor, with all Your frightful power — You hate me.* You Who by nature are merciful have, inexplicably, become — toward me — cruel and hating (*Metzudos*).

22. תִּשָּׂאֵנִי אֶל־רוּחַ תַּרְכִּיבֵנִי וּתְמֹגְגֵנִי תֻּשִׁיָּה — *You have lifted me up, buffeted me with the winds, have melted me down into helplessness.* The translation follows *Metzudos.* תֻּשִׁיָּה, from תָּשַׁשׁ, *to be weak.*

Rashi translates the first phrase: *You have handed me over to malevolent spirits* (רוּחַ = שֵׁד). This interpretation assumes particular significance in the commentary of *R' Yosef Kara,* who writes: You have handed me over to to spirits and specters, as it is written, *HASHEM said to the Satan, 'See he is in your hands!'* This would constitute a direct reference to the events recorded at the beginning of the book, and would perhaps indicate that Iyov had, at least, an inkling of what took place in the Heavenly Court. But, nowhere in the book is there any indication that Iyov ever discovered the real cause for his suffering. Indeed, as we will discuss (see 42:5-6 and fn. ad loc.), the logic of the entire book requires that Iyov should never be told of the challenge which the Satan had thrown at God.

23. כִּי־יָדַעְתִּי מָוֶת תְּשִׁיבֵנִי וּבֵית מוֹעֵד לְכָל־חָי — *So that I know full well that You are inclining me toward death, the ultimate destination of all that lives.* My weakness (previous verses) convinces me that I am not far from death (*Metzudos*). See commentary to next verse.

24. אַךְ לֹא־בְעִי יִשְׁלַח־יָד אִם־בְּפִידוֹ לָהֶן שׁוּעַ — *But, let Him not stretch forth His hand in absolute fury, for, even when destruction is their lot — there is also some relief.* The translation follows *Rashi*: עִי denotes *destruction* (see also *Rashi* to *Numbers* 21:11); פִּיד is *breakage* (see also *Proverbs* 24:22); and שׁוּעַ derives from שַׁעֲשַׁע, *to delight.*

In the latter section, Iyov is bringing proof from God's direction of history. When He turns His fury upon any one nation, He always bestows His favors upon another. Let God now do the same to him, let him merit some softness. Why must God turn His full fury upon him?

While *Rashi* does not say so in so many words, it appears that he takes verses 23-25 as one unit. In verse 23 Iyov seems almost to have given up his struggle. The second half of the verse appears to be an attempt to soften the blow of his inevitable death. Iyov is saying: I know full well that You intend to have me die. I could reconcile myself to this fate, by contemplating the fact that death is, after all, the end of every life. If it must ultimately come to me, I can accept that it come sooner rather

20 If I scream to You, You do not answer me, if I keep silent, You do
not consider me. 21 You have turned into my tormentor, with all
Your frightful power — You hate me. 22 You have lifted me up,
buffeted me with the winds, have melted me down into
helplessness. 23 So that I know full well that You are inclining me
toward death, the ultimate destination of all that lives. 24 But, let
Him not stretch forth His hand in absolute fury, for, even when
destruction is their lot — there is also some relief. 25 Did I not weep
for the one who was heavily burdened, did I not sorrow for the
destitute? 26 I had hoped for happiness — but trouble came; looked
forward to light — but darkness came. 27 My innards boiled, could
find no rest, but days of affliction have come to meet me.
28 Blackened — but not by the sun — I make my way, I rise in
public and scream. 29 I feel like a brother to the jackals, at one with
the owls. 30 My skin is blackened upon me, my bones are heated by
the fever. 31 My harp has turned to mourning, my lute to the sound
of weeping.

than later (v. 23). But, now that I have accepted Your judgment, may I not ask You to soften the blow a little? Why must all my troubles come upon me at once? Am I to receive no relief at all (v. 24)? And, indeed, I deserve at least some consideration. One who was so loving toward the helpless and the poor, one who shed so many tears at the sorrow of others, may surely lay some claim to mercy (v. 25)!

R' Yosef Kara takes עי as *a pile*, and פִּיד as *something that comes in little doses* (see also *Rashi* to *Avodah Zarah* 4a). The sense of the verse is: Do not send all my suffering in one unbearable lot. If it came to me piecemeal I would delight in it.

25. אִם־לֹא בָכִיתִי לִקְשֵׁה־יוֹם עָגְמָה נַפְשִׁי לָאֶבְיוֹן — *Did I not weep for the one who was heavily burdened, did I not sorrow for the destitute?* See commentary to previous verse.

26. כִּי טוֹב קִוִּיתִי וַיָּבֹא רָע וַאֲיַחֲלָה לְאוֹר וַיָּבֹא אֹפֶל — *I had hoped for happiness — but trouble came; looked forward to light — but darkness came.* I had hoped that my caring attitude would find its reward. Instead I appear to have been punished (*Rashi*).

27. מֵעַי רֻתְּחוּ וְלֹא־דָמּוּ קִדְּמֻנִי יְמֵי־עֹנִי — *My innards boiled, could find no rest, but days of affliction have come to meet me.* The Torah (*Genesis* 43:30) uses the idiom נִכְמְרוּ רַחֲמָיו, with נִכְמָרָה connoting *heat*, to describe *pity*. רָתַח, *to boil*, would carry the same meaning. This verse picks up the theme of verse 25. In spite of the fact that Iyov had felt such overwhelming pity for the defenseless, he is still faced with days of affliction (*Metzudos*).

28. קֹדֵר הִלַּכְתִּי בְּלֹא חַמָּה קַמְתִּי בַקָּהָל אֲשַׁוֵּעַ — *Blackened — but not by the sun — I make my way, I rise in public and scream.* The tan made by the sun will go away when some time is spent in the shade. Iyov has no hope that the blackness which envelops him will ever leave. If his suffering had been the result of sin, there would have been the expectation that penitence would bring relief. But, he is guiltless. How then should he hope ever to be able to change his fate? He is resigned to make his way through life, forever disfigured; but will scream out against his unwarranted agonies (*Metzudos*).

29. אָח הָיִיתִי לְתַנִּים וְרֵעַ לִבְנוֹת יַעֲנָה — *I feel like a brother to the jackals, at one with the owls.* These creatures, too, cry out. In my screams I feel a sense of unison with them (*Metzudos*).

30. עוֹרִי שָׁחַר מֵעָלָי וְעַצְמִי־חָרָה מִנִּי־חֹרֶב — *My skin is blackened upon me, my bones are heated by the fever.* The heat which engulfed me did not only blacken my skin. It penetrated to my very bones, burning them in its fierce fires.

31. וַיְהִי לְאֵבֶל כִּנֹּרִי וְעֻגָבִי לְקוֹל בֹּכִים — *My harp has turned to mourning, my lute to the sound of weeping.* This verse brings the elegy section of this second *mashal* to an end. See Introductory Remarks to this chapter.

לא/א־ו א־ב בְּרִית כָּרַתִּי לְעֵינָי וּמָה אֶתְבּוֹנֵן עַל־בְּתוּלָה: וּמֶה ׀
ג חֵלֶק אֱלוֹהַּ מִמָּעַל וְנַחֲלַת שַׁדַּי מִמְּרֹמִים: הֲלֹא־
ד אֵיד לְעַוָּל וְנֵכֶר לְפֹעֲלֵי אָוֶן: הֲלֹא־הוּא יִרְאֶה דְרָכָי
ה וְכָל־צְעָדַי יִסְפּוֹר: אִם־הָלַכְתִּי עִם־שָׁוְא וַתַּחַשׁ עַל־
ו מִרְמָה רַגְלִי: יִשְׁקְלֵנִי בְמֹאזְנֵי־צֶדֶק וְיֵדַע אֱלוֹהַּ תֻּמָּתִי:

XXXI.

In this last part of the second *mashal*, Iyov presents a litany of his personal modesty and probity, arguing that one as righteous as he should certainly be spared the suffering to which he is being subjected.

That this list is separate from the one in 29:12-17, seems to bear out our perception of the nature of that passage. There Iyov is simply saying that, conscious of the respect which his community paid him, he richly repaid it by exerting his influence for the good of the people. The issue is not whether he, personally, was a good man, but that with a sense of *noblesse oblige*, he acted responsibly for the public good.

Here, Iyov's personal goodness is the issue.

However, even in this list, Iyov speaks only of those things that he did *not* do. There is no sense at all of a loving relationship to God, nothing about what Iyov *is*, only about the way he had carried himself.[1]

Berachos 17a reports that R' Yochanan, after studying the book of *Iyov*, was wont to say among other things, 'Happy is he whose ... [actions are motivated by the desire] to give God pleasure (עֹשֶׂה נַחַת רוּחַ לְיוֹצְרוֹ).' Perhaps it was the contemplation of Iyov's attitude which was engaging R' Yochanan's thought. In the commentary to 6:2 we compared Iyov's reaction to his suffering to that which is reported of Nachum Ish Gamzu. Where Iyov has only plaintive questions, Nachum fervently asserts that far from spurning his troubles, he welcomes them. He is a sinner and they will purge him of all that makes him impure. The source of these differing perceptions may well lie in the respective attitudes which these two men had toward their God. Did they do good out of a sense of duty or out of a feeling of love? Iyov contemplates his life and sees a record of obligations conscientiously discharged, with never a slip into the forbidden. What more can be asked of him, he feels. Nachum, permeated with a burning love, must always see himself as falling short. There is so much more that he could have done.

In this chapter, Iyov will list those of his meritorious deeds and attitudes which, he feels, should have protected him from his suffering. These are: He never associated with frauds and practiced no deceit (v. 5); he was careful never to commit any sins (v. 7); he never allowed himself to be attracted by women and made sure that his wife too, lived in chastity (vs. 9 and 10); he was fair to his servants (v. 13); he was generous in helping the needy (vs. 16,17 and 19); he did not oppress the orphans (v. 21); he was not enamored of his wealth (vs. 4 and 25); he served no idols (vs. 26 and 27); he did not rejoice at his enemy's downfall (v. 29); he fulfilled all the obligations attendant upon tilling his lands (vs. 38 and 39).

1. בְּרִית כָּרַתִּי לְעֵינָי וּמָה אֶתְבּוֹנֵן עַל־בְּתוּלָה — *I have made a covenant with my eyes; why would I contemplate [regarding] a virgin.* Iyov had, as it were, made a covenant with his eyes, exacting a guarantee that they would not look upon a married woman since she is forbidden to him. The second phrase takes his modesty further. He would not even contemplate a virgin — a woman who was not married, to whom he might feel a natural attraction since he might one day take her as his wife (*Rashi*).

Our verse is worded differently than all the others which describe the meritorious acts which we listed in the Introductory narrative. These all begin with ... אִם, and then continue with, either a form of curse — if I did such and

1. The question of whether he served God from love or from fear is one which we raise constantly throughout the commentary — see particularly at chapters 2 and 9. We saw that it is *Ramban's* opinion that Iyov undergoes a gradual process wherein fear turns gradually to love. We noted that *Rashi* interprets many passages in such a way that, as we would expect, the two attitudes war constantly with one another for ascendancy. There are times when Iyov soars to the heights of adoration, there are others where we can find only a surly acceptance of what must be borne but can never be understood.

Our interpretation of this passage places it between the two extremes which we have noted. We have the conscientious fulfillment of duty, but miss the soaring affirmations of adoration.

1 *I have made a covenant with my eyes; why would I contem-*
plate [regarding] a virgin. 2 *Now why this lot which God*
has apportioned to me from above, why this fate which Shad-
dai has allotted to me from the heights! 3 *Disaster is approp-*
riate only to the wicked, unheard-of tragedy to those who
commit sins. 4 *Does He not see my paths, does He not count*
my steps? 5 *Whether I walked with empty frauds, or if my*
feet hastened to take part in deceit. 6 *Let Him weigh me with*
honest scales, God will be aware of my unquestioning integrity.

such, then such and such should happen to me — or with an explanation — I would never have done such and such, because ... This verse is an exception. It stands alone, proud, unexplained and unadorned, apparently able to support itself as a ringing affirmation of absolute merit.

What is so special about the covenant which Iyov made with his eyes and, in particular, in what way is this merit substantively different from those mentioned in verses 9 and 10, which seem to cover the same ground, but which are a part of the general grouping?

In Torah thought, control of the eyes plays a very special role. *Zevachim* 118b addresses the fact that in Shilo, the Tabernacle which stood in Joseph's portion of the land, the aura of sanctity extended as far as the eye could see, while in the Temple it was limited to the confines of Jerusalem: Let the eye which refused to nourish itself and to enjoy a sight which was not appropriate to it [that is, Joseph, who refused to look upon Potiphar's wife] spread its aura of sanctity as far as the eye can see.

Perhaps Iyov reasoned that the perfect control which he exercised over his eyes should, more than anything else, spread a protective curtain, which would not allow access to the malevolent spirits whom he identified with his sickness.

2. וּמֶה חֵלֶק אֱלוֹהַּ מִמָּעַל וְנַחֲלַת שַׁדַּי מִמְּרֹמִים — *Now why this lot which God has apportioned to me from above, why this fate which Shaddai has allotted to me from the heights!* The translation follows *Rashi* and *Metzudos.*

Ramban has this verse bridge between the previous one and the next. Together they explain why Iyov would not consider allowing his eyes to wander where they ought not to look. What, after all, does God on high do (our verse), but mete out punishment to the wicked (v. 3). Iyov would not want to incur God's wrath by allowing his eyes free reign.

3. הֲלֹא־אֵיד לְעַוָּל וְנֵכֶר לְפֹעֲלֵי אָוֶן — *Disaster is appropriate only to the wicked, unheard-of tragedy to those who commit sins.* The translation follows *Rashi.* For *Ramban's* perception, see commentary to previous verse.

נֵכֶר from נָכַר, *to be strange.* Experiences which have never happened to anyone before.

4. הֲלֹא־הוּא יִרְאֶה דְרָכָי וְכָל־צְעָדַי יִסְפּוֹר — *Does He not see my paths, does He not count my steps? Rashi* and *Ramban* agree that this verse is to be read together with the following one. God knows me well enough to judge *whether I walked with empty frauds.*

5. אִם־הָלַכְתִּי עִם־שָׁוְא וַתַּחַשׁ עַל־מִרְמָה רַגְלִי — *Whether I walked with empty frauds, or if my feet hastened to take part in deceit.* שָׁוְא is short for אַנְשֵׁי שָׁוְא (*Metzudos*). וַתַּחַשׁ, from חוּשׁ, *to hasten.*

6. יִשְׁקְלֵנִי בְמֹאזְנֵי־צֶדֶק וְיֵדַע אֱלוֹהַּ תֻּמָּתִי — *Let Him weigh me with honest scales, God will be aware of my unquestioning integrity. Rashi* is silent to this verse, but *Ramban* combines it with the earlier ones. Let God, who has all the necessary information (v. 4) weigh me on a fair scale (v. 6), and He will find out that I need not feel guilty about having spent my time on futility.

Once more we have Iyov's insistence upon his *temimus* (see Introductory Remarks to chapter 27 and commentary to v. 5, there). This may give us a hint at the true meaning of this, Iyov's first claim in the litany of meritorious deeds. What precisely does he mean when he says that he did not consort with frauds, that he eschewed deceit?

Iyov wishes his philosophy of life to be taken seriously. There is no lack of shallow theologians whose ideas tax no beliefs, challenge no ideas. Iyov, had he been less committed to the truth, had he been less of a *tam,* would have had far less trouble in his travails. But, he did not take the easy road. Why then should he be made to suffer?

It is indeed very understandable that Iyov should put this claim above all others in his list. Everything which he will still have to say, will ultimately stand or fall on whether or not this, his first claim, is valid.

ז אִם־תִּטֶּה אַשֻּׁרִי מִנִּי הַדָּרֶךְ וְאַחַר עֵינַי הָלַךְ לִבִּי וּבְכַפַּי
ח דָּבַק מְאוּם: אֶזְרְעָה וְאַחֵר יֹאכֵל וְצֶאֱצָאַי יְשֹׁרָשׁוּ:
ט־י אִם־נִפְתָּה לִבִּי עַל־אִשָּׁה וְעַל־פֶּתַח רֵעִי אָרָבְתִּי: תִּטְחַן
יא לְאַחֵר אִשְׁתִּי וְעָלֶיהָ יִכְרְעוּן אֲחֵרִין: כִּי־°הוּא זִמָּה °וְהִיא — °הִיא ק׳
יב עָוֺן פְּלִילִים: כִּי אֵשׁ הִיא עַד־אֲבַדּוֹן תֹּאכֵל וּבְכָל־ — °וְהוּא ק׳
יג תְּבוּאָתִי תְשָׁרֵשׁ: אִם־אֶמְאַס מִשְׁפַּט עַבְדִּי וַאֲמָתִי בְּרִבָם
יד עִמָּדִי: וּמָה אֶעֱשֶׂה כִּי־יָקוּם אֵל וְכִי־יִפְקֹד מָה אֲשִׁיבֶנּוּ:

7. אִם־תִּטֶּה אַשֻּׁרִי מִנִּי הַדֶּרֶךְ וְאַחַר עֵינַי הָלַךְ לִבִּי וּבְכַפַּי דָּבַק מאוּם — *If my footsteps had ever strayed from the road, if my heart had ever followed my eyes, if anything reprehensible had ever stuck to my hands.* Iyov's undeviating honesty was not limited to his theological stance. His actions were governed by the same stringent standards. They did not put his theories to shame. Had it been otherwise he would have deserved to be punished, as explicated in the next verse.

The א in מְאוּם is extra. The word is to be read as though it were written מוּם, *blemish* (*Rashi*).

8. אֶזְרְעָה וְאַחֵר יֹאכֵל וְצֶאֱצָאַי יְשֹׁרָשׁוּ — *Then I would deserve to plant and have strangers consume, my produce pulled out by the roots.* Iyov does not say that he should be punished by having his fields destroyed. Rather, his produce should be utterly consumed by strangers. It would seem that he deems just this as an appropriate punishment for his own deviations. *Leviticus* 19:29 talks of the earth being untrue to its owners (וְתִזְנֶה הָאָרֶץ) in punishment for certain shortcomings. This זְנוּת of the land is accomplished by its yielding its fruits to strangers (see *Rashi* there). Iyov declares that if he would have been untrue to his own principles, then he would expect his lands to be untrue to him also.

9. אִם־נִפְתָּה לִבִּי עַל־אִשָּׁה וְעַל־פֶּתַח רֵעִי אָרָבְתִּי — *If I ever allowed my heart to be allured by a woman, if I ever lay in ambush at my neighbor's door.* Iyov has talked of his mind and of his hands. His ideas measure up to the stringent standards of truth, his actions do not belie them. What of his heart? Iyov knows full well that a person's theological stance can be unflawed, his actions in the marketplace of human contact, impeccable; and still his heart may lust and make a shambles of his good intentions. Full of loathing for himself — his mind knows, after all, the depravity of what he does — he may yet lie in ambush at his neighbor's door, may yet violate his neighbor's wife.

Iyov knows himself to be free of any such taint. His heart is as guiltless as the standards mandated by his intellect demand.

10. תִּטְחַן לְאַחֵר אִשְׁתִּי וְעָלֶיהָ יִכְרְעוּן אֲחֵרִין — *Let my wife grind for another, let strangers kneel over her.* We have followed *Metzudos* in his translation. The sentence describes the punishment which Iyov feels he would deserve if he had acted as described in the previous verse. His wife would have to do other men's menial work, and thus exposed, would surely be violated by them.

Rashi quotes the tradition of the Sages that טָחַן is used here as a euphemism for the conjugal act. According to this, the translation would be: *Let other men grind [that is, have relations with] my wife.* We have elected to go with *Metzudos'* rendering, since it seems likely that the Sages offered their interpretation as *d'rash* rather than as *p'shat.*

11. כִּי־הִיא זִמָּה וְהוּא עָוֺן פְּלִילִים — *For such would have meant sinful planning, a punishable crime.* At *Ezekiel* 16:43, *Rashi* writes: The word זִמָּה in Scripture must always be understood as a *plan.* This may have either good or bad connotations. Accordingly, *Rashi* would understand our verse as follows: The misdeeds described in verse 9 could never have been committed without careful planning. This I would never have done.

פְּלִילִים from פָּלַל, *to judge.* Hence, a crime for which the courts would certainly assign a punishment (*Metzudos*).

12. כִּי אֵשׁ הִיא עַד־אֲבַדּוֹן תֹּאכֵל וּבְכָל־תְּבוּאָתִי תְשָׁרֵשׁ — *For it is a conflagration, consuming totally, destroying all my accomplishments.* Iyov is still explaining why he had never permitted himself to lust after another woman. Such lust is a fire which never allows itself to be quenched. It rages on, until it has taken over the person completely and destroyed all that is good within him.

It is difficult to accommodate the idea of תְּבוּאָה as *produce* in this context. *Metzudos* renders the word with this, its usual connotation, and reads the phrase as describing the punishment which Iyov would have merited

*7 If my footsteps had ever strayed from the road, if my heart
had ever followed my eyes, if anything reprehensible had
ever stuck to my hands. 8 Then I would deserve to plant and
have strangers consume, my produce pulled out by the roots. 9 If
I ever allowed my heart to be allured by a woman, if I ever lay
in ambush at my neighbor's door. 10 Let my wife grind for another, let strangers kneel over her. 11 For such would have meant
sinful planning, a punishable crime. 12 For it is a conflagration,
consuming totally, destroying all my accomplishments. 13 Never
did I arrogantly ignore my servant's or my maid-servant's rights,
when they laid claim against me. 14 What would I do were God
to arise, what would I answer Him if He were to inquire of me?*

had he allowed himself to lust. He would have deserved to have all his grain uprooted. *R' Meyuchas* thinks that the term refers to Iyov's *seed*, his children: Iyov feels that if he would have succumbed to such evil, he would have deserved to be punished by *kares*, being cut off from his people and having his children die.

Rashi does not explain the expression תְּבוּאָה. He limits himself to writing that the conflagration mentioned in the first part of the verse would have *uprooted* it. The use of this term in Scripture is not confined to agricultural products. Thus, for example, *Proverbs* 18:20 refers to pithy speech as תְּבוּאַת פִּיו, *the product of his mouth* (parallel to פְּרִי פִי אִישׁ). Accordingly, it seems to denote any positive accomplishment, and this is how we have translated it.

Iyov devotes four full verses to this assertion of innocence. He appears to care very much that it should be absolutely clear that he never had any inappropriate lustful designs. This appears strange in the light of the fact that never once was Iyov accused of such behavior. Even in Eliphaz's third speech, in which many serious accusations were leveled against Iyov, we find no whisper of allegations of any lustful impropriety. Why then did Iyov feel the need to clear himself so vigorously?

We note that Iyov does not protest that he never violated his neighbor's wife. It is not the act of violation of which he feels the need to clear himself, but of the suspicion that he might have felt attracted to a strange woman, might have had the intention of taking her. *If I ever allowed my heart to be* allured *by a woman, if I ever lay in ambush at my neighbor's door.* Eliphaz did not accuse Iyov of immoral behavior because even he realized that Iyov was above any such depravity. Iyov makes the point that even in his heart — something that Eliphaz could never know — he was entirely pure. Had it not been so, then indeed, he could have understood the suffering which had become his lot.

For, in contrast to other sins in which only the illicit action is reprehensible, impurity wreaks its pernicious havoc even when it is confined to the mind. Anyone who allows his mind to dwell upon immoral thoughts — his strength deserts him (*Sanhedrin* 92b, and see *Rashi* there). Iyov's suffering would have come upon him because, having allowed his mind — the seat of his contact with the Divine — to become tainted, he would have forfeited God's protection.

In claiming innocence from tainted thoughts, Iyov affirms his right to the enjoyment of God's protective grace.

13. אִם־אֶמְאַס מִשְׁפַּט עַבְדִּי וַאֲמָתִי בְּרִבָם עִמָּדִי — *Never did I arrogantly ignore my servant's or my maid-servant's rights, when they laid claim against me.* If the members of my household felt mistreated and summoned me to court, I would go with them to litigation even though I had the power to ignore them (*Metzudos*).

Iyov has now tested his mind, his hands and his heart, and found them to his satisfaction (see commentary to v. 9). In this section he describes his relationship to others. He begins with his own household and then goes on to the poor (vs. 16, 19, 21), who while they were not his direct responsibility, nevertheless benefited from his largess.

14. וּמָה אֶעֱשֶׂה כִּי־יָקוּם אֵל וְכִי־יִפְקֹד מָה אֲשִׁיבֶנּוּ — *What would I do were God to arise, what would I answer Him if He were to inquire of me?* I would tell myself that it would be wrong to take advantage of my servants' weakness. I could, indeed, deal with them from my superior strength, but what would I do if God, in their defense, would rise up against me? (*Rashi* and *Metzudos*).

טו־טז הֲלֹא־בַבֶּטֶן עֹשֵׂנִי עָשָׂהוּ וַיְכוּנֶנּוּ בָּרֶחֶם אֶחָד׃ אִם־אֶמְנַע
יז מֵחֵפֶץ דַּלִּים וְעֵינֵי אַלְמָנָה אֲכַלֶּה׃ וְאֹכַל פִּתִּי לְבַדִּי וְלֹא־
יח אָכַל יָתוֹם מִמֶּנָּה׃ כִּי מִנְּעוּרַי גְּדֵלַנִי כְאָב וּמִבֶּטֶן אִמִּי
יט אַנְחֶנָּה׃ אִם־אֶרְאֶה אוֹבֵד מִבְּלִי לְבוּשׁ וְאֵין כְּסוּת לָאֶבְיוֹן׃
כ־כא אִם־לֹא בֵרְכוּנִי חֲלָצָו וּמִגֵּז כְּבָשַׂי יִתְחַמָּם׃ אִם־הֲנִיפוֹתִי
כב עַל־יָתוֹם יָדִי כִּי־אֶרְאֶה בַשַּׁעַר עֶזְרָתִי׃ כְּתֵפִי מִשִּׁכְמָה
כג תִפּוֹל וְאֶזְרֹעִי מִקָּנָה תִשָּׁבֵר׃ כִּי־פַחַד אֵלַי אֵיד אֵל וּמִשְּׂאֵתוֹ
כד לֹא אוּכָל׃ אִם־שַׂמְתִּי זָהָב כִּסְלִי וְלַכֶּתֶם אָמַרְתִּי מִבְטַחִי׃
כה־כו אִם־אֶשְׂמַח כִּי־רַב חֵילִי וְכִי־כַבִּיר מָצְאָה יָדִי׃ אִם־אֶרְאֶה
כז אוֹר כִּי יָהֵל וְיָרֵחַ יָקָר הֹלֵךְ׃ וַיִּפְתְּ בַּסֵּתֶר לִבִּי וַתִּשַּׁק יָדִי לְפִי׃

15. הֲלֹא־בַבֶּטֶן עֹשֵׂנִי עָשָׂהוּ וַיְכוּנֶנּוּ בָּרֶחֶם אֶחָד — *Did not He who formed me in the belly form him too? Was it not One, Who laid our foundations in the womb*? We have translated according to *Rashi. Metzudos* reads the last phrase: *Were our foundations not laid in the same womb?* The sense is, since all of mankind is descended from Adam and Eve, why should the accidental difference in our station in life make me more significant than my servant?

16. אִם־אֶמְנַע מֵחֵפֶץ דַּלִּים וְעֵינֵי אַלְמָנָה אֲכַלֶּה — *Never did I withhold their desires from the destitute, nor make the widow's eyes long in vain.* כָּלָה, as in כִּלְיוֹן עֵינַיִם, denotes an unrequited longing.

17. וְאֹכַל פִּתִּי לְבַדִּי וְלֹא־אָכַל יָתוֹם מִמֶּנָּה — *Nor have my meal in solitude, so that the orphan might not eat of it.* If indeed Iyov acted so mercifully toward the orphan, it seems strange that, at verse 21 he finds it necessary to point out that he never struck the orphan, secure in the knowledge that the courts would not punish him.

18. כִּי מִנְּעוּרַי גְּדֵלַנִי כְאָב וּמִבֶּטֶן אִמִּי אַנְחֶנָּה — *For from my youth it has nurtured me as would a father, I have practiced it from the moment I left my mother's belly.* My instinctive rectitude has, like a father, guided me from birth (*Rashi*).

19-20. אִם־אֶרְאֶה אוֹבֵד מִבְּלִי לְבוּשׁ וְאֵין כְּסוּת לָאֶבְיוֹן — *If I would see one who is destitute without any clothes, a poor man without a garment.* אִם־לֹא בֵרְכוּנִי חֲלָצָו וּמִגֵּז כְּבָשַׂי יִתְחַמָּם — *Surely his loins would bless me, as he warms himself with the wool of my sheep.* In the earlier passage, the grateful reaction of the beneficiaries of Iyov's largess is not described.

21. אִם־הֲנִיפוֹתִי עַל־יָתוֹם יָדִי כִּי־אֶרְאֶה בַּשַּׁעַר עֶזְרָתִי — *If I raised my hand against an orphan, secure that I would be helped by the courts.* See commentary to verse 17.

22. כְּתֵפִי מִשִּׁכְמָה תִפּוֹל וְאֶזְרֹעִי מִקָּנָה תִשָּׁבֵר — *Let then my upper arm drop from the shoulder, my lower arm snap from its shaft.* The punishment is to be מִדָּה כְּנֶגֶד מִדָּה, *measure for measure.* If he lifted his arm against the orphan, that arm should fall off.

כָּתֵף and שְׁכֶם are used interchangeably in Scripture. Thus, for example, one carries upon the כָּתֵף (*Isaiah* 49:22), and also on the שְׁכֶם (*Genesis* 24:15). Nevertheless, since כָּתֵף is also used as a synonym for *end* (for example, *II Kings* 11:11) it seems likely that the word describes the *ends* of the shoulder. At *Bechoros* 9a we have the expression, שָׁמַט כְּתֵפֶיהָ, *his* כָּתֵף *was dislocated.* There, *Rashi* equates כָּתֵף with פֶּרֶק הַשֶּׁכֶם, *the joint of the* שֶׁכֶם. We have rendered *upper arm* to reflect the sense of the expression. The literal translation would be, *Let then my shoulder-joint drop from its shoulder.*

23. כִּי־פַחַד אֵלַי אֵיד אֵל וּמִשְּׂאֵתוֹ לֹא אוּכָל — *For I am terrified by the fate that God might bring against me, I am rendered paralyzed by His grandeur.* Perhaps there is a special punishment in store for those who abuse orphans. God, at *Psalms* 68:6, is described as the *father of orphans, the judge Who protects widows from abuse.* Iyov knows that had he indeed raised his hand against the orphan he would have to reckon with God's fury.

24. אִם־שַׂמְתִּי זָהָב כִּסְלִי וְלַכֶּתֶם אָמַרְתִּי מִבְטַחִי — *Did I place my trust in gold, or create a fortress with my wealth*? We have followed *Rashi* in the translation of this verse and the next. The sense is that Iyov never lorded it over the poor. He did not allow his riches to erect a barrier between them and him, nor did he ever make them feel bad at the great differences between their station and his.

[15] Did not He who formed me in the belly form him too? Was it not
One, Who laid our foundations in the womb? [16] Never did I withhold
their desires from the destitute, nor make the widow's eyes long
in vain. [17] Nor have my meal in solitude, so that the orphan might
not eat of it. [18] For from my youth it has nurtured me as would a
father, I have practiced it from the moment I left my mother's
belly. [19] If I would see one who is destitute without any clothes,
a poor man without a garment, [20] Surely his loins would bless me,
as he warms himself with the wool of my sheep. [21] If I raised my
hand against an orphan, secure that I would be helped by the courts.
[22] Let then my upper arm drop from the shoulder, my lower arm
snap from its shaft. [23] For I am terrified by the fate that God might
bring against me, I am rendered paralyzed by His grandeur. [24] Did
I place my trust in gold, or create a fortress with my wealth? [25] Did
I flaunt my joy at my abundant wealth, at the affluence which
my hand had wrought? [26] If, when I saw the sun bursting forth with
brightness, the moon its glory on the rise. [27] I permitted my inner
heart to be persuaded, only clapping my hand over my mouth.

Metzudos hews more closely to the literal meaning of the words: With all my wealth, I never made the mistake of putting my trust in my money. Never did my riches wean me away from my trust in God. This would be a fitting introduction to the next section in which Iyov asserts that he never allowed his heart to stray after idol-worship. The two ideas are closely linked. For a man who idolizes his possessions, the path to real idolatry is neither far nor difficult.

25. אִם־אֶשְׂמַח כִּי־רַב חֵילִי וְכִי־כַבִּיר מָצְאָה יָדִי — *Did I flaunt my joy at my abundant wealth, at the affluence which my hand had wrought.* Thus *Rashi.* אִם אֶשְׂמַח does not mean, *I was not happy,* but *I did not flaunt my joy in a way that would have upset the poor people.*

26. אִם־אֶרְאֶה אוֹר כִּי יָהֵל וְיָרֵחַ יָקָר הֹלֵךְ — *If, when I saw the sun bursting forth with brightness, the moon its glory on the rise.* In this passage, Iyov prides himself on never having followed the lure of idolatry. In the footnote to 1:1 we took this as one of the indications that it is likely that the Iyov saga is to be placed within a patriarchal framework. It seems unlikely that, once the Torah had been given, great merit would have attached to one who did not bow down before the heavenly bodies.

In such a context we can appreciate Iyov's pride in not allowing himself to be attracted to the idol-worship which proliferated all around him. If he had the inner strength to train himself not to see his wealth as a fortress, in itself no small feat, then it would have been natural to at least crave some tangible insurance against the dangers which, in the thought-world of the pagans, lurked in every corner. The idea that there is an all-able deity, one which can be seen and felt and which accordingly exists within a frame of reference which can be readily grasped, one which, since it has a physical reality can presumably be bribed or appeased, must have exerted a very powerful attraction.

That Iyov stood strong in an uncompromising monotheistic stance, is indeed worthy of recognition.

27. וַיִּפְתְּ בַּסֵּתֶר לִבִּי וַתִּשַּׁק יָדִי לְפִי — *I permitted my inner heart to be persuaded, only clapping my hand over my mouth. Rashi* is silent on the second phrase and we have followed *Metzudos.* Iyov asserts that not only his lips but also his heart was free from any taint of idol-worship. It could so well have been otherwise. It could have been that while he would be sure to *clap his hand over his mouth,* allowing no overt indication of an attraction to idol-worship to escape him, that nevertheless in his heart of hearts, he ascribed some validity to such an attractive theological system.

But Iyov knows, and proudly asserts, that he did not succumb. He can stand straight before his God, in the knowledge that he had ever remained loyal.

כח־כט גַּם־הוּא עָוֺן פְּלִילִי כִּי־כִחַשְׁתִּי לָאֵל מִמָּעַל׃ אִם־אֶשְׂמַח
ל בְּפִיד מְשַׂנְאִי וְהִתְעֹרַרְתִּי כִּי־מְצָאוֹ רָע׃ וְלֹא־נָתַתִּי
לא לַחֲטֹא חִכִּי לִשְׁאֹל בְּאָלָה נַפְשׁוֹ׃ אִם־לֹא אָמְרוּ מְתֵי
לב אָהֳלִי מִי־יִתֵּן מִבְּשָׂרוֹ לֹא נִשְׂבָּע׃ בַּחוּץ לֹא־יָלִין גֵּר
לג דְּלָתַי לָאֹרַח אֶפְתָּח׃ אִם־כִּסִּיתִי כְאָדָם פְּשָׁעָי לִטְמוֹן
לד בְּחֻבִּי עֲוֺנִי׃ כִּי אֶעֱרוֹץ | הָמוֹן רַבָּה וּבוּז־מִשְׁפָּחוֹת יְחִתֵּנִי
לה וָאֶדֹּם לֹא־אֵצֵא פָתַח׃ מִי יִתֶּן־לִי | שֹׁמֵעַ לִי הֶן־תָּוִי שַׁדַּי
לו יַעֲנֵנִי וְסֵפֶר כָּתַב אִישׁ רִיבִי׃ אִם־לֹא עַל־שִׁכְמִי אֶשָּׂאֶנּוּ

28. גַּם־הוּא עָוֺן פְּלִילִי כִּי־כִחַשְׁתִּי לָאֵל מִמָּעַל — *That too would have been a punishable crime, that I would have denied God, above.* Iyov recognizes that an attraction toward the heavenly bodies would have been tantamount to a denial of God. Now, idolatry in its most sophisticated form does not at all posit the non-existence of God. On the contrary, it is built upon the assumption that one pays the most ideal homage to the One God by doing obeisance to His creatures (see *Rambam, Avodah Zarah* chapter 1). Nevertheless, the absolute uniqueness of God is so clear to Iyov that he knows without any doubt that any compromising of that concept is in fact the equivalent of the peak of heresy.

The very purity of Iyov's beliefs explains the terrible frustrations which his sufferings imposed upon him. Had there been room in his religious thought for any entity other than God Himself, he would have been able to ascribe his fate to some other, malevolent power. His struggle with God might have been avoided. As it is, he knows absolutely that there is none at all beside Him. The God Whom he was able to love so much had, he thinks, somehow betrayed that love.

29. אִם־אֶשְׂמַח בְּפִיד מְשַׂנְאִי וְהִתְעֹרַרְתִּי כִּי־מְצָאוֹ רָע — *Did I ever rejoice at my enemy's downfall, make a move when evil times befell him?* For פִּיד see 30:24.

Rashi is silent to the second half of the verse. *Metzudos* explains: Even when evil times overtook my enemy and I might well have taken that opportunity to do him harm on the assumption that once a person begins to slip it is easy to push him further, I did not do so.

30. וְלֹא־נָתַתִּי לַחֲטֹא חִכִּי לִשְׁאֹל בְּאָלָה נַפְשׁוֹ — *I would not give my mouth free reign to make him sin, to trap his soul by means of an oath.* The translation follows *Metzudos*. When my enemy was in trouble I could easily have brought more problems upon him by calling in a debt which he owed me, and thereby trapping him into making a false oath. This, I never did.

31. אִם־לֹא אָמְרוּ מְתֵי אָהֳלִי מִי־יִתֵּן מִבְּשָׂרוֹ לֹא נִשְׂבָּע — *Have the men of my household not said, 'Who will give us of his flesh, that we might devour, never being satisfied!'* Iyov's servant's hated him. They resented the numerous guests, all needing attention, who were constantly present because of Iyov's determination that his house be open to all comers (next verse). They wished for nothing more than that they could destroy Iyov, consuming his very flesh, never even feeling satiated.

32. בַּחוּץ לֹא־יָלִין גֵּר דְּלָתַי לָאֹרַח אֶפְתָּח — *No stranger ever slept outside, my door was ever open to the guest.* Iyov built his house in a way that no poor man was ever impeded from entering. No porter's lodge or hidden entryway here. Doors were open to every side (*Rashi*).

33. אִם־כִּסִּיתִי כְאָדָם פְּשָׁעָי לִטְמוֹן בְּחֻבִּי עֲוֺנִי — *Did I with human frailty cover my sins, conceal my transgression in my hideaway?* This verse must be read together with the next. Had I indeed put on a false front, hiding my frailties from sight, it would be no more than justice that my true weakness should now be revealed by the terrors with which the most low-born can frighten me. But it was not so. I was always forthright, readily admitting my shortcomings. Why then should I now be afraid to leave my house?

34. כִּי אֶעֱרוֹץ הָמוֹן רַבָּה וּבוּז־מִשְׁפָּחוֹת יְחִתֵּנִי וָאֶדֹּם לֹא־אֵצֵא פָתַח — *So that I who was wont to subdue huge crowds, am now frightened by the most low-born, silenced so that I dare not go out the door.* The translation follows *Rashi* and *Metzudos*.

Ramban reads the verse as a continuation of Iyov's protestation of innocence: I never concealed my sins (previous verse) so that I never had any reason to fear that the multitudes might have discovered something about me that I had wished to hide. Nor had I ever done anything shameful to a family that I would have to fear their vengeance, afraid to show my face beyond my door.

28 That too would have been a punishable crime, that I would have
denied God, above. 29 Did I ever rejoice at my enemy's downfall,
make a move when evil times befell him? 30 I would not give my
mouth free reign to make him sin, to trap his soul by means of an
oath. 31 Have the men of my household not said, 'Who will give us
of his flesh, that we might devour, never being satisfied!' 32 No
stranger ever slept outside, my door was ever open to the guest.
33 Did I with human frailty cover my sins, conceal my transgres-
sion in my hideaway? 34 So that I who was wont to subdue huge
crowds, am now frightened by the most low-born, silenced so that
I dare not go out the door. 35 Who will grant that someone would
listen to me. Come, let my record be inscribed, let Shaddai answer
me. And let my opponent make a written record. 36 Would I then

R' Meyuchas takes עָרִץ in the sense, *to be subdued.* This verse is a direct continuation of the subject begun in the previous one. I never was interested in concealing my shortcomings, but would, on the contrary, willingly subdue and humble myself by admitting my guilt in front of the crowds. I would stand in awe before even the most lowly person, gladly owning up to any wrongdoing of which he might accuse me, so embarrassed that I would not go out to the door of my house.

35-37. These three verses appear to be the culmination of this, Iyov's second *mashal.* [See below for the explanation for the appearance of verses 38-40, seemingly out of place.] What do they say, and what is their significance in the structure of the book?

As *Rashi* takes them, they appear to be an outright bid for an ally in Iyov's fight for justice. If only someone were willing to listen and assist in recording his contentions, Iyov would show him every kind of honor, share with him the most intimate details of his life (verses 36 and 37).

A glance back at this long soliloquy will yield that it is precisely tailored to elicit just this result — that others should be moved to take up the cudgels for him. Chapters 29 and 30 provided a heart-rending contrast between Iyov's erstwhile life, a life lived with confidence born of the respect which his community paid him and the loving care which, in recompense, he lavished upon it; and the dreadful reality which now bounds his woeful hold on life. Our chapter then demonstrates, beyond the possibility of any cavils, that Iyov deserved none of this. There had been nothing mean, nothing ugly or petty in his life. He has every right to protest — and to inveigle others to join him in his battle for justice.

When we consider the central role which the three friends, or better, which the idea of friendship, have played in this book, the implications of our passage are absolutely crucial to the development of the Iyov saga. Iyov is looking for new friends! He needs friends who will understand, not condemn him, who will stand side by side with him advancing his just cause, rather than impeding and frustrating him with contrived and convoluted theologies which, he knows, have no bearing on his reality.

Eliphaz, Bildad and Tzophar have failed. Elihu will take their place.

This, indeed, appears to be the significance of this passage. It opens the way for Elihu to appear. Iyov had asked for an understanding friend — Elihu offers to fill that position. But — and here will lie the beginnings of Iyov's salvation — he will not be the friend whom Iyov had sought. He will not be uncritical, will not be supportive. He will, in fact, say much the same as the trio had said before him. But, he will show that true friendship does not have to be based upon slavish emulation. Sharp criticism, stated understandingly and lovingly, can be the fruit of the strongest love of all.

And that love will conquer Iyov. He will accept from Elihu what he rejected from the friends. That acceptance will, in turn, ready the way for the culminating experience of the saga. God Himself will appear to Iyov — and Iyov will at last find comfort.

35. מִי יִתֶּן־לִי שֹׁמֵעַ לִי הֶן־תָּוִי שַׁדַּי יַעֲנֵנִי וְסֵפֶר כָּתַב אִישׁ רִיבִי — *Who will grant that someone would listen to me. Come, let my record be inscribed, let Shaddai answer me. And let my opponent make a written record.* We have followed *Rashi's* second rendering, inasmuch as it obviates the necessity of having recourse to *aggadic* material for translating this verse.

תָּו is a *mark* (*Rashi* to *Ezekiel* 9:4, where those who were destined to die in the siege of

לא/לז־מ לז אֶעֶנְדֶנּוּ עֲטָרוֹת לִי: מִסְפַּר צְעָדַי אַגִּידֶנּוּ כְּמוֹ־נָגִיד
לח־לט אֲקָרְבֶנּוּ: אִם־עָלַי אַדְמָתִי תִזְעָק וְיַחַד תְּלָמֶיהָ יִבְכָּיוּן: אִם־
מ כֹּחָהּ אָכַלְתִּי בְלִי־כָסֶף וְנֶפֶשׁ בְּעָלֶיהָ הִפָּחְתִּי: תַּחַת חִטָּה
יֵצֵא חוֹחַ וְתַחַת־שְׂעֹרָה בָאְשָׁה תַּמּוּ דִּבְרֵי אִיּוֹב:
לב/א א וַיִּשְׁבְּתוּ שְׁלֹשֶׁת הָאֲנָשִׁים הָאֵלֶּה מֵעֲנוֹת אֶת־אִיּוֹב

Jerusalem were to have a *mark* placed on their forehead), derived from the root תִּוָה, *to outline* (*Rashi* to *I Samuel* 21:14). Hence: Iyov demands, 'Allow me and my impeccable record (אוֹתִי וְאֶת כִּשְׁרִי) to be inscribed!'

Iyov wishes that there were someone willing to join his fight, in the first place by recording in writing all that he is and all that he has done. In the second half of the verse he offers his opponent the same privilege. He too should write down that of which he accuses Iyov.

The contrast between the use of תָּוִי, and סֵפֶר כָּתַב ..., is striking. As we have seen, תָּו is first and foremost a mark that is placed upon the person himself. By using this expression to make the request that his contentions should be recorded in writing, Iyov appears to be saying: My righteousness is so much a part of me, defining my entire being (אוֹתִי), that my actions (כִּשְׁרִי) automatically flow from my nature. All this is so clear and obvious that it will imprint itself, as it were, upon a written record. I and the record of my innocence are essentially one. By contrast, my opponent will have to write a סֵפֶר, *written record*. That which he has to say are ideas which lie outside himself. He will write down dispassionately whatever he feels to be relevant. *Rashi's* first rendering: O that God would testify that which He Himself has *written* about me at the beginning of this book ... *For there is no one like him on earth, a man of unquestioning integrity coupled with a probing mind, who fears God and eschews evil* (1:8). Also Moses who wrote the Torah and also this book [based on *Bava Basra* 14b which ascribes the authorship of *Job* to Moses] let him come to testify for me.

Metzudos takes תָּו as short for תָּאו, *to desire*. Hence: *Who will help me gain that for which I crave — that Shaddai might answer me.*

36. אִם־לֹא עַל־שִׁכְמִי אֶשָּׂאֶנּוּ אֶעֶנְדֶנּוּ עֲטָרוֹת לִי — *Would I then not carry him upon my shoulders, bind it upon me as a crown.* We follow *Rashi*. Iyov would pay honor to the person who would help him write his brief by bearing him upon his shoulder, and would regard the brief itself as a crown wrapped about his head.

עָנַד, *to tie* or *bind* around the head.

37. מִסְפַּר צְעָדַי אַגִּידֶנּוּ כְּמוֹ־נָגִיד אֲקָרְבֶנּוּ — *I would tell him the very number of my steps, would draw him close, as one would a prince.* Where at 14:16 Iyov had resented the fact that God was *numbering* his footsteps, here, he would willingly grant that privilege to a friend who would truly care for him.

38-40. The position of this passage is remarkable. It is clearly a part of the litany of protestations of decency and innocence which have formed the bulk of this chapter. Surely then, it belongs together with them. By every criterion we would have expected it to precede verses 35-37.

Why does Iyov, after he has brought his soliloquy to its culmination, once more revert to an assertion of his blameless and conscientiously lived life?

Iyov, as an active participant, is about to leave the stage. Except for short reactions to God's speeches, he has nothing more to say (תַּמּוּ דִּבְרֵי אִיּוֹב). Clearly, he would wish his final words to encompass that which is most important to him.

By ending his speech on this note, Iyov is saying: There are many things about which I care a great deal. I would wish to be healthy, have a family, have friends, have a God Whom I can understand and with Whom I could commune in times of need. All these are important to me. But, most significant of all is my own integrity. If I can have nothing else at all, I wish, at least, to be able to assure myself and others that there is nothing in my history of which I need to feel ashamed.

Iyov leaves us as we originally found him — a *tam*, steadfastly true to the principles according to which he has lived his life.

38. אִם־עָלַי אַדְמָתִי תִזְעָק וְיַחַד תְּלָמֶיהָ יִבְכָּיוּן — *If my fields were to call out against me, if all the furrows, together, would weep. Metzudos* assumes that the next verse will be the explanation of this one: If my field were to testify against me that I had stolen it; if my furrows would accuse me of having withheld the wages of the laborers who plowed them.

Rashi: If my field were to cry out against me for having left my obligations to the poor unfulfilled. If it were to say that I had not left them the gleanings, the forgotten sheaves and the corner. If my furrows were to cry out be-

31/37-40 *not carry him upon my shoulders, bind it upon me as a crown.* [37] *I*
would tell him the very number of my steps, would draw him
close, as one would a prince. [38] *If my fields were to call out against*
me, if all the furrows, together, would weep. [39] *If I consumed its*
energy without payment, or disappointed the spirit of its owners.
[40] *Let thistles grow instead of wheat, and noxious weeds instead of*
barley. The words of Iyov have come to an end.

32/1 [1] *These three men then refrained from answering Iyov further,*

cause I had plowed them with an ox and an ass harnessed together to the plow, in contravention of the Torah's laws.

39. אִם־כֹּחָהּ אָכַלְתִּי בְלִי־כָסֶף וְנֶפֶשׁ בְּעָלֶיהָ הִפָּחְתִּי — *If I consumed its energy without payment, or disappointed the spirit of its owners.* The first part of our verse explains the second part of the earlier one: If I had not paid the workers who had toiled to make my field yield its bounty. The second part of our verse goes back onto the first part of the previous one: If I had taken the field from its owners without paying for it.

Rashi continues with the ideas he applied in the previous verse. The payment in the first phrase refers to the obligatory tithes that are to be given of the produce; the second, to the wages of the workers.

40. תַּחַת חִטָּה יֵצֵא חוֹחַ וְתַחַת־שְׂעֹרָה בָאְשָׁה תַּמּוּ דִּבְרֵי אִיּוֹב — *Let thistles grow instead of wheat, and noxious weeds instead of barley. The words of Iyov have come to an end.*

בָאְשָׁה from בְּאַשׁ, *to stench.*

Metzudos feels that the last phrase, *The words of Iyov have come to an end,* are also part of Iyov's speech. There is nothing more that Iyov can add to what he has already said. At this point he must rest his case.

XXXII.

◆§ Elihu's First Speech

The words of Iyov have come to an end (31:40). The debate is over, the protagonists are ready to leave. The furious passions, the unassuaged pain, the anger, the frustrations, the soaring eloquence, all are about to be lost in brooding silence. The mysteries of God's stewardship of human affairs have remained inviolate under the onslaught of the keenest intellects, the most sincere questings, the gropings for historical insights and theological verities. None have made a breach.

Then, unexpectedly, the young stranger Elihu appears and provides the light his seniors had been groping to find.

What are we to learn from the fact that the ultimate solution to the problems which earlier had seemed so intractable, is provided by a bystander who seems to appear out of nowhere, and who, once he has had his say, returns once more to the background?

Perhaps we are to learn that not for everyone, and not always, will the answer be given. Had Elihu not appeared, Iyov and the friends might well have been left unenlightened, at one with the untold millions who have had to live as best they could with the forces which seem to play havoc with man and his expectations.

Through Elihu, the book points a way. Enough that one Iyov found his Elihu, and through him, his way to God. Enough that one struggling questing human being found his travail rewarded. No poor sufferer will ever, after this, be entirely alone. Iyov, who so desperately needed comfort, has become the comforter for wretched, ignorant nonplused man. Somewhere, each of us may now feel, there is my Elihu. Somehow, in some form and at some level, I too may find my way to God.

1. וַיִּשְׁבְּתוּ שְׁלֹשֶׁת הָאֲנָשִׁים הָאֵלֶּה מֵעֲנוֹת אֶת־אִיּוֹב כִּי הוּא צַדִּיק בְּעֵינָיו — *These three men then refrained from answering Iyov further, for in his own eyes he was righteous.* The use of אֲנָשִׁים, the neutral *men,* instead of רֵעֵי אִיּוֹב, *Iyov's friends* (2:11), seems significant. Inasmuch as it echoes Elihu's perception of the friends, as spelled out in verse 5, we may surmise that the expression was chosen because the narrative now takes on the coloration of Elihu's perspective. Elihu has listened carefully to the debate, but has heard it as an outsider. He has held back his own ideas, not because he realizes that friends, able as they are to empathize in a way

ב כִּי הוּא צַדִּיק בְּעֵינָיו׃ וַיִּחַר אַף ׀ אֱלִיהוּא בֶן־
בַּרַכְאֵל הַבּוּזִי מִמִּשְׁפַּחַת רָם בְּאִיּוֹב חָרָה אַפּוֹ עַל־צַדְּקוֹ
ג נַפְשׁוֹ מֵאֱלֹהִים׃ וּבִשְׁלֹשֶׁת רֵעָיו חָרָה אַפּוֹ עַל אֲשֶׁר לֹא־
ד מָצְאוּ מַעֲנֶה וַיַּרְשִׁיעוּ אֶת־אִיּוֹב׃ וֶאֱלִיהוּ חִכָּה אֶת־אִיּוֹב
ה בִּדְבָרִים כִּי זְקֵנִים־הֵמָּה מִמֶּנּוּ לְיָמִים׃ וַיַּרְא אֱלִיהוּא כִּי
ו אֵין מַעֲנֶה בְּפִי שְׁלֹשֶׁת הָאֲנָשִׁים וַיִּחַר אַפּוֹ׃ וַיַּעַן ׀
אֱלִיהוּא בֶן־בַּרַכְאֵל הַבּוּזִי וַיֹּאמַר צָעִיר אֲנִי לְיָמִים
וְאַתֶּם יְשִׁישִׁים עַל־כֵּן זָחַלְתִּי וָאִירָא ׀ מֵחַוֺּת דֵּעִי אֶתְכֶם׃

no stranger ever could, might be better comforters, but because they were older, and presumably wiser, than he. He may not even have known who the debaters were, much less what their earlier relationship with Iyov had been. He saw them from the point of view of what they said, not what they were. Accordingly, to him they are simply *men*.

At 2:11-13 we suspected that one of the themes of the book might be to point to the pitfalls which lie in the path of friends who are would-be comforters. Occasionally, the disinterested bystander might be in a better position to choose the words which will resonate in the sufferer's soul. The use of אֲנָשִׁים here might tend to bear out this thesis.

The debate has reached an impasse. The friends are convinced that suffering can only come as a result of sin (*Ramban*), and they therefore cannot believe Iyov's assertions that he is guiltless. But Iyov, who knows no explanation for his terrible fate, but refuses to be dishonest with himself and His God, stoutly maintains that he has not sinned. Neither side can budge without compromising their theological stance. The debate would simply continue on without an end (*R' Yosef Kara* — אם כֵּן אֵין לְדָבָר סוֹף) and, accordingly, the friends disengage themselves from further argument.

2. וַיִּחַר אַף אֱלִיהוּא בֶן־בַּרַכְאֵל הַבּוּזִי מִמִּשְׁפַּחַת רָם בְּאִיּוֹב חָרָה אַפּוֹ עַל־צַדְּקוֹ נַפְשׁוֹ מֵאֱלֹהִים — *The anger of Elihu son of Barachel the Buzzite, from the Ram family, flared up. It flared up [against Iyov] because he considered himself to be more in the right than God*. *Ramban* explains why the family name is given. In the tradition of the Sages, *Ram* is Abraham. Thus Elihu came from a family thoroughly steeped in the tradition of faith in God, and the apprehension of His ways. For the man who, in *Ramban's* opinion — see below — has the right answer to Iyov's problems, no better introduction would be possible.

Ramban makes the point that Elihu would not have been angry at Iyov if he had simply maintained his own innocence. Nowhere does Elihu claim that Iyov was a sinner. He objected only to the fact that Iyov had claimed numerous times that God had, in his case, perverted justice. Elihu will assert that Iyov was innocent and that, nevertheless, God was not unjust in making him suffer How these two propositions can coexist is the problem with which *Ramban* grapples in his commentary to the Elihu chapters. See below.

3. וּבִשְׁלֹשֶׁת רֵעָיו חָרָה אַפּוֹ עַל אֲשֶׁר לֹא־מָצְאוּ מַעֲנֶה וַיַּרְשִׁיעוּ אֶת־אִיּוֹב — *And, against his three friends, his anger flared, because they were unable to find an appropriate answer, thus pronouncing Iyov wicked*. At this stage, Elihu thinks of them as *friends* of Iyov rather than as the *men* of verses 1 and 5. This is because Elihu sees the ties of friendship as being the cause of their failure to act as comforters.

The relationship between the phrases, עַל אֲשֶׁר לֹא־מָצְאוּ מַעֲנֶה and וַיַּרְשִׁיעוּ אֶת־אִיּוֹב lends itself to a number of different interpretations. *Ramban* (as implied both in his *D'rashah al Koheles*, and in *Toras HaAdam*) understands as follows: Because they found no way to react to Iyov's plaints other than to accuse him of evildoing. According to *Metzudos*: They caused Iyov to sin even more than he had done before because by begging off from further debate they made him believe that they had finally agreed with him.

In *Toras HaAdam*, *Ramban* adds an extremely significant dimension to the criticism of the friends. By focusing their theological theories too narrowly, they made it impossible for Iyov to accept them. This, as follows: They, who were not privy to the explanation which Elihu will ultimately give — see at 32:4 and onwards — could conceive of no manner in which God's justice might be defended other than to assume that suffering can only come as a result of sin, and that therefore Iyov must really be wicked. This left Iyov no room for maneuvering. He knew himself to be righteous and, as far as the friends' theology was

for in his own eyes he was righteous. 2 *The anger of Elihu son of*
Barachel the Buzzite, from the Ram family, flared up. It flared up
[against Iyov] because he considered himself to be more in the right
than God. 3 *And against his three friends, his anger flared, because*
they were unable to find an appropriate answer, thus pronouncing
Iyov wicked. 4 *Elihu bided his time to address Iyov, for they were*
older than he. 5 *Elihu noticed that the three men had no approp-*
riate answer, and so his anger flared. 6 *So Elihu son of Barachel*
the Buzzite declared, 'I am young in days and you are old. Because
of this I trembled and was afraid of declaring my ideas to you.

concerned, could view his suffering only as a proof that God, far from being just, acted with capriciousness and cruelty, or, perhaps, was not at all concerned with human fate. Had they, more modestly, said simply that God's ways are beyond our understanding — that we simply cannot know why He does what He does, but that we must submit and accept His will — then they would not have driven Iyov into a corner from which he could not hope to extricate himself. In a sense, it was they who created Iyov's problem.

Both *Rashi* and *Metzudos* bring a tradition of the Sages that our phrase is an example of תִּקּוּן סוֹפְרִים, that is, that Scripture substitutes a phrase in order to avoid an expression that would be disrespectful to God. The real meaning of the phrase is that by not arguing further they seemed to confirm Iyov's strictures against God. The object of the phrase would therefore have had to be *God*. In order to avoid a wording with such terrible connotations, *Iyov* was substituted for *God*.

4. וֶאֱלִיהוּ חִכָּה אֶת־אִיּוֹב בִּדְבָרִים כִּי זְקֵנִים־הֵמָּה מִמֶּנּוּ לְיָמִים — *Elihu bided his time to address Iyov, for they were older than he.* The translation follows *Metzudos*. Ever since Iyov began his complaints, Elihu had been aching to answer him. He had felt diffident about voicing his ideas; Iyov and the three friends were older than he. Now that they had all had their say, he felt free to say what was on his mind.

5. וַיַּרְא אֱלִיהוּא כִּי אֵין מַעֲנֶה בְּפִי שְׁלֹשֶׁת הָאֲנָשִׁים וַיִּחַר אַפּוֹ — *Elihu noticed that the three men had no appropriate answer, and so his anger flared.* This verse must be seen as a continuation of the previous one and an explanation of verse 3. Elihu had waited until Iyov finished his last speech. He was still able to anticipate that, perhaps, the friends would react in some way. When he *noticed* (our verse) that they had no intention of saying anything he became angry (v. 3).

6. וַיַּעַן אֱלִיהוּא בֶן־בַּרַכְאֵל הַבּוּזִי וַיֹּאמַר צָעִיר אֲנִי לְיָמִים וְאַתֶּם יְשִׁישִׁים עַל־כֵּן זָחַלְתִּי וָאִירָא מֵחַוֹּת דֵּעִי אֶתְכֶם — *So Elihu son of Barachel the Buzzite declared, 'I am young in days and you are old. Because of this I trembled and was afraid of declaring my ideas to you.* Do not think that I had nothing to say earlier, and formulated my ideas only on the basis of what you have said. From the very beginning I have had a clear outlook on the matters under discussion. It is only my youth which made me wait until you had finished (*Metzudos*).

Why, if the book of *Iyov* is a *mashal*, is Elihu projected as a young man who must keep silent until the oldsters have had their say? Why, indeed, does his appearance wait until the other three have finished? Why is he not introduced at the beginning of the book together with Eliphaz, Bildad and Tzophar?

On a purely technical level, *R' Zerachiah* suggests, these questions can be readily answered. Elihu is separated from the friends because, where they go down in ignominious defeat, he succeeds in the task which he sets himself. This difference can best be highlighted by having him appear only after they have left the stage. But, if he would have been their age, there would have been no logic in denying him a platform together with the others. Therefore, Elihu is presented as a younger man. This provides a ready and logical framework for the author of the *mashal* to leave him until the end.

Are there perhaps other reasons for Elihu's youth, more intrinsic to the message of the book?

In our discussion of the role which friendship plays in the Iyov saga (2:11-13) we noted a number of significant aspects to Elihu's intervention into the debate: In contrast to the other three he is not introduced as a friend, but appears to be simply a bystander who gets drawn into the discussion by his feelings of frustration with both Iyov and his opponents. After his initial remarks which are addressed

ז־ח אָמַרְתִּי יָמִים יְדַבֵּרוּ וְרֹב שָׁנִים יֹדִיעוּ חָכְמָה: אָכֵן רוּחַ־
ט הִיא בֶאֱנוֹשׁ וְנִשְׁמַת שַׁדַּי תְּבִינֵם: לֹא־רַבִּים יֶחְכָּמוּ וּזְקֵנִים
י יָבִינוּ מִשְׁפָּט: לָכֵן אָמַרְתִּי שִׁמְעָה־לִּי אֲחַוֶּה דֵעִי אַף־אָנִי:
יא הֵן הוֹחַלְתִּי לְדִבְרֵיכֶם אָזִין עַד־תְּבוּנֹתֵיכֶם עַד־תַּחְקְרוּן
יב מִלִּין: וְעָדֵיכֶם אֶתְבּוֹנָן וְהִנֵּה אֵין לְאִיּוֹב מוֹכִיחַ עוֹנֶה אֲמָרָיו
יג מִכֶּם: פֶּן־תֹּאמְרוּ מָצָאנוּ חָכְמָה אֵל יִדְּפֶנּוּ לֹא־אִישׁ:

to Iyov he casts his thought in the third person talking to wise men in general (34:2), but not to Iyov directly.

Both these factors may be combined in explaining the third, highly significant, hallmark of Elihu's presentation — that nowhere does he accuse Iyov of any wrongdoing. The book appears to present Elihu's views as disinterested, as opposed to the personal gritty relationship of exaggerated caring which is the byproduct of very close friendship. Where the friends focused upon Iyov the person as they attempted to pummel him into the thought-frame which they considered correct, with little concern for the suffering they were causing along the route of their determination, Elihu wants only to defend his and Iyov's God. He does not want to educate Iyov but to proclaim the truth. It is significant that, at the end of the book, when God criticizes the friends and declares Iyov justified, He makes no mention at all of Elihu. There is no need to mention him. His significance lies not in his person but in the truth which he conveys — a truth which will find its fruition in God's subsequent appearance.

With exquisite sensitivity Elihu moves Iyov away from the contemplation of his own predicament, to the larger truths which, if they are but given the chance, can inspire and elevate.

With this, he accomplishes two very significant results: Iyov, not bristling under attack, is willing to hear and to weigh, and finally to allow himself to be convinced. The silence with which he greets Elihu's words is eloquent testimony to the effectiveness of the speeches. But, even more significantly, by drawing Iyov out of his obsessive concern with his own predicament, he readies him for the overwhelming experience of God's revelation from out of the whirlwind.

This appears to be Elihu's role in the saga and, as we have delineated it, it is absolutely pivotal in bringing the story to its ringing climax.

Now, all this depends upon a distancing of Elihu from Iyov which makes his objectivity possible. This can best be accomplished by presenting him as someone with whom Iyov, the dignified, awe-inspiring magisterial figure whom we know from his own descriptions of his past, would have had no contact at all. And thus, sensitive, inspired wisdom, solidly based in family tradition, can accomplish what the friends, with all their good intentions, could not.

Earlier (Introductory Notes to chapter 4 and elsewhere) we saw from the *Zohar* that the friends failed not because they had nothing worthwhile to say, but because they had not taken the trouble to think through the best way of saying it. Elihu shows what can be done with the requisite degree of sensitivity.

7. אָמַרְתִּי יָמִים יְדַבֵּרוּ וְרֹב שָׁנִים יֹדִיעוּ חָכְמָה — *I had thought, "Let days have their say, let years dispense wisdom."* The friends had never demonstrated the slightest doubt about their own ability to understand and explain Iyov's predicament. It seems very possible that Elihu's diffidence about speaking his thoughts helped to endear him to Iyov and make his teachings more palatable.

8. אָכֵן רוּחַ־הִיא בֶאֱנוֹשׁ וְנִשְׁמַת שַׁדַּי תְּבִינֵם — *But truly it is a kind of prophecy in man, the breath of Shaddai inspires them with understanding.* Elihu had waited for the oldsters to end their debate, assuming that they, by virtue of their years, were the repository of true wisdom. Now that he sees that they have failed, he realizes that wisdom is not the property of years, but comes as a gift from God, to whomever — even a youngster — He wishes to grant it (*R' Yosef Kara*).

We have rendered *a kind of prophecy*, in order to accord with *Targum* who translates: רוּחַ נְבוּאֲתָא.

9. לֹא־רַבִּים יֶחְכָּמוּ וּזְקֵנִים יָבִינוּ מִשְׁפָּט — *Therefore there are not many who are truly wise, oldsters do not necessarily understand justice.* We have translated in accordance with *Metzudos*.

10. לָכֵן אָמַרְתִּי שִׁמְעָה־לִּי אֲחַוֶּה דֵעִי אַף־אָנִי — *Therefore I said, "Listen to me! I too will declare my ideas."* My youth is no impediment. But that alone does not give Elihu the right to be heard. In the next verses he will

*[7] I had thought, "Let days have their say, let years dispense
wisdom." [8] But truly it is a kind of prophecy in man, the breath of
Shaddai inspires them with understanding. [9] Therefore there are
not many who are truly wise, oldsters do not necessarily understand justice. [10] Therefore I said, "Listen to me! I too will declare
my ideas." [11] See I held off until you had spoken, listened carefully
to your wisdom, waited until you had thought through your words.
[12] I weighed your thoughts carefully, but see, Iyov has not found
one who might make things clear to him, one among you who can
answer his speeches. [13] Do not tell yourselves that you have
discovered the path of wisdom. God, not man, has smitten him!*

explain that he has earned the right to have his say.

11. הֵן הוֹחַלְתִּי לְדִבְרֵיכֶם אָזִין עַד־תְּבוּנֹתֵיכֶם עַד־תַּחְקְרוּן מִלִּין — *See I held off until you had spoken, listened carefully to your wisdom, waited until you had thought through your words.* I have listened to you carefully, have given you every chance to weigh your words so that they should have the maximum possible impact.

12. וְעָדֵיכֶם אֶתְבּוֹנָן וְהִנֵּה אֵין לְאִיּוֹב מוֹכִיחַ עוֹנֶה אֲמָרָיו מִכֶּם — *I weighed your thoughts carefully, but see, Iyov has not found one who might make things clear to him, one among you who can answer his speeches.* מוֹכִיחַ we have rendered, *One who might make things clear to him*, in accordance with *Rashi* to 6:26 who writes: Every appearance of תוֹכָחָה in the book of *Iyov* is to be understood as an act of *clarification*, a *correcting of wrong assumptions*.

Now, as the Elihu speeches unfold before us, we shall see that the difference between his thoughts and those of the friends appears to be minimal (save only as *Ramban* understands him — see below), a matter of form rather than of substance. But, and this is the only thing that matters, Elihu succeeds where the others failed. Even the best of ideas will clarify nothing at all if they are not couched in a form which will make them palatable to the listener.

Rashi to *Jeremiah* 2:19 teaches us that יָכַח can also mean to *admonish* (מוּסָר), and at *Psalms* 94:10 he renders, *chastise* (יִיַּסֵּר). Since these meanings share the root with the base-meaning, to *clarify*, we may say that they connote a very special kind of admonition and chastisement: One that leaves the person who is being admonished and chastised with a new understanding; which help him appreciate that if the experience of being punished was unpleasant, it was nevertheless justified and helpful in purging him of wrong.

It seems likely that these undertones are also present in Elihu's use of the term. With all the kindness that Elihu will bring to his task, he pulls no punches in severely admonishing Iyov where he deems this necessary. But, it will always be a carefully directed admonition, a precisely weighed chastisement, and withal it will so clearly be a part of an understanding sensitivity to Iyov's plight, that he will never be offended by it.

The administration of such admonishment is a difficult task. Elihu, in our verse, feels that none of the friends have lived up to it.

13. פֶּן־תֹּאמְרוּ מָצָאנוּ חָכְמָה אֵל יִדְּפֶנּוּ לֹא־אִישׁ — *Do not tell yourselves that you have discovered the path of wisdom. God, not man, has smitten him*! Here, as *Rashi* reads the verse, Elihu takes the friends to task for dropping out of the debate. He suspects that they have stopped arguing because they thought silence under these circumstances was the path of wisdom. Where nothing is to be gained there is no purpose in further talk. But, Elihu points out, that is not so simple. God's honor is at stake. By remaining silent the friends are implying that Iyov's strictures against Divine Providence are justified. That must not be allowed to happen.

The significance of the concern which Elihu voices in this matter should be understood as follows: As we study the Elihu speeches we shall see that he too, just as the friends, has much to criticize in Iyov. The difference lies in the focus of the criticism. Their's reaches back to before Iyov's calamities struck. Nothing of all this would have happened if you had not been sinful. Nowhere does Elihu make such allegations. However, he does object to Iyov's reaction to his problems. He cannot abide the self-righteousness and pugnacity which somehow questions the fairness of God's providence.

He now castigates the friends for their

לב/יד־כב יד־טו וְלֹא־עָרַךְ אֵלַי מִלִּין וּבְאִמְרֵיכֶם לֹא אֲשִׁיבֶנּוּ: חַתּוּ
טז לֹא־עָנוּ עוֹד הֶעְתִּיקוּ מֵהֶם מִלִּים: וְהוֹחַלְתִּי כִּי־לֹא
יז יְדַבֵּרוּ כִּי עָמְדוּ לֹא־עָנוּ עוֹד: אַעֲנֶה אַף־אֲנִי חֶלְקִי אֲחַוֶּה
יח־יט דֵעִי אַף־אָנִי: כִּי מָלֵתִי מִלִּים הֱצִיקַתְנִי רוּחַ בִּטְנִי: הִנֵּה
כ בִטְנִי כְּיַיִן לֹא־יִפָּתֵחַ כְּאֹבוֹת חֲדָשִׁים יִבָּקֵעַ: אֲדַבְּרָה
כא וְיִרְוַח־לִי אֶפְתַּח שְׂפָתַי וְאֶעֱנֶה: אַל־נָא אֶשָּׂא פְנֵי־
כב אִישׁ וְאֶל־אָדָם לֹא אֲכַנֶּה: כִּי לֹא יָדַעְתִּי אֲכַנֶּה כִּמְעַט
לג/א א יִשָּׂאֵנִי עֹשֵׂנִי: וְאוּלָם שְׁמַע־נָא אִיּוֹב מִלָּי וְכָל־דְּבָרַי

skewered values. You seem more intent upon finding fault in Iyov than in fighting for God's vindication. In your eyes the problem lies in the past. When you saw that nothing would move Iyov to admit prior guilt, you felt that your task was done. The truth is that God's integrity is under attack. Every effort must still be made to set Iyov straight on that score.

14. וְלֹא־עָרַךְ אֵלַי מִלִּין וּבְאִמְרֵיכֶם לֹא אֲשִׁיבֶנּוּ — *He did not address his speeches to me, I would not have answered him with your words.'* The translation follows *Rashi*. Elihu bemoans the fact that Iyov had not addressed his speeches to him. Had he done so he would have been able, as the friends were not, to set him straight.

Elihu's language seems to bear out the teaching of the *Zohar*, that the objection to the friends' handling of the situation was more one of form than of substance. Elihu distances himself from their method, not their thoughts.

15. חַתּוּ לֹא־עָנוּ עוֹד הֶעְתִּיקוּ מֵהֶם מִלִּים — *They were defeated, unable to debate further. Words were lost to them.* Elihu feels constrained to criticize the friends harshly — he would not have used their method (v. 14), because it had failed utterly to do the job. However, with exquisite sensitivity he does not address the friends directly, but changes to the third person — as though explaining to the bystanders his reason for making his own way.

16. וְהוֹחַלְתִּי כִּי־לֹא יְדַבֵּרוּ כִּי עָמְדוּ לֹא־עָנוּ עוֹד — *I waited in vain but they did not speak, they stopped and debated no further.* I did not jump to the conclusion that they were defeated quickly or carelessly. I gave them every chance to continue the verbal battle. But, I waited in vain.

17. אַעֲנֶה אַף־אֲנִי חֶלְקִי אֲחַוֶּה דֵעִי אַף־אָנִי — *I, too, am determined to give voice to my contribution, even I will declare my ideas.* Elihu is acutely aware of his deficiencies. But, coupled with a highly developed sense of modesty, there is also the confidence born of the justice of his cause. These two forces within him will interact, allowing him to argue forcefully while maintaining his sensitivity towards the people whom he feels called upon to criticize.

18. כִּי מָלֵתִי מִלִּים הֱצִיקַתְנִי רוּחַ בִּטְנִי — *For I am filled with words, the wind within my belly makes me feel constricted.* Perhaps it is Elihu's youth speaking here. Perhaps, too, it is his Abrahamic antecedents which leave him no peace. The truth must out!

19. הִנֵּה בִטְנִי כְּיַיִן לֹא־יִפָּתֵחַ כְּאֹבוֹת חֲדָשִׁים יִבָּקֵעַ — *See, my belly is like a barrel of wine that has not been opened, like new flagons, ready to split.* As long as the wine-barrel has not been opened, the wine retains its full strength — able to split the barrel open; so too my words (*Metzudos*).

20. אֲדַבְּרָה וְיִרְוַח־לִי אֶפְתַּח שְׂפָתַי וְאֶעֱנֶה — *I shall speak — I will feel relieved, I will open my lips so that I may respond.* The first half of the sentence continues the metaphors begun in the two earlier ones. For the second phrase, *Metzudos* explains: I need only open my lips, the words will come tumbling out of their own accord.

21. אַל־נָא אֶשָּׂא פְנֵי־אִישׁ וְאֶל־אָדָם לֹא אֲכַנֶּה — *I shall pander to no man, dissemble for no mere human.* When Elihu admonishes he will pull no punches. Only exaggerations and personal animus can hurt, but never the unvarnished truth. Elihu will have no need to dissemble.

כָּנָה has the meaning, *to call something by a name other than its own*. Thus, הַמְכַנֶּה ... שֵׁם לַחֲבֵרוֹ, *one who calls his friend by a nickname*. When someone chastises another, he may occasionally substitute a fictitious name for the real one in order not to cause embarrassment (*Metzudos*). The author of the book, himself, used such a method at verse 3 where he substituted *Iyov* for *God* (see commentary there). Elihu will have

32/14-22 [14] *He did not address his speeches to me, I would not have*
answered him with your words. [15] *They were defeated, unable to*
debate further. Words were lost to them. [16] *I waited in vain but*
they did not speak, they stopped and debated no further. [17] *I, too,*
am determined to give voice to my contribution, even I will declare
my ideas. [18] *For I am filled with words, the wind within my belly*
makes me feel constricted. [19] *See, my belly is like a barrel of wine*
that has not been opened, like new flagons, ready to split. [20] *I shall*
speak — I will feel relieved, I will open my lips so that I may
respond. [21] *I shall pander to no man, dissemble for no mere human.*
[22] *For I am not able to dissemble, it were likely that He Who made*
me would burn me up!'

33/1 [1] *However, Iyov, hear, I beg you, what I have to say, listen*

recourse to no such conduct (*Rashi*).

That Elihu at verse 15 had the sensitivity to switch to the third person, as we explained there, has no bearing on his determination to admonish without resorting to ambiguity. There, his meaning, and to whom his criticism was directed, was perfectly clear. To be clear one does not have to be unfeeling.

22. כִּי לֹא יָדַעְתִּי אֲכַנֶּה כִּמְעַט יִשָּׂאֵנִי עֹשֵׂנִי — *For I am not able to dissemble, it were likely that He Who made me would burn me up!* The translation follows *Metzudos*.

The rules are now laid down. Elihu has made very clear where he stands. He is modest but determined. He promises not to go over past mistakes — the approach which the friends had chosen has been thoroughly discredited (v. 14). He will be sensitive but honest. He represents neither Iyov nor the friends — he is on the side of God, determined to protect His honor (v. 13). He will be the admonisher whom Iyov has, up till now, missed so sorely.

XXXIII.

1. וְאוּלָם שְׁמַע־נָא אִיּוֹב מִלָּי וְכָל־דְּבָרַי הַאֲזִינָה — *However, Iyov, hear, I beg you, what I have to say, listen closely to all my words.* Elihu addresses Iyov directly by name, something which none of the friends has ever done. Moreover, he invites his attention in a non-threatening, non-belligerent way. שְׁמַע נָא, *hear, I beg you,* again a thoughtfulness which we cannot detect in a single one of the speeches which the friends had made.

Clearly, Elihu wants to set a tone which will make Iyov receptive to what he has to say. We feel the use of Iyov's name is particularly effective in this context. 'Iyov,' Elihu appears to be saying, 'you mean something as a person, not just as a theological problem which needs to be solved.' Elihu must have heard how Iyov had previously bemoaned his reduced state in a society which earlier had paid him all manner of respect. With exquisite sensitivity Elihu picks up Iyov's need to feel that in spite of his losses and his brokenness Elihu sees him as he had always been — a human being deserving of recognition and respect.

We, the readers, know more of what is in store in this speech than does Iyov. In the previous chapter we learned that Iyov had provoked Elihu's anger because, . . . *he considered himself to be more in the right than God.* Iyov does not yet know that this is to be Elihu's target, but surely realizes that Elihu feels strongly that he, Iyov, has erred badly in something. This, because in the previous chapter Elihu had complained bitterly that the friends had backed out of the argument too early. Evidently, then, the end of the debate, in Elihu's eyes, signaled only the defeat of the friends, not the victory of Iyov. However, Elihu has made clear in verse 14, *'He did not address his speeches to me, I would not have answered him with your words,'* that his intention is not simply to rehash what the friends have already said. Iyov, then, must now wonder what Elihu will have to say. What would Elihu find to criticize which the friends had not already reacted to? What home-truths would he be told by one who is determined to say the truth even though it may hurt, who refuses to dissemble on anyone's account?

In spite of all this tension, Iyov is willing to listen. Elihu has made a friendly beginning. Perhaps there is really something to learn!

ב־ג הַאֲזִינָה: הִנֵּה־נָא פָּתַחְתִּי פִי דִּבְּרָה לְשׁוֹנִי בְחִכִּי: יֹשֶׁר־
ד לִבִּי אֲמָרָי וְדַעַת שְׂפָתַי בָּרוּר מִלֵּלוּ: רוּחַ־אֵל עָשָׂתְנִי
ה וְנִשְׁמַת שַׁדַּי תְּחַיֵּנִי: אִם־תּוּכַל הֲשִׁיבֵנִי עֶרְכָה לְפָנַי
ו הִתְיַצָּבָה: הֵן־אֲנִי כְפִיךָ לָאֵל מֵחֹמֶר קֹרַצְתִּי גַם־
ז אָנִי: הִנֵּה אֵימָתִי לֹא תְבַעֲתֶךָּ וְאַכְפִּי עָלֶיךָ לֹא־יִכְבָּד:
ח־ט אַךְ אָמַרְתָּ בְאָזְנָי וְקוֹל מִלִּין אֶשְׁמָע: זַךְ אֲנִי בְּלִי
י פֶשַׁע חַף אָנֹכִי וְלֹא עָוֺן לִי: הֵן תְּנוּאוֹת עָלַי יִמְצָא
יא יַחְשְׁבֵנִי לְאוֹיֵב לוֹ: יָשֵׂם בַּסַּד רַגְלָי יִשְׁמֹר כָּל־אָרְחֹתָי:

2. הִנֵּה־נָא פָּתַחְתִּי פִי דִּבְּרָה לְשׁוֹנִי בְחִכִּי — *Hardly have I opened my mouth, but that my tongue speaks of its own upon my palate.* The translation follows *Metzudos.* Clearly, from the fact that the subject of the first phrase is *I,* while that of the second is *my tongue,* this verse does not follow the parallelism of the other verses in this speech. Accordingly, the sense is that the tongue speaks, as it were, of its own volition. Without my willing it, it forms words in interaction with the palate.

Given this rendering, we readily understand why, indeed, the structure of this verse lacks the stylized parallelism of the others. The structure is designed to accord with its content. Not only what Elihu says, but how he says it, conveys the idea of a torrent of words pouring out beyond his ability to control.

3. יֹשֶׁר־לִבִּי אֲמָרָי וְדַעַת שְׂפָתַי בָּרוּר מִלֵּלוּ — *My words are an expression of the sound convictions of my heart, my lips express unclouded knowledge.* Heart (לִבִּי) and mind (דַּעַת), feeling and intellect, are unanimous in their avowal of a loving, caring God. יְשָׁרוּת and בְּרִירוּת, *soundness of understanding* and *clarity of vision,* both contribute to the unashamed and unambiguous affirmation of Elihu's creed.

4. רוּחַ־אֵל עָשָׂתְנִי וְנִשְׁמַת שַׁדַּי תְּחַיֵּנִי — *The wind of God made me, the breath of Shaddai sustains me in life.* Just as you are, I, too, am only human, dependent upon God to keep me alive. Do not feel overwhelmed by me, I am no stronger than you *(Rashi, R' Yosef Kara* and *R' Meyuchas).*

Iyov had earlier expressed his fear that, even if God were to grant him a hearing, he would be too afraid to speak up — see particularly 9:14ff. Accordingly Elihu hastens to set his mind at rest. From me you have nothing to fear. If, indeed, you have something to say (next verse), there is no reason that you should feel inhibited.

Indeed, this insight may help us understand the structure of the book according to *Ramban,* whose understanding of Elihu's contribution we shall discuss below. We shall find that in *Ramban's* view, Elihu provides the one true answer to Iyov's questions, and that this answer is associated with the concept of *Gilgul HaNeshamos* (see introduction before verse 14 here). Now, why could this same answer not have been given by God Himself in His appearance from out of the whirlwind? Throughout, Iyov had constantly asked for a confrontation with God. What would have been more natural than for God to accede to his request and to reveal to him the truth which he had so tenaciously sought?[1]

The answer may well be that Iyov needed Elihu to prepare the way for God's appearance. Had God come to him while he was still angry and rebellious he might indeed have been overwhelmed with the terror inherent in such a confrontation. It was only after he had become reconciled to the truth which Elihu, softly with love and tact, taught him, that he was ready for the heady moment of absolute revelation.

Metzudos reads our verse as an explanation of why Elihu feels so involved. God has granted him life, and he therefore feels obligated to defend Him.

5. אִם־תּוּכַל הֲשִׁיבֵנִי עֶרְכָה לְפָנַי הִתְיַצָּבָה — *If you feel able — then answer me, marshal your arguments and stand up against me.* None of the friends had ever seriously suggested that Iyov might have anything to say in defense of his position. Their approach had been entirely judgmental and condemnatory.

The whole tenor of Elihu's speech suggests

1. This problem would not arise according to the alternative understanding of the function of Elihu's contribution as we have understood it. From that standpoint Elihu succeeds where the friends had failed, not because he reveals a profound truth to which they had not been privy, but because he was considerate where they were overbearing, kind and understanding where they had been capable of only stricture and condemnation. Clearly this role can be fulfilled only by a human.

closely to all my words. 2 *Hardly have I opened my mouth, but*
that my tongue speaks of its own upon my palate. 3 *My words*
are an expression of the sound convictions of my heart, my
lips express unclouded knowledge. 4 *The wind of God made*
me, the breath of Shaddai sustains me in life. 5 *If you feel able*
— then answer me, marshal your arguments and stand up against
me. 6 *See it is I who, as you requested, represent God, sculpted,*
as you have been, from clay. 7 *See, no fear of me need terrorize*
you, from my part, no imposition will weigh upon you. 8 *But,*
you spoke to my ears, I heard your prattle. 9 *I am blameless,*
without wanton sin, I am pure, no fault ought be ascribed to me.
10 *See, He seeks to find pretexts against me, considers me to be His*
enemy. 11 *Places my feet in the stocks, stalks my every path.*

that this is not a sarcastic put-down, but a serious offer. Iyov is to feel entirely free to marshal any argument he wishes. Elihu is human (previous and following verses), and as such, prone to error.

6. הֵן־אֲנִי כְפִיךָ לָאֵל מֵחֹמֶר קֹרַצְתִּי גַם־אָנִי — *See it is I who, as you requested, represent God, sculpted, as you have been, from clay.* See commentary to verse 4. On the one hand, Iyov had very much wanted to have a chance to lay his case before God. On the other hand, there was something in him which knew that in the unlikely case that he would be granted his wish, he would in all probability be so overwhelmed by the Divine Presence that he would at best become confused, at worst, admit to guilt which he did not feel. He realized that, after all, some human arbitrator, who would treat both sides equally and fairly, would in any case be best for him (9:33).

Elihu offers himself in this position.

7. הִנֵּה אֵימָתִי לֹא תְבַעֲתֶךָּ וְאַכְפִּי עָלֶיךָ לֹא־יִכְבָּד — *See, no fear of me need terrorize you, from my part, no imposition will weigh upon you. Ramban* suggests that אַכְפִּי is related to כָּפַף *to bend down.* Thus, that which causes another to bend down, *an imposition.*

Alternatively, *Ramban* suggests (as does *Radak* in *Sefer HaShorashim*) that the א in אַכְפִּי is extra, and that the word is to be read as כַּפִּי, *my hand.* At 13:21 Iyov had asked, כַּפְּךָ מֵעָלַי הַרְחַק וְאֵמָתְךָ אַל־תְּבַעֲתַנִּי, *Distance Your coercion [hand] from me, let fear of You not terrify me!* Elihu is reassuring Iyov — from me, you have nothing at all to fear.

8. אַךְ אָמַרְתָּ בְאָזְנָי וְקוֹל מִלִּין אֶשְׁמָע — *But, you spoke to my ears, I heard your prattle.* We have translated קוֹל מִלִּין as *prattle,* in accordance with *Metzudos.* What you say is simply *words* spoken without appropriate consideration.

9. זַךְ אֲנִי בְּלִי פָשַׁע חַף אָנֹכִי וְלֹא עָוֺן לִי — *I am blameless, without wanton sin, I am pure, no fault ought be ascribed to me.* This and the next two verses describe those of Iyov's ideas with which Elihu has a quarrel. At 32:2 we learned that Elihu's anger *flared up against Iyov because he considered himself to be more in the right than God.* Elihu will attempt to show that there is no justification for such an attitude.

10. הֵן תְּנוּאוֹת עָלַי יִמְצָא יַחְשְׁבֵנִי לְאוֹיֵב לוֹ — *See, He seeks to find pretexts against me, considers me to be His enemy. Rashi* here equates תְּנוּאָה [from נוא] with תּוֹאֲנָה, *pretext* [from אָנָה] (*Judges* 14:4). However, throughout Scripture *Rashi* takes תְּנוּאָה as הֲסָרָה, *removal* (see at *Numbers* 14:34 and 30:6). Accordingly, he would have been able to understand the word here as does *Radak* in *Sefer HaShorashim* s.v. נוא: *the breaking of matters and thoughts, and their frustration.* Thus, ... *He frustrates my intentions. Ramban* agrees with *Rashi's* rendering, and adduces 14:17 which he appears to translate: *You seek to make sins stick to me.*

The second phrase in our verse, that God considers Iyov as an enemy, together with the next verse, is a quote from verses 24 and 27 of Iyov's response to Tzophar's first speech, at chapter 13. See there in commentary to verse 27 for an analysis of the fact that from among all the harsh thoughts which Iyov has expressed, Elihu finds these words to be the most objectionable.

11. יָשֵׂם בַּסַּד רַגְלָי יִשְׁמֹר כָּל־אָרְחֹתָי — *Places my feet in the stocks, stalks my every path.* This verse is a verbatim quote from Iyov's speech at 13:27.

See commentary above at 32:2. Elihu objects to Iyov's accusations, although, since he nowhere alleges that Iyov was guilty of any earlier wrongdoing, he appears to agree with Iyov that he does not deserve his terrible fate.

יב־יג הֶן־זֹאת לֹא־צָדַקְתָּ אֶעֱנֶךָּ כִּי־יִרְבֶּה אֱלוֹהַּ מֵאֱנוֹשׁ: מַדּוּעַ
יד אֵלָיו רִיבוֹתָ כִּי כָל־דְּבָרָיו לֹא יַעֲנֶה: כִּי־בְאַחַת יְדַבֶּר־אֵל

It will be our task to understand how Elihu can maintain these two apparently contradictory propositions. If Iyov had not previously sinned, how can we reconcile what happened to him with the concept of a just God?

12. הֶן־זֹאת לֹא־צָדַקְתָּ אֶעֱנֶךָּ כִּי־יִרְבֶּה אֱלוֹהַּ מֵאֱנוֹשׁ — *Now, I must declare to you: In this you are not correct. For God is much greater than man.* I challenge you only in *this*! I do not accuse you as did the friends of having been wicked. I am willing to grant that you may have been a צַדִּיק גָּמוּר, *a totally righteous* man. But even if you were a צַדִּיק in the way you carried yourself, you are not a צַדִּיק [צָדַק, *to be correct*] in the claims which you are now making. God is infinitely greater than man and would never stoop to considering a human being as an enemy, and therefore having an interest in entrapping him (*Ramban*).

13. מַדּוּעַ אֵלָיו רִיבוֹתָ כִּי כָל־דְּבָרָיו לֹא יַעֲנֶה — *Why have you made a claim against Him because He does not answer all man's questions.* Iyov, at 13:23, had challenged God to accuse him of specific transgression: *Inform me of my iniquity and my transgression.* Evidently he expected to hear detailed charges. Elihu chides Iyov for the impropriety of such demands. God answers not according to your prescription, but in the way in which He chooses. This will be explained in the next verse (*Metzudos*).

Elihu has now come to the end of his criticism of Iyov. In preparation of his own contribution he has stressed that he is not accusing Iyov of any evil prior to the onset of his suffering. He has promised not to retread the paths which the friends had taken, but he has asserted God's greatness together with the necessary corollary of God's absolute justice. The duty now devolves upon him to solve the enigma.

With the next verse we enter into a new phase of the book. The mysteries of Iyov's travail are about to be unraveled.

Our goal throughout the commentary has been to present the story through the eyes of two commentators: *Rashi* is representative of the opinion that the book of *Iyov* is not, strictly speaking, the depiction of a theological debate concerning reward and punishment, good and evil, providence and happenstance and the like; but that rather it seeks to delve into the soul of the sufferer, to understand his roiling passions and furies, thereby the better to learn the skills of friendship, of empathy and sensitivity, and ultimately the consummate wisdom required of him who dares to offer comfort. *Ramban* represents the overwhelming majority of commentators who, each in his own way, see the book as a vehicle by means of which the author grapples with the thorny problems which are posed by the exigencies of real life in apparent collision with theoretical theological verities. The object of the book, as they see it, is to find answers, ultimately to know the elusive truth of life.

Up to this point, the difference in approach between the two commentators has caused only minor differences in interpretation. The thrust of this or another speech, the odd passage or sentence, even the occasional word, each of these has yielded to disparate insights growing out of disparate views of the purpose and direction of the book.

But, by and large, we have had more congruences than disparities.

As we now come to the substantive contribution which Elihu wishes to make to the solution of Iyov's predicament, a radical change sets in. *Ramban's* approach moves absolutely and irrevocably away from that of *Rashi.* In the hands of these two commentators, the book takes on completely divergent coloration.

And, indeed, it must be so. A book devoted to theological debate must, to be true to itself, eventually provide a solution to the conundrums which the protagonists raise. To do otherwise would be to throw the whole exercise into question. Why record a debate which centers upon matters of which, ultimately, we can have no understanding.

If, on the other hand, our book is person, rather than issue-centered, then the placing of a new solution into Elihu's mouth would defeat the very purpose of the presentation. The friends failed not because they knew too little but because they cared too little; Elihu wins Iyov's confidence because he understands deeply the turmoil which rages inside him — and tailors his thought accordingly. It is precisely because his solutions are not new, that Elihu has a significant role to play. He is to teach us that even a sufferer in the epic mode can find comfort, if only those who shoulder the responsibility of providing it will take the trouble to do it correctly.

And so, *Ramban,* given the system which he has chosen for interpreting the book, has no choice but to find a solution to its problems in Elihu's words.

[12] *Now, I must declare to you: In this you are not correct. For God is much greater than man.* [13] *Why have you made a claim against Him because He does not answer all man's questions.* [14] *For God will grant one communication, and even a second*

What is this solution concerning which *Ramban* writes: This explanation is true and beautiful; it leaves no possible room for anyone to have any questions (commentary to verse 30).

Before we provide the answer, we quote *Ramban* from his Introduction to the book: But, to tell the truth, this matter belongs among the deep mysteries of the Torah (סוֹד גָּדוֹל מִסּוֹדוֹת הַתּוֹרָה). Intellect could never discover it. Only one who has deserved such merit, one who studies with a teacher who carries a tradition reaching back to Moses at Sinai, who himself received it from God, [can know of it] — this is what Elihu has to say.

Ramban himself, in his commentary, is very cautious with words. We owe our limited understanding of the mysteries with which he deals to the exposition in the *Kad HaKemach* of *Rabbeinu Bachya*. It transpires that Elihu's contribution is the revelation of the *Sod Halbur* or *Gilgul HaNeshamos* (*Chavel*). As we shall see when we get to the individual verses, this doctrine asserts that people who lived less than perfect lives will, after death, be returned to this world in a different incarnation in which they may be subjected to suffering to atone for wrongs committed in their earlier life, even if in their present incarnation they are absolutely righteous. Clearly, this proposition eliminates any difficulty from the suffering of the righteous, as indeed also, from the well-being of the wicked. All can be explained on the basis of residual debts to be paid from an earlier existence.

The details of *Ramban's* ideas will become clear in the course of the commentary to the individual verses. After that we will consider his solution to the enigma of the book from the perspective of two issues which still require clarification. The first is that this proposition seems irrelevant to Iyov's own predicament. *Ramban* does not suggest, nor does it seem implied, that Elihu is explaining Iyov's own suffering on the basis of sins committed in an earlier incarnation. Indeed, that would contradict the prologue in which it is clearly stated that they resulted from the Satan's challenge (but see commentary to 34:2). How then does this have a bearing on Iyov's complaints? Surely we are not to conclude that Elihu was deceiving Iyov by revealing a mystery to him which, in the event, has no bearing on his case.

Secondly, and more profoundly, we need to examine the proposition that an open passage in Scripture cannot be explained except through recourse to mysteries of the Torah which are the purview of an initiated few, but can never talk to the multitudes.[1]

While it is well known that *Ramban*, in his commentary to the Torah, frequently offers explanations which he identifies as being עַל דֶּרֶךְ סוֹד, these are invariably suggested as alternatives to other possibilities of interpretation. This, indeed, is a manifestation of the multi-layered all-encompassing truth of the Torah which addresses us through פְּשָׁט, *textual meaning;* רֶמֶז, *hint;* דְּרוּשׁ, *homiletic interpretation;* and סוֹד, *hidden secret meaning.* But, nowhere do we find סוֹד encroaching into the realm of פְּשָׁט, effectively usurping its place. Is it possible that Elihu cannot be understood except in the context of סוֹד?

We shall return to these issues after we have learned the individual verses.

14. כִּי־בְאַחַת יְדַבֶּר־אֵל וּבִשְׁתַּיִם לֹא יְשׁוּרֶנָּה — *For God will grant one communication, and even a second one for him who will not see.* We have translated according to *Metzudos* on the assumption that *Rashi,* who is silent on this verse, would agree.

Ramban, in order to lead up to the answer which, in his view, settles all the issues once and for all, renders the verse in exactly the opposite way: *For God does answer in one, unambiguous way. There is no need for Him to demonstrate a second possibility.*

Metzudos takes שְׁתַּיִם as an alternative to אַחַת. For the person who will not listen to God's first communication, there is a second one in store. If you do not listen to the dream, you may yet listen to the pain. Suffering is a *second* form of communication.

Since *Rashi* is silent on this verse, we may suggest an alternative interpretation which, if it is

1. We note that in his Introduction to the book of *Iyov, Ramban* shows that many of the problems which troubled Iyov are also discussed in *Psalms* 73. In the course of his explication of that psalm he notes that it too, just as Elihu does here, offers the explanation of *Gilgul HaNeshamos.* But again, this is done only through a רֶמֶז, *hint,* in verse 20 there. Once more, we have the mystery of *Gilgul HaNeshamos* hidden from the multitude and made accessible only to the few who have the wisdom to pick up this veiled reference.)

טו וּבִשְׁתַּיִם לֹא יְשׁוּרֶנָּה: בַּחֲלוֹם ׀ חֶזְיוֹן לַיְלָה בִּנְפֹל תַּרְדֵּמָה
טז עַל־אֲנָשִׁים בִּתְנוּמוֹת עֲלֵי מִשְׁכָּב: אָז יִגְלֶה אֹזֶן אֲנָשִׁים
יז וּבְמֹסָרָם יַחְתֹּם: לְהָסִיר אָדָם מַעֲשֶׂה וְגֵוָה מִגֶּבֶר יְכַסֶּה:

true, can open up an entirely new perspective upon the role which Elihu plays in the saga, in particular, and upon the structure of the book, in general.

There is an alternative: שְׁתַּיִם does not relate to אַחַת as does a second method to a first, but as a two-pronged method relates to a single-faceted one. For him who cannot comprehend the dream as it comes to him unadorned, it needs to be accompanied by suffering. Then, even one who might be deaf to the dream-communication on its own, can, if he but wills it, begin to hear it plainly.

Elihu appears to be propounding an as yet untouched aspect of the educational function of suffering.

We must analyze this function and then see whether the words which Elihu uses will justify the assumption that this is, indeed, what he means.

We go to *Gra* in his comments to *Proverbs* 3:11-12: מוּסַר ה׳ בְּנִי אַל תִּמְאָס וְאַל תָּקֹץ בְּתוֹכַחְתּוֹ. כִּי אֶת אֲשֶׁר יֶאֱהַב ה׳ יוֹכִיחַ וּכְאָב אֶת בֵּן יִרְצֶה, *Do not, my son, disparage chastisement from* HASHEM *and do not feel repulsed by His admonition. For* HASHEM *admonishes those whom He loves, then shows good-will toward him as a father would do to a son. Gra* interprets the מוּסַר of the first verse as *suffering* and תּוֹכָחָה as *verbal admonition.* The sense of the verse seems to be that it is necessary to accept the suffering sent by God, so as to be able to accept His admonition. Thus: Do not disparage God's chastisement *so that* you will not feel repulsed by His admonition. The sense of the second verse would then be similar. God chastises only those whom He loves exceedingly and whose actions therefore matter to Him greatly. He wishes, as any father would, to shower His child with goodness. But He can do this only after the child is ready to listen, and this occasionally requires that he be chastised in order to break the natural rebellion within him.

It is instructive to quote *Gra* in his famous letter to his wife: Sometimes a person may sow upon stony ground, and that is the heart of stone into which nothing can enter. Then, the stone must be beaten so that it might be smashed into pieces. Therefore, I exhort you to hit our children if they refuse to listen to you . . .

At 32:12 Elihu bemoaned the fact that Iyov had not found a מוֹכִיחַ, and we rendered that word as, *one who might make things clear to him.* With *Gra* in mind (see also *Gra* to *Proverbs* 1:23) we might render: *One who would be able to make* מוּסַר, *that is, suffering, palatable to him.*

In verse 16 we have the expression, וּבְמֹסָרָם יַחְתֹּם. The use of חָתַם, *to seal,* in this connection is obscure. See below for various possibilities. In the context of our discussion, we would interpret the word as it stands within the connection between verses 15 and 16. Verse 15 had told how God will appear to man as he lies asleep on his bed with the purpose of communicating with him (v. 16a). The sense of the final phrase would then be that where the person is so self centered, his mind so blocked, that he is insensitive to these revelations, then God will *inhibit* (חתם) these self-indulgent forces within him, through the medium of pain. Through this, his *ear will be opened,* he will become sensitized to the communication which is taking place.

Now the contents of this communication may vary with the needs of the person who is being addressed. Certainly the principle which Elihu is enunciating is a general one, not limited to Iyov. In fact, in verses 17-18 the message is assumed to be one which might turn a person who had been wicked and had incurred death-guilt, away from his evil path, so that he might be saved.

But this is clearly not the case with Iyov himself. In his case the message would surely be a different one.

Is there a clue in the text which could teach us what it might be?

In the context of the Iyov saga, the solution lies at hand. The *dream* is the vision which in the end was granted Iyov, of God addressing him from out of the whirlwind.

Elihu has indeed broken new and exciting ground. Iyov has erred badly. Not, as the friends had claimed, in being a sinner who deserved the suffering to which he was subject, as Elihu never arrogates to himself the right to make such a judgment. But, he has erred in his reaction to the suffering. With his constant self-righteous carping at the perceived injustice of his fate, he has obstructed the purpose of his suffering. He has not learned the lesson which the passage from *Proverbs,* which we quoted above, seeks to teach. He has *disparaged* suffering, has been *repulsed,* by the admonition contained within it, and has consequently forgotten that suffering is first and foremost addressed to one whom God loves, so that he might yet merit the

one for him who will not see. [15] *In a dream, a vision of the night,*
when slumber envelops man, when he dozes upon the bed. [16] *Then*
does He make Himself heard by man, or shackle him with pain.
[17] *To immobilize man from action, to place pride beyond his reach.*

manifestation of God's *good-will.*

In the Introductory Remarks to verse 14 we made the point that, according to *Rashi,* we will not expect Elihu to provide Iyov with an answer to his problems. And this remains true. The ultimate answer is left to God — and what it is, we shall have to leave to an examination of the vision from out the whirlwind.

But, Elihu's immeasurable contribution is the lesson which he teaches Iyov concerning the correct reaction to the terrible fate which has overtaken him.

And Elihu has indeed taught well. The silence with which Iyov greets his words is ample proof that he was able to make his point. That God immediately afterwards appeared to Iyov, attests eloquently to the correctness of his thesis. Once Iyov allowed himself to inhibit his obsessive involvement with his own blamelessness (וּבְמֹסְרָם יַחְתֹּם) God did indeed appear to him (אָז יִגְלֶה אֹזֶן אֲנָשִׁים) and his problems were solved.

15. בַּחֲלוֹם חֶזְיוֹן לַיְלָה בִּנְפֹל תַּרְדֵּמָה עַל־אֲנָשִׁים בִּתְנוּמוֹת עֲלֵי מִשְׁכָּב — *In a dream, a vision of the night, when slumber envelops man, when he dozes upon the bed. Metzudos,* and perhaps *Rashi,* takes this verse as an introduction to the next verse in which we learn of the two methods by which God communicates with man. These are likely to take place at night while he is asleep. *Metzudos* notes that תַּרְדֵּמָה is a *heavy sleep,* while תְּנוּמָה is a light *dozing.*

Ramban notes that the answer which Elihu will offer has come to us through the medium of prophecy. This is the meaning of this verse and the next.

16. אָז יִגְלֶה אֹזֶן אֲנָשִׁים וּבְמֹסָרָם יַחְתֹּם — *Then does He make Himself heard by man, or shackle him with pain.* We have followed *Rashi* here. For the first part of the verse he writes: As God did to Avimelech as he dreamt during the night. Reference is to the story told in *Genesis* chapter 20, in which the Philistine king who had taken Sarah into his house thinking that she was Abraham's sister, was warned by God as to the true state of affairs and was thereby saved from sinning with another man's wife.

This is the first method by which God communicates with man.

The second is addressed in the latter half of the verse. If the person whom God attempted to help in his dream does not respond, God will yet try to help him by sending him suffering. His pains might pull him up short in his headlong rush to destruction. In this interpretation we can understand יַחְתֹּם in one of two ways. Either, as *Rashi* takes it: God will *tie him up* (חָתַם, *to seal,* hence to prevent movement), or as *Ramban* suggests: God will *seal* the decree which is issued against him.

The above exposition assumes that *Rashi* would understand this verse essentially as does *Metzudos.* Above, in the commentary to verse 14, we have suggested an alternative way in which *Rashi* might understand our verse.

The sense of the section would be to answer the plaint mentioned in verse 13. God does, in fact communicate with man in His own way. He chooses to do so through the medium of dreams and chastisement.

Ramban notes that the commentators have been unable to find Elihu producing any thoughts which had not already been suggested by the friends, excepting only this, that God will occasionally communicate with people in their dreams, or through chastisement, in order to prevent incipient sin. However, *Ramban* cannot accept this. This very idea had already been suggested by Eliphaz (5:19-26), and been rejected by Iyov for the very simple reason that chastisement can be educational only when administered in reasonable and bearable measure (6:11-12). Moreover, this theory will help not at all in regard to the problem of the well-being of the wicked, which had occupied such an important position in the second round of the debates.

The suggestions which we made in the commentary to verse 13 would, of course, obviate these questions. If the interpretation which we offered there is correct, then Elihu would in fact have broken very new ground.

Ramban, therefore, offers an alternative interpretation: This and the previous verse are to be taken together. They make the point that the truth which Elihu is about to reveal could be known only by means of prophecy. For the last part of the verse he suggests; The pangs which the recipient of the prophecy suffers bear the signature (חָתַם, *to seal*) of God himself. The truth derives directly from Him.

17. לְהָסִיר אָדָם מַעֲשֶׂה וְגֵוָה מִגֶּבֶר יְכַסֶּה — *To immobilize man from action, to place pride beyond his reach.* In the commentary to verse 13 we made the point that the description

יח־יט יַחְשֹׂךְ נַפְשׁוֹ מִנִּי־שָׁחַת וְחַיָּתוֹ מֵעֲבֹר בַּשָּׁלַח: וְהוּכַח
כ בְמַכְאוֹב עַל־מִשְׁכָּבוֹ °וריב עֲצָמָיו אֵתָן: וְזִהֲמַתּוּ °וְרוֹב ק׳
כא חַיָּתוֹ לָחֶם וְנַפְשׁוֹ מַאֲכַל תַּאֲוָה: יִכֶל בְּשָׂרוֹ מֵרֹאִי
כב °ושפי עַצְמֹתָיו לֹא רֻאוּ: וַתִּקְרַב לַשַּׁחַת נַפְשׁוֹ וְחַיָּתוֹ °וְשֻׁפּוּ ק׳
כג לַמְמִתִים: אִם־יֵשׁ עָלָיו ׀ מַלְאָךְ מֵלִיץ אֶחָד מִנִּי־אָלֶף
כד לְהַגִּיד לְאָדָם יָשְׁרוֹ: וַיְחֻנֶּנּוּ וַיֹּאמֶר פְּדָעֵהוּ מֵרֶדֶת שָׁחַת
כה מָצָאתִי כֹפֶר: רֻטֲפַשׁ בְּשָׂרוֹ מִנֹּעַר יָשׁוּב לִימֵי עֲלוּמָיו:

given in this verse and the next, of the message which the dream might seek to convey, does not refer to Iyov but to someone who had, because of his wickedness, incurred death-guilt. It is meant merely to demonstrate how revelation and chastisement can work in tandem. Indeed, the fact that Elihu chooses to illustrate the idea which he has enunciated by an example, rather than by addressing Iyov's particular and unique predicament, is itself a part of the extreme sensitivity which he has shown throughout his dealings with Iyov.

A man's pride, the dangerous quality which so often is the cause of sin, comes about from a sense of control, a feeling of power. There is nothing like the immobilizing paralysis of sickness to drain a person of his conceit and make him aware of his vulnerability and dependence. In this sense, sickness can open a person's ears to God's messages which will hold him back from the precipice of sin which, unless he turns back, will spell his doom.

In *Ramban's* view, we now learn what prophecy (the previous verses) has to say about the doctrine of *Gilgul HaNeshamos.* To do so he must translate crucial terms in this verse quite differently than does *Rashi.* Thus, while *Rashi* understands the phrase, אָדָם מַעֲשֶׂה, as though it were written אָדָם מִמַּעֲשֶׂה, that is, as we have rendered, ... *from action, Ramban* creates a construct term from the two terms: אָדָם מַעֲשֶׂה, *utilitarian man, the part of man that is only a tool.* The expression denotes the body which is only a tool for the soul, which is man's essential component. Thus, the phrase exactly parallels גֵּוָה, which is not to be taken as does *Rashi,* as *pride,* but as a shortened form of גְּוִיָּה, the *human body.*

The prophetic lesson teaches that the physical part of the person, his body, is transient and can easily be removed (לְהָסִיר), leaving the soul to function in another context, with a different body to serve it.

The groundwork for the doctrine of *Gilgul HaNeshamos* has thus been laid.

18. יַחְשֹׂךְ נַפְשׁוֹ מִנִּי־שָׁחַת וְחַיָּתוֹ מֵעֲבֹר בַּשָּׁלַח — *Thereby, He spares him the grave, his life, from being subject to the sword.* שָׁלַח connotes,*weapons.* Thus, in *Rashi's* view: The suffering to which God subjects man is for his own good. By preventing him from committing sins, by smashing his conceit (v. 17), God saves him from the grave, makes sure that his life will not be submitted to the sword of the Angel of Death.

Or, as we suggested in the commentary to verse 13, man is saved from the ugly fates described in our verse because his suffering alerts him to the communication which God vouchsafes him in his dreams. This message will guide him along the correct path, and he will be saved from the grave.

Ramban continues with the development of his own thesis. חָשַׂךְ does not denote a *withholding* which would imply that a given situation will never take place, but rather, that the condition will not be without end. God makes sure that the grave-experience of the soul, once it is freed from its body (v. 17), will not be without end. The time will come at which God will resurrect man from the grave (יַחְשֹׂךְ נַפְשׁוֹ מִנִּי שַׁחַת), to bring him back into this world. This, in order that he will not be subject to eternal perdition (וְחַיָּתוֹ מֵעֲבֹר בַּשָּׁלַח), but will be able to cleanse himself from former sins through the suffering which he is called upon to bear in his present incarnation (v. 19).

19. וְהוּכַח בְּמַכְאוֹב עַל־מִשְׁכָּבוֹ וְרוֹב עֲצָמָיו אֵתָן — *Pain admonishes him upon his bed, it attacks the many bones from which he derives his strength.* The thrust of verses 19-22 is the same according to *Rashi* and *Ramban.* They describe the terrible suffering to which the sinner is to be subjected. The difference lies only in the timing of these agonies. In *Rashi's* view, they occur as a person sins, and their purpose is to save him from his own wickedness. In *Ramban's* view, they occur in the second incarnation in order to atone for the shortcomings of the first.

The second phrase is difficult. We have translated it as does *Rashi. Ramban* suggests that אֵתָן is to be taken as describing מַכְאוֹב of

18 Thereby, He spares him the grave, his life, from being subject to
the sword. 19 Pain admonishes him upon his bed, it attacks the
many bones from which he derives his strength. 20 His being will
find all food loathsome, his soul the finest delicacies. 21 His flesh is
consumed to invisibility, his bones become dislocated to deformity.
22 His soul will approach the grave, his being, the killers. 23 If there
be even one defending angel among a thousand, to assert this
man's righteousness in his behalf. 24 Then He will grant him grace
and say, 'Deliver him from having to descend into the grave. I
have found cause to grant atonement!' 25 His flesh has revived
from its trembling, he is set to return to the days of his youth.

the earlier part of the verse. The many bones are attacked by strong (אֵתָן) pain.

20. וְזִהֲמַתּוּ חַיָּתוֹ לָחֶם וְנַפְשׁוֹ מַאֲכַל תַּאֲוָה — *His being will find all food loathsome, his soul the finest delicacies.* זָהַם, *to be foul* or *loathsome.* As part of his sickness, he will derive no pleasure from even the most delicious food.

21. יִכֶל בְּשָׂרוֹ מֵרֹאִי וְשֻׁפּוּ עַצְמֹתָיו לֹא רֻאוּ — *His flesh is consumed to invisibility, his bones become dislocated to deformity.* The translation follows *Rashi.* We have rendered לֹא רֻאוּ as *to deformity* to reflect *Rashi's* interpretation: *To the extent that they lose their appearance and form.*

22. וַתִּקְרַב לַשַּׁחַת נַפְשׁוֹ וְחַיָּתוֹ לַמְמִתִים — *His soul will approach the grave, his being, the killers.* His suffering will be so great that it will bring him to the very brink of the grave.

מְמִתִים, *the killers,* are the minions of the Angel of Death (*Metzudos*).

23. אִם־יֵשׁ עָלָיו מַלְאָךְ מֵלִיץ אֶחָד מִנִּי־אָלֶף לְהַגִּיד לְאָדָם יָשְׁרוֹ — *If there be even one defending angel among a thousand, to assert this man's righteousness in his behalf.* If, among a thousand accusing angels, there be but one who is willing to take up the cudgels for him (*Rashi*).

If there be but one angel who will testify to the fact that his suffering has brought him to repentance (*Ramban*).

24. וַיְחֻנֶּנּוּ וַיֹּאמֶר פְּדָעֵהוּ מֵרֶדֶת שַׁחַת מָצָאתִי כֹפֶר — *Then He will grant him grace and say, 'Deliver him from having to descend into the grave. I have found cause to grant atonement!'* פְּדָעֵהוּ is to be understood as though it were written פְּדָאֵהוּ, from פָּדָה, *to redeem.*

God will command the single angel who has taken up cudgels for the sick man, to redeem him from the hands of the thousands of minions which the Angel of Death has thrown into the field. The object here is to demonstrate God's merciful disposition: He will listen to a single advocate, although there are thousands of accusers (*Ramban*).

This will be the result of suffering borne as it should be — with the full knowledge that it is a gift from God to enable man to erase a past which would otherwise cling to him for all eternity.

Elihu has now reached the end of his explanation for the suffering which strikes the righteous. He now moves on to the next aspect of his presentation. Here again *Rashi* and *Ramban* will part ways.

25. רֻטֲפַשׁ בְּשָׂרוֹ מִנֹּעַר יָשׁוּב לִימֵי עֲלוּמָיו — *His flesh has revived from its trembling, he is set to return to the days of his youth.* As *Rashi* reads this passage it describes what, in an ideal state, would happen after God has communicated with recalcitrant man, by way of suffering. His ordeal past, he will return to a healthful vigorous youth.

In *Ramban's* view this verse goes back to verse 18. There we learned — as *Ramban* reads that verse, see above — that God makes sure that the grave-experience not be eternal, but that there will be a resurrection with a view to producing a reincarnation. The intervening verses have described the suffering to which the subject would be exposed in that second incarnation, so that he should be able to atone for the sins of his earlier life. Now the actual reincarnation is being described.

With different perspectives concerning the function of this verse, come different interpretations of the difficult expressions.

For רֻטֲפַשׁ, *Rashi* offers a French word which according to *Foreign Words in Rashi-Tanach, J. Greenberg, Jerusalem,* translates as [lit. *shaken, roused*] *revived.* נֹעַר also translates as *to shake,* hence the trembling caused by the sickness.

Ramban renders רֻטֲפַשׁ with צָמַח, *to sprout.* He also believes the word to be a contraction of two roots, רָטַב, *to be moist,* and פָּשָׁה, *to*

כו יֶעְתַּר אֶל־אֱלוֹהַּ ׀ וַיִּרְצֵהוּ וַיַּרְא פָּנָיו בִּתְרוּעָה וַיָּשֶׁב
כז לֶאֱנוֹשׁ צִדְקָתוֹ: יָשֹׁר ׀ עַל־אֲנָשִׁים וַיֹּאמֶר חָטָאתִי וְיָשָׁר
כח הֶעֱוֵיתִי וְלֹא־שָׁוָה לִי: פָּדָה °נפשי מֵעֲבֹר בַּשָּׁחַת °וחיתי °נַפְשׁוֹ ק׳
כט בָּאוֹר תִּרְאֶה: הֶן־כָּל־אֵלֶּה יִפְעַל־אֵל פַּעֲמַיִם שָׁלוֹשׁ °וְחַיָּתוֹ ק׳
ל עִם־גָּבֶר: לְהָשִׁיב נַפְשׁוֹ מִנִּי־שָׁחַת לֵאוֹר בְּאוֹר הַחַיִּים:

spread. Instead of the dry shriveled skin of the oldster who has died, a moist, plump flesh will once more cover the skeleton, מִנֹּעַר, beginning once more from childhood (נער, *to be young*).

26. יֶעְתַּר אֶל־אֱלוֹהַּ וַיִּרְצֵהוּ וַיַּרְא פָּנָיו בִּתְרוּעָה וַיָּשֶׁב לֶאֱנוֹשׁ צִדְקָתוֹ — *When he entreats God, thus eliciting His favor, appearing before Him in prayer, then will He recompense man according to his righteousness. Rashi* limits his commentary to pointing out that תְּרוּעָה is to be rendered, *prayer.* For the meaning of the verse as we assume *Rashi* would take it, we go to *Metzudos*: When the former invalid now turns to God in prayer to thank Him for having delivered him from his sickness, then God will recompense him for all his good deeds, without taking off any part of his reward for having saved him from his illness.

In *Ramban's* view, the *righteousness* for which the person will be recompensed is that which he has performed in his new incarnation. We recall that the subject of our passage is one who, in his present life, has been absolutely blameless, and is being made to suffer for sins committed in an earlier life. Once he has gracefully accepted his suffering, and demonstrated his penitence for earlier wrongdoings by approaching God in prayer, he will be able to receive the reward for his current righteousness.

27. יָשֹׁר עַל אֲנָשִׁים וַיֹּאמֶר חָטָאתִי וְיָשָׁר הֶעֱוֵיתִי וְלֹא־שָׁוָה לִי — *He will contemplate men and declare, 'I have sinned, I have made crooked that which was straight, but it benefited me not at all.'* We have translated according to *Ramban*, taking יָשֹׁר from שור, *to see. Ramban* writes: He will look upon men who had been in a similar position to his own, and who were lost. He will say, 'I too have sinned, but my sin has helped me not at all. It was not through it that I was saved, but it was my righteousness which stood me in good stead.'

שָׁוָה from שָׁוֶה, *to have worth,* as in *Proverbs* 8:11.

Yoma 87a teaches that if one has offended one's friend and attempted without success to appease him, he must try three separate times, in the presence of a row of three men, to win him over. He bases this upon our verse, taking יָשֹׁר as being related to שׁוּרָה, *a row.* Thus: *He shall place men into rows ...* This is the interpretation which *Rashi* offers. We have not used it in the translation, on the assumption that it is meant as a דְּרָשָׁה, rather than as the simple meaning of the word. See footnote to 28:4.

28. פָּדָה נַפְשׁוֹ מֵעֲבֹר בַּשָּׁחַת וְחַיָּתוֹ בָּאוֹר תִּרְאֶה — *He will have delivered his soul from passing through the grave, his being will behold light.* The confession contained in the previous verse will have had the desired effect: The former sinner will, because of it, have delivered his life from the grave, and will have ensured that he will yet bask in the light of eternal life (*Metzudos*).

In *Ramban's* view our verse describes the person who will have made full use of his reincarnation. If he has repented for his earlier evil, he will have saved himself from immediate death, and will have ensured that when, eventually, he will die, he will not have to go through another incarnation. Rather, he will be able to enjoy the eternal light which is the lot of the righteous after their death.

29. הֶן־כָּל־אֵלֶּה יִפְעַל־אֵל פַּעֲמַיִם שָׁלוֹשׁ עִם־גָּבֶר — *All this God will do for man, even two or three times.* If man is obdurate and continues to sin after the first warning, God will bring suffering upon him up to two or three times. Each of these times he will be brought to the very brink of death in the hope that the suffering will have some salutary effect upon him. If after all this he does not listen, he must be prepared to face perdition. There is a limit to the number of warnings which God is prepared to give him (*Rashi*).

According to *Ramban* we have here the number of times that God would resurrect a person in order to give him the opportunity to make up for the shortcomings of earlier existences. Occasionally it will be done only twice, sometimes, three times.

30. לְהָשִׁיב נַפְשׁוֹ מִנִּי־שָׁחַת לֵאוֹר בְּאוֹר הַחַיִּים — *To deflect his soul from the grave, to allow him to bask in life-giving light.* According to both *Rashi* and *Ramban*, the *life-giving light* could refer either to a joyous life in this world, or to the basking in the ultimate

[26] *When he entreats God, thus eliciting His favor, appearing before
Him in prayer, then will He recompense man according to his
righteousness.* [27] *He will contemplate men and declare, 'I have
sinned, I have made crooked that which was straight, but it
benefited me not at all.'* [28] *He will have delivered his soul from
passing through the grave, his being will behold light.* [29] *All
this God will do for man, even two or three times.* [30] *To deflect
his soul from the grave, to allow him to bask in life-giving light.*

eternal light of the World to Come.

With this verse, as *Ramban* sees it, Elihu comes to the end of his shattering revelation. In the course of a few sentences he has laid bare the mysteries of Divine Providence and done away with every one of the seemingly insurmountable difficulties which had so troubled Iyov.

◆§ The Glimpses of an Answer

We quote *Ramban* in his concluding remarks to this chapter:

> Clearly, Elihu has now solved the mystery of the suffering righteous, and from this base comes also the solution to the problem of the well-being of the wicked. The two can really be solved with the self-same assumptions. The reason why Elihu has concentrated on the one rather than the other is because the well-being of the wicked can always be ascribed to God's kindness, while the suffering of the righteous, had it been undeserved, would have constituted injustice. Now I have laid bare this matter. The verses and language of the passage all fit well into this theme and, in fact, indicate it clearly and precisely. The theory itself, too, is true and appealing. After these assumptions are accepted, no rational human can be left with any questions, and it is for this reason that Iyov kept silent and offered no rebuttal to Elihu.

Ramban appears to find it necessary to make the point that his proposition can be effortlessly read from the passage: *The verses and language of the passage all fit well into this theme and, in fact, indicate it clearly and precisely.* This posture seems to indicate that, while he feels that the text may well yield what he suggests, his ideas are, perhaps, not the only possible way of reading the passage.

This insight may help us solve the difficulties which we left unanswered in the Introductory Remarks to verse 14.

We wondered there about the relationship between פְּשַׁט, *p'shat* and סוֹד, *sode*. While we recognized that interpretations based on *sode* are frequently offered in tandem with those based upon *p'shat*, we asserted that we never find them as the sole legitimate explanation of any passage. Is it possible, we wondered, that a section in Scripture should be accessible only to those privy to the mysteries of *sode*?

If our reading of *Ramban's* words is correct, then, indeed, he does not maintain that the interpretation based upon the proposition of *Gilgul HaNeshamos* is the only possible one for our passage. We may well conclude that readers who know nothing of *Gilgul HaNeshamos* may nevertheless read and understand Elihu's speech without penetrating to the inner layer.

We suspect that if there is indeed such a legitimate option for understanding our passage, that reading would yield the one which we have recognized to be *Rashi's* interpretation.

We conclude that in *Ramban's* reading, the words which Elihu chose for his speech address us at two levels. At the surface level they have the meaning which *Rashi* attaches to them. At a sub-surface level they talk of *Gilgul HaNeshamos.*

But, we must ask, is this possible? *Ramban* had argued that the structure of the book requires that a solution to Iyov's problems be found. If we are correct in our assertion that the answer of *Gilgul HaNeshamos* exists only at the sub-surface level, then, at the level of פְּשַׁט, we are left without a solution. Is this acceptable from the point of view of the structure of the book?

We are forced to conclude that the bi-leveled structure of the answer is itself a part of the answer. Elihu was telling Iyov as follows: Human suffering can be explained at several levels — all of them true. At one level they can be interpreted as a means by which a person is being readied to be receptive to messages which God may be wishing to convey to him [*Rashi's* reading. In itself this is not a satisfying solution to Iyov's problems but, as we shall develop it in future passages, it will be the

לג/לא-לג לא-לב הַקְשֵׁב אִיּוֹב שְׁמַע־לִי הַחֲרֵשׁ וְאָנֹכִי אֲדַבֵּר: אִם־יֵשׁ־מִלִּין
לג הֲשִׁיבֵנִי דַּבֵּר כִּי־חָפַצְתִּי צַדְּקֶךָּ: אִם־אַיִן אַתָּה שְׁמַע־
לד/א-ב א-ב לִי הַחֲרֵשׁ וַאֲאַלֶּפְךָ חָכְמָה: וַיַּעַן אֱלִיהוּא וַיֹּאמַר:

opening by which Iyov will eventually make peace with his fate.] But, there is also a deeper truth, not accessible except to the initiated, and that is the proposition of *Gilgul HaNeshamos.*

We have now gained a new perspective upon Elihu's answer to Iyov as *Ramban* understands it. We should not understand Elihu as telling Iyov: The explanation of the suffering of the righteous is to be found in the proposition of *Gilgul HaNeshamos.* Rather, we should interpret his answer as follows: All suffering can be justified. Truth is not single-faceted but multi-faceted. There is an overt truth and there is a covert truth. You, Iyov, are not living in a world of judicial chaos, but in one in which, at every level of experience, God, in His benign stewardship, provides man with the experiences which are best for him.

With this realization in hand, we are now in a position to grapple with the other question which we had left unanswered. How is the mystery of *Gilgul HaNeshamos* relevant to Iyov, whose suffering had its cause in the challenge of the Satan rather than in sins committed in an earlier incarnation?

The answer is as follows: Elihu never maintains that he has understood Iyov's personal predicament. Rather he has attempted to paint the picture of a benign, rather than antagonistic, world in which everything has its explanation. Elihu does not know — indeed cannot know — the reason for Iyov's travail. What he does know is that what happens in this world is never the result of blind happenstance. Just as millions of people who suffer may know nothing of *Gilgul HaNeshamos* and thus not understand what is happening to them, so too must you, Iyov, realize that there are levels of truth to which even we who can grasp the awesome mysteries of *Gilgul HaNeshamos,* are not privy.

In the event, he was, of course, right. Iyov's suffering came about for excellent reasons which neither he nor Iyov himself ever knew.

31. הַקְשֵׁב אִיּוֹב שְׁמַע־לִי הַחֲרֵשׁ וְאָנֹכִי אֲדַבֵּר — *Be attentive Iyov and listen to me, keep silent so that I might speak.* Here Elihu lays the groundwork for his next speech. The implication of our verse is: See, I have already made much headway in removing some of the difficulties with which you have grappled. You have every reason to listen attentively to all the other things which I have to say (*Metzudos*).

32. אִם־יֵשׁ־מִלִּין הֲשִׁיבֵנִי דַּבֵּר כִּי־חָפַצְתִּי צַדְּקֶךָּ — *If you have something to say, then answer me. Speak up for I wish to justify you.* Before he goes on to his next speech, Elihu urges Iyov to consider well whether he has any rebuttals for that which Elihu has already said. He implies that he is more than willing to discuss any difficulties which Iyov might raise. He has no reason to lose patience with Iyov's arguments, since he is motivated by no other wish than to find Iyov blameless (*Metzudos*).

33. אִם־אַיִן אַתָּה שְׁמַע־לִי הַחֲרֵשׁ וַאֲאַלֶּפְךָ חָכְמָה — *If not, then do you listen to me, keep silent so that I may teach you wisdom.* This verse does not appear to add anything to verse 31. However, a careful reading does yield a development to the theme of that verse. There, Elihu had asked Iyov to keep silent so that, ... *I might speak.* Here he urges him to be quiet so that, ... *I may teach you wisdom.* The difference may have come about because of what was said in verse 32. There Elihu had urged Iyov to consider carefully whether there was any rebuttal that he might wish to offer. Once Iyov had indeed given the matter his careful consideration and realized that there were no difficulties which he could raise, he would be that much more convinced that Elihu's words were indeed the pearls of wisdom which Elihu claimed them to be.

XXXIV.

⤛ Elihu's Second Speech

Elihu, the consummately skillful comforter, now dares to risk the next stage in his education of Iyov. He manages to do that which has so frustratingly eluded the friends — to admonish Iyov sternly for that which he has done wrong.

Each time that the friends had attempted a similar approach, it had foundered upon Iyov's intractable insistence upon his innocence. Not once, not a single time, in all the myriads of words which have poured out from this tragic figure, will we find so much as a hint that perhaps

33/31-33 [31] *Be attentive Iyov and listen to me, keep silent so that I might*
speak. [32] *If you have something to say, then answer me. Speak up*
for I wish to justify you. [33] *If not, then do you listen to me, keep*
silent so that I may teach you wisdom.

34/1-2 [1] *Then Elihu proclaimed and said.* [2] *O wise men, hear my*

somehow, somewhere, he had erred. It was as though some invisible armor of righteousness, or, perhaps, self-righteousness, was able to deflect any and all criticisms. It is not so much that Iyov was able to marshal defenses against the accusations which the friends kept hurling at him, as that he did not seem even to hear them.

And now, all this has changed. Elihu is as forthright, as unbending and accusatory as any of the friends (with the exception of Eliphaz in his last speech) had ever been, and Iyov, by his silence, clearly accepts all that he has to say.

What is the secret which Elihu knows, and of which the friends appear to have been so painfully ignorant?

In the first place, the difference lies, of course, in the fact that Elihu's castigations hit the truth. Since he never once accuses Iyov of any wrongdoing prior to the onset of his illness, but criticizes only Iyov's reaction to the suffering, there is little that Iyov can object to. After all, Iyov himself was never sanguine about his denials of Divine justice. Again and again during his speeches we saw fierce denials in active and constant counterpoint with fervent and longing affirmations. We noted often that there was no theological consistency in Iyov's stance. Agony and frustration kept pulling him one way, while all the time he well knew that his heart was telling him the truth: There is a loving and caring God. Somehow, somewhere there must be a satisfying explanation for his predicament.

And so — Iyov is psychologically ready for Elihu's strictures. In a sense they reflect the promptings of his own conscience. Had Elihu indulged in overkill, had he wantonly made accusations not based on knowledge or facts, as the friends had done, simply in order to fit reality into some preconceived theological system, then surely even those parts of his argument which were justified would have been lost in Iyov's angry denials.

The wise and loving Elihu did not fall into this trap. Limiting himself skillfully to demonstrable faults, he found an accepting and contrite ear.

But there is more than this.

Never once does Elihu permit personal pique to dictate his words. To say that he presents his arguments calmly and dispassionately would be wrong. On the contrary. The absolute truth of what he has to say animates and inspires him to lyric hyperbole. He is full and bursting with the excitement of his message. But — his enthusiasm is not for himself as the bearer of the truth, but for God in Whose hands he sees himself as a passive tool. The messenger disappears. He, as it were, fuses not only with the message but also with Him Who sent him. It is his mouth which forms the words — but they are God's, not his (see at v. 33 and further at v. 36)

And so, with this speech another stone is added to the edifice of truth for which Elihu is laying the foundations, and which, in the end, will be crowned with the absolute clarity of God's own intervention.

While the general thrust of this speech, as delineated in the commentary to verse 2, is clear, the general structure presents many problems. In these Introductory Remarks we shall suggest a possible system which, if correct, will provide a logical and smooth flow to Elihu's words.

We postulate that three different audiences are addressed: The חֲכָמִים of verse 2 who are the wise men, from whose ranks Elihu originally came, who have gathered around Iyov and the friends to listen to the debate; the אַנְשֵׁי לֵבָב of verse 10, who are the understanding people among the general populace; and finally, Iyov himself as introduced at verse 16.

Elihu has something to say to each of these separately. At the end of the speech — see verses 33 and 34 — he groups them together so that they all might hear his final thoughts.

We break down the speech as follows:

In verses 2-9 Elihu addresses the wise men, explaining to them the danger of the philosophy which Iyov has propounded. This section culminates with verse 9: *Saying that man derives no*

ג שִׁמְעוּ חֲכָמִים מִלָּי וְיֹדְעִים הַאֲזִינוּ לִי: כִּי־אֹזֶן מִלִּין תִּבְחָן
ד וְחֵךְ יִטְעַם לֶאֱכֹל: מִשְׁפָּט נִבְחֲרָה־לָּנוּ נֵדְעָה בֵינֵינוּ מַה־
ה־ו טּוֹב: כִּי־אָמַר אִיּוֹב צָדַקְתִּי וְאֵל הֵסִיר מִשְׁפָּטִי: עַל־מִשְׁפָּטִי

benefit from living in consonance with God's wishes — the high, or low, point of Iyov's erroneous view of God and man.

From verse 10 to verse 15 Elihu then turns to men everywhere who may have been harmed by Iyov's negative approach to Divine Providence, and seeks to set them right. In these six verses he makes a general statement asserting that God is just and explaining why it is ridiculous to impute any unfairness to Him.

Elihu is not yet finished with this segment of his audience. He plans to paint a graphic picture of the inevitable punishment which lies in wait for the wicked. This will begin at verse 24 and continue till verse 32.

But first, he interrupts the flow of his words in order to exhort Iyov to pay attention to what he has to say. If he has any sense at all (v. 15) Iyov will realize that if he continues to display a belligerent attitude towards God's justice, he must give up all hope of any eventual cure (v. 16). Elihu takes the opportunity of having gained Iyov's attention by addressing him directly, to convince him of the essential justice of God. This continues up to verse 24, at which point he turns back once more to his previous audience.

At verse 33 he readies himself for the finale of his speech.

The commentary will refer back to this general introduction at the appropriate places.

2. שִׁמְעוּ חֲכָמִים מִלָּי וְיֹדְעִים הַאֲזִינוּ לִי — *O wise men, hear my words, and you who have knowledge, listen to me.* While in the first speech Elihu had addressed Iyov directly, in this, his second speech, he directs his words to the wise and understanding among the bystanders (see also at vs. 10, 16 and 34), talking, for the most part, about Iyov (vs. 5, 35 and 36), but not to him.

This observation throws new light upon the last verses in the previous chapter (vs. 31-33), *Be attentive Iyov and listen to me, keep silent so that I might speak. If you have something to say, then answer me. Speak up for I wish to justify you. If not, then do you listen to me, keep silent so that I may teach you wisdom.* Clearly, Elihu is exhorting Iyov to listen further to what he has to say but, as we now realize, not as the sole addressee but as part of a whole group of interested bystanders. [This, unless we assume that Elihu is already thinking ahead to chapter 35ff. in which he once more turns to Iyov directly.]

What are we to learn from this change of direction in Elihu's remarks?

For a correct understanding, we will need to analyze precisely what point Elihu is making in this speech.

In a survey which *Ramban* provides of Elihu's three speeches (at 33:11), he defines each of them as reacting to a particular misconception from which Iyov appears to suffer. The first speech addresses itself to Iyov's contention that God considers him as an enemy (v. 10), which we might paraphrase as a part of the general question of צַדִּיק וְרַע לוֹ, *the suffering of the righteous.* Elihu's answer to that was, as we saw above, the revelation of the doctrine of *Gilgul HaNeshamos.* The second speech, *Ramban* asserts, deals with Iyov's apparent denial of Divine Providence (see at v. 9), while the third takes up Iyov's argument that, inasmuch as God is neither served by our good deeds, nor harmed by our shortcomings, there is no reason for either reward or punishment, and that therefore we must assume that man's fate is the result of happenstance.

Now *Ramban,* in his commentary to our chapter, appears to see the main thrust of Elihu's contention to be the assertion that all suffering, including that of Iyov, comes as a result of sin (but see Introductory Remarks to 33:14, and also commentary to 33:30). This is to be Elihu's defense of the doctrine of Divine Providence, which he assumed was under attack by Iyov: Sins do not go unpunished; the righteous life brings appropriate rewards; suffering is never out of proportion to the crimes which brought it about. In Iyov's case, where no sins worthy of such punishment had been committed, the assumption is to be that atonement is required for shortcomings in an earlier incarnation.

Now, what is *Rashi* to make of all this? We have earlier pointed out (see at 32:13) that in contrast to the friends, Elihu never accuses Iyov of having sinned before calamity struck. His criticisms of Iyov center upon the latter's reaction to his troubles. But, is this not contradicted by this, Elihu's second speech? Do all those references adduced by *Ramban,* that suffering is the wages of sin, imply that Elihu

words, and you who have knowledge, listen to me. [3] *For the ear is*
able to discern the meaning of speech, just as the palate can savor
food. [4] *Let us choose to deliberate, let us decide among ourselves*
what is good. [5] *In that Iyov has claimed, 'I am in the right! God has*
failed to meet my claim to justification. [6] *Because of my unfulfilled*

is indeed accusing Iyov of prior sin?

The solution may lie in the fact, noted above, that it is the bystanders, not Iyov, to whom this speech is addressed. Had it been Elihu's intention to accuse Iyov of prior sin, we may assume that he would have talked to him directly, as he did when he apprised him, in the earlier speech, about the efficacy of suffering for opening man to Divine communication. That he does not do so, persuades us that the thrust of the speech is quite different.

Indeed, there would be no logic to ascribing Iyov's suffering to prior sin, since, in the earlier speech, Elihu had already offered a different explanation. Rather, Elihu is bent upon neutralizing damage which, he feels, Iyov had caused by his ill-considered reaction to his travail.

Clearly, Elihu postulates a just world in which, precisely as *Ramban* has noted, crime is followed by punishment and, as a corollary to this assumption, where there is suffering, there is a strong assumption of prior sin. *Rashi* differs from *Ramban* only in that the latter seems to argue that there is never any cause for suffering other than sin, while *Rashi*, as he read the previous speech, asserts that occasionally it might be used as a prelude to Divine communication. But this is the exception, not the rule. In Iyov's case, although Elihu does not know it, there is a third cause: the challenge of the Satan. Elihu's intention is not to explain every instance of suffering, but to argue that all that happens in our world, contrary to what we might think through superficial observation, has a good and sufficient reason.

Now Iyov, with his grumbling, may well have weakened people's belief in Divine Providence. By denying any grounds for his own troubles — justified by his own lights because he knew himself to be innocent of any real wrongdoing and had not been aware of the alternative explanation offered by Elihu in the previous speech, or indeed of any of the other possibilities — he may have convinced listeners that there was indeed no justice in the world.

Elihu is determined to correct this impression. His impassioned second speech is designed to educate the masses (see particularly at v. 36). To do so, he demonstrates the relationship of suffering to sin. Not because he believes this to be the explanation of Iyov's own troubles, but because that is indeed the norm, and the faith upon which the masses must base their religious equilibrium.

3. כִּי־אֹזֶן מִלִּין תִּבְחָן וְחֵךְ יִטְעַם לֶאֱכֹל — *For the ear is able to discern the meaning of speech, just as the palate can savor food.* In the next verse we shall see that Elihu will not be satisfied by winning an argument. He wants to shake his listeners out of their complacency, and have the courage to change their lives. For this he needs their careful concentration. Just as the trained palate can savor the subtle nuances of a wide variety of flavors, so too can the attentive ear pick up whole philosophies from words which may be simple in their meaning but explosive in their implications.

4. מִשְׁפָּט נִבְחֲרָה־לָּנוּ נֵדְעָה בֵינֵינוּ מַה־טּוֹב — *Let us choose to deliberate, let us decide among ourselves what is good.* For בָּחַר, *Ramban* suggests two possible alternatives. It could, as it is used elsewhere in Scripture, be a synonym for בָּחַן, *to examine*, or it could be taken as *Targum* does, as indicating *want*. We have tried to incorporate both meanings in our rendering.

The decision as to what is *good* carries responsibilities with it. We quote *Ramban*: Let us find out which is the *good* path and then take it, strong in the faith of God. (See commentary to verse above.)

As we have understood *Rashi's* approach to this chapter, we would take the verse as follows: Elihu is talking to all the interested bystanders, including Iyov in his capacity as a wise and understanding person, and exhorting them to take steps to counteract damage to the community which Iyov's complaining may have done: Let us, all of us together, become clear in our own minds concerning what is right and what is wrong, in order to be able to bring about necessary corrections. See further, below.

5. כִּי־אָמַר אִיּוֹב צָדַקְתִּי וְאֵל הֵסִיר מִשְׁפָּטִי — *In that Iyov has claimed, 'I am in the right! God has failed to meet my claim to justification.* We have rendered in accordance with *Rashi* who understands מִשְׁפָּטִי as הוֹכָחַת דְּבָרִים, a *presenting of proof or justification. Metzudos* would render: *God has denied me my due.*

ז אֲכַזֵּב אָנוּשׁ חִצִּי בְלִי־פָשַׁע: מִי־גֶבֶר כְּאִיּוֹב יִשְׁתֶּה־לַּעַג
ח כַּמָּיִם: וְאָרַח לְחֶבְרָה עִם־פֹּעֲלֵי אָוֶן וְלָלֶכֶת עִם־אַנְשֵׁי־
ט־י רֶשַׁע: כִּי־אָמַר לֹא יִסְכָּן־גָּבֶר בִּרְצֹתוֹ עִם־אֱלֹהִים: לָכֵן ׀
יא אַנְשֵׁי לֵבָב שִׁמְעוּ לִי חָלִלָה לָאֵל מֵרֶשַׁע וְשַׁדַּי מֵעָוֶל: כִּי
יב פֹעַל אָדָם יְשַׁלֶּם־לוֹ וּכְאֹרַח אִישׁ יַמְצִאֶנּוּ: אַף־אָמְנָם
יג אֵל לֹא־יַרְשִׁיעַ וְשַׁדַּי לֹא־יְעַוֵּת מִשְׁפָּט: מִי־פָקַד עָלָיו
יד אַרְצָה וּמִי שָׂם תֵּבֵל כֻּלָּהּ: אִם־יָשִׂים אֵלָיו לִבּוֹ רוּחוֹ
טו וְנִשְׁמָתוֹ אֵלָיו יֶאֱסֹף: יִגְוַע כָּל־בָּשָׂר יָחַד וְאָדָם עַל־
טז עָפָר יָשׁוּב: וְאִם־בִּינָה שִׁמְעָה־זֹּאת הַאֲזִינָה לְקוֹל מִלָּי:
יז הַאַף שׂוֹנֵא מִשְׁפָּט יַחֲבוֹשׁ וְאִם־צַדִּיק כַּבִּיר תַּרְשִׁיעַ:

6. עַל־מִשְׁפָּטִי אֲכַזֵּב אָנוּשׁ חִצִּי בְלִי־פָשַׁע — *Because of my unfulfilled claim, I declare a miscarriage of justice, I am gravely ill from my wounds, on account of no guilt.'* We once more follow *Rashi* who renders this verse in consonance with his understanding of the previous one. *Metzudos* takes אֲכַזֵּב, from כָּזַב, *to be interrupted,* and understands the sentence as follows: *Apart from my due which has been withheld from me, I also suffer from my wound without any guilt.* The sense is: Not only are my rights withheld, I am even punished without any justification.

Ramban takes כָּזַב as *to disappoint.* Thus: I am disappointed at the justice that has been dealt to me.

7. מִי־גֶבֶר כְּאִיּוֹב יִשְׁתֶּה־לַּעַג כַּמָּיִם — *Where is there another man to be found like Iyov, drinking cynicism like so much water.* We have translated according to *Metzudos. Ramban* takes לַעַג, not as the cynicism which Iyov displays toward values which ought to be treated with respect, but as the disdain with which right-thinking people would look upon the theories which Iyov is propounding.

8. וְאָרַח לְחֶבְרָה עִם־פֹּעֲלֵי אָוֶן וְלָלֶכֶת עִם־אַנְשֵׁי־רֶשַׁע — *Who treads a path that leads to common cause with perpetrators of sin, to walking with men permeated by evil. Ramban* reads this verse together with the previous one: Iyov's words deserve derision because, in his old age, he is treading a path which leads to common cause with sinners who deny God and His justice.

9. כִּי־אָמַר לֹא יִסְכָּן־גָּבֶר בִּרְצֹתוֹ עִם־אֱלֹהִים — *Who says that man derives no benefit from living in consonance with God's wishes.* In his commentary to 33:11, *Ramban* identifies this verse as being central to Elihu's second speech. He accuses Iyov of undermining belief in הַשְׁגָּחָה, the doctrine of *Divine Providence.* For, as *Ramban* explains our verse, if Iyov's suffering has overtaken him through no fault or shortcoming of his own (v. 6), then it necessarily follows that good deeds, too, will remain unrewarded. If what Iyov says is true, then indeed God has no interest in either man's goodness or his misdeeds.

10. לָכֵן אַנְשֵׁי לֵבָב שִׁמְעוּ לִי חָלִלָה לָאֵל מֵרֶשַׁע וְשַׁדַּי מֵעָוֶל — *Therefore understanding men, listen to me! It is sacrilegious to ascribe injustice to the Almighty, iniquity to Shaddai.* Having explained his worries to the wise men who surrounded the debaters, Elihu now turns to the multitudes whom he feels called upon to protect from Iyov's pernicious views concerning Divine Providence. See Introductory Remarks.

We have rendered אַנְשֵׁי לֵבָב as *understanding men,* in accordance with *Ramban* and *Metzudos.* In particular, *Ramban* makes the point that the distancing of any iniquity from God is a matter of logic. Anyone with a sound mind would be able to grasp this. If our perception of *Rashi's* approach, that Elihu's concern is that people in general should not be weakened in their belief in Divine Providence, is correct, then perhaps the term should be rendered, *men of conscience,* or *men of courage,* men who are concerned with society's well-being.

Metzudos believes that רֶשַׁע describes the withholding of earned merit, while עָוֶל would be the exposing of the righteous to suffering, and of allowing the wicked to prosper.

Ramban includes the thought that if God were not interested in man at all, and left his fate to happenstance, that too would be considered *iniquity.* Elihu, then, postulates a world in which absolute justice reigns.

11. כִּי פֹעַל אָדָם יְשַׁלֶּם־לוֹ וּכְאֹרַח אִישׁ יַמְצִאֶנּוּ — *For, He recompenses man in accordance with*

claim, I declare a miscarriage of justice, I am gravely ill from my wounds, on account of no guilt. [7] *Where is there another man to be found like Iyov, drinking cynicism like so much water.* [8] *Who treads a path that leads to common cause with perpetrators of sin to walking with men permeated by evil.* [9] *Who says that man derives no benefit from living in consonance with God's wishes.* [10] *Therefore understanding men, listen to me! It is sacrilegious to ascribe injustice to the Almighty, iniquity to Shaddai.* [11] *For, He recompenses man in accordance with his deeds, will expose him to experiences which accord with the path which he has followed.* [12] *Certainly, God will do nothing wicked, Shaddai will not pervert justice.* [13] *Who ordered His involvement with the earth, who established the entire world?* [14] *If it were in His heart to harm him, then He could gather to Himself his spirit and soul which He had placed into him.* [15] *All flesh would perish together, humanity would return to the dust.* [16] *If you wish to understand, hear this. Listen to what I have to say.* [17] *Can it be expected that He would heal one who hates justice? Would you undertake to declare the Most Righteous at fault?*

his deeds, will expose him to experiences which accord with the path which he has followed. As we have noted above, *Ramban* views this statement as absolute: Suffering is invariably the result of sin. *Rashi*, as we have understood him, would take a softer approach: God administers our world with justice. In most cases suffering will be the wages of sin, though occasionally, there may be other purposes at work.

12. אַף־אָמְנָם אֵל לֹא־יַרְשִׁיעַ וְשַׁדַּי לֹא־יְעַוֵּת מִשְׁפָּט — *Certainly, God will do nothing wicked, Shaddai will not pervert justice. Metzudos* maintains that the verse is to be understood as though it read, . . . אַף כִּי אָמְנָם, a formulation which introduces an *a fortiori* argument: Most certainly God would not make the righteous suffer, if He even invariably makes sure that they receive their just rewards.

13. מִי־פָקַד עָלָיו אָרְצָה וּמִי שָׂם תֵּבֵל כֻּלָּהּ — *Who ordered His involvement with the earth, who established the entire world*? God need give an accounting to no one. There is none who ordered His involvement with humankind, or who, indeed, had a hand in creating the world. Under such circumstances, what possible reason could there be for God to deal with man in any but the most just manner? (*Rashi*).

14. אִם־יָשִׂים אֵלָיו לִבּוֹ רוּחוֹ וְנִשְׁמָתוֹ אֵלָיו יֶאֱסֹף — *If it were in His heart to harm him, then He could gather to Himself his spirit and soul which He had placed into him.* We have followed *Rashi.* The spirit and soul within each man comes to him from God. They therefore belong to God and He can withdraw them whenever He wishes. He has no need to exercise caprice in making man suffer.

15. יִגְוַע כָּל־בָּשָׂר יָחַד וְאָדָם עַל־עָפָר יָשׁוּב — *All flesh would perish together, humanity would return to the dust.* The verse continues from the previous one. As readily as God might choose to cause the death of a single person, He could elect to have all flesh perish. There is nothing and no one to stop Him (*Rashi*).

16. וְאִם־בִּינָה שִׁמְעָה־זֹּאת הַאֲזִינָה לְקוֹל מִלָּי — *If you wish to understand, hear this. Listen to what I have to say.* שִׁמְעָה is in the singular. At this point Elihu turns to Iyov himself, attempting to save him from his own indifference (see Introductory Remarks).

17. הַאַף שׂוֹנֵא מִשְׁפָּט יַחֲבוֹשׁ וְאִם־צַדִּיק כַּבִּיר תַּרְשִׁיעַ — *Can it be expected that He would heal one who hates justice? Would you undertake to declare the Most Righteous at fault*? We have followed *Rashi* who takes חָבַשׁ as *to bind*, as in binding up a wound. Hence, *to heal*. The sense of the verse is as follows: There are only two alternatives: Either you deserve to suffer, in which case your unreasonable and inexcusable rebellion eliminates any chance that God would wish to heal you. Or, you must claim that your suffering is undeserved. In that case you are accusing the Most Righteous [כַּבִּיר is a synonym for מְאֹד, *very* (*Rashi*)] of having missed the mark. Clearly this is unacceptable.

יח־יט הַאֲמֹר לְמֶלֶךְ בְּלִיָּעַל רָשָׁע אֶל־נְדִיבִים: אֲשֶׁר לֹא־נָשָׂא ׀
פְּנֵי שָׂרִים וְלֹא נִכַּר־שׁוֹעַ לִפְנֵי־דָל כִּי־מַעֲשֵׂה יָדָיו כֻּלָּם:
כ רֶגַע ׀ יָמֻתוּ וַחֲצוֹת לָיְלָה יְגֹעֲשׁוּ עָם וְיַעֲבֹרוּ וְיָסִירוּ אַבִּיר
כא־כב לֹא בְיָד: כִּי־עֵינָיו עַל־דַּרְכֵי־אִישׁ וְכָל־צְעָדָיו יִרְאֶה: אֵין־
כג חֹשֶׁךְ וְאֵין צַלְמָוֶת לְהִסָּתֶר שָׁם פֹּעֲלֵי אָוֶן: כִּי לֹא עַל־
כד אִישׁ יָשִׂים עוֹד לַהֲלֹךְ אֶל־אֵל בַּמִּשְׁפָּט: יָרֹעַ כַּבִּירִים לֹא־
כה חֵקֶר וַיַּעֲמֵד אֲחֵרִים תַּחְתָּם: לָכֵן יַכִּיר מַעְבָּדֵיהֶם וְהָפַךְ
כו־כז לַיְלָה וְיִדַּכָּאוּ: תַּחַת־רְשָׁעִים סְפָקָם בִּמְקוֹם רֹאִים: אֲשֶׁר
כח עַל־כֵּן סָרוּ מֵאַחֲרָיו וְכָל־דְּרָכָיו לֹא הִשְׂכִּילוּ: לְהָבִיא
כט עָלָיו צַעֲקַת־דָּל וְצַעֲקַת עֲנִיִּים יִשְׁמָע: וְהוּא יַשְׁקִט ׀ וּמִי
יַרְשִׁעַ וְיַסְתֵּר פָּנִים וּמִי יְשׁוּרֶנּוּ וְעַל־גּוֹי וְעַל־אָדָם יָחַד:

[We have translated according to *Rashi* although it is difficult to see how the threat that healing would be withheld from the rebel is germane to Elihu's argument in this chapter. The flow of the argument seems better served as the other commentators take this verse — see below.]

Other commentators take חָבַשׁ as *to rule.* Thus: *Is it conceivable that the administration of justice would be handed over to one who hates justice?* If indeed you were correct that your suffering has no justification, that would mean that God hates justice. Could we conceive of such a one controlling the destiny of man? *Would you accuse the Most Righteous of such an aberration?* Thus *Metzudos.* Or: *Would you accuse the Most Righteous Who so clearly acts justly in all other cases, of acting unfairly just toward you?* (*Ramban*).

18. הַאֲמֹר לְמֶלֶךְ בְּלִיָּעַל רָשָׁע אֶל־נְדִיבִים — *Should the king be accused of wantonness, should princes be called wicked?* This verse is to be read together with the next which will explain why such accusations would be inappropriate (*Ramban*). The reader is expected to supply the *a fortiori* ending: Certainly, then, the most just King of all, God Himself, ought not to be slandered.

19. אֲשֶׁר לֹא־נָשָׂא פְּנֵי שָׂרִים וְלֹא נִכַּר־שׁוֹעַ לִפְנֵי־דָל כִּי־מַעֲשֵׂה יָדָיו כֻּלָּם — *Who shows no favor to rulers, before whom we perceive no difference between the aristocrat and the pauper, for they all are His creatures.* The *king* of the previous verse is being described.

At *Isaiah* 32:5 שׁוֹעַ is paralleled with נָדִיב. Hence, *a noble* or an *aristocrat.*

20. רֶגַע יָמֻתוּ וַחֲצוֹת לָיְלָה יְגֹעֲשׁוּ עָם וְיַעֲבֹרוּ וְיָסִירוּ אַבִּיר לֹא בְיָד — *In just one second they can die, at midnight a people can fall into turmoil and pass on, their strength gone — and not by human hands.* The first phrase apparently refers to the *rulers* and the *aristocrats* of the previous verse. God is totally unimpressed by their exalted standing. If they deserve it, He will destroy them in an instant.

Rashi reads the reference in the second phrase to the Egyptians who were destroyed at midnight. Perhaps the phrase is meant to back up what was said in the previous one. If God, for sufficient cause, is prepared to destroy an entire people, then certainly the nobility of an individual will not stay His hand.

For לֹא בְיָד, *not by human hands,* we have followed *R' Meyuchas* who adds, *not by human hands,* but by means of the Divine Spirit (אֶלָּא בְרוּחַ הַקּוֹדֶשׁ). Reference is evidently to the death at midnight of the first-born in Egypt.

21. כִּי־עֵינָיו עַל־דַּרְכֵי־אִישׁ וְכָל־צְעָדָיו יִרְאֶה — *For His eyes follow man's paths, He observes all his footsteps.* Elihu continues with his argument that God is just and demands a reckoning for all man's deeds. Iyov has no business to ascribe his suffering to happenstance.

22. אֵין־חֹשֶׁךְ וְאֵין צַלְמָוֶת לְהִסָּתֶר שָׁם פֹּעֲלֵי אָוֶן — *There is no darkness, nor gloom, in which evildoers can hide.* The argument from the previous verse continues. Sin will inevitably be punished.

23. כִּי לֹא עַל־אִישׁ יָשִׂים עוֹד לַהֲלֹךְ אֶל־אֵל בַּמִּשְׁפָּט — *He would not impose additional suffering upon man, that there were a purpose in going to God for litigation.* God is just. He would never punish man more than he deserves [עוֹד here is to be understood as *something extra,* a punishment beyond actual culpability].

For the second phrase we have followed *Metzudos.* If God were occasionally unfair, burdening the sinner with undeserved punishment, there would be some point in, as it

18 Should the king be accused of wantonness, should princes
be called wicked? 19 Who shows no favor to rulers, before whom
we perceive no difference between the aristocrat and the pauper,
for they all are His creatures. 20 In just one second they can die,
at midnight a people can fall into turmoil and pass on, their
strength gone — and not by human hands. 21 For His eyes
follow man's paths, He observes all his footsteps. 22 There is
no darkness, nor gloom, in which evildoers can hide. 23 He would
not impose additional suffering upon man, that there were a
purpose in going to God for litigation. 24 He smashes the mighty
beyond ken, replacing them with others. 25 Because He is aware
of their wiles, He brings down darkness to crush them. 26 Because
of their evil He smashed them, where all could see. 27 Because
they had deserted Him, unable to comprehend His ways. 28 To
punish each one of them for the cries of the poor, the cries of
the destitute which He would hear. 29 Were He to decree tran-
quility — who could cause turmoil? Were He to hide His face
— who could gaze upon Him? Nation or individual — all together.

were, summoning Him to judgment. But such is not the case.

The personal exhortation to Iyov has now come to an end. Elihu will now pick up once more his speech to the אַנְשֵׁי לֵבָב of verse 10. See Introductory Remarks.

24. יָרֹעַ כַּבִּירִים לֹא־חֵקֶר וַיַּעֲמֵד אֲחֵרִים תַּחְתָּם — *He smashes the mighty beyond ken, replacing them with others.* In the earlier section of the speech which was addressed to the *understanding men,* Elihu had contented himself with delineating God's justice in general terms. Now, apparently in order to shake them loose from any complacency which might have been induced by Iyov's denigration of the concept of Divine Providence, he launches into a graphic description of the destruction which is the inevitable lot of the wicked.

25. לָכֵן יַכִּיר מַעְבָּדֵיהֶם וְהָפַךְ לַיְלָה וְיִדַּכָּאוּ — *Because He is aware of their wiles, He brings down darkness to crush them. Rashi* understands the phrase, הָפַךְ לַיְלָה, as producing a state of nocturnal darkness and sorrow, where ordinarily there would have been light.

26. תַּחַת־רְשָׁעִים סְפָקָם בִּמְקוֹם רֹאִים — *Because of their evil He smashed them, where all could see. Rashi* thinks that this verse introduces a description of the downfall of Sodom which God destroyed because of the evil which was perpetrated there. Elihu draws upon this historical event to illustrate his thesis that the wicked are bound to be punished. See commentary at 22:15.

27. אֲשֶׁר עַל־כֵּן סָרוּ מֵאַחֲרָיו וְכָל־דְּרָכָיו לֹא הִשְׂכִּילוּ — *Because they had deserted Him, unable to comprehend His ways.* This distancing from God's ways was expressed by the cruelty which was displayed towards the poor, as described in the next verse (*Rashi*).

God's *ways* are clearly the paths of kindness and empathy which, if they could but have grasped them, would have made their social philosophy impossible.

28. לְהָבִיא עָלָיו צַעֲקַת־דָּל וְצַעֲקַת עֲנִיִּים יִשְׁמָע — *To punish each one of them for the cries of the poor, the cries of the destitute which He would hear.* We have followed *Metzudos* who maintains that the singular עָלָיו is used in order to stress that every one of the wicked oppressors would be subject to punishment.

29. וְהוּא יַשְׁקִט וּמִי יַרְשִׁעַ וְיַסְתֵּר פָּנִים וּמִי יְשׁוּרֶנּוּ וְעַל־גּוֹי וְעַל־אָדָם יָחַד — *Were He to decree tranquility — who could cause turmoil? Were He to hide His face — who could gaze upon Him? Nation or individual — all together.* God's omnipotence is being described. The very poor whose piercing cries for help were mentioned in the previous verse, may at other times, by Divine decree, enjoy perfect tranquility. When this is God's will, all their oppressors are impotent to create a disturbance. When, on the other hand, He chooses to hide His face, that is, to leave them unprotected to their fate, then He remains hidden — utterly. His power extends to nations and individuals. All are in His hands (*Rashi*).

ל־לא מִמְּלֹךְ אָדָם חָנֵף מִמֹּקְשֵׁי עָם: כִּי אֶל־אֵל הֶאָמַר נָשָׂאתִי
לב לֹא אֶחְבֹּל: בִּלְעֲדֵי אֶחֱזֶה אַתָּה הֹרֵנִי אִם־עָוֶל פָּעַלְתִּי לֹא
לג אֹסִיף: הֲמֵעִמְּךָ יְשַׁלְּמֶנָּה כִּי־מָאַסְתָּ כִּי־אַתָּה תִבְחַר וְלֹא־
לד אָנִי וּמַה־יָּדַעְתָּ דַבֵּר: אַנְשֵׁי לֵבָב יֹאמְרוּ לִי וְגֶבֶר חָכָם
לה שֹׁמֵעַ לִי: אִיּוֹב לֹא־בְדַעַת יְדַבֵּר וּדְבָרָיו לֹא בְהַשְׂכֵּיל:
לו אָבִי יִבָּחֵן אִיּוֹב עַד־נֶצַח עַל תְּשֻׁבֹת בְּאַנְשֵׁי־אָוֶן:

30. מִמְּלֹךְ אָדָם חָנֵף מִמֹּקְשֵׁי עָם — *Removing hypocrites from kingship, who came to power through the sins of the people.* Our verse is an example of the *tranquility* which God decreed upon the poor of the previous verse. This *tranquility* might take the form of making certain that a hypocritical king — a disaster for the people — not continue to rule over them (*Rashi*).

For the second part of the verse, we understand *Rashi* as interpreted by *R' Yosef Kara*: מֹקְשֵׁי עָם are the sins of the people. Only these could have caused that such a catastrophic ruler should have attained power in the first place.

31. כִּי אֶל־אֵל הֶאָמַר נָשָׂאתִי לֹא אֶחְבֹּל — *Thus, it is appropriate to say to God, 'I will bear it, I will not wound myself!* Now that Elihu has asserted the absoluteness of God's justice, he begins to draw conclusions. Clearly the best that a sufferer can do is to accept his fate philosophically, declaring himself ready to bear anything which God might demand of him. Any other attitude would be the equivalent of inflicting a wound upon oneself (*Rashi*).

We may surmise that the meaning of the second phrase is as follows: As long as the sufferer brings the correct attitude to bear upon his fate, the pain which he is called upon to bear is not in vain. Far from *wounding* him, it has a salutary effect. It is only when he refuses to subjugate himself to God's will that it becomes a *wound*.

32. בִּלְעֲדֵי אֶחֱזֶה אַתָּה הֹרֵנִי אִם־עָוֶל פָּעַלְתִּי לֹא אֹסִיף — *Besides what I have on my own, do You instruct me. If I have sinned, I shall do so no more.'* This verse continues to instruct the sufferer. He is to ask God for understanding, over and above that which he could have grasped on his own. Moreover, he is to criticize himself ruthlessly: If in the past he has fallen short of doing God's will, he must make a firm resolution that the future will be different.

With this exhortation, Elihu's charge to the men of understanding is completed. He has tried to do what he can to counteract the negative influences of Iyov's belligerency.

Elihu will now turn to Iyov in uncharacteristic sarcasm. For the first time, Elihu allows some anger to show. Perhaps he permits this to happen because, in all honesty, Iyov cannot take exception to his criticism. When the friends had taken him to task for imagined wrongs which he had allegedly committed prior to his suffering, Iyov reacted negatively. The charges were simply not true. But Elihu's criticism zeroes in upon a demonstrable carelessness on Iyov's part. People have been harmed by his thoughtless pugnaciousness (v. 37), and honesty demands that he shoulder the blame.

33. הֲמֵעִמְּךָ יְשַׁלְּמֶנָּה כִּי־מָאַסְתָּ כִּי־אַתָּה תִבְחַר וְלֹא־אָנִי וּמַה־יָּדַעְתָּ דַבֵּר — *Should He have consulted with you before exacting payment,* [*thus, that His not having done so*] *would have justified your loathing. Would you, rather than I, choose? What can you know that you should speak?* Elihu sees as particularly pernicious, Iyov's tendency towards death-wishes in the face of his travail. At 6:9 Iyov had prayed: *O that God would but wish to crush me, let loose His hand so that He would destroy me,* and at 7:16 he had declared: *I am sickened; I shall not live forever, leave me be for my days are nothing* (*Rashi*). That attitude is destructive, and undermines any hope that the sufferer might bow before God's justice and accept it with love, as Elihu had recommended in the previous two verses.

And so, Elihu is determined to excise this inexcusable *loathing* of life from Iyov's mind-set. For this excision he does not hesitate to use even the finely honed scalpel of sarcasm. This may, indeed, be hurtful to Iyov (see at v. 36), but this consideration cannot hold Elihu back from protecting the innocent victims of Iyov's errors (see at v. 37).

In the commentary to the previous verse we noted that sarcasm and anger do not come easily to Elihu. As we have recognized at 32:6, a major aspect of Elihu's contribution to the saga is the exquisite sensitivity which he brings to bear upon his difficult task. It is just because of his calm, dispassionate approach that he avoids the pitfalls which had made such pathetic shambles of the friends' best efforts, and succeeds in instructing Iyov without angering him.

*30 Removing hypocrites from kingship, who came to power through
the sins of the people. 31 Thus, it is appropriate to say to God, 'I will
bear it, I will not wound myself! 32 Besides what I have on my own,
do You instruct me. If I have sinned, I shall do so no more.' 33 Should
He have consulted with you before exacting payment, [thus
that His not having done so] would have justified your loathing.
Would you, rather than I, choose? What can you know that you
should speak? 34 Understanding men will agree with me, wise
people will listen to me. 35 Iyov does not speak wisely, his points
are not made with intelligence. 36 O father! That Iyov might be
tested to all eternity, so that the sinners might find their answer.*

Is this passage, then, in contradiction to all that for which Elihu stands? How are we to remain with a consistent and cohesive understanding of Elihu, and yet accommodate this seeming aberration?

The answer may lie in the fusing of Elihu's concerns with those of God, which is evidenced in the shocking wording of the second phrase: *Would you, rather than I, choose?* Suddenly Elihu speaks — for God — in the first person. His voice, and God's, become one (thus *Rashi*).

We may well surmise that Elihu chose this mode of speech in order to diffuse any resentment which Iyov might have felt. It is as though he is saying to Iyov: 'Pardon my use of sarcasm and my expression of anger. It is not on my own behalf, but on God's, that I speak. You, Iyov, are important to me, but my loyalty is first and foremost to God. His will is mine, His needs speak through my mouth.' See further at verse 36.

All this, according to *Rashi* who takes this middle phrase as a rhetorical question. *Ramban* reads it as a declamation: *You* would do yourself a favor were you to *choose* the agonies which you have suffered in the knowledge that you require them in order to assuage your guilt, *more than I am doing* for you by trying to find your good points.

Ramban goes on to say that this interpretation is a perfect reflection of the simple meaning of the words. However, in consonance with his interpretation of Elihu's contribution, he notes that interpreted with an ear to the mysteries of the Torah (עַל דֶּרֶךְ הָאֱמֶת), the verse should be understood as follows: The time will come in which you yourself will crave such suffering, and you will beg that you be exposed to more and more such experiences so that you might redeem your soul from having to pass through the lower depths (בַּשַּׁחַת), and so that your soul (וְחַיָּתְךָ) may yet merit the light.

Clearly, the reference here, too, is to the doctrine of *Gilgul HaNeshamos*.

34. אַנְשֵׁי לֵבָב יֹאמְרוּ לִי וְגֶבֶר חָכָם שֹׁמֵעַ לִי — *Understanding men will agree with me, wise people will listen to me.* As noted above in Introductory Remarks to this chapter, Elihu plans to end his second speech by summoning the attention and agreement of both the groups whom he had previously addressed. He asks them to affirm the truth of the points which he will make in the next three verses.

35. אִיּוֹב לֹא־בְדַעַת יְדַבֵּר וּדְבָרָיו לֹא בְהַשְׂכֵּיל — *Iyov does not speak wisely, his points are not made with intelligence.* As we have noted many times above, Elihu never accuses Iyov of any wrongdoing prior to his suffering. Even at his most accusatory, Elihu addresses himself only to Iyov's damaging attitudes.

36. אָבִי יִבָּחֵן אִיּוֹב עַד־נֶצַח עַל־תְּשֻׁבֹת בְּאַנְשֵׁי־אָוֶן — *O father! That Iyov might be tested to all eternity, so that the sinners might find their answer.* Thus *Rashi*. Elihu is making the point to Iyov upon which we elaborated in the commentary to verse 33. Precious as Iyov is to Elihu, and with all the love and sensibility which he has shown toward him, Elihu loves the truth more. Iyov must understand that he may not purchase relief at the expense of heresy. No encouragement may be given to those who would deny Divine Providence!

That Elihu prefaces this shocking statement with the exclamation, אָבִי! is highly significant. It confirms our interpretation of the fusion of his and God's wishes in verse 33, as *Rashi* there understands it. It is as though Elihu is begging that God not condemn him for the roughness with which he is handling Iyov: It is only for You, my father, that I do this. There is no personal pique involved.

Rashi in his second interpretation, and *Metzudos* take אָבִי as deriving from אָבָה, *to desire.* They render: *It is my wish . . .*

Ramban writes that עַל דֶּרֶךְ הָאֱמֶת the meaning of our phrase is clear, but does not specify what it is. We quote *Chavel's* understanding of

לד/לז לז כִּי יֹסִיף עַל־חַטָּאתוֹ פֶשַׁע בֵּינֵינוּ יִסְפּוֹק וְיֶרֶב אֲמָרָיו
לה/א־ה א־ב לָאֵל: וַיַּעַן אֱלִיהוּ וַיֹּאמַר: הֲזֹאת חָשַׁבְתָּ
ג לְמִשְׁפָּט אָמַרְתָּ צִדְקִי מֵאֵל: כִּי־תֹאמַר מַה־יִּסְכָּן־
ד לָךְ מָה־אֹעִיל מֵחַטָּאתִי: אֲנִי אֲשִׁיבְךָ מִלִּין וְאֶת־רֵעֶיךָ
ה עִמָּךְ: הַבֵּט שָׁמַיִם וּרְאֵה וְשׁוּר שְׁחָקִים גָּבְהוּ מִמֶּךָּ:

Ramban's view: [Elihu asks that] Iyov's soul be tested for all eternity, never returning to its source, but required to undergo *Gilgul HaNeshamos.*

37. כִּי יֹסִיף עַל־חַטָּאתוֹ פֶשַׁע בֵּינֵינוּ יִסְפּוֹק וְיֶרֶב אֲמָרָיו לָאֵל — *For, by holding forth among us, he adds rebellion to his transgressions, piling up words against God.* We have followed *Rashi* who ascribes a meaning to ספק not found anywhere else: It is an expression denoting abundant speech, spoken loudly. The sense of the verse is that by constantly harping upon the injustice of his fate, Iyov is turning a חֵטְא, *an inadvertent sin,* into a פֶּשַׁע, *an act of rebellion.* His erroneous accusations against God can be termed inadvertent, a mistaken theological outlook. But, by constantly reiterating his accusations in public, he is exacerbating the situation. The silence of the bystanders is equivalent to acquiescence. For dragging them with him into the mire of his errors there can be no excuse.

Ramban suggests that ספק is used here in the sense of *creating doubt.* By voicing his fulminations in public he is weakening the faith of those who hear him.

XXXV.

◆§ Elihu's Third Speech

By the sensitivity which Elihu has displayed in the earlier speeches, he has earned the right to be brutally frank. With the precision of a surgeon probing for malignancies, he exposes layer upon layer of faulty theology in Iyov's ready and facile assumptions. And his scalpel does not hesitate to cut — deeply and painfully — where excision is the only hope that a wholesome, pulsating spiritual life might be maintained.

And so, Elihu sets out to tackle some of the thorny issues with which man — Iyov as Everyman in *Rashi's* view — has to grapple in his relationship with God: Is God bound by human concepts and standards of morality? Is there efficacy in prayer — when experience seems to teach us otherwise? Does God care — can a God firmly ensconced in heaven, far, far removed from any possibility of human influence, care — about whether we are good or evil? What are His concerns? Can we fathom the purpose of the Torah's commands and interdictions? Why, in the final analysis, should man struggle to live a life of probity and morality?

All these issues are touched upon and explored fearlessly by Elihu, in the view of the three commentators whom we have chosen to follow in the interpretation of this difficult speech.

The solutions which Elihu offers are, apparently, of such a nature that Iyov might have been expected to have understood them of his own accord. Because he did not, but instead complained in a way that was destructive to himself and to all those who came into contact with him, Elihu castigates him mercilessly. That Iyov accepted these stern strictures in silence, making no attempt at all to defend himself against them, is a mark of Elihu's exquisite sensitivity. Once he had established himself as a non-threatening lover of the truth for its own sake, he was able to educate Iyov in truths which he would never have accepted from the friends.

Rashi and *Ramban* part ways sharply in their respective interpretations to this difficult chapter. The translation follows *Rashi*, but we will note *Ramban's* ideas where appropriate.

To which of Iyov's heresies does Elihu address himself here?

First, *Rashi*: Iyov feels that he *and* all of mankind has a legitimate gripe against God — a claim which, if there were but a possibility to test it, could stand up in a court of justice. A life of consistent probity and goodness has not yielded the expected fruits. He cannot imagine that, had he been wicked instead of righteous, he would have been exposed to any worse fate.

God, Iyov feels, has no defense against this contention. Demonstrably Iyov was good, and demonstrably this helped him not at all. This is not fair. God has an obligation to reward

34/37 [37] *For, by holding forth among us, he adds rebellion to his transgressions, piling up words against God.*

35/1-5 [1] *Elihu declaimed and said:* [2] *Did you consider this that you say, 'My righteousness is superior to that of God!' to be a justified claim.* [3] *That you wondered, 'What have you gained?' 'Why am I better off than if I would have sinned?'* [4] *I will find words to set you right, together with your friends.* [5] *Look up into the heavens and see, observe the skies which tower above you.*

goodness. If He does not do so, says Iyov, He is morally deficient. No such objection can be made to the way Iyov has carried himself throughout his life.

Now, *Ramban*: The initial phrase, אָמַרְתָּ צִדְקִי מֵאֵל, does not refer specifically to that aspect of Iyov's heresy which Elihu tackles in this chapter. It is a catch-all phrase which encompasses various complaints which Iyov has leveled against God. Elihu's earlier two speeches had each tackled one of these: The first, that God considers Iyov to be His enemy, and sets out consciously to harm him; the second, that there is no הַשְׁגָּחָה, no *Divine Providence*. That, in short, all human life is left to happenstance.

In our chapter, Elihu addresses himself to a third issue. Does God value human endeavors to come close to Him? Iyov thinks that He does not and he is convinced that his own experience confirms this. He has made every effort to correct any small wrongdoings which he may have committed. He has not been obstinate, has not denied his guilt where appropriate, has honestly craved to fear God as he should — and all to absolutely no avail. God has in no wise reacted to any of his efforts. Silent, cold and distant, He appears to be oblivious to human longings.

2. הֲזֹאת חָשַׁבְתָּ לְמִשְׁפָּט אָמַרְתָּ צִדְקִי מֵאֵל — *Did you consider this that you say, 'My righteousness is superior to that of God!' to be a justified claim.* Thus *Rashi*. מִשְׁפָּט, here, is used in the sense of *a claim pressed in litigation*. It is a claim that, really, all mankind might justifiably make (מִשְׁפַּט הַבְּרִיּוֹת נֶגֶד יוֹצְרָם). אָמַרְתָּ צִדְקִי מֵאֵל is in apposition to זֹאת (*Daas Mikra*), precisely as we have rendered it. The next verse is to make clear why Iyov feels justified in claiming moral superiority over God.

Ramban would understand מִשְׁפָּט as *an acceptable idea*. Do you really believe that you have any justification in making such a preposterous claim? As in my previous speeches, I have shown up the mistakes in your other assumptions, and I will now show how wrong you are in the claim described in the next verse.

3. כִּי־תֹאמַר מַה־יִּסְכָּן־לָךְ מָה־אֹעִיל מֵחַטָּאתִי — *That you wondered, 'What have you gained?' 'Why am I better off than if I would have sinned?'* In *Rashi's* view, לָךְ refers to Iyov. [This is evident from *R' Yosef Kara*. The printed *Rashi* in this section appears particularly deficient and can be understood best with reference to *Kara's* commentary]. The sense of Iyov's ruminations is that he has gained nothing from a life lived in probity. We have rendered the verse in such a way that it reports two different thoughts which have crossed Iyov's mind. This because it is unlikely that he would have used both second and first person, relative to himself, in one sentence. The מ in מֵחַטָּאתִי, is comparative: *Than if I would have sinned.*

Iyov implied such ideas in verses such as 10:15: אִם רָשַׁעְתִּי אַלְלַי לִי וְצָדַקְתִּי לֹא אֶשָּׂא רֹאשִׁי שְׂבַע קָלוֹן וּרְאֵה עָנְיִי, which *R' Yosef Kara* understands: *If I were wicked I would have to mourn, but, even if I was righteous, You nonetheless see fit to make me suffer ...*

Ramban takes לָךְ as referring to God. Is there anything at all that gives God any pleasure? What effective steps can I possibly take to seek atonement for my sins? [מֵחַטָּאתִי is equivalent to, עַל חַטָּאתִי.] Man seems to be incapable of doing anything at all to please God. Witness — that all Iyov's penitential gestures appear to have been rejected.

This is reflected in Iyov's cry: חָטָאתִי מָה אֶפְעַל לָךְ נֹצֵר הָאָדָם, which *Ramban* here is inclined to render: *If I sinned what can I possibly do to You that You would once more wish to cherish me?*

4. אֲנִי אֲשִׁיבְךָ מִלִּין וְאֶת־רֵעֶיךָ עִמָּךְ — *I will find words to set you right, together with your friends.* The friends, by their silence, appear to have acquiesced with Iyov's claim (*Rashi*).

5. הַבֵּט שָׁמַיִם וּרְאֵה וְשׁוּר שְׁחָקִים גָּבְהוּ מִמֶּךָּ — *Look up into the heavens and see, observe the skies which tower above you.* Nothing that you could possibly do can affect God in any way.

ו אִם־חָטָאתָ מַה־תִּפְעָל־בּוֹ וְרַבּוּ פְשָׁעֶיךָ מַה־תַּעֲשֶׂה־לּוֹ:
ז־ח אִם־צָדַקְתָּ מַה־תִּתֶּן־לוֹ אוֹ מַה־מִיָּדְךָ יִקָּח: לְאִישׁ־כָּמוֹךָ
ט רִשְׁעֶךָ וּלְבֶן־אָדָם צִדְקָתֶךָ: מֵרֹב עֲשׁוּקִים יַזְעִיקוּ יְשַׁוְּעוּ

He is too exalted for you to be able to touch Him. Why then should you boast of your righteousness (*Rashi*)?

God, then, owes man nothing at all for his righteous behavior. He is not like another person from whom, logically, a return could be demanded for favors rendered. Why then should you be disappointed that your good deeds appear to go unrewarded (thus *R' Yosef Kara* to v. 8).[1]

For *Ramban* this verse introduces an analysis of the nature of that which we call *good* and *evil*. This might refer to the *mitzvos* of the Torah, if we postulate that it had already been given, or to the moral behavior which was expected of mankind from the times of Adam. Since, clearly, God remains unaffected by anything we do, we must look for a different rationale, for the need to act correctly.

This rationale can only be that ultimately it is man who stands to benefit from moral behavior. This could mean that through the performance of *mitzvos*, he refines his brute nature, learning to eschew all those acts which would normally be motivated by his base instincts (see *Ramban* to *Deuteronomy* 22:6), or it could mean that society is the better for them. The poor and the weak are protected by the prohibitions which the Torah places upon the actions of the strong, and the common weal is enhanced by responsible behavior.

Given this, the ground is laid for explaining why God seemed to be rejecting Iyov's best efforts, implying that He was not receptive to his penitential prayers. It is possible that a person pray with absolute purity of heart, but his prayers are still rejected because at some time he caused suffering to others. The cries of these victims will drown out, as it were, the supplications of the oppressor. This theme is to be developed from verse 9 onward.

6. אִם־חָטָאתָ מַה־תִּפְעָל־בּוֹ וְרַבּוּ פְשָׁעֶיךָ מַה־תַּעֲשֶׂה־לּוֹ — *Were you to have transgressed how would you have affected Him? Even if your rebellions were numerous what would you have done to Him?* If you would wish to sin so that you might anger your Creator, you could not affect Him in any way, so that He might be annoyed, for the skies (שְׁחָקִים) which constitute the Throne of Glory are much higher than you. It is impossible to approach Him (*R' Yosef Kara*).

7. אִם־צָדַקְתָּ מַה־תִּתֶּן־לוֹ אוֹ מַה־מִיָּדְךָ יִקָּח — *Were you to have been righteous how would you have benefited Him, indeed what would He take from your hand.* You are unable to hand Him even a simple gift. Clearly your actions can affect only other humans (next verse) but never Him (*R' Yosef Kara*).

8. לְאִישׁ־כָּמוֹךָ רִשְׁעֶךָ וּלְבֶן־אָדָם צִדְקָתֶךָ — *Your wickedness can affect only another human being, your righteousness another man.* Now this being so, how can any human make a belligerent case against the Creator, claiming that he is owed reward? What has he contributed that he should be justified in demanding payment? Certainly among men it makes sense that a gift should eventually be recom-

1. Elihu's argument, simple enough on the surface, has troubling theological implications.

The idea that a life well lived and obligations conscientiously performed should be rewarded, would seem to find sanction in the Torah. Although no one familiar with the Torah needs to be told that God is above any personal needs, or would make the ludicrous mistake of thinking that his righteousness or wickedness affects God in any way, a claim for reward can still be based upon the promises which the Torah itself makes. Is Iyov not justified in demanding recognition for his righteousness based upon the principle of reward and punishment, which inheres in the very fabric of Torah as it has been revealed to us?

It would appear that Elihu, here, must be understood in terms of the points made in footnote 1 p. 9 to 1:6-12. It is true that the Torah promises temporal rewards for the righteous life, but these have the nature of a פְּרָס, a kind of *bonus* which God grants to help us along our rocky path in this world. The true reward — the one which seems to be intuitively expected from a moral and just God — is left for *Olam Haba*, the *World to Come*. See there for a fuller discussion.

Given these assumptions, we can understand Elihu as follows: If our righteousness could indeed touch God, if we would really benefit Him when we are good, then we would have earned our reward in this world, and God would have been, as it were, under a moral obligation not to withhold it nor in any way to inhibit our enjoyment of it. Then, indeed, Iyov would have an actionable claim. But this is not the case. God owes us nothing at all in this world. The reward which we nevertheless expect comes to us as a gift, never as a right. Accordingly it is subject to review. If, for educational or other reasons, God deems it appropriate to withhold it, no violence has been done to justice or morality.

6 Were you to have transgressed how would you have affected
Him? Even if your rebellions were numerous, what would you
have done to Him? 7 Were you to have been righteous how
would you have benefited Him, indeed what would He take from
your hand? 8 Your wickedness can affect only another human
being, your righteousness another man. 9 See, they make their
numerous victims scream; they cry out because of the bullying

pensed. But as for God, what possible claims could you have to Him Who has received nothing at all from your hands (*R' Yosef Kara*).

In the last three verses we have quoted extensively from *R' Yosef Kara*, on the assumption that his interpretation, expansively stated, is congruent with that of *Rashi* whose comments here are sparse and do not really convey an accurate insight as to the way he understands this section. However, in the next section he and *Rashi* part ways, and we shall note his thoughts together with those of *Rashi* and *Ramban*.

Ramban has this verse express the credo upon which, as we saw above, he expands at *Deuteronomy* 22:6: ... הָא לֹא נִתְּנוּ הַמִּצְוֹת אֶלָּא לְצָרֵף בָּהֶם אֶת הַבְּרִיּוֹת, *Mitzvos were given us [not because God has any need of anything which we might do but] solely that through their performance humans might attain a state of purity* (*Bereishis Rabbah* 42:1). God's concern is with man and the society within which he lives and functions. Thus, if man somehow offended against this purpose by causing undeserved suffering to others, he will have frustrated God's will and must expect that, as long as the wrong which he has caused is not redressed, his prayers, be they ever so sincere, will be rejected.

❧ ❧ ❧

This passage is variously interpreted by each of the three commentators whom we have been following in this chapter.

Rashi reads it as addressing Iyov's complaint that God seems inaccessible to his prayers, demands and challenges. Elihu argues that God is under no obligation to answer prayers immediately. Even those who have been terribly wronged by their fellow men must occasionally wait for Divine reaction to their entreaties. If God has an obligation to relieve them of their undeserved suffering, He cares deeply about the sinner too, waiting as long as a reasonable balance is maintained to give him a chance to repent. Surely, then, one whose complaints are directed at God Himself must expect to have to wait for satisfaction.

The connection between the two halves of the speech is self-evident. Iyov had felt that he had a right to expect his day in court. Somehow God, by denying him the chance for a confrontation, by not being receptive to his legitimate cravings was, in Iyov's view, acting immorally. Elihu demonstrates that on the contrary, even when God appears at His most distant, His apparent lack of interest is itself prompted by exquisite moral sensitivity. His love and concern for the oppressor is no less than that which He has for the victim. Their needs must be balanced; the one may be called upon to wait for the satisfaction of his claim, so that the other might have the chance to put his spiritual house in order.

R' Yosef Kara feels that the passage seeks to anticipate a mistake which Iyov might make, based upon Elihu's earlier assertions. If, as we have just learned, God remains unaffected both by man's pieties and by his sins, would it not be reasonable to argue that He has no interest at all in human affairs, and that therefore any man might oppress his fellow with impunity? Is it not true to say that God simply does not care? Elihu demonstrates that this is not the case. Those who oppress others will find their own pieties rejected by God.

As *Ramban* reads our chapter, Elihu is still in the middle of his argument. He has shown that God desires only the good of mankind. Why then does it occur that people cry to Him and are not answered? The explanation is that they may previously have wronged another person. Their victim's cries may well block out their own, possibly sincere, prayers.

9. מֵרֹב עֲשׁוּקִים יַזְעִיקוּ יְשַׁוְּעוּ מִזְּרוֹעַ רַבִּים — *See, they make their numerous victims scream; they cry out because of the bullying of their many oppressors.* According to all three commentators, this verse says less than it wishes to imply, relying upon the reader to supply the missing words. According to both *Rashi* and *R' Yosef Kara* the passage is switching to a description of what certain oppressors — the latter identifies these as the people of

י מִזְּרוֹעַ רַבִּים: וְלֹא־אָמַר אַיֵּה אֱלוֹהַּ עֹשָׂי נֹתֵן זְמִרוֹת
יא־יב בַּלָּיְלָה: מַלְּפֵנוּ מִבַּהֲמוֹת אָרֶץ וּמֵעוֹף הַשָּׁמַיִם יְחַכְּמֵנוּ: שָׁם
יג יִצְעֲקוּ וְלֹא יַעֲנֶה מִפְּנֵי גְּאוֹן רָעִים: אַךְ־שָׁוְא לֹא־יִשְׁמַע ׀
יד אֵל וְשַׁדַּי לֹא יְשׁוּרֶנָּה: אַף כִּי־תֹאמַר לֹא תְשׁוּרֶנּוּ דִּין לְפָנָיו
טו וּתְחוֹלֵל לוֹ: וְעַתָּה כִּי־אַיִן פָּקַד אַפּוֹ וְלֹא־יָדַע בַּפַּשׁ מְאֹד:

Noah's generation and the inhabitants of Sodom — did to their victims. These oppressors are not identified in the text [the verse uses יַזְעִיקוּ, *they . . . make scream* but never tell us who *they* are] and the reader must supply the subject.

According to *Ramban* the reader is called upon to supply the actual argument of the verses. The sense of the verse is that God's severity in dealing with apparently righteous people is due to the fact that the cries of their victims makes their own entreaties unacceptable to God. But the text never makes this argument explicit. *Ramban* would translate our verse: *It comes about because of the cries . . .*, with *It* standing for the fact that God may occasionally not accept the prayers of the righteous. *Ramban* notes that our's is a מִקְרָא קָצֵר, *a shortened verse.*

10. וְלֹא־אָמַר אַיֵּה אֱלוֹהַּ עֹשָׂי נֹתֵן זְמִרוֹת בַּלָּיְלָה — *Who never bother to ask, 'Where is my God, my Creator, He Who executes judgments by night?'* This verse describes the oppressors who were introduced in the previous verse.

Rashi takes זְמִרוֹת as deriving from, זָמַר, *to prune.* Thus, *to cut off*, or, as we have rendered it, *to execute judgment.* The wicked oppressors feel no fear of God. If they had at all stood in awe before Him they would have wanted to know something of Him so that they might express their adoration. They would have remembered Amrafel, the Egyptians and Senecharib, all of whom were cut off during the night, and changed their ways.

R' Yosef Kara understands the verse essentially as does *Rashi.* He differs in taking זְמִרוֹת from זֶמֶר, *song.* The phrase is to be rendered: *To Whom,* in gratitude, I should offer *songs of praise at night* as well as during the day.

Ramban sees the songs of jubilation as though offered by nature itself. The slumbering night, with its glorious starry sky, is meant to project God's omnipotence as is the turbulent and active day. Certainly it was not meant to provide cover for deeds of violence which the oppressors have perpetrated.

11. מַלְּפֵנוּ מִבַּהֲמוֹת אָרֶץ וּמֵעוֹף הַשָּׁמַיִם יְחַכְּמֵנוּ — *'Who teaches us so that we might be different from the animals which roam the earth, Who made us wise beyond the birds of heaven.'* All this, the wicked do not consider. They refuse to draw conclusions from the vast wisdom with which God has endowed mankind. They act like animals although, clearly, by giving them so much understanding, God had shown that He expected different behavior from them.

Ramban renders the verse as do the other commentators, but adds the following: Because Iyov had compared man to the animals and the birds, in the sense that he had denied Divine Providence over human destiny, Elihu injects this thought so as to demonstrate the error of this position. An infinite chasm divides the brutish animal world from intelligent man. Each individual human is the object of God's caring concern.

12. שָׁם יִצְעֲקוּ וְלֹא יַעֲנֶה מִפְּנֵי גְּאוֹן רָעִים — *See there! They cry out because of the arrogance of the oppressors, but He will not answer.* The translation follows *Rashi.* As mentioned in the Introductory Remarks to these verses, Elihu is going to argue that Iyov has no right to expect immediate answers from God, Who occasionally does not answer immediately even those with more pressing claims. This argument is begun in our verse and will be developed in the subsequent verses.

R'Yosef Kara has the verse referring to the oppressors mentioned earlier. The time will come when, because of the suffering which will overtake them, they too, as had their victims before them, will cry out to God for help. They will cry in vain. God will not answer them. Clearly, then, God cares about what happens in this world. The fact that He is not affected by our pieties or sins does not mean that human fate does not matter to Him.

According to *Ramban,* Elihu's point has already been made. He has explained why God appears to be deaf to Iyov's entreaties. In this verse, which he understands essentially as does *R' Yosef Kara,* the fate of the oppressors is described.

13. אַךְ־שָׁוְא לֹא־יִשְׁמַע אֵל וְשַׁדַּי לֹא יְשׁוּרֶנָּה — *But it is for nothing! God will not listen, Shaddai refuses to observe.* Even the justified prayers

of their many oppressors. 10 *Who never bother to ask, 'Where*
is my God, my Creator, He Who executes judgments by night?'
11 *'Who teaches us so that we might be different from the animals which roam the earth, Who made us wise beyond the*
birds of heaven.' 12 *See there! They cry out because of the*
arrogance of the oppressors, but He will not answer. 13 *But it is*
for nothing! God will not listen, Shaddai refuses to observe.
14 *Certainly then, when you say, you cannot see Him! Make*
your case before Him — and place your hope in Him. 15 *And*
now, the anger which He visited upon you is as nothing, is as though He were unaware of the enormous weight of your guilt.

of the afflicted appear to be for nothing. God does not answer them immediately because He wishes to give the oppressors time to repent. Therefore even those who have every right to expect relief must occasionally wait for it (*Rashi*).

R' Yosef Kara takes שָׁוְא as short for אַנְשֵׁי שָׁוְא, *deceitful men*. God is unwilling to listen to the prayers of the wicked oppressors who have led a life of dishonesty.

14. אַף כִּי־תֹאמַר לֹא תְשׁוּרֶנּוּ דִּין לְפָנָיו וּתְחוֹלֵל לוֹ — *Certainly then, when you say, you cannot see Him! Make your case before Him — and place your hope in Him.* The translation follows *Rashi*. Iyov, whose troubles came to him from God's hands, has less right to expect an immediate answer than those who were oppressed by humans — and who still have to wait. It therefore behooves him to stop searching for a face to face confrontation with God, and instead turn to Him and hope that his sufferings will come to an end.

R' Yosef Kara renders as follows: As for you — it is inexcusable for you to demand a confrontation. For this you will be forced to make a reckoning before Him (דִּין לְפָנָיו), and you should tremble (תְּחוֹלֵל from חִיל, *to tremble*) in anticipation of the punishment which is in store for you.

Ramban renders as follow: Now that Elihu has demonstrated that God will listen to the prayers of the oppressed, but reject those of the oppressors, it is patently ridiculous to accuse Him, as Iyov has done when complaining about רָשָׁע וְטוֹב לוֹ, *the tranquility of the wicked*, of ignoring the evil of evildoers. God's stewardship of the world is built on justice (דִּין לְפָנָיו) and it behooves you to wait patiently for this to become revealed.

15. וְעַתָּה כִּי־אַיִן פָּקַד אַפּוֹ וְלֹא־יָדַע בַּפַּשׁ מְאֹד — *And now, the anger which He visited upon you is as nothing, is as though He were unaware of the enormous weight of your guilt.* The translation follows *Rashi*. With all his compassion, Elihu was serious when he chided Iyov with undermining the simple faith of the bystanders. However innocent Iyov may have been before catastrophe struck, his present belligerence has laden him with guilt. He deserves more punishment than he received. God has treated him less harshly than He might have done. It is as though God has purposely averted His eyes from major aspects of Iyov's guilt.

פַּשׁ from פָּשָׂה, *to spread*, denotes *a large amount*.

R' Yosef Kara takes פַּשׁ as deriving from נָפַשׁ, *to rest*. He takes the verse as describing one of Iyov's main complaints. The next verse will then react to this claim and expose its bankruptcy. His rendering is as follows: *And now* as to your claim that *He has visited his anger upon me for absolutely no reason, I know no rest* from my travail . . .

Ramban takes the first part of the verse as does *Rashi*. Iyov really deserves more punishment than he received. In the second section he deviates from *Rashi* and renders as follows; Iyov does not even know the great punishments which he must yet anticipate in accordance with the multitude of his sins. It behooves Iyov to be very concerned about what the future holds for him.

Ramban takes note of the fact that Iyov, by his silence, appears to accept Elihu's condemnation, while he had, unequivocally, rejected the same thesis when it was propounded by the friends. The answer must lie in the interpretation which *Ramban* has offered for Elihu's contribution to the debate. Iyov had been unable to accept the friends' strictures because he knew himself to be innocent. Now, however, that Elihu has revealed the secret of *Gilgul HaNeshamos*, Iyov has no problem with accepting the idea that he may indeed be carrying guilt from a previous incarnation.

לה/טז טז־א וְאִיּוֹב הֶבֶל יִפְצֶה־פִּיהוּ בִּבְלִי־דַעַת מִלִּין יַכְבִּר: וַיֹּסֶף
לו/א־ה ב אֱלִיהוּא וַיֹּאמַר: כַּתַּר־לִי זְעֵיר וַאֲחַוֶּךָּ כִּי־עוֹד לֶאֱלוֹהַּ
ג־ד מִלִּים: אֶשָּׂא דֵעִי לְמֵרָחוֹק וּלְפֹעֲלִי אֶתֵּן־צֶדֶק: כִּי־
ה אָמְנָם לֹא־שֶׁקֶר מִלָּי תְּמִים דֵּעוֹת עִמָּךְ: הֶן־אֵל כַּבִּיר

16. וְאִיּוֹב הֶבֶל יִפְצֶה־פִּיהוּ בִּבְלִי־דַעַת מִלִּין יַכְבִּר — *As for Iyov, his mouth speaks nonsense, he piles up words without understanding. Rashi* presumably reads this verse as a general assessment of Iyov's attitudes to which Elihu has addressed himself in this speech.

R' Yosef Kara, as we saw above, has this verse refer to the particular complaint which he read into the previous verse.

Ramban notes that the *piling up* of words refers to the three different heresies with which the three speeches of Elihu have dealt: The contention that God appears to regard Iyov as an enemy, the contention that there is no Divine Providence, and the contention that there is no purpose in piety and no harm in doing evil since man's actions can in no way affect God.

XXXVI.

⤜ Elihu's Fourth Speech

None of the friends had spoken more than three times — Elihu speaks a fourth time.

That Elihu's speeches can be numbered at all is noteworthy. When the friends had engaged Iyov in debate, each one of their speeches had been stimulated by Iyov's rejoinder to the previous one. We were able to isolate a first, second and third round of debate. But, from the first moment that Elihu began talking, Iyov has kept silent. In what sense then was there a first, second, third, and now even a fourth, speech? What separates the one from the others?

In the matter of the first three speeches we might have suggested an adequate solution. Each of them, as indicated in the commentary, demonstrably deals with a clearly defined and discrete problem. It is not unreasonable that a different speech be devoted to each. But this will not help us with the fourth. It appears to have no central theme tying its disparate parts together. There seems to be little connection between an apparently conventional theory of suffering and the riotous canvas which Elihu paints of lowering sky, lashing torrents, rolling thunderclaps, and flashing lightning — all testimony to the omnipotence of Him Who controls these titans, all eloquent witness to the puniness of man who can never aspire to understand even a fraction of all this grandeur.

We are inclined to believe that we were mistaken in our assumptions concerning the differentiation of the first three speeches into discrete entities. Precisely as had those of the friends, each of Elihu's speeches comes about as a reaction to Iyov's response to the earlier one. The difference is only that, whereas in the earlier debates, Iyov had responded with speech, here he responds with silence. Each of Iyov's silences, each acceptance of the bitter medicine which Elihu was offering, provided the momentum for a further foray into ever more frightening theological thickets.

When Iyov kept silent even after the third speech, the one which probed most painfully, which exposed most ruthlessly, which played havoc with Iyov's most cherished assumptions and which Elihu the peacemaker dared to end with the brutally contemptuous, *As for Iyov, his mouth speaks nonsense, he piles up words without understanding,* Elihu knew that victory was at hand. Iyov is ready for rehabilitation. And this, as the commentary will make clear, is what this fourth and last speech will attempt to do. Iyov is helped to look outwards and upwards. He is to be brought to the point at which, finally, he is ready to meet his Maker.

The introductory וַיֹּסֶף [from יָסַף, *to add*] clearly indicates that this speech strikes a new path. It is, as it were, in addition to what was said before (*Rashi*).

What marks it as different?

Rashi notes that it is possible to see the first three of Elihu's speeches as paralleling the three rounds of debate in which the friends had engaged Iyov. This would mark this fourth speech as something belonging uniquely to Elihu. In the course of the commentary we shall have to determine what precisely it is that Elihu has to contribute.

Ramban writes as follows: In this speech Elihu does not take Iyov to task for any wrongdoings.

35/16 [16] *As for Iyov, his mouth speaks nonsense, he piles up words*
without understanding.

36/1-5 [1] *Once more, Elihu spoke.* [2] *Give me a little time, that I may*
instruct you, for, there is more to say in God's behalf. [3] *I will*
spread my ideas afar, will yet ascribe justice to Him Who formed
me. [4] *For, my words are certainly not false, they address your*
conviction of being absolutely in the right. [5] *See the Almighty is so*

He has already done this systematically in the earlier speeches. From now on, Elihu does what the friends had done: He speaks God's praises and affirms His providence over the physical world. From this, he says, we can readily deduce His providential interest in man. Man, after all, is the only one among all creatures who can relate to God. Everything else exists only for his sake. Further, Elihu will make the point that quite apart from the ultimate answer which he has already offered to Iyov — and which indeed has the power to lay all doubts to rest — it makes sense to ascribe fairness to the Creator of all, in view of the fact that we can observe Him as being a mighty monarch, a righteous judge, Who extends providential care to all beings.

We appear then to have, once more, a diversion between the approaches of *Rashi* and *Ramban*. *Rashi* will certainly find Elihu breaking new, as yet unexplored ground, while *Ramban* will attempt only to find ideas which have already been enunciated by the friends. In the course of the commentary we shall have to examine why, in this view, Elihu is successful in persuading Iyov of truths which he had rejected when they had been offered by the friends.

1. וַיֹּסֶף אֱלִיהוּ וַיֹּאמַר — *Once more, Elihu spoke.* See Introductory Remarks for the implication of the opening, ... וַיֹּסֶף.

2. כַּתַּר־לִי זְעֵיר וַאֲחַוֶּךָּ כִּי־עוֹד לֶאֱלוֹהַּ מִלִּים — *Give me a little time, that I may instruct you, for, there is more to say in God's behalf.* Most commentators take כַּתַּר as an Aramaic root with the meaning, *to wait*. *Ibn Ezra* suggests a Hebrew derivation: כָּתַר, *to crown*. Thus: Look upon me with a little respect, and listen to what I have to say.

חָוָה, *to tell*. Cf. *Rashi* to *Psalms* 19:3.

The translation of the final phrase follows *Rashi*. לֶאֱלוֹהַּ is to be understood as *one who speaks for God*.

3. אֶשָּׂא דֵעִי לְמֵרָחוֹק וּלְפֹעֲלִי אֶתֵּן־צֶדֶק — *I will spread my ideas afar, will yet ascribe justice to Him Who formed me*. *Rashi* is silent. *R' Yosef Kara*, whose ideas are frequently congruent with those of *Rashi*, understands as follows: When I cast my mind far back in history, analyzing what has happened from the very earliest times, my research invariably serves to underscore God's righteousness.

Metzudos offers: I will spread my ideas to the farthest reaches of society, so that anyone who feels that I am incorrect will have the opportunity to make his opinion known.

Ramban has רָחוֹק refer to depths of truth which the human mind can never plumb. The sense of the verse is as follows: I have offered you good and sufficient answers to your questions. Clearly what I have said is the truth, but not the whole truth. There are many levels of reality to which we can have no access. Nevertheless, when you consider that which you do understand, you will certainly conclude that God's justice obtains at even the most profound level of truth.

4. כִּי־אָמְנָם לֹא־שֶׁקֶר מִלָּי תְּמִים דֵּעוֹת עִמָּךְ — *For, my words are certainly not false, they address your conviction of being absolutely in the right.* The translation follows *Rashi* [עִמָּךְ, *I deal with you because of your contention that* ...]. Other possibilities are: I agree with your idea [עִמָּךְ, *I am of your opinion*] concerning God's total omnipotence (*R' Yosef Kara*); or, from all that I have revealed to you, you will certainly realize that all that God does to you [עִמָּךְ, *His relationship with you*] derives from His absolute perfection.

5. הֶן־אֵל כַּבִּיר וְלֹא יִמְאָס כַּבִּיר כֹּחַ לֵב — *See the Almighty is so powerful, He has no need to distance [the poor]. He is strong, courageous of heart.* For the first phrase *Rashi* has: God possesses both wisdom and mercy in such abundance that he has no need to distance the poor.

מָאַס generally connotes *looking upon something with disgust*. We have followed *Targum* who renders, יִרְחַק, *distance*. For the second phrase: He is sufficiently strong and courageous, that He has no need to pander to the wicked, as expressed in the next verse.

ו וְלֹא יִמְאָס כַּבִּיר כֹּחַ לֵב: לֹא־יְחַיֶּה רָשָׁע וּמִשְׁפַּט עֲנִיִּים
ז יִתֵּן: לֹא־יִגְרַע מִצַּדִּיק עֵינָיו וְאֶת־מְלָכִים לַכִּסֵּא וַיֹּשִׁיבֵם
ח לָנֶצַח וַיִּגְבָּהוּ: וְאִם־אֲסוּרִים בַּזִּקִּים יִלָּכְדוּן בְּחַבְלֵי־עֹנִי:
ט־י וַיַּגֵּד לָהֶם פָּעֳלָם וּפִשְׁעֵיהֶם כִּי יִתְגַּבָּרוּ: וַיִּגֶל אָזְנָם לַמּוּסָר
יא וַיֹּאמֶר כִּי־יְשֻׁבוּן מֵאָוֶן: אִם־יִשְׁמְעוּ וְיַעֲבֹדוּ יְכַלּוּ יְמֵיהֶם
יב בַּטּוֹב וּשְׁנֵיהֶם בַּנְּעִימִים: וְאִם־לֹא יִשְׁמְעוּ בְּשֶׁלַח יַעֲבֹרוּ

6. לֹא־יְחַיֶּה רָשָׁע וּמִשְׁפַּט עֲנִיִּים יִתֵּן — *He will not grant the wicked longevity, will grant the poor their due.* This conclusion follows upon the truths established in the previous verse. See above. Our rendering of יְחַיֶּה follows *Ibn Ezra.*

7. לֹא־יִגְרַע מִצַּדִּיק עֵינָיו וְאֶת־מְלָכִים לַכִּסֵּא וַיֹּשִׁיבֵם לָנֶצַח וַיִּגְבָּהוּ — *He will not withhold His concern from the righteous. They, together with kings, will occupy the throne. There, elevated, they will sit forevermore.* Elihu continues to describe God's benign stewardship of human affairs. He will not, even for one moment, forsake the righteous to happenstance, and will, on the contrary, protect them from all evil and arrange their lives so that they will sit with the rulers of the earth.

This is God's method with those who are wholly good. Others need to be educated, and it is to their experiences that Elihu now turns.

8. וְאִם־אֲסוּרִים בַּזִּקִּים יִלָּכְדוּן בְּחַבְלֵי־עֹנִי — *And even if they are shackled by chains, caught up in the cords of poverty.* Admittedly there is the occasional *tzaddik* who is exposed to terrible suffering. But this can be readily explained, as Elihu will continue in the next verse.

9-17. In the next nine verses, Elihu will offer a theology of pain. It is the means which God occasionally chooses in order to make the sinner aware of his shortcomings. Accepted in the right spirit, it will save him from the agonies of *Gehinnom* and enable him to bask in the full measure of bliss which lies in store for him in the World to Come.

As an introduction to this section, *Rashi* writes: Elihu has no sharp words of criticism for Iyov. He offers only unadulterated comfort. He tries to persuade Iyov that he should not allow his agonies to depress him as they were sent to him entirely for his own benefit.

Ramban quotes *Rashi*, but questions the assertion. What, he asks, is the real difference between what Elihu has to say here, and that which each one of the friends had already said before — and had been rejected out of hand? Eliphaz at 5:17ff., Bildad at 8:5ff., and Tzophar at 11:13ff. had, each in his own way, maintained the same principle (see, especially, footnote to Introductory Remarks to chapter 11). In what way had they been more offensive than Elihu? Had they, perhaps, raised their voices, while Elihu spoke quietly?

It is instructive to quote *Ramban's* explanation: But, the truth of the matter is as I have explained previously. Elihu had offered good and adequate answers to Iyov's problems and, because of this, Iyov had accepted his words in silence. Following this, Elihu continues to speak along the lines which the friends had already taken, for he had no real way of knowing whether Iyov was indeed an absolute *tzaddik*. Therefore he explains that there could be many different reasons for suffering in this world — each of them grounded in God's absolute justice. Occasionally suffering might come about because of the mystery (*Gilgul HaNeshamos*) explored above. Sometimes the reason may be completely beyond us, but it is incumbent upon us to assume that even then it comes about for good and adequate reasons (based on *Ramban's* explanation of verse 3, see there). And, occasionally, it will come about in order to chastise man, thereby to wean him away from his sins. All this, because Elihu in no way claims that the friends' contentions are false. Rather, his ideas are based upon the assumption that they are not universally applicable. Men may experience suffering for many different reasons.

Ramban, then, feels that Elihu's way was paved by the satisfactory explanations which he had given for Iyov's predicament. His advantage over the friends lies in the fact that he does not claim that the thoughts which he offers here are the only explanation. Iyov had rejected similar thoughts before, because he knew that they had no validity for him. Once this obstacle is removed, he has no difficulty in accepting these, in themselves valid, ideas.

How does *Rashi* cope with *Ramban's* objections?

From *Rashi's* commentary to this section, it does appear that Elihu has something very new to say. Verse 16, for the very first time in the book, makes specific reference to *Gehinnom*

powerful, He has no need to distance [the poor]. He is strong,
courageous of heart. 6 *He will not grant the wicked longevity, will*
grant the poor their due. 7 *He will not withhold His concern from*
the righteous. They, together with kings, will occupy the throne.
There, elevated, they will sit forevermore. 8 *And even if they are*
shackled by chains, caught up in the cords of poverty. 9 *It is only*
because thereby He makes them aware of what they have done,
that their rebellions may have been overwhelming. 10 *He opened*
their ears to discipline, exhorting them to make their way back
from sin. 11 *If they pay attention and subjugate themselves, they*
will live out their days in comfort, their years with pleasantness.
12 *But, if they do not pay attention they will pass on by the sword,*

and the World to Come.[1]

In this, Elihu veers sharply away from what the friends had argued earlier. It is true that they too, as *Ramban* has pointed out, maintained that suffering may have a salutary effect upon the sufferer, and that Iyov should take a positive view of his experiences. But, they never once had recourse to the idea that suffering in this world might be the means of assuring a blissful, pain-free existence in *Olam Haba.*

In this sense we might even say that in this speech Elihu is propounding a specifically Jewish doctrinal response to suffering.

The doctrine that the righteous must be purged of sin in this world, so that they might enjoy unimpaired bliss in the next, is a truth attested to, albeit indirectly, by the Torah itself. *Deuteronomy* 7:10 reads: *But He pays back His enemies to their face, to destroy them.* The sense of this verse, as rendered by *Targum* and understood in our tradition, is that God will reward the wicked for any good which they might have done, in this world [*to their face*], so that they might be totally destroyed in the next. Now, while there is no specific verse which makes the same assertion for the suffering of the righteous — that is, that they are punished in this world for any sins which they might have committed, so that their reward in the next world might be untainted — the analogy is clearly made by the Sages. Thus, in *Yerushalmi, Pe'ah* 1:1, we learn: If a man has many merits but few sins, he is punished for these small shortcomings in this world, so that his reward might be untainted in the next. If he has committed many sins but has a few merits, he is rewarded for these insignificant good deeds in this world, so that his punishment might be unlimited in the next.

We recall that at 32:2, Elihu was introduced as being a scion of the family of Ram — the patriarch Abraham — see commentary there. It comes as no surprise that it should be he, among all the protagonists, who introduces this specifically Jewish concept into the discussion.

9. וַיַּגֵּד לָהֶם פָּעֳלָם וּפִשְׁעֵיהֶם כִּי יִתְגַּבָּרוּ — *It is only because thereby He makes them aware of what they have done, that their rebellions may have been overwhelming.* Even though we are dealing with a *tzaddik* whose merits are many and whose sins are few, he must still be brought up short. Even small transgressions may well turn into an avalanche of sin (*Metzudos*).

10. וַיִּגֶל אָזְנָם לַמּוּסָר וַיֹּאמֶר כִּי־יְשֻׁבוּן מֵאָוֶן — *He opened their ears to discipline, exhorting them to make their way back from sin.* Perhaps לַמּוּסָר, literally, *to the discipline,* rather than לְמוּסָר, *to discipline,* is used to stress that the degree and nature of the suffering will be tailored precisely to the needs of the instruction.

11. אִם יִשְׁמְעוּ וְיַעֲבֹדוּ יְכַלּוּ יְמֵיהֶם בַּטּוֹב וּשְׁנֵיהֶם בַּנְּעִימִים — *If they pay attention and subjugate themselves, they will live out their days in comfort, their years with pleasantness.* This verse appears to describe this-worldly bliss. Verses 12, 13 and 14 then tell of the fate which awaits those who refuse to be swayed by God's benign chastisement. Verse 15 returns to the advantages of suffering — this time, to be reaped in the World to Come.

12. וְאִם־לֹא יִשְׁמְעוּ בְּשֶׁלַח יַעֲבֹרוּ וְיִגְוְעוּ בִּבְלִי־דָעַת — *But, if they do not pay attention they will pass on by the sword, they will die for never having*

1. *Ramban* in *Toras HaAdam* points out that there have been various hints to a World to Come and a *Gehinnom* in the earlier speeches. He identifies these as occurring at: 10:22, 13:19,20 and at 20:26. However, none of these references are more than hints, and the concept cannot in any way be regarded as central to the arguments which have been made.

יג וִיגְוְעוּ בִּבְלִי־דָעַת: וְחַנְפֵי־לֵב יָשִׂימוּ אָף לֹא יְשַׁוְּעוּ
יד־טו כִּי אֲסָרָם: תָּמֹת בַּנֹּעַר נַפְשָׁם וְחַיָּתָם בַּקְּדֵשִׁים: יְחַלֵּץ
טז עָנִי בְעָנְיוֹ וְיִגֶל בַּלַּחַץ אָזְנָם: וְאַף הֲסִיתְךָ | מִפִּי־צָר
רַחַב לֹא־מוּצָק תַּחְתֶּיהָ וְנַחַת שֻׁלְחָנְךָ מָלֵא דָשֶׁן:
יז־יח וְדִין־רָשָׁע מָלֵאתָ דִּין וּמִשְׁפָּט יִתְמֹכוּ: כִּי־חֵמָה פֶּן־
יט יְסִיתְךָ בְשָׂפֶק וְרָב־כֹּפֶר אַל־יַטֶּךָּ: הֲיַעֲרֹךְ שׁוּעֲךָ לֹא בְצָר
כ וְכֹל מַאֲמַצֵּי־כֹחַ: אַל־תִּשְׁאַף הַלָּיְלָה לַעֲלוֹת עַמִּים
כא תַּחְתָּם: הִשָּׁמֶר אַל־תֵּפֶן אֶל־אָוֶן כִּי עַל־זֶה בָּחַרְתָּ מֵעֹנִי:

understood. The translation follows *Metzudos.* יַעֲבֹרוּ refers to *passing* from the world, that is, *dying,* and the second phrase provides the reason. The people who refuse to listen have incurred death-guilt because of their obduracy.

13. וְחַנְפֵי־לֵב יָשִׂימוּ אָף לֹא יְשַׁוְּעוּ כִּי אֲסָרָם — *But those who delude themselves stir up fury, they offer no entreaties even after He shackled them. Ramban* understands the unique combination, חַנְפֵי לֵב, to connote, *those who are hypocritical in their own heart,* that is, those, perhaps including Iyov, who delude themselves into thinking that they are free of sin and who therefore refuse to be swayed by their suffering. Such obduracy angers God. He had hoped to help the sinner to better his ways, and has been rejected. The sinner, instead of availing himself of the healing balm of prayer, is lost in his obstinate silence.

14. תָּמֹת בַּנֹּעַר נַפְשָׁם וְחַיָּתָם בַּקְּדֵשִׁים — *Mayhem will attend them as they die, as their life-force leaves them among the unchaste. Rashi* usually renders נֹעַר with תַּשְׁנוּק (*Isaiah* 33:9), which at *Exodus* 14:27 he identifies with the Hebrew טֵרוּף, *confusion. Ramban* and other commentators take נֹעַר in our verse as connoting *youth. They will die in their youth.*

With *Rashi's* rendering we can readily understand the connection to the end of the verse. We must recall that this section of Elihu's speech is dealing with essentially righteous people for whom suffering is meant to serve as a reminder to repent upon the few sins which they may have committed. Elihu warns that if they ignore the message of their suffering, they will be unlikely to maintain the high spiritual standing which they had already attained. By the time they die, they will have sunk to the very lowest depths; their deaths attended by violence will take place in the most sordid of surroundings, among prostitutes — the very dregs of society.

קְדֵשִׁים from קָדֵשׁ, *to set aside.* Hence people who are available to others for prostitution. See *Deuteronomy* 23:18.

15. יְחַלֵּץ עָנִי בְעָנְיוֹ וְיִגֶל בַּלַּחַץ אָזְנָם — *But, He will reclaim the pauper through his suffering, will use oppression to reach their ear.* The *pauper* in this verse is not one who is actually poor, but one who, unlike those who had been described in the previous verses, considered himself sufficiently in need to have turned to God in prayer (*Rashi*).

God will *reclaim* this *pauper* from the terrors of *Gehinnom* by making him suffer in this world (*Rashi*).

16. וְאַף הֲסִיתְךָ מִפִּי־צָר רַחַב לֹא־מוּצָק תַּחְתֶּיהָ וְנַחַת שֻׁלְחָנְךָ מָלֵא דָשֶׁן — *Moreover, He has distanced you from that which has a narrow entrance but has unbounded width beneath. This, so that the fare upon your table might be rich.* The first part of the sentence describes *Gehinnom.* Its entrance is narrow so that the heat generated in the unlimited vastness of its bowels might not escape. The suffering of the righteous will save him from experiencing the terrors of *Gehinnom,* and will, moreover, enable him to enjoy the bliss of the World to Come — *the fare upon your table . . .*

The translation of מוּצָק as *narrow,* and thus לֹא מוּצָק as *unbounded,* follows *Metzudos.*

This and the previous verse have now moved Elihu into the new dimension which, as we have discussed above, is the main contribution of this speech as *Rashi* presumably sees it — that suffering in this world may have the function of readying the sufferer for his share in the World to Come.

17. וְדִין־רָשָׁע מָלֵאתָ דִּין וּמִשְׁפָּט יִתְמֹכוּ — *Therefore, if you have fully experienced the fate of the wicked, that just fate will be your support.* Elihu now turns to Iyov in order to exhort him to draw the correct conclusion from the theories which Elihu has now propounded. Iyov is to realize that as terrible as his experiences may have been, they are to be regarded as no more than God's means of saving him from the horrors of *Gehinnom.*

they will die for never having understood. [13] *But those who delude*
themselves stir up fury, they offer no entreaties even after He
shackled them. [14] *Mayhem will attend them as they die, as their*
life-force leaves them among the unchaste. [15] *But, He will reclaim*
the pauper through his suffering, will use oppression to reach their
ear. [16] *Moreover, He has distanced you from that which has a*
narrow entrance but has unbounded width beneath. This, so that
the fare upon your table might be rich. [17] *Therefore, if you have*
fully experienced the fate of the wicked, that just fate will be your
support. [18] *For wrath will come! Let your feelings not goad you to*
excessive talk. Let the biggest gain not turn you aside. [19] *Ought then*
your prayers make you free of care, and from all overwhelming
experiences? [20] *Do not crave that night, when nations, firmly en-*
sconced, met their death. [21] *O take care that you should not incline*
to iniquity! For, it is this which you have chosen over submission.

18. כִּי־חֵמָה פֶּן־יְסִיתְךָ בְשָׂפֶק וְרָב־כֹּפֶר אַל־יַטֶּךָּ — *For wrath will come! Let your feelings not goad you to excessive talk. Let the biggest gain not turn you aside.* The translation follows *Rashi.* שָׂפֶק, *to be sufficient* (see at *I Kings* 20:10). The final phrase has the sense: Now that God's fury has struck at you, do not try to avoid it even if this should appear to win you the greatest reward. It is for your benefit that you have been submitted to your agonies. You should by no means squander the experience.

19. הֲיַעֲרֹךְ שׁוּעֲךָ לֹא בְצָר וְכֹל מַאֲמַצֵּי־כֹחַ — *Ought then your prayers and make you free of care, from all overwhelming experiences?* The translation follows *Rashi.* עָרַךְ, *to arrange one's prayers;* שָׁוַע, *to pray.* It would not be good for even the most sincere prayers to free one from all suffering. Difficult times are needed to collect on accrued debts of sin.

20. אַל־תִּשְׁאַף הַלָּיְלָה לַעֲלוֹת עַמִּים תַּחְתָּם — *Do not crave that night, when nations, firmly ensconced, met their death.* History knows many examples of nations which, blessed with all manner of riches, allowed their success to go to their heads, and were then unceremoniously pushed from the stage of human affairs. Your desire to live a pain-free life puts you in line to experience catastrophes similar to those which overtook these nations. Better to suffer a little than to bask in unmarred pleasures, only eventually to lose everything (*Metzudos*).

21. הִשָּׁמֶר אַל־תֵּפֶן אֶל־אָוֶן כִּי עַל־זֶה בָּחַרְתָּ מֵעֹנִי — *O take care that you should not incline to iniquity! For, it is this which you have chosen over submission.* Up to this point, Iyov has chosen belligerent pugnaciousness over humble submission to God's exhortations. Elihu begs him not to continue along this path of iniquity (*Metzudos*).

❦ ❦ ❦

With the previous verse, Elihu appears to have completed his argument, that pain and suffering are sent by God to guide the sinner back to the paths of righteousness. From verse 27 onwards, he will launch into an ecstatic paean extolling the sheer wonder of the lashing rains, the cloud-bedecked skies, the roaring thunder and the flashing lightning. The unchecked, untrammeled power of the titans of nature grips his imagination, and leads him unerringly to the adoration of the Almighty who carries all this in His hand.

What precisely is the role of the intervening five verses?

Although the point is not made expressly by the commentators, it is tempting to view this section as an introductory hymn to the Song of the Rain. The exclamatory flourish with which both verses 22 and 26 begin — the earlier with הֶן אֵל יַשְׂגִּיב, *See, God . . . will raise up;* the latter with הֶן אֵל שַׂגִּיא, *God is exalted* — appear to bracket them together. Moreover, the fact that the earlier ends with a rhetorical question, מִי כָמֹהוּ מוֹרֶה, *Who can offer guidance as He does?* while the second ends with a simple statement, מִסְפַּר שָׁנָיו וְלֹא חֵקֶר, *the number of His years, beyond inquiry,* suggests a logical progression from a starting-point to an end-point.

If then, with *Targum,* we take אֲשֶׁר שֹׁרְרוּ אֲנָשִׁים of verse 24 to mean, . . . *of which men sing,* we have a number of indicators that here, indeed, Elihu is giving voice to a song of jubilation celebrating God's omnipotence.

In such a context, we would not really be

כב־כג הֶן־אֵל יַשְׂגִּיב בְּכֹחוֹ מִי כָמֹהוּ מוֹרֶה: מִי־פָקַד עָלָיו דַּרְכּוֹ
כד וּמִי־אָמַר פָּעַלְתָּ עַוְלָה: זְכֹר כִּי־תַשְׂגִּיא פָעֳלוֹ אֲשֶׁר שֹׁרְרוּ
כה־כו אֲנָשִׁים: כָּל־אָדָם חָזוּ־בוֹ אֱנוֹשׁ יַבִּיט מֵרָחוֹק: הֶן־אֵל שַׂגִּיא
כז וְלֹא נֵדָע מִסְפַּר שָׁנָיו וְלֹא־חֵקֶר: כִּי יְגָרַע נִטְפֵי־מָיִם יָזֹקּוּ
כח־כט מָטָר לְאֵדוֹ: אֲשֶׁר־יִזְּלוּ שְׁחָקִים יִרְעֲפוּ עֲלֵי ׀ אָדָם רָב: אַף
ל אִם־יָבִין מִפְרְשֵׂי־עָב תְּשֻׁאוֹת סֻכָּתוֹ: הֵן־פָּרַשׂ עָלָיו אוֹרוֹ
לא וְשָׁרְשֵׁי הַיָּם כִּסָּה: כִּי־בָם יָדִין עַמִּים יִתֶּן־אֹכֶל לְמַכְבִּיר:

constrained to interpret the words of these five verses to have any direct reference to the arguments which Elihu made at the beginning of this speech. Nevertheless, in the interpretation we will follow *Ramban,* who renders the various phrases in the context of Elihu's present concerns.

We will translate these verses and offer the primary interpretation in accordance with *Ramban,* since his perceptions lend themselves best to the role which we have suggested for these five introductory verses. It is more difficult to see how *Rashi* understood their function.

22. הֶן־אֵל יַשְׂגִּיב בְּכֹחוֹ מִי כָמֹהוּ מוֹרֶה — *See, God, in His Omnipotence will raise up. Who can offer guidance as He does?* The translation follows *Ramban.* יַשְׂגִּיב is transitive with the object, *those whom He has made to suffer,* implied. He instructs (מוֹרֶה) the sinners concerning the path they are to follow.

Rashi renders as follows: *See, God is almighty, who will, as He does, offer warnings?* The sense is as follows: God, if He wishes to punish someone, will first offer a warning. Someone weak would not do this, afraid that his intended victim might escape. God, in this matter, can be magnanimous. He knows that no one can escape Him.[1]

23. מִי־פָקַד עָלָיו דַּרְכּוֹ וּמִי־אָמַר פָּעַלְתָּ עַוְלָה — *Who ever directed Him upon a path? Who said to Him, 'You have acted unjustly!'?* A human king will usually act only upon the advice of his counselors. If he ever does something on his own, his advisors may well chide him for not having sought their advice. None of this happens with God, Who is responsible to no one for His actions (*Metzudos*).

24. זְכֹר כִּי־תַשְׂגִּיא פָעֳלוֹ אֲשֶׁר שֹׁרְרוּ אֲנָשִׁים — *Consider, so that you might extol His deeds, beyond any of which men sing.* The translation follows *Ramban.*

Rashi renders the second phrase: *Those which men were able to observe.* It is noteworthy that here, once more, Elihu hints at depths which the human mind cannot grasp, and therefore cannot praise. See commentary to verse 3 for *Ramban's* perception of that verse.

25. כָּל־אָדָם חָזוּ־בוֹ אֱנוֹשׁ יַבִּיט מֵרָחוֹק — *All were able to apprehend this concerning Him. From the vantage point of distance, [frail] mortal is able to observe.* The translation follows *Ramban.* Each man, according to his own perceptiveness, is able to apprehend the righteousness and rightness of God's deeds. Even though man is unable to approach God closely, his wisdom will enable him to see all this.

As *Rashi* reads it, רָחוֹק connotes the distant past. From the beginning of history, the wisdom of God's stewardship has been obvious.

We have rendered אֱנוֹשׁ as *frail mortal* since this term [from אנש, *to be weak*] for man is generally used to describe him at his most vulnerable. See *Wertheimer's, Biur Sheimos HaNirdafim B'Tanach.*

26. הֶן־אֵל שַׂגִּיא וְלֹא נֵדָע מִסְפַּר שָׁנָיו וְלֹא־חֵקֶר — *God is exalted beyond our ken, the number of His years, beyond inquiry.* From the awareness of God's inscrutability, Elihu now moves to the wonders of the heavens through which His omnipotence becomes apparent.

☙ The Song Of The Rain

27. כִּי יְגָרַע נִטְפֵי־מָיִם יָזֹקּוּ מָטָר לְאֵדוֹ — *He multiplies the water-droplets, the [heavens]*

1. We suspect that *Rashi* offers this interpretation as *d'rash* rather than as the simple meaning of the verse (see fn. at 28:4 and commentary to 33:27). This, because *Rashi* brings our verse in his commentary to *Exodus* 4:23 in a clearly homiletical context. There, immediately upon coming to Pharaoh to demand the release of the Israelites, Moses is commanded to warn him that failure to comply would result in the death of the Egyptian firstborn. This was destined to be the final one of the plagues. Why then mention it to Pharaoh from the very beginning? *Rashi* offers our verse, as interpreted here, as a justification.

*[22] See, God, in His Omnipotence will raise up. Who can offer
guidance as He does? [23] Who ever directed Him upon a path?
Who said to Him, 'You have acted unjustly!'? [24] Consider, so
that you might extol His deeds, beyond any of which men sing.
[25] All were able to apprehend this concerning Him. From the
vantage point of distance, [frail] mortal is able to observe. [26] See!
God is exalted beyond our ken, the number of His years, beyond
inquiry. [27] He multiplies the water-droplets, the [heavens] pour
rain into His clouds. [28] That the heavens might flow rain, pour
down upon the human masses. [29] Certainly man cannot grasp
the spread of the clouds, the impenetrable darkness of His canopy.
[30] See, over it He has spread His rains, has used it to cover the
fount of the sea. [31] Through them He passes judgment upon the
nations, but grants sustenance to the man of great responsibilities.*

pour rain into His clouds. See at 15:4 for *Rashi's* perception of גָּרַע as *to increase.* There is the possibility that *Rashi* understands this phrase as does *R' Yosef Kara*: The stress is on the fact that the rain comes down in myriad drops rather than as a single sheet of water. Were it to do so, all growing things would be inundated with water and drown.

יָזֹקּוּ, from זָקַק, *to refine,* also apparently used in the sense of *to pour* — see *Radak, Sefer HaShorashim.* However, *Rashi* to *Taanis* 9b seems to believe that the word is a variant of יָצַק, *to pour. Rashi's* interpretation of אֵד as *cloud* is also attested in his commentary to *Taanis* 9b, although there is some ambiguity in his commentary to *Genesis* 2:6. He takes the word *heaven* as understood as the subject of יָזֹקּוּ.

28. אֲשֶׁר־יִזְּלוּ שְׁחָקִים יִרְעֲפוּ עֲלֵי אָדָם רָב — *That the heavens might flow rain, pour down upon the human masses. Rashi* is silent on this verse. We have followed *R' Yosef Kara* for אָדָם רָב, an interpretation also attested by *Ramban.*

29. אַף אִם־יָבִין מִפְרְשֵׂי־עָב תְּשֻׁאוֹת סֻכָּתוֹ — *Certainly man cannot grasp the spread of the clouds, the impenetrable darkness of His canopy. Rashi* appears to render אַף with a soft, *or.* However, it is not impossible that he understands the verse as does *R' Yosef Kara*: The אַף, as it does throughout Scripture, introduces a *kal vachomer,* an *a fortiori* argument. The earlier verse had followed on to verse 27 which had talked of God's inscrutability, and had thus implied that man can have no understanding of how the rain descends benignly in droplets, granting rain to thirsty humanity. If even such an apparently simple and constantly observable phenomenon is beyond our ken, how much more the *spread of clouds* and the *impenetrable darkness* that surrounds God's כִּסֵּא הַכָּבוֹד, His *Throne of Glory.*

30. הֵן־פָּרַשׂ עָלָיו אוֹרוֹ וְשָׁרְשֵׁי הַיָּם כִּסָּה — *See, over it He has spread His rains, has used it to cover the fount of the sea. It* seems to refer to the עָב of the previous verse. *Rashi* does not make clear whether אוֹרוֹ, here, is to be understood as *light* or *rain.* See *Ibn Ezra.* Either way it is difficult to understand the precise imagery of this verse.

Daas Mikra takes the word as *light,* that is, the *lightning,* and interprets as follows: One of the inscrutable facets of the *spread of the clouds* mentioned in the previous verse is God's ability to light up their darkness with the lightning as it flashes across the sky. Furthermore he takes שָׁרְשֵׁי הַיָּם literally, as *roots of the sea,* and believes that it describes the line of the horizon at which the clouds appear to touch the waves. To the casual observer, that is the point from which the sea appears to grow, as a tree grows from its roots. God's lightning brightens up even that distant point.

31. כִּי־בָם יָדִין עַמִּים יִתֶּן־אֹכֶל לְמַכְבִּיר — *Through them He passes judgment upon the nations, but grants sustenance to the man of great responsibilities.* The clouds are the means by which God punishes the wicked and sustains the deserving. He may either withhold blessed rainfall, or have the clouds pour fire and brimstone upon those whom He wishes to punish. The righteous poor, those who have numerous [כָּבַר, *to be much or many*] children to support, will find them to be the source from which they may expect to be helped.

לב־לג עַל־כַּפַּ֥יִם כִּסָּה־א֑וֹר וַיְצַ֥ו עָ֝לֶ֗יהָ בְמַפְגִּֽיעַ׃ יַגִּ֣יד עָלָ֣יו רֵע֑וֹ
א מִ֝קְנֶ֗ה אַ֣ף עַל־עוֹלֶֽה׃ אַף־לְ֭זֹאת יֶחֱרַ֣ד לִבִּ֑י וְ֝יִתַּ֗ר
ב־ג מִמְּקוֹמֽוֹ׃ שִׁמְע֣וּ שָׁ֭מוֹעַ בְּרֹ֣גֶז קֹל֑וֹ וְ֝הֶ֗גֶה מִפִּ֥יו יֵצֵֽא׃ תַּֽחַת־
ד כָּל־הַשָּׁמַ֥יִם יִשְׁרֵ֑הוּ וְ֝אוֹר֗וֹ עַל־כַּנְפ֥וֹת הָאָֽרֶץ׃ אַחֲרָ֤יו ׀
יִשְׁאַג־ק֗וֹל יַ֭רְעֵם בְּק֣וֹל גְּאוֹנ֑וֹ וְלֹ֥א יְ֝עַקְּבֵ֗ם כִּֽי־יִשָּׁמַ֥ע
ה קוֹלֽוֹ׃ יַרְעֵ֤ם אֵ֣ל בְּ֭קוֹלוֹ נִפְלָא֑וֹת עֹשֶׂ֥ה גְ֝דֹל֗וֹת וְלֹ֣א נֵדָֽע׃
ו כִּ֤י לַשֶּׁ֨לַג ׀ יֹאמַ֗ר הֱוֵ֫א אָ֥רֶץ וְגֶ֥שֶׁם מָטָ֑ר וְ֝גֶ֗שֶׁם מִטְר֥וֹת
ז עֻזּֽוֹ׃ בְּיַד־כָּל־אָדָ֥ם יַחְתּ֑וֹם לָ֝דַ֗עַת כָּל־אַנְשֵׁ֥י מַעֲשֵֽׂהוּ׃

32. עַל־כַּפַּיִם כִּסָּה־אוֹר וַיְצַו עָלֶיהָ בְמַפְגִּיעַ — *He hides the rain over the cloudlets, will release it as entreaties are offered. Rashi* suggests that clouds are called כַּפַּיִם from כַּף, *hand,* because the occasional cloud is often no larger than the human hand. פָּגַע, *to meet* or *to reach,* is often used to describe *prayer.* Thus, the מַפְגִּיעַ is *one who prays.*

Once more, one wonders whether *Rashi* is here offering the simple meaning of the verse or whether his rendering is to be considered as *d'rash* (*Rashi's* source is *Taanis* 7b where both the interpretation of אוֹר as *rain* and of מַפְגִּיעַ as *one who prays* is offered in an *aggadic* context). *Daas Mikra* suggests a meaning for the verse as follows: Once more, אוֹר is to be translated as *lightning* rather than as *rain.* Elihu looks upon lightning as a spear hurled at a mark by the hands of a warrior. But, the hands of God which, as it were, dispatch the spear are invisible. The lightning, as it were, *covers* them up. We know only that God, as One who is a מַפְגִּיעַ, determined that the mark be *reached,* has sent off the lightning.

This rendering may hold true even if אוֹר is understood as *rain.* God dispatches it so that it should fall in the precise place in which He wishes it to water the thirsty earth.

See further in the next verse.

33. יַגִּיד עָלָיו רֵעוֹ מִקְנֶה אַף עַל־עוֹלֶה — *As a caring friend will express their needs, he asserts their rights, directs them upwards.* This verse is among the most obscure in the book. Once more we translate as *Rashi* appears to do, although it appears unlikely that the rendering accords with the simple meaning of the words. רֵעוֹ is taken as *a friend,* one who is great and wise and is able to tell God of the troubles which his people have to bear, and of their needs. He is the מַפְגִּיעַ of the previous verse. מִקְנֶה, from קָנָה, *to acquire,* is meant to express the idea that it is through the intercession of the righteous man that the right to rain is asserted. The idea of the final phrase appears to be that these prayers will not only elicit the expected rain but also serve to stimulate the people to spiritual growth — עַל is taken as *upwards.*

For an interpretation which might more closely hew to the simple meaning of the words, we go to *Ramban* who bases his understanding on *Ibn Ezra.* רֵעוֹ derives from רעע, *to produce sound,* and is to be translated as *His thunder.* An analogy is *Exodus* 32:17. Thus, *The thunder announces the approaching rain.* מִקְנֶה in the second half of the verse is *the cattle,* who tend to act in specific ways as rain approaches and can therefore be used as indicators of a coming downpour. These behavorial patterns come early, often preceding the rising of the actual cloud (אַף עַל עוֹלֶה) and are therefore particularly useful for predicting the weather.

XXXVII.

1. אַף־לְזֹאת יֶחֱרַד לִבִּי וְיִתַּר מִמְּקוֹמוֹ — *It is because of this that my heart quakes, leaping from its place.* The combination of חָרַד with לֵב occurs twice more in Scripture. At *I Samuel* 4:13 it describes the *anxiety* which Eli felt concerning the Holy Ark, and at 28:5 (there) it tells of the *terror* which gripped Saul when he saw the mighty Philistine camp. Here it could connote either of the two meanings. As *Rashi* took the previous verses, the expression might well describe the *anxiety* which Elihu feels in the knowledge that the bounty of rain must be deserved. Will it come his way? Have his prayers been offered with sufficient fervor?

As *Ramban* and many others take the earlier verses — that they describe the thunderclaps which announce a coming deluge, Elihu might well be telling of the *terror* which he feels when the heavens suddenly begin to roar.

The idiom of the heart leaping from its place does not recur in Scripture. The quickening heartbeat which we experience at times of heightened tension might well suggest a leaping, skipping motion.

36/32-33 [32] *He hides the rain over the the cloudlets, will release it as entreaties are offered.* [33] *As a caring friend will express their needs, he asserts their rights, directs them upwards.*

37/1-7 [1] *It is because of this that my heart quakes, leaping from its place.* [2] *O hearken as, in fury, He gives voice, speech issuing from His mouth.* [3] *As, under all the heavens He sends it upon its unswerving path, as its light reaches the corners of the earth.* [4] *A roaring peal comes right after, crashing in majestic thunder. It is not that He holds it back — if only its sound were heard.* [5] *Through His voice God gives sound to wonders. What other mighty deeds, forever beyond our ken, does He perform?* [6] *He orders the snow to be upon the ground, and the pouring rain! The rain — mighty lashing of His power!* [7] *It can effectively incarcerate anyone. Thus, that all recognize His deeds.*

2. שִׁמְעוּ שָׁמוֹעַ בְּרֹגֶז קֹלוֹ וְהֶגֶה מִפִּיו יֵצֵא — *O hearken as, in fury, He gives voice, speech issuing from His mouth.* רֹגֶז can have the meaning, *to be angry*, or, *to shiver with fear.* We have followed *R' Meyuchas.* The thunder sounds to us as though it were an expression of God's fury. *R' Yosef Kara* takes the second meaning. He renders: *O Hearken, tremblingly, to His voice!*

His mouth might refer to God, in which case the sense of the verse would be that the thunder is described as speech issuing from His mouth. This is how we have rendered it. *Ramban* has it refer to the thunder. הֶגֶה is the lightning which is pictured as the speech of the thunder.

3. תַּחַת־כָּל־הַשָּׁמַיִם יִשְׁרֵהוּ וְאוֹרוֹ עַל־כַּנְפוֹת הָאָרֶץ — *As, under all the heavens He sends it upon its unswerving path, as its light reaches the corners of the earth.* We have followed *Metzudos* in taking יִשְׁרֵהוּ from יָשָׁר, *to be straight.* Reference is to the lightning.

4. אַחֲרָיו יִשְׁאַג־קוֹל יַרְעֵם בְּקוֹל גְּאוֹנוֹ וְלֹא יְעַקְּבֵם כִּי־יִשָּׁמַע קוֹלוֹ — *A roaring peal comes right after, crashing in majestic thunder. It is not that He holds it back — if only its sound were heard.* The sense of the verse is that the lightning is immediately followed by the roaring thunder. The second phrase, as *Metzudos* understands it, informs us that the sound of thunder comes about in the very second that the flash of light occurs. God does not hold back [עָקֵב as in עָקֵב, *the heel, that which comes in the end*]. It is only because our ears are slower to pick up sounds than are our eyes in perceiving light, that it appears to us that there is a time lapse between thunder and lightning.

Rashi, who at 36:32 read a reference to a pious supplicant into the verse, sees our verse as continuing that theme. כִּי יִשָּׁמַע קוֹלוֹ has the voice of that prayerful person in mind.

5. יַרְעֵם אֵל בְּקוֹלוֹ נִפְלָאוֹת עֹשֶׂה גְדֹלוֹת וְלֹא נֵדָע — *Through His voice God gives sound to wonders. What other mighty deeds, forever beyond our ken, does He perform?* The translation follows *Metzudos.* The rhetorical question with which the verse ends is the conclusion reached on the basis of what was said in the earlier phrase. The awesome roar of the thunder directs our mind to other, altogether unknowable miraculous deeds.

6. כִּי לַשֶּׁלֶג יֹאמַר הֱוֵא אָרֶץ וְגֶשֶׁם מָטָר וְגֶשֶׁם מִטְרוֹת עֻזּוֹ — *He orders the snow to be upon the ground, and the pouring rain! The rain — mighty lashing of His power!* Elihu continues to describe the wonders which God performs.

According to *Wertheimer's Biur Sheimos HaNirdafim,* the difference between מָטָר and גֶּשֶׁם is as follows: מָטָר describes any kind of a heavy downpour, not at all limited to rain. In Scripture we have it used in connection with hail, sulphur and brimstone, and the like. By contrast, גֶּשֶׁם is used exclusively for rain, and normally depicts the soft refreshing variety. Our translation attempts to reflect this difference.

7. בְּיַד־כָּל־אָדָם יַחְתּוֹם לָדַעַת כָּל־אַנְשֵׁי מַעֲשֵׂהוּ — *It can effectively incarcerate anyone. Thus, that all recognize His deeds.* We have translated in accordance with *R' Meyuchas,* as being closest to the simple meaning of the words. The sheer power of the rains in effectively preventing any real work from being done, demonstrates beyond any doubt just how powerful God is. אַנְשֵׁי is irregular and should be read, אֲנָשִׁים.

Rashi in an *aggadic* reference renders as follows: He elicits everyman's signature (חָתַם,

ח־ט וַתָּבוֹא חַיָּה בְמוֹ־אָרֶב וּבִמְעוֹנוֹתֶיהָ תִשְׁכֹּן: מִן־הַחֶדֶר
י תָּבוֹא סוּפָה וּמִמְּזָרִים קָרָה: מִנִּשְׁמַת־אֵל יִתֶּן־קָרַח וְרֹחַב
יא־יב מַיִם בְּמוּצָק: אַף־בְּרִי יַטְרִיחַ עָב יָפִיץ עֲנַן אוֹרוֹ: וְהוּא
מְסִבּוֹת | מִתְהַפֵּךְ בְּתַחְבּוּלֹתָו לְפָעֳלָם כֹּל אֲשֶׁר יְצַוֵּם |
יג עַל־פְּנֵי תֵבֵל אָרְצָה: אִם־לְשֵׁבֶט אִם־לְאַרְצוֹ אִם־לְחֶסֶד
יד יַמְצִאֵהוּ: הַאֲזִינָה זֹּאת אִיּוֹב עֲמֹד וְהִתְבּוֹנֵן | נִפְלְאוֹת אֵל:

to sign) so that when, after his death, man is confronted with the sins which he has committed, his own handwriting will condemn him.

8. וַתָּבוֹא חַיָּה בְמוֹ־אָרֶב וּבִמְעוֹנוֹתֶיהָ תִשְׁכֹּן — *The wild animal will enter its lair, crouching in its den.* Not only man becomes incarcerated because of the rain (previous verse). The wild animals, too, unable to forage, retire to their lairs to await the clearing weather (*R' Meyuchas*).

9. מִן־הַחֶדֶר תָּבוֹא סוּפָה וּמִמְּזָרִים קָרָה — *Tempests issue forth from the inner chamber, the constellations usher in the cold.* In מְזָרִים, the *reish* replaces the more usual *lamed* of מַזָּל, a *constellation.* Thus, *Metzudos.*[1]

Rashi quotes the tradition of the Sages that *Mezarim* is the name of a celestial *storage house* [or, as *Pirkei d'R'Eliezer* 6 has it, a *window*] from which the cold issues forth. At 38:32 the word in the feminine form, מַזָּרוֹת, appears in a context which clearly indicates the rendering, *constellation.* That is how *Rashi,* too, renders it there.

10. מִנִּשְׁמַת־אֵל יִתֶּן־קָרַח וְרֹחַב מַיִם בְּמוּצָק — *By God's breath ice is formed, the expanses of water, constrained.* The translation follows *Metzudos* who takes מוּצָק in the sense of *narrowness,* as it was used at 36:16. As God's *breath* produces the ice, the waters are *constrained* beneath it, since they are prevented by it from gushing forth.

11. אַף־בְּרִי יַטְרִיחַ עָב יָפִיץ עֲנַן אוֹרוֹ — *Even when the weather is mild He will burden the clouds, spreading the cloud formations which bear His rains.* The translation follows *Metzudos.* בְּרִי derives from בָּרַר, *to cleanse.* Even when the skies are clean and no rain is in sight or, indeed, seems possible, God fills the clouds with water so that they will be ready to do His bidding when the time comes when He wishes to have rain pour down upon the earth.

Rashi notes the tradition of the Sages that אַף בְּרִי is the name of the angel appointed over rainfall (see *Tefillas Geshem* for *Shemini Atzeres* and *Artscroll* commentary there). It is he who burdens the clouds with water so that, in accordance with his duties, he might cause God's rain to spread over the world.

12. וְהוּא מְסִבּוֹת מִתְהַפֵּךְ בְּתַחְבּוּלֹתָו לְפָעֳלָם כֹּל אֲשֶׁר יְצַוֵּם עַל־פְּנֵי תֵבֵל אָרְצָה — *Good reasons direct its movements, cunningly it pursues its task. All at His orders [that the rain might fall] where people dwell.* The translation follows *Metzudos.* The subject of the verse is the cloud formation of the previous one. Its movements around the heavens are not to be considered as undirected happenstance, but are, on the contrary, skillfully planned so that God's purpose might most readily be filled.

In *Rashi's* view, the verse describes the activities of the heavenly אַף־בְּרִי of the previous verse. He arranges the rainfall so that its bounty will be either benign or destructive. *Rashi* quotes the Rabbinic tradition as follows: Assume that on Rosh Hashanah Israel were judged entirely righteous and God ordained that they should be granted rain. Subsequently they sinned. The amount of rain will not be reduced. However, now that they are no longer deserving, it will fall at the wrong times and at the wrong locations. Similarly, if they changed for the better, the little rain which had been apportioned to them will now fall judiciously so that its benefit will be maximized.

13. אִם־לְשֵׁבֶט אִם־לְאַרְצוֹ אִם־לְחֶסֶד יַמְצִאֵהוּ — *It might be a punishing rod, it might be directed to His land, it might be pure kindness — He will produce it.* Both *Rashi* and *Metzudos* read this verse as describing the various ways in which rainfall might be bestowed — either benignly or in anger. They differ in the precise meaning of the middle phrase, אִם לְאַרְצוֹ. This will also influence the interpretation of the third phrase. *Rashi* takes לְאַרְצוֹ as describing the natural, neutral way in which the rain might fall: neither for punishment, as in the first phrase, nor as reward, as in the third. *Metzudos* sees a progression between the second and third

1. *Ramban* to *Mishpatim* 22:15 adduces numerous examples for both Scriptural and Rabbinic usage where the letters *lamed* and *reish* are interchanged. Thus, for example: נִמְלְצוּ/נִמְרְצוּ (*Psalms* 119:103/*Job* 6:25), or, the Rabbinic שַׁלְשֶׁלֶת which replaces the Scriptural, שַׁרְשֶׁרֶת. See further at verse 16.

8 The wild animal will enter its lair, crouching in its den. 9 Tempests issue forth from the inner chamber, the constellations usher in the cold. 10 By God's breath ice is formed, the expanses of water, constrained. 11 Even when the weather is mild He will burden the clouds, spreading the cloud formations which bear His rains. 12 Good reasons direct its movements, cunningly it pursues its task. All at His orders [that the rain might fall] where people dwell. 13 It might be a punishing rod, it might be directed to His land, it might be pure kindness — He will produce it. 14 Give ear to this, O Iyov, stand still and consider the wonders of the Almighty.

phrases. The second describes the rain falling upon *His*, God's land, that is upon the righteous people who merited rainfall by living their lives in accordance with God's will. The third phrase goes even further. It envisions a rainfall dictated by pure kindness, where a small amount of rain is directed so precisely, that not a single drop is wasted — each one an individual blessing.

14. הַאֲזִינָה זֹּאת אִיּוֹב עֲמֹד וְהִתְבּוֹנֵן נִפְלְאוֹת אֵל — *Give ear to this, O Iyov, stand still and consider the wonders of the Almighty. Daas Mikra* points out that זאת is a neutral term and could refer to the *Song of the Rain* which Elihu has now completed, or to that which is about to follow.

We are inclined to think that Elihu has both the forgoing and the following, in mind. The style in which the next few verses is written is quite different from that which went before and, accordingly, marks them as constituting a new direction in Elihu's thought. Nevertheless, for illustrations of what he has in mind, Elihu still reaches back to the Divine grandeur and omnipotence evinced in the wonders of the rainfall. It is likely, therefore, that Elihu wishes to say: 'Consider well, Iyov, that which I have said up to this point, so that that which I have yet to tell you can make the requisite impact.'

At 33:1 we noted how wise and sensitive Elihu had been in addressing Iyov by name. By this simple act of thoughtfulness he had conveyed to Iyov that he was more to him than a thorny theological problem. Iyov was a human being to whom feelings and dignity were as important as answers to his questions — and Elihu's respect for this need paved the way to successful communication.

What are these final thoughts with which Elihu is going to leave Iyov before returning to the anonymous oblivion from which he came?

At the commentary to 33:4 we wondered in what sense Elihu is crucial to the Iyov saga. Why, as *Ramban* understands Elihu's contribution, could not God Himself, from out of the whirlwind, have informed Iyov of the mystery of *Gilgul HaNeshamos*? We surmised that if God had come to him immediately after the debacle of the debate with the friends, Iyov, angry and frustrated, confirmed in his pathetic illusion that no one could ever understand him, would have been unprepared to receive with the requisite love the unprecedented gift of God's communication.

Elihu, then, soft and sensitive, uncensorious and nonjudgmental, tries to restore Iyov's faith in man, so that, rehabilitated, he might be ready to trust and to meet his God.

But Elihu does not satisfy himself with simply preparing Iyov for God's appearance. As we saw at 34:33 and 36, his ecstasy is able to goad him to peaks where distinctions blur, and Elihu's very identity is fused into that of His God. He is nothing but the medium through which absolute truth is purveyed. He becomes invisible behind his message. And so now, in these last few verses, he assumes the precise style of rhetoric which will mark God's address to Iyov. [Compare הֲתֵדַע, Have you any idea, with אֵיפֹה הָיִיתָ, *Where were you*, at 38:4; and הֲבָאתָ עַד נִבְכֵי יָם, *Have you penetrated to the inaccessible abysses of the sea*, at 38:16 and throughout God's speech.] He challenges, he hectors, he forces Iyov to search the deepest recesses of his being — just as God will when finally He is ready to reveal Himself. It is a tone which might well have offended the fragile sensitivities of the sorely battered Iyov. But, coming from Elihu whom he has learned to trust, Iyov understands the motivations behind the demanding tone. He understands that it is a sign of returning health. He is becoming ready to absorb the impact of unadulterated truth. Elihu, as it were, is taking him by the hand, leading him to the threshold of rebirth. Beyond the horizon of his agony, he is able to see the image of renewal to which he can now, once more, aspire.

טו־טז הֲתֵדַע בְּשׂוּם־אֱלוֹהַּ עֲלֵיהֶם וְהוֹפִיעַ אוֹר עֲנָנוֹ: הֲתֵדַע
יז עַל־מִפְלְשֵׂי־עָב מִפְלְאוֹת תְּמִים דֵּעִים: אֲשֶׁר־בְּגָדֶיךָ
יח חַמִּים בְּהַשְׁקִט אֶרֶץ מִדָּרוֹם: תַּרְקִיעַ עִמּוֹ לִשְׁחָקִים
יט חֲזָקִים כִּרְאִי מוּצָק: הוֹדִיעֵנוּ מַה־נֹּאמַר לוֹ לֹא־נַעֲרֹךְ
כ מִפְּנֵי־חֹשֶׁךְ: הַיְסֻפַּר־לוֹ כִּי אֲדַבֵּר אִם־אָמַר אִישׁ כִּי
כא יְבֻלָּע: וְעַתָּה | לֹא רָאוּ אוֹר בָּהִיר הוּא בַּשְּׁחָקִים וְרוּחַ
כב עָבְרָה וַתְּטַהֲרֵם: מִצָּפוֹן זָהָב יֶאֱתֶה עַל־אֱלוֹהַּ נוֹרָא הוֹד:
כג שַׁדַּי לֹא־מְצָאנֻהוּ שַׂגִּיא־כֹחַ וּמִשְׁפָּט וְרֹב־צְדָקָה לֹא
כד יְעַנֶּה: לָכֵן יְרֵאוּהוּ אֲנָשִׁים לֹא־יִרְאֶה כָּל־חַכְמֵי־לֵב:

15. הֲתֵדַע בְּשׂוּם אֱלוֹהַּ עֲלֵיהֶם וְהוֹפִיעַ אוֹר עֲנָנוֹ — *Have you any idea how God imposes upon them, how He makes his rain-clouds appear?* *Rashi* supplies the object of שׂוּם. It is God's binding covenant which makes the heavenly bodies subservient to His will.

16. הֲתֵדַע עַל־מִפְלְשֵׂי־עָב מִפְלְאוֹת תְּמִים דֵּעִים — *Have you any idea of what occurs above the cloud-spread, the inscrutable acts of the All-understanding?* The translation follows *Metzudos.* מִפְלְשֵׂי is to be understood as מִפְרְשֵׂי from פָּרַשׂ, *to spread*, with the *lamed* substituting for the *reish* (see commentary to verse 9). The sense is as follows: You do not understand the cloud formations. How much more, then, must that which happens above the cloud-spread (עַל מִפְלְשֵׂי עָב) be forever hidden from you!

17. אֲשֶׁר־בְּגָדֶיךָ חַמִּים בְּהַשְׁקִט אֶרֶץ מִדָּרוֹם — *Why your clothes feel warm when the land is becalmed from the south?* *Metzudos* points out that this verse, too, is to be understood as though it began with the word הֲתֵדַע, *Have you any idea?* The north wind brings cold in its wake. But when the wind is from the south, there is a calm softness in the air which makes the very clothes feel warm. This too is seen as one of the wonders which God, in His infinite and inscrutable wisdom, performs.

Clearly the reaction which is expected from Iyov as he is faced with all these rhetorical questions is to know deep-down that God's wisdom must forever lie beyond his ken. The more he will allow himself to be overwhelmed by the sheer grandeur of God's design, the more he will make peace with his place within it.

18. תַּרְקִיעַ עִמּוֹ לִשְׁחָקִים חֲזָקִים כִּרְאִי מוּצָק — *Have you helped Him spread out the sky, firm as a mirror, cast?* *Metzudos* points out that the *lamed* in לִשְׁחָקִים substitutes for the accusative אֶת.

In the next verse Elihu reverts to Iyov's oft-repeated dream that, if only he were given a chance to meet face to face with God, he could make his case and demonstrate the unfairness of his fate. Elihu will show the futility of such mental meanderings. Clearly our verse is meant to buttress the argument offered there. Iyov is made to recognize his own puny insignificance in the face of God's omnipotence. Does he really believe that it would be appropriate for him to face-off against God?

19. הוֹדִיעֵנוּ מַה־נֹּאמַר לוֹ לֹא־נַעֲרֹךְ מִפְּנֵי־חֹשֶׁךְ — *Please tell us what we should say to Him. We are unable to lay out our case because of the darkness.* If there were some possibility of success, it would not be necessary for you to argue your case on your own. I, too, would join in making your defense. But — what is there that we could possibly tell God? (*Metzudos*).

The *darkness* of the second phrase, is either that which surrounds God's celestial throne, preventing anyone from approaching (*Rashi*), or a symbol of man's obtuseness which would surely prevent him from making any meaningful case (*Metzudos*).

20. הַיְסֻפַּר־לוֹ כִּי אֲדַבֵּר אִם־אָמַר אִישׁ כִּי יְבֻלָּע — *Must He be informed of what I speak, must everything man says be revealed?* The translation follows *Rashi.* However, *Rashi* is unique among the commentators in rendering בלע as *to reveal.* He himself says this nowhere else, and even the verse from *II Samuel* which he adduces here, he translates differently in his commentary there.

Metzudos takes בלע in its more usual meaning, *to cover.* He renders our verse as follows: *Must He be informed of what I speak? Is then anything that man says hidden from Him?*

21. וְעַתָּה לֹא רָאוּ אוֹר בָּהִיר הוּא בַּשְּׁחָקִים וְרוּחַ עָבְרָה וַתְּטַהֲרֵם — *And now alas! They have seen nothing! Like the cloudlets in the sky which a passing wind scatters.* The translation follows

*15 Have you any idea how God imposes upon them, how He makes
his rain-clouds appear? 16 Have you any idea of what occurs above
the cloud-spread, the inscrutable acts of the All-understanding?
17 Why your clothes feel warm when the land is becalmed from the
south? 18 Have you helped Him spread out the sky, firm as a mirror,
cast? 19 Please tell us what we should say to Him. We are unable to
lay out our case because of the darkness. 20 Must He be informed of
what I speak, must everything man says be revealed? 21 And now
alas! They have seen nothing! Like the cloudlets in the sky which
a passing wind scatters. 22 By way of the north, gold issues forth,
from before God, awesome in splendor! 23 As for Shaddai we have
not found His force beyond tolerance. There is due measure, there
is much charity. He does not torment. 24 Therefore men stand in awe
of Him, and as for Him — He does not even glance upon the wise.*

Rashi. As he comes to the end of his speeches, Elihu once more bemoans the obduracy of the friends. When all has been said, in spite of all their herculean efforts, they have understood nothing at all. They are like the stillborn fetus who never saw the light of wisdom. They are like the bright cloudlets [*Rashi* here coins a new word, using the adjective בָּהִיר, *bright*, as a noun meaning *bright clouds*] which promise rain, only to disappoint as they are blown away by the wind. [וַתְּטַהֲרֵם, from טֹהַר, *to cleanse*, means literally, *to cleanse the sky* (*of the clouds*).]

22. מִצָּפוֹן זָהָב יֶאֱתֶה עַל־אֱלוֹהַּ נוֹרָא הוֹד — *By way of the north, gold issues forth, from before God, awesome in splendor*! The north wind blows, driving away the clouds so that the golden sun becomes visible. The wind issues forth from before God, who is permeated by the awesome splendor of His majesty (*Rashi*).

What, at this late stage of his speeches, is Elihu trying to convey? Why just here does he describe God's awesome majesty?

With *Daas Mikra* we are inclined to see these last few verses as being said with the intention of preparing Iyov for God's appearance from out of the whirlwind. Elihu, perhaps still in the grip of his earlier ecstasies, looks up into the sky bathed in the sun's golden rays — and is suddenly aware of a brilliance within the brilliance. With mounting excitement he realizes that this is no ordinary light. The beauty is too exquisite, the splendor altogether unbearable. This cannot be anything but the first intimations of experiences yet to come, undreamed of and unimaginable. The impossible is about to happen. Iyov is to be granted his aspiration!

23. שַׁדַּי לֹא־מְצָאנֻהוּ שַׂגִּיא־כֹחַ וּמִשְׁפָּט וְרֹב־צְדָקָה לֹא יְעַנֶּה — *As for Shaddai we have not found His force beyond tolerance. There is due measure, there is much charity. He does not torment.* On the assumption that *Rashi's* rendering is *aggadic* rather than at the simple level, we have rendered the verse such that it might accord most closely with our perception of the previous verse.

First then, *Rashi* as we have it: *We have not found Shaddai overly demanding* in the requests which He makes of His creatures. Rather, what He asks, He asks in mercy: They are able to attain atonement with small sacrifices within everyone's reach — a fistful of flour (for the *minchah* offering), half a *shekel*, two pigeons or doves, cattle or sheep. He has never demanded exotic animals. Even when He exposes His people to suffering (וּמִשְׁפָּט) He does so in a measured way, not tormenting them unnecessarily.

In the context of our explanation of the previous verse, we may surmise the following meaning: Having surmised from the golden heavens that God is about to appear, Elihu finds it important to reassure Iyov that he has nothing to fear. If God does appear, it will not be with the intention to overwhelm. The insights about to be vouchsafed Iyov will be in *due measure* [For מִשְׁפָּט as something *appropriately apportioned*, see *I Kings* 5:8.] The fact of God's appearance is to be viewed as an abundance of charitable good-will, not as a means by which to torment Iyov.

24. לָכֵן יְרֵאוּהוּ אֲנָשִׁים לֹא־יִרְאֶה כָּל־חַכְמֵי־לֵב — *Therefore men stand in awe of Him, and as for Him — He does not even glance upon the wise.* *Ramban* has this final verse refer to all the wonders which Elihu has described in this speech. All that he has said leads to one inescapable conclusion — Iyov has erred terribly. In challenging God to face him at a bar of justice, in accusing Him of unfairness or worse, in daring to believe that God might view him as an enemy, might indeed take perverse joy in making him suffer — in all this Iyov has, perhaps inadvertently, attempted to cut God to human size. Nothing could be further from the truth. Imagine, Elihu suggests, that God and man were looking toward one another. Man could only be overwhelmed with awe. God, looking upon man — even upon the very wisest among us — would see nothing to impress Him.

Elihu has had his say. With this final verse he disappears once more into the oblivion from which he had come. His entire being has exhausted itself in his message.

Elihu's fourth speech is, perhaps, his most remarkable. As we saw above at 34:2, it is relatively simple to assign each of the first three speeches to a particular theological topic. Their's is a tidy structure, their messages persuasively presented with tact and sensitivity. But what of this fourth, and last, speech — the one which, as we saw in Introductory Remarks to chapter 36, is uniquely his own? The first part of the speech is simple enough to understand. As we have interpreted in the commentary to chapter 36, it makes extremely significant contributions to Elihu's presentation. But what of the *Song of the Rain*? It is unexpected and appears unconnected. Why would Elihu, whose avowed intention was only to set Iyov and the friends straight, suddenly burst into such a paean of exultation?

We are inclined to answer that this is one final example of Elihu's consummate human touch. He knows that he has convinced Iyov, sees that Iyov intends to remain silent, has allowed himself to be captivated by the mixture of sound theology and the sensitive, feeling humanity which Elihu has projected. He feels now that Iyov is ready for the next stage. If Iyov is to be ready to apprehend the vision of God from out of the whirlwind, then he must first be drawn out of his obsessive concern with his own predicament. Elihu slowly, with infinite care, guides Iyov's vision outwards and upwards. 'Allow yourself, O Iyov, to see the mighty splendor of God's universe,' Elihu appears to be saying, 'And you will be ready for even greater visions!'

His task accomplished, Elihu fades forever from our consciousness.

◆§ Epilogue: Elihu From the Family of Ram

Alone among the protagonists in this enigmatic story, Elihu is identified as coming from Jewish stock: *The family of Ram* — the family of the patriarch Abraham (*Targum*).

Ramban points out just how appropriate this is. Elihu's success where the friends, older and perhaps wiser than he, had failed, must be traced to this fortuitous circumstance. Steeped in an abiding faith, privy to a tradition in which the reality of God, mighty, just and merciful, permeated every aspect of life, Elihu was able to find the path to Iyov's heart which had so frustratingly eluded the others.

The precise contribution which Elihu made to the solution of Iyov's problems has been dealt with exhaustively in the commentary to the four speeches. Both *Rashi's* idea that Elihu's was a human victory, and that of *Ramban* that it was granted him to reveal the mystery of *Gilgul HaNeshamos,* were examined and traced to their respective sources. See particularly chapter 33, Introductory Remarks to verse 14ff.

No verse-to-verse commentary can possibly plumb the infinity of nuance, the constant stimulants pricking away at our intuitive mental reflexes, with which a work of the extraordinary complexity of Elihu's speeches is laced. Again and again the commentary has touched upon issues which cry for further elaboration. In this epilogue we will examine some of those areas and, perhaps, gain some additional insights into Elihu's contribution to the ultimate *denoument* of the Iyovian drama.

Olam Haba — a Specifically Jewish Concept: In no matter is Elihu's Abrahamian descent more evident than in his introduction of the concept of *Olam Haba, the World to Come,* into the discussion (see detailed analysis in Introductory Remarks to 36:9ff.). As we read the book up to the point at which Elihu suggests that suffering may have the purpose of cleansing man in this world from any sins which he might have committed, in order that he might enjoy unimpeded bliss in *Olam Haba,* we are astounded that an idea which so permeates Jewish thinking, should be entirely absent in a book which wishes to grapple with the problematic, deeply disturbing problem of suffering in the context of *Kisvei HaKodesh* (the Scriptures).

We thought that, perhaps, neither Iyov nor the friends had had recourse to this concept, because the context of their discussion was a gentile one (see fn. to 1:1). *Olam Haba,* or at least the notion that God might bring suffering upon a person so that he might remain untainted there, is a specifically Jewish idea — one of which the protagonists may simply not have known, or which they may have considered inapplicable to the problem at hand.

But, if this is so, it would imbue Elihu's injection of this idea into the thought-world of the drama, with unbounded significance. Baldly stated it would mean no less than that Jewish tradition and doctrine has the power to create a degree of order out of chaos, of making sense of a world in which justice or, indeed, fairness, seem to have little or no bearing on the affairs of man. If the assumption which we made throughout is correct — that Iyov was a non-Jew and that certain ideas addressed in the book are addressed to non-Jews — we have a confrontation between a gentile and a Jewish world-view. The protagonists are Elihu from the family of Ram (representing a *tradition* based on prophecy), and Iyov from the land of Utz (representing the *intellect* — see quote from *Rambam, Moreh Nevuchim* 3:22 at 1:1 s.v. בְּאֶרֶץ עוּץ). With nothing more substantial than the power of truth firing the art of sensitive persuasion, Elihu carries the day.

Taken thus, the implications of the book are phenomenal. The story becomes, in microcosm, a paradigm for the resolution of world-history. תִּקּוּן עוֹלָם בְּמַלְכוּת שַׁדַּי, the point at which history will have run its course, becomes that point at which the gentile world, will at last be willing to accept the God of Israel. A new revelation lies ahead! It comes from out of the whirlwind to teach of a natural order which, in every one of its myriad miracles, proclaims the wisdom and omnipotence of God. The sun-washed dawn; the ferocious lion mauling its prey; the mindless ostrich forsaking its eggs; the arching neck of the snorting, war-wise stallion poised for battle, the soaring eagle painting fluid movement upon the vast canvas of the sky, all proclaim a truth which, in the end, will turn man's gaze beyond themselves to the God Whose messengers they all are.

Olam Hazeh — An Antechamber: Once the doctrine of *Olam Haba* is established, a new perspective is brought to bear upon our own, physical world. Iyov's travails had taken place against the background of an idyllic *Olam Hazeh* which had given him everything which it had in its power to bestow. Wealth, children and good health had been his in abundance (see fn. to 1:3). *Olam Hazeh* had been the center and focus of his life. It was, in his eyes, a self-justifying entity — and his philosophy demanded that it be predictable and consistent within its own categories. When catastrophe struck, when with dreadful thoroughness and consistency, without any logic that he could fathom, he had been brutally stripped of his all, he became bewildered and disoriented. The verities which had anchored his life's work disintegrated. He was left adrift in a sea of frustration and recrimination.

Elihu, with his introduction of the concept of *Olam Haba,* hands Iyov the chance to reconsider. If indeed there is an *Olam Haba,* then *Olam Hazeh* can no longer be viewed in the terms to which he had become accustomed. Far from being self-sufficient and self-justifying, it now becomes no more than an antechamber to an infinitely different, infinitely finer, world. Its bounties would now have to be measured against a sterner standard. What contributes towards a firm progression to *Olam Haba* is useful and desirable, what hinders such a progression becomes that much useless dross.

This proposition granted, radically new perceptions blow through the mind, sweeping out old ideas which had served well enough in the now discredited context. The concept that righteousness bestows rights, that wealth and health ought, by definition, to follow upon a life lived positively and responsibly, ceases to be valid. Indeed good deeds ought to be rewarded, indeed the wicked ought to perish — but logic demands that these axioms hold true for the ultimate, the true world, the World to Come. In this world, it becomes clear that שְׂכַר מִצְוָה בְּהַאי עַלְמָא לֵיכָּא, ultimate reward is not to be expected. Such pleasantness as comes my way is in the form of a פְּרָס, a *bonus,* to make life easier, to help me towards greater efforts. My education, not my well-being, is the crucial issue. And if my education demands that I be exposed to suffering, if my physical being must be broken so that my soul might be more receptive to a light which is not of the here and now, then there is no logic which would demand that the righteous never suffer. [For a wide-ranging analysis of this concept, see fn. to Introductory Remarks, chapter 1:6-12.]

Elihu has granted Iyov a new perspective upon life. Iyov's tormented mind picks up the first intimations of possible comfort.

Righteousness May Be Its Own Reward: Now if indeed we must await the reward for our meritorious deeds in eternity, if in this world even a life of goodness is no guarantee against the most terrible vicissitudes, what can, in the short run, motivate us to act as we ought? Is it not human nature to crave some tangible result for one's good deeds? Do we not court a dispirited lethargy if nothing that we do seems, in the immediate sense, to matter?

And worse. How is man to find God in a world in which there is no discernible pattern, in which the derisive face of undeserved suffering grins from every corner, in which unearned well-being smirks from the faces of the wicked, who, basking in luxury, reveling in power, make a travesty of the notion that it is somehow better to be good than to be evil? Is there to be any meaning to our intuitive certainty that man stands at the center of creation, that he is not *as the fish of the sea* but has infinite personal and individual value, when alone among all God's creatures he is left to toss like so much flotsam in a seemingly uncaring sea of happenstance, subject to no apparent predictable law, at the mercy of forces which seem to care for him not at all? Will not the very orderliness in nature of which God will talk when He finally appears, seem like a cruel mockery to man who seems destined to be able to observe and affirm it — but never, in his own experiences, to share in it?

To this quandary, too, Elihu has an answer: לְאִישׁ כָּמוֹךָ רִשְׁעֶךָ וּלְבֶן אָדָם צִדְקָתֶךָ, *Your wickedness can affect only another human being your righteousness another man.*. While in the commentary (35:8) we have offered a different explanation, it seems well within the bounds of possibility that the meaning is as follows: The two previous verses had asked: *Were you to have transgressed how would you have affected Him? Even if your rebellions were numerous, what would you have done to Him? Were you to have been righteous how would you have benefited Him, indeed what would He take from your hand*? The conclusion is inevitable. Indeed, God is in no way touched by what you do, but you, as a person in the here and now, are profoundly changed. If you have sinned it is yourself whom you have harmed; your good deeds reward you by having made you good.

No man need ever feel that his actions do not matter. While it is true that they do not always affect his immediate fate — he may well have been good and yet have to suffer grievously, and the wicked may indeed often prosper — yet his soul will mark the difference. There are dimensions to life which are not limited to the experiences which our physical senses are able to locate. Our souls are attuned to a different song.

And so, while it is true that *true reward is not to be found in this world* (*Kiddushin* 39b), our good deeds are not lost even here. The righteous feel richly repaid by the sense and feel of their own integrity; the wicked, though outwardly sleek and well-satisfied, know deep down that they are damned, and suffer a thousand deaths. Neither are fooled by the apparent capriciousness of fate. The righteous, buttressed by their inner strength, can find the patience to outwait the chaos, knowing that understanding will not forever elude them; the wicked cannot delude themselves by their good fortune. Intuitively they realize that it will turn to ashes in their mouths.

Elihu Disappears Without a Trace: After Elihu has had his say, we do not hear of him again. At 42:7ff., where God makes known His assessment of the performances of the various protagonists, He praises Iyov and condemns the friends, but Elihu seems not to exist for Him. The explanation would seem to lie in the fusing of man and idea which we recognized in Elihu (see commentary to 34:33,36 and 37:14). As the truth of which Elihu speaks gathers more and more momentum, as the sheer force of its persuasiveness, clarity and conviction sweeps away all possible objections, the man disappears behind the message. The ultimate truth is an objective and self-sustaining entity. It does not need to be identified with the person of him who had been called upon by destiny to be the medium through which it was revealed.

And that, itself, may well be part of the message of the book: Truth is absolute only when we can divorce it totally from the man who proclaims it. The friends had never succeeded in placing themselves entirely into the background. Again and again they had allowed personal pique and frustration to find expression in their polemic. What was ostensibly a defense of God became, in their hand, a justification of their own deeply ingrained theological theories — and ultimately, of themselves as purveyors of those ideas. [See Introductory Remarks to chapter 34, *Elihu's Second Speech.*] In allowing themselves to be human they fell prey to the most endemic of human frailties. They simply had no room in their minds for Iyov as an aching, suffering personality, in need of understanding and empathy. He became no more than a foil for their ideas, an object rather than a subject, a specimen to be examined, rather than a brother to be loved.

And so they failed — ignominiously. Their best arguments fell on absolutely deaf ears. The entire theological edifice which they had so carefully and thoughtfully erected, crashed to the ground. It had not touched Iyov in the least, had helped him not at all. Bitter frustration usurped the place of exalted love. They have become the paradigms of — how not to comfort.

Elihu, lover of truth for its own sake, became — instead of them — the carrier of comfort and conviction. It is his hand, proffered in disinterested friendship, which leads Iyov to meet his God.

XXXVIII.

◈ The First Speech From Out of the Whirlwind

We have reached the climax of the book.

Clearly with God's appearance from out of the whirlwind — itself surely a reward for Iyov's relentless and non-compromising search for the truth — the *denoument* of this complex and gripping saga is about to begin. And indeed the cumulative impact of God's two speeches will yield its fruit. Iyov will find the inner peace which has so long eluded him. With his family rebuilt and his wealth restored, he will live out his days in the tranquility which his uncompromising integrity has earned.

But how do God's speeches accomplish all this?

The speeches do not at all spell out what really happened. No mention is made of the session of the Heavenly Court with which the book had opened. Never once does Iyov hear of Satan's preposterous demands. No word of explanation for his suffering, no hint that it had all been a test — a God-sent opportunity to prove his constancy. God does not even once address the burning issues which had so occupied the minds of all the protagonists. The suffering of the righteous, the tranquility of the wicked — all these issues are simply ignored.

There is only the haunting beauty of the vaulting sky, the mystery of the roiling seas, the grace, the energy, the invigorating independence, and yes, even the beauty vested in the mindless cruelty of the animal-world. And that is all.

How can this vision help Iyov out of his predicament?

Perhaps *Rambam* can help us here. In chapter 2 of *Yesodei HaTorah* he writes as follows:

> We are commanded to love and to stand in awe of . . . God.
>
> And how are we to attain this love and fear?
>
> When man considers God's deeds and His wondrous and mighty creatures, apprehending through them God's immeasurable and boundless wisdom — immediately he will be filled with love, praise and exultation, longing deeply to know more of this great God. This, as David wrote, *My soul thirsts for God, the living Almighty!* (*Psalms* 42:3).
>
> And when he ponders these matters further he immediately recoils in awe and is filled with terror at the realization that he is nothing but a tiny lowly creature, smothered in darkness, standing in utter ignorance in the presence of the all-Knowing. This, as David said: *When I see Your heavens, that which Your fingers wrought — what is man that You should take heed of him!* (*Psalms* 8:4).

The wonders of nature, then, have the power to wrench us away from the egocentrism which limits our vision, cramps our thoughts and undermines the sound instincts which should be able to perceive God in every aspect of creation.

But — there is a condition. We must *consider,* must be willing to *ponder,* must look upwards and outwards.

This is what the vision from out of the whirlwind accomplished. *The voice of God is in the power, the voice of God is in the form* (*Psalms* 29:4) [see Introductory Remarks to chapter 9]. For the first time since his troubles began, Iyov was willing to hear. The first steps along the road to spiritual recovery have been taken.

❦ ❦ ❦

It is remarkable that much of what has troubled Iyov throughout the book seems also to have disturbed the chorister, Asaf, in *Psalms* 73.

> *As for me, my feet had almost strayed, my steps were nearly led off course. For I envied the wanton, I saw the wicked at ease. Death has no pangs for them; their bodies are healthy. They have no part in the travail of men; they are not afflicted like the rest of mankind. So pride adorns their necks, lawlessness enwraps them as a mantle. Fat shuts out their eyes, their fancies are extravagant. They scoff, and plan evil; from their eminence they plan wrongdoing. They set their mouths against heaven and their tongues range over the earth. So they pound His people again and again until they are drained of their very last tear. Then they say, 'How God know? Is there knowledge with the Most High?' Such are the wicked, ever tranquil they amass wealth.*
>
> *It was for nothing that I kept my heart pure and washed my hands in innocence. Seeing that I have been constantly afflicted, that each morning brings new punishments . . .*

No punches are pulled here. The troubling reality of a world in which — in the face of all that we know of the Torah's promises of equitable reward for the righteous and punishment for the wicked — moral anarchy appears to hold sway, is spelled out with the same clarity — we might say with the same degree of bitterness — as in the book of *Iyov.*

What solution did the psalmist find?

Till I entered God's Sanctuary and reflected upon their fate!

When Asaf entered the Sanctuary, his problems faded, his agony was assuaged.

But why? Nothing had changed in the wide world outside. We might almost say that the groans of the suffering righteous, the raucous hilarity of the evildoers could easily have penetrated the thin walls of the *Mishkan* (Tabernacle) as it stood in Asaf's time. And still, the ears of this chorister, this maker of Divine music, although assaulted by this ugly cacophony, were attuned to a different frequency — the sweet melody of absolute rightness which is refracted in the world of *Psalms* — that part of our Torah which allows us to divert our look from form to essence, from appearance to reality.[1]

Asaf found no answers to his questions, but by exposing himself to the light of the Sanctuary, he gained the ability to view his world from a radically new perspective. We feel that, essentially, Asaf's experience parallels that of Iyov. Both were granted entry into the world of *shirah* — that world in which mighty songs of jubilation sweep away the timidity of doubting, the temerity of arrogant questioning.

The difference between the two lies in the difference between an Asaf — scion of a people who had found themselves sufficiently in tune with the Divine reality that permeates the world to have been able to declare נַעֲשֶׂה וְנִשְׁמָע. We have no doubts, attach no conditions, *We will do* under all circumstances, and need only to *hear* so that we might become acquainted with our task. Then there is an Iyov, son of a more timorous tradition. The question, מַה כְּתִיב בָּהּ, *What is written in it?* reflects more than a weak faith. It betrays a basic sense of alienation, and insecurity in the sub-surface world of God's absolute truth. [For the assertion that the book of *Iyov* is addressed to those who had asked, מַה כְּתִיב בָּהּ, see footnote 2 to 1:1 and commentary to 6:2.]

And thus, the *shirah* which Asaf heard was different to the one to which Iyov became privy. Asaf heard the inner *shirah* of the Sanctuary — Iyov the surface *shirah* of nature. The one more deep, more profound — closer to the ultimate truth; the other — the thundering proclamation of God's glory through the heavens (*Psalms* 19:1ff.) — as meaningful to an Iyov.

In the event, this first of the speeches from out of the whirlwind proved to be not quite enough. It was greeted by Iyov's silence — not by his wholehearted acquiescence. That will come only after the second speech.

The moment for which Iyov had so desperately hoped, seems to have finally arrived. He had constantly demanded that he be permitted to face God — and God, apparently in answer to that challenge, appears to him from out of the whirlwind. Surely an experience unique in the annals of human experience!

But, careful reflection does not bear out this perception of the events. Iyov had not asked for a vision but for a confrontation (see for example at 9:33), had wanted to meet God as an equal, as it were, before a bar of justice, not as an omnipotent Being before Whom he would have to yield in silent impotence and grudging submission.

We may wonder whether this vision would not have made Iyov even more frustrated than before. Until God appeared to him, he could have told himself that justification eluded him only because of God's inaccessibility. No human being can expect to meet God — therefore his craving for litigation must remain a dream. Certainly — so he would have told himself — if a meeting were possible, it would be on his terms. Of such pipe-dreams, he is now disabused. He does indeed meet God, but not at all as he had expected. Far from being vindicated, he is forced to wallow in the awareness of utter and irredeemable insignificance.

---

1. Reference is to the thesis propounded by Bieberfeld's, *David King of Israel* in which he makes the point that *Psalms* sees the world as it is essentially, rather than as its phenomena appear to us. The individual enemy who pursues David at a given point becomes paradigmatic of all enemies of David — and of God. His personal joys become manifestations of all God's goodness; his disappointments, the universal cry of anguish torn out of each man's soul when dreams are shattered and reality looms large and threatening.

Psalms is the book of ultimate truth.

So we would suppose.

Whether or not this construction accords with what actually happened, depends to a large extent upon an accurate understanding of the structure of the speeches which we are about to study.

We shall see that *Ramban* does not understand the matter as we have, but that the sparseness with which *Rashi* treats this section leaves open the possibility of accommodating our thesis.

We begin our analysis by examining the unexpected terseness with which the narrative moves from Elihu's speeches to those of God. During the earlier debates, the movement from one speaker to another was natural and needed no special introduction. Iyov spoke and the friends responded in a manner entirely consistent with our expectations. When, at the end of the debate, Elihu begins to speak, the matter is not so simple. His appearance requires an explanation. Why, if the debate is over, need anything more be said? The beginning of chapter 32 addresses this issue. Elihu asserts that neither the friends nor Iyov were correct in their attitudes. It is up to him to reveal the truth.

But, what of God's speeches? If, indeed, Elihu has already said what needed to be said, why should God speak again? And, if there was something missing in Elihu's presentation, why are we not given some sort of explanation to parallel that given in chapter 32?

The answer would seem to lie in a correct understanding of the role which Elihu plays in the saga. In Introductory Remarks to chapter 34 and in the commentary to verse 33 there, we saw that Elihu's persona seems to fade away behind the ecstasy of his message. The man fuses with the message, and he becomes no more than God's mouthpiece. Moreover, we have noted again and again that Elihu's purpose is to prepare Iyov for the vision from out of the whirlwind (see at 32:6, 33:4, 37:14 and 22). Accordingly we may say as follows: God's speech needs no introduction because, in a sense, it is no more than a continuation of Elihu's. Already at 37:14 we noted how, toward the end of his last speech, Elihu assumes the precise form of rhetoric which will be the hallmark of God's speeches. There is enough similarity between Elihu's arguments and those which God will muster to make the transition smooth and seamless.

This given, before we continue our analysis of the structure of God's speeches we must ask ourselves why the vision from out of the whirlwind was at all necessary. What does God's description of the wonders of nature add to that which Elihu has already said? In his *Song of the Rain* Elihu has already pointed out to Iyov his sheer puniness and insignificance in the face of God's omnipotence. Since this appears to be the theme of, at least, God's first speech, it seems to add little to what Iyov had already accepted from Elihu.

But, this itself is something which we ought to question. Did Iyov, in fact, accept Elihu's ideas? It is true that he keeps silent — and in view of his vociferous reactions to the friend's speeches [which he of course rejected — see at 33:30, Introductory Remarks to chapter 36 and at 37:24], we might well take that silence as acquiescence. However, there is another side to that coin. As true as it is that he made no bones of voicing his disagreement with the friends, so it is true that when God has spoken, Iyov admits freely that he has been convinced. What, then, are we to make of his silence in reaction to Elihu's speeches?

We are inclined to interpret silence as something more than rejection, but something less than outright acceptance. Elihu's arguments were persuasive — at least according to *Ramban's* interpretation of Elihu's role — and Iyov saw no way of rejecting them. However, only his intellect, not his emotions, were engaged. What his mind readily grasped did not have the power to remove the dreadful scars which his suffering had left upon him. To reconcile, to rebuild, to help him find once more his pristine faith and joy in life, more was needed. It required the overwhelming experience of revelation to heal Iyov's shattered being. [For *Ramban's* perception of why Iyov required a revelation from God even after he had apparently been satisfied by what Elihu had told him, see commentary to verse 1.]

We are now ready to continue our analysis. To do this, we should consider Iyov's reaction to God's first speech. Was it positive or was it negative?

Certainly, if our suggestion that God's speech is really no more than a continuation of that which Elihu had so successfully begun is correct, we would have supposed that Iyov should accept with unbounded joy everything that God is now willing to reveal to him.

But is this, indeed, what happened?

This question brings us to another one. Why was it necessary for God to deliver two speeches?

At this point we recognize a possible parting of ways between *Rashi* and *Ramban*. We have spoken of two speeches delivered by God. Strictly speaking there appear to have been three; the one consisting of just one sentence at 40:2.

Since *Rashi* is silent on this issue, we shall first examine *Ramban's* ideas:

First, *Ramban's* translation of 40:2: *Is it to be assumed that he who found fault with Shaddai will now continue to quarrel? That he who had earlier seen fit to scold God will even now have something to say?* The sense is as follows: God understands why Iyov, while he was still ignorant of the truths which he had recently learned, would have felt justified in haranguing God. Now, however, that he has learned of the mystery of *Gilgul HaNeshamos* from Elihu [and had it confirmed by God — see below at v. 13], and of God's omnipotence in God's first speech, there is surely no reason for Iyov to continue in his confrontational stance.[1]

Ramban prefaces his commentary to this verse with the following remarks: Once God has completed this [first] speech, and Iyov has kept silent, God comes back once more, appearing to him in a still quiet voice (קוֹל דְּמָמָה דַקָּה), rather than in a storm or a whirlwind. This, so that Iyov should not be frightened by God's awesomeness, as he had previously begged, *Let fear of You not terrify me* (13:21). In *Ramban's* view, this tiny speech, uttered quietly, is indeed fully persuasive. Iyov accepts his fate and, as we shall see in the commentary, God's next speech turns to other matters.

Apparently, then, the appearance from out of the whirlwind could not really satisfy the need of the moment. Iyov would be overwhelmed with terror — precisely as he had earlier feared.

Why, then, did God choose to appear in this form?

At 40:6, God begins what, according to *Ramban*, is His third speech. This one too is said *from out of the whirlwind. Ramban* offers an explanation why, after God had already addressed Iyov with the still quiet voice, He found it necessary to revert to an appearance from within a raging storm. We quote: 'Even though Iyov had already agreed that now there was nothing left about which he could have anything left to say, knowing that God is fully righteous, [God appeared once more from out the whirlwind] because Iyov had not yet confessed that he had earlier been at fault . . .'

Clearly, then, an appearance *from out of the whirlwind* is viewed as indicating a degree of displeasure. This is understandable for the third speech, after Iyov had been less than totally forthcoming even after the second, kindly approach. But why was the first speech made *from out of the whirlwind*?

Here, there is some slight ambiguity in *Ramban*. At 38:1, where the *whirlwind* is first introduced, he appears to interpret it as an indication that the level of prophecy which Iyov attained was a relatively low one. He demonstrates from many passages in Scripture that even the greatest prophets, Elijah and Ezekiel, were initially accosted by a mighty storm which *preceded* their prophecies. This rudimentary manifestation of the Divine was then followed by the actual prophecy — see at *I Kings* 19:11-12: . . . *And behold, HASHEM passed by and there was a mighty wind uprooting mountains and smashing rocks before HASHEM — but HASHEM was not in the wind! After the wind there was an earthquake — but HASHEM was not in the earthquake! After the earthquake came a fire — but HASHEM was not in the fire! But, after the fire a still, quiet voice.* Iyov never attains the highest level of prophecy. The voice which he is permitted to hear comes from the whirlwind.

Now, since in his introduction to chapter 40, *Ramban* maintains that the second speech was in fact delivered in a *still, quiet voice* — see above — it would have seemed logical to have perceived the first speech, from out of the whirlwind, as an introduction to that prophecy. Certainly in *Ramban's* perception that tiny speech was the most significant of the three — it was that one which finally convinced Iyov — and such a structure would have been eminently logical.

However, *Ramban* does not make this point and chooses instead to see the original appearance from out of the whirlwind as an indication of the low level of Iyov's prophecy, and the still quiet voice of the second one as mitigating the terror which Iyov would certainly have felt at the original vision.

We may now sum up *Ramban's* perception of the structure of God's speeches as follows: Initially God appears from out of the whirlwind to bring Elihu's ideas to a conclusion. Elihu had

1. It is noteworthy that of the two arguments which are claimed to be sufficient to have changed Iyov's stance, the one — the mystery of *Gilgul HaNeshamos* — was revealed by Elihu [God in His speech only alludes to it, as see below in commentary to verse 13, but it is certainly not the central part of God's argument]; the other — God's omnipotence — by God Himself.

This might tend to confirm the theory which we propounded in these Introductory Remarks. *Gilgul HaNeshamos* is a fact which, once revealed, can satisfy on the intellectual level. For this purpose, Elihu is enough. However, the projection of God's omnipotence is not something that Iyov did not know before. Rather, it was necessary that he be confronted with it on an emotional level, in the context of an experience which would be able to wrench his entire being into a new, positive and happy existence. This Elihu could never have done.

informed Iyov of *Gilgul HaNeshamos*, and God now wishes to convince him of His omnipotence and goodness, while at the same time confirming the doctrine of *Gilgul HaNeshamos* — see below in commentary to verse 13. This is done through the medium of a storm because Iyov's level of prophecy reached no further. This first speech is then followed by the tiny second speech — delivered in a still quiet voice — which finally convinces Iyov that he has no right to question God. However, Iyov does not yet manage to confess that his initial reaction was wrong. In order to bring Iyov to this level of submission, God appears once more from out of the whirlwind to deliver the third speech.

Now, of the main pillars of *Ramban's* interpretation — the notion that the middle speech was delivered in a still quiet voice; the assumption that Iyov was fully mollified after that small second speech; the concept and function of the whirlwind — *Rashi* says nothing at all. Accordingly we are left with the task of attempting to understand how he perceived the function and structure of God's speeches.

It is not only the structure, but also the content of God's speeches, which presents difficulties. What, precisely, does God wish to accomplish with His first speech? If, as one would tend to assume from even a superficial reading, the purpose is to demonstrate the meticulous order which obtains throughout the natural world — G-d's omnipotence and caring stewardship — and then to lead to an *a fortiori* argument that certainly in human affairs there can be no assumption of happenstance, then we have a troublesome problem: Why does God choose to limit His arguments to His stewardship over nature? Why is there not a single illustration of God's loving kindness in human affairs? From our own experiences we can testify how moved we are when, in our lives or in the lives of our acquaintances, some obvious experience of Divine Providence is manifest. How we rejoice when seemingly intractable problems are solved by fortuitous circumstances which — we know intuitively — could only have come about through God's intervention. How we weep when God's hand — it is so clear to us — falls heavily upon a friend and plunges him into mourning. Would such examples of direct Divine intervention not have proved more helpful to Iyov than the pictures from nature which, however vividly drawn, remain at best outside his own experience?

Again, what is the point of constantly reminding Iyov that he is unable to do that which God can do. If his pride needs to be broken, is this the way to do it? Does a normal human being really feel inadequate because he is unable to duplicate God's acts of creation. If, indeed, Iyov suffered from some unpardonable pride, that would have derived from actions which he deemed meritorious. It seems unlikely that awareness of God's omnipotence would cure him of this.

God's second [or perhaps, third] speech seems to veer away from the arguments used in the first. But, again we are troubled. Why taunt Iyov with his human frailties? What is he expected to conclude from the fact that God can do more than he? And, above all, why, in this second speech, at verse 15, does God revert to the arguments of the first speech? Would not the description of *behemoth* and *livyathan* have fit better into the first speech? Are they not of a kind with the other pictures from nature drawn there? Why come back to these ideas after a new topic had already been broached?

For a correct understanding, much will depend on the precise interpretation of 40:2 and its relationship to the earlier speech. *Ramban*, as we saw above, interprets this single verse as a self-contained speech. We would assume that *Rashi*, who does not explicate this, has a different view. Moreover, it is important to understand Iyov's response at 40:4-5. How does this reaction to G-d's first speech relate to the response to the second speech, at 42:2-6?

It is possible that *Rashi* shares the view of *Metzudos* to 40:1: God broke off His original speech so as to give Iyov a chance to respond to it. When Iyov remained silent and did not answer, God continued.

Against this background, we may readily understand *Rashi's* interpretation of 40:2 (see commentary for details). *Does fighting with Shaddai confer privilege? One who presumes to wrangle with God has the obligation to respond*! God is chiding Iyov for his silence in face of His first speech. Does he consider himself so privileged that he is relieved from the obligation of responding? Does one who arrogates to himself the right to argue with God not have an obligation to respond in some way when God addresses him?

Why, indeed, did Iyov remain silent?

At the beginning of these Introductory Remarks we surmised that Iyov may well have been disappointed at God's appearance from out of the whirlwind. He had hoped for a confrontation on equal terms — and, instead, was being overwhelmed by what he perceived to be an avalanche of words designed to crush him in the awareness of his own puniness and inadequacy. This, we feel, is expressed in his response at 40:4-5 which contrasts sharply with that to the second speech

א־ב וַיַּעַן־יהוה אֶת־אִיּוֹב °מִנהסערה וַיֹּאמַר: מִי זֶה | מַחְשִׁיךְ
°מִן | הַסְּעָרָה ק׳ ג עֵצָה בְמִלִּין בְּלִי־דָעַת: אֱזָר־נָא כְגֶבֶר חֲלָצֶיךָ וְאֶשְׁאָלְךָ

at 42:2-6. That latter one, as we shall see in the commentary there, is full of contrition and adoration. By contrast, the one here seems almost sulky in tone. Iyov appears to be saying: 'Why should I bother to answer? You have shown me that I am nothing. So I will be nothing and stop making my case. You have made Your point and obtained my silence. But — and this by implication — not my understanding nor my contrite acceptance!'

Such a negative reaction could only come about through a radical misunderstanding of God's intention in His first speech.

What, indeed, was God's purpose in this first speech? Above we noted that it could hardly have been to convince Iyov of his folly or to break his pride. These objectives could have been accomplished more readily by different means. Rather, we should assume as follows: At our concluding remarks to chapter 37 we thought that Elihu, by describing the wonders of nature to Iyov, was attempting to draw him out from his obsessive concern with his own predicament and to guide his vision outwards and upwards. Certainly we should assume that this, too, is God's purpose in this first speech. With infinite patience and understanding He attempts to help Iyov to a mind-set which will enable him to make his way back to a healing of the spirit.

But, Iyov misread God's intentions. The vision, coming as it did from out of the whirlwind, was fraught with terror. For Iyov, vulnerable as he had become through all his suffering, it seemed to confirm his worst fears. God had come not to help, but to browbeat him into submission. Instead of luring him into a constructive and ultimately uplifting contemplation of God's wonders, the descriptions of God's omnipotence seemed designed to mock his impotence. No wonder that he retreated into silence, and that even after God demanded a response, his words reflect a churlish capitulation rather than a loving acceptance.

But, needless to say, he had been totally mistaken. In the first part of the second speech, God demonstrates to him what His words would have been had He really wanted to intimidate Iyov. But, nothing had been further from His mind. Accordingly, at 40:15 with the description of the *livyathan*, He reverts once more to the subject of the earlier speech. It is infinitely meaningful that He introduces that section with the words, . . . הִנֵּה נָא. He is imploring Iyov, as it were, to accept the vision in the sense that it is meant, and not to allow himself to be hurt.

This time Iyov is convinced and, at the end of the second speech, responds with the final, absolute acceptance of his fate.

See commentary for a possible explanation of the fact that God chose to appear to Iyov from out of the whirlwind.

1. וַיַּעַן־ה׳ אֶת־אִיּוֹב מִן הַסְּעָרָה וַיֹּאמַר — *Then* *HASHEM responded to Iyov from out of the whirlwind, saying*: We quote *Ramban*: Iyov has now attained prophecy. He merited this because he was of unquestioning integrity coupled with a probing mind and eschewed evil. Moreover, he had been exposed to a test. Now, although he sinned when he unwisely expressed doubt concerning God's justice, still his experiences were effective in bringing him close to God — witness the fact that he accepted Elihu's arguments and admitted that they solved his problems. Therefore he was now once more God-fearing, and completely righteous.[1]

What is the subject of this prophecy?

As *Ramban* sees it, it is twofold. Firstly, it is to demonstrate the ludicrousness of Iyov's presumption in thinking that he could have an opinion concerning God's stewardship of

1. *Ramban* uses the expression, יְרֵא אֱלֹהִים וְצַדִּיק תָּמִים, *God-fearing and wholly righteous.* This raises a vastly significant question for the correct understanding of the Iyovian saga. Did Iyov in fact pass the Satan's test? Was God, in the end, satisfied with the man whom He had described in such glowing terms? There is no doubt that at some points during the debate, Iyov strayed perilously close to blasphemy. On the other hand, there were always mitigating circumstances (see fn. to 9:22-24), and we must recall Rava's dictum that אֵין אָדָם נִתְפָּס בִּשְׁעַת צַעֲרוֹ, *no man should be blamed for statements uttered in the throes of his agony* (*Bava Basra* 16b).

It appears significant that, in the end, when God vindicates Iyov (42:7-8) He says only that — in contrast to the friends who had erred — he had spoken correctly. There is not even a hint to an accolade similar to the one which He had made after Iyov had passed the first test, וְעֹדֶנּוּ מַחֲזִיק בְּתֻמָּתוֹ, *he still keeps his unquestioning integrity* (2:3). We have the impression that Iyov has not totally fulfilled God's hopes for him.

For one approach to the question whether or not Iyov is perceived as having passed his test, see *R' Yosef Kara* in commentary to verse 2, below.

[1] Then HASHEM responded to Iyov from out of the whirlwind, saying: [2] Who is this who has such murky ideas, speaking without due consideration! [3] Come, gird your loins like a warrior. I

human affairs. If nature, in all its wonderful, variegated complexities, is hopelessly beyond his ken, then surely there is no way at all in which he could have any understanding of God's justice.

Secondly, God wishes to endorse Elihu's thesis of the doctrine of *Gilgul HaNeshamos.* Elihu himself had suggested it only as a possibility. No man can be sure of such a premise unless it is directly received from God (רַק בְּדֶרֶךְ קַבָּלָה). In this speech God will offer the required confirmation. See commentary at verse 13.

It seems significant that the introductory verse to God's speeches reads: *Then HASHEM responded to Iyov.* In all the other speeches the introductory formula had invariably been, וַיַּעַן ... וַיֹּאמַר, *responded and said,* without the addressee being mentioned. The impression was always that the protagonists were not really responding to one another at all. They were talking *at* each other rather than *to* each other. God, of course, is different. He knows Iyov and cares for him as an individual. Every word which He utters is honed specifically for Iyov's ear. No wonder, then, that Iyov, too, at 40:3 and 42:1 reciprocates and addresses his remarks directly to God.

Throughout this section of the book we shall be seeing the exquisite sensitivity with which God approaches Iyov's problem, the wisdom which finally breaks down the barriers and draws Iyov out of the slough of his despondency. This introductory verse already sets the tone which makes it all possible.

2. מִי זֶה מַחְשִׁיךְ עֵצָה בְמִלִּין בְּלִי־דָעַת — *Who is this who has such murky ideas, speaking without due consideration!* The combination, חָשַׁךְ in the *hiphil, to darken,* with עֵצָה, *plans* or *ideas,* is unique. *Rashi* suggests: An עֵצָה which is *dark and foolish.* See further at 42:3.

Ramban and *Metzudos* think that עֵצָה here refers to God's deeply laid plans. *Ramban* notes that עֵצָה implies any idea which is generated with particular care and wisdom, but the logic of which is not easily understood. The sense of the phrase is: *Who dares cast aspersions upon God's deeply laid plans!*

As *Rashi* interprets the phrase, it appears to parallel Elihu's words at 34:35. But, where Elihu uses Iyov's name — something which throughout we have understood as a mark of respect and sensitivity — God, after His initial address (see above), uses wording which seems to be designed to make Iyov feel small. God cannot even be bothered to mention his ame. Just a rhetorical, *Who is this ...* (*Daas Mikra*).

God may have chosen this mode of address, even though He clearly wants to help Iyov out of his despondency as we have discussed in Introductory Remarks to this chapter, because it is of a piece with the thrust of the whole speech. Iyov is to be forced to come to grips with his puniness in the face of the omnipotence demonstrated by God in His acts of creation. Only once Iyov has admitted that there is something, outside himself, infinitely greater than he, will he be able to shed his obsessive self-involvement.

In a profoundly significant interpretation, *R' Yosef Kara* renders as follows: *You have frustrated My plan* which I had taken *in consultation* with My *Phamalia* (Heavenly counsel) whereby I would have sanctioned the joining of My name to yours (אֱלֹהֵי אִיּוֹב), precisely as that is done with the three patriarchs — and this because of the four qualities (תָּם, יָשָׁר, יְרֵא אֱלֹהִים, סָר מֵרָע) which you possess. But they required that I put you to the test to see if you could be steadfast, just as the patriarchs had been tested. Now, I have tested you, **but you have failed,** *because you acted without intelligence.* This interpretation is also reflected in *Rashi.*

The basis for this interpretation is the *Pesikta Rabbasi* which is quoted above in commentary to 1:1 and footnote to 9:14. The significance of *R' Yosef Kara's* interpretation is that he reads this *Pesikta* as an assessment that Iyov in fact failed the test which God, upon the instigation of the Satan, had given him — see footnote to verse 1 above.

R' Yosef Kara will interpret 42:3 to say that Iyov contests this charge. He will claim that he said what he said only because he was unaware of certain truths which he had since learned. He contends that he has, in fact, passed the test (see commentary there).

3. אֱזָר־נָא כְגֶבֶר חֲלָצֶיךָ וְאֶשְׁאָלְךָ וְהוֹדִיעֵנִי — *Come, gird your loins like a warrior. I will put questions to you and you will enlighten Me.* Iyov is to ready himself for a serious confrontation. Wearing one's belt is an indication of readiness and enthusiasm (*Metzudos*). *Rashi* understands the first phrase as a hint that Iyov is to be cured of his illness: *You will yet be able*

לח/ד־יג

ד וְהוֹדִיעֵנִי׃ אֵיפֹה הָיִיתָ בְּיָסְדִי־אָרֶץ הַגֵּד אִם־יָדַעְתָּ
ה בִינָה׃ מִי־שָׂם מְמַדֶּיהָ כִּי תֵדָע אוֹ מִי־נָטָה עָלֶיהָ קָּו׃
ו־ז עַל־מָה אֲדָנֶיהָ הָטְבָּעוּ אוֹ מִי־יָרָה אֶבֶן פִּנָּתָהּ׃ בְּרָן־יַחַד
ח כּוֹכְבֵי בֹקֶר וַיָּרִיעוּ כָּל־בְּנֵי אֱלֹהִים׃ וַיָּסֶךְ בִּדְלָתַיִם יָם
ט בְּגִיחוֹ מֵרֶחֶם יֵצֵא׃ בְּשׂוּמִי עָנָן לְבֻשׁוֹ וַעֲרָפֶל חֲתֻלָּתוֹ׃
י־יא וָאֶשְׁבֹּר עָלָיו חֻקִּי וָאָשִׂים בְּרִיחַ וּדְלָתָיִם׃ וָאֹמַר עַד־
יב פֹּה תָבוֹא וְלֹא תֹסִיף וּפֹא־יָשִׁית בִּגְאוֹן גַּלֶּיךָ׃ הֲמִיָּמֶיךָ
יג צִוִּיתָ בֹּקֶר יִדַּעְתָּה °שחר מְקֹמוֹ׃ לֶאֱחֹז בְּכַנְפוֹת הָאָרֶץ

°הַשַּׁחַר ק׳

to wear your belt as any healthy person would!

R' Yosef Kara believes that at this point, Iyov is actually cured. He was given the health of one who had never been sick in his life, so that he would be at the peak of his energies and thus have no excuse if he will not be able to challenge what God is about to say to him. This, because at 9:34 Iyov had said, *That He might remove his cudgel from me . . .*, implying that if only he were healthy he would be able to assert his claims against God aggressively. He is now to be given every chance — and will still keep silent.

The second phrase seems to be meant to shake Iyov out of his smug involvement with his own problems. Certainly the questions which God will now put are rhetorical. No real answer from Iyov is expected.

4. אֵיפֹה הָיִיתָ בְּיָסְדִי־אָרֶץ הַגֵּד אִם־יָדַעְתָּ בִינָה — *Where were you when I laid the foundations for the earth? Pray tell — if you are so wise*! The system whereby Iyov is made aware of God's greatness by means of rhetorical questions which draw his attention to the wonders of nature, was begun by Elihu at 37:15.

The rhetorical questions begun here will continue till the end of God's first speech, through chapter 39. There, taking the entire speech together, we shall try to understand what Iyov is to conclude from the fact that he was not present when God created the world, and that the wonders of nature are beyond human ken.

We have seen above that *Ramban's* understanding of the thrust of this speech is to demonstrate that Iyov cannot possibly hope to *understand* God's stewardship of human affairs. As *R' Yosef Kara* interprets our verse, it is not Iyov's understanding but his *rights* which are being contested: Were you then My fellow-worker when I laid the foundations of the earth, that you arrogate to yourself the right to quarrel with My judgment? In everyday life, when two people are fellow-workers, and one does something without consulting the other, his fellow may voice a protest . . . But, you who were not present when I laid the foundations of the earth, what right have you to quarrel with Me? Is not the whole world Mine? I created the world, and I [alone] am its judge!

5. מִי־שָׂם מְמַדֶּיהָ כִּי תֵדָע אוֹ מִי־נָטָה עָלֶיהָ קָּו — *Who determined its dimensions — would you know? Or, who measured it with a line*? Was it you or I who determined its dimensions? Clearly it was I, since you have no knowledge of them (*Ramban*).

6. עַל־מָה אֲדָנֶיהָ הָטְבָּעוּ אוֹ מִי־יָרָה אֶבֶן פִּנָּתָהּ — *Wherein are its sockets sunk, or who set its cornerstone*? The earth is described as being supported upon pillars. These pillars, in turn, are inserted into *sockets*. [For אֶדֶן as *socket*, see *Exodus* chapter 26 and throughout the description of Moses's Tabernacle.] Iyov is being asked whether he knows into what material these sockets are sunk [טָבַע, *to sink*] in order to give them support.

7. בְּרָן־יַחַד כּוֹכְבֵי בֹקֶר וַיָּרִיעוּ כָּל־בְּנֵי אֱלֹהִים — *When all the morning stars sang in unison, when all the angels shouted*? The imagery of nature raising its voice in songs of praise to God is prevalent throughout *Psalms* and also, especially, in *Isaiah*.

8. וַיָּסֶךְ בִּדְלָתַיִם יָם בְּגִיחוֹ מֵרֶחֶם יֵצֵא — *Damming in the sea behind doors, as its flow issues forth from the womb*? The waters which gush forth from the *womb* — the very depths — of the sea, would normally engulf the dry land. By surrounding the sea with sand, God effectively contained its waters as though He had surrounded it with a mighty wall through which it is impossible to pass without doors (*Metzudos*).

גיחו from גָּחָה or גוח means, *to flow*. See for example at *Michah* 4:10.

From the earth and the heavens, we have now moved on to the seas. The challenge hurled at Iyov in verse 4, *Where were you . . .*, covers the creation and consolidation of all three elements. This sequence continues up to

will put questions to you and you will enlighten Me. 4 *Where*
were you when I laid the foundations for the earth? Pray tell — if
you are so wise! 5 *Who determined its dimensions — would you*
know? Or, who measured it with a line? 6 *Wherein are its sockets*
sunk, or who set its cornerstone? 7 *When all the morning stars sang*
in unison, when all the angels shouted? 8 *Damming in the sea*
behind doors, as its flow issues forth from the womb? 9 *When I*
clothed it in clouds, swaddled it in mists. 10 *I hemmed it in by*
moats, providing bolts and gates. 11 *Saying, 'Up to here you shall*
come and no further. Only here will your crests flaunt their
majesty!' 12 *Have you ever ordered up the morning, told the dawn*
its place? 13 *That it might take hold of the corners of the earth,*

verse 12 where a new rhetorical question is introduced.

9. בְּשׂוּמִי עָנָן לְבֻשׁוֹ וַעֲרָפֶל חֲתֻלָּתוֹ — *When I clothed it in clouds, swaddled it in mists. Rashi* has this refer to the sea which surrounds the earth. It is surrounded by clouds much as a garment surrounds the body. The verse may be a continuation of the previous one, in which case a boundary function would be ascribed to the clouds — they and the darkness which surrounds the sea prevent the waters from washing over the dry land as do the *doors* of verse 8. Or, our verse could belong to the series of rhetorical questions beginning in verse 4.

Daas Mikra suggests that the metaphor *swaddled* is appropriate here, because earlier the sea had been described as issuing forth from the *womb.*

Within the context of a description of the sea we have assumed that עֲרָפֶל, which means *darkness,* refers to the lowering mists which rise from the sea.

The following three verses are in the first person. In this they are unique in this extremely long speech. Perhaps, already at this early stage, God wishes to draw Iyov's thoughts upwards. It is as though God is saying, 'In pounding you with all these questions, My purpose is not to impress you with your own impotence, but rather to allow yourself to be uplifted by the contemplation of My omnipotence.'

10. וָאֶשְׁבֹּר עָלָיו חֻקִּי וָאָשִׂים בְּרִיחַ וּדְלָתָיִם — *I hemmed it in by moats, providing bolts and gates. Rashi* takes the root שבר to indicate a *breaking* of the ground, that is, the digging of a moat. He adduces *Joshua* 7:5 where he takes שְׁבָרִים as meaning *a moat.* חוק would be used in its sense of *boundary.* The use of this metaphor, though strictly speaking not really appropriate for keeping in the waters of the sea, would be justified since *doors* and *bolts* have also been used. [We may still wonder at its use. The usual function of a moat would be to keep people out of the city, rather than to hold back the citizens from leaving.]

R' Yosef Kara thinks that שבר is used in the sense that God *breaks* the waves and prevents them from engulfing the dry land. He adduces *Psalms* 65:8 and 89:10, where שבח is used in the same context. Apparently he feels that the ר and ח are interchangeable.

Daas Mikra suggests that חוק might be used here in two meanings. It could mean *a boundary,* and that is how *Rashi* has understood it. But with *Metzudos,* we could also interpret the word as *law.* God imposes His law upon the seas. In such a context שבר would be used in the sense *to execute* a law, in much the same way as כרת is used with בְּרִית.

11. וָאֹמַר עַד־פֹּה תָבוֹא וְלֹא תֹסִיף וּפֹא־יָשִׁית בִּגְאוֹן גַּלֶּיךָ — *Saying, 'Up to here you shall come and no further. Only here will your crests flaunt their majesty!'* When we think of waves we think of motion. Nothing so clearly demonstrates God's might as the towering foam-spun wave, one minute rearing upwards and forwards in seemingly wild abandon, and the next lapping softly and harmlessly at the seashore.

12. הֲמִיָּמֶיךָ צִוִּיתָ בֹּקֶר יִדַּעְתָּה הַשַּׁחַר מְקֹמוֹ — *Have you ever ordered up the morning, told the dawn its place?* The position of the sun vis-a-vis the earth changes every day. It does not rise today at the precise location at which it rose yesterday. Clearly, Iyov would be at a loss to tell the sun where it should rise (*Ramban*).

13. לֶאֱחֹז בְּכַנְפוֹת הָאָרֶץ וְיִנָּעֲרוּ רְשָׁעִים מִמֶּנָּה — *That it might take hold of the corners of the earth, so that the wicked might be shaken from it.* Both *Ibn Ezra* and *Ramban* have the *dawn* of the previous verse as the subject of this one. The spreading light is pictured as taking hold of the corners of the earth. The breaking day signals the destruction of the wicked. This may

יד וְיִנָּעֲרוּ רְשָׁעִים מִמֶּנָּה׃ תִּתְהַפֵּךְ כְּחֹמֶר חוֹתָם וְיִתְיַצְּבוּ
טו כְּמוֹ לְבוּשׁ׃ וְיִמָּנַע מֵרְשָׁעִים אוֹרָם וּזְרוֹעַ רָמָה תִּשָּׁבֵר׃
טז־יז הֲבָאתָ עַד־נִבְכֵי־יָם וּבְחֵקֶר תְּהוֹם הִתְהַלָּכְתָּ׃ הֲנִגְלוּ לְךָ
יח שַׁעֲרֵי־מָוֶת וְשַׁעֲרֵי צַלְמָוֶת תִּרְאֶה׃ הִתְבֹּנַנְתָּ עַד־רַחֲבֵי־
יט אֶרֶץ הַגֵּד אִם־יָדַעְתָּ כֻלָּהּ׃ אֵי־זֶה הַדֶּרֶךְ יִשְׁכָּן־אוֹר וְחֹשֶׁךְ

well be because the natural element of the wicked is the darkness of the night — see 24:13ff. In the bright morning light they must soon succumb.

In an alternative interpretation, *Ramban* reads this and the next verse as God's affirmation of Elihu's doctrine of *Gilgul HaNeshamos.* It is true that Elihu had already made this point and that Iyov, as indicated by his silence, had already accepted it. However, Elihu could not possibly have been certain of the truth of his assertion. By its nature the doctrine is one which can only be known through revelation and tradition. This verification God now provides.

Ramban at 33:29 had made the following point. The doctrine as enunciated by Elihu had dealt with only one half of the problem — the suffering of the righteous. This, because it had been that aspect of the difficulty which, in a practical way, had most troubled Iyov. The tranquility of the wicked was less of a problem because that might well be explained as a manifestation of God's overwhelming goodness, vouchsafed even when least deserved. Once the doctrine had been established as far as the suffering of the righteous is concerned, it can be used as a model for the solution of the other.

Because the former problem had already been dealt with by Elihu, God in His treatment here concentrates upon the latter.

Our verses, then, are designed to solve the mystery of the well-being of the wicked.

How, then, are we to understand verses 13 and 14?

The sense appears to be as follows: Verse 13 teaches that whatever tranquility the wicked enjoy will certainly come to an end. When the precise time comes, they will be *shaken* from the earth. Verse 14 then goes on to say that after this will have occurred, the earth will take on a new appearance (תִּתְהַפֵּךְ כְּחֹמֶר חוֹתָם), because it will become populated by new forms, as these same wicked people will reappear upon it, changed into other personalities, changed as thoroughly as one who is unrecognizable because he is wearing different clothes (וְיִתְיַצְּבוּ כְּמוֹ לְבוּשׁ).

Although *Ramban* discusses this matter repeatedly — in the Introduction to Iyov, in the commentary, in the *D'rashah al Divrei Koheles* and in *Toras HaAdam,* he never makes completely clear how the doctrine of *Gilgul HaNeshamos* justifies the tranquility of the wicked. He never says, in so many words, that it might be explained on the basis of merits earned in an earlier incarnation — and it seems unlikely that this is what he means.

The closest *Ramban* comes to an explication of the matter is when he offers his analysis of *Psalms* 73 in the Introduction to Iyov. There, at verse 20, after the psalmist had described his confusion at the tranquility of the wicked and the suffering of the righteous which seem to fly in the face of all his theological assumptions, we read: כַּחֲלוֹם מֵהָקִיץ ה׳ בָּעִיר צַלְמָם תִּבְזֶה, which, as *Ramban* understands it, we might translate: *When they reawaken in the city as from a dream, God will render their visage odious.* In explanation of this verse, *Ramban* writes: After they will have reawakened in the city, their visage, having earlier been one that inspires respect will become odious. This, in contrast to the righteous man who will not have to be returned to the crucible, but will remain eternally in the presence of His God, as it says: וַאֲנִי תָמִיד עִמָּךְ אָחַזְתָּ בְּיַד יְמִינִי, *still, I was always loyal You, You grasped my right hand* (v. 23, there).

Ramban appears to be untroubled by the tranquility of the wicked in one incarnation, as long as in the next one, the suffering which is his due will come upon him. Accordingly we may say as follows: The tranquility of the wicked should never disturb us. If they seem to be contented there is presumably some good reason for it. As for the suffering which is their due, they will experience it in another incarnation.

14. תִּתְהַפֵּךְ כְּחֹמֶר חוֹתָם וְיִתְיַצְּבוּ כְּמוֹ לְבוּשׁ — *It changes radically, as does clay exposed to the seal, they stand revealed as through a garment.* Most commentators read this verse as a reference to the doctrine of תְּחִיַּת הַמֵּתִים, the ultimate *Resurrection of the Dead.* However, this doctrine seems to have little to do with the general thrust of this speech, and we assume that the various *aggadic* sources for this interpretation are meant in a homiletic sense, and are not

38/14-19 so that the wicked might be shaken from it. [14] It changes radically, as does clay exposed to the seal, they stand revealed as through a garment. [15] Thus, the wicked will have their light withheld, and the power of the haughty will be smashed. [16] Have you penetrated to the inaccessible abysses of the sea, have your critical searchings taken you to the deepest depths? [17] Are the gates of death familiar to you? Are you able to look upon the portals leading to the dread shadows? [18] Have you considered the wide expanses of the earth? Pray tell if you know it all! [19] Where is the road which leads to the light's abode, and as for the darkness,

offered as the simple meaning — see footnote to 28:4. Accordingly we have translated, as does *Daas Mikra*, according to the *p'shat*, but will also bring *Rashi's* homiletical interpretation.

As *Daas Mikra* understands the verse, the subject of תִּתְהַפֵּךְ is the earth. It is compared to wet clay which receives impressions from the artisan's seal — in this case the breaking dawn. The sense of the simile is that just like the clay takes on an entirely new form when it is stamped by the seal, so too the earth, in the morning's light, looks quite different than it did when it was still shrouded in darkness. Its topography takes on fresh contours, becomes clothed, as with a fresh *garment* in unanticipated shapes and forms.

For *Rashi's* homiletic explanation we go to *Rashi* in *Sanhedrin* 38a where his language is clearer than it is here. חוֹתָם is the human face, so called because it is stamped in the image of Adam. This visage changes (תִּתְהַפֵּךְ) into amorphous clay (חֹמֶר) as the body disintegrates in the grave. One day, when the dead will be resurrected, this body will once more arise, like a fresh garment.

15. וְיִמָּנַע מֵרְשָׁעִים אוֹרָם וּזְרוֹעַ רָמָה תִּשָּׁבֵר — *Thus, the wicked will have their light withheld, and the power of the haughty will be smashed.* We continue with *Daas Mikra*. Since the wicked are afraid of the light they will have to hide during the day and thus reap none of its benefits. Those, on the other hand, who arrogantly decide to brave the dangers which it poses, will ultimately be caught and have their power smashed.

16. הֲבָאתָ עַד־נִבְכֵי־יָם וּבְחֵקֶר תְּהוֹם הִתְהַלָּכְתָּ — *Have you penetrated to the inaccessible abysses of the sea, have your critical searchings taken you to the deepest depths?* For *Rashi's* interpretation of נִבְכֵי as *something which is locked away*, see also at *Exodus* 14:3 and commentary to 28:11, above.

Verses 8-11 had already described God's prowess over the sea. Verses 12-15 had then moved on to the rising dawn and its devastating effect upon the wicked. Why come back to the sea once more?

We must assume that the thrust of this passage is quite different from the earlier one. Here the picture is not one of peerless power, of God imposing His will upon the roaring, bucking waves. Here we are given an intimation of impenetrable mysteries lurking deep in the abyss, of arcane riddles the solution for which must be sought in the deepest depths. The נִבְכֵי יָם (*inaccessible abysses of the sea*) and the תְּהוֹם (*deepest depths*) of our verse seem intimately connected with the שַׁעֲרֵי מָוֶת (*gates of death*) and the שַׁעֲרֵי צַלְמָוֶת (*portals leading to the dread shadows*) of the next. These terms, as *Rashi* understands them, deal with *Gehinnom*, a nether world forever beyond human ken. Clearly, with our verse a new section is begun, one which is in no way connected with the earlier description of the sea.

17. הֲנִגְלוּ לְךָ שַׁעֲרֵי־מָוֶת וְשַׁעֲרֵי צַלְמָוֶת תִּרְאֶה — *Are the gates of death familiar to you? Are you able to look upon the portals leading to the dread shadows?* See at 3:4 for צַלְמָוֶת as *dread shadows.*

Rashi thinks that the *gates of death* refers to *Gehinnom*. *Ramban* thinks that the question might be: Do you have any knowledge of those who have already died?

18. הִתְבֹּנַנְתָּ עַד־רַחֲבֵי־אָרֶץ הַגֵּד אִם־יָדַעְתָּ כֻלָּהּ — *Have you considered the wide expanses of the earth? Pray tell if you know it all!* Just as you are not privy to the secrets of the depths, so too can you claim no knowledge of the widths of the earth (*Daas Mikra*).

We have rendered רַחֲבֵי as *wide expanses*, since the plural form [similar to גָּבְהֵי שָׁמַיִם] is used to indicate abundance (*Daas Mikra*).

19. אֵי־זֶה הַדֶּרֶךְ יִשְׁכָּן־אוֹר וְחֹשֶׁךְ אֵי־זֶה מְקֹמוֹ — *Where is the road which leads to light's abode, and as for the darkness, where is its place?* In the poet's mind, light and darkness are pictured

כ אֵי־זֶה מְקֹמוֹ׃ כִּי תִקָּחֶנּוּ אֶל־גְּבוּלוֹ וְכִי תָבִין נְתִיבוֹת
כא־כב בֵּיתוֹ׃ יָדַעְתָּ כִּי־אָז תִּוָּלֵד וּמִסְפַּר יָמֶיךָ רַבִּים׃ הֲבָאתָ
כג אֶל־אֹצְרוֹת שָׁלֶג וְאוֹצְרוֹת בָּרָד תִּרְאֶה׃ אֲשֶׁר־
כד חָשַׂכְתִּי לְעֶת־צָר לְיוֹם קְרָב וּמִלְחָמָה׃ אֵי־זֶה הַדֶּרֶךְ
כה יֵחָלֶק אוֹר יָפֵץ קָדִים עֲלֵי־אָרֶץ׃ מִי־פִלַּג לַשֶּׁטֶף
כו תְּעָלָה וְדֶרֶךְ לַחֲזִיז קֹלוֹת׃ לְהַמְטִיר עַל־אֶרֶץ לֹא־
כז אִישׁ מִדְבָּר לֹא־אָדָם בּוֹ׃ לְהַשְׂבִּיעַ שֹׁאָה וּמְשֹׁאָה
כח וּלְהַצְמִיחַ מֹצָא דֶשֶׁא׃ הֲיֵשׁ־לַמָּטָר אָב אוֹ מִי־הוֹלִיד
כט אֶגְלֵי־טָל׃ מִבֶּטֶן מִי יָצָא הַקָּרַח וּכְפֹר שָׁמַיִם מִי יְלָדוֹ׃

as dwelling at particular locations, and it is from there that they spread out over the world (*Daas Mikra*).

However, we may consider the possibility that *light* and *darkness* in this verse are metaphors for good and evil, this, because it seems likely that our verse relates to verse 18 as does verse 17 to verse 16. Just as there we saw that the *abyss* and the *depths* are associated with the gates of death mentioned in the next verse, so too, in verse 18 the ends of the earth implied in רַחֲבֵי אָרֶץ might well be those heavenly chambers from which bliss and sorrow emanate.

20. כִּי תִקָּחֶנּוּ אֶל־גְּבוּלוֹ וְכִי תָבִין נְתִיבוֹת בֵּיתוֹ — *That you could take it to its boundary, and do you really think that you know the paths that lead to its house?* The object of תקח is the *light* from the previous verse. It takes wisdom to be able to take the light from its abode and to bring it to where the darkness is, so that it might illuminate that place. Clearly Iyov does not have the requisite knowledge (*Metzudos*).

21. יָדַעְתָּ כִּי־אָז תִּוָּלֵד וּמִסְפַּר יָמֶיךָ רַבִּים — *Did you know all this? Then surely you were born even then, and surely the years of your life are many!* The tone of this verse, as *Rashi* appears to take it, is slightly mocking. Apparently Iyov needs to be shaken out of his moral complacency.

22. הֲבָאתָ אֶל־אֹצְרוֹת שָׁלֶג וְאוֹצְרוֹת בָּרָד תִּרְאֶה — *Did you ever penetrate to the vaults where the snow is kept? Have you seen into the repositories of the hail?* A new series of rhetorical questions begins with the same introductory הֲבָאתָ . . . of verse 16.

23. אֲשֶׁר־חָשַׂכְתִּי לְעֶת־צָר לְיוֹם קְרָב וּמִלְחָמָה — *Which I withheld in anticipation of a day of trouble, for a day when battle is to be joined.* Snow and hailstones are considered to be weapons which God uses against His enemies. The Sages see hints in our verse to the devastating hail which fell upon the five kings at Giveon (*Joshua* 10:11) [לְעֵת צָר, *a time of trouble*], and which will, one day, lay waste the hoards of Gog, king of Magog (*Ezekiel* 38:22) [לְיוֹם קְרָב וּמִלְחָמָה] (*Rashi*).

24. אֵי־זֶה הַדֶּרֶךְ יֵחָלֶק אוֹר יָפֵץ קָדִים עֲלֵי־אָרֶץ — *Which path leads to the point at which the light is refracted, where the sunlight diffuses out upon the earth.* The translation follows *Rashi.* The first phrase focuses upon the sunlight as it divides into rays. In the second phrase קָדִים, *east*, is used as a metaphor for the *sun* which rises in the east.

25. מִי־פִלַּג לַשֶּׁטֶף תְּעָלָה וְדֶרֶךְ לַחֲזִיז קֹלוֹת — *Who opened a canal for the rushing waters, or made a path for the clouds which carry the crashing of the thunder?* In this poetic version, the torrential rain is seen as guided by means of a canal which directs it to the desired location.

For חֲזִיז as *cloud*, see *Rashi* to *Zechariah* 10:1.

26. לְהַמְטִיר עַל־אֶרֶץ לֹא־אִישׁ מִדְבָּר לֹא־אָדָם בּוֹ — *That the rain might fall upon uninhabited land, a wilderness with no one in it.* The rain occasionally falls upon arid land which could produce nothing and which therefore never supported any life. As a result of the rainfall it becomes productive. This would be another of the wonders of nature which Iyov clearly cannot duplicate. Thus, apparently, *Metzudos.*

Ramban's comments are very brief and, while extremely significant for the understanding of the thrust of this speech, they lend themselves to two possible explanations. In this verse and the next he remarks simply that rain that falls in uninhabited areas clearly falls for the benefit of the wild animals which are the only ones who live there.

Now, what is the correct conclusion to draw from this?

R' Yosef Kara apparently understands the verses as does *Ramban*, but elaborates further: If, God says, I act mercifully towards even the

where is its place? 20 *That you could take it to its boundary, and do*
you really think that you know the paths that lead to its house?
21 *Did you know all this? Then surely you were born even then, and*
surely the years of your life are many! 22 *Did you ever penetrate to*
the vaults where the snow is kept? Have you seen into the
repositories of the hail? 23 *Which I withheld in anticipation of a day*
of trouble, for a day when battle is to be joined. 24 *Which path leads*
to the point at which the light is refracted, where the sunlight
diffuses out upon the earth. 25 *Who opened a canal for the rushing*
waters, or made a path for the clouds which carry the crashing of
the thunder? 26 *That the rain might fall upon uninhabited land, a*
wilderness with no one in it. 27 *To bring plenty where there was only*
desolation, to bring forth a verdant sprouting. 28 *Does rain then*
have a father? Who gave birth to the dew-springs? 29 *From whose*
womb did the ice issue forth? Who gave birth to the frost of heaven?

wild animals, sustaining them in their desolate surroundings, then surely I would be considerate of man who was created in My image. How then can you have the temerity of accusing Me of having treated you unfairly?

It also seems possible that *Ramban* may have had in mind the interpretation which *Daas Mikra* offers for these verses: From the fact that rain falls even in desolate areas in which the only beneficiaries are the wild animals, it is clear that man is not the only creature upon whom Divine Providence is showered. Man is not God's only concern. If the earth produces its bounty, it is not exclusively for him.

Now, if this latter explanation is the correct one, then the passage fits comfortably into the rest of the speech as *Ramban* understands it — see commentary to verse 1. The less than central position which man occupies in the hierarchy of nature precludes his understanding anything of God's stewardship of his affairs.

But, as *R' Yosef Kara* understands the argument, this passage would seem to have a substantively different purpose than have any of the other passages. Its purpose is to convince Iyov that God is not vindictive but merciful. This has not been the thrust of the speech as *Ramban* has read it. However, this idea would be in consonance with the thrust of the speech as *R' Yosef Kara* has understood it. See above in commentary to various verses for his apparent perception of God's speech.

27. לְהַשְׂבִּיעַ שֹׁאָה וּמְשֹׁאָה וּלְהַצְמִיחַ מֹצָא דֶשֶׁא — *To bring plenty where there was only desolation, to bring forth a verdant sprouting.* This verse is to be taken as an elaboration of the previous one. We have followed *Metzudos* for שֹׁאָה וּמְשֹׁאָה. See above at 30:3 for a different rendering.

28. הֲיֵשׁ־לַמָּטָר אָב אוֹ מִי־הוֹלִיד אֶגְלֵי־טָל — *Does rain then have a father? Who gave birth to the dew-springs?* The sources of the rainfall are a mystery which Iyov will never be able to penetrate.

We have followed *Metzudos* for אֶגְלֵי. He believes that the א is pleonastic, that is, that it is added to the word without any apparent reason (see at 21:23, 31:7 and 33:7). The word is identical in meaning with גֻּלָּה, which at *Joshua* 15:19 means *a spring.*

Rashi (as explicated also at *Chagigah* 12b) believes that the ל of אֶגְלֵי has replaced a נ (see above at 37:9) and that the word is the same as, אַגָּן, *a bowl* (see *Exodus* 24:6). Thus: *pools of dew.*

Ramban understands the sense of the verse as follows: Do rain, dew, ice and frost have parents which produce offspring in their own likeness? Who, if not God, determined that the one should appear in this form, the other, in that?

R' Yosef Kara is interested in the phenomenon that the rain, which in its original state is presumably one amorphous body of water, falls down as separate drops which never touch one another. Do these drops have a father who took them from the body of water and separated them, or were they created as discrete entities?

29. מִבֶּטֶן מִי יָצָא הַקָּרַח וּכְפֹר שָׁמַיִם מִי יְלָדוֹ — *From whose womb did the ice issue forth? Who gave birth to the frost of heaven?* All this, Iyov can never know.

לח/ל־מ ל־לא כָּאֶבֶן מַיִם יִתְחַבָּאוּ וּפְנֵי תְהוֹם יִתְלַכָּדוּ: הַתְקַשֵּׁר מַעֲדַנּוֹת
לב כִּימָה אוֹ־מֹשְׁכוֹת כְּסִיל תְּפַתֵּחַ: הֲתֹצִיא מַזָּרוֹת בְּעִתּוֹ
לג וְעַיִשׁ עַל־בָּנֶיהָ תַנְחֵם: הֲיָדַעְתָּ חֻקּוֹת שָׁמָיִם אִם־
לד תָּשִׂים מִשְׁטָרוֹ בָאָרֶץ: הֲתָרִים לָעָב קוֹלֶךָ וְשִׁפְעַת־מַיִם
לה־לו תְּכַסֶּךָּ: הַתְשַׁלַּח בְּרָקִים וְיֵלֵכוּ וְיֹאמְרוּ לְךָ הִנֵּנוּ: מִי־שָׁת
לז בַּטֻּחוֹת חָכְמָה אוֹ מִי־נָתַן לַשֶּׂכְוִי בִינָה: מִי־יְסַפֵּר שְׁחָקִים
לח בְּחָכְמָה וְנִבְלֵי שָׁמַיִם מִי יַשְׁכִּיב: בְּצֶקֶת עָפָר לַמּוּצָק
לט וּרְגָבִים יְדֻבָּקוּ: הֲתָצוּד לְלָבִיא טָרֶף וְחַיַּת כְּפִירִים
מ תְּמַלֵּא: כִּי־יָשֹׁחוּ בַמְּעוֹנוֹת יֵשְׁבוּ בַסֻּכָּה לְמוֹ־אָרֶב:

30. כָּאֶבֶן מַיִם יִתְחַבָּאוּ וּפְנֵי תְהוֹם יִתְלַכָּדוּ — *Like a stone, the waters are concealed, the very depths are imprisoned.* Just like a stone which falls into the water is forthwith concealed from the human eye, so too the waters, once covered by the ice, cannot be seen and are indeed imprisoned underneath it.

31. הַתְקַשֵּׁר מַעֲדַנּוֹת כִּימָה אוֹ־מֹשְׁכוֹת כְּסִיל תְּפַתֵּחַ — *Would you undertake to tie the bonds of Kimah, or to loosen the shackles of K'sil?* According to *Berachos* 58b, the constellation *Kimah* is the source of cold, while *K'sil* is the source of heat. *Kimah's* bonds must be tied because, without restraint, the cold which it would release could destroy the whole world. *K'sil*, on the other hand, must be let loose so that its warmth might temper the frigid *Kimah* (*Rashi*).

מַעֲדַנּוֹת usually means *delights*, from עֵדֶן, *to luxuriate*. As *bonds*, it is unique in Scripture although it is attested in Rabbinic literature — see *Succah* 13b (*Radak, Sefer HaShorashim*). It is noteworthy that the root עָנַד, that is, with the ד and נ interchanged, does indeed mean *to bind*.

32. הֲתֹצִיא מַזָּרוֹת בְּעִתּוֹ וְעַיִשׁ עַל־בָּנֶיהָ תַנְחֵם — *Would you be able to bring forth the constellations, each in its own time? Is it you who leads Ayish along with her dependents?* For מַזָּרוֹת instead of מַזָּלוֹת, that is, a substitution of ר for ל, see at 37:9 and 16.

Berachos 58b teaches that the constellation *Ayish* is tail-shaped, that is, that it seems to be pulling along a slew of smaller stars in its wake. These are the *children* or *dependents* of our verse.

33. הֲיָדַעְתָּ חֻקּוֹת שָׁמָיִם אִם־תָּשִׂים מִשְׁטָרוֹ בָאָרֶץ — *Do you understand the laws which govern the heavens? Is it you who subjects earth to their dominion?* The constellations control the climate of the earth, determining cold and heat, summer and winter (*Rashi*).

R' Yosef Kara cites *Bereishis Rabbah*: R' Siman taught: Not a single blade of grass will grow until a constellation in heaven whips it and tells it, 'Grow!'

34. הֲתָרִים לָעָב קוֹלֶךָ וְשִׁפְעַת־מַיִם תְּכַסֶּךָּ — *Do you give orders to the cloud, or cause avalanches of water to drench you? Rashi* joins the two phrases with *or* [lit. *Do you raise your voice to the cloud or have avalanches of water cover you up*]?

The orders given the cloud would have the purpose of commanding them to gather together in order to form the dark, lowering, cloud-cover from which torrential rains would descend.

35. הַתְשַׁלַּח בְּרָקִים וְיֵלֵכוּ וְיֹאמְרוּ לְךָ הִנֵּנוּ — *Do you dispatch the lightning so that it goes upon its way, saying to you, 'We have done Your bidding!' Rashi* appears to understand the verse as describing God's omnipresence. God is as much at the point to which the lightning is dispatched, as He is at the point from which it leaves. The *Shechinah* is everywhere.

36. מִי־שָׁת בַּטֻּחוֹת חָכְמָה אוֹ מִי־נָתַן לַשֶּׂכְוִי בִינָה — *Who gave the kidneys wisdom? Who imbued the heart with understanding?* טֻחוֹת are *kidneys* from טָחָה, *to cover*, because the kidneys are covered by body fats (*Ramban*). That the kidneys are considered to be the seat of wisdom is attested by *Psalms* 16:7, *By night my kidneys chastise me* (*Ramban*). The heart, which throughout Scripture is viewed as being the seat of *understanding*, is called שֶׂכְוִי, from סָכָה, *to look afar* (*Rashi, Bereishis* 11:29).

The commentators do not make clear by what logic this verse is inserted here. Verse 37 appears to belong to the description of God's stewardship over the heavenly forces.

Rosh Hashanah 26a reports a linguistic usage whereby the rooster, wise of heart because he is able to distinguish between night and day, the rainy season and the summer (*R' Meyuchas*), was called שֶׂכְוִי. This is how *Berachos* 60b seems to take it. There, we learn that upon hearing the rooster's call in the morning,

30 *Like a stone, the waters are concealed, the very depths are impris-*
oned. 31 *Would you undertake to tie the bonds of Kimah, or to loosen*
the shackles of K'sil? 32 *Would you be able to bring forth the constel-*
lations, each in its own time? Is it you who leads Ayish along with
her dependents? 33 *Do you understand the laws which govern the*
heavens? Is it you who subjects earth to their dominion? 34 *Do you*
give orders to the cloud, or cause avalanches of water to drench you?
35 *Do you dispatch the lightning so that it goes upon its way,*
saying to you, 'We have done Your bidding!' 36 *Who gave the kid-*
neys wisdom? Who imbued the heart with understanding? 37 *Who,*
with wisdom, makes the firmament shine? Who makes heaven's
cloud-flagons lie low? 38 *When the earth was cast into a firm mass,*
and the clods were joined. 39 *Are you prepared to trap prey for the*
lion? Can you supply the needs of a pride of lions? 40 *That they*
are able to crouch in their lairs, lie low in ambush in their dens.

we are to recite the blessing: אֲשֶׁר נָתַן לַשֶּׂכְוִי בִינָה לְהַבְחִין בֵּין יוֹם וּבֵין לָיְלָה. However, *Rosh* there explains as follows: In that blessing, too, the true meaning of שֶׂכְוִי is *heart* — it is, after all, the understanding lodged in the heart whereby we have the faculty to differentiate between light and darkness — and therefore we are to make this blessing even when we have not heard the rooster crow. However, since this Hebrew word is similar in sound to the Arabic word for rooster, the Sages instituted this blessing in conjunction with the cock's crow, because for one who is sleeping in a dark room with no windows, it is only this song which makes him aware of the breaking day.

37. מִי־יְסַפֵּר שְׁחָקִים בְּחָכְמָה וְנִבְלֵי שָׁמַיִם מִי יַשְׁכִּיב — *Who, with wisdom, makes the firmament shine? Who makes heaven's cloud-flagons lie low?* The translation follows *Ramban* and *Metzudos* who take יְסַפֵּר from סַפִּיר, *a sapphire stone*, and see the verse as describing the brightness of the sky. *Rashi* takes the word from סַפֵּר, *to tell*, thus: Who tells the heavens what to do?

The clouds are described as flagons because they contain the water which will later come down as rain (*Rashi*).

38. בְּצֶקֶת עָפָר לַמּוּצָק וּרְגָבִים יְדֻבָּקוּ — *When the earth was cast into a firm mass, and the clods were joined.* Our rendering of מוּצָק as *a firm mass* follows *Radak, Sefer HaShorashim.* It also appears to be *Rashi's* opinion since he has this phrase refer to the central core (לִיסוֹד עוֹלָם בְּאֶמְצָעִיתוֹ) from which the earth was built.

39. הֲתָצוּד לְלָבִיא טָרֶף וְחַיַּת כְּפִירִים תְּמַלֵּא — *Are you prepared to trap prey for the lion? Can you supply the needs of a pride of lions?* *Ramban* understands the first phrase to deal with the lion's instinctive knowledge of how to catch his prey. The question is: Would you be able to teach the lion his hunting skills?

There is also the possibility that the point of this description is to demonstrate God's benign concern for the lion's — and particularly for his cub's — food supply. In contrast to the vulture — the last of the animals to be described in this speech, see 39:27 — the lion is not equipped with the faculty of seeking out its own food. If the animals upon which it feeds do not come into the vicinity of his lair, he will starve. That God places an adequate food-supply within reach of the lion, is a mark of His concern.

This would make the description of the lion of a piece with that of the raven in verse 41. There, too, the point is that God looks after the little ones whom the parents are apt to ignore.

For חַיָּה we have also followed *Ramban* who adduces *II Samuel* 23:13, where חַיַּת פְּלִשְׁתִּים, according to all commentators, means *a group of the Philistines. R' Meyuchas* here, as also *Ibn Ezra*, takes the word to mean the *living force*, the *soul* or craving of the wild beasts.

The change from God's stewardship over the mighty heavens to His caring concern for the much narrower animal-world is seamless and sudden. There are no limits to the range of God's concerns. Great and small merit His loving attention.

40. כִּי־יָשֹׁחוּ בַמְּעוֹנוֹת יֵשְׁבוּ בַסֻּכָּה לְמוֹ־אָרֶב — *That they are able to crouch in their lairs, lie low in ambush in their dens.* The lions know instinctively how to trap their prey into a sense of security. They lie low in their dens, so that the animals which they are stalking will not be aware of the danger (*Metzudos*).

לח/מא מא מִי יָכִין לָעֹרֵב צֵידוֹ כִּי־יְלָדָו אֶל־אֵל יְשַׁוֵּעוּ יִתְעוּ
לט/א־ט א לִבְלִי־אֹכֶל: הֲיָדַעְתָּ עֵת לֶדֶת יַעֲלֵי־סָלַע חֹלֵל אַיָּלוֹת
ב תִּשְׁמֹר: תִּסְפֹּר יְרָחִים תְּמַלֶּאנָה וְיָדַעְתָּ עֵת לִדְתָּנָה:
ג־ד תִּכְרַעְנָה יַלְדֵיהֶן תְּפַלַּחְנָה חֶבְלֵיהֶם תְּשַׁלַּחְנָה: יַחְלְמוּ
ה בְנֵיהֶם יִרְבּוּ בַבָּר יָצְאוּ וְלֹא־שָׁבוּ לָמוֹ: מִי־שִׁלַּח
ו פֶּרֶא חָפְשִׁי וּמֹסְרוֹת עָרוֹד מִי פִתֵּחַ: אֲשֶׁר־שַׂמְתִּי
ז עֲרָבָה בֵיתוֹ וּמִשְׁכְּנוֹתָיו מְלֵחָה: יִשְׂחַק לַהֲמוֹן קִרְיָה
ח תְּשֻׁאוֹת נוֹגֵשׂ לֹא יִשְׁמָע: יְתוּר הָרִים מִרְעֵהוּ וְאַחַר
ט כָּל־יָרוֹק יִדְרוֹשׁ: הֲיֹאבֶה רֵּים עָבְדֶךָ אִם־יָלִין עַל־

41. מִי יָכִין לָעֹרֵב צֵידוֹ כִּי־יְלָדָיו אֶל־אֵל יְשַׁוֵּעוּ יִתְעוּ לִבְלִי־אֹכֶל — *Who prepares nourishment for the raven, when its children cry out to God, confused without food?* Little ravens are hatched white. The parents, sure that these are not their own offspring, neglect to feed them. God makes tiny worms grow in the body-wastes of the offspring, and it is from these that they receive their sustenance (*Rashi* from *Tanchuma, Eikev* 2).

XXXIX.

1. הֲיָדַעְתָּ עֵת לֶדֶת יַעֲלֵי־סָלַע חֹלֵל אַיָּלוֹת תִּשְׁמֹר — *Can you fathom when the mountain-goat will yean? Can you anticipate the labor pangs of the gazelle? Ramban* introduces this chapter, as follows: It is the purpose of all the descriptions which follow to convince Iyov that God has full knowledge even of the individuals within the animal-world, and looks after them so that His world might be filled through them. This would counter the heresies which Iyov had occasionally propounded — that God neither knows nor cares about what happens in this world.

Ramban feels that both the ravens at the end of the previous chapter and the mountain-goat here are chosen because they are of no immediate use to man — the raven in his blackness even seems repulsive to us. God's caring providence extends even to such.

Rashi quotes *Bava Basra* 16b. The mountain-goat has no feeling for its young and, when about to give birth, it ascends a rock so that the new-born calf will fall to the ground and be killed. At the precise moment of the drop, God brings an eagle to the spot to catch the little one upon its wings.

The gazelle's womb is extremely narrow. It cannot provide safe passage for its young. At the precise moment at which the lamb is about to pass through, God has a scorpion bite the mother. The pain and shock causes the opening to widen, and birth becomes possible.

Rashi continues by quoting the *Gemara.* Both these efforts at saving the young require split-second timing. If I were off by even one short moment, all would be lost. If, now, I am capable of such precision, does it stand to reason that I would confuse אִיּוֹב with אוֹיֵב, that I would carelessly consider you to be my enemy? (see at 1:1 for Iyov's claim that God seemed to have confused the two).

2. תִּסְפֹּר יְרָחִים תְּמַלֶּאנָה וְיָדַעְתָּ עֵת לִדְתָּנָה — *Counting the months to the fullness of her term, foreseeing the moment of birth?* So that you might function towards them as would a midwife (*Metzudos*).

3. תִּכְרַעְנָה יַלְדֵיהֶן תְּפַלַּחְנָה חֶבְלֵיהֶם תְּשַׁלַּחְנָה — *When they crouch to bring forth their young, ridding themselves of their agonies.* פָּלַח means *to cleave* — see at 16:13. It is used here to describe the contractions which open up the passage through which the young can be expelled. With the birth accomplished, the pains which had wracked the mother's body are no more.

4. יַחְלְמוּ בְנֵיהֶם יִרְבּוּ בַבָּר יָצְאוּ וְלֹא־שָׁבוּ לָמוֹ — *Their young will grow to robust health, will fatten in the meadows. They have gone, never more to return to them.* יַחְלְמוּ from חָלַם, *to grow strong.* יִרְבּוּ from רָבָה, *to increase;* thus, in our case, to widen their girth by fattening.

One of the miracles of creation is the ability of the newborn, in the animal-world, to fend for themselves, and quickly to gain independence from their mothers.

5. מִי־שִׁלַּח פֶּרֶא חָפְשִׁי וּמֹסְרוֹת עָרוֹד מִי פִתֵּחַ — *Who set the wild ass free? Who loosened the fetters of the onager? Targum* to *Jeremiah* 2:24 uses עָרוֹד to render [א] פֶּרֶה. They evidently

38/41 [41] *Who prepares nourishment for the raven, when its children cry*
out to God, confused without food?

39/1-9 [1] *Can you fathom when the mountain-goat will yean? Can you*
anticipate the labor pangs of the gazelle? [2] *Counting the*
months to the fullness of her term, foreseeing the moment of birth?
[3] *When they crouch to bring forth their young, ridding themselves*
of their agonies. [4] *Their young will grow to robust health, will*
fatten in the meadows. They have gone, never more to return to
them. [5] *Who set the wild ass free? Who loosened the fetters of the*
onager? [6] *It is the wilderness which I have designated as his home,*
his dwelling is upon the salt-flats. [7] *He scorns the teeming*
cities, will never hear the clamoring of the taskmaster. [8] *He scouts*
the mountains for his pasture, searches out all greenery. [9] *Would*
the wild ox be willing to serve you? Would he spend time at

describe the same animal. We have used different words in order to reflect the Hebrew in the text.

Rashi explains that the wild ass is *free* in the sense that it will not permit itself to be domesticated and thus will never be forced to work for anyone.

6. אֲשֶׁר־שַׂמְתִּי עֲרָבָה בֵּיתוֹ וּמִשְׁכְּנוֹתָיו מְלֵחָה — *It is the wilderness which I have designated as his home, his dwelling is upon the salt-flats.* The description of the ass's unfettered freedom continues. It makes its home — through God's providence — where it can never be tamed by man.

7. יִשְׂחַק לַהֲמוֹן קִרְיָה תְּשֻׁאוֹת נוֹגֵשׂ לֹא יִשְׁמָע — *He scorns the teeming cities, will never hear the clamoring of the taskmaster.* City dwelling confines. One is hemmed in by the crowds, deafened by the noise. The wilderness permits uninhibited movement and release.

8. יְתוּר הָרִים מִרְעֵהוּ וְאַחַר כָּל־יָרוֹק יִדְרוֹשׁ — *He scouts the mountains for his pasture, searches out all greenery.* The wild ass is beholden to no one for its food. The huge expanses of greenery are its table.

In this piece, too, the stress seems to be upon the utter self-justifying existence of the wild ass, uncaring of and unresponsive to the needs of man. As earlier, in the case of the ravens and the mountain-goat, Iyov is being told in no uncertain terms that he is only part of a vast whole. While his fate may not be understandable when viewed only from the constraints of a narrow, self-centered perspective, it may be eminently reasonable in the context of a universal plan. A tiny screw may find the wrenching twists to which it is subjected unfair, only as long as it does not realize that it is there to hold together a mighty machine.

An example of how such a view of the individual's suffering might tend to make Iyov's fate more understandable could be found with reference to the tradition of the Sages, quoted repeatedly in chapter 1, that the Satan had been concerned that God's interest in Iyov might presage a rejection of Abraham and the Jewish people. The broader picture, though not Iyov's own life-experience, thus demanded that he be put to the test.

9. הֲיֹאבֶה רֵים עָבְדֶךָ אִם־יָלִין עַל־אֲבוּסֶךָ — *Would the wild ox be willing to serve you? Would he spend time at your feeding trough?* God moves on to another denizen of the wilds who will never permit himself to be harnessed to man's needs.

רֵים here is used as a shortened form of רְאֵם.

As *Aryeh Kaplan* in *The Living Torah* has shown, the רְאֵם is variously identified as either a unicorn or rhinocerous (*Radak, Sefer HaShorashim*), the white antelope (*R' Saadyah Gaon*), the wild ox, aurochs or bison. Our context which connects this animal to the activities surrounding the field and the threshing floor would apparently favor the latter group.

There is, of course, the domesticated ox which serves man willingly enough. The point being made here is that we could never succeed in extending our dominion to the wild variety. These contemptuously reject the bribe of our feeding-trough, opting instead for a life that is free from our yoke.

יָלִין from לון, *to stay overnight*, is used here to describe the state of being connected with anything with some degree of permanence (*Metzudos*).

י אֲבוּסֶךָ: הֲתִקְשָׁר־רֵים בְּתֶלֶם עֲבֹתוֹ אִם־יְשַׂדֵּד עֲמָקִים
יא אַחֲרֶיךָ: הֲתִבְטַח־בּוֹ כִּי־רַב כֹּחוֹ וְתַעֲזֹב אֵלָיו יְגִיעֶךָ:
יב־יג הֲתַאֲמִין בּוֹ כִּי־°ישוב זַרְעֶךָ וְגָרְנְךָ יֶאֱסֹף: כְּנַף־רְנָנִים (יָשִׁיב ק׳)
יד נֶעֱלָסָה אִם־אֶבְרָה חֲסִידָה וְנֹצָה: כִּי־תַעֲזֹב לָאָרֶץ בֵּצֶיהָ
טו וְעַל־עָפָר תְּחַמֵּם: וַתִּשְׁכַּח כִּי־רֶגֶל תְּזוּרֶהָ וְחַיַּת הַשָּׂדֶה
טז תְּדוּשֶׁהָ: הִקְשִׁיחַ בָּנֶיהָ לְּלֹא־לָהּ לְרִיק יְגִיעָהּ בְּלִי־פָחַד:
יז־יח כִּי־הִשָּׁהּ אֱלוֹהַּ חָכְמָה וְלֹא־חָלַק לָהּ בַּבִּינָה: כָּעֵת
יט בַּמָּרוֹם תַּמְרִיא תִּשְׂחַק לַסּוּס וּלְרֹכְבוֹ: הֲתִתֵּן לַסּוּס
כ גְּבוּרָה הֲתַלְבִּישׁ צַוָּארוֹ רַעְמָה: הֲתַרְעִישֶׁנּוּ כָּאַרְבֶּה הוֹד
כא נַחְרוֹ אֵימָה: יַחְפְּרוּ בָעֵמֶק וְיָשִׂישׂ בְּכֹחַ יֵצֵא לִקְרַאת־
כב נָשֶׁק: יִשְׂחַק לְפַחַד וְלֹא יֵחָת וְלֹא־יָשׁוּב מִפְּנֵי־חָרֶב:

10. הֲתִקְשָׁר־רֵים בְּתֶלֶם עֲבֹתוֹ אִם־יְשַׂדֵּד עֲמָקִים אַחֲרֶיךָ — *Could ropes hitch the wild ox to your plow? Would he follow you as he breaks the valley's clods?* The true meaning of תֶּלֶם is *furrow*. It is used here as a metaphor for the plow — that which makes the furrow.

11. הֲתִבְטַח־בּוֹ כִּי־רַב כֹּחוֹ וְתַעֲזֹב אֵלָיו יְגִיעֶךָ — *Would you rely on him for his strength is great, and leave to him [the fruits of] your toil?* הֲתִבְטַח from בָּטַח, *to trust*. Thus: Would you ever be justified in depending upon it for help?

12. הֲתַאֲמִין בּוֹ כִּי־יָשִׁיב זַרְעֶךָ וְגָרְנְךָ יֶאֱסֹף — *Could you trust him to bring in your plantings, gather the produce of your threshing-floor?* With his voracious appetite, he would consume your entire harvest. It is only I, God, Who can supply him with the food that he needs (*Metzudos*).

13. כְּנַף־רְנָנִים נֶעֱלָסָה אִם־אֶבְרָה חֲסִידָה וְנֹצָה — *Song-wings exult! Even the plumed pinions of the stork!* For this verse we have followed *R' Yosef Kara* because his rendering is simpler than that of *Rashi*.

Rashi thinks that רְנָנִים, חֲסִידָה and נֹצָה are all names of birds. He describes the רְנָנִים as a *large bird* — perhaps, as some commentators suggest, the ostrich.[1]

Metzudos thinks that it is a bird which delights (נֶעֱלָסָה) in the rich colors of its plumage — thus, perhaps the peacock. The sense of the verse is to challenge Iyov to consider the usage of these wondrous birds and to realize how little he really knows about their exotic world. *Rashi* takes אֶבְרָה, which normally means *pinion*, as a word describing *birds* in general.

Since it is simpler to understand the passage if it deals with only one species, we have followed *R' Yosef Kara* who takes רְנָנִים as deriving from רָנַן, *to sing*. It describes the music made by the whirring wings of the bird in flight. אֶבְרָה is not taken as a metaphor for bird, but as the actual *pinion*. נֹצָה is the *plumage* as the term is used in *Ezekiel* chapter 17.

14. כִּי־תַעֲזֹב לָאָרֶץ בֵּצֶיהָ וְעַל־עָפָר תְּחַמֵּם — *For she ignores her eggs upon the ground, leaving the earth to heat them.* The translation follows *Metzudos*. The sense of the passage will be that the only hope for these forsaken youngsters

1. *Dr. Yehudah Feliks* in *The Animal World of the Bible* demonstrates how precisely the description in this passage fits what is known about the habits of the ostrich. We quote:

> The ostrich is called *Kenaph Renanim, Its wing rejoices*, i.e. its lovely plumage is an aesthetic feast to the eye. The verse goes on, *But, are her pinions and feathers kindly?* — it has wings but is unable to fly. The Hebrew word חֲסִידָה [in Arabic, *thorns*] is probably a reference to the strong spikes in the chest which it uses to steady the body before leaping forward. Verses 14-15: *For she ignores her eggs upon the ground, leaving the earth to heat them. Forgetting that they will be crushed by feet, ground under by the field-animals* — the blazing hot sand hatches the eggs and thus they are exposed to the danger of being trampled under the feet of passing travelers. The next verse says: *She has disavowed her children* .... The male mates with a number of females and he cares for their young. He transfers (הִקְשִׁיחַ) the young of one female into the nest of the other. This biological fact might have branded the ostrich with cruelty (see *Lamentations* 4:3). The description continues: *For God has denied her wisdom, did not grant her understanding.* The ostrich is considered a very stupid, timid bird [as indicated by the disproportionately small head]. *When the time is ripe she will simply fly off, making sport of horse and rider.* The speed of the ostrich, the result of its powerful, long strides, is such that it distances a man on horseback. It is caught only of exhaustion after a long pursuit by a chain of fast riders.

39/10-22 *your feeding trough?* 10 *Could ropes hitch the wild ox to your plow?*
Would he follow you as he breaks the valley's clods? 11 *Would you*
rely on him for his strength is great, and leave to him [the fruits of]
your toil? 12 *Could you trust him to bring in your plantings, gather*
the produce of your threshing-floor? 13 *Song-wings exult! Even the*
plumed pinions of the stork! 14 *For she ignores her eggs upon the*
ground, leaving the earth to heat them. 15 *Forgetting that they*
will be crushed by feet, ground under by the field-animals.
16 *She has disavowed her children as though they were not her*
own, unafraid that her labor will go to waste. 17 *For God has*
denied her wisdom, did not grant her understanding. 18 *When the*
time is ripe she will simply fly off, making sport of horse and
rider. 19 *Do you give the horse its power, do you imbue its neck*
with menace? 20 *Can you make it prance as the locusts leap,*
snorting regally — total terror! 21 *His hooves plow up the valley-*
floor, exulting in its brawn it strains towards battle. 22 *It scoffs*
at fear, never trembles, does not recoil from before the sword.

lies in God's benign providence.

15. וַתִּשְׁכַּח כִּי־רֶגֶל תְּזוּרֶהָ וְחַיַּת הַשָּׂדֶה תְּדוּשֶׁהָ — *Forgetting that they will be crushed by feet, ground under by the field-animals.* תְּזוּרֶהָ from זָרָה, *to smash* — see *Rashi* to *Exodus* 32:20. תְּדוּשֶׁהָ from דוּשׁ, *to thresh.*

16. הִקְשִׁיחַ בָּנֶיהָ לְּלֹא־לָהּ לְרִיק יְגִיעָהּ בְּלִי־פָחַד — *She has disavowed her children as though they were not her own, unafraid that her labor will go to waste.* קָשַׁח in the *hiphil* has the meaning, *to harden the heart* — see *Rashi* to *Isaiah* 63:17.

17. כִּי־הִשָּׁהּ אֱלוֹהַּ חָכְמָה וְלֹא־חָלַק לָהּ בַּבִּינָה — *For God has denied her wisdom, did not grant her understanding.* הִשָּׁהּ, from נָשָׁה, *to forget.* The root is also used in the sense, *to withhold.* See, for example, *Genesis* 41:51 (*Daas Mikra*).

18. כָּעֵת בַּמָּרוֹם תַּמְרִיא תִּשְׂחַק לַסּוּס וּלְרֹכְבוֹ — *When the time is ripe she will simply fly off, making sport of horse and rider.* מרא does not recur in Scripture, and the sense of תַּמְרִיא must be inferred from the context. *Rashi* believes the word to denote an irresponsible wanderlust which can seduce a person to leave home and culture behind, in order to roam the world.

Once the stork has taken off, it can afford to laugh at horse and rider whom it can easily outstrip (*Ramban*).

Daas Mikra suggests that the man on the horse might be a hunter attempting to catch the stork. With all his advantages he has no chance of catching it. The message to Iyov is that even so foolish a bird may still easily elude man. Clearly he is not as significant in the scheme of things as Iyov's self-centered preoccupation with his own affairs would have implied.

19. הֲתִתֵּן לַסּוּס גְּבוּרָה הֲתַלְבִּישׁ צַוָּארוֹ רַעְמָה — *Do you give the horse its power, do you imbue its neck with menace?* It seems likely that the description of the war-horse is now taken up because of the mention of the horse in the previous verse (*Daas Mikra*).

רַעַם is *thunder. Rashi* adds בְּעָתָה, *fear,* apparently assuming that it is the terror which thunder inspires which explains its use here. The arching neck of the rearing war-horse is certainly an awe-inspiring sight.

The use of לָבַשׁ, *to clothe,* in this context is typical Hebrew idiom which has no real parallel in English. The sense derives from the fact that the clothes which a person wears convey a particular impression about him.

20. הֲתַרְעִישֶׁנּוּ כָּאַרְבֶּה הוֹד נַחְרוֹ אֵימָה — *Can you make it prance as the locusts leap, snorting regally — total terror!* נָחַר, *to snort* (*Jeremiah* 6:29), thus, נַחַר, *a snorting,* and נָחִיר, *the nostril* (41:12).

21. יַחְפְּרוּ בָעֵמֶק וְיָשִׂישׂ בְּכֹחַ יֵצֵא לִקְרַאת־נָשֶׁק — *His hooves plow up the valley-floor, exulting in its brawn it strains towards battle.* For חָפַר, *to dig,* we have followed *Daas Mikra. Rashi* and *Metzudos* render, *to spy out,* because valleys are the ideal places for cavalry to reconnoiter. *R' Yosef Kara* renders, *to be trusting* — see at 11:18. The horse gallops sure-footedly along the valley.

22. יִשְׂחַק לְפַחַד וְלֹא יֵחָת וְלֹא־יָשׁוּב מִפְּנֵי־חָרֶב — *It scoffs at fear, never trembles, does not recoil from before the sword.* Perhaps there is a lesson here for Iyov. Just as the flashing sword

כג־כד עָלָיו תִּרְנֶה אַשְׁפָּה לַהַב חֲנִית וְכִידוֹן: בְּרַעַשׁ וְרֹגֶז
כה יְגַמֶּא־אָרֶץ וְלֹא־יַאֲמִין כִּי־קוֹל שׁוֹפָר: בְּדֵי שֹׁפָר ׀ יֹאמַר
הֶאָח וּמֵרָחוֹק יָרִיחַ מִלְחָמָה רַעַם שָׂרִים וּתְרוּעָה:
כו־כז הֲמִבִּינָתְךָ יַאֲבֶר־נֵץ יִפְרֹשׂ כְּנָפָו לְתֵימָן: אִם־עַל־
כח פִּיךָ יַגְבִּיהַּ נָשֶׁר וְכִי יָרִים קִנּוֹ: סֶלַע יִשְׁכֹּן וְיִתְלֹנָן
כט עַל־שֶׁן־סֶלַע וּמְצוּדָה: מִשָּׁם חָפַר־אֹכֶל לְמֵרָחוֹק עֵינָיו
ל יַבִּיטוּ: וְאֶפְרֹחָו יְעַלְעוּ־דָם וּבַאֲשֶׁר חֲלָלִים שָׁם הוּא:

intimidates only such as allow themselves to be frightened, so too, the terrors of sickness and pain break only those too weak to rise to the challenge of battle.

23. עָלָיו תִּרְנֶה אַשְׁפָּה לַהַב חֲנִית וְכִידוֹן — *Let the quiver clash against him, the flash of spear and javelin.* The arrows in the quiver rattle against one another, producing a frightening sound (*Rashi*).

24. בְּרַעַשׁ וְרֹגֶז יְגַמֶּא־אָרֶץ וְלֹא־יַאֲמִין כִּי־קוֹל שׁוֹפָר — *With furious energy he swallows the earth, never heeding the trumpet sounds.* The fluid speed with which he gallops along makes it appear as though he is swallowing up the ground (*Metzudos*). The implied threat of the trumpet-blasts of the opposing army leaves him cold. He refuses to be intimidated by them and, instead, rushes headlong into the fray.

25. בְּדֵי שֹׁפָר יֹאמַר הֶאָח וּמֵרָחוֹק יָרִיחַ מִלְחָמָה רַעַם שָׂרִים וּתְרוּעָה — *As the trumpet's sounds increase, he says, 'Aha!,' scents battle from afar, the tumult of captains and trumpet blasts.* דֵּי, *a sufficiency* (*Rashi*). The more the trumpet blasts are directed against him, the more he neighs in delight at the pending confrontation. The accouterments of war, far from intimidating him, spur him to inspired frenzy.

Each of the previous descriptions seems to have been inspired by one of two themes, neither of which seems to underlie the picture of the war-horse drawn here. There were those in which God's concern for the young, who might otherwise go unprotected and hungry, was prominent. Clearly, these were drawn so that Iyov might have God's benign concern for all creatures brought home to him. The others pictured such animals as are totally independent of man, unwilling to trade their freedom for any pittance of which servitude might assure them. These were apparently chosen so that Iyov might be disabused of his concept that only man and his concerns are important.

But, why the war-horse? The selfless enthusiasm with which it serves its masters would seem to affirm rather than undermine those of Iyov's ideas which, it would appear, had led him astray in his thinking.

Perhaps the message concerns the degree of adaptability of which God's creatures are capable. It is the nature of the wild horse to rebel bitterly against the imposition of a human environment — man's touch, man's control, man's bridle and saddle. It is not for nothing that we talk of *breaking* a horse. Nevertheless, once it is broken we see the war-horse savoring its role upon the battlefield — an alien world of human presence, human sounds, human domination, of which, in nature, it knows nothing at all. Its adaption to situations that by disposition it would find hateful, is total. Iyov should have done no less. True that by his losses his world had been turned topsy-turvy. But, might he not consider that those same sterling qualities which had stood him in such good stead during better times, might just as well be turned to good advantage in his present, so sadly reduced, state? Why can he not demand of himself that he adapt to the new reality?

26. הֲמִבִּינָתְךָ יַאֲבֶר־נֵץ יִפְרֹשׂ כְּנָפָו לְתֵימָן — *Is it by your insight that the hawk hovers, spreads its wings southward?* According to *Dr. Yehudah Feliks* in *The Animal World of the Bible*, the נֵץ is the *sparrow-hawk*. It is not a permanent resident of the Land of Israel, but stays awhile on its migration from the northern climes to the south. Hence our phrase, ... *spreads its wings southward.*

Unlike other hawks who pick their prey off the ground, the sparrow-hawk *hovers* in the air, catching its prey, the small warbler, in flight. אֵבֶר, *wing*; hence, יַאֲבֶר־נֵץ.

27. אִם־עַל־פִּיךָ יַגְבִּיהַּ נָשֶׁר וְכִי יָרִים קִנּוֹ — *Is it by your orders that the vulture soars, making its nest on high? Feliks* identifies the נֶשֶׁר as the *vulture* rather than as the *eagle* as has often been assumed. This, on the basis of our verse 30 from which it is apparent that it feeds on carrion rather than on live prey. He believes that the name נֶשֶׁר, from נָשַׁר, *to fall out*, derives from the vulture's bald neck which conveys the impression of feathers having fallen out.

[23] Let the quiver clash against him, the flash of spear and javelin.
[24] With furious energy he swallows the earth, never heeding the
trumpet sounds. [25] As the trumpet's sounds increase, he says,
'Aha!,' scents battle from afar, the tumult of captains and trumpet
blasts. [26] Is it by your insight that the hawk hovers, spreads its
wings southward. [27] Is it by your orders that the vulture soars,
making its nest on high? [28] It makes its home upon the cliffs and
roosts there, on outcrops and fortress-like rocks. [29] From there it
spies out food, its eyes sweeping the distances. [30] Its young gulp
blood. Where the carrion is, there too is he.

28. סֶלַע יִשְׁכֹּן וְיִתְלֹנָן עַל־שֶׁן־סֶלַע וּמְצוּדָה — *It makes its home upon the cliffs and roosts there, on outcrops and fortress-like rocks. R' Meyuchas* to this verse stresses the inaccessibility of the vulture's home. Perhaps he thinks that the vulture was chosen for description because — in contrast to the war-horse which precedes it — it lives totally removed from any human contact. The vulture does not serve man, nor is it dependent upon him. It does not even affect him negatively by preying upon his livestock — since it feeds off the carrion in the field. From man's point of view the vulture inhabits a world of its own — might as well inhabit a different planet. Surely it is the ultimate contradiction to the ethnocentricity of Iyov's thought.

מְצוּדָה is usually understood as *tower* or *fortress. Daas Mikra* points out that its use in conjunction with סֶלַע parallels *II Samuel* 22:2-3.

29. מִשָּׁם חָפַר־אֹכֶל לְמֵרָחוֹק עֵינָיו יַבִּיטוּ — *From there it spies out food, its eyes sweeping the distances.* This is in sharp and direct contrast to the lion with whom the description of the animal world had begun. There God's benign providence is manifest by the way in which He makes sure that the animals upon which the lion feeds pass by close to his lair. The lion has no mechanism by which he might detect his prey further afield. Here, that same providence expresses itself in the sharp eyesight which enables the vulture to spot, from huge distances, the carrion upon which it feeds.

The message is the same. God cares passionately not only for man but for all His creatures.

30. וְאֶפְרֹחָו יְעַלְעוּ־דָם וּבַאֲשֶׁר חֲלָלִים שָׁם הוּא — *Its young gulp blood. Where the carrion is, there too is he. Rashi* takes יְעַלְעוּ as onomatopoeic. עַל עַל conveys the sound of someone gulping down a liquid.

✾ ✾ ✾

The crashing voice from out of the whirlwind ceases as abruptly as it had begun. Iyov's mind is left reeling. Images of a world in formation, of light and darkness, of seething waters, pelting rains, frigid ice, snow and frost, of lurking lions, croaking cries of ravens, of the graceful gazelle writhing in the agonies of birthing, of the onager rejoicing in the wild abandon of its freedom, of the wild ox spurning the pittance which one might offer him to purchase his awesome power, of the foolish stork abandoning its young, of the prancing menacing war-horse chafing at the bit as it strains to rush into battle, of the ferocious birds of prey; all these chase each other around in his mind's eye. The last picture, the one apparently designed to leave the most searing image, is of the vulture chicks gulping down blood, of the adults astride their prey tearing at the carrion's innards,

What is Iyov to make of all this?

The brooding silence reverberates with the echoes of questions and challenges: Where were you . . .?, Have you ever ordered . . .?, Have you considered . . .?, Did you know . . .?, Did you ever penetrate . . .?, Would you undertake . . . be able . . .?, Do you understand . . .?, Do you give orders . . . dispatch . . .?, Are you prepared . . .?, Can you fathom . . .?, and many more.

Is Iyov expected to answer? Does God indeed expect an answer when He says: . . . *I will put questions to you and you will enlighten Me* (38:3).

But, in truth, all these questions are only subsections of the one, overwhelming, crushing query with which God begins His speech: מִי זֶה מַחְשִׁיךְ עֵצָה בְמִלִּין בְּלִי דָעַת, *Who is this who has such murky ideas, speaking without due consideration?* (38:2). It is the relentless מִי which must be pounding within Iyov's mind. *Who*! *Who* am I? *Who* is it really, who has persisted in challenging God, in arrogating to himself the right to pass judgment over the Divine stewardship of human affairs? If Iyov could only identify that *who* — and distance himself from him, then perhaps he will find surcease from his agonies.

Would we not have expected a more loving,

א־ב וַיַּעַן יהוה אֶת־אִיּוֹב וַיֹּאמַר: הֲרֹב עִם־שַׁדַּי יִסּוֹר מוֹכִיחַ

a more conciliatory tone, to one who has suffered so terribly and who has throughout — in spite of occasional lapses into non-acceptable frustration — remained loyal to an incomprehensible God?

The answer lies in the base-question — *Who . . .?*

To *Genesis* 2:7 where we learn how God breathed life into the earthen form of man which He had created, *Rashi* quotes the *midrash*: In man, God combined both the lower and the upper spheres — his body from the lower, his soul from the upper. This, because on the first day heaven [upper] and earth [lower] were formed; on the second day — the firmament [upper]; on the third day — the sea and the dry land [lower]; on the fourth day — the heavenly bodies [upper]; and on the fifth day — the teeming animal world of the sea [lower]. Therefore, in order to avoid jealousy between the upper and the lower spheres, that one should not have one day more than the other allotted to them, God created man — a combination of the upper and the lower — on the sixth day.

Unique, then, among all of God's creatures, man must cope with a crisis of identity. He is combined from two, basically antagonistic, elements. He is neither angel nor beast, can feel fully at home in neither world. Clearly, in order to function positively and productively he must make peace with both his disparate halves. One must dominate, the other must subsume itself so that it can interact in harmonious and constructive counterpoint.

Which half is to preponderate? Is man to identify with his soul, his nonmaterial essence, and have his body serve as loyal handmaiden in pursuit of the goals of the spirit, or is his real place among the creatures of the lower sphere, to which the spiritual longings of his soul must defer?

The answer seems clear enough. *Olam Hazeh*, this physical world, is but an antechamber before *Olam Haba*, the World to Come. *Prepare yourself in the antechamber so that you will be able to enter the palace* (*Avos* 4:21)! This teaching of the Sages, and many more like it, seem to make an unambiguous case for the ascendancy of the spirit over the body.

But, there is also another teaching of the Sages: To *Psalms* 36:7, . . . *Man and animal will God deliver*, they teach: This refers to people who are extremely intelligent, but act simply as though they were [but] animals (*Chullin* 5b). Apparently, then, there are areas in which it were better for man to deny himself the surgical precision of his sharply honed intellect and, instead, to accept unquestioningly the fate which God wishes for him.

This may be the meaning of the accusing, *Who*! in God's opening sentence: *Who is this who has such murky ideas, speaking without due consideration*! Perhaps He meant to shake Iyov out of his complacency and bring him to the realization that it was the wrong part of his being which he had engaged in his search for the truth. A stranger has intruded upon the relationship between God and His servant. This stranger must be driven out — harshly. *Who* — which part of you is making your belligerent claims? Can you not see that by involving your intellect in attempting to fathom God's ways, you are placing yourself outside the pale? See before you a world of the most wondrous creatures, all without complaint, harmonizing into the symphony of praise to God which is the song of the physically functioning world.

How readily you could have joined this chorus had you but been willing to admit the limitations to which your humanness is subject.

XL.

◆ God's Final Speech

The chapter begins with a small exchange of words between God and Iyov. *Rashi* and *Ramban* part ways sharply in their respective interpretations of this exchange — the commentary deals with the details of these divergent approaches.

After that, there is still some unfinished business. According to *Ramban*, Iyov, while finally having accepted that he had been in the wrong, has not yet verbalized his contrition. True repentance must be reflected in the soul-wrenching mortification of confession — and of this Iyov has as yet proved himself incapable. According to *Rashi* even more is still missing. Iyov, as indicated by his earlier silence and subsequent surliness, has been intellectually convinced but not yet emotionally won over. This is not enough. More *can* be accomplished and, therefore, *must* be accomplished. Iyov deserves that he not be left in the slough of defeat. He must be helped to become a victor — over the enemy within himself.

[1] Then HASHEM challenged Iyov, saying: [2] Does fighting with Shaddai confer privilege? One who presumes to wrangle with

Ramban does not point out any essential difference between this speech and the earlier one. Accordingly, we are left with no clear picture of why Iyov should have been brought to confession by it.

We may surmise that it was a matter of form rather than of content. As we will see at verse 6, the whirlwind which accompanied this last speech was of lesser intensity than the first one had been. Iyov must have wondered why. The fact that the speech came from out of a whirlwind where the second one had been made in a *still, quiet voice,* must have alerted him to the fact that all was not well. The fact that the whirlwind was less forceful than the earlier one would have told him that he was at least on the road to ultimate rehabilitation. Aware that amends were still expected of him, but, at the same time encouraged by the fact that his efforts appeared to bear fruit, Iyov drew the correct conclusions and was able to bring himself to confess his errors.

For understanding *Rashi,* we feel that the crucial element in the speech is the change from second to third person at 41:1. As we explain this change in the commentary, it signals the fact that God was willing to leave any adversarial stance behind Him, and henceforth to regard Iyov as a partner in His contemplation of the world's wonders. Iyov's switch from churlish submission to adoring acceptance is the direct result of the euphoria borne of the fact that — against all expectations — God was willing to trust him.

From that point on, Iyov is gently drawn to the full realization of how, ideally, man might cope with the vicissitudes which life hurls at him. His instruction — in the context of a book where wholesale failure at comforting has been traced again and again to insensitivity — is importantly accomplished by indirection. God, rather than imposing ideas, draws Iyov into His thought-world. He encourages him to draw his own conclusions. This He does by permitting him a glimpse into the mythical, a world of terribly harsh but ultimately triumphant beauty. The *leviathan,* the very name of which implies an *accompaniment,* a *drawing along* (see at 40:29), will by the sheer power of its savage grace serve as Iyov's guide to a recognition of his own vast potential.

1. וַיַּעַן ה׳ אֶת־אִיּוֹב וַיֹּאמַר — *Then HASHEM challenged Iyov, saying.* עָנָה, *to declare* can be used with many different nuances. As delineated in Introductory Remarks to chapter 38, we feel that *Rashi* would agree to *Metzudos'* understanding of what happened here. God, upon ending His first speech, expects a response from Iyov. When none is forthcoming (for reasons which we have discussed in detail there), He challenges him. We have tried to reflect this in our translation.

2. הֲרֹב עִם־שַׁדַּי יִסּוֹר מוֹכִיחַ אֱלוֹהַּ יַעֲנֶנָּה — *Does fighting with Shaddai confer privilege? One who presumes to wrangle with God has the obligation to respond!* *Rashi* appears to assume that the ס in יִסּוֹר replaces a ש, and that the word derives from שָׂרַר, *to exercise rulership. Rashi's* comments to both halves of this verse are not entirely clear but, based on our assumption in the commentary to verse 1, that he agrees with *Metzudos* that God's words here are meant to express surprise and dissatisfaction at Iyov's silence, it would seem that our translation has caught *Rashi's* meaning.

In a similar vein, *Metzudos* renders: *Have you, who had the temerity to quarrel with Shaddai, not been sufficiently chastised [by His answer]? Clearly one who argues with God, has the obligation to respond [to His words]. [Why, then, do you keep silent?]*

In Introductory Remarks to chapter 38 we have discussed why, indeed, Iyov kept silent in the face of the glorious panorama of nature which God had painted for him. We thought that — as reflected in his almost sulky answer (vs. 4-5) — Iyov had gravely misunderstood God's meaning. Where God had intended to help him towards a more balanced perspective — one which would have allowed him to wean himself away from the excessive egocentrism which lay at the bottom of his inability to find comfort — he had felt himself pushed into a recognition of his own frailty and futility. It was this misunderstanding — we felt — which made God's second speech necessary.

As we pointed out there, *Ramban* has a radically different perception of our verse. He views it as a small speech in its own right and renders it: *Is it to be assumed that he who found fault with Shaddai will now continue to quarrel? That he who had earlier seen fit to scold God will even now have something to say?* The sense of the argument is that now that Iyov has learned of the mystery of *Gilgul HaNeshamos,* it could surely be supposed that he would not continue his argument with God. If he had previously *found fault with Shaddai* that was

ג־ד אֱלוֹהַ יַעֲנֶנָּה׃ וַיַּעַן אִיּוֹב אֶת־יהוה וַיֹּאמַר׃ הֵן
ה קַלֹּתִי מָה אֲשִׁיבֶךָּ יָדִי שַׂמְתִּי לְמוֹ־פִי׃ אַחַת דִּבַּרְתִּי וְלֹא
ו אֶעֱנֶה וּשְׁתַּיִם וְלֹא אוֹסִיף׃ וַיַּעַן־יהוה אֶת־
ז אִיּוֹב °מִנסְעָרָה וַיֹּאמַר׃ אֱזָר־נָא כְגֶבֶר חֲלָצֶיךָ אֶשְׁאָלְךָ
ח וְהוֹדִיעֵנִי׃ הַאַף תָּפֵר מִשְׁפָּטִי תַּרְשִׁיעֵנִי לְמַעַן תִּצְדָּק׃

°מִן ו סְעָרָה ק׳

only because he had not yet learned the truth. Surely now that he knows better, he will desist.

As we saw there, *Ramban* feels that it is this small speech, delivered without the terrifying accompaniment of the whirlwind, which tipped the scales and finally won Iyov's absolute contrition and submission. God's third speech is needed only because, in spite of everything, Iyov has not yet admitted fault. This will come in chapter 42.

3. וַיַּעַן אִיּוֹב אֶת־ה׳ וַיֹּאמַר — *Iyov responded to* HASHEM, *saying.* The context requires a different rendering for וַיַּעַן than in verse 1.

4. הֵן קַלֹּתִי מָה אֲשִׁיבֶךָּ יָדִי שַׂמְתִּי לְמוֹ־פִי — *Truly I am of little worth. What can I answer you? I have put my hand to my mouth. Rashi* is silent on this verse. We continue with the assumption that he would agree with *Metzudos* for the general meaning of the section.

There is a parting of the ways here between *Metzudos* and *Ramban.* As *Metzudos* sees it, this verse is simply an answer to God's query. God had wondered why Iyov had not seen fit to react in any way to the first speech. Iyov answers that, very simply, he had nothing to say. His inferiority has been made so obvious to him, that there seemed little point in continuing the discussion. There is no sense of contrition here; simply a recognition of the reality of his position.

Ramban sees the matter differently. The impact of God's words had been overwhelming. Iyov now realizes that God knows, cares, and does kindness, justice and charity in the land (. . . כִּי הֵבִין שֶׁהָאֵ־ל יוֹדֵעַ וּמַשְׁגִּיחַ וְעוֹשֶׂה חֶסֶד מִשְׁפָּט וּצְדָקָה בָּאָרֶץ). *Ramban* makes clear that Iyov's change of heart derived directly from the tiny speech which God had just delivered in *a small still voice.* The next speech will add nothing new, but will bring about the next and final stage in Iyov's rehabilitation. He will go a step beyond recognition and confess the error of his earlier stance.

5. אַחַת דִּבַּרְתִּי וְלֹא אֶעֱנֶה וּשְׁתַּיִם וְלֹא אוֹסִיף — *I have said little — but I shall declare no more; only two things — but I will not continue. Rashi* equates אַחַת with something small and insignificant (מְעַט). Our translation conveys the sense of the verse as *Rashi* would render it at the *p'shat* level.

Rashi also brings the tradition of the Sages that אַחַת and שְׁתַּיִם, respectively, refer to statements which Iyov had made containing those words. The first at 9:22 — אַחַת הִיא עַל כֵּן אָמַרְתִּי תָּם וְרָשָׁע הוּא מְכַלֶּה, *There is a thing — because of which I said: 'He destroys the constant with the wicked!'* The second, at 13:20 — אַךְ שְׁתַּיִם אַל תַּעַשׂ עִמָּדִי אָז מִפָּנֶיךָ לֹא אֶסָּתֵר, *If only You would not do these two to me, then I will not conceal myself from Your presence.*

The impression is that these two statements, among all the many near-blasphemies which Iyov had uttered throughout his many speeches, are particularly heinous. We have discussed the nature of the first one at 9:24 — see there.

For the second passage, we may suggest as follows:

At 13:15 we noted that *Ramban* understands the passage at 13:20 as expressing Iyov's terror at the thought that God might deny him the bliss of the World to Come, as He had already mistreated him in this world. We could well understand that Iyov's conscience is much troubled for having entertained such a thought. One who accepts the idea of an afterlife can never be absolutely adamant in his denial of God's justice. Given the complexity of rendering absolute justice amid the conflicting needs and claims of teeming humanity there may be any number of reasons why the righteous man did not, in this world, receive his due. But, there is always the valid assumption that God would make it up to him in *Olam Haba.*[1]

Thus, Iyov's willingness to consider the possibility that he may never receive his due, moves his temerity into a new and frightening framework. Up to this point his many complaints could have been interpreted as a grumbling at why God could not have found some

1. *R' Elchanan Wasserman* in his *Kovetz Maamarim* makes this point. He cites the example of a single righteous person who lives among many wicked people whose actions cause God to deny them the blessing of rain. Certainly God will not, under normal circumstances, bring rain upon the one field owned by the *tzaddik* while the rest of the area is subject to a drought. Rather, this *tzaddik's* undeserved losses will be made up to him in *Olam Haba.*

God has the obligation to respond! 3 Iyov responded to HASHEM,
saying: 4 Truly I am of little worth. What can I answer you? I have
put my hand to my mouth. 5 I have said little — but I shall declare
no more; only two things — but I will not continue. 6 So HASHEM
responded to Iyov from out the whirlwind, saying. 7 Come,
gird your loins like a warrior. I will put questions to you and
you will enlighten Me. 8 Would you go so far as to undermine
My judgment, put Me in the wrong so that you might be right?

means to make even his temporal existence more pleasant. With this thought, however, he broaches the abyss of absolute heresy.

But, as we saw at 13:20, *Rashi* does not take that passage as does *Ramban*. Why, in his perception, does Iyov choose his regret at having made that particular statement, as illustrating his change of heart?

Perhaps, a careful reading of that passage will yield a rather different insight into Iyov's meaning here. It is not so much an expression of regret at inexcusable liberties taken, as a sour reflection upon the futility of earlier hopes.

The passage in question is one of those in which Iyov allows himself to dream how wonderful it would be if only he were given a chance to confront God with the justice of his cause. Surely, there is a part of him which knows that his imaginings are unrealistic. There is just no way in which man can summon God to the bar of justice. But notwithstanding this perception, the thought is real enough to Iyov as long as it occupies his mind. He feels — indeed knows — that if only God would not do these *two* to him, if He would not release His power to crush Iyov and if He would not allow fear of Him to terrorize Iyov, then he could make a creditable case, could persuade God of his legitimate claims.

Now that God has actually appeared to him, Iyov regrets his earlier outburst. Not because, as is the case with the passage from chapter 9, he now realizes how blasphemous such words can be, but because the futility of his dreams finally hits him. He has had his wish. God has, in fact, appeared to him. And he has had no chance at all to put into practice any of his carefully-laid plans. Instead of him overwhelming God by the justice of his cause, God has crushed him by the sheer force of His majesty.

As we saw above, Iyov has not read God's first speech correctly. As his silence indicates, he feels vanquished rather than loved, defeated rather than uplifted. Never again will he make the error of dreaming that he might win vindication by confronting God.

This perception of Iyov's ruminations at this point, provides the background for the correct understanding of the first part of God's next speech. See below.

6-14. As we noted before (Introductory Remarks to chapter 38), these opening verses of God's next speech appear to escalate the severity with which Iyov is being addressed. We thought that, according to *Rashi*, the explanation of this intensification is as follows: God has seen that His attempt to wean Iyov away from his excessive egocentrism, and thus to help him come to grips with his fate, has failed. By his silence Iyov has shown that he has entirely misunderstood God's purpose. He feels smothered by the glorious panorama of nature which has only now been passed before him, rather than elevated. He has been cudgeled into silence rather than having been electrified into an adoring ecstasy. Because of this, God's first task is to show Iyov how He would have talked had His intention really been to intimidate him. After that comes the loving reconciliatory tone (הִנֵּה נָא . . .) of verse 15, which will finally yield the fruit of Iyov's loving acceptance.

6. וַיַּעַן־ה׳ אֶת־אִיּוֹב מִן סְעָרָה וַיֹּאמַר — *So HASHEM responded to Iyov from out of the whirlwind, saying.* See Introductory Remarks to chapter 38 for a discussion of why this speech, too, was said from out of the whirlwind.

Ramban points out that מִן סְעָרָה lacks the definite article which had been used at 38:1. Apparently, then, this second whirlwind was less terrifying than the first. See Introductory Remarks to this chapter.

7. אֱזָר־נָא כְגֶבֶר חֲלָצֶיךָ אֶשְׁאָלְךָ וְהוֹדִיעֵנִי — *Come, gird your loins like a warrior. I will put questions to you and you will enlighten Me.* This is the precise form in which God's first speech began (see commentary at 38:3). By using the same words it is as though God were saying: Come, let us start again at the beginning — but notice what I could have said had I really wanted to intimidate you.

8. הַאַף תָּפֵר מִשְׁפָּטִי תַּרְשִׁיעֵנִי לְמַעַן תִּצְדָּק — *Would you go so far as to undermine My judgment, put Me in the wrong so that you might be right?* *Ramban*, after examining a number of other

ט־י וְאִם־זְרוֹעַ כָּאֵל ׀ לָךְ וּבְקוֹל כָּמֹהוּ תַרְעֵם׃ עֲדֵה־נָא
יא גָאוֹן וָגֹבַהּ וְהוֹד וְהָדָר תִּלְבָּשׁ׃ הָפֵץ עֶבְרוֹת אַפֶּךָ
יב וּרְאֵה כָל־גֵּאֶה וְהַשְׁפִּילֵהוּ׃ רְאֵה כָל־גֵּאֶה הַכְנִיעֵהוּ
יג וַהֲדֹךְ רְשָׁעִים תַּחְתָּם׃ טָמְנֵם בֶּעָפָר יָחַד פְּנֵיהֶם חֲבֹשׁ
יד־טו בַּטָּמוּן׃ וְגַם־אֲנִי אוֹדֶךָּ כִּי־תוֹשִׁעַ לְךָ יְמִינֶךָ׃ הִנֵּה־נָא

possibilities, feels that in this verse God picks up on the heresies which Iyov has uttered in the past. From the fact that Iyov has not yet seen fit to ask forgiveness for the errors which he made in the past, it is clear that the silence with which Iyov greeted the first speech did not constitute absolute submission. There is something in him which still refuses to acknowledge how absolutely wrong he had been. Accordingly, God now instructs him in the hope that Iyov will yet take that final step in his rehabilitation.

9. וְאִם־זְרוֹעַ כָּאֵל לָךְ וּבְקוֹל כָּמֹהוּ תַרְעֵם — *Do you have strength comparable to that of God? Can you, like He, produce the thunder's clap?* Now Iyov had never claimed — could never have thought — that he was in any way comparable to God. Why should God thus labor the obvious?

Our perception of the Sages' interpretation of verse 5 may help us here. As we saw there, Iyov, in his earlier response, seemed to be grumbling at the fact that his request for a confrontation with God had not been granted. He was still dreaming that if only he had been given the opportunity, he could have vindicated himself. There is an arrogance in such an assertion and it assumes an equal standing with God. In such a context, the criticism contained in this and the next verses would appear justified.

Ramban has the following: In arguing that God's stewardship of the world is unjust, you appear to claim greater wisdom than God's for yourself. Is your strength also greater than His?

10. עֲדֵה־נָא גָאוֹן וָגֹבַהּ וְהוֹד וְהָדָר תִּלְבָּשׁ — *Come, adorn yourself with majesty and grandeur, clothe yourself in splendor and magnificence.* It is pure folly for a human to aspire to the grandeur which rightfully belongs only to God. When man tries to emulate His majesty, he succeeds only in making himself ridiculous (*Ramban*).

11. הָפֵץ עֶבְרוֹת אַפֶּךָ וּרְאֵה כָל־גֵּאֶה וְהַשְׁפִּילֵהוּ — *Let the hot fury of your anger spew forth. Look upon the haughty one so that you might diminish him.* God's challenge that Iyov attempt to subdue the wicked is the subject of the next four verses. If we were to consider verses 9 and 10 as unconnected to this passage, there would be a striking disproportion in the amounts of space devoted to the three statements which God appears to aim at Iyov's arrogance.

Accordingly we read verses 9 and 10 together with the passage beginning with our verse — as follows:

Be the reasons what they may, we have seen (particularly in the second round of the debates between Iyov and the friends) that of the two problems — the suffering of the righteous and the tranquility of the wicked — it is the latter which holds center-stage. It was to that issue that Iyov addressed his devastating critique of the friends' dream-perception of the world, in his response to Tzophar in chapter 21.

Accordingly God, in our section, addresses Iyov's attitude to that issue.

He wishes to show Iyov that he too, were he endowed with even all the possible and necessary powers and abilities required for such a task, would still find it impossible to smash the wicked as readily as he demands of God.

The qualities mentioned in verses 9 and 10 are those with which one who would wish to administer justice as Iyov would have it done, would have to be equipped. Verse 9 deals with the brute power which would be necessary to subdue the wicked; verse 10, with the *majesty, grandeur, splendor* and *magnificence* which are expressions of the exaltedness of one who stands above creation and society and who, from this vantage point, sees the world at his feet, its patterns and relationships open to his scrutiny.[1]

The sense of the entire verse would then be as follows: God wishes to impress upon Iyov that things are not as simple as he believes. Nothing exists in a vacuum and the complex interrelationships which are the warp and woof of society may well make it desirable and

1. Thus, for example, for גֹּבַהּ, we have *Isaiah* 5:16, *Then* HASHEM *Tzevaos will be exalted* (וַיִּגְבַּהּ) *in justice*, to which *Yalkut* remarks: When will *HaKadosh Baruch Hu* be exalted in His world? When, at the end of days, He will exercise justice against the gentile nations. Again, the הוֹד וְהָדָר of the second phrase is familiar to us from *Psalms* 104:1, where it introduces God as the One from Whom system and order flow in the natural world.

40/9-15 9 *Do you have strength comparable to that of God? Can you, like He,*
produce the thunder's clap? 10 *Come, adorn yourself with majesty*
and grandeur, clothe yourself in splendor and magnificence. 11 *Let*
the hot fury of your anger spew forth. Look upon the haughty
one so that you might diminish him. 12 *Look upon the haughty*
one and force him into submission, trample the wicked in their
place. 13 *Hide them all together in the earth, drive their faces down*
into the hidden depths. 14 *I too will join in your praise, when your*
right hand will have stood you in good stead. 15 *Consider, I beg you,*

necessary that the wicked continue to function unperturbed until such a time as justice can overtake them.

The flourishing of the wicked, then, is not a sign of God's impotence, but rather, it derives from His carefully balanced stewardship of human affairs.

This point would then be illustrated by the description of the *behemoth* and the *leviathan* which follows. Both are mighty animals which have the power to wreak untold violence and harm upon their surroundings. Nevertheless, while the *leviathan* is indeed a fearsome predator which strikes terror into the hearts of all who approach it, the *behemoth,* for all its strength, is herbivorous and threatens no one at all. Both these monsters are legitimate denizens of the natural world-order. The vicious *leviathan,* fulfilling the role assigned to it by its Creator, contributes to the harmonious beauty of nature no less than the lumbering, benign, *behemoth.*[1]

It is the same with the wicked people who function within, and serve to balance and to complete, human society. Iyov must learn to live with the limitations which the real world of physical and interdependent existence, imposes upon the idea of pure justice.

12. רְאֵה כָל־גֵּאֶה הַכְנִיעֵהוּ וַהֲדֹךְ רְשָׁעִים תַּחְתָּם — *Look upon the haughty one and force him into submission. Trample the wicked in their place.* תַּחְתָּם from תַּחַת, *underneath,* implies, *into that which is below them,* that is, the place upon which they are standing.

13. טָמְנֵם בֶּעָפָר יָחַד פְּנֵיהֶם חֲבֹשׁ בַּטָּמוּן — *Hide them all together in the earth. Drive their faces down into the hidden depths.* We might have rendered, חֲבֹשׁ as, *[to] veil* which is the usual meaning of the root, חָבַשׁ. However, *Targum* renders כְּבוֹשׁ, from כָּבַשׁ, *to subdue,* and appears to take the expression as analogous to the rabbinic usage, כָּבַשׁ פָּנָיו בְּקַרְקַע (*Sanhedrin* 19b).

There is another rabbinic usage for כָּבַשׁ which is, *to hide.* [When your students are young, תְּהֵא מְכַבֵּשׁ לִפְנֵיהֶם דִּבְרֵי תוֹרָה, *hide the Torah from them,* in contrast to, תְּהֵא מְגַלֶּה לָהֶם, *reveal it to them,* which is recommended for older students (*Shir HaShirim Rabbah* 1). Taken thus, חָבַשׁ in the second phrase would parallel טָמַן in the first.

14. וְגַם־אֲנִי אוֹדֶךָּ כִּי־תוֹשִׁעַ לְךָ יְמִינֶךָ — *I too will join in your praise, when your right hand will have stood you in good stead.* There is heavy sarcasm here. God is making it very clear that Iyov's pretensions to a superior moral standing are ridiculous indeed.

15-24. The first of the two monsters to be paraded before Iyov in this, God's final speech, is the *behemoth.*

Ramban thinks that the plural form of בְּהֵמָה implies that reference is not to any individual creature, but to the entire set of massive beasts which constitute the brawn and terror of the animal world. However, he takes note of the tradition of the Sages (*Bava Basra* 74b) that the *behemoth* is a primordial creature, the שׁוֹר הַבָּר, *wild ox,* of *aggadic* literature, which God created together with man on the sixth day of creation, and which He has preserved for the delight of the *tzaddikim* when the Messiah will have come.[2]

Rashi, too, assumes the Rabbinic tradition for the elucidation of some of the following verses.

At the *p'shat* level it has been recognized that much of the material used in the descrip-

1. This perception of the passage explains the disproportion in the length of the respective descriptions of the two monsters. The word-picture of the *behemoth* takes up just ten verses, while that of the *leviathan* spreads over thirty-four.

The explanation is simple: It is the *leviathan* which requires a defense. Iyov would have no problem accepting the *behemoth* into nature's scheme. It is the predatory *leviathan* which causes him problems.

2. For a detailed discussion and a listing of the relevant *aggadic* sources, see *ArtScroll, Akdamus* pp. 127-135.

טז בְהֵמוֹת אֲשֶׁר־עָשִׂיתִי עִמָּךְ חָצִיר כַּבָּקָר יֹאכֵל׃ הִנֵּה־נָא
יז כֹחוֹ בְמָתְנָיו וְאוֹנוֹ בִּשְׁרִירֵי בִטְנוֹ׃ יַחְפֹּץ זְנָבוֹ כְמוֹ־אָרֶז
יח גִּידֵי פַחֲדָו יְשֹׂרָגוּ׃ עֲצָמָיו אֲפִיקֵי נְחֻשָׁה גְּרָמָיו כִּמְטִיל
יט־כ בַּרְזֶל׃ הוּא רֵאשִׁית דַּרְכֵי־אֵל הָעֹשׂוֹ יַגֵּשׁ חַרְבּוֹ׃ כִּי־בוּל
כא הָרִים יִשְׂאוּ־לוֹ וְכָל־חַיַּת הַשָּׂדֶה יְשַׂחֲקוּ־שָׁם׃ תַּחַת־
כב צֶאֱלִים יִשְׁכָּב בְּסֵתֶר קָנֶה וּבִצָּה׃ יְסֻכֻּהוּ צֶאֱלִים צִלְלוֹ
כג יְסֻבּוּהוּ עַרְבֵי־נָחַל׃ הֵן יַעֲשֹׁק נָהָר וְלֹא יַחְפּוֹז יִבְטַח ׀

tion of the *behemoth* would fit the hippopotamus precisely. Its huge size and girth would make it the ideal model for the awesome proportions with which this terrifying beast is endowed. It is herbivorous (vs. 15,20), is an excellent swimmer and thus spends much of its time in the river with only the top of its head above the water (v. 23), but comes up onto the dry land to sleep in the protective shade of the vegetation which proliferates near the river (v. 22) (*Feliks, The Animal World of the Bible*).

15. הִנֵּה־נָא בְהֵמוֹת אֲשֶׁר־עָשִׂיתִי עִמָּךְ חָצִיר כַּבָּקָר יֹאכֵל — *Consider, I beg you, the behemoth which I created together with you, it feeds on grass, as the cattle do.* After God has demonstrated that Iyov is no match for the wicked of the earth, he is now challenged by the description of the much less powerful denizens of the animal world. He is to realize that even these animals, though they subsist entirely upon vegetation and are therefore not fighters by nature, are far mightier than he. He has no chance at all to overpower them (*Ramban*). [See commentary to verse 11 above for an alternative explanation of why God chooses to describe the *behemoth* and the *leviathan* in this speech.]

At the *p'shat* level, *Ibn Ezra* suggests that עִמָּךְ, *with you*, implies that this monster lives *with you* upon the dry land. This in contrast to the *leviathan* which makes its home in the water. *R' Yosef Kara* suggests: Consider the *behemoth*, which although it feeds only on grass is still *equal to you* in strength.

Mindful of the Sages' interpretation, commentators offer various other explanations: It was created *together with you* on the sixth day of creation (*R' Meyuchas*); or: Although it entered the world during the six days of creation, it is still alive *with you*, since God has preserved it for the Messianic era (*Metzudos*).

16. הִנֵּה־נָא כֹחוֹ בְמָתְנָיו וְאוֹנוֹ בִּשְׁרִירֵי בִטְנוֹ — *See, then the brawn in its loins, the power in its belly.* At the *p'shat* level, Iyov is invited to contemplate the impression of sheer brute power which animates the mighty girth of loins and belly.

Rashi interprets in accordance with the tradition of the Sages recorded at *Bava Basra* 74b. The *behemoth*, in common with the rest of the animal world, were created as a pair, male and female. God, seeing that if they were allowed to propagate normally, their offspring would soon overpopulate the earth, neutered the male and rendered the female frigid. The first phrase describes the male: Its brawn, that is its seed, must now remain in its loins. The second phrase describes the female: Its power, that is the young which it might have born, remain in its frustrated belly.

שְׁרִיר is taken by most commentators as the *umbilicus*. This is attested at *Shir HaShirim* 7:3.

17. יַחְפֹּץ זְנָבוֹ כְמוֹ־אָרֶז גִּידֵי פַחֲדָו יְשֹׂרָגוּ — *Does it wish — its tail stands strong like the cedar, its testicles are bound by twisted cords.* We have followed *R' Meyuchas* for חָפֵץ because he takes it at its most frequent usage — *to desire*.

Rashi and *Metzudos* both suggest that the ץ replaces a ז. חפז is taken respectively as, *to harden — It hardens its tail like a cedar* (*Rashi*); or, *to hasten — Its tail is thick as a cedar and still moves it with utmost speed* (*Metzudos*).

פַּחַד as *testicle* is attested at *Leviticus* 21:20. See *Targum* and *Rashi* there. For שָׂרַג as *twisted*, see *Rashi* at *Eichah* 1:14.

18. עֲצָמָיו אֲפִיקֵי נְחֻשָׁה גְּרָמָיו כִּמְטִיל בַּרְזֶל — *Its skeleton is hard as brass, its large bones are like iron weights.* We have followed *Wertheimer* in his *Biur Sheimos HaNirdafim B'Tanach.* He shows that עֶצֶם is used for the totality of bones, both large and small, while גֶּרֶם always describes the larger bones in the skeletal structure. Thus, even the skeleton of the *behemoth*, which has to take into account even the smaller, softer bones is *hard as brass*. The larger, stronger bones of the *behemoth* can be compared to — even — iron.

מְטִיל does not recur in Scripture. *Rashi*, without adducing any source, renders, *burden*. [But, compare *Targum* to *Isaiah* 13:1 who renders מַשָּׂא as מַטְלָא]. *Mabit* suggests, a *pillar* or

the behemoth which I created together with you, it feeds on grass,
as the cattle do. 16 *See, then the brawn in its loins, the power in its*
belly. 17 *Does it wish — its tail stands strong like the cedar, its*
testicles are bound by twisted cords. 18 *Its skeleton is hard as brass,*
its large bones are like iron weights. 19 *It is the choicest of God's*
creations, only He who made it can bring the blade up close.
20 *For the hills offer it their bounty, there, where all the*
field-animals frolic. 21 *Can it find rest under the shade trees,*
in a bower made from reeds and rushes? 22 *Can the shade tree*
cover it, providing shade? Can the river's stalks surround it?
23 *See, it plunders the river without ever rushing, knows well that*

beam. Ramban thinks of the huge iron sledgehammers which are used to crush rocks. He believes מְטִיל to derive from נָטַל, *to lower* or *swing downward.*

19. הוּא רֵאשִׁית דַּרְכֵי־אֵל הָעֹשׂוֹ יַגֵּשׁ חַרְבּוֹ — *It is the choicest of God's creations, only He who made it can bring the blade up close.* רֵאשִׁית does not only mean *that which is first,* but also, *the choicest* — see, for example at *Amos* 6:6. It is thus that *Ibn Ezra* and *R' Meyuchas* take it, and the simple *p'shat* demands this rendering.

Rashi and others, who interpret the section in accordance with its midrashic meaning, take the word to mean, *first.* The *behemoth* was the very first of the animal world to be created on the sixth day.

Commentators appear to be unanimous in their interpretation of the second phrase. The *behemoth* is so mighty that no mere human can expect to subdue it. Only God Himself can slay it. In the midrashic context this refers to the tradition that when the Messiah comes, and the *tzaddikim* will be ready to delight in their meal, it will be God who slaughters the *behemoth* for them.

❦ ❦ ❦

The printed editions of the book of *Iyov* have a notation here that *Rashi's* commentary stops here. It is not clear from whose pen the concluding commentary comes — although it has much in common with the commentary of *R' Yosef Kara.* From here on we shall refer to this commentary as *The Commentator.*

20. כִּי־בוּל הָרִים יִשְׂאוּ־לוֹ וְכָל־חַיַּת הַשָּׂדֶה יְשַׂחֲקוּ־שָׁם — *For the hills offer it their bounty, there, where all the field-animals frolic.* It derives its strength from the fact that there is always plenty of food for it to eat. It does not need to hunt — the verdure of the hills is readily available. In spite of its enormous strength, none of the field animals stand in fear of it. It never harms them in any way (*Metzudos*).

The Commentator, in the midrashic tradition, makes reference to *Psalms* 50:10, *Behemoth among the thousand hills* . . .. As the Sages tell it, the *behemoth* daily consumes the growth of a thousand hills, and these miraculously replenish themselves overnight (*Pirkei d'R' Eliezer* 11).

21. תַּחַת־צֶאֱלִים יִשְׁכָּב בְּסֵתֶר קָנֶה וּבִצָּה — *Can it find rest under the shade trees, in a bower made from reeds and rushes?* We have translated this and the next verse as rhetorical questions in accordance with *Metzudos* and *Radak, Sefer HaShorashim.* The tenor of the passage seems to require such an interpretation. A description of the tranquil *behemoth* resting under a lotus tree would be dissonant in a passage which appears to be intent upon describing its fearsome qualities.

We have rendered צֶאֱל as a shade tree in accordance with *R' Saadyah Gaon, Ibn Janach, Radak, Sefer HaShorashim* and others who assume the word to describe a specific tree. This in contrast to *the Commentator* who takes the word as an extended form of צֵל, *shade.* The translation of the next verse is rendered more simple if we assume the word to describe a particular tree.

22. יְסֻכֻּהוּ צֶאֱלִים צִלְלוֹ יְסֻבּוּהוּ עַרְבֵי־נָחַל — *Can the shade tree cover it, providing shade? Can the river's stalks surround it?* Another rhetorical question — see commentary to previous verse. The *behemoth* is too mighty to be readily helped by any covering which nature might provide. God created it in such a way that, unprotected, it can tolerate the fierce sun.

23. הֵן יַעֲשֹׁק נָהָר וְלֹא יַחְפּוֹז יִבְטַח כִּי־יָגִיחַ יַרְדֵּן אֶל־פִּיהוּ — *See, it plunders the river without ever rushing, knows well that it can gulp down the Jordan into its mouth.* Here the picture turns to hyperbole. The *behemoth* drinks such vast amounts of water that it is as though it wishes to plunder the reserves of an entire river. This,

כד כִּֽי־יָגִ֣יחַ יַרְדֵּ֣ן אֶל־פִּֽיהוּ׃ בְּעֵינָ֥יו יִקָּחֶ֑נּוּ בְּ֝מוֹקְשִׁ֗ים יִנְקָב־
כה־כו אָֽף׃ תִּמְשֹׁ֣ךְ לִוְיָתָ֣ן בְּחַכָּ֑ה וּ֝בְחֶ֗בֶל תַּשְׁקִ֥יעַ לְשֹׁנֽוֹ׃ הֲתָשִׂ֣ים
כז אַגְמֹ֣ן בְּאַפּ֑וֹ וּ֝בְח֗וֹחַ תִּקֹּ֥ב לֶֽחֱיֽוֹ׃ הֲיַרְבֶּ֣ה אֵ֭לֶיךָ תַּחֲנוּנִ֑ים
כח אִם־יְדַבֵּ֖ר אֵלֶ֣יךָ רַכּֽוֹת׃ הֲיִכְרֹ֣ת בְּרִ֣ית עִמָּ֑ךְ תִּ֝קָּחֶ֗נּוּ
כט לְעֶ֣בֶד עוֹלָֽם׃ הַֽתְשַׂחֶק־בּ֭וֹ כַּצִּפּ֑וֹר וְ֝תִקְשְׁרֶ֗נּוּ לְנַעֲרוֹתֶֽיךָ׃

even when it is drinking slowly, not gulping the water down in a hurry (*Metzudos*).

The Commentator understands the root גוח from which יָגִיחַ is formed as meaning *to draw out*. See, for example, *Ezekiel* 32:2. *Radak*, *Sefer HaShorashim*, understands it as *to extract*.

24. בְּעֵינָיו יִקָּחֶנּוּ בְּמוֹקְשִׁים יִנְקָב־אָף — *He will subdue it with His eyes, perforate its nose with hooks.* We follow *The Commentator*. When the time comes, God will just have to look at the *behemoth* in order to subdue it. He will hook its nose to drag it to its fate.

[In the Introductory Remarks to verses 15-24 we saw that *Ramban* thought that *behemoth* might be regarded as a generic term covering all the massive denizens of dry land. He suggests the same for the *leviathan*. The following passage may have a whole range of sea-monsters in mind.

However, *Ramban* concluded that it was better to follow the tradition of the Sages that *behemoth* is the primordial *wild ox* of which the *aggadah* speaks. By the same token, he takes *leviathan* as the mythical fish from which, in Messianic times, the *tzaddikim* will have their meal prepared.

At the *p'shat* level we note that much of the description contained in our and the next chapter (40:25-41:26) seems to fit the crocodile. This is particularly true of 41:7-8 which speaks of the thick scales which allow not even air to pass through, and which make the *leviathan* impervious to attacks by spear. See also, at verse 29 of our chapter.]

25. תִּמְשֹׁךְ לִוְיָתָן בְּחַכָּה וּבְחֶבֶל תַּשְׁקִיעַ לְשֹׁנוֹ — *Can you pull leviathan by a hook, can you embed a line in its tongue?* It is instructive to contrast the ambience of the *leviathan* section, with that of the passage which had been devoted to the *behemoth*.

The picture with which we are left of the *behemoth* is that of massive strength coupled with a surprisingly benign temperament. This titan is pictured as living its life with no reference to any struggle with man. It browses on the hills, tolerates wildlife in its surroundings, stretches out to sleep in the sun and seems to be in conflict with no one at all. When we are taught that only its Creator could ever *bring the blade up close*, that is simply a testimonial to its enormous strength, not a measure of any meanness of spirit or anti-social pugnaciousness.

The image of the *leviathan* is quite different. With no other introduction at all, we are immediately confronted with the picture of a bucking, pitching colossus, spitting forth man's puny tackle, fiercely resisting capture, utterly contemptuous of man's need to dominate it.

Where the *behemoth* follows its own path, untouched by any human agenda, the *leviathan* expresses its vitality in confrontation with man — proudly free and untrammeled, never the supplicant (v. 27a), never even the soft-spoken cooperator, certainly never the slave of a system, foreign to its nature, which wishes to entrap it (v. 28).

Thus in these two prototypes, silent witnesses to man's struggle from Eden to the Messianic utopia (see *Metzudos's* understanding of עִמָּךְ in v. 15), lurkers, skulking, as it were behind the facades of history, we have two devastating critiques of any thesis which would grant the well-being of human society an exclusive stance at the center of God's concerns. Both these creatures, the one totally oblivious of, the other irredeemably antagonistic to humankind, are no less important to God than is man himself.[1]

Stewardship of the world, then, is a question of balances. There is room for the *behemoth* and for the *leviathan*, for nature's victims and its snarling predators.[2]

Iyov must understand that absolute justice in a physical world can never be more than a theoretical construct. In a real world of con-

1. For a critique of those who would say that man stands at the center of creation and that all that exists is there only for his sake, see *Rambam*, *Moreh Nevuchim* 3:13. We quote a short section:

"Therefore, what I believe to be the correct attitude from the point of view of the Torah, one which coincides with the ideas which philosophy would affirm, is that we should not suppose that all that exists finds its justification in man's existence. Rather that all that exists has its own justification, never that it is here only because of the needs of another . . ."

2. . . . and the world would lack in beauty if wild animals would not prey upon their victims (*Chazon Ish*, *Emunah U'Bitachon*)

40/24-29 *it can gulp down the Jordan into its mouth.* [24] *He will subdue it with His eyes, perforate its nose with hooks.* [25] *Can you pull leviathan by a hook, can you embed a line in its tongue?* [26] *Can you fasten a hook in its nose, pierce its cheek with a barb?* [27] *Will it beset you with entreaties, will it speak to you softly?* [28] *Will it make a pact with you so that you might take it as an indentured servant?* [29] *Will you sport with it as with a bird, tether it for your maidens?*

flicting claims and the concomitant need for balance, the longevity and tranquility of the wicked may also contribute to a greater good which is beyond the ken of man. *All that there is, God created for His greater glory — even the wicked marking time toward the day when evil will overtake them* (*Proverbs* 16:4).

26. הֲתָשִׂים אַגְמֹן בְּאַפּוֹ וּבְחוֹחַ תִּקֹּב לֶחֱיוֹ — *Can you fasten a hook in its nose, pierce its cheek with a barb?* אַגְמֹן is the *bullrush.* It is used to describe the bowing of the head (*Isaiah* 58:5). Hence, *a hook* which is a bent piece of metal. חוֹחַ is a *thorn* and therefore an appropriate name for the *barb* designed to pierce the cheek (*Metzudos*).

27. הֲיַרְבֶּה אֵלֶיךָ תַּחֲנוּנִים אִם־יְדַבֵּר אֵלֶיךָ רַכּוֹת — *Will it beset you with entreaties, will it speak to you softly?* The *leviathan* is man's implacable foe. There is no hope at all that it would ever allow itself to be subjugated. See commentary to verse 25.

28. הֲיִכְרֹת בְּרִית עִמָּךְ תִּקָּחֶנּוּ לְעֶבֶד עוֹלָם — *Will it make a pact with you so that you might take it as an indentured servant?* Other animals might become servants to man's ambitions. The *leviathan* will never let itself be subdued. It has its own agenda, will never become a part of man's.

29. הַתְשַׂחֶק־בּוֹ כַּצִּפּוֹר וְתִקְשְׁרֶנּוּ לְנַעֲרוֹתֶיךָ — *Will you sport with it as with a bird, tether it for your maidens? Psalms* 104:26 speaks of God creating the *leviathan* in order that *He might disport Himself with it.* Could you, as does God make a playmate out of this vicious monster? (*R' Yosef Kara*).[1]

It is not out of place to discuss briefly an alternative meaning for the verse in *Psalms* — one which can help us to a deeper insight into the use of the *leviathan* symbol in our context.

The full verse in *Psalms* reads as follows: *There the ships travel, with this leviathan whom You have created for entertainment.* Now when we consider that לִוְיָתָן, is a proper noun deriving from the root, לָוָה, *to accompany*, there is the distinct possibility that the psalmist is painting an extremely evocative picture. We see a ship making its lonely way across the oceans, the sailors lonesome and dispirited within their tiny, unnatural world. Suddenly they cheer up. They are not so alone after all. A friendly school of dolphins frisks and frolics around the ship, sent there by God, as it were, to *accompany* them along their solitary trek.

This picture of the *leviathan* as a friendly companion contrasts sharply with the vicious beast portrayed here.

Nevertheless, our לִוְיָתָן, too, is a creature which *accompanies* us. Why is it here? What does it accomplish for us?

It is here to teach us that none of God's creatures owes us an explanation. None is forced to give an accounting of its usefulness in terms which we can grasp.

Perhaps this is precisely the lesson which Iyov and we are to draw from the detailed depiction of the anti-social qualities of the *leviathan.* This monster has apparently nothing at all to contribute to our well-being. That God values it and nurtures it is proof-positive that He has considerations of His own, which need not nor do they coincide with our own.

It is for this reason that the *leviathan* accompanies us through history, until he may be finally consumed by the *tzaddikim* when the Messiah comes. Until that moment of ultimate clarification comes upon us, we need to be reminded of our place in the variegated Eden of God's creation. Only then, when, *The world will be full of the understanding of God just as the water covers the sea-bed,* will the doubts and questions which trouble us in our benighted ignorance pose no more problems.

Metzudos believes that שָׂחֵק here is used in the sense, *to make fun of.* Animals can be caught by laying down a trail of food which they will follow and which leads them into the trap. The *leviathan* is too cunning to be caught by such subterfuge.

1. The idea of God entertaining Himself, as it were, with the *leviathan,* derives from *Avodah Zarah* 3b and clearly belongs to that category of *aggadah* which is beyond our comprehension.

מ/ל-לב ל-לא יִכְרוּ עָלָיו חַבָּרִים יֶחֱצוּהוּ בֵּין כְּנַעֲנִים: הַתְמַלֵּא
לב בְשֻׂכּוֹת עוֹרוֹ וּבְצִלְצַל דָּגִים רֹאשׁוֹ: שִׂים־עָלָיו כַּפֶּךָ
מא/א-ג א זְכֹר מִלְחָמָה אַל־תּוֹסַף: הֵן־תֹּחַלְתּוֹ נִכְזָבָה הֲגַם
ב אֶל־מַרְאָיו יֻטָל: לֹא־אַכְזָר כִּי יְעוּרֶנּוּ וּמִי הוּא
ג לְפָנַי יִתְיַצָּב: מִי הִקְדִּימַנִי וַאֲשַׁלֵּם תַּחַת כָּל־הַשָּׁמַיִם

30. יִכְרוּ עָלָיו חַבָּרִים יֶחֱצוּהוּ בֵּין כְּנַעֲנִים — *Can friends make a feast of it, can they divide it up among the merchants?* For the first phrase we follow Radak, *Sefer HaShorashim* and *R' Meyuchas* here, who take חַבָּרִים as *members of a group* (בְּנֵי חֲבוּרָה) and יִכְרוּ from כָּרָה, *to give a feast* (see at *II Kings* 6:23).

The Commentator has חַבָּרִים mean *sorcerers*, and derives יִכְרוּ from כָּרָה, *to dig*. Fishermen apparently would often use some kind of sorcery to lure the fish into their nets or into the trenches which they had especially dug for them. None of this would help for the huge and vicious *leviathan*.

31. הַתְמַלֵּא בְשֻׂכּוֹת עוֹרוֹ וּבְצִלְצַל דָּגִים רֹאשׁוֹ — *Could you riddle its skin with barbs, capture its head in a fish-trap?* We have followed *Daas Mikra* in the rendering of this difficult verse. שֻׂכּוֹת are *barbs* or *arrows* as in *Numbers* 33:55, לְשִׂכִּים בְּעֵינֵיכֶם. The context requires that the unknown צִלְצַל be understood as one of the implements used in catching fish.

Malbim, in the footsteps of *Ralbag*, renders: *Could you slice its skin with knives* [מַלֵּא from, מָלַל, *to sunder*; שֻׂכּוֹת, an unusual form of שַׂכִּין, *knife*], *or sever its head with a cleaver?*

The Sages (*Bava Basra* 75a), basing themselves upon our verse, teach: Rabba said in the name of R' Yochanan: God will one day fashion a booth for the *tzaddikim* from the skin of the *leviathan*. Most early commentators interpret שֻׂכּוֹת in line with this tradition — as a *booth*. This could refer to a hut upon the beach in which, protected from the sun, the fish that are caught are laid until they can be removed. It was customary to use the skin of the fish to build these enclosures. The skin of the *leviathan* could never be used to build such a hut, nor its head to cast shade [צִלְצַל an unusual form of צֵל, *shadow*] upon the fish which are stored there (*R' Saadyah Gaon*); or, the *booth* might be an enclosure which would be lowered into the water, so that when the fish swim inside it they would be trapped, and the צִלְצַל would be a similar coop designed to ensnare the fish's head (*Mabit*).

32. שִׂים־עָלָיו כַּפֶּךָ זְכֹר מִלְחָמָה אַל־תּוֹסַף — *Were you but to place your hand upon it, you need anticipate no more battles.* This, because you will surely be killed if you but dare to place a hand upon this fierce monster (*Ramban*).

Metzudos explains along similar lines: One attempt to place your hand upon it will teach you never to contemplate any more battles against it. He will react so fiercely that you will be convinced that it is best to keep your distance.

XLI.

1. הֵן־תֹּחַלְתּוֹ נִכְזָבָה הֲגַם אֶל־מַרְאָיו יֻטָל — *How disillusioned he is concerning his ambitions! Its very appearance fells him!* This verse follows directly upon the previous chapter. There we had seen just how invincible this fierce beast really is, and how even touching it would inevitably bring sudden death. Our verse continues with this theme by describing the frustration which the *leviathan's* would-be conqueror must surely suffer. What possible hope can he have of ever achieving his goal if just contemplating the *leviathan's* dreadful visage throws him to the ground.

However, although, as we have seen, this verse is a direct continuation from the previous one, there is a major change in tone. Up to this point, God has addressed Iyov directly, in the second person, daring him to imagine himself locked in combat with the *leviathan*. From this point on, only the third person is used. Where till now the word-picture places Iyov together with the *leviathan* in center-stage, with God, as it were, a spectator reflecting upon the futility of man's delusions of power, Iyov is now, as it were, to join God in His ruminations. He is no more the pathetic figure of the puny hunter, but has become the wise philosopher who, detached from the tumult of the battle can, together with his God, contemplate the scene and draw wisdom from it.

Why the change?

In the commentary to verses 2-4 we shall see that those difficult verses lend themselves to two possible interpretations. We have rendered them as God's challenge to whomever has the temerity to wish to confront God and to chal-

40/30-32 30 *Can friends make a feast of it, can they divide it up among the*
merchants? 31 *Could you riddle its skin with barbs, capture its*
head in a fish-trap? 32 *Were you but to place your hand upon it,*
you need anticipate no more battles.

41/1-3 1 *How disillusioned he is concerning his ambitions! Its very ap-*
pearance fells him. 2 *None is so cruelly determined that he*
would awaken it. 'Who then would dare stand up to Me! 3 *Whoever*
anticipated Me — I will reward him. All that is under the heavens

lenge Him. If man can never stand up to even one of God's creatures, how could he presume to question God? There is also, as we shall see, the possibility that these verses are the *leviathan's* own words, and are simply a continuation of the description of its might.

According to the first of these two explanations we could understand the change to third person as follows: God has no wish to browbeat Iyov. The purpose of the speech, as we have seen on numerous occasions, is not to intimidate Iyov but to draw him out of himself through love. God could have said: 'How foolish you are to think that you can best Me!' Instead he chooses to allow Iyov himself to come to that conclusion by an elliptical approach. He is not derided for his own temerity, but invited to contemplate a third person. 'Iyov,' God is saying, 'You have seen the power of the *leviathan* and are aware of man's puniness in its face. What would you say if this same hunter who only now trembled in front of the *leviathan*, were now to attempt to challenge God. Do you see the folly of his ways?'

What explanation can we offer if the second interpretation of the next few verses is the correct one?

We may surmise that, in that case, the sensitivity displayed by God is even more exquisite. Midway in the description of the *leviathan* God is signaling to Iyov that He feels sure that the earlier parts of the speech have had their effect. God is displaying His trust in Iyov. Only moments before Iyov had seemed to be the object of God's ridicule. Now he is called upon to join God in the contemplation of the wonders of His creation.

We may surmise that this moment is the crucial one in Iyov's metamorphosis from sulky submission to adoring acceptance. By a simple change of tone in God's speech, his sense of worth has been restored to him. The dreadful losses which he has sustained become bearable because he has lost neither himself nor his God.

We have had occasion to quote *Rashi* from *Bava Basra* that the purpose of the book of *Iyov* is to teach: ... *answers which might be given to those who feel unfairly treated by God's justice.* Here we have our lesson clearly spelled out: Raise your friend from out of the slough of his despondency! Assure him that he has lost neither his value as a human being nor your regard, nor yet, more importantly, your love. His spirit will remain healthy, will be able to fight off the destructive cancers of depression, self-doubt and despair.

In the commentary to 2:11-13 we surmised that the friends failed in their efforts at comfort mainly because they failed, ... *to convey the message that he was not alone, that smashed by debilitating illness and prostrated by the loss of his all, he was nevertheless a man of goodness and integrity, and, above all, of worth.* By the use of that very formula, God seems now to have started Iyov along the path of spiritual resurrection.

יֻטָל from טוּל, *to hurl.*

2. לֹא־אַכְזָר כִּי יְעוּרֶנּוּ וּמִי הוּא לְפָנַי יִתְיַצָּב — *None is so cruelly determined that he would awaken it. 'Who then would dare stand up to Me!* The commentators part ways in the interpretation of the second half of the verse. Is the speaker God or the *leviathan*?

If the former, the logic is as follows: If no one has the courage to face the *leviathan* by awakening it [יְעוּרֶנּוּ from עוֹרֵר, *to awaken*, or perhaps the rendering is; *to challenge it to war*, based on the usage of עוּרִי at *Zechariah* 13:7 (*Daas Mikra*)] how could anyone presume to attempt to stand up against Me.

R' Yosef Kara and most commentators assume this meaning.

Ramban, while also considering this possibility, makes room for an alternative rendering. The second phrase is spoken by the *leviathan*: it is issuing a challenge to whomever would be inclined to accept it. The challenge continues in the next verses.

3. מִי הִקְדִּימַנִי וַאֲשַׁלֵּם תַּחַת כָּל־הַשָּׁמַיִם לִי־הוּא — *Whoever anticipated Me — I will reward him. All that is under the heavens is Mine!* If God is talking the meaning might be: Is there perhaps

ד־ה לִי־הוּא: °לא־אַחֲרִישׁ בַּדָּיו וּדְבַר־גְּבוּרוֹת וְחִין עֶרְכּוֹ: מִי־
לו ק' ו גִלָּה פְּנֵי לְבוּשׁוֹ בְּכֶפֶל רִסְנוֹ מִי יָבוֹא: דַּלְתֵי פָנָיו מִי פִתֵּחַ
ז סְבִיבוֹת שִׁנָּיו אֵימָה: גַּאֲוָה אֲפִיקֵי מָגִנִּים סָגוּר חוֹתָם
ח־ט צָר: אֶחָד בְּאֶחָד יִגַּשׁוּ וְרוּחַ לֹא־יָבֹא בֵינֵיהֶם: אִישׁ־
י בְּאָחִיהוּ יְדֻבָּקוּ יִתְלַכְּדוּ וְלֹא יִתְפָּרָדוּ: עֲטִישֹׁתָיו תָּהֶל
יא אוֹר וְעֵינָיו כְּעַפְעַפֵּי־שָׁחַר: מִפִּיו לַפִּידִים יַהֲלֹכוּ כִּידוֹדֵי
יב־יג אֵשׁ יִתְמַלָּטוּ: מִנְּחִירָיו יֵצֵא עָשָׁן כְּדוּד נָפוּחַ וְאַגְמֹן: נַפְשׁוֹ
יד גֶּחָלִים תְּלַהֵט וְלַהַב מִפִּיו יֵצֵא: בְּצַוָּארוֹ יָלִין עֹז וּלְפָנָיו
טו תָּדוּץ דְּאָבָה: מַפְּלֵי בְשָׂרוֹ דָבֵקוּ יָצוּק עָלָיו בַּל־יִמּוֹט:

someone who went out to fight the *leviathan* even before I threw down My challenge? I would reward him as well. I own all that there is and would have no difficulty in rewarding anyone who deserves it (*Ramban*).

If the *leviathan* is talking we would have to translate: *Whoever bests me, I will reward him.* This is the kind of boast which is common among all who joust with one another (*Ramban*).

4. לוֹ־אַחֲרִישׁ בַּדָּיו וּדְבַר־גְּבוּרוֹת וְחִין עֶרְכּוֹ — *I will not suppress his boastings, his heroism nor his impressive worth.'* The verse has the same meaning whether it is God or the *leviathan* who is talking. Each, in the context of what went before, is promising that, should anyone have the gallantry to fight the *leviathan,* they would pay him all the respect due to such heroism and publicize his deeds.

For בַּדָּיו, *Ramban,* as also *Radak, Sefer HaShorashim,* suggest כְּזָבָיו, *his falsehoods.* In the context this would be meaningless if an outright lie were meant. Accordingly we have translated, *boastings.* It is normal for someone who has accomplished an unusually heroic feat to wish to embellish his account. Nevertheless, there is usually a grain of truth in what he says, and the promise is made here not to obscure even such descriptions of his exploit.

Metzudos points out that חִין has the same meaning as חֵן, *the finding of favor in another's eyes.* He adduces examples of similar words being occasionally expanded with an added י.

עֶרְכּוֹ from עָרַךְ, *to estimate.*

5. מִי־גִלָּה פְּנֵי לְבוּשׁוֹ בְּכֶפֶל רִסְנוֹ מִי יָבוֹא — *Who has succeeded in peeling off the surface of its garment? Who dares enter the folds ready for the halter?* Together now, as it were, God and Iyov contemplate the invincible *leviathan.* The description begins with the scales which cover its body.

פָּנִים is the *face,* that which is clearly visible. Thus the surface of its garment — the scales in which it is clothed. No one has ever succeeded in removing it. גִּלָּה, from גָּלָה, *to reveal,* would here mean to take the scales off the body (*R' Meyuchas*).

רֶסֶן is the *halter* normally placed in the animal's mouth in order to control it. The *folds* are the two [from כָּפַל, *to double*] lips which would normally surround the halter — if only it could be inserted. See next verse.

6. דַּלְתֵי פָנָיו מִי פִתֵּחַ סְבִיבוֹת שִׁנָּיו אֵימָה — *Who could pry open its face's portals? Around its fangs — terror. Metzudos* understands this verse as a continuation of the previous one. No halter has ever controlled the *leviathan* because no one was ever able to pry open its jaws in order to insert it.

7. גַּאֲוָה אֲפִיקֵי מָגִנִּים סָגוּר חוֹתָם צָר — *Arrogant because of the strength of its shields; closed, tightly sealed.* No part of the *leviathan's* body is vulnerable. The scales are so tightly packed as to leave no chink into which a weapon might penetrate.

8. אֶחָד בְּאֶחָד יִגַּשׁוּ וְרוּחַ לֹא־יָבֹא בֵינֵיהֶם — *Each single one converges upon the other, even air cannot come between them.* An alternative rendering of the second phrase might be, . . . *so that no air might come between them.*

9. אִישׁ־בְּאָחִיהוּ יְדֻבָּקוּ יִתְלַכְּדוּ וְלֹא יִתְפָּרָדוּ — *Each hugs the other closely, they are interlocked, will never come apart.* There seems a certain redundance here. This verse, even allowing for poetic license, seems to add nothing to the previous one.

We may surmise that God is purposely overemphasizing the protective qualities of the *leviathan's* scales so that Iyov might derive a lesson from them. Even as God has provided the *leviathan* with an armor which has made it impervious to attack from the outside, so too can you, Iyov, learn to protect yourself from the exigencies of life. Armed with the correct attitudes, man need not feel

is Mine! 4 *I will not suppress his boastings, his heroism nor his*
41/4-15 *impressive worth.'* 5 *Who has succeeded in peeling off the surface*
of its garment? Who dares enter the folds ready for the halter?
6 *Who could pry open its face's portals? Around its fangs — terror.*
7 *Arrogant because of the strength of its shields; closed, tightly*
sealed. 8 *Each single one converges upon the other, even air cannot*
come between them. 9 *Each hugs the other closely, they are*
interlocked, will never come apart. 10 *Its sneezings flash light, its*
eyes are like the blush of dawn. 11 *Torches spew from its mouth,*
fire-sparks are released. 12 *Smoke belches from its nostrils, like a*
seething pot, like the mist of the marshes. 13 *Its breath fires coals,*
flame shoots from its mouth. 14 *Power is ensconced in its neck,*
before it worry turns to joy. 15 *The droopings of its flesh cleave*
together, each molded upon the other so that it shall not move.

vulnerable to the vagaries of his fate.

10. עֲטִישֹׁתָיו תָּהֶל אוֹר וְעֵינָיו כְּעַפְעַפֵּי־שָׁחַר — *Its sneezings flash light, its eyes are like the blush of dawn.* When the *leviathan* sneezes, the water spouts up about him (*Ramban*) and catches the sun's rays (*Daas Mikra*).

For עַפְעַפֵּי שָׁחַר see at 3:8.

11. מִפִּיו לַפִּידִים יַהֲלֹכוּ כִּידוֹדֵי אֵשׁ יִתְמַלָּטוּ — *Torches spew from its mouth, fire-sparks are released.* כִּידוֹד does not recur in Scripture. *Metzudos*, from the context, surmises that *spark* is the correct translation.

12. מִנְּחִירָיו יֵצֵא עָשָׁן כְּדוּד נָפוּחַ וְאַגְמֹן — *Smoke belches from its nostrils, like a seething pot, like the mist of the marshes.* We have followed *Ibn Ezra* in the rendering of אַגְמֹן. He relates the word to אֲגַם, *marshland.* Other commentators think that the word describes another kind of pot used in the kitchen, thus paralleling דוּד.

13. נַפְשׁוֹ גֶּחָלִים תְּלַהֵט וְלַהַב מִפִּיו יֵצֵא — *Its breath fires coals, flame shoots from its mouth.* Breath issuing from the nose is called נֶפֶשׁ (*Ramban*).

In the last four verses, the fire-breathing qualities of the *leviathan* have been described. We have the impression of a poetic description of the terror which this monster inspires, rather than a recording of actual physical properties. This would certainly be the case if the crocodile is meant (see at 40:24), but, one feels, it would hold true even if the *leviathan* of the *Aggadah* is being described.

Accordingly, we may surmise that God is teaching Iyov another lesson in how to react to life's exigencies. See, He tells Iyov, how our perceptions are influenced by our preconceived notions. Because we stand in terror of the *leviathan*, we imbue it with impossibly frightening properties. With a correct, more objective perspective, we are more readily able to cope. True, a crocodile is sufficiently frightening just as it really is, but there is no need to see fire belching from its mouth. Suffering, too, may be shorn of some of its terror when one is willing to admit the incontestable goodness and justice of the God Who sent it. With an awareness of its true nature it becomes a difficult, but manageable challenge.

14. בְּצַוָּארוֹ יָלִין עֹז וּלְפָנָיו תָּדוּץ דְּאָבָה — *Power is ensconced in its neck, before it worry turns to joy.* The neck is normally the weakest, most vulnerable part of the animal. That of the *leviathan* is strong and impregnable (*Metzudos*).

It is noteworthy that the verse does not say that the neck is powerful. Such a formulation would be impressive but, in the context, not sufficiently overwhelming. Rather, we have the pure concept, *power*, in all its unadulterated force, ensconced within the *leviathan*.

לְפָנָיו, *before it*, might mean, before the *leviathan* (*R' Yosef Kara*), or, it could be the chest which lies *before* the neck (*Metzudos*). Either way the sense is the same. Situations which might well be perceived as dangerous and therefore worrisome to the *leviathan*, are instead viewed as invigorating challenges. This mighty beast fears nothing at all.

15. מַפְּלֵי בְשָׂרוֹ דָבֵקוּ יָצוּק עָלָיו בַּל־יִמּוֹט — *The droopings of its flesh cleave together, each molded upon the other so that it shall not move.* מַפָּל, from נָפַל, *to fall*. Thus, the chunks of flesh hanging down because of the excessive fat, appearing as though they were falling off (*Radak, Sefer HaShorashim*). These chunks lie upon one another, closely packed as though they were cast together, thus that the one never moves away from the other (*The Commentator*).

טז־יז לִבּוֹ יָצוּק כְּמוֹ־אָבֶן וְיָצוּק כְּפֶלַח תַּחְתִּית: מִשֵּׂתוֹ יָגוּרוּ
יח אֵלִים מִשְּׁבָרִים יִתְחַטָּאוּ: מַשִּׂיגֵהוּ חֶרֶב בְּלִי תָקוּם חֲנִית
יט מַסָּע וְשִׁרְיָה: יַחְשֹׁב לְתֶבֶן בַּרְזֶל לְעֵץ רִקָּבוֹן נְחוּשָׁה:
כ־כא לֹא־יַבְרִיחֶנּוּ בֶן־קָשֶׁת לְקַשׁ נֶהְפְּכוּ־לוֹ אַבְנֵי־קָלַע: כְּקַשׁ
כב נֶחְשְׁבוּ תוֹתָח וְיִשְׂחַק לְרַעַשׁ כִּידוֹן: תַּחְתָּיו חַדּוּדֵי חָרֶשׂ
כג יִרְפַּד חָרוּץ עֲלֵי־טִיט: יַרְתִּיחַ כַּסִּיר מְצוּלָה יָם יָשִׂים
כד כַּמֶּרְקָחָה: אַחֲרָיו יָאִיר נָתִיב יַחְשֹׁב תְּהוֹם לְשֵׂיבָה:

16. לִבּוֹ יָצוּק כְּמוֹ־אָבֶן וְיָצוּק כְּפֶלַח תַּחְתִּית — *Its heart is tough as stone, firm as the nether millstone.* The *heart* may be the actual organ or the middle part of the body which covers the heart. The toughness may refer to the physical hardness which can deflect any weapon, or it might be a metaphor for the *leviathan's* lack of fear (*Daas Mikra*).

The upper millstone is the one which rotates when grinding the grain. The lower stone stands firm and immovable (*Daas Mikra*). Alternatively, the nether millstone is not perforated and is therefore stronger than the upper one which has a hole through which the corn is poured (*Metzudos*). Or, the lower millstone is harder than the upper one which is the softer of the two (*R' Yosef Kara*).

R' Yosef Kara points out that the description of the *leviathan* moves in a logical direction. First its outer covering, the scales, were described; then the flesh which is beneath them, and now the heart which lies beneath the flesh.

17. מִשֵּׂתוֹ יָגוּרוּ אֵלִים מִשְּׁבָרִים יִתְחַטָּאוּ — *Its awe makes the mightiest afraid, the very breakers are found wanting.* מִשְׁבָּר is *a wave* — see *Psalms* 42:8, 93:4. יִתְחַטָּאוּ is *to be lacking* — see *Rashi,* אֲחַטֶּנָּה to *Genesis* 31:39. The association comes from the fact that the *leviathan* is a sea monster. As it flashes through the sea, it is as though it breaks off chunks from the waves so that they do not have their full complement of water.

God has dealt with the *leviathan's* impregnable scales, his fiery breath, and now, with the enormous strength — which has the ability to turn potential worries into exhilarating challenges. God may well have wished to instruct Iyov in the correct way to meet life's troubles. Observe, He says to Iyov, how confidence in one's inner power can change reality. None of life's vicissitudes have a life of their own. Whether they are implacable foes or opportunities with potential for growth, depends entirely upon how you perceive yourself. Trust yourself — and nothing in life can ultimately be a threat to you.

18. מַשִּׂיגֵהוּ חֶרֶב בְּלִי תָקוּם חֲנִית מַסָּע וְשִׁרְיָה — *No triumph for those who join it in combat with the sword, not with the hurled spear nor the javelin.* מַשִּׂיגֵהוּ, from נשג which appears only in the *hiphil* and the meaning of which is, *to reach* or, *to overtake.* קום has many meanings, among them, *to prevail,* cf. *Proverbs* 19:21.

Radak, Sefer HaShorashim brings two possible meanings for, מַסָּע. The first, that it, as well as שִׁרְיָה are types of weapons. The second, that מַסָּע derives from, נָסַע, *to travel* and that the word goes together with חֲנִית and means, *a spear which travels.* We have translated according to this second meaning and have therefore also rendered שִׁרְיָה as *javelin* since the context seems to demand a projectile.

19-21. יַחְשֹׁב לְתֶבֶן בַּרְזֶל לְעֵץ רִקָּבוֹן נְחוּשָׁה — *It treats iron like straw, brass like rotted wood.* לֹא־יַבְרִיחֶנּוּ בֶן־קָשֶׁת לְקַשׁ נֶהְפְּכוּ־לוֹ אַבְנֵי־קָלַע — *It will not flee before an arrow, for it, the sling's stones turn to straw.* כְּקַשׁ נֶחְשְׁבוּ תוֹתָח וְיִשְׂחַק לְרַעַשׁ כִּידוֹן — *It looks upon the catapult as so much straw, laughs at the swish of the dart.* The sense of the three verses is the same. Conventional weapons are no threat at all to the *leviathan.*

בֶּן קֶשֶׁת is an unusual expression for *arrow.* The arrow issues forth from the bow as the child comes out of the mother (*Metzudos*).

תּוֹתָח does not recur in Scripture. We have rendered *catapult* in accordance with *Metzudos.*

Now weapons are hurled by people — and this section demonstrates to Iyov with what disdain it is possible to look upon adversaries when the ordinance which they carry threatens not at all. Iyov had complained bitterly about the abuses heaped upon him by his friends, and, at 30:1 and 9-12 about the careless contempt which has replaced the awe in which he was once regarded in his community. Clearly, Iyov regarded as important the attitude with which others viewed him. Perhaps, with this section, God is attempting to wean him from the excessive dependence upon the good-will of others. What, in the

16 Its heart is tough as stone, firm as the nether millstone. 17 Its awe
makes the mightiest afraid, the very breakers are found wanting.
18 No triumph for those who join it in combat with the sword,
not with the hurled spear nor the javelin. 19 It treats iron like
straw, brass like rotted wood. 20 It will not flee before an arrow,
for it, the sling's stones turn to straw. 21 It looks upon the cata-
pult as so much straw, laughs at the swish of the dart. 22 Beneath
it, a burnished sword flashing like the sun, a golden couch
spread over the mud. 23 It churns up the depths as in a seething
cauldron, turns the sea, like a spice mixture, into a ferment. 24 In its
wake the path sparkles, the depths appear venerable with old age.

final analysis, can the sneer, the spittle or the scowl do to you. Why cannot you, as does the *leviathan*, shrug off the impotent weapons with which your enemies believe that they can hurt you?

22. תַּחְתָּיו חַדּוּדֵי חָרֶשׂ יִרְפַּד חָרוּץ עֲלֵי־טִיט — *Beneath it, a burnished sword flashing like the sun, a golden couch spread over the mud.* The translation follows *The Commentator, R' Yosef Kara* and *R' Meyuchas.* Reference is to the fins of the *leviathan* which shine brightly in the water. חַדּוּד from חָדַד, *to be sharp* is the sword, which when burnished brightly flashes in the sun. חָרֶשׂ is *the sun,* as at 9:7, above.

רָפַד, means, *to spread out,* usually a bed or couch. חָרוּץ can be used for *gold,* as in *Proverbs* 3:14 and elsewhere.

Ramban and *Metzudos* understand the verse quite differently. חַדּוּדֵי חָרֶשׂ are *jagged shards of earthenware,* and חָרוּץ describes the uneven teeth of a saw — as at *Isaiah* 28:27 or *Amos* 1:3. The sense of the verse is that the *leviathan's* body is so well protected that it can lie down on jagged shards without being hurt, and it can make its bed upon the river's mud, although it is riddled with sharp protruding teeth.

We have chosen to follow the first, rather than the latter, rendering because this makes it possible to interpret the final section of the speech — that is verses 22-26 — as a single grouping, with the beauty and majesty of the *leviathan* as the subject. As we have seen throughout the commentary to this chapter, such groupings have been the norm in this final section of God's speech. According to the latter interpretation, there seems little cohesion between our verse and the next.

23. יַרְתִּיחַ כַּסִּיר מְצוּלָה יָם יָשִׂים כַּמֶּרְקָחָה — *It churns up the depths as in a seething cauldron, turns the sea, like a spice mixture, into a ferment.* The cauldron is a relatively small receptacle and it does not take much heat to have it seethe. The *leviathan* is able to boil up the huge ocean as easily (*R' Yosef Kara*).

רָקַח is the act of mixing spices together. The מֶרְקָחָה is the mixture or the spice-pot in which the mixing is done.

The previous verse — as interpreted by *R' Yosef Kara* — had spoken of the gilded loveliness of the *leviathan's* fins. The following verse will describe the sparkling light which follows in its wake. Within this context it would make sense to interpret our verse too, although this is not explicated, as addressing itself to some aspect of the *leviathan's* beauty. This could be understood either in the sense that the brute power with which this monster slashes through the waves, raising them to the boil, carries its own grace and comeliness, or because the roiling waters catch the sun's glint and sparkle turning the waters into a riot of color. If this second interpretation is the correct one, we assume that the following verse ought to be seen as an explanation of this one — see below.

24. אַחֲרָיו יָאִיר נָתִיב יַחְשֹׁב תְּהוֹם לְשֵׂיבָה — *In its wake the path sparkles, the depths appear venerable with old age.* As the *leviathan* leaps out of the water, its shine (זִוּו) casts a light upon the path which it has traveled (*R' Yosef Kara*).

The second phrase is particularly difficult. Taking into account that *Metzudos* takes the phrase as referring to the white hairs of the sage — deep waters look black, but the shallow waters which remain after the *leviathan* has emptied out the river with the speed of his passage look white — it seems possible to interpret the phrase, with *Daas Mikra,* as referring to the white topped foam which tops the waves after the water has been roiled up by the furious progress of the rushing monster.

מא/ כה־כו אֵין־עַל־עָפָר מָשְׁלוֹ הֶעָשׂוּ לִבְלִי־חָת: אֵת־כָּל־גָּבֹהַּ
כה־כו א יִרְאֶה הוּא מֶלֶךְ עַל־כָּל־בְּנֵי־שָׁחַץ: וַיַּעַן
מב/א־ד ב אִיּוֹב אֶת־יהוה וַיֹּאמַר: יָדַעְתָּ כִּי־כֹל תּוּכָל וְלֹא־
ג יִבָּצֵר מִמְּךָ מְזִמָּה: מִי זֶה ׀ מַעְלִים עֵצָה בְּלִי דָעַת לָכֵן
ד הִגַּדְתִּי וְלֹא אָבִין נִפְלָאוֹת מִמֶּנִּי וְלֹא אֵדָע: שְׁמַע־נָא

25. אֵין־עַל־עָפָר מָשְׁלוֹ הֶעָשׂוּ לִבְלִי־חָת — *None on earth can emulate its total control — made utterly without fear.* The translation combines the two trends among the commentators. There are those, among them *Ramban,* who take מָשְׁלוֹ from מָשָׁל, *to compare.* Thus: *There is none on earth who could be compared to him.* The idea, as *Ramban* understands it, is that although the *leviathan* is a sea creature which, because it dwells in the water and does not have the same food supply as do land-based animals, might be supposed to be weaker, it nonetheless is mightier than anything on land. The other commentators, of whom *R' Yosef Kara* is representative, take the word from מָשַׁל, *to govern.* That is: *There is none on earth whose rulership is as powerful as that of the leviathan.* Or, as *The Commentator* takes it: *There is none on earth who can rule over it.*

When we consider the next verse which explicitly describes the *leviathan* as *king,* and the fact that, moreover, the earlier verses had made a point of the gilded aura and glistening colors which are a part of it and which might well be taken as the beauty which is associated with royalty (see *Isaiah* 33:17), we are inclined to the second interpretation. As we noted above, there is every reason to interpret our passage in such a way that it presents a cohesive whole — rather than a set of discrete descriptions of various qualities of the *leviathan* — as do all the other sections in this second half of God's final speech. As we shall point out in the commentary to the next verse, the subject of this final section would be the majestic royal bearing which is the *leviathan's,* and which, by implication, could be Iyov's too.

26. אֶת־כָּל־גָּבֹהַּ יִרְאֶה הוּא מֶלֶךְ עַל־כָּל־בְּנֵי־שָׁחַץ — *The greatest heights lie open before it, it is king over all the most arrogant.* In spite of the fact that the *leviathan* is a sea monster and consequently really lies lower than all the creatures of the land, still the fact that in its own eyes it is king, elevates it beyond its station so that, indeed, all lies open before it.

God's speech ends with unexpected abruptness. We would have expected that the lesson which most of the commentators feel is implied in this speech — that if God has such wondrous creatures in His world then surely it is inexcusable temerity on Iyov's part to presume to argue with Him — would have been explicated by God Himself.

In fact, of course, God's silence at this point is a powerful part of the exquisite feeling with which God is affecting Iyov's rehabilitation. It belongs to the same category of sensitivity which made God — at the beginning of this chapter — switch from the second to the third person, as we explained it there. It states more eloquently than any words could have done that Iyov is now no longer in an adversarial relationship with God but is rather a partner with Him in contemplating and taking delight in the wonders of creation. The word-picture which God draws is so graphic, the images pack so much impact, are so evocative, that, inevitably Iyov, without any prompting at all, will draw his own conclusions.

And what is Iyov to learn from this final picture with which God leaves him?

The answer is simple. There is beauty, there is splendor, there is the dignity of majesty for him who makes himself invulnerable to the slings and arrows of life's vicissitudes.

Here is the *leviathan,* God appears to be saying, invincible behind the fortress of his protective armor, secure in the awareness of his absolute superiority to any potential enemy. He fears no one, cares for no one, makes his life according to his own agenda with supreme indifference to the obstacles which would daunt or break lesser creatures. And all this translates into — majesty!

But, Iyov, consider this. None of all the wondrous properties with which the *leviathan* is endowed are of his own making. He has won no battles with the greatest and most fearsome enemy of all — his own feelings of inadequacy and vulnerability. He has never lived with the total loss of all that was dear to him, has never felt disgust at the putrid rotting of his own body, has never felt alienated by the inexorable falling away of all the friends who — when they were really needed — proved to be no friends at all.

And yet — he is beautiful and kingly!

What dignity, then, can you, Iyov, not

41/25-26 [25] *None on earth can emulate its total control — made utterly without fear.* [26] *The greatest heights lie open before it, it is king over all the most arrogant.*

42/1-4 [1] *Iyov responded to HASHEM and said:* [2] *I have known all along that You are all-able, that no aspect of wisdom is beyond You.*
[3] *'Who is this who through lack of knowledge obscures the facts of purposeful design!' That being so I declare: 'I can understand nothing. It is beyond me. I shall never know!'* [4] *'Listen I beg You*

attain if you will but wrest victory from the broken shambles which your life has become. You too can be invulnerable, you too can lift yourself beyond the pinpricks of a fate which has no relevance to your essence, of disloyalties of men whose smallness of spirit need be no threat to the infinite splendor of your real being!

This is the message which God leaves Iyov to absorb — on his own. Nothing which God could have said at this point could possibly have been as eloquent as the silence of trust with which God departs the stage. He has not yet restored Iyov's children, nor his cattle or his flocks. But, He has given him — or better, has allowed Iyov to recapture — the sense of worth, of mattering, which had been snatched from him in his travail.

The words of submission with which Iyov, in the next chapter, will finally make peace with his fate, are no less sublime than those with which, when tragedy first struck, he had accepted his new reality (see at 1:20-21). But, significantly, here he does not prostrate himself as he did there. It is no more in the negation of his own worth but in its assertion that he is able to offer himself to his God.

XLII.

1. וַיַּעַן אִיּוֹב אֶת־ה׳ וַיֹּאמַר — *Iyov responded to HASHEM and said:* At 38:1 we noted that with God's first speech, the introductory formula changes. Where before, we invariably had: *So and so responded and said,* without the addressee being mentioned, that speech is introduced with the words, *Then HASHEM responded to Iyov ...* We saw this change as ushering in the period of Iyov's healing. At last someone — or better, Someone — cares about him enough to talk to him directly. He has changed from a symbol in a theological debate to an individual. Inevitably, faced with the reality of his own worth, he will take the necessary steps towards rehabilitation.

Iyov has reacted to God's sensitivity. No more does he simply express his own tortured thoughts without paying any real attention to what his opponents had said. He has listened carefully to God's words — and here, as at 40:2, is ready to say what must be said — to God.

2. יָדַעְתִּי כִּי־כֹל תּוּכָל וְלֹא־יִבָּצֵר מִמְּךָ מְזִמָּה — *I have known all along that You are all-able, that no aspect of wisdom is beyond You.* The full implications of this verse can be understood only in conjunction with the next. See below.

3. מִי זֶה מַעְלִים עֵצָה בְּלִי דָעַת לָכֵן הִגַּדְתִּי וְלֹא אָבִין נִפְלָאוֹת מִמֶּנִּי וְלֹא אֵדָע — *'Who is this who through lack of knowledge obscures the facts of purposeful design!' That being so I declare: 'I can understand nothing. It is beyond me. I shall never know!'* The first phrase of this verse is clearly a paraphrase of God's opening sentence at 38:2: מִי זֶה מַחְשִׁיךְ עֵצָה בְמִלִּין בְּלִי דָעַת, *Who is this who has such murky ideas, speaking without due consideration!*, and is thus understood by many commentators of whom *Metzudos* is representative. Iyov is quoting the accusation which God had hurled at him, in the sheer horror of the realization of how low he has sunk. Is it really possible that these words were addressed to me? Had I really been so foolish?

Shaken up by the shock of recognition — this sorry target of God's derision and bitter denunciation was he and no other — Iyov realizes that he must first and foremost make amends.

לָכֵן, *That being so*: I recognize now that I have been sick. I must, before anything else, purge myself of the arrogance which was the cause of my sickness.

הִגַּדְתִּי, *I declare*: The use of the past tense as a declaratory, as at *Deuteronomy* 26:3: *I declare this day ...* (*Daas Mikra*).

וְלֹא אָבִין, that *I can understand nothing*: The *vav* replaces a כִּי, as in דַּבֵּר אֶל בְּנֵי יִשְׂרָאֵל וְיִסָּעוּ (*Exodus* 14:15) (*Daas Mikra*).

The explanation of how this could have

ה וְאָנֹכִי אֲדַבֵּר אֶשְׁאָלְךָ וְהוֹדִיעֵנִי: לְשֵׁמַע־אֹזֶן שְׁמַעְתִּיךָ
ו וְעַתָּה עֵינִי רָאָתְךָ: עַל־כֵּן אֶמְאַס וְנִחַמְתִּי עַל־עָפָר וָאֵפֶר:

happened must wait till later. Iyov will pick up this issue at verse 5. In the meantime his mind is taken up by the sheer grotesqueness of his earlier folly. Bemused by what has transpired, Iyov will, in the next verse, once more pass one of God's other challenges before his mind's eye.

The full impact of Iyov's meaning can best be realized when we contrast the יָדַעְתִּי of verse 2 with the בְּלִי דָעַת of our verse. How can both statements be true? How can Iyov say of himself, *I have known all along ...*, when God accuses him of obfuscation deriving from בְּלִי דָעַת, *lack of knowledge*?

It has suddenly dawned upon Iyov. Intellectual apprehension means nothing at all! Indeed it is true that he had *known* everything all along. He was acquainted with every one of the wondrous creatures which God had passed before him. Sky and sea, thunder and rain had all been a part of his experience. But — he now understands — this knowledge led him nowhere at all. It was a *knowledge* which was really a *lack of knowledge*. As long as the heart is not engaged, as long as understanding comes through the *ear* instead of through the *eye* (see below, commentary to verse 5) man, the true man who matters, is left untouched, unchanged and ultimately unredeemed.

4. שְׁמַע־נָא וְאָנֹכִי אֲדַבֵּר אֶשְׁאָלְךָ וְהוֹדִיעֵנִי — *'Listen I beg You and I will speak!' 'I will put questions to you and you will enlighten Me!'* We have put both phrases into quotes because they appear to refer to different snatches of speech taken from what either Iyov or God had said earlier.

The first phrase, as *R' Yosef Kara* takes it, is a paraphrase of the latter part of 13:22, *Then call out, and I shall respond, or, let me speak, and give an answer*. Iyov, looking back now, cannot believe that he had been so presumptuous.

R' Yosef Kara believes that the second phrase, אֶשְׁאָלְךָ וְהוֹדִיעֵנִי, is a paraphrase of 10:2, הוֹדִיעֵנִי עַל מַה תְּרִיבֵנִי ..., which we rendered, ... *tell me, why do You pick a fight with me?* Again Iyov is shocked at his temerity. How could he have had so little sensitivity as to challenge God in such crude language.

Inasmuch as the phrase is a verbatim quote from God's first speech (see at 38:3) and, moreover, since we have Iyov quoting God's words in the previous verse, we are inclined to suggest that this too is a quote from God's opening speech. We might paraphrase this verse as follows: Iyov, now that he can step back and view the past in an objective manner, is nonplused by what has occurred. What kind of an atmosphere was this, he asks himself, in which challenges flew back and forth between God and myself? Here I am, challenging God to answer me, here is God demanding that I enlighten Him. Is this really the kind of person I was? Is it possible that I, in my folly, maneuvered myself into an adversarial stance vis-a-vis my God?

The next two verses — the last which Iyov as the hero of this drama will utter — tell the tale. In lyric adoration born of his newfound wisdom, he is finally reconciled with himself, his fate and finally and most importantly, with his God.

5-6. לְשֵׁמַע־אֹזֶן שְׁמַעְתִּיךָ וְעַתָּה עֵינִי רָאָתְךָ — *It was through fame by hearsay that I heard of You, but now my eye has beheld You!* עַל־כֵּן אֶמְאַס וְנִחַמְתִּי עַל־עָפָר וָאֵפֶר — *Therefore I revile. Were my lot to be dust and ashes I would not mind!* We have arrived! The words contained in these two sentences are the ones towards which the entire exercise, the vast and heroic efforts of the friends, of Elihu and finally of God, were directed. Our understanding of the book of *Iyov* will ultimately depend upon our perception of what they express.

It was not granted us to know how *Rashi* would have explained these verses. The closest we can come is to assume that *R' Yosef Kara* was sufficiently under his master's aura, that his interpretation can be taken as reflecting — at least in its general contours — *Rashi's* ideas. In the event, *R' Yosef Kara's* interpretation is that which we find also in *The Commentator*. These ideas seem to be substantively different to those of *Ramban*, and in analyzing the two interpretations we will be consistent with our approach to the commentary of the entire book. We set it as our goal to view *Rashi* and *Ramban* as paradigmatic of two schools of thought concerning the meaning of the book of *Iyov* — and we will be true to that goal at this, the final *denoument* of the drama.

First, then, *R' Yosef Kara*:

לְשֵׁמַע אֹזֶן שְׁמַעְתִּיךָ: I have heard of Your fame on numerous occasions.

וְעַתָּה עֵינִי רָאָתְךָ: [My eye] has beheld Your *Shechinah*.

עַל כֵּן אֶמְאַס: Because I had the merit to behold Your *Shechinah*, I *revile* my life.

וְנִחַמְתִּי עַל עָפָר וָאֵפֶר: I would be able to find comfort even if it were my lot to go to the grave and thus return to the dust and ashes from which I was originally taken.

and I will speak!' 'I will put questions to you and you
will enlighten Me!' [5] *It was through fame by hearsay that I*
heard of You, but now my eye has beheld You! [6] *Therefore I*
revile. Were my lot to be dust and ashes I would not mind!

Now *Ramban*:

לְשֵׁמַע אֹזֶן שְׁמַעְתִּיךָ: I knew of You only through tradition.

וְעַתָּה עֵינִי רָאָתְךָ: But now I have attained the level of prophecy and have come to know the essential truth of existence (אֲמִתַּת הַמְּצִיאוּת). That You exist, that You are all-knowing and caring, and that You are a fair judge, with an abundance of kindness and truth.

עַל כֵּן אֶמְאַס: Therefore I now revile that which till now I had craved, namely this-worldly life and the tranquility which I had desired, concerning the loss of which I would have grumbled.

וְנִחַמְתִּי עַל עָפָר וָאֵפֶר: עָפָר וָאֵפֶר refers to the human body ... The meaning is that now he has regrets concerning the body which he had held in such high esteem, having equated life with God's kindness, while death for the righteous was seen as doing violence to their rights. Now I can well do without the body's needs, would wish only to cleave to You and find light in the shine of Your face, and that my soul might be joined to You in a bond of life.

We begin with an analysis of *Ramban.*

We recall that in *Ramban's* view, it is God's tiny speech at the beginning of chapter 40 which had finally tipped the scales. After it, Iyov had realized that, *God knows, cares, and does kindness, justice and charity in the land* (... כִּי הֵבִין שֶׁהָאֵל יוֹדֵעַ וּמַשְׁגִּיחַ וְעוֹשֶׂה חֶסֶד מִשְׁפָּט וּצְדָקָה בָּאָרֶץ) — precisely that which *Ramban* has listed here under וְעַתָּה עֵינִי רָאָתְךָ. God's third speech, as *Ramban* understands it, had been required only in order that Iyov might be brought to the final step of openly confessing that he had been in the wrong. The second speech had been effective where the first had not, because it was made in a *small, still voice* and had not intimidated Iyov as had the first speech from out of the whirlwind.

Iyov's actual change of heart, then, came about because of the first speech, which required the second, tiny speech only to clear away the daunting terror of the whirlwind.

Thus, when Iyov, in our passage, explains what had finally convinced him, he is referring to the first of God's speeches. The linchpin of that speech had been God's affirmation of Elihu's doctrine of *Gilgul HaNeshamos* (see Introductory Remarks to chapter 38 and commentary to verse 13, there). Although Iyov had already accepted this (in *Ramban's* view, the ultimate answer from Elihu), this acceptance had been only tentative. Elihu himself could not have been fully certain of his ground — by its nature this doctrine cannot be discovered by logic but requires tradition or revelation to substantiate it — and therefore, for its final impact it had to await God's confirmation.

Looking now at *Ramban's* rendering of our verse, we discover that this is clearly what he has in mind. Iyov had known of the essential truths concerning God even before God's speech. But, his source had been tradition [by way of Elihu] and therefore had lacked the absolute authority which can come only through prophecy. This prophecy had now been finally vouchsafed him, and his problems have been solved.

This appears to be *Ramban's* understanding of our verse. The units which are being contrasted to one another are *tradition* [which can go a long way in convincing but can never, by its very nature be absolute] and *prophecy.*

But these are not the units which are contrasted as *R' Yosef Kara* [and, perhaps, *Rashi*] reads the verse.

As he understands it, Iyov contrasts the ear [*I have heard ...*] with the eye [*My eye has beheld ...*], *hearing* to *seeing*. The difference in impact between oral and visual cognizance cannot be overstated. Sound perception provides a one-dimensional simulation which still allows the imagination full play in fleshing out those details which simply cannot be conveyed orally. Sight, by its very vividness, sternly imposes strict limits upon subjectivity. It provides a rounded image which engraves itself indelibly upon the mind. It demands acquiescence to the contours and colorations which it projects.

There was nothing in God's speeches which Iyov had not known before. He was certainly no stranger to the wonders of nature, knew absolutely that they were the work of God's hands — miracles of perfection which no human could ever hope to emulate. But he had known all this by way of observation and tradition, his intellect had been engaged. He had accepted God's omnipotence but had never experienced it.

Iyov, in short, had discovered God not through revelation but through speculation. Inevitably, God the untrammeled, the all-free,

ז וַיְהִי אַחַר דִּבֶּר יְהוָה אֶת־הַדְּבָרִים הָאֵלֶּה אֶל־אִיּוֹב וַיֹּאמֶר
יְהוָה אֶל־אֱלִיפַז הַתֵּימָנִי חָרָה אַפִּי בְךָ וּבִשְׁנֵי רֵעֶיךָ כִּי לֹא
דִבַּרְתֶּם אֵלַי נְכוֹנָה כְּעַבְדִּי אִיּוֹב׃

the all-perfect, removed wholly from such human shortcomings as vindictiveness or cruelty, had become cramped and corrupted in the narrow prism of human conceptualization. Iyov, who in some of his speeches had accused God of just such utterly human frailties had, understandably, created a God in his own image. [See Introductory Remarks to chapter 9. See also at 13:1.]

All these distortions were now dispelled, exploded in the ecstasy of revelation, consumed in the searing blaze of a Divine Presence which, by blinding the physical eye, opened the mind to the recognition of infinity.

Iyov had experienced God.

In that moment of absolute adoration Iyov's problems disappear. Not because he has received cogent explanations for all that had troubled him so much — not a word has been said which addresses even one of the knotty issues which had once appeared so intractable. But because there are no more questions. An ambience of trust and adoration has been established which absolutely obviates the need for any justification. It is enough for Iyov that he has seen what he has seen. The carping, assertive, ever challenging Iyov has given way to one who, having been vouchsafed a glimpse of eternity, has nothing more to ask of life.[1]

This, indeed, is *R' Yosef Kara's* perception of the second verse as we understand him. וְנִחַמְתִּי עַל עָפָר וָאֵפֶר: *I would be able to find comfort even if it were my lot to go to the grave and thus return to the dust and ashes from which I was originally taken.* The one moment of total rapture which he has been granted is sufficient justification for Iyov's life. He needs no more, he asks no more. He is ready to die.[2]

We conclude that the Iyov saga finds its resolution when the intellect gives way to the heart, when the eye supplies that which the ear has failed to produce. We have suggested that the vision of God from out of the whirlwind was itself the reward which Iyov won in return for the integrity which would not allow him to compromise his determined questing — see at 14:15 and in Introductory Remarks to chapter 38 — and thus, this climax has indeed something to teach all of us. An uncompromising adherence to the truth, a determined refusal to become a pandering hypocrite — even in search of some assumed theological verity — will in the end yield a reward. Surely it will not always be, as it was in Iyov's paradigmatic case, an actual revelation. But, a relationship can be established with God which can make problems less cruel, questions less pressing. Each of us can enter into a relationship with God in which loving, unquestioning acceptance is a viable option.

We have been true to the goal which we had set ourselves — to attempt to understand the book through the eyes of *Rashi* and *Ramban*. We have up till now, as far as the commentary is concerned, left aside the ideas of *Rambam*, for reasons which we have discussed in the Introductory Remarks to the book. However, at this seminal point we would be remiss if we did not consider his pro-

1. Our insights should help us to a solution of one of the abiding mysteries of the book. Why, at no stage, is Iyov ever apprised of what really happened? Why, after he has passed his test, has repented, has confessed, has, in short, vindicated God's trust in him, is he not told of the Satan's challenge and his own success in withstanding it (see at 30:22)?

As we understand these crucial verses, the solution is simple. Had Iyov indeed been told the true explanation of his dreadful experiences, this would have vitiated the entire message of the book. It would have implied that somehow, in some form and at some stage, an answer to the problems raised could be necessary and useful. The message of the book is the exact opposite. No answer is necessary. The solution to our problems lies not in the mind but in the heart. We are to learn to live with life's vicissitudes not because we know their cause, but because we do not feel the need to ask.

2. It seems significant that, taken thus, Iyov's final words precisely parallel his first speech at chapter 3. There, too, he had spoken concerning the allures of the grave, had wished so desperately that he might already have found his way there.

But what a difference!

There he had spoken as a broken man betrayed and disillusioned, wanting only to die.

Here, intoxicated with the untold beauty of what life has to offer, he feels that his cup is already overflowing, he has no right to demand more. The few moments of communion with his God have been justification enough. If he were to die in the next moment, he would believe that all his travail had been worthwhile.

42/7 [7] *After* HASHEM *had spoken these words to Iyov,* HASHEM *said to Eliphaz the Temanite, 'My anger is seething against you and against your two friends, because in your defense of Me you did not speak as appropriately as had My servant Iyov.*

found interpretation of the *denoument* of the Iyovian saga

Rambam appears to understand the difference between *the hearing ear* and the *seeing eye* as the difference between the uncritical, unsophisticated tradition-based faith of the man in the street (עַל פִּי קַבָּלָה כְּדֶרֶךְ שֶׁיּוֹדְעִים אוֹתוֹ הֲמוֹן הַתּוֹרָתִיִּים), and the refined insightful understanding of the philosopher (בְּדֶרֶךְ הָעִיּוּן).[1]

In *Rambam's* view, Iyov had earlier erred in his perception of God's relationship with the world (see Introductory Remarks to the book). He had believed that God simply did not care about man. But, this had been true only as long as he had not known anything beyond what tradition had taught him. At that stage he was no different than the unsophisticated multitudes. Now, however, having been vanquished in debate and thus forced to delve beneath the surface and to find the absolute truth through philosophical conjecture, a new world had opened up to him.

We quote:

> But when he came to know God correctly, he realized that true bliss — which is the knowledge of God — is available to whomever knows Him. No suffering can ever dim its luster. However, in the past, as long as Iyov had known God only by tradition, he had thought health, wealth and children — in themselves temporal values — had absolute worth. All this, and his confusions and the words which he had spoken, held sway only as long as he had not become a philosopher (לְשֵׁמַע אֹזֶן שְׁמַעְתִּיךָ). Now, however (וְעַתָּה עֵינִי רָאָתְךָ) I decry all those things which earlier I had valued (עַל כֵּן אֶמְאַס) and no longer mind the dust and ashes in which, during my sickness, I had to wallow (וְנִחַמְתִּי עַל עָפָר וָאֵפֶר).

In *Rambam's* view, then, Iyov never understands — or indeed seeks to understand — the reason for his suffering. The bright light of wisdom which illuminates the world of the philosopher blinds him to the smaller worries. The man whose intellect has finally grasped the ineffable will be concerned only about such matters which might cast a shadow upon his delight. Nothing that is temporal can ever matter very much.

7. וַיְהִי אַחַר דִּבֶּר ה׳ אֶת־הַדְּבָרִים הָאֵלֶּה אֶל־אִיּוֹב וַיֹּאמֶר ה׳ אֶל־אֱלִיפַז הַתֵּימָנִי חָרָה אַפִּי בְךָ וּבִשְׁנֵי רֵעֶיךָ כִּי לֹא דִבַּרְתֶּם אֵלַי נְכוֹנָה כְּעַבְדִּי אִיּוֹב — *After* HASHEM *had spoken these words to Iyov,* HASHEM *said to Eliphaz the Temanite, 'My anger is seething against you and against your two friends, because in your defense of Me you did not speak as appropriately as had My servant Iyov.* Why, *After* HASHEM *had spoken these words to Iyov?* Why not, *After this ...,* that is, after Iyov's answer?

We may perhaps surmise that God's words to Eliphaz are in reality meant more for Iyov's benefit than for the friends' atonement. This as follows: God knows that His final speech will have the desired effect. Iyov will grasp the opportunity and achieve final rehabilitation. But, God knows also that words come cheap and that the mere fact that Iyov verbalizes his new-found insights will not guarantee that the change in his outlook will be permanent. Good resolutions are notoriously short-lived. God wishes that Iyov be given the opportunity to translate his change of heart into action. Once embodied into a practical application there is a greater chance that good intentions will lead to good living — see *Sforno* to *Leviticus* 1:2 concerning the obligation for the person who brings the sacrifice to perform the act of סְמִיכָה, *laying his hands upon the animal.* For, says *Sforno,* by this act he actualizes his penitential

1. *R' Yosef Kapah* makes reference to *Moreh Nevuchim* 3:51 where *Rambam* offers his famous parable of the different groups of people who are searching for the king. After he has disposed of the people who are entirely outside the capital city, and of those who are inside the city but have their backs to the palace — groups which *Rambam* considers to be outside the pale — he describes those who are facing towards the palace but are so distant that they have not yet even seen the wall. These, *Rambam* thinks, are the decent religious *men in the street* who are, however, without any theological sophistication (הֵם הֲמוֹנֵי אַנְשֵׁי הַתּוֹרָה כְּלוֹמַר עַמֵּי הָאָרֶץ הָעוֹסְקִים בְּמִצְוֹת). The group which has reached the palace courtyard are those wise men who know the truth, but only by way of tradition, while the ones who have actually entered the courtyard are the true philosophers (אוֹתָם אֲשֶׁר הִתְעַסְּקוּ בְּעִיּוּן בִּיסוֹדוֹת הַדָּת).

At this stage of the Iyov saga, Iyov has clearly reached the last stage. It is not entirely clear whether before this, *Rambam* would have classed him with the religious simpletons or with the more sophisticated believers who nevertheless fall short of true philosophical conjecture.

ח וְעַתָּה קְחוּ־לָכֶם שִׁבְעָה־פָרִים וְשִׁבְעָה אֵילִים וּלְכוּ ׀
אֶל־עַבְדִּי אִיּוֹב וְהַעֲלִיתֶם עוֹלָה בַּעַדְכֶם וְאִיּוֹב עַבְדִּי
יִתְפַּלֵּל עֲלֵיכֶם כִּי אִם־פָּנָיו אֶשָּׂא לְבִלְתִּי עֲשׂוֹת
עִמָּכֶם נְבָלָה כִּי לֹא דִבַּרְתֶּם אֵלַי נְכוֹנָה כְּעַבְדִּי אִיּוֹב׃

thoughts into some physical act of submission.

Iyov is to be given a chance to turn his new-found love of God into a much more difficult, much more demanding, love of man. He is called upon to pray for forgiveness on behalf of the friends — who had been so unwilling to forgive him for the wrongs which they had falsely imputed to him. That he was able to do so with a full heart — had it been otherwise his prayers would surely not have been answered — provided an act of expiation which contained the promise of permanence for his *teshuvah* (repentance).

Iyov had talked *correctly*, appropriately; the friends had not.

In what sense was Iyov *correct*?

Ramban suggests as follows: Iyov had maintained throughout that he was innocent. This had been the bone of contention between him and the friends. In this Iyov had been completely correct. He had, in fact, done nothing which would have made him deserve his terrible fate. The difficulty was that, given his innocence, there was nothing which could logically justify his suffering. Once this missing logic was supplied by Elihu, the problem was solved, the way to Iyov's penitence for his belligerence was open, and once Iyov had taken that path, nothing more stood in the way of his total rehabilitation. Iyov is now rightly called עַבְדִּי, *God's loyal servant*, because his penitence has earned him that title.

R' Yosef Kara sees the *correctness* of Iyov's stance in the light of Rava's teaching in *Bava Basra* that אֵין אָדָם נִתְפָּס עַל צַעֲרוֹ, no man can be blamed for excesses of which he was guilty when these were caused by the terrible agonies which he was forced to bear. Iyov had indeed said many things that would have been better left unsaid. But, he need not carry any blame for this. These dreadful words were forced out of him by his suffering.

Rambam (see above, commentary to previous verses) rejects this interpretation. While he admits that this idea is indeed mentioned in the Talmud (Rava's statement in *Bava Basra*) he feels that this cannot be the true intent of the Iyov saga. This is surely because *Rambam* had seen Iyov's error not as one of intemperate speech — in which case Rava's rationalism would have been eminently reasonable — but of philosophical unsophistication. Iyov had simply been wrong in his perception of God and man. No amount of suffering can excuse such callow simplicity. Accordingly *Rambam* maintains that Iyov's *correctness* lies in his newly found knowledge. Iyov had finally recognized the truth.

How did the friends fail in their appointed task? In what way did they not speak *correctly*? [See our discussion of the *Zohar's* position, in the Introductory Remarks to chapter 4 and in many subsequent places. Much of our commentary has been based upon the assumption that the friends simply did not bring sufficient sensitivity to their difficult task of comforting a distraught sufferer. The fact that both *Ramban* and *R' Yosef Kara*, whom we shall quote below, offer different explanations at this point may indicate that their understanding of the book was not based upon the assumptions made by the *Zohar*.]

First *Ramban*: The friends were too sure of their position. Suffering is the wages of sin — there can be no other explanation. By leaving no room for any alternative, they practically forced Iyov, or anyone who, like Iyov, knows himself to be guiltless of any wrongdoing, into a denial of God's justice. The mathematics became simple: Suffering has no justification except as an act of retribution. I have not sinned, deserve no punishment. Therefore my agonies have no justification. God must be vindictive and unjust. How much better it would have been if the friends, instead of staking out a non-negotiable theological position, had simply told Iyov the truth: The ways of God are beyond us. We can never really second-guess Him. However, all our observations, all our experiences point to a just and loving God. Do you, Iyov, therefore trust Him that what He has done, He has done for the best.

Ramban also considers another aspect of the friends' part in the saga for which they can justly be faulted. At one point of the argument they simply gave up. Their silence appears to imply that in some way, to some degree, they had been won over to Iyov's position. But — Iyov was wrong. Fundamentally and terribly wrong. Iyov had now redeemed himself by repenting upon his earlier excesses and confessing his error. He had once more won for himself the title, עַבְדִּי אִיּוֹב, *My servant Iyov*, with which God had described him at the

8 So now take seven bullocks and seven rams and go to My servant Iyov that he might sacrifice them up for you. Then My servant Iyov will pray for you, and I will look upon him with goodwill in order that I not be forced to deal with you improperly. This, because in your defense of Me you did not speak as appropriately as had My

beginning of the book (1:8). But the friends, to the extent that they were now identified with Iyov's discredited positioı., remained unredeemed and unforgiven.

R' Yosef Kara introduces an entirely new dimension, one which we suspected long ago (see Introductory Remarks 11-13 to chapter 2) might be germane to the issue but which the commentators, up to this point, have not developed. The friends, instead of being critical of Iyov, should have comforted him. With trenchant brevity *R' Yosef Kara* writes: *Were Iyov's troubles and suffering not of sufficient magnitude, that you, by your insensitive badgering, had to add to them!* [See also *Elihu-From the Family of Ram*].

The friends, then, failed at the most crucial test of friendship. First and foremost a friend must love, must empathize, must by word and deed show the stricken sufferer that he has not lost dignity or worth or, most importantly, friendship. By hectoring Iyov with weak, unproven theological theories, instead of acting as friends should act, they produced the opposite result of that which they had intended. [See *The First Round* for a wide-ranging discussion.]

We recall that *Bava Metziah* 59b uses the friends' thoughtless patter as a paradigm for *Ona'as Devarim, the use of speech to subject a person to suffering* (see Introductory Remarks 11-13 to chapter 2). This failing of the friends in their self-appointed task is certainly a significant sub-plot of the story. Throughout the commentary we have quoted the assertion of *Rashi* to *Bava Basra* that the purpose of the book is to teach us appropriate answers to one who grumbles against his lot in life. It teaches us also what kind of approaches are inappropriate (see also at Introductory Remarks to chapter 20).

See *Elihu — From the Family of Ram*, under *Elihu Disappears Without a Trace* (p. 322), for our explanation of the fact that Elihu is not mentioned at all in our passage.

8. וְעַתָּה קְחוּ־לָכֶם שִׁבְעָה־פָרִים וְשִׁבְעָה אֵילִים וּלְכוּ אֶל־עַבְדִּי אִיּוֹב וְהַעֲלִיתֶם עוֹלָה בַּעַדְכֶם וְאִיּוֹב עַבְדִּי יִתְפַּלֵּל עֲלֵיכֶם כִּי־אִם פָּנָיו אֶשָּׂא לְבִלְתִּי עֲשׂוֹת עִמָּכֶם נְבָלָה כִּי לֹא דִבַּרְתֶּם אֵלַי נְכוֹנָה כְּעַבְדִּי אִיּוֹב — *So now take seven bullocks and seven rams and go to My servant Iyov that he might sacrifice them up for you. Then My servant Iyov will pray for you, and I will look upon him with goodwill in order that I not be forced to deal with you improperly. This, because, in your defense of Me you did not speak as appropriately as had My servant Iyov.'* The friends had sinned — but unwittingly. Because of this they are able to find atonement through the bringing of sacrifices. Their shortcoming could have been one of two things. By their uncompromising insistence that suffering can only be the wages of sin, they opened up God — to Whose defense they had rushed — to charges of injustice. Or, by backing down too soon they seem to have associated themselves with some of Iyov's errors. While he, through his plea of ignorance (vs. 5-6) had achieved forgiveness, they had gone through no such catharsis. Accordingly, they need the cleansing of sacrifice to attain forgiveness (*Ramban*).

Iyov was to be the *kohen* who would bring their sacrifices (וְהַעֲלִיתֶם ... בַּעַדְכֶם) because God saw him as fit for this exalted task, and it would be by way of his hands that the offerings would be received with goodwill upon God's altar (*Ramban*).

Each of the friends had, at one time or another, urged Iyov to pray to God (see fn. to Introductory Remarks to chapter 11 and commentary to 5:8). Little did they think, at that time, that he would indeed one day turn to God in prayer, but that *they*, not he, would be the beneficiaries of his supplications. It must have been terribly hard for the friends — and especially for Eliphaz, who in his third speech had overstepped all bounds of propriety in his condemnation of Iyov — to see their chances of rehabilitation in God's eyes dependent upon Iyov's intercession. God, as it were, intensifies their shame by referring to Iyov — three times in this single verse — as עַבְדִּי, *My loyal servant*, he who throughout his tribulations remained true to Me.[1]

1. Our assertion that עַבְדִּי describes Iyov even as he was during the debate with the friends, would not hold true according to *Ramban*. At verse 7 we saw that he maintains that Iyov earned this title only as a result of his penitence.

However, it may well be that according to *R' Yosef Kara's* understanding of verse 7's assertion that Iyov

ט וַיֵּלְכוּ אֱלִיפַז הַתֵּימָנִי וּבִלְדַּד הַשּׁוּחִי צֹפַר הַנַּעֲמָתִי וַיַּעֲשׂוּ
כַּאֲשֶׁר דִּבֶּר אֲלֵיהֶם יהוה וַיִּשָּׂא יהוה אֶת־פְּנֵי אִיּוֹב׃

We have, on many occasions, contrasted the approaches of those commentators of whom we have taken *Ramban* as paradigmatic, who see the purpose of the book as depicting a debate concerning some theological issues, with those of whom we have taken *Rashi* as paradigmatic, who see it as a story of suffering and well-meaning but disastrously executed comforting. According to the former view, this demeaning of the friends does not seem to be germane to the purpose of the book. It is difficult to see why it should have been included. According to the latter view, the scene of the chastened friends begging Iyov's help is an integral part of the saga.

Ramban explains the term נְבָלָה as *a disgraceful act*, as follows: God will be happy not to have to punish the friends. They had, after all, engaged in what they perceived to be His defense. They had erred — but not wantonly. If now they were to be punished, this would appear to people to be a נְבָלָה.

9. וַיֵּלְכוּ אֱלִיפַז הַתֵּימָנִי וּבִלְדַּד הַשּׁוּחִי צֹפַר הַנַּעֲמָתִי וַיַּעֲשׂוּ כַּאֲשֶׁר דִּבֶּר אֲלֵיהֶם ה׳ וַיִּשָּׂא ה׳ אֶת־פְּנֵי אִיּוֹב — *Then Eliphaz the Temanite, Bildad the Shuhite, and Tzophar the Naamathite went, and did as* HASHEM *had told them, and* HASHEM *looked with goodwill upon Iyov's prayers.* Each one of the friends made the trek to Iyov's door, ready to debase himself and beg for Iyov's intercession in his behalf.

It appears significant that the conjunction *vav* is missing from Tzophar. We have צֹפַר הַנַּעֲמָתִי, not, as seems expected, ... וְצֹפַר. This seems to bear out the thesis which we propounded in Introductory Remarks and commentary to chapter 20. There, for both stylistic and contextual considerations, we thought that in his second speech, Tzophar had distanced himself from the friends. Already, he speaks for himself alone, has cut himself loose from the earlier association with the other two. He bids Iyov farewell and disappears from the stage. In the third round he has nothing at all to say. From that point onwards, Tzophar must be considered on his own merits and not be bracketed together with the friends. The omission of the *vav* accomplishes this distancing emphatically.

As we bid good-bye to Eliphaz, Bildad and Tzophar, we wonder what happened to the precious friendship which had made them, together with Iyov, the paradigm for all that is best in human relationships — see the discussion at the end of chapter 2. Did they once more wear the crowns or nurture the trees which had been the symbol of all that had forged these four men into a single whole? Was this, Iyov's most wonderful possession, restored to him even as were his children, his cattle and his sheep?

We are told nothing of this. Perhaps we do not really need to know. But, perhaps, the issue is significant. The Sages do, after all, make a major issue of this paradigmatic friendship and, we would suppose from this perspective, the question is a weighty one.

The fissures which had torn the friendship asunder had run deep indeed. [For a tracing of the various stages in the relationship between Iyov and the three friends, see 19:21.] At 8:20-22 Bildad had described himself and his colleagues as *evildoers* and *those who hate you*, in Iyov's eyes. He had anticipated that if Iyov were ever to be vindicated, he would crow over the downfall of those who had so single-mindedly insisted upon seeing him in the worst of all possible lights.

Clearly, in this, Bildad was mistaken. Far from crowing over the comeuppance of the friends, Iyov poured out his sincere prayers in their behalf.

But, what had motivated these prayers? If we can isolate Iyov's feelings at the moment of his supplication, we should be able to make an assessment of what he now thought of his erstwhile friends.

In the next verse we learn that Iyov was fully

had spoken appropriately — see commentary above — the appellation could apply equally to the pugnacious, assertive Iyov of the debates. In his excesses he had not sinned — Rava had taught that he cannot be blamed for these — and if he had not sinned, then indeed he had been an exceedingly loyal servant to God. For, as we demonstrate at 13:6-11, Iyov, in spite of his questioning, had never at any point compromised his perception of God as the repository of pure and unadulterated truth. On the contrary — his very vision of God as all-just, all-good, had left him no alternative but to question and to probe and to lash out against the appearance of injustice which threatened to topple the whole edifice of his beliefs. Not so the friends. They had created a puny God, in their own narrow image. A God Who will feel flattered by their insincerities, Who will wish to hide behind the wall of bland theology which they have erected for His protection.

Indeed it was Iyov, and Iyov only, who had remained loyal to the true God.

servant Iyov.' 9 Then Eliphaz the Temanite, Bildad the Shuhite, and Tzophar the Naamathite went, and did as HASHEM *had told them, and* HASHEM *looked with goodwill upon Iyov's prayers.*

rehabilitated *when he prayed for his friend.* Clearly, then, there is a relationship between the two. It was only because he was able to bring himself to pray that he was returned to his earlier happiness.

How does the one lead to the other?

For this we have two different midrashic sources.

First, *Pesikta Rabbasi* 38: . . . Throughout the time that Iyov was pitted against his friends and his friends were against him, there could be no mercy for him. Thus, we find Iyov complaining, *And now, those that are younger than I in days, such whose fathers I would have regarded to be unworthy of serving with my sheep dogs, sneer at me.* And they asserted to him, *We have among us such as have white hairs, even such as are very aged, with many more days than even your father.* However, immediately when he allowed himself to show goodwill towards them and prayed on their behalf, at that very moment the Holy One Blessed is He came back to him, as it is written, *HASHEM restored Iyov's fortunes.* When? *When he prayed for his friend.*

Now, *Bava Kamma* 92b: . . . What is the source for the saying of the Sages, *Whoever, while requiring that very thing, prays for his friend [rather than for himself], he will be answered first*? From Iyov . . . Or, as *Aggados Bereishis* 28 puts it: As long as you show mercy to your fellowman, God too will show mercy to you, but, if you do not show mercy to your fellowman, God will not show mercy to you. We can illustrate this from Iyov. As long as Iyov was holding forth against his friends and they against him, he was unable to elicit mercy . . . but, immediately when he prayed for them, he found goodwill with God . . .

In the first source the crucial issue appears to be the hatred that had soured the relationship between Iyov and the friends. It is that which caused mercy to be withheld from Iyov. Once friendship had been restored, there was nothing to stand in the way of God's mercy. The implication is that as a result of Iyov's prayers the old relationship between the four men was once more in place. We may assume that there had been no permanent damage to the friendship.

However, according to the second source, there is no talk of a return to a friendly relationship. The concept is simply that an act of mercy elicits reciprocal mercy from God. No hint here of a restored friendship.

We catch a final glimpse of Iyov living out a long life, surrounded by his former friends, with vast herds and flocks, in the midst of a family made up of seven sons and three beautiful daughters, fat, sleek and — to the extent that the text seems to yield — totally empty.

Did Iyov still feel the responsibility of looking after the poor and the unprotected? (see detailed account in chapter 29). Did he continue to be the benign and respected leader of his community (ibid.)? Did he maintain the high standards of modesty which, in earlier times he had set himself (29:1)? Did his sons continue to carouse in each others houses week after week after week so that Iyov felt constrained to offer up sacrifices for them in case, in drunken stupor, they had blasphemed God (1:4-5)?

Of all this, we are told nothing at all. Only of wealth and longevity — as though a good life consisted only of these.

If we continue in the footsteps of the Sages and, as they did (see footnote 1, p. 5 to 1:1), examine Iyov's life in contrast to that of the patriarch Abraham, we could do worse than to contemplate the phrase which the Torah uses to describe Abraham's ripe old age, וְאַבְרָהָם זָקֵן בָּא בַּיָּמִים, *Abraham was old, well on in years* (*Genesis* 24:1), and compare it with our book's description of Iyov's death, זָקֵן וּשְׂבַע יָמִים, *old and satiated with days* (v. 17). Tradition views the phrase בָּא בַּיָּמִים as indicating that Abraham *came with his days* — that is, he brought along into his old age *all* of his days. Not one moment of his life was wasted or spent on anything but service to his Creator. The ambience of the phrase is one of giving, of a life fully lived in the sense that it was dedicated to something worth preserving and, as it were, handing it to God with a feeling of well deserved pride: See! I have used well the gifts which You have bestowed upon me!

By contrast, שְׂבַע יָמִים, *satiated with days,* conveys an aura of taking, of swallowing up, of a life lived only for oneself.[1]

1. The only other place where שְׂבַע יָמִים is used in Scripture is in connection with David at *I Chronicles* 23:1. However, there are good reasons why the connotations there are not as negative as they seem to us to be here. In the first place, the phrase there parallels וְהַמֶּלֶךְ דָּוִד זָקֵן בָּא בַּיָּמִים — the identical expression which the Torah uses to describe Abraham's full life. Again, and this is surely the reason why in *Chronicles* the

מב/י־יא
שְׁבוּת ק׳

י וַיהוָה שָׁב אֶת־°שבית אִיּוֹב בְּהִתְפַּלְלוֹ בְּעַד רֵעֵהוּ
יא וַיֹּסֶף יהוָה אֶת־כָּל־אֲשֶׁר לְאִיּוֹב לְמִשְׁנֶה: וַיָּבֹאוּ אֵלָיו
כָּל־אֶחָיו וְכָל־אַחְיֹתָיו וְכָל־יֹדְעָיו לְפָנִים וַיֹּאכְלוּ עִמּוֹ
לֶחֶם בְּבֵיתוֹ וַיָּנֻדוּ לוֹ וַיְנַחֲמוּ אֹתוֹ עַל כָּל־הָרָעָה

How are we to explain to ourselves this disappointing outcome of the Iyov saga?

In footnote 2 p. 6 to 1:3 we noted that in the tradition of the Sages, Iyov is portrayed as a man of the here and now — one who, as perceived by *Maharal*, has no portion in the World to Come.

We shall see that these assumptions can serve to help us understand our section.

Earlier, at verse 5, we saw that in the view which we sought to identify as that of *Rashi*, the point at which Iyov finally became reconciled and rehabilitated was the point at which the ear gave way to the eye; tradition and intellect, to experience of the Godly.

The ascendancy of sight over sound, of seeing over hearing may be one more of those many areas in which the ways of Iyov and Abraham diverge. In *Psalms* 45:11 we read: *Hear, O maiden, see and incline your ear, forget your people and your father's house* .... *Midrash Rabbah* to *Bereishis* has this verse hint at God's first appearance to Abraham at which time He commanded him, *Go from your land, from your birthplace and from your father's house to the land which I shall show you.* [... *Forget your people and your father's house*]. Now a careful analysis of the first phrase in this verse forces us to come to grips with the concept that there are two levels of absorbing by way of the ear. *Hear, O maiden* precedes *see and incline your ear* follows it. Apparently, then, there is a superficial first hearing, followed by the experience of sight, and this in turn is followed by another, more profound *inclining of the ear*.

Abraham, then, also was vouchsafed a vision [*See!*]. But this was not the point at which his experience with the Divine would stop. He would be called upon to examine carefully the implications of his vision, to *incline his ear* to those whispers which might, at the first superficial hearing, have eluded him. And — profoundly significant — what he hears upon this second, more careful listening is the command to forsake all the verities which had anchored him in life — his land, his birthplace and his father's house — to follow God and to trek into the unknown.

What a contrast to Iyov! Iyov is vouchsafed a vision, leaves it at that, and forthwith settles himself to enjoy the comfortable life depicted in our section. Abraham sees — but probes further. The result — the precise opposite. He forsakes a life of comfort to find his inspiration in the unknown.

Our passage bears out the assumptions which we made in the commentary and footnotes to chapter 1. Indeed Iyov is a man of the here and now. He is a man for whose spiritual development the appropriate setting is *Olam Hazeh* (This World) in all the perfection of which it is capable. If we feel a sense of letdown upon seeing the end to which Iyov's heroism led, if we ask ourselves if this is to be all there is to his vindication, whether the struggle was worthwhile — then that is because we are scions of a more worthy tradition. As children of Abraham, the paradigm for the appropriate reaction to pain and suffering is not Iyov but Nachum Ish Gamzu (see comm. to 6:2).

10. וַה׳ שָׁב אֶת־שְׁבוּת אִיּוֹב בְּהִתְפַּלְלוֹ בְּעַד רֵעֵהוּ וַיֹּסֶף ה׳ אֶת־כָּל־אֲשֶׁר לְאִיּוֹב לְמִשְׁנֶה — *Then, when Iyov prayed for his friend,* HASHEM *restored to him that which had been taken from him. Moreover* HASHEM *increased all that Iyov had so that it was doubled.* We have left the translation of שָׁב שְׁבוּת vague, in order to allow for the various nuances which the commentators respectively see in the phrase.

שְׁבוּת, from שָׁבָה, *to capture*, is normally rendered *captivity*, as at *Deuteronomy* 30:3. Thus our phrase would mean that God brought back to Iyov that which had been captured from him. But what could that mean?

Ibn Ezra, with daring insight into the dynamics of the Iyov saga, has it refer to Iyov himself. He had, as it were, been captured by the Satan who had been given permission to do

expression is changed to שְׂבַע יָמִים, the context in which this expression is used is one in which David decides to take steps which will lay the foundations for the Temple service during Solomon's reign. In such a context the implication of the idiom is certainly that David, recognizing that his reign was nearing its close — he was *satiated* by days, and realized that his end was near — had to consider now what would happen after his death.

That is quite different than the use of the expression here, where it is given as an assessment of Iyov's life, without any glance into the future.

[10] *Then, when Iyov prayed for his friend,* HASHEM *restored to him that which had been taken from him. Moreover* HASHEM *increased all that Iyov had so that it was doubled.* [11] *Then all his brothers, his sisters and his former acquaintances came to him to eat a meal with him in his house, they recalled his mourning and comforted*

with him as he wished. Iyov was now removed from that pernicious control. Although *Ibn Ezra* does not make the point, we may surmise that his perception of Iyov *held captive* by the Satan, could explain some of the excesses contained in Iyov's earlier speeches. Had he not been enthralled by the powers of evil, he might never have spoken thus.

Ramban first suggests that the phrase might refer to the oxen which, according to 1:15, the Sabeans had captured but not killed. But, since the phrase seems to be used here to describe the restoration of Iyov's fortunes in their fullest sense, including also the sons and daughters who were restored to him, *Ramban* finds here the source for his radical understanding of the entire episode (see commentary at 1:12) — that none of the tragedies described there actually happened. He points to the fact that we never witness the killings and robberies — we only hear about them through the words of a מַלְאָךְ, a term which invariably connotes a *messenger* who was *sent* by someone for a specific purpose. Accordingly, we assume that these messengers were sent by the Satan in order to deceive Iyov into believing that indeed all that he had possessed was lost. In fact, the Satan had only hidden his children and possessions pending the outcome of the test. He now returned all of them to Iyov.

Ramban quotes opinions which he ultimately rejects, that שְׁבוּת need not mean *that which had been captured,* but simply, *that which is being restored.* Thus it is appropriate for describing all that was now being given to Iyov — sons, daughters, cattle and flocks — although these were not identical with the ones which he had lost.

At *Hosea* 6:11 and *Eichah* 2:14, *Rashi* believes that שְׁבוּת describes the *wildness* associated with extreme youth and lack of discipline. שָׁב שְׁבוּת or הֵשִׁיב שְׁבוּת would be the eliminating of this recklessness by education or other means. It seems barely possible that *Rashi* would understand our phrase, too, in the same way. God now helped Iyov to rid himself of the character traits which had allowed him to make some of the intemperate remarks which had peppered and besmirched some of his earlier speeches.

For רֵעֵהוּ in the singular, rather than the expected רֵעָיו, *his friends,* the commentators offer: *Each individual among the three friends.* This usage appears to be significant. In Introductory Remarks to chapter 20 — Tzophar's second speech — we noted that, in contrast to all the friends in the earlier speeches who had always thought about themselves as a group, he was suddenly talking only from his own perspective and did not any longer view himself as part of a group. We concluded there that at that point Tzophar had broken his association with the others, refused to be a part of their mindless condemnations any more and, looking upon Iyov from his own perspective, wanted only to part from him on a friendly and constructive note.

We may formulate the conclusions which we can draw from these insights by asserting that the problems which the friends encountered in their abortive attempt at comforting Iyov derived from their sense of functioning as a group. Such a mentality tends to exacerbate any small misunderstandings and to freeze people into attitudes which, in a different context, they would readily recognize as being untenable. Now that they were about to elicit atonement from God, they would have to do so as individuals. Iyov did not intercede for the friends as a group but considered each as an individual deserving compassion.

The doubling of the flocks is no doubt meant to teach Iyov the boundless love which God felt for him. It was not to be a grudging return of what had been taken away from him, but rather an openhanded gesture of kindness.

It seems significant that only the livestock — not the children — was doubled. [See below on the various opinions concerning this. *Metzudos* and *Rashi*, based on *Bava Basra* 16b, seem to assume that the number of sons was indeed doubled.] Each of the children is of infinite individual worth — not because it is one child but because it is this person. To double the number of sons and daughters would have been to trivialize their individuality. This was an important lesson for Iyov to learn — see below to verse 14.

11. וַיָּבֹאוּ אֵלָיו כָּל־אֶחָיו וְכָל־אַחְיֹתָיו וְכָל יֹדְעָיו לְפָנִים וַיֹּאכְלוּ עִמּוֹ לֶחֶם בְּבֵיתוֹ וַיָּנֻדוּ לוֹ וַיְנַחֲמוּ אֹתוֹ עַל כָּל־הָרָעָה אֲשֶׁר־הֵבִיא ה׳ עָלָיו וַיִּתְּנוּ־לוֹ אִישׁ קְשִׂיטָה אֶחָת וְאִישׁ נֶזֶם זָהָב אֶחָד — *Then all his brothers, his sisters and his former acquaintances came to*

אֲשֶׁר־הֵבִיא יְהוָה עָלָיו וַיִּתְּנוּ־לוֹ אִישׁ קְשִׂיטָה אֶחָת
יב וְאִישׁ נֶזֶם זָהָב אֶחָד: וַיהוָה בֵּרַךְ אֶת־אַחֲרִית אִיּוֹב
מֵרֵאשִׁתוֹ וַיְהִי־לוֹ אַרְבָּעָה עָשָׂר אֶלֶף צֹאן וְשֵׁשֶׁת
יג אֲלָפִים גְּמַלִּים וְאֶלֶף־צֶמֶד בָּקָר וְאֶלֶף אֲתוֹנוֹת: וַיְהִי־
יד לוֹ שִׁבְעָנָה בָנִים וְשָׁלוֹשׁ בָּנוֹת: וַיִּקְרָא שֵׁם־הָאַחַת
יְמִימָה וְשֵׁם הַשֵּׁנִית קְצִיעָה וְשֵׁם הַשְּׁלִישִׁית קֶרֶן הַפּוּךְ:

him to eat a meal with him in his house, they recalled his mourning and comforted him for all the dreadful things which HASHEM had brought upon him. Each of them gave him one kesitah and one golden nose-ring. For a discussion of who these friends were who had so cravenly deserted him in the time of his greatest need, the nature of their friendship and Iyov's attitude towards people in general, see commentary to 30:1.

For נוד see at 2:11. There the meaning is clearly that the three friends came to mourn with Iyov; here, that they mentioned the earlier troubles only in order that the present state of well-being might be appreciated all the more.

For the use of the coin, *kesitah*, which we know only from patriarchal times, see footnote 2 to 1:1. *Targum* renders חוּרְפָא, *a young lamb.*

The text does not indicate why the friends felt called upon to shower Iyov with these trinkets. *Tzavaoth Iyov* (a collection of *midrashim* on Iyov) preserves a tradition that the friends asked Iyov what they could do for him. He answered that he wanted nothing for himself but would be happy if he could once more feed and clothe the poor. Accordingly the friends gave him this money (or these lambs) so that he could pass them on to the poor.

12. וַה׳ בֵּרַךְ אֶת־אַחֲרִית אִיּוֹב מֵרֵאשִׁתוֹ וַיְהִי־לוֹ אַרְבָּעָה עָשָׂר אֶלֶף צֹאן וְשֵׁשֶׁת אֲלָפִים גְּמַלִּים וְאֶלֶף־צֶמֶד בָּקָר וְאֶלֶף אֲתוֹנוֹת — *Now HASHEM blessed Iyov's latter time more than his beginnings, and he had fourteen thousand small-stock, six thousand camels and one thousand span of oxen and one thousand she-asses.* In the original account of Iyov's well-being his children (1:2) were mentioned before his livestock (1:3). Why is the order reversed here?

According to those commentators who believe that the number of children were not doubled, the answer seems obvious. God's blessing — the subject of the passage — was more apparent in the one than in the other. The livestock, by right, is considered before the children.

However there are opinions — thus, for example, *The Commentator* and *Metzudos* — that the unusual שִׁבְעָנָה in the following verse indicates that the children too were doubled.

Perhaps the unexpected sequence is meant to draw our attention to another contrast between Iyov and Abraham. Abraham too had been blessed by God — . . . *And HASHEM blessed Abraham with everything* [בַּכֹּל] (*Genesis* 24:1). But what a difference in the language! We know nothing of the numbers of Abraham's livestock. How much is *everything*? Did he have more than Iyov or less? Clearly it makes no difference at all. If what he has is perceived as *everything*, then the numbers play no role at all. By contrast, the very fact that Iyov's flocks are numbered makes their size somehow forever — inadequate. Were they doubled? Why were they not tripled! Clearly, they were not *everything*.

By giving the livestock pride of position, the first of Iyov's blessings to be mentioned after the soaring, adoring profession of faith of verses 5 and 6, the book is conveying an assessment of its hero. Inescapably, ultimately and absolutely he remains a man of *Olam Hazeh*.

13. וַיְהִי־לוֹ שִׁבְעָנָה בָנִים וְשָׁלוֹשׁ בָּנוֹת — *Further, he had [twice] seven [of] sons and three daughters.* The נ in שִׁבְעָנָה is irregular and the commentators address this issue each in his own way.

Ibn Ezra sees it as simply an idiosyncrasy of the language. He adduces *Hosea* 10:6 where we also find a נ added in the middle of a word for no apparent reason. In *Ibn Ezra's* view there is nothing here to indicate that the number of Iyov's sons was doubled.

The Commentator, *Metzudos* and *R' Yosef Kara* all believe that the unusual form of שִׁבְעָה indicates a twosome of sevens. Accordingly they assume that the blessing of God which had doubled Iyov's livestock did the same for Iyov's sons. The daughters, it is true, were not doubled in number. But for them, too, God's blessing had its effect because their beauty increased remarkably. The names which Iyov gave them (v. 14) reflect this great beauty (*Bava Basra* 16b).

Ramban subscribes to that opinion which holds that the number of the children was not doubled. He believes that the extra נ indicates that a *specific* seven is meant here. He believes

him for all the dreadful things which HASHEM had brought
upon him. Each of them gave him one kesitah and one golden
nose-ring. 12 *Now HASHEM blessed Iyov's latter time more than*
his beginnings, and he had fourteen thousand small-stock,
six thousand camels and one thousand span of oxen and one
thousand she-asses. 13 *Further, he had [twice] seven [of] sons and*
three daughters. 14 *He gave the one, the name Yemimah, the*
second, the name Ketziah, and the third, the name Keren HaPuch.

that the usage of this irregular form supports his contention that the sons had in fact never died. The Satan had simply hidden them. Accordingly, we are told that the seven sons which he had now were the particular set of seven sons whom he had earlier thought dead.

If we do not accept *Ramban's* theory — and most commentators say nothing which would indicate that they share it — we are somehow offended by the concept that children can simply be replaced as was the livestock. Certainly those opinions which hold that the number of sons, too, was doubled seem to trivialize the humanity of the individual, as if the pain at the loss of any unique and precious soul could somehow be vitiated by replacing it with two others. Could we imagine Jacob finding comfort for the loss of Joseph, had he fathered two other sons in his stead? Would David's cries of anguish when he lost his wicked Absalom have somehow been quieted with the birth of other children?

The truth is that we cannot really understand, let alone sympathize, with the relationship which Iyov appears to have had with his children. We meet them only in a constant state of revelry (see commentary to 1:4), carousing from one house to the next seeking only their own company — never that of their father. Iyov seems to have accepted this way of living passively. We observe him hovering, as it were, on the periphery of their lives, seeking to appease with offerings a God Who might have been angered by their blasphemy, but showing neither the fatherly devotion, nor indeed concern, which might have weaned them away from their profligacy.

Never once, among the avalanche of words which pours out from Iyov's anguished heart during the time of his trial, do we find a specific reference to this or any of his children. Again and again he comes back to the putrid filthy mess into which he has sunk as a result of his sickness. But of his children, of warmth, of love, of hopes and dreams, of the sense of familial rightness which derives from the knowledge of filial devotion, daughterly sensitivity — of all this there is never a word.

In our careful analysis of Iyov's own assessment of life as he had lived it during his heyday (see commentary to 30:1), we discovered a man who, it appears, had not much room for love in his life. We saw a man appreciated for his wisdom, one with a highly developed sense of *noblesse oblige* towards all segments of his community, charitable and beyond when the occasion demanded it, unbending and dignified with those who considered themselves — and whom, so it is implied, he considered — his inferiors. A man of stern demeanor and iron discipline — but not of warmth or softness.

Perhaps such attitudes extended into Iyov's family life. His children are depicted in the narrative more as extensions of his personality than as individuals of infinite worth in their own right.

Perhaps this too is a function of life lived within the orbit of *Olam Hazeh.* Perhaps for a paradigm for the ideal relationship between father and children we must look to Abraham and his descendants.

14. וַיִּקְרָא שֵׁם־הָאַחַת יְמִימָה וְשֵׁם הַשֵּׁנִית קְצִיעָה וְשֵׁם הַשְּׁלִישִׁית קֶרֶן הַפּוּךְ — *He gave the one, the name Yemimah, the second, the name Ketziah, and the third, the name Keren HaPuch.* The names are apparently designed to spell out the particular beauty of each of the three daughters. According to *Bava Basra* 16b יְמִימָה derives from יוֹם, *day,* and is a description of the glow of her face which reminded one of the sun (*Rashi* there). קְצִיעָה is the name of a spice, and this daughter had a similar, pleasant aroma. קֶרֶן הַפּוּךְ is the receptacle in which פּוּךְ, *a face-powder* of delightful color, was kept. The coloration of this third daughter was particularly pleasing.

Why are the names of the daughters given?

We surmise as follows: We have seen throughout the commentary that Iyov had, in the past, been excessively involved with himself. By drawing his attention to the wonders of nature, God had succeeded in orienting Iyov outward, nursing him as it were to a more balanced view of himself vis-a-vis society as a

טו וְלֹא נִמְצָא נָשִׁים יָפוֹת כִּבְנוֹת אִיּוֹב בְּכָל־הָאָרֶץ וַיִּתֵּן
טז לָהֶם אֲבִיהֶם נַחֲלָה בְּתוֹךְ אֲחֵיהֶם׃ וַיְחִי אִיּוֹב אַחֲרֵי־זֹאת
מֵאָה וְאַרְבָּעִים שָׁנָה וַיַּרְא אֶת־בָּנָיו וְאֶת־בְּנֵי בָנָיו
יז אַרְבָּעָה דֹּרוֹת׃ וַיָּמָת אִיּוֹב זָקֵן וּשְׂבַע יָמִים׃

whole, and also, perhaps, of his relationship to his family.

Iyov's rehabilitation had been accomplished when he managed to bring himself to pray for his broken friends. He had become merciful — that is, able to perceive the other's need — and because of that had merited mercy from on high. See commentary above.

It may well be that towards his children, too, Iyov had fallen short of the ideal attitude. In the narrative at the beginning of the book, the daughters had no personality at all. They were simply a group who were welcomed to the house of whichever brother happened to be hosting the feast that week. They were granted no individualism at all.

The new Iyov would change that. Grateful for the lovely beauty with which they had been endowed, he called each an individual name. He perceived each of them as a person — and became thereby a better father.

15. וְלֹא נִמְצָא נָשִׁים יָפוֹת כִּבְנוֹת אִיּוֹב בְּכָל־הָאָרֶץ וַיִּתֵּן לָהֶם אֲבִיהֶם נַחֲלָה בְּתוֹךְ אֲחֵיהֶם — *Throughout the land no women could be found as beautiful as Iyov's daughters. Their father granted them an inheritance among their brothers.* The irregular masculine form לָהֶם at the end of the verse may bear out the thesis which we suggested in the previous verse. The individuality of these daughters was now recognized, with rights granted to them which were equivalent to those of their brothers.

16. וַיְחִי אִיּוֹב אַחֲרֵי־זֹאת מֵאָה וְאַרְבָּעִים שָׁנָה וַיַּרְא אֶת־בָּנָיו וְאֶת־בְּנֵי בָנָיו אַרְבָּעָה דֹּרוֹת — *After this, Iyov lived one hundred and forty years. He saw his children and children's children —*

15 Throughout the land no women could be found as beautiful as
Iyov's daughters. Their father granted them an inheritance among
their brothers. 16 After this, Iyov lived one hundred and forty
years. He saw his children and children's children — four
generations. 17 Then Iyov died, old and satiated with days.

four generations. Iyov's years, too, were doubled. We derive this from the fact that the normal human life-span was seventy years. We are not told the total number of years which he lived because Iyov's personal story is not really of interest to us. The purpose of this account is only to let us know how the tests to which he had been subjected turned out to be for his own good (*Ramban*).

17. וַיָּמָת אִיּוֹב זָקֵן וּשְׂבַע יָמִים — *Then Iyov died, old and satiated with days.* Our final glimpse of Iyov once more underlines the fact that he did not belong to the Jewish people. In contrast to the patriarchs whose death is expressed with the phrase, וַיִּגְוַע וַיָּמָת ... וַיֵּאָסֶף אֶל עַמָּיו, *He breathed his last, died and was gathered to his people,* this formula is not used here because, ... *He did not belong to the Holy People whose portion is in eternal life* (*Ramban*).

For the expression וּשְׂבַע יָמִים, we can do no better than to go to *Ramban* in his Commentary to the Torah where he teaches us the implications of this phrase. It will leave us with a picture of Iyov as a man whose mighty struggles finally yielded their fruit.

He experienced all his heart's desires, and was satiated with all manner of good ... and had no expectation that further life would add anything to that which was already his ... This is a description of God's kindness to the righteous and depicts an admirable quality that they do not crave luxuries ... In contrast to other more ordinary people who, since they love money, can never be satiated by it. As the Rabbis taught: No man dies with even half his cravings fulfilled.

Appendices

◆§ Appendix: The Authorship of the Rashi Commentary

We assume that the commentary printed in the standard editions under the name of *Rashi*, was indeed penned by him.

This assumption is not without its problems. *Chida* in his *Shem HaGedolim* under רש"י writes as follows:

> *Seder HaDoros* ... writes that in the *Rashi* Commentary which we have, *Rashi* is mentioned [by name]. Clearly then the commentary to *Iyov* is not *Rashi's*. I, however, have not, up to this point found this [naming of *Rashi*]. So also the linguistic style in the *Iyov* commentary does not appear to be that of *Rashi*.

As against this we have *Rashi's* contemporary, *R' Yosef Kara* quoting *Rabbeinu Shlomo* [that is, of course *Rashi*] five times in the course of his *Iyov* commentary [see Introduction to *Moshe Arends* edition of *R' Yosef Kara* to *Iyov*], and the comments which he quotes are all verbatim in our *Rashi*. *Ramban*, too, quotes *Rabbeinu Shlomo* several times throughout his *Iyov* commentary.

I have found some thirty places in which *Rashi* to *Iyov* interprets words differently than he does in other places. This is particularly noteworthy in cases in which *Rashi* elsewhere adduces the *Iyov* verse as a proof for an interpretation other than the one offered here, or where, in the *Iyov* commentary *Rashi* adduces a verse from a different part of Scripture, but in his commentary there offers a different meaning.

Herewith some examples.

At 29:4 *Rashi* interprets חָרְפִּי as, *my early days*, adducing the Aramaic, חָרְפָא which is used in the Talmud to describe, the *early* market, *early* seeds, and the like. However, at *Bava Metzia* 106b, *Rashi* explains that חוֹרֶף, *winter* is so called because it is the *strength* and coldest part of the fall season. He adduces our verse and renders חָרְפִּי as, חִזְקִי וְעִקְּרִי.

Rashi's interpretation here, that חָרְפִּי is related to *youth*, appears verbatim in the commentary of *R' Yosef Kara*, which raises the possibility that, at least, this particular *"Rashi"* may really be an interpolation by *R' Yosef Kara*.

A more complex example, one in which *R' Yosef Kara* will not serve as a putative source, can be found at 6:25 on the phrase, מַה נִּמְרְצוּ אִמְרֵי יֹשֶׁר. In commenting on נִמְרְצוּ, *Rashi* adduces *I Kings* 2:8, קְלָלָה נִמְרֶצֶת, as also, נִמְלְצוּ לְחִכִּי of *Psalms* 119:103. This, on the basis of the asumption that in the earlier two cases [the examples from *Iyov* and *Kings*] the ר was substituted for a ל, and that all the three words are an expression of מְלִיצָה. *Rashi* does adduce a meaning for מְלִיצָה but quotes *Proverbs* 25:11, דָּבָר דָּבֻר עַל אָפְנָיו, which clearly means, *an expression appropriate to its purpose*. Thus, our phrase is to be rendered: *How fitting would straight talk be!*

Now *Rashi* to the *Psalms* passage equates נִמְלְצוּ with נִמְתְּקוּ, *sweet*.

At the *Kings* passage, *Rashi* defines נִמְרֶצֶת as מְפוֹרֶשֶׁת, adducing the *Iyov* but not the *Psalms* verse, and without bringing the *Proverbs* verse to explain the sense.

Clearly, then, both places which *"Rashi"* adduces here [*Kings* and *Psalms*], are explained differently by *Rashi* himself at their respective locations, [*Psalms*, נִמְתְּקוּ, *Kings*, מְפוֹרֶשֶׁת].

The best way of coping with problems such as these, would be to assume that, perhaps, the basic commentary on *Iyov* is indeed by *Rashi*, but that it is riddled with interpolations. This would account for the stylistic unfamiliarity which worried *Chida*, and still explain why both *R' Yosef Kara* and *Ramban* clearly adduce the commentary to *Rashi*.

⁂ Appendix: Eliphaz's Two Speeches

A

Speech 1

Chapter 4

2. Do you tire of one hurdle set against you; who would be capable of withholding speech.
3. Mark well! You have chided many, steadying hands that were weak.
4. Your words would raise him who had stumbled, you would brace buckling knees.
5. So now do you weary when it befalls you, it touches you, and you become confused?
6. Was then your reverence not your folly, so too your hopes and the constancy of your ways.

Speech 2

Chapter 15

2. Would a wise man hold forth with bluster, fill his belly with the east wind?
3. Indulge in arguments from which he will gain nothing, in words which help him not at all.
4. Certainly you will subvert awe, through that you inflate speech before God.
5. It is the evil within you which coaches your mouth, you should have chosen the language of the wise.
6. Let your mouth pronounce you wicked — not I, let your lips testify against you.
7. Were you the first man ever to be born, were you formed before the hills?
8. Are you privy to God's mysteries, appropriating all wisdom for yourself?
9. What can you know that we do not know, what fathom that we do not possess?
10. We have among us such as have white hairs, even such as are very aged, with many more days than even your father.
11. Do you deem God's consoling gestures, inadequate? His serene bearing towards you?
12. Whither does your heart prompt you, what do your eyes intimate?
13. That you respond to God with wind-thoughts, speak [wind]-words from your mouth

B

7. Do recall I beg you: Who is the innocent who was ever lost without a trace, who

14. What power can man command that he could ever win his case? Could he

Speech 1

the upright ones who were blotted out.
8. Even as I observed, that those who plow sin and plant weariness must harvest it.
9. Just a puff from God, and they perish; by the breath of His nostrils they come to their end.
10. By the lion's roar, the lionet's yelp, the fangs of the cub, they lose their bearings.
11. By the lion straying without a kill, by the lion's whelps who roam loose.
12. As for me, a message stole up upon me, my ear picked up just a mite of it . . . (to end of chapter).

Speech 2

who is born of woman ever be in the right?
15. See! Even his holy ones He does not trust, the very heavens are not unsullied in His eyes.
16. Certainly, then, one who is loathsome and tainted, who drinks iniquity like water.

C

Chapter 5

1. Cry out — will any answer you — to whom among the saintly can you turn.
2. For frustration will kill the fool; anger will slay the simple minded.
3. As for me, I saw a fool strike roots, but presaged a curse upon his home.
4. May fortune elude his children; let them be crushed at the gate with no one to help.
5. May the famished consume his harvest; gathering it from among the brambles, the parched will gulp their riches.
6. For injury does not spring from the dust, nor does the earth bring forth weariness.
7. For man is born to weariness, while the spirits soar in flight.
8. But, as for me, I would search out the Almighty, direct my speech to God.
9. Who performs great deeds beyond comprehension, wonders beyond numbering.
10. Who brings rain upon the earth, sends waters over the open country.
11. So that the lowly will be raised on high, the shriveled uplifted by deliverance.

Speech 1

D

12. He frustrates the plottings of the cunning, so that their hands will not produce results.
13. He traps the wise in their trickery, and the plans of the devious turn to folly.
14. Even by day they encounter darkness, grope around at midday, as in the night.
15. He delivers from the sword — [from] their mouths, the destitute from the hands of the powerful.
16. For the miserable it constitutes hope; wrongdoing must clamp up its mouth.

E

17. See, how happy the man whom God disciplines, never loathe the chastisement of Shaddai.
18. For He inflicts pain but will assuage; wounds, but His hands will heal.
19. From six straits He will save you, and at the seventh, no harm shall come to you.
20. During famine he rescued you from death, during war — from the sword.
21. When calumny roams, you shall be concealed, you need have no fear when destruction threatens.
22. You can smile at violence and famine, need have no fear of the wild beasts in the land.
23. For you have struck a treaty with the boulders of the field, the wild beasts of the field will be at peace with you.
24. So you will be secure that there is peace in your tent, you will contemplate your home — and never err.
25. You will know that your seed is manifold, your descendants as the grass of the field.
26. You will go to the grave in ripe old age, as the sheaf is taken in, in its time.
27. See, all this we have considered, it is

Speech 2

17. I will instruct you. Hear Me! I have observed this and will recount —
18. That the wise are willing to tell, will not conceal from their fathers.
19. To them alone will the land have been given, no interloper will pass through it.

20. But all the days of the wicked are spent in fretting, the sum of the years allotted to the oppressor.
21. The sounds of terror are in his ears, even in times of tranquility he anticipates the pillager.
22. He cannot believe that he will escape the dark, [knows] that he is destined for the sword.
23. [Knows] that he must roam [to find] where bread might be, knows that he is fated for a day of darkness.
24. Distress and straits frighten him, overpower him, like a king destined to the flames.
25. For he turned his hand against God, [wished] to rear himself up over Shaddai.
26. Dashed against Him with neck [held high], [secure] in the massive bulk of his shields.
27. For his face is covered by his fat, it was [folded] mouth-like over his loins.
28. He dwelt in cities which had been laid waste, in houses which had no inhabitants — had been destined to be mounds.
29. He will never be wealthy, his possessions will not endure, their aspirations

Speech 1

so. O hear it. And, as for you — absorb it!

Speech 2

will never reach earth.

30. He will never shake off darkness, a flame will dry out his sapling so that it will be gone by the breath of His mouth.
31. He who meanders around to no good purpose will never believe that his exertions will produce — vanity.
32. Before its time it will be stunted, no freshness in its bower.
33. He will cut off — as the vine its unripe grapes, throw off — as the olive tree its flowers.
34. For the hypocrite's clan will be forlorn, fire will consume tents [built from] bribes.
35. To conceive sin is to bear iniquity, their womb prepares — deceit!

In the second, as in the first round of the debate, each of the three friends has his say. We should be able to trace some parallel between each of these second round speeches and the one made by that protagonist in the first round. This because there would be no reason to have three friends, instead of just one, come to comfort Iyov, unless each has his own discrete role in the drama (see footnote to 11:13-15).

The accompanying breakdown of the structure of Eliphaz's first and second speeches reveals an unmistakable similarity in general design, which makes the differences in length — and therefore in emphasis — of the individual components all the more striking. Eliphaz's disenchantment with the attitudes displayed by Iyov in his earlier speeches clearly colors what he has to say.

If we break down the first speech into five components (A-E), we find that the second one has parallels for each of them, except C.

Thus: A is an introduction, castigating Iyov for perceived faults. B is a reasoned argument, designed to convince Iyov of some point. C is an expression of friendly concern, in which Eliphaz attempts, by the power of his eloquence, to guide Iyov along a more acceptable path. D, in speech 1, describes the fate of the wicked, and in speech 2 admires the righteous. E reverses the subjects — speech 1 describes the bliss of the righteous; speech 2, the downfall of the wicked.

A: The castigation in the second speech is much longer than in the first (twelve verses as against five) and is also much more vehement in tone. Where in the first speech Eliphaz reminds Iyov of past accomplishments, presumably (at least in part) to challenge him to rise to his former heights, here we have only out and out condemnation.

B: In the first speech (15 verses to the end of the chapter) Eliphaz makes a genuine attempt to convince Iyov of the essential justice of God's stewardship over the affairs of man — even to the extent of sharing with him the vision from high which had been vouchsafed him. Here, in a curt three verses, he dismisses out of hand Iyov's wistful longings for a confrontation with God. Where a more sensitive ear might have caught the whimsy in Iyov's musings — the yearning of an aching heart, not always in consonance with strict logic — Eliphaz will have none of that. With the self-righteousness of the shallow listener, he wields the rapier of legalistic reasoning to shred — a dream.

C: This section has no parallel in the second speech. It is a sharing of experiences, a revealing of the inner self to a friend, an ardent urging to transcend misfortune and discover the inner spark which can animate even a maimed and broken body. It is, in short, the single passage in which something of the old, now forgotten love shines through. In this second round, Eliphaz cannot find it within himself any more to communicate at this level.

D and E: In both speeches, the D section is much shorter than the E. The structural scheme is self-explanatory. In both instances, the main thrust is the longer E section. Even without the disparity in length, its position at the end of the speech — the part which will leave the most vivid mark on the listener's mind — makes clear that this is the impression with which the speaker wishes to leave his audience. In the first speech the earlier, less significant part deals with the destruction of the wicked. Eliphaz wishes to believe that Iyov is more accurately described by the end passage — the one which sings so lyrically of the grace with which the righteous can expect to be blessed. In the second speech (as *Rashi* understands it — see commentary) the order is reversed. Eliphaz, in the D section, does indeed pay lip-service to the possibility that Iyov may yet admit his fault. The main thrust of his thinking, though (and this is evidenced both by the inordinate length of the E section and by the important end position which it occupies), is that Iyov must be told what happens to the obdurate and obstinate. Manifestly, by this time, Eliphaz has come to feel that Iyov belongs in this category.

This volume is part of
THE ARTSCROLL SERIES®
an ongoing project of
translations, commentaries and expositions
on Scripture, Mishnah, Talmud, Halachah,
liturgy, history and the classic Rabbinic writings;
and biographies, and thought.

For a brochure of current publications
visit your local Hebrew bookseller
or contact the publisher:

Mesorah Publications, ltd

4401 Second Avenue
Brooklyn, New York 11232
(718) 921-9000